2.1.5 Advance human rights and social and economic justice: 2, 4, 5, 7
a. Understand the forms and mechanisms of oppression and discrimination 1-5, 7, 9, 13
b. Advocate for human rights and social and economic justice 1-3, 5, 7, 9, 13
c. Engage in practices that advance social and economic justice 2, 3, 5, 7, 9, 13

2.1.6 Engage in research-informed practice and practice-informed research:
a. Use practice experience to inform scientific inquiry 7
b. Use research evidence to inform practice 3, 4, 6, 7, 11

2.1.7 Apply knowledge of human behavior and the social environment: All chapters
a. Utilize conceptual frameworks to guide the processes of assessment, intervention, and evaluation All chapters
b. Critique and apply knowledge to understand person and environment All chapters

2.1.8 Engage in policy practice to advance social and economic well-being and to deliver effective social work services:
a. Analyze, formulate, and advocate for policies that advance social well-being 4, 6, 7, 9, 13, 16
b. Collaborate with colleagues and clients for effective policy action 7, 13

2.1.9 Respond to contexts that shape practice:
a. Continuously discover, appraise, and attend to changing locales, populations, scientific and technological developments, and emerging societal trends to provide relevant services 1, 3, 4, 6, 7
b. Provide leadership in promoting sustainable changes in service delivery and practice to improve the quality of social services 13

2.1.10 Engage, assess, intervene, and evaluate with individuals, families, groups, organizations and communities: 1
a. Substantively and affectively prepare for action with individuals, families, groups, organizations, and communities 4, 7, 11
b. Use empathy and other interpersonal skills 7, 9
c. Develop a mutually agreed-on focus of work and desired outcomes 3
d. Collect, organize, and interpret client data 4, 7, 9, 11
e. Assess client strengths and limitations 1-5, 7, 9, 11, 13
f. Develop mutually agreed-on intervention goals and objectives
g. Select appropriate intervention strategies 2-4, 6-9, 11, 13
h. Initiate actions to achieve organizational goals 4, 6
i. Implement prevention interventions that enhance client capacities 2, 4, 6, 7, 9
j. Help clients resolve problems 3, 4, 7-9, 11, 13
k. Negotiate, mediate, and advocate for clients 1, 2, 6, 7, 9
l. Facilitate transitions and endings 9
m. Critically analyze, monitor, and evaluate interventions 4

B2.2 Generalist Practice: 1
For more information about the standards themselves, and for a complete policy statement, visit the Council on Social Work Education website at www.cswe.org.

Adapted with permission from the Council on Social Work Education

5 REASONS

to buy your textbooks and course materials at

CENGAGE**brain**.com

1 **SAVINGS:**
Prices up to 75% off, daily coupons, and free shipping on orders over $25

2 **CHOICE:**
Multiple format options including textbook, eBook and eChapter rentals

3 **CONVENIENCE:**
Anytime, anywhere access of eBooks or eChapters via mobile devices

4 **SERVICE:**
Free eBook access while your text ships, and instant access to online homework products

5 **STUDY TOOLS:**
Study tools* for your text, plus writing, research, career and job search resources
*availability varies

Find your course materials and start saving at:
www.cengagebrain.com

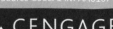

Cengage Learning
Empowerment Series

TENTH EDITION

Understanding Human Behavior and the Social Environment

Charles H. Zastrow
University of Wisconsin–Whitewater
Professor Emeritus

Karen K. Kirst-Ashman
University of Wisconsin–Whitewater
Professor Emerita

CENGAGE
Learning·

Australia · Brazil · Mexico · Singapore · United Kingdom · United States

CENGAGE
Learning®

Cengage Learning Empowerment Series:
*Understanding Human Behavior and the
Social Environment*, **Tenth Edition**
Charles H. Zastrow and
Karen K. Kirst-Ashman

Product Director: Jon-David Hague

Product Manager: Gordon Lee

Content Developer: J.L. Hahn Consulting
Group-Ted Knight

Product Assistant: Stephen Lagos

Associate Media Developer: John Chell

Marketing Director: Jennifer M Levanduski

Art and Cover Direction, Production
Management, and Composition: Lumina
Datamatics, Inc.

Manufacturing Planner: Judy Inouye

Cover

Image 1: © Izzet Keribar/Lonley Planet
Images/Getty Images
Dufy Room, Museum of Modern Art, Paris,
Ile-de-France, France, Europe

Image 2: © Annareichel/Shutterstock
violet ethnic pattern

Interior art (common)

Title Page, FM, EM:
Cover Art (image 1): © Izzet Keribar/
Lonley Planet Images/Getty Images

Image 2: credit: Annareichel/Shutterstock
Bright ethnic pattern

Chapter Opener
Credit: Annareichel/Shutterstock
Bright orange ethnic pattern

Unless otherwise noted, all items
© Cengage Learning

Library of Congress Control Number: 2014950545

ISBN: 978-1-305-10191-3

Cengage Learning
20 Channel Center Street
Boston, MA 02210
USA

Cengage Learning is a leading provider of customized learning solutions with office locations around the globe, including Singapore, the
United Kingdom, Australia, Mexico, Brazil, and Japan. Locate your local
office at **www.cengage.com/global.**

Cengage Learning products are represented in Canada by
Nelson Education, Ltd.

To learn more about Cengage Learning Solutions, visit
www.cengage.com.

Purchase any of our products at your local college store or at our preferred online store **www.cengagebrain.com.**

Printed in Canada
Print Number: 01   Print Year: 2015

To Danny, Becca, and Maggie Kirst, Laura and Daniel Allen; and Kathy Zastrow

Brief Contents

1   Introduction to Human Behavior and the Social Environment   1

PART I   Infancy and Childhood

2   Biological Development in Infancy and Childhood   62

3   Psychological Development in Infancy and Childhood   112

4   Social Development in Infancy and Childhood   178

5   Ethnocentrism and Racism   254

PART II   Adolescence

6   Biological Development in Adolescence   295

7   Psychological Development in Adolescence   333

8   Social Development in Adolescence   376

9   Gender, Gender Identity, Gender Expression, and Sexism   423

PART III   Young and Middle Adulthood

10   Biological Aspects of Young and Middle Adulthood   469

11   Psychological Aspects of Young and Middle Adulthood   498

12   Sociological Aspects of Young and Middle Adulthood   549

13   Sexual Orientation   617

PART IV   Later Adulthood

14   Biological Aspects of Later Adulthood   654

15   Psychological Aspects of Later Adulthood   685

16   Sociological Aspects of Later Adulthood   715

Contents

Preface   xxi

About the Authors   xxv

CHAPTER 1

Introduction to Human Behavior and the Social Environment   1

A Perspective   3

Learning Objectives   4

Explain the Importance of Foundation Knowledge for Social Work with an Emphasis on Assessment   5

The Profession of Social Work   6

The Process of Social Work: The Importance of Assessment   6

✦ **Highlight 1.1**   Generalist Social Work Practice   7

Identifying and Evaluating Alternative Courses of Action   7

✦ **Highlight 1.2**   Case Example: Unplanned Pregnancy   8

Review the Organization of This Book That Emphasizes Life-Span Development   8

✦ **Highlight 1.3**   Bio-Psycho-Social Developmental Dimensions Affect Each Other   9

Common Life Events   9

Normal Developmental Milestones   10

Describe Important Concepts for Understanding Human Behavior   11

Human Diversity, Cultural Competency, Oppression, and Populations-at-Risk   11

✦ **Highlight 1.4**   Culture and the Importance of Cultural Competency   12

Focus on Empowerment, the Strengths Perspective, and Resiliency   13

✦ **Highlight 1.5**   Assessing Your Strengths   17

Critical Thinking About Ethical Issues   18

✦ **Highlight 1.6**   Ethics in Social Work at the International Level: Human Rights and Social Justice Issues   20

✦ **Highlight 1.7**   Application of Values and Ethics to Bio-Psycho-Social Assessments   21

Employing Conceptual Frameworks for Understanding Human Behavior and the Social Environment: A Person-in-Environment Perspective   22

Employ a Conceptual Framework for Understanding Human Behavior and the Social Environment: Ecosystems Theory   23

Understanding Key Concepts in Systems Theories   23

✦ **Highlight 1.8**   Goals of Social Work Practice   24

✦ **Highlight 1.9**   A Summary of Some of the Other Theoretical Perspectives Addressed in This Book   26

Application of Systems Concepts to a Case Example of Child Abuse   29

Understanding Key Concepts in the Ecological Perspective   33

Recognize People's Involvement with Multiple Systems in the Social Environment   35

Micro, Mezzo, and Macro Systems   36

Interactions Between Micro Systems and Macro Systems   36

Examine Human Behavior in the Context of Community Macro Systems   38

Community Conceptual Frameworks   38

Traditional Models of Community Change 43

✵ Spotlight on Diversity 1.1 Latino and Hispanic
Communities Promote Strengths and Empowerment 45

✦ Highlight 1.10 Characteristics of Three Models of
Community Change 48

Contemporary Conceptual Frameworks of Community
Change 49

**Examine Human Behavior in and with Organizational
Macro Systems 49**
What Are Organizations? 50
The Exceptional Problems of Social Service
Organizations 51

**Recognize Social Worker Roles in Organizational and
Community Systems 52**
Enabler 53
Mediator 53
Coordinator 53
Manager 53
Educator 53
Evaluator 53
Broker 53
Facilitator 54
Initiator 54
Negotiator 54
Advocate 54

Chapter Summary 54
✦ Highlight 1.11 Knowledge, Skills, and Values Needed for
Social Work Practice 55

Competency Notes 58

Web Resources 61

PART I
Infancy and Childhood

CHAPTER 2

**Biological Development in Infancy and
Childhood 62**
A Perspective 63

Learning Objectives 63

Describe the Dynamics of Human Reproduction 63
Conception 64
Diagnosis of Pregnancy 65
Fetal Development During Pregnancy 65
Prenatal Influences 66
Prenatal Assessment 69
Problem Pregnancies 70

✦ Highlight 2.1 Social Workers Can Assist Women in
Getting Prenatal Care: Implications for Practice 71

The Birth Process 72

✦ Highlight 2.2 An International Perspective on Low-Birth-
Weight Infants 76

Early Functioning of the Neonate 77

**Explain Normal Developmental Milestones for Infants and
Children 77**
Growth as a Continuous, Orderly Process 78
Specific Characteristics of Different Age Levels 78
Individual Differences 78
The Nature-Nurture Controversy 78
Relevance to Social Work 79

**Profiles of Normal Development for Children Ages
4 Months to 11 Years 79**
Age 4 Months 79
Age 8 Months 79
Age 1 Year 80
Age 18 Months 81
Age 2 Years 81
Age 3 Years 82
Age 4 Years 82
Age 5 Years 83
Ages 6 to 8 Years 84
Ages 9 to 11 Years 85
A Concluding Note 85

Significant Issues and Life Events 85

**Examine the Abortion Controversy: Impacts of Social and
Economic Forces 85**
✦ Highlight 2.3 Case Example: Single and Pregnant 87

The Impacts of Macro-System Policies on Practice and Access
to Services 88

✵ Spotlight on Diversity 2.1 International Perspective on
Abortion Policy 90

✦ Highlight 2.4 Intact Dilation and Extraction (Late-Term
Abortion) 94

Incidence of Abortion 95
Reasons for Abortion 95
Methods of Abortion 96
The Importance of Context and Timing 97

✵ Spotlight on Diversity 2.2 Effects of Abortion on Women
and Men 97

Arguments for and Against Abortion 97
Social Worker Roles and Abortion: Empowering
Women 98
Abortion-Related Ethical Dilemmas in Practice 99

✦ Highlight 2.5 More Abortion-Related Ethical Dilemmas in
Practice 100

Explain Infertility 101
Causes of Infertility 102

✦ Highlight 2.6 Aging Affects a Woman's Fertility 102

Psychological Reactions to Infertility 102
Treatment of Infertility 103

Assessment of Infertility   103
Alternatives Available to the Infertile Couple   104
Social Work Roles, Infertility, and Empowerment   107

✦ **Highlight 2.7** The Effects of Macro Systems on Infertility   108

Chapter Summary   108

❋ Spotlight on Diversity 2.3   A Feminist Perspective on Infertility Counseling and Empowerment   109

Competency Notes   110

Web Resources   111

CHAPTER 3

Psychological Development in Infancy and Childhood   112
A Perspective   113

Learning Objectives   113

Summarize Psychological Theories About Personality Development   114

The Psychodynamic Conceptual Framework   114

✦ **Highlight 3.1** Definitions of Common Defense Mechanisms Postulated by Psychoanalytic Theory   116

Critical Thinking: Evaluation of Psychodynamic Theory   118
Neo-Freudian Psychoanalytic Developments   118
Behavioral Conceptual Frameworks   119
Phenomenological Conceptual Frameworks: Carl Rogers   119
Feminist Conceptual Frameworks   122

❋ Spotlight on Diversity 3.1   Diversity in Feminism   124

Critical Thinking About the Relevance of Theory to Social Work   127

✦ **Highlight 3.2** Use Critical Thinking to Evaluate Theory   127

Examine Piaget's Theory of Cognitive Development   129

❋ Spotlight on Diversity 3.2   Relate Human Diversity to Psychological Theories   130

The Sensorimotor Period   134
The Preoperational Thought Period   134
The Period of Concrete Operations   136
The Period of Formal Operations   136
Critical Thinking: Evaluation of Piaget's Theory   137

Review the Information-Processing Conception of Cognitive Development   138

Attention   139
Memory   139
Development of Information-Processing Strategies   140

Apply Vygotsky's Theory of Cognitive Development   141

❋ Spotlight on Diversity 3.3   Sociocultural Learning of Interdependence Versus Independence   142

The Zone of Proximal Development   142
Scaffolding   143
Private Speech   143
Critical Thinking: Evaluation of Vygotsky's Theory   143

Explain Emotional Development   144

Infants' Emotions   144
Infants and Temperament   145
Attachment   147

❋ Spotlight on Diversity 3.4   Cross-Cultural Diversity in Expectations and Temperament   148

Examine Self-concept, Self-esteem, and Empowerment   150

❋ Spotlight on Diversity 3.5   Cross-Cultural Differences in Attachment   151

✦ **Highlight 3.3** The Effects of Positive and Negative Self-Concepts   151

Significant Issues and Life Events   152

Discuss Intelligence and Intelligence Testing   152

Cattell's Fluid and Crystallized Intelligence   153
Sternberg's Triarchic Theory of Intelligence   153
Intelligence Testing   154
Targeting Special Needs   156
Other Potential Problems with IQ Scores   157

❋ Spotlight on Diversity 3.6   Explain Cultural Biases and IQ Tests   157

Analyze Intellectual Disabilities and the Importance of Empowerment   158

Defining Intellectual Disability   158

❋ Spotlight on Diversity 3.7   What Are People with Intellectual Disabilities Like?   159

The Significance of Empowerment by Support Systems   161
Macro-System Responses to Intellectual Disabilities   161

❋ Spotlight on Diversity 3.8   The Americans with Disabilities Act: The Pursuit of Social and Economic Justice   162

Social Work Roles   164

Examine Learning Disabilities   164

❋ Spotlight on Diversity 3.9   Empowerment and a Consumer-Directed Approach   165

Common Problems Involved in Learning Disabilities   166

❋ Spotlight on Diversity 3.10   Other Disabilities That Can Affect Children   167

What Causes Learning Disabilities?   169
Effects of Learning Disabilities on Children   169
Treatment for Learning Disabilities   170

Policies to Achieve Social Justice for Children Who Have Learning and Other Disabilities 171

Discuss Attention Deficit Disorder 172
Treatment for ADHD 172
Social Work Roles 173

Chapter Summary 173

Competency Notes 175

Web Resources 177

CHAPTER 4

Social Development in Infancy and Childhood 178

A Perspective 179

Learning Objectives 179

Explain the Concept of Socialization 180

Analyze the Family Environment 180
Membership in Family Groups: Variations in Family Structure 181
Positive Family Functioning 182
Macro Systems, Families, and the Pursuit of Social and Economic Justice 183
The Dynamics of Family Systems 184

Apply Systems Theory Concepts to Families 185
Systems 185
Homeostasis 185
Subsystems 186
Boundaries 186
Input 186
Output 187
Feedback 187
Entropy 188
Negative Entropy 188
Equifinality 188
Differentiation 188

Assess the Family Life Cycle 189
✹ Spotlight on Diversity 4.1 Explain Diverse Perspectives on the Family Life Cycle 190

Describe Learning Theory 194
Critical Thinking: Evaluation of Theory 195
Respondent Conditioning 195
Modeling 196
Operant Conditioning 197
The ABCs of Behavior 197
✦ Highlight 4.1 Consequences and Recurring Behavior 198
Reinforcement 198
Punishment 199
Extinction 200

Apply Learning Theory Concepts to Practice 201
The Use of Positive Reinforcement 202

The Use of Punishment 207
Additional Issues 210
✦ Highlight 4.2 Accidental Training 211
A Specific Treatment Situation: Time-Out from Reinforcement 213

Examine Common Life Events That Affect Children 215
Membership in Family Systems 215
Membership in Sibling Subsystems 216
✹ Spotlight on Diversity 4.2 Cultural Context and Parenting Style 217
✹ Spotlight on Diversity 4.3 Recognize Ethnic and Cultural Differences in Families: Empowerment Through Appreciation of Strengths 218
Gender-Role Socialization 222

Assess Relevant Aspects of the Social Environment 222
The Social Aspects of Play with Peers 222
Bullying 226
The Influence of Television and Other Media 228
The School Environment 230
✹ Spotlight on Diversity 4.4 Educational Programming That Responds to Cultural Values 232

Examine Child Maltreatment 233
Incidence of Child Maltreatment 234
Physical Child Abuse 234
✹ Spotlight on Diversity 4.5 Diverse Cultural Contexts: Discipline or Abuse? 235
Child Neglect 237
Psychological Maltreatment 240
Macro-System Responses to Child Maltreatment 241
Sexual Abuse 243
✦ Highlight 4.3 Suggestions for Talking to Children Victimized by Sexual Assault 247
✦ Highlight 4.4 Use of Cognitive-Behavioral Techniques with Children Who Have Been Sexually Abused 248

Chapter Summary 249

Competency Notes 251

Web Resources 253

CHAPTER 5

Ethnocentrism and Racism 254

A Perspective 255

Learning Objectives 255

Define and Describe Ethnic Groups, Ethnocentrism, Race, Racism, Prejudice, Discrimination, Oppression, and Institutional Discrimination 255

Ethnic Groups and Ethnocentrism 255

Race and Racism 256

❀ Spotlight on Diversity 5.1   Violence Against Minorities in the United States 257

Aspects of Social and Economic Forces: Prejudice, Discrimination, and Oppression 258

Racial and Ethnic Stereotypes 259

Racial and Ethnic Discrimination Is the Problem of Whites 259
White Privilege 260
Hate Crimes 260

Race Is a Social Concept 260

❀ Spotlight on Diversity 5.2   Discrimination Against Arab Americans and American Muslims 261

Institutional Values and Racism: Discrimination in Systems 263
Discrimination and Oppression in Organizational Macro Systems 263
Discrimination and Oppression in Community Macro Systems 264

Outline the Sources of Prejudice and Discrimination 264

Sources of Prejudice and Discrimination 264
Projection 265
Frustration-Aggression 265
Countering Insecurity and Inferiority 265
Authoritarianism 265
History 265
Competition and Exploitation 265
Socialization Patterns 266
Belief in the One True Religion 266
White Supremacy 266
Evaluation of Discrimination Theories 267

Summarize the Effects and Costs of Discrimination and Oppression and Describe the Effects of Discrimination on Human Growth and Development 267

Impacts of Social and Economic Forces: The Effects and Costs of Discrimination and Oppression 267

❀ Spotlight on Diversity 5.3   Is Racial Discrimination Based on Criminal Thinking? 268

Stereotyping and Multiculturalism: A Perspective 270

Intersectionality of Multiple Factors 271

The Effects of Discrimination on Human Growth and Development 271
History and Culture of African Americans 272
Effects of Discrimination on Development of Self-Concept 274
The Afrocentric Perspective and Worldview 274

❀ Spotlight on Diversity 5.4   Kwanzaa 275

Suggest Strategies for Advancing Social and Economic Justice 276

Community Strategies to Promote Social and Economic Justice 276
Mass Media Appeals: Striving to Change Institutional Values 276
Greater Interaction Between Minority Groups and the Majority Group 277
Civil Rights Laws: Changing the Legal Macro System 277
Activism 277

❀ Spotlight on Diversity 5.5   Rosa Parks's Act of Courage Sparked the Civil Rights Movement 278

Affirmative Action: A Macro-System Response 278
Confronting Racist Remarks and Actions 281
Minority-Owned Businesses 281

Asset-Based Community Development 281

◆ Ethical Dilemma   Are Native American Casinos a Benefit or a Detriment? 282

Human Rights and Social Justice 284

Outline Some Guidelines for Social Work Practice with Racial and Ethnic Groups 285

Social Work Practice with Racial and Ethnic Groups 285
Ethnic-Sensitive Practice 285
Empowerment 286
Strengths Perspective 286
Culturally Competent Practice 286
Social Work Roles for Countering Discrimination 290

Forecast the Pattern of Race and Ethnic Relations in the United States in the Future 291

The Future of U.S. Race and Ethnic Relations 291

Chapter Summary 292

Competency Notes 293

Web Resources 294

**PART II
Adolescence**

CHAPTER 6

Biological Development in Adolescence 295

A Perspective 296

Learning Objectives 296

Define Adolescence 297

Describe Major Physical Changes During Adolescence 297

Puberty   297
The Growth Spurt   298
The Secular Trend   298
Primary and Secondary Sex Characteristics   298
❋ **Spotlight on Diversity 6.1**   Diversity and Menarche   299

Explain Psychological Reactions to Physical Changes   300
Body Image and Self-Concept   300
Early and Late Maturation in Boys   301
Early and Late Maturation in Girls   302
Brain Development During Adolescence   302
Adolescent Health, and Substance Use and Abuse   303

Significant Issues and Life Events   305

Describe Sexual Activity in Adolescence   305
✦ **Highlight 6.1**   Masturbation   306

❋ **Spotlight on Diversity 6.2**   Racial and Other Differences in Adolescent Sexual Activity   307

Unplanned Pregnancy in Adolescence   307
Teenage Fathers   308
✦ **Highlight 6.2**   Portrait of a Single Father   309
Why Do Teens Get Pregnant?   310

Assess Sex Education and Empowerment   310
Sex Education by Parents   311
Current Policy and Sex Education Programs   312
Abstinence-Only-Before-Marriage Sex Education Programs   312
Comprehensive Sex Education Programs   313

❋ **Spotlight on Diversity 6.3**   Empowerment Through Sex Education for Native Americans   315

Identify Sexually Transmitted Infections   316
Chlamydia   316
Gonorrhea   316
Syphilis   317
Pubic Lice   318
Scabies   318
Trichomoniasis   318
Genital Herpes   318
Human Papillomavirus (HPV)   319
HIV (Human Immunodeficiency Virus)   319
Preventing STIs   319

Explain Major Methods of Contraception   320
The Pill   320
The Birth Control Patch and Vaginal Ring   322
Depo-Provera Injections   323
Hormonal Implants   323
Emergency Contraception (EC)   323
Vaginal Spermicides   324
Condoms for Men   325
The Female Condom   325
The Diaphragm and Cervical Cap   326
The Birth Control Sponge   327
The IUD (Intrauterine Device)   327
Withdrawal   328

Fertility Awareness Methods   328
Sterilization   329
Contraceptive Methods of the Future   329

Chapter Summary   330

Competency Notes   331

Web Resources   332

CHAPTER 7

Psychological Development in Adolescence   333
A Perspective   334

Learning Objectives   334

Explore Identity Formation in Adolescence   334
Erikson's Psychosocial Theory   334
Implications of Identity Formation in Adolescence   337
✦ **Highlight 7.1**   How to Determine Who You Are   337
Marcia's Categories of Identity   339
Critical Thinking: The Evaluation of Theory and Application to Client Situations   340

Examine Race, Culture, Ethnicity, and Identity Development   340
❋ **Spotlight on Diversity 7.1**   Lesbian and Gay Adolescents: The Need for Empowerment   341

An Alternative Model of Racial and Cultural Identity Development   343
Communities and Schools Can Strengthen Racial and Cultural Identity Development for Adolescents   344

Explore Moral Development   345
Moral Development: Kohlberg's Theory   345
Critical Thinking: Evaluation of Kohlberg's Theory   346
Moral Development and Women: Gilligan's Approach   347
Critical Thinking: Evaluation of Gilligan's Theory   348
Ethical Applications of Gilligan's Theory to Client Situations   349
Moral Development: A Social Learning Theory Perspective   349

Review Fowler's Theory of Faith Development   350
Fowler's Seven Stages of Faith Development   351
Critical Thinking: Evaluation of Fowler's Theory   352
Social Work Practice and Empowerment Through Spiritual Development   353

❋ **Spotlight on Diversity 7.2**   Evidence-Based Practice and Spirituality   354

Significant Issues and Life Events: Assertiveness and Suicide   355

Assess Empowerment Through Assertiveness and Assertiveness Training   355
The Relevance of Assertiveness   355

✦ **Highlight 7.2**   Each of Us Has Certain Assertive Rights   356

Nonassertive, Assertive, and Aggressive
Communication 356
The Advantages of Assertiveness 358
Assertiveness Training 358
Application of Assertiveness Approaches to Social Work
Practice 359

Explore Suicide in Adolescence 360
Incidence of Suicide 360
Causes of Adolescent Suicide 360

✦ **Highlight 7.3** Joany: A Victim of Suicide 361

Lesbian and Gay Adolescents and Suicide 362
Suicidal Symptoms 362

✦ **Highlight 7.4** Suicide Notes 363

How to Use the SAD PERSONS
Scale 365

❋ **Spotlight on Diversity 7.3** Suicide and Adolescent
Hispanic Females 366

✦ **Highlight 7.5** The SAD PERSONS Scale 366

Guidelines for Helping Suicidal People 367
Community Empowerment: Suicide Prevention and Crisis
Intervention 369

Chapter Summary 371

Competency Notes 371

Web Resources 375

CHAPTER 8

Social Development in Adolescence 376

A Perspective 377

Learning Objectives 378

Describe the Social Development Changes That
Adolescents Undergo 378

Social Development Changes in Adolescence 378
Movement from Dependence to Independence 378
Is Adolescent Rebellion a Myth? 379
Interaction in Peer Group Systems 379

✦ **Highlight 8.1** Interaction in Families:
Effective Communication Between Parents and
Children 380

Empowerment of Homeless Youth 382

Describe Some Major Problems Encountered by This Age
Group: Eating Disorders 383

Social Problems 383
Eating Disorders 383

Understand Theoretical Material on the Causes and
Treatments of These Problems 388
Causes 388
Impacts of Social Forces 389
Treatment 389

Describe Some Major Problems Encountered by This Age
Group: Emotional and Behavioral Problems 390
Emotional and Behavioral Problems 390

✦ **Highlight 8.2** Major Mental Disorders According to the
American Psychiatric Association 392

Understand Theoretical Material on the Causes and
Treatments of These Problems 394
Assessing and Treating Unwanted Emotions: Application of
Theory to Client Situations 394

✦ **Highlight 8.3** Format for Rational Self-Analysis 396

✦ **Highlight 8.4** A Rational Self-Analysis to Combat
Unwanted Emotions Following the Ending of a Romantic
Relationship 397

✦ **Highlight 8.5** Our Thinking Determines Our Behavior and
Our Emotions 400

Describe Some Major Problems Encountered by This Age
Group: Crime and Delinquency 400
Macro-System Problems: Crime and Delinquency 400

Understand Theoretical Material on the Causes and
Treatments of These Problems 401
Causes 401

Describe Some Major Problems Encountered by This Age
Group: Delinquent Gangs 401
Macro-System Problems: Delinquent Gangs 401

✦ **Highlight 8.6** Self-Talk Explanation for Columbine
Massacre 402

Four Types of Gangs 402

Understand Theoretical Material on the Causes and
Treatments of These Problems 404
Sociological Theories: Applications of Theories to
Gangs 404

Understand Material on Social Work with Groups,
Including Theories About Group Development and
Theories About Group Leadership 406

Empowerment Through Social Work with Groups 406
Types of Groups 407

❋ **Spotlight on Diversity 8.1** The RAP Framework for
Leading Multiracial Groups 410

Models of Group Development over Time 411

✦ **Highlight 8.7** Case Example: Therapy Group for Spouses
of Adults with Cancer 412

Task and Maintenance Roles 415
Leadership Theories 416

The Servant Leadership Approach 419

Chapter Summary 420

Competency Notes 421

Web Resources 422

CHAPTER 9

Gender, Gender Identity, Gender Expression, and Sexism   423

A Perspective   424

Learning Objectives   424

Define Gender, Gender Identity, Gender Expression, and Gender Roles   425

Discuss the Social Construction of Gender   425

Examine the Complexities of Gender, Gender Identity, and Gender Expression   426

Evaluate Traditional Gender-Role Stereotypes over the Life Span   429

   ✵ Spotlight on Diversity 9.1   Other Forms of Gender Expression   430

   Childhood   431
   Adolescence   431
   Adulthood   432

   ✵ Spotlight on Diversity 9.2   Cross-Cultural Perspectives on Gender-Role Development   433

   ✦ Highlight 9.1   The Special Issues and Needs of Men   435

Assess Some Differences Between Men and Women   435

   Ability Level   435
   Communication Styles   436
   People as Individuals   437

Significant Issues and Events in the Lives of Women   437

   ✵ Spotlight on Diversity 9.3   Gender/Racial Comparison of Median Annual Earnings   437

Discuss Economic Inequality Between Men and Women   437

Examine Sexual Harassment   440

   The Definition of Sexual Harassment   441
   Strengthening the Definition: A Macro-System Response   442
   The Extent of Sexual Harassment   442
   Effects of Sexual Harassment   443

Review Sexist Language   444

   ✦ Highlight 9.2   Confronting Sexual Harassment   445

   ✦ Highlight 9.3   Using Nonsexist Language   446

Examine Rape and Sexual Assault   446

   Incidence of Rape   447
   Theoretical Views of Rape   447
   Common Myths About Rape   448
   Profile of a Rapist   449

   ✦ Highlight 9.4   Suggestions for Rape Prevention   450

   Date Rape   452
   Survivors' Reactions to Rape   452

   Suggestions for Counseling Rape Survivors: Keys to Empowerment   453

Explore Domestic Violence and Battered Women   455

   The Abusive Perpetrator   456
   The Battering Cycle   457
   Why Does She Stay?   457

   ✵ Spotlight on Diversity 9.4   Battering in Gay and Lesbian Relationships   459

   Community Responses to Empower Battered Women: Their Alternatives   459

Identify Means of Empowering Women   463

Chapter Summary   464

   ✵ Spotlight on Diversity 9.5   Strategies for Empowering Women and Achieving Sexual Equality   465

Competency Notes   467

Web Resources   468

PART III
Young and Middle Adulthood

CHAPTER 10

Biological Aspects of Young and Middle Adulthood   469

A Perspective   470

Learning Objectives   470

Recognize the Contributions of Physical Development, Health Status, and Other Factors to Health During Young Adulthood   471

Young Adulthood   471

   Physical Development   471
   Health Status   471
   Breast Cancer   472

   ✦ Highlight 10.1   Early Detection of Breast Cancer   476

   Lifestyle and Good Health   476

Describe the Physical Changes in Middle Adulthood, Including Those Affecting Physical Appearance, Sense Organs, Physical Strength and Reaction Time, and Intellectual Functioning   477

Middle Adulthood   477

   Physical Changes in Middle Age   477

   ✵ Spotlight on Diversity 10.1   Differential Incidence of Death   478

   ✦ Highlight 10.2   An Identity Crisis: When the Applause Stops   480

Describe the Midlife Crises Associated with Female Menopause and Male Climacteric   482

Female Menopause 482

❋ Spotlight on Diversity 10.2 Cultural Differences in Women's Experience of Menopause 483

✦ Highlight 10.3 Osteoporosis 484

Male Climacteric 485
Midlife Crisis: True or False? 486

Summarize Sexual Functioning in Middle Age 487
Sexual Functioning in Middle Age 487

✦ Highlight 10.4 Five Languages of Love 489

Describe AIDS—Its Causes and Effects; How It Is Contracted; How Its Spread Can Be Prevented; and Understand AIDS Discrimination 491

People Living with AIDS: A Population-at-Risk 491
What Causes AIDS? 492
How Is AIDS Contracted? 492
Diagnosis 493
The Effects of HIV 493
Treatment and Prevention of AIDS 494
Impacts of Social and Economic Forces: AIDS Discrimination and Oppression 494

❋ Spotlight on Diversity 10.3 AIDS: A Global Epidemic 495

Professional Values and AIDS 495

◆ Ethical Dilemma Do You Have a Duty to Inform a Person Who Is at Risk of Acquiring HIV? 496

Chapter Summary 496

Competency Notes 497

Web Resources 497

CHAPTER 11
_____

Psychological Aspects of Young and Middle Adulthood 498

A Perspective 499

Learning Objectives 499

Describe Erickson's Theories of Psychological Development During Young and Middle Adulthood 500

Intimacy Versus Isolation 500

Generativity Versus Stagnation 501

Describe Peck's Theory of Psychological Development During Middle Adulthood 501

Peck's Theories of Psychological Development 501

✦ Highlight 11.1 The Key to Success in Work, and in Life—Be Focused 502

Describe Levinson's Theories of Life Structure, Life Eras, and Transitions During Adulthood 503

Levinson's Theories of Life Structure, Life Eras, and Transitions for Men 503

Summarize Maslow's Theory on Hierarchy of Needs 505

Maslow's Hierarchy of Needs 505

❋ Spotlight on Diversity 11.1 Application of Levinson's Theories to Women: An Evaluation 506

Describe Emotional Intelligence and Social Intelligence 507

Emotional Intelligence 507

Social Intelligence 508

Describe Nonverbal Communication Cues 509

Mezzo-System Interactions: Nonverbal Communication 509
The Functions of Nonverbal Communication 509
Posture 510
Body Orientation 510
Gestures 510

✦ Highlight 11.2 Eye-Accessing Cues 511

Touching 512
Clothing 513
Personal Space 513
Territoriality 515
Facial Expressions 515
Physical Appearance 516
The Environment 517

Summarize Glasser's Choice Theory of Human Behavior 518

Choice Theory 518

✦ Highlight 11.3 The Impact of Thoughts on Physiological Functioning 521

Describe Gawain's Theories About Intuition and How Human Behavior Is Affected by It 522

Intuition 522

Understand the Issue of Substance Abuse 523

Chemical Substance Use and Abuse 523
Specific Drugs: What They Are and What They Do 524

✦ Highlight 11.4 Drugs of Abuse: Facts and Effects 525

✦ Highlight 11.5 Drug-Related Deaths of Famous People 528

✦ Highlight 11.6 Date-Rape Drugs 529

✦ Highlight 11.7 Babies Who Are Crack Exposed 532

✦ Highlight 11.8 Use of Performance-Enhancing Drugs in Baseball 538

Dependence on Alcohol and Other Drugs 538

Interaction in Family Systems: A Theoretical Approach to
Drug Abuse   539
The Application of Theory to Client Situations: Treatment
for the Chemically Dependent Person and His or Her
Family   540

✦ **Highlight 11.9**   An AA Meeting   542

✦ **Highlight 11.10**   Motivational Interviewing with Alcoholic
Clients Who Are in Denial   544

Understanding and Treating Codependency   546
The Relationship Between Knowledge and Assessment   546

⬣ **Ethical Dilemma**   Punishing or Treating Users of
Prohibited Drugs?   547

Chapter Summary   547

Competency Notes   548

Web Resources   548

CHAPTER 12

**Sociological Aspects of Young and Middle
Adulthood   549**

A Perspective   550

Learning Objectives   550

**Describe the Following Lifestyles and Family Forms That
Young Adults May Enter Into: Marriage, Cohabitation,
Single Life, Parenthood, and the Life of a Childless
Couple   550**

**Interaction in Family Systems: Choosing a Personal
Lifestyle   550**
Marriage   551

✦ **Highlight 12.1**   Theories About Why People Choose Each
Other as Mates   551

⬣ **Ethical Dilemma**   Should You Marry Someone You Are
Not in Love With?   551

✦ **Highlight 12.2**   Predictive Factors Leading to Marital
Happiness/Unhappiness   552

Cohabitation   553

✦ **Highlight 12.3**   Romantic Love Versus Rational Love   554

✦ **Highlight 12.4**   Guidelines for Building and Maintaining a
Happy Marriage   555

Single Life   555
Parenthood   556

✦ **Highlight 12.5**   Parental Gender Preferences   556

Childless Couples   557

**Describe Three Major Sociological Theories About Human
Behavior: Functionalism, Conflict Theory, and
Interactionism   558**

Macro-Social-System Theories   558

The Functionalist Perspective   559
The Conflict Perspective   560
The Interactionist Perspective   561

**Understand Three Social Problems That Young and
Middle-Aged Adults May Encounter: Poverty, Empty-Shell
Marriages, and Divorce. One-Parent Families, Blended
Families, and Mothers Working Outside the Home Will
Also Be Discussed.   563**

**Poverty: Impacts of Social and Economic
Forces   563**

❋ **Spotlight on Diversity 12.1**   Personal Income Disparities
Are Astounding   563

The Rich and the Poor   563
The Problem   564
Who Are the Poor?   565

✦ **Highlight 12.6**   The Ideology of Individualism   566

What Causes Poverty?   566

❋ **Spotlight on Diversity 12.2**   Poverty Perpetuates
Poverty   567

The Culture of Poverty: Evaluation of the Theory and Its
Application to Client Situations   568
Poverty Is Functional   569
Application of Functionalism to Poverty   570
Application of Conflict Theory to Poverty   571
Application of Interactionist Theory to Poverty   571

Family Mezzo-System Problems   572
Empty-Shell Marriages   572

✦ **Highlight 12.7**   Conflict Resolution Strategies   573

Divorce   576

✦ **Highlight 12.8**   Analyzing Love Relationships   577

✦ **Highlight 12.9**   Facts About Divorce   579

✦ **Highlight 12.10**   The Effects of a Divorce on Children
Depend on What Happens After the Divorce   582

One-Parent Families   583
Blended Families   584

✦ **Highlight 12.11**   Temporary Assistance for Needy Families
(TANF)   585

Mothers Working Outside the Home   589
The "Sandwich" Generation   590

**Understand Material on Assessing and Intervening
in Family Systems   590**

Assessing and Intervening in Family Systems   590
Verbal and Nonverbal Communication   590
Family Norms   591
Family System Assessment: The Ecomap   592
Family System Assessment: The Genogram   595
Family Problems and Social Work Roles   597

**Summarize Material on Social Work with Organizations,
Including Several Theories of Organizational
Behavior   600**

Social Work with Organizations 600
The Autocratic Model 600
The Custodial Model 600

✦ **Highlight 12.12** Analyzing a Human Services
Organization 601

The Scientific Management Model 602
The Human Relations Model 602
Theory X and Theory Y 603
The Collegial Model 604
Theory Z 604
Management by Objectives 605
Total Quality Management 605
Summary Comments About Models of Organizational
Behavior 606

✦ **Highlight 12.13** Value Conflicts Between a Helping
Professional and Bureaucracies 607

**Value Orientations in Organizational Decision
Making 609**

**Describe Liberal, Conservative, and Developmental
Perspectives on Human Service Organizations 611**

**Liberal, Conservative, and Developmental Perspectives on
Human Service Organizations 611**
Conservative Perspective 611

⬤ **Ethical Dilemma** Are the Poor to Blame for Being Poor?
612

Liberal Perspective 612
Developmental Perspective 613

Chapter Summary 614

Competency Notes 616

Web Resources 616

CHAPTER 13

Sexual Orientation 617

A Perspective 619

Learning Objectives 619

Explain Sexual Orientation 619
Homosexuality and Bisexuality 619

✦ **Highlight 13.1** Review Stereotypes About Lesbian and
Gay People 620

What Does Being a Homosexual Mean? 621
Bisexual People 622

✦ **Highlight 13.2** The Ethical Problems of Conversion
Therapy 623

✳ **Spotlight on Diversity 13.1** Transsexual and Transgender
People 624

Numbers of Lesbian and Gay People 626

**Discuss Conceptual Frameworks Concerning Sexual
Orientation 626**
Biological Theories 627
Psychosocial Theories 628
The Evaluation of Theory: What Is the Answer? 628
Interactionist Theory 628
Ethical Issues Related to Theory 629
Other Research on the Origins of Homosexuality 629

✳ **Spotlight on Diversity 13.2** Address Discrimination and
the Impacts of Homophobia 630

Describe Lesbian and Gay Lifestyles 631
Lesbian and Gay Relationships 631
Sexual Interaction 633

**Explore Significant Issues and Life Events for Lesbian and
Gay People 633**
The Impacts of Social and Economic Forces: Legal
Empowerment and Social Justice 633

✳ **Spotlight on Diversity 13.3** Recognize Gay and Lesbian
Pride, Empowerment, and a Sense of Community 634

✦ **Highlight 13.3** Same-Sex Marriage on a Global
Basis 638

Community Responses: Violence Against LGBT People 640
Coming Out 642

✳ **Spotlight on Diversity 13.4** Ethnicity and Sexual
Orientation 644

✦ **Highlight 13.4** Cheryl's Exploration of Her Self-Identity
and Sexual Orientation 645

Lesbian and Gay Adolescents 645
Empowering Lesbian and Gay Parents 646
As Lesbians and Gay Men Age 648
Gay and Lesbian People and AIDS 649

✳ **Spotlight on Diversity 13.5** Social Work with LGBT
People: Promoting Optimal Well-Being 650

Chapter Summary 650

Competency Notes 651

Web Resources 653

**PART IV
Later Adulthood**

CHAPTER 14

Biological Aspects of Later Adulthood 654

A Perspective 656

Learning Objectives 656

Define Later Adulthood 657

What Is Later Adulthood? 657

✦ Spotlight on Diversity 14.1 Noted Individuals Prove That Age Need Not Be a Barrier to Productivity 657

A New View of Aging 658

Describe the Physiological and Mental Changes That Occur in Later Adulthood 658

Senescence 658

✦ Highlight 14.1 Values and Aging: The Myth of Senility 661

Understand Contemporary Theories on the Causes of the Aging Process 665

What Causes Aging? 665

Describe Common Diseases and Major Causes of Death Among Older Adults 666

Diseases and Causes of Death Among Older People 666

Factors That Influence the Aging Process 666

● Ethical Dilemma Is Genetic Testing Desirable? 667

✦ Highlight 14.2 Health Practices and Longevity 668

✦ Highlight 14.3 Leading Causes of Death Among Older People 668

✦ Highlight 14.4 Alzheimer's Disease 669

Life Expectancy 671

Understand Material on Stress Management and on Other Ways to Maintain Good Physical and Mental Health Throughout Life 672

Wellness: The Strengths Perspective 672

✦ Spotlight on Diversity 14.2 Longevity: Cross-Cultural Research on Centenarians 673

Physical Exercise 673

Mental Activity 673

Sleep Patterns 674

Nutrition and Diet 674

Stress and Stress Management 675

✦ Highlight 14.5 Conceptualizing Stressors, Stress, and Stress-Related Illnesses 676

✦ Highlight 14.6 Traumas and Stress Disorders 678

✦ Highlight 14.7 Law of Attraction, and Becoming All That You Can Be 680

✦ Highlight 14.8 A Strategy to Improve Your Self-Concept 682

Chapter Summary 683

Competency Notes 684

Web Resources 684

CHAPTER 15

Psychological Aspects of Later Adulthood 685
A Perspective 686

Learning Objectives 686

Describe the Developmental Tasks of Later Adulthood 687

Developmental Tasks of Later Adulthood 687

Understand Theoretical Concepts About Developmental Tasks in Later Adulthood 689

Theoretical Concepts About Developmental Tasks in Later Adulthood 689

Integrity Versus Despair 689

Three Key Psychological Adjustments 689

Life Review 690

Self-Esteem 690

Life Satisfaction 690

Low Status and Ageism 691

Depression 691

✦ Spotlight on Diversity 15.1 Triple Jeopardy: Being Female, African American, and Old 692

Spirituality and Religion 693

✦ Spotlight on Diversity 15.2 Spirituality and Religion 694

Summarize Theories of Successful Aging 696

Theories of Successful Aging: The Strengths Perspective 696

Activity Theory 696

Disengagement Theory 697

Social Reconstruction Syndrome Theory 698

Understand the Impact of Key Life Events on Older People 699

The Impact of Life Events on Older People 699

Marriage 699

Death of a Spouse 699

Widowhood 700

Never Married 700

Remarriage 700

Gay and Lesbian Relationships 700

Family System Relationships 700

Understand Guidelines for Positive Psychological Preparations for Later Adulthood 703

Guidelines for Positive Psychological Preparation for Later Adulthood: The Strengths Perspective 703

✦ Highlight 15.1 Jimmy Carter: Stumbled as President, Excelled in Later Adulthood 704

Summarize Material on Grief Management and Death Education 704

Grief Management and Death Education   704
Death in Our Society: The Impact of Social Forces   705

✵ Spotlight on Diversity 15.3   The Cultural-Historical Context of Death and Bereavement   705

The Grieving Process   706
How to Cope with Grief   708
Application of Grief Management Theory to Client Situations   708

✦ Highlight 15.2   Celebration of Life Funerals   709

How to Relate to a Dying Person   709
How to Relate to Survivors   710
How to Become Comfortable with the Idea of Your Own Eventual Death: The Strengths Perspective   710

✦ Highlight 15.3   Questions About Grief, Death, and Dying   711

● Ethical Dilemma   Whether to Insert a Feeding Tube   712

✦ Highlight 15.4   Life After Life   713

Chapter Summary   713

Competency Notes   714

Web Resources   714

CHAPTER 16

Sociological Aspects of Later Adulthood   715
A Perspective   717

Learning Objectives   717

Summarize the Specific Problems Faced by Older People and the Causes of These Problems   717

Older People: A Population-at-Risk   717

Problems Faced by Older People   718
Emphasis on Youth: The Impact of Social and Economic Forces   719

✵ Spotlight on Diversity 16.1   High Status for Older People in China, Japan, and Other Countries   719

The Increasing Older Population   719
The Fastest-Growing Age Group: Old-Old   720
Early Retirement: The Impact of Social and Economic Forces   721
Financial Problems of Older People   722
The Social Security System   723
Death   724
Elder Abuse   724

● Ethical Dilemma   A Right to Die?   725

Housing   726
Transportation   727
Crime Victimization   727
Malnutrition   727
Health Problems and Cost of Care   727

✦ Highlight 16.1   The Tea Party Movement and Federal Funding of Social Programs   728

Describe the Current Services to Meet These Problems and Identify Gaps in These Services   729

Current Services: Macro-System Responses   729
Older Americans Act of 1965   729
Old Age, Survivors, Disability, and Health Insurance (OASDHI)   729
Supplemental Security Income (SSI)   730
Medicare   730
Prescription Drug Assistance for Seniors   730
Medicaid   731
Obama's Health-Care Reform   731
Food Stamps   731
Adult Protective Services   731

✦ Highlight 16.2   Adult Protective Services   732

Additional Programs   733
Nursing Homes   733

Social Work with Older People   735

Understand the Emergence of Older People as a Significant Political Force in Our Society   736

Older People: A Powerful Political Force   736

Describe a Proposal to Provide Older People with a Meaningful, Productive Social Role in Our Society   737

Changing a Macro System: Finding a Social Role for Older People   737

✦ Highlight 16.3   John Glenn, One of the Many Productive Older People   739

Chapter Summary   739

Competency Notes   740

Web Resources   740

Bibliography   741

Name Index   781

Subject Index   795

Introduction and What's New in the Tenth Edition

An 18-year-old man, who sees no reason to live anymore, threatens to kill himself. A couple suddenly separates after 23 years of marriage. A young family plagued by unemployment is evicted from their apartment, and moves into a tent. A demonstration is staged because a local factory refuses to hire African American workers.

Why do people do what they do? The main focus of this text is on assessment—that is, this text presents material to help readers understand the underlying reasons why people act the way they do, and to help them evaluate the strengths and deficits in their biological, psychological, and social development. A variety of theories and research about human growth and development is presented. The theories cover both the internal and external variables that influence human behavior.

Understanding Human Behavior is especially written for undergraduate and graduate courses in human behavior and the social environment (HBSE). The Council on Social Work Education (CSWE), the national accrediting body, provides the following guidelines for HBSE content in its Educational Policy and Accreditation Standards (EPAS):

> ***Educational Policy 2.1.7—Apply knowledge of human behavior and the social environment**. Social workers are knowledgeable about human behavior across the life course; the range of social systems in* which people live; and the ways social systems promote or deter people in maintaining or achieving health and well-being. Social workers apply theories and knowledge from the liberal arts to understand biological, social, cultural, psychological, and spiritual development. Social workers
>
> ● *utilize conceptual frameworks to guide the processes of assessment, intervention, and evaluation; and*
> ● *critique and apply knowledge to understand person and environment.*[1]

The EPAS (2008) also requires that a wide range of additional content be incorporated into the social work curriculum. Examples of this content are: social work professional roles; social work ethical principles; applying critical thinking to inform and communicate professional judgments; human diversity; human rights and social and economic justice; mechanisms of oppression and discrimination; research-informed practice and practice-informed research; evidence-based interventions; policy practice to advance social and economic well-being and to deliver effective social work services; contexts that shape practice; and engagement, assessment, intervention, and evaluation with individuals, families,

---

[1]Council on Social Work Education, *Educational Policy and Accreditation Standards* (Alexandria, VA: Council on Social Work Education, 2008).

groups, organizations, and communities. Content on all of these topics is presented in this text.

For a number of years, social work programs have struggled to develop an HBSE curriculum that covers the extensive content mandated in the EPAS. This text is designed to facilitate the coverage of such content. The text has the following thrusts:

- It presents a vast array of theories and research that seek to explain and describe human development and behavior. It focuses on individual functioning within systems of various sizes (including families, groups, organizations, and communities).
- It presents substantial information on human diversity, including material on groups distinguished by age, class, color, disability, ethnicity, gender, gender identity and expression, immigration status, political ideology, race, religion, sex, and sexual orientation.
- It uses a life-span approach that allows for a description of human growth and development from conception through adulthood.
- It identifies biological, psychological, sociological, cultural, and spiritual factors that influence development for each age group.[2] Interactions among these systems are discussed in some depth. For many of the biopsychosocial theories described, content about values and ethical issues is included.
- It presents material on strategies that promote social and economic justice.
- It describes normal developmental tasks and milestones for each age group.
- It describes the impact of social and economic forces on individuals, social systems, and societies.
- It presents material on the attainment and maintenance of optimal mental and physical health and well-being. It also describes the ways in which systems promote or deter health and well-being.
- It presents material, using a four-faceted approach, to evaluate theory, and describes how diverse theories can be applied to client situations.

---

[2]In some cases, the biological, psychological, and sociological variables overlap. For example, a midlife crisis often involves a combination of biological, psychological, and sociological variables. Therefore, the authors may, rather arbitrarily, cover some material under one heading (e.g., biological aspects) when a strong case can be made that it should be covered under some other heading (e.g., psychological aspects or sociological aspects).

A major thrust of this text is to present the material in a readable fashion. Numerous case examples, photographs, and illustrations are used in presenting provocative and controversial issues about human behavior. As much as possible, jargon-free language is used so that the reader can readily grasp theory.

The following new and expanded content has been added on a chapter-by-chapter basis:

Chapter 1

- Specification of the goals of social work practice
- Description of the profession of social work
- Discussion of the knowledge, skills, and values inherent in generalist practice

Chapter 2

- The effects of maternal stress on fetal development
- Current NASW policy statement on reproductive rights and abortion
- Updated information on the legal aspects of abortion
- Policy changes concerning stem cells research
- Recent violence against abortion clinics
- Updated information and statistics on infertility treatments

Chapter 3

- Intersectionality and gender
- The information-processing conceptualization of cognitive development
- Updated content on intellectual disabilities that reflects the new information presented in the American Psychiatric Association's *Diagnostic and statistical Manual (DSM-5)*

Chapter 4

- New and updated information on variations in family structure
- New content on multicultural parenting styles including parents of Caribbean heritage
- New suggestions for discouraging and stopping bullying in schools
- Use of a cognitive-behavioral approach to the treatment of children who have been sexually abused

Chapter 5

- Asset-based community development

Chapter 6

- Adolescents' use of mind-altering substances
- New and updated content on sex education including new policies and current status
- New and updated content on contraception including that on the contraceptive pill and emergency contraception
- New and updated content on sexually transmitted infections including that on human Papillomavirus (HPV)

Chapter 7

- Updated statistics and content about suicide

Chapter 8

- *DSM-5* classification of major mental disorders according to the American Psychiatric Association
- Stopping a perpetrator from continuing to commit a specific crime

Chapter 9

- New content on the gender spectrum, new terms, and cultural diversity concerning the gender spectrum
- Updated and new content on cross-cultural perspectives concerning gender-role development including subject matter on Arab and Muslim Americans, and African Americans
- Updated facts about women in politics
- New content on sexual harassment in the workplace and in educational settings
- Updated content about the reporting of rapes and rape survivors' treatment in the legal system

Chapter 10

- New content on breast cancer
- Five languages of love

Chapter 11

- The key to success in work, and in life—be focused
- Drug-related deaths of famous people
- Use of performance-enhancing drugs in baseball
- Babies who are crack exposed

Chapter 12

- Surviving and thriving in a bureaucracy
- Value conflicts between a helping professional and bureaucracies

Chapter 13

- Commentary on the use of identity labels
- Suggestions for effective social work practice with LGBT people
- Updated content on lesbians and gay men in the military
- Updated content on lesbian and gay marriage
- New content on legalized same-sex marriage around the world
- New content on hate crimes against GLBTQ people

Chapter 14

- Law of attraction, and becoming all that you can be
- A strategy to improve your self-concept

Chapter 15

- Celebration of life funerals

Chapter 16

- The Tea Party Movement and Federal Funding of Social Programs

Charles H. Zastrow, MSW and PhD, is professor emeritus in social work at the University of Wisconsin-Whitewater. He chaired the Social Work Department for 6 years at this campus. He has also been the assistant director and professor in the Social Work Program at George Williams College of Aurora University at Williams Bay, Wisconsin. He has worked as a practitioner in a variety of public and private social welfare agencies and has chaired 28 social work accreditation site visit teams for the Council on Social Work Education (CSWE). He has served two terms as a commissioner on the Commission on Accreditation of CSWE. He has been a board member of the Association of Baccalaureate Social Work Program Directors, Inc. (BPD). He has chaired The Commission on Educational Policy of CSWE. Dr. Zastrow is a licensed clinical social worker in the state of Wisconsin. He received his MSSW degree in 1966 and his PhD in social welfare in 1971 from the University of Wisconsin–Madison. He is the author of nine books, of which four are social work textbooks. He has also authored more than 45 articles in professional journals. His other social work texts are *Introduction to Social Work and Social Welfare* (11th ed.), *Social Work with Groups* (9th ed.), and *The Practice of Social Work* (10th ed.).

Karen K. Kirst-Ashman, BSW, MSSW, and PhD, was a full professor and a former chairperson in the Social Work Department at the University of Wisconsin–Whitewater, where she taught for 28 years. She is certified as a licensed clinical social worker in the state of Wisconsin. She earned her BSW degree in 1972 and MSSW in 1973 at the University of Wisconsin–Madison, and her PhD in Social Work at the University of Illinois at Urbana–Champaign. She has worked as a practitioner and administrator in child welfare and mental health agencies. She received the University of Wisconsin–Whitewater's Excellence in Teaching Award in 1986 and the University Outstanding Teaching Award in 2007. She has been a member of the board of directors of the Council on Social Work Education in addition to being an accreditation site visitor. She is also a current member of BPD and NASW. She has served on the editorial board of *Affilia: Journal of Women and Social Work*, and as a consulting editor for many social work journals, including the *Journal of Social Work Education*. She is the author of numerous publications, articles, and reviews concerning social work and women's issues. Other books she has authored or coauthored include *Introduction to Social Work and Social Welfare: Critical Thinking Perspectives* (4th ed.); *Human Behavior in the Macro Social Environment: An Empowerment Approach to Understanding Communities, Organization, and Groups* (4th ed.); *Generalist Practice with Organizations and Communities* (5th ed.); *The Macro Skills Workbook* (2nd ed.); and *Understanding Generalist Practice* (7th ed.).

INTRODUCTION TO HUMAN BEHAVIOR AND THE SOCIAL ENVIRONMENT

Why do people behave the way they do? Are behavior and personality caused mainly by a person's genetic makeup and given nature? Or are they due to the environment and a person's treatment in that environment?

Human behavior and its dynamics can be remarkably complex. A fascinating example concerns the case of a boy, sometimes referred to as "the wild boy of Aveyron," who grew up alone in the Aveyron forest of southern France at the end of the eighteenth century (Papalia, Olds, & Feldman, 2007). On various occasions, French villagers sighted the boy, who was naked, filthy, and covered with scars, as he roamed through the wilderness, foraging for roots, nuts, and whatever other food he could find (Yousef, 2001).

In January 1800, the boy, eventually named Victor, was caught burrowing for vegetables in a tanner's garden in the French village of Saint-Sernin. Although he was only about four and a half feet tall, he appeared to be about 12 or 13 (Lane, 1976). He had "delicate white skin, a round face, long eyelashes, a long, slightly pointed nose, an average-sized mouth, a rounded chin, generally agreeable features, and an engaging smile." Externally he appeared much like any other boy; however, he could make "only weird, meaningless cries," could not speak, vehemently refused to wear clothing, and rejected any prepared food (Saskatchewan Psychology Portal, n.d.; Shattuck, 1980). Victor also failed to respond to others, neither communicating with them nor paying attention to what they were doing. It was apparent that Victor had been abandoned at an early age and, without human company, had learned to fend for himself in his own way.

Victor was eventually sent to Paris, where he came to the attention of two important Parisian physicians. A basic question they addressed was, Why was Victor behaving that way? This focused on the nature-nurture controversy. In other words, was Victor's behavior the result of nature (i.e., inborn traits), or was it a consequence of nurture (i.e., the influence of his background, experience, and environment)? One physician, the early psychiatrist Philippe Pinel, determined that Victor was not really wild, but rather mentally deficient and an "incurable idiot" (Human Intelligence, 2004). He believed that nature caused Victor's pattern of behavior. The other physician, Jean-Marc Gaspard Itard, chief physician at the National Institution for Deaf-Mutes in Paris, disagreed. Itard credited Victor for his self-sufficiency and survival, asserting that Victor's deprivation of human interaction had denied him the opportunity to learn how to fit into society. Itard believed that Victor could learn to interact, communicate, and conform if he were taught to do so. Itard argued that Victor's behavior resulted from the nurturance, or lack thereof, he received from his environment.

More specific questions can be raised. Why couldn't Victor speak? He had a horizontal scar across his throat, apparently caused by a knife, that may have damaged his vocal cords (Yousef, 2001). However, he could utter some sounds, which suggested that his vocal cords were not damaged. Could Victor hear? He would often ignore human speech and even the sound of a gunshot (Human Intelligence, 2004), yet would react to the sound of a walnut being cracked behind him, an unseen dog barking outside, or a door creaking open in the dark (Yousef, 2001). Was Victor autistic (a condition characterized by intense inner-directedness that is discussed further in Chapter 3)? Some believe he presents the first documented case of autism (FeralChildren.com, 2005; Human Intelligence, 2004).

Far ahead of his time, Itard worked with Victor for five years, using behavior modification principles to teach and reinforce desired behavior (Chapter 4 elaborates on behavior modification concepts and techniques). Victor learned to "read and speak a few words, demonstrated affection for his caretakers, and could carry out simple commands" (Human Intelligence, 2004). Consider what great accomplishments these were! However, Itard was greatly disappointed that Victor could not achieve much more and become "normal." Victor never learned to communicate well nor cared much about interpersonal interactions. His focal point continued to be his own desires. He couldn't survive independently in the civilized world as he had in the wild. Victor spent the remainder of his life being cared for by Madame Guerin, who had been Itard's housekeeper. He was in his early forties when he died in 1828.

Ethical Question 1.1¹

Was it ethical for Dr. Itard and the others to remove Victor from the wild against his will?

EP 2.1.2

Victor's story raises many questions about how human behavior and personality develop. Why do we behave the way we do? How much of our behavior is a product of our genetic heritage? To what extent do we think, feel, and interact the way we do because we've been taught to do just that by other people, our family, school, the media, our culture, and our government? Understanding Human Behavior will explore various dimensions of human behavior to enhance your understanding of why people have developed as they have and why they behave the way they do.

A Perspective

The goals of this book are to explore the dynamics of human behavior and prepare a foundation of knowledge upon which to build social work practice skills. What do we mean, exactly, by human behavior and the social environment, the title of this book? First, let's break down and define the terminology. Human behavior involves people's actions, conduct, and responses as they go through life. Individuals, of course, demonstrate human behavior. Groups of people ranging from couples to families to communities to nations also exhibit human behavior. People then behave within the context of their environment. An environment includes "the surroundings or conditions" in which people or other organisms live and function (Lindberg, 2007, p. 460). For our purposes, the social environment involves the systems of other people, including economic, political, legal, social, spiritual, and cultural, with whom any individual interacts as he or she operates within the encompassing environment.

Why is understanding human behavior and the social environment important for social workers and other helping professionals? Social workers help people solve problems and get access to resources. They must recognize what conditions people are faced with in their social environments and how these conditions affect people's behavior and functioning. The social environment may vary on many levels. It may be urban or rural. It may be wealthy with many resources or impoverished with very few. It may be liberal or conservative. On an international level, it may be democratic, socialist, or communist. Social workers must understand the social environment in order to help people figure out what options are available to them so people can get what they need.

One of the primary steps in the helping process—and the focus of this book—is assessment, the identification and exploration of variables affecting people's behavior, functioning, and well-being. Assessment for social workers entails investigating people's strengths,

---

¹Ethics are standards that guide behavior. Ethical questions such as this will be raised throughout this book to encourage students to engage in ethical decision making by addressing professional values and using professional ethical standards.

problems, needs, and issues to begin understanding how to help people and improve their lives.

Human behavior can be fascinating and, sometimes, quite puzzling. For example, I (Karen Kirst-Ashman) once got home from work, walked into the master bedroom, and observed my partner ironing the mattress. Befuddled, I thought to myself, "This is a new one. What in the world is he doing?" Mattress ironing had never been part of my repertoire of logical behavior. As it turned out, my partner, who is an engineer, explained his actions quite rationally. We had recently bought a new mattress, and its covering was so slippery that neither a mattress cover nor sheets would stay in place. This was quite annoying when we were trying to sleep. My partner was using the iron to attach a sheet with Stitch Witchery, a bonding tape that melts and secures materials like hems after heat is applied to it. It's an easy way to get cloth materials to stick together if you don't want to bother with needle and thread. My partner's idea was that we'd put another sheet over the one bonded to the mattress; in effect, the bonded sheet would be a permanent—and nonslippery—mattress cover. As it turned out, his plan worked. The sheets no longer slipped off. This experience reinforced my hypothesis that people always have a reason for doing what they do, as baffling as it might appear at the time.

Social work is unique in that it emphasizes a focus that stretches far beyond that of an individual. Assessment in social work addresses all aspects of a client's situation. Many times it's not the client's fault that problems exist. Rather, something outside the client may be instigating the problem. The client's whole family may not be functioning well. There may be difficulties beyond the client's control in his or her workplace. Existing social service organizations may not be providing what clients need. Resources may be too difficult to obtain, inadequate, or even nonexistent. Organizational policies or laws affecting the client may be unfair. As part of assessment, social workers focus on families, work groups and environments, social agencies, organizations, neighborhoods, communities, and even local, state, and national government in addition to the individual. Figuring out what to do about any specific problem may directly involve any of these entities.

Learning Objectives

This chapter will help prepare students to:

EP 2.1.7,
2.1.7a,
2.1.7b

LO 1-1 *Explain the importance of foundation knowledge for social work with an emphasis on assessment*

LO 1-2 *Review the organization of this book that emphasizes life-span development*

LO 1-3 *Describe important concepts for understanding human behavior (that are stressed throughout the book and include human diversity, cultural competency, oppression, populations-at-risk, empowerment, the strengths perspective, resiliency, human rights, and critical thinking about ethical issues)*

LO 1-4 *Employ a conceptual framework for understanding human behavior and the social environment: ecosystems theory*

LO 1-5 *Recognize people's involvement with multiple systems in the social environment*

LO 1-6 *Examine human behavior in the context of community macro systems*

LO 1-7 *Examine human behavior in and with organizational macro systems*

LO 1-8 *Recognize social worker roles in organizational and community systems*

LO 1-9 *Identify knowledge, skills, and values necessary for generalist social work practice.* *

LO 1-1 Explain the Importance of Foundation Knowledge for Social Work with an Emphasis on Assessment**

In order to recognize the significance of foundation knowledge, including that presented in this book, the purpose and process of social work must be understood. Social work may be viewed as having three major thrusts (Baer & Federico, 1978, p. 68). First, social workers can help people solve their problems and cope with their situations. Second, social workers can work with systems, such as social agencies, organizations, communities, and government bureaucracies, so that people can

have better access to the resources and services they need. Third, social workers can "link people with systems" (Baer & Federico, 1978, p. 68), so that clients themselves have access to resources and opportunities. Much of social work, then, involves social functioning.

People interact with other people, with organizations (such as social service agencies), and with small groups (such as families and colleagues in the workplace). Social work targets not only how individuals behave, but also how these other systems and people affect each other.

An example is a family of five in which both parents work at low-paying jobs in order to make a marginal living. The father works at a small, non-unionized leather-processing plant. The mother works as a waitress at a short-order diner. Suddenly, the father is laid off. For a short time, the family survives on unemployment compensation. When that runs out, they face a serious financial crisis. Despite a great effort, the father is unable to find another job. In desperation, the family applies for public assistance. Due to some unidentified error in the lengthy application process, the payments are delayed for two months.

Meanwhile, the family is forced to eat poorly and is unable to pay rent and utility bills. The phone is disconnected, the electricity is turned off, and the landlord threatens to evict them. Reacting to the externally imposed stress, the parents begin to fight verbally and physically. The children complain because they are hungry. This intensifies the parents' sense of defeat and disillusionment. As a result of stress and frustration, the parents hit the children to keep them quiet.

Although this example has not been presented in detail, it illustrates that people are integrally involved with other systems in their environment.

---

*Note that **"helping hands" icons** of two hands embracing a sun are located next to the learning objectives just cited and other content throughout the book. Accredited social work programs must demonstrate that they're teaching students to be proficient in 10 core competencies that are operationalized by 41 practice behaviors designated by the Council on Social Work Education (CSWE) Educational Policy and Accreditation Standards (EPAS). Students require knowledge in order to develop skills and become competent. Our intent here is to specify what chapter content and knowledge coincides with the development of specific competencies and practice behaviors. (This ultimately is intended to assist in a social work program's accreditation process.) Throughout each chapter, icons such as those located on this page call attention to the location of EPAS-related content. Each icon identifies what competency or practice behavior is relevant by specifying the designated Educational Policy (EP) reference number beneath it. "Competency Notes" are provided at the end of each chapter that describe how EPAS competencies and practice behaviors are related to designated content in the chapter. EPAS competencies and their alphabetized practice behaviors are cited in the inside covers of this book.

**Note that content headings in chapters throughout the book are tagged with learning objectives [e.g., LO 1-1, LO 1-4]. These indicate what content relates to which learning objective.

A social worker reviewing this case might assess how the family and other systems in the environment have had an impact on each other. First, the father's life is seriously affected by his place of employment, the leather factory, when he is laid off. He then seeks unemployment compensation, which affects that system by dipping into its funds. When those benefits cease, the family then affects the public assistance system by drawing on its funds. The public assistance system, in turn, impacts the family by delaying their payments. The resulting frustration affects all family members, as the parents are unable to cope with their stress. The entire situation can be viewed as a series of dynamic interactions between people and their environment.

The Profession of Social Work

EP 2.1.1

The National Association of Social Workers (NASW) is the primary professional organization for social workers in the United States. NASW (1982) defines *social work* as follows:

> *Social work is the professional activity of helping individuals, groups, or communities to enhance or restore their capacity for social functioning and to create societal conditions favorable to their goals.*
>
> *Social Work practice consists of the professional application of social work values, principles, and techniques to one or more of the following ends: helping people obtain tangible services; providing counseling and psychotherapy for individuals, families, and groups; helping communities or groups provide or improve social and health services; and participating in relevant legislative processes.*

The profession of social work is the profession that is recognized as having the primary responsibility to implement society's mandate to provide safe, constructive, and effective social services. Social work is thus distinct from other professions (such as psychology and psychiatry) because it has the responsibility and mandate to provide social services.

A social worker needs training and expertise in a wide range of areas to effectively handle problems faced by individuals, groups, families, organizations, and the larger community. Although most professions are increasingly becoming more specialized (e.g., most medical doctors now specialize in one or two areas), social work continues to emphasize a generic (broad-based) approach. The practice of social work is analogous to the old general practice of medicine. A general (or family) practitioner has professional education to handle a wide range of common medical problems; a social worker has professional education to handle a wide range of common social and personal problems.

The foundation of social work is described in Highlight 1.1. The knowledge, skills, and values needed for generalist social work practice are described in greater detail later in the chapter.

The Process of Social Work: The Importance of Assessment

Accurate assessment is a critically important step in the social work process. Information about the problem or situation needs to be gathered, analyzed, and interpreted. Regardless of the specific type of situation, careful thought is necessary in order to

EP 2.1.10

make effective decisions about how to proceed. Assessment also involves basic knowledge and assumptions about human behavior. There are always reasons why people behave the way they do.

For example, a social worker who is trying to help a potentially suicidal adolescent needs certain types of information. The worker needs to know some of the reasons why people commit suicide so that he or she knows what questions to ask, how to react to and treat the person, and what alternatives and supports to pursue.

Additionally, the worker must be able to identify what resources are readily available to suicidal adolescents. How can the crises be addressed immediately, simply to keep them alive? What supportive resources are available to keep them from suicidal thoughts in the future? Where can a social worker refer them to get help? (Chapter 7 explores adolescent suicide in greater depth.)

HIGHLIGHT 1.1

Generalist Social Work Practice

There used to be an erroneous belief that a social worker was a caseworker (who worked with individuals and families), a group worker (who worked with groups), or a community organizer (who worked on people's behalf in organizations and communities). Practicing social workers know that such a belief is faulty because every social worker is a change agent working with individuals, groups, families, organizations, and the larger community. Social workers today are generalists. A *generalist* practitioner is one who uses a wide range of knowledge and skills to help people with an extensive array of problems and issues. These include anything from personal issues that affect an individual to extensive, far-reaching problems that involve entire communities. The amount of time spent at these levels varies from worker to worker, but every worker will, at times, work at each of these levels and therefore needs training in all of them.

The Council on Social Work Education (CSWE, the national accrediting entity for baccalaureate and master's programs in social work) requires that all bachelor's and master's programs train students in generalist social work practice. MSW programs, in addition, usually require students to select and study in an area of concentration. They generally offer several choices, such as family therapy, administration, corrections, or clinical social work.)

The Council on Social Work Education (2008), in *Educational Policy and Accreditation Standards*, defines generalist practice:

> *Generalist practice is grounded in the liberal arts and the person and environment construct. To promote human and social well-being, generalist practitioners use a*

range of prevention and intervention methods in their practice with individuals, families, groups, organizations, and communities. The generalist practitioner identifies with the social work profession and applies ethical principles and critical thinking in practice. Generalist practitioners incorporate diversity in their practice and advocate for human rights and social and economic justice. They recognize, support, and build on the strengths and resiliency of all human beings. They engage in research-informed practice and are proactive in responding to the impact of context on professional practice.

This text focuses on the generalist-practice approach in social work by describing a variety of assessment strategies. Once you have learned these strategies, you can select the approaches that hold the most promise in facilitating positive changes in your clients.

In working with individuals, families, groups, organizations, and communities, social workers use a problem-solving approach. The process can be described in a variety of ways but includes these steps:

1. *Identify as precisely as possible the problem or problems; in other words, conduct an assessment of the situation.*
2. *Generate possible alternative solutions, evaluate their potential effectiveness, and establish a plan of action for intervention.*
3. *Implement the plan and carry out the intervention.*
4. *Evaluate the intervention's effectiveness.*
5. *Terminate the process.*

Identifying and Evaluating Alternative Courses of Action

Clients come to social workers with problems and needs. The worker must understand these problems and needs in order to help the client. One primary task for the practitioner is to help the client define the alternatives available to him or her. Often people have tunnel vision. Because of stress or habit or lack of experience, people fail to realize that various alternatives exist. Not only must alternatives be defined, but they also must be evaluated. The positive and negative consequences of each alternative should be clearly stated and weighed. Figure 1.1 illustrates the process of evaluating alternatives.

Much of generalist social work practice involves individual clients and small groups. Highlight 1.2, "Case Example: Unplanned Pregnancy," shows how an individual client might be helped to identify the various alternatives available, evaluate the consequences of each, and finally select a course of action.

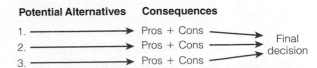

FIGURE 1.1 Social Workers Help Clients Identify Alternatives and Evaluate the Consequences of Each

HIGHLIGHT 1.2

Case Example: Unplanned Pregnancy

Mona, 16, is a high school sophomore who just found out that she is two months pregnant. The father is Fred, a 17-year-old high school junior.

Mona and Fred have been going steady for two years. They think they love each other. Mona is a vivacious, outgoing cheerleader, and Fred is a muscular, handsome quarterback on the school football team. They are both involved in school activities and have never thought very much about the future.

Mona hasn't told Fred about being pregnant. She's very confused about what to do. She doesn't know how he'll react. Mona hasn't told her parents either. They're very religious, and Mona is afraid they'll be terribly disappointed in her. She doesn't know what to do.

Mona finally gets up enough courage to talk to the school social worker, Ms. Peterson. Ms. Peterson is a warm, empathetic individual who encourages Mona to talk about her situation. Mona shares her shock and dismay over her situation. She had simply avoided thinking about contraception or possible pregnancy. It had been easier not to worry about it.

With Ms. Peterson's encouragement, Mona considers her alternatives. One alternative would be to have an abortion. The positive consequence of that would be a relatively fast termination of the problem and its implications. The negative consequences would include the cost, any difficulty she might encounter in setting up an appointment, and any physical discomfort the procedure would cause. The most serious negative consequence for Mona would be the guilt she says she would feel. She believes that abortion is morally wrong.

A second alternative would be to keep the baby and raise it herself. The positive consequence would be the fact that she would accept responsibility for the child she has conceived. The negative consequences would be the financial, social, and educational difficulties she would have to face in order to support and care for her child.

A third alternative would be to keep the child and marry Fred. Mona feels that this is a rather uncertain alternative. She doesn't know if Fred would want to get married. Although the positive consequence would be a two-parent home for the baby, Mona doesn't feel that either she or Fred is ready for the responsibilities of marriage.

A fourth alternative would be to have the baby and give it up for adoption. The positive consequences would be that her baby would live and have a home. The negative consequences would be that she would have to face the social consequences of being a pregnant high school sophomore. The other major negative consequence would be the pain and regret she would experience when she gave up her baby.

Ms. Peterson should not, nor does she want to, make Mona's decision for her. It is up to Mona to weigh the positive and negative consequences of each alternative and make a decision. However, Ms. Peterson helps Mona think through her situation and her various alternatives.

Mona finally decides to have the baby and give it up for adoption. After weighing each positive and negative consequence within her own personal value system, she decides that this is the best route for her to take. She knows she will have to talk to Fred and to her parents first, but feels that at least she has defined her own perspective.

LO 1-2 Review the Organization of This Book That Emphasizes Life-Span Development

EP 2.1.7

Understanding and assessing human behavior includes being knowledgeable about human development. It also involves comprehension of the wide range of issues facing people as they progress through life. For a coherent approach to changes that take place during a person's life span, this text will assume a chronological perspective. The life span is divided up into four main phases: *infancy and childhood, adolescence, young and middle adulthood, and later adulthood.* Three chapters, respectively focusing on biological, psychological, and social development, address each life phase.

Biological development and theories concern the physical aspects of a person's life. For example, biological dimensions for children include when they begin to walk and develop coordination. For adolescents, biological development includes puberty and the physical changes related to it. Biological aspects for older adults concern the physical changes that normally occur as people age.

Psychological development and theories emphasize individuals' functioning and cognitive or thought processes. Psychological aspects concern how people think about themselves, others, and the environment around them. For children, this includes the gradual development from more concrete to more abstract thought. Development of a sense of morality is involved. As life progresses, people may make great intellectual contributions involving scientific discovery or artistic expression. They may also experience issues concerning mental health, such as depression or eating disorders.

Finally, *social* development and theories address people's interaction with others around them in the social environment. Children live within the social context of their family. They develop their social lives as they start interacting and playing with other children. As people continue through life, social dimensions include interaction with friends and participation in work groups. They may find significant others as partners and/or start families of their own. Many join organizations for political, social, recreational, or professional reasons. Some become great leaders who initiate and implement major social change.

Considered together, these aspects of development may be referred to as *bio-psycho-social* development. As Highlight 1.3 explains, these three dimensions integrally affect each other. Sometimes, the dividing lines among them are not clear-cut. For instance, where does psychological development end and social development begin? Consider young people who attend school. Children attend school when they reach a certain biological age. A goal is to learn

and develop thinking ability, a psychological dimension. Yet, school also provides a major social context in which people develop communication and interaction skills. People *psychologically* think about both gaining knowledge and developing their *social* relationships during this period of *biological* development.

Because of the importance of human diversity and its effects on human behavior, three chapters on this topic are interspersed throughout the book. These chapters focus on ethnocentrism and racism, gender roles, and sexual orientation. (Note that content on various aspects of human diversity, including aspects of cultural and spiritual development, are also infused throughout the chapters on biological, psychological, and social development.) Figure 1.2 summarizes the chapter layout of this book.

Common Life Events

Throughout each of the life periods—infancy and childhood, adolescence, young and middle adulthood, and later adulthood—people tend to experience common life events related to biological, psychological, and social development that occur at certain times of life. For example, adolescence is a time when people establish an identity. Adolescents strive for independence and search for a place to fit into social peer groups. Sometimes adolescence is even more stressful. It may be marked by running away from home or by delinquency.

 HIGHLIGHT 1.3

Bio-Psycho-Social Developmental Dimensions Affect Each Other

Because people are complex, social workers should focus on the dynamic interaction among biological, psychological, and social aspects of development. Various aspects of development act together to affect an individual's overall growth and maturity.

Consider a depressed adolescent. Although his psychological state, or depression, may be the presenting problem, problems related to other systems may also be evident. His psychological depression may cause him to withdraw from others and become isolated. Thus, his social interaction may be drastically affected. He may stop eating and/or exercising, which would have a significant impact on his biological system. (Chapter 6 explores the biological development and Chapter 7 the psychological development of adolescents in much greater detail.)

Another example involves an alcohol-addicted adult. Her drinking affects her biological, psychological, and social development. Biologically, she loses weight and has frequent physical problems such as severe hangover headaches. Her physical health affects her psychological health in that she frequently becomes disgusted with herself. Her psychological condition affects her interactions with those close to her, and they begin to avoid her. Hence, her social interaction and development are affected. Social isolation, in turn, enhances her psychological desire to drink and escape, and her physical condition continues to deteriorate. (Chapter 11 discusses further the dynamics of alcoholism and its effects.)

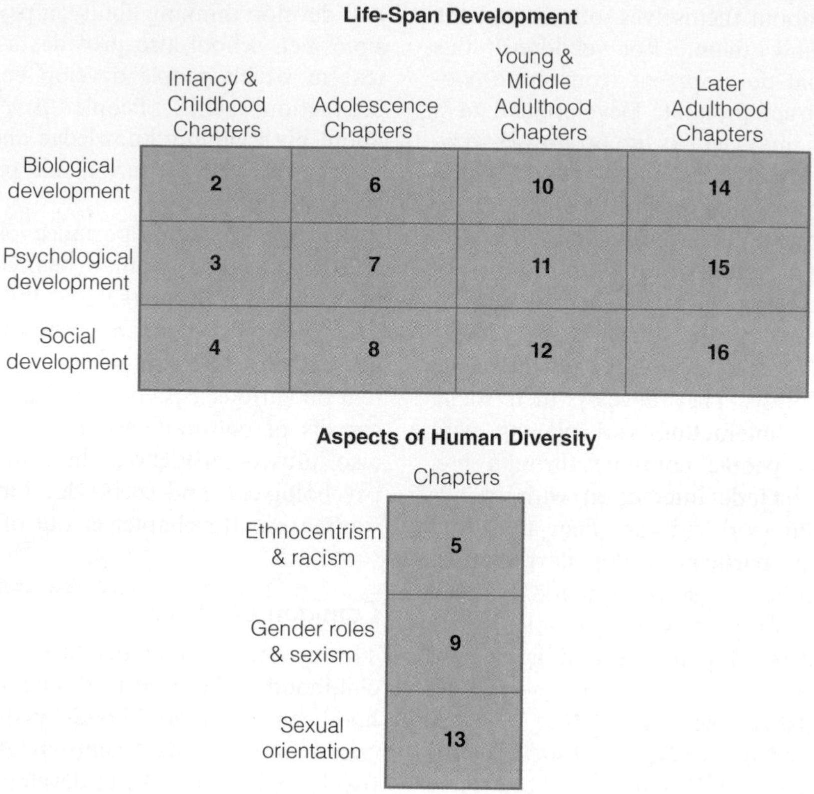

Life-Span Development

	Infancy & Childhood Chapters	Adolescence Chapters	Young & Middle Adulthood Chapters	Later Adulthood Chapters
Biological development	2	6	10	14
Psychological development	3	7	11	15
Social development	4	8	12	16

Aspects of Human Diversity

	Chapters
Ethnocentrism & racism	5
Gender roles & sexism	9
Sexual orientation	13

FIGURE 1.2 Organization of the Text

Marriage and having children are often characteristic events of early and middle adulthood. Sometimes people face unplanned pregnancy and single parenthood during this time of life. Some people must deal with divorce. Life events in later adulthood include retirement and readjustments to married life when children leave home. Many older adults remain deeply involved in family and community life, as predicted by activity theory. However, disengagement theory predicts that others will become increasingly isolated and detached from society (Santrock, 2012b). Additionally, many older adults must cope with increasingly more serious health problems and illnesses.

These experiences or life events—identity crises, marriage and children, retirement, and detachment—all tend to happen during certain periods of life. Each of these common events will be addressed within the context of the time of life when it generally occurs. The variety of experiences that may be considered typical is great. However, there are certain life events that social workers are frequently

called upon to help people cope with. We will arbitrarily select and focus on some of these experiences because of their relevance to practice.

Normal Developmental Milestones

Normal developmental milestones include those significant biological, psychological, emotional, intellectual, and social points of development that normally occur in a person's life span. This category focuses on the individual as a distinct entity. It provides a perspective on what can be considered normal. Topics include motor development, personality development, motivation, social development, and learning.

For example, consider a young child's normal motor development. By age three or four, most children begin to jump, hop, run, navigate a tricycle, employ a fork effectively, and use a pair of scissors (Berk, 2012a). (Chapter 2 profiles normal developmental milestones for children.) Or consider the normal developmental occurrences for older adults.

Older persons tend to have important changes in their sleeping patterns, such as taking longer to fall asleep and typically sleeping for shorter time periods at night (Ancoli-Israel & Alessi, 2005; Kail & Cavanaugh, 2013). (Chapter 14 further discusses the changes in sleeping patterns commonly experienced by older people.)

In order to distinguish between what is normal and what is pathological, one must have a clear understanding of normal developmental milestones at any age. The term *normal* is used here to refer to levels of functioning that are considered appropriate for a particular age level. Social work practitioners must be able to distinguish between situations that merit intervention and those that do not. Much time and effort can be wasted on trying to solve problems that are really not problems at all. For instance, it is needless to worry about a baby who is not walking at the age of 12 months. However, it may merit investigation if that baby is still not beginning to walk by the age of 24 months. Likewise, consider the older adult with sleeping problems. It may be senseless to worry about a tendency to sleep lightly when that is simply a normal sign of age. Social workers may help people adjust their expectations so that they are more reasonable. People can be helped to stop worrying about what is really the normal state of things. On the other hand, sleeping problems at the age of 50 may merit further exploration. At this earlier point in life, such problems may be caused by stress or some physiological problem.

Normal developmental milestones provide a baseline for assessing human behavior. The extent of the problem or abnormality can be assessed only to the extent that it deviates from what is normal or typical.

LO 1-3 Describe Important Concepts for Understanding Human Behavior

Because of their significance in assessing and understanding human behavior, we will spend some time introducing several major concepts here. They involve themes that will be addressed throughout the book. The first cluster of ideas includes human diversity, cultural competency, oppression, and populations-at-risk, all of which are somewhat related. The second grouping entails empowerment, the strengths perspective, and resiliency, which are also interconnected. The third important dimension discussed here involves critical thinking about ethical issues.

Human Diversity, Cultural Competency, Oppression, and Populations-at-Risk

EP 2.1.4

Social workers must be aware of human differences and the effects they have on human behavior. *Human diversity* is the vast range of differences among groups, including those related to "age, class, color, culture, disability, ethnicity, gender, gender identity and expression, immigration status, political ideology, race, religion, sex and sexual orientation" (Council on Social Work Education [CSWE], 2008). Highlight 1.4 elaborates on the importance of one aspect of human diversity—culture.

EP 2.1.5a

Anytime a person can be identified as belonging to a group that differs in some respect from the majority of others in society, that person is subject to the effects of that diversity, including discrimination and oppression. *Discrimination* is the act of treating people differently because they belong to some group (e.g., racial or religious) rather than on merit. Oppression involves putting unfair and extreme limitations and constraints on members of an identified group. Picture a woman in an all-male business establishment. Think of a 62-year-old person applying for a sales job in a department store where everyone else is under 30. Or consider an African American applying for membership in a country club that has no other members who are people of color. (People of color "is a collective term that refers to the major groups of African, Latino, Asian, and First Nations Peoples [Native Americans] who have been distinguished from the dominant society by color" [Lum, 2011, p. 129]). A *population-at-risk*, then, is any group of "people who share some identifiable characteristic that places them at greater risk of social and economic deprivation and oppression than the general mainstream of society" (Kirst-Ashman, 2007, p. 57).

Culture and the Importance of Cultural Competency

EP 2.1.4

One significant aspect of human diversity is *culture*, the configuration of shared attitudes, values, goals, spiritual beliefs, social expectations, arts, technology, and behaviors that characterize a broader society in which people live. It's vital for social workers to learn to understand and appreciate the various cultural values, beliefs, and practices of their clients. A goal is to achieve *cultural competency*, "the mastery of a particular set of knowledge, skills, policies, and programs used by the social worker that address the cultural needs of individuals, families, groups, and communities" (Lum, 2005, p. 4). Cultural competency involves cross-cultural understanding, the ability to appreciate and compare differences and similarities between and among different cultures, including your own. Winkelman (2005) explains the significance of cultural competency:

> A general cross-cultural orientation covers the general dynamics of intercultural interactions…. [It provides]

perspectives for developing productive and less-stressful relations with members of different cultures by understanding the dynamics of cross-cultural contact…. A central aspect of general cross-cultural orientation is an understanding of the culturally relative nature of beliefs and behavior. This perspective provides a basis for acceptance of other cultures as meaningful and rational. Another important aspect is development of cultural self-awareness, particularly of one's values, prejudices and beliefs. Effective intercultural relations require an awareness of one's cultural biases that can block acceptance and understanding of other cultures. Specific cross-cultural orientations provide information about a particular culture, region or ethnic group, covering information such as the group's history, cultural system, normative social behavior, politics, beliefs and other information necessary for successful adaptation to interpersonal interaction with people from that culture. (p. 13)

Privilege, Power, and Acclaim

EP 2.1.4a

People in any society might be placed on a continuum based on social status and the amount of influence they have over others. People who experience discrimination and oppression might be placed on one end of the continuum. People who have exceptional "privilege, power, and acclaim" might be situated on the other (CSWE, 2008, EP 2.1.4a). *Power* is "the ability to achieve one's goals despite the opposition of others"; in other words, power involves "the ability to do whatever you want because no one can stop you" (Leon-Guerrero, 2011, p. 48). Power may entail using "force, authority, manipulation, or persuasion" to make others alter their behavior (Eitzen, Zinn, & Smith, 2014, p. 45).

Privilege entails special rights or benefits enjoyed because of elevated social, political, or economic status. Privilege is often related to *prestige*, "the amount of social respect or standing given to an individual based on occupation. We assign higher prestige to occupations that require specialized education or training [e.g., physicians], … or that make more money [e.g., CEOs of major corporations]"

(Leon-Guerrero, 2011, p. 48). *Acclaim* is "enthusiastic approval or praise" (Nichols, 1999, p. 8). People who experience acclaim, such as high-level politicians and famous entertainers, maintain broad influence over what other people think. People who have privilege and acclaim have greater power to influence and control the destinies of others.

Eitzen and his colleagues (2014) make several points regarding power, wealth, and status in the United States:

- "The inequality gap in the United States is the widest of all the industrialized nations. The gap continues to grow especially because of tax benefits for the affluent….
- These tax policies, in addition to increasing the unequal distribution of wealth, increase the national debt, reduce government spending for programs to help the less fortunate, and weaken public institutions[2] that benefit [all members of] society. The widening gap increases the political influence of the wealthy….

---

[2]In this context, an *institution* is a well-established custom or cultural expectation in a society; examples are public education and public assistance (welfare).

● The power elite in society (those who control the government and the largest corporations) tend to come from backgrounds of privilege and wealth. Their decisions tend to benefit the wealthy disproportionately. The power elite is not organized and conspiratorial, but the interests of the wealthy are served, nevertheless, by the way in which society is organized. This bias occurs through influence over elected and appointed officials, ... [social and economic policies that affect the distribution of wealth, and prestige and acclaim that serve as a] control of the masses." (p. 52)

Group Membership and Values

Membership in any group provides a certain set of environmental circumstances. A Chicano adolescent from a Mexican American inner-city neighborhood has a different social environment from that of an upper-middle-class adolescent of European descent living in the well-to-do suburbs of the same city.

Sensitivity to group differences is critical in understanding any individual's behavior. This is important from two perspectives. First, the values or orientation of a particular group will affect how an individual behaves. For instance, an individual with a sexual orientation for the same gender may very well choose to participate in social activities with others of the same orientation. The individual might tend to avoid bars and nightclubs where heterosexual singles meet and might join activities or social clubs aimed at helping people with a sexual orientation toward the same gender meet each other.

The Societal Perspective on Group Differences

There is a second important perspective concerning sensitivity to group differences. The first perspective focused on how the group member feels and chooses to act. The second perspective directs attention to how other people and groups in the social environment view the (diverse) group in question. The diverse group may be the object of *prejudgments* (predetermined assumptions made without assessing facts) and *stereotypes* (standardized views about people who belong to some group that do not take into account individual qualities and differences). Each group member tends to lose his or her individual identity and assume the group identity in the eyes of others in the environment. To these outsiders, the characteristics of the group become the characteristics of the individual, whether or not the individual actually has them.

For example, consider a young, single, African American mother of three young children who is receiving public aid. She applies for a service job behind the counter of a local delicatessen. The deli is run by a lower-middle-class white family that holds many of the larger society's traditional values. These values include the outdated ideas that the head of the household must be a man and that women should stay home and take care of the children. The owner of the deli, a man and head of the family, interviews the young woman and makes several assumptions.

The first assumption is that the woman has no business not being married. The second is that she should be staying at home with her children. The third assumption is that the woman, because of her color, is probably lazy and undependable. He uses the excuse that she has no experience in this particular job and refuses to hire her. This young woman has run up against serious difficulties in her job search. In addition, she may have problems getting adequate day care for her young children. Taken together, all these difficulties may prevent her from finding a job and getting off public aid.

In assessing behavior, one must be aware of limitations imposed by the environment. Otherwise, impossible alternatives might be pursued. In practice, a social worker who does not understand these things might continue to pressure the young woman in the example to go out and get a job. Since she was already trying and failing, this additional pressure might make her turn against the social worker and the social service system. She might just give up.

Awareness of how prejudgments and stereotypes affect people is important because it involves professional values, one of the foundation blocks of social work. Adherence to basic social work values should be stressed. These values include respect for each individual and that individual's right to self-determination; the importance of confidentiality; commitment to social justice, advocacy, and positive social change; the appreciation of human diversity; and the right to equal treatment and equal opportunity (CSWE, 2008; Reamer, 2013).

Focus on Empowerment, the Strengths Perspective, and Resiliency

The second cluster of vital concepts for understanding human behavior includes empowerment, the strengths perspective, and resiliency. They constitute ongoing themes stressed throughout social work practice.

Empowerment

Empowerment is the "process of increasing personal, interpersonal, or political power so that individuals can take action to improve their life situations" (Gutierrez, 2001, p. 210). The empowerment approach is a perspective on practice that provides "ways of thinking about and doing practice" (Lee, 2001, p. 32). Throughout the assessment process and our quest to understand human behavior, it's critical to emphasize, develop, and nurture strengths and positive attributes in order to empower people. Empowerment aims at enhancing the power and control that individuals, groups, families, and communities have over their destinies.

We have also determined that some groups of people suffer from stereotypes, discrimination, and oppression. It is social work's task to empower clients in general and members of oppressed groups in particular.

Cowger and Snively (2002) explain:

Promoting empowerment means believing that people are capable of making their own choices and decisions. It means not only that human beings possess the strengths and potential to resolve their own difficult life situations, but also that they increase their strength and contribute to the well-being of society by doing so. The role of the social worker is to nourish, encourage, assist, enable, support, stimulate, and unleash the strengths within people; to illuminate the strengths available to people in their own environments; and to promote equity and justice at all levels of society. To do that, the social worker helps clients articulate the nature of their situations, identify what they want, explore alternatives for achieving those desires and then achieve them. (p. 110)

The Strengths Perspective

EP 2.1.10e

Focusing on strengths can provide a sound basis for empowerment. Sometimes referred to as the *strengths perspective*, this orientation focuses on client resources, capabilities, knowledge, abilities, motivations, experience, intelligence, and other positive qualities that can be put to use to solve problems and pursue positive changes.

Assessment of human behavior establishes the basis for understanding people's problems and issues, and subsequently helping them improve their lives. Social workers address people's problems every day, but it's the identification of people's strengths that provides clues for how to solve their problems and improve their life situations. Saleebey (2013, pp. 17–20) cites at least four principles involved in the strengths perspective:

1. *Every individual, group, family, and community has strengths.* The case example in the next section concerning the Fernandez family will illustrate this idea.

2. *Trauma and abuse, illness and struggle may be injurious, but they may also be sources of challenge and opportunity.* Have you ever experienced a serious problem or disappointment that turned out to have opened other, perhaps better, opportunities for you? Days after my 16th birthday, I was in a car accident in which my face was crushed. (It happened at about midnight on Friday the 13th, amazingly enough.) My injuries were painful and required four years of plastic surgery. This experience taught me the value and superficiality of exterior beauty, gave me a much more realistic approach to viewing and understanding people, and made me tougher.

    Another trauma occurred when I applied for a second master's degree after receiving my MSW, and was turned down. I was devastated. However, the experience forced me to get out of school and into social work practice, which turned out to be by far the more gratifying and constructive choice.

3. *Assume that you do not know the upper limits of the capacity to grow and change, and take individual, group, and community aspirations seriously.* You don't have a crystal ball telling you what opportunities and choices will confront you in your life. So many students come to me worrying about their choice of major or what will happen after they graduate. It's important to appreciate the strengths you have and to grasp opportunities as they occur. You don't yet know what chances will present themselves to you or where your career will take you.

4. *Every environment is full of resources.* Resources can provide great strengths. One of social workers' major roles is to link clients with the resources they need to empower them to improve their lives.

Multiple Sources of Strengths: A Case Example

As mentioned, empowerment through focusing on strengths can occur on the individual, family, group, organizational, and community levels (Saleebey, 2013). For instance, consider the following case situation of a family coming to the attention of a social service agency (Haulotte & Kretzschmar, 2001, pp. 30–31). This provides an example of how a strengths perspective is helpful in assessment:

The Fernandez family consists of Carmen, the 35-year-old wife and mother, Juan, the 36-year-old husband and father, and their two daughters—Oralia, 13, and Mari, 14. The family had immigrated to the United States seven years ago from Mexico. Both Carmen and Juan had finished primary school, which is equivalent to attaining a sixth grade education. In this country they had been taking English lessons and were becoming quite fluent. Oralia and Mari both attended the same school and were doing reasonably well. When Juan and Carmen immigrated here, they had high hopes of attaining a better life for themselves and their daughters.

Three months ago U.S. Citizenship and Immigration Service officers found Juan doing construction work at a site near the Fernandez apartment. After determining that his papers were not in order, the officers then deported Juan to Mexico.

Carmen is finding it very difficult making ends meet without her husband being with her. Juan did get a low-paying, part-time job in a Mexican border town. He is sending his family some money, but not much. He also must support himself and is trying to save money to return to the United States. Carmen works as a checker in a grocery store and just got a second part-time job as a janitor. She thus works from 6:30 a.m. until 11:00 p.m. on most days. Fortunately, bus transportation to and from work is readily available. Although the family has always experienced financial problems, these problems got much worse when Juan had to leave.

The current crisis is that right after Carmen got home last night, a police officer arrived at her door with Oralia. He had found Oralia alone in a nearby park, which violated the local curfew. Apparently, Oralia and Mari had been arguing intensively about something when Oralia stomped off. (Now neither of them could remember what the argument was about.) Carmen told the officer

that she was sick to death of listening to the girls' continuous squabbling. She threw up her hands and said she didn't know what to do. Carmen had to work long hours to keep the family afloat. She was forced to expect the girls to take care of themselves when she was gone.

The Fernandez family has no relatives in town. They did have friends in the neighborhood. Juan and Carmen had attended services at a local Pentecostal church. However, they had not made the final decision to become members. At one point the couple met with the church's pastor who suggested that counseling for the girls might help the family. He had referred them to a local social service agency that provides a range of services to immigrants including counseling, legal advice, and help in finding employment. Carmen emphasized, however, that she wanted no one to ask questions about the family's immigration status.

Carmen finally decides to seek outside help. She is experiencing horrible headaches from all of the stress. She is considering going to see a neighborhood currandera *(a traditional unlicensed healer who typically uses herbal remedies and traditional cultural healing practices). Carmen is already taking* manzanilla *(Chamomile, an ingredient found in herbal teas that is thought to calm anxiety in addition to easing stomach aches and intestinal cramping). She also plans to contact the social services agency that provides help to immigrants.*

Problems in this case are fairly obvious. They include fighting between Carmen and the girls, financial difficulties, immigration status, Juan's absence, and Carmen's headaches. However, focusing on the Fernandezes' strengths can provide clues for how to deal with the issues.

Individual strengths include the facts that both Juan and Carmen have completed middle school and are literate; both had been attending English classes; both have jobs (this is also a family strength as it directly affects the family's well-being); both Oralia and Mari are doing fairly well in school; and Carmen is motivated to seek family counseling.

Family strengths include strong family bonds, mutual concern among family members for each other's welfare, and the parents' pride in their daughters and high hopes for their futures.

Group strengths include any support and help family members can get from friends and others at work, school, and church, and in the neighborhood. Organizational strengths include the fact that the family plans to become involved with the agency serving immigrants, is willing to get counseling, and can use this agency as a resource to help Juan return to the States. Another organizational strength is that family members can be involved with a church if they choose to do so.

Community strengths include having a social services agency, a church, public bus transportation, and access to a *curandera* to provide alternative health care. (Note the importance of appreciating cultural differences when focusing on natural support networks such as the *curandera*. A *natural support network* or *helping network* is a group of people—including family, friends, neighbors, work colleagues, and fellow members in organizations such as churches and other community groups—who informally provide help and support.) Communities and their significance are covered in greater depth later in this chapter. Can you see any other strengths in the Fernandez example that have been missed?

Consider also that sometimes a strength may overlap two or more categories. For example, spiritual involvement with a church may reflect individual, family, group, organizational, and community strengths. How the strength is labeled is not important. The essential thing is to consider all potential categories of strength when trying to understand human behavior.

Individual Empowerment

Individual strengths can include educational background, work history, problem-solving and decision-making skills, personal qualities and characteristics, physical and financial resources, and positive attitudes (Jones & Biesecker, 1980; Kirst-Ashman & Hull, 2012b). This text will explore many aspects of empowerment with individuals. Examples include infertility counseling (Chapter 2); appreciation of ethnic and cultural strengths in families (Chapter 4); culturally competent practice (Chapter 5); sex education for Native Americans (Chapter 6); spiritual development (Chapter 7); women and sexual equality (Chapter 9); persons living with AIDS (Chapter 10); promoting optimal well-being for lesbian and gay people (Chapter 13); and theories of successful aging (Chapter 15).

Understanding yourself enhances your ability to understand others. Other people deal with many of the same feelings, issues, and problems that you do. Recognizing strengths in yourself is just as important as recognizing them in others. How would you answer the questions about your personal strengths posed in Highlight 1.5?

Empowerment Through Groups

An example of using strengths to pursue empowerment for people from a group perspective involves the use of *support groups*. These are made up of people with similar problems or issues who come together and provide each other with support, information about how to cope with difficulties, and suggestions for resources (Toseland & Rivas, 2012). Such groups emphasize the identification and use of strengths. Examples given by Toseland and Rivas include:

- "A group of children meeting at school to discuss the effects of divorce on their lives.
- A group of people diagnosed with cancer, and their families, discussing the effects of the disease and how to cope with it.
- A group of recently discharged psychiatric patients discussing their adjustment to community living.
- A group of single parents sharing the difficulties of raising children alone." (p. 20)

Chapter 8 elaborates more fully on empowerment through social work with groups.

Organizational and Community Empowerment

Kretzmann and McKnight (1993) suggest a strengths perspective for enhancing communities and empowering community residents. They stress using potential community assets, including: citizens' "religious, cultural, athletic, [and] recreational" associations; "private businesses; public institutions such as schools, libraries, parks, police and fire stations; [and] nonprofit institutions such as hospitals and social service agencies" to improve a community's functioning and quality of life (pp. 6–8).

McKnight and Block (2010) refer to "the abundant community" that is full of potential and strength (p. 65). They describe communities as unique entities, each having special characteristics and strong points. "A competent community … takes advantage of its abundance" (p. 65). Its residents strive to identify the community's positive attributes and use them in creative ways to improve the quality of life.

HIGHLIGHT 1.5

Assessing Your Strengths

EP 2.1.1b

How would you answer the following questions in assessing your own array of strengths?

Individual Strengths
● What are your best qualities?
● What are you most proud of about yourself?
● What skills do you have (e.g., educational, work, leadership, communication, social, technological)?

Family Strengths
● To what extent do you receive support from your family of origin, current family, or significant other?
● In what ways do you rely on family members for help?
● What are the best characteristics about your family?

Group Strengths
● How do your friends, neighbors, colleagues at work, or fellow students help and support you?
● Do you belong to any social, recreational, or counseling groups?

● If so, how does each serve to meet your needs, provide support, or offer opportunities for self-fulfillment, new experiences, or pleasure?

Organizational Strengths
● Do you currently belong to any organizations, or have you in the past?
● If so, what benefits and support do or did you receive?
● Do you receive any special advising, support, or financial help from school? If so, in what form?
● If you're working, what are the strengths in your work environment?

Community Strengths
● What services and resources are available to you in your community?
● What do you like best about your community?
● What cultural opportunities are available in your community that you appreciate?

What other strengths do you have that you can draw upon as you interact with others in your environment? Who and/or what helps you pursue your plans and dreams? Who and/or what helps you get through each day and, hopefully, make the most of it?

The following are examples of using the strengths of an abundant community (Kretzmann & McKnight, 1993):

● "About 60 youth leaders are trained to teach a youth empowerment curriculum to 700 younger kids. The curriculum, which develops self-esteem through a variety of nontraditional classes, offers youth alternatives to crime, gangs, and drugs. The project is sponsored jointly by a community college and the neighborhood police precinct." (p. 37)

● "Seniors organize and convince the Department of Aging to open an alternative nutrition site after two have already been closed down." (p. 56)

● "A group of homeless women with children are working together to create a housing cooperative in which they will provide care for each other's children and also share in community meal preparation several days a week. Their combined effort means that they will be involved in every

aspect of planning, purchasing, remodeling, and maintaining their new home." (p. 89)

● "A group of recently graduated college students created an association that collected information from the people in their neighborhood who were willing to teach others what they knew, either for pay or for free. The group identified thousands of things local people could teach, from how to play a guitar to the works of Aristotle. This "library" of community knowledge became a major new resource for local learning, discussion, and recreation." (p. 136)

● "A coalition of local churches provides sanctuary for refugees from Central America." (p. 149)

Resiliency: Using Strengths to Fight Adversity

A concept related to the strengths perspective and empowerment is resiliency. *Resiliency* is the ability of an individual, family, group, community, or organization to recover from adversity and resume functioning even when suffering serious trouble, confusion, or hardship. Whereas the "strengths perspective focuses on capabilities, assets, and positive attributes rather than problems and pathologies," resiliency emphasizes the use of strengths to cope with adversity and survive, despite difficulties (Greene & Conrad, 2012; Gutheil & Congress, 2000, p. 41).

The following scenarios provide an illustration of the concept of resiliency:

> When a pitched baseball hits a window, the glass usually shatters. When that same ball meets a baseball bat, the bat is rarely damaged. When a hammer strikes a ceramic vase, it too usually shatters. But when that same hammer hits a rubber automobile tire, the tire quickly returns to its original shape. The baseball bat and the automobile tire both demonstrate resiliency. (Norman, 2000, p. 3)

Resiliency involves two dimensions: risk and protection (Greene & Conrad, 2012; Norman, 2000). In this context, risk involves "stressful life events or adverse environmental conditions that increase the *vulnerability* [defenselessness or helplessness] of individuals" or other systems (p. 3). *Protection*, on the other hand, concerns those factors that "buffer, moderate, and protect against those vulnerabilities" (Norman, 2000, p. 3).

On the individual level, an example of a resilient child is one who, despite being shunted from one foster home to another during childhood, still completes high school, enters college, and later begins a healthy family of her own. Regardless of the risks to which she's been exposed, she uses her strengths to protect her and struggle through her adversity. Such strengths might include positive self-esteem and self-worth, good problem-solving ability to address the difficulties confronting her, a positive sense of direction, the ability to empathize with others' situations, the use of humor, high expectations for personal performance, and the ability to distance herself from the dysfunctional people and negative events around her (Norman, 2000). A key to stressing resiliency is the identification and use of clients' strengths to overcome problems.

Examples of resiliency on the individual level can also include older adults (Lewis & Harrell, 2012). For example,

> 79-year-old Steven R has been lovingly caring for his 80-year-old wife in their home since she was diagnosed with Alzheimer's disease 2 years ago.

> 68-year-old Juan T., having vowed to rebuild his business after it burned to the ground, reopened to great fanfare. 73-year-old Eudora B. has been raising her two teenage grandchildren since their mother died. 87-year-old Rose N. continues to write and publish short stories despite her recent stroke which left her wheelchair-bound and nearly totally blind. (Gutheil & Congress, 2000, p. 41)

An example of resiliency at the organizational level is a public university experiencing budget cuts of several million dollars. That university is resilient to the extent that it responds to the risk of loss, protects its most important functions, makes plans to adapt to the shortfall of resources, and continues providing students with a quality education. Resiliency involves focusing on its strengths to maintain basic functioning.

Resiliency in a community is illustrated by a group of urban neighborhoods that address increasing crime and drug use, problems that put the community at risk of disorganization and destruction. Community strengths include availability of organizations that provide resources, residents' expectations for appropriate and positive behavior, and opportunities for "neighborhood youths to constructively participate in the community" (Greene & Livingston, 2002, p. 78). A resilient community might use its concerned citizens to form neighborhood organizations that oversee community conditions and upkeep, work with public services to improve conditions, and advocate for increased resources (Homan, 2011). Neighborhood Watch Programs may be formed in which residents volunteer to keep careful watch on each other's premises to prevent and combat crime. Community residents might work with local police and schools to establish drug education and prevention programs for young people. They might also advocate for more police to increase the surveillance and apprehension of drug dealers. A resilient community uses its strengths to address the risks threatening it and to protect its residents.

Critical Thinking About Ethical Issues

Another important dimension necessary for understanding human behavior and social work practice involves critical thinking about ethical issues. Values and ethics serve as a major foundation of the social work knowledge base. *Values* are perceptions and opinions held by individuals, professions, and cultures about "what is *good* and *desirable*"

(Dolgoff, Harrington, & Loewenberg, 2012, p. 25). For example, our culture values education and offers it to everyone. Similarly, you value college or you wouldn't be here. *Ethics* are principles based on values that guide behavior and determine "what is *right* and *correct*" (Dolgoff et al., 2012, p. 25). Values are concerned with ideas, while ethics have to do with the appropriate behavior based on those ideas.

EP 2.1.2b

Social workers must be vigilant concerning their adherence to professional values. The National Association of Social Workers (NASW, 2008) has a professional *Code of Ethics* that specifies the following six basic ethical principles to guide practitioners' behavior (access the entire Code at http://www.socialworkers. org/pubs/code/code.asp):

1. *"Social workers' primary goal is to help people in need and to address social problems."*
2. *"Social workers challenge social injustice."*
3. *"Social workers respect the inherent dignity and worth of the person."*
4. *"Social workers recognize the central importance of human relationships"*
5. *"Social workers behave in a trustworthy manner."*
6. *"Social workers practice within their areas of competence and develop and enhance their professional expertise."*

Although the NASW *Code of Ethics* is the code followed by social workers in the United States, note that other ethical codes also are available (CSWE, 2008). Consider, for example, the Canadian Association of Social Workers (CASW) *Code of Ethics*, available at http://www.caswacts.ca/sites/default/files/attachements/CASW_Code%20of%20Ethics_0.pdf. Highlight 1.6 addresses the ethical responsibilities of social workers at the international and global levels and discusses an international social work code of ethics.

EP 2.1.2c

Throughout a social work career, professionals must face and address *ethical dilemmas*, situations in which ethical principles conflict and all solutions are imperfect. Social workers must learn to "tolerate ambiguity in resolving ethical conflicts" (CSWE, 2008, EP 2.1.2c). For example, a 16-year-old client tells her social worker that she hates her stepfather and plans to poison him. The social worker is supposed to maintain *confidentiality* (being trustworthy and keeping information in confidence). However, this is a situation where a person's life may be in danger, which must take precedence over confidentiality. In this case, the worker decides to break confidentiality in order to preserve the person's life.

Consider another example of an ethical dilemma:

A client told the [social work] field student intern that she was pregnant and was planning to marry the father of the baby. The student also was working with this client's mother, who had told the student about her own sexual relationship with the same man that her daughter was going to marry. The mother did not want to tell her daughter that she was having a sexual relationship with her daughter's boyfriend. (Abels, 2001, p. 9)

What should the student intern do? Tell the daughter about her mother's relationship with her boyfriend? Or maintain confidentiality, remaining silent and letting the family work it out for themselves?

The social work student decided to "ask the mother to consider telling the daughter about her relationship, and to ask the boyfriend to do the same. Neither agreed. Because the daughter was 18, the agency could not identify a legal violation of sex with minors" (Abels, 2001, p. 9). The student social worker had tried her best. Maybe things would work out over time. Eventually, "the mother told her boyfriend that she was no longer going to see him" (p. 9).

EP 2.1.3

As this story illustrates, social workers are bound to run into problems with no perfectly satisfactory solution. When this occurs, they must use critical thinking to determine the best course of action. *Critical thinking* is "the careful examination and evaluation of beliefs and actions" to establish an independent decision about what is true and what is not (Gambrill & Gibbs, 2009, p. 4). Gibbs and Gambrill (1999) explain:

Critical thinkers question what others take for granted. They may ask people to support assumptions that others believe to be self-evident, but which are far from being self-evident. They ask, "What's the evidence for———?" Critical thinking encourages open dialogue and the consideration of

HIGHLIGHT 1.6

Ethics in Social Work at the International Level: Human Rights and Social Justice Issues

EP 2.1.5b

Social workers should attend to and advocate for the basic rights of all people. National Association of Social Workers (NASW) policy states that social workers must be prepared "to advocate for the rights of vulnerable people and must condemn policies, practices, and attitudes of bigotry, intolerance, and hate that put any person's human rights in grave jeopardy. The violation of human rights on the basis of race, ethnicity, gender, gender identity or expression, sexual orientation, age, disability, immigration status, or religion are examples" (NASW, 2012, p. 206). *Human rights* involve the premise that all people, regardless of race, culture, or national origin, are entitled to basic rights and treatment. Such essential entitlements include those "basic *civil rights* recognized in democratic constitutions such as life, liberty, and personal security" (Barker, 2003, p. 203). They also include "people's rights to have paid employment, adequate food, education, shelter, health care, as well as the right to freedom from violence and freedom to pursue their dreams" (NASW, 2012, p. 204). Human rights are based on the concept of *social justice*, the idea that in a perfect world all citizens would have identical "rights, protection, opportunities, obligations, and social benefits" (Barker, 2003, p. 405).

Human rights and social justice are global issues. NASW (2012) reports:

Human rights violations are prevalent throughout the world, including the United States. Civilians are injured, maimed, and killed in times of conflict, far outnumbering military personnel. Refugees and immigrants are fleeing their countries in record numbers. Women everywhere continue to be treated as second-class citizens and subjected to violence in epidemic proportions. The social situation of children and [older adults] ... alike is of grave concern the world over and appears to be deteriorating. There has been a resurgence of violence and oppression against ethnic and racial minority groups, and against lesbian, gay, bisexual, and transgender people in many regions of our globe, and poverty is endemic, fueling the fires of unrest and making a sham of the very concept of human rights. (p. 205)

EP 2.1.2b

When addressing ethical issues on an *international* (involving two or more nations) or *global* (involving the entire world) level, social workers may consult an international social work code of ethics (CSWE, 2008). Two important international organizations that have developed an *Ethics in Social Work, Statement of Principles* are the International Federation of Social Workers (IFSW) and the International Association of Schools of Social Work (IASSW). IFSW "is a global organisation striving for social justice, human rights and social development through the promotion of social work, best practice models and the facilitation of international cooperation" (IFSW, 2013b). IASSW "promotes the development of social work education throughout the world, develops standards to enhance quality of social work education, encourages international exchange, provides forums for sharing social work research and scholarship, and promotes human rights and social development through policy and advocacy activities" (IASSW, 2013). Both organizations actively engage social workers around the globe.

The *Ethics in Social Work, Statement of Principles*, concurrently supported by both organizations, consists of the following five parts:

1. Preface
2. Definition of social work
3. International conventions (various organizations' statements of human rights)
4. Principles
5. Professional conduct (IASSW, 2004; IFSW, 2013a)

The "principles" in the *Ethics in Social Work, Statement of Principles* include "human rights and human dignity" and "social justice." The former indicates that "social work is based on respect for the inherent worth and dignity of all people, and the rights that follow from this. Social Workers should uphold and defend each person's physical, psychological, emotional and spiritual integrity and well-being." The latter suggests that "Social workers have a responsibility to promote social justice, in relation to society generally, and in relation to the people with whom they work"; this involves "challenging negative discrimination," "recognizing diversity," "distributing resources equitably," "challenging unjust policies and practices," and "working in solidarity" (i.e., social workers have the responsibility to confront social injustice).

Information about IFSW is available at http://www.ifsw.org/ and about IASSW at http://www.iassw-aiets.org/

opposing views. It involves taking responsibility for claims made and arguments presented. It requires flexibility and a readiness to admit, even welcome, the discovery of mistakes in your thinking. Critical

thinking is independent thinking—thinking for yourself. Critical thinkers question values and positions that may be common in a society, in a group, or in their own family. (p. 13)

Just because someone else says something is true doesn't mean it is. Just because you read something in a book or a newspaper doesn't mean it's accurate. Just because it's documented as a law doesn't mean it's right and just. Critical thinking means not taking things at face value but rather making a determination about their accuracy yourself.

Ethical decision making involves critical thinking. Social workers must assess potential problems and make a decision regarding what is the most ethical thing to do. This book's purpose is not to teach you *how* to do social work. Social work practice books do that and explore ethical practice issues in much greater depth. However, this book does intend to encourage you to begin to think critically about ethical issues. Ethical questions are incorporated throughout to encourage you to use critical thinking to determine your own answers and opinions.

For example, consider the story of the wild boy of Aveyron that introduced this chapter. The ethical question posed there was, Was it ethical for Itard and the others to remove Victor from the wild against his will? Did they have the right to take his freedom from him and place him in captivity where he never learned to function independently? Does it matter that he was only 12 or 13 instead of being an adult? What do you critically think about these issues?

Questions ripe for critical thinking are endless:

- Should the life-preserving feeding tube be removed from a person who is brain-dead and will never regain consciousness?
- Should existing limited public funding be used to finance the military abroad, save Social Security, or provide scholarships and no-interest loans to finance higher education?
- Should prayer be allowed in public schools?

Highlight 1.7 explores further the application of values and ethics to bio-psycho-social assessments.

HIGHLIGHT 1.7

Application of Values and Ethics to Bio-Psycho-Social Assessments

EP 2.1.2b

Social workers assess problems and attempt to understand human behavior within the context of social work values and ethics. The National Association of Social Workers (NASW) *Code of Ethics* (2008) focuses on six areas involving how a worker should behave in a professional role. These include ethical responsibilities (1) *to clients*, (2) *to colleagues*, (3) *in practice settings*, (4) *as professionals*, (5) *to the social work profession*, and (6) *to the broader society*.

Social workers should always keep in mind their clients' rights and well-being. We have established that to the best of their ability, social workers should strive to abide by professional ethical principles, respect the rights and needs of others, and make decisions about right and wrong consistent with their professional ethics. This sounds simple.

But consider the following scenarios, all occurring within the context of social work assessment.

EP 2.1.2c

Scenario 1: *You are a social worker at a shelter for runaways, assessing an unmarried, pregnant 15-year-old who has been living on the streets. She is in her seventh month of pregnancy. She is addicted to cocaine, which she has been using throughout the pregnancy (prenatal influences will be discussed in Chapter 2). She has been informed of the potential side effects of her cocaine use on the fetus, which is likely to result in an infant who will require more attention than that given to infants born to nonaddicted mothers. She adamantly states that she will keep the baby and figure out what to do with her addiction after it's born. You have serious concerns for the infant's well-being. You personally feel that the young woman should place the baby for adoption or at least in foster care until she can solve her own problems. What is the ethical thing to do?*

Scenario 2: *You are a hospital social worker assessing a client with AIDS. (AIDS is covered in Chapter 10.) He tells you that he has had unprotected intercourse with dozens of women since he received his positive HIV diagnosis. He has shared his diagnosis with none of these women. He boldly states that he is incredibly angry that he has the disease and plans to continue having intercourse with as many women as he can. You believe that it is both unethical and hazardous to his sex partners for him not to tell them about their potential exposure to the disease. Clients are supposed to be able to make choices about their own behavior. You are supposed to keep the interactions between you and your client confidential. But what about the unsuspecting victims of your client's choices? What is the ethical thing to do?*

(continued)

HIGHLIGHT 1.7 (continued)

Scenario 3: You are an Adult Protective Services social worker. Your job is to make assessments and pursue interventions to make certain that vulnerable older adults with limited ability to take care of their basic needs get the help and resources they require. You are assessing an older woman in her own home. Her physical and intellectual health is deteriorating. The woman lives alone in a rundown apartment in a poor section of town. She has no close family. She insists that she wants to remain in her home. Your agency supervisor has told you that older adults deemed unable to take care of themselves must be placed in a nursing home facility. However, you also know that the only nursing home facilities available to poor older people in the area are run-down, understaffed, and offer a minimal quality of life. Ethically, your client has the right to make her own decisions. However, you fear that she may fall and remain helpless, turn the gas stove on and forget to light the flame, or have some other accident. What is the ethical thing to do?

Each of these situations portrays an ethical dilemma. Dilemmas involve problematic situations for which possible solutions are imperfect and unsatisfactory. Many such dilemmas are encountered in social work practice.

Three basic suggestions can guide your critical thinking process. They are made within the context of assessing human behavior in order to lay the groundwork for determining what intervention to pursue.

EP 2.1.2d

1. Put your theoretical and factual knowledge base about human behavior to work. (This text intends to provide you with such a base.)
2. Identify your own values concerning the issues and then distinguish between your values and professional ethics.
3. Weigh the pros and cons of each alternative available to you and your client, and then proceed with the alternative you determine is the most positive.

There are no perfect answers. Following is an example of how these suggestions might be applied to scenario 1.

In scenario 1 (the pregnant, unmarried, 15-year-old cocaine addict), first gather the knowledge you need. You need to know the effects of cocaine on prenatal development (described in Chapter 2), the dynamics of drug addiction (discussed in Chapter 11), and the needs of newborn infants in general (addressed in Chapters 2, 3, and 4). Such information can give you clues regarding what types of information you need to know in order to plan interventions.

The second step is to recognize clearly your own personal values and biases. You should not impose your values on your client. Strive to make decisions that coincide as much as possible with professional ethics.

Finally, as depicted earlier in Figure 1.1, identify the alternatives available to you, weigh the pros and cons of each, and make the decision you consider to be the most ethical. Knowledge of human behavior in the areas cited above can lead you to the questions you need to ask in order to make an effective, ethical decision along with your client. Questions in scenario 1 might include:

EP 2.1.2a

- What are the client's drug-using behaviors?
- What are the potential effects on the child?
- How motivated is the client to enter a drug treatment program?
- What resources for drug treatment and other supportive services for unmarried teen mothers are available?
- If not available, can needed services be initiated and developed?
- What resources can you turn to in order to maximize the child's well-being?

You can address the dilemmas posed in scenarios 2 and 3 in a similar manner. What theoretical and factual knowledge do you have about human behavior that can be applied to your understanding of the situation? What personal values and biases do you hold concerning the client and the client's situation? What alternatives are available to you and your client? What are the pros and cons of each? Answers to these questions will guide you to the alternative that is the most ethical to pursue.

Employing Conceptual Frameworks for Understanding Human Behavior and the Social Environment: A Person-in-Environment Perspective

We have established that this book uses the organizing framework of a life-span approach for studying human development and behavior. We've also emphasized important concepts that will be stressed throughout the book (including human diversity, cultural competency, oppression, populations-at-risk, empowerment, the strengths perspective, resiliency, and critical thinking about ethical issues). Subsequent sections will examine the book's theoretical orientation based on ecosystems theory.

A *theory* is a coherent group of principles, concepts, and ideas organized to explain some observable

EP 2.1.7a

occurrence or trend. Theories provide conceptual frameworks for how to view the world. They direct your attention and indicate on what aspects of a situation you should focus when trying to understand why people behave the way they do. (Note that the terms *theory, theoretical perspective, and conceptual framework* are often used interchangeably.) In this book, *ecosystems theory* incorporates concepts from both systems theories and the ecological perspective, which focuses on the environment. One definition of ecosystems theory is "systems theory used to describe and analyze people and other living systems and their transactions" (Beckett & Johnson, 1995, p. 1391). Ecosystems theory fits well with the concept *person-in-environment*, a foundation notion in social work practice and our basis for understanding the dynamics of human behavior (Greene, 1999; Sheafor & Horejsi, 2012). Kirst-Ashman and Hull (2012b) explain:

> *A person-in-environment focus sees people as constantly interacting with various systems around them. These systems include the family, friends, work, social services, politics, religion, goods and services, and educational systems. The person is portrayed as being dynamically involved with each. Social work practice then is directed at improving the interactions between the person and the various systems. This focus is referred to as improving person-in-environment fit. (p. 12)*

Greene (1999, p. 17) describes the importance of the person-in-environment concept as an underlying principle of social work practice:

> *The person-in-environment perspective has been a central influence on the professions theoretical base and its approach to practice. This perspective is based on the belief that the profession's basic mission requires a dual focus on the person and the environment and a common structured approach to the helping process (Gordon, 1962). By serving as a blueprint or an organizing guide for social work assessment and intervention at a multiple systems level, the person-[in-]environment focus has allowed for social workers to intervene effectively "no matter what their different theoretical orientations and specializations and regardless of where or with what*

> *client group they practice" (Meyer, 1987, p. 409).... In short, the person-[in-]environment perspective has established social work's conceptual reference point and has delineated the practitioner's role.*

> (Greene & Watkins, 1998)

Highlight 1.8 discusses social workers' goals as they work with people in the context of their environment.

LO 1-4 Employ a Conceptual Framework for Understanding Human Behavior and the Social Environment: Ecosystems Theory

In the following pages, we explain the various concepts involved in ecosystems theory. First, we define significant conceptions in systems theory. We then present a case example involving child abuse that demonstrates the application of these concepts in practice. Next, we discuss important concepts inherent in the ecological perspective that also contribute to ecosystems theory, stressing people's involvement with multiple systems in the environment.

Note that multitudes of other theories may be applied to various aspects of human development and behavior. Such theories are explained throughout the book in one of two contexts—either a specific developmental phase of life or people's interaction with the encompassing social environment. Highlight 1.9 provides a summary of these theories and the chapters in which they are addressed.

Understanding Key Concepts in Systems Theories

A number of terms are important to an understanding of systems theories and their relationship to social work practice. These include *system, boundaries, subsystem, homeostasis, role, relationship, input, output, feedback, interface, differentiation, entropy, negative entropy,* and *equifinality.*

A *system* is a set of elements that are orderly and interrelated to make a functional whole. A large nation, a public social services department, and a newly married couple are all examples of systems. We will refer primarily to social systems—that is, those systems that are composed of people and affect people.

HIGHLIGHT 1.8

Goals of Social Work Practice

The National Association of Social Workers (1982) has conceptualized social work practice as having the following four major goals followed by a fifth goal posed by the Council on Social Work Education (2008):

Goal 1: "Enhance People's Problem-Solving, Coping, and Developmental Capacities"

Social work emphasizes the person-in-environment conceptualization. This conceptualization views every person as interacting with a number of systems: such systems include (but are not limited to) political system; educational system; family system; religious system; employment system; social service system; and goods and services system. A depiction of this person-in-environment conceptualization is presented Figure 1.3.

Using the person-in environment concept, social work practice at this level focuses on the "person." With this focus, a social worker serves primarily as an *enabler*. In this role, the worker may take on the activities of a counselor, teacher, caregiver (providing supportive services to those who cannot fully solve their problems and meet their own needs), and behavior changer (i.e., changing specific parts of a client's behavior).

Goal 2: "Link People with Systems That Provide Them with Resources, Services, and Opportunities"

Using the person-in-environment concept, the focus of social work practice at this level focuses on the relationships between individuals and the systems they interact with. In this situation, a social worker serves primarily as a *broker*.

Goal 3: "Promote the Effective and Humane Operation of Systems That Provide People with Resources and Services"

Using the person-in-environment concept, the focus of social work practice at this level is on the systems people interact with. One role a worker may fill at this level is an *advocate*. Additional roles include:

Program developer: The worker seeks to promote or design programs or technologies to meet social needs.

Supervisor: The worker seeks to increase the effectiveness and efficiency of the delivery of services through supervising other staff.

Coordinator: The worker seeks to improve a delivery system by increasing communications and coordination between human service resources.

Consultant: The worker seeks to provide guidance to agencies and organizations by suggesting ways to increase the effectiveness and efficiency of services.

(Social work roles that practitioners may assume as they work with larger systems are discussed more thoroughly later in the chapter.)

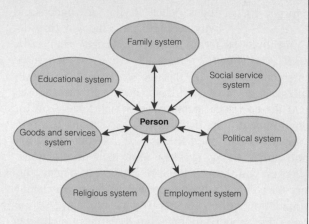

FIGURE 1.3 Person-in-Environment Conceptualization

Goal 4: "Develop and Improve Social Policy"

Similar to goal 3, social work practice at this level focuses on the systems people interact with. The distinction between goal 3 and goal 4 is that the focus of goal 3 is on the available resources for serving people. Goal 4 works on the statutes and broader social policies that underlie such resources. The major roles at this level are *planner* and *policy developer*. In these roles, workers develop and seek adoption of new statutes or policies and propose elimination of ineffective or inappropriate ones. In these planning and policy development processes, social workers may take on an advocate role and, in some instances an activist role.

The Council on Social Work Education (CSWE) is the national accrediting body for social work education in the United States. It describes the purpose of social work as follows (CSWE, 2008):

> *"The purpose of the social work profession is to promote human and community well-being. Guided by a person and environment construct, a global perspective, respect for human diversity, and knowledge based on scientific inquiry, social work's purpose is actualized through its quest for social and economic justice, the prevention of conditions that limit human rights, the elimination of poverty, and the enhancement of the quality of life for all persons."*

This description of the purpose of social work is consistent with the four goals of social work mentioned earlier. One additional goal of social work involves the following:

Additional Goal 5: "Promote Human and Community Well-Being"

The social work profession is committed to enhancing the well-being of all human beings and to promoting community

HIGHLIGHT 1.8 (continued)

well-being. It is particularly committed to alleviating poverty, oppression, and other forms of social injustice. Almost 16 percent of the U.S. population has an income below the poverty line (Bishaw, 2012). Social work has always advocated for developing programs to alleviate poverty, and many practitioners focus on providing services to the poor.

Poverty is the condition of "not having enough money to buy things that are considered necessary and desirable" (Kornblum & Julian, 2012, p. 196). Poverty is global as every society has members who are poor. In some societies, as much as 95 percent of the population lives in poverty. Social workers are committed to alleviating poverty not only in the United States but also worldwide. Alleviating poverty is obviously complex and difficult. Social work professionals work with a variety of systems to make progress in alleviating poverty, including educational systems, health-care systems, political systems, business and employment systems, religious systems, and human services systems.

Oppression is the condition of putting unfair and extreme limitations and constraints on members of an identified group. In our society, numerous groups have been oppressed—including African Americans, Latinos, Chinese Americans, Native Americans, women, persons with disabilities, gays and lesbians, various religious groups, and people living in poverty. (The listing of these groups is only illustrative and certainly not

exhaustive.) Social injustice occurs when some members of a society have less protection, fewer basic rights and opportunities, or fewer social benefits than other members of that society. Social work is a profession that is committed not only to alleviating poverty but also to combating oppression and other forms of social injustice.

Social justice is an ideal condition in which all members of a society have the same basic "rights, protection, opportunities, obligations, and social benefits" (Barker, 2003, p. 405). *Economic justice* is also an ideal condition in which all members of a society have the same opportunities to attain material goods, income, and wealth. Social workers have an obligation to help populations-at-risk increase their personal, interpersonal, socioeconomic, and political strength and influence through improving their circumstances. Populations-at-risk are any group of people who share some identifiable characteristic that places them at greater risk of social and economic deprivations and oppression than the general mainstream of society. Empowerment-focused social workers seek a more equitable distribution of resources and poverty among the various groups in society. Diverse groups that may be at risk include those distinguished by "age, class, color, culture, disability, ethnicity, gender, gender identity and expression, immigration status, political ideology, race, religion, sex, and sexual orientation" (CSWE, 2008).

CONCEPT SUMMARY

Important Concepts Stressed in This Book

Critical thinking: "The careful examination and evaluation of beliefs and actions" to establish an independent decision about what is true and what is not (Gambrill & Gibbs, 2009, p. 4).

Cultural competency: "The mastery of a particular set of knowledge, skills, policies, and programs used by the social worker that address the cultural needs of individuals, families, groups, and communities" (Lum, 2005, p. 4).

Economic justice: An ideal condition in which all members of a society have the same opportunities to attain material goods, income, and wealth.

Empowerment: "The process of increasing personal, interpersonal, or political power so that individuals can take action to improve their life situations" (Gutierrez, 2001, p. 210).

Ethical dilemmas: Situations in which ethical principles conflict and all solutions are imperfect.

Human diversity: The vast range of human differences and the effects they have on human behavior.

Human rights: The premise that all people, regardless of race, culture, or national origin, are entitled to basic rights and treatment.

Oppression: The condition of putting unfair and extreme limitations and constraints on members of an identified group.

Populations-at-risk: Any group of people who share some identifiable characteristic that places them at greater risk of social and economic deprivations and oppression than the general mainstream of society.

Poverty: The condition of "not having enough money to buy things that are considered necessary and desirable" (Kornblum & Julian, 2012, p. 196).

Resiliency: The ability of an individual, family, group, community, or organization to recover from adversity and resume functioning even when suffering serious trouble, confusion, or hardship.

Social justice: An ideal condition in which all members of a society have the same basic "rights, protection, opportunities, obligations, and social benefits" (Barker, 2003, p. 405).

HIGHLIGHT 1.9

A Summary of Some of the Other Theoretical Perspectives Addressed in This Book

EP 2.1.7a

The following are some of the conceptual frameworks and theoretical perspectives provided in this book. For ease of location, they are listed in alphabetical order. Some theories related to a specific topic are listed under that topic.

Theoretical Perspective	Chapter
Afrocentric perspective and worldview	5
Aging theories	
Activity theory	14
Disengagement theory	14
Genetic theories	14
Nongenetic cellular theories	14
Physiological theories	14
Social reconstruction syndrome theory	14
Behavioral theories	3
Choice theory by Glasser	11
Community (macro) change models	1
Community conceptual frameworks	
Human ecology perspective	1
Social systems perspective	1
Sociopsychological perspective	1
Structural perspective	1
Conflict perspective	12
Erikson's psychosocial theory	7, 11, 15
Feminist theories	3
Fowler's theory of faith development	7
Functionalist perspective	12
Gangs and sociological theories	8
Gilligan's theory of moral development for women	7
Group development models	
Bales model	8
Garland, Jones, and Kolodny model	8
Schiller model	8
Tuckman model	8
Interactional model addressing emotional and behavioral problems	8
Interactionist perspective	12

Theoretical Perspective	Chapter
Kohlberg's theory of moral development	7
Leadership theories	
Distributed-functions approach	8
Position approach	8
Style approach	8
Trait approach	8
Learning theory	4
Levinson's theories of life structure and transitions for men	11
Marcia's hierarchy of needs	11
Medical model addressing emotional and behavioral problems	8
Motivational interviewing	10
Neo-Freudian psychoanalytic perspectives	3
Organizational theories	
Autocratic model	12
Collegial model	12
Conservative perspective	12
Custodial model	12
Developmental perspective	12
Human relations model	12
Liberal perspective	12
Scientific management model	12
Theories X and Y	12
Theory Z	12
Parten's theory of children's play development	4
Peck's theory of psychological development	11
Phenomenological theories	3
Piaget's theory of cognitive development	3
Psychodynamic theory	3
Racial/cultural identity development model (by Howard-Hamilton & Frazier)	7
Sexual orientation development theories	
Biological theories	13
Interactionist theories	13
Psychological theories	13
Social construction of gender	9
Social intelligence	10
Social learning theory and moral development	7

Boundaries are the borders or margins that separate one entity from another. For example, your skin provides a boundary between you as an independent, living system and the external environment. Similarly, a boundary encompasses the students enrolled in the class that's using this book. You're either part of the class or you're not.

A boundary may exist between parents and their children. Parents maintain family leadership and provide support and nurturance to their children. (Chapter 4 discusses more thoroughly the application of this and other systems concepts to family systems.) A boundary may also exist between the protective service workers in a large county social service agency and those who work in financial assistance. These are orderly and interrelated groups set apart by specified boundaries in terms of their designated job responsibilities and the clients they serve, yet each group is part of the larger social services agency.

A *subsystem* is a secondary or subordinate system that is a component of a larger system. Obvious examples of subsystems are the parental and sibling subsystems within a family. The group of protective services workers in the large social services agency forms one subsystem, and the financial assistance workers another. These subsystems are set apart by designated boundaries, yet still are part of the larger, total system.

Homeostasis is the tendency for a system to maintain a relatively stable, constant state of balance. If something disturbs the balance, the system will readjust itself and regain stability. A homeostatic family system is one that is functioning in such a way that it can continue to function and stay together. A homeostatic social services agency is one that works to maintain its ongoing existence. However, neither the family nor the agency is necessarily functioning as well or as effectively as possible. Homeostasis merely means maintaining the status quo.

This family illustrates the concept of homeostasis. Despite its members' diverse ages and interests, the family stays together and functions effectively.

Edgardo Contreras/Getty Images

Sometimes that status quo can be ineffective, inefficient, or seriously problematic.

A *role* is the culturally established social behavior and conduct expected of a person in any designated interpersonal relationship. Each individual involved in a system assumes a role within that system. For instance, a person in the role of social worker is expected to behave in certain "professional" ways as defined by the profession's *Code of Ethics*. Each of us probably fulfills numerous roles because we are involved in multiple systems. The social worker may also assume the roles of spouse and parent within his or her own family system. Additionally, that person may assume the role of executive director within the National Association of Social Workers state chapter, the role of Little League coach, and the role of Sunday school teacher.

A *relationship* is a reciprocal, dynamic, interpersonal connection characterized by patterns of emotional exchange, communication, and behavioral interaction. For example, a social worker may have a professional relationship with a client. They communicate and interact in order to meet the client's needs. Relationships may exist between systems of any size. A client may have a relationship with an agency; one agency may have a relationship with another agency.

Input involves the energy, information, or communication flow received from other systems. A parent may receive input from a child's grade school principal, noting that the child is doing poorly in physical education. A public agency may receive input from the state in the form of funding.

Output, on the other hand, is the response of a system, after receiving and processing input, that affects other systems in the environment. For instance, output for a social services agency for people who are substance abusers might be 150 hours of individual counseling, 40 hours of group counseling, 30 hours of family counseling, 10 hours of drug education at local schools, and 50 hours of liaison work with other agencies involved with clients. (Chapter 11 discusses substance abuse and its effects on family systems in greater detail.)

Note that the term *output* is qualitatively different from *outcome*, a term frequently used in social work education. Output is a more general term for the result of a process. Outcomes are specified variables that are measured for the purpose of evaluation. For example, outcomes for the social services agency just

mentioned might include clients' decreased use of addictive substances, enhanced communication among family members receiving treatment, and decreased use of drugs and alcohol by students receiving drug education. Output is what is done, which may or may not have value. Outcomes measure positive effects of a system's process.

An issue that this text will continue to address is the importance of evaluating whether a system's outputs are worth the inputs. Is an agency, for example, achieving the outcomes it hopes to? Is the agency using its resources efficiently and effectively? Or can those resources be put to a better use by providing some other type of service (output)?

If clients receiving treatment from the substance abuse counseling agency described previously continue to abuse drugs and alcohol at the same rate, to what extent is the treatment effective? Since treatment is expensive, is the agency's output worth its input? Is the agency achieving its outcomes? If the agency typically sees little progress at the end of treatment for clients, we have to question the agency's usefulness. Should the agency's treatment process be changed to achieve better outcomes? Or should the agency be shut down totally so that resources (input) can be better invested in some other agency or treatment system?

Feedback is a special form of input in which a system receives information about its own performance. As a result of *negative feedback* involving problematic functioning, the system can choose to correct any deviations or mistakes and return to a more homeostatic state. For example, a supervisor may tell a social work supervisee that he or she is filling out an important agency form incorrectly. This allows the worker the opportunity to correct his or her behavior and complete the form appropriately.

Positive feedback is also valuable. This involves a system's receiving information about what it is doing correctly in order to maintain itself and thrive. Getting a 97 percent on a history exam provides a sixth grader with the information that she has mastered most of the material. An agency that receives a specific federal grant has gotten the feedback that it has developed a plan worthy of such funding.

An *interface* is the point at which two systems (individuals, families, groups, organizations, or communities) come into contact with each other or communicate. For example, one interface is the written contract established between a field instructor in an adoptions agency and a student intern placed under his or her supervision. At the beginning of the semester, they discuss plans and goals for the semester. What tasks will the student be given, and what levels of performance are expected? With the help of the student's field liaison (i.e., the student's university professor), a written contract is established that clarifies these expectations. Contracts generally involve written, oral, or implied agreements between people concerning their goals, procedures, techniques, time frames, and reciprocal responsibilities during some time period in their relationship.

At his midterm evaluation, the student receives a grade of D. Although he is devastated, he still has half a semester to improve. Focusing on the interface between the field instructor and field intern (in this case, the contract they established at the beginning of the semester) provides direction concerning what to do about the problem of poor performance in his internship. By reviewing the terms specified in the contract, the instructor and student, with the liaison's help, can elaborate upon problems and expectations. Where did the student go wrong? Which of the student's expectations did the field instructor fail to fulfill? They can then establish a new contract concerning the student's performance for the remainder of the semester.

It is still up to the student to "make or break" his field experience. However, the interface (contract) provides a clearly designated means of approaching the problem. Having the field instructor and field liaison vaguely tell the student that he needs "to improve his performance" would probably accomplish little. Rather, identifying and using the interface in the form of the student-instructor contract provides a specific means for attacking the problem. Interfaces are not limited to those between individual systems. Interfaces can characterize interactions among systems of virtually any size. For example, there is an interface between the adoptions agency providing the student placement and the university social work program that places the student intern. This interface involves the specified agreements concerning each of these two larger systems' respective responsibilities and expectations.

Differentiation is a system's tendency to move from a simpler to a more complex existence. Relationships, situations, and interactions tend to get more complex over time. For example, in the life of any particular family, each day adds new experiences. New information is gathered, and new options are explored. The family's life becomes more complex. And as a social services agency continues over time, it may develop more detailed policies and programs.

Entropy is the tendency of a system to progress toward disorganization, depletion, and death. Nothing lasts forever. People age and eventually die. Young families get older, and children leave to start their own families. As time passes, older agencies and systems are eventually replaced by new ones.

Negative entropy is the process of a system toward growth and development. In effect, it is the opposite of entropy. Individuals develop physically, intellectually, and emotionally as they grow. Social service agencies grow and develop new programs and clientele.

Equifinality refers to the fact that there are many different means to the same end. It is important not to get locked into only one way of thinking. In any situation, there are alternatives. Some may be better than others, but nonetheless there are alternatives. For instance, as a social worker you may get needed resources for a family from a variety of sources. These may include financial assistance, housing allowances, food stamps, grants, or private charities. You may have to choose among the alternatives available from a variety of agencies.

Application of Systems Concepts to a Case Example of Child Abuse

The following case example concerning the Horney family involves potential child abuse. The discussion applies various systems concepts (italicized) to the assessment and beginning treatment of the family. Note that child abuse is just one of a wide range of practice situations in which systems concepts can be applied to help understand the dynamics involved. Other issues that you may encounter include unwanted pregnancy, drug and alcohol abuse, potential suicide, severe illness, poverty, intellectual disability (formerly referred to as mental retardation), domestic violence, racial discrimination, and grief over illness or death.

The Presenting Problem

As she was baking Christmas cookies, Mrs. Green overheard Mr. Horney in the next apartment screaming at his son, Jimmy. Mrs. Green became very disturbed. Jimmy, who was only 6, was crying. Next, Mrs. Green heard sharp cracks that sounded like a whip or a belt. This was not the first time; however, she hated to interfere in her neighbor's business. She recalled that last summer she had noticed strange-looking bruises on Jimmy's arms and legs, as well as on those of his 4-year-old sister, Sherry. She just couldn't stand it anymore. She finally picked up the phone and reported what she knew to the public Social Services Department. She asked that the Horneys not be told who had called to report the situation. She was assured that the report would remain confidential. State law protects persons who report suspected child abuse or neglect by ensuring their anonymity if they wish.

The Investigation

Ms. Samantha Chin was the Protective Services worker assigned to the case. She visited the Horney home the day after Mrs. Green made the report. Both Mr. and Mrs. Horney were home. Ms. Chin explained to them that she had come to investigate potential child abuse.

She then proceeded to assess the functioning of the family *system*. Mr. and Mrs. Horney formed a parental *subsystem* within that system. Ms. Chin solicited *input* from that subsystem.

Harry Horney was 38 years old. He was a tall, slightly overweight, balding man dressed in an old blue shirt and coveralls. He spoke in a gruff voice, but expressed a strong desire to cooperate. He also had a faint odor of beer on his breath.

Marion Horney was a pale, thin, soft-spoken woman of 32. Mrs. Horney looked directly at the worker, shook her head in a determined manner, and stated that she was eager to cooperate. However, she often deferred to Mr. Horney when spoken to or asked a question.

Ms. Chin asked to examine the children. Together, the children formed a sibling *subsystem* within the larger family *system*. She found slashlike bruises on their arms and legs. When Mr. Horney was asked how the children got these bruises, he replied that they continually made noise when he was trying to watch the football game on television or sleep. He stated they had to learn discipline in order to survive in life. He just strapped them a little now and then to teach them a lesson. It was no different from his treatment at the hands of his own father. He also stated that his neighbors could just keep their noses out of the way he wanted to raise his kids. This comment reflected how the family itself was a *subsystem* of the larger *community system* and did not escape notice.

Ms. Chin replied that the state's intent was to protect the children from abuse or neglect. The *interface* between the state and the family was Ms. Chin's contact. She explained that citizens were encouraged to make a report even if abuse or neglect was only suspected. Ms. Chin added that the anonymity of people who made reports was protected by state law.

When asked how she felt about discipline, Mrs. Horney said she agreed with her husband regarding how he chose to punish the children. Mr. Horney was the main disciplinarian, and Mrs. Horney felt all he was doing was teaching the children a lesson or two in order to maintain control and respect.

The Children

Jimmy was an exceptionally nonresponsive child of relatively small stature for his age. When he was asked a question, he tended to avoid eye contact and mumbled only one-word answers. When his father asked him to enter or leave the room, he did so immediately and quietly. His mother mentioned that he was having some problems with reading in school.

Sherry, on the other hand, was an extremely eager and aggressive child. When asked to do something, she initially ignored the request and continued her own activities. She refused to comply until her parent raised his or her voice. At that point she would look up and very slowly do what she was told, often requiring several proddings. At other times, Sherry would aggressively pull at her parents' clothing, trying to get their attention. She would also scream at them loudly and ask for things such as food, even though this interrupted their ongoing conversation.

Parental History and Current Status

In order to do an accurate assessment, Ms. Chin asked the Horneys various questions about themselves, their histories, and their relationship with each other. Mr. Horney came from a family of 10. His father drank a lot and frequently used a belt to discipline his children. He remembered being very poor and having to work most of his life. At age 16, he dropped out of high school because he was able to get a job in a steel mill.

Mrs. Horney came from a broken family; her father had left when she was 3. This reflected a state of *entropy* or disorganization. She had two older brothers who, she felt, often teased and tormented her. She described her mother as being a quiet, disinterested woman who rarely stated her own opinions and liked to keep to herself. The family had always been on welfare. Mrs. Horney dropped out of high school to marry Mr. Horney when she was 17. At that time, Mr. Horney was 23 and had already held six different jobs since he started working at the steel mill seven years before.

The Horneys' marriage had not been an easy one. It was marked by poverty, frequent unemployment, and frequent moves. Mr. Horney had been laid off 19 months earlier from his last assembly-line job at a local tractor factory. He stated that he was "very disgusted" that the family had to rely on welfare. Despite his frequent job changes, he had always been able to make it on his own without any assistance. Yet this time he had just about given up getting another job. He stated that he didn't like to talk to Mrs. Horney very much about his problems because it made him feel weak and incompetent. He didn't really have any buddies he liked to talk to or do things with either. All he seemed to be doing lately was watching television, sleeping, and drinking beer. He was even starting to watch the daytime reality shows.

Mrs. Horney was resigned to her fate. She did pretty much what her husband told her to do. She told Ms. Chin that she never did have much confidence in herself. She said that she and Mr. Horney were never really able to talk much.

The Horneys had been living in their current apartment for six months. However, as usual, they were finding it hard to keep up with the rent and thought they'd have to move soon. The family's output was surpassing its input. This deficit could affect the family's homeostasis, or stability, and ability to function effectively. Moving so often made it hard to get involved and make friends in any neighborhood. Mrs. Horney said she'd always been a lonely person.

The Assessment of Human Behavior

Factors that must be considered in the assessment of a child abuse case include physical and behavioral indicators, and certain aspects of social functioning that tend to characterize abusive families. Before Ms. Chin could plan an appropriate and effective intervention, she needed to understand the dynamics of the behavior involved in this family situation. Additionally, she needed to know what resources or *input* were available to help the family.

Physical Indicators of Abuse   Although definitions vary depending on medical, social, and legal emphases, simply put, physical child abuse is "non-accidental injury inflicted by a caregiver" (Crosson-Tower, 2014, p. 86). Physical indicators of abuse include bruises and welts, burns, lacerations and abrasions, skeletal injuries, head injuries, and internal injuries (Crosson-Tower, 2014; Downs, Moore, & McFadden, 2009).

Often it is difficult to determine whether a child's injury is the result of abuse or a simple accident. For instance, a black eye may indeed have been caused by being hit by a baseball instead of a parent's fist. However, certain factors suggest child abuse. These include an inconsistent medical history, injuries that do not seem to coincide with developmental ability (e.g., it is not logical that an 18-month-old girl broke her leg when running and falling when she is not yet old enough to walk well), and odd patterns of injuries (e.g., a series of small circular burns from a cigarette or a series of bruises healed to various degrees).

In Jimmy's and Sherry's case, slashlike bruises were apparent on their arms and legs. Upon further investigation, the worker established that these did result from disciplinary beatings by the children's family. Cases of discipline often involve a discretionary decision on the part of the worker. The issue concerns parental rights to discipline versus children's rights and well-being. The worker must assess the situation and determine whether abuse is involved.

Behavioral Indicators of Abuse   Ms. Chin needed to know not only what types of physical indicators are involved in child abuse but also the behavioral indicators of abused children. These types of behaviors differ from "normal" behavior. She needed to know the parameters of normal behavior in order to distinguish it from the abnormal behavior typically displayed by abused children.

Abused children are sometimes overly compliant and passive (Crosson-Tower, 2013, 2014). If a child acts overly eager to obey and/or is exceptionally quiet and still, this may be a reaction to abuse. Such children may be seeking to avoid further abuse by maintaining a low profile and avoiding notice by the abuser. Jimmy manifested some of these behaviors. He was afraid of being disciplined and so maintained as innocuous a profile as possible. This was a logical approach for him to take in order to avoid being hurt.

Sherry, on the other hand, assumed an aggressive, attention-getting approach, another behavior pattern frequently displayed by abused children (Crosson-Tower, 2013, 2014; Miller-Perrin & Perrin, 2013). She frequently refused to comply with her parents' instructions until they raised their voices, and often demanded additional prodding. She also tried to get their attention by pulling at them and screaming requests at them. This approach is also typical of certain abused children. Since Sherry was not getting the attention she needed through other means, she was acting aggressively to get it, even though such behavior was inappropriate. Ms. Chin needed to be knowledgeable about the normal attention needs of a 4-year-old in order to understand the dynamics of this behavior.

One other symptom typical of abused children involves lags in development (Crosson-Tower, 2013, 2014; Kolko, 2002; LeVine & Sallee, 1999). They might also regress to an earlier developmental stage, displaying such behaviors as "[b]aby talk, wetting the bed, and sucking fingers or thumb" in order to "cope with their situations" (Crosson-Tower, 2014, p. 97). Jimmy was small for his age and was having difficulty in school. Ms. Chin needed to be aware of the normal parameters of development for a 6-year-old in order to be alert to developmental lags. She also needed to know that such lags were potential indicators of abuse.

Family Social Functioning Not only the children but also the parents must be assessed. A worker must understand the influence of both personal and environmental factors on the behavior of the parents. Only then can these factors be targeted for intervention and the abusive behaviors be changed.

Personal parental factors that are related to abuse include unfulfilled needs for nurturance and dependence, isolation, and lack of nurturing child-rearing practices (Barnett, Miller-Perrin, & Perrin, 2011; Crosson-Tower, 2014). Ms. Chin discovered in her interview that both parents were isolated and alone. They had no one to turn to for emotional support. There was no place where they could appropriately and harmlessly vent their frustrations. Nor had either parent learned appropriate child-rearing

practices in their families of origin. Mr. Horney had learned excessive discipline—to be strict and punitive. Mrs. Horney had learned compliance and passivity—to be helpless and to believe she could have no effect on others, no matter what she did.

Environmental factors are equally important in the assessment of this case. Specific factors related to abuse often include lack of support systems, marital or cohabiting problems, and life crises (Barnett et al., 2011; Tower, 2014). Life can become more difficult and complicated. *Differentiation*, in a negative sense, can occur.

Neither parent had been able to develop an adequate support system. Due to frequent moves, they had not been able to develop *relationships* with neighbors or others in the community *systems* of which they were part. Nor could they turn to each other for emotional support. They had never learned how to communicate effectively within a marital relationship. Finally, they were plagued by the serious life crises of poverty and unemployment. All of these things contributed to the abusive situation.

Making Connections with Available Resources

Ms. Chin considered several treatment directions. *Equifinality* is reflected in the range of options available. Of course, resource availability in the client's community system is critically important. If resources had not been available, Ms. Chin might have faced quite a dilemma. Should she work to help get appropriate resources developed? If so, what kind? How should she proceed? This would involve focusing on aspects of the larger social systems in which her clients lived.

However, the Horneys' community had a number of resource input possibilities. A Parents Anonymous group and various social groups were available to decrease the Horneys' social isolation. (Parents Anonymous is a self-help organization, similar to Alcoholics Anonymous, for parents who have abused or neglected their children.) Individual and marital counseling were available to improve the Horneys' personal self-images and to enhance marital communication. A visiting homemaker could encourage Mrs. Horney to more assertively undertake her homemaking and child-rearing tasks. She could also provide personal support. Parent Effectiveness Training could be used to teach the Horneys parenting skills and alternatives to harsh discipline. Finally,

Mr. Horney could be encouraged to get re-involved in a job search. An employment specialist at the agency could help him define and pursue alternative employment possibilities. The intent was to help the Horneys achieve *negative entropy*.

Ms. Chin discussed these alternatives with the Horneys. In essence, she provided them with *input* and *feedback*. Together they determined which were possible and realistic. They then decided which should be pursued first. Mr. Horney admitted that he could use some help in finding a job, which he stated was his highest priority. He agreed to contact the agency job specialist to help him reinstitute his job search. Mrs. Horney liked the idea of having a visiting homemaker. She felt that this would help her get her work done, and it would also give her someone to talk to. Both agreed to attend a Parents Anonymous group on a trial basis. They were not interested in pursuing marriage counseling or Parent Effectiveness Training now, but would keep it in mind for the future.

Ethical Questions 1.2

EP 2.1.2 *When child maltreatment is suspected, should children be allowed to remain in their own home? How much risk of child maltreatment is too much risk? What effect does it have on children to be removed from their home?*

Understanding Key Concepts in the Ecological Perspective

In addition to terms taken from systems theories, concepts from the ecological perspective also contribute to ecosystems theory. In some ways, the ecological perspective might be considered an offshoot or interpretation of systems theories. An ecological approach provides a more specific view of the world within a social work perspective. It tends to place greater emphasis on individuals' and individual family systems' functioning within their environments. It also brings to ecosystems theory many terms such as coping that are very important in understanding human behavior. Systems theories, on the other

hand, can assume a broader perspective. They can be used to describe the dynamics in a social service agency or the functioning of an entire government.

Note that some systems and ecological terms, such as interface and the input of energy, overlap. In essence, their meanings are very similar, especially when relating specifically to people functioning within their environments.

Some of the major terms employed in the ecological perspective and defined here include *social environment, transactions, energy, interface, adaptation, coping, and interdependence.*

Social Environment

The social environment involves the conditions, circumstances, and human interactions that encompass human beings. Individuals must have effective interactions with this environment in order to survive and thrive. The social environment includes the actual physical setting that the society or culture provides. This involves the type of home a person lives in, the type of work a person does, the amount of money that is available, and the laws and social rules people live by. The social environment also includes the individuals, groups, organizations, and systems with which a person comes into contact, including family, friends, work groups, and governments. Social institutions such as health care, housing, social welfare, and educational systems are yet other aspects of this social environment.

Transactions

People communicate and interact with others in their environments. These interactions are referred to as transactions. Transactions are active and dynamic because something is communicated or exchanged. They may be positive or negative. An example of a positive transaction is the revelation that the one you dearly love also loves you in return. Another positive transaction is the receipt of a paycheck after two weeks of work. An example of a negative transaction is being laid off from a job that you've had for 15 years. Another example of a negative transaction is an irritable neighbor complaining to the police about your dog barking too much.

Energy

Energy is the natural power of active involvement between people and their environments. Energy can take the form of input or output. Input is the form of energy coming into a person's life and adding to that life. For example, an older adult whose health is failing may need input in the form of substantial physical assistance and emotional support in order to continue performing the daily tasks necessary to stay alive. (Chapters 15 and 16 discuss the importance of energy and input from the environment to maintain health and quality of life.) Another example of input is a teacher giving a student feedback on a term paper.

Output, on the other hand, is a form of energy going out of a person's life or taking something away from it. For instance, parents may expend tremendous amounts of energy in taking care of their young children. So may a person who volunteers time and effort to work on the campaign of a politician he or she supports.

Interface

The *interface* in the ecological perspective is similar to that in systems theory. It is the exact point at which the interaction between an individual and the environment takes place. During an assessment, the interface must be clearly in focus in order to target the appropriate interactions for change. For example, a couple entering marriage counseling initially state that their problem concerns disagreements about how to raise their children. Upon further exploration, however, the real problem is discovered—namely, their inability to communicate feelings to each other. The actual problem, the inability to communicate, is the interface where one individual affects the other. If the interface is inaccurately targeted, much time and useless energy can be wasted before getting at the real problem. (Chapter 12 describes the importance of communication within the context of couples and families.)

The ecological perspective, however, differs from systems theories in its tendency to emphasize interfaces concerning individuals and small groups such as families. It is more difficult to apply the ecological perspective's conception of interfaces to those involving only larger systems such as communities and organizations.

Adaptation

Adaptation refers to the capacity to adjust to surrounding environmental conditions. It implies change. A person must change or adapt to new conditions and circumstances in order to continue functioning effectively. Social workers frequently help people in their process of adaptation to a new marriage partner, a new job, or a new neighborhood. Adaptation usually requires energy in the form of effort. Social workers often help direct people's energies so that they are most productive.

Not only are people affected by their environments, but environments are also affected by people in their process of adaptation. People change their environments in order to adapt successfully. For instance, a person might find it hard to survive a winter in Montana in the natural environment without shelter. Therefore, those who live in Montana manipulate their environment by clearing land and constructing heated buildings. They change their environment in order to survive in it. Therefore, adaptation is often a two-way process involving both the individual and the environment.

Coping

Coping is a form of adaptation that implies a struggle to overcome problems. Although adaptation may involve responses to new conditions that are either positive or negative, coping refers to the way people deal with the negative experiences they encounter. For example, a person might have to cope with the sudden death of a parent, a primary family wage earner losing a job, gangs that are vandalizing the community, or vital public assistance payments that are significantly decreased.

At least five types of coping skills are important for people to develop (Barker, 2003). First, people need to solicit and obtain the types of information they need to function well. For instance, an older adult who becomes sick needs to know how to obtain Medicare benefits (see Chapter 16). Second, people need to have coping skills for thinking about and planning for the future. For example, a person who loses a job needs to develop a plan for finding another one. Third, coping skills involve controlling emotions. For example, a minor disagreement with a significant other should not result in a major battle involving screaming, scratching, and punching. Fourth, people need coping skills to control their needs for immediate gratification. For instance, a family needs to budget its income so that there is food on the table at the end of the week, instead of spending money on a new television set. Finally, coping skills involve identifying alternative ways of approaching a problematic situation and evaluating the pros and cons of each alternative.

CONCEPT SUMMARY

Systems and Ecological Perspective Concepts Prominent in Ecosystems Theory

Systems Theory Concepts

System: A set of elements that are orderly and inter-related to make a functional whole.

Boundaries: The borders or margins that separate one entity from another.

Subsystem: A secondary or subordinate system that is a component of a larger system.

Homeostasis: The tendency for a system to maintain a relatively stable, constant state of balance.

Role: The culturally established social behavior and conduct expected of a person in any designated interpersonal relationship.

Relationship: A reciprocal, dynamic interpersonal connection characterized by patterns of emotional exchange, communication, and behavioral interaction.

Input: The energy, information, or communication flow received from other systems.

Output: The response of a system, after receiving and processing input, that affects other systems in the environment.

Feedback: A special form of input in which a system receives information about its own performance (either negative or positive).

Interface: The point where two systems of any size come into contact with each other or communicate.

Differentiation: A system's tendency to move from a simpler to a more complex existence.

Entropy: The tendency of a system to progress toward disorganization, depletion, and death.

Negative entropy: The process of a system toward growth and development.

Equifinality: The fact that there are many different means to the same end.

Ecological Perspective Concepts

Social environment: The conditions, circumstances, and human interactions that encompass human beings.

Transactions: The means by which people communicate and interact with others in the environment.

Energy: The natural power of active involvement between people and their environments.

Interface: The exact point at which the interaction between an individual and the environment takes place.

Adaptation: The capacity to adjust to surrounding environmental conditions.

Coping: A form of adaptation that implies a struggle to overcome problems.

Interdependence: The mutual reliance of each person on every other person.

Social workers are frequently called upon to help clients develop coping skills. A major theme in the helping process involves working with clients to evaluate alternatives and to choose the one that's best for them. Evaluating alternatives was addressed earlier in this chapter.

Interdependence

The final ecological concept is that of *interdependence*, the mutual reliance of each person on every other person. An individual is interdependent or reliant on other individuals and groups of individuals in the social environment.

A person cannot exist without other people. The businessperson needs the farmer to produce food and the customer to purchase goods. The farmer needs the businessperson to provide money to buy seed, tools, and other essentials. The farmer becomes the customer for the businessperson. People, especially in a highly industrialized society, are interdependent; they need each other to survive.

LO 1-5 Recognize People's Involvement with Multiple Systems in the Social Environment

We have established that people are constantly and dynamically involved in interactions with their social environment. Social work assessment tries to answer the question, What is it in any particular situation that causes a problem to continue despite the client's expressed wish to change it? An ecosystems approach provides a perspective for assessing many aspects of a situation. Clients are

EP 2.1.10

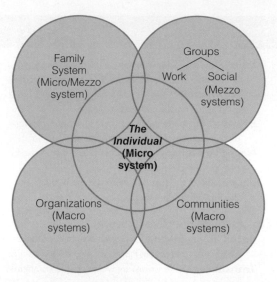

Each individual is involved in multiple systems consisting of families, groups, organizations, and communities.

FIGURE 1.4 Human Behavior Involves Multiple Systems

affected by and in constant dynamic interactions with other systems, including families, groups, organizations, and communities. Figure 1.4 portrays the dynamic interactions of clients with other systems in the social environment.

Micro, Mezzo, and Macro Systems

A system is a set of elements that are interrelated to make a functional whole. For our purposes, we will distinguish three basic types of systems throughout this text: micro, mezzo, and macro systems. *Micro system* refers to an individual. In a broad sense, a person is a type of system that entails biological, psychological, and social systems. All of these systems interact. A micro orientation to social work practice involves focusing on an individual's needs, problems, and strengths. It also stresses how that individual might address issues, generate solutions, and make the best, most effective choices possible. Micro practice, then, involves working with an individual and enhancing that person's functioning. Issues concerning micro systems are addressed throughout the text. Examples include dimensions of physical and psychological development and maturity (all chapters on biological and psychological systems throughout the life span), women's resilience after violence (Chapter 9), identity development as a gay or lesbian person (Chapter 13), and grief management (Chapter 15).

Mezzo system refers to any small group, including family, work groups, and other social groups. Sometimes for assessment purposes it is difficult to clearly differentiate between issues involving a micro system (individual) and a mezzo system (small group) with which the individual is involved. This is because individuals are so integrally involved in interactions with others close to them. In many cases, we will make an arbitrary distinction between an issue concerning a micro system and one concerning a mezzo system. Examples of content about mezzo systems in this text include the importance of play with peers and participation in school for children (Chapter 4), empowerment through social work with groups (Chapter 8), the functions of nonverbal communication (Chapter 11), and family issues for older adults (Chapter 15).

Macro system refers to a system larger than a small group. A macro orientation involves focusing on the social, political, and economic conditions and policies that affect people's overall access to resources and quality of life. Macro practice in social work, then, involves striving to improve the social and economic context in which people live. Examples of content in this text about macro systems and how they affect people include the impacts of policies concerning abortion (Chapter 2), legislation regarding people with disabilities (Chapter 3), strategies to promote social and economic justice (Chapter 5), community responses to battered women (Chapter 9), and current services for older adults (Chapter 16).

Interactions Between Micro Systems and Macro Systems

Individual micro systems are also continuously and seriously affected by the macro systems with which they interact within the social environment. Two major types of macro systems impact individual clients: *communities and organizations*. The two are intertwined.

A *community* is "a number of people with something in common that connects them in some way and that distinguishes them from others"; the common feature might be a neighborhood where people live, an activity people share such as jobs, or other connections such as "ethnic identification" (Homan, 2011, p. 8).

Organizations are structured groups of people who come together to work toward some mutual goal and perform established work activities that

People and the environment are affected by social, political, and economic conditions at the macro level. Here, auto workers march against Wall Street.

are divided among various units. Organizations generally have a clearly defined membership in terms of knowing who is in and who is out.

We have emphasized the importance of clients' interactions with the many systems engulfing them. It is easy for practitioners, especially those who are new to the field, to focus on micro and mezzo systems. Assuming a "clinical" approach targets trying to change individuals within the context of small groups and families.

We have also emphasized that a unique and vital aspect of social work is assessing the effects of macro systems on individual client systems. Two broad theoretical perspectives that most clearly underlie practice with large systems are organizational theory and community theory.

Organizational theory includes specific attempts to understand how organizations function, what improves or impairs the ability of an organization to accomplish its mission, and what motivates people to work toward organizational goals. Some approaches to organizational theory have focused on management or leadership style; others have dealt with structural issues such as organizational hierarchy, planning, staffing patterns, and budgeting. Groups considered as organizations include virtually every structure with staff, policies, and procedures whose purpose is to continue operation in order to attain certain goals. For example, schools, public social welfare departments, and an agency operating four group homes for adults with intellectual disabilities are all types of organizations.

The second theoretical framework, *community theory*, has two primary components. First, it involves perspectives on the nature of communities. What constitutes a particular community? How are its boundaries defined? You may think of a community as having specific geographical boundaries, like Muleshoe, Texas, or Mattawamkeag, Maine, or Devil's Den, Wyoming. However, a community may also be a group of people with shared ideas, interests, and allegiance, like the professional social work community, the military community, or a virtual community.

The second thrust of community theory involves how social workers practice within the community context. How can practitioners improve community services and conditions? What skills must social workers acquire to enhance clients' quality of life within their community?

Communities and community theories will be discussed in the following sections. Organizations will be addressed later in this chapter and organizational theories described in Chapter 12.

LO 1-6 Examine Human Behavior in the Context of Community Macro Systems

EP 2.1.10

Human behavior always occurs within the context of a community. We have defined a community as "a number of people with something in common that connects them in some way and that distinguishes them from others" (Homan, 2011, p. 8). People live and develop throughout life while interacting with others. Their behavior constantly affects and is affected by people around them. Because of the significance of community macro systems as a context for living throughout the life span, we will spend some time describing community theories and work within communities here.

Note that the definition of community is tremendously broad in terms of whom and what a community can include. Does a community include all the people living on one city block? Or is the community a group of people with common issues, problems, and concerns? For example, there is the social work community and the community of people with physical disabilities. Does the word community connote a certain ethnic, cultural, or racial group? How large or small should a

community be? Can the United States be considered a community?

Because of the wide range of possible meanings, we will focus here on three major concepts inherent in our broad definition. First, we have a designated group of people, and we could thus establish a list of the individuals involved in a particular community. Second, this group has something in common. Such commonality may include values, resources, services, interests, or location. Third, because of the community's commonality, individuals interact in some way or have the potential to do so.

From a social work perspective these concepts are very important. A community can be organized so that its citizens can work together to empower each other, solve their mutual problems, or improve their overall quality of life. Social workers can use their macro practice skills to mobilize citizens within communities in order to accomplish the goals they define for themselves.

This book will stress the importance of communities in various contexts. Examples include community provision of sex education (Chapter 6), community strategies to improve social and economic justice (Chapter 5), the sense of pride and community for gay and lesbian people (Chapter 13), and community treatment of older adults (Chapter 15).

Community Conceptual Frameworks

Communities vary widely. Think of a mammoth 20-story urban public housing project. In contrast, consider suburban neighborhoods that require each home to be built on a minimum of four acres at a minimum cost of $750,000. Now contemplate neigh-

EP 2.1.7a

borhoods in New York City where thousands of people work, buy groceries, eat, sleep, and play within a few city blocks of each other. Finally, consider rural farm communities where individual farmers keep livestock and harvest thousands of bushels of grain.

Despite these broad contrasts, we can use a variety of theoretical perspectives to examine communities and gain greater understanding of how they work. Here we will focus on geographically based communities and view them in four ways. These theoretical perspectives include structural, sociopsychological, human ecology, and social systems (Fellin, 2001a,

2001b; Kirst-Ashman, 2014; Martinez-Brawley, 1995; Rothman, 1987).

Structural Perspective

Structure refers to the boundaries that define and the rules that govern any particular community. The *structural perspective* focuses on how individuals fit into their community environment and are linked to those who govern them. Three dimensions of communities are emphasized.

First, communities are *political entities*, organized public units such as a town, city, village, neighborhood, or province (Martinez-Brawley, 1995; Streeter, 2008). Local governments exert control over their citizens, state or provincial governments over local, and national over all units below. As political entities, communities perform numerous political, economic, and social functions; they serve as mediators between government units and the actions of individual citizens (Martinez-Brawley, 1995).

The second dimension related to the political is *power* (Homan, 2011). As just stated, the structural perspective focuses on how larger units exert power and control over their smaller units or subsystems. The structural perspective on communities implies an unequal allocation of power to influence and make political decisions, inequitable class standing among citizens, and disproportionate access to financial resources in the community (Rothman, 1987). As communities are subsystems of larger governmental units having greater amounts of power in varying degrees, so citizens as subsystems of communities have unequal power. Wealthier citizens who are bank presidents, business chief executive officers (CEOs), or physicians likely wield greater power and influence over what happens in a community than do poor, unemployed citizens. Similarly,

Communities provide an important context for human interaction and cultural celebrations. Here a crowd awaits the Chinese New Year's parade in front of the main entrance to the Los Angeles Chinatown.

elected officials have greater power than do citizens not holding office.

The third dimension inherent in the structural approach involves *geographical organization* of communities. Is the population concentrated in some areas, or more evenly distributed throughout? Where are business and residential areas located? How are streets and highways plotted? What are the boundaries that distinguish one community from another?

Sociopsychological Perspective

A *sociopsychological perspective* of a community involves how its members feel about themselves and interact with one another (Longres, 2008; Martinez-Brawley, 1995). People's feelings about their relationship to and with their community are paramount. To what extent do residents feel that they are part of their community? Do they interact frequently with neighbors, or do they feel isolated and alone? Do they feel that they fit in? Do they suffer racial or other discrimination, enhancing alienation from the community? How safe do they feel? Do they perceive themselves as victims of discrimination, crimes, and violence, or do they consider themselves productive members of a community who are in control of their environment?

An example comes to mind that can be viewed from a sociopsychological perspective. Fabian, age 42, lived in a modest home on Main Street in Butterbrickle, a small midwestern village at the edge of a large city. He had cerebral palsy, a disability resulting from damage to the brain at birth and manifested by muscular incoordination and speech disturbances. As his mobility was seriously restricted, he had made his home readily accessible for his wheelchair. He was a bright, personable, assertive individual who comfortably felt an integral part of his community. From a sociopsychological perspective, he experienced a sense of being a significant part of something larger than himself, his community. He understood how to negotiate his environment. He felt comfortable with the support and caring of the townspeople around him.

Fabian's disability, limited mobility, and special bathroom needs made it difficult for him to find employment, especially in tiny Butterbrickle. Thus, he was dependent on his SSI (Supplemental Security Income) payments, which were adequate to meet his monthly house payments and basic living expenses but left little for recreation or amenities. He loved to putter in his small garden and became quite an effective gardener. Each summer neighbors praised the beauty, color, and lushness of his flowers. Suddenly, Fabian came up with an idea: What about turning his hobby into a profitable business? Why not sell his flowers and significantly enhance his meager income? "Fabian's Fabulous Flowers" became a reality as he put up a sign and arranged plank shelves on sawhorses in his front yard, covering them with dozens of potted plants. Many customers responded to the dazzling display, and Fabian found himself making a small supplemental income.

However, his immediate neighbors were enraged that Fabian had turned a residential plot into commercial property that devalued the worth of their own properties and intensified parking congestion. Instead of applauding his flowers, neighbors demanded Fabian stop his commercial enterprise immediately. He refused. As a result, the neighbors complained to the village administrator that this "continuous yard sale" violated zoning regulations. The administrator subsequently contacted Fabian and told him to terminate his business unless he received a special permit.

Fabian decided to advocate for himself, submitted the necessary information to the village board of appeals for such a permit, and requested the required hearing. All neighbors were notified and attended the event. After many questions and much fiery debate, the board ultimately decided to grant Fabian his special permit. One of their considerations in making this decision was Fabian's difficulty in finding work elsewhere because of his special physical needs.

Fabian's neighbors remained irate, stopped speaking to him, and ignored his existence. He had increased his economic status and enhanced his independence. However, from a sociopsychological perspective, his social acceptance and standing in his immediate community were strikingly diminished. He no longer felt part of the "we" along with his community neighbors.

•••• Ethical Questions 1.3

EP 2.1.2

Was it right that Fabian was allowed to continue to sell his flowers? To what extent were his neighbors' rights violated? What would the best solution have been?

Human Ecology Perspective

A *human ecology perspective* of a community "focuses on the relationship of populations to their environment, especially in regard to spatial organization—that is, how people and services are distributed. Emphasis is placed on the 'division of labor' within a community—types of occupational groups, and how a structure of occupational stratification emerges through an interdependence within and between communities" (Fellin, 2001b, p. 119). The ecological approach considers how the environment affects human development, interaction, and quality of life.

This view emphasizes both how population is distributed within a geographical area and how individuals interact with others in their social environment. Part of this interaction involves access to resources. In any community, some population groups inevitably will have greater access than others. We discussed some ecological concepts earlier in the chapter. Additional ecological concepts that apply to community macro systems include *competition, segregation*, and *integration* (Fellin, 2001b, p. 119; Streeter, 2008, p. 354).

Competition concerns how community members vie for "the use of land ... [and] seek an 'advantage of place' for commercial, industrial, institutional, and residential purposes" (Fellin, 2001b, p. 119). Each community has only so much space and so many resources available. People therefore compete to attain their share, or at least enough to survive. As we know, huge inequities exist in terms of individuals' resources. Some may be rich and powerful, while others are bereft and homeless.

Segregation is the detachment or isolation of some group having certain common characteristics (such as race, ethnicity, or religion) through social pressure, restrictive laws, or personal choice. *Integration*, on the other hand, refers to the process of bringing together and blending a range of groups (including people of different races and ethnic backgrounds) into a unified, functional whole.

Such ecological concepts as competition, segregation, and integration can help you as a social worker analyze a community in terms of its fairness and supportiveness to all of its members. Fellin (2001b) explains that "membership in these groups affects the quality of life of people in positive and negative ways. People benefit or suffer as a result of their social positions within communities, through differential life chances, employment opportunities, access to social and material resources, and social relationships" (p. 121).

Viewing communities from a human ecology perspective helps you to focus on the inequities and problems faced by people who have fewer resources (in effect, less energy) than do others in the community. It provides a useful assessment mechanism for understanding why people act as they do within the context of the larger community macro system. An example concerns the life circumstances and reactions of people brought up in two families from diverse backgrounds within the same metropolitan community. Fred and Ed were brothers, both in their 30s. They grew up in the rural outskirts of the Milwaukee area. Both benefited from a good school system, a middle-class upbringing with adequate financial support, and a college education. Both worked full-time and could afford to purchase a home, make house and car payments on time, and even put a little away in savings.

Ed was married to Ursula, 23, who had a younger brother Doug, 19. Ursula and Doug grew up in a single-parent home in a poor urban neighborhood on the south side of Milwaukee. Resources were scarce. Their schools, having access to few resources, were unable to provide them with the academic skills necessary to pursue a college education successfully. Doug dropped out of high school as soon as he could at the age of 16. Ursula finished high school. Both worked at fast-food establishments earning minimum wage. Ursula's economic state improved considerably when she married Ed. Doug lived in a one-room apartment where he shared a bathroom with eight other men who lived on the same floor.

In their early years, Fred and Ed were separated from Ursula and Doug by social class. *Social class* "refers to inequalities among people measured in such terms as socioeconomic status and life-style" (Fellin, 2001b, p. 121). In turn, indicators of social class usually include job type, educational level, amount of income, and typical manner of living. After her marriage, Ursula was integrated into a higher social class.

A family gathering at Fred's brought Ed, Ursula, Doug, and an array of other relatives and in-laws together. This event became the interface where the individuals met. After several hours of eating and drinking, Doug began to reveal his anger. He raged about how he never had the chances that

Fred and Ed had, and how he never would. Ed and Ursula tried to calm Doug down. Nothing seemed to work. Finally, Doug pounded on the hood of Fred's 2009 red Mustang, cursing and swearing. Then he stomped over to his decrepit 1999 Dodge Neon and drove off before his concerned sister and brother-in-law could stop him.

As this story shows, access to resources within a community can have profound impacts on human behavior. Communities and people's status within them are critically significant to their quality of life. Some might think that Doug should have tried to improve his position in life. How difficult would it have been for Doug to achieve the lifestyle enjoyed by Fred and Ed? How likely was it that Doug could have attained a quality of life similar to that of his brother-in-law?

As a postscript to this story, Doug developed a drinking problem. He eventually got into a violent fight with another man at a bar, who shot him in the kneecap. Doug consequently had a permanent partial disability that seriously curtailed his potential to maintain most employment available at minimum wage. Fred had the dents in his car repaired for about $3,500, of which he had to pay the $500 deductible on his collision insurance. Ed and Ursula thereafter maintained only minimal contact with Doug, fearing his violent eruptions.

•••• Ethical Questions 1.4

EP 2.1.2

To what extent is economic inequality fair? Did Doug have the right to vent his anger in such a violent manner? What, if anything, could be done to improve Doug's economic and ecological status?

As a social worker, you have the responsibility to examine the community macro environment in which your clients reside. Certainly, you are concerned about how specific clients function as individuals. However, the effects of the environment in which they live cannot be ignored. Assessment of human behavior within the community context is necessary to propose solutions that address the larger issues affecting a broad range of clients. A subsequent section will explain some specific goals that you as a practitioner may develop within community environments.

Social Systems Perspective

The *social systems perspective* emphasizes analyzing how the various social subsystems within the community interact with each other. It helps you view clients in the context of the larger community system. Homan (2011) comments on how social systems theory applies to communities:

> *Each organism—a city, a neighborhood, an individual—is a system that requires ongoing input in the form of nutrients and other energy. The system takes in energy to grow, produce, and sustain life and to maintain its equilibrium. Maintaining equilibrium or balance is one of the core concerns of any system. A system acts when it feels out of balance. Though a system may act to regain balance, it may do so without adequately addressing the need or discomfort that created the imbalance to begin with. It can be a temporary adjustment or fix [for example, filling cracks in roads badly in need of total replacement, or opening a free food pantry for people living in poverty when what they really need are jobs], leading the system to respond with temporary fixes to chronic conditions that the system doesn't recognize or feel able to deal with. A system will more likely take radical action when it is more aware of conditions that affect it and when the imbalance has achieved the level of crisis [for example, escalating deaths resulting from car accidents on poor roads, or mounting starvation among children]....*
>
> *As the system processes the input it receives, this energy is converted to productive output, which is expressed in activity (such as work), in seeking new input [such as financial investments, business development, or home building and renovation], or in discarding used input as waste [for example, tearing down dilapidated homes in dying neighborhoods]. (pp. 35–36)*

A strength of the systems perspective on communities is the emphasis on interconnections. Primary social units or subsystems within communities include "formal organizations, such as businesses, governmental units, churches, schools, health-care organizations, and social welfare agencies" in addition to informal subsystems such as families and social groups (Fellin, 1995, p. 32). The dynamic interaction between clients and other community subsystems is an important focus of social work assessment. Each subsystem is integrally involved with other subsystems in the community. Family members work in organizations and businesses, attend school, socialize with friends, work out at health clubs, receive health and dental care, and pursue myriad activities within their community. Homan (2011) reflects:

> *In healthy communities members are able to meet their needs sufficiently well that energy can be directed beyond matters of basic survival to those of personal and community development (Kesler, 2000). Healthy communities provide ways for members not only to survive but to grow; not only to receive but to contribute. (p. 38)*

For social workers, the community context can be the focus of attention. How does the community affect the client? Is the client receiving the resources (input) needed for optimum health and well-being? Is affordable housing adequate to meet the client's needs? Are jobs available that correspond with the client's skills? Is the community growing and thriving, or is it shriveling and dying? Are adequate resources available in the forms of social services and health care? Answers to these questions can provide clues about what you can do to help clients. Working with community subsystems to provide needed services and advocating for resources when services are inadequate are fundamental dimensions of social work.

Traditional Models of Community Change

EP 2.1.7a

Various approaches have been developed for community practitioners to bring about community change. Traditionally, they have been categorized into three conceptual frameworks: *locality development, social planning*, and *social action* (Rothman, 2001). These models are "ideal types." Actual approaches to community change have tendencies or emphases that categorize them in one of the three models; yet most approaches also have components characteristic of one or both of the other models. Advocates of the social planning model, for example, may at times use community change techniques (such as wide discussion and participation by a variety of groups) that are characteristic of the other two models. We will not deal with the mixed forms, but for analytical purposes will instead view the three models as "pure" forms.

Locality Development Model

The *locality development model* (also called *community development*) asserts that community change can best be brought about through broad participation of a wide spectrum of people at the local community level. The model seeks to involve a broad cross section of people (including the disadvantaged and the power structure) in identifying and solving their problems. Some themes emphasized in this model are democratic procedures, a consensus approach, voluntary cooperation, development of indigenous leadership, and self-help.

The roles of the community practitioner in this approach include enabler, catalyst, coordinator, and teacher of problem-solving skills and ethical values. The approach assumes that conflicts that arise between various interest groups can be creatively and constructively handled. It encourages people to express their differences but assumes people will put aside their self-interests to further the interests of their community. The basic theme of this approach is "Together we can figure out what to do and then do it." The approach seeks to use discussion and communication between different factions to reach consensus about the problems to focus on and the strategies to resolve these problems. A few examples of locality development efforts include neighborhood work programs conducted by community-based agencies; Volunteers in Service to America; village-level work in some overseas community development programs, including the Peace Corps; and a variety of activities performed by self-help groups. A case example of the locality development model is the following.

Robert McKearn, a social worker for a juvenile probation department, noticed that an increasing number of school-age children were being referred to his office by the police department, school system, and parents from a small city of 11,000 people in the county served by his agency. The charges included status offenses (such as truancy from school) and delinquent offenses (such as shoplifting and burglary). Mr. McKearn noted that most of these children were from single-parent families.

Mr. McKearn contacted the community mental health center, the self-help organization Parents Without Partners, the pupil services department of the public school system, the county social services department, some members of the clergy, and the community mental health center in the area. Nearly everyone he contacted saw an emerging need to better serve children in single-parent families. The pupil services department mentioned that such children were performing less well academically and tended to display more serious disciplinary problems.

Mr. McKearn arranged a meeting of representatives from the groups and organizations that he contacted.

At the initial meeting a number of concerns were expressed about the problematic behaviors being displayed by children who had single parents. The school system considered these children to be at risk for higher rates of truancy, dropping out of school, delinquent activities, suicide, emotional problems, and unwanted pregnancies. Although numerous problems were identified, no one at this initial meeting was able to suggest a viable strategy to better serve single parents and their children. The community was undergoing an economic recession; therefore, funds were unavailable for an expensive new program.

Three more meetings were held. At the first two, numerous suggestions for providing services were discussed, but all were viewed as either too expensive or impractical. At the fourth meeting of the group, a single parent representing Parents Without Partners mentioned that she was aware that Big Brothers and Big Sisters programs in some communities were of substantial benefit to children in single-parent families. This idea seemed to energize the group. Suggestions began to piggyback. The group, however, determined that funds were unavailable to hire staff to run a Big Brothers and Big Sisters program. However, Rhona Quint, a social worker in the pupil services department, noted that she was willing to identify at-risk younger children in single-parent families and that she would be willing to supervise qualified volunteers in a "Big Buddy" program.

Mr. McKearn mentioned that he was currently supervising a student in an undergraduate field placement for an accredited social work program from a college in a nearby community. He noted that perhaps arrangements could be made for undergraduate social work students to be Big Buddies for

their required volunteer experience. Rhona Quint said she would approve of the suggestion if she could have the freedom to screen the applicants for Big Buddies. Arrangements were made over the next two months for social work students to be Big Buddies for at-risk younger children from single-parent families. After a two-year experimental period, the school system found the program sufficiently successful that it assigned Ms. Quint half-time to supervise the program, which included selecting at-risk children, screening volunteer applicants, matching children with Big Buddies, monitoring the progress of each matched pair, and conducting follow-up to ascertain the outcome of each pairing.

In summary, locality development focuses on communities helping themselves. It stresses participation by as many community residents as possible, who work together to solve problems and achieve mutually beneficial goals. Social workers tend to serve as catalysts, facilitators, coordinators, and teachers of problem-solving skills.

Spotlight 1.1 provides some examples of how Hispanic communities have focused on their strengths through locality development.

Social Planning Model

The second model, the *social planning* approach, emphasizes a technical process of problem solving. The approach assumes that community change in a complex industrial environment requires highly trained and skilled planners who can guide complex change processes. The role of the expert is stressed in this approach. The expert or planner is generally employed by a segment of the power structure, such as area planning agency, city or county planning department, mental health center, United Way board, or Community Welfare Council. There is a tendency for the planner to serve the interests of the power structure that employs him or her. Building community capacity or facilitating radical social change is generally not an emphasis in this approach.

The planner's roles in this approach include gathering facts, analyzing data, and serving as program designer, implementer, and facilitator. Community participation may vary from little to substantial, depending on the community's attitudes toward the problems being addressed. For example, an effort to design and obtain funding for a community center for older adults may or may not result in substantial involvement by interested community groups,

Latino and Hispanic Communities Promote Strengths and Empowerment

EP 2.1.4

Historically, Hispanic people have frequently been involved in community development and social action (Weil & Gamble, 1995). For example, consider La Raza Unida, a "political movement and party, comprising mostly Mexican American people and others of Spanish-speaking heritage, that advocates for policies and candidates favorable to the needs of Hispanic people" (Barker, 2003, p. 241; Green, 1999). Various Hispanic organizations have worked to improve political, economic, and social conditions in numerous development and action projects (Weil & Gamble, 1995).

Consider, for instance, the "Comunidad de Bienestar" (community of wellness) in the middle of the Chicago Puerto Rican community (Kelley, 2007). This is a community-sponsored initiative intended to promote communication among residents, celebrate Puerto Rican and other Hispanic cultures, enhance ethnic pride, improve the living environment, and address health and other "basic needs (food, water, shelter, income, safety, work)" for all community residents (p. 3). Community leaders emphasize political advocacy and actively seek political representation to address these community goals. A striking example of community progress involves the development of a length of Western Division Street into an area called Paseo Boricua. This has become "a Puerto Rican culinary, cultural and entertainment district. This nearly mile long area is anchored by two 45 ton steel Puerto Rican flags ... and has a Puerto Rican Walk of Fame and beautiful murals depicting history and culture. It becomes a social space for people to walk together, shop, eat—socialize—while also getting services from places such as Vida Sida—a culturally tailored HIV/AIDS prevention and control program" (p. 3). The Comunidad de Bienestar also has developed an attractive park to serve as a setting for family activities and an annual cultural festival, Fiesta Boricua.

Garcia (2011) examines another means by which Hispanic communities can empower their residents. This concerns a program aimed at enhancing Latino families' relationship with community schools, thereby helping children to do well in school:

The family-centeredness that characterizes Latino culture is interwoven with a concern for and emphasis on the collective. This emphasis can be used by workers to provide educational, informational, and problem-focused services by using group formats. In particular, the use of parent groups to inform parents about school policy or to address special topics, if driven by a culturally

sensitive format, can be especially effective. Because so many Latino families immigrate to this country to ensure good educational resources for their children, developing services in collaboration with schools to strengthen the relationship between parents and the school systems is a critical need area. (p. 327)

Delgado, Jones, and Rohani (2005) provide another example of how a Hispanic community developed a program to enhance children's performance in school:

The Hispanic Committee of Virginia, through its school alliance program titled "Alianza Escolar," seeks to provide educational services that promote learning and encourage youth to stay in school while also assisting parents to participate in their children's education and expand their own potential. The program matches Latino children who attend targeted elementary and middle schools with adult volunteers for tutoring and other mentoring activities. The program works with students whose environment puts them at risk of dropping out of school. Teachers and counselors identify Latino students in the fourth through eighth grades for the program. After being selected, students are matched with a volunteer mentor. Throughout the school year, the students meet with their mentors one evening a week for one-hour sessions. The mentors help the students with their schoolwork, concentrate on verbal and math skills, and provide activities that promote the students' achievement. (p. 106)

A Brief Note About Terms

The preceding paragraphs have used the terms *Puerto Rican*, *Latino*, and *Hispanic*. It is important to clarify terms as much as possible when referring to these populations. Weaver (2005) explains:

The terms Spanish, Hispanic, Latino, *and* Chicano *have all been used as labels to represent people in the United States who trace their history and culture back to areas colonized by Spain. Some terms are more inclusive than others. These terms have somewhat different connotations, and people often have strong feelings about which terms they prefer. Issues of identity are situated within a historical and political context and are closely tied to the choice of ethnic labels such as* Latino, Hispanic, Chicano, *and* Rican.... *The right to choose a name is empowering.*

The term Hispanic *was introduced in the 1970s and used by the U.S. Census Bureau for those with cultural*

(continued)

SPOTLIGHT ON DIVERSITY 1.1 *(continued)*

origins in Mexico, Puerto Rico, Cuba, Central America, and other Latin American countries. This term sometimes includes Spaniards and Brazilians [Brazil's primary language is Portuguese]. Although Hispanic *is the term officially used and created by the U.S. Census Bureau, many people do not accept this label to represent themselves....*

Some people prefer the label Latino *as more representative of the amalgam of people linked by the Spanish colonial history.... However, given the extensive diversity among the people grouped under this label, when speaking of a specific group, it is preferable to use terms based on national origin (e.g., Ecuadoran, Dominican) rather than more encompassing terms such as* Hispanic *or* Latino.... *When referring exclusively to women, the term* Latina *is used. (pp. 140–141)*

Note that the terms *Chicano* and *Chicana* have often been used to refer to people of Mexican descent (Barker, 2003).

An example of the complexity of this issue comes to mind: A social worker who identified herself as Hispanic was actively involved in advocacy on behalf of Hispanic people in

general and poor women in particular. She was interested in joining an organization that advocated for the rights of Hispanics, the Chicano Initiative (CI). Originally from Argentina, she expressed serious concern regarding her membership in a Chicano/Chicana organization because she was not of Mexican descent. Members of the organization, however, valued her interest, input, and efforts. They indicated that their intent was to involve a broad-based membership of people who originated from countries with a Spanish heritage. The members welcomed all people, regardless of their origins, who were interested in CI's cause. The social worker joined the organization and became quite a dynamo in getting things done.

EP 2.1.1b, 2.1.4b

The important thing for social workers is to be sensitive to the ethnic and cultural background of their clients. Practitioners should respect clients' preferred group identification.

In this book when it is not practical to refer to specific countries of origin, we will arbitrarily use the terms Latino/Latina to refer to the wide range of ethnic groups within this population (Garcia, 2011; Lum, 2005; Weaver, 2005).

---

depending on the politics surrounding such a center. Much of the focus of the social planning approach is on identifying needs and on arranging and delivering goods and services to people who need them. The change focus of this approach is "Let's get the facts and take the next rational steps." A case example of the social planning model follows.

The mayor and city council of a medium-sized midwestern city became increasingly concerned about the deterioration of community living in the northeast area of the city. The mayor and city council passed a resolution directing the City Planning Department to develop an approach to combat a variety of social ills (including rising rates of crime, racial conflict, and a lack of recreational resources for children and adults) in this section of the city. The planning department assigned Jose Cruz (an MSW social worker with 11 years of social planning experience) to develop a proposal to improve the community.

Mr. Cruz first contacted and introduced himself to community leaders in this neighborhood: city aldermen, county board supervisors, members of the clergy, administrators of community service agencies, and business leaders. He then arranged and led five focus groups in this neighborhood with these

community leaders. (Focus groups provide one method for gathering data. A *focus group* is a gathering of people who meet to discuss a specific topic or issue, evaluate it in depth, share information, and when appropriate, propose solutions or plans of action. They typically include 6 to 12 members who meet to discuss and brainstorm about an issue and are usually led by a moderator who keeps the group on task.) Mr. Cruz's first focal topic was "What do you see as the major problems in this community?" Common responses were a deteriorating community, high rates of crime, lack of community resources, racial conflict, and lack of a sense of community among the residents. Mr. Cruz also led several focus groups of citizens in the community who were invited to the meetings by members of the clergy in the neighborhood. Responses of the citizens were similar to those identified by community leaders.

Once the major concerns were identified, Mr. Cruz invited those who attended the first focus groups to attend one of a second set of focus groups. At these he asked, "Given the fact that this neighborhood is experiencing high rates of crime, racial conflict, single-parent families, lack of recreational resources for children and adults, and a lack of community pride, what can we do to combat these problems?" A number of focus group members suggested building a neighborhood center in a neighborhood park to provide a variety of cultural, recreational, social, and educational programs.

Mr. Cruz then urged interested community leaders and citizens to form a Neighborhood Center Planning Committee. Thirty-three community residents agreed to be on this committee. Mr. Cruz worked with the committee to prepare an architectural design for the Center. This committee, with Mr. Cruz's assistance, then prepared a budget to build and operate the Center, with funding from a variety of sources—federal funding, city funding, neighborhood fundraising, and a contribution from the United Way. Mr. Cruz and the Neighborhood Center Planning Committee then presented the proposal to the City Planning Department, which rapidly approved it. The proposal was then presented to the mayor and the city council, who deliberated about it for 14 months but eventually approved it. Groundbreaking for the Center will soon begin.

In summary, social planning involves the use of experts to assist communities in solving problems. Such experts gather facts and apply skills to propose and implement solutions that benefit community residents. Social work roles in social planning include expert planner, fact gatherer, program developer, and implementer.

Social Action Model

The third model, the *social action* approach, assumes there is a disadvantaged (often oppressed) segment of the population that needs to be organized, perhaps in alliance with others, in order to pressure the power structure for increased resources or for treatment more in accordance with democracy or social justice. Social action approaches at times seek basic changes in major institutions or seek changes in basic policies of formal organizations. Such approaches often seek redistribution of power and resources. Whereas locality developers envision a unified community, social action advocates see the power structure as the opposition—the target of action.

Perhaps the best known social activist was Saul Alinsky (1972), who advised, "Pick the target, freeze it, personalize it, and polarize it" (p. 130).

The roles of the community practitioner in this approach include advocate, agitator, activist, partisan, broker, and negotiator. Tactics used in social

One means of empowerment is for people from various cultural groups to attain positions of political and economic power. Here Governor Deval Patrick of Massachusetts delivers his eighth State of the Commonwealth speech.

Barry Chin/The Boston Globe /Getty Images

action projects include protests, boycotts, confrontation, and negotiation. The change strategy is "Let's organize to overpower our oppressor" (Alinsky, 1969, p. 72). The client population is viewed as being "victims" of the oppressive power structure. Examples of the social action approach include boycotts during the civil rights movement in the 1960s, strikes by unions, protests by antiabortion groups, and protests by African American and Native American groups.

The social action model is not widely used by social workers at present. Many workers find that being involved in social action activities may lead their employing agencies to penalize them with unpleasant work assignments, low merit increases, and denial of promotions. Many agencies will accept minor and moderate changes in their service delivery systems but are threatened by the prospect of the radical changes often advocated by the social action approach.

Saul Alinsky (1972) provides the following example of a creative social action effort:

I was lecturing at a college run by a very conservative, almost fundamentalist Protestant denomination. Afterward some of the students came to my motel to talk to me. Their problem was that they couldn't have any fun on campus. They weren't permitted to dance or smoke or have a can of beer. I had been talking about the strategy of effecting change in a society and they wanted to know what tactics they could use to change their situation. I reminded them that a tactic is doing what you can with what you've got. "Now, what have you got?" I asked. "What do they permit you to do?" "Practically nothing," they said, "except—you know—we can chew gum." I said, "Fine. Gum becomes the weapon. You get 200 or 300 students to get two packs of gum each, which is quite a wad. Then you have them drop it on the campus walks. This will cause absolute chaos. Why, with 500 wads of gum I could paralyze Chicago, stop all the traffic in the Loop." They

looked at me as though I was some kind of nut. But about two weeks later I got an ecstatic letter saying, "It worked! It worked! Now we can do just about anything so long as we don't chew gum." (pp. 145–146)

In summary, social action involves pressuring the power structure to provide resources or improve the treatment of oppressed populations who are victims. In the pursuit of social justice, the power structure is viewed as the adversary, so conflict, confrontation, and direct action are often used. Social workers pursuing social action often serve as advocates, activities, brokers, and negotiators, all social work roles described later in the chapter.

Highlight 1.10 summarizes the three traditional models of community change just discussed.

HIGHLIGHT 1.10

Characteristics of Three Models of Community Change

Characteristic	Locality Development	Social Planning	Social Action
1. Goals	Self-help; improve community living; emphasis on process goals.	Use problem-solving approach to resolve community problems; emphasis on task goals.	Shift power relationships and resources to an oppressed group, create basic institutional change; emphasize task and process goals.
2. Assumptions concerning community	Everyone wants community living to improve and is willing to contribute to that improvement.	Social problems in the community can be resolved through the efforts of planning experts.	The community has a power structure and one or more oppressed groups, so social injustice is a major problem.
3. Basic change strategy	Broad cross section of people involved in identifying and solving problems.	Experts using fact-gathering and problem-solving approach.	Members of oppressed groups organize to take action against the power structure—i.e., the enemy.
4. Characteristic change tactics and techniques	Consensus: communication among community groups and interests; group discussion.	Consensus or conflict.	Conflict or contest: confrontation, direct action, negotiation.
5. Practitioner roles	Catalyst; facilitator; coordinator; teacher of problem-solving skills.	Expert planner; fact gatherer; analyst; program developer; and implementer.	Activist; advocate; agitator; broker; negotiator; partisan.
6. Views of power structure	Members of power structure are collaborators in a common venture.	Power structure is employers and sponsors.	Power structure is external target of action; oppressors to be coerced or overturned.
7. Views of client population	Citizens.	Consumers.	Victims.
8. Views of client role	Participant in a problem-solving process.	Consumer or recipient.	Employer or constituent.

Contemporary Conceptual Frameworks of Community Change

EP 2.1.3b,
2.1.7a,
2.1.7b,
2.1.9a

Rothman (2007) proposes a newer outlook concerning the traditional models of locality development, social planning, and social action that calls for "multi modes of intervention" (p. 11). Two new ideas predominate.

One major initiative is that the traditional three community organization methods should be updated to reflect a modification in focus. First, "social advocacy" should replace social action (Rothman, 2007, p. 12). "*Social advocacy* deems the application of pressure as the best course of action to take against people or institutions that may have [brought about] ... the problem or that stand in the way of its solution—which frequently involves promoting equity or social justice. When interests clash in this way, conflict is a given" (p. 12). Advocacy becomes the focus of attention.

"Planning and policy practice" then replace the traditional social planning approach (Rothman, 2007, p. 12). Planning continues to involve "proposing and enacting particular solutions" (p. 12). *Policy practice* entails "efforts to change policies in legislative, agency, and community settings, whether by establishing new policies, improving existing ones, or defeating the policy initiatives of other people" (Jansson, 2011, p. 15). Changing policy often becomes an objective.

"Community capacity development" is substituted for community development (Rothman, 2007, p. 12). "*Community capacity development* assumes that change is best accomplished when the people affected by problems are empowered with the knowledge and skills needed to understand their problems, and then work cooperatively together to overcome them. Thus there is a premium on consensus as a tactic and on social solidarity [unity including diverse community groups that is based on mutual interests, support, and goals] as [a means] ... and outcome" (p. 12). Here community capacity (the potential use of the community's inherent strengths, resources, citizen participation, and leadership) is stressed.

The second primary initiative posed for contemporary macro practice involves the flexibility of mixing various aspects of these three approaches to get things done. Rothman (2007) reflects that macro practice is often a complex process that requires emphasizing various aspects of these three approaches depending on the situation. For example, planning and policy practice may require varying degrees of social advocacy. *Advocacy*, of course, involves stepping forward on the behalf of the client system in order to promote fair and equitable treatment or gain needed resources. *Policy advocacy* is "policy practice that aims to help powerless groups, such as women, children, poor people, persons of color, gay men and lesbians, and people with disabilities to improve their resources and opportunities" (Jansson, 2012, p. 522).

Rothman (2007) provides an example of a person undertaking policy advocacy to improve policies that affect groups at risk of harm:

> *Wilbur Cohen, a former secretary of the Department of Health, Education, and Welfare, vividly exemplifies a policy advocate who spent a lifetime in public service. During the Depression-era administration of Franklin D. Roosevelt and his New Deal he helped draft the 1936 act that established the Social Security System.... In 1956 he was instrumental in instituting disability insurance. Continuing as a prime designer of America's "welfare state," under the Johnson administration in 1965 he set up the Medicare system.... Johnson described him as the "planner, architect, builder, and repairman" for most of the social legislation of "The Great Society" [the period during Johnson's presidency that referred to major social welfare initiatives aimed at pursuing a War on Poverty (Barker, 2003)]. (p. 20)*

LO 1-7 Examine Human Behavior in and with Organizational Macro Systems

Just as communities are vital contexts for human behavior in the social environment, so are organizations. Organizations provide the structure and physical facilities in which people work. They also provide the settings in which goods and services are provided. It's important for you to understand the environment in which social workers practice and clients go to receive services. Therefore, our focus here is on organizations that provide social services. *Social services* include the work that social work practitioners and other

EP 2.1.10

A homeless shelter is an example of an activity system within the context of an organization. Here volunteers feed homeless people in Detroit, Michigan.

helping professionals perform for improving people's physical and mental health; promoting self-determination and independence; fortifying family bonds; enhancing quality of life; and seeking the effective functioning of individuals, families, groups, and communities. One type of social services organization frequently referred to in the social work field is the *social agency*. This is an organization providing social services overseen by a board of directors[3] and usually staffed by various personnel including social workers, members of other professions, paraprofessionals, and clerical staff (Barker, 2003). The terms *social services*, *human services*, and sometimes *social welfare* are often used interchangeably when referring to organizations, agencies, and agency personnel.

Organizations are particularly important to you for two reasons. First, most likely you will be employed by one. Your organization's policies, goals, and restrictions will directly affect what work you can and cannot do with clients. The second reason for their significance is that often the organization, not the client, may be the source of the problem. (We will discuss this later in greater

depth.) Therefore, you will need to evaluate for yourself how well your own organization is functioning in order to do your work effectively.

To assess the effectiveness of any organization, you need to understand some basic organizational concepts. Here we will define the concept of organization and explain how organizations provide or fail to provide services and resources to clients.

What Are Organizations?

Because organizations are systems, all of the systems concepts discussed earlier apply to them. Organizations are in constant interaction with other systems in the environment. Some systems provide organizations with resources (e.g., public funds, fees, or grants). Other systems are their clients who receive their services and output resources.

Organizations are "(1) social entities that (2) are goal-directed, (3) are designed as deliberately structured and coordinated activity systems, and (4) are linked to the external environment" (Daft, 2013, p. 12). Four elements stand out in this definition.

First, organizations are *social entities*. That is, organizations are made up of people with all their strengths and failings. Organizations dictate how people should behave and what responsibilities employees must assume as they do their jobs.

---

[3]A *board of directors* is an administrative "group of people authorized to formulate the organization's mission, objectives, and policies in addition to overseeing the organization's ongoing activities" (Kirst-Ashman, 2014, p. 145).

Individuals bring to their jobs their own values and personalities affecting how they behave in the organizational environment.

Second, organizations are *goal-directed*. They exist for some specified purpose. An organization specializing in stockbroking exists to help clients develop financial packages that make money. Social service organizations exist to provide services and resources to help people with designated needs. An organization must clearly define its goals so that workers can evaluate the extent to which it achieves these goals.

The third key concept in the definition is that organizations are *deliberately structured and coordinated activity systems*. Activity systems are clusters of work activities performed by designated units within an organization. Such systems are guided by the practical application of knowledge to achieve desired ends. Organizations coordinate the functioning of various activity systems to enhance efficiency in attaining desired goals. They have structures that include policies for how the organization should be run, hierarchies of how personnel are supervised and by whom, and different units working in various ways to help the organization function.

A homeless shelter in a large city is an example of an activity system. Staff include intake workers, care supervisors, vocational counselors, social workers, administrative staff, and support staff. They work together to provide short-term emergency shelter for people in need and transitional help toward independence. People receive food, shelter, showers, and clothing on an emergency basis; transitional services aim to help people assimilate back into the community by providing education about practical skills, help in locating housing, and counseling when needed (Johnson, 1995; Wong, 2008). The shelter has an established policy manual concerning staff and client procedures to keep things running smoothly. There is a clear delineation regarding various staffers' responsibilities and who reports to whom in the supervisory hierarchy.

The fourth concept inherent in the definition of organizations is *linkage to the external environment*. Thus, an organization is in constant interaction with other systems in the social environment, including individuals, groups, other organizations, and communities. Agencies providing social services interact dynamically with clients, funding sources, legislative and regulatory agencies, politicians, community leaders, and other social service agencies.

It is imperative that social workers have an extensive knowledge of organizations. Surviving and thriving in organizations are skills in which social workers are expected to have expertise. Chapter 12 summarizes several theories of organizational behavior. The text also describes service provision taking place within the organizational context. For example, Child Protective Services address child maltreatment (Chapter 4), and various programs provide resources to older adults (Chapter 16).

The following section describes some common problems encountered by practitioners working within organizations. These include the shifting external environment, vagueness of process, and vagueness of goals.

The Exceptional Problems of Social Service Organizations

Numerous problems that do not affect private business plague social service organizations. Most are based on the fact that working with people is infinitely more complicated than working with materials.

EP 2.1.9a

As populations continue to expand worldwide, resources continue to shrink. The shrinking of resources means that funding becomes more difficult to obtain. It also means that competition becomes more intense. The result is that organizations producing higher quality products at lower costs requiring less input will be more likely to survive than those that are less effective and efficient.

Before you as a practitioner can begin to assess the effectiveness of organizations for your clients, you need to understand some of the problems afflicting these organizations. Organizational problems are almost never easy to address or change. As already indicated, these organizational problems include uncertainties in the environment, vague processes, and vague goals.

The Shifting Environment

The environment in which social service organizations strive to exist is constantly in flux. Social forces affect other macro organizations and influence political policies, which, in turn, modify the availability of funding. Organizations must often respond dramatically to funding cuts by reorganizing staff and drastically cutting back programs. Community opinions concerning services and funding can change over relatively short periods of time. New legislation can change policies that govern how agencies operate. Incorporation of rapidly expanding new technology may increase costs and affect how an agency can provide services.

Social forces can jar social service organizations unpredictably and severely. To survive and effectively meet their goals of helping clients, these organizations must be keenly aware of external influences and their effects. Organizations must be able to react quickly to changing needs and demands.

Vagueness of Process

Interventions performed by a variety of individual practitioners and other staff are difficult to measure and monitor. They are unlike manufacturing machines that punch out slabs of metal that can be measured. Raw materials are predictably uniform. Effectiveness can be evaluated in terms of a machine's accuracy and efficiency (i.e., how fast the machine can punch out slabs). Work routines are predictable, repetitive, and relatively easy to monitor and control.

Professional staff in social services organizations vary widely. Clients vary even more. Therefore, social service organizations have multiple, immeasurable, human factors involved in the intervention process. Because people vary a great deal more than do inanimate materials such as metal slabs, practitioners who work with people must have much more flexibility than metal-slab punchers. Workers in organizations need to have some degree of discretion, or ability to make decisions, in working with their clients. This, in turn, makes the monitoring of the intervention process even more difficult.

Vagueness of Goals

Accountability is critically important to social work practitioners today. *Accountability* is a practitioner's responsibility to clients, community, and agency for ethical and effective practice. Individual practitioners and whole agencies are called upon to prove that their performance is productive and valuable. A way to do this is to define specific, measurable goals and monitor the extent to which they are achieved.

Superficially, this sounds simple. However, how can a practitioner prove that a client has been helped? For instance, if you are teaching child management techniques to physically abusive parents, how do you know when you've been successful? When they can pass a written test quizzing them on the specific techniques? Or when they strike their children only on the hands and rump instead of on the head? Or when they hit their children only once each day instead of a dozen times? Human behavior is difficult to define and measure.

Evaluating the outcomes of an entire organization or even of a program, including goals, effectiveness, and efficiency, is much more difficult than evaluating the outcomes of micro or mezzo interventions. This is due to the increased number of variables involved. In order to evaluate program outcomes, the services provided must be clearly defined, consistent in their provision, and proven to be effective.

LO 1-8 Recognize Social Worker Roles in Organizational and Community Systems

Social workers conduct their practice as they work in and for organizations. Organizations, social workers, and their clients all function within the context of the larger community macro system. Social workers assume a wide range of roles as they work

EP 2.1.1c

with clients in organizations and communities. In this context, *roles* are the expected behaviors and professional tasks considered important as social workers go about their work in macro social environments. Roles provide blueprints for how social workers can function to help clients, provide services, and improve agency service provision. Understanding the roles used in practice helps set the stage for skill acquisition and helps tie knowledge to practice.

The following sections describe some of the roles workers use at various levels of practice. Some roles are more useful in a macro system context; others relate primarily to micro or mezzo systems. Many can be applied at all three levels of generalist practice. Keep in mind that for any particular intervention, a worker may assume a number of roles, often at the same time. Generalist practitioners need to be flexible and capable of working with multiple systems.

Roles especially useful for macro system intervention include *enabler, mediator, coordinator, manager, educator, evaluator, broker, facilitator, initiator, negotiator,* and *advocate* (Kahn, 1995; Kirst-Ashman, 2014; Yessian & Broskowski, 1983).

Enabler

In the *enabler* role, a worker helps a client cope with various stresses ranging from crisis situations like divorce or job loss to community issues such as inadequate housing or day care. Skills used in the enabler role include "conveying hope, reducing resistance and ambivalence, recognizing and managing feelings, identifying and supporting personal strengths and social assets," breaking down problems into more manageable parts, emphasizing goals, and identifying ways to attain them (Barker, 2003, p. 143). Enablers are helpers. Practitioners can function in the role of enabler for micro, mezzo, or macro systems.

This definition of *enabler* is very different from that used in the area of chemical dependency. There *enabler* refers to a family member or friend who helps the substance abuser continue to use and abuse the drug of his or her choice.

Mediator

EP 2.1.10k

The *mediator* role involves resolving arguments or conflicts among micro, mezzo, or macro systems. At the macro level, the mediator helps various factions (subsystems) within a community, or a community and some other system, work out their differences. At the micro and mezzo levels, mediation is becoming increasingly important in resolving divorce and child custody cases.

The mediator role may involve improving communication among dissident individuals or groups and helping those involved come to a compromise. A mediator remains neutral and does not side with either party in the dispute. Mediators make sure they understand the positions of both parties. They may help to clarify positions, recognize miscommunication about differences, and help those involved present their cases clearly.

Coordinator

Coordination involves bringing components together in some kind of organized manner. Coordinators

can bring people together and organize them to pursue any number of goals. Such group goals might include advocating for policy changes at the agency, state, or national level, or forming a task group to achieve some designated goal (e.g., improving the agency's recordkeeping system).

Manager

Management in social work involves having some level of administrative responsibility for a social agency or other unit in order to accomplish the following: establish organizational goals; administer social service programs; improve agency effectiveness and efficiency; obtain financial resources; solicit community support; and coordinate the work of agency staff. Management tasks include supervising other staff, planning programs, getting and distributing resources, developing and establishing organizational structures and processes, developing budgets, evaluating programs, and implementing program changes when needed.

Educator

The *educator* role involves giving information and teaching skills to client and other systems. To be an effective educator, the worker must first be knowledgeable. Additionally, the worker must be a good communicator so that information is conveyed clearly and is understood by the client or macro system.

Evaluator

An *evaluator* determines whether a program, agency, or policy is effective. This can occur in an organizational or community context. Generalist social workers with a broad knowledge of how various systems function can analyze or evaluate how well such systems enhance the quality of people's lives. They can also evaluate the effectiveness of their own interventions.

Broker

A *broker* helps link clients (individuals, groups, organizations, or communities) with community resources and services. A broker may help a client obtain emergency food or housing, legal aid, or other needed resources. A broker can also help put different community groups or organizations in touch with each other so that they can work together and achieve mutual goals. In micro and mezzo systems, the role of broker requires that the worker be familiar with community services, have general knowledge about eligibility requirements, and be sensitive to client needs.

Facilitator

A *facilitator* is one who guides and directs a group encounter or gathering. The group may be a family therapy group, a task group, a sensitivity group, an educational group, a self-help group, or a group with some other focus. A facilitator can also work with groups in organizational and community settings to enhance communication, initiate meetings, contribute to plan development, solicit needed resources, provide information, and pursue goals.

Initiator

The *initiator* is the person or persons who call attention to an issue. The issue may be a problem existing in the community, a need, or simply a situation that can be improved. It is important to recognize that a problem does not have to exist before the initiator steps in. Often, preventing problems or enhancing existing services is satisfactory reason for a change effort. A social worker may recognize that a policy is creating problems for particular clients and bring this to the supervisor's attention. A client may identify ways that service could be improved. In each case, the person is playing the role of initiator. Usually, this role must be followed up by other kinds of work, because pointing out existing or potential problems doesn't guarantee that they will be solved.

Negotiator

EP 2.1.10k

A *negotiator* represents an organization, a group, or an individual that is trying to gain something from another group or system. Somewhat like mediation, negotiation involves finding a middle ground that all sides can live with and achieving consensus whenever possible. Unlike mediators, who play a neutral role, negotiators clearly ally themselves with one of the sides involved.

Advocate

An *advocate* is one who speaks out on the behalf of individuals, groups, or communities "to promote fair and equitable treatment or gain needed resources" (Kirst-Ashman, 2010, p. 96). The advocate role often entails stepping forward and speaking on behalf of the client system. This may be especially appropriate when a client

EP 2.1.10

system has little power to get what it needs. Advocacy often involves expending more effort than is absolutely necessary to accomplish the job. It also may entail taking risks, especially when advocating on behalf of a client who faces a larger, more powerful system.

The advocate role is one of the most important roles a generalist social worker can assume, despite its potential difficulties. It is often undertaken when the client system is in desperate need of help.

Highlight 1.11 describes the knowledge, skills, and values necessary for undertaking generalist practice and assuming these roles.

Chapter Summary

The following summarizes this chapter's content as it relates to the learning objectives presented at the beginning of the chapter. Chapter content will help prepare students to:

LO 1-1 Explain the importance of foundation knowledge for social work with an emphasis on assessment.

This book provides a knowledge base in preparation for social work practice. Social workers need knowledge in order to understand the dynamics of human behavior and conduct client assessments. The social work process then involves helping clients identify and evaluate available alternatives to select the best plan of action.

LO 1-2 Review the organization of this book that emphasizes life-span development.

This book is organized using a life-span approach. The life span is divided into four phases: infancy and childhood, adolescence, young and middle adulthood, and later adulthood.

Chapters on biological, psychological, and social (bio-psycho-social) aspects of development portray common life events, normal developmental milestones, and relevant issues for each life phase.

HIGHLIGHT 1.11

Knowledge, Skills, and Values Needed for Social Work Practice

In *Educational Policy and Accreditation Standards (EPAS)*, the Council on Social Work Education (2008) identified knowledge, skills, and values that accredited baccalaureate and master's degree programs are mandated to convey to social work students. *EPAS* is based on a competency approach. The following material is reprinted with permission from *EPAS* (CSWE, 2008).

The BSW curriculum prepares its graduates for generalist practice through mastery of the core competencies. The MSW curriculum prepares its graduates for advanced practice through mastery of the core competencies augmented by knowledge and practice behaviors specific to a concentration.

Educational Policy 2.1—Core Competencies

Competency-based education is an outcome performance approach to curriculum design. Competencies are measurable practice behaviors that are comprised of knowledge, values, and skills. The goal of the outcome approach is to demonstrate the integration and application of the competencies in practice with individuals, families, groups, organizations, and communities. The 10 core competencies are listed below [EP 2.1.1–EP 2.1.10(d)], followed by a description of characteristic knowledge, values, skills, and the resulting practice behaviors that may be used to operationalize the curriculum and assessment methods.

Programs may add competencies consistent with their missions and goals.

Educational Policy 2.1.1—Identify as a Professional Social Worker and Conduct Oneself Accordingly

Social workers serve as representatives of the profession, its mission, and its core values. They know the profession's history. Social workers commit themselves to the profession's enhancement and to their own professional conduct and growth. Social workers

- advocate for client access to the services of social work;
- practice personal reflection and self-correction to assure continual professional development;
- attend to professional roles and boundaries;
- demonstrate professional demeanor in behavior, appearance, and communication;
- engage in career-long learning; and
- use supervision and consultation.

Educational Policy 2.1.2—Apply Social Work Ethical Principles to Guide Professional Practice

Social workers have an obligation to conduct themselves ethically and to engage in ethical decision making. Social workers are knowledgeable about the value base of the profession, its ethical standards, and relevant law. Social workers

- recognize and manage personal values in a way that allows professional values to guide practice;
- make ethical decisions by applying standards of the National Association of Social Workers *Code of Ethics* (NASW, 2008) and, as applicable, of the International Federation of Social Workers/International Association of Schools of Social Work *Ethics in Social Work, Statement of Principles* (IFSW, 2013a);
- tolerate ambiguity in resolving ethical conflicts; and
- apply strategies of ethical reasoning to arrive at principled decisions.

Educational Policy 2.1.3—Apply Critical Thinking to Inform and Communicate Professional Judgments

Social workers are knowledgeable about the principles of logic, scientific inquiry, and reasoned discernment. They use critical thinking augmented by creativity and curiosity. Critical thinking also requires the synthesis and communication of relevant information. Social workers

- distinguish, appraise, and integrate multiple sources of knowledge, including research-based knowledge, and practice wisdom;
- analyze models of assessment, prevention, intervention, and evaluation; and
- demonstrate effective oral and written communication in working with individuals, families, groups, organizations, communities, and colleagues.

Educational Policy 2.1.4—Engage Diversity and Difference in Practice

Social workers understand how diversity characterizes and shapes the human experience and is critical to the formation of identity. The dimensions of diversity are understood as the intersectionality of multiple factors including age, class, color, culture, disability, ethnicity, gender, gender identity and expression, immigration status, political ideology, race, religion, sex, and sexual orientation. Social workers appreciate that, as a consequence of difference, a person's life experiences may include oppression, poverty, marginalization, and alienation as well as privilege, power, and acclaim. Social workers

- recognize the extent to which a culture's structures and values may oppress, marginalize, alienate, or create or enhance privilege and power;
- gain sufficient self-awareness to eliminate the influence of personal biases and values in working with diverse groups;
- recognize and communicate their understanding of the importance of difference in shaping life experiences; and
- view themselves as learners and engage those with whom they work as informants.

(continued)

HIGHLIGHT 1.11 *(continued)*

Educational Policy 2.1.5—Advance Human Rights and Social and Economic Justice

Each person, regardless of position in society, has basic human rights, such as freedom, safety, privacy, an adequate standard of living, health care, and education. Social workers recognize the global interconnections of oppression and are knowledgeable about theories of justice and strategies to promote human and civil rights. Social work incorporates social justice practices in organizations, institutions, and society to ensure that these basic human rights are distributed equitably and without prejudice. Social workers

- understand the forms and mechanisms of oppression and discrimination;
- advocate for human rights and social and economic justice; and
- engage in practices that advance social and economic justice.

Educational Policy 2.1.6—Engage in Research-Informed Practice and Practice-Informed Research

Social workers use practice experience to inform research, employ evidence-based interventions, evaluate their own practice, and use research findings to improve practice, policy, and social service delivery.

Social workers comprehend quantitative and qualitative research and understand scientific and ethical approaches to building knowledge. Social workers

- use practice experience to inform scientific inquiry; and
- use research evidence to inform practice.

Educational Policy 2.1.7—Apply Knowledge of Human Behavior and the Social Environment

Social workers are knowledgeable about human behavior across the life course; the range of social systems in which people live; and the ways social systems promote or deter people in maintaining or achieving health and well-being. Social workers apply theories and knowledge from the liberal arts to understand biological, social, cultural, psychological, and spiritual development. Social workers

- utilize conceptual frameworks to guide the processes of assessment, intervention, and evaluation; and
- critique and apply knowledge to understand person and environment.

Educational Policy 2.1.8—Engage in Policy Practice to Advance Social and Economic Well-Being and to Deliver Effective Social Work Services

Social work practitioners understand that policy affects service delivery, and they actively engage in policy practice.

Social workers know the history and current structures of social policies and services; the role of policy in service delivery; and the role of practice in policy development. Social workers

- analyze, formulate, and advocate for policies that advance social well-being; and
- collaborate with colleagues and clients for effective policy action.

Educational Policy 2.1.9—Respond to Contexts That Shape Practice

Social workers are informed, resourceful, and proactive in responding to evolving organizational, community, and societal contexts at all levels of practice. Social workers recognize that the context of practice is dynamic, and use knowledge and skill to respond proactively. Social workers

- continuously discover, appraise, and attend to changing locales, populations, scientific and technological developments, and emerging societal trends to provide relevant services; and
- provide leadership in promoting sustainable changes in service delivery and practice to improve the quality of social services.

Educational Policy 2.1.10(a)–(d)—Engage, Assess, Intervene, and Evaluate with Individuals, Families, Groups, Organizations, and Communities

Professional practice involves the dynamic and interactive processes of engagement, assessment, intervention, and evaluation at multiple levels. Social workers have the knowledge and skills to practice with individuals, families, groups, organizations, and communities. Practice knowledge includes identifying, analyzing, and implementing evidence-based interventions designed to achieve client goals; using research and technological advances; evaluating program outcomes and practice effectiveness; developing, analyzing, advocating, and providing leadership for policies and services; and promoting social and economic justice.

Educational Policy 2.1.10(a)—Engagement

Social workers

- substantively and affectively prepare for action with individuals, families, groups, organizations, and communities;
- use empathy and other interpersonal skills; and
- develop a mutually agreed-on focus of work and desired outcomes.

HIGHLIGHT 1.11 (continued)

Educational Policy 2.1.10(b)—Assessment
Social workers

- collect, organize, and interpret client data;
- assess client strengths and limitations;
- develop mutually agreed-on intervention goals and objectives; and
- select appropriate intervention strategies.

Educational Policy 2.1.10(c)—Intervention
Social workers

- initiate actions to achieve organizational goals;
- implement prevention interventions that enhance client capacities;
- help clients resolve problems;
- negotiate, mediate, and advocate for clients; and
- facilitate transitions and endings.

Educational Policy 2.1.10(d)—Evaluation
Social workers critically analyze, monitor, and evaluate interventions.

Educational Policy B2.2—Generalist Practice
Generalist practice is grounded in the liberal arts and the person and environment construct. To promote human and social well-being, generalist practitioners use a range of prevention and intervention methods in their practice with individuals, families, groups, organizations, and communities. The generalist practitioner identifies with the social work profession and applies ethical principles and critical thinking in practice. Generalist practitioners incorporate diversity in their practice and advocate for human rights and social and economic justice. They recognize, support, and build on the strengths and resiliency of all human beings. They engage in research-informed practice and are proactive in responding to

the impact of context on professional practice. BSW practice incorporates all of the core competencies.

Educational Policy M2.2—Advanced Practice
Advanced practitioners refine and advance the quality of social work practice and that of the larger social work profession. They synthesize and apply a broad range of interdisciplinary and multidisciplinary knowledge and skills. In areas of specialization, advanced practitioners assess, intervene, and evaluate to promote human and social well-being. To do so they suit each action to the circumstances at hand, using the discrimination learned through experience and self-improvement. Advanced practice incorporates all of the core competencies augmented by knowledge and practice behaviors specific to a concentration.

Educational Policy 2.3—Signature Pedagogy: Field Education
Signature pedagogy represents the central form of instruction and learning in which a profession socializes its students to perform the role of practitioner. Professionals have pedagogical norms with which they connect and integrate theory and practice (Shulman, 2005). In social work, the signature pedagogy is field education. The intent of field education is to connect the theoretical and conceptual contribution of the classroom with the practical world of the practice setting. It is a basic precept of social work education that the two interrelated components of curriculum—classroom and field—are of equal importance within the curriculum, and each contributes to the development of the requisite competencies of professional practice. Field education is systematically designed, supervised, coordinated, and evaluated based on criteria by which students demonstrate the achievement of program competencies."

This text provides content on most of the above knowledge, skills and values needed for social work practice.

LO 1-3 Describe important concepts for understanding human behavior (that are stressed throughout the book and include human diversity, cultural competency, oppression, populations-at-risk, empowerment, the strengths perspective, resiliency, human rights, and critical thinking about ethical issues).

Human diversity is the vast range of human differences among groups, including those related to age, class, color, culture, disability, ethnicity, gender, gender identity and expression, immigration status, political ideology, race, religion, sex, and sexual orientation. Cultural competency is "the mastery of

a particular set of knowledge, skills, policies, and programs used by the social worker that address the cultural needs of individuals, families, groups, and communities" (Lum, 2005, p. 4).

Discrimination is the act of treating people differently because they belong to some group rather than on merit. Oppression involves putting unfair and extreme limitations and constraints on members of an identified group. A population-at-risk is any group of people who share some identifiable characteristic that places them at greater risk of social and economic deprivation and oppression than the general mainstream of society.

Empowerment is "the process of increasing personal, interpersonal, or political power so that individuals can take action to improve their life situations" (Gutierrez, 2001, p. 210). The strengths perspective is an orientation that focuses on client resources, capabilities, knowledge, abilities, motivations, experience, intelligence, and other positive qualities that can be put to use to solve problems and pursue positive changes. Empowerment based on strengths can occur at the individual, group, organizational, and community levels. Resiliency is the ability of an individual, family, group, community, or organization to recover from adversity and resume functioning even when suffering serious trouble, confusion, or hardship.

Human rights involve the premise that all people, regardless of race, culture, or national origin, are entitled to basic rights and treatment.

Critical thinking can be used to address ethical issues and dilemmas. Critical thinking is "the careful examination and evaluation of beliefs and actions" to establish an independent decision about what is true and what is not (Gambrill & Gibbs, 2009, p. 4). Ethical dilemmas are situations where ethical principles conflict and all solutions are imperfect. Critical-thinking questions about ethical issues are interspersed throughout the book.

LO 1-4 Employ a conceptual framework for understanding human behavior and the social environment: ecosystems theory.

Ecosystems theory is "systems theory used to describe and analyze people and other living systems and their transactions" (Beckett & Johnson, 1995, p. 1391). It offers a framework for viewing human behavior that incorporates concepts from systems theories and the ecological perspective, and provides this book's theoretical orientation. Relevant systems theory concepts include system, boundaries, subsystem, homeostasis, role, relationship, input, output, feedback, interface, differentiation, entropy, negative entropy, and equifinality. Pertinent concepts from the ecological perspective include social environment, transactions, energy, interface, adaptation, coping, and interdependence.

LO 1-5 Recognize people's involvement with multiple systems in the social environment.

People are involved with multiple systems in their environment. A micro system is an individual. A mezzo system is a small group. A macro system is a system larger than a small group. Macro systems that are primary contexts for human behavior include communities and organizations.

LO 1-6 Examine human behavior in the context of community macro systems.

A community is "a number of people with something in common that connects them in some way and that distinguishes them from others" (Homan, 2011, p. 8). Theoretical perspectives on communities include the structural, sociopsychological, human ecology, and social systems perspectives. Traditional models of community change include locality development, social planning, and social action. Updated models of macro-level change include social advocacy, planning and policy practice, and community capacity development (Rothman, 2007).

LO 1-7 Examine human behavior in and with organizational macro systems.

Organizations are structured groups of people who come together to work toward some mutual goal and perform established work activities that are divided among various units. Organizations are important to social workers who work within social service organizations that provide services to clients. Problems sometimes experienced by organizations include the shifting environment, vagueness of process, and vagueness of goals.

LO 1-8 Recognize social worker roles in organizational and community systems.

Social workers can perform the following roles as they practice in the context of organizations and communities: enabler, mediator, coordinator, manager, educator, evaluator, broker, facilitator, initiator, negotiator, and advocate.

LO 1-9 Identify Knowledge, Skills, and Values Necessary for Generalist Social Work Practice.

The 10 competencies and their respective 41 practice behaviors necessary for effective generalist social work practice are cited.

COMPETENCY NOTES

This section relates chapter content to the Council on Social Work Education's (CSWE) *Educational Policy and Accreditation Standards* (EPAS) (CSWE, 2008).

One major goal of social work education is to facilitate students' attainment of the EPAS-designated 10 core competencies and their 41 related practice behaviors so that students develop into competent practitioners. "Competencies are measurable practice behaviors that are comprised of knowledge, values, and skills. The goal of the outcome approach is to demonstrate the integration and application of the competencies in practice with individuals, families, groups, organizations, and communities" (CSWE, 2008, EP 2.1).

Students require knowledge in order to develop skills and become competent. Our intent here is to specify what chapter content and knowledge coincides with the development of specific competencies and practice behaviors. (This ultimately is intended to assist in the accreditation process.) Therefore, the following listing first cites the various Educational Policy (EP) core competencies and their related practice behaviors (which are alphabetized beneath competencies) that are relevant to chapter content. Note that most of the listing follows the order that competencies and practice behaviors are cited in the EPAS.

EP 2.1

We have established that "helping hands" icons such as that illustrated in this paragraph are interspersed throughout the chapter indicating where relevant accompanying content is located. Page numbers noted below indicate where icons are placed in the chapter. Following the icon's page number is a brief explanation of how the content accompanying the icon relates to the specified competency or practice behavior.

The content of this chapter prepares students to apply knowledge of human behavior and the social environment. This entire chapter and book address competency Educational Policy (EP) EP 2.1.7 and its respective practice behaviors EP 2.1.7a and EP 2.1.7b (as cited below). (Note that icons representing these are introduced on p. 5.)

EP 2.1.7 Apply knowledge of human behavior and the social environment.

EP 2.1.7a Utilize conceptual frameworks to guide the processes of assessment, intervention, and evaluation. (Such conceptual frameworks will typically be identified by a "helping hands" icon.)

EP 2.1.7b Critique and apply knowledge to understand person and environment.
Other EP competencies and practice behaviors addressed in this chapter include the following:

EP 2.1 Core Competencies.
(p. 59): Competencies are introduced and explained.

EP 2.1.1 Identify as a professional social worker and conduct oneself accordingly.
(p. 6): The profession of social work is described.

EP 2.1.1b Practice personal reflection and self-correction to assure continual professional development.
(p. 17): Assessment of personal and professional strengths in addition to improving areas of weakness is an important aspect of professional identity in social work.
(p. 46): Social workers must continuously assess their perspective on diverse groups and work on understanding their clients' preferred group identification.

EP 2.1.1c Attend to professional roles and boundaries.
(p. 52): Widely ranging professional roles are described that social workers might assume when working in the macro social environment.

EP 2.1.2 Apply social work ethical principles to guide professional practice.
(pp. 3, 33, 40, 42): Ethics are standards that guide behavior. Ethical questions such as these will be raised throughout this book to encourage students to engage in ethical decision-making by addressing professional values and using ethical standards.

EP 2.1.2a: Recognize and manage personal values in a way that allows professional values to guide practice.
(p. 22): Social workers must identify and deal with their own values so that these values don't interfere with professional practice.

EP 2.1.2b: Make ethical decisions by applying standards of the National Association of Social Workers [NASW] *Code of Ethics* and, as applicable, of the International Federation of Social Workers [IFSW]/International Association of Schools of Social Work [IASSW] Ethics in Social Work, Statement of Principles.
(p. 19): The NASW *Code of Ethics* is introduced.

(p. 20): The IFSW/IASSW Ethics in Social Work, Statement of Principles is introduced.

(p. 21): Ethical responsibilities according to the NASW *Code of Ethics* are identified.

EP 2.1.2c: Tolerate ambiguity in resolving ethical conflicts.

(p. 19): Social workers must tolerate the uncertainty and lack of clarity often posed by ethical dilemmas in order to achieve acceptable resolution.

(p. 21): Ethical dilemmas are posed that require readers to struggle with ambiguity and imperfection in order to arrive at an ethical conclusion.

EP 2.1.2d: Apply strategies of ethical reasoning to arrive at principles decisions.

(p. 22): Suggestions are made regarding how to address ethical dilemmas.

EP 2.1.3 Apply critical thinking to inform and communicate professional judgments.

(p. 19): Critical thinking is defined and its relationship to ethical decision-making discussed.

EP 2.1.3b Analyze models of assessment, prevention, intervention, and evaluation.

(p. 49): Social workers should analyze conceptual frameworks for community change to determine which is most appropriate and helpful in the planned change process.

EP 2.1.4 Engage diversity and difference in practice.

(p. 11): Human diversity refers to many differences among people, including those identified here.

(p. 12): Culture is one important dimension of human diversity.

(p. 45): Ethnicity, color, and culture are aspects of diversity.

EP 2.1.4a Recognize the extent to which culture's structures and values may oppress, marginalize, alienate, or create or enhance privilege or power.

(p. 12): Social workers must understand how oppression, on the one hand, and privilege, power, and acclaim, on the other, can dramatically affect people's well-being and quality of life.

EP 2.1.4b Gain sufficient self-awareness to eliminate the influence of personal biases and values in working with diverse groups.

(p. 46): Social workers should strive to improve self-awareness to eliminate personal biases concerning diverse groups.

EP 2.1.5a Understand the forms and mechanisms of oppression and discrimination.

(p. 11): Oppression and discrimination are defined.

EP 2.1.5b Advocate for human rights and social and economic justice.

(p. 20): Human rights and social justice are defined, and the importance for advocacy on their behalf is stressed.

EP 2.1.7 Apply knowledge of human behavior and the social environment.

(p. 8): Social workers must be "knowledgeable about human behavior across the life course." They should "understand geological, social, cultural, psychological, and spiritual development."

EP 2.1.7a Utilize conceptual frameworks to guide the processes of assessment, intervention, and evaluation.

(p. 23): Ecosystems theory that incorporates concepts from both systems theory and the ecological perspective is a useful conceptual framework for understanding human behavior and the social environment.

(p. 26): Numerous conceptual frameworks and theoretical perspectives are examined in this book.

(p. 38): The structural, sociopsychological, human ecology, and social systems perspectives are useful conceptual frameworks for understanding communities.

(p. 43): Locality development, social planning, and social action conceptual frameworks provide models for macro-level change.

(p. 49): A newer conceptual framework for understanding and undertaking community change entails the concepts of social advocacy, planning and policy practice, and community capacity development.

EP 2.1.7b Critique and apply knowledge to understand person and environment.

(p. 49): Social workers must critique models of community change to determine which are most applicable to understanding the current social environment.

EP 2.1.9a Continuously discover, appraise, and attend to changing locales, populations, scientific and technological developments, and emerging societal trends to provide relevant services.

(p. 49): Practitioners should explore how the dynamics of community change are transformed over time to provide relevant services.

(p. 51): Social workers should strive to understand how the macro social environment is changing.

Issues include the shifting environment, vagueness of process, and vagueness of goals.

EP 2.1.10 Engage, assess, intervene, and evaluate with individuals, families, groups, organizations, and communities.

(p. 6): Social workers must be competent in assessing individuals, families, groups, organizations, and communities.

(p. 35): Social work practice requires understanding people's involvement with multiple systems in the environment.

(p. 38): Social workers should have engagement, assessment, intervention, and evaluation skills with respect to communities.

(p. 49): Social workers should have engagement, assessment, intervention, and evaluation skills with respect to organizations.

EP 2.1.10e Assess clients' strengths and limitations.

(p. 14): Assessing client strengths is an important part of the intervention process. Core competencies form the basis for generalist practice, the foundation of the social work curriculum (see EP 2.0 and EP B2.2). Generalist practitioners "recognize, support, and build on the strengths and resiliency of all human beings" (EP B2.2).

EP 2.1.10k Negotiate, mediate, and advocate for clients.

(p. 53): Social workers should be competent in the mediator role.

(p. 54): Practitioners should be competent in the negotiator role.

(p. 54): Social workers should be competent in the advocate role.

WEB RESOURCES

See this text's companion website at *www.cengage brain.com* for learning tools such as chapter quizzing, videos, and more.

BIOLOGICAL DEVELOPMENT IN INFANCY AND CHILDHOOD

Camille Tokerud/Taxi /Getty Images

Juanita lovingly watched her 1-year-old Enrico as he lay in his crib playing with his toes. Enrico was her first child, and Juanita was very proud of him. She was bothered, however, that he could not sit up by himself. Living next door was a baby about Enrico's age, whose name was Teresa. Not only could she sit up by herself, but she could crawl, stand alone, and was even starting to walk. Juanita thought it was odd that the two children could be so different and have such different personalities. That must be the reason, she thought. Enrico was just an easygoing child. Perhaps he was also a bit stubborn. Juanita decided that she wouldn't worry about it. In a few weeks, Enrico would probably start to sit up.

Knowledge of normal human development is critical in order to understand and monitor the progress of children as they grow. In this example, Enrico was indeed showing some developmental lags. He was in need of an evaluation to determine his physical and psychological status so that he might receive help.

A Perspective

The attainment of normal developmental milestones has a direct impact on the client. Biological, psychological, and social development systems operate together to affect behavior. This chapter will explore some of the major aspects of infancy and childhood that social workers must understand in order to provide information to clients and make appropriate assessments of client behavior.

Learning Objectives

This chapter will help prepare students to:

**EP 2.1.7,
2.1.7a,
2.1.7b**

LO 2-1 *Describe the dynamics of human reproduction (including conception, the diagnosis of pregnancy, fetal development, prenatal influences and assessment, problem pregnancies, and the birth process)*

LO 2-2 *Explain normal developmental milestones for infants and children*

LO 2-3 *Examine the abortion controversy (in addition to the impacts of social and economic forces)*

LO 2-4 *Explain infertility (including the causes, the psychological reactions to infertility, the treatment of infertility, the assessment process, alternatives available to infertile couples, and social work roles concerning infertility)*

LO 2-1 Describe the Dynamics of Human Reproduction

Chuck and Christine had mixed emotions about the pregnancy. It had been an accident. They were both in their mid-30s and already had a vivacious 4-year-old daughter named Hope. Although Hope had been a joy to both of them, she had also placed serious restrictions on their lifestyle. They were looking forward to her beginning school. Christine had begun to work part-time and was planning to go full-time as soon as Hope turned 5.

Now all that had changed. To complicate the matter, Chuck, a university professor, had just received an exciting job offer in Hong Kong—the opportunity of a lifetime. They had always dreamed of spending time overseas.

The unexpected pregnancy provided Chuck and Christine with quite a jolt. Should they terminate the pregnancy and go on with their lives in exotic Hong Kong? Should they have the baby overseas? Questions concerning foreign prenatal care, health conditions, and health facilities flooded their thoughts. Would it be safer to remain in the United

States and turn down this golden opportunity? Christine was 35. Her reproductive clock was ticking away. Soon risk factors concerning having a healthy, normal baby would begin to skyrocket. This might be their last chance to have a second child. Chuck and Christine did some serious soul-searching and fact-searching to arrive at their decision.

Yes, they would have the baby. Once the decision had been made, they were filled with relief and joy. They also decided to take the job in Hong Kong. They would use the knowledge they had about prenatal care, birth, and infancy to maximize the chance of having a healthy, normal baby. They concluded that this baby was a blessing who would improve, not impair, the quality of their lives.

The decision to have children is a serious one. Ideally, a couple should examine all alternatives. Children can be wonderful. Family life can bring pleasurable activities, pride, and fullness to life. On the other hand, children can cause stress. They demand attention, time, and effort and can be expensive to care for. Information about conception, pregnancy, birth, and child rearing can only help people make better, more effective decisions.

Conception

Sperm meets egg; a child is conceived. But in actuality, it is not quite that simple. Many couples who strongly desire to have children have difficulty conceiving. Many others whose last desire is to conceive do so with ease. Some amount of chance is involved.

Conception refers to the act of becoming pregnant. Sperm need to be deposited in the vagina near the time of ovulation. *Ovulation* involves the ovary's release of a mature egg into the body cavity near the end of one of the fallopian tubes. Fingerlike projections called *fimbriae* at the end of the fallopian tube draw the egg into the tube. From there, the egg is gently moved along inside the tube by tiny hairlike extensions called *cilia*. Fertilization actually occurs in the third of the fallopian tube nearest the ovary.

If a sperm has gotten that far, conception may occur. After *ejaculation*, the discharge of semen by the penis, the sperm travels up into the uterus and through the fallopian tube to meet the egg. Sperm are equipped with a tail that can lash back and forth, propelling them forward. The typical ejaculate, an amount of approximately one teaspoon, usually contains 200 to 400 million sperm; however

only 1 in 1,000 of these will ever make it to the area immediately surrounding the egg (Rathus, Nevid, & Fichner-Rathus, 2014). Unlike females, who are born with a finite number of eggs, males continually produce new sperm. Fertilization is therefore quite competitive. It is also hazardous. The majority of these sperm don't get very far (Hyde & DeLamater, 2014; Rathus et al., 2014). Many spill out of the vagina, drawn by gravity. Others are killed by the acidity of the vagina. Still others swim up the wrong fallopian tube, meaning the one without the egg. Only about 2,000 sperm make it up the right tube. By the time a sperm reaches the egg, it has swum a distance 3,000 times its own length; an equivalent swim for a human being would be more than 3 miles (Hyde & DeLamater, 2014).

Although sperm are healthiest and most likely to fertilize an egg during the first 24 hours after ejaculation, they may survive up to 72 hours in a woman's reproductive tract; an egg's peak fertility is within the first 8 to 12 hours after ovulation, although it may remain viable for fertilization for up to 24 hours, and some may remain viable for up to five days (Greenberg, Bruess, & Conklin, 2014; Yarber & Sayad, 2013). Therefore, sexual intercourse should ideally occur not more than five days before or one day after ovulation for fertilization to take place (Yarber & Sayad, 2013).

In the fallopian tube, the egg apparently secretes a chemical substance that attracts sperm. The actual fertilization process involves sperm reaching the egg, secreting an enzyme, and depositing it on the egg. This enzyme helps dissolve a gelatinous layer surrounding the egg and allows for the penetration of a sperm. After one sperm has penetrated the barrier, the gelatinous layer undergoes a physical change, thus preventing other sperm from entering it.

Fertilization occurs during the exact moment the egg and sperm combine. Eggs that are not fertilized by sperm simply disintegrate. The genetic material in the egg and sperm combine to form a single cell called a *zygote*.

Eggs contain an X chromosome. Sperm may contain either an X or a Y chromosome. Eggs fertilized by a sperm with an X chromosome will result in a female; those fertilized by sperm with a Y chromosome will result in a male.

The single-celled zygote begins a cell division process in which the cell divides to form two cells, then four, then eight, and so on. Within a week, the new mass of cells, called a *blastocyst*, attaches itself to the lining of the uterus. If attachment does not occur, the newly formed blastocyst is simply expelled. From the point of attachment until eight weeks of gestation, the *conceptus*, or product of conception, is called an *embryo*. From eight weeks until birth, it is referred to as a *fetus*. *Gestation* refers to the period of time from conception to birth.

Diagnosis of Pregnancy

Pregnancy can be diagnosed by using laboratory tests, by observing the mother's physical symptoms, or by performing a physical examination. Many women first become aware of the pregnancy when they miss a menstrual period. However, women also can miss periods as a result of stress, illness, or worry about possible pregnancy. Some pregnant women will even continue to menstruate for a month or even more. Therefore, lab tests are often needed to confirm a pregnancy. Such lab tests are 98 to 99 percent accurate and can be performed at a Planned Parenthood agency, a medical clinic, or a physician's office (Hyde & DeLamater, 2014; Rathus et al., 2014).

Most pregnancy tests work by detecting human chorionic gonadotropin (HCG) in a woman's urine or blood. HCG is a hormone secreted by the *placenta* (the tissue structure that nurtures a developing embryo). Laboratory tests can detect HCG as early as eight days after conception (Greenberg et al., 2014).

The use of home pregnancy tests (HPTs) has become quite common. Like some laboratory tests, they measure HCG levels in urine. They are very convenient, relatively inexpensive and can be used as early as the first day a menstrual period was supposed to start. However, they are more likely to be accurate if administered after more time has passed.

Most HPTs function in a similar fashion. The user holds a stick in the urine stream or collects urine in a cup and dips the stick into it. Most tests have a results window indicating whether a woman is pregnant or not. Most tests also stress retaking the test a few days or a week later to confirm its accuracy.

Because HCG increases as the pregnancy progresses, HPTs become more accurate as time goes on. "Many home pregnancy tests claim to be 99 percent accurate on the day you miss your period. Although research suggests that most home pregnancy tests don't consistently spot pregnancy this early, home pregnancy tests are considered reliable when used according to package instructions one week after a missed period" (Mayo Clinic, 2013c).

Although HPTs can be highly accurate, there is room for error. If instructions are not followed perfectly, results can be faulty. For instance, exposure to sunlight, accidental vibrations, using an unclean container to collect urine, or examining results too early or too late all can end in an erroneous diagnosis. False negatives (i.e., showing that a woman is not pregnant when she really is) are more common than false positives (i.e., showing that a woman is pregnant when she really is not). Regardless, it is suggested that a woman confirm the results either by waiting a week and administering another HPT or by having a laboratory diagnosis performed. Early knowledge of pregnancy is important either to begin early health care or to make a decision about terminating a pregnancy.

Fetal Development During Pregnancy

An average human pregnancy lasts about 280 days (Steinberg, Bornstein, Vandell, & Rook, 2011a). It is most easily conceptualized in terms of trimesters, or three periods of three months each. Each trimester is characterized by certain aspects of fetal development.

The First Trimester

The first trimester is sometimes considered the most critical. Because of the embryo's rapid differentiation and development of tissue, the embryo is exceptionally vulnerable to the mother's intake of noxious substances and to aspects of the mother's health.

By the end of the first month, a primitive heart and digestive system have developed. The basic initiation of a brain and nervous system is also apparent. Small buds that will eventually become arms and legs are appearing. In general, development starts with the brain and continues down through the body. For example, the feet are the last to develop. In the first month, the embryo bears little resemblance to a baby because its organs have just begun to differentiate.

The embryo begins to resemble human form more closely during the second month. Internal organs become more complex. Facial features including eyes, nose, and mouth begin to become identifiable.

The 2-month-old embryo is less than an inch long and weighs about one-third of an ounce.

The third month involves the formation of arms, hands, legs, and feet. Fingernails, hair follicles, and eyelids develop. All the basic organs have appeared, although they are still underdeveloped. By the end of the third month, bones begin to replace cartilage. Fetal movement is frequently detected at this time.

During the first trimester, the mother experiences various symptoms. This is primarily due to the tremendous increase in the amount of hormones her body is producing. Symptoms frequently include tiredness, breast enlargement and tenderness, frequent urination, and food cravings. Some women experience nausea, referred to as morning sickness.

It might be noted that these symptoms resemble those often cited by women when first taking birth control pills. In effect, the pill, by introducing natural or artificial hormones that resemble those of pregnancy, tricks the body into thinking it is pregnant, thus preventing ovulation. The pill as a form of contraception is discussed more thoroughly in Chapter 6.

The Second Trimester

Fetal development continues during the second trimester. Toes and fingers separate. Skin, fingerprints, hair, and eyes develop. A fairly regular heartbeat emerges. The fetus begins to sleep and wake at regular times. Its thumb may be inserted into its mouth.

For the mother, most of the unappealing symptoms of the first trimester subside. She is more likely to feel the fetus's vigorous movement. Her abdomen expands significantly. Some women suffer edema, or water retention, which results in swollen hands, face, ankles, or feet.

The Third Trimester

The third trimester involves completing the development of the fetus. Fatty tissue forms underneath the skin, filling out the fetus's human form. Internal organs complete their development and become ready to function. The brain and nervous system become completely developed.

An important concept that becomes relevant during the sixth and seventh months of gestation is *viability*. This refers to the ability of the fetus to survive on its own if separated from its mother. Although a fetus reaches viability by about the middle of the second trimester, many infants born at 22–25 weeks

"do not survive, even with intensive medical care, and many of those who do experience chronic health or neurological problems" (Sigelman & Rider, 2012, p. 100).

The viability issue becomes especially critical in the context of abortion. The question involves the ethics of aborting a fetus that, with external medical help, might be able to survive. This issue underscores the importance of obtaining an abortion early in the pregnancy when that is the chosen course of action.

For the mother, the third trimester may be a time of some discomfort. The uterus expands, and the mother's abdomen becomes large and heavy. The additional weight frequently stresses muscles and skeleton, often resulting in backaches or muscle cramps. The size of the uterus may exert pressure on other organs, causing discomfort. Some of the added weight can be attributed to the baby itself, amniotic fluid, and the placenta. Other normal weight increases include those of the uterus, blood, and breasts as part of the body's natural adaptation to pregnancy.

Prenatal Influences

Numerous factors can influence the health and development of the fetus. These include the mother-to-be's nutrition, drugs and medication, alcohol consumption, smoking habits, age, maternal stress, and a number of other factors.

EP 2.1.10i

Nutrition

A pregnant woman is indeed eating for two. In the past, pregnant women were afraid of gaining too much weight. But a woman should usually gain 25 to 35 pounds during her pregnancy (Berk, 2013; Kail & Cavenaugh, 2013; Sigelman & Rider, 2012). She typically requires 300 to 500 additional calories daily to adequately nurture the fetus (Papalia & Feldman, 2012). The optimal weight gain depends on the individual, her height, and her weight prior to pregnancy. For example, a woman who is underweight before pregnancy might require a greater weight gain to maintain a healthy pregnancy.

Being underweight or overweight poses risks to the fetus. Too little weight gain due to malnutrition can result in low infant birth weight, increased risk of mental or motor impairment, and a higher infant mortality rate (Berk, 2013; Newman & Newman, 2012). Being overweight either before or during pregnancy can increase the risk of miscarriage and other complications during pregnancy and birth (Chu et al., 2008), in addition to birth defects (Stothard, Tenant, Bell, & Rankin, 2009).

Not only does a pregnant woman need to eat more, but also the quality of food needs careful monitoring and attention. It is especially important for pregnant women to get enough protein, iron, calcium, folic acid (B vitamin), in addition to other vitamins and minerals (Berk, 2013; Kail & Cavenaugh, 2013). Hyde and DeLamater (2014) explain:

> *Protein is important for building new tissues. Folic acid is also important for growth; symptoms of folic acid deficiency are anemia [low red blood cell count] and fatigue. A pregnant woman needs much more iron than usual, because the fetus draws off iron for itself from the blood that circulates to the placenta. Muscle cramps, nerve pains, uterine ligament pains, sleeplessness, and irritability may all be symptoms of a calcium deficiency. (p. 130)*

Drugs and Medication

Because the effects of many drugs on the fetus are unclear, pregnant women are cautioned to be wary of drug use. Drugs may cross the placenta and enter the bloodstream of the fetus. Any drugs should be taken only after consultation with a physician. The effects of such drugs usually depend on the amount taken and the gestation stage during which they are taken. This is especially true for the first trimester, when the embryo is very vulnerable.

Teratogens are substances, including drugs, that cause malformations in the fetus. Certain drugs can cause malformations of certain body parts or organs. The so-called thalidomide babies of the early 1960s provide a tragic example of the potential effects of drugs. Thalidomide, a type of tranquilizer, was found to produce either flipperlike appendages in place of arms or legs, or no arms or legs at all.

A variety of prescription drugs can produce teratogenic effects. These include antibiotics such as tetracycline and streptomycin, Accutane (an acne drug), and some antidepressants (Rathus et al., 2014; Santrock, 2012b). Generally speaking, women should avoid taking drugs or medications during pregnancy and while breast-feeding unless such medication is absolutely necessary.

Even nonprescription, over-the-counter drugs such as aspirin or caffeine should be consumed with caution (Santrock, 2012b). Aspirin can cause bleeding problems in the fetus (Steinberg et al., 2011a). Coffee, tea, colas, and chocolate all contain caffeine. The research findings concerning the effects of caffeine on a fetus have been mixed (Maslova, Bhattacharya, Lin, & Michels, 2010; Minnes, Lang, & Singer, 2011; Rathus, 2014a). However, some research results have revealed a higher risk of miscarriage and low birth weight (Rathus, 2014a; Santrock, 2013). Even vitamins should be consumed with care and only under a physician's supervision (Rathus et al., 2014; Steinberg et al., 2011a). An expectant mother's best bet is to be cautious.

Addiction to such drugs as barbiturates, heroin, and amphetamines can result in numerous problems. Newborn children of drug addicts tend to be addicted themselves at birth. Potential problems include birth defects, low birth weight, abnormal crying, irritability, sleeping and feeding difficulties, and muscle tremors (Newman & Newman, 2012; Rathus, 2014b; Santrock, 2013). Note, however, that it is difficult to separate out the direct effects of specific drugs because of the numerous other factors involved (e.g., an impoverished environment or use of other potentially harmful substances by the mother).

Ethical Questions 2.1

EP 2.1.2 *Should a pregnant woman who consumes illegal drugs that damage her child be punished as a criminal? Should her child be taken from her? If so, with whom should the child be placed?*

Alcohol

Alcohol consumption during pregnancy can have grave effects on a fetus. The condition is termed *fetal alcohol syndrome (FAS)*. Babies of women who were heavy drinkers during pregnancy have "unusual facial characteristics [including widely spaced eyes, short nose, and thin upper lip], small head and body size, congenital heart defects, defective joints, and intellectual and behavioral impairment" (Yarber & Sayad, 2013, p. 373). Effects stretch into childhood and even adulthood. They include difficulties in paying attention, hyperactivity, lower-than-normal intelligence, and significant difficulties in adjustment and social interaction (Shaffer & Kipp, 2010). The severity of defects increases with the amount of alcohol consumed during pregnancy (Shaffer & Kipp, 2010). However, there is evidence that even more moderate alcohol consumption, such as one or two drinks a day, can harm the fetus (Rathus et al., 2014; Shaffer & Kipp, 2010; Steinberg et al., 2011a). *Fetal alcohol effects (FAE)* is a condition that manifests relatively less severe (yet still significant) problems, presumably resulting from lower levels of alcohol consumption during pregnancy.

Smoking

Numerous studies associate smoking with low birth weight, preterm births, breathing difficulties, fetal death, and crib death (Rathus, 2014a; Santrock, 2013; Shaffer & Kipp, 2010; Yarber & Sayad, 2013). Even secondhand smoke is thought to pose a danger to the fetus (Rathus, 2014a). Some research found a relationship between a mother's smoking during pregnancy and a child having behavioral and emotional problems when the child reaches school age (Papalia & Feldman, 2012; Rathus, 2014a).

Age

The pregnant woman's age may affect both the woman and the child. Women "between ages 16 and 35 tend to provide a better uterine environment for the developing fetus and to give birth with fewer complications than do women under 16 or over 35" (Newman & Newman, 2012, p. 115). Women aged 35 and older account for more than 16 percent of all births in the United States (U.S. Census Bureau, 2011). For example, although a woman who is aged 16 to 34 has a very low risk of having a baby with Down syndrome,[1] the likelihood increases to about 1 in 100 when she reaches age 40, and almost 1 in 10 at age 50 (Santrock, 2013). It is thought that a contributing factor to Down syndrome is deterioration of the female's egg or the male's sperm as people age

(Newman & Newman, 2012). Mothers aged 40 and over "are also at slightly higher risk for maternal death, premature delivery, cesarean sections, and low-birth-weight babies (London, 2004). As women age, chronic illnesses such as high blood pressure and diabetes may also present pregnancy- and birth-related complications" (Yarber & Sayad, p. 375).

Teen mothers account for about 12 percent of all U.S. births (U.S. Census Bureau, 2011). Their infants have twice the mortality rates of infants born to mothers in their 20s (Santrock, 2012b). Their infants are more likely to be underweight and experience a greater risk of health problems and disabilities (Papalia & Feldman, 2012). Problems are often due to an immature reproductive system, inadequate nutrition, poor or no prenatal care, and poverty (Santrock, 2013; Smithbattle, 2007).

Maternal Stress

Maternal stress is another factor that can affect fetal development (Kail & Cavenaugh, 2014; Rathus, 2014a). Bjorklund and Blasi (2014) explain:

> Women who experience high levels of stress during pregnancy are more apt to have premature births and low-weight babies (Mulder [et al.], 2002). It is important to note that stress is not some phantom effect but quite real in its physical effects; it causes decreased nutrients and oxygen to the fetus and weakens the mother's immune system, making the fetus more vulnerable as well. Stress in the mother can cause hormone imbalances in the placenta. In addition, women with high levels of stress are more apt to engage in behaviors that are harmful to the fetus, such as tobacco and alcohol use. (pp. 108–109)

Other Factors

Other factors have been found to affect prenatal and postnatal development. For example, lower income level and socioeconomic class can pose health risks to any mother and her fetus (Newman & Newman, 2012). Illness during pregnancy may damage the developing fetus. Rubella (German measles) can cause physical or mental disabilities in the fetus if a woman contracts it during the first three months of pregnancy (Yarber & Sayad, 2013). Prevention of rubella is possible by vaccination; however, this should not be done during pregnancy because it can harm the fetus.

Sexually transmitted infections (STIs) may also be transmitted from mother to newborn in the

---

[1]*Down syndrome* is a congenital condition resulting from a chromosomal abnormality. It is characterized by intellectual disability and by physical features including thick folds at the corners of the eyes, making them appear slanted; short stature; a wide, short skull; broad hands with short fingers; and wide spaces between the first and second toes (Friend, 2008; Mish, 2008). People with the most common type of Down syndrome, trisomy 21, have an extra chromosome.

womb, during birth, or afterward. Pregnant women should be tested for "chlamydia, gonorrhea, hepatitis B, HIV, and syphilis" (described in Chapter 6; Yarber & Sayad, 2013, p. 374). Transmission can often be prevented or infants treated successfully. For example, acquired immune deficiency syndrome (AIDS), which is transmitted by human immunodeficiency virus (HIV), can infect a fetus through the placenta or an infant, at birth if there is contact with the mother's blood, or through breast milk. However, certain drugs such as administration of azidothymidine (AZT) to the mother during pregnancy and to the infant after birth, in addition to performing a cesarean section (surgical removal of the infant from the womb), has radically decreased HIV transmission rates in the United States (Santrock, 2013; Yarber & Sayad, 2013).

Prenatal Assessment

EP 2.1.10e

Tests are available to determine if a developing fetus has any of a variety of defects. These tests include *ultrasound sonography, fetal MRI, amniocentesis, chorionic villus sampling, and maternal blood tests.*

"The development of brain imaging techniques has led to increasing use of *fetal MRI* to diagnose fetal malformations (Schmid & others, 2011).... MRI (magnetic resonance imaging) uses a powerful magnet and radio images to generate detailed images of the body's organs and structures" (Santrock, 2013, p. 68). Ultrasound sonography is generally the first and much more common option for fetal screening because it's cost-effective and safe. However, when a clearer image or more information is required to provide an accurate diagnosis and effective treatment planning, an MRI can be used. Frequently, ultrasound sonography will identify a potential abnormality and a subsequent MRI will offer a more comprehensive, clearer picture of what's involved (Mangione et al., 2011). "Among the fetal malformations that fetal MRI may be able to detect better than ultrasound sonography are certain central nervous system, chest, gastrointestinal, genital/urinary, and placental abnormalities (Nemec & others, 2011; Triulzi, Managaro, & Volpe, 2011; [Amini,] Wikstrom, Ahlstrom, & Axelsson, 2011)" (Santrock, 2013, p. 68).

Amniocentesis involves the insertion of a needle through the abdominal wall and into the uterus to obtain amniotic fluid for determination of fetal

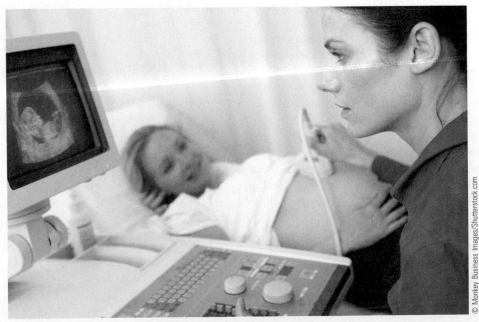

A physician and pregnant mother examine an ultrasound of the fetus.

gender or chromosomal abnormalities. The amniotic fluid contains fetal cells that can be analyzed for a variety of birth defects including Down syndrome, muscular dystrophy,[2] and spina bifida.[3] The gender of the fetus can also be determined. Amniocentesis is recommended if a woman has had a baby with a birth defect, may be a genetic carrier of such a defect, or is over age 35. A disadvantage of amniocentesis is that the test is usually performed about the 16th or 17th week of pregnancy (Charlesworth, 2014). Results are available in about 2 weeks after that (Santrock, 2012b). If a serious problem is discovered, people don't have much time to decide whether to terminate the pregnancy. Another danger is a small risk of miscarriage (Rathus, 2014a; Santrock, 2013).

Chorionic villus sampling (CVS) is another method of diagnosing defects in a developing fetus. It involves the insertion of a thin plastic tube through the vagina or a needle through the abdomen into the uterus. A sample of the chorionic villi (tiny fingerlike projections on the membrane that surrounds the fetus) is taken for analysis of potential genetic irregularities (National Institutes of Health [NIH], 2012). It can be performed between the 10th and 12th weeks of pregnancy with results received within about two weeks (NIH, 2012). An advantage of CVS is that it can be done earlier in the pregnancy than amniocentesis. Couples may have a different perspective on whether to abort or keep a defective fetus at this early stage of the pregnancy. A disadvantage of CVS, as with amniocentesis, is an increased risk of miscarriage (Charlesworth, 2014; NIH, 2012; Rathus, 2014a).

Maternal blood tests done between the 16th and 18th weeks of gestation can detect a variety of conditions (Santrock, 2013). For instance, the amount of a substance called alpha-fetoprotein (AFP) can be measured. High levels of AFP forewarn about abnormalities of the brain and spinal cord. Testing AFP levels can also detect Down syndrome. Ultrasound sonography or amniocentesis can then be used to verify the presence of such congenital conditions.

In addition to a pregnant woman's behavior and condition, numerous other variables in the macro environment and in a woman's personal situation also directly affect the fetal condition. Highlight 2.1 discusses how social workers can help pregnant women access and maximize the use of prenatal care.

Problem Pregnancies

In addition to factors that can affect virtually any pregnancy, other problems can develop under certain circumstances. These problems include ectopic pregnancies, toxemia, and Rh incompatibility. Spontaneous abortions also happen periodically.

Ectopic Pregnancy

When a fertilized egg begins to develop somewhere other than in the uterus, it is called an *ectopic pregnancy* or *tubal pregnancy*. In most cases, the egg becomes implanted in the fallopian tube. Much more rarely, the egg is implanted outside the uterus somewhere in the abdomen.

Ectopic pregnancies most often occur because of a blockage in the fallopian tube. The current rate of ectopic pregnancy has increased dramatically from what it was 30 years ago (Hyde & DeLamater, 2014). This may be attributed partially to increasing rates of STIs that result in scar tissue (Hyde & DeLamater, 2014). Others have hypothesized that this increase in ectopic pregnancies may be due to the increased use of fertility drugs and escalating external stresses in the environment (Kelly, 2008).

Ectopic pregnancies in the fallopian tubes "may spontaneously abort and be released into the abdominal cavity, or the embryo and placenta may continue to expand, stretching the tube until it ruptures" (Hyde & DeLamater, 2014, p. 142). In the latter case, surgical removal is necessary to save the mother's life.

Toxemia

Toxemia (also called *preeclampsia*) is an abnormal condition involving a form of blood poisoning. Carroll (2013b) explains:

> In the last 2 to 3 months of pregnancy, 6% to 7% of women experience **toxemia** … or **preeclampsia**.… Symptoms include rapid weight gain, fluid retention, an increase in blood pressure [hypertension],

---

[2]*Muscular dystrophy* is a group of hereditary diseases characterized by progressive wasting of muscles.
[3]*Spina bifida* is a condition in which the spinal column has not fused shut, and consequently some nerves remain exposed.

Social Workers Can Assist Women in Getting Prenatal Care: Implications for Practice

Prenatal care is considered vital "because it provides social workers and other health professionals with opportunities to identify pregnant women who are at risk of premature or low-weight births, and to deliver the medical, nutritional, educational, or psychosocial interventions that can promote positive pregnancy outcomes" (Perloff & Jeffee, 1999, p. 117). Early prenatal care is especially significant because of the developing fetus's vulnerability. It is important not to assume that all women's knowledge about prenatal care and easy access to such care is equal.

Barriers to obtaining prenatal care may include a number of factors. Women may be struggling with numerous other life issues (e.g., poverty, stress, and demands on their time for other things). Clinics and services may not be readily available and easy for them to reach. Pregnant women may experience difficulties in getting transportation for services or be struggling with other work and child-care demands. They may distrust the health-care system generally. They may have had previous bad experiences with respect to other health-care issues. They may have faced long waiting periods, crowded conditions, and inconvenient hours while trying to get services (Sable & Kelly, 2008).

There are several implications for social work practice. First, workers can help women navigate a complex health-care system, making certain they have ready access to available insurance and Medicaid payments. Second, practitioners can advocate with clinics to improve their internal environments. Providing child care, magazines, comfortable furniture, and refreshments can significantly improve the clinic experience. Third, workers can assist pregnant women "in gaining access to clinic resources (for example, appointments, laboratory tests, and educational seminars) through regular, ongoing contact with clients" (Cook, Selig, Wedge, & Baube, 1999, p. 136). Fourth, practitioners can "develop innovative service delivery models," including screening women during their initial visit to identify those at greatest risk, mailing or calling reminders of clinic appointments, and participating in community outreach (p. 136). Outreach might entail conducting door-to-door case finding of pregnant women to expedite early initiation of prenatal care. This could involve sharing information about risks posed without care, benefits of care, and the availability of services.

EP 2.1.5b, 2.1.10k

---

and protein in the urine. If toxemia is allowed to progress, it can result in **eclampsia**, *which involves convulsions, coma, and in approximately 15% of cases, death.... Overall, [African American] ... women are at higher risk for eclampsia than White or Hispanic women ... (p. 319.)*

Rh Incompatibility

People's red blood cells differ in their surface structures and can be classified in different ways (Santrock, 2013). One way of distinguishing blood type involves categorizing it as either A, B, O, or AB. Another way to differentiate blood cells involves the Rh factor, which is positive if the red blood cells carry the marker or negative if they don't (Santrock, 2013). If the mother has Rh-negative blood and the father Rh-positive blood, the fetus may also have Rh-positive blood. This results in *Rh incompatibility* between the mother's and fetus's blood, and the mother's body forms antibodies in defense against the fetus's incompatible blood. Problem pregnancies and a range of defects in the fetus

may result. Problems are less likely to occur in the first pregnancy than in later ones, because antibodies have not yet had the chance to form. The consequence to an affected fetus can be intellectual disability,[4] anemia, or death.

Fortunately, Rh incompatibility can be dealt with successfully. The mother is injected with a serum, RhoGAM, that prevents the development of future Rh-negative sensitivity. This must be administered within 72 hours after the first child's birth or after a first abortion. In those cases where Rh sensitivity already exists, the newborn infant or even the fetus within the uterus can be given a blood transfusion.

---

[4]Note that here we use the term *intellectual disability* to refer to the condition formerly referred to as *mental retardation* (Hallahan, Kauffman, & Pullen, 2009). This is a condition in which a person has intellectual functioning that is significantly below average and has accompanying deficits in adaptive functioning, both of which occur before age 18. The term *intellectual disability* carries a less negative connotation than *mental retardation*.

Spontaneous Abortion

A *spontaneous abortion* or *miscarriage* is the termination of a pregnancy due to natural causes before the fetus is capable of surviving on its own. About 15 to 20 percent of all diagnosed pregnancies result in spontaneous abortion (Carroll, 2013b; Friebe & Arck, 2008). Thus, a woman may not even be aware of the pregnancy when the miscarriage occurs. Sometimes it is perceived as an extremely heavy menstrual period. The vast majority of miscarriages occur within the first trimester, with only a small minority occurring during the second or third trimester.

Most frequently, spontaneous abortions occur as a result of a defective fetus or some physical problem of the expectant mother. The body for some reason knows that the fetus is defective or that conditions are not right, and expels the fetus. Maternal problems may include a uterus that is "too small, too weak, or abnormally shaped, … maternal stress, nutritional deficiencies, excessive vitamin A, drug exposure, or pelvic infection" (Carroll, 2013b, p. 318). Some evidence indicates that faulty sperm may also be to blame (Carrell et al., 2003).

The Birth Process

The birth process itself involves three stages. During the first stage of labor, *dilation*, the cervix is dilated, or opened, in preparation for the baby to pass through it. Early on, contractions may come between 5 and 20 minutes apart; as labor progresses they continue to build in frequency, duration, and intensity (MFMER, 2009). Three other signs may indicate that labor has begun (NWHIC, 2010a). These include a bloody mucus discharge (which is the plug that blocked the cervix during pregnancy), lower back pain that doesn't stop, and having one's "water break." The latter involves membranes that rupture preceding the birth, resulting in anything from "a gush" to "a slow trickle of amniotic … fluid" (NWHIC, 2010a).

Note that "[m]any women, especially first-time mothers-to-be think they are in labor when they're not. This is called *false labor*. 'Practice' contractions called Braxton Hicks contractions are common in the last weeks of pregnancy or earlier" (emphasis added) (NWHIC, 2010a).

The first stage of labor, which is the longest, typically lasts about 12 to 19 hours, although "how labor progresses and how long it lasts are different for every woman" (NWHIC, 2010a). The first stage may be shorter for women who have had a prior vaginal delivery (MFMER, 2009).

The second stage of labor, *expulsion*, marks the time when the baby is actually born. This stage, which typically lasts 20 minutes to 2 hours, involves pushing between contractions to facilitate the baby's movement out of the uterus (NWHIC, 2010a). Each contraction also helps move the baby farther along. The cervix is completely dilated, and the baby begins to move through the vagina. The head usually emerges first. However, depending on the baby's position, some other body part may appear first.

Although most women don't need it, sometimes an episiotomy is performed during the second stage (NWHIC, 2010a). An *episiotomy* involves making a small incision in the skin just behind the vagina. Its purpose is to relieve pressure on the strained tissues and help to provide a larger opening through which the baby can emerge. Theoretically, an episiotomy should also prevent tearing of the mother's tissues that can result in difficulty when healing.

CONCEPT SUMMARY

Problem Pregnancies

Ectopic pregnancy: The circumstance when a fertilized egg becomes implanted and begins to develop somewhere other than the uterus (usually in a fallopian tube).

Toxemia: A pregnant woman's abnormal condition involving a form of blood poisoning that results in rapid weight gain, fluid retention, hypertension, and protein in the urine.

Rh incompatibility: The condition when a mother and fetus have opposite Rh factors (positive versus negative), resulting in the mother's blood forming antibodies against the fetus's incompatible blood.

Spontaneous abortion: The termination of a pregnancy due to natural causes before the fetus is capable of surviving on its own.

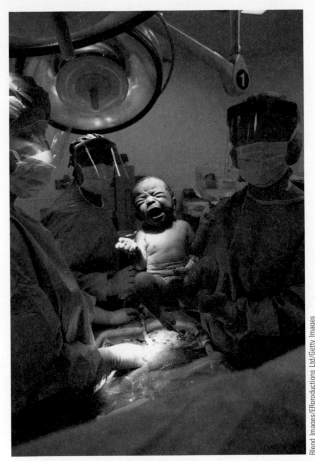

The birth process is an amazing experience.

Blend Images/ERproductions Ltd/Getty Images

After the baby completely emerges, the umbilical cord, which still attaches the baby to its mother, is clamped and severed about three inches from the baby's body. Because there are no nerve endings in the cord, this does not hurt. The small section of cord remaining on the infant gradually dries up and simply falls off.

The third stage of labor, the *afterbirth*, involves delivery of the placenta and other remaining fetal material. It lasts 5 to 30 minutes, beginning about 30 minutes after the birth (NWHIC, 2010a). The afterbirth detaches itself from the uterine walls and is expelled with the help of a few contractions. Finally, the episiotomy, if performed, is stitched up.

Birth Positions

The majority of babies are born with their heads emerging first. Referred to as a *vertex presentation*, this is considered the normal birth position and most often requires no assistance with instruments. Figure 2.1 depicts various birth positions.

About 4 percent of babies are born in a *breech presentation* (Santrock, 2013). Here, the buttocks and feet appear first and the head last as the baby is born. This type of birth may merit more careful attention. Often a cesarean section is performed (Santrock, 2013).

A *cesarean section*, or *C-section*, is a surgical procedure in which the baby is removed by making an incision in the abdomen through the uterus. Cesarean sections account for over 32 percent of all births in the United States (U.S. Census Bureau, 2011). Note that more cesarean sections are carried out in the United States than in any other nation (Santrock, 2013). Cesarean sections are necessary when the baby is in a difficult prenatal position, when the baby's head is too large to maneuver out of the uterus and vagina, when fetal distress is detected, or when the labor has been extremely long and exhausting. Today it is usually safe with only minimal risks to the mother or infant. The mother's recovery, however, will be longer because the incisions must heal.

Finally, about 1 percent of babies are born with a *transverse presentation* (Dacey, Travers, & Fiore, 2009). Here the baby lies crossways in the uterus. During birth, a hand or arm usually emerges first in the vagina. As such positions also merit special attention, a cesarean section is typically performed (Santrock, 2013).

In the United States, 98.8 percent of all births occur in hospital settings, and a doctor is usually present (Martin et al., 2012). However, it's quite a different scene throughout much of the world, where home births and *midwifery* (the practice of having a person who is not a physician assist a mother in childbirth) are much more common. Although midwives are present for only 8.1 percent of births in the United States (American College of Nurse-Midwives, 2012), this reflects a significant increase from the less than 1 percent evident in 1975 (Martin et al., 2005).

Natural Childbirth

In natural childbirth, the emphasis is on education for the parents, especially the mother. The intent is to maximize her understanding of the process and to minimize her fear of the unknown. Natural childbirth also emphasizes relaxation techniques.

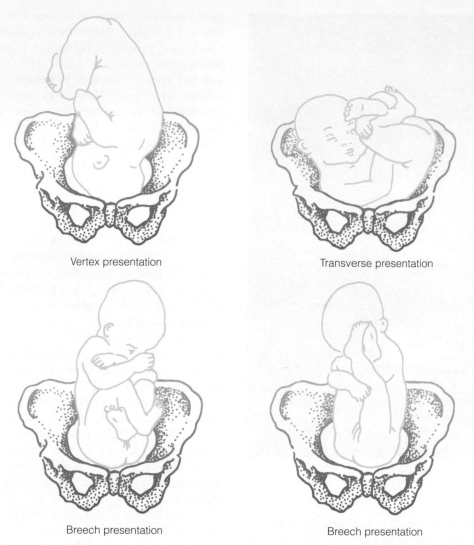

Vertex presentation

Transverse presentation

Breech presentation

Breech presentation

FIGURE 2.1 Forms of Birth Presentation

Mothers are encouraged to tune in to their normal body processes and learn to consciously relax when under stress. They are taught to breathe correctly and to facilitate the birth process by bearing down in an appropriate manner. The Lamaze method is currently popular in the United States, although other methods are also available. Most "emphasize education, relaxation and breathing exercises, and support" in addition to the partner's role as a labor coach" (Santrock, 2013, p. 116).

Many women prefer natural childbirth because it allows them to experience and enjoy the birth to the greatest extent possible. When done correctly, pain is minimized. Anesthetics are usually avoided so that

maximum feeling can be attained. It allows the mother to remain conscious throughout the birth process.

Newborn Assessment

Birth is a traumatic process that is experienced more easily by some newborns, often referred to as neonates, and with more difficulty by others. Evaluation scales have been developed to assess an infant's condition at birth. The sooner any problems can be attended to, the greater the chance of having the infant be normal and healthy. Two such scales are the Apgar and the Brazelton.

EP 2.1.10e

In 1953, Virginia Apgar developed a scale, commonly known as an Apgar scale, that assesses the following five variables (note the acronym):

1. **A**ppearance: Skin color (ranging from bluish-gray to good color everywhere).
2. **P**ulse: Heart rate (ranging from no heart rate to at least 100 beats per minute).
3. **G**rimace: Reflex response (ranging from no response while the airways are being suctioned to active grimacing, pulling away, and coughing).
4. **A**ctivity: Muscle tone (ranging from limpness to active motion).
5. **R**espiration: Baby's breathing (ranging from not breathing to normal breathing and strong crying) (Apgar, 1958; Berk, 2013; Steinberg et al., 2011a).

Each of these five variables is given a score of 0 to 2. Evaluation of these signs usually occurs twice—at one minute and at five minutes after birth. A maximum score of 10 is possible. Scores of 7 through 10 indicate a normal, healthy infant. Scores of 4 through 6 suggest that some caution be taken and that the infant be carefully observed. Scores of 4 or below warn that problems are apparent. In these cases, the infant needs immediate emergency care.

A second scale used to assess the health of a newborn infant is the Brazelton (1973) Neonatal Behavioral Assessment Scale. Whereas the Apgar scale addresses the gross or basic condition of an infant immediately after birth, the Brazelton assesses more extensively the functioning of the central nervous system and behavioral responses of a newborn. Usually administered 24 to 36 hours after birth, the scale focuses on finer distinctions of behavior. It includes a range of 28 behavioral items and 18 reflex items that evaluate such dimensions as motor system control, activity level, sucking reflex, responsiveness while awake or sleeping, and attentiveness to the external environment (Brazelton Institute, 2005). Extremely low scores can indicate brain damage or a brain condition that, given time, may eventually heal (Santrock, 2013).

Birth Defects

Birth defects refer to any kind of disfigurement or abnormality present at birth. Birth defects are much more likely to characterize fetuses that are miscarried. *Miscarriage* provides a means for the body to prevent seriously impaired or abnormal births. The specific types of birth defects are probably infinite; however, some tend to occur with greater frequency.

Down syndrome is a disorder involving an extra chromosome that results in various degrees of intellectual disability. Accompanying physical characteristics include a broad, short skull; widely spaced eyes with an extra fold of skin over the eyelids; a round, flattened face; a flattened nose; a protruding tongue; shortened limbs; and defective heart, eyes, and ears. We've already noted that a woman's chances of bearing a child with Down syndrome increase significantly with her age.

Spina bifida is a condition in which the spinal column has not fused shut and consequently some nerves remain exposed. Surgery immediately after birth closes the spinal column. Muscle weakness or paralysis and difficulties with bladder and bowel control often accompany this condition. Frequently occurring along with spina bifida is hydrocephalus, in which an abnormal amount of spinal fluid accumulates in the skull, possibly resulting in skull enlargement and brain atrophy. Spina bifida has a prevalence rate of 3.49 per 10,000 births (Centers for Disease Control [CDC], 2011).

Low-Birth-Weight and Preterm Infants

Low birth weight and preterm status (prematurity) pose grave problems for newborns. *Low birth weight* is defined as 5 pounds 8 ounces or less; "about 1 in every 12 babies in the United States is born with low birth weight" (March of Dimes, 2012). Primary causes for low birth weight are premature birth and fetal growth restriction (i.e., being small for gestational age due to any of a number of reasons); other maternal factors increasing risk for low birth weight include chronic health conditions (such as those involving high blood pressure, diabetes, or lung and kidney problems), some infections (especially those involving the uterus), troubles with the placenta (resulting in inadequate nutrients provided to the fetus), inadequate weight gain during pregnancy, and the pregnant mother's behavior and experience (e.g., smoking, drinking, poor nutrition, chronic maternal health problems, and lack of access to adequate resources) (March of Dimes, 2012).

Preterm or *premature* babies, born before the 37th week of gestation, often experience low birth weight.

HIGHLIGHT 2.2

An International Perspective on Low-Birth-Weight Infants

EP 2.1.5a

Santrock (2013) reflects on the circumstances of low-birth-weight infants in various countries around the world:

The incidence of low birth weight varies considerably from country to country. In some countries, such as India and Sudan, where poverty is rampant and the health and nutrition of mothers are poor, the percentage of low birth weight babies reaches as high as 31 percent.... In the United States, there has been an increase in low birth weight infants in the last two decades. The U.S. low birth weight rate of 8.2 percent in 2007 is considerably higher than that of many other developed countries (Hamilton & others, 2009). For example, only 4 percent of infants born in Sweden, Finland, Norway, and Korea are low birth weight, and only 5 percent of those born in New Zealand, Australia, and France are low birth weight.

The causes of low birth weight also vary (Mortensen & others, 2009). In the developing world, low birth weight stems mainly from the mother's poor health and nutrition (Christian, 2009). For example, diarrhea and malaria, which are common in developing countries, can impair fetal growth if the mother becomes affected while she is pregnant. In developed countries, cigarette smoking during pregnancy is the leading cause of low birth weight (Fertig, 2010). In both developed and developing countries, adolescents who give birth when their bodies are not fully matured are at risk of having low birth weight babies (Malamitsi-Puchner & Boutsikou, 2006). In the United States, the increase in the number of low birth weight infants is due to such factors as the use of drugs, poor nutrition, multiple births, reproductive technologies, and improved technology and prenatal care, resulting in a higher survival rate of high-risk babies (Chen & others, 2007). Nonetheless, poverty still is a major factor in preterm birth in the United States.... (p. 121)

A full-term pregnancy is considered to last between 37 and 42 weeks, with most babies being born at about 40 weeks; about one in eight of all babies born in the United States are preterm (Centers for Disease Control [CDC], 2013d). Premature infants tend to weigh less because they haven't had the necessary time to develop. Risk factors for premature birth include having born a prior premature baby, being part of a multiple birth scenario, and uterine or cervical abnormalities (CDC, 2013d). Other risk factors resemble those involved in infants having a low birth weight (CDC, 2013d).

Both low birth weight and preterm status place infants at higher risk for a range of problems (CDC, 2013d; March of Dimes, 2012). However, note that most low-birth-weight babies eventually function normally (Santrock, 2013; Wilson-Costello et al., 2007; Xiong et al., 2007). The earlier infants are born and the lower their birth weight, the greater their potential for developmental delays and long-term disabilities (CDC, 2013d; Santrock, 2013).

Due to modern technology and care, low-birth-weight babies are much more likely to survive than they were in the past. Yet, early on, they are also more likely to experience problems involving

breathing, bleeding, heart problems, intestinal difficulties, and potential loss of vision (March of Dimes, 2012). There is some indication that by school age, low-birth-weight children are more likely to experience learning and attention difficulties[5] or breathing problems such as asthma (Anderson et al., 2011; Berk, 2013; Santo, Portuguez, & Nunes, 2009; Santrock, 2013). Increasing evidence indicates that low-birth-weight infants have greater difficulties socializing as adults (Berk, 2013; Moster, Lie, & Markestad, 2008). Be aware, however, that it is difficult to distinguish the direct effects of low birth weight from the effects of other variables such as an impoverished or abusive environment. Highlight 2.2 addresses the circumstances of low-birth-weight infants internationally.

Social work roles that are used to help pregnant women bear healthy infants might include that of a broker to help women get the resources they need.

---

[5]One type of attention difficulty involves *attention deficit hyperactivity disorder (ADHD)*. This is a syndrome of learning and behavioral problems beginning in childhood that is characterized by a persistent pattern of inattention, excessive physical movement, and impulsivity that appears in at least two settings. ADHD is discussed further in Chapter 3.

EP 2.1.1c

These resources include access to good nutrition and prenatal care. If such resources are unavailable, especially to poor women, social workers might need to advocate on the women's behalf. Funding sources and services might need to be developed.

Treatment for low-birth-weight babies includes immediate medical attention to meet their special needs and provision of educational and counseling support. Group counseling for parents and weekly home visits to teach parents how to care for their children, play with them, and provide stimulation to develop cognitive, verbal, and social skills also appear to be helpful.

Early Functioning of the Neonate

The average full-term newborn weighs about 7½ pounds and is approximately 20 inches long (most weigh from 5½ to 10 pounds, and measure from 18 to 22 inches long). Girls tend to weigh a bit less and to be shorter than boys. Many parents may be surprised at the sight of their newborn, who does not resemble the cute, pudgy, smiling, gurgling baby typically shown in television commercials. Rather, the baby is probably tiny and wrinkled with a disproportionate body and squinting eyes. Newborns need time to adjust to the shock of being born. Meanwhile, they continue to achieve various milestones in development. They gain more and more control over their muscles and are increasingly better able to think and respond.

First, newborn babies generally spend much time sleeping, although the time spent decreases as the baby grows older. Second, babies tend to respond in very generalized ways. They cannot make clear distinctions among various types of stimuli, nor can they control their reactions in a precise manner. Any type of stimulation tends to produce a generalized flurry of movement throughout the entire body.

Several reflexes that characterize newborns should be present in normal neonates. First, there is the *sucking reflex*. This obviously facilitates babies' ability to take in food. Related to this is a second basic reflex, rooting. Normal babies will automatically move their heads and begin a sucking motion with their mouths whenever touched even lightly on the lips or cheeks beside the lips. The *rooting reflex* refers to this automatic movement toward a stimulus.

A third important reflex is the *Moro reflex*, or *startle reflex*. Whenever infants hear a sudden loud noise, they automatically react by extending their arms and legs, spreading their fingers, and throwing their heads back. The purpose of this reflex is unknown, and it seems to disappear after a few months of life.

Five additional reflexes are the *stepping reflex*, the *grasping reflex*, the *Babinski reflex*, the *swimming reflex*, and the *tonic neck reflex*. The *stepping reflex* involves infants' natural tendency to lift a leg when held in an upright position with feet barely touching a surface. In a way, it resembles the beginning motions involved in walking. The *grasping reflex* refers to a newborn's tendency to grasp and hold objects such as sticks or fingers when placed in the palms of their hands. The *Babinski reflex* involves the stretching, fanning movement of the toes whenever the infant is stroked on the bottom of the foot. The *swimming reflex* involves infants making swimming motions when they're placed face down in water. Finally, the *tonic neck reflex* is the infant's turning of the head to one side when laid down on its back, the extension of the arm and leg on the side it's facing, and the flexing of the opposite limbs. Sometimes, this is referred to as the "fencer" pose as it resembles just that.

LO 2-2 Explain Normal Developmental Milestones for Infants and Children

As infants grow and develop, their growth follows certain patterns and principles. At each stage of development, people are physically and mentally capable of performing certain types of tasks. *Human development* is the continuous process of growth and change, involving physical, mental, emotional, and social characteristics, that occurs over a life span. Human development is predictable in that the same basic changes occur sequentially for everyone. However, enough variation exists to produce individuals with unique attributes and experiences.

Four major concepts are involved in understanding the process of human development: (1) growth as a continuous, orderly process, (2) specific characteristics of different age levels, (3) the importance of individual differences, and (4) the effects of both heredity and the social environment.

Growth as a Continuous, Orderly Process

People progress through a continuous, orderly sequence of growth and change as they pass from one age level to another. This has various implications. For one thing, growth is continuous and progressive. People are continually changing as they get older. For another thing, the process is relatively predictable and follows a distinct order. For example, an infant must learn how to stand up before learning how to run. All people tend to follow the same order in terms of their development. For instance, all babies must learn how to formulate verbal sounds before learning how to speak in complete sentences.

Several subprinciples relate to the idea that development is an orderly process. One is that growth always follows a pattern from simpler and more basic to more involved and complex. Simple tasks must be mastered before more complicated ones can be undertaken.

Another subprinciple is that aspects of development progress from being more general to being more specific. Things become increasingly more differentiated. For example, infants initially begin to distinguish between human faces and other objects such as balloons. This is a general developmental response. Later they begin to recognize not only the human face, but also the specific faces of their parents. Eventually, as they grow older they can recognize the faces of Uncle Horace, Mr. Schmidt the grocer, and their best friend Joey. Their recognition ability has progressed from being very basic to being very specific.

Two other subprinciples involve cephalocaudal development and proximodistal development. *Cephalocaudal development* refers to development from the head to the toes. Infants begin to learn how to use the parts of the upper body such as the head and arms before their legs. *Proximodistal development* refers to the tendency to develop aspects of the body trunk first and then later master manipulation of the body extremities (e.g., first the arms and then the hands).

Specific Characteristics of Different Age Levels

A second basic developmental principle is that each age period tends to have specific characteristics. During each stage of life, from infancy throughout adulthood, "normal" people are generally capable of performing certain tasks. Capabilities tend to be similar for all people within any particular age category. Developmental guidelines provide a very general means for determining whether an individual is progressing and developing normally.

Individual Differences

The third basic principle of development emphasizes that people have individual differences. Although people tend to develop certain capacities in a specified order, the ages at which particular individuals master certain skills may show a wide variation. Some people may progress through certain stages faster. Others will take more time to master the same physical and mental skills. Variation may occur in the same individual from one stage to the next. The specific developmental tasks and skills that characterize each particular age level may be considered an average of what is usually accomplished during that level. Any average may reflect a wide variation. People may still be "normal" if they fall at one of the extremes that make up the average.

The Nature-Nurture Controversy

A fourth principle involved in understanding human development is that both heredity and the surrounding environment affect development. Individual differences, to some extent, may be influenced by environmental factors. People are endowed with some innate ability and potential. In addition, the impinging environment acts to shape, enhance, or limit that ability.

For example, take a baby who is born with the potential to grow and develop into a normal adult, both physically and intellectually. Nature provides the individual baby with some prospective potential. However, if the baby happens to be living in a developing country during a famine, the environment or nurture may have drastic effects on the baby's development. Serious lack of nourishment limits the baby's eventual physical and mental potential.

Given the complicated composition of human beings, the exact relationship between hereditary potential and environmental effects is unclear. It is impossible to quantify how much the environment affects development compared to how much development is affected by heredity. This is often referred to as the *nature-nurture controversy*. Theorists assume stands at both extremes. Some state that nature's heredity is the most important. Others hypothesize that the environment imposes the crucial influence.

You might consider that each individual has a potential that is to some extent determined by inheritance. However, this potential is maximized or minimized by what happens to people in their particular environments.

Former president Ronald Reagan maintained only a C average in college. Yet he was able to attain the most powerful position in the country. It is difficult to determine how much of his success was due to innate ability and how much to situations and opportunities he encountered in his environment.

Our approach is that a person develops as the result of a multitude of factors including those that are inherited and those that are environmental.

Relevance to Social Work

EP 2.1.10e

Knowledge of human development and developmental milestones can be directly applied to social work practice. Assessment is a basic fact of intervention throughout the life span. In order to assess human needs and human behavior accurately, the social worker must know what is considered normal or appropriate. He or she must decide when intervention is necessary and when it is not. Comparing observed behavior with what is considered normal behavior provides a guideline for these decisions.

This book will address issues in human development throughout the life span. A basic understanding of every age level is important for generalist practice. However, an understanding of the normal developmental milestones for young children is especially critical. Early assessment of potential developmental lags or problems allows for maximum alleviation or prevention of future difficulties. For example, early diagnosis of a speech problem will alert parents and teachers to provide special remedial help for a child. The child will then have a better chance to make progress and possibly even catch up with peers.

Profiles of Normal Development for Children Ages 4 Months to 11 Years

Children progress through an organized sequence of behavior patterns as they mature. Research has established indicators of normality such as when children typically say their first word, run adeptly, or throw a ball overhand. These milestones reflect only an average indication of typical accomplishments. Children need not follow this profile to the letter. Normal human development provides for much individual variation. Parents do not have to be concerned if their child cannot yet stand alone at 13 months instead of the average 12 months. However, serious lags in development or those that continue to increase in severity should be attended to. This list can act as a screening guide to determine if a child might need more extensive evaluation.

Each age profile is divided into five assessment categories. They include motor or physical behavior, play activities, adaptive behavior that involves taking care of self, social responses, and language development. All five topics are addressed together at each developmental age level in order to provide a more complete assessment profile.

Occasionally, case vignettes are presented that describe children of various ages. Evaluate to what extent each of these children fits the developmental profile.

Age 4 Months

Motor: Four-month-old infants typically can balance their heads at a 90-degree angle. They can also lift their heads and chests when placed on their stomachs in a prone position. They begin to discover themselves. They frequently watch their hands, keep their fingers busy, and place objects in their mouths.

Adaptive: Infants are able to recognize their bottles. The sight of a bottle often stimulates bodily activity. Sometimes teething begins this early, although the average age is closer to 6 or 7 months.

Social: These infants are able to recognize their mothers and other familiar faces. They imitate smiles and often respond to familiar people by reaching, smiling, laughing, or squirming.

Language: The 4-month-old will turn his or her head when a sound is heard. Verbalizations include gurgling, babbling, and cooing.

Age 8 Months

Motor: Eight-month-old babies are able to sit alone without being supported. They usually are able to assist themselves into a standing position by pulling themselves up on a chair or crib. They can reach for

Children achieve their developmental milestones step by step.

an object and pick it up with all their fingers and a thumb. Crawling efforts have begun. These babies can usually begin creeping on all fours, displaying greater strength in one leg than the other.

Play: The baby is capable of banging two toys together. Many can also pass an object from one hand to the other. These babies can imitate arm movements such as splashing in a tub, shaking a rattle, or crumpling paper.

Adaptive: Babies of this age can feed themselves pieces of toast or crackers. They will be able to munch instead of being limited to sucking.

Social: Babies of this age can begin imitating facial expressions and gestures. They can play pata-cake, peekaboo, and wave bye-bye.

Language: Babbling becomes frequent and complex. Most babies will be able to attempt copying the verbal sounds they hear. Many can say a few words or sounds such as *mama* or *dada*. However, they don't yet understand the meaning of words.

Age 1 Year

Motor: By age 1 year, most babies can crawl well, which makes them highly mobile. Although they usually require support to walk, they can stand alone without holding onto anything. They eagerly reach out into their environments and explore things. They can open drawers, undo latches, and pull on electrical cords.

Play: One-year-olds like to examine toys and objects both visually and by touching them. They typically like to handle objects by feeling them, poking them, and turning them around in their hands. Objects are frequently dropped and picked up again one time after another. Babies of this age like to put objects in and take them out of containers. Favorite toys include large balls, bottles, bright dangling toys, clothespins, and large blocks.

Adaptive: Because of their mobility, 1-year-olds need careful supervision. Because of their interest in exploration, falling down stairs, sticking forks in electric sockets, and eating dead insects are constant possibilities. Parents need to scrutinize their homes and make them as safe as possible.

Babies are able to drink from a cup. They can also run their spoon across their plate and place the spoon in their mouths. They can feed themselves with their fingers. They begin to cooperate while being dressed by holding still or by extending an arm or a leg to facilitate putting the clothes on. Regularity of both bowel and bladder control begins.

Social: One-year-olds are becoming more aware of the reactions of those around them. They often vary their behavior in response to these reactions. They enjoy having an audience. For example, they tend to repeat behaviors that are laughed at. They also seek attention by squealing or making noises.

Language: By 1 year, babies begin to pay careful attention to the sounds they hear. They can understand simple commands. For instance, on request they often can hand you the appropriate toy. They begin to express choices about the type of food they will accept or about whether it is time to go to bed. They imitate sounds more frequently and can meaningfully use a few other words in addition to *mama* and *dada*.

Case Vignette A: To what extent does this child fit the developmental profile?

Wyanet, age 1 year, is able to balance her head at a 90-degree angle. She can also lift her head when placed on her stomach in a prone position. She is not yet able to sit alone. She can recognize her bottle and her mother. Verbalizations include gurgling, babbling, and cooing.

Age 18 Months

Motor: By 18 months, a baby can walk. Although these children are beginning to run, their movements are still awkward and result in frequent falls. Walking up stairs can be accomplished by a caregiver holding the baby's hand. These babies can often descend stairs by themselves but only by crawling down backward or by sliding down by sitting first on one step and then another. They are also able to push large objects and pull toys.

Play: Babies of this age like to scribble with crayons and build with blocks. However, it is difficult for them to place even three or four blocks on top of each other. These children like to move toys and other objects from one place to another. Dolls or stuffed animals frequently are carried about as regular companions. These toys are also often shown affection such as hugging. By 18 months, babies begin to imitate some of the simple things that adults do such as turning pages of a book.

Adaptive: Ability to feed themselves is much improved by age 18 months. These babies can hold their own glasses to drink from, usually using both hands. They are able to use a spoon sufficiently to feed themselves.

By this age, children can cooperate in dressing. They can unfasten zippers by themselves and remove their own socks or hats. Some regularity has also been established in toilet training. These babies

often can indicate to their parents when they are wet and sometimes wake up at night in order to be changed.

Social: Children function at the solitary level of play. It is normal for them to be aware of other children and even enjoy having them around; however, they don't play with other children.

Language: Children's vocabularies consist of more than 3 but less than 50 words. These words usually refer to people, objects, or activities with which they are familiar. They frequently chatter using meaningless sounds as if they were really talking like adults. They can understand language to some extent. For instance, children will often be able to respond to directives or questions such as "Give Mommy a kiss," or "Would you like a cookie?"

Case Vignette B: To what extent does this child fit the developmental profile?

Luis, age 18 months, can crawl well but is unable to stand by himself. He likes to scribble with crayons and build with blocks. However, it is difficult for him to place even three or four blocks on top of each other. He can say a few sounds, including mama and dada, but he cannot yet understand the meaning of words.

Age 2 Years

Motor: By age 2, children can walk and run quite well. They also can often master balancing briefly on one foot and throwing a ball in an overhead manner. They can use the stairs themselves by taking one step at a time and by placing both feet on each step. They are also capable of turning pages of a book and stringing large beads.

Play: Two-year-olds are very interested in exploring their world. They like to play with small objects such as toy animals and can stack up to six or seven blocks. They like to play with and push large objects such as wagons and walkers. They also enjoy exploring the texture and form of materials such as sand, water, and clay. Adults' daily activities such as cooking, carpentry, or cleaning are frequently imitated. Two-year-olds also enjoy looking at books and can name common pictures.

Adaptive: Two-year-olds begin to be capable of listening to and following directions. They can assist in dressing rather than merely cooperating. For example, they may at least try to button their clothes, although they are unlikely to be successful.

They attempt washing their hands. A small glass can be held and used with one hand.

They use spoons to feed themselves fairly well. Two-year-olds have usually attained daytime bowel and bladder control with only occasional accidents. Nighttime control is improving but still not complete.

Social: These children play alongside each other, but not with each other in a cooperative fashion. They are becoming more and more aware of the feelings and reactions of adults. They begin to seek adult approval for correct behavior. They also begin to show their emotions in the forms of affection, guilt, or pity. They tend to have mastered the concept of saying no, and use it frequently.

Language: Two-year-olds can usually put two or three words together to express an idea. For instance, they might say, "Daddy gone," or "Want milk." Their vocabulary usually includes more than 50 words. Over the next few months, new vocabulary will steadily increase into hundreds of words. They can identify common facial features such as eyes, ears, and nose. Simple directions and requests are usually understood. Although 2-year-olds cannot yet carry on conversations with other people, they frequently talk to themselves or to their toys. It's common to hear them ask, "What's this?" in their eagerness to learn the names of things. They also like to listen to simple stories, especially those with which they are very familiar.

Case Vignette C: To what extent does this child fit the developmental profile?

Kenji, age 2 years, can walk well but still runs with an awkward gait. He likes to play with and push large objects such as wagons and walkers. He also likes to play alongside other children but is not able to play with them in a cooperative fashion. His vocabulary includes about 25 words, but he is not yet very adept at putting two to three words together to express an idea.

Age 3 Years

Motor: At age 3, children can walk well and also run at a steady gait. They can stop quickly and turn corners without falling. They can go up and down stairs using alternating feet. They can begin to ride a tricycle. Three-year-olds participate in a lot of physically active activities such as swinging, climbing, and sliding.

Play: By age 3, children begin to develop their imagination. They use books creatively such as making them into fences or streets. They like to push toys such as trains or cars in make-believe activities. When given the opportunity and interesting toys and materials, they can initiate their own play activities. They also like to imitate the activities of others, especially those of adults. They can cut with scissors and can make some controlled markings with crayons.

Adaptive: Three-year-olds can actively help in dressing. They can put on simple items of clothing such as pants or a sweater, although their clothes may be on backward or inside out. They begin to try buttoning and unbuttoning their own clothes. They eat well by using a spoon and have little spilling. They also begin to use a fork. They can get their own glass of water from a faucet and pour liquid from a small pitcher. They can wash their hands and face by themselves with minor help. By age 3, children can use the toilet by themselves, although they frequently ask someone to go with them. They need only minor help with wiping. Accidents are rare, usually happening only occasionally at night.

Social: Three-year-olds tend to pay close attention to the adults around them and are eager to please. They attempt to follow directions and are responsive to approval or disapproval. They also can be reasoned with at this age. By age 3, children begin to develop their capacity to relate to and communicate with others. They show an interest in the family and in family activities. Their play is still focused on the parallel level where their interest is concentrated primarily on their own activities. However, they are beginning to notice what other children are doing. Some cooperation is initiated in the form of taking turns or verbally settling arguments.

Language: Three-year-olds can use sentences that are longer and more complex. Plurals, personal pronouns such as I, and prepositions such as above or on are used appropriately. Children are able to express their feelings and ideas fairly well. They are capable of relating a story. They listen fairly well and are very interested in longer, more complicated stories than they were at an earlier age. They also have mastered a substantial amount of information including their last name, their gender, and a few rhymes.

Age 4 Years

Motor: Four-year-olds tend to be very active physically. They enjoy running, skipping, jumping, and performing stunts. They are capable of racing up and down stairs. Their balance is very good, and they can carry a glass of liquid without spilling it.

Play: By age 4, children have become increasingly creative and imaginative. They like to construct things out of clay, sand, or blocks. They enjoy using costumes and other pretend materials. They can play cooperatively with other children. They can draw simple figures, although they are frequently inaccurate and without much detail. Four-year-olds can also cut or trace along a line fairly accurately.

Adaptive: Four-year-olds tend to be very assertive. They usually can dress themselves. They've mastered the use of buttons and zippers. They can put on and lace their own shoes, although they cannot yet tie them. They can wash their hands without supervision. By age 4, children demand less attention while eating with their family. They can serve themselves food and eat by themselves using both spoon and fork. They can even assist in setting the table. Four-year-olds can use the bathroom by themselves, although they still alert adults of this and sometimes need assistance in wiping. They usually can sleep through the night without having any accidents.

Social: Four-year-olds are less docile than 3-year-olds. They are less likely to conform, in addition to being less responsive to the pleasure or displeasure of adults. Four-year-olds are in the process of separating from their parents and begin to prefer the company of other children over adults. They are often social and talkative. They are very interested in the world around them and frequently ask "what," "why," and "how" questions.

Language: The aggressiveness manifested by 4-year-olds also appears in their language. They frequently brag and boast about themselves. Name calling is common. Their vocabulary has experienced tremendous growth; however, they have a tendency to misuse words and some difficulty with proper grammar. Four-year-olds talk a lot and like to carry on long conversations with others. Their speech is usually very understandable with only a few remnants of earlier, more infantile speech remaining. Their growing imagination also affects their speech. They like to tell stories and frequently mix facts with make-believe.

Case Vignette D: To what extent does this child fit the developmental profile?

Chaniqwa, age 4 years, is very active physically. She enjoys running, skipping, jumping, and performing stunts. She can use the bathroom by herself. She has a substantial vocabulary, although she has a tendency to misuse words and use improper grammar.

Age 5 Years

Motor: Five-year-olds are quieter and less active than 4-year-olds. Their activities tend to be more complicated and more directed toward achieving some goal. For example, they are more adept at climbing and at riding a tricycle. They can also use roller skates, jump rope, skip, and succeed at other such complex activities. Their ability to concentrate is also increased. The pictures they draw, although simple, are finally recognizable. Dominance of the left or right hand becomes well established.

Play: Games and play activities have become both more elaborate and competitive. Games include hide-and-seek, tag, and hopscotch. Team playing begins. Five-year-olds enjoy pretend games of a more elaborate nature. They like to build houses and forts with blocks and to participate in more dramatic play such as playing house or being a space invader. Singing songs, dancing, and playing DVDs are usually very enjoyable.

Adaptive: Five-year-olds can dress and undress themselves quite well. Assistance is necessary only for adjusting more complicated fasteners and tying shoes. These children can feed themselves and attend to their own toilet needs. They can even visit the neighborhood by themselves, needing help only in crossing streets.

Social: By age 5, children have usually learned to cooperate with others in activities and enjoy group activities. They acknowledge the rights of others and are better able to respond to adult supervision. They have become aware of rules and are interested in conforming to them. Five-year-olds also tend to enjoy family activities such as outings and trips.

Language: Language continues to develop and becomes more complex. Vocabulary continues to increase. Sentence structure becomes more complicated and more accurate. Five-year-olds are very interested in what words mean. They like to look at books and have people read to them. They have begun learning how to count and can recognize colors. Attempts at drawing numbers and letters are begun, although fine motor coordination is not yet well enough developed for great accuracy.

Case Vignette E: To what extent does this child fit the developmental profile?

Sheridan, age 5 years, can draw simple although recognizable pictures. Dominance of her left hand has become well established. She can readily dress and undress herself. She enjoys playing in groups of other children and can cooperate with them quite well. She has a vocabulary of about 50 words. She can use pronouns such as I and prepositions such as on and above appropriately. She can put two or three words together and use them appropriately, although she has difficulty formulating longer phrases and sentences.

Ages 6 to 8 Years

Motor: Children ages 6 to 8 years are physically independent. They can run, jump, and balance well. They continue to participate in a variety of activities to help refine their coordination and motor skills. They often enjoy unusual and challenging activities, such as walking on fences, which help to develop such skills.

Play: These children participate in much active play such as kickball. They like activities such as gymnastics and enjoy trying to perform physical stunts. They also begin to develop intense interest in simple games such as marbles or tiddlywinks and collecting items. Playing with dolls is at its height. Acting out dramatizations becomes very important; these children love to pretend they are animals, horseback riders, or jet pilots.

Adaptive: Much more self-sufficient and independent, these children can dress themselves, go to bed alone, and get up by themselves during the night to go to the bathroom. They can begin to be trusted with an allowance. They are able to go to school or to friends' homes alone. In general, they become increasingly more interested in and understanding of various social situations.

Social: In view of their increasing social skills, they consider playing skills within their peer group increasingly important. They become more and more adept at social skills. Their lives begin to focus around the school and activities with friends. They are becoming more sensitive to reactions of those around them, especially those of their parents. There is some tendency to react negatively when subjected to pressure or criticism. For instance, they may sulk.

Language: The use of language continues to become more refined and sophisticated. Good pronunciation and grammar are developed according to what they've been taught. They are learning how to put their feelings and thoughts into words to express themselves more clearly. They begin to understand more abstract words and forms of language. For

Children ages 6 to 8 love action play. They can run, jump, and balance well.

©istockphoto.com/monkey business images

example, they may begin to understand some puns and jokes. They also begin to develop reading, writing, and numerical skills.

Ages 9 to 11 Years

Motor: Children continue to refine and develop their coordination and motor skills. They experience a gradual, steady gain in body measurements and proportion. Manual dexterity, posture, strength, and balance improve. This period of late childhood is transitional to the major changes experienced during adolescence.

Play: This period frequently becomes the finale of the games and play of childhood. If it has not already occurred, boys and girls separate into their respective same-gender groups.

Adaptive: Children become more and more aware of themselves and the world around them. They experience a gradual change from identifying primarily with adults to formulating their own self-identity. They become more independent. This is a period of both physical and mental growth. These children push themselves into experiencing new things and new activities. They learn to focus on detail and accomplish increasingly difficult intellectual and academic tasks.

Social: The focus of attention shifts from a family orientation to a peer orientation. They continue developing social competence. Friends become very important.

Language: A tremendous increase in vocabulary occurs. These children become adept at the use of words. They can answer questions with more depth of insight. They understand more abstract concepts and use words more precisely. They are also better able to understand and examine verbal and mathematical relationships.

A Concluding Note

We emphasize that individuals vary greatly in their attainment of specific developmental milestones. The developmental milestones provide a general baseline for assessment and subsequent intervention decisions. If a child is assessed as being grossly behind in terms of achieving normal developmental milestones, then immediate intervention may be needed. On the other hand, if a child is only mildly behind his or her normal developmental profile, then no more than close observation may be appropriate.

In the event that the child continues to fall further behind, help can be sought and provided.

Significant Issues and Life Events

Two significant issues will be discussed that relate to the decision of whether to have children. They have been selected because they affect a great number of people and because they often pose a serious crisis for the people involved. The issues are abortion and infertility.

LO 2-3 Examine the Abortion Controversy: Impacts of Social and Economic Forces

Many unique circumstances are involved in any unplanned pregnancy. Individuals must evaluate for themselves the potential consequences of each alternative and assess the positive and negative consequences of each.

A basic decision involved in unplanned pregnancy is whether to have the baby. If the decision is made to have the baby, and the mother is unmarried, a subset of alternatives must then be evaluated. One option is to marry the father (or to establish some other ongoing relationship with him). A second alternative is for the mother to keep the baby and live as a single parent. In the past decade, the media have given increasing attention to fathers who seek custody. Perhaps joint custody is a viable option. Or the mother's parents (the child's grandparents) or other relatives could either keep the baby or assist in its care. Still another option is to have the baby and place it for adoption. Each choice involves both positive and negative consequences.

Abortion is the termination of a pregnancy by removing an embryo or fetus from the uterus before it can survive on its own outside the womb. Social workers may find themselves in the position of helping their clients explore abortion as one possibility open to them. Highlight 2.3 provides a case example of how one young woman struggled with her dilemma.

The concept of abortion inevitably elicits strong feelings and emotions. These feelings can be very positive or negative. People who take stands against abortion often do so on moral and ethical grounds. A common theme is that each unborn child has the

Kevin Dietsch/UPI/Landov

The abortion issue is one of the most controversial in the country. Here, opposite sides confront each other at a demonstration.

right to life. On the opposite pole are those who feel strongly in favor of abortion. They feel that women have the right to choice over their own bodies and lives.

The issue concerning unplanned and, in this context, unwanted pregnancy provides an excellent example of how macro-system values affect the options available to clients. In June 1992, the U.S. Supreme Court ruled that states have extensive power to restrict abortions, although they cannot outlaw all abortions. If abortions are illegal or unavailable to specific groups in the population, then women's choices about what to do are much more limited.

The abortion issue illustrates how clients function within the contexts of their mezzo and macro environments. For example, perhaps a woman's parents are unwilling to help her with a newborn, or the child's father shuns involvement. In both these instances, some of the woman's potential mezzo system options have already been eliminated.

Options are also affected by macro environments. If abortion is illegal, then social agencies are unable to provide them. Another possibility is that states can legally allow abortion only under extremely limited circumstances. For instance, it may be allowed

only if the conception is the product of incest or rape, or if the pregnancy and birth seriously endanger the pregnant woman's life.

Even if states allow abortions, the community in which a pregnant woman lives can pose serious restrictions on her options. For instance, a community renowned for having a strong and well-organized anti-abortion movement may be supportive of actions (including legal actions) to curtail abortion services. Abortion clinics can be picketed, patients harassed, and clinic staff personally threatened. Such strong community feelings can force clinics to close.

Additionally, the abortion issue provides an excellent opportunity to distinguish between personal and professional values. Each of us probably has an opinion about abortion. Some of us most likely have strong opinions either one way or the other.

EP 2.1.2a

In practice, our personal opinions really don't matter. However, our professional approach does. As professionals, it is our responsibility to help clients come to their own decisions. Our job is to assist clients in assessing their own feelings and values, in identifying available alternatives, and in evaluating

HIGHLIGHT 2.3

Case Example: Single and Pregnant

Roseanne was 21 years old and two months pregnant. She was a junior at a large midwestern state university, majoring in social work. Hank, the father, was a 26-year-old divorcé she met in one of her classes. He already had a 4-year-old son named Ronnie.

Roseanne was filled with ambivalent feelings. She had always pictured herself as being a mother someday—but not now. She felt she loved Hank but had many reservations about how he felt in return. She'd been seeing him once or twice a week for the past few months. Hank didn't really take her out much, and she suspected that he was also dating other women. He had even asked her to babysit for Ronnie while he went out with someone else.

That was another thing—Ronnie. She felt Ronnie hated her. He would snarl whenever she came over and make nasty, cutting remarks. Maybe he was jealous that his father was giving Roseanne attention.

The pregnancy was an accident. She simply didn't think anything would happen. She knew better now that it was too late. Hank had never made any commitment to her. In some ways she felt he was a creep, but at least he was honest. The fact was that he just didn't love her.

The problem was, What should she do? A college education was important to her and to her parents. Money had always been a big issue. Her parents helped her as much as they could, but they also had other children in college. Roseanne worked odd, inconvenient hours at a fast-food restaurant for a while. She also worked as a cook several nights a week at a diner.

What if she kept the baby? She was fairly certain Hank didn't want to marry her. Even if he did, she didn't think she'd want to be stuck with him for the rest of her life. How could she possibly manage on her own with a baby? She shared a two-bedroom apartment with three other female students. How could she take care of a baby with no money and no place to go? She felt dropping out of college would ruin her life. The idea of going on welfare instead of working in welfare was terrifying.

What about adoption? That would mean seven more months of pregnancy while she was going to college. She wondered what her friends and family would say about her giving up a child. She thought about how difficult that would be—she would always wonder where her child was and how he or she was doing. She couldn't bear the thought of pursuing this option.

Yet, the idea of an abortion scared her. She had heard so many people say that it was murder.

Roseanne made her decision, but it certainly was not an easy one. She carefully addressed and considered the religious and moral issues involved in terminating a pregnancy. She decided that she would have to face the responsibility and the guilt. In determining that having a baby at this time would be disastrous both for herself and for a new life, she decided to have an abortion.

Fourteen years have passed. Roseanne is now 35. She is no longer in social work although she finished her degree. She does have a good job as a court reporter. This job suits her well. She's been married to Tom for three years. Although they have their ups and downs, she is happy in her marriage. They love each other very much and enjoy their time together.

Roseanne thinks about her abortion once in a while. Although she is using no method of contraception, she has not yet gotten pregnant. Possibly she never will. Tom is 43. He has been married once before and has an adult child from that marriage. He does not feel it is a necessity for them to have children.

Roseanne is ambivalent. She is addressing the possibility of not having children and is looking at the consequences of that alternative. She puts it well by saying that sometimes she mourns the loss of her unborn child. Yet, in view of her present level of satisfaction and Tom's hesitation about having children, she feels that her life thus far has worked out for the best.

---

as objectively as possible the consequences of each alternative.

The National Association of Social Workers (NASW) has established issue and policy statements on family planning and reproductive choice that include its stance on abortion. A *policy* is a clearly stated or implicit procedure, plan, rule, or stance concerning some issue that serves to guide decision making and behavior. The statements read:

"As social workers, we support the right of individuals to decide for themselves, without duress and according to their own personal beliefs and convictions, whether they want to become parents, how many children they are willing and able to nurture, the opportune time for them to have children, and with whom they may choose to parent.... To support self-determination, ... reproductive health services, including abortion services, must be legally, economically, and geographically accessible to all who need them.... Denying people with low income access to the full range of contraceptive methods, abortion, and sterilization services, and the educational programs that explain them, perpetuate

poverty and the dependence on welfare programs and support the status quo of class stratification.... NASW supports....

- *[A] woman's right to obtain an abortion, performed according to accepted medical standards and in an environment free of harassment or threat for both patients and providers.*
- *[R]eproductive health services, including abortion services, that are confidential, available at a reasonable cost, and covered in public and private health insurance plans on a par with other kinds of health services (contraceptive equity).*
- *[I]mproved access to the full range of reproductive health services, including abortion services, for groups currently underserved in the United States, including people with low income and those who rely on Medicaid[6] to pay for their health care...."* (NASW, 2012, pp. 131, 133)

Seven aspects of abortion are discussed here. First, we describe the current impact of legal and political macro systems. Second, we note the incidence of abortion and provide a profile of women who have abortions. Third, we explore reasons why women seek abortions. Fourth, we explain the abortion process itself and the types of abortion available. Fifth, we briefly examine some of the psychological effects of abortion. Sixth, we compare and assess the arguments for and against abortion. Seventh, we describe a variety of social work roles with respect to the abortion issue.

The Impacts of Macro-System Policies on Practice and Access to Services

EP 2.1.7

People's values affect laws that, in turn, regulate policy regarding how people can make decisions and choose to act. Government and agency policies specify and regulate what services organizations can provide to women within communities.

---

[6]*Medicaid* is a public assistance program, established in 1965 and funded by federal and state governments, that pays for medical and hospital services for eligible people, determined to be in need, who are unable to pay for these services themselves.

Subsequently, whether services are available or not controls the choices available to most pregnant women.

The abortion debate focuses on two opposing perspectives, antiabortion and pro-choice. Carroll (2013b) describes the antiabortion stance as the belief "that human life begins at conception, and thus an embryo, at any stage of development, is a person. [Therefore,] ... aborting a fetus is murder, and... the government should make all abortions illegal" (p. 366).

Pro-choice advocates, on the other hand, focus on a woman's right to choose whether to have an abortion. They believe that a woman has the right to control what happens to her own body, to navigate her own life, and to pursue her own current and future happiness.

For more than four decades, the political controversy over abortion has been raging. In 1973, the U.S. Supreme Court decision known as *Roe v. Wade* overruled state laws that prohibited or restricted a woman's right to obtain an abortion during the first three months of pregnancy. States were allowed to impose restrictions in the second trimester only when such restrictions related directly to the mother's health. Finally, during the third trimester states could restrict abortions or even forbid them, excluding those necessary to preserve a woman's life and health. Women, in essence, won the right to "privacy," or in other words, "the right to be left alone" (Hartman, 1991, p. 467). This, of course, is a pro-choice stance.

The courts have gotten increasingly more conservative concerning abortion. In *Planned Parenthood v. Casey* (1992), the Supreme Court ruled that states had the right to restrict abortions as they saw fit, except that they could not outlaw all abortions. Additionally, the Court has put restrictions of increasing severity into place. In *Harris v. McRae* (1980), the Court confirmed that both Congress and individual states could legally refuse to pay for abortions. This significantly affected poor women.

In *Webster v. Reproductive Health Services* (1989), the Supreme Court upheld a restrictive Missouri law. This law "prohibits performing abortions in public hospitals unless the mother's life is in danger; forbids the spending of state funds for counseling women about abortion; and requires doctors to add an expensive layer of testing before performing abortions after twenty weeks if they feel it will help them determine whether a fetus would be viable outside the womb" (Wermiel & McQueen, 1989, p. 1).

Since this decision, many states have passed bills imposing restrictions on abortions that will be discussed in more detail later (e.g., requiring waiting periods or parental consent for teens). Kirk and Okazawa-Rey (2013) reflect on the gradual chipping away of abortion rights:

> *For nearly forty years, well-funded anti-abortion groups have worked strategically to undermine and overturn the right to abortion. They have used public education, mainstream media, protests and direct action-including attacks on clinics and their staffs.... They have financed and elected anti-choice political candidates at city, state, and congressional levels. Republican congresspersons have introduced bills session after session to whittle away at the legality of abortion and elevate the unborn child, even as a "nonviable fetus," to the status of "personhood" with rights equal to or greater than those of the mother. If the Supreme Court overturns* Roe v. Wade, *legal jurisdiction will revert to the states, many of which are poised to ban abortion or to re-criminalize it.... This issue is central to women's autonomy and will continue to be highly contentious. (p. 217)*

EP 2.1.2a, 2.1.2c

The abortion debate continues. New decisions are made daily at the state and federal levels. However, numerous issues remain in the forefront when assessing the impacts on clients' rights and on their ability to function. Several have surfaced in recent years and will probably continue to characterize the abortion debate. We will discuss a number of them here: restricting access through legal barriers, limiting financial support, the mother's condition, the fetus's condition, violence against clinics, stem cell research, and intact dilation and extraction (often referred to by opponents as "partial-birth abortion"). Spotlight 2.1 presents some international perspectives on abortion policy.

Restricting Access

There are several ways legislation can restrict access to abortion (Center for Reproductive Rights [CRR], 2009). First, states can enact mandatory delays before an abortion can be performed. For example, a state may require a 24-hour waiting period from the time a woman initiates the abortion process to the time the procedure is completed. The decision to abort can be very painful for many reasons, and a waiting period can result in significant stress. Critics indicate that such rules aim to impose obstacles in getting abortions, thus discouraging women from doing so. This rule makes access to abortion especially difficult for poor women from rural areas who have to travel significant distances for the abortion and have little or no money for lodging.

A second type of restriction requires women to receive designated material that may present a negative view of abortion or counseling prior to undergoing an abortion. Critics of this legislation maintain that it only encourages women to delay an abortion procedure; "intrudes on a woman's autonomy and dignity; interferes with the physician's professional practice; and corrupts the informed consent process" (CRR, 2009).

The following summarizes state waiting periods and mandatory counseling requirements (Guttmacher Institute, 2013c):

- Thirty-five states require that women receive counseling prior to receiving an abortion.
- Twenty-six of these states also require that a specified period of time, usually 24 hours, elapse between counseling and the actual abortion.
- Ten states require two separate visits to the facility, one for counseling and another to begin the waiting period.

A third legal barrier concerns requiring teenagers to either notify one or both parents or receive consent from one or both parents before getting an abortion. Some states also allow minors to seek a court order to exempt them from parental involvement. Thirty-nine states have enacted parental involvement laws (Guttmacher Institute, 2013f). Fear of confronting parents may cause many young women to delay making the decision to have an abortion. Receiving court permission, where allowed, may also result in difficult delays.

Other legal barriers can also be established. In 2013 Texas passed a law that "requires doctors performing abortions to have admitting privileges at a... hospital" that must be located within 30 miles of the clinic (Liptak, 2013). Although a number of abortion rights groups and clinics subsequently sought the attention of the U.S. Supreme Court, the Court refused to address and rule on the law.

SPOTLIGHT ON DIVERSITY 2.1

International Perspective on Abortion Policy

EP 2.1.5

Abortion incidence and policy vary around the world as the following facts explain (Guttmacher Institute, 2012b). Generally speaking on a global level, abortion rates declined sharply between 1995 and 2003, but remained relatively stable between 2003 and 2008. However, rates vary significantly among countries, especially between *developed* and *developing* nations. In 2008 6 million abortions were performed in developed nations and 38 million in developing countries. Globally, almost half of the abortions that are performed are unsafe. However, almost 98 percent of all abortions performed in developing nations are unsafe compared to 6 percent in developed countries. Women who are poor that live in developing countries have little access to family planning services and few economic resources to pay for safe abortions. As a result, they are more likely to encounter health problems related to unsafe abortion practices. In places where abortion is legal, it tends to be much safer. On the other hand, where abortion is forbidden, it is less safe. That makes sense as legality offers the opportunity for trained, knowledgeable, and skilled personnel to perform abortions.

Huge variations exist around the world in abortion policy (Cohen 2009):

> Throughout Europe, except for Ireland and Poland, abortion is broadly legal, widely available and safe.... China was the first large developing country to enact a liberal abortion law—in 1957. The Soviet Union and the central and western Asian republics enacted similar laws in the 1950s. Over the next 50 years, abortion become legal on broad grounds in a wide range of less developed countries, including Cuba (1965), Singapore (1970), India (1971), Zambia (1972), Tunisia (1973), Vietnam (1975), Turkey (1983), Taiwan

(1985), Mongolia (1989), South Africa (1996) and Cambodia (1997). Indeed, the worldwide trend in abortion law has continued to be toward liberalization. And since 1997, another 21 countries or populous jurisdictions have liberalized their laws, including Colombia, Ethiopia, Iran, Mexico City, Nepal, Portugal, and Thailand. During this same period, only three countries—El Salvador, Nicaragua, and Poland—have increased restrictions.

> Today, 60% of the world's 1.55 billion women of reproductive age (15–44) live in countries where abortion is broadly legal.

> The remaining 40% live where abortion is highly restricted, virtually all in the developing world. In Africa, 92% of women of reproductive age live under severely restrictive laws; in Latin America, 97% do.

Also consider the following global facts (Cohen, 2009):

- Unsafe abortions take the lives of 70,000 women annually (or 12.5 percent of all deaths related to pregnancy).
- Around the world, seven women die from an unsafe abortion every hour.
- Eight million women experience complications from abortion that can be very serious.
- Almost 3 million women who experience serious complications related to abortion receive no medical attention.

Cohen (2009) makes the following conclusions. The most effective way to address unwanted pregnancy is to provide readily available contraception to prevent pregnancy from occurring to begin with. However, in developing nations where resources are scarce, this is now a difficult, perhaps impossible, goal. Women who are desperate will resort to abortion whether it is legal or not. In places where abortion is not legal, it is likely unsafe and potentially deadly.

As a result, the law effectively closed 36 abortion clinics, left 24 counties without such services, and prevented "some 20,000 women a year from access to safe abortions" (Liptak, 2013).

Bill and Karen Bell (National Abortion Federation, 2004) tell the story of their "beautiful, vibrant, 17-year-old daughter Becky [who] died suddenly, after a six-day illness." The diagnosis was a form of pneumonia "brought about by an illegal abortion." Bill and Karen couldn't believe that this

had happened to their daughter. Why didn't she tell them she was pregnant? They could have helped and supported her. They learned the heartbreaking answer by talking to Becky's friends. Becky's parents reflected, "Becky had told her girlfriends that she believed we would be terribly hurt and disappointed in her if she told us about her pregnancy. Like a lot of young people, she was not comfortable sharing intimate details of her developing sexuality with her parents." A parental consent law was in effect in Becky's state. Although a request to the court was an option, the presiding judge had never granted a request for an abortion in over a decade. Desperate, Becky opted for an illegal, unsafe "back-alley abortion."

The U.S. military also restricts access to abortion. Medical treatment facilities in the Department of Defense are prohibited from performing abortions for U.S. military personnel unless the life of the mother is endangered or the pregnancy is a result of rape or incest (Montgomery, 2013).

Limiting Financial Support

One clear trend since 1973 has been the antiabortion factions' pressure to limit, minimize, and eventually prohibit any public financial support for abortion. This significantly affects poor women. Only 17 states provide Medicaid funding for all medically necessary abortions (Guttmacher Institute, 2013i). (*Medicaid* is a public assistance program, established in 1965 and funded by federal and state governments, that pays for medical and hospital services for eligible people, determined to be in need, who are unable to pay for these services themselves.) The Hyde amendment, introduced to Congress in 1977, abolished federal funding for abortion unless a woman's life was in danger. Congress has renewed this legislation annually, imposing various restrictions on abortion funding. Since 1993, Medicaid can fund an abortion only in the case of rape, incest, or a life-threatening situation; 32 states and the District of Columbia abide by this standard (Guttmacher Institute, 2013i). "Even when a woman's health is jeopardized by her pregnancy to the extent that it will leave her incapacitated, unable to care for her children or hold down a job, she is still not eligible for Medicaid funding in many states" (CRR, 2003, July 8).

Nabha and Blasdell (2002) provide an example:

31-year-old "Alina" had bi-polar disorder [a mental disorder involving extreme moods including manic frenzy, severe depression, or both] and obsessive-compulsive disorder [a mental disorder involving an obsession with organization, neatness, perfectionism, and control], and was taking psycho-tropic medications known to cause fetal anomalies. She also had fibromyalgia, a disease that causes weakness, exhaustion, numbness, and dizziness, in addition to other symptoms. As a result of these circumstances, Alina chose to have an abortion. Although Alina was enrolled in Medicaid during this period, the program in her state refused to cover abortions necessary to protect a woman's health, so she was unable to receive any public funds.

Another approach for limiting financial support involves the concept of a *gag rule*—that is, banning federal funding to agencies that allow staff to talk to pregnant women about abortion as an alternative. Depending on the stance of various administrations, gag rules have been supported or rebuffed. For example, at one point Planned Parenthood said it would give up its federal funding rather than fail to discuss all options available to clients, including abortion. (*Planned Parenthood* is an international organization dedicated to promoting the use of family planning and contraception.) The gag rule also has the potential to prohibit giving federal money to international groups that perform abortions or provide abortion information.

Eight states forbid private insurance plans from covering abortion; 18 states restrict insurance coverage of abortions for public employees (Guttmacher Institute, 2013g).

Condition of the Mother

Some people support the idea that abortion is acceptable under specific conditions. One involves the mother's health. Should an abortion be performed if carrying the fetus to full term will kill the mother? Whose life is more important, that of the mother or that of the fetus?

Another issue is this: Should a woman impregnated during rape or incest be forced to carry the fetus to term? Is it fair for a woman who has undergone the horror of a sexual assault to be forced to live with the assault's result, an unwanted child, for the rest of her life?

Fetal Condition

The condition of the fetus illustrates another circumstance in which some people consider abortion acceptable. If the fetus is severely damaged or defective, should the mother have to carry it to term? If the woman is forced to bear the child, shouldn't she be provided with resources to care for herself and the child before and after birth? To what extent would a mother forced to bear a severely disabled child also be forced to provide the huge resources necessary for maintaining such a child?

Ethical Questions 2.2

What are your personal views about abortion? Under what, if any, circumstances do you think it might be performed?

EP 2.1.2

Violence Against Clinics

The abortion controversy has been fraught with violence. Statistics on violence against abortion clinics have been recorded for over 30 years (NAF, 2010). In 2010, there were 187 incidents of violence against abortion providers in the United States and Canada; these included arson, attempted bombings, invasions, vandalism, trespassing, anthrax threats, assault and battery, death threats, burglary, and stalking ("the persistent following, threatening, and harassing of an abortion provider, staff member, or patient away from the clinic") (NAF, 2010). Several recent attacks reflect extreme aggression by people who stand strongly against abortion (LeClaire, 2013). One incident involved a man who broke into an Indiana Planned Parenthood clinic and caused massive destruction with an ax. Another event concerned someone detonating an explosive device outside a central Wisconsin Planned Parenthood clinic. Yet another occurrence involved someone demolishing a family planning clinic in Florida with a Molotov cocktail.

Abortion clinics and pro-choice groups stress that they are functioning legally and need protection from harassment and violence. In 1994, a legal decision and legislation served to help

> *safeguard women's right to access their legal rights. After the public outcry associated with the public harassment, wounding, and death of abortion services providers, and the vandalism and bombing of various clinics, the Supreme Court ruled in* Madsen et al. v. Women's Health Center, Inc. [1994] *to allow a buffer zone around clinics to permit patients and employees access and to control noise around the premises. The same year the Freedom of Access to Clinic Entrances (FACE)*

> *Act made it a federal crime to block access, harass, or incite violence in the context of abortion services. (Shaw & Lee, 2012, p. 308)*

The Freedom of Access to Clinic Entrances (FACE) Act prohibits such activities as trespassing, physical violence such as shoving, "vandalizing a reproductive health care facility by gluing locks or spraying butyric acid" (an acid used in disinfectants and other pharmaceuticals), threatening violence, stalking employees, and making bomb or arson threats (Blasdell & Goss, 2004).

To the extent that violence against clinics and harassment of clinic staff and patients continue, women's access to legal abortions may be significantly curtailed. For whatever reason, the number of U.S. abortions performed has reached its record low since 1980 (U.S. Census Bureau, 2011).

Stem Cell Research

An ongoing controversial issue related to abortion involves the use of fetal tissue (stem cells) for health research and treatment. *Stem cells* are

> *unspecialized human or animal cells that can produce mature specialized body cells and at the same time replicate themselves.... Medical researchers are interested in using stem cells to repair or replace damaged body tissues because stem cells are less likely than other foreign cells to be rejected by the immune system when they are implanted in the body. (Tissue and organ rejection is a major problem following transplant surgery, for example.) Embryonic stem cells have the capacity to develop into every type of tissue found in an adult. Stem cells have been used experimentally to form the blood-making cells of the bone marrow and heart, blood vessel, muscle, and insulin-producing tissue. (Kail & Cavanaugh, 2014, p. 26)*

Significant research has focused on the potential for using stem cells to combat spinal cord injuries, Parkinson's disease,[7] juvenile diabetes,[8] heart

---

[7] *Parkinson's disease* is a progressive disease of the nervous system, usually occurring later in life, that is characterized by muscular weakness, tremors, and a shuffling gait.
[8] *Juvenile diabetes* is a severe, chronic disease affecting children and young adults, in which the body fails to produce enough insulin, resulting in increased sugar in the bloodstream, extreme thirst, frequent urination, and gradual deterioration (Berube, 2002).

disease, and Alzheimer's disease;[9] more than 100 million Americans suffer from some form of disease that could potentially benefit from stem cell research (Kalb & Rosenberg, 2004). Maggie, age 4, provides an example of someone suffering from juvenile diabetes who is in need of help. "Ten to 15 times a day, Maggie's blood sugar must be checked. And the little blond ballerina has to wear a portable insulin pump, which delivers insulin through a tube inserted into her abdomen or lower back. She carries the device to preschool in a fanny pack decorated with yellow and green ladybugs" (Kalb & Rosenberg, 2004, p. 44).

Although research has focused on a few different types of cells with some potential to function as stem cells (the discussion of which is beyond the scope of this book), much attention and research has centered on embryonic stem cells. *Embryonic stem cells* are cells taken from a 3-to-5-day-old embryo that has been developed during an in vitro fertilization process. *In vitro* is Latin for "in glass," referring to something done in an artificial environment, such as in a laboratory dish or test tube; *in vitro fertilization*[10] (discussed later in this chapter) refers to a procedure that unites the egg and sperm in a laboratory; stem cells "are not derived from eggs fertilized in a woman's body" (NIH, 2013b). When such cells were no longer needed for the in vitro fertilization process, "they were donated for research with the informed consent of the donor" (NIH, 2013b). Sometimes, you might hear the term *embryonic stem cell lines*. This refers to embryonic stem cells that "have been cultured under in vitro conditions" for continuous cell division and specialization (as they develop into more specific types of tissue) and are studied "for months to years" (NIH, 2013b).

Many people have strong opinions about stem cell research. An issue at the heart of the debate concerns whether the study and use of human embryonic tissue reflects the obliteration of human life. "Religious conservatives argue that using those stem cells means deriving benefit from the destruction of human embryos—fertilized eggs in early stages of development—in their eyes no less a crime than abortion" (Lacayo, 2001, p. 17).

People who support embryonic stem cell research contend that it has incredible positive potential.

The National Institutes of Health (2013b) reports on "the promise of stem cells":

> *Studying stem cells will help us understand how they transform into the dazzling array of specialized cells that make us what we are. Some of the most serious medical conditions, such as cancer and birth defects, are due to problems that occur somewhere in this process. A better understanding of normal cell development will allow us to understand and perhaps correct the errors that cause these medical conditions.*
>
> *Another potential application of stem cells is making cells and tissues for medical therapies. Today, donated organs and tissues are often used to replace those that are diseased or destroyed. Unfortunately, the number of people needing a transplant far exceeds the number of organs available for transplantation.… [S]tem cells offer the possibility of a renewable source of replacement cells and tissues to treat a myriad of diseases, conditions, and disabilities including Parkinson's disease, amyotrophic lateral sclerosis, spinal cord injury, burns, heart disease, diabetes, and arthritis.*

The debate rages in the national and state political arenas. Depending on the political orientation of those in power at the national and state levels, stem cell research may or may not receive various degrees of support. Research may be encouraged or prohibited. Funding may be provided or withdrawn.

Consider recent shifting national policy (Research America, 2013). Former president George W. Bush limited stem cell research by allowing federal funding for study only involving already established stem cell lines (stem cells already cultured in vitro and ready for use in research). Subsequently, President Barack Obama issued an executive order in 2009 negating the prior mandate, allowing federal funding for potential study of new stem cell lines, and thereby expanding stem cell research. However, since this mandate has not been signed into law, the future of stem cell research remains uncertain. It depends on national leadership and the political climate.

Note that "[i]ndividual states have the authority to pass laws to permit human embryonic stem cell research using state funds" instead of or in addition to federal funds (NIH, 2010). Numerous states have taken steps to support stem cell research through funding (e.g., grants), such mechanisms as technical assistance, and encouragement of inter-agency and inter-state cooperation (NIH, 2010).

---

[9]*Alzheimer's disease* is a degenerative brain disorder that gradually causes deterioration in intelligence, memory, awareness, and ability to control bodily functions.

[10]*In vitro fertilization*, discussed later in the chapter, is a process in which eggs are removed from a woman's body, fertilized with sperm in a laboratory, and then implanted in the woman's uterus.

EP 2.1.1e

Stem cell research provides an example of how the ever-changing political context affects what can be and is done. As with many other issues influencing the human condition, social workers should keep abreast of such circumstances in their ongoing learning about human behavior. Participating in a career-long learning process is part of their professional responsibility.

•••• Ethical Questions 2.3

EP 2.1.2

What is your opinion about using embryonic stem cells for research? Should the possibility of helping many seriously ill people through stem cell research be pursued? Or is an embryo several days old a human being that should be respected as such? How do you feel about embryonic tissue that is discarded after use at fertility clinics?

Highlight 2.4 addresses another very controversial issue—the late-term abortion procedure known as intact dilation and extraction (referred to by some as "partial-birth abortion").

Commentary

We have just scratched the surface of some of the debates currently raging. Social workers need to understand the issues and the context in which opposing views are raised in order to help clients make difficult decisions. The abortion issue with its potent pro-choice and antiabortion factions in the political arena illustrates the impact that macro systems can have on individual lives. The extent to which national policies limit the availability of abortion relates directly to service accessibility. Organizations in the macro environment must have the sanction of the national and state macro systems in order to provide women with free choice.

The next sections describe the incidence of abortion, reasons for abortion, common abortion procedures, and the pros and cons of abortion. Finally,

---

◆ HIGHLIGHT 2.4

Intact Dilation and Extraction (Late-Term Abortion)

Intact dilation and extraction (D&X) is "a late-term abortion involving partial delivery of a viable fetus before extraction" (Berube, 2002, p. 1014). It is performed after "20 weeks and before viability" (Crooks & Baur, 2014, p. 323). Although physicians refer to it as *intact dilation and extraction*, its opponents often refer to it as *partial-birth abortion* (DiNitto, 2005, p. 462). Opponents view the procedure as "the interference with the birth of a live baby, rather than the termination of a pregnancy" (Greenberg, Bruess, & Conklin, 2011, p. 264). In practice, it has been "reserved for situations when serious health risks to the woman, or severe fetal abnormalities, exist" (Crooks & Baur, 2014, p. 323).

In November 2003, President Bush "signed into law the first ban on a specific abortion procedure," namely the D&X, making it "a criminal offense for doctors to perform the procedure, even to preserve the woman's health" (DiNitto, 2005, p. 462). In April 2007, the Supreme Court upheld this law that "includes no health exception" and prohibits the procedure from being used (Guttmacher Institute, 2013a).

The following facts reflect the current state of partial-birth abortion (Guttmacher Institute, 2013a):

- At the time of this writing, 32 states have established bans on "partial-birth" abortion, 19 of which are in effect and 13 of which have been blocked by a court.

- The definition of "partial-birth" abortion varies widely from one state to another.
- All 32 state laws incorporate some kind of exception.

In reality, the majority (61.2 percent) of abortions are performed at less than 9 weeks' gestation, and 88.6 percent at or before 12 weeks (U.S. Census Bureau, 2011).

•••• Ethical Questions 2.4

EP 2.1.2

What is your opinion about intact dilation and extraction? Should it be legally allowed if the pregnant woman faces serious health risks with continued pregnancy? If the woman risks death? If the fetus suffers from serious mental or physical abnormalities?

various social work roles concerning the issue are discussed.

Incidence of Abortion

Over 1.2 million abortions were performed in 2007 in the United States, down from over 1.6 million in 1990 and over 1.3 million in 2000 (U.S. Census Bureau, 2011). "Nearly half of pregnancies among American women are unintended, and four in 10 of these [unintended pregnancies] are terminated by abortion. Twenty-two percent of all pregnancies (excluding miscarriages) end in abortion" (Guttmacher Institute, 2010b). As Table 2.1 indicates, about one-third of all abortions were performed for women ages 20 to 24. Almost three-quarters of all abortions were for women between the ages of 15 and 29, which makes sense in terms of maximum female fertility. The largest number of women having abortions (41 percent) had not had any children. This was followed by those

TABLE 2.1	FACTS ABOUT WOMEN HAVING ABORTIONS*
AGE	**TOTAL ABORTIONS (%)**
14 years or less	0.5
15 to 19 years	16.2
20 to 24 years	32.6
25 to 29 years	24.4
30 to 34 years	14.4
35 to 39 years	8.8
40 years and over	3.1
Number of previous childbirths	
None	40.9
One	27.1
Two	19.1
Three	8.3
Four or more	4.6
Number of previous abortions	
None	53.9
One	26.2
Two or more	19.9

*These facts were gleaned from the U.S. Census Bureau's *Statistical Abstract of the United States: 2012* (2011).

having had one previous child (27 percent) and two previous children (20 percent). Few had three or more children. A majority had had no previous abortions (53 percent), followed by those who had previously had one abortion (27 percent) or two or more abortions (20 percent). "Fifty-four percent of women who have abortions had used a contraceptive method (usually the condom or the pill) during the month they became pregnant" (Guttmacher Institute, 2013e).

Almost 84 percent of women having abortions are unmarried (U.S. Census Bureau, 2011). Abortions are spread across races. Thirty-six percent of abortions occur to non-Hispanic white women, 30 percent to non-Hispanic African American women, 25 percent to Hispanic women, and 9 percent to women of other races (Guttmacher Institute, 2013e). Thirty-seven percent of women having an abortion state they are protestant and 28 percent Catholic (Guttmacher Institute, 2013e). Women having abortions tend to be poor. Forty-two percent of women having abortions have incomes below the federal poverty line, and another 27 percent have incomes of 100 to 199 percent of the poverty line (Guttmacher Institute, 2013e).

Reasons for Abortion

Unplanned or accidental pregnancy has three basic causes. First, the couple may not use contraception at all. Second, they may use it ineffectively, inconsistently, or incorrectly. Third, no method of contraception is perfect; each has a failure rate. (Chapter 6 discusses contraception in greater detail.)

Women give several reasons for having an abortion. "Three-fourths of women cite concern for or responsibility to other individuals; three-fourths say they cannot afford a child; three-fourths say that having a baby would interfere with work, school or the ability to care for dependents; and half say they do not want to be a single parent or are having problems with their husband or partner" (Guttmacher Institute, 2013e). Many abortions are also performed annually in the United States following a rape.

No one desires to have an unwanted pregnancy that ends in abortion. It is a difficult choice to make among a range of alternatives, all of which have negative consequences. One implication is the importance of readily accessible contraception and family planning counseling so that the difficult alternative of abortion is no longer necessary.

Methods of Abortion

Several different procedures are used to perform abortions, depending on how far the pregnancy has progressed. The cost for an abortion during the first trimester ranges from about $300 to $1,700 depending on the length of gestation, where you get services, and what type of services they are (Planned Parenthood, 2013). Costs are higher when the abortion occurs later in the pregnancy. The two major kinds of abortion are a medication abortion (sometimes referred to as an "abortion pill") and abortion procedures performed within a clinic. Methods used early in pregnancy include vacuum aspiration and medication abortion. Procedures used later on include dilation and evacuation, and intact dilation and evacuation (discussed in Highlight 2.4). Illegal abortion will also be mentioned.

Medication Abortion

A *medication abortion* is an abortion induced by taking certain drugs. The most commonly used drug in the United States, *mifepristone* (formerly referred to as RU-486), triggers a deterioration of the uterine lining (Planned Parenthood, 2013). It was approved by the U.S. Food and Drug Administration (FDA) for use as an abortion drug in 2000, and has been used in several European countries for over a decade earlier. The process involves taking mifepristone and then taking a dose of *misoprostol* (a prostaglandin that triggers uterine contractions) up to three days later. As mentioned, mifepristone causes the uterine lining to break down, which makes it unable to support a fetus. The subsequent dose of misoprostol then causes uterine contractions that expel the fetus. A medication abortion can be performed up to 63 days (9 weeks) after the first day of a woman's last period and costs from $300 to $800; note that some states restrict the period of use to 49 days (Planned Parenthood, 2013).

A majority of women abort within four or five hours of taking misoprostol; overall, the process is 97 percent effective (Planned Parenthood, 2008a). Potential side effects include dizziness, severe cramping, nausea, diarrhea, abdominal pain, and mild fever or chills (most of which can be reduced by taking Tylenol or ibuprofen [e.g., Advil], not aspirin)

(Planned Parenthood, 2013). In 2008, about 17 percent of all abortions (and about 25 percent of abortions performed prior to nine weeks' gestation) were medication abortions (Guttmacher Institute, 2013e).

Vacuum Aspiration

Vacuum aspiration (also referred to as *vacuum curettage* or *suction curettage*) is a procedure used up to 16 weeks after a missed period (Planned Parenthood, 2013). The cervical entrance is enlarged, and the contents of the uterus are evacuated through a suction tube. Usually done under local anesthesia, the procedure involves first dilating the cervix (i.e., widening the opening into the uterus) by inserting a series of rods with increasing diameters. Then a small tube is inserted into the vagina and subsequently through the cervix into the uterus. The tube is connected to a suction machine that vacuums out the fetal tissue from the uterus. Sometimes, *curettage* (scraping with a small, spoon-shaped instrument called a curette) is used afterward (Planned Parenthood, 2013). The entire procedure takes about 5 to 10 minutes in addition to preparation time (Planned Parenthood, 2013).

Most abortions are performed in clinics, where staff usually require that a patient remain for a couple hours following an abortion. Primary side effects include some bleeding and cramping, which are considered normal. Vacuum aspiration is considered a very safe procedure and rarely has complications.

Dilation and Evacuation

Second-trimester abortions are more complicated and involve greater risks. An abortion method that can be used during the fourth and fifth months of pregnancy is dilation and evacuation (D&E). This method resembles vacuum aspiration in that fetal material is initially suctioned out of the uterus and then usually scraped out with a curette. However, because a D&E is performed later in pregnancy, a greater amount of fetal material must be removed. General anesthesia instead of local is used. Potential complications include those associated with vacuum aspiration and those resulting from general anesthesia.

Illegal Abortion

Many women turn to unsafe illegal abortions when safe procedures are illegal or inaccessible. We have established that 40 percent of women of reproductive age live in nations where abortion is highly restricted or prohibited (Cohen, 2009). In desperation, many women turn to unregulated, unqualified abortionists who may use unclean or unsafe instruments. Other women try to abort themselves by using some sharp object or ingesting some harmful substance. We have also established that 70,000 women around the world die annually from dangerous illegal abortions (Cohen, 2009).

The Importance of Context and Timing

Although abortion is considered a very safe medical practice in the United States, the further a woman is into her pregnancy, the greater the risk of death; only one death occurs for every million abortions performed before eight weeks of pregnancy, one death for every 29,000 abortions during weeks 16 to 20 of pregnancy, and one death per 11,000 abortions performed at 21 or more weeks of pregnancy (Guttmacher Institute, 2013e). Problems are also less likely to occur when the woman is healthy, conditions are clean and safe, and follow-up care is readily available. Women are about 11 times more likely to die in childbirth than from an abortion performed during the first 20 weeks of pregnancy (Planned Parenthood, 2013).

Risks from abortion complications are negligible; less than 0.5 percent of women having an abortion require subsequent hospitalization for complications (Guttmacher Institute, 2013e). Risks such as allergic reactions to medication or sedation, infection, blood clots, or heavy bleeding are very rare in first-trimester abortions, but increase in probability as the pregnancy continues (Planned Parenthood, 2013).

Spotlight 2.2 explores the psychological effects of abortion on both women and men.

Arguments for and Against Abortion

Numerous arguments have been advanced for and against permitting abortions. Many of these views are related to how facts are interpreted and presented. Following is a sampling of arguments in favor of abortion rights:

- Permitting women to obtain an abortion corresponds with the principle of self-determination and allows women to have greater freedom of choice concerning their own bodies and lives.
- If abortions were prohibited, women would seek illegal abortions as they did in the past. No law

SPOTLIGHT ON DIVERSITY 2.2

Effects of Abortion on Women and Men

EP 2.1.4

Research indicates that most women demonstrate positive adjustment a year after an abortion and rarely suffer long-term psychological effects from an abortion (Hyde & DeLamater, 2014; Munk-Olsen et al., 2011). Many women "report feeling relieved, satisfied, and relatively happy, and say that if they had the decision to make over again they would do the same thing"; there is little support for the existence of a "postabortion syndrome" characterized by traits similar to those of posttraumatic stress disorder* (Hyde & DeLamater, 2014, p. 181).

However, Kelly (2008) cautions:

Although serious emotional complications following abortion are quite rare, some women and their male partners experience some degree of depression, grieving, regret, or sense of loss. These reactions tend to be even more likely in second or third abortions. Support and counseling from *friends, family members, or professionals following an abortion often help to lighten this distress, and it typically fades within several weeks after the procedure. Counseling often helps in cases where the distress does not become alleviated in a reasonable time. (p. 324)*

A frequently ignored psychological aspect of abortion is the male's reaction to the process. Many men experience feelings of "residual guilt, sadness, and remorse" (Yarber & Sayad, 2013, p. 355). A man may feel ambivalent about the pregnancy and the abortion similar to that felt by his pregnant partner. Many clinics now provide counseling for male partners of women seeking abortion (Yarber & Sayad, 2013). Both partners should receive the counseling they need to make difficult decisions and to cope with whatever feelings they are experiencing.

*Posttraumatic stress disorder is a condition in which a person continues to reexperience an excessively traumatic event, such as a bloody battle or a sexual assault.

has ever stopped abortion, and no law ever will. Performed in a medical clinic or hospital, an abortion is relatively safe; but performed under unsanitary conditions, perhaps by an inexperienced or unskilled abortionist, the operation is extremely dangerous and may even imperil the woman's life.

- If abortions were prohibited, some women would attempt to self-induce abortions. Such attempts can be life-threatening. Women have tried such techniques as severe exercise, hot baths, and pelvic and intestinal irritants, and have even attempted to lacerate the uterus with such sharp objects as nail files and knives.
- No contraceptive method is perfectly reliable. All have failure rates and disadvantages. Contraceptive information and services are not readily available and accessible to all women, particularly teenagers, the poor, and rural women.
- Abortions are necessary in many countries with soaring birthrates. Contraceptives may be inadequate, unavailable, or beyond what people can afford. Abortion appears to be a necessary population control technique to preserve the quality of life. (In some countries, the number of abortions is approaching the number of live births.)

Opponents of abortion argue:

- The right of a fetus to life is basic and should in no way be infringed.
- Abortion is immoral and against certain religious beliefs. For example, former Pope John Paul II condemned abortion as a sign of the "encroaching 'culture of death' that threatens human dignity and freedom" (Woodward, 1995, p. 56).
- A woman who chooses to have an abortion is selfish. She prefers her own pleasure over the life of her unborn child.
- In a society where contraceptives are so readily available, there should be no unwanted pregnancies and therefore no need for abortion.
- People supporting abortion are antifamily. People should take responsibility for their behavior, cease nonmarital sexual intercourse, and bear children within a family context.

Professional social workers must be aware of arguments on both sides of the issue. Only then can they assist a client in making the decision that is right for her.

Social Worker Roles and Abortion: Empowering Women

EP 2.1.1c

Social workers can assume a variety of roles when helping women with unwanted pregnancies. Among them are enabler, educator, broker, and advocate. First, as *enablers*, social workers can help women make decisions about what they will do. This involves helping clients identify alternatives and evaluate the pros and cons of each. Chilman (1987) reflects upon how social workers can counsel women concerning abortion:

> *The ultimate decision… should be made chiefly by the pregnant woman herself, preferably in consultation with the baby's father and family members. To make the decision that is best for the couple and their child, the pregnant woman—ideally, with the expectant father—needs to view each option in the context of the couple's present skills, resources, values, goals, emotions, important interpersonal relationships, and future plans. The counselor's role is to support and shape a realistic selection of the most feasible pregnancy resolution alternative. (p. 6)*

A second role social workers can assume is that of *educator*. This involves providing the pregnant woman with accurate information about the abortion process, adoption, fetal development, and options available to her. The educator role may also entail providing information about contraception to avoid subsequent unwanted pregnancies.

A third social work role involves being a *broker*. Regardless of her final decision, a pregnant woman will need to acquaint herself with the appropriate resources. These include abortion clinics, prenatal health counseling, and adoption services. A social worker can inform her of available resources, explain them, and help her obtain them.

Finally, a social worker can function as an *advocate* for a pregnant woman. A woman might want an abortion, yet live in a state that severely restricts them; if she is poor, her access to an abortion is even further restricted. A worker can advocate on this woman's behalf to improve her access to abortion or to financial support for abortion services. Another form of advocacy would be to work to change the laws and policies that inhibit women from getting the services they need. If a woman decides against an abortion, a social worker can advocate for the resources and services the woman needs to support herself and her pregnancy.

Abortion-Related Ethical Dilemmas in Practice

EP 2.1.2a–d

Picture yourself as a professional social worker in practice. What happens when your own personal values seriously conflict with those expressed by your client? A basic professional value clearly specified in the NASW *Code of Ethics* is the right of clients to make their own decisions.

By definition, an ethical dilemma involves conflicting principles. When two or more ethical principles oppose each other, it is impossible to make a "correct" decision that satisfies both or all principles involved. There is no perfect solution. For example, if a 15-year-old client tells you that he plans to murder his mother, you are caught in an ethical dilemma. It is impossible to maintain confidentiality with your client (a basic social work professional value) and yet do all you can to protect his mother from harm.

A wide range of situations involving abortion can force workers to address ethical dilemmas. Social workers should first consider what principles in the NASW *Code of Ethics* might help to guide their practice and make decisions. We have emphasized that professional values should take clear precedence over personal values about issues.

Dolgoff, Harrington, and Loewenberg (2012) have formulated a hierarchy of ethical principles, the "Ethical Principles Screen (EPS)," to provide a guide for making difficult decisions. They suggest which principle should have priority over the other when two ethical principles conflict. The hierarchy can be helpful in working through difficult situations. If the *Code of Ethics* does not directly apply or a significant amount of ambiguity exists, the worker may turn to the EPS described next.

The EPS hierarchy involves the following seven principles (pp. 80–82):

- *Principle 1: Protection of life* is of utmost importance. This might include provision of adequate food, shelter, clothing, or health care. It might concern acting in response to a person's suicide threat or threat of physically harming another. This principle applies not only to clients but also to others whose survival is imperiled.
- *Principle 2*: After protection of life, social workers should strive to *nurture equality and address inequality*. On the one hand, groups should be treated equally and have equal access to resources. On the other hand, groups who are oppressed or hold lesser status should be treated specially so that their rights are not violated. For example, consider a child abuse situation. Because the child does not hold an equal position with that of an abusive parent, "the principles of confidentiality and autonomy with respect to the abusing adult are of a lower rank order than the obligation to protect the child … , even when it is not a question of life and death" (p. 81).
- *Principle 3*: Social workers should make practice decisions that *"foster a person's self-determination, autonomy, independence, and freedom"* (p. 81). People should be allowed to make their own choices about their lives. However, this should not be at the expense of their own or someone else's life as Principle 1 prescribes. Maintaining autonomy should not be pursued if equality supported by Principle 2 would be sacrificed.
- *Principle 4*: Social workers should pursue an option that results in the *least harm* to those involved in the decision and its results.
- *Principle 5*: Social workers should make practice decisions that promote a *better quality of life for all people*. People's overall well-being is important. This involves not only the well-being of an individual or family, but also that of entire communities.
- *Principle 6*: Social workers should *respect people's privacy and maintain confidentiality*. However, this principle is superseded when people's quality of life is endangered.
- *Principle 7*: Practice decisions should allow workers to *be honest and disclose all available information*. Workers should be able to provide any information that they deem necessary in any particular situation. However, the "truth" should not be told for its own sake when it violates a client's confidentiality, which is championed by Principle 6.

The following scenario poses an ethical dilemma concerning abortion that a worker might face in practice. Next, we give an example of how Dolgoff

HIGHLIGHT 2.5

More Abortion-Related Ethical Dilemmas in Practice

Apply the hierarchy of ethical principles to each of the following case examples.

Scenario A

A 45-year-old woman becomes pregnant. She already has seven children and numerous grandchildren. Her personal physician refused to prescribe birth control pills for her because of her age and other health reasons. Nor did he discuss other forms of contraception with her or offer her the alternative of sterilization. Physically, it would be hazardous for her to have more children. She comes to you, distraught and crying. She doesn't know what to do.

Scenario B

A 32-year-old woman with a severe intellectual disability becomes pregnant. She is unable to take care of herself independently. She has a history of numerous sexual encounters. Her genetic background indicates that she would probably have a child with an intellectual disability. It is clear that she would be unable to care for a child herself.

Scenario C

A 19-year-old college student is six weeks pregnant. She has been going with her boyfriend for seven months. For the past three months they have been seeing only each other, but they do not consider themselves serious as yet. She had been using a diaphragm and contraceptive cream, but they failed to protect her. She doesn't want a baby right now. However, she feels terribly guilty about getting pregnant.

Scenario D

A married 24-year-old woman is pregnant. She already has one child with a genetic defect. She and her husband have been through genetic evaluation and counseling at a local university. The conclusion is that because both parents have a history of significant genetic problems, the chances for a normal child are extremely small. The couple was deciding upon a sterilization procedure when she became pregnant.

Scenario E

A married 28-year-old medical technician has been unaware of being pregnant until now, the seventh week of gestation. Throughout her pregnancy she has been exposed to dangerous X-rays. The possibility that her fetus has been damaged from the radiation is very high. She and her husband want children at some time, but they dread the thought of having a baby with a serious impairment.

Scenario F

Four months ago, a married man of 42 had a vasectomy. His 41-year-old wife just found out that she is five weeks pregnant. Some sperm had apparently still been present in his semen. The couple already have three children in their teens. They do not want more.

Scenario G

A 14-year-old girl is pregnant. It happened one night when she was out drinking. She had never really considered using contraception. She's shocked that she's pregnant and is having difficulty thinking about the future.

and colleagues' hierarchy of ethical principles might be applied in this case. Highlight 2.5 provides several more scenarios for you to work out on your own. Remember, there are no easy or perfect answers.

Scenario A

A 16-year-old girl was raped by a middle-aged man as she walked home from school one night and became pregnant. Both she and her parents are horrified and plagued with worry. They come to you for help. The girl desperately wants an abortion.

Application of Ethical Principles in Scenario A

Consider Principle 1, the need to protect life. If you personally adopt an antiabortion stance and feel that

abortion is murder, what do you do? A professional social worker's personal values must be acknowledged yet put aside in professional situations. The young woman and her parents want her to have the abortion.

We then look at Principle 2, which calls for the nurturance of equality and the combating of inequality. According to this principle, people should be treated equally. In this case they should have equal access to services. A neighboring state, its border only 25 miles away, allows abortions for all women who want them within the first trimester. Is this fair? Is this ethical? Should you help the young woman and her parents seek an abortion in a state that has different rules? Or should you work actively in your own state to advocate for change so that abortion would be a legal alternative for clients such as this?

Now consider Principle 3, which stresses people's right to autonomy, independence, and freedom. The young woman has the right to make her own decision. Your state might legally allow abortions for all women seeking them, or it might restrict them to only those women who have been raped or sexually abused. Or your state might ban all abortions unless the life of the mother is critically endangered.

If an abortion is legal in your state for a teenager like this, you as a worker can help her get one. She has made her decision. It is her legal right. However, if your state does not allow her to have a legal abortion, you are confronted with another dilemma.

Principle 4 refers to choosing options that result in the least harm to those involved. Principle 5 reflects the importance of maintaining an optimum quality of life. If this young woman is prevented from having an abortion, will her future be harmed? In what ways might she lose control over her life? How will her short-term and long-term quality of life be affected?

This discussion simply raises questions and issues. Each case is unique. Circumstances and attitudes vary widely. It is a professional social worker's ethical responsibility to resolve dilemmas and help clients solve problems to the best of that worker's ability. Each client should be helped to identify alternatives, evaluate the pros and cons of each, and come to a final decision. There are no absolute answers or perfect solutions.

LO 2-4 Explain Infertility

Ralph and Carol, both age 28, had been married for five years. Ralph was a drill press operator at a large bathroom fixture plant. Carol was a waitress at a Mexican restaurant. They both liked their jobs well enough. They were earning enough to purchase a small three-bedroom house and to enjoy some pleasurable amenities such as going out to dinner occasionally, taking annual camping vacations, and having cable television.

However, they felt something was wrong. Although Carol had stopped taking birth control pills more than three years before, she had still not gotten pregnant. She had read in an article in *Cosmopolitan* that women over age 35 had a much

greater chance of having a child with an intellectual disability or birth defects. Although she still had a few years, she was concerned. She and Ralph had always wanted to have as large a family as they could afford. This meant that they had better get going.

The couple really didn't talk much about the issue. Neither one wanted to imply that something might be wrong with the other one. The idea that one or both might be infertile was not appealing. It was almost easier to ignore the issue and hope that it would resolve itself in a pregnancy. After all, they still had a few years.

Infertility is the inability to conceive despite trying for 1 year, or 6 months for women age 35 or older (CDC, 2013c). Women who are unable to sustain their pregnancies and experience miscarriage are also considered to have an infertility problem. Although many people assume that they will automatically initiate a pregnancy if they don't use contraception, this is not always the case.

It is estimated that infertility affects 6.7 million American women ages 15 to 44, or almost 11 percent of this group (CDC, 2013b). However, this is an aggregate statistic that does not take into account the effects of age or a wide range of other conditions. Therefore, the 11 percent figure is probably not useful to individual couples seeking infertility counseling. Many other factors should be considered.

For example, consider the statement that older women tend to experience increased infertility. "With increasing age, the quality and quantity of a woman's eggs begin to decline. In the mid-30s, the rate of follicle loss accelerates, resulting in fewer and poorer quality eggs, making conception more challenging and increasing the risk of miscarriage" (Mayo Clinic, 2013b).

Several other factors also tend to increase infertility (Mayo Clinic, 2013b). Smoking increases the risk of miscarriage and *ectopic pregnancy* (a condition where a fertilized egg implants itself somewhere other than in the uterus, usually in a fallopian tube). Smoking may also age and diminish eggs prematurely, making it more difficult to become pregnant. Being overweight or extremely underweight, and heavy consumption of alcohol or caffeine (e.g., six cups of coffee or more each day) increases infertility. Contraction of STIs can damage the fallopian tubes, also making it harder to conceive.

Causes of Infertility

Of all infertility cases, males are responsible for approximately one-third and females for about one-third; the remaining third involves a mixture of male and female factors, or unknown causes (Mayo Clinic, 2013b). The following sections explore some of the major causes of infertility in both men and women.

Female Infertility

A primary cause of infertility in women involves difficulties with ovulation (CDC, 2013c; Mayo Clinic, 2013b). Highlight 2.6 summarizes how age affects a woman's fertility.

Whether ovulation has occurred can be detected by daily monitoring of a woman's morning temperature. Basal body temperature charts can be used for this purpose. A woman may experience a slight dip in body temperature on the day before ovulation. Immediately after ovulation, the body temperature rises slightly. There should be "a temperature shift of at least .4 degrees over a 48-hour period to indicate ovulation" (Fertilityplus, 2010).

Another cause of infertility in women involves blocked fallopian tubes (CDC, 2013c). *Pelvic inflammatory disease (PID)* is an infection of the female reproductive tract (especially the fallopian tubes) that can cause inflammation and scar tissue that blocks tubes. It often results from STIs such as gonorrhea and chlamydia (both described in Chapter 6). Tumors or various congenital abnormalities can also cause blocked tubes.

Other conditions affecting a woman's fertility include physical abnormalities in the uterine wall and benign fibroid tumors (ASRM, 2010). Endometriosis—the growth of tissue resembling that of the uterine lining outside the uterus, which often results in severe pain—can also cause infertility.

Male Infertility

Common causes of male infertility are low sperm count and decreased sperm motility (sperm's ability to maneuver quickly and vigorously) (CDC, 2013c). Another frequent cause of male infertility is a condition called varicocele, pronounced (VIAR-ih-koh-seel) (Hyde & DeLamater, 2014; NWHIC, 2009). Here the veins on a man's testicle(s) are enlarged, thereby producing too much heat and affecting sperm production. Numerous conditions can affect sperm count. Age, environmental toxins, declining health conditions, medical problems, smoking, use of drugs or alcohol, use of some medications, and radiation treatment and chemotherapy for cancer have all been blamed as contributors to infertility (NWHIC, 2009).

Couple-Related Causes of Infertility

Sometimes infertility results from a mixture of conditions and behaviors shared by a couple. It may involve timing and frequency of intercourse or specific coital techniques used. Occasionally, infertility is a consequence of antibodies produced by a woman that attack the man's sperm (Hyde & DeLamater, 2014).

Psychological Reactions to Infertility

Some people experience serious reactions to infertility. They may show signs of depression, guilt, deprivation, frustration, or anger as they pursue infertility counseling. They may feel that their lives are out of their control. In many ways feelings resemble those of grieving, including denial, anger, bargaining, depression, and finally, acceptance (Greenberg et al., 2014; Kübler-Ross, 1969).

Especially for those who really desire to have children, infertility can be associated with failure.

HIGHLIGHT 2.6

Aging Affects a Woman's Fertility

As a woman ages, five conditions affect her fertility (American Society for Reproductive Medicine, 2012a; CDC, 2013c):

1. Her ovaries' ability to release eggs ready for fertilization declines.

2. The number of eggs has decreased.
3. The health of the eggs themselves weakens.
4. A woman is more likely to experience other health problems that negatively affect fertility.
5. Her risk of miscarriage increases.

Van Den Akker (2001) studied 105 people who were infertile and found that three-quarters of them were "devastated" by their infertility "diagnosis" (p. 152). Sixty-four percent of the female and 47 percent of the male respondents indicated happiness was an impossibility without having children. One respondent elaborated, "I was angry ... there isn't anything else in my life that I've worked that hard at really, that I didn't get ... I deserved to have succeeded. I didn't have the energy to do anything else, I just couldn't do it anymore. But I was really angry. It was like, this isn't the way it was supposed to end" (p. 131).

An infertility problem is compounded by the fact that even the most intimate partners often don't feel comfortable talking about their sexuality, let alone that something may be wrong with it. Some men associate their potency with their ability to father children. Traditionally, women have placed great importance on their roles as wife and mother. Hopefully, with the greater flexibility of women's roles today, the technological advances aimed at improving fertility, and the new options available to infertile couples, the negative psychological reactions to infertility will be minimized.

Treatment of Infertility

A wide range of scenarios may reflect individual variations of infertility. One involves listening to the infamous ticking of the biological clock, an example of which Meadows (2004) describes:

Heather Pansera and her husband, Anthony, started trying to have a baby as soon as they got married [A year later] they settled into a new house in Canton, Ohio, with plenty of room to raise a family. One year passed, and Heather, 32, didn't think much about it. Another year passed and she panicked.

"We were a couple for five years by the time we got married, so we decided to let nature take its course," she says. "It never crossed our minds that getting pregnant would be so difficult."

"It seemed like everyone else was having babies," says Anthony, 39. "I have three brothers and three sisters, and they all had kids. You're happy for other people, but you want to experience it, too."

The Panseras decided to pursue fertility treatments. After five unsuccessful attempts, Heather finally became pregnant.

Treatment for infertility depends, of course, on the specific problem involved and its seriousness. It is not necessarily an easy or effective process. It can also be very expensive.

After a year of trying to conceive, both partners should pursue a medical evaluation to help determine if anything is physically wrong. When a woman is age 35 or older and has been trying unsuccessfully to get pregnant for six months, or when there is already some indication of a fertility problem, a couple may want to pursue treatment more aggressively before a year is up (see Highlight 2.6).

The first thing to be done in the case of suspected infertility is to bring the matter out into the open. People need to talk about their ideas and feelings. Only then can the various alternatives be identified and a plan of action determined. The couple's sexual practices concerning pregnancy should also be discussed to make certain they have accurate and specific information.

Assessment of Infertility

The assessment of infertility usually begins with a general physical examination to evaluate the couple's overall health; potential physical problems that might be inhibiting fertility are also investigated (ASRM, 2010). Additionally, the couple is asked about their sexual behavior to determine whether it is conducive to conception (ASRM, 2010).

Subsequently, infertility assessment typically involves a regimen of tests (Greenberg et al., 2014; NWHIC, 2009). Assessment of the male entails tests that evaluate the number, normality, and mobility of sperm. Sometimes hormonal tests are also conducted.

The first step in assessing female infertility usually involves evaluating whether the woman is ovulating each month. This can be done by monitoring her own body temperature fluctuations each day, by using home ovulation test kits that can be purchased over the counter at drug or grocery stores, or by a physician administering blood tests to establish hormone levels or taking ultrasounds of the ovaries. If it is determined that the woman is ovulating regularly, additional tests may include X-rays of the fallopian tubes and uterus after injecting dye (*hysterosalpingography*). The X-ray indicates whether the tubes are open and profiles the shape of the uterus. A laparoscopy may also be performed, in which a thin, tubular instrument is inserted into the body cavity to examine the female reproductive organs directly for any abnormalities.

Alternatives Available to the Infertile Couple

EP 2.1.10g

Alternatives available to the infertile couple include adoption, conventional treatment using surgery or drugs, in vitro fertilization, and various forms of assisted reproductive technology, all of which are explained in the following sections.

Adoption

Adoption is the legal act of taking in a child born to other parents and formally making that child a full member of the family. To provide a home and family for a child who has none is a viable and beneficial option for infertile couples.

Currently, there is an emphasis on encouraging parents to adopt children with special needs—that is, children who require additional support in the form of medical or financial help for adoptive placement; factors involved in special needs may include race, age, being part of a sibling group, or having a physical or mental disability (Barth, 2008). People pursuing the adoption alternative also often seek the adoption of foreign-born children (Barth, 2008; Crosson-Tower, 2013).

Surgery and Fertility Drugs

Conventional treatments including surgery or drugs are generally used first to treat infertility in 85 to 90 percent of all cases (Greenberg et al., 2014). Microsurgery has been used to correct blocked fallopian tubes, and remove pelvic adhesions and patches of tissue supporting endometriosis; examples of microsurgery for infertile men are vasectomy reversal and repairing varicose veins in the scrotum and testes (Hyde & DeLamater, 2014).

For women who have problems ovulating, drugs such as Clomid or Seraphine (taken orally), Repronex, or Gonal-F (both given by injection) may be prescribed to stimulate ovulation (Mayo Clinic, 2013b). Note, however, that such "fertility drugs" can result in multiple births, which may cause greater problems for both mothers and infants (American Society for Reproductive Medicine, 2012b). Infants may be born prematurely and experience health problems such as breathing difficulties, bleeding blood vessels in their brains, low birth weight, and other birth defects.

Mothers may have difficulties during pregnancy including high blood pressure, diabetes, and low blood count (anemia). They may also encounter problems during the delivery of multiple infants.

Unfortunately, drug treatment for male infertility is much less advanced.

Intrauterine Insemination

Intrauterine insemination (IUI) (also referred to as *artificial insemination [AI]*) is the process of "injecting the woman with sperm from her partner or a donor" (Yarber & Sayad, 2013, p. 381). It tends to be used when the male's infertility problems are mild or the cause of a couple's infertility is unknown (CDC, 2013c). During IUI, sperm are deposited directly into the uterus instead of the vagina. This tends to enable pregnancy in cases where sperm have difficulty penetrating cervical mucus, as it allows it to bypass that barrier. Additionally, it gives sperm a head start.

Human sperm can be frozen for up to 10 years, thawed, and then used to impregnate (Carroll, 2013b). For a fee, a sperm bank collects and maintains sperm either for the donors themselves or for nondonors, depending on the arrangement made by the donor.

The sperm used in AI may be the husband's or partner's. This procedure might also be used for family planning purposes—for example, a man might deposit his sperm in the bank, then undergo a vasectomy, and later withdraw the sperm to have children. High-risk jobs or onset of a serious illness might prompt a man to make a deposit in case of impending sterility. It is possible to pool several ejaculations from a man with a low sperm count and to inject them simultaneously into the uterus or vaginal canal.

A second type of artificial insemination is by a donor other than the husband or partner. This practice has been used for several decades to circumvent male infertility and also when the partner is a carrier of a genetic disease (e.g., a condition such as hemophilia).[11]

In recent years, an increasing number of single women have requested the services of a sperm bank. A woman requests the general genetic characteristics she wants from the father, and the sperm bank then tries to match the request from the information

---

[11]*Hemophilia* is any of several genetic disorders mostly affecting males in which blood fails to clot normally because of a defective clotting factor. Hemophiliacs must be wary of even slight injuries because these may cause excessive bleeding.

known about its donors. Donors are paid for their sperm and remain anonymous.

A third type of artificial insemination has received considerable publicity. Some married couples, in which the wife is infertile, may contract with another woman to be artificially inseminated with the husband's sperm. Under the terms of the contract, this surrogate mother is paid and expected to give the infant to the married couple shortly after birth.

A number of ethical and legal questions have been raised about artificial insemination. Many religious leaders claim that God did not mean for people to reproduce this way. In the case of using another donor's sperm, certain psychological stresses may be placed on partners and on marriages, as the procedure emphasizes the husband's infertility and involves having a baby that he has not fathered. On a broader dimension, artificial insemination raises such questions as, What are the purposes of marriage and of sex? What will happen to male-female relationships if a couple does not even have to see each other to reproduce?

There are other possible legal implications. What happens if the sperm at a bank is not paid for? Would it become the property of the bank? Could it be auctioned off? If a woman was artificially inseminated by a donor and the child was later found to have genetic defects, could the parents bring suit against the physician, the donor, or the bank? What about frozen sperm used to inseminate a woman after the donor's death? Could such children be considered the donor's heirs?

• • • • Ethical Questions 2.5

EP 2.1.2

Does a child resulting from artificial insemination by an unknown donor have the right to know who that donor was? What if this knowledge is necessary for some medical reason, such as diagnosing a hereditary disease? What if the donor does not want the child to know who he is?

Assisted Reproductive Technology

Assisted reproductive technology (ART) involves procedures to promote pregnancy that involve handling both the sperm and the egg (CDC, 2013g).

Artificial insemination is not considered ART because the egg is not manipulated. The results of ART procedures are often referred to as test-tube babies. However, this phrase is inaccurate because ART has nothing to do with a test tube. Earlier, we established that *in vitro* is Latin for "in glass" (Hyde & DeLamater, 2014). In vitro fertilization, gamete intrafallopian transfer, zygote intrafallopian transfer, and direct sperm injection are ART procedures discussed in this section.

In Vitro Fertilization   *In vitro fertilization (IVF)* is a process in which eggs are removed from a woman's body, fertilized with sperm in a laboratory dish, and then implanted in the woman's uterus. Before egg removal, the woman is given fertility drugs to encourage multiple egg production. The process can be helpful for women whose fallopian tubes are damaged, blocked, or even absent, so that the normal process of fertilization is difficult or impossible.

The first successful IVF procedure took place in Oldham, England, in 1978. Baby Louise, weighing 5 pounds, 12 ounces, was born to her parents Lesley and John Brown. The world was stunned by such a feat. The physicians who developed the technique, Patrick Steptoe and Robert Edwards, had attempted the process more than 30 times before they achieved this first success.

As with artificial insemination, the ethical issues, legal complications, and other potential problems with IVF are numerous. For example, a Dutch woman underwent IVF after trying to conceive unsuccessfully for five years. The process was successful; twins were born—one black and one white. The University Hospital at Utrecht deemed "the mix-up 'a deeply regrettable mistake,' and took responsibility for accidentally fertilizing the woman's eggs with sperm from a man from Aruba, as well as that of her husband" (American Association of Sex Educators, Counselors, and Therapists [AASECT], 1995).

Assisted reproductive technology's effectiveness varies tremendously from couple to couple. As mentioned, variables include the viability of the eggs and sperm, the mother's age, and the mother's structural capacity to maintain a pregnancy. Mulrine (2004) describes the situation for some of the most difficult cases who seek help from the Sher Institutes for Reproductive Medicine in Las Vegas:

They have... graduated to advanced treatments beyond their wildest calculations. Most of them have already undergone two or more in vitro fertilization attempts with other doctors and some 75 percent of them have traveled from out of state to try again. It is an arduous process, not without its embarrassments. One couple speaks of feeling ridiculous racing through rush-hour traffic to deliver sperm gathered at home to the clinic; another describes an earlier treatment when the doctor, in a lame effort at humor, dressed in a bunny suit on egg retrieval day, in preparation for his "Easter hunt." (p. 61)

Gamete Intrafallopian Transfer (GIFT) In *gamete intrafallopian transfer (GIFT)*, collected eggs and sperm are placed directly into a fallopian tube. Resulting embryos can then drift into the uterus. GIFT differs from IVF only where fertilization takes place. In IVF, fertilization occurs in a petri dish; in GIFT, fertilization occurs in the fallopian tube. All other aspects of the two processes are alike. Both allow natural implantation to take place in the uterus. GIFT can be performed only in those cases in which the fallopian tubes are clear and healthy. It may be used successfully with women who have endometriosis or when no specific cause for infertility has been identified. GIFT is not useful for women with blocked fallopian tubes, a common cause of female infertility.

Zygote Intrafallopian Transfer (ZIFT) *Zygote intrafallopian transfer (ZIFT)* is similar to GIFT. In the ZIFT procedure, eggs and sperm are first combined in a laboratory dish to form a zygote. The zygote is then immediately transferred to the fallopian tube. An advantage of this technique is that fertilization is known to have taken place, whereas GIFT couples can only hope that it will take place. Natural implantation in the uterus can then occur.

Direct Sperm Injection (ICSD) In *intracytoplasmic sperm injection (ICSD)*, or direct sperm injection, a physician, using a microscopic pipette (a narrow tube into which fluid is drawn by suction), injects a single sperm into an egg. The resulting zygote is subsequently placed in the uterus. This technique can be used when the male has a low sperm count or the couple has failed to conceive using traditional in vitro insemination (Rathus et al., 2014). The first successful birth using ICSD occurred late in 1994 (Sparks & Syrop, 2005).

Embryo Transplants Embryo transplants may be used for women who do not have healthy ova (eggs) themselves, often due to age or ovarian failure

(Carroll, 2013b; Rathus et al., 2014). Rathus and his colleagues (2014) explain:

Embryonic transfer can be used with women who do not produce ova of their own. A woman volunteer is artificially inseminated by the male partner of the infertile woman, or by donor sperm. Five days later the embryo is removed from the volunteer and inserted within the uterus of the mother-to-be, where it is hoped that it will become implanted. (p. 299)

Success Rates of ART Note that the effectiveness of ART procedures varies from clinic to clinic. The Fertility Clinic Success Rate and Certification Act of 1992 requires all clinics practicing artificial reproduction technology to report their success rates annually to the Centers for Disease Control (CDC). The CDC, in turn, publishes an annual report, which details the success rate for each clinic (CDC, 2013g). (Note that success rates usually refer to pregnancy rates per cycle. A cycle involves a two-week period during which ART is undertaken, usually beginning with administration of a fertility drug [CDC, 2005]).

According to the 2011 CDC national summary on ART, the average percentage of ART cycles that led to a successful implantation in the uterus were:

- 35.6 percent in women aged 34 or younger
- 27.3 percent in women aged 35–37
- 17.3 percent in women aged 38–40
- 9.4 percent in women aged 41–42
- 4.5 percent in women aged 43–44
- 1.2 percent in women aged 45 or older (CDC, 2013a)

Surrogate Motherhood

Thousands of married couples who want children but who are unable to reproduce because the woman is infertile have turned to surrogate motherhood. A surrogate can give birth to a baby conceived by artificial insemination using the sperm of the husband. Or a woman can function as a surrogate without using her own genetic material. For example, any egg fertilized using the GIFT or ZIFT process may be transferred to the surrogate mother's fallopian tube.

On birth, the surrogate mother terminates her parental rights, and the child is legally adopted by the donor(s) of the egg and/or sperm. Agencies sponsoring surrogacy stress the need for clearly established contractual agreements. However, various ethical issues are involved in surrogacy, many of which are currently being debated in the courts. Ethical Questions 2.6 addresses some of them.

Ethical Questions 2.6

EP 2.1.2

What if the surrogate mother changes her mind shortly before birth or right after birth and decides to keep the baby?

If the child is born with severe mental or physical disabilities, who will care for the child and pay for the expenses? Should it be the surrogate mother, the contracting adoptive couple, or society?

Should the best interests of the resulting children rather than their procreators be taken into account? At some point in the children's lives, should they be told that they have a surrogate mother somewhere? How might this affect their own psychological well-being?

Acceptance of Childlessness

For some infertile couples, accepting childlessness may be the most viable option. Each alternative has both positive and negative consequences that need to be evaluated. The positive aspects of childlessness need to be identified and appreciated. Increasing numbers of people are choosing to remain childless for various reasons. Not having children allows the time and energy that children would otherwise demand to be devoted to other activities and accomplishments. These include work, career, and recreational activities. A couple might also have more time to spend with each other and invest in their relationship as a couple. Children are expensive and time-consuming.

On the one hand, children can provide great joy and fulfillment. On the other hand, they also can cause problems, stress, and strain. Infertile couples (as well as fertile couples) may benefit from evaluating both sides of the issue.

Highlight 2.7 discusses the effects of macro systems on infertility.

Social Work Roles, Infertility, and Empowerment

Social workers may assume a number of roles to empower and help people address infertility: enabler, mediator, educator, broker, analyst/evaluator, and advocate. Social workers can enable people in making their decisions concerning the options available to

EP 2.1.1c

CONCEPT SUMMARY

Technological Procedures to Assist in Reproduction

Intrauterine Insemination (IUI) (Artificial insemination [AI]): The "process of injecting the woman with sperm from her partner or a donor" (Yarber & Sayad, 2013, p. 381).

Assisted reproductive technology (ART): Procedures to promote pregnancy that involve handling both the sperm and the egg.

In vitro fertilization (IVF): A process in which eggs are removed from a woman's body, fertilized with a sperm in a laboratory dish, and then implanted in the woman's uterus.

Gamete intrafallopian transfer (GIFT): A procedure in which collected eggs and sperm are placed directly into a fallopian tube where fertilization, hopefully, will take place.

Zygote intrafallopian transfer (ZIFT): A procedure in which eggs and sperm are first combined in a laboratory dish to form a zygote, which is then transferred immediately to the fallopian tube.

Direct sperm injection (intracytoplasmic sperm injection [ICSD]): A process in which a physician, using a microscopic pipette, injects a single sperm into an egg, hopefully resulting in a zygote, which is subsequently placed in the uterus.

Embryo transplant: "A method of conception in which a woman volunteer is artificially inseminated by the male partner of the intended mother, after which the embryo is removed from the volunteer and inserted within the uterus of the intended mother" (Rathus et al., 2014, p. 299).

Surrogate motherhood: The procedure in which an egg fertilized using the GIFT or ZIFT process is transferred to the fallopian tube of a surrogate mother (a woman who will bear a child for another woman).

HIGHLIGHT 2.7

The Effects of Macro Systems on Infertility

**EP 2.1.5a–c;
2.1.7**

Unlike abortion issues, which are fairly well crystallized and articulated, the issues, ethics, and values concerning infertility and reproductive technologies are only now being discovered and defined. Abortion has been available for a long time. However, modern technology has allowed sophisticated means of artificial fertilization to be undertaken for only a few decades. Additionally, new developments are rapidly advancing.

A major issue is that most fertility enhancement techniques are expensive. They may be available, but not to poor people and the uninsured. Organizations within the community will provide services only if they are paid. Is this fair or appropriate? Should infertile wealthy people be allowed to enjoy such advances when infertile poor people are not? Should these expensive advances be pursued at all in view of the world's exploding population? Vital philosophical and ethical issues are involved here. Once again, there are no easy answers.

infertile people. In cases in which the members of a couple disagree for some reason, a social worker can assume a mediator role to help them come to some compromise or mutually satisfactory decision. The social worker as educator can inform clients about options and procedures with specific and accurate data. The broker role is used to connect clients with the specific resources and infertility procedures they need.

The role of analyst/evaluator might be used to evaluate the relative effectiveness of different fertility clinics and the appropriateness of different assisted reproductive technologies to meet a couple's or individual's needs. As an advocate, a social worker might need to speak on behalf of clients if they are being denied services or if the process for receiving infertility treatment is overly cumbersome or expensive.

Spotlight 2.3 addresses client empowerment by using a feminist perspective on fertility counseling.

Chapter Summary

The following summarizes this chapter's content as it relates to the learning objectives presented at the beginning of the chapter. Chapter content will help prepare students to:

LO 2-1 Describe the dynamics of human reproduction (including conception, diagnosis of pregnancy, fetal development, prenatal influences and assessment, problem pregnancies, and the birth process).

Human reproduction is a complex process involving ovulation, ejaculation, and conception.

Prenatal influences that affect the fetus include the mother's nutrition, drugs and medication, alcohol usage, smoking habits, age, maternal stress, and other factors such as specific illnesses (e.g., rubella or AIDS) during pregnancy.

Methods of prenatal assessment include ultrasound sonography, fetal MRI, amniocentesis, chorionic villus sampling, and maternal blood tests.

Conditions that cause problem pregnancies are ectopic pregnancies, toxemia, and Rh incompatibility. Spontaneous abortions also occur periodically.

Stages in the birth process include initial contractions and dilation of the cervix, the actual birth, and afterbirth.

Birth positions include the most common vertex position, breech presentations, and transverse presentations.

Newborn assessment approaches include the Apgar scale and the Brazelton (1973) Neonatal Behavioral Assessment Scale.

Birth defects include Down syndrome and spina bifida. Other factors affecting development include low birth weight, prematurity, and anoxia.

LO 2-2 Explain normal developmental milestones for infants and children.

Children pass many developmental milestones as they grow older. Typical motor, play, adaptive, social, and language profiles for children at various age levels provide guidelines for assessment, although individual variations must be appreciated.

SPOTLIGHT ON DIVERSITY 2.3

A Feminist Perspective on Infertility Counseling and Empowerment

EP 2.1.7a

Feminist principles can be applied to counseling women who discover themselves to be infertile (Georgiades & Grieger, 2003; Solomon, 1988). The medical establishment tends to view infertility as a medical problem that needs to be solved, as dysfunctional equipment that needs to be fixed.

Social attitudes tend to support this medical view in four basic ways (Georgiades & Grieger, 2003; Solomon, 1988). First, most people in society aren't aware of the immense impact the crisis of infertility has on a woman. Second, people tend to look down on infertile women as if a woman can't possibly live a well-rounded, worthwhile life without bearing children. Third, infertile women experience feelings such as denial, anger, and depression, as do people confronted with any serious loss (Carroll, 2013b). Fourth, infertility can pose a major life crisis for a woman (Yarber & Sayad, 2013). People in crisis are generally more vulnerable, more suggestible, and more easily manipulated than they are during more normal times.

A two-pronged approach to infertility treatment is proposed (Solomon, 1988). First, social workers and other helping professionals should address infertility as a very personal issue (Georgiades & Grieger, 2003). Women who are experiencing the crisis of infertility should be treated as people with other crises are treated. A woman needs to be encouraged to identify and express her feelings, even when they hurt, come to accept her situation, and eventually make decisions about how she wants to proceed. Too frequently, infertile women are told

what to do by medical professionals and are led to follow extensive, expensive, complicated, time-consuming procedures that may have little chance of success. It should be acknowledged that the infertile woman is more vulnerable and more likely to respond to medical direction than when she is not experiencing a crisis. Instead, the infertile woman may need specific information about the options available to her, the risks, the amount of effort required to pursue treatment, and help in evaluating which alternative is to her individual best advantage. Each woman needs to evaluate if she really wants to put forth the amount of effort needed. Infertile women need to be empowered to make their own choices.

The second level involved in a feminist approach concerns the more general social attitudes about women (Hyde, 2008), in this case infertile women and their treatment. Infertile women are stigmatized. They are viewed by society as having something wrong with them, as being incomplete. These attitudes need to be changed.

EP 2.1.5b

The positive qualities of any life choice need to be emphasized. Women need to recognize their value as individual human beings, not as a failure or success because of their ability or lack of ability to bear children. People as citizens, advocates, and social workers can form pressure groups to encourage more extensive research into the causes and treatment of infertility and to alter the traditional manner in which fertility treatment is done. Women need to be and feel empowered, and to have their choices maximized.

LO 2-3 Examine the abortion controversy (in addition to the impacts of social and economic forces).

Macro-system policies and the battle between pro-choice and antiabortion forces affect service delivery.

Controversial issues include restricting access through legislation, limiting financial support, condition of the mother, fetal condition, violence against clinics, stem cell research, and intact dilation and extraction (often referred to by opponents as partial-birth abortion).

Significantly fewer abortions are performed today than in past decades.

Methods of abortion include medication abortion, vacuum aspiration, and dilation and evacuation. Illegal abortions pose significant health risks around

the world. Major physical complications from legal abortion are rare.

Women who have had abortions generally experience no serious long-term psychological effects, although the decision to terminate a pregnancy is often a difficult and complex one. Men may also experience psychological distress following an abortion, a fact that is often ignored.

Proponents and opponents of abortion have developed arguments in support of their respective stances.

Many women face serious ethical dilemmas with respect to unwanted pregnancy. Professional social workers have an obligation to assist pregnant clients in evaluating the various alternatives open to them to empower them to make their own decisions.

LO 2-4 *Explain infertility (including the causes, the psychological reactions to infertility, the treatment of infertility, the assessment process, alternatives available to infertile couples, and social work roles concerning infertility).*

Almost 11 percent of all U.S. couples are infertile. Leading causes of women's infertility are difficulties with ovulation, blocked fallopian tubes, and physical abnormalities such as fibroid tumors and endometriosis. Most male infertility is caused by a low sperm count, decreased sperm motility, and varicocele. Sometimes infertility results from a mixture of conditions shared by a couple.

People may suffer serious psychological reactions to infertility.

Treatment of infertility includes fertility drugs, microsurgery, intrauterine insemination (IUI) (also referred to as artificial insemination [AI]), and assisted reproductive technology (ART), which can involve in vitro fertilization (IVF), gamete intrafallopian transfer (GIFT), zygote intrafallopian transfer (ZIFT), intracytoplasmic sperm injection (ICSD), and embryo transplants. Other alternatives include surrogate motherhood, adoption, and acceptance of childlessness.

An ethical issue is the cost of treatment, which limits access for those who are not wealthy. Social workers may assume many roles in helping people choose alternatives.

A feminist approach to treating infertile women emphasizes empowerment by dealing with the issue on a personal level and addressing general social attitudes about women and infertility.

COMPETENCY NOTES

The entire chapter addresses competency Educational Policy (EP) EP 2.1.7 and its respective practice behaviors EP 2.1.7a and EP 2.1.7b (as cited below). (See p. 63.)

EP 2.1.7 Apply knowledge of human behavior and the social environment.

EP 2.1.7a Utilize conceptual frameworks to guide the processes of assessment, intervention, and evaluation. (Such conceptual frameworks will typically be identified by a "helping hands" icon.)

EP 2.1.7b Critique and apply knowledge to understand person and environment.
Other EP competencies and practice behaviors addressed in this chapter include the following:

EP 2.1.1c Attend to professional roles and boundaries.
(p. 77): Social work roles regarding helping pregnant women bear healthy infants are identified.
(p. 98): Social work roles with respect to women and abortion are reviewed.
(p. 107): Social work roles with respect to working with infertile couples are explained.

EP 2.1.1e Engage in career-long learning.
(p. 94): The circumstances of stem cell research is an example of the many issues social workers should attend to in order to keep abreast of current developments.

EP 2.1.2 Apply social work ethical principles to guide professional practice.
(pp. 67, 92, 94, 94, 105, 107): Ethical questions are raised.

EP 2.1.2a Recognize and manage personal values in a way that allows professional values to guide practice.
(p. 86): The abortion issue is a useful one to analyze and discuss because people have personal opinions, often very strong ones, about it. It sets the stage for social workers to assess their own personal values and explore how those values should not interfere with professional practice.
(p. 89): Social workers must explore their personal values on a range of controversial issues in order to remain objective in their work with clients.
(p. 99): Social workers must distinguish between personal and professional values, so that personal values don't interfere with professional behavior. Because of strong and varied opinions concerning the abortion issue, it provides a fertile ground for recognizing personal opinions, distinguishing them from professional values, and addressing ethical dilemmas in a professional manner.

EP 2.1.2b Make ethical decisions by applying standards of the National Association of Social Workers (NASW) Code of Ethics and, as applicable, of the International Federation of Social Workers/International Association of Schools of Social Work Ethics in Social Work, Statement of Principles.
(p. 99): The NASW *Code of Ethics* stresses that it is clients' right to make their own decisions.

EP 2.1.2c Tolerate ambiguity in resolving ethical conflicts.
(p. 89): The controversial issues described in the following sections may be ambiguous in terms of

the best solution. Social workers must learn to tolerate such ambiguity as they seek to resolve ethical conflicts.

(p. 99): As they practice, social workers often confront ambiguity in the context of ethical dilemmas.

EP 2.1.2d Apply strategies of ethical reasoning to arrive at principled decisions.

(p. 99): A hierarchy is described for addressing ethical dilemmas. Various ethical dilemmas in practice are presented. Ethical principles are applied to Scenario A.

EP 2.1.4 Engage diversity and difference in practice.

(p. 97): Gender is a dimension of diversity. Men are often overlooked in terms of how an abortion may affect them psychologically.

EP 2.1.5 Advance human rights and social and economic justice.

(p. 90): Social workers should be knowledgeable about the global ramifications of human rights involving many issues, including abortion, health and safety, and self-determination.

EP 2.1.5a Understand the forms and mechanisms of oppression and discrimination.

(p. 76): It is important to understand the global interconnections of oppression in terms of the relationship between poverty and low birth weight.

(p. 108): It is important to appraise the inequities of access to infertility services.

EP 2.1.5b Advocate for human rights and social and economic justice.

(p. 71): Social workers can advocate for improved policies and services that meet pregnant women's needs.

(p. 108): Social workers should advocate for policies that are fair and equitable.

(p. 109): Social workers should advocate for improving general social attitudes toward infertile women.

EP 2.1.5c Engage in practices that advance social and economic justice.

(p. 108): Social workers should engage in practices that advance social and economic justice on behalf of people with infertility problems.

EP 2.1.7 Apply knowledge of human behavior and the social environment.

(p. 88): Social workers must be knowledgeable about the wide range of social systems in which people live, including the effects of macro systems upon people's ultimate health and well-being.

(p. 108): Macro systems affect the alternatives available to infertile people.

EP 2.1.7a Utilize conceptual frameworks to guide the processes of assessment, intervention, and evaluation.

(p. 109): A feminist conceptual framework can be useful in working with infertile women.

EP 2.1.10e Assess clients' strengths and limitations.

(p. 69): Tests that assess the strengths and weaknesses of a fetus are described.

(p. 74): Two assessment approaches for newborns are described.

(p. 79): Social workers must be knowledgeable about normal developmental milestones in order to provide clients with the services they need.

EP 2.1.10g Select appropriate intervention strategies.

(p. 104): It is important to know what options are available in order to help infertile clients select appropriate intervention strategies.

EP 2.1.10i Implement prevention interventions that enhance client capacities.

(p. 66): It is important to understand factors that influence the health and development of the fetus in order to avoid behaviors that can cause subsequent problems.

EP 2.1.10k Negotiate, mediate, and advocate for clients.

(p. 71): Social workers can advocate for services that pregnant clients need.

WEB RESOURCES

See this text's companion website at *www.cengage brain.com* for learning tools such as chapter quizzing, videos, and more.

CHAPTER 3

PSYCHOLOGICAL DEVELOPMENT IN INFANCY AND CHILDHOOD

blue jean images/Getty Images

"Hey, Barry, wha'd ya get on that spelling test?"
"I got an 87. How about you?"
"Aw, I got a 79. If I get a C in spelling, my ma will kill me."
*"Yeah, Marta got a 100 again. She always ruins it for the rest of us by getting straight A's.
I'm so sick of Ms. Butcherblock comparing us to her."*
"I hear Billy flunked again. He's never going to make it into fifth grade."
"Yeah, Bill's an okay guy, but he sure isn't very smart."
"Only 10 more minutes to recess. I'm gettin' out there first and get the best ball."
"Wanna bet? I'll race ya!"

Psychology is defined as the science of mind and behavior. Human psychological development involves personality, cognition, emotion, and self-concept. Each child develops into a unique entity with individual strengths and weaknesses. At the same time, however, some principles and processes apply to the psychological development of all people. Likewise, virtually everyone is subject to similar psychological feelings and reactions that affect their behavior.

This example portrays two schoolboys discussing their current academic careers. Numerous psychological concepts and variables are affecting even this simple interaction. The boys are addressing their own and their peers' ability to learn and achieve. Learning is easier for some children and more difficult for others. Personality characteristics also come into play. Some children are more dominant and aggressive. Others are more passive. Some young people are more motivated to achieve and win. Others are less interested and enthusiastic. Finally, some children feel good about themselves, and others have poor self-concepts.

A Perspective

Psychological variables interact with biological and social factors to affect an individual's situation and behavior. Their interaction influences the potential courses of action available to a person at any point in time. This chapter focuses on some of the psychological concepts that critically impact children as they grow up. There are four major thrusts. The first presents a perspective on how personalities develop. The second provides a basic understanding of how children think and learn. The third focuses on emotion, and the fourth on self-concept.

Learning Objectives

This chapter will help prepare students to:

**EP 2.1.7,
2.1.7a,
2.1.7b**

LO 3-1 *Summarize psychological theories about personality development (including psychodynamic, neo-Freudian psychoanalytic, behavioral, phenomenological, and feminist theories)*

LO 3-2 *Use critical thinking to evaluate theory*

LO 3-3 *Relate human diversity to psychological theories*

LO 3-4 *Examine Piaget's theory of cognitive development*

LO 3-5 *Review the information-processing conception of cognitive development*

LO 3-6 *Apply Vygotsky's theory of cognitive development*

LO 3-7 *Explain emotional development (including the development of temperament and attachment)*

LO 3-8 *Examine self-concept, self-esteem, and empowerment*

LO 3-9 *Discuss intelligence and intelligence testing*

LO 3-10 *Explain cultural biases and IQ tests*

LO 3-11 *Analyze intellectual disabilities and the importance of empowerment*

LO 3-12 *Examine learning disabilities*

LO 3-13 *Discuss attention deficit disorder*

LO 3-1 Summarize Psychological Theories About Personality Development

EP 2.1.7a

How many times have you heard someone make statements such as the following: "She has a great personality," or "He has a personality like a wet dishrag." *Personality* is the complex cluster of mental, emotional, and behavioral characteristics that distinguish a person as an individual. The term may encompass a wide array of characteristics that describe a person. For instance, a person may be described as aggressive, dominant, brilliant, or outgoing. Another individual may be characterized as slow, passive, mousy, or boring. Because personality can include such varying dimensions of personal characteristics, explaining its development can be difficult.

This section reviews a number of psychological theories that aim to provide conceptual frameworks for explaining why individual personalities develop as they do. Many more psychological theories exist. Theories addressed in this text were chosen because of their historical significance, widespread use, and relevance to social work assessment and practice. They include psychodynamic theory, neo-Freudian psychoanalytic theory, phenomenological theories, and feminist theories. Behavioral theory is mentioned only briefly here; Chapter 4 covers it extensively within the context of its application to effective parenting. Chapter 7 addresses other psychological theories in depth, including those of Erik Erikson and Lawrence Kohlberg, and applies them to adolescence and young adulthood.

The Psychodynamic Conceptual Framework

Sigmund Freud is perhaps the best known of all personality theorists. This section discusses psychodynamic theory in some detail because of its historical significance. Arlow (1995) explains: "Originating as a method for treating psychoneurotic disorders, psychoanalysis has come to serve as the foundation for a general theory of psychology. Knowledge derived from the treatment of individual patients has led to insights into art, religion, social organization, child development, and education" (p. 15).

Adler (2006) describes Freud as the

theoretician who explored a vast new realm of the mind, the unconscious: a roiling dungeon of painful memories clamoring to be heard and now and then escaping into awareness by way of dreams, slips of the tongue and mental illness.... [He was the] philosopher who identified childhood experience, not racial destiny or family fate, as the crucible of character.... Not many still seek a cure on a psychoanalyst's couch four days a week, but the vast proliferation of talk therapies—Jungian and Adlerian analyses, cognitive behavioral and psychodynamic therapy—testify to the enduring power of his idea. (p. 43)

Freud's conception of the mind was two dimensional, as indicated in Figure 3.1. One dimension of the mind consisted of the *conscious*, the *preconscious*, and the *unconscious*. Freud thought that the mind was composed of thoughts (ideas), feelings, instincts, drives, conflicts, and motives. Most of these elements in the mind were thought to be located in the unconscious or preconscious. Elements in the preconscious area had a fair chance to become conscious, whereas elements in the unconscious were unlikely to arise to a person's conscious mind. The small conscious cap at the top of Figure 3.1 indicates Freud's theory that a person was aware of only a fraction of the total thoughts, drives, conflicts, motives, and feelings in the mind.

The repressed area was a barrier under which disturbing material (primarily thoughts and feelings) had been placed by the defense mechanism of repression. *Repression* is a process in which unacceptable

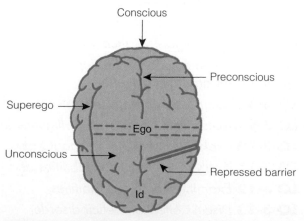

FIGURE 3.1 Freud's Conception of the Mind

desires, memories, and thoughts are excluded from consciousness by sending the material into the unconscious under the repressed barrier. Freud thought that once a material has been repressed, it has energy and acts as an unconscious irritant, producing unwanted emotions and bizarre behavior, such as anger, nightmares, hallucinations, and enuresis.

The Id, Superego, and Ego

The second dimension of the mind was composed of the *id*, *superego*, and *ego*. These parts are interrelated and impact the functioning of each other.

The *id* is the primitive psychic force hidden in the unconscious. It represents the basic needs and drives on which other personality factors are built. The id involves all of the basic instincts that people need to survive. These include hunger, thirst, sex, and self-preservation. The id is governed by the pleasure principle; that is, the instincts within the id seek to be expressed regardless of the consequences. Freud believed that these basic drives, or instincts, involved in the id provide the main energy source for personality development. When the id is deprived of one of its needs, the resulting tension motivates a person to relieve the discomfort and satisfy the need. The id's relationship with the ego allows a person to rationally determine a means to fulfill the need.

The *ego* is the rational component of the mind. It begins to develop, through experience, shortly after birth. The ego controls a person's thinking and acts as the coordinator of personality. Operating according to the reality principle, the ego evaluates consequences and determines courses of action in a rational manner. The id indicates to a person what is needed or wanted. The ego then helps the person figure out how to get it.

The third component of this dimension of the mind is the *superego* or conscience. Normally developing between the ages of 3 and 5, it consists of the traditional values and mores of society that are interpreted to a child by the parents. The superego's main function is to determine whether something is right or wrong. When an instinctual demand strives for expression that the superego disapproves of, the superego sends a signal of anxiety as a warning to the ego to prevent the expression of the instinct. The emotion of guilt is said to originate from the superego. Without the superego to provide a sense of right and wrong, a person would be completely selfish. That is, a person would use the ego to rationally determine a means of getting what the id wanted, regardless of the consequences on other people.

An example of how the id, ego, and superego might function together is provided in the case of a 9-year-old girl looking at CDs in her favorite store. Although the girl adores Nasal Thrusters and Sleek Spit (a group hitting the top of the charts), she has only $7.67 to her name. Her id, functioning by the pleasure principle, urges her to get that newly released CD. Her ego reasons that she could slip the CD under her jacket and race out of the store. Her ego also encourages her to look to see if anyone, especially those "nosy" clerks, are anywhere around. She's just about to do it when her superego propels itself into action. Clearly reminding her that stealing is wrong, it raises questions such as what her parents would think about her if she were to get caught. They would be terribly disappointed. Maybe she would even be kicked out of Girl Scouts. As a result, the girl gives the CD one last lingering look, sighs, and starts on her way home. Her ego has already begun to work on how much lawn mowing she will have to do to earn the money needed to purchase the CD.

Psychosexual Development

Freud came to realize that many people had sexual conflicts, and he made sexuality a focus of his theories. The term he used for the energy of the id's biological instincts was *libido*. This energy was primarily conceived as being sexual energy. Freud thought sexuality included physical love, affectionate impulses, self-love, love for parents and children, and friendship associations.

Freud further conceptualized that people in their development of personality progressed through five consecutive phases. During any one of the earlier phases, conflicts or disturbances could arise that, if not resolved, could fixate that person in some ways at that particular level of development. According to Freud, the term *fixated* meant that a person's personality development was largely, though not completely, halted at a particular stage. In order to develop optimal mental health, an individual would either have to resolve these crises and/or use one of several defense mechanisms. A *defense mechanism* involves any unconscious attempt to adjust to conditions that are painful. These conditions may

Definitions of Common Defense Mechanisms Postulated by Psychoanalytic Theory

Compensation: struggling to make up for feelings of inferiority or areas of weakness. For example, a stock market analyst's intense, aggressive competitiveness might be geared to compensating for internal feelings of inferiority. Or a man who was a weakling as a child might work to become a Mr. Atlas competition bodybuilder as an adult to compensate for his former weakness.

Repression: mechanism through which unacceptable desires, feelings, memories, and thoughts are excluded from consciousness by being sent down deep into the unconscious. For example, you might repress an unpleasant incident, such as a fight with your best friend, by blocking it from your conscious memory.

Sublimation: mechanism whereby consciously unacceptable instinctual demands are channeled into acceptable forms for gratification. For example, aggression can be converted into athletic activity.

Denial: mechanism through which a person escapes psychic pain associated with reality by unconsciously rejecting reality. For example, a mother may persistently deny that her child has died.

Identification: mechanism through which a person takes on the attitudes, behavior, or personal attributes of another person whom he or she had idealized (parent, relative, popular hero, etc.). Reaction formation: blocking out

"threatening impulses or feelings" by acting out an "opposite behavior"; for example, a mother who resents her children might emphasize how much she loves them and could never live without them (Coon, 2002, p. 413).

Regression: mechanism that involves a person falling back to an earlier phase of development in which he or she felt secure. Some adults when ill, for example, will act more childish and demanding, with the unconscious goal of having others around them give them more care and attention.

Projection: mechanism through which a person unconsciously attributes his or her own unacceptable ideas or impulses to another. For example, a person who has an urge to hurt others may feel that others are trying to hurt him.

Rationalization: mechanism by which an individual, faced with frustration or with criticism of his or her actions, finds justification for them by disguising from him- or herself (as he or she hopes to disguise from others) his or her true motivations. Often, this is accomplished by a series of excuses that are believed by the person. For example, a student who fails an exam may blame it on poor teaching or having long work hours, rather than consciously acknowledging the real reasons—for instance, that she had "partied hardy" the night before.

---

include anxiety, frustration, or guilt. Defense mechanisms are measures through which a person preserves his or her self-esteem and softens the blow of failure, deprivation, or guilt. Some of these mechanisms are positive and helpful. Others only help avoid positive resolution of conflict. Highlight 3.1 defines common defense mechanisms postulated by Freud.

Freud's phases of psychosexual and personality development include the oral, anal, phallic, latency, and genital stages.

Oral Stage   This phase extends from birth to approximately 18 months. It is called oral because the primary activities of a child are centered around feeding and the organs (mouth, lips, and tongue) associated with that function. Feeding is considered to be an important area of conflict, and a child's attention is focused on receiving and taking. People fixated at this stage were thought to have severe

personality disorders, such as schizophrenia or psychotic depression.

Anal Stage   Between the ages of 18 months and 3 years, a child's activities are mainly focused on giving and withholding, primarily connected with retaining and passing feces. Bowel training is an important area of conflict. People fixated at this stage have such character traits as messiness, stubbornness, rebelliousness; or they may have a reaction formation and have such opposite traits as being meticulously clean and excessively punctual.

Phallic Stage   From ages 3 through 5, the child's attention shifts to the genitals. Prominent activities are pleasurable sensations from genital stimulation, showing off one's body, and looking at the bodies of others. Also, a child's personality becomes more complex during this stage. Although self-centered, the child wants to love and be loved and seeks to be admired. Character traits that are apt to develop from fixation at this stage are pride, promiscuity, and self-hatred.

Boys and girls experience separate complexes during this stage. Boys encounter an *Oedipus complex.* This is the dilemma faced by every son at this age when he falls sexually in love with his mother. At the same time he is antagonistic toward his father, whom he views as a rival for her affections. As the intensity of both these relationships mount, the son increasingly suffers from *castration anxiety*; that is, he fears his father is going to discover his "affair" with his mother and remove his genitals. Successful resolution of the Oedipus complex occurs through defense mechanisms. A typical resolution is for the son to first *repress* his feelings of love for his mother and his hostile feelings toward his father. Next, the son has a *reaction formation* in which he stops viewing his father negatively, and turns this around and has positive feelings toward his father. The final step is for the son to *identify* with his father, and thereby seek to take on the attitudes, values, and behavior patterns of his father.

Girls, on the other hand, undergo an *Electra complex* during this phallic stage. Freud believed girls fall sexually in love with their father at this age. Meanwhile, they also view their mother with antagonism. Because of these relationships, girls also suffer from castration anxiety, but the nature of this anxiety is different from that of boys. Castration anxiety in a girl results from the awareness that she lacks a penis. She then concludes she was castrated in infancy and blames her mother for this. Freud went on to theorize that because girls believe they have been castrated they come to regard themselves as inferior to boys (i.e., they have penis envy). Therefore, they perceive that their role in life is to be submissive and supportive of males. Freud did not identify the precise processes for resolution of the Electra complex in girls.

Latency Stage   This stage usually begins at the time when the Oedipus/Electra complexes are resolved and ends with puberty. The sexual instinct is relatively unaroused during this stage. The child can now be socialized and become involved in the education process and in learning skills.

Genital Stage   This stage, which occurs from puberty to death, involves mature sexuality. The person reaching this stage is fully able to love and

to work. Again, we see Freud's emphasis on the *work ethic*, the idea that hard work is a very important part of life, in addition to being necessary to attaining one's life goals. This ethic was highly valued in Freud's time. Freud theorized that personality development was largely completed by the end of puberty, with few changes thereafter.

Psychopathological Development

Freud theorized that disturbances can arise from several sources. One source was traumatic experiences that a person's ego is not able to cope with directly and therefore strives to resolve using such defense mechanisms as repression. Breuer and Freud (1895) provide an example of a woman named Anna O. who developed a psychosomatic paralysis of her right arm. Anna O. was sitting by her father's bedside (her father was gravely ill) when she dozed off and had a nightmare that a big black snake was attacking her father. She awoke terrified and hastily repressed her thoughts and feelings about this nightmare for fear of alarming her father. During the time she was asleep, her right arm was resting over the back of a chair and became "numb." Freud theorized that the energy connected with the repressed material then took over physiological control of her arm, and a psychological paralysis resulted.

In addition to unresolved traumatic events, Freud thought that internal unconscious processes could also cause disturbances. There was a range of possible sources. An unresolved Electra or Oedipus complex could lead to a malformed superego and thus lead a person to have a variety of sexual problems—such as frigidity, promiscuity, sexual dysfunctions, excessive sexual fantasies, and nightmares with sexual content. Unresolved internal conflicts (e.g., an unconscious liking and hatred of one's parents) might cause such behavioral problems as hostile and aggressive behavior and such emotional problems as temper tantrums. Fixations at early stages of development were another source that largely prevented development at later stages and led the person to display such undesirable personality traits as messiness or stubbornness.

As indicated earlier, the main source of anxiety was thought to be sexual frustrations. Freud thought that anxiety would arise when a sexual instinct sought expression, but was blocked by the ego. If the instinct was not then diverted through defense mechanisms, the energy connected with sexual instincts was transformed into anxiety.

An *obsession* (a recurring thought such as a song repeatedly on your mind) and a *compulsion* ("an act a person feels driven to repeat, often against his or her will," such as an urge to step on every crack of a sidewalk) were thought to be mechanisms through which a person was working off energy connected with disturbing unconscious material (Coon, 2002, pp. 448–449).

Unconscious processes were thought to be the causes for all types of mental disorders. These unconscious processes were almost always connected with traumatic experiences, particularly those in childhood.

Critical Thinking: Evaluation of Psychodynamic Theory

EP 2.1.3

We have established that *critical thinking* is "the careful examination and evaluation of beliefs and actions" to establish an independent decision about what is true and what is not (Gibbs & Gambrill, 1999, p. 3). It entails the ability to evaluate carefully the validity of an assumption and even of a so-called fact. Critical thinking can be used concerning almost any issue, condition, statement, or theory, including psychodynamic theory.

Freud was virtually the first to focus on the impact of the family on human development. He was also one of the earliest, most positive proponents of good mental health. However, he was a product of the past century, and many of his ideas are subject to serious contemporary criticisms.

First, research does not support either the existence of his theoretical constructs or the effectiveness of his therapeutic method. Part of this lack may be due to the abstract nature of his concepts. It is very difficult, if not impossible, to pinpoint the location and exact nature of the superego.

The second criticism involves the lack of clarity in many of his ideas. For instance, although Freud asserts that the resolution of a boy's Oedipus complex results in the formation of the superego, he never clarifies how this occurs. Nor does he ever clearly explain the means by which girls might resolve the Electra complex.

The Electra complex leads us to a third criticism of Freud's theories. Women never really attain either an equal or a positive status within the theory. Essentially, women are left in the disadvantaged position of feeling perpetual grief at not having a penis, suffering eternal inferiority with respect to men, and being doomed to the everlasting limbo of inability to resolve an Electra complex.

Neo-Freudian Psychoanalytic Developments

Since Freud's time, many other theorists have modified and expanded on his ideas. These theorists, often referred to as neo-Freudians, or ego psychologists, include Carl Jung, Erich Fromm, Alfred Adler, and Harry Stack Sullivan, among others. In general, they are more concerned with the ego and the surrounding social environment than the role of instincts, libido, and psychosexual stages, which were central to Freud's perspective.

Carl Jung, who lived from 1875 to 1961, was a Swiss psychologist originally associated with Freud. He later developed his own approach to psychology, called *analytic psychology*. Jung thought of the mind as more than merely a summation of an individual's past experiences. He proposed the idea of an inherited "collective unconscious." Each person's individual experiences somehow melded into this collective unconscious, which was part of all people. He theorized that this gave people a sense of their goals and directions for the future. Jung stressed that people have a religious, mystical component in their unconscious. Jung was fascinated with people's dreams and the interpretation of their meaning. He also minimized the role that sexuality plays in emotional disorders.

Erich Fromm came to the United States from Germany in 1934. Whereas Freud had a primarily biological orientation in his analysis of human behavior, Fromm had a social orientation. In other words, he hypothesized that people are best understood within a social context. He focused on how people interact with others. Individual character traits then evolve from these social interactions. Fromm used psychoanalysis as a tool for understanding various social and historical processes and the behavior of political leaders.

Alfred Adler was also associated with Freud in his earlier years. After breaking with Freud in 1911 because of his basic rejection of Freud's libidinal theory, he went on to develop what he called "individual psychology," which emphasized social interaction.

Adler saw people as creative, responsible individuals who guide their own growth and development through interactions with others in their social environment (Mosak & Maniacci, 2011). Adler theorized that each person's unique striving process or lifestyle "is sometimes self-defeating because of inferiority feelings. The individual with 'psychopathology' is discouraged rather than sick, and the therapeutic task is to encourage the person to activate his or her social interest and to develop a new lifestyle through relationship, analysis, and action methods" (Mosak & Maniacci, 2011, p. 67). This social interest, an inborn trait, guides each person's behavior and stresses cooperation with others.

Of all the neo-Freudians, Harry Stack Sullivan, an American psychiatrist who lived from 1892 to 1949, made perhaps some of the most radical deviations from Freudian theory. He abandoned many of the basic Freudian concepts and terms. Like Adler, Sullivan emphasized that each individual personality developed on the basis of interpersonal relationships. He proposed that people generally have two basic needs, one for security and one for satisfaction. Whenever a conflict arose between these two needs, the result was some form of emotional disturbance. He emphasized that to improve interaction, communication problems must be overcome. Sullivan placed "greater emphasis upon developmental child psychology" than did Adler and proposed six developmental stages ranging from infancy to late adolescence (Mosak, 1995; Mosak & Maniacci, 2011, p. 72).

Neo-Freudians have had a great impact on the way we think about ourselves and on the ways in which we view psychotherapy. However, they have not produced hypotheses that are specific enough to be tested scientifically. Most of these theorists were psychotherapists and writers focusing on philosophical interest rather than scientists who conducted rigorous research. Therefore, their major usefulness may involve providing ideas and ways to think about human behavior rather than contributing to the scientific foundation of psychology.

Behavioral Conceptual Frameworks

Behavioral or learning theories differ from many other personality theories in one basic way. Instead of focusing on internal motivations, needs, and perceptions, behavioral theories focus on specific observable behaviors.

Behavioral theories state that people learn or acquire their behaviors. This learning process follows certain basic principles. For example, behavior can be increased or strengthened by receiving positive reinforcement.

Behavioral theories encompass a vast array of different perspectives and applications. However, they all focus on behavior and how it is learned. More recently, greater attention has been given to the complex nature of social situations and how people react in them (Kazdin, 2008b, 2013; Wilson, 2011). This involves people's perceptions about different situations and their ability to distinguish between one and another. More credit is given to people's ability to think, discriminate, and make choices. This perspective in behavioral theory is frequently called *social learning or social behavioral theory*. Behavior is seen as occurring within a social context. Chapter 4 discusses social learning theory in depth and applies it to effective parenting. Therefore, it is addressed only briefly here.

Phenomenological Conceptual Frameworks: Carl Rogers

Phenomenological or self theories of personality focus on particular individuals' perceptions of the world, and how these individuals feel about these experiences. A person is viewed as having various experiences and developing a personality as a result of these subjective experiences, rather than as being born with a specified personality framework. These theories assert that there are no predetermined patterns of personality development. Rather, phenomenological theories recognize a wider range of options or possibilities for personality development, depending on the individual's life experiences. Uniqueness of the individual personality is emphasized. Each individual has a configuration of personal experiences that will produce a personality unlike any other. This is a relatively positive theoretical approach in that it focuses on growth and self-actualization.

One of the best-known self theorists, Carl Rogers, is the founder of *person-centered* (previously known as *client-centered*) therapy, which is based on his self theory.[1] One of Rogers's basic concept is the self, or self-concept. Rogers defines these terms as the

---

[1]This material on person-centered therapy was originally adapted from Charles Zastrow, *The Practice of Social Work*, 3rd ed., 1989, pp. 357–360. © 1989 Wadsworth Publishing Company.

"organized, consistent, conceptual gestalt composed of perceptions of the characteristics of the 'I' or 'me' and the perceptions of the relationships of the 'I' or 'me' to others and to various aspects of life, together with the values attached to these perceptions" (Raskin, Rogers, & Witty, 2011; Rogers, 1959, p. 200). In other words, self-concept is a person's perception of and feelings about him- or herself, including his or her personality, strengths weaknesses, and relationships with others. A person is the product of his or her own experience and how he or she perceives these experiences. Life, therefore, provides a host of opportunities to grow and thrive.

Rogers maintains that there is a natural tendency toward *self-actualization*—that is, the tendency for every person to develop capacities that serve to maintain or enhance the person (Raskin et al., 2011; Rogers, 1959). People are naturally motivated toward becoming fulfilled through new experiences.

In contrast to Freud, who viewed the basic nature of human beings as evil (having immoral, asocial instincts), Rogers views humans as being inherently good. Rogers believes that if a person remains relatively free of influence attempts from others, the self-actualization motive will lead to a sociable, cooperative, creative, and self-directed person.

The driving force in personality development is seen by client-centered theorists as the "self-actualization motive," which seeks to optimally develop a person's capacities. As an infant grows, the infant's "self-concept" begins to be formed. The development of the self-concept is highly dependent on the individual's *perceptions* of his or her experiences. The person's perceptions of experiences are influenced by the "need for positive regard" (to be valued by others). The need for positive regard is seen as a universal need in every person (Raskin et al., 2011; Rogers, 1959). Out of the variety of experiences of frustration or satisfaction of the need for positive regard, the person develops a "sense of self-regard"—that is, the learned perception of self-worth that is based on the perceived attention and esteem received from others.

Although self-actualization is a natural process as people mature, they often encounter barriers. Ivey, D'Andrea, Ivey, and Simek-Morgan (2002) introduce the dynamics involved:

A critical issue in Rogerian counseling is the discrepancy that often occurs between the real self [the person one actually is] and the ideal self [the person one would like to be]. Individuals need to see themselves as worthy. Often individuals lose sight of what they really are in an effort to attain an idealized image. . . . This discrepancy between thought and reality, between self-perception and others' perceptions, or between self and experience leads to incongruities. These incongruities in turn result in areas in which individuals are not truly themselves. . . . The objective of therapy . . . is to resolve the discrepancies between ideal and real self, thus eliminating the tension and substituting forward-moving self-actualization. (pp. 248–249) (emphasis added)

One type of barrier to self-actualization involves a child's *introjection* (taking on) of others' values that are inconsistent with his or her self-actualizing motive. The introjection of values inconsistent with one's self-actualizing motive results in *conditions of worth*—a person's perceptions that he or she is only valuable when behaving as others expect and prefer him or her to act. A person, then, is only worthy (of value) under the *condition* that he or she behaves as expected. Good and Beitman (2006, p. 30) explain:

[Emotional and intellectual] growth is interfered with by conditions of worth outside of their awareness. Specifically, as children grow up and seek positive regard from others, they experience conflicts between their inner wishes and those of their caregivers. Children gradually internalize their caregivers' appraisals of them, thereby developing conditions of worth (beliefs like "I am worthy when I do what others expect of me"). However, these conditions of worth occasionally are incongruous with people's true inner selves. Hence, conflicts and discrepancies develop between people's conscious, introjected values (taken in from others as one's own) and their unconscious genuine values. As an example, a child growing up in a racist-homophobic community may experience criticism if he or she does not reflect the views of those around [him or her].... The child may introject ... the discriminatory views of others as his/her own, even though such views conflict with his/her unconscious appreciation of diverse people.

Another example of incongruence involves a child who introjects values from her parents that sex is dirty or that dancing is bad. When that child reaches adolescence, she may feel morally righteous and view herself as being a value setter for refusing to dance or date. This reflects her *ideal self*, the person she would like to be. However, she may then experience that peers relate to her as being a prude with archaic values. Although her introjected values forbid her from dancing or dating, her *real self* may have a strong desire to participate. *Incongruence* occurs when a discrepancy exists between a person's ideal self and real self, or self-concept and experience, resulting in tension, anxiety, and internal confusion.

An individual responds to incongruence between aspects of self and experiences in a variety of ways. One way is to use various defense mechanisms. A person may deny that experiences are in conflict with his or her self-concept. Or the person may distort or rationalize the experiences so that they are perceived as being consistent with his or her self-concept. If a person is unable to reduce the inconsistency through such defense mechanisms, the person is forced to face the fact that incongruences exist between self and experiences. This leads the person to feel unwanted emotions (such as anxiety, tension, depression, guilt, or shame) and potentially experience psychological maladjustment.

An individual then might enter therapy to resolve these problems and incongruences. Person-centered therapy emphasizes the positive aspects of human nature and a person's assets. Corey (2013) explains:

Because of the belief that the individual has an inherent capacity to move away from maladjustment and toward psychological health and growth, the therapist places the primary responsibility on the client.... Therapy is rooted in the client's capacity for awareness and self-directed change in attitudes and behavior.

In the person-centered approach the emphasis is on how clients act in their world with others, how they can move forward in constructive directions, and how they can successfully deal with obstacles (both from within themselves and outside of themselves) that are blocking their growth. By promoting self-awareness and self-reflection, clients learn to exercise choice. Humanistic therapists emphasize a discovery-oriented approach in which clients are the experts on their own inner experience (Watson, Goldman, & Greenberg, 2011), and they encourage their clients to make changes that

will lead to living fully and authentically, with the realization that this kind of existence demands a continuing struggle.... [B]ecoming self-actualizing individuals is an ongoing process rather than a final destination....

Person-centered theory holds that the therapist's function is to be present and accessible to clients and to focus on their immediate experience. First and foremost, the therapist must be willing to be real in the relationship with clients. By being congruent [in this context, meaning genuine or real], accepting, and empathic, the therapist is a catalyst for change. Instead of viewing clients in preconceived diagnostic categories, the therapist meets them on a moment-to-moment experiential basis and enters their world. Through the therapist's attitude of genuine caring, respect, acceptance, support, and understanding, clients are able to loosen their defenses and rigid perceptions and move to a higher level of personal functioning. When these therapist attitudes are present, clients then have the necessary freedom to explore areas of their life that were either denied to awareness or distorted....

Therapeutic change depends on clients' perceptions both of their own experience in therapy and of the counselor's basic attitudes. If the counselor creates a climate conducive to self-exploration, clients have the opportunity to explore the full range of their experience, which includes their feelings, beliefs, behavior, and worldview [how one perceives the world and one's place in it]. What follows is a general sketch of clients' experiences in therapy.

Clients come to the counselor in a state of incongruence; that is, a discrepancy exists between their self-perception and their experience in reality. For example, Leon, a college student, may see himself as a future physician, yet his below-average grades could exclude him from medical school. The discrepancy between how Leon sees himself (self-concept) or how he would like to view himself (ideal self ...) and the reality of his poor academic performance [experience] may result in anxiety and personal vulnerability, which can provide the necessary motivation to enter therapy. Leon must perceive that a problem exists or, at least, that he is uncomfortable enough with his present psychological adjustment to want to explore possibilities for change. (pp. 178–180)

CONCEPT SUMMARY

Self Theory

Self-concept: a person's perception of and feelings about him- or herself, including his or her personality, strengths weaknesses, and relationships with others.

Self-actualization: the tendency for every person to develop capacities that serve to maintain or enhance the person.

Need for positive regard: the need to be valued by others.

Sense of self-regard: the learned perception of self-worth that is based on the perceived attention and esteem received from others.

Real self: the person one actually is.

Ideal self: the person one would like to be. Conditions of worth: a person's perception that he or she is only valuable when behaving as others expect and prefer him or her to act (only worthy under certain conditions).

Incongruence: a discrepancy between a person's ideal self and real self, or self-concept and experience, resulting in tension, anxiety, and internal confusion.

Psychological maladjustment: the condition in which a person experiences significant incongruence between self and experiences, resulting in emotional and psychological problems.

Feminist Conceptual Frameworks

Feminist theories are based on the concept of feminism and the basic themes involved in that definition. Feminism is the "doctrine advocating social, political, and economic rights for women equal to those of men" and the "movement for the attainment of such rights" (Nichols, 1999, p. 483). They are included here with other theories of personality development because they provide a context for women's development and experience throughout the life span.

Hyde and Else-Quest (2013) remark on the development of feminist theories:

Feminist theories were created by no single person. Instead, numerous writers have contributed their ideas, consistent with the desire of feminists to avoid power hierarchies and not to have a single person become the sole authority. But it also means that the feminist perspective … has been drawn from many sources. (p. 50)

Because of the multiple origins and ongoing nature inherent in their development, we refer to feminist theories instead of feminist theory. At least nine principles underlie these approaches.

First, feminist theories emphasize the "*elimination of false dichotomies*" (Van Den Bergh & Cooper, 1986, p. 4). That is, people should critically evaluate the way thought and behavioral expectations are structured within the culture. Western culture emphasizes separating people, things, and events into mutually exclusive categories. For example, people are classified as either *male or female* on the basis of biology. These categories are "viewed as mutually exclusive entities that should be manifest for one gender but not the other. Distinctions between the sexes, rather than commonalities, are emphasized" (Van Den Bergh & Cooper, 1986, p. 4). A traditional Western view stresses that men and women should have different traits such as women being emotional, social caregivers and men being strong, working, decision makers. In contrast, a feminist perspective emphasizes acknowledging and appreciating a balance of these traits for each male or female as an individual.

A second principle underlying feminist theories is "*rethinking knowledge*" (Hunter College Women's Studies Collective, 1995, p. 63). In some ways, this is related to the first principle because they both involve *how* people think and view the world. Rethinking knowledge involves critically evaluating not only how you think about something, but also *what* you think about. It involves which ideas and thoughts are considered to reflect "facts" and which are thought to have value. Consider the following point:

Not only have topics of interest to women, but of less interest to men, such as rape, the sexual abuse of children, employment patterns among women, or the histories of women's lives, been simply left out of traditional disciplines, but the very concepts and assumptions with which inquiry has proceeded have reflected a male rather than a universal point of view. (The Hunter College Women's Studies Collective, 1995, p. 63)

A third dimension characterizing feminist theories is the recognition that *differences exist in male and female experiences* throughout the life span (Hyde, 2008; Land, 1995). One aspect of this dimension is the feminist focus on the impact of gender-role socialization. A *gender role* is the cluster of "culturally defined expectations that define how people of one gender ought to behave" (Hyde & DeLamater, 2014, p. 592). *Socialization* is the developmental process of teaching members of a culture the appropriate and expected pattern of values and behavior. Hyde and Else-Quest (2013) elaborate:

From their earliest years, children are socialized to conform to these roles.... Essentially, gender roles tell children that there are certain things they may not do, whether telling a girl that she cannot be a physicist or a boy that he cannot be a nurse. Because gender roles shut off individual potential and aspirations, feminists believe that we would be better off without such roles or at least they need to be radically revised. (p. 52)

Gilligan's (1982) work on the moral development of women, described in Chapter 7, provides a good example of work focusing on gender-related differences in life experience. Her proposed sequence of levels and transitions differ significantly from the traditional stages of moral development proposed by Kohlberg (1963, 1968, 1969, 1981a, 1981b), arguing that the latter relate primarily to the experience of men.

A fourth principle inherent in feminist theories is *egalitarianism*, a philosophy that people should be treated equally as individuals without focusing on gender (Hyde, 2008). This approach diverges from the traditional emphasis on hierarchies of power, where some (historically, men) have greater power and control over others. An egalitarian perspective is democratic, emphasizing the use of consensus building, collaboration, and the sharing of tasks (Hyde, 2008).

The fifth feminist principle, closely related to that of ending patriarchy, is that of *empowerment* (Hyde, 2008; Land, 1995; Netting & O'Connor, 2003), defined as the "process of increasing personal, interpersonal, or political power so that individuals can

take action to improve their life situations" (Gutierrez, 2001, p. 210). A feminist perspective emphasizes the need to empower women, enhance their potential for self-determination, and expand opportunities. Means of empowerment include assertiveness training, enhancing self-esteem, improving communication and problem-solving skills, and learning conflict resolution and negotiating skills (Van Den Bergh & Cooper, 1986).

A sixth concept underlying feminist theories is that of *"valuing process equally with product"* (Hyde, 2008; Van Den Bergh & Cooper, 1986, p. 6). It is not only important *what* you get done, but *how* you get it done. A traditional patriarchal approach stresses the importance of the end result. For example, the fact that a male chief executive officer of a large oil company has amassed amazing wealth is considered significant. The traditional view would not consider how he had hoarded his wealth as significant (by ruthlessly stepping on competitors, breaking environmental regulations, and consistently making decisions on his own, not the employees' nor the public's, best interests). Feminist theories focus on decision making based on equality and participation by all. The concept of "having power over" others is irrelevant. Thus, feminist theories focus on aspects of process such as making certain all participants have the chance to speak and be heard, adhering to principles of ethical behavior, working toward agreement or consensus, and considering personal issues as important.

A seventh underlying principle in feminist theories is the idea that *"the personal is political"* (Bricker-Jenkins & Lockett, 1995, p. 2531; GlenMaye, 1998; Hyde, 2008). Personal experience is integrally intertwined with the social and political environment. *Sexism* is "prejudice or discrimination based on sex, especially discrimination against women" that involves "behavior, conditions, or attitudes that foster stereotypes of social roles based on sex" (Mish, 2008, p. 1141). Feminist theories maintain that sexism is the result of the social and political structure. It does not simply involve problems experienced by isolated individuals.

Another implication of this principle is that the political environment can be changed and improved by personal actions. Thus, personal experience can be used to alter the political environment, which in turn can improve the personal experience. For example, individual women can collectively campaign for a candidate who supports women's issues, thus applying their personal actions to the political arena. As a result, the candidate gets elected and seeks to improve her supporters' work environments and access to resources, a political result that affects women's personal lives.

An eighth feminist principle involves *unity and diversity* (Bricker-Jenkins & Hooyman, 1986; Bricker-Jenkins & Lockett, 1995; Hyde, 2008). Women working together can achieve a better quality of life for all. In order to remain unified, women must appreciate each other's differences. Diversity is viewed as a source of strength.

A ninth dimension inherent in feminist theories is the importance of *advocating for positive change on women's behalf* (Hyde, 2008). Feminist theories go beyond the simple recognition of inequities in cultural expectations, individual rights, and options. Feminist frameworks stress the importance of making structural and attitudinal changes to attain equality and enhance opportunity for everyone.

EP 2.1.5b, 2.1.5c

Spotlight 3.1 discusses the diversity of feminist theories that vary in their relative emphasis on these nine concepts.

 SPOTLIGHT ON DIVERSITY 3.1

Diversity in Feminism

Hyde and Else-Quest (2013) categorize five major approaches among feminist theorists. These include liberal feminism, cultural feminism, Marxist or socialist feminism, radical feminism, and postmodern feminism. Note, however, that these categories are presented only to stimulate your thinking about these issues. In reality, each individual has his or her own views that may involve some blend of these and many other perspectives.

Liberal Feminism

"*Liberal feminism* holds that women should have opportunities and rights equal to those of men" (Hyde & Else-Quest, 2013, p. 53). This is a relatively optimistic view that American society is founded on a sound basis of positive values including "justice and freedom for all" (Hyde & Else-Quest, 2013, p. 53). However, liberal feminism also acknowledges that injustice on the basis of gender does indeed exist for women. Therefore, there should be an ongoing pursuit of legal, social, and educational change that pursues real equality for women. The National Organization for Women (NOW) generally reflects a liberal feminist perspective.

Some of the issues that have been addressed by liberal feminism include pay inequities in the workplace (e.g., women earn significantly less than men), gender segregation (e.g., women tend to be clustered in lower-paying occupations and men in higher ones), and hitting the *glass ceiling* (i.e., a barrier involving psychological perception and decision making by those in power that prevents women from progressing higher in a power structure just because they are women). Another issue liberal feminism speaks to is the role of men and women in family caregiving (Lorber, 2010). If men and

women are equal, to what extent do they and should they assume equal responsibilities in that arena?

Cultural Feminism

"*Cultural feminism* argues that women have special, unique qualities that differentiate them from men" (Hyde & Else-Quest, 2013, p. 53). This contrasts with liberal feminism, which views women and men as being essentially the same because they're both human beings. Cultural feminism emphasizes placing greater importance on the positive qualities typically manifested by women, including "nurturing, connectedness, and intuition" (Hyde & Else-Quest, 2013, p. 53). The ongoing goal is to achieve equal but different respect, power, and appreciation.

Marxist or Socialist Feminism

"*Marxist* or *socialist feminism* … views the oppression of women as just one instance of oppression," women being downgraded as one of various classes of people devalued by a capitalistic society (Hyde & Else-Quest, 2013, pp. 53–54). Such devaluation serves those in power well. For example, consider the significant difference in wages typically earned by women and men (discussed more thoroughly in Chapter 9). "What would happen to the average American corporation if it had to start paying all of its secretaries as much as plumbers earn? (Both jobs require a high school education and a certain amount of manual dexterity and specific skills)" (Hyde & Else-Quest, 2013, p. 54). Marxist feminism seeks a total transformation of the current capitalist system such that wealth would be spread much more equally across classes, including women and other oppressed populations.

Marxist feminism contends that there are "two solutions to women's exploitation in capitalism: wages for housework and government subsidization of wives and children" (Lorber, 2010, p. 48). This calls for women working in the home to be paid for that work because it is work, just as others are paid for working outside the home (Lorber, 2010).

Radical Feminism

Radical feminism perceives "liberal feminism and cultural feminism as entirely too optimistic about the sources of women's oppression and the changes needed to end it" (Hyde & Else-Quest, 2013, p. 54). From this perspective, "men's control" over women "manifests itself in gender roles, family relationships, heterosexuality, and male violence against women, as well as the wider male-dominated world of work, government, religion, and law… For radical feminists, women's liberation requires the eradication of patriarchy and the creation of women-centered ways of living" (Kirk & Okazawa-Rey, 2010, p. 12). "Collective political and social action [is] … essential. Given the difficulty of changing social institutions, radical feminists sometimes advocate separatist communities in which women can come together to pursue their work free of men's oppression" (Hyde & Else-Quest, 2013, p. 54).

Postmodern Feminism

"*Postmodern feminism* is not focused on social action, but rather is an academic movement that seeks to reform thought and research within colleges and universities" (Hyde & Else-Quest, 2013, p. 54). "It is particularly concerned with the issue of *epistemology*, which is the question of how people—whether lay-people or scientists—know. How do we know about truth and reality?" (Hyde & Else-Quest, 2013, p. 54). "*Postmodern feminism* claims that gender and sexuality are performances, and that individuals modify their displays of masculinity and femininity to suit their own purposes. Males can masquerade as women, and females can pass for men. Postmodern feminism argues that, like clothing, sexuality and gender can be put on, taken off, and transformed" (Lorber, 2010, p. 195).

Lorber (2010) explains:

Postmodern feminism examines the ways societies create beliefs about gender at any time (now and in the past) with discourses embedded in cultural representations or texts. Not just art, literature, and the mass media, but anything produced by a social group, including newspapers, political pronouncements, and religious liturgy, is a text. A text's discourse is what it says, does not say, and hints at (sometimes called a subtext). The historical and social context and the material conditions under which a text is produced become part of the text's discourse. If a movie or

newspaper is produced in a time of conservative values or under a repressive political regime, its discourse is going to be different from what is produced during times of openness or social change. Who provides the money, who does the creative work, and who oversees the managerial side all influence what a text conveys to its audience. The projected audience also shapes any text, although the actual audience may read quite different meanings from those intended by the producers. Deconstruction is the process of teasing out all these aspects of a text. (pp. 268–269)

Deconstruction can be applied to any set of beliefs. In a way, it is a form of critical thinking. Deconstruction involves analysis of underlying meanings and assumptions when presented with an occurrence, trend, or so-called fact. It focuses on not how the phenomenon is objectively represented or portrayed, but rather on subjective interpretation within the phenomenon's social, political, and economic context.

Lorber (2010) continues:

Soap operas and romance novels are "read" by women … action films and war novels are the stuff of men's spectator-ship. Postmodern feminism deconstructs cultural representations of gender, as seen in movies, video, TV, popular music, advertising—whether aimed at adults, teenagers, or children—as well as paintings, operas, theater productions, ballet, and the Olympics. These are all discourses that overtly and subliminally tell us something about female and male bodies, sexual desire, and gender roles. A romantic song about the man who got away glorifies heterosexuality…. These discourses influence the way we think about our world, without questioning the underlying assumptions about gender and sexuality. They encourage approved-of choices about work, marriage, and having children by showing them as normal and rewarding and by showing what is disapproved of as leading to a "bad end."

By unpacking the covert as well as more obvious meanings of texts, postmodern deconstruction reveals their messages. We can then accept or reject them, or use them for our own purposes. The memoirs and the life histories of transgendered people, and the activities of gay men and lesbian women, as depicted in the media, create a different discourse. (p. 269)

Diversity and Intersectionality

Still another perspective on feminism questions the usefulness of clustering all women together. To what extent are the issues faced by lesbians, white women, and women of color the same or different? Some have criticized various feminist perspectives for giving lesser priorities to the issues confronting

(continued)

SPOTLIGHT ON DIVERSITY 3.1 *(continued)*

female groups other than white women (Hyde & Else-Quest, 2013; Lorber, 2010). Newer trends in feminist research and thinking involve a broader perspective on the human condition (Hyde & Else-Quest, 2013; Lorber, 2010). Examining "women and men across different racial ethnic groups, social classes, religions, nationalities, residencies, [and] occupations" reflects a trend of the future (Lorber, 2010, p. 306).

The concept of intersectionality applies here. *Intersectionality* is "the idea that people are complex and can belong to multiple, overlapping diverse groups" (Kirst-Ashman, 2013, p. 67). "The intersectional perspective acknowledges the breadth of human experiences, instead of conceptualizing social relations and identities separately in terms of either race *or* class *or* gender *or* age *or* sexual orientation"; rather, an intersectional approach focuses on the "*interactive* effects" of belonging to multiple groups (Murphy, Hunt, Zajicek, Norris, & Hamilton, 2009, p. 2). "Race, class, and gender are inseparable determinants of inequalities" that interconnect to generate numerous aspects of oppression; the resulting great burden of oppression can affect interpersonal relationships, people's rights, how people are treated, and how they go about their daily lives (Murphy et al., 2009, p. 7). For example, "the meaning of womanhood for a middle-class, middle-age, African American woman is different than that held by a working-class, older, White woman" (Murphy et al., 2009, p. 10). (Intersectionality is addressed further in Chapter 5.)

The Feminist Future

The special needs of women and the issues they face must continue to be addressed. The issues, gender roles, and

cultural expectations for women of color merit ongoing attention (Hyde & Else-Quest, 2013). Additionally, more awareness, research, and concentrated effort should focus "on adjustment problems in women, particularly on depression, anxiety, alcoholism, and eating disorders, because they can be so devastating. We need to know what causes depression and what can be done to prevent it (e.g., changing child-rearing practices, school policy, violence against women, or family roles)" (Hyde & Else-Quest, 2013, p. 358).

The development of feminist theories is anything but stagnant. There is a dynamic, rapidly growing body of research and ideas that focus on the importance of understanding women's gender roles, issues, qualities, and oppression. (Chapter 9 addresses women's needs and issues in much greater depth.)

•••• **Ethical Questions 3.1**

EP 2.1.2

What are your views about the various approaches to feminism? What is the fair way to treat women and men? What kinds of efforts, if any, do you think should be undertaken to improve current conditions?

Feminist Identity Development

How do people become feminists? One study focused on students enrolled in women's studies courses, which are, of course, feminist based. Attending such classes tends to modify the attitudes and perceptions of both women and men, although perhaps more significantly for women. Five steps in the development of a feminist identity emerged for women (Bargad & Hyde, 1991; Hyde, 2002; Hyde & Else-Quest, 2013, pp. 358–359):

1. *Passive acceptance.* During this stage, women simply don't think critically about gender issues or oppression. They passively accept that the way things are is the way they should be.
2. *Revelation.* This stage is characterized by the "Aha!" experience that yes, indeed, inequities

do exist between women and men. A woman begins to confront issues and think more deeply about oppression. Common reactions during this stage include heated anger and resentment toward men.

3. *Embeddedness.* At this stage a woman becomes emotionally linked with other women, and receives support and sustenance from them. She begins to feel stronger in her identity as a woman.
4. *Synthesis.* Now a woman begins to assume a "positive feminist identity" that goes beyond focusing on gender-role differences. She gains greater understanding of herself as a woman and no longer resents men. Rather, she assesses her relationships with men as individuals.
5. *Active commitment.* During this stage, a woman's feminist identity is firmly established.

She uses her confidence to advocate on behalf of women to address inequities, oppression, and women's issues.

Critical Thinking About the Relevance of Theory to Social Work

EP 2.1.3a,
2.1.7a

We have reviewed a number of psychological theories about human behavior that can help us better understand how people function. This section examines how theories are relevant to social work practice, and Highlight 3.2 proposes an approach for evaluating theory.

In Chapter 1, we defined the term *theory* or *conceptual framework* as a coherent group of principles, concepts, and ideas organized to explain some observable occurrence or trend. In effect, theory provides a way for people to view the world. It helps them sort out and make sense of what they see. Likewise, it aids them in understanding how and why things are the way they are and work the way they do. Different theories provide us with different explanations.

For instance, consider the differences between systems theory and the medical model in trying to explain the reasons for human behavior. From the 1920s to the 1960s, social work programs used a medical model approach to human behavior. The *medical model*, developed by Sigmund Freud, views clients as "patients." The task of the social worker providing services is to first diagnose the causes of a patient's problems and then provide treatment. The patient's problems are viewed as being inside the patient.

✦ HIGHLIGHT 3.2

LO 3-2 Use Critical Thinking to Evaluate Theory

The Evaluation of Theory

EP 2.1.3,
2.1.3a,
2.1.3b,
2.1.7a

There are many ways to evaluate theory. This is partly because theories can concern virtually anything from the best method of planting a garden to whether intelligent extraterrestrials exist. Four major approaches for evaluating theory are provided here. The approaches are applied to various theories throughout the text and are not necessarily presented in the order of importance. Different theories may require different orders and emphases in terms of how they can best be evaluated.

EP 2.1.7b

1. *Evaluate the theory's application to client situations.* In what ways is the theory relevant to social work? In what ways does the theory provide a means to help us think about our clients and how to help them? For example, a theory about the mating patterns of gorillas would probably be very difficult to apply to any practice situation. However, a theory that hypothesizes how interpersonal attraction occurs between people might help you to work with an extremely shy, lonely young adult with serious interpersonal problems.

2. *Evaluate the research supporting the theory.* Research often involves singular, obscure, or puzzling findings. Such findings may be vague and may or may not be true. For example, the sample of people studied in a particular research project may have been extremely small. Thus, results may have been due primarily to chance. Or the sample may not have resembled the entire population very well. Therefore, the results should be applied only to the sample studied and not to anything or anybody else. (Consider this a commercial for why you need to take a research course!) On the one hand, it's important to be cautious about assuming that any research study establishes a *fact*. On the other hand, when more and more studies continue to support each other, a fact (or as close as we can come to a fact) may begin to develop.

EP 2.1.6b

A student once complained to me about her textbook. She said that the author confused her by presenting "facts"—in reality, research findings—that were contradictory. She said she hated such contradictions and wanted the author to tell her what was or was not a fact. My response was that I didn't think the world was like that. It cannot be so clearly divided, even though it sometimes seems that it would be more convenient that

(continued)

HIGHLIGHT 3.2 (continued)

way. Facts are the closest estimation of the truth we can come to based on the limited information we have. For example, people believed that the world was flat until somebody discovered that it was round. They believed that the northern lights were reflections of sunlight off the polar ice cap until someone discovered that they are really the effect of solar radiation on the earth's ionosphere.

Research can help establish whether theories portray facts or not. In other words, research can help determine how accurate and useful any particular theory is. We need theories to guide our thinking and our work so that we may undertake research-informed practice.

However, there are at least two problems with evaluating research in support of a theory. First, you might not have access to all, most, or any of the relevant research. Research findings (which often are interpreted as facts) can be found in thousands of journals. Second, there may be no research specifically directed at finding the specific facts you need to help you verify a theory in your own mind.

EP 2.1.2b

3. *Evaluate the extent to which the theory coincides with social work values and ethics.* Does the theory involve an underlying assumption that coincides with the mission of social work. According to the National Association of Social Workers' (NASW) Code of Ethics, "the primary mission of the social work profession is to enhance human well-being and help meet the basic human needs of all people, with particular attention to the needs and empowerment of people who are vulnerable, oppressed, and living in poverty" (NASW, 2008).

One example of how a theory can support or contradict professional ethics involves the ethical standard that social workers must be "sensitive to cultural and ethnic diversity and strive to end discrimination, oppression, poverty, and other forms of social injustice" (NASW, 2008). Consider a theory that one group of people is by nature more intelligent than another group. This theory obviously conflicts with professional values. Therefore, it should not be used or supported by social workers.

Another example is the theory that women are too emotional, flighty, and lacking in intellectual capability

to vote or hold a political office. This theory was espoused by the powerful majority of men who held public office until 1920, when women finally won the right to vote after a long, drawn-out battle for this right. This theory, too, stands in direct opposition to professional values and ethics.

Another section discusses the importance of being sensitive to human diversity when examining psychological theories. It also introduces several concepts that are useful in that process.

4. *Evaluate the existence and validity of other comparable theories.* Are there other theories that adhere better to the first three evaluation criteria? If so, which theory or theories should be chosen to guide our assessments and practice?

The medical model and systems theory were compared earlier. The social work profession now subscribes to systems theory, which provides a better perspective for respecting people's dignity and rights and for targeting the macro environment in order to effect change, reduce oppression, and improve social conditions.

Sometimes, two or more theories will have basic similarities. Recall the discussion concerning the differences between systems theory and the ecological model in Chapter 1. Both approaches provide frameworks for how to analyze the world and what to emphasize. Many of the concepts they employ are similar or identical. It was concluded that the ecological model is an offshoot of *systems* theory. This text assumes a systems theory perspective, yet adopts some ecological concepts. For instance, the term system is used in both. Both *social environment* and *coping* are ecological terms. Thus, many times it may be determined that a combination of theories provides the best framework for viewing the world within a social work context. Each social worker needs to determine the theoretical framework or combination of frameworks best suited for his or her practice context.

At other times, no theory will be perfectly applicable. Perhaps you will decide that only one or two concepts make any sense to you in terms of working with clients. The quest for the perfect theory resembles the pursuit of the perfect fact. It's very difficult to achieve perfection. Thus, when evaluating theories, be flexible. Decide which concepts in any particular theory have the most relevance to you and your work with clients.

The medical model conceptualizes emotional and behavioral problems as "mental illnesses." People with such problems are given medical labels such as *schizophrenic, psychotic, manic depressive,* or *insane.* Adherents of the medical approach believe the disturbed person's mind is affected by some generally unknown, internal condition, thought to be due to a variety of possible causative factors inside the person. These include genetic endowment, metabolic disorders, infectious diseases, internal conflicts, unconscious uses of defense mechanisms, and traumatic early experiences that cause emotional fixations and prevent future psychological growth.

In the 1960s, social work began questioning the usefulness of the medical model. Environmental factors were shown to be at least as important as internal factors in causing a client's problems. Also, research demonstrated that psychoanalysis was probably ineffective in treating clients' problems (Stuart, 1970). Social work shifted at least some of its emphasis to a reform approach. A reform approach seeks to change *systems* to benefit clients. Antipoverty programs such as Head Start[2] and Job Corps[3] are examples of efforts to change systems to benefit clients.

In the past several decades, social work has increasingly focused on using a systems approach to viewing clients and the world surrounding them. This approach integrates both treatment and reform by emphasizing the dysfunctional transactions between people and their physical and social environments. Human beings are viewed as being in constant interaction with other micro, mezzo, and macro systems within their social environment.

Social workers started to explore both causes and solutions in the environment encompassing any individual client instead of blaming the client. For instance, consider a person who is unemployed and poverty stricken. A social worker assuming a systems perspective would assess the client in situation. This worker would assess not only the problems and abilities of the client but also the client's interactions with the multiple systems affecting him or her. What services are available to help the person develop needed job skills? What housing is available in the meantime? What aspects of the macro systems in the environment are contributing to the high unemployment and poverty rates? What services need to be developed in order to respond to these needs?

In contrast, the medical model might orient a worker to try to cure or "fix" the individual by providing counseling to help him or her develop a better attitude toward finding a job. There would be an underlying assumption that it was the individual micro system that was somehow at fault.

Thus, theory helps social workers decide how to go about helping people. The medical model versus systems theory is only one example. Throughout this text, a broad range of theories will be presented concerning various aspects of human development and behavior. Evaluation of their relevance will often be provided. You, as a future social worker, will be expected to learn how to evaluate theories for yourself in order to apply them to your practice situations. Highlight 3.2 provides some suggestions for how to do this. Spotlight 3.2 stresses the importance of being sensitive to diversity when evaluating theories.

LO 3-4 Examine Piaget's Theory of Cognitive Development

EP 2.1.7a

Specific theories and conceptual frameworks concerning how people develop their capacities to think and understand have also been developed. *Cognition* involves the ability to take in information, process it, store it, and finally retrieve and use it. In other words, cognition involves the ability to learn and to think. The most noted of the cognitive theorists is probably Jean Piaget. Piaget (1952) proposed that people go through various stages in learning how to think as they develop from infancy into adulthood. His theory, which concerns the stages through which people must progress in order to develop their cognitive or thinking ability, was derived from careful observations of his own children's growth and development.

Piaget postulates that virtually all people learn how to think in the same way. That is, as people develop they all go through various stages of how they think. In infancy and early childhood, thinking is very basic and concrete. As children grow, thinking progresses and becomes more complex and abstract. Each stage of cognitive development is characterized by certain principles or ways in which an individual thinks.

The following example does an exceptionally good job of illustrating how these changes occur. In his studies, Piaget would show children of various ages two glass containers filled with a liquid. The containers were identical in size and shape, and

---

[2]*Head Start* is a program providing preschoolers with "recreational, educational, and health programs" throughout the year (Jansson, 2009, p. 298).

[3]*Job Corps* is a federal program created to recruit impoverished youth from disadvantaged urban and rural communities and provide them with job training (Jansson, 2009).

SPOTLIGHT ON DIVERSITY 3.2

LO 3-3 Relate Human Diversity to Psychological Theories

EP 2.1.4a

Psychological theories of development often focus on prescribed stages through which people progress throughout their lives. Such theories are also oriented to expectations about what is normal and what is abnormal during each stage. An issue facing us as we evaluate psychological theories is the rigidity with which some attempt to structure human development. In reality, people experience different worlds as they progress through their lives and time. We have established that their experiences are altered by many aspects of diversity and the intersectionality of factors. Such factors include "age, class, color, culture, disability, ethnicity, gender, gender identity and expression, immigration status, political ideology, race, religion, sex, and sexual orientation" (EP 2.1.4, CSWE, 2008). A woman will experience life differently than a man because of variables related to being a woman. An American of Asian background will encounter different treatment and issues than will an American of Northern European origins moving through the same time. Thus, it is critically important to be sensitive to the vast differences people can experience because of their membership in certain groups or other characteristics.

For decades, social work has been moving to view clients and the world from a less rigid, more open-minded perspective that is sensitive to diversity and individual differences. The field has worked "to encompass new perspectives on women's development and roles and the unique experiences, characteristics, strengths, and coping strategies of African Americans, Latinos, Asians, and other people of color and of other oppressed groups such as gay men and lesbians," in addition to incorporating principles such as empowerment (Goldstein, 2008). It is up to us as social workers to be sensitive to people's varying perspectives and needs. We must not make value judgments based on rigid assumptions about how people are *supposed* to behave. Rather, we must maintain flexibility thinking about human behavior and nurture our appreciation of differences.

People's progress through life involves much more than distinct, predefined periods tied and limited to a person's age and development. Rather, we should view life stages and circumstances as the result of integral interaction with many aspects of the environment. Various transitional points are experienced differently depending on an individual's life context as characterized by the many variables described earlier (Devore & Schlesinger, 1999). The life course may be divided into seven transitional points—entry, childhood, adolescence, emerging adulthood, adulthood, later adulthood, and old age (Devore & Schlesinger, 1999, pp. 68–69). Persons with divergent characteristics and backgrounds can experience these transitional points in distinctly different ways.

For example, during the childhood transitional period, children's psychological profiles are shaped by the ideas of their parents and of other people around them. This social context, in turn, is the product of culture. Berk (2012a) provides an example:

Culture influences emotional self-regulation. In a striking illustration, researchers studied children in two collectivist [that emphasizes the importance of group well-being above that of the individual] subcultures in rural Nepal. In response to stories about emotionally charged situations (such as peer aggression or unjust parental punishment), Hindu children more often said they would feel angry but would try to mask their feelings. Buddhist children, in contrast, interpreted the situation so that they felt OK, rather than angry. "Why be angry?" they explained. "The event already happened." In line with this difference, Hindu mothers reported that they often teach their children how to control their emotional behavior, whereas Buddhist mothers pointed to the value their religion places on a calm, peaceful disposition (Cole & Tamang 1998; Cole, Tamang, & Shrestha, 2006). Compared to both Nepalese groups, U.S. children preferred conveying anger verbally in these situations; for example, to an unjust punishment, they answered, "If I say I'm angry, he'll stop hurting me!" (Cole, Bruschi, & Tamang, 2002). Notice how this response fits with the Western individualistic emphasis on personal rights and self-expression. (p. 491)

Other examples of life-course differences involve the adolescent transitional period. Adolescents raised in different cultural environments with different experiences and treatment view their developing life, gender roles, and sexuality in very diverse ways. A female Puerto Rican adolescent learns her expected role by closely observing her mother and caring for the family's children; however, there often is no mention of sex (Devore & Schlesinger, 1999). Kelly (2008) comments on Japanese adolescent sexuality:

In Japan, sexuality has been minimized and regulated as being tangential to the performance of responsible duty. Japanese youth consider chastity very important. There is less teenage sexual activity and far less single motherhood than in the United States, although abortion is quite accessible. Japanese youth often rush into sexual activity during late adolescence, as if making up for their more chaste earlier years. As the age of marriage becomes even later, the rate of premarital pregnancies and "shotgun" weddings has been increasing. (p. 159)

The transitional period of emerging adulthood provides more examples of diverse life course experiences. Young people experience this as a time of decision making about

✳ SPOTLIGHT ON DIVERSITY 3.2 *(continued)*

marrying or remaining single and pursuing a work or career path. Devore and Schlesinger (1999) remark:

> *For young Jewish women … [t]he plan to work continues a tradition established long ago by grandmothers and mothers whose diverse occupations were important to the survival of the family. Jewish tradition more easily accepts employment of women. In the present, however, the emerging Jewish woman has choice. The Jewish value of education is traditional but in the past was more reserved for men. Women now attend college in equal numbers with men but may experience conflict as they make the choice. "As a young Jewish woman I am achievement oriented, committed to individual achievement, accomplishment and career—but, I am equally committed to marriage. What then of my children? If I am to be a responsible mother then I must remain at home with my young children." … Such is the ethnic dilemma shared by Italians and Slavic young women.*
>
> *A young married Navajo woman expects to hold to the traditions of the past. Her husband is the formal head of the household, but she has as much, or perhaps even more, influence in the family management due to a reverence for matrilineal descent [heritage based on the female line]. This tradition provides her with support from the extended family, with her brothers assuming responsibility in the teaching and discipline of their nieces and nephews. Women and men, sisters and brothers participate in the retention of the ethnic reality. (pp. 77–78)*

The important point here is the need for sensitivity to diversity when evaluating human behavior, regardless of which theory you apply.

Other concepts are also helpful when examining and evaluating psychological theories and their application to diverse populations. They include worldview (Choudhuri, Santiago-Rivera, & Garrett, 2012; Diller, 2015; Lum, 2007), spirituality (Canda, 2008; Canda & Furman, 2010, Cunningham, 2012), and the strengths perspective (Kim, 2008; Saleebey, 2013).

Worldview

A concept helpful for appreciating diversity when applying psychological theory to behavior is the *worldview* perspective. Worldview concerns people's perceptions of the world around them and how they fit into that world. Perceptions include awareness of the surrounding environment, social status, social roles, legal rights, and economic status, among the many other variables characterizing people's lives. Not only do worldviews consist of "our attitudes, values, opinions, and concepts, but they also affect how we think, define events, make decisions, and behave" (Sue & Sue, 2008, p. 294).

Understanding that people have different worldviews involves looking beyond the narrow boundaries of our daily existence. It means developing an openness and awareness of

The African American worldview is characterized by a strong achievement and work orientation.

life in other neighborhoods, counties, states, and countries. It also requires developing an appreciation of differences instead of fear and aversion. It encourages us to allow new perceptions of the world to penetrate our consciousness instead of clinging doggedly to what we already know. There are many other ways to live than the way we are accustomed to.

Sue and Sue (2008) reflect:

EP 2.1.1b, 2.1.1e, 2.1.5c

> *For marginalized groups in America, a strong determinant of worldviews is very much related to the subordinate position assigned to them in society. Helping professionals who hold a worldview different from that of their clients, and who are unaware of the basis for this difference, are most likely to impute negative traits to*

(continued)

SPOTLIGHT ON DIVERSITY 3.2 *(continued)*

clients. In most cases, for example, clients of color are more likely to have worldviews that differ from those of therapists [and social workers]. Yet many therapists [and social workers] are so culturally unaware that they respond according to their own conditioned values, assumptions, and perspectives of reality without regard for other views. Without this awareness, counselors [and social workers] who work with culturally diverse groups may be engaging in cultural oppression. (p. 294)

Spirituality

EP 2.1.4

A second concept important in understanding human diversity and psychological development is *spirituality*. Spirituality "includes one's values, beliefs, mission, awareness, subjectivity, experience, sense of purpose and direction, and a kind of striving toward something greater than oneself" (Frame, 2003, p. 3). The spiritual domain is an important means by which many people organize their view of the world. The spiritual dimension is part of their reality. Therefore, it must be considered when you assess human behavior from a psychological perspective even though you may have very different beliefs concerning spirituality than your clients or your colleagues.

Spiritual beliefs can provide people with hope, support, and guidance as they progress through life. Spirituality, including Fowler's (1981) seven stages of faith, will be discussed further in Chapter 7. Chapter 15 explores spirituality and some of the major religions.

The Strengths Perspective

The strengths perspective is a third concept that is useful in increasing sensitivity to human diversity, and understanding people from various ethnic and cultural backgrounds. Chapter 1 introduced the concepts of empowerment and strengths-based social work practice. Norman (2005) explains:

EP 2.1.10e

Strengths-based social work practice focuses on helping client systems tap into the strengths within them.... Potential strengths include cultural values and traditions, resources, coping strategies, family, friends, and community support networks. Past successful experiences need to be linked to solving current problems.... The client is the expert in identifying past success and in developing solutions based on past experiences. Focusing on concrete tasks and objectives ... works better for people of color than more abstract methods....

Even when we are talking the same language, our perceptions of an interaction are culturally influenced.... Different groups of people translate nonverbal communication, such as spatial observance, handshaking, and eye contact, in different ways.... Mastering cross-cultural communication is the key to effective practice with individuals, families, groups, and communities of color. This requires sharpening observation and listening skills as well as learning about clients' cultural beliefs and traditions. (pp. 403, 407)

held an equal amount of liquid (see Figure 3.2). Children inevitably would agree that each container held the same amount of liquid. Piaget then would take the liquid from one of the containers and pour it into another taller, narrower glass container. Interestingly enough, he found that children under age 6 would frequently say that the taller glass held more even though the amount of liquid in each was identical. Children approximately age 6 or older, however, would state that despite the different shapes, both containers held the same amount of liquid. Later studies established that the results of this experiment were the same for children of various backgrounds and nationalities.

This example demonstrated how children in different cognitive stages thought about or conceptualized the problem. Younger children tended to rely directly on their visual perceptions to make a decision about which glass held more or less liquid. Older children, however, were able to do more logical thinking about the problem. They thought about how liquid could take various forms and how the same amount could look different depending on its container. The older children illustrated a higher, more abstract level of cognitive development. This particular concept involving the idea that a substance can be changed in one way (e.g., shape) while remaining the same in another (e.g., amount) is called *conservation*.

These ways of thinking about and organizing ideas and concepts depending on one's level of cognitive development are called *schema*. A person perceives the world at an increasingly more abstract level during each stage. In other words,

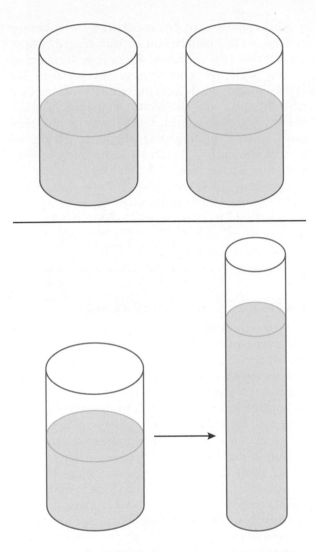

Children under age 6 would say that the taller glass holds more, even though the amount of liquid in each is identical.

FIGURE 3.2 Conservation

different aspects of the environment are emphasized depending on a person's cognitive level of development.

Piaget hypothesizes that all people go through the cognitive stages in the same order. An individual progresses through them in a continuous manner. In other words, a child does not wake up one morning and suddenly state, "Aha, I'm now in the preoperational stage of development!" Rather, children gradually progress through each stage with smooth and continual transitions from one stage to the next. Each stage acts as a foundation or prerequisite for

the next. Three other concepts that are also important are adaptation, assimilation, and accommodation.

Adaptation refers to the capacity to adjust to surrounding environmental conditions. It involves the process of changing in order to fit in and survive in the surrounding environment. Piaget would say that adaptation is composed of two processes, assimilation and accommodation.

Assimilation refers to the taking in of new information and the resulting integration into the schema or structure of thought. In other words, when a person is exposed to a new situation, event, or piece of information, not only is the information received and thought about at a conscious level, but it is also integrated into a way of thinking. The information is stored in such a way that it can be used later in problem-solving situations.

For example, go back to the situation in which young children observe and judge the quantities of liquid in glass containers. Younger children, those under age 6, assimilate information at a level using only their observations. Items and substances are only as they appear before their eyes. These children could not think of items as changing, as being somewhere else, or as being in a different context. They could not yet assimilate such information using higher, more logical levels of thought in which some qualities of a substance can change while others remain the same. Children of age 6 or older can think about substances or items that are not immediately before their eyes. They can think about other different circumstances and situations.

Accommodation refers to the process by which children change their perceptions and actions in order to think using higher, more abstract levels of cognition. Children assimilate (take in) new information and eventually accommodate it. That is, they build on the schema they already have and use new, more complex ways of thinking. Children age 6 or older have accommodated the information about the liquid-filled glass containers. Furthermore, they can think about changes in substance in a more abstract way. They can think of the liquid not only as being held in a container of a specific shape and size, but also as it may be held in other containers of other shapes and sizes.

Piaget describes four major stages of cognitive development: the sensorimotor period, the preoperational thought period, the period of concrete operations, and the period of formal operations. Each stage will be described next.

The Sensorimotor Period

The *sensorimotor period* extends from birth to approximately 2 years of age. During this period, a child progresses from simple thoughtless reflex reactions to a basic understanding of the environment. Three major accomplishments are made during the sensorimotor period. First, children learn that they have various senses through which they can receive information. Additionally, they begin to understand that they can receive different kinds of sensory information about the same object in the environment.

For example, initially an infant may see and hear her parents squabbling over who will take the new Ford Mustang GT with air-conditioning on a 99-degree summer day and who will take the old Ford Escort in which the air-conditioning doesn't work. Even though she will hear and see them squabbling, she will not be able to associate the two types of sensory information as referring to the same aspect of her environment—namely, her parents. By the end of the sensorimotor period, she will understand that she can both hear and see her parents at the same time. She will perceive their interaction through both modes of sensory input.

A second major accomplishment during the sensorimotor period is the exhibition of *goal-directed* behavior. Instead of displaying simple responses randomly, the child will purposefully put together several behaviors in order to accomplish a simple goal. For example, a child will reach for a piece of a wooden puzzle and try to place it into its appropriate slot. The child will plan to put the puzzle together. However, because a child's thinking during the sensorimotor period is still very concrete, the ability to plan very far ahead is extremely limited.

The third major accomplishment during the sensorimotor period is the understanding that objects are permanent. This is the idea that objects continue to exist even when they are out of sight and out of hearing range. The concept of *object permanence* is the most important schema acquired during the sensorimotor period. Initially, children immediately forget about objects as soon as they no longer can perceive them. By age 2, children are generally able to think about the image of something that they can't see or hear, and can solve a simple problem in relationship to that image. Children begin to use *representation*—the visual imagining of an image in their minds—which allows them to begin solving problems.

For example, take 2-year-old Ricky who is very attached to his "blanky," an ancient, ragged, yellow blanket that he loves dearly. Ricky is in the midst of playing with his action garage toy set with his blanky placed snugly next to him. Ricky's mother casually walks into the room, gently picks up the blanky, and walks down the hallway to the bedroom. Instead of forgetting about the blanky as soon as it's out of sight, Ricky immediately gets up and starts actively seeking out his blanky, calling for it relentlessly. Even though he can't presently see it and he doesn't know exactly where his mother put it, Ricky is able to think of the blanky and begin a quest in search of it. Furthermore, he is able to run around the house and look for it in various nooks and crannies, thinking about where it might be.

The Preoperational Thought Period

Piaget's second stage of cognitive development, the *preoperational thought period*, extends from approximately ages 2 to 7. Some overlap from one stage to another should be expected. A child's thinking continues to progress to a more abstract, logical level. Although children are still tied to their physical and perceptual experiences, their ability to remember things and to solve problems continues to grow.

During the preoperational stage, children begin to use symbolic representations for things in their environment. Children are no longer bound to actual concrete perception. They can think in terms of symbols or mental representations of objects or circumstances.

Words provide an excellent example of symbolic representation. Children may symbolize an object or situation with words and then reflect on the object or situation later by using the words. In other words, language can be used for thought even when objects and situations are not present.

Barriers to the Development of Logical Thinking

Despite children's progress toward more abstract thinking, three major obstacles to logical thinking exist during the preoperational period: egocentrism, centration, and irreversibility.

Egocentrism In egocentrism, a child is unable to see things from anybody else's point of view. The child is aware only of himself or herself; the needs and perspectives of others don't exist.

Piaget illustrated this concept by showing a child a doll in a three-dimensional scene. With the child remaining in the same position, the doll could be moved around the scene so that the child could observe it from different perspectives. The child would then be shown various pictures and asked what the scene would look like from the doll's perspective or point of view. Piaget found that the child would often choose the wrong picture. The child would continue to view the scene from his or her own perspective. It was difficult if not impossible for the child to imagine that the doll's perspective or point of view could be any different from the child's own.

Centration Centration refers to a child's tendency to concentrate on only one detail of an object or situation and ignore all other aspects.

To illustrate centration, refer back to the example in which a child is asked to evaluate the amounts of liquid in two glasses. The child would observe the same amount of liquid being poured into two different shaped containers. One container was short and squat, and the other, tall and thin. When asked which container held more liquid, the child would frequently answer that the tall, thin container did. In this situation, the child was focusing on the concept of height instead of width. She was unable to focus on both height and width at the same time. Only one aspect of the situation was used to solve the problem. This is a good example of how centration inhibits more mature, logical thought.

Irreversibility Irreversibility refers to a child's ability to follow and think something through in one direction without being able to imagine the relationship in reverse. For example, 4-year-old Gary might be asked, "Who are your cousins?" Gary might then reply, "Sherrie, Donna, Lorrie, and Tanya." If Gary is then asked who is Sherrie's cousin, he will probably say he doesn't know. Gary is able to think through a situation in one direction, but is unable to reverse his train of thought. He knows that Sherrie is his cousin. However, he is unable to see the reverse of that relationship—that he is also Sherrie's cousin.

Developing Cognitive Ability

Despite barriers to the development of logical thought, several concepts illustrate ways in which children progress in their ability to think. Major changes concerning these concepts occur between the onset of the preoperational thought period and the culmination of adult logical thinking. Children gradually improve their perceptions and grasp of these concepts.

Classification Classification refers to a child's ability to sort items into various categories according to certain characteristics. The characteristics might include shape, color, texture, or size. Children gradually develop the ability to distinguish differences between objects and categorize them to reflect these differences.

For example, 2½-year-old Kwan is given a bag of red, blue, and green "creepy crawlers." In this case, the creepy crawlers consist of soft, plastic lizards, all of which are the same size and shape. When asked to put all the red lizards together in a heap, Kwan is unable to do so. She cannot yet discriminate between the colors in order to categorize or classify the lizards according to their color. However, when Kwan is given the same task at age 7, she is easily able to put the red, blue, and green lizards into their respective heaps. She has acquired the concept of classification.

Seriation Seriation refers to a child's ability to arrange objects in order according to certain characteristics. These characteristics might include size, weight, volume, or length.

For example, a child is given a number of soda straws cut to various lengths. The child's ability to arrange such objects from shortest to longest improves as the child's cognitive ability develops. By age 4 or 5, a child is usually able to select both the longest and the shortest straws. However, the child still has difficulty discriminating among the middle lengths. By age 5 or 6, the child will probably be able to order the straws one by one from shortest to longest. However, this would probably be done with much concentration and some degree of difficulty. By age 7, the task of ordering the straws would probably be much easier.

The ability to apply seriation to various characteristics develops at different ages depending on a specific characteristic. For example, children are usually unable to order a series of objects according to weight until age 9. Seriation according to volume is typically not possible until approximately age 12.

Conservation Conservation, discussed earlier, refers to a child's ability to grasp the idea that while one aspect of a substance (e.g., quantity or weight) remains the same, another aspect of that same substance (e.g., shape or position) can be changed.

For example, 4-year-old Bart is given two wads of Silly Putty of exactly equal volume. One wad is then rolled into a ball, and the other is patted into the shape of a pancake. When asked which wad has a greater among of material in it, Bart is likely to say that the pancake does. Even though Bart initially saw that the two wads were exactly equal, he focused on only the one aspect of area. In terms of area alone, the pancake appeared to Bart as if it had more substance. However, by the time Bart reached age 6 or 7, he would probably be able to state that both wads had equal substance. He would know that matter can take different forms and still have the same amount of material.

As with seriation, children achieve the ability to understand conservation at different ages depending on the characteristic to be conserved (Papalia, Olds, & Feldman, 2009). For example, whereas conservation of substance is typically attained by age 7 or 8, conservation of weight is usually not achieved until age 9 or 10, and conservation of volume not until age 11 or 12.

The Period of Concrete Operations

The period of *concrete operations* extends from approximately age 7 to 11 or 12 years. During this stage, a child develops the ability to think logically at a concrete level. In other words, a child has mastered the major impediments to logical thinking that were evident during earlier stages of cognitive development.

The child now develops the capacity to see things from other people's points of view. Understanding and empathy are substantially increased during this period.

More complex thinking is developed. Situations and events can be viewed and examined in terms of many variables. The child gradually becomes less limited by centration. A child is no longer limited to solving a problem in terms of only one variable; rather, a number of variables can be taken into account. In the glass example, the child would begin to think in terms of height, volume, substance, and shape all at the same time.

A child also develops the ability to conceptualize in terms of reversibility during this period. Relationships begin to be understood from various perspectives. Returning to an example presented earlier, Gary would now understand that not only was Sherrie his cousin, but also that he was her cousin.

The concepts of classification, seriation, and conservation would also be mastered. During the period of concrete operations, a child gains much flexibility in thinking about situations and events. Events are appraised from many different points of view.

Additionally, children develop their use of symbols to represent events in the real world. Their ability to understand math and to express themselves through language greatly improves. Correspondingly, their memories become sharper.

Despite the great gains in cognitive development made during the stage of concrete operations, a child is still somewhat limited. Although events are viewed from many perspectives, these perspectives are still tied to concrete issues. Children think about things they can see, hear, smell, or touch. Their focus is on thinking about *things* instead of *ideas*. Children must enter the final stage of cognitive development, the period of formal operations, before they can fully develop their cognitive capability.

The Period of Formal Operations

The final stage of cognitive development is the period of *formal operations*. This period, beginning at approximately age 11 or 12 and extending to approximately age 16, characterizes cognitive development during adolescence. Technically, this chapter addresses childhood and not adolescence. However, for the purposes of continuity, Piaget's fourth period of cognitive development will be discussed here.

Abstract thought reaches its culmination during the period of formal operations. Children become capable of taking numerous variables into consideration and creatively formulating abstract hypotheses about how things work or about why things are the way they are. Instead of being limited to thought about how things are, children begin to think about how things could be. They begin to analyze why things aren't always as they should be.

For example, Meredy, age 10, is still limited by the more concrete type of thinking that characterizes the period of concrete operations. She is aware that a nuclear bomb was dropped on Hiroshima near the close of World War II. When asked about why this happened, she might say that the United States had to defend its own territory and this was a means of bringing the war to an end. She can conceptualize the situation and analyze it in terms of some variables. In this case, the variables might include the fact that the United States was at war and had to take actions to win that war. Her ability to think through the situation might extend no further than that. When asked the same question at age 15, Meredy might have quite a different answer. She might talk about what a difficult decision such a step must have been in view of the tremendous cost in human life. She might describe the incident as one of the various tactical strategies that might have been taken. She also might elaborate on the political fallout of the event. In other words, Meredy's ability to consider multiple dimensions when assessing an idea or event would improve drastically during the period of formal operations.

Three major developments, then, characterize adolescent thought. First, the adolescent is able to identify numerous variables that affect a situation—an issue can be viewed from many perspectives. Second, the adolescent can analyze the effects of one variable on another—that is, can hypothesize about relationships and think about changing conditions. Third, an adolescent is capable of *hypothetical-deductive* reasoning. In other words, an adolescent can systematically and logically evaluate many possible relationships in order to arrive at a conclusion. Various possibilities can be scrutinized in a conditional "if-then" fashion. For instance, the adolescent might begin thinking in terms of: if certain conditions exist, then certain consequences will follow.

Critical Thinking: Evaluation of Piaget's Theory

EP 2.1.3b

Criticisms of Piaget's theory have addressed his general approach and also raised questions about specific concepts. One general criticism is that the vast majority of his suppositions are based on his observations of his own children rather than on scientific studies conducted under laboratory conditions. Questions have been raised about the manner in which he observed and interviewed his children,

the language he used to obtain information from them, and personal biases that may have emerged. His findings were primarily based on only three subjects, his own children, instead of on a variety of subjects from different backgrounds.

A second general criticism involves the fact that Piaget focuses on the "average" child. Questions can be raised regarding who the average child really is. Cultural, socioeconomic, and ethnic differences were not taken into account.

Consideration of only limited dimensions of human development poses yet a third general criticism. Little is said of personality or emotional growth except in specific instances where they relate directly to cognitive development. The effects of social interaction are virtually ignored. Piaget concentrates on how children see and think of objects instead of the people closest to them.

Piaget (1972) has offered several responses to these criticisms. First, an individual's social environment may influence cognitive development. Persons from deprived environments may not be offered the types of stimulation and support necessary to achieve high levels of cognition. Second, individual differences might have to be taken into account. Some persons might not have the necessary ability to attain the levels of thought that characterize the formal operations period. Finally, even if a person develops a capacity for formal operational thought, this capacity may not be versatile in its application to all problems. In other words, some individuals might be unable to use formal operations with some problems or in some situations.

Questions have also been raised regarding the meaning and appropriate age level attributed to some of Piaget's specific concepts (Steinberg, Borstein, Vandell, & Rook, 2011a). He appears to have erred by underestimating children's abilities concerning various conceptual achievements. Some research replicates Piaget's in terms of principle. However, by simplifying the language used to communicate with children and by using words and concepts with which they are familiar, other researchers have found higher levels of performance at a given age. In other words, sometimes when children can relate better to the experiment, they better understand what is expected from them and thus can perform better.

For example, consider research that involves object permanence, the concept that objects continue to exist even when they're out of sight. According to Piaget, children don't attain this skill until nearing age 2, at the end of the sensorimotor period. However, Baillargeon (1987) cleverly adapted his experimental procedure to eliminate the need for infants to have a higher level of muscular coordination than is developmentally possible at their age in order to respond appropriately. He found that by 4½ months, and sometimes by age 3½ months, babies indicated that they were aware of object permanence.

Piaget's examination of egocentricity has also received some criticism. Egocentrism involves the concept that a child is unable to see things from anyone else's perspective but his own.

The idea that children in this age group are so self-centered may be overly harsh. Many parents can think of instances in which their young children appeared to show genuine empathic ability. For example, 4-year-old Johnnie approaches his father after finding a robin's egg that fell from the nest. He states, "Daddy, poor birdie. She lost her baby."

Additionally, there is some evidence that children are not quite as egocentric as Piaget initially claimed and that their thinking is much more complex (Dacey, Travers, & Fiore, 2009; Papalia & Feldman, 2012). A child's ability to empathize with others depends somewhat on the circumstances and the issues involved. For example, children living in families that encourage discussion of feelings are more adept at recognizing other people's emotions.

Piaget initially investigated egocentricity by having children observe three fabricated "mountains" of unequal heights placed on a table. Children were able to walk around the table and look at the mountains from various perspectives. They were then asked to sit on a chair at the table. A doll was placed in a chair on the opposite side of the table. The children were then shown a variety of photographs of the "mountains," which illustrated how they looked from a number of perspectives. Piaget asked the children to select the picture that best showed how the mountains looked from where the doll sat. Children in the preoperational stage would choose the picture that best showed the mountains from where they themselves sat, not from where the doll sat. Piaget concluded, then, that the children had not yet worked through the barrier of egocentrism because they couldn't comprehend the view of the mountains from the doll's perspective.

When a variation of the mountain task was used, the results were quite different (Hughes, 1975; Papalia & Feldman, 2012). Instead of "mountains," a child was seated in front of a square table with dividers on the top to divide it into four equal sectors. The researcher placed a doll in one of the sectors and a police officer figure in another sector. The child was then asked if she thought the police officer could see the doll from where he stood. The task was then complicated by placing another police officer figure somewhere on the table. The researcher then asked the child to place the doll somewhere on the table where she thought neither police officer could see her. Of 30 children aged 3½ to 5 years, 90 percent responded correctly. Most of these young children could clearly see the situation from another's perspective. These results differ significantly from Piaget's. Perhaps children had trouble understanding the concept of fake "mountains" on a table, with which they were unfamiliar. On the other hand, perhaps children could better relate to and understand the concepts of police officers and dolls, both of which were familiar to them.

These and other studies indicate that the cognitive development of children is a very complicated process, perhaps much more so than Piaget could guess. It's interesting to note that a major thrust of these more recent studies is to emphasize what young children *can* do rather than what they *cannot* do.

Regardless of the various criticisms, Piaget must be given great credit. Decades ago, he provided us with a foundation for thinking about cognitive development and has tremendously influenced research in this area. Additionally, he set the stage for establishing appropriate expectations regarding what types of things children at various age levels can realistically accomplish.

LO 3-5 Review the Information-Processing Conception of Cognitive Development

A newer perspective on cognitive development involves the *information-processing* approach. This conceptual framework focuses on the processes an individual uses to think and solve problems. It relates human thought to how computers function with both hardware and software. Kail and Cavanaugh (2014) explain:

Information-processing theorists draw heavily on how computers work to explain thinking and how it develops through childhood and adolescence. Just as computers consist of both hardware (disk drives, central processing unit, etc.) and software (the programs they run), ***information-processing theory*** *proposes that human cognition consists of mental hardware and mental software. Mental hardware refers to [physical] cognitive structures ... [that allow thought to take place and memories to be stored.] Mental software includes organized sets of cognitive processes [mental "programs"] that enable people to complete specific tasks, such as reading a sentence, playing a video game, or hitting a baseball. For example, an information-processing psychologist would say that, for a student to do well on an exam, she must encode the information as she studies, store it in memory, and then retrieve the necessary information during the test.*

According to information-processing psychologists, developmental changes in thinking reflect better mental hardware and mental software in older children and adolescents than in younger children. For example, older children typically solve math word problems better than younger children because they have greater memory capacity to store the facts in the problem and because their methods for performing arithmetic operations are more efficient. (p. 12)

Three facets of information processing that are especially significant include attention, memory, and information-processing strategies (Kail & Cavanaugh, 2014; Rathus, 2014a).

Attention

Attention is "a process that determines which sensory information receives additional cognitive processing" (Kail & Cavanaugh, 2014, p. 103). As children mature, they develop the ability to focus on the more relevant aspects of a situation or problem and "screen out distractions" (Rathus, 2014a, p. 385). This involves selectively directing their attention. Eventually, children can attend to numerous facets of a problem at the same time, thus allowing them to solve more difficult problems and think

at a more complex level. Rathus (2014a) provides an example of selective attention developing as children get older:

An experiment by Strutt and colleagues (1975) illustrates how selective attention and the ability to ignore distraction develop during middle childhood. The researchers asked children between 6 and 12 years of age to sort a deck of cards as quickly as possible on the basis of the figures depicted on each card (e.g., circle versus square). In one condition, only the relevant dimension (form) was shown on each card. In another condition, a dimension not relevant to the sorting also was present (e.g., a horizontal or vertical line in the figure). In a third condition, two irrelevant dimensions were present (e.g., a star above or below the figure, in addition to a horizontal or vertical line in the figure).... [T]he irrelevant information interfered with sorting ability for all age groups, but older children were much less affected than younger children. (p. 385)

Note that improvements in selective attention are related to brain development (Nelson, Thomas, & de Haan, 2006). However, a "child's environment and experiences with parents are also important... Children from stimulating homes with warm, responsive parents gain control of their attention earlier than do children from less supportive homes. Why? One reason may be that frequent conversations with parents provide young children with guided opportunities to observe and practice concentration and self-regulation" (Steinberg, Bornstein, Vandell, & Rook, 2011a, p. 210).

Memory

Memory involves "the processes of storing and retrieving information" (Rathus, 2013, p. 285). Memory entails three basic types—sensory, short term, and long term (Rathus, 2013, 2014a).

Sensory Memory

Sensory memory is "a subconscious process of picking up sensory information from the environment (sights, sounds, smells, and touch). Sensory memory consists of fleeting impressions. This information is either forgotten or transferred to *working memory*: conscious representations of what a person is actively thinking about at a given time" (Steinberg et al., 2011a,

p. 211). In order for a person to remember a sensory memory, the person needs to focus on it and probably relate it to other thoughts. Rathus (2013) explains:

> When we look at an object and then blink our eyes, the visual impression of the object lasts for a fraction of a second in what is called sensory memory. Then the "trace" of the stimulus decays. The concept of sensory memory applies to all the senses. For example, when we are introduced to somebody, the trace of the sound of the name also decays, but we can remember the name by focusing on it. (p. 285)

Short-Term Memory (Working Memory)

Short-term (or working) memory is "[t]he structure of memory that can hold a sensory stimulus for up to 30 seconds after the trace decays" (Rathus, 2013, p. G-13). Steinberg and colleagues (2011a) explain that short-term memory involves:

> conscious, short-term representations of what a person is actively thinking about at a given time. It depends on the child (or adult) paying attention and encoding the impression in some way—for example, attaching it to a known word or image. Working memory improves during early childhood from recall of two numbers at age 2½ years to five numbers at age 7, and about seven numbers in adulthood.
>
> Part of the reason for the improvements in working memory is biological; part, social.... [The portions of the brain] that provide the "hardware" for short-term memory ... are developing during early childhood and provide the capacity that supports an expanded working memory (Nelson et al., 2006). And, as is the case with attention, the development of working memory is accelerated by warm, stimulating interactions with parents at home and by attending preschools or child-care centers that are high quality. (p. 211)

Long-Term Memory

Long-term memory is "[t]he structure of memory capable of relatively permanent storage of information" (Rathus, 2013, p. G-8). Rathus (2013) explains:

> Think of long-term memory as a vast storehouse of information containing names, dates, places, what Johnny did to you in second grade, what Alyssa said about you when you were 12. Long-term memories may last days, years, or, for practical purposes, a lifetime.
>
> There is no known limit to the amount of information that can be stored in long-term memory. From time to time, it may seem that we have forgotten, or lost, a long-term memory, such as the names of elementary- or high-school classmates. But it is more likely that we cannot find the right cues to retrieve it. It is lost in the same way we misplace an object but know it is still in the house. (p. 287)

Development of Information-Processing Strategies

As children grow older, they increase their abilities to process information and solve problems. They gradually get better at taking into account multiple variables, thinking about potential solutions, making decisions, and working out answers to problems. Children develop information-processing strategies to "store information in permanent [long-term] memory and retrieve it when needed later. To illustrate, how do you try to learn the information in a textbook? If you're like many college students, you probably use some combination of highlighting key sentences, outlining chapters, taking notes, writing summaries, and testing yourself. These are all effective learning strategies that make it easier for you to store information permanently" (Kail & Cavanaugh, 2014, p. 160).

Other strategies include repetition, organization, elaboration, and the use of external supportive techniques (Kail & Cavanaugh, 2014). At age 7 or 8, children use simpler strategies like repetition. Repetition involves repeating some information over and over again to establish it more firmly in one's memory. As they get older, children start to manage their information by using more complex strategies. Organization concerns "structuring information to be remembered so that related information is placed together" (Kail & Cavanaugh, 2014, p. 160). A child might group facts or concepts in categories according to some common variable. For example, a sixth grader studying for a history test might remember historical events geographically by relating them to the state or country in which they occurred. Similarly, that sixth grader might organize historical information chronologically according to the dates when events occurred.

Another more advanced information-processing approach involves elaboration. ***Elaboration is "[a] method for increasing retention of new information by relating it to well-known information"*** (Rathus, 2013, p. G-4). *For example, a teacher might help a student remember new vocabulary words by placing them in the context of a sentence (Rathus, 2014a). Another example involves relating a new concept or word to other familiar words that sound similar. For instance, a child living in Juneau, Alaska, might be able to remember the word juniper (a type of evergreen shrub, pronounced joo-ne-per) by associating it with the word "Juneau."*

LO 3-6 Apply Vygotsky's Theory of Cognitive Development

EP 2.1.7a

Lev Vygotsky proposed an alternative sociocultural theory of cognitive development to that developed by Piaget. Kail and Cavanaugh (2013) explain:

Human development is often referred to as a journey that takes people along many different paths. For Piaget … children make this journey alone. Other people (and culture in general) certainly influence the direction that children take, but fundamentally the child is a solitary adventurer-explorer, boldly forging ahead. Lev Vygotsky (1896–1934), a Russian psychologist, proposed a very different account: Development is an apprenticeship, in which children advance when they collaborate with others who are more skilled. According to Vygotsky (1934/1986), children rarely make much headway on the developmental path when they walk alone; they progress when they walk hand in hand with an expert partner, [emphasis omitted] (p. 144)

Unfortunately, Vygotsky died at the age of 37 from tuberculosis so never had time to fully develop his ideas. However, he has had a major impact on the understanding of cognitive development. He stressed that "children's thinking does not develop in a vacuum, but is influenced by the sociocultural context in which children grow up" (Kail & Cavanaugh, 2013, p. 16).

Several important principles underlie Vygotsky's theory (Vander Zanden, Crandell, & Crandell, 2007).

First, a child's development will differ depending on what's going on around that child. In other words, children will develop differently depending on the social and cultural circumstances and expectations evident in where they grow up. Second, children develop as they are exposed to various social situations and changes to which they must respond. Third, development occurs as part of children's interaction in group activities. Fourth, children develop by observing others and learning from the activities and performance of those around them. Fifth, children must use a scheme of symbols such as language in order to process what they see and learn new skills. Sixth, children learn cultural values through their interaction with others around them.

According to Vygotsky, then, children interact with others and observe these interactions. They frame these interactions in their minds by thinking about them through the use of language. They then develop their ability to think and learn in the context of interpersonal interaction and understanding this interaction through language.

Vander Zanden and his colleagues (2007) provide an example of this process:

The child, according to Vygotsky, will observe something happening between others and then will be able to take that observation and mentally incorporate it. One of Vygotsky's examples is the way children use language. First, a child will be told "Say please and thank you" by his or her parents. The child will also see people saying "Please" and "Thank you" to each other. Then the child will begin to say these words aloud. By saying "Please" and "Thank you" aloud, the child is internalizing the words and the concepts they stand for in a social setting. Only after assimilating the words' meaning can the child individually start to act in a polite manner. It follows that development is always a social process for Vygotsky, and the child—adult interaction plays an important role (Berk & Winsler, 1995). So it should come as no surprise that for Vygotsky, the way to understand development is to observe the individual in a social activity. (p. 55)

Spotlight 3.3 illustrates how values can be shaped depending on the cultural environment in which a child is raised.

At least three concepts are important in understanding Vygotsky's perspective: the zone of

SPOTLIGHT ON DIVERSITY 3.3

Sociocultural Learning of Interdependence Versus Independence

EP 2.1.4

North American culture encourages independence on the part of children (Vander Zanden et al., 2007). From birth on, children usually sleep in a room apart from their parents. Children are often placed out of the home in day care while their parents work. "Parents also reinforce a preference for objects rather than people to be used as means of comforting in times of distress. Children are supplied and rely on 'blankies,' pacifiers, and stuffed animals rather than parents or other people to console them when they are upset or conflicted. Parents and children become adversaries over sleeping arrangements as children get older. The 'terrible twos' revolve around the young child's eventual demand for independence" (Vander Zanden et al., 2007, p. 55). The culture generally encourages independence and competition. Children compete in school. Young adults compete for college admission. Workers compete for raises and advancement in their workplace environments.

In contrast, Vander Zanden and his colleagues (2007) describe how other cultures may encourage interdependence instead of independence:

Child-rearing practices in many other cultures stress interdependence, sometimes called collectivism, over independence or individualism, with the focus on ties to family. Children are socialized to think of themselves as being part of a group or community, rather than an individual at odds with those in the vicinity. For example, in the Pacific Island nation of Kiribati, an infant is in constant contact with some member of the extended family during the first year of life—sleeping with, eating with, and tagging along to work with a family member. These infants are socially involved in all of the day-to-day activities of the mother and father. Three generations of a family will gather around the baby to sing traditional songs while the infant is initiated into the social and cultural rhythms of the community. Rather than battling parents over issues of independence, the caregivers support the needs of the infant as they carry out the routine activities—there is no battle of the wills. (p. 55)

proximal development, scaffolding, and private speech (Vygotsky, 1934/1986).

The Zone of Proximal Development

The *zone of proximal* (meaning "near") *development* is "the difference between what a learner can accomplish independently and what he or she can accomplish with the guidance and encouragement of a more skilled partner" (Shaffer & Kipp, 2010, p. 283; Vygotsky, 1978). In other words, the zone "refers to a range of tasks that the child cannot yet handle alone but can do with the help of ... [others who are better at performing the activity.] To understand this idea, think of a sensitive adult ... who introduces a child to a new activity. The adult picks a task that the child can master but that is challenging enough that the child cannot do it by herself. Or the adult capitalizes on an activity that the child has chosen. The adult guides and supports, adjusting the level of support offered to fit the child's current level of performance. As the child joins in the interaction and picks up mental strategies, her competence increases,

and the adult steps back, permitting the child to take more responsibility for the task. This form of teaching—known as *scaffolding* [discussed in the next section]—promotes learning at all ages" (Berk, 2012a, p. 224).

The zone of proximal development, then, reflects the level of thinking a child can master when participating in an activity by him- or herself, compared to the higher level of learning that can occur by watching and interacting with others who know more about the activity. Consider the following example (Shaffer & Kipp, 2010):

Tanya, a 4-year-old, has just received her first jig-saw puzzle. She attempts to work the puzzle but gets nowhere until her father sits down beside her and gives her some tips. He suggests that it would be a good idea to put together the corners first, points to the pink area at the edge of one corner piece and says, "Let's look for another pink piece." When Tanya seems frustrated, he places two interlocking pieces near each other so that she will notice them, and when Tanya succeeds, he offers words of encouragement. As Tanya gradually gets the hang of it, he steps back and lets her work more and more independently. (p. 283)

Scaffolding

One means by which children learn in the zone of proximal development is a process called scaffolding. In commonplace language, a scaffold implies a structure of support. Vygotsky defined *scaffolding* as the process whereby "adults help children learn how to think by 'scaffolding,' or supporting, their attempts to solve problems or discover principles" (Coon & Mitterer, 2009, p. 126; Daniels, 2005). Caregivers use scaffolding as they adjust their level of guidance and support to the level of help the child needs. In effect, the child and the caregiver are adjusting their behavior by responding reciprocally to each other.

Santrock (2013) elaborates:

For example, in the game peek-a-boo, parents initially cover their babies, then remove the covering and register "surprise" at the babies' reappearance. As infants become more skilled at peek-a-boo, infants gradually do some of the covering and uncovering. In addition to peek-a-boo, pat-a-cake and "so-big" are other caregiver games that exemplify scaffolding and turn-taking sequences. (p. 223)

Private Speech

Consider Timmy, a 4-year-old who talks to himself intensively as he draws a picture of his house. Vygotsky emphasized the significance of *private speech*, "comments that are not intended for others but are designed to help children regulate their own behavior" (Kail & Cavanaugh, 2013, p. 146; Vygotsky, 1934/1986).

Kail and Cavanaugh (2013) describe the significance of private speech:

Vygotsky viewed private speech as an intermediate step toward self-regulation of cognitive skills (Fernyhough, 2010). At first, children's behavior is regulated by speech from other people that is directed toward them. When youngsters first try to control their own behavior and thoughts, without others present, they instruct themselves by speaking aloud. Private speech seems to be children's way of guiding themselves, of making sure that they do all the required steps in solving a problem.

Finally, as children gain ever greater skill, private speech becomes inner speech, *which was Vygotsky's term for thought (p. 150).*

Dacey and his colleagues (2009) provide an illustration:

For example, think of a 5-year-old girl asked to get a book from a library shelf. The book is just out of her reach, and as she tries to reach it, she mutters to herself, "Need a chair." After dragging a chair over, she climbs up and reaches for the book. "Is that the one?" "Just a little more." "OK." Note how speech accompanies her physical movements, guiding her behavior. In two or three years, the same girl, asked to do the same thing, will probably act the same way, with one major exception: She won't be talking aloud. Vygotsky believed she would be talking to herself, using inner speech to guide her behavior, and for the difficult tasks she undoubtedly would use inner speech to plan her behavior. (p. 134)

Critical Thinking: Evaluation of Vygotsky's Theory

Vygotsky's theory stresses the importance of social interaction and how a person functions within the environmental context, concepts basic to social work practice. This contrasts with Piaget's theory, which proposes that all children progress through predefined phases in essentially the same way.

At least two positive implications of Vygotsky's theory are important (Newman & Newman, 2012). First, it allows for appreciation of diverse cultures. How people think about and perceive things in one culture may differ radically from how they think about and perceive those same things in another culture. Whereas Piaget "viewed the emergence of logical thought as largely a universal process, Vygotsky considered the nature of reasoning and problem solving as culturally created" (Newman & Newman, 2012, p. 40). This focuses attention on the importance of family and social influence on the early development of ideas.

A second positive implication of Vygotsky's theory is that "individuals can promote their own cognitive development by seeking interactions with others who can help draw them to higher levels of functioning within their zone of proximal development" (Newman & Newman, 2012, p. 40). Thus, children can learn by interacting with others around them who are more skilled.

There are also criticisms of Vygotsky's sociocultural theory. For example, interactions that "rely heavily on the kinds of verbal instruction that Vygotsky emphasized may be less adaptive in some cultures or less useful for some forms of learning than for others. A young child learning to stalk prey in Australia's outback or to plant, care for, and harvest rice in Southeast Asia may profit more from observation and practice than from verbal instruction and encouragement. Other investigators are finding that collaborative problem solving among peers does not always benefit the collaborators and may actually undermine task performance if the more competent collaborator is not very confident about what he knows or if he fails to adapt his instruction to a partner's level of understanding" (Shaffer & Kipp, 2010, p. 291).

Berk (2012a) provides other criticisms:

Vygotsky's emphasis on culture and social experience led him to neglect the biological side of development. Although he recognized the importance of heredity and brain growth, he said little about their role in cognitive change. Furthermore, Vygotsky's focus on social transmission of knowledge meant that, compared with other theorists, he placed less emphasis on children's capacity to shape their own development. Followers of Vygotsky stress that children actively participate in the conversations and social activities from which their development springs. From these joint experiences, they not only acquire culturally valued practices but also modify and transform those practices (Nelson, 2007; Rogoff, 2003). Contemporary sociocultural theorists grant the individual and society balanced, mutually influential roles. (p. 25)

Vygotsky appears to be the recipient of less criticism than Piaget. There are at least two reasons for this. First, his approach fits well with the social work person-in-environment focus. Second, Vygotsky died very young, before being able to develop his theory to the fullest. Perhaps greater specificity would have allowed more options for detailed criticism.

LO 3-7 Explain Emotional Development

Both the concepts of *personality* and *cognition* and the relationship between them are complex and abstract. It is not clear exactly how thinking affects personality or how personality affects thinking. The tremendous amount of variation from one individual to another, and even one individual's varying reactions from one situation to another, makes it even more difficult to comprehend these concepts.

Emotions are also involved in a person's development. They complicate the profile of an individual's personality even further. For our purposes, *emotion* is the complex combination of feelings and moods that involves subtle psychological reactions and is expressed by displaying characteristic patterns of behavior. For example, a 4-year-old boy's goldfish might be found floating belly-up one morning. On hearing the unhappy news, the boy might become upset. His heart might start beating faster, and his breathing might accelerate. Finally, he might run to his room and start to cry. In this case, the boy has experienced an emotion. His body responded as he became upset. Finally, the behavior of crying clearly displayed his emotional state.

Infants' Emotions

Bridges (1932), a very early researcher of infants' emotions, claimed that infants initially showed only one basic emotion—excitement. J. B. Watson (1919), another early researcher, felt that infants were capable of three basic emotions: love, rage, and fear. Each of these emotions, according to Watson, was emitted as a reflex reaction to a specific stimulus. For example, an infant would experience love if stroked softly and spoken to gently by a parent, rage if physically restrained, and fear if suddenly startled by an unexpected loud noise.

Immediately upon birth, infants can express general interest, disgust, and distress. Other emotions, including surprise, anger, and sadness, occur approximately during the third to fourth month of life. Fear is displayed during months 5 through 7. Emotions that reflect *self-awareness* tend to develop later, sometimes not until the second year. *Self-awareness* is the realization that one is a unique entity distinctly separate from the surrounding environment and is involved in interaction with people and things in that environment. Such emotions include shyness, jealousy, pride, and shame.

Crying

One means by which babies can clearly display their emotions is through crying. Infants demonstrate at least three types of crying (Papalia & Feldman, 2012; Santrock, 2013). First, there is the basic cry (also referred to as the *hunger cry*). This is a "rhythmic pattern that usually consists of a cry, followed by a briefer silence, then a shorter … whistle that is somewhat higher in pitch than the main cry, then another brief rest before the next cry. Some infancy experts stress that hunger is one of the conditions that incite the basic cry" (Santrock, 2012b, p. 305). The second type is the *angry cry*, an exceptionally loud cry in which the baby forces a large column of air through the vocal cords. The third type, the *cry of pain*, is characterized by an initial loud wail with no preceding sniffling or moaning. The cry may be followed by the baby holding its breath for a long period.

Kail and Cavanaugh (2013) explain the significance of crying: "Crying represents the newborn's first venture into interpersonal communication. By crying, babies tell their parents that they are hungry or tired, angry or hurt. By responding to these cries, parents are encouraging their newborn's efforts to communicate" (p. 84).

According to Berk (2012a):

Although parents do not always interpret their baby's cry correctly, their accuracy improves with experience…. Fortunately, there are many ways to soothe a crying baby when feeding and diaper changing do not work…. The technique that Western parents usually try first, lifting the baby to the shoulder and rocking or walking, is most effective. (p. 148)

Different societies use different techniques to comfort crying babies (Berk, 2012b). For example, in the harsh altitudes of the Andes Mountains, a Peruvian mother covers her infant's body, including the head, with layers of blankets and clothing, and then places the infant's pouch on her back. The warmth and the rhythmic motion of the mother's walking serve to soothe the infant and encourage sleep. The desert !Kung people of Botswana carry their infants in hip slings made of animal skins. This positioning allows infants to view what's going on around them and also to "nurse at will" (p. 149). Infants in cultures that promote extensive close contact with their mothers tend to cry less than North American babies (Barr, 2001).

Smiling and Laughing

Babies can also express themselves emotionally through smiling and laughing. Infants smiling at their parents and their parents smiling back provide a major means of fostering the primary relationship between children and parents.

Infants tend to progress through several basic phases of smiling (Martin & Fabes, 2009; Papalia & Feldman, 2012; Santrock, 2012b). Initially, involuntary reflex smiling occurs, often while sleeping, as an automatic function of central nervous system development. After a few weeks, infants begin smiling in response to "visual, tactile, and auditory stimulation"; by 6 to 8 weeks of age, social smiling occurs where "the infant smiles upon seeing Mother's or Father's face or hearing her or his voice" (Martin & Fabes, 2009, p. 208). "From 2 to 6 months, infants' social smiling increases considerably, both in self-initiated smiles and in smiles in response to others' smiles" (Santrock, 2012b, p. 306). The smiling process reflects infants' gradual orientation toward other people and social relationships.

Laughing may begin at the fourth month (Martin & Fabes, 2009; Papalia & Feldman, 2012). "At first laughing occurs in response to physical stimulation, such as tickling or being swooped up high in Mom's or Dad's arms … After 6 months of age, infants increasingly laugh at visual and social stimuli, such as playing peek-a-boo or seeing a sister make a funny face" (Martin & Fabes, 2009, p. 208).

Infants and Temperament

It's difficult to refer to personality with respect to infants. Personality implies a complex mixture of attitudes, expressions, and behaviors that develop over time and characterize a specific individual. Infants don't yet have enough breadth or ability for expression to portray the complexity inherent in personality. Rather, psychologists tend to refer to an infant's temperament instead of personality. *Temperament* is each individual's distinguishing mental and emotional nature that results in a characteristic pattern of responses to people and situations.

Researchers have identified the following six concepts involved in temperament:

1. "Fearful distress, reflecting a child's tendency to withdraw and become distressed in new situations or circumstances
2. Anger/frustration, reflecting the degree to which a child becomes angry or frustrated when his or her needs or desires are not met

3. Positive affect, reflecting the amount of positive emotion, pleasure, and excitement shown by a child
4. Activity level, reflecting a child's level of gross motor activity and energy
5. Attention span/persistence, reflecting a child's ability to maintain focus and interest
6. Regularity, reflecting the predictability of a child's behavior" (Martin & Fabes, 2009, pp. 214–215; Putnam, Gartstein, & Rothbart, 2006; Rothbart & Mauro, 1990)

Psychologists often use three basic categories of temperament to characterize children (Rathus, 2011a; Santrock, 2012b; Sigelman & Rider, 2012; Thomas & Chess, 1977, 1989, 1991). Easy children are those whose lives have a relatively predictable, rhythmic pattern. They are generally cheerful and easy to get along with. They accept change well and are interested in new situations. The second category of child temperament includes *difficult* children. These children are frequently irritable, show much irregularity in their daily pattern of activities, and have much difficulty adapting to new situations. They can have intense reactions when confronted with something unfamiliar. Finally, there are the *slow-to-warm-up* children. They tend to have a generally low level of activity, a mild temperament, and moderate reactions to new situations and experiences. They often withdraw from the unfamiliar, at least initially, and are slow to make changes in themselves.

Rathus (2014b) comments on the stability of temperament over time:

There is at least moderate consistency in the development of temperament from infancy onward (Elliot & Thrash, 2010; Zuckerman, 2011). The infant who is highly active and cries in novel situations often becomes a fearful toddler. An anxious, unhappy toddler tends to become an anxious, unhappy adolescent. The child who refuses to accept new foods during infancy may scream when getting the first haircut, refuse to leave a parent's side during the first day of kindergarten, and have difficulty adjusting to college as a young adult. Difficult children in general are at greater risk for developing psychological disorders and adjustment problems later in life (Pauli-Pott et al., 2003; Roth-bart et al., 2004). A longitudinal study tracked the progress of infants with a difficult temperament from 1½ through 12 years of age

(Guerin et al., 1997). Temperament during infancy was assessed by the mother. Behavior patterns were assessed by both parents during the third year through the age of 12 and by teachers from the ages of 6 to 11. A difficult temperament correlated significantly with parental reports of behavioral problems from ages 3 to 12, including problems with attention span and aggression. Teachers concurred that children who had shown difficult temperaments during infancy were more likely to be aggressive later on and to have shorter attention spans. (pp. 246–247)

Note, however, that temperament and adjustment are very complex. Consider that the relationships between a child's temperament and later adjustment are questionable in that they're based on only a few studies (Santrock, 2012b).

Additionally, more than a third of children do not fit neatly into any of these three categories (Berk, 2012b). An infant's temperament involves emotionality, activity, and sociability. Many children show a combination of difficult and easy characteristics, yet still fall clearly within the realm of what is considered normal. For instance, a child may have an extremely irregular sleeping schedule, yet reach out and adapt quickly to new, unfamiliar people. Likewise, a child may be cheerful and easygoing most of the time, but horribly stubborn and difficult to live with on some occasions, such as when visiting relatives. The research points to some general tendencies; however, each infant, child, and adult is a unique person.

Theorists generally concur that an infant's temperament results from both hereditary and environmental factors (Berk, 2012b; Santrock, 2013; Steinberg et al., 2011a). Some research found that identical twins were more likely to reflect a similar temperament than were fraternal twins (Buss & Goldsmith, 2007; Santrock, 2013; Steinberg, Vandell, & Bornstein, 2011b). Yet, the relationship is neither perfect nor clear.

Why does temperament change for many people as they age? People modify their behavior and attitudes as they encounter new experiences. A major variable related to overall adjustment may be the "goodness of fit" between the individual and the expectations in the social environment (Papalia & Feldman, 2012; Santrock, 2012b; Sigelman & Rider, 2012). For instance, take parents who expect to have a dynamic, motivated child who is eager for new

An infant's temperament involves emotionality, activity, and sociability.

experiences. If they discover that their child is mild mannered, hesitant, and somewhat shy, they may be very disappointed. They may even place inordinate pressure on the child to be very different than he or she naturally is. On the other hand, take parents who sustain a family climate where moods are intense, daily routines are irregular, and changes are assimilated only slowly. A difficult child's fit in such a family may be good. The family may not view the child as difficult at all, but rather as normal.

If parents recognize that their child has a temperament of his or her own that may be very different from their own temperaments, they can make adjustments in their own behavior and expectations to help that child along. For instance, a slow-to-warm-up child can be given more time to adjust to new situations. Likewise, parents of a difficult child who has trouble organizing her day in a predictable manner can help her by providing structure and helping her learn how to make plans and carry them out. Spotlight 3.4 discusses cross-cultural expectations and temperament.

Attachment

Attachment "is a strong affectional tie that binds a person to an intimate companion and is characterized by affection and a desire to maintain proximity" (Sigelman & Rider, 2012, p. G-2). Attachment theory, originally developed by John Bowlby (1969), provides a major perspective on initial human relationships. Kail and Cavanaugh (2013) remark:

According to Bowlby, children who form an attachment to an adult—that is, an enduring socio-emotional relationship—are more likely to survive. *This person is usually the mother but need not be; the key is a strong emotional relationship with a responsive, caring person. Attachments can form with fathers, grandparents, or someone else.* (p. 170)

Attachment theory emphasizes the importance of interaction between the parent (or other caregiver) and the child that results in emotional bonding. The infant is viewed as an active participant in the relationship-building process. This perspective differs from Freud's oral stage, which stresses the infant's passivity and dependence on the caregiver.

Stages of Attachment

Based on Bowlby's conceptual framework, attachment develops in four stages, progressing from a fondness for people in general to an attachment to specific individuals who care for them (Berk, 2012b;

(image credit, rotated) John Henley/Jupiter Images

SPOTLIGHT ON DIVERSITY 3.4

Cross-Cultural Diversity in Expectations and Temperament

EP 2.1.4

Parental and social expectations that vary dramatically from one culture to another can affect the development of temperament. Malaysian infants tend to be less flexible and responsive to new situations and more reactive to outside stimuli than American infants; this may be due to the fact that Malaysian parents shelter children from new conditions that necessitate adaptability, on the one hand, and promote sensitivity to new sensations such as the need for a diaper change, on the other (Banks, 1989; Papalia & Feldman, 2012).

Sigelman and Rider (2009) comment on an example posed by the Masai in East Africa:

> *In most settings, an easy temperament is likely to be more adaptive than a difficult one, but among the Masai during famine, babies with difficult temperaments outlived easy babies. Why? Perhaps because Masai parents believe that difficult babies are future warriors or perhaps because babies who cry loud and long get noticed and fed. As this example suggests, a particular temperament may be a good fit to the demands of one environment but maladaptive under other circumstances. (p. 315)*

One cross-cultural study of Canadian and Chinese 2-year-olds found significant differences in temperament, with Chinese children generally being much shyer and more withdrawn than Canadian children (Chen et al., 1998).

Canadian mothers were much more punitive and overprotective in orientation with shy children, whereas Chinese mothers supported and encouraged introverted behavior. Perhaps, this difference is due to the expectation in Western countries such as Canada that children should be more outgoing and assertive if they're ever going to get anywhere in this world. Mothers might react to shy behavior either with cold rejection or with coddling. In contrast, introversion and self-control are valued in China. Therefore, mothers might encourage this sort of temperament and discourage more aggressive behavior.

Another example involves a group of Mayans in southern Mexico, the Zinacantecos (Greenfield & Childs, 1991). Their infants tend to be very quiet and relatively immobile as newborns. Bernstein, Penner, Clarke-Stewart, and Roy (2008) explain that Mayan mothers

> *reinforce this innate predisposition toward restrained motor activity by swaddling their infants and by nursing at the slightest sign of movement. . . . This combination of genetic predisposition and cultural reinforcement is culturally adaptive: Quiet Mayan infants do not kick off their covers at night, which is important in the cold highlands where they live; inactive infants are able to spend long periods on their mother's back as she works at the loom; infants who do not begin to walk until they can understand some language do not wander into the open fire at the center of the house. (p. 480)*

Kail & Cavanaugh, 2013; Steinberg et al., 2011a). They include:

Stage 1: "Preattachment." During the first two months of life, infants learn to distinguish between people and things. Subsequently, they respond increasingly more to people in general by smiling and vocalizing.

Stage 2: "Attachment in the making." From age 2 to 8 months, infants learn to distinguish between primary caregivers and strangers. They respond more positively to caregivers and display enthusiasm and excitement during their interactions. They also demonstrate upset when the caregiver leaves. The complex process of emotional attachment develops as the infant and caregiver learn how to respond to each other.

Stage 3: "True attachment." From age 8 to 18 months, infants search out their caregivers and

try to stay close to them. As crawling and mobility increase, infants maintain periodic eye contact with their caregiver as they explore their environment. They begin paying closer attention to the caregivers' reactions to their behavior and often respond accordingly. For example, an infant might smile if the caregiver is near and giving the child close attention. Or the infant might quickly return to the caregiver if he or she perceives that the caregiver is too far away. Infants continue to develop a more detailed internal picture of the caregiver, his or her behavior, and his or her expectations. Infants become more adept at interpreting the caregiver's reactions and anticipating how the caregiver will respond to their distress.

Stage 4: "Reciprocal relationships." Beginning at age 18 months, children develop increased

Attachment theory emphasizes the importance of interaction between parent (or other caregiver) and child that results in emotional bonding.

Camille Tokerud/Photographer's Choice RF/Getty Images

sensitivity to their dynamic interaction with the caregiver. Children begin showing affection while seeking the love, attention, and physical contact they need. Children might ask their caregiver to read them a bedtime story or give them a hug. They develop increasing sensitivity to their caregivers' feelings and goals (Kail & Cavanaugh, 2013, p. 170).

Qualities of Attachment

Four factors contribute to the attachment between the child and the caregiver (Cassidy, 1999; Colin, 1996; Newman & Newman, 2012):

1. Significant amount of time spent together.
2. Alert reactions to the child's needs and the provision of attentive care.
3. The caregiver's emotional responsiveness and depth of commitment to the child.
4. Being readily available in a child's life over a long period of time.

These variables make sense. The more responsive the care, attentiveness, and emotional commitment demonstrated by a caregiver are, the more intense the relationship with the child will be. Such qualities also provide the child with more opportunities to respond positively to the caregiver's overtures.

Positive responses can reinforce the dynamic interpersonal interaction between the caregiver and the child, resulting in an ever-increasing level of attachment.

Patterns of Attachment

Infants and caregivers have various degrees of attachment that are distinguished by the closeness and quality of the relationship. Four patterns have been established: secure attachment, anxious-avoidant attachment, anxious-resistant attachment, and disorganized attachment. Most infants form a *secure attachment* with their mother (or other primary caregiver or caregivers) (Thompson, 1998). Newman and Newman (2012) explain:

> *Infants who have a* secure *attachment actively explore their environment and interact with strangers while their mothers are present. After separation, the babies actively greet their mothers or seek interaction. If the babies were distressed during separation, the mothers' return reduces their distress and the babies return to exploration of the environment....*
>
> *Infants who show an* anxious-avoidant *attachment avoid contact with their mothers during the reunion segment following separation or ignore their efforts to interact. They appear to expect that their mothers will not be there when needed. They show less distress at being alone than other babies. Mothers of babies who were characterized as anxious avoidant seem to reject their babies. It is almost as if they were angry at their babies. They spend less time holding and cuddling their babies than other mothers, and more of their interactions are unpleasant or even hurtful ...*
>
> *Infants who show an* anxious-resistant *attachment are very cautious in the presence of the stranger. Their exploratory behavior is noticeably disrupted by the caregiver's departure. When the caregiver returns, the infants appear to want to be close to the caregiver, but they are also angry, so that they are very hard to soothe or comfort. Infants who are characterized as anxious-resistant have mothers who are inconsistent in their responsiveness....*
>
> *In the* disorganized *attachment, babies' responses are particularly notable in the reunion sequence. These babies have no consistent strategy for managing their distress. They behave in contradictory, unpredictable ways that seem to convey feelings of extreme fear or utter confusion....*

Some mothers are negative, intrusive, and they frighten their babies in bursts of intense hostility. Other mothers are passive and helpless, rarely showing positive or comforting behaviors. (pp. 165–166)

The characteristics of both the infant and the caregiver contribute to the development of attachment. Caregivers who are sensitive to a child's needs and demonstrate the factors related to attachment discussed previously may facilitate the attachment process (Newman & Newman, 2012; Papalia & Feldman, 2012). Infant characteristics such as irritability may make the attachment process more difficult, although research indicates that caregivers' responsive, positive approaches to meeting infants' needs tend to override infant characteristics in the attachment process (Berk, 2012b).

Long-Term Effects of Attachment

One research review examined 63 studies exploring the relationship between parent-child attachment and children's subsequent development of social relationships with peers (Schneider, Atkinson, & Tardif, 2001). Children who manifested secure attachment with caregivers early on tended to have more positive social interactions with peers as they got older and formed closer friendships. It follows that children who learn how to trust and interact positively as young children can apply these skills when they develop other social relationships later on.

Attachment and Day Care

When considering the importance of attachment and interaction, some working parents worry about the effects that day care might have on their children. Coon and Mitterer (2011) address this issue:

Does commercial day care interfere with the quality of attachment? *It depends on the quality of day care. Overall, high-quality day care does not adversely affect attachment to parents (National Institute of Child Health and Human Development, 1999). In fact, children in high-quality day care tend to have better relationships with their mothers and fewer behavior problems. They also have better cognitive skills and language abilities (Burchinal et al., 2000; Vandell, 2004). (pp. 100–101)*

However, note that poor-quality day care has just the opposite effects (Coon & Mitterer, 2011). It can actually encourage behavior problems to develop

(Pierrehumbert, Ramstein, Karmaniola, Miljkovitch, & Halfon, 2002).

What constitutes good day care? Parents should assess at least five aspects when considering a daycare center or provider (Howes, 1997). First, there should be a small staff-child ratio so that children receive adequate personal attention. Second, the size of the total group present should be no more than 12 to 15 children. Once again, the importance of personal attention is stressed. Third, caregivers should be trained in various relevant areas such as child development and child management to best meet children's needs. Fourth, staffing should be stable with little turnover so that children can be secure in their relationships with caregivers and suffer minimal disruption. Fifth, the daily experience should be steady and predictable, with clearly established procedures and effectively planned activities. Coon and Mitterer (2011) note that parents should also probably "avoid any child-care center with the words *zoo, menagerie,* or *stockade* in its name" (p. 101).

Spotlight 3.5 addresses cross-cultural differences in attachment.

LO 3-8 Examine Self-concept, Self-esteem, and Empowerment

All individuals form impressions about who they think they are. It's almost as if each person develops a unique theory regarding who exactly she feels she is. This personal impression of one's own "unique attributes and traits," both "positive and negative," is referred to as the self-*concept* (Sigelman & Rider, 2012, p. 348). The idea of self-concept was introduced earlier in a discussion of Carl Rogers's self theory. A related idea is that of self-esteem. *Self-esteem* refers to a person's judgment of his or her own value. Although self-concept may include more aspects about the self than just value, the two terms are often used interchangeably.

Self-concept is an important theme throughout mental health literature. Improving one's self-concept is often seen as a therapeutic goal for people with adjustment problems and as a means of empowerment. One's self-concept is important throughout life. In order to continue working, living, striving, and positively interacting with others, one must have a positive self-concept. In other words, one must feel good enough about oneself to continue

SPOTLIGHT ON DIVERSITY 3.5

Cross-Cultural Differences in Attachment

EP 2.1.4

As with temperament, social expectations adopted by parents (or other caregivers) for children's levels of attachment, dependence, activity, or autonomy may affect how attachment develops. Berk (2012b) reflects:

> *German infants show considerably more avoidant attachment than American babies do. But German parents encourage their infants to be nonclingy and independent, so the baby's behavior may be an intended outcome of cultural beliefs and practices (Grossmann et al., 1985). In contrast, a study of infants of the Dogon people of Mali, Africa, revealed that none showed avoidance attachment to their mothers (True, Pisani, & Oumar, 2001). Even when grandmothers are primary caregivers (as they are with firstborn sons). Dogon mothers remain available to their babies, holding them close and nursing them promptly in response to hunger and distress. (p. 268)*

A high proportion of Japanese infants demonstrate anxious-resistant attachment. They are quite wary of strangers (Berk, 2012b), perhaps because Japanese mothers keep their infants very close to them. Japanese parents value infants' dependence on them and expect infants to resist separation; thus, anxious-resistant attachment is a normal expectation for the development of the Japanese parent-child relationship (Rothbaum, Weisz, Pott, Miyake, & Morelli, 2000).

Finally, although cultural variations in attachment do exist, secure attachment still tends to be the norm in most infant-caregiver relationships (van IJzendoorn & Sagi, 1999).

---

living and being productive. This is just as true for children as it is for adults. Highlight 3.3 demonstrates the effects of positive and negative self-concepts in children.

The self-concept is an abstract idea. It is difficult to explain exactly what it involves. However, it is still an important factor in a person's ability to function. People of virtually any age need to feel good about themselves in order to be confident and enjoy life's experiences.

Theoreticians have emphasized the social significance of the self-concept and have labeled it "the meeting ground of the individual and society" (Markus & Nurius, 1984, p. 147). Middle childhood is the period when children are confronted with social expectations and demands. They become

HIGHLIGHT 3.3

The Effects of Positive and Negative Self-Concepts

Two 5-year-old girls, one with a good self-concept and the other with a relatively poor self-concept, illustrate the enormous effects of self-concept. Julie, who has a positive perception of self, is fairly confident in new situations. When she enters kindergarten, she assertively introduces herself to her peers and eagerly makes new friends. She frequently becomes a leader in their games. She often volunteers to answer her teacher's questions. Her teacher considers her happy and well adjusted.

In contrast, Mary has a relatively poor self-concept. She does not think very highly of herself or her abilities. On her first day of kindergarten, she usually stays by herself or lingers on the fringes of activities. She speaks little to others out of fear that they might criticize her. She really wants to be liked but is worried that there is nothing to like about her. Thus, it is easier for her to remain quiet and unobtrusive. For

example, one day the teacher brings out pieces of colored clay for the children to play with. Being so quiet and afraid, Mary does not rush up to her teacher to get hers even though playing with clay is one of her favorite pastimes. Rather, she waits until all the other children have their clay and are returning to their seats.

By the time Mary approaches the teacher, all the clay has been handed out. Instead of clay her teacher gives her a coloring book and some crayons. Mary takes them passively and begins to color a big yellow duck. All the while she is crying silently to herself. She is very disappointed that she did not get any clay. She also is hoping no one will notice that she is different from everyone else. Mary has a poor self-concept. She is afraid of others and what they might think. She does not have much self-esteem.

aware of the importance of the social setting and begin evaluating how they fit in.

One way of exploring the issue of self-esteem or self-worth stems from Harter's work (1987, 1988, 1990, 1993, 1998, 1999, 2006). (For the purposes of our discussion, the terms *self-esteem* and *self-worth* will be used interchangeably.) Harter postulates that children develop a sense of *global self-worth*, an overall view of how positively they feel about themselves, in two ways. First, self-worth is based on how competent children perceive themselves to be. Second, self-esteem depends on the amount of social support they receive from those around them. Children tend to establish positive or negative perceptions of themselves by about age 5, but they are unable to describe this awareness in words until about age 8 (Papalia & Feldman, 2012).

In exploring self-worth, Harter asked elementary-school children how competent and confident they felt about five different areas of their lives. The first, scholastic competence, involved how well children felt they performed in doing schoolwork. The second area concerned athletic competence, the children's perception of their sports prowess. Third, children were asked about their social competence—that is, how well accepted and popular they felt they were. The fourth area of competence concerned behavioral conduct, or how the children felt others viewed their behavior. The fifth area was physical appearance, how attractive they felt they appeared to others and how they felt about their specific physical characteristics (such as height, weight, hair, or facial attractiveness). In addition to these five areas, Harter asked questions directed at the children's overall sense of global self-worth.

Harter's research resulted in at least three major findings. First, the most significant variable contributing to self-esteem was how much positive regard children felt from people around them. The most important people were parents and classmates, followed by friends and teachers. It is interesting that these children rated classmates above friends in terms of importance. Perhaps they felt more social pressure and experienced more painful criticism from peers they were not close to. It is also interesting that children at all grade levels rated their parents high in importance. This contradicts the idea that as children grow up, their peers become more significant to them and their parents lose ground.

A second research finding was the ranking of the five areas. For both younger children (grades 3 through 5) and older children (grades 6 through 8), physical appearance was the most important, and behavioral conduct was the least important.

A third significant result involved the relationship between self-worth and affect (emotional mood). Children who felt a more positive global self-worth tended to be happier. They also were more likely to involve themselves in activities, trust in their own beliefs, express a high level of self-confidence, and handle criticism better. Those children who had a poorer sense of global self-worth were less happy, sad, and even depressed. They tended to hold themselves back from activities and be watchers rather than doers. They also were more likely to criticize themselves and experience frustration more easily. The implications of this research are that it is important to enhance children's self-esteem, especially those children with exceptionally low levels.

Significant Issues and Life Events

Several issues and life events that can affect children are discussed in this section. They were selected based on the importance of the effects they have on children and on the probability that social workers will encounter these issues in practice. The issues are intelligence testing, along with its potential problems and cultural biases; intellectual disabilities (mental retardation); learning disabilities; and attention deficit hyperactivity disorder. The content focuses on both characteristics and treatment.

LO 3-9 Discuss Intelligence and Intelligence Testing

Intelligence may be defined as the ability to understand, to learn, and to deal with new, unknown situations. Beyond this general definition, little is known about the origins of intelligence. Attempts to refine and clarify the definition have ranged from primitive measurement of head size, referred to as *phrenology*, to the listing of specific mental abilities that are supposed to be involved in intelligence (e.g., the ability to perceive spatial relationships, perceptual speed, memory, word fluency, reasoning, numerical ability, and verbal ability) (Thurstone, 1938).

Cattell's Fluid and Crystallized Intelligence

Cattell (1971) identifies two different types of intelligence: fluid and crystallized. *Fluid intelligence* is an individual's natural aptitude for solving highly conceptual problems as well as other problems, remembering facts, attending to the task at hand, and calculating numerical figures. This type of intelligence is innate and, therefore, theoretically not subject to change over the life span. Such native aspects of intelligence include the ability to perform abstract computations and memory capabilities. *Crystallized intelligence*, on the other hand, includes intellectual abilities that emphasize verbal communication and involve the ability to learn from others in the social environment through education and interaction. For instance, a person can learn a language or increase vocabulary. The person can also acquire new information and benefit from what has been learned through experience.

It would logically follow, then, that fluid intelligence would remain relatively constant throughout the life span, but that crystallized intelligence has the potential to increase.

Sternberg's Triarchic Theory of Intelligence

Sternberg (1984, 1985, 1986, 1987, 1990, 1996, 2000a, 2000b, 2004, 2008, 2009) has proposed a triarchic theory of human intelligence that emphasizes the context in which behavior occurs. He believes that three major components are involved in intelligence. These components are integrally related to a person's adaptive behavior—that is, what is relevant in the individual person's environment. For example, Bill Klumpe's business was to install septic tanks around small towns and rural farmlands in southeastern Wisconsin. Septic tanks were necessary because public sewers were unavailable throughout the area. Bill's reading skills were so poor that he had barely passed the written test to get his driver's license. The advent of calculators was a blessing to him because he was not adept at adding and subtracting numbers when figuring out what his customers owed him.

However, Bill was the best septic tank installer people in the area had ever seen. He had learned the business as a teenager, and now, in his 50s, he knew just about everything about septic tanks. He could look at a piece of schedule 40 PVC piping and know immediately if it was the right size for the proper drainage capacity. His gaskets were perfect, and his pipe couplings never leaked. His buddies at the bowling alley tavern sometimes would tease him, "You don't have a brain in your head, but you sure can dig!" Sternberg would say that what Bill had was intelligence. He had the capability to use his mind extremely well in those areas that were most significant to him.

Thus, Sternberg's model emphasizes the relevance of what people think about. The three specific components of intelligence are the componential, experiential, and contextual elements. The *componential* element involves how people think about, process, and analyze information to solve problems and evaluate their results. People who have high levels of componential intelligence also score highly on intelligence tests and are good at debate and formulating arguments.

The second component of intelligence, according to Sternberg, is the *experiential* element. This involves a person's actual doing of a task. It is the insightful, perceptive facet of intellect that enables an individual to put together information in new and creative ways. For example, Einstein conceptualized a theory of relativity. Part of this has to do with being able to master some tasks so that they become almost automatic. The mind can then devote greater attention to solving new parts of a problem or to working on new and better ways of accomplishing a task.

For example, Ruth, a medical transcriber at a large suburban hospital, types all the technical medical reports that physicians dictate on tape so that the information becomes part of each patient's permanent medical record. Over her many years of experience, she has identified a large body of technical medical words that are used repeatedly. In order to save time and make herself more efficient, she has developed a coding system that uses symbols or abbreviations to represent technical words and has encoded these into her word-processing software. For instance, when she types the letters *cd*, the computer interprets the letters to mean *cephalopelvic disproportion*, which the processor automatically prints. This system allows Ruth to concentrate more closely on the new, unknown, or most difficult terminology.

Sternberg's third component of intelligence is the *contextual* element. This involves the practical aspect of how people actually adapt to their environment. Within an individual's personal situation, it involves what knowledge is learned and how that knowledge can best be put to use in a practical sense.

To illustrate these three components, consider three undergraduate social work students: Jackie, Danielle, and Sara. Jackie had gotten almost straight A's in high school. In college, she was a whiz at taking both multiple-choice and true-or-false exams. However, she did not do nearly as well on essay exams, especially when they involved applications to problem situations in practice (e.g., how a social worker would intervene in a family where alcohol abuse was involved). She also had a terrible time when she entered her first social work practice course where she had to learn and apply interviewing skills in role plays. Eventually, she switched her major to sociology. She felt she could best apply her interest in working with people if she went on to graduate school in sociology and eventually did social research.

Danielle, on the other hand, did extremely well on essay exams but not as well on the objective multiple-choice and true-or-false tests. She got A's in the social work practice courses, which involved articulating how she would help people solve problems in the field. Her instructors praised her for her creativity and ideas. When she got into her field internship, she performed relatively well. She was able to apply her knowledge and skills to practice situations. She had some difficulty, however, working with clients who came from socioeconomic and ethnic backgrounds radically different than hers. Her final grade in field was an A–.

Sara barely got her college application accepted. She was in the lowest 25 percent of her high school graduating class, which meant she had to begin college on probation. She barely squeaked by each semester with the minimal cumulative grade point necessary. She also managed to attain the required grade point necessary to get into her advanced social work courses and continue on in the major. However, when she finally got into her field placement, her social work supervisor raved about what an excellent student she was. Sara was able to take on difficult cases early in the semester and required relatively little supervision. Sara's personal manner was such that she established relationships quickly with clients. She was able to make clear applications of the practice skills she had learned in her courses. It almost seemed like working with people as a social worker came naturally to her. She seemed to have a natural sense of what to do in situations that were completely foreign to her. She received an A in fieldwork, which contrasted with her C+ cumulative grade. The agency later enthusiastically hired her.

Each of these three individuals is strong in one component in Sternberg's model of intelligence. Jackie was strong in the componential aspect of intelligence. She could conceptualize extremely well at abstract levels and clearly remember facts and details. Danielle's strength lay in the experiential component of intelligence. She was creative and insightful. She could take recommendations for what to do in a specific situation and clearly apply them. Sara excelled in the contextual aspect of intelligence. She could adapt virtually to any situation and solve problems in a very practical sense.

In real life, people can be strong in any or all of these components. They have an intellectual mixture of strengths and weaknesses.

Intelligence Testing

We have established that no absolutely clear definition of intelligence exists. Therefore, it is important to recognize the relationship between the more global concept of intelligence and the intelligence quotient, commonly referred to as IQ. Many mistakenly assume that an IQ represents the absolute quantity of intelligence that a person possesses. This is not true. An IQ really stands for how well an individual might perform on a specific intelligence test in relation to how well others perform on the same test. The IQ, then, involves two basic facets. One is the score that a person attains on a certain type of test. The second is the person's relative standing within the peer group.

An IQ score is the best thing available for attempting to measure whatever intelligence is there. Such a statement may not inspire confidence in the value of one's IQ. However, perhaps it should elicit caution. IQ scores can be used to determine grade school placement, admission to special programs, and encouragement or lack thereof to attend college. A person who is aware of having a low IQ score may establish lower expectations. These lower expectations may act as a barrier to what the person could actually achieve. She might become the victim of a self-fulfilling prophecy—that is, what she expects is what she gets.

This could have been the case, for example, for a returning college student who was the mother of three children. She was also receiving social insurance benefits because of a permanent disability. Her vocational counselor told her that her IQ was not nearly high enough for success in college. He suggested that she stay home and enjoy her moderate financial benefits. Although his statements discouraged her, she had the courage and stamina to enroll with a full course load at a well-respected state university. Her final grade report after her first semester indicated that she had achieved a perfect 4.0 average. She immediately returned to her vocational counselor and requested financial assistance for a computer to assist her in her course work. He mumbled in an embarrassed manner that that might be a good idea.

Intelligence testing is done in both group and individual formats. Many school systems use group testing because it is less time consuming and cheaper. Individual tests, however, tend to be more precise and useful in targeting specific areas of need. The most frequently used tests in the English language include the Stanford-Binet Test and the Wechsler Intelligence Scale, which are described in the next sections (Kalat, 2011).

The Stanford-Binet IQ Test

A common intelligence test is the Stanford-Binet IQ test. First used in 1905, it has continued to be refined. Schools frequently use the Stanford-Binet to determine program and grade placement and potential academic success.

The Stanford-Binet test can be administered to individuals age 2 through later adulthood (Coon & Mitterer, 2011; Roid, 2003). Scores can be obtained in five areas that measure both *verbal* ability (related to the use and understanding of language) and *nonverbal* ability (related to problem solving and thinking in ways that do not use language, such as completing pictures) (Roid, 2003). The five aspects of reasoning assessed include: "*fluid reasoning* (e.g., completing verbal analogies, such as 'hot is to cold as _____ is to low'), *knowledge* (e.g., defining words, detecting errors in pictures), *qualitative reasoning* (e.g., solving math problems), *visual-spatial processing* (e.g., assembling a puzzle), and *working memory* (e.g., repeating a sentence). Each of the five abilities is measured by one verbal and one nonverbal subtest, so it is possible to calculate a core for each of

the five abilities, a total score on all the verbal tests, a total score on all the nonverbal tests, and an overall score for all ten tests combined" (Bernstein, 2011, p. 277).

"Stanford-Binet IQ scores are computed from tables set up to ensure that a given IQ score means the same at different ages. The mean [or average] IQ for each age is 100" (Kalat, 2011, p. 321). Thus, half of all scores are higher than 100 and half are lower (Bernstein, 2014). About two-thirds of all scores range from 85 to 115; about one-sixth fall below 85 and another one-sixth above 115 (Nevid, 2009). "A 6-year-old with an IQ score of, say, 116 has performed better on the test than 84% [about 5/6] of other 6-year-olds. Similarly, an adult with an IQ score of 116 has performed better than 84% [about 5/6] of other adults" (Kalat, 2011, p. 321).

In the past, the Stanford-Binet was criticized because of its heavy emphasis on verbal ability. Children whose verbal ability was not strong for some reason may not have had their actual intellectual ability adequately reflected. However, the current edition diminishes that bias and focuses more on other avenues of reasoning. For example, a child might be asked to define several words, such as *banana* or *pencil*, as part of the verbal assessment, and then be asked to draw a course through a maze to test other aspects of thinking ability. The test is also designed to be more evenly responsive to a broad range of groups differing significantly in geographic location, ethnicity, and gender. Newly designed approaches stress nonverbal performance for people with "limited English, deafness, or communication disorders" (Roid, 2003).

The Wechsler Tests

Two commonly used variations of the Wechsler tests are the Wechsler Adult Intelligence Scale—Fourth Edition (WAIS-IV) and the Wechsler Intelligence Scale for Children—Fourth Edition (WISC-IV) (Kalat, 2011). Kalat explains that both tests:

produce the same average, 100, and almost the same distribution of scores as the Stanford-Binet. The WISC is given to children up to age 16, and the WAIS is for everyone older....

A Wechsler test provides an overall score and four major subscores. One is the Verbal Comprehension Index, based on such items as "Define the word letter" and "How are a peach and a plum similar?" A second part is the Perceptual Reasoning Index, which calls for nonverbal answers. For example, the examiner might arrange four blocks in a particular pattern and then ask the child to arrange four other blocks to match the pattern.…

A third part, the Working Memory Index, includes such items as "Listen to these numbers and then repeat them: 3 6 2 5" and "Listen to these numbers and repeat them in reverse order: 4 7 6." The fourth part is Processing Speed. An example of an item is "Here is a page full of shapes. Put a slash (/) through all the circles and X through all the squares." This task is simple, but the question is how quickly someone can proceed accurately. (p. 321)

Comparing verbal and performance scores as well as reviewing scores on specific subtests can be especially useful in detecting specific learning problems. For example, if a child performs significantly better on the performance segments than on the verbal ones, a learning disability (discussed later in the chapter) or some other perceptual deficit may be present.

Ethical Questions 3.2

Should children be informed of their IQ? Should parents be told of their child's results? What are the reasons for your answers?

EP 2.1.2

Targeting Special Needs

Perhaps one of the most beneficial uses of IQ tests is in targeting special needs. For example, IQ is one of the measures used to identify both gifted people and people with intellectual disabilities (historically referred to as mental retardation).

Gifted People

Giftedness has been defined in many ways. However, five dimensions have emerged that characterize the majority of the definitions (Friend, 2011, p. 470; Hardman, Drew, & Egan, 2014; P.L. 95-561, Title IX, [a]; Reis & Housand, 2008, p. 66; Smith & Tyler, 2010, p. 468); these include:

1. *Intellectual ability.* We have defined intelligence as the ability to understand, to learn, and to deal with new, unknown situations. Gifted people may have an exceptional intellectual ability.
2. *Specific academic aptitude.* Gifted people may excel in some academic area or areas. Academic dimensions, of course, include educational studies related to math, science, verbal expression, and social sciences, among many others.
3. *Creative or productive thinking.* Creativity involves "the capacity for innovation, originality, expressiveness, and imagination and the ability to manipulate ideas in fluent, flexible, elaborate, and original ways" (Friend, 2011, p. 471). Productive thinking concerns generating ideas that are exceptionally useful, practical, or applicable.
4. *Leadership ability.* "*Leadership* is a process whereby an individual influences a group of individuals to achieve a common goal" (Northouse, 2010, p. 3). Thus, a gifted individual may be exceptionally good at influencing others.
5. *Visual and performing arts.* People may be gifted in artistic ways. They may be exceptionally adept at creating visual displays such as painting or sculpture. Or they may be unusually talented in performing theatrical or physical activity.

Once identified, gifted people can be nurtured to develop their gift or talent. Although not consistently available due to differences in funding and philosophy, a range of educational services may be offered to gifted students (Smith & Tyler, 2010).

In the past, IQ was often the only means used to identify gifted people. However, as the definition of giftedness implies, it is now one of a range of measures used. Areas of giftedness might include *analytic* (the ability to carefully analyze a problem or issue, dissect it, and understand it—a quality measured by traditional intelligence tests); *synthetic* (the ability to be insightful, creative, perceptive, and imaginative—qualities often manifested by people excelling in the arts and sciences); and *practical* (the ability to function exceptionally well in daily life experiences and situations—a quality often demonstrated by people with flourishing careers) (Hallahan, Kauffman, & Pullen, 2012, p. 431; Sternberg, 1997). About 6.7 percent of all American students are considered gifted (National Center for Education Statistics, 2009). However, note that the actual numbers may vary radically, depending on the definition of giftedness used.

IQ tests also can be used as an indicator for people who fall below the "normal" range of intelligence so that they can receive the special help they need. A later section will address this in depth.

Other Potential Problems with IQ Scores

The use of IQ tests alone to categorize people is problematic for several reasons. One is cultural bias, discussed in Spotlight 3.6. Another is that the definition of IQ is arbitrary. At its most basic level, an IQ score reflects how well people perform on an IQ test. It does not provide a reliable indication of competence in the real world.

Another problem with IQ tests is that placing IQ labels on people may become self-fulfilling prophecies. An individual with a low IQ score may stop trying to reach his or her true potential. A person labeled with a high IQ may develop an inappropriately superior, even arrogant, attitude. We all probably know people like this.

Another potential problem with IQ scores is that they do not take motivation into account. A person with a lower IQ score who works hard and is motivated may attain much higher levels of achievement and success than a person with a higher IQ who is not motivated to use it. Simply having the ability does not necessarily mean that it will be put to use.

Many aspects of an individual's personality, ability to interact socially, and adapt to society are not directly related to IQ. In effect, IQ is only one facet of an individual. People have numerous other strengths and weaknesses that make up their unique personalities. Each person is an individual whose worth and dignity merit appreciation.

 SPOTLIGHT ON DIVERSITY 3.6

LO 3-10 Explain Cultural Biases and IQ Tests

EP 2.1.4a

It is critical to be vigilant about the potential for cultural biases in IQ tests. White middle- and upper-class children historically have had an unfair advantage over non-white children on these tests. Similarly, urban children have had advantages over rural children, and middle-class children over lower-class children in general. Biases can involve the use of words, concepts, and contexts that are more familiar to some children than to others.

For example, Kail and Cavanaugh (2013, p. 219) discuss the question, "A conductor is to an orchestra as a teacher is to what?" They pose the possible answers as "book," "school," "class," or "eraser." Children who have been exposed to the concept of "orchestra," perhaps having attended a concert, are more likely to provide the correct answer than children who have little or no idea what orchestras or conductors are.

What is considered significant by members of a culture can influence what children consider important, and hence how they answer questions on IQ tests. Plotnik and Kouyoumdjian (2011) comment on how other cultures perceive the concept of intelligence differently by emphasizing other aspects of human behavior and existence:

For example, the Taiwanese conception of intelligence emphasizes how one understands and relates to others, including when and how to show intelligence (R. J. Sternberg & Yang, 2003). In Zambia (Africa), parents describe the intelligence of their children as including cognitive abilities as well as showing social responsibility, which is considered equally important (Serpell, 2003). In Micronesia, people demonstrate remarkable navigational skills as they sail long distances using only information from stars and sea currents (Ceci et al., 1997). These navigational abilities certainly indicate a high degree of intelligence that would not be assessed by traditional Western IQ tests. Thus, the definition of intelligence differs across cultures. (p. 291)

Even testing situations and children's comfort level in them can affect IQ test results. Specific variables include the test-takers' relationship with the test-giver, their ability to sit quietly and respond to instructions, and their understanding of the dynamics involved in taking tests successfully, such as going through the entire test first, answering the questions they know, pacing themselves, and then returning to the more difficult items so that they are able to complete most of the test (Ceci, 1991).

Much attention has been paid to *cultural fairness* in IQ tests. Culture-fair IQ tests try to include test items and terms that are familiar to children from as many cultural and socioeconomic backgrounds as possible. However, because a totally "culture-free" test (i.e., one with no culturally biased content at all) is impossible to achieve, it is important to remain sensitive to fairness and strive to make tests as "culture fair" as possible.

LO 3-11 Analyze Intellectual Disabilities and the Importance of Empowerment

EP 2.1.4

Intellectual disability (formerly referred to as *mental retardation*) is a condition characterized by intellectual functioning that is significantly below average and accompanying deficits in adaptive functioning, both of which occurred before reaching adulthood (American Psychiatric Association [APA], 2013a, 2013b). Note two important points about the terms intellectual disability and mental retardation. First, the term *intellectual disability* has a less negative connotation than the term *mental retardation*. Second, it is important to refer to people with intellectual disabilities as *people* before referring to any disability they might have. For example, referring to them as *intellectually, mentally, or cognitively challenged people* tends to emphasize the disability because the disability is stated first. Our intent is simply to respect their right to equality and dignity. (Note that some states may use other terms for people with intellectual disabilities. Terms might include *cognitive impairment, cognitive disability, mental impairment, mental disability,* or *mental handicap*; more consistent and positive changes in terminology should occur over time to better understand and appreciate these people [Friend, 2011, p. 235].)

Individuals with intellectual disabilities, to some degree, are unable intellectually to grasp concepts and function as well and as quickly as their peers. The exact prevalence of intellectual disability is unknown; however, the American Psychiatric Association estimate is approximately 1 percent of the population (APA, 2013b). This figure "suggest[s] that school-age children with intellectual disabilities are possibly underidentified" (Friend, 2011, p. 237). The following sections will elaborate on the definition of intellectual disability, the significance of support systems, and what people who have intellectual disabilities are like (see Spotlight 3.7).

Defining Intellectual Disability

There are three major parts in the definition of *intellectual disability* (referred to as *mental retardation*) in the *DSM-5* (APA, 2013a). First, a person must score significantly below average in general intellectual functioning. Although this determination was historically based on IQ tests, it now involves "both clinical assessment and individualized, standardized intelligence testing" (APA, 2013a, p. 33). In general, intellectual disability is thought to characterize people whose intelligence levels fall at least two standard deviations below the norm; this means having an IQ of 70 or below (APA, 2013b).

A second part of the definition of intellectual disability involves impairment in *adaptive functioning*, that is, how a person thinks about his or her situation, interacts with others, and masters daily life activities (APA, 2013a). Adaptive activities fall within three dimensions—conceptual, social, and practical (APA, 2013b). The *conceptual* dimension concerns the ability to think, remember, solve problems, and perform academically. The *social* dimension involves the ability to communicate with others, form relationships, and understand people's emotional and other needs. The *practical* dimension entails conducting necessary daily tasks like attending to self-care and personal hygiene, holding a job, managing money, and fulfilling other educational and work responsibilities.

The third part of the definition of intellectual disability concerns the fact that the condition is identified or diagnosed "during the developmental period," that is, the time before a person reaches adulthood (APA, 2013b). In the past, this meant turning age 18 but now other factors such as adaptive functioning may be taken into account (APA, 2013b). One intent of this part of the definition is to rule out people who become brain damaged (e.g., in a car accident) or experience some other mental impairment when they are adults. In those incidences, people would probably fall under other *DSM-5* diagnostic categories.

Spotlight 3.7 recognizes the four traditional categories of intellectual disability, which historically emphasized IQ scores. The categories are noted here with their traditional IQ scores (APA, 2000, p. 42):

Mild	IQ of 50–55 to approximately 70
Moderate	IQ of 35–40 to 50–55
Severe	IQ of 20–25 to 35–40
Profound	IQ below 20 or 25

SPOTLIGHT ON DIVERSITY 3.7

What Are People with Intellectual Disabilities Like?

There are huge differences in the capabilities of people who have intellectual disabilities, depending on their strengths and level of functioning. Therefore, it is important to maintain a strengths perspective and consider each person as an individual with his or her own special abilities and potential. Compared to people who have "normal" IQs, people with intellectual disabilities tend to experience deficits in six basic areas: *attention, memory, language, self-regulation, motivation,* and *social development* (Hallahan et al., 2012, p. 113). It is important to remember that not all people with intellectual disabilities have deficits in all areas.

This discussion on problems associated with intellectual disabilities is negatively oriented. It focuses on people's deficits instead of their strengths. However, you need to understand where people with intellectual disabilities are likely to experience problems in order to emphasize and enhance their strengths in those and other areas.

People with intellectual disabilities may have trouble paying *attention* to ongoing activities and events as carefully as other people do. They may be easily distracted or pay attention to things other than what they are supposed to attend to.

Research has established that people with intellectual disabilities experience difficulty with *memory*, the second problem area. They may be weaker in their ability to remember things recently told to them or experienced by them. Complex ideas are more difficult for them to retain than simpler concepts.

Language development is the third area of difficulty that is evident in many people with intellectual disabilities. They usually take longer to master language skills. They will probably require more time to understand ideas and concepts. They may display speech and pronunciation problems.

Self-regulation, a fourth problematic area, is a person's ability to organize thinking and plan ahead. People with intellectual disabilities may have less ability to organize their thoughts. For instance, when "normal" students take essay exams, they may use acronyms (words formed from the initial letter or letters of each of the successive parts of some complex term or succession of steps) to help them remember a series of steps or ideas. People with intellectual disabilities likely would not.

The fifth area of possible difficulty is *motivation*. People with intellectual disabilities generally do poorly in school compared with their peers and may develop a long history of defeat and failure. If they think that they will fail no matter how hard they try, they may not try to succeed at all.

Poor *social development* is a sixth area of potential difficulty. This may be due to low levels of self-esteem and poor self-concept. It may be due to having more difficulty learning how to respond appropriately in social situations. It also may result in more disruptive behavior than that of their peers.

If children with intellectual disabilities have difficulties in learning, especially in academic settings, disruptive behavior may be a way for them to get attention or amuse themselves.

People with intellectual disabilities are often placed in categories called mild, moderate, severe, and profound according to the American Psychiatric Association's *Diagnostic and Statistical Manual* (5th ed.) *(DSM-5)* (APA, 2013a). The following profiles of each category are based on descriptions in *DSM-5*. The intent is to provide you with some general ideas about the types of support people may need.

The majority of people with intellectual disabilities fall within the *mild* category. In the past, these people were referred to as "educable" in that they often achieved academic skills up to a sixth-grade level. As preschoolers, people with mild intellectual disabilities often develop social and communication

Empowerment is essential for people with disabilities. Here, Gena Killinger, an athlete from Nebraska, raises her hand in victory after winning a 25-yard backstroke in a Special Olympics event held in Ames, Iowa.

AP Photo/The Ames Tribune, Andrew Rullestad

(continued)

skills, demonstrate minimal sensory or motor impairment, and generally fit in fairly well with their peers. In fact, the majority of people with intellectual disabilities are very similar to everybody else except that they are a bit slower in learning and don't progress quite as far as others in the "normal" population. Their limitations usually become more evident as they advance in school. As adults, they usually gain employment "in jobs that don't emphasize conceptual skills" (APA, 2013a, p. 34). They often require assistance in making health and legal decisions, and frequently need support to fulfill the necessary functions involved in raising a family.

People with *moderate* intellectual disabilities progress more slowly in academic pursuits and require more assistance. They tend to view issues and experiences more concretely than their peers. They likely have difficulty in reading and in managing finances by themselves. These people "show marked differences from peers in social and communicative behavior across development" (APA, 2013a, p. 35). They usually can form successful relationship ties with family members and with friends having abilities similar to their own. They tend to have difficulty accurately interpreting social cues. "Significant social and communicative support is needed in work settings for success" (APA, 2013a, p. 35). They generally can assume responsibility for daily self-care tasks, but require substantial teaching and support in order to master household tasks. They can gain employment in jobs requiring "limited conceptual and communication skills," but need significant support. Additionally, they require substantial help in "scheduling, transportation, health benefits, and money management" (APA, 2013a, p. 35). They can enjoy a range of recreational activities with adequate "supports and learning opportunities" (APA, 2013a, p. 35). They can potentially function well in their communities with enough support, usually living in a supervised environment.

People with *severe* intellectual disabilities develop little, if any, speech in early childhood. As childhood progresses, they can develop some speech capability and skills to take personal care of themselves. Conceptual and problem-solving skills are lacking. They generally can eventually develop very basic skills in uncomplicated social speech. They can enjoy family members and other people with whom they're familiar. People with severe intellectual disabilities require substantial help in virtually all areas of life including decision making and self-care tasks. They need extensive, ongoing support in their daily life activities and living arrangements. They often live with their families or in some other closely supervised, structured setting.

People with *profound* intellectual disabilities most often have additional motor and sensory problems that prevent them from manipulating many objects effectively. They view the world as a very concrete place. They have major difficulties with conceptualization and formulation of ideas. Communication is primarily through nonverbal gestures instead of words, although they may learn to understand some simple words and directions. They can experience pleasure through interaction with family members and familiar others close to them. People with profound intellectual disabilities are "dependent on others for all aspects of daily physical care, health, and safety," although many can learn to partake in some activities with assistance (e.g., removing dishes from the dinner table) (APA, 2013a, p. 36). They can generally enjoy and participate in basic recreational ventures with extensive supervision. Such pursuits might include listening to music, taking walks, watching television, or being in a swimming pool.

People with intellectual disabilities have strengths and weaknesses just like the rest of us. Each is a unique individual. Most people with intellectual disabilities are pretty much like everybody else, but they have less intellectual potential. They have similar feelings, joys, and needs. And they have rights.

The ranges in each category reflected the varying results that can be attained on different IQ tests, the 5 percent measurement error in the tests themselves, and the importance of taking adaptive functioning into account (APA, 2000). For example, a person scoring 40 on an IQ test but suffering from serious deficits in adaptive ability might be placed in the "Severe" category. On the other hand, another person scoring 40 who has many adaptive strengths might be placed in the "Moderate" category.

Highlighting adaptive ability and achievement allows the individual to be evaluated as a unique functioning being. Older definitions of intellectual disability placed greater importance on IQ alone, which does not necessarily provide an accurate

picture of someone's ability to function and make decisions on a daily basis.

The new *DSM-5* is the primary diagnostic tool used in the United States for mental and emotional disorders. New diagnostic procedures stress both clinical assessment of intellectual ability and extensive evaluation of adaptive functioning in addition to standardized IQ tests. The American Association on Intellectual and Developmental Disabilities (AAIDD, 2013) also emphasizes the use of adaptive skill areas when evaluating an individual's ability to function independently. Additionally, the AAIDD (2013) stresses that the community social environment, "linguistic diversity," and "cultural differences in the way people communicate" and behave be taken into account when assessing intellectual disability.

EP 2.1.2

Do people with intellectual disabilities have the right to have children?

The Significance of Empowerment by Support Systems

EP 2.1.4a

In addition to highlighting adaptive skill areas, it is important to evaluate the configuration and intensity of support an individual needs—"intermittent," "limited," "extensive," or "pervasive"—besides considering IQ and adaptive skill acquisition (Hallahan, Kauffman, & Pullen, 2009, p. 148; Kirk, Gallagher, Coleman, & Anastasiow, 2012; Lightfoot, 2009a). *Intermittent support* is the occasional provision of support whenever it is needed. People needing only intermittent support function fairly well by themselves; they need help from family, friends, or service-providing agencies only sporadically. This usually occurs when they are experiencing periods of stress or major life transitions (such as a health crisis or job loss). *Limited support* is intensive help or training provided for a limited time to teach specific skills, such as job skills, or to assist in major life transitions such as moving from one's parental home. *Extensive support* is long-term, continuous support that usually occurs daily and affects major areas of life both at home and at work. Finally, *pervasive support* is continuous, consistent, and concentrated. People need pervasive support for ongoing survival.

It's important to remember that identification of the support level needed "must not limit the planning and opportunities developed" for a person with intellectual disabilities (Kirk et al., 2012, p. 180). These people are individuals who may demonstrate a wide range of strengths. The emphasis on, discovery of, and use of such strengths is an ongoing process.

The support systems perspective coincides well with social work values in at least four ways (DeWeaver,

1995). First, instead of labeling people as having mild, moderate, severe, or profound intellectual disabilities, it stresses people's ability to function and achieve for themselves with various levels of support from others. It looks at what people can do with some help, rather than what they cannot do. Second, it refutes the sole focus on medical labeling and related issues as the primary concern. Medical labels are not necessarily useful when determining what you can do to help people. For example, labeling a person as having severe intellectual disability or mental retardation is not as useful as saying that this person requires extensive support. Third, the support systems perspective shifts the primary assessment focus from IQ to adaptive skills. Fourth, because of its focus on individual strengths, it encourages assessment and emphasis on ethnic, cultural, and linguistic differences and qualities. The professionals involved in assessment are not limited to examining one or two variables. Rather, they are encouraged to explore virtually any aspect of the individual's environment.

Macro-System Responses to Intellectual Disabilities

The programs available for people with intellectual disabilities depend on policies that dictate where public funds should and will be spent. Once again, we see how policy (such as federal and state laws) affects social work practice. Policies provide the rules for how organizations can spend money and what services they can provide. Social workers must do their jobs within the context of the organizations they work for. Spotlight 3.8 discusses current legislation concerning people with disabilities.

Services for people who have intellectual disabilities or designated other disabilities are paid for primarily by federal and state programs, the majority of which are administered through programs under the U.S. Department of Health and Human Services. The rest are administered through the Department of Education.

Here, we address two issues involved in developing programs and providing services for people with intellectual disabilities: deinstitutionalization and community-based services. The important thing to remember throughout our discussion is that intelligence, although an important variable in terms of daily living and ability, is only one of many factors affecting people's lives. Limited intelligence

The Americans with Disabilities Act: The Pursuit of Social and Economic Justice

EP 2.1.5a–c

The intent of the Americans with Disabilities Act (ADA) of 1990 was to provide the millions of Americans who have disabilities access to public places, work settings, and "the mainstream of public life" (Jimenez, 2010; Smolowe, 1995a, p. 54; U.S. Department of Justice, 2005). "Unemployment and economic stress are major concerns" for people with disabilities (Segal, 2010, p. 112). The ADA "was intended as a sweeping civil rights law that works to eliminate discrimination against people with disabilities in the areas of employment, public accommodations, state and local government, transportation and communications" (Lightfoot, 2009b, p. 449; U.S. Department of Justice, 2005).

The ADA includes under its umbrella people who have intellectual disabilities, other developmental disabilities (various serious chronic conditions), and physical disabilities. "An individual with a disability is defined by the ADA as a person who has a physical or mental impairment that substantially limits one or more major life activities, a person who has a history or record of such an impairment, or a person who is perceived by others as having such an impairment. The ADA does not specifically name all of the impairments that are covered" (U.S. Department of Justice, 2005).

The ADA is one attempt by a national macro system to improve the lives of people with disabilities and provide them with greater social and economic justice. The ADA consists of four major provisions (U.S. Department of Justice, 2005). Title I forbids job and employment discrimination against people with disabilities and requires employers to provide "the full range of employment-related opportunities available to others." It "prohibits discrimination in recruitment, hiring, promotions, training, pay, social activities, and other privileges of employment." It also restricts an employer's questions about a person's disability prior to making a job offer.

Title I requires employers with 15 or more employees to provide qualified individuals with disabilities an equal opportunity to benefit from the full range of employment-related opportunities available to others. For example, it prohibits discrimination in recruitment, hiring, promotions, training, pay, social activities, and other privileges of employment. It restricts questions that can be asked about an applicant's disability before a job offer is made, and it requires that employers make reasonable accommodation to the known physical or mental limitations of otherwise qualified individuals with disabilities, unless it results in undue hardship.

Title II requires all state and local governments to provide equal opportunities to people with disabilities. Applicable services include those involved in "public education, employment, transportation, recreation, health care, social services, courts, voting, and town meetings." These governing bodies are also required to make buildings accessible, modify policies to avoid discrimination, and provide communication channels for people with "hearing, vision, or speech disabilities." Title II also prohibits "public transportation services, such as city buses and public rail transit (e.g., subways, commuter rails, Amtrak)" from discriminating against people with disabilities. This often entails making services accessible or providing individualized transportation when needed.

Title III requires that "businesses and nonprofit service providers" that offer goods and services to the public provide equal opportunities to people with disabilities. These include "restaurants, retail stores, hotels, movie theaters, private schools, convention centers, doctors' offices, homeless shelters, transportation depots, zoos, funeral homes, day-care centers, and recreation facilities including sports stadiums and fitness clubs." Such accommodation often includes making locations accessible and making opportunities (e.g., for credentials requiring testing) or information available to people with disabilities.

Title IV requires that state and national telecommunication relay services accommodate people with hearing and speech impairments. These entities must allow people with such disabilities communications access 24 hours a day, 7 days a week. "Title IV also requires closed captioning of federally funded public service announcements."

In summary, the ADA requires "universal access to public buildings, transit systems, and communications networks" (Smolowe, 1995a, p. 54). Significant gains have been made in terms of curb ramps, wide bathroom stalls, and public vehicles with lifts for wheelchairs for persons with physical disabilities.

However, employers and public agencies must make only "reasonable accommodation." In reality, they are not compelled to provide such access or encouragement if the ensuing costs would result in "undue hardship," often in the form of "undue financial and administrative burdens." Because of the vagueness in terminology and lack of specification regarding how changes must be implemented, gains have been limited (Karger & Stoesz, 2013). What do the words *reasonable accommodation, undue hardship, and undue administrative and financial burdens* mean? What kind of accommodation is reasonable? How much money is unduly excessive? How can discrimination against capable people with intellectual or other specific disabilities be prohibited and equal opportunity enforced?

People with disabilities often experience "exclusion from typical activity and opportunity afforded to those who are

SPOTLIGHT ON DIVERSITY 3.8 *(continued)*

not considered disabled" (DePoy & Gilson, 2004, p. 41; Mackelprang, 2008; Mackelprang & Salsgiver, 2009). Consider the following economic facts about people with disabilities (U.S. Census Bureau, 2013):

● Only 33 percent are employed.
● The median earnings for people with a disability are $19,735 compared to $30,285 for people without a disability.
● Twenty-three percent of people with disabilities live in poverty compared to 15 percent without a disability living in poverty.

Additionally, bear in mind the following about people with disabilities (National Organization on Disability, 2004, 2011; Patchner & DeWeaver, 2008):

● Twenty-two percent report that they have been victims of discrimination in some situation.
● Twenty-two percent of those who are employed report having been victimized by discrimination on the job.
● The extent of disability directly impacts quality of life in virtually every aspect of living. Jimenez (2010) describes more recent ADA amendments:

The ADA Amendments Act of 2008 was designed to enlarge coverage of the ADA by overturning a series of U.S. Supreme Court cases, which limited the number of persons who could demonstrate they were disabled.

These new amendments call for "the definition of disability to be construed in favor of broad coverage of individuals," shifting the burden of proof to those who would deny disabled persons the protection of the law. The amendments favor broad coverage of conditions that interfere with activities of daily living, as well as thinking and learning, working, lifting, and speaking. Unfortunately, the amendments did not clarify the important question in the ADA of what are "reasonable accommodations" that employers must make for . . . persons [with disabilities]. Under the amendments, Congress recognized that . . . persons [with disabilities] are often denied the right to participate fully in society because of social prejudice, as well as due to the existence of societal and institutional barriers. (p. 193)

The battle for equal access and opportunity for people with disabilities has not been won. Much of the public attention to the act has focused on people with physical disabilities, many of whom require wheelchairs for transportation. Where do people with intellectual and other developmental disabilities fit in? The ADA "will be successful only to the extent that these individuals [with disabilities] and those who advocate on their behalf learn about the ADA and use it as a means to ensure employment [and other] opportunities" (Kopels, 1995, p. 345).

For additional information, go to the ADA homepage at http://www.ada.gov.

---

may reduce some of the alternatives available to an individual. However, other alternatives are available for that person to construct a rich, satisfying, and fulfilling life. A basic task of the social worker might be to help that person identify alternatives and weigh the various consequences of each.

Deinstitutionalization

Deinstitutionalization is the process of relocating people who need a significant level of care (e.g., people with intellectual disabilities, physical disabilities, or mental illness) from a structured institutional residence to a typical community setting. An assumption is that supportive community-based services and resources will take the institution's place in meeting people's needs.

Deinstitutionalization is supported by a number of rationales (Segal, 2008). First, the oppression caused by institutional living has been extensively documented. Second, costs of institutionalizing people are

high. Third, social research continues to document that total institutionalization is frequently ineffective. Fourth, social values have increasingly emphasized the civil rights of all citizens, including people with intellectual disabilities; institutionalization severely inhibits civil rights. Fifth, other policies have been developed to provide aid to people in ways other than placing them in large residential facilities.

Historically, most federal money has been spent on maintaining people with intellectual disabilities in institutional settings. Worse, most of these institutions were actually intended for housing people who had mental illnesses (Segal, 2008). Current legislation, however, supports deinstitutionalization and the development of alternative services.

Concerns about deinstitutionalization have focused on lack of sufficient resources to provide adequate services and care outside of institutions (Hallahan et al., 2012; Segal, 2008). If deinstitutionalization is to work effectively, community, state, and national macro systems must invest enough resources to provide adequate levels of support for people with varying needs.

Community-Based Services

If a trend is to move people with intellectual disabilities out of institutional settings and into communities, the subsequent question is, "Where?" Hallahan and his colleagues (2012) describe *community residential facilities (CRFs)* (also referred to as community-based residential facilities [CBRFs]) as:

> *group homes [that]… accommodate small groups (three to ten people) in houses under the direction of "house parents." Placement can be permanent, or it can serve as a temporary arrangement to prepare the individuals for independent living. In either case, the purpose of the CRF is to teach independent living skills in a more normal setting than a large institution offers.*
>
> *Some professionals question whether CRFs go far enough in offering opportunities for integration into the community. They recommend **supported living**, in which persons with intellectual disabilities receive supports to live in more natural, noninstitutional settings, such as their own home or apartment. (pp. 125–127)*

The key is to maximize self-determination while still providing adequate, necessary support. Much may depend on the individual's potential level of functioning.

An important concept related to community-based services is *normalization*. This means arranging the environmental context for people with intellectual disabilities so that it is as "normal" as possible. The lives of people who have intellectual disabilities should be as similar to those of people in the "normal," overall population as they can be.

⦁⦁⦁⦁ / Ethical Questions 3.4

EP 2.1.2 *Should people with intellectual disabilities be mainstreamed (i.e., be integrated into regular school classes) or be provided separate special education to meet their special needs? What are the pros and cons of each approach?*

Social Work Roles

Social workers can perform many roles when working with people who have intellectual or other developmental disabilities. Social workers can function as *enablers*, helping people with intellectual disabilities and their families make decisions and solve problems. Social workers can be *brokers*, linking clients to the resources (e.g., transportation, job placements, or group homes) they need in order to go about their daily lives. *Educator* is another major role. People who have intellectual disabilities may need information about employment, interpersonal relationships, and even personal hygiene. Social workers can also function as *coordinators* who oversee a range of support services that clients need.

EP 2.1.1c

Social workers can also fulfill roles within the macro-system context. They can assume administrative functions as *general managers* within agencies providing services to clients and their families. In this capacity, they can *evaluate* the effectiveness of the services provided. Are clients getting what they really need? Is service provision as efficient as possible? Finally, social workers can serve as *initiators*, *negotiators*, and *advocates*. In communities and states where needed services are not readily available or are nonexistent, practitioners can work with organizational, community, and government macro systems to change policies so that clients can have access to what they need.

Spotlight 3.9 discusses the importance of empowering people with disabilities to advocate for themselves and get control of their own lives.

LO 3-12 Examine Learning Disabilities

Learning disabilities are commonly defined in one of two ways—the federal definition established in P. L. 94-142 and the definition adopted by the National Joint Committee on Learning Disabilities (NJCLD) (Friend, 2011; Hallahan et al., 2012). The federal definition is as follows:

> *Specific learning disability means a disorder in one or more of the basic psychological processes involved in understanding or in using language, spoken or written, which disorder may manifest itself in the*

SPOTLIGHT ON DIVERSITY 3.9

Empowerment and a Consumer-Directed Approach

**EP 2.1.10c,
2.1.10e**

Mackelprang and Salsgiver (2009) call for social workers and other human services professionals to emphasize the empowerment of people with disabilities. They stress the importance of identifying and focusing on the strengths and abilities of people with disabilities and the necessity of supporting their self-advocacy. They focus on the need to recognize and appreciate human difference rather than problems in functioning. Such an empowerment stance highlights the following six principles:

1. "People with disabilities are capable, have potential, and are important members of society.
2. Devaluation and a lack of resources, not individual pathology, are the primary obstacles facing persons with disabilities.
3. Disability, like race and gender, is a social construct, and intervention with people with disabilities must be political in nature.
4. There is a Disability culture and history that professionals should be aware of in order to facilitate the empowerment of persons with disabilities.
5. There is a joy and vitality to be found in disability.
6. Persons with disabilities have the right to self-determination and the right to guide professionals' involvement in their lives" (Mackelprang & Salsgiver, 2009, pp. xv–xvii).

Lightfoot (2009b) elaborates on the importance of *consumer-directed services* (services that maximize the choice and self-determination of consumers, in this case, people with disabilities):

A growing trend in the area of disability policy is for people with disabilities to direct their own services. The move toward consumer-directed services, also known as consumer-controlled services, emanates from the concern that agency-controlled services often do not meet the individual needs of people with disabilities and further increase the dependence on professionals and systems that people with disabilities experience. When agencies control services, people with disabilities have little choice over the personnel providing services, including services that are quite personal in nature. Consumer-directed services allow people with disabilities to hire, train, supervise, and fire their own staff with public money. . . . [T]here are consumer-directed demonstration projects across the country that allow people of all ages who have disabilities to control the services they use (Benjamin, Matthias, & Franke, 2000; Mahoney, Simone, & Simon-Rusinowitz, 2000). Public social services policies for people with disabilities are likely to increasingly allow consumer-directed options, particularly as baby boomers age and desire more control over the supports they receive (p. 457).

---

imperfect ability to listen, think, speak, read, write, spell, or do mathematical calculations, including conditions such as perceptual disabilities, brain injury, minimal brain dysfunction, dyslexia, and developmental aphasia.... Disorders not included[:]... Specific learning disability does not include learning problems that are primarily the result of visual, hearing, or motor disabilities, of mental retardation, of emotional disturbance, or of environmental, cultural, or economic disadvantage. (Individuals with Disabilities Education Act [IDEA], 20 U.S.C. §1401 [2004], 20 CFR §300.8[c][10]) (U. S. Department of Education, n.d.)

The NJCLD is an organization made up of representatives from a range of professional organizations that deal with students who have learning disabilities (Hallahan et al., 2012). The NJCLD found the abovementioned federal definition lacking in several ways (Hallahan et al., 2012). First, the definition makes no reference to causal factors, whereas the NJCLD considers "central nervous system dysfunction within the individual" as the cause (p. 187). Second, there is no mention of adults and the fact that a learning disability is a lifelong condition. Third, the definition fails to indicate that people with learning disabilities often experience difficulties regulating their own behavior (including problem solving) and face problematic issues in social interaction. Fourth, the definition includes terms that are hard to define and understand (e.g., "perceptual handicaps" or "minimal brain dysfunction"). Fifth, the definition includes spelling, which NJCLD feels falls under the umbrella of writing. Sixth, it fails to note that learning disabilities may occur concurrently with other disabilities (Friend, 2011).

Therefore, the NJCLD (2010) defines learning disabilities as follows:

Learning disabilities is a general term that refers to a heterogeneous group of disorders manifested by significant difficulties in the acquisition and use of listening, speaking, reading, writing, reasoning, or mathematical abilities. These disorders are intrinsic to the individual, presumed to be due to central nervous system dysfunction, and may occur across the life span. Problems in self-regulatory behaviors, social perception, and social interaction may exist with learning disabilities but do not by themselves constitute a learning disability. Although learning disabilities may occur concomitantly with other handicapping conditions (for example, sensory impairment, mental retardation, serious emotional disturbance), or with extrinsic influences (such as cultural differences, insufficient or inappropriate instruction), they are not the result of those conditions or influences.

Both of these definitions are complex. Friend (2011) cites the following fundamental dimensions that characterize learning disabilities in general:

Learning disabilities comprise a heterogeneous group of disorders. Students with learning disabilities may have significant reading problems (dyslexia), difficulty in mathematics (dyscalculia), or a disorder related to written language (dysgraphia). They may have difficulty with social perceptions, motor skills, or memory. Learning disabilities can affect young children, students in school, and adults. No single profile of a person with a learning disability can be accurate because of the interindividual differences [relating to an individual's unique interacting traits] in the disorder.

- *Learning disabilities are intrinsic to the individual and have a neurobiological basis. Learning disabilities exist because of some type of dysfunction in the brain, not because of external factors such as limited experience or poor teaching.*
- *Learning disabilities are characterized by unexpected underachievement. That is, the disorder exists when a student's academic achievement is significantly below her intellectual potential even after intensive, systematic interventions have been implemented to try to reduce the learning gap….*

- *Learning disabilities are not a result of other disorders or problems, but individuals with learning disabilities may have other special needs as well. For example, being deaf cannot be considered to be the basis for having a learning disability. However, some students who are deaf also have learning disabilities. (Emphasis omitted.) (p. 129)*

A learning disability is different from either intellectual disability or emotional disturbance. Rather, learning disabilities entail a breakdown in processing information of some type. Difficulties involve either absorbing information in the first place or subsequently using this information to communicate and participate in activities. Spotlight 3.10 describes some other disabilities that can have an impact on children.

Children with learning disabilities currently make up just under 5 percent of schoolchildren ages 6 to 17, and about half of all students identified as needing placement in special education classes (Hallahan et al., 2012). Boys are three times more likely to have learning disabilities than girls (Hallahan et al., 2012; Santrock, 2012b).

It is often difficult to identify learning disabilities because the children in question function normally in other areas. The first clue is commonly a problem in academic work. Other symptoms include a lack of attentiveness in classes; thoughtless, impulsive, overly active behavior; frequent mood shifts; difficulties in remembering symbols; lack of motor coordination in writing or play activities; apparent problems in speaking or listening; and other difficulties in completing academic work. These difficulties are often vague enough to raise questions about a child's emotional health, family life, motivation to achieve, or intellectual level. Once a learning disability is suspected, assessment may involve standardized tests, such as achievement tests, as well as a range of other evaluative approaches, administered by teachers, that focus on individual work and progress.

Common Problems Involved in Learning Disabilities

Although people "with learning disabilities typically have average or above-average intelligence," they may experience weaknesses in one or more areas; a learning disability may involve cognitive, academic,

SPOTLIGHT ON DIVERSITY 3.10

Other Disabilities That Can Affect Children

EP 2.1.4

People with disabilities are at risk of being oppressed, discriminated against, ignored, ridiculed, and denied equal rights. Intellectual disabilities and learning disabilities are only two of the many disabilities that can affect children. Other disabilities arbitrarily mentioned here (considered developmental disabilities) include autistic spectrum disorders, cerebral palsy, hearing problems, vision problems, and epilepsy.

Autistic spectrum disorders (ASDs) "can cause significant social, communication and behavioral challenges" (CDC, 2010b). People with ASDs have brains that process information in ways unlike the brains of other people. Such a disorder reflects a lifelong condition that begins before age 3. Because ASDs involve a *spectrum*, people can experience aspects characterizing ASDs in different ways, ranging from mild to severe. People with ASDs typically demonstrate intense inner-directedness and a number of other symptoms (CDC, 2010b). These include difficulties in social skills, such as problems communicating and lack of normal emotional reactions to others, including attachment. They often have trouble talking about their own feelings or being aware of other people's feelings. People with ASDs may avoid eye contact and being physically touched. They frequently demonstrate sensory distortion such as underreacting to pain and overreacting to noise. They may engage in repetitive, self-stimulating movements and behavior such as hand flapping, spinning their bodies, or rocking back and forth.

Two types of autistic spectrum disorders are autistic disorder (also called classic autism) and Asperger syndrome (CDC, 2010b). People with *autistic disorder* or *autism* experience more severe symptoms, including difficulties in social interaction and bizarre behaviors. Often they also have an intellectual disability. *Asperger syndrome* involves a milder form of ASDs where people manifest fewer or less extreme symptoms. They may demonstrate difficulties in social interaction or some unusual behaviors, but generally have no problems

with language. They usually do not have an intellectual disability.

Cerebral palsy (CP) is a disability involving problems in muscular control and coordination resulting from damage to the brain's muscle-control centers before or during birth, or in the first years of life. Variations in muscle tone may result in movements that are very stiff and difficult, jerky, unbalanced, or floppy. Depending on the extent of damage, lack of balance, difficulty walking, tremors, involuntary movements, problems with precise motions, and difficulty talking or eating can result.

Hearing problems range from mild hearing losses to total deafness. They can result from any part of the ear not functioning normally and effectively. At least 50 percent of hearing problems in children are due to genetic causes, 25 percent to "maternal infections during pregnancy, complications after birth, and head trauma," and 25 percent to unknown factors (CDC, 2010d). Symptoms in infants may involve failure to respond to sounds and in young children delayed speech.

Vision impairment "means that a person's eyesight cannot be corrected to a 'normal' level. Vision impairment may be caused by a loss of visual acuity, where the eye does not see objects as clearly as usual. It may also be caused by a loss of visual field, where the eye cannot see as wide an area as usual without moving the eyes or turning the head" (CDC, 2010e). The severity of vision impairment may be classified in different ways. To be eligible for designated educational or federal programs in the United States, "blindness" is legally defined as visual acuity that is 20/200 or worse (i.e., when a person sees at 20 feet what a person with normal vision can see at 200 feet) (CDC, 2010e).

Epilepsy (commonly referred to as seizure disorder) consists of various disorders marked by disturbed electrical rhythms of the central nervous system and manifested in convulsive attacks. Symptoms range from periods of unconsciousness resembling daydreaming to violent convulsions.

Concurrent disabilities are also common. For example, a person with intellectual disabilities might also have a hearing impairment and/or epilepsy.

or social/emotional characteristics (Friend, 2011, p. 133). Remember that each individual is unique, and so could experience only one of these difficulties or any number of them. The categories often overlap, as cognitive characteristics and processing problems are integrally related to performance in other areas. Many examples and references presented here concern students and educational settings, because this is often where learning disabilities are discovered and addressed.

Cognitive Characteristics

These include "attention, perception, memory" (Friend, 2011, p. 133), and the organization and generalization of information (Smith & Tyler, 2010). People with learning disabilities may have trouble paying *attention* to what they're supposed to. They may be easily distracted by someone screaming in the hallway or a noisy vehicle traveling down the street. They may have difficulty discriminating between what is important in their immediate environment and what is not, what they should focus on and what they should ignore.

A second potential cognitive characteristic of a person with a learning disability involves perceptual difficulties. "*Perception* does not pertain to whether a student sees or hears but rather to how her brain interprets what is seen or heard and acts on it. For example, a student with a visual perception problem may see perfectly well the words on a page. However, when asked to read the words, the student may skip some of them" (Friend, 2011, p. 133). Another scenario is that a student might perceive items or symbols reversed from what they really are.

Perceptual difficulties may also involve understanding spatial relationships. Children might judge distances between one item and another inaccurately.

Perceptual problems may entail auditory processing difficulties. Some children have trouble paying attention to what is being said; the problem concerns being able to focus on the sounds most important in conveying meaning. Other children have trouble discriminating between one sound and another. For example, instead of hearing the word *bed*, a child may hear the word *dead*. The result is confusion for the child and difficulty in understanding and following instructions. Still, other children have trouble recalling what they have heard being said in the correct sequence. This also makes it difficult to follow instructions correctly. They cannot understand the proper order in which they are supposed to do things. These children have special difficulties in remembering content in a series format (e.g., months of the year).

A third cognitive characteristic for children with learning disabilities concerns *memory* and recall. Such children find it difficult to remember accurately what they have seen or heard. They commonly misspell words and forget where they placed objects.

A fourth cognitive trait often involved in learning disabilities entails lacking the ability to organize information received and generalize it to other scenarios. The *organization* of information concerns "classifying, associating, and sequencing" it so that it can be retrieved and generalized (Smith & Tyler, 2010, p. 164). *Generalization* involves the application of what you've already learned to new situations. For example, if you learn how to organize information and write a paper in your English course, you

could generalize this skill to writing a paper in your social welfare policy course.

Academic Characteristics

Learning disabilities involve cognitive characteristics and processing issues as were just discussed. However, learning disabilities become more readily apparent in academic performance. Difficulties may surface in "reading, spoken language, written language, mathematics, or any combination of these" (Friend, 2011, p. 134; Hallahan et al., 2012). Academic achievement deficits reflect the most common problem found in learning disabilities.

Some students have difficulty *reading*. They may have difficulties in processing that interfere with their ability to use language and reasoning. They might be unable to grasp the meanings of words or how words relate to each other in terms of grammatical position. They may have trouble comprehending what they've read, such as being unable to answer questions about a story after reading it. They often are unable to read efficiently and smoothly.

Oral language is another potential problematic area for people with learning disabilities. They may have difficulty "using the correct sounds to form words" (Friend, 2011, p. 134). They may not grasp grammar, discriminate among similar words, comprehend the meaning of words, or participate readily in conversations (Friend, 2011). They may have trouble saying what they mean or would like to say. Sometimes this involves having difficulty remembering the words they want to say. Still others have trouble telling a story so that it makes sense or describing an event or situation so that the listener can understand it.

Written language may also pose problems. Spelling, punctuation, capitalization, or understanding word forms (such as possessives or tenses) may be very difficult for them (Friend, 2011). As discussed earlier, students may have trouble organizing information into stories or term papers.

Still, other people with learning disabilities experience extreme difficulty with math. They can have problems grasping basic *math* fundamentals, fractions, calculation, measurement, time, or geometry (Friend, 2011; Hallahan et al., 2012).

Having a learning disability may involve *social/emotional characteristics* that increase the risk of social and emotional problems (Friend, 2011; Hallahan et al., 2012; Smith & Tyler, 2010). "For example, [children with learning disabilities] ... are at a greater risk for depression, social rejection, suicidal thoughts, and loneliness (Al-Yagon, 2007; Bryan, Burstein, & Ergul, 2004; Daniel et al., 2006; Maag & Reid, 2006; Margalit, 2006)" (Hallahan et al., 2012, p. 149).

Hallahan and his colleagues (2012) explain a possible rationale for social/emotional characteristics:

> *One plausible reason for the social problems of some students with learning disabilities is that these students have deficits in social cognition. That is, they misread social cues and may misinterpret the feelings and emotions of others. Most children, for example, can tell when their behavior is bothering others. Students with learning disabilities sometimes act as if they are oblivious to the effect their behavior is having on their peers. They also have difficulty taking the perspective of others, of putting themselves in someone else's shoes. (p. 150)*

What Causes Learning Disabilities?

The specific causes of learning disabilities in most children are unknown. As discussed earlier, it is thought the disabilities involve neurological dysfunction (Hallahan et al., 2012).

Potential causes tend to fall into three categories (Hallahan et al., 2012). The first involves genetic factors (Friend, 2011; Smith & Tyler, 2010). There is a tendency for learning disabilities to be more common in some families. This may be due to heredity or to the family being exposed to some causative agent in the environment. Second, *teratogens* (substances that can cause damage such as drugs causing malformation in the fetus) may cause learning disabilities. Malnutrition or poisoning by lead-based paint may also result in learning disabilities (Friend, 2011). Third, medical conditions such as premature birth or childhood AIDS may be directly related to the development of learning disabilities (Hallahan et al., 2012).

More extensive research concerning these possibilities is necessary to establish causes. The broad range of behaviors clustered under the title "learning disabilities" and their frequently vague descriptions make it difficult to pinpoint causal relationships.

Effects of Learning Disabilities on Children

Learning disabilities may psychologically affect children in several ways, including learned helplessness, low self-esteem, and lack of social competence.

EP 2.1.4c

The *learned helplessness reaction* is one way of responding to a learning disability (Friend, 2011; Hallahan et al., 2012; Smith & Tyler, 2010). This is the situation where children have failed so often that they no longer want to try to learn; instead they depend on others to do things for them. In other words, they lose their motivation to try and just give up. Because the child refuses to take any new risks, potential progress is halted. Children may also use the fact that they cannot do some things to get out of doing other things they are capable of doing. The vague and complicated nature of learning disabilities does not help this situation. For example, a mother may ask her daughter to do her homework. The daughter responds, "Gee, Mom, I don't know how." The daughter's learning disability involves reading. Her homework is an arithmetic assignment that she has no more difficulty completing than her peers. However, because of her learning disability, the daughter is perceived as being helpless in her mother's eyes. As a result, the mother does not make the daughter do her homework.

Another possible reaction of a child with learning disabilities is *low self-esteem* (Friend, 2011; Smith & Tyler, 2010). These children are likely to see other children do things they cannot. Perhaps others make critical comments to them. Teachers and parents may show at least some impatience and frustration at the children's inability to understand or perform in the areas affected by their learning disabilities. These children are likely to internalize their failures. The result may be that they feel inferior to others, and they may develop low self-esteem.

Research indicates that children with learning disabilities often suffer from a lack of social competence (Burden, 2008; Friend, 2011; Gumpel, 2007; Smith & Tyler, 2010). "*Social competence* is the ability to perceive and interpret social situations, generate appropriate social responses, and interact with others" (Smith & Tyler, 2010, p. 166). We've already established that some social/emotional learning disabilities may be related to the inability to interpret appropriately and accurately other people's interaction and communication. It makes sense that this would affect one's social competence and, in effect, popularity. For example, consider Melvin, a third grader, who's waiting in line to leave the classroom and go out for recess. The other kids are excitedly talking about what games they're going to play and who's going to get to the best playground equipment first. Melvin, oblivious, simply states, "I'm going to visit Uncle Harry on Sunday. He works for a cell phone company." Needless to say, this does not grab his peers' interest. Instead, they roll their eyes and start to make fun of him. Melvin didn't have a clue regarding what might have been a more appropriate thing to say in order to "fit in" better with his peers.

Note that certainly not all or even most people with learning disabilities experience these negative emotional and social effects. We've established that learning disabilities vary widely and are highly individualized. Many children with learning disabilities are happy, well adjusted, and well liked (Meadan & Halle, 2004). Much depends on the classroom climate, the actions of teachers and other professionals, and the establishment of a positive, supportive classroom and family environment. At school, emphasis should be placed on mutual respect and productive learning instead of focusing only on problems.

What are the long-term effects of learning disabilities? Some people with learning disabilities may continue to experience problems in work and social adjustment as adults. However, how people with learning disabilities are treated and accepted is critical in terms of their satisfaction and achievement as adults. Their coping skills and motivation are also important. The best predictors for successful transition into adulthood include the following:

- "An extraordinary degree of perseverance
- The ability to set goals for oneself
- A realistic acceptance of weaknesses coupled with an attitude of building on strengths
- Access to a strong network of social support from friends and family
- Exposure to intensive and long-term educational intervention
- High-quality on-the-job or postsecondary vocational training
- A supportive work environment
- Being able to take control of their lives." (Hallahan et al., 2012, p. 162)

Treatment for Learning Disabilities

There are two dimensions to treatment for learning disabilities. One concerns the educational environment and planning. The second involves parents' and others' treatment of a person with learning disabilities in the home and other social settings.

Educational treatment for children with learning disabilities focuses on designing an individualized educational program for the child to emphasize strengths and minimize weaknesses. For a child with a visual perceptual disorder, emphasis might be placed on providing material that the child can hear rather than see. For example, instead of reading an assignment in a textbook, the child might be given an audio recording of the assignment. Another means of tailoring an individualized educational program is breaking down tasks into smaller, more workable units so that children will more likely understand the process and achieve success.

Within the educational context, cognitive training and direct instruction are two major approaches to individualized instruction (Hallahan et al., 2012, pp. 151–154). *Cognitive training* is a method that focuses on procedures to teach children with learning disabilities how to change their patterns of thinking by emphasizing three tactics: "(1) changing thought processes, (2) providing strategies for learning, and (3) teaching self-initiative" (p. 151). The emphasis is on changing thinking patterns rather than observable external behavior.

One specific cognitive training technique is *self-instruction*, the process of making "students aware of the various stages of problem-solving tasks while they are performing them and to bring behavior under verbal control" (Hallahan et al., 2012, p. 151). Here, the idea is to develop the child's ability to attend to a task by breaking it up into a series of steps, modeling the task for the child, and then carefully supervising until he or she learns the process. For example, a five-step procedure for learning how to solve math word problems entails "saying the problem out loud, looking for important words and circling them, drawing pictures to help explain what was happening, writing the math sentence, and writing the answer" (Hallahan et al., 2012, p. 152).

A second major approach to individualized instruction is *direct instruction*. This method, usually used to improve math and reading skills, emphasizes drilling and practicing. It stresses "maximizing not only the quantity of instruction students receive but also the quality" (Friend, 2011, p. 152). Teachers instruct small groups of children with clearly specified lessons and provide them with immediate feedback, correcting wrong answers and praising right ones.

Outside the educational arena, children with learning disabilities need help within their family and other social settings. Some of the suggestions

**EP 2.1.10g,
2.1.10j**

for helping children in educational settings also apply to many social contexts. For example, the development of self-esteem and a positive self-concept is important in both educational and social environments (Raines, 2006). First, the positive things that children do should be emphasized. Problems are easy to see, but good behaviors and accomplishments often go unnoticed. Second, children should feel loved not for their behavior, but rather for whom they are. Third, confidence can be developed in children by giving them responsibility for things they are capable of accomplishing. Success at tasks helps them develop faith in themselves. Fourth, comparisons to others and what they accomplish should be avoided. The child's own accomplishments should be the focus of attention. Finally, structure in the form of clear guidelines for behavior is helpful. If the child knows what is acceptable and what is not, he or she is less likely to make mistakes. The child will also probably respond to the fact that someone cares enough to put forth the effort to provide structure.

Other forms of treatment are also used to enhance social functioning in families with a child who has learning disabilities. Educating both the child with a learning disability and those around that person can help all involved understand what the disability entails and modify their expectations accordingly. Individual and family counseling can improve communication and increase family members' understanding of how others view the disability. It can also help them develop problem solving strategies to improve a child's behavior and cope with interpersonal irritations.

Policies to Achieve Social Justice for Children Who Have Learning and Other Disabilities

EP 2.1.5b

Major legislation has positively affected educational programming for children with learning and other disabilities in the past few decades (Lightfoot, 2009b; Mackelprang, 2008). Mackelprang and Salsgiver (2009) explain:

The All Handicapped Children Act of 1975 is one of the few pieces of legislation known to professionals in human services and education by its original number, Pub. L. No. 94-142. The All Handicapped Children Act of 1975 went through several levels of evolution and was renamed the Individuals with Disabilities Education Act (IDEA) in 1990, and most recently the Individuals with Disabilities Education Improvement Act, which Congress last modified in 2004 ... Individuals from birth up through the age of twenty-one years are covered under this historic act. IDEA stipulates that "free appropriate public education" be provided at public expense to all children, including children with disabilities from age three through twenty-one years. The education of children with disabilities should be provided in the most open and "normal" environment possible (the least restrictive environment). When children need to be diagnosed, be evaluated, and receive prescriptions, the diagnosis, evaluation, and prescription should not produce stigmatization and discrimination. Parents and the child need to be primary players in any remedial or pedagogical plan established for the child's education (Albrecht, 1992; Altschuler, 2007).

The original legislation provided for the establishment of an Individual Education Program (IEP). IDEA maintains the IEP as the central process in the education of a child with a disability. These plans should delineate the current level of education of the child, the goals and objectives of the child's educational process, specific services needed and when they need to be provided, and the method by which the plan's implementation will be evaluated ...

Part C ... of IDEA mandates that participating states provide early intervention services to children with developmental disabilities from birth to their third birthday. In addition, Part C covers children and youths to age twenty-one....

It is important ... to understand some of the unique qualities of IDEA as a disability law. First, it covers... youths [with disabilities] through age twenty-one or until high school graduation, whichever comes first. Second, it mandates public support of substantial services placing financial and service responsibility on states and schools. Third, it mandates substantial involvement of both ... individuals [with disabilities] and their families. Fourth, IDEA is entitling legislation: not only are people eligible for services, but schools and states are responsible for providing services. (pp. 144–145)

Children with learning, intellectual, and other developmental disabilities are thus guaranteed the right to an education. States and communities cannot ignore or reject children with learning and other disabilities. Excuses such as high costs or lack of existing facilities are no longer acceptable. This illustrates how legislation forces state, community, and organizational macro systems to respond to a social need and seek social justice.

LO 3-13 Discuss Attention Deficit Disorder

One other condition merits attention because of its significance and prevalence for children of school age. It has been labeled, studied, and given much public attention. *Attention deficit hyperactivity disorder (ADHD)*, a psychiatric diagnosis, is a syndrome of learning and behavioral problems beginning before age 12 that is characterized by a persistent pattern of inattention, excessive physical movement, and impulsivity that appears in at least two settings (including home, school, work, or social contexts) (APA, 2013a). It is estimated that about 5 percent of all children and 2.5 percent of adults in most cultures have ADHD (APA, 2013a). Note that "ADHD often occurs simultaneously with other behavioral and/or learning problems such as learning disabilities or emotional or behavioral disorders" (Hallahan et al., 2012, p. 182). ADHD is more likely to affect boys more than girls by an estimated 3:1 ratio (Barkley, 2006; Kail & Cavanaugh, 2013).

The definition of ADHD has several dimensions. First, a child manifests a pattern of ADHD symptoms before the age of 7, although the pattern may not be identified until much later. A second dimension of ADHD is that it occurs in multiple settings, not just in one context or with one person. It involves uncontrollable behavior that is not necessarily related to a particular context. Finally, three primary clusters of behavior characterize ADHD. The first is *inattention*. Behavioral symptoms include messy work, carelessly handled tasks, frequent preoccupation, easy distractibility, aversion to tasks that require attention and greater mental exertion, serious problems in organizing tasks and activities, and difficulties attending to ongoing conversations. The second cluster of behaviors concerns *hyperactivity*, excessive physical activity that is difficult to control, resulting from an "impaired ability to sit or concentrate for long periods of time" (Smith & Tyler, 2010, p. 203). That is difficult to control (hyperactivity). This involves almost constant action, squirming or being unable to sit down at all, demonstrating great difficulty in attending to quiet activities, and talking nonstop. The third batch of behaviors falls under the umbrella of *impulsivity*. This is characterized by extreme impatience, having great difficulty in waiting for one's turn, and making frequent interruptions and intrusions.

Treatment for ADHD

ADHD has been treated for decades by using drugs that "stimulate the parts of the brain that normally inhibit hyperactive and impulsive behavior. Thus, stimulants [e.g., Ritalin] actually have a calming influence for many youngsters with ADHD, allowing them to focus their attention" (Kail & Cavanaugh, 2013, p. 227). However, some questions have been raised about the effectiveness of long-term drug use (Hardman et al., 2014; Kail & Cavanaugh, 2013). Other treatment methods such as family intervention and provision of special treatment to children along with drug therapy are also frequently used.

Additional techniques suggested to help children who have ADHD involve providing a structured classroom environment with minimal distracting stimuli. For example, the student with ADHD might be given "a desk or work area in a quiet, relatively distraction-free area of the classroom. Other physical accommodations can include pointers or bookmarks to help a student track words visually during reading exercises, timers to remind students how much time is left before an assignment must be finished, [and] visual cues as prompts to change behavior (e.g., turning the classroom lights off to indicate that the noise level is too high)" (Smith & Tyler, 2010, p. 214). Other suggestions for the classroom include providing "directions that are clear, concise, and thorough (even better when they are presented both visually and orally)" and immediate, periodic praise for completing tasks successfully (Smith & Tyler, 2010, p. 214).

Behavior modification also offers techniques that are helpful for children with ADHD (Friend, 2011). Chapter 4 discusses behavior modification techniques with respect to effective parenting. For ADHD children, behavior modification focuses on specifying and reinforcing good behavior and decreasing poor behavior by monitoring and structuring each behavior's consequences.

A major ongoing study initiated in the 1990s and sponsored by the National Institute of Mental Health is being conducted to evaluate the effectiveness of both drug and psychosocial treatment (i.e., psychologically and behaviorally oriented intervention with child and family) (Richters et al., 1995). Kail and Cavanaugh (2013) summarize findings. Initial results indicate that medication can often be effective in treating hyperactivity as such. However, related issues including specific academic problems, social skill development, and working in conjunction with parents are addressed slightly better when medication is administered along with the provision of psychosocial treatment. It should also be noted that medication is only effective when it is closely monitored with consistent visits to health-care providers and there is ongoing communication with school staff about the drug's effects and the child's behavior.

Friend (2011) expresses a number of factors to consider before using ADHD drug treatment, including the following:

- "The child's age
- Prior attempts at other interventions and their impact on the behaviors of concern
- Parent and child attitudes toward using medication…
- Severity of symptoms
- Availability of adults in the household to supervise use of medications, ensuring that medications are taken regularly and as prescribed." (p. 182)

Social Work Roles

**EP 2.1.1c,
2.1.5b**

Social work roles with respect to clients with both ADHD and learning disabilities are similar to those used with clients who have intellectual disabilities. Social workers function as brokers to help link clients with resources. In the school setting, "besides participating in the multidisciplinary team conferences and consultation, social workers coordinate IEP [Individualized Education Program] and IFSP [Individualized Family Service Plan] conferences, serve as trained mediators,… lead parent education and informational groups, function

as case managers, and facilitate the development of relationships that link the services of the school with those found in the community" (Atkins-Burnett, 2010, p. 187). Practitioners also function as advocates to effect positive change in macro systems that are not responsive to clients' needs.

Chapter Summary

The following summarizes this chapter's content as it relates to the learning objectives presented at the beginning of the chapter. Chapter content will help prepare students to:

LO 3-1 Summarize psychological theories about personality development (including psychodynamic, neo-Freudian psychoanalytic, behavioral, phenomenological, and feminist theories).

Freud's psychoanalytic theory, the predominant psychodynamic theory, emphasizes concepts including the id, superego, ego, libido, fixation, defense mechanisms, Oedipus complex, and Electra complex. His proposed stages of psychosexual development are oral, anal, phallic, latency, and genital. Freud's phases of psychosexual and personality development include the oral, anal, phallic, latency, and genital stages. Criticisms of psychoanalytic theory include a lack of supportive research, poor clarity of ideas, and failure to adequately address the status of women.

The neo-Freudian psychoanalytic theorists include Carl Jung, Erich Fromm, Alfred Adler, and Harry Stack Sullivan. Theoretical emphases include analytic psychology for Jung, a social context for Fromm, individual psychology for Adler, and individual personality development based on interpersonal relationships for Sullivan.

Behavioral theories, one of the most useful conceptual frameworks for understanding human behavior, are discussed more thoroughly in Chapter 4. They focus on specific observable behaviors instead of on internal motivations, needs, and perceptions.

The self theory of Carl Rogers is a phenomenological approach that emphasizes the ideas of self-concept, self-actualization, ideal self, incongruence between self and experience, the need for positive regard, and conditions of worth, among others.

Feminist theories are based on the concept of feminism and reflect a range of theories. Major underlying principles include the elimination of false dichotomies, rethinking knowledge, differences in male and female experiences throughout the life span, egalitarianism, empowerment, valuing process equally with product, the personal as political, unity and diversity, and the importance of advocating for positive change on women's behalf. Diverse feminist theories include liberal feminism, cultural feminism, Marxist or socialist feminism, radical feminism, and postmodern feminism. People progress through several phases in the process of feminist identity development.

LO 3-2 Use critical thinking to evaluate theory.

Determining theories' relevance to social work involves evaluating each theory's application to client situations, the research supporting the theory, the extent to which the theory coincides with social work values and ethics, and the existence and validity of other comparable theories.

LO 3-3 Relate human diversity to psychological theories.

It is important to be sensitive to diversity when examining psychological theories. Important concepts are worldview, spirituality, and the strengths perspective.

LO 3-4 Examine Piaget's theory of cognitive development.

Piaget's theory of cognitive development includes four stages: the sensorimotor period, the preoperational thought period, the period of concrete operations, and the period of formal operations. Important concepts include conservation, schema, adaptation, assimilation, accommodation, object permanence, representation, egocentrism, centration, irreversibility, classification, and seriation. Criticisms of Piaget's theory include the fact that it was based on observations of his own children, its focus on the "average child," and its limited consideration of other dimensions of human development.

LO 3-5 Review the information-processing conception of cognitive development.

The information-processing approach to cognitive development relates human thought to how computers function with both hardware and software. The physical cognitive structure in the brain is compared to computer hardware. Established processes regarding how thought takes place in the brain is related to software programs. As children mature, they increase their ability to process information and solve problems. Important concepts include attention, memory (including sensory, short-term, and long-term), and information-processing strategies.

LO 3-6 Apply Vygotsky's theory of cognitive development.

Vygotsky's theory of sociocultural cognitive development emphasizes how children develop differently depending on the social and cultural circumstances and expectations evident in their environment. Children learn as they interact with and observe others, framing their development with the use of language. North American culture emphasizes the development of independence, whereas many other cultures encourage mutual dependence. Important concepts include the zone of proximal development, scaffolding, and private speech. Positive aspects of the theory include the appreciation of diversity and the potential for individuals to promote their own cognitive development. Criticisms include its neglect of aspects of learning other than verbal and its inattentiveness to the biological side of development.

LO 3-7 Explain emotional development (including the development of temperament and attachment).

People begin displaying their emotions and temperament in infancy. Early behaviors include crying, smiling, and laughing. A major variable related to overall adjustment may be the "goodness" or "poorness" of fit between the individual and the impinging environment. Cultural values affect the development of temperament.

Infants tend to pass through various stages as they form social and emotional attachments with adults. Secure attachment is the most common pattern of attachment. Other patterns include anxious-avoidant attachment, anxious-resistant attachment, and disorganized attachment. Being in quality day care does not interfere with the attachment process between child and parents. Cross-cultural differences in attachment exist.

LO 3-8 Examine self-concept, self-esteem, and empowerment.

One's self-concept is the personal impression of one's own unique attributes and traits, both positive and negative. Self-esteem is a person's judgment of his or her own value. It is important to strengthen children's self-concepts and enhance their self-esteem, especially for those children with exceptionally low self-esteem.

LO 3-9 Discuss intelligence and intelligence testing.

Intelligence is the ability to understand, learn, and deal with new, unknown situations. Cattell identifies two types of intelligence: fluid and crystallized. Sternberg's triarchic theory of intelligence emphasizes componential, experiential, and contextual elements.

LO 3-10 Explain cultural biases and IQ tests.

Intelligence tests include the Stanford-Binet IQ test and the Wechsler Intelligence Scale tests. Giftedness involves analytic, synthetic, and practical abilities. It is critical to be vigilant concerning the potential for cultural biases and other potential problems in IQ tests.

LO 3-11 Analyze intellectual disabilities and the importance of empowerment.

Intellectual disability is a condition characterized by intellectual functioning that is significantly below average and accompanying deficits in adaptive functioning, both of which occur before reaching adulthood. Support systems are important for people with intellectual disabilities. Problem areas for people with intellectual disabilities include attention, memory, language development, self-regulation, motivation, and social development. Macro-system responses to intellectual disabilities include deinstitutionalization, community-based services, and the Americans with Disabilities Act.

LO 3-12 Examine learning disabilities.

Learning disabilities involve a heterogeneous group of neurological disorders resulting in perceptual processing problems in learning to read, communicate verbally, understand math, perceive social interactions, use motor skills, or maintain memory. They may involve one or more of these areas and are characterized by underachievement. Although learning disabilities are not the result of other disorders, people with learning disabilities may have other disorders. Characteristics of learning disabilities include cognitive, academic, or social/emotional aspects.

Specific causes of learning disabilities are as yet unknown, although they are thought to involve neurological dysfunction. Learning disabilities may psychologically affect children in several ways,

including learned helplessness, low self-esteem, and lack of social competence. Treatment approaches may involve the school or family and social settings. The Individuals with Disabilities Education Improvement Act (IDEA) has expanded educational opportunities for children with learning and other disabilities.

Other conditions that can affect children include autistic spectrum disorders, cerebral palsy, hearing problems, vision impairment, and epilepsy. People may have concurrent disabilities.

LO 3-13 Discuss attention deficit disorder.

Attention deficit hyperactivity disorder (ADHD) is a syndrome of learning and behavioral problems beginning in childhood that is characterized by a persistent pattern of inattention, excessive physical movement, and impulsivity occurring before age 12 that appears in at least two settings. Treatment may involve medical drugs and/or family intervention and special treatment.

COMPETENCY NOTES

The entire chapter addresses competency Educational Policy (EP) EP 2.1.7 and its respective practice behaviors EP 2.1.7a and EP 2.1.7b (as cited below). (See p. 113.)

EP 2.1.7 Apply knowledge of human behavior and the social environment.

EP 2.1.7a Utilize conceptual frameworks to guide the processes of assessment, intervention, and evaluation,
(Such conceptual frameworks will typically be identified by a "helping hands" icon.)

EP 2.1.7b Critique and apply knowledge to understand person and environment.
Other EP competencies and practice behaviors addressed in this chapter include the following:

EP 2.1.1b Practice personal reflection and self-correction to assure continual professional development.
(p. 131): As an ongoing process, social workers must continue to reflect on their own worldviews and distinguish these from the worldviews of others.

EP 2.1.1c Attend to professional roles and boundaries.
(p. 164): Social work roles with respect to people who have intellectual or other developmental disabilities are described.

(p. 173): It is important for social workers to attend to the appropriate roles when working with people who have ADHD and learning disabilities. These roles are comparable to those assumed when working with people who have intellectual disabilities.

EP 2.1.1e Engage in career-long learning.
(p. 131): Learning about the worldviews of others is a career-long process.

EP 2.1.2 Apply social work ethical principles to guide professional practice.
(pp. 126, 156, 161, 164): Ethical questions are raised.

EP 2.1.2b Make ethical decisions by applying standards of the National Association of Social Workers (NASW) Code of Ethics and, as applicable, of the International Federation of Social Workers/International Association of Schools of Social Work Ethics in Social Work, Statement of Principles.
(p. 128): Theories should be evaluated regarding how they coincide with the NASW Code of Ethics.

EP 2.1.3 Apply critical thinking to inform and communicate professional judgments.
(p. 118): Psychodynamic theory is evaluated.
(p. 127): A means of evaluating theory is provided.

EP 2.1.3a Distinguish, appraise, and integrate multiple sources of knowledge, including research-based knowledge, and practice wisdom.
(p. 127): The relevance of theory to social work is examined.
(p. 127): Social workers should consider and evaluate a wide range of theories to determine which have the most effective application in practice.

EP 2.1.3b Analyze models of assessment, prevention, intervention, and evaluation.
(p. 127): A model for critically thinking about and assessing the relevance of a theory is described.
(p. 137): Piaget's conceptual framework for assessing cognitive development is evaluated.

EP 2.1.4 Engage diversity and difference in practice.
(p. 132): Religion and spirituality are dimensions of diversity.

(p. 142): Culture is a significant aspect of diversity regarding how children learn to be interdependent or independent.
(p. 148): Culture, an aspect of diversity, affects children's development of temperament.
(p. 151): Attachment levels differ depending on culture, a dimension of diversity.
(p. 158): Intellectual disabilities are included under the umbrella of disability, an aspect of diversity.
(p. 167): There is a wide range of diversity in disability.

EP 2.1.4a Recognize the extent to which culture's structures and values may oppress, marginalize, alienate, or create or enhance privilege and power.
(p. 130): Social workers should evaluate how psychological theories are sensitive to various characteristics involved in human diversity.
(p. 157): Culture is a facet of diversity that can negatively affect people's performance on IQ tests.
(p. 161): Societal support is critical in crushing the oppression experienced by and enhancing the well-being of people with intellectual disabilities.

EP 2.1.4c Recognize and communicate their understanding of the importance of difference in shaping life experiences.
(p. 169): Learning disabilities are an aspect of diversity that shapes life experiences.

EP 2.1.5a Understand the forms and mechanisms of oppression and discrimination.
(p. 162): The ADA seeks to enhance social and economic justice for people with disabilities by fighting oppression and discrimination, and providing equitable treatment.

EP 2.1.5b Advocate for human rights and social and economic justice.
(p. 124): Feminist conceptual frameworks emphasize advocating for equal rights and enhanced opportunities.
(p. 162): Practitioners should support legislation that advances social and economic justice for persons with disabilities.
(p. 171): Social workers should advocate for policies that advance social and economic justice on the behalf of people with learning disabilities and ADHD.
(p. 173): Social workers should advocate for the human rights of people with disabilities.

EP 2.1.5c Engage in practices that advance social and economic justice.

(p. 124): Feminist theories stress working for improved structural and attitudinal changes to enhance social and economic justice.

(p. 131): To seek social and economic justice for clients, social workers must be aware of their clients' worldviews.

(p. 162): Social workers should engage in practices that advance social and economic justice for people with disabilities.

EP 2.1.6b Use research evidence to inform practice.

(p. 127): Social workers should utilize research on practice effectiveness to guide their practice.

EP 2.1.7a Utilize conceptual frameworks to guide the processes of assessment, intervention, and evaluation.

(p. 114): Psychodynamic, neo-Freudian psychoanalytic, phenomenological, and feminist conceptual frameworks are described, with a brief mention of a behavioral approach.

(p. 127): A brief history of conceptual frameworks used in social work is discussed and critiqued.

(p. 129): Piaget's theory provides a conceptual framework for understanding cognitive development.

(p. 141): Vygotsky provides another conceptual framework for understanding cognitive development.

EP 2.1.7b Critique and apply knowledge to understand person and environment.

(p. 127): A procedure for critiquing the application of knowledge to social work practice is provided.

EP 2.1.9a Continuously discover, appraise, and attend to changing locales, populations, scientific and technological developments, and emerging societal trends to provide relevant services.

(p. 127): Practitioners must continuously respond to and appraise new theories and developments that may affect practice.

EP 2.1.10c Develop a mutually agreed-on focus of work and desired outcomes.

(p. 165): A consumer-directed approach means that clients use self-determination and make their own decisions with the worker's assistance, rather than being told what they should do by the worker.

EP 2.1.10e Assess clients' strengths and limitations.

(p. 132): Social workers should assess, appreciate, and emphasize clients' strengths.

(p. 165): A consumer-directed approach emphasizes the assessment and use of clients' strengths.

EP 2.1.10g Select appropriate intervention strategies.

(p. 171): When working with people who have learning disabilities and their families, practitioners should select appropriate interventions.

EP 2.1.10j Help clients resolve problems.

(p. 171): Social workers may help people with learning disabilities and their families resolve problems.

WEB RESOURCES

See this text's companion website at www.cengage brain.com for learning tools such as chapter quizzing, videos, and more.

CHAPTER 4

SOCIAL DEVELOPMENT IN INFANCY AND CHILDHOOD

Yellow Dog Productions/Getty Images.

"My dad could punch out your dad, I bet!" Jimmy yelled at Harry, the neighborhood bully. Harry had just bopped Jimmy in the nose. Jimmy, who was small for his age, felt hurt. So he resorted to name calling as he edged away from his aggressor. Since his own house was a full two blocks away, Jimmy had to do some fast thinking about how to get there without everybody thinking he was chicken. The worst thing was that Harry was also a pretty fast runner.

To Jimmy's surprise and delight, Harry was apparently losing interest in this particular quarry. Somebody called out from the next block and was trying to interest Harry, a good fullback, in a game of football.

Scowling, Harry shouted back to Jimmy, "Oh, get out of here, you nose wad. Your dad sucks eggs!" He then darted down the block and into the sunset.

That last remark did not make much sense, although Harry's intent was to be as nasty as possible (intellect was not his strong suit). The important thing, however, was that Harry was running in the other direction. Any of the other guys who happened to witness this incident might just think that it was Harry who was running scared. Nonetheless, Jimmy thought it best not to reply, just in case Harry decided to change his mind.

"Whew!" thought Jimmy. "That was a close one." He was usually pretty good at staying far out of Harry's way. This meeting was purely an accident. He was on his way home from a friend's house after working on a class project. That was another story. Their project involved growing bean plants under different lighting conditions. The bean plants that were supposed to be growing good beans weren't. Jimmy secretly suspected that his partner was eating the beans.

Anyway, Jimmy had better things to do now. He had to finish his homework. His parents had promised to buy him an Xbox if he maintained at least a B+ average for the whole year. Harry would probably flunk this year anyhow. He was big, but he was also pretty stupid.

Jimmy hightailed it down the street. He imagined hearing the tones of Ear Discharge, his favorite hip-hop group. The horrible Harry affair was soon forgotten.

A Perspective

The attainment of primary social developmental milestones and the significant life events that usually accompany them have tremendous impacts on the developing individual and that individual's transactions with the environment. Family and peer group mezzo systems are dynamically involved in children's growth, development, and behavior. Social interaction in childhood provides the foundation for building an adult social personality. Children and their families do not function in a vacuum. Macro systems within the environment, including communities, government units, and agencies, can provide necessary resources to help families address issues and solve problems typically experienced by children. Impinging macro systems within the social environment can either help or hinder family members in fulfilling their potential.

Learning Objectives

This chapter will help prepare students to:

**EP 2.1.7,
2.1.7a,
2.1.7b**

LO 4-1 *Explain the concept of socialization*

LO 4-2 *Analyze the family environment (including variations in family structures, positive family functioning, macro systems and the pursuit of social and economic justice, and family system dynamics)*

LO 4-3 *Apply systems theory concepts to families*

LO 4-4 *Assess the family life cycle*

LO 4-5 *Explain diverse perspectives on the family life cycle*

LO 4-6 *Describe learning theory*

LO 4-7 *Apply learning theory concepts to practice (including positive reinforcement, punishment, issues related to the application of learning theory, and time-out from reinforcement)*

LO 4-8 *Examine common life events that affect children (including treatment of children in families, sibling subsystems, and gender-role socialization)*

LO 4-9 *Recognize ethnic and cultural differences in families*

LO 4-10 *Assess relevant aspects of the social environment (including the social aspects of play with peers, bullying, the influence of television and the media, and the school environment)*

LO 4-11 *Examine child maltreatment (including incidence, physical child abuse, child neglect, psychological maltreatment, Child Protective Services, treatment approaches for child maltreatment, and sexual abuse)*

LO 4-1 Explain the Concept of Socialization

Socialization is the process whereby children acquire knowledge about the language, values, etiquette, rules, behaviors, social expectations, and all the subtle, complex bits of information necessary to get along and thrive in a particular society.

Although socialization continues throughout life, most of it occurs in childhood. Children need to learn how to interact with other people. They must learn which behaviors are considered acceptable and which are not. For example, children should learn that they must abide by the directives of their parents, at least most of the time. They must learn how to communicate to others what they require in terms of food and comfort. On the other hand, they must also learn what behaviors are not considered appropriate. They need to learn that breaking windows and spitting in the eyes of other people when they don't get their way will not be tolerated.

Because children start with knowing nothing about their society, the most awesome socialization occurs during childhood. This is when the fundamental building blocks of their consequent attitudes, beliefs, and behaviors are established.

LO 4-2 Analyze the Family Environment

Because children's lives are centered initially within their families, the family environment becomes the primary agent of socialization. The family environment involves the circumstances and social climate within families. Because each family is made up of different individuals in a different setting, each family environment is unique. The environments can differ in many ways. For example, one obvious difference is socioeconomic level. Some families live in luxurious 24-room estates, own a Mercedes and an SUV in addition to the family minivan, and can afford to have shrimp cocktail for an appetizer whenever they choose. Other families subsist in two-room shacks, struggle with payments on their used 1998 Chevy, and have to eat macaroni made with processed cheese four times a week.

This section addresses several aspects of the family environment. They include variations in family structures, positive family functioning, impacts of social forces and policies on family systems, and the application of systems theory principles to families.

Membership in Family Groups: Variations in Family Structure

Families in the United States today are no longer characterized by two first-time married parents who live blissfully together with their 2.5 children. The traditional nuclear family included heterosexual parents married one time, with one or more children. Today's families are more likely to reflect a varied medley of structures and configurations. *Family structure* is "the nuclear family as well as those non-traditional alternatives to nuclear family which are adopted by persons in committed relationships and the people they consider to be 'family'" (Commission of the Council on Social Work Education, 2002). Scrutinizing this definition shows how flexible the notion of family has become.

A family is a *primary group* defined as people who have close personal relationships, interact often with each other, have shared expectations regarding how members in the group should behave, and are exposed to the same ongoing forces and experiences (Barker, 2014). Thus, family members as members of a primary group have significant influence on each other. They have mutual commitment and responsibility for other family members. Additionally, they interact frequently with each other, often living together.

Families, then, may consist of intact two-parent families with or without children, single-parent families, blended families, stepfamilies, or any other configuration that fits our definition. Some of these terms are defined as follows.

A *single-parent family* is a family household in which one parent resides with the children but without the other parent. (Note that a *household* "comprises all persons who occupy a 'housing unit,' that is, a house, an apartment or other group of rooms, or a single room that constitutes 'separate living quarters'" [U.S. Census Bureau, 2009, p. 6].) Almost 30 percent of all households with their own children under age 18 are headed by single parents; more than 79 percent of these single-parent families are headed by women (U.S. Census Bureau, 2009).

Stepfamilies are families in which one or both parents reside with children from prior marriages or unions. Members may include stepmothers, stepfathers, and any children either may have from prior marriages. Stepfamilies may also include children

The family environment involves the unique circumstances and social climate within a family.

born to the currently married couple. Stepfamilies have become extremely common because about half of all marriages end in divorce. Stepfamilies may also become very complex when one or both spouses have been married more than once and/or have children from a variety of relationships.

A *blended family* is any nontraditional configuration of people who live together, are committed to each other, and perform functions traditionally assumed by families. Such relationships may not involve biological or legal linkages. The important thing is that such groups *function* as families.

Several other changes from traditional patterns characterize today's family life (Mooney, Knox, & Schacht, 2013):

- *Marrying later or not at all.* Both men and women are waiting much longer to marry. In 1960, the median age for men to marry was 23 and women 20; now men marry at the median age of 28 and women at 26 (Mooney et. al., 2013). At present, 13.8 percent of women and 20.4 percent of men in the 40 to 44 age group have never been married; this is the highest percentage ever in the United States (Mooney et al., 2013).
- *Living together without being married.* Heterosexual and same-gender cohabitation without marriage has escalated significantly in recent years (Mooney et al., 2013). *Cohabitation* is the situation where two adults share the same residence and have a sexual relationship, without the legality of marriage.

    One recent study revealed the following results:

    — In more recent years, women were increasingly likely to cohabit with a partner as a first union rather than to marry directly: 48% of women interviewed in 2006–2010 cohabited as a first union, compared with 43% in 2002 and 34% in 1995.
    — The rise in cohabitation as a first union over this time period led to a lower percentage of women aged 15–44 whose first union was a marriage: 23% in 2006–2010 compared with 30% in 2002 and 39% in 1995.
    — An increase in cohabitation as a first union for all Hispanic origin and race groups occurred between 1995 and 2006–2010, except among Asian women. The percentage of women who cohabited as a first union increased 57% for

Hispanic women, 43% for white women and 39% for black women over this time period. (Copen, Daniels, & Mosher, 2013, p. 3)

- *Being together but living separately.* This new phenomenon involves couples who are married or "together" emotionally and sexually, but live in different cities or states. Many of these couples live apart because of being employed in different locations; however, some choose to live apart to maintain a sort of freedom and avoid daily conflicts resulting from too much intimacy (Mooney et al., 2013). This phenomenon has been observed not only in the United States, but also in various Western European nations (Levin, 2004).
- *Increased births to single women.* Of all births, the percentage to unmarried women is 40.7 percent; this reflects a rise from 18 percent in 1980, to 33 percent in 1994, to between 32 and 34 percent in 2002 (ChildStats.gov, 2013). In almost 75 percent of all births to women under age 25, the women were unmarried (ChildStats.gov, 2013).
- *Higher divorce rates and more stepfamilies.* Divorce will terminate between 40 and 50 percent of all marriages (Cherlin, 2010). A majority of divorced people will remarry and form stepfamilies (Mooney et al., 2013). Over 40 percent of adults living in the United States have a minimum of one person in their family that is a step-relative (Parker, 2011).
- *More mothers being employed.* About 72 percent of single women with children under age 18 and almost 70 percent of married women with such children are employed outside the home (U.S. Census Bureau, 2011). These figures have increased from 52 percent and more than 54 percent, respectively, since 1980 (U.S. Census Bureau, 2011). Note that women with small children are also likely to work. Almost 68 percent of single women and 61.6 percent of married women who have children under age 6 work outside the home (U.S. Census Bureau, 2011).

Positive Family Functioning

In view of the vast range of family configurations, it is extremely difficult to define a "healthy" family. However, at least two concepts are important when assessing the effectiveness of a family. These include how well *family functions* are undertaken and how well family members *communicate* with each other.

Family functions include a wide range of caregiving functions, including nurturing and socializing children, providing material and emotional support, and assuming general responsibility for the well-being of all members. Children must be nurtured and taught. All family members need adequate resources to thrive. Additionally, family members should be able to call on each other for help when necessary.

Good communication is the second characteristic of "healthy" families. Communication and autonomy are closely related concepts. Good communication involves clear expression of personal ideas and feelings even when they differ from those of other family members. On the other hand, good communication also involves being sensitive to the needs and feelings of other family members. Good communication promotes compromise so that the most important needs of all involved are met. In families that foster autonomy, boundaries for roles and relationships are clearly established. All family members are held responsible for their own behavior. Under these conditions, family members much less frequently feel the need to tell others what to do or "push each other around." (Family communication is discussed more thoroughly in Chapters 8 and 12.)

Negotiation is also clearly related to good communication and good relationships. When faced with decisions or crises, healthy families involve all family members, so as to come to solutions for the mutual good. Conflicts are settled through rational discussion and compromise instead of open hostility and conflict. If one family member feels strongly about an issue, healthy families work to accommodate his or her views in a satisfactory way. Both unhealthy and healthy families suffer conflict and disagreements, but a healthy family deals with conflict much more rationally and effectively.

Families can be compared and evaluated on many other dimensions and variables. The specific variables are not as important as the concept that children are socialized according to the makeup of their individual family environments. The family teaches children what types of transactions are considered appropriate. They learn how to form relationships, handle power, maintain personal boundaries, communicate with others, and feel that they are an important subset of the whole family system.

Macro Systems, Families, and the Pursuit of Social and Economic Justice

EP 2.1.5,
2.1.8a

We have established that families provide an immediate, intimate social environment for children as they develop. However, families do not exist in a vacuum. They are in constant interaction with numerous other systems permeating the macro social environment. Families can provide care and nurturance only to the extent that other macro systems in the environment, including communities and organizations, provide support and empower them.

For example, unemployment may soar because of an economic slump. Political decisions such as increasing business taxes may have sparked the slump. Ideologically, the general public may feel that in "a free country" of rugged individualists, it is each person's responsibility to find and succeed in work. The public may not support political decisions to subsidize workers by providing long-term unemployment benefits or developing programs for job retraining. At the same time, legislators concerned about the increasing unemployment rate and their reelection may hesitate to impose increasing restrictions on business and industry such as more stringent (and more costly) pollution control regulations. Thus, the physical environment suffers.

This example, of course, is overly simplistic. Volumes have been written on each aspect of the political, economic, environmental, and ideological dimensions of the social environment. However, the point is that it is impossible to comprehend a family's situation without assessing that family within the context of the macro social environment. For example, economic downturns and unemployment may leave a parent jobless and poverty-stricken. That parent will then be less able to provide the food, shelter, health care, and other necessities for a family environment in which children can flourish.

Likewise, the resources available to agencies and communities for dispersal to clients depend on legislative and organizational policies. For instance, U.S. society is structured such that all citizens have the right to receive a high school education. This idea is based in ideology that, in turn, is reflected by legislative and administrative policy that regulates how that education is provided.

Public day care or child care, on the other hand, is not provided to working parents on a universal basis. Day care involves an agency or a program that provides supervision and care for children while parents or guardians are at work or otherwise unavailable. There are many historical ideological reasons for this lack. For one, traditional thought is that a woman's place is in the home and that she should be the primary caretaker of the children (Spakes, 1992). However, we have established that a strong majority of women, many with children under age 6, work outside the home (U.S. Census Bureau, 2011). Massive evidence suggests that although most women in heterosexual relationships work, they still continue to carry the overwhelming responsibility for child care and other household tasks (Kesselman, McNair, & Schniedewind, 2008; Kirk & Okazawa-Rey, 2013; Lorber, 2010; Shaw & Lee, 2012). We have noted that although most people marry, a significant number of marriages end in divorce. More than 79 percent of all single-parent families are headed by women (U.S. Census Bureau, 2011). (Many of these issues will be discussed more thoroughly in Chapter 9.)

In summary, a number of facts point to the need for adequate day care to serve the nation's children. First, most women work outside the home because of economic necessity. Second, the majority have the additional burden of being primary homemakers. Third, many women have no mate to help with child care.

Day-care facilities are clearly inadequate to meet the nation's needs (Kirk & Okazawa-Rey, 2013; Lein, 2008). Parents often struggle to find adequate, affordable, and accessible day care for their children. Many day-care centers refuse to accept small infants because of the difficulty of caring for them. Furthermore, numerous children in the United States are provided day care in private homes, unregulated by public standards.

Why doesn't the government require that facilities be developed to meet the day-care need? There is no clear answer. Cost may be one possibility. Low priority may be another.

• • • • ▏**Ethical Questions 4.1**

EP 2.1.2

As a student social worker, what do you think about the nation's day-care situation? How critical is it, especially for women? To what extent might you be willing to seek out answers for how to solve this problem and others like it?

The Dynamics of Family Systems

In order to understand family functioning, it's helpful to view the family within a systems perspective. Systems theory applies to a multitude of situations, ranging from the internal mechanisms of a computer to the bureaucratic functioning of a large public welfare department to the interpersonal relationships within a family. Regardless of the situation, understanding systems theory concepts helps you to understand dynamic relationships among people. Systems theory helps to conceptualize how a family works. Basic systems theory concepts were introduced in Chapter 1. The next section reviews those concepts and shows how they can be applied to family systems.

Systems theory helps us understand how a family system is intertwined with many other systems. Each member of a family is affected by what happens to any of the other members. Each member and the family as a whole are also affected by the many other systems in the family's environment. For instance, if Johnny flunks algebra, the family works with the school system to help him make improvements. The entire family might have to cancel their summer vacation because Johnny has to attend summer school. The school system directly affects the family system.

A second example concerns Shirl, Johnny's mother and the family's primary breadwinner. She works as an engineering supervisor for Bob Bear, a corporation based in Racine, Wisconsin, that makes tractors. New World International, an immense conglomerate corporation, owns Bob Bear. What if New World International decides to close down the Bob Bear plant in Racine because of inadequate profits and to move the large plant to Bonetraill, North Dakota? Bonetraill is a far cry from small, but urban, Racine. One possibility for the family is to move two states away to a totally different environment because Shirl has been offered a comparable position in Bonetraill. Lennie, Johnny's father, is a journalist for the local paper. In the event of a move, he would have to find a new job. The whole family would have to leave their neighborhood and friends. Another alternative is for Shirl to seek a new job in the Racine area. However, the economy there is depressed, and she would have difficulty finding a position with a salary anywhere near the one she is currently earning. Thus, the family system is seriously affected by the larger Bob Bear system, and the Bob Bear system by the even larger New World International system.

Another important reason can be given for understanding systems theory as it relates to families. Intervention in families with problems is a major concern of social work. Family therapy is intervention by a social worker or other *family therapist* with members of a family to improve communication and interaction among members and to pursue other changes and goals they wish to pursue. Family therapy is based on the idea that the family is a system. In finding solutions to problems within a family, the target of intervention is the family system.

Whether a particular problem is initially defined as an individual member's or as the entire family's, a family therapist views this problem as one involving the entire family system. The entire family should be the focus of treatment. In family therapy, the specific relationships between various family members in the family system need to be closely observed. Family interaction is discussed more thoroughly in Chapter 12.

LO 4-3 Apply Systems Theory Concepts to Families

EP 2.1.7a

A number of the basic systems theory concepts introduced in Chapter 1 will be briefly redefined here and then applied to examples of family situations.

Systems

A *system* is a set of elements that form an orderly, interrelated, and functional whole. Several aspects of this definition are important. The idea that a system

is a "set of elements" means that a system can be composed of any type of things as long as these things have some relationship to each other. Things may be people, or they may be mathematical symbols. Regardless, the set of elements must be orderly. In other words, the elements must be arranged in some order or pattern that is not simply random. The set of elements must also be interrelated. They must have some kind of mutual relationship or connection with each other. Additionally, the set of elements must be functional. Together they must be able to perform some regular task, activity, or function and fulfill some purpose. Finally, the set of elements must form a whole.

Families are systems. Any particular family is composed of a number of individuals, the elements making up the system. Each individual has a unique relationship with the other individuals in the family. Spouses normally have a special physical and emotional relationship with each other. In a family with seven children, the two oldest sisters may have a special relationship with each other that is unlike their relationship with any of the other siblings. Regardless of what the relationships are, together the family members function as a family system. These relationships, however, are not always positive and beneficial. Sometimes, a relationship is negative or even hostile. For example, a 3-year-old daughter may be fiercely jealous of and resentful toward her newborn brother.

Homeostasis

Homeostasis refers to the tendency of a system to maintain a relatively stable, constant state of equilibrium or balance. A homeostatic family system functions effectively. The family system is maintaining itself and may even be thriving. However, a homeostatic family system is not necessarily a perfect family. Mother may still become terribly annoyed at father for never wanting to go out dancing. Ten-year-old Bobby may still be maintaining a D average in English. Nonetheless, the family is able to continue its daily existence, and the family system itself is not threatened.

Homeostasis is exceptionally important in determining whether outside therapeutic intervention is necessary. Absolute perfection is usually unrealistic. However, if the family's existence is threatened, the system may be in danger of breaking apart.

In these instances, the family system no longer has homeostasis.

For instance, an 89-year-old maternal great-grandmother, Tula, no longer can care for herself. She has been living alone since the death of her husband 20 years earlier. Her eyesight is failing, and her rheumatoid arthritis puts her in constant pain. She remains fairly alert, however, with only some minor forgetfulness. Tula had raised her only grandchild, Jasmine, now age 35, since Jasmine was 3 when her own mother was killed in a car accident. Jasmine's father left before Jasmine was born, never to be heard from again. Tula and Jasmine have always been very close.

Jasmine refuses to place Tula in a nursing home. She feels responsible for Tula because Jasmine is the only grandchild, and she would like to "pay back" all the care she received when she was young.

Jasmine's husband, Hank, however, hates the idea of having Tula move in. Tula, he feels, has always tried to intervene in his marriage. He feels that she takes sides with his wife and constantly tells him what to do. He also feels she talks incessantly and is so hard of hearing that she listens to old *Brady Bunch* reruns loud enough to deafen him, even when he's working down in the basement. Hank also feels that Tula's presence in the home would seriously disrupt his own children's lives. His son Bill is 11 and Bob is 8.

Hank relents, and Tula moves in. Jasmine and Hank start quarreling more and more over Tula. Soon they seem to be quarreling over everything. Jasmine has to quit her job because Tula requires more care and attention than Jasmine expected. The family had just purchased a new home with high mortgage payments. Without Jasmine's salary, money becomes scarce for food, clothing, and other necessities. Jasmine and Hank fight over the financial situation; each blames the other for buying the expensive new home to begin with. Bill's and Bob's grades in school start dropping, and they begin to display some behavior problems. Hank simply threatens to leave if things don't improve. The family system's homeostasis is threatened.

At this point, intervention might take the form of family counseling to help the family clearly identify their problems, voice their opinions, and come to some mutually agreed-upon resolutions. Couple's counseling might be involved to improve the communication between Jasmine and Hank. Social services might be needed to help Tula and the family decide what her best care alternative might be, including consideration of placement in a nursing home. In order for the family to survive, homeostasis must be restored and maintained.

Subsystems

A *subsystem* is a secondary or subordinate system—a system within a system. The most obvious examples are the parental and sibling subsystems. Other more subtle subsystems may also exist depending on the boundaries established within the family system. A mother might have a daughter to whom she feels especially close. These two might form a subsystem within a family system, apart from other family members. Sometimes subsystems exist because of more negative circumstances within family systems. A subsystem might exist within a family with an alcoholic father. Here the mother and children might form a subsystem in coalition against the father.

Boundaries

Boundaries are repeatedly occurring patterns of behavior that characterize the relationships within a system and give that system a particular identity. In a family system, boundaries determine who are members of that particular family system and who are not. Parents and children are within the boundaries of the family system. Close friends of the family are not.

Boundaries may also delineate subsystems within a system. For instance, boundaries separate the spouse subsystem within a family from the sibling subsystem. Each subsystem has its own specified membership. Either a family member is within the boundaries of that subsystem or he is not.

Input

Input can be defined as the energy, information, or communication flow received from other systems. Families are not isolated, self-sufficient units. Each family system is constantly interacting with its environment and with other systems. For example, one type of input into a family system is the money received for the parents' work outside the home. Another type of input involves the communication and supportive social interaction family members receive from friends, neighbors, and relatives. Schools

AJA Productions/Getty Images

Family systems involve powerful interpersonal connections and dynamics. A subsystem may be subtle—a mother might feel especially close to one child.

also provide input in the form of education for children and progress reports concerning that education.

Output

Output is the energy, information, or communication emitted from a system to the environment or to other systems. Work, whether it be in a job situation, a school setting, or in the home, can be considered output. Financial output is another form. This is necessary for the purchase of food, clothing, shelter, and the other necessities of life.

An important thing to consider about output is its relationship to input. If a family system's output exceeds its input, family homeostasis may be threatened. In other words, if more energy is leaving a family system than is coming in, tensions may result and functioning may be impaired. For example, in a multiproblem family troubled by poverty, illness, lack of education, isolation, loneliness, and delinquency, tremendous amounts of effort and energy may be expended simply to stay alive. At the same time, little help and support may be coming in. The result would be severely restricted family functioning and lack of homeostasis.

Feedback

Feedback is a system's receipt of information from an outside source about its own performance or behavior. Feedback can be given to an entire family system, a subsystem (such as a marital pair), or an individual within the family system.

Feedback can be information obtained from outside the system. For example, a family therapist can provide a family with information about how it is functioning. Feedback can also be given by one individual or subsystem within the family system to another. For example, the sibling subsystem might communicate to the alcoholic mother that they are suffering from the consequences of her alcoholic behavior. Finally, a system, subsystem, or individual within a system can give feedback to those outside the family system. For instance, a family might contact their landlord and notify him that their kitchen sink is backing up. They might also add that he won't see another rent check until it's fixed.

Feedback can be either positive or negative. Positive feedback involves information about what a system is doing right in order to maintain itself and thrive. Positive feedback can provide specific information so that members in a family system are aware of the positive aspects of their functioning. For example, a mother works outside her home as a computer programmer. During her job performance evaluation, her supervisor may tell her that she has maintained the highest accuracy record in the department. This indicates to her that her conscientiousness in this respect is valued and should be continued.

Negative feedback can also be valuable. Negative feedback involves providing information about problems within the system. As a result of negative feedback, the system can choose to correct any deviations or mistakes and return to a more homeostatic state. For example, the mother mentioned earlier who works as a computer programmer can receive negative feedback during the same job evaluation. Her supervisor indicates that she tends to fall behind on her weekly written reports. Although she feels the reports are extraordinarily dull and tedious to complete, her supervisor's feedback gives her the information she needs to perform her job better.

Perhaps the most relevant example for social workers concerning feedback is its application in a family treatment setting. When a family comes in for help about a particular problem, feedback can raise their awareness about their functioning. It can help them correct areas where they are making mistakes. It can also encourage them to continue positive interactions. For example, if every time a husband and wife discuss housework responsibilities, they yell at each other about what the other does not do, a social worker can give them feedback that their yelling is accomplishing nothing. Constructive suggestions might then be given about how the couple could better resolve their differences over who takes out the garbage, who makes waffles for breakfast, and who separates the colors from the whites in the laundry.

Positive feedback might also be given. The husband and wife may not be aware that when asked a question about their feelings for each other or about how they like to raise their children, they are very supportive of each other. They immediately look to each other to check out the other's feelings. They smile at each other and encourage the other's opinions. Giving them specific positive feedback about these interactions by describing their behaviors to them may be helpful. Such feedback may encourage them to continue these positive interactions. It may also suggest to them that they could apply similar positive means to resolving other differences.

Entropy

Entropy is the natural tendency of a system to progress toward disorganization, depletion, and, in essence, death. The idea is that nothing lasts forever. People age and eventually die. Young families get older, and children leave to start their own families.

Homeostasis itself is dynamic in that it involves constant change and adjustment. Families are never frozen in time. Family members are constantly changing and responding to new situations and challenges.

Negative Entropy

Negative entropy is the process of a system moving toward growth and development. In effect, it is the opposite of entropy. Goals in family treatment often involve striving to make conditions and interactions better than they were before. A relationship between quarreling spouses can improve. Physical abuse of a child can be stopped. Negative entropy must be kept in mind when helping family systems grow and develop to their full potential.

Equifinality

Equifinality refers to the idea that there are many different means to the same end. It is important not to get locked into only one way of thinking, because in any particular situation, there are alternatives. Some may be better than others, but there are alternatives. It's easy to get trapped into tunnel vision in which no other options are apparent. Frequently, family systems need help in defining and evaluating the options available to them.

Consider, for instance, a family in which the father abruptly loses his job. Instead of wallowing in remorse, they might pursue other alternatives. The family might consider relocating someplace where a similar position is available. The mother, who previously had not worked outside the home, might look into finding a job herself, to help the family's financial situation. Moving to less expensive housing might be considered. Finally, the father might look into other types of work, at least temporarily. There are always alternatives. The important thing is to recognize and consider them.

Differentiation

Differentiation is a system's tendency to move from a more simplified to a more complex existence. In other words, relationships, situations, and interactions tend to get more complex over time instead of more simplified.

For example, two people fall in love, marry, and begin to establish their lives together. They have three children, and both parents work full-time in order to save enough for a modest home of their own. As time goes on, marital problems and disputes develop as their lives grow more complicated with children and responsibilities. Their initial simple life becomes clouded with children's illnesses, car

CONCEPT SUMMARY

Systems Theory Concepts

System: A set of elements that form an orderly, inter-related, and functional whole.

Homeostasis: The tendency for a system to maintain a relatively stable, constant state of equilibrium or balance.

Subsystem: A secondary or subordinate system—a system within a system.

Boundaries: Repeatedly occurring patterns of behavior that characterize the relationships within a system and give that system a particular identity.

Input: Energy, information, or communication flow received from other systems.

Output: Energy, information, or communication emitted from a system to the environment or to other systems.

Feedback: A system's receipt of information from an outside source about its own performance or behavior.

Entropy: The natural tendency of a system to progress toward disorganization, depletion, and, in essence, death.

Negative entropy: The process of a system moving toward growth and development.

Equifinality: The idea that there are many different means to the same end.

Differentiation: A system's tendency to move from a more simplified to a more complex existence.

---

payments, job stresses, and so on. Systems theory provides a framework for viewing this couple's relationship. It provides for the acknowledgment of increasing complexity. From a helping perspective, the basic fact of the couple's affection for and commitment to each other may need to be identified and emphasized.

LO 4-4 Assess the Family Life Cycle

Several decades ago, the traditional family life cycle was conceptualized as having six major phases (Carter & McGoldrick, 1980). Each phase focused on some emotional transition in terms of intimate relationships with other people and on changes of personal status. The six stages were:

1. Separating an unattached young adult from his or her family of origin
2. Marrying and establishing an identity as part of a couple, rather than as an individual
3. Having and raising young children
4. Dealing with adolescent children striving for independence, and refocusing on the couple relationship as adolescents gain that independence
5. Sending children forth into their own new relationships, addressing midlife crises, and coping with the growing disabilities of aging parents
6. Adjusting to aging and addressing the inevitability of one's own death

Today, our perspective on family life cycles is much more adaptable and varied. McGoldrick, Carter, and Garcia-Preto (2011) propose a contemporary framework for considering family life cycles that emphasizes flexibility and diversity. Spotlight 4.1 explores this new conceptualization of diverse family life cycles. Although the stages resemble those in the traditional approach, discussion focuses on the variability within each stage. Families are significantly affected by a wide range of conditions and issues. The stages described in Spotlight 4.1 may occur, but not necessarily in that order or at all. Rather, each family experiences a complex existence, as a system and as a collection of individuals, within an environmental context involving "race, ethnicity, class, gender, sexual orientation, religion, age, family status" and "disability" (p. 18). Additionally, "current or longstanding social, political, and economic issues" directly affect family life and the family life cycle; such matters include "random violence, affirmative action, de facto school and neighborhood segregation, gay and lesbian adoption or marriage, welfare reform, abortion rights, the education of all our children, prejudice against legal and illegal immigrants, health care and insurance, tax cuts, layoffs, social services to [older adults] … and other groups, cost and availability of infertility treatments, and physician-assisted suicide" (p. 18).

Within the context of the family system's life cycle, we will now turn our attention back to the social development of young children. We will

SPOTLIGHT ON DIVERSITY 4.1

LO 4-5 Explain Diverse Perspectives on the Family Life Cycle

EP 2.1.4a,
2.1.4c,
2.1.5a,
2.1.7,
2.1.7a

McGoldrick and her colleagues (2011) articulate the following seven family life-cycle stages; these proposed stages may be considered as a "map" for examining and assessing how families respond to their widely diverse issues and circumstances (pp. 16–17).

Stage 1: Leaving Home: Emerging Young Adults

Early young adulthood arbitrarily extends from age 18 to 21, and older young adulthood from 22 to about 30 or older (Arnett, 2007; Fulmer, 2011). In the past, young adulthood marked the cessation of the dependence upon family of origin and the entrance into the world of independent living and work. Now, however, the concept of "breaking ties" with the family of origin is no longer so important. Whereas that old model "overemphasized separation," the new perspective "blends separation and attachment by recognizing the need for individuation while retaining cross-generational relationships" (Fulmer, 2011, p. 176).

Stage 1 is often characterized by entrance into the self-supporting work world, formulation of intimate friendships and relationships, and possibly experimentation with mind-altering substances (Fulmer, 2011). However, these experiences are affected by a number of factors. For example, "poor urban groups have easier access to stronger drugs in their neighborhoods than do college students"; this may put such urban youth who are poor into high-risk groups for drug addiction and the negative repercussions resulting from addiction (Fulmer, 2011, p. 179). College students, on the other hand, may just use drugs "recreationally," not necessarily suffering such dire consequences.

Another example of diverse circumstances concerns chronic illness and its effects on a family with an emerging young adult. Rolland (2011) explains:

> If illness onset coincides with the launching . . . phases of the family life cycle [Stage 1], it can derail a family's natural momentum. Illness or disability in a young adult may requires a heightened dependency and return to the family of origin for disease-related caretaking. The autonomy ad individuation of parents and child are in jeopardy, and separate interests and priorities may be relinquished or put on hold. Family dynamics as well as disease severity will influence whether the family's reversion to a child-rearing-like structure is a temporary detour or a permanent reversal. (p. 357)

Stage 2: Joining of Families Through Marriage/Union

To varying degrees, marriage can require adjustment, compromise, and struggle. Even small issues like how to arrange cereal boxes on the shelf, make spaghetti, or take out the garbage can require communication and cooperation. People going through Stage 2 may form a commitment with each other and readjust their relationships with friends and family as they establish themselves as a couple (McGoldrick, 2011).

However, numerous issues can make a couple's adjustment to each other more difficult (McGoldrick, 2011). These include inadequate jobs or resources, differences in "religious, racial, ethnic, or class background," disparities in "financial power, socioeconomic status, education, career option or skills," and "issues with family of origin" (e.g., poor relationships with parents or siblings, financial dependence on parents, or living too far away or too close) (p. 210).

Gay and lesbian couples may face additional issues, including the inability to marry legally in most states. Furthermore, "the stigmatizing of homosexual couples by our society means that their relationships are often not validated by their families or communities and they must cope with prejudice on a daily basis. The AIDS crisis produced a terrible trauma for the gay community and its impact on a whole generation of gay men at the point of forming couple relationships cannot be underestimated" (McGoldrick, 2011, p. 201).

Stage 3: Families with Young Children

Cultural values significantly affect how children are socialized, what values they acquire, and what behaviors they learn. "One cannot view the socialization of certain behaviors independently from the cultural context. Cultures define the basic values and ideals as well as the agents who teach the values and the settings in which they are taught" (Gardiner, Mutter, & Kosmitzki, 1998, p. 148). Greder and Allen (2007) reflect that "cultural traditions shape parenting by influencing childrearing practices, expectations of roles of children at different ages and stages of development, where families live, family structure, and roles and responsibilities of adults in families" (p. 123). Spotlights 4.2 and 4.3 discuss further the influence of culture.

Greder and Allen (2007) continue that economic hardship also severely affects parenting ability:

> Households headed by single mothers, individuals, and families from ethnic minority groups and families with pre-school children are overrepresented among those in the population who live in poverty…. Geography and generations also play important roles in determining who becomes poor, as do factors such as adolescent parenting, insufficient education, lack of job training, and chronic unemployment. Limited access to health care (and resulting poor health outcomes), inadequate housing and homelessness and violent or unsupportive neighborhoods all contribute to the economic barriers confronting poor families. (p. 125)

Stage 4: Families with Adolescents

In the United States, adolescence can be a difficult period. Adolescents strive to establish their own identities, which often results in conflict with parents. Parents often struggle to maintain control while adolescents vehemently resist it. Ethnic diversity and cultural values can add to the complexity of these scenarios.

As later chapters will explore, identity development is very important in adolescence. It, too, is subject to diverse factors. Preto (2011) addresses identity development for adolescents of color:

> *For African Americans, Latinos, Asians, and other adolescents of color, forming an identity goes beyond values and beliefs about gender, since they have to first cope with how society defines them, marginalizes, and oppresses them. For African Americans, forming a positive identity as a Black male or Black female in a racist society in which being Black has been demeaned for centuries poses a grave challenge for adolescents and their parents.... Although there has been an increased visibility of African Americans in the popular culture, even more so since the election of Barack Obama as president the insidious effects of racism on the everyday lives of Blacks in this country hasn't gone away. (p. 236)*

Social class also impacts the conditions surrounding and the opportunities provided for adolescents. For example, families in the upper-level social classes, who have higher levels of education and greater income potential, view adolescents as needing attention, direction, and safekeeping; in contrast, working-class and poor families regard their adolescents as active participants needed to help with important family responsibilities such as washing, cooking, and babysitting (Kliman, 2011).

Stage 5: Launching Children and Moving on at Midlife

When children leave home to be on their own, family life often changes dramatically in many ways (McGoldrick et al., 2011). The original couple must reestablish itself as its own system. Relationships are developed with grown children, their partners, and grandchildren. The couple may establish new interests, activities, and relationships to replace the time no longer needed for child-care duties. The couple system's own parents may require help and attention as they themselves age.

However, Stage 5 is also characterized by great diversity (Preto & Blacker, 2011). People may be married or in permanent couple systems, divorced, single, or remarried (possibly multiple times) by this stage of life. Some people are well adjusted. Others may face the clichés of a "midlife crisis" or "the empty nest syndrome." People with greater assets and higher socioeconomic status often enter midlife in good health, eagerly seeking out new and exciting experiences. However, people in the lower socioeconomic classes frequently experience economic hardship, especially with diminishing availability of jobs, industrial downsizing and movement of production to other countries, and work environments characterized by escalating technology.

Stage 6: Families in Late Middle Age

Families in late middle age often face a range of conditions (Walsh, 2011). Stage 6 is often characterized by retirement and grandparenthood. Many people remain vibrant and healthy. As with other stages in life, socioeconomic status and available resources dramatically affect the quality of life in late middle age. People with many resources can experience travel, recreational pursuits, and good living conditions. People with inadequate resources may be forced to keep working, sometimes taking minimum-wage jobs to keep them afloat. Such people may not have adequate housing, food, or health care.

Other aspects of diversity, including race, also affect late middle age. For instance, increasing numbers of African American grandparents are assuming responsibility for their grandchildren (Brownell & Fenley, 2009; Cox, 2002, 2005; Diller, 2015; Misiewicz, 2012; Sue & Sue, 2008). Primary reasons include crack cocaine or alcohol addiction, incarceration for drug- or alcohol-related crimes, mental illness, and unwillingness to surrender custody of grandchildren to public foster care (Cox, 2002, 2005). "Surrogate parenting has been a pattern for African American grandparents in U.S. society" (Cox, 2002, p. 46).

These grandparents experience undue pressures when assuming such responsibility and are "prone to an increased incidence or exacerbation of depression and insomnia, hypertension, back and stomach problems,... as well as increased use of alcohol and cigarettes .... In addition, grandparents tend to ignore their problems and associated stresses to meet the needs of their grandchildren" (Cox, 2002, p. 46).

Cox (2002) calls for *empowerment practice* on their behalf and explains: "The immediate goals of empowerment practice are to help clients achieve a sense of personal power, become more aware of connections between individual and community problems, develop helping skills, and work collaboratively toward social change" (p. 46, citing Gutierrez, GlenMaye, & DeLois, 1995).

Cox calls for providing grandparents with information on a range of relevant topics and teaching them various skills to empower them. The recommended curriculum includes the following content: "(1) introduction to empowerment; (2) importance of self-esteem; (3) communicating with grandchildren; (4) dealing with loss and grief; (5) helping grandchildren deal with loss; (6) dealing with behavior problems; (7) talking to grandchildren about sex, HIV/AIDS, and drugs; (8) legal and entitlement issues; (9) developing advocacy skills; (10) negotiating systems; [and] (11) making presentations" so that they can share their knowledge with others (p. 47).

Stage 7: Families Nearing the End of Life

Facing the reality that life is coming to an end is important for families (McGoldrick et al., 2011). Often, this involves

(continued)

people dealing with losses, including the deaths of partners and friends. Preparing for one's own death and legacy is also part of this stage. Decisions may be made about where to reside as health declines and increased supportive care is required.

Great diversity characterizes this stage. Depending on your cultural background, there are numerous ways of viewing and dealing with old age and death. For example, Dhooper and Moore (2001) maintain:

Native American* [older adults]…, those aged 65 and above, are more traditional in their philosophy and values and have a deeper understanding of racism and oppression against Native people as a result of having a longer history of experience with these forces. [Early in the last century]… the BIA [Bureau of Indian Affairs] sanctioned field agents to alter Native customs. "Forbidden were the wearing of long hair by males, face painting of both sexes, and wearing Indian dress" (Hirschfelder & Kreipe de Montano, 1993, p. 22)…. The [older adults] … have been the vanguards of their culture and have passed down their traditions and cultural beliefs throughout the generations. Through the [older adults] … "traditional values are sustained…. The ancient languages are spoken and taught, traditional ceremonies are observed and baskets are woven" (L. Hall, 1997, p. 755). As such they are held in high regard by their people and are treated respectfully. "Generally Native American traditional values consist of sharing, cooperation and a deep respect for elders" (Garrett, 1999, p. 87). (p. 191)

Similarly, various cultures view and deal with death very differently. Consider the approach assumed by the Lebanese:

Lebanese families are generally very expressive in their response to death, even after several generations of living in the United States. Extreme displays of emotion are common, and it is not unusual for older family members to ask the deceased to get up and perform a favored deed one last time (i.e., to dubkee, a Lebanese dance, or cook a favored meal). After the deceased is unable to respond to the request, the grief of the family is amplified and followed by wailing and crying. For immigrant Lebanese several decades ago, it was not uncommon to jump into the grave at the cemetery if a child had preceded a parent in death. In recent times Lebanese American reactions to death are less dramatic but still highly emotional and demonstrative. Calmness at wakes is perceived as a lack of love for the deceased, and emotional outbursts are perceived as respect for the deceased. Because of the strong bonds and emotional attachments of Lebanese families, wakes and funerals are highly charged experiences. (Simon, 1996, p. 374)

The Hindu perception and treatment of death involves the following:

Death is a particularly potent symbolic event among Hindus, given their beliefs about karma [destiny]…. As with weddings, traditional rituals associated with death and mourning are likely to be modified when Indians live in the United States.

Mourning cycles vary, but … customs include a 10- to 12-day mourning ritual … in addition to requiring extensive absence from work. In keeping with Indian sex-role traditions, widows are expected to perform many rituals of sacrifice glorifying the family, whereas widowers and other family members are not required to observe such rites. (Almeida, 1996, p. 408)

Mindell (2007) explains Jewish families' view and handling of death:

Judaism, regardless of denomination—Reform, Conservative, or Orthodox—has the overriding values of honoring the dead and comforting the mourners. Burial is usually within twenty-four hours after the death and the funeral service begins with the cutting of a garment or a black ribbon attached to the mourners, the immediate family of the deceased. This ritual is a visual representation of the individual being separated—cut away—from the loved one. The period of mourning at home after the burial lasts for one week. This ritual is called Shiva, the Hebrew word for seven. Friends, family, and neighbors visit the mourners in the home during Shiva, which provides the opportunity to share stories about the deceased, how his or her life touched others, and provide the bereaved a supportive environment to also share memories and to grieve. The first thirty days, referred to as Sheloshim, the Hebrew word for thirty, after the funeral is a time when the family might attend morning and evening services. Mourning ends after the first year, the anniversary of the death, when a tombstone is dedicated. At each anniversary of the death, the Yahzeit, the family lights a special twenty-four-hour memorial candle.

---

*"Note that *American Indian* and *Native American* are both accepted terms for referring to indigenous peoples of North America, although *Native American* is a broader designation because the U.S. government includes Hawaiians and Samoans in this category. There are close to 450 Native groups" (American Psychological Association, 2010, p. 75). Another term used to refer to indigenous peoples of North America is *First Nations Peoples*. Lum (2003) comments that "there is no consensus about which term is best, yet some Native people have strong preferences for one term over the others. These terms all include many different groups of distinct people. Use of such broad terms tends to obscure diversity. Generally, when speaking of a particular Native person or nation (such as Comanche or Oneida), it is best to employ the specific label used by those people rather than a more general term such as *Native American*" (p. 197).

Mourning is seen as a process that has stages and takes time. Rituals enable the living to remember the dead.

The religious customs that are practiced during the continuum of an individual's life allow one to cope with difficult happenings, experiences, and emotions, in a supportive, emotional "home" as she or he struggles to make sense out of events that seem to have no meaning. The manner in which the struggle is done, the emotions expressed, and how the community supports its members reflect the religious and cultural history of the group and help to define the identity of the members of the group. (pp. 231–232)

Additional Issues Affecting Multiple Phases of the Family Life Cycle

Many other dimensions of diversity affect the life cycle of families and individuals. We will arbitrarily address two additional issues here that affect various life-cycle stages—adults who remain single and families dealing with immigration status.

Single Adults

Simply put, many adults for various reasons neither marry nor commit themselves to long-term intimate partnerships. The seven-stage family life cycle just described doesn't really apply to them. The demographic picture has changed. More people remain single now than in past decades, people who do marry do so later than before, people often delay childbearing, and many people live much longer than they have in the past (Berliner, Jacob, & Schwartzberg, 2011).

Berliner and her colleagues (2011) describe four life-cycle stages often encountered by people who remain single. First, during their 20s, people establish their adult status. They make the transition from being dependent on their family of origin to starting their independent lives. They develop new contexts for living by establishing work status and friendship relationships.

During the second stage in their 30s, single adults may face "the single crises" (Berliner et al., 2011, p. 166). They contend with the condition that they are single and may remain so. They may develop new life objectives and possibilities that don't include marriage. They may consider having children.

In their third phase of midlife, single adults may accept the fact that they may indeed neither marry nor have children. The dream of "the perfect family" may not materialize. They may take a new look at the status of work in their lives and attend to their financial future as single adults. They determine to view their status as single adults as valid and positive. Establishing social networks of friends for emotional support is also important.

The fourth phase entails "putting it all together" (Berliner et al., 2011, p. 166). This concerns single adults making decisions about work and their financial future. It means stressing the positive aspects of being free and independent. It also involves planning for future living conditions in the case of

failing health. Finally, they cope with the decreasing health and death of people important to them.

Immigration Status

Immigration status is "a person's position in terms of legal rights and residency when entering and residing in a country that is not that person's legal country of origin" (Kirst-Ashman & Hull, 2012b, p. 26). Migrating from one country to another can powerfully affect a family's life cycle.

People who migrate can assume any of the following statuses:

- *Immigrants* are "those individuals who depart their country of origin voluntarily in search of better economic and living arrangement" (Delgado, Jones, & Rohani, 2005, p. 5). They may be either permanent or temporary (e.g., students or seasonal workers); they may have either legal or illegal status, as described next (Potocky, 2008).
- *Undocumented immigrants* "are those individuals who enter this country without proper (legal) documentation, and have done so for reasons similar to those who are in this country as immigrants" (Delgado et al., 2005, p. 5). They sometimes are referred to as *illegal aliens*.
- *Refugees* "are those individuals who are forced to leave their country because of human rights violations and threats to safety" (Delgado et al., 2005, p. 5). They may also be victims of natural or man-made disasters (Potocky, 2008).

Migration to a new country and environment can dramatically affect a family's life cycle (Falicov, 2011). Regardless of where a family is in its life cycle, migration forces family members to face major changes and disruptions. It also involves experiencing the losses of the known and familiar patterns of their old existence. "The age at the time of migration, the stage of personal development, and the length of stay in the adopted country alter how migration is constructed and lived over time" (Falicov, 2011, p. 337). Ability to adapt to new circumstances varies widely depending on the family member's age. The experience will be very different for babies, "school-age children, adolescents, young adults," and older adults (Falicov, 2011, p. 337). For example, young children generally have the ability to acquire a new language much more easily than older adults (Potocky, 2008).

There are many dimensions to the migration experience and many questions to ask about how the experience affects various family members. Garcia (2009) raises issues and questions to address in order to understand the family's circumstances at whatever phase of the life cycle they're in:

1. *The process of immigration: Was the move voluntary or involuntary? Anticipated or not anticipated? What were the points of transit on the way to the United States? Who was left behind, what separations occurred with family members? What is the status of immigration documentation?*

(continued)

SPOTLIGHT ON DIVERSITY 4.1 *(continued)*

2. *Social power changes and coping: Have there been socio-economic, educational, occupational adjustments? Shifts in new employment or unemployment status? Shifts in family decision making due to structural family changes? What are the effects of language and literacy fluency in the new country? Is the immigrant facing workplace-related stressors? Is so, what types of stressors (e.g., supervisory, interpersonal, xenophobic [involving an intense dislike or fear of foreigners or foreign customs], immigration authorities)?*

3. *Economic and housing resources: What are the immigrant's debt commitments and assets? What is the status of housing (e.g., quality), transportation, access to communication technology?*

4. *Physical and psychological health status: Are the immigrant's basic needs for food and shelter being met? Can the immigrant utilize and/or access professional health*

providers and/or cultural healers? Are there any antecedent health conditions prior to immigration, during the immigration process (e.g., loss of health, limb)? What is the immigrant's current health status?

5. *Family system and social networks: What are the family constellations, structures, communication patterns, multigenerational experiences, and coping abilities? What social support systems, if any, is the family involved with (e.g., extended family, friends, religious, community, political, recreational)? To what degree is the individual or family isolated and/or active with social contacts?*

6. *Cultural: Profile and qualities of individuals' social identity? In what ways and to what degree is the individual identified with his or her traditional culture, with the new American culture, and/or with other cultures (e.g., religious, people with disabilities, gender orientation)? (pp. 84–85)*

---

focus on how children become integrated into their family system and how they learn to behave (or misbehave). Learning theory provides a relevant, conceptual base for understanding how socialization and learning occur. Thus, we will emphasize the theoretical basis for learning theory and its applications to practical parenting.

LO 4-6 Describe Learning Theory

EP 2.1.7a

"Mom! I want a candy bar! You promised! I want one right now! Mom!" Four-year-old Huey screamed as loudly as he possibly could. He and his mother were standing in the checkout line at the local supermarket. An older adult woman was checking out in front of them. Two other women and a man were waiting in line behind them.

Huey's mother saw everybody looking at her and her young son. Huey simply would not stop screaming. She tried to shush him. She scolded him in as much of a whisper as she could muster. She threatened that he would never see the inside of a McDonald's again. Absolutely nothing would work. Huey just kept on screaming.

Finally, in total exasperation, his mother grabbed the nearest candy bar off the shelf, ripped off the wrapper, and literally stuck the thing into Huey's

mouth. A peaceful silence came over the grocery store. All witnessing the event breathed a sigh of relief. Huey stood there with a happy smile on his sticky face. One might almost say he was gloating.

The family environment has already been established as the primary agent of children's socialization. It provides the critical social environment in which children learn. The next logical question to address concerns how children learn. The social and emotional development of children is frequently a focus of social work intervention. Children sometimes create behavior problems. They become difficult for parents and other supervising adults to manage. When they enter school, these management problems often continue. Teachers and administration find some children difficult to control. Frequently, as children get older, problems escalate.

Children can learn how to be affectionate, considerate, fun-loving, and responsible. But they can also learn how to be selfish, spoiled, and inconsiderate. This latter state is not good for parents and other supervising adults, nor for the children themselves. Children need to cooperate with others. They need to know how to get along in social settings in order to become emotionally mature, well-adjusted adults. Learning theory concepts are useful for recognizing why anyone, child or adult, behaves the way he does. However, the concepts are especially helpful when addressing the issue of behavior management.

Critical Thinking: Evaluation of Theory

EP 2.1.3a

In order to change behavior, it first must be understood. *Learning theory* is a theoretical orientation that conceptualizes the social environment in terms of behavior, its preceding events, and its subsequent consequences. It posits that behavior can be learned, and therefore maladaptive behavior can be unlearned. Learning theory provides a framework for understanding how behavior develops. We will focus on learning theory for several reasons. First, it emphasizes the social functioning of people within their environments. The total person in dynamic interaction with all aspects of the environment is the focus of attention. This is in contrast to many other theoretical approaches that focus primarily on the individual's personality or isolated history.

Second, learning theory emphasizes the importance of assessing observable behaviors. It also stresses the use of behaviorally specific terms in defining behaviors. This helps to make any particular behavior more clearly understandable.

Finally, learning theory provides a positive approach. The underlying idea is that behaviors develop through learning them, and therefore undesirable behaviors can be unlearned. This allows for positive behavioral changes. Instead of individuals being perceived as victims of their personal histories and personality defects, they are seen as dynamic living beings capable of change.

EP 2.1.6b

Behavior modification involves the therapeutic application of learning theory principles. Much evidence supports the effectiveness of behavioral techniques for a wide variety of human problems and learning situations (Degangi & Kendall, 2008; Kazdin, 2013; Miltenberger, 2012; Spiegler & Guevremont, 2010; Sundel & Sundel, 2005; Wilson, 2011).

Respondent Conditioning

One view of understanding behavior focuses on a stimulus and the response resulting from that stimulus. A *stimulus* is "an object or event that can be detected by one of the senses, and thus has the potential to influence the person" (Miltenberger, 2012, p. 66). A particular stimulus elicits a particular response. The stimulus can be a word, a sight, or a sound.

Lobster and German chocolate cake *(Unconditioned stimulus)* → Martha's salivation *(Response)*

FIGURE 4.1 A Stimulus-Response Relationship

For example, Martha, who has been on a strict diet for a week, stops by to visit her friend Evelyn. Evelyn is in the process of preparing a lobster dinner. She is also baking a German chocolate cake for dessert. Martha begins salivating at the thought of such appetizing food. Martha's response, salivation, occurs as a result of the stimulus, witnessing Evelyn's preparation of the wonderful, albeit fattening, food. Figure 4.1 portrays this relationship.

Much respondent behavior is unlearned; that is, a response is naturally emitted after exposure to a stimulus. This stimulus is called an *unconditioned* (naturally occurring) *stimulus*. *Respondent conditioning* (also called *classical or Pavlovian conditioning*) occurs when a person learns to respond to a new stimulus that does not naturally elicit a response. This new stimulus is called a *conditioned* (learned) *stimulus*. In order to accomplish this, the new stimulus is paired with the stimulus that elicited the response naturally. The person then learns to associate the new stimulus with a particular response even though it had nothing to do with that response originally.

For example, Mr. Bartholomew, a third-grade teacher, slaps students very hard on the hand when they talk out of turn. (This punitive physical behavior, of course, could get Mr. Bartholomew into a LOT of trouble.) As a result of this stimulus, the slapping, students fear Mr. Bartholomew. By associating Mr. Bartholomew with getting a slap on the hand, the students eventually learn to fear Mr. Bartholomew even when he isn't slapping them. Mr. Bartholomew himself has been paired with the hand slapping until he elicits the same response that the slapping did. Figure 4.2 helps to illustrate this relationship.

Some behavioral techniques used by social workers involve the principles of respondent conditioning. *Systematic desensitization* provides an example. Systematic desensitization is a procedure in which a person with a phobia practices relaxation while imagining scenes of the fear-producing stimulus. A *phobia* is "a fear in which the level of anxiety or escape and avoidance behavior is severe enough to

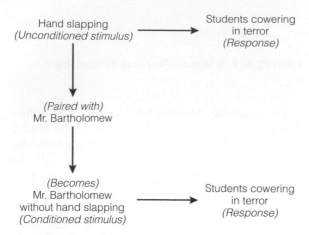

Hand slapping
(*Unconditioned stimulus*) → Students cowering in terror
(*Response*)

(*Paired with*)
Mr. Bartholomew

(*Becomes*)
Mr. Bartholomew
without hand slapping
(*Conditioned stimulus*) → Students cowering in terror
(*Response*)

FIGURE 4.2 Respondent Conditioning

disrupt the person's life" (Miltenberger, 2012, p. 552). The extreme fear or anxiety may involve almost anything. Examples include snakes, enclosed places, or school.

Systematic desensitization usually has two major thrusts. First, the client is exposed very gradually to the thing he or she fears. Second, while the client is being exposed to the fearful item or event, he or she is also taught an incompatible response. The incompatible response must be something that cannot occur at the same time as the anxiety and fear. A good example of an incompatible response is progressive relaxation.

For example, the client first learns how to control his or her body and relax. Then the standard procedure is that he or she is exposed to the feared item or event in increasing amounts or degrees. A person who fears rats might first be shown a picture of a rat in the distance while, at the same time, using his or her newly acquired relaxation skills. Anxiety and fear cannot occur while the individual is in a relaxed state. They are incompatible responses.

The individual might then be shown an 8-by-10-inch photo of a rat. Once again, the individual would use relaxation techniques to prevent anxiety from occurring. The client would be exposed to rats in a more and more direct manner until the client could actually hold a laboratory rat in his or her hand. The client would gradually learn to use the incompatible relaxation technique to quell any anxiety that rats might once have elicited.

A variety of techniques based on respondent conditioning have also been used to treat enuresis, or bed-wetting, overeating, cigarette smoking, alcohol consumption, and sexual deviations (Kazdin, 2001, 2008a, 2013; Sundel & Sundel, 2005). However, they are not nearly as abundant nor are they as common as those behavioral techniques based on operant conditioning, discussed in a later section.

Modeling

A second perspective on understanding behavior and learning involves *modeling*, the learning of behavior by observing another individual engaging in that behavior. In order to learn from a model, an individual does not necessarily have to participate in the behavior. An individual only needs to watch how a model performs the behavior. For obvious reasons, modeling is also called *observational learning*. A behavior can be learned simply by observing its occurrence.

Modeling is important within the context of practical parenting. Parents can model appropriate behavior for their children. For example, a father might act as a model for his son concerning how to play baseball. The father can teach his son how to throw and catch a ball by doing it himself. The child can learn by watching his father.

In social work intervention, modeling can be used to model appropriate treatment of children so that parents may observe. For example, 5-year-old Larry, who frequently has behavior problems, may pick up a pencil that the social worker accidentally dropped and return it to the social worker. The social worker may then model for the parent how the child can be positively reinforced for his good behavior. The social worker may say, "Thank you for picking up my pencil for me, Larry. That was very helpful of you."

Another example of modeling within a social work practice context is *role playing*, practicing behavior through a trial run in preparation for a later situation in which some goal is to be achieved (such as gaining greater understanding of another's position or learning more effective communication skills). For example, a social worker might ask a mother who has trouble controlling her son to role-play that son and mimic his behavior. She is instructed to act the way she thinks her son would act. The social worker may then model for the parent some appropriate, effective things to say to the son when the son behaves in that way. Such modeling provides the opportunity for the parent to learn new ways of responding to her son.

Modeling can also teach children inappropriate and ineffective behavior. For example, consider a mother who strikes other family members whenever she gets the least bit irritated with them. She is likely to act as a model for that type of behavior. Her children may learn that striking others is the way to express their anger.

Some classic research studied the effects of positive and negative consequences on modeling (Bandura, 1965). Children were shown a film of an adult hitting and kicking a large doll, obviously modeling aggressive behavior. Afterward, the children were divided into three groups. Each group then observed the model experiencing different respective consequences. One group of children viewed the model being punished for the aggressive behavior. Another group of children saw the model being rewarded for the same behavior. A third group of children saw the model being ignored. The children were then placed in situations where they could display aggression. Children who saw the model receive a reward for aggressive behavior and those who saw him experience no consequences clearly displayed more aggressive behavior than those children who saw the model punished. It was ascertained that all the children had learned the aggressive behavior; when they were told they would receive a reward for being aggressive, they all could indeed be aggressive. The conclusion is that modeling behavior can be affected both by consequences to the model and to the observer.

Other conditions can also affect the effectiveness of modeling or the degree to which modeling works. These conditions include "the similarity of the model to the observer; the prestige, status, and expertise of the model; and the number of models observed. As a general rule, imitation of a model by an observer is greater when the model is similar to the observer, more prestigious, and higher in status and expertise than the observer and when several models perform the same behavior" (Kazdin, 2008a, pp. 24–25; Miltenberger, 2012; Sundel & Sundel, 2005).

Modeling has been used in a variety of clinical settings, including the control of fear and the development of social skills. Usually, it's used in conjunction with other behavioral techniques.

Operant Conditioning

Operant conditioning is one of the dominant types of learning focused on in the United States. It allows for the easiest and most practical understanding of behavior. Many treatment applications are based on the principles of operant conditioning.

Operant conditioning is "a type of learning in which behaviors are influenced primarily by the consequences that follow them" (Kazdin, 2008a, p. 458; 2013). New behaviors can be shaped, weak behaviors can be strengthened, strong behaviors can be maintained, and undesirable behaviors can be weakened and eliminated. The emphasis lies on the consequences of behavior. What follows a particular behavior affects how frequently that behavior will occur again, as illustrated in Highlight 4.1.

The ABCs of Behavior

One way of conceptualizing operant behavior is to divide it into its primary parts, known as antecedents, behaviors, and consequences. Another way of referring to them is the *ABCs of behavior*.

Antecedents are the events occurring immediately before the behavior itself. These events set the stage for the behavior to occur. For instance, some individuals state that they are able to quit smoking cigarettes except when they are socializing at a party. The party conditions act as a stimulus for smoking behavior, whereas other environments do not. In other words, the party setting acts as an antecedent for smoking behavior.

Behavior is "any observable and measurable response or act…. Behavior is occasionally broadly defined to include cognitions, psychophysiological reactions, and feelings, which may not be directly observable but are defined in terms that can be measured by means of various assessment strategies" (Kazdin, 2008a, p. 450; Miltenberger, 2012). The important phrase here is that behavior is "defined in terms that can be measured." Therefore, even thoughts and feelings can be changed as long as words can be found to clearly describe what they are. For instance, specific messages that people send to themselves can be altered as long as these messages can be clearly defined and measured. A woman who frequently tells herself "I am so fat," can have that message changed to "I am a worthwhile person." Each time she tells herself this message, it can be noted, so that the overall frequency can be measured.

Most behavior involved in operant conditioning is observable. Even thoughts and feelings frequently

---

◆ **HIGHLIGHT 4.1**

Consequences and Recurring Behavior

The Johnsons hired their neighbor, 9-year-old Eric, to mow their lawn once a week during the summer. Eric, not being sophisticated in the ways of money management, failed to discuss how much he would be paid per hour. Eric slaved away for four hours one Saturday afternoon when he would rather have been playing baseball.

When Eric had finished, Mr. Johnson came out, complimented Eric on what a fine job he had done, and gave him $12 for his trouble. Unfortunately, $12 worked out to be $3 per hour. Mr. Johnson thought this was more than adequate. Mr. Johnson himself had been paid only a grand total of $1 for doing a similar job when he was a boy. Eric, however, felt this was more than chintzy on Mr. Johnson's part. He knew that $12 would barely begin to cover the brand new Xbox of his dreams.

The consequences for Eric's lawn-mowing behavior were not positive. He did not receive his expected $32. Thus, Eric never mowed Mr. Johnson's lawn again. Instead he turned to other, more generous and benevolent neighbors to upgrade his financial future. He also learned to make salary one of the first items on his business agenda. If Mr. Johnson had given him his expected rate of $8 an hour, Eric would have been a dependable and industrious worker for him throughout the summer. In other words, more favorable consequences for Eric would have encouraged his lawn-mowing behavior. He would have been conditioned to mow Mr. Johnson's lawn. As it turned out, Mr. Johnson was doomed to mowing his own lawn for the remainder of the summer.

---

occur with accompanying behaviors. For example, Ieasha is a 6-year-old who has been clinically diagnosed as depressed. Any thoughts she has about being depressed are not noticeable. However, she makes frequent statements about what a bad girl she is, how her parents don't like her, and what it would be like to die. These statements can be observed and noted. Such statements might be used as indicators for childhood depression.

Ieasha's statements can also be measured; that is, the types of statements she makes and how often she makes them can be counted and evaluated. She might make a statement concerning what a bad girl she is 12 times per day, about how her parents dislike her 5 times per day, and about her own death 16 times per day. When her depression begins to subside, these types of verbal statements may decrease in frequency and severity. For example, Ieasha may make derogatory remarks about herself only 4 times per day instead of 12. She may say only once each day that her parents dislike her. Statements about death may disappear altogether.

In addition to verbal behavior, physical behavior or actions may also be observed and measured. Besides making statements that indicate she's depressed, Ieasha may spend much of her time sitting in a corner, sucking her thumb, and gazing off into space. The exact amount of time she spends displaying these specific behaviors may be observed and measured. For example, Ieasha initially may spend five hours each day sitting in a corner. When depression begins to wane, she may spend only half an hour in the corner.

The final component as a basis for operant conditioning involves the consequences of the behavior. A *consequence* may be either something that is given or something that is withdrawn or delayed. In other words, something happens as a direct result of a particular behavior. Consequences are best described in terms of reinforcement and punishment.

Reinforcement

Reinforcement refers to a procedure or consequence that increases the frequency of the behavior immediately preceding it. If the behavior is already occurring at a high level of frequency, then reinforcement maintains the behavior's frequency. A behavior occurs under certain antecedent conditions. If the consequences of the behavior serve to make that behavior occur more often or be maintained at its current high rate, then those consequences are considered reinforcing. Reinforcers strengthen behaviors and make them more likely to occur in the future.

Positive Reinforcement

Reinforcement can be either positive or negative. *Positive reinforcement* refers to positive events or consequences that follow a behavior and strengthen it. In other words, something is added to a situation and encourages a particular behavior. For example, 8-year-old Herbie receives a weekly allowance of $15 if he straightens up his room and throws all of his dirty laundry down the clothes chute. Receiving his allowance serves to strengthen, or positively reinforce, Herbie's cleaning behavior.

Negative Reinforcement

Negative reinforcement is the removal of a negative event or consequence that serves to increase the frequency of a behavior. There are two important aspects of this definition. First, something must be removed from the situation. Second, the frequency of a particular behavior is increased. In this manner, positive and negative reinforcement resemble each other. Both function as reinforcement that, by definition, serves to increase or maintain the frequency of a behavior.

A good example of negative reinforcement is a seat-belt buzzer in a car. The car door is opened, and a loud and annoying buzzer is activated. It will not stop until the driver's seat belt is fastened. Conceptually, the buzzer functions as a negative reinforcer because it increases the frequency of buckling seat belts. The buzzer is also negative or aversive. It increases seat-belt buckling behavior because people are motivated to stop (remove) it.

To take another example of negative reinforcement, suppose Orlando, a college sophomore, is trying to study in his dorm room one Thursday night. His next-door neighbor, Gavin, has decided that Thursday nights are much better for partying than for studying. Gavin, therefore, decides to invite a bunch of his friends over to take some illegal substance. Gavin cranks up his CD player to the highest vibration level it can tolerate.

Orlando tries to ignore this nuisance and continues trying to study until he can't stand it anymore. In a state of fury, he stomps up to the wall between the rooms, smashes his fist on it several times, and screams, "Shut the #$@*$%& up in there!"

On the other side of the wall, Gavin says to his buddies, "That guy is such a dweeb. If I don't turn it down, he'll probably narc on me to the hall director. Let's go somewhere else." He turns off his CD player and leaves with his friends.

Evaluating this scenario with learning theory leads to several conclusions. First, Orlando's screaming behavior served as negative reinforcement for Gavin's turning off his CD player and leaving the room. Orlando's screaming was aversive to Gavin. In order to terminate it, Gavin turned off his music and left. Moreover, from then on, Gavin made it a point to turn off his CD player whenever Orlando was around and leave his room when he wanted to party. Thus, Orlando's (aversive) screaming reinforced (increased the frequency of) Gavin's turning off his CD player and leaving his room when he wanted to party.

Looking at his situation from another perspective, Gavin's room-leaving behavior served as positive reinforcement for Orlando's screaming behavior. Orlando was positively reinforced for screaming because he got what he wanted—namely, peace and quiet. Orlando became much more likely to scream at Gavin in the future (i.e., Orlando was reinforced), because he immediately received something positive as a result of his behavior.

Although at first glance this may appear obvious and simplistic, it is easy to become confused about the type of reinforcement that is occurring. In any particular situation, both positive and negative reinforcement may be taking place at the same time. Consider, for instance, the example given initially to illustrate learning theory. It involved 4-year-old Huey and his mother at the supermarket. Huey yelled for a candy bar. His mother finally gave in and thrust one into his mouth. His crying immediately stopped. Both positive and negative reinforcement were occurring in this example. Mother's giving Huey the candy bar served as a positive reinforcer. Huey received something positive that he valued. At the same time he learned that he could get exactly what he wanted from his mother by screaming in the supermarket. Giving him the candy bar positively reinforced his bad behavior. Therefore, that type of behavior would be more likely to occur in the future.

At the same time, negative reinforcement was occurring in this situation. Mother's giving-in behavior was encouraged or strengthened. She learned that she could stop Huey's obnoxious yelling by giving him what he wanted—in this case, a candy bar. Huey's yelling, therefore, acted as negative reinforcement. It increased his mother's giving-in behavior by motivating her to stop—or to escape from—his yelling.

Punishment

Punishment and negative reinforcement are frequently mistaken for each other. Perhaps this is because they both concern something negative or aversive. However, they represent two distinctly different concepts.

Punishment is the presentation of an aversive event or the removal of a positive reinforcer, which results in a decrease in the frequency of a behavior. Two aspects of this definition are important. First, the result of punishment is a decrease in a behavior's frequency. This is in direct opposition to negative reinforcement, which increases a behavior's frequency.

Second, punishment can be administered in two different ways. One way involves presenting a negative or aversive event immediately after a behavior occurs. Negative events may include spankings, scoldings, electric shocks, additional demands on time, or embarrassing criticisms. For example, 10-year-old Susie hadn't studied for her social studies exam. Her parents had already complained about the last report card. She just hadn't given the test much thought until Ms. McGuilicutte was handing out the test papers. Susie looked over her test paper and gasped. Nothing looked even vaguely familiar. She was sitting next to Juana, whom she considered the class genius. She figured that just a few brief glances at Juana's paper wouldn't hurt anybody. However, Susie was wrong. Ms. McGuilicutte immediately noticed Susie's wandering attention. Ms. McGuilicutte swooped down on Susie and confiscated her test paper. In front of the entire class Susie was told that cheating resulted not only in an F grade, but also in two weeks of detention after school. Susie was mortified. She vowed to herself that she would never cheat again.

Susie received extremely aversive consequences as the result of her cheating behavior. The consequences included not only a failing test grade and two weeks of detention, but also humiliation in front of her peers. Her cheating behavior decreased in frequency to zero.

The second way in which punishment can be administered is by withdrawing a positive reinforcer. Once again, the result may be a decrease in the frequency of a particular behavior. For example, 7-year-old Robbie thought it was funny to belch at the table during dinner. Several times his parents asked him to stop belching. Each time Robbie was quiet for about a minute and then started belching again. Finally, his mother stated firmly that such belching was considered rude behavior and that, as

punishment, Robbie would not receive the banana split she had planned for his dessert. Robbie whined and pleaded, but his mother refused to give it to him. Robbie loved desserts, and banana splits were his favorite. Robbie never belched at the table again, at least not purposefully. Removal of the positive reinforcer—the banana split—had served as punishment. The punishment resulted in an abrupt decrease in belching behavior.

It should be emphasized that the term *punishment* as it is used in learning theory does not necessarily mean physical punishment. For some of us, the word may bring to mind pictures of parents putting children over their knees and spanking them. Punishment does not have to be physical. Verbal reprimands such as a mother saying how disappointed she is that she caught her daughter "making out" with her boyfriend in the family room can also serve as punishment. The reprimand functions as a punishment if the behavior decreases. Likewise, withdrawal of a valued activity, such as not allowing a child to go to a popular movie, can be a punishment if it acts to decrease or stop some negative behavior.

Extinction

Extinction is the process whereby reinforcement for a behavior stops, resulting in the eventual decrease in frequency and possible eradication of that behavior. Reinforcement simply stops; nothing is actively taken away. Note that extinction and punishment are two separate concepts "In extinction, a *consequence that was previously provided no longer follows the response.* An event or stimulus (money, noise) is neither taken away nor presented. In punishment, some aversive event follows a response (a reprimand) or some positive event (money) is taken away" (Kazdin, 2008a, p. 58; 2013). In everyday life, extinction often takes the form of ignoring a behavior that was previously reinforced with attention.

An example of extinction concerns the reduction of tantrum behaviors in a 21-month-old child. When put to bed, the child screams until his parents return to the room to comfort him. This provides positive reinforcement for the child's behavior. The parents are instructed to put the child to bed, leave the room, and ignore his screaming. The first night, the child screams for 45 minutes. However, the next night when the parents leave the room, no screaming occurs. Eventually, withdrawing the

Here the differences between positive reinforcement, negative reinforcement, punishment, and extinction are summarized. Important differences involve what happens and what results with each behavioral approach.

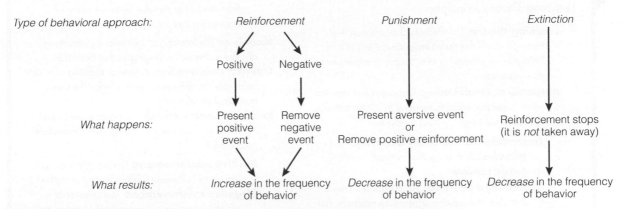

FIGURE 4.3 Positive Reinforcement, Negative Reinforcement, Punishment, and Extinction

positive reinforcer of attention results in the total elimination of the child's tantrums. Ignoring, therefore, can be used as an effective means of extinction.

Extinction occurs with many other reinforcers in various daily situations. For example, if putting a dollar in a coffee machine results in nothing but a gush of clear, hot water without the cup, use of that coffee machine will probably be extinguished. Likewise, say you're having difficulty in your biology lab course. You don't understand what the professor is saying during lectures, and you're not sure what he wants from you on exams (you've already received a D+ on two of them). Three times you try to see your professor during his office hours, and each time he is not there. Eventually, you stop trying to see him, despite your frustration. Your behavior involved in seeing him to get help has been extinguished.

One other aspect of extinction is important to note. Frequently, when reinforcement is initially stopped, a brief increase in the frequency or intensity of the behavior may occur. This is referred to as an *extinction burst*. For example, consider again tantrums in a small child. When the reinforcement of attention is withdrawn, the child's behavior may escalate temporarily. If in the past the child has always received positive reinforcement through attention for his behavior, it may be very confusing suddenly to receive no attention for that very same behavior. The child may try exceptionally hard to get the attention to which he was accustomed. The intensity of the undesirable behavior can seriously strain the patience

and tolerance of parents. However, eventually the child will learn that the tantrums are not reinforced and are therefore simply not worth the effort. Thus, the tantrum behavior is extinguished.

The relationships between positive reinforcement, negative reinforcement, punishment, and extinction are summarized in Figure 4.3.

LO 4-7 Apply Learning Theory Concepts to Practice

As children become socialized, they learn and assimilate various behaviors. Because learning is a complicated process, sometimes the behaviors they learn are not those that their parents would prefer. Behavior management is a major issue for many parents.

EP 2.1.6b, 2.1.10g, 2.1.10j

Parents have various alternative ways of responding to a child's behavior. At any point, an individual can follow alternative plans of action. For each alternative, there are consequences. The critical task is to evaluate each alternative and select the one with the most advantageous results. Learning theory concepts provide parents with a means of understanding the alternatives open to them and predicting the potential consequences of each alternative. It can help them gain control over their children's behavior.

CONCEPT SUMMARY

Learning Theory Principles

Learning theory: The theoretical orientation that conceptualizes the social environment in terms of behavior, its preceding events, and its subsequent consequences.

Respondent conditioning: Responses that develop when a person learns to respond to a new stimulus that does not naturally elicit a response.

Unconditioned (naturally occurring) stimulus: A stimulus that naturally results in specific response.

Conditioned (learned) stimulus: A stimulus that does not result in a response naturally, but does result in a response after being paired with an unconditioned stimulus that elicits the response naturally (i.e., a person learns to respond to a conditioned stimulus).

Systematic desensitization: The procedure whereby a person with a phobia practices relaxation while imagining scenes of the fear-producing stimulus, with the intent of decreasing that fear.

Modeling: The learning of behavior by observing another individual engaging in that behavior.

Operant conditioning: A type of learning in which behaviors are influenced primarily by the consequences that follow them.

Reinforcement: A procedure or consequence that increases the frequency of the behavior immediately preceding it.

Positive reinforcement: Positive events or consequences that follow a behavior and strengthen it.

Negative reinforcement: The removal of a negative event or consequence that serves to increase the frequency of a behavior.

Punishment: The presentation of an aversive event or the removal of a positive reinforcer, which results in a decrease in the frequency of a behavior.

Extinction: The process whereby reinforcement for a behavior stops, resulting in the eventual decrease in frequency and possible eradication of that behavior.

An example of parental alternatives in response to behavior is provided by Tung, age 4. At the dinner table, Tung nonchalantly and without warning says an unmentionable four-letter word. Tung's parents are shocked. At this point, they can respond in several different ways. They can ignore the fact that Tung said the word. Without being given undue attention, saying the word may be stopped. A second alternative is to tell Tung calmly that the word is not considered a very nice word. They might add that some people use it when they're angry and that other people don't really like to hear it. They might also ask him not to use the word anymore. A third alternative is for the parents to display their horror and disbelief, scream at Tung never to say that word again, and send him to bed without being allowed to finish his supper.

When this incident actually occurred, the parents opted to respond as described in the third alternative. Poor Tung really didn't understand what the word meant. He had just heard it on the playground that afternoon. He was amazed at the response of his parents and at the attention he received. His mother reported that for the following two years, he continued to repeat that unmentionable four-letter word virtually everywhere. He said it to the dentist, to the grocer, to the police officer, and even to his grandmother. His mother reported that after a while she would have been willing to pay Tung to stop using that word, if such a strategy would have worked.

In Tung's situation, his parents' attention became a strong positive reinforcer. Perhaps if they had stopped and thought in terms of learning theory principles, they could have gained immediate control of the situation and never thought another thing of it.

The Use of Positive Reinforcement

Positive reinforcement is based on the very fundamental idea that behavior is governed by its consequences. If the consequences of a particular behavior are positive or appealing, then the individual will tend to behave that way. In other words, the frequency of that behavior will be increased.

Positive reinforcement provides a valuable means of behavioral control. It has been established as an appropriate technique for achieving positive behavioral changes in numerous situations (Degangi & Kendall, 2008; Kazdin, 2013; Miltenberger, 2012). The use of positive reinforcement helps to reduce

The manner in which parents use reinforcement and punishment directly affects children's behavior.

the risk that clients will begin associating the negative effects of punishment, for example, with the therapist, resulting in an aversion to therapy. Positive reinforcement can also teach individuals exactly how to improve their behavior.

Various aspects of positive reinforcement will be discussed here. First, we'll examine the types of reinforcers available. The differences between positive reinforcement and the use of rewards will be explained. Finally, we'll offer suggestions for maximizing the effectiveness of positive reinforcement.

Types of Positive Reinforcers

Reinforcers can be separated into two major categories, primary and secondary. *Primary* or *unconditioned reinforcers* are rewarding in themselves, without any association with other reinforcers. They include objects and activities that people naturally find valuable. Food, water, candy, and sex are examples of primary reinforcers. Individuals respond positively to them naturally, without having to learn their value.

Secondary reinforcers, on the other hand, have values that are learned through association with other reinforcers. The key idea is that they must be learned. Alone they have no intrinsic value. Money perhaps is the most easily understood example. A $1,000 bill in itself is nothing but a small piece of high-quality paper with printed symbols on it. However, it is associated with things of value. It can be used to purchase actual items ranging from diamonds to pistachio nuts. Money is valuable only because it is associated with other, concrete primary reinforcers.

The concepts of primary and secondary reinforcers can be readily applied to treatment situations. For example, a child with a developmental disability may not initially value verbal praise. He may not yet have learned to associate verbal praise with his actual behavior. A social worker may be working with the child concerning his ability to dress himself. Initially, saying, "That's good," may mean nothing to the child. However, saying, "That's good," while at the same time giving the child a small chocolate star, may eventually give the verbal praise some meaning. The child learns to associate verbal praise with the positive value of the candy. Eventually, the praise itself becomes reinforcing to the child, even without the candy. This technique involves pairing a primary reinforcer, the chocolate star, with a secondary reinforcer, verbal praise. The secondary reinforcer becomes valuable to the child through its initial association with the candy.

Categories of Secondary Reinforcers

Four major types of secondary reinforcers will be addressed here: (1) material reinforcers and nonfood consumables, (2) activities, (3) social reinforcers, and (4) tokens (Fischer & Gochros, 1975; Kazdin, 2001, 2008a, 2013; Spiegler & Guevremont, 2010).

Material Reinforcers and Nonfood Consumables

Material reinforcers are specific objects or substances that can be used as rewards to increase specific behaviors. Eight-year-old Herbie received an allowance for cleaning his room. Herbie's cleaning behavior was strengthened or reinforced by receiving an allowance.

Money might be considered an object (a specific, tangible thing) that reinforces a behavior. Other objects that might have been used as tangible reinforcers for Herbie include CDs and toys. Each of these items would have acquired their value through learning. Therefore, they would be considered secondary reinforcers.

Food has already been established as a primary reinforcer along with a number of other things that are naturally reinforcing; learning is not involved. In addition, people can learn to value some nonfood consumables. Examples include cigarettes, gum, and chewing tobacco. Although these are not naturally desired, a taste for them can be acquired. Because they are material substances, they are included in this category of secondary reinforcers.

Activities Activities make up the second category of secondary reinforcers. *Activities* are tangible events whose value has been learned. Positively reinforcing activities for children might include watching rented movies, playing with friends, staying up late at night, being read to, going shopping, or visiting the stock-car races.

For example, 12-year-old Gina hates doing her homework at night. However, she loves going to the movies on Saturdays. Her parents positively reinforce her for doing an hour's worth of homework five nights per week by giving her money to go to the movies on Saturday. Going to the movies is an activity that serves as positive reinforcement for Gina's doing her homework.

Premack (1965) recognized that people have hierarchies of preferred behavior. In other words, any individual when given a choice will choose one behavior over another behavior. For instance, if given a choice, an individual might prefer to plant flowers in the garden over doing the laundry. The *Premack Principle* states that "the opportunity to engage in a high-probability behavior (a preferred behavior) as a consequence for a low-probability behavior (a less-preferred behavior)" will "increase the low-probability behavior," but never vice versa (Miltenberger, 2012, p. 68). Thus, more-preferred activities can be used to reinforce less-preferred activities. Consider the person who prefers garden work over laundry. Allowing him to plant the garden after he completes the laundry will serve to reinforce the laundry-related behavior. He will be more likely to do the laundry if he knows he can plant the garden afterward.

We've established that enjoyable, exciting activities can serve as secondary reinforcers if they are indeed valued and enjoyed by the person involved. The Premack Principle implies that activities needn't be special or extremely valued but simply preferred in order to act as a secondary reinforcer. The garden work might not be something the same individual would choose if a weekend in Las Vegas were also given as an option. However, he still would choose the garden over the laundry. Therefore, the garden could be used as a secondary reinforcer for the

laundry. Following the same line of thinking, a trip to Las Vegas could be used as a secondary reinforcer for working in the garden or doing the laundry.

One of the implicit assumptions here is that each individual will have a different hierarchy of preferred activities. For example, on camping trips, Nick prefers the following specific activities in this order, from most preferred to least preferred: reading *Peterson's 4-Wheel & Off-Road* magazine; cooking the food; doing the dishes; reading science fiction, especially space horror stories. Karen, on the other hand, prefers the specified camping activities in this order: reading science fiction, especially space horror stories; doing the dishes; cooking the food; reading *Peterson's 4-Wheel & Off-Road* magazine ("Winch Wisdom," the title of the leading article, doesn't excite her at all). For Karen, reading science fiction would function as a secondary reinforcer for any of the other three activities. She would be more likely to do any of them if she could read science fiction afterward. For Nick, however, the science fiction would not serve to reinforce any of the other activities, whereas reading *Peterson's 4-Wheel & Off-Road* magazine would.

Social Reinforcers Material reinforcers and activities are not the only things that people learn to value. Various aspects of social interaction can also be considered valuable. *Social reinforcers* include words and gestures used to indicate caring and concern toward another person. These can be communicated in one of two ways, by giving either verbal or physical praise. Verbal praise involves words or phrases that indicate approval or appreciation of someone's specific behavior, such as "Good job," "You did that very well," or "That's terrific!"

Effective verbal praise is directed at a specific behavior or activity. The person receiving the praise should be clearly aware of what the praise concerns. For instance, 8-year-old Linda did the dishes without being asked for the two days her mother was out of town attending a professional conference. Her mother, on her return home, stated, "Thank you very much for helping out and doing the dishes. I understand you did them without even being told. I really appreciate your help." Linda's mother made it very clear exactly what Linda did that was appreciated. When such praise acts to strengthen Linda's dish-washing behavior in the future, it is positive reinforcement. If Linda's mother instead had said, "You're a very good girl," it might not have been clear to Linda exactly why she was good. The positive regard communicated by such a statement, of course, is valuable in itself. However, Linda might have understood her mother to mean that she was good because she didn't cry when her mother left or because she stayed up only one half hour past her bedtime. Linda might not have understood that her mother appreciated her washing dishes, and thus might never have done so again without being told.

The second type of social reinforcement is physical praise. Physical praise involves communicating appreciation or praise through physical gestures or body posture. This may simply involve a smile or a nod of the head. Hugging, clapping, or even winking can also indicate praise.

Consider, for example, how a smile might acquire significance. An infant may not initially value her mother's smile. However, the infant may soon learn to associate the smile with comfort, warmth, and food. Eventually, the smile itself becomes reinforcing. It is a secondary reinforcer. The infant learns to value it. The smile is valued not because it is of value itself, but because the infant has learned to associate it with things of value.

The effects of social reinforcement are illustrated by Beverly, age 5, who had acquired a role in the kindergarten play. Her part involved playing a duck whose job was to waddle back and forth across the stage. Beverly was extremely nervous about her part because she was an exceptionally shy child. She even had to get a new yellow dress and wear red boots to help characterize her role. She had been practicing her waddling for days before the play. Finally, the critical night arrived. It was almost time to initiate her waddle and dare to venture out on the stage. At the last minute, she almost backed down and started crying. However, she looked out into the audience and saw her parents in the second row, looking directly at her. They were both smiling proudly and nodding their heads. With such encouragement, she waddled across that stage like no one had ever waddled before. Her parents' obvious approval and encouragement had served to positively reinforce her acting and waddling behavior. After this experience, she was much more likely to volunteer to participate in activities that required performing before an audience.

Tokens Tokens provide the fourth category of secondary reinforcers. *Token reinforcers* are designated symbolic objects reflecting specific units of value that an individual can exchange for some other commodity that he or she wants. Tokens can include poker chips, artificial coins, points, checkmarks, or gold stars. In and of themselves, they mean nothing. However, they can be associated with something of value and eventually be exchanged for that item or activity.

A practical application of tokens is the use of a token economy in child management. For example, a new bicycle might serve as a strong positive reinforcer for a particular child. However, it is absurd to give the child a new bicycle every time the child cleans his or her room. Rather, a system can be designed in which a child can earn tokens. The child can be told that if he or she earns a certain number of tokens, he or she can exchange them for a new bicycle. Tokens become a secondary reinforcer. A large sum of tokens can be used to acquire a new bicycle, the item of real value.

Reinforcers Versus Rewards

A distinction must be made between reinforcers and rewards. A reward is not necessarily a positive reinforcer. A reward is something that is given in return for a service or a particular achievement. It may or may not increase the frequency of a particular behavior. A soldier might receive a medal of honor at the end of a war for shooting down 27 enemy aircraft. This is a reward. This reward does not, however, increase the frequency of this individual's shooting down more aircraft during his civilian life.

Reinforcers, by definition, increase the frequency of a behavior. Receiving an A on an exam is a positive reinforcer for studying behavior if it serves to increase the frequency of a particular student's studying in preparation for exams. However, the student may not value the grade very much. The A may not serve to motivate him to increase or maintain studying behavior. The student becomes bored with studying and receives C and D grades on the next two exams. In this case, the A grade might be considered a reward for performance on one exam. However, the grade is not a positive reinforcer because it neither maintained nor increased the frequency of his studying.

By definition, something serves as reinforcer only if it increases behavior. A positive reinforcer needs to be valued by an individual for it to be effective. Not all items, activities, and social interactions are reinforcing to all people. A roller-coaster ride at Disney World may be positively reinforcing for a third grader whose dream it is to visit Disney World. However, that same ride may not be at all reinforcing to the third grader's father who tends to become ill on roller coasters.

Suggestions for Using Positive Reinforcement

Four suggestions to enhance the use of positive reinforcement involve the quality, the immediacy, the frequency of positive reinforcement, and the use of small steps for shaping behavior.

Quality of Positive Reinforcement

In order to be considered reinforcement, an item or event must actually increase the frequency of some behavior. We've already established that what is reinforcing for one person may not be reinforcing for another.

A more subtle issue, however, involves the varying degrees of reinforcement value of any particular reinforcer. A particular positive reinforcer might be more reinforcing in one form than in another.

A high school senior working as a part-time janitor at a small inner-tube factory provides an example. The young man, Jorge, is working to save for a down payment on a car. The idea of owning a car is very reinforcing to him. Because of the tremendous costs involved in purchasing a car, Jorge had decided to be satisfied with almost anything that he could reasonably afford. However, when he found a 2005 tomato-red Mustang with black racing trim for sale, his working behavior sharply increased. He asked if he could double his working hours. To Jorge, the Mustang served as a much stronger positive reinforcer than an older, beat-up van.

Immediacy of Positive Reinforcement

Positive reinforcement has a greater effect on behavior if it is administered immediately or shortly after the behavior occurs (Miltenberger, 2012; Spiegler & Guevremont, 2010). It's important that the behavior and the positive reinforcement occur very close to each other in time. Positive reinforcement loses its effect if it is delayed too long. For example, one morning a 5-year-old boy brushes his teeth without being told. Praising him for this behavior immediately after he's finished or even while he's brushing will have a much greater effect on whether he brushes his teeth again on his own than if he's praised when he gets into bed at night. By bedtime, it becomes more difficult for him to associate the praise with the specific teeth-brushing behavior.

Frequency of Positive Reinforcement

The most effective way to increase a particular behavior is to reinforce it every time it occurs. This is referred to as *continuous reinforcement*. For example, Kaitlyn, age 12, is supposed to do her math homework every night. If Kaitlyn's teacher collects the assignments every morning and gives Kaitlyn credit for doing them, Kaitlyn is likely to complete her homework every night. However, if Kaitlyn's teacher collects only the Thursday-night homework, Kaitlyn is less likely to do her homework every night.

Continuous reinforcement is the most effective in establishing a particular behavior. However, if the positive reinforcement stops for some reason, the behavior is likely to extinguish rapidly. For example, Kaitlyn's teacher collects her homework every morning for two months. Suddenly, the teacher decides that it's no longer necessary to collect the homework. As a result, there is a fairly strong likelihood that Kaitlyn will stop doing her homework if she no longer gets credit for it.

An alternative to continuous reinforcement is *intermittent reinforcement*. In this case, a behavior is not reinforced every time it is performed, but is reinforced only occasionally. In the real world, continuous reinforcement is difficult to administer. It is difficult to be with a person every minute of the day in order to observe that person's behavior. Sometimes intermittent reinforcement is a viable alternative.

Intermittent reinforcement is not as powerful in initially establishing a behavior. It may take longer to establish the behavior, and the behavior may not occur as regularly as it would under the conditions of continuous reinforcement. For example, Kaitlyn might not do her homework every night because of the chance it wouldn't be collected the next day.

However, intermittent reinforcement is less subject to extinction. That is, suppose Kaitlyn's teacher had only occasionally collected her homework. Suddenly, she no longer collects the homework. Kaitlyn would be more likely to continue doing the homework after an intermittent schedule of reinforcement than after a continuous schedule. When she was accustomed to intermittent reinforcement, Kaitlyn would be more likely to continue doing her homework on the chance that it might be collected again. If homework collection stops abruptly after continuously being collected, Kaitlyn would probably think that her teacher no longer liked to collect it. As a result, Kaitlyn would probably stop doing her homework.

Each type of intermittent reinforcement dictates a different procedure for how frequently or in what order reinforcement should be administered (e.g., every third time or randomly). These various procedures are referred to as *schedules of reinforcement.*

Shaping Behavior

Sometimes the behavior that's supposed to be positively reinforced never occurs. It is impossible to reinforce a behavior that isn't there. In such cases, a technique called shaping can be used. *Shaping* refers to the reinforcement of successive approximations—that is, small steps of progress made toward the final desired behavior.

For example, 7-year-old Ralph is terrified of the water. His mother thinks that it would be valuable for him to learn to swim. However, swimming behavior cannot be reinforced because Ralph simply refuses to enter a swimming pool. In this case, it might be useful to break down the specific behavior into smaller, more manageable pieces of behavior: going to the beach and playing far away from the water, playing several feet away from the water, playing while sitting in an inch of water, wading, entering the water waist deep, moving arms around in the water, briefly dunking head beneath the water, and finally starting to practice beginning swimming strokes. At each step, Ralph could be positively reinforced with praise, attention, or toys for participating in that step. Eventually, his behavior could be shaped so that he would participate in behavior resembling swimming. Specific swimming techniques could then be initiated and reinforced.

The Use of Punishment

Punishment is frequently and often unwillingly chosen as the first alternative in controlling children's behavior. Often punishment is used in the name of discipline. Punishment involves either the application of an aversive consequence or the removal of a positive reinforcer. In either case, the result is a decrease in the frequency of a behavior.

Potential Negative Consequences

Before using punishment as a means of behavioral management, it's important to consider the potential negative consequences. Five of them will be mentioned here (Kazdin, 2001, 2008a, 2013; Miltenberger, 2012; Sundel & Sundel, 2005). First, punishment tends to elicit a negative emotional response. The child may come to dislike the learning situation. For example, if a child is punished for spelling some words wrong in a composition, the child may no longer want to write at all. The child may also have a negative reaction toward the person administering the punishment.

For example, a young woman in junior high school was walking through the crowded halls from study hall to her next class. The gruff varsity football coach grabbed her by the shoulder and shouted, "Act like a lady!" She had no idea what he was referring to. However, from that time on, she avoided both crowded hallways and that football coach whenever she could. She had developed an intense dislike for the man.

This example also illustrates the second possible negative side effect of punishment: avoidance of either the punishing person or the punitive situation. In homes where physical punishment is used freely and regularly, children may try to stay away from the home as much as possible. Lying may provide another effective means of avoiding punitive situations. (Children sometimes learn to lie because parents set the price for honesty too high.)

The third possible negative effect of punishment is that it can teach children to be aggressive. Another way of saying this is that a punishing agent models aggressive behavior. Children can learn that the way to deal with frustration or with not getting their own way is to hit or scream. This can carry over to their interactions with peers, siblings, or adults. An example is an adolescent who had been labeled as having severe emotional and behavioral problems. When he was a small child, physical punishment was used frequently in the home. By the time he reached age 16 and had grown to be 6 feet 3 inches tall, a different problem became apparent in the home. The boy began to physically assault his mother whenever they had disagreements. He had learned to be aggressive.

The fourth potential problem with using punishment, specifically physical punishment, is the possibility of physically harming the child. A parent may lose control or not be aware of his or her real strength. Without initial intent, physical damage may result.

Finally, there is a fifth reason for questioning the use of punishment. Punishment teaches people what they *should* not do but gives them no indication as to what they *should* do. Scolding a child for being impolite when visiting Aunt Edna does not help the child know how she could have treated Aunt Edna more appropriately.

In summary, all five of these considerations involve losing control of the consequences of punishment. The outcome of punishment is unpredictable, and therefore it should be used with extreme care.

The Nature of Punishment

Punishment has several characteristics (Kazdin, 2001, 2008a, 2008b, 2013; Miltenberger, 2012). First, a decrease in the frequency of a behavior usually occurs relatively soon after the punishment is presented. If the behavior doesn't decrease almost immediately after the supposed punishment starts, there is a good possibility it never will. Thus, it is not wise to continue punishment if it doesn't work almost immediately.

For example, 1-year-old Tyrone was crawling happily on his mother's kitchen floor when he discovered the electric socket. His mother, who was watching him out of the corner of her eye, ran over to him, slapped his hand, and raised her voice in a loud, "No!" He looked at her and returned his attention immediately to the socket. After this occurred four times, his mother slapped him even harder. He then started crying, and she removed him to another room. In this incident, scolding and hitting were not effective. Instead, the mother's attention appeared to positively reinforce Tyrone's playing with the electric socket. Since scolding and hitting were not effective even after several attempts, it was not likely that they would ever work. Calmly diverting Tyrone's attention might have been a more effective approach to controlling Tyrone's behavior.

Another characteristic of punishment is that its effects, although often immediate, frequently do not last very long. Relatively soon after receiving punishment, a person often reverts to the old behavior. For example, a driver may receive a speeding ticket for driving 87 mph on a 55-mph expressway. For a while he takes care to drive within the speed limit. However, he soon finds it too restrictive and time consuming to drive so slowly. His speeds gradually creep up to the old levels of 85 to 90 mph.

A third characteristic of punishment is that its effects are frequently limited to the conditions under which the punishment occurred. In other words, punishment tends to work only in the specific situation in which it occurred or only with the particular person who administered the punishment. For example, Trudy, age 7, likes to spit at people as they pass by her on the sidewalk. Her mother spanks her when she sees this behavior. Therefore, Trudy never spits in front of her mother. However, when her mother is in the house or at the grocery store, or when Trudy is at the babysitter's, she continues to spit at passersby. The babysitter spanked her twice, but it didn't change Trudy's behavior. Spanking functioned as punishment for Trudy only when her mother was present and only when her mother administered it.

The Effectiveness of Punishment

Miltenberger (2012) comments that "authority figures such as governments, police, churches, or parents impose punishment to inhibit inappropriate behavior—that is, to keep people from breaking laws or rules. Punishment may involve prison time, the electric chair, fines, the threat of going to hell, spanking, or scolding. However, the everyday meaning of punishment is very different from the technical definition of punishment used in behavior modification" (p. 104).

Sundel and Sundel (2005) reflect:

Despite the disadvantages of punishment and the stringent requirements for ensuring its effectiveness, punishment is still commonly used as a behavioral control technique. One reason for this is that punishment usually works immediately to suppress undesired behavior. Therefore, the short-term consequences are reinforcing for the individual who administers the punishment. For example, Mel spanked his daughter Terri when she complained about eating her vegetables. Terri stopped complaining; thus, her father was reinforced for spanking her. (p. 133)

This everyday scenario focuses on the immediate, short-term effects of punishment, not on long-term effects or consequences other than the immediate cessation of the targeted behavior. Kazdin (2008a) discusses the use of punishment as a means of behavior modification:

> There has been extensive debate within the profession regarding the use of aversive events…. Many of the discussions have focused on self-injurious (e.g., head banging, face slapping) and aggressive behavior (e.g., fighting). Behaviors that are dangerous warrant immediate attention and require complete elimination if at all possible. Early in the development of behavior modification, electric shock was used (brief, mild, and delivered on few occasions) and was shown to be effective in eliminating self-injurious behavior. This was significant because in a number of instances, the behavior was long-standing and had not responded to other treatments. Over the past several years, significant advances have been made in devising alternative procedures to reduce and eliminate dangerous behaviors. (p. 415)

In summary, punishment may be effective when used to curb extremely self-destructive or aggressive behavior in cases in which other treatment approaches have failed. The problematic behavior's dynamics should be carefully assessed to determine the appropriateness and potential effectiveness of punishment. Serious thought should go into the method of punishment to be used. It should be the least severe possible to be effective. The well-being of the person experiencing the behavioral program should always be of paramount importance. Finally, the potential side effects of punishment, mentioned earlier, should be cautiously considered.

Suggestions for Using Punishment

When the decision is made to use punishment, follow three suggestions for maximizing its effectiveness (Kazdin, 2001, 2008a; Miltenberger, 2012; Spiegler & Guevremont, 2010; Sundel & Sundel, 2005). First, intervention should occur early; that is, punishment should be administered as soon as possible after the behavior that is to be punished occurs.

For example, 10-year-old Santiago had been stealing CDs for about six months. One afternoon, he decided to shoplift a CD from Wal-Mart. Although he made it out to the parking lot, his friend, Maynard, was not so lucky. A huge male clerk grabbed Maynard by the wrist as he was hoisting a CD under his T-shirt. Santiago, although feeling very bad that his friend got caught, also felt relieved that he himself did not.

Two weeks later Santiago's father received a phone call from the police. Apparently under duress and with the promise of a lesser punishment, Maynard had relented and given the police Santiago's name. Santiago's punishment was being grounded for the next month. Being grounded involved reporting in by 8:00 p.m. every night including weekends. Although Santiago was not particularly happy about his situation, he was more unhappy about being caught than about stealing a CD. He interpreted his punishment to mean "Don't get caught." The punishment had virtually no effect on his CD-stealing behavior. He continued to steal CDs, but did so with exceptional care. In this situation, because the punishment was not administered soon after the stealing behavior occurred, it had little effect.

A second suggestion for using punishment is to administer the punishing consequences every time the behavior occurs. In Santiago's situation, he was punished only once. Many other times his stealing behavior was positively reinforced by his getting and enjoying the CDs he wanted. Receiving a punishment every time a behavior occurs helps to strengthen the idea that the consequence of that particular behavior is unappealing.

The third suggestion concerning the use of punishment is the most important. At the same time that punishment is used, a complementary program should be used to reinforce other, more appropriate behaviors. Punishment has been found to be most effective when an individual is being reinforced for adopting more appropriate behaviors at the same time. For example, a therapeutic goal for a child with profound intellectual disabilities was to walk instead of crawl (O'Brien, Azrin, & Bugle, 1974). Punishment for crawling involved restraining him from movement for five seconds. However, this did not really serve as punishment because the child's crawling behavior didn't decrease. Nor did his walking behavior increase. Eventually, a new approach was tried. While the child was being restrained from crawling, he was also encouraged or positively reinforced for moving his body. This included being helped to walk. As a result, his walking behavior increased, and his crawling behavior decreased. In this case, punishment was effective when the child was reinforced for a more appropriate behavior at the same time. It has been found that the negative side effects of punishment, such as resentment toward the punitive person, aggressive behavior, and avoidance of the punitive situation, are not nearly as great when reinforcement for alternative appropriate behaviors is used (Carey & Bucher, 1986).

Additionally, Patterson (1975) makes a fourth suggestion for using punishment: Remain calm while administering it. Excessive attention directed at a particular behavior may serve as a positive reinforcer for that behavior rather than as a punishment. For example, 18-month-old Petey discovered a book of matches lying on the coffee table. He immediately sat down and started to play with them. His mother saw him, ran over to him, and spanked him. She also took away the matches. Because both of Petey's parents smoked, it was fairly likely that Petey would find more matchbooks lying around the house. In fact, he found some the next day. His mother responded in a similar manner. Petey learned that he could get attention from his mother by playing with matches. As a result, he loved to find matches and play with them. Although his mother's attention was negative, it was forceful enough to serve as positive reinforcement. Petey continued to play with matches every chance he got.

Ethical Questions 4.2

EP 2.1.2

What are your thoughts about punishing children? What was your experience with punishment as a child? If punishment was used, in what ways were you punished? Did punishment work or not? Why?

Additional Issues

In addition to the focus on positive reinforcement and punishment, three additional issues merit attention here. They concern common elements encountered in practice. The additional issues include accidental training, the use of behaviorally specific terminology, measuring improvement, and the importance of parental attention.

Accidental Training

Thus far, the discussion has emphasized planned behavioral change. However, many times reinforcement and punishment affect behavior without conscious planning. Behavior can be increased or decreased without intention. When attempting to understand the dynamics of behavior, it's important to understand that accidental training does occur.

Negative attention is frequently an effective means of providing accidental training. Attention, even in the form of yelling, can function as positive reinforcement. Even though it is supposed to be negative, the social reinforcement value can be so strong that the behavior will be strengthened instead of weakened. For example, if Ethan's mother yells at him for picking her favorite peonies, then Ethan may learn that picking those peonies will make his mother yell. If Ethan continues to pick the peonies and his mother continues to yell at him for it, the yelling has served to reinforce his peony-picking behavior. Highlight 4.2 provides another example of accidental training.

Behaviorally Specific Terminology

EP 2.1.3c

A major advantage of conceptualizing behavior in terms of learning theory is the emphasis on *specificity*. A behavior must be clearly and concisely defined. A clear description of behavior allows for all involved in the behavioral management of a child to understand exactly what behavior, including problem behavior, involves.

For example, Jessica, age 9, was described by her teachers as too passive. It is difficult to know what is meant by "too passive." The word passive is relatively abstract. The image of a passive Jessica is quite vague. However, if Jessica's passivism is defined in terms of her behavior, as it would be with a learning theory conceptualization, the image of Jessica becomes more distinct. Jessica's passivism might be described behaviorally in the following way:

Jessica sits quietly by herself during classes and recesses at school. She avoids social contact with

HIGHLIGHT 4.2

Accidental Training

Tommy was an only child. His parents, who were in their late 30s, had tried to have children for years without success. When Tommy came along, they were overjoyed. Both parents thought almost everything Tommy did was "simply darling." One time, when Tommy was 3 years old, he approached some dinner guests and asked for money. He had learned that money bought ice cream and other good things. Two things occurred. First, his parents thought it was cute, so they laughed. Then they appropriately told him that asking for money was not a good thing to do. But they maintained happy, smiling faces all the while. Tommy thus received massive social reinforcement in the form of praise and attention for his begging behavior. Second, Tommy did receive $2, which he later spent for mocha fudge ice cream. The guests were not quite as entertained by Tommy's behavior as his

parents were. But they felt he was a cute kid and gave him money to avoid embarrassment in front of his parents.

The next time Tommy's parents had guests, Tommy did the same thing. He came out for display, said hello, and then asked them if he could have some money. He received a similar reaction. As time went on, Tommy consistently continued his begging behavior in front of guests. His parents became less entertained as the years passed. They discovered that an 8-year-old Tommy coming out and asking guests for money was no longer as cute as a 3-year-old doing the same thing. However, by the time Tommy was 8, they were having a terrible time trying to decrease or extinguish his begging behavior. For an extended period of time, Tommy had accidentally been trained to beg. Such extensive accidental training had become very difficult to extinguish.

peers during recess by walking to the far side of the playground away from the other children. She does not volunteer information during class. When asked a question, she typically shrugs her shoulders as if she does not know the answer. She then avoids eye contact and looks down toward the ground. She is consistently standing last in lines for lunch, for recess, or for returning to school. When other children push her out of their way, she allows herself to be pushed without comment.

Learning theory mandates clear behavioral descriptions in order to conceptualize any particular behavior. The antecedents, the behavior itself, and the consequences of the behavior must be clearly defined in order to make changes in the behavior. The behavioral description of Jessica provides a much clearer picture than merely labeling Jessica as being "too passive."

Measuring Improvement

EP 2.1.10m

Observation of behavior becomes much easier when it has been specifically described. Subsequently, improvements in behavior become more clearly discernable. For example, it might be difficult to establish if Jessica is becoming less passive. However, it is much easier to determine the number

of times Jessica assertively raises her hand to answer a question in class.

Behavior must be observable in order to measure if it has improved. In other words, it must be clear when the behavior occurs and when it does not. In Jessica's situation, the frequency of hand-raising in class has been targeted as a behavior that involves passivism. If Jessica never raises her hand to answer a question, she will be considered passive. If she raises her hand frequently, on the other hand, she will not be considered passive.

For the sake of this illustration, hand-raising is used as a means to measure passivism. Clearly stated behaviors can be counted. For example, in Jessica's case, each time she raises her hand above shoulder level after her teacher has asked the class a question could count as one hand-raising behavior. In an actual situation, Jessica's other behaviors could also be used. These might include behaviors such as the amount of time she spends talking to peers or the number of times she answers her teacher's questions. Her improvement might be measured by using a summation of several measures.

The first step, then, is targeting a behavior to change. The next step is determining how severe the problem is in the first place. This must be known in order to tell when improvements have been made. In Jessica's case, the hand-raising must be counted and a baseline established. A *baseline* is the frequency with which a behavior occurs before behavior modification begins. After a baseline is established, it is easy to determine when a change in the frequency of the behavior has occurred. The change is the difference between how frequently that behavior occurred at the baseline and how frequently the behavior occurs after the behavior modification program has begun.

For example, during the first month of school, Jessica raises her hand to answer a question zero times per school day. However, by the seventh month of school, she raises her hand to answer a question an average of six times per day. If one of the means of measuring passivism is the number of times Jessica raises her hand in class, then Jessica can easily be described as less passive during the seventh month of school than during the first.

The final point concerning behavioral specificity involves how the behaviors are counted in the first place—who keeps track of the frequency of the behavior and how this is done. Behavior checklists and charts can be developed for this purpose. A behavior checklist simply allows for a place to make note of when a behavior occurs. For example, a two-dimensional chart might have each day of the week listed on the horizontal axis. Each day might be broken down into individual hours on the vertical axis on the left-hand side. Table 4.1 illustrates how this might be applied to Jessica's situation.

Whenever Jessica raised her hand in class, her teacher would make a note of it on her behavior checklist. The total number of times could be counted. It could thus be clearly established if an improvement occurred.

We have not addressed the specific types of treatment that could be used to decrease Jessica's passivism. A treatment program could be established in various ways. For example, positive reinforcement could be administered whenever she raises her hand. This could take the form of verbal praise, a piece of candy, or a token that could be used to buy something she really wanted.

The Importance of Parental Attention

One of the criticisms of the application of learning theory has been that it is a rigid and somewhat cold dissection of human behavior. Warmth, caring, and human concern are not readily evident. This certainly does not have to be the case. The importance of parents' communicating with their children and genuinely showing spontaneous concern for them should not be overlooked. Learning theory provides a framework for analyzing and gaining control over behavior. Other important aspects of human relationships can occur concurrently with programs based on learning theory.

For example, active listening is often emphasized in suggestions for effective parenting (Ivey, Ivey, & Zalaquett, 2012, 2014). *Active listening* is the process in which the receiver of a communication pays close attention to what the sender of the communication is saying, and subsequently reflects back what was heard to make sure the "message has been accurately understood" (Sheafor & Horejsi, 2006, p. 148). A parent and a child often have different ways of saying things. Each has a different perspective. Active listening encourages a parent to stop for a moment and consciously examine what the child is saying. The idea is for the parent to look at the issue

TABLE 4.1	BEHAVIOR CHART: NUMBER OF TIMES JESSICA RAISES HER HAND				
	MON.	TUES.	WED.	THURS.	FRI.
8:00–8:59 a.m.	0	0	0	0	0
9:00–9:59 a.m.	0	0	0	0	0
10:00–10:59 a.m.	0	0	0	0	0
11:00–11:59 a.m.	0	0	0	0	0
12:00–12:59 p.m.	0	0	0	0	1
1:00–1:59 p.m.	0	1	1	0	1
2:00–3:00 p.m.	0	0	1	3	3

from the child's perspective. This may not be clear from the particular words the child has spoken. The parent then is urged to reflect these feelings back to the child. The end result of a parent's taking the time to understand a child should be an enhancement of the warmth and caring between them.

Charlene and her mother provide an example of active listening. Charlene, age 7, comes home after school, crying. She says to her mother, "Betty invited everybody but me to her birthday party." Instead of passing it off as a simple childhood disappointment, Charlene's mother stops for a moment and thinks about what this incident might mean to Charlene. She replies to Charlene, "You really feel left out and bad about this, don't you?" Charlene comes into her mother's arms and replies, "I sure do, Mom." In this instance, her mother simply reflected to Charlene her empathy and concern. As a result, Charlene felt that her mother really understood. Warmth and feeling were apparent in their interchange.

Although this interaction is not structured within learning theory terms, it certainly illustrates the basic components of warmth and empathy necessary in the parent-child relationship. Feelings and communication are ongoing, dynamic parts of that relationship. They occur simultaneously along with the ongoing management of children's behavior.

A Specific Treatment Situation: Time-Out from Reinforcement

Extensive volumes have been written about the various aspects of learning theory and its applications. Specific concepts have already been discussed. We have selected a specific treatment situation to illustrate the application of these concepts using specific techniques. It focuses on concepts frequently used by social work practitioners. The treatment situation presented here involves the use of a time-out from reinforcement procedure.

The term *time-out* refers to a *time-out from reinforcement*. In this procedure, previous reinforcement is withdrawn, with the intended result being a decrease in the frequency of a particular behavior. Kazdin (2008a) explains why time-outs are a form of punishment instead of extinction:

The defining feature of time-out is based on a period of time and the unavailability of reinforcement during that time period. Of course, time-out is also a punishment procedure. Something is withdrawn (availability of reinforcers) contingent on behavior. Extinction is not a punishment procedure. In extinction, a response that has been reinforced (e.g., praise for smiling) is no longer reinforced. The key feature of extinction is that a previously reinforced behavior is no longer reinforced. There is no time interval or period involved in extinction. When the response occurs, no consequence follows. In contrast, during time-out, when a response to be suppressed occurs, a period is invoked in which no reinforcers can be provided for any behavior. (pp. 210–211)

Instead of applying some aversive consequences such as a spanking after a behavior occurs, a child is simply removed from the reinforcing circumstances. If a child gets no attention or positive reinforcement for a behavior, that behavior will eventually diminish.

For example, 4-year-old Vernite loves to play with her Legos®. However, Vernite has difficulty sharing them with other children. When another child picks up one of the pieces, Vernite will typically run over to that child, pinch him, take the toy, and place it in a pile with the rest of her own Legos®. As a result, other children don't like Vernite very much.

The goal here might be to decrease Vernite's selfish behavior. Selfish behavior is defined as the series of behaviors involved in pinching and taking toys away from other children. A time-out from reinforcement procedure can be used to control Vernite's selfish behavior. Whenever Vernite pinches another child or takes a Lego away from that child, her mother immediately picks her up and puts her in a corner behind a screen for three minutes. At the end of that time, her mother picks up Vernite again and puts her back in the play situation. What happens from Vernite's perspective is that the positively reinforcing situation filled with fun, Legos, and other children is removed. (In actuality, of course, it is Vernite who is removed.) Without receiving the reinforcement of having the toys for herself, Vernite's selfish behavior should eventually disappear. She should learn that such behavior is inappropriate and, in effect, not worth its consequences. Vernite's selfish behavior should eventually be extinguished.

Improving the Effectiveness of Time-Outs

EP 2.1.6b

Several aspects of time-outs tend to improve their effectiveness. The following are suggestions for using time-outs:

1. A time-out should be applied immediately after the targeted behavior occurs in order for it to be effective.

2. Time-outs should be applied consistently. A time-out should occur as a consequence every time the targeted behavior occurs.

3. Time-outs should usually extend from 1 to 10 minutes (Miltenberger, 2012). Such short periods of time have been shown to be effective (Kazdin, 2001, 2008a, 2008b, 2013; Sundel & Sundel, 2005). "However, if the client is engaging in problem behaviors in the time-out area at the end of the time-out period, time-out is extended for a brief time (typically 10 seconds to 1 minute) until the client is no longer engaging in problem behaviors" (Miltenberger, 2012, p. 347). Extending time-outs for longer periods of time does not increase the effectiveness of the time-out (Kazdin, 2001, 2008a, 2008b, 2013). The relationship between the targeted behavior and the time-out becomes too distant. An extended timeout of an hour, for instance, may also take on some of the potential negative consequences of a more severe form of punishment such as resentment toward the person administering the time-out.

4. The time-out should take place in a very boring place. An ideal time-out should provide absolutely no positive reinforcement. It might take place in a chair facing a corner or in a room devoid of stimulating objects and pictures. If the time-out location is exciting or stimulating, it may positively reinforce a negative target behavior rather than extinguish it.

5. The person, frequently a parent, who is administering the time-out should be careful not to give the child positive reinforcement in the form of attention while the time-out is taking place. A parent might simply state to the child, "Timeout." The child should then be removed to the time-out location with as little show of emotion as possible. No debate should take place.

6. A child should be told ahead of time exactly which behaviors will result in a time-out. The length of the time-out should also be specified. The intent is to help the child understand exactly what he or she is doing wrong and what the resulting consequences will be.

7. If the child refuses to go to the time-out location, he or she may have to be physically taken there. This should be done with as little show of emotion as possible. The child should be gently restrained from all activity until the time-out can begin.

8. The most important thing to remember about using the time-out procedure is that positive reinforcement should be used to reinforce more appropriate replacement behaviors for the same situation. Appropriate behavior should be praised as soon as it occurs after the time-out has taken place. For example, when Vernite is returned to the play scene, she should be praised for playing with her own toys and not taking them away from other children. Her mother might simply say, "Look how well you're playing and sharing now, Vernite. Good girl."

A simple anecdote taking place in a supermarket illustrates the ingenuity and creativity with which a time-out might be used. A mother was shopping, with her 2-year-old sitting in a shopping cart. Suddenly for no apparent reason the child began to scream. Much to the surprise of onlooking shoppers, the mother calmly removed her raincoat and placed it over the child's head for 20 seconds. People who are unfamiliar with the time-out technique may have thought she was trying to suffocate the child. However, she performed the procedure calmly and gently. When she removed the raincoat, there sat a peaceful and quiet child. The mother had no further problems with screaming behavior in the supermarket that day. What this mother did was to remove the child from all positive reinforcement for a brief period of time. The child learned that screaming led to no positive consequences. Thus, the screaming stopped.

Grounding

One other thing should be noted regarding the use of time-outs. Frequently, parents use grounding or sending children to their rooms to curb children's behavior. Although superficially these techniques might resemble time-outs, they don't seem to be very effective. Perhaps too many positive reinforcers are available in a child's room. Often this form of time-out is administered long after the actual behavior occurs. The actual time of restriction is certainly longer than the recommended time period of a maximum of several minutes.

LO 4-8 Examine Common Life Events That Affect Children

Some basic aspects of family functioning have already been examined. These included a conceptualization of family systems and an examination of learning theory applied to parenting situations.

Several other social aspects of childhood merit attention. Common events or situations involving the family that frequently affect the lives of children are discussed here. These include membership in sibling subsystems and gender-role socialization. Ethnic and cultural differences in families, the social aspects of play with peers, the influence of television, and the school environment are also examined. The incidence and dynamics of physical abuse, neglect, emotional maltreatment, and sexual abuse of children are explored. Finally, the treatment of child abuse and neglect is explained.

Membership in Family Systems

The family environment is of crucial importance to a child. Even though as children grow they become more and more involved with their peers, the family itself remains very important (McGoldrick et al., 2011). A good family environment provides nurturance, support, guidance, and a safe, secure place to which children can turn.

EP 2.1.7

Baumrind conducted an interesting series of studies to evaluate how parents actually go about their business of parenting (Baumrind, 1971, 1978, 1991a, 1991b, 1993, 1996; Lamanna & Riedmann, 2009; Rathus, 2014b). Three basic styles of parenting emerged. First, *permissive* parents are very nondirective and avoid trying to control their children. Permissive parents may be either overly indulgent or rejecting-neglecting. "*Permissive-indulgent* parents ... are easygoing and unconventional. Their brand of permissiveness is accompanied by high nurturance (warmth and responsiveness)"; permissive *rejecting-neglecting* parents shun or ignore their children, thereby leaving children to fend for themselves (Rathus, 2014b, p. 316). Such parents show little if any affection and responsiveness.

The second parenting style is *authoritarian*. Parents adopting this style have definite ideas about how children should behave. These parents do not hesitate to make rules and tell their children what to do. They emphasize control and conformity.

The third parenting style is *authoritative*. Parents using this style are neither permissive nor authoritarian, but somewhere in the middle. On the one hand, they provide control and consistent support. On the other hand, they involve their children in decision making and encourage the development of independence.

Which parenting style is the most effective? There is some support that an authoritative approach to parenting is preferable (Lamanna & Riedmann, 2009). Dacey and Travers (2006) describe this style: "Authoritative parents are high on control (they have definite standards for their children), high on clarity of communication (the children clearly understand what is expected of them), high in maturity demands (they want their children to behave in a way appropriate for their age), and high in nurturance (a warm, loving relationship exists between parents and children)" (pp. 206–207).

Rathus (2013) reflects that the research suggests that it's best for parents to avoid either of the more extreme permissive or authoritarian styles in their parenting approach. He suggests using a number of effective techniques that coincide with the application of learning-theory principles. Effective parents should:

- "Reward good behavior with praise, smiles, and hugs.
- Give clear, simple, realistic rules appropriate to the child's age.
- Enforce rules with reasonable consequences.
- Ignore annoying behavior such as whining and tantrums….
- Be consistent." (Rathus, 2013, p. 231).

Ethical Questions 4.5

What type of parenting style do you think is best, and why? What style did your parents use? To what extent was it effective, and why?

EP 2.1.2

One potential problem with the conclusion that an authoritative style is best is that it may not clearly reflect the values and effective child-rearing practices evident in other cultures. Spotlight 4.2 addresses the importance of cultural context in the assessment of the effectiveness of parenting style. Spotlight 4.3 explores ethnic and cultural differences in families.

A variety of other issues involving children and families will be discussed in Chapter 12. These include single-parent families, families of divorce, blended families, mothers working outside the home, family communication, family interaction, and common problems facing families.

Membership in Sibling Subsystems

Siblings compose a child's most intimate and immediate peer group. Brothers and sisters will affect the development and behavior of a child. Siblings learn how to play with each other. They act as models for each other. They also learn how to fight with each other.

The Coming of a New Baby

Picture a 3½-year-old girl waiting patiently for her mother to come home from the hospital with her new baby sister. When Mom arrives, imagine her surprise when she sees her beloved mother holding a blanket that looks like it has a tiny doll in it. Her mother is smiling and cooing down at the "doll." The little girl thinks to herself, "That must be my baby sister." She feels surprise, wonderment, happiness, and worry all at once, but is unable to articulate these feelings. Her general impression of the whole new situation is, "Now what?"

The coming of a new baby changes a child's family environment. Children's reactions to the change in circumstances vary dramatically. Some may withdraw into themselves and regress to more babylike behavior. Others may show open hostility toward the new baby and suggest giving it back. One 3-year-old boy was found holding a safety pin near his new infant brother, contemplating poking him in the eye. Still other children happily and proudly accept the family's new addition and enjoy holding and playing with the baby.

Because of the complexity of the issue and the lack of clear-cut research, it is difficult to propose how to make the transition as easy as possible. Dr. Benjamin Spock (Spock, 1976; Spock & Rothenberg, 1985), the famous pediatrician who gave several generations of parents advice about how to raise their children, provided some logical suggestions.

SPOTLIGHT ON DIVERSITY 4.2

Cultural Context and Parenting Style

**EP 2.1.1e,
2.1.4c,
2.1.4d**

Various ethnic groups have markedly different parenting styles that don't fit neatly into the permissive/authoritarian/authoritative classification system. Specific variations involve how parents perceive and demonstrate caring and control. For example, Chinese American parents are generally viewed as more demanding concerning control of their children's behavior (Berk, 2012a; Papalia & Feldman, 2012). For one thing, "most Chinese parents strictly control their children's aggressive behavior" and demand "that their children display no aggressive behavior under any circumstances" (Ou & McAdoo, 1999, p. 255). The Baumrind system emphasizes control as characterizing an authoritarian parenting style. However, this approach suggests a somewhat different intent and purpose than that of the Western authoritarian parenting style. "High control [in Chinese culture] reflects the Confucian belief in strict discipline, respect for elders, and socially desirable behavior, taught by deeply involved parents" (Berk, 2013, p. 582). Chinese tradition emphasizes that a "child, no matter how old, should remain emotionally and financially attached to the parents," and there are "strong indications of a lack of independence training in child rearing" (Lin & Liu, 1999, p. 238). The Chinese view control of children as a means to teach "obedience and cooperation," the "values most emphasized."... "Frequent receiving and giving of help between generations is seen by Chinese as an indication of family solidarity. Most children are expected to turn their earnings over to their parents to be used for general family needs" (p. 238).

So what Western eyes might view as an authoritarian trait is really a demonstration of warmth, support, and caring from the Chinese perspective. These latter values more closely characterize authoritative parents in Baumrind's classification system, but without stressing the American values of rugged individualism and free choice (Papalia & Feldman, 2012). Berk (2013) reflects:

In Hispanic, Asian Pacific Island families, and Caribbean families of African and East Indian origin, firm insistence on respect for parental authority is paired with high parental warmth—a combination suited to promoting competence and strong feelings of family loyalty (Harrison, Wilson, Pine, Chan, & Buriel, 1994; Roopnarine & Evans, 2007). In one study, Mexican-American mothers living in poverty who adhered strongly to their cultural traditions tended to combine warmth with strict, even somewhat harsh, control—a style that served a protective function, in that it was associated with reduced child and adolescent conduct problems (Hill, Bush, & Roosa, 2003). Although at one time viewed as coercive, contemporary Hispanic fathers typically spend much time with their children and are warm and sensitive (Garcia Coll & Pachter, 2002; Jambunathan, Burts, & Pierce, 2000). In Caribbean families that have immigrated to the United States, fathers' authoritativeness—but not mothers'—predicted preschoolers' literacy and math skills, probably because Caribbean fathers take a larger role in guiding their children's academic progress (Roopnarine, Krishnakumar, Metindogan, & Evans, 2006)." (p. 582)

African American mothers also tend to require immediate and rigorous compliance with their directions (Berk, 2012a). Their approach, however, combines caring and affection with strict discipline and rarely involves physical punishment. This no-nonsense tactic is viewed as a means of helping children regulate their behavior and keep themselves safe even when in a treacherous environment; children view such parental control as a means of caring for their welfare (Brody & Flor, 1998).

In summary, it is important to recognize the cultural context of child rearing, parental expectations, and social responsibilities before stating unilaterally that one parenting style is "best." Learning from clients about their culture and cultural expectations concerning parenting style is a career-long process.

First, children should be told in advance about all the changes they are to experience. Changes might include sharing a bedroom or having the new baby use their old high chair. Preparing them in this way is supposed to minimize surprises. Not knowing what's going to happen is scary for children. Second, Spock suggested continuing to talk to older children and emphasizing how much they are loved and valued. Finally, children should be encouraged to express their feelings, including the negative ones, so that parents can allay their children's fears and address problems as they occur.

Sibling Interaction

Approximately 80 percent of children in the United States have at least one brother or sister (Berk, 2012a; Santrock, 2012b). Sibling interaction involves a multitude of behaviors and feelings. Siblings fight with each other but they also play with each other, work together, and show affection such as hugging each other.

SPOTLIGHT ON DIVERSITY 4.3

LO 4-9 Recognize Ethnic and Cultural Differences in Families: Empowerment Through Appreciation of Strengths

**EP 2.1.1e,
2.1.4c,
2.1.4d,
2.1.10e**

The father's role in the family, the availability and nature of support systems, and perspectives on disciplining children vary greatly among cultures (Santrock, 2008). Despite these variations, research on 186 cultures throughout the world revealed a pattern of successful parenting (Santrock, 2008; Whiting & Edwards, 1988). The variables that emerged are *consistency* in the form of supportive control and genuine caring for children.

When assessing the dynamics of families from various cultures, three factors are important. First, cultural variations involving expectations and values reflect each culture. Second, people of different cultures living in the United States and Canada experience varying degrees of assimilation into the majority culture simply by living there. Third, people not of European origin frequently experience discrimination and oppression because of their differences.

Two other perspectives are helpful when thinking about multicultural diversity in families: cultural pluralism and internal variations or subgroups within a culture. In conceptualizing a multicultural nation, it is helpful to think in terms of *cultural pluralism* instead of a melting pot. A melting pot implies that all people blend together into one uniform whole. Cheese fondue comes to mind, where the cheese and other ingredients blend together in one bubbling mass. This is not really the case with a multicultural society. Rather, people from different cultures come together, and each cultural group retains its own rich spirit and customs. This is cultural pluralism. One of those huge lollipops made up of multicolored swirls comes to mind. It is one mammoth piece of candy,

yet it is made up of distinct swirls of brilliant blue, red, yellow, orange, pink, and green blending together to various degrees.

Still another perspective useful in understanding cultural diversity involves respecting and appreciating the differences within large groups. For example, among Native Americans, there are far more than 500 specific groups (Weaver, 2008).

Social workers should strive to learn from clients about their diverse cultures. To be effective, this is a career-long process. Here we discuss some of the values, beliefs, and perspectives assumed by three cultural groups in American society: Hispanics, Native Americans, and Asian Americans.

Hispanic Families

Chapter 1 established that the terms *Hispanic* and *Latino* have generally been used to refer to people originating in countries where Spanish is spoken. However, we also noted that the terms in reality refer to people originating in a number of places. No one term is acceptable to all the groups of Spanish-speaking people.

The U.S. Census Bureau collects information by having people identify themselves as being Hispanic or not.

Persons of Spanish/Hispanic/Latino origin are those who classified themselves in one of the specific Hispanic origin categories listed on the questionnaire—Mexican, Puerto Rican, Cuban, as well as those who indicated that they were of Other Spanish/Hispanic/Latino origin (persons whose origins are from Spain, the Spanish-speaking countries of Central or South America, or the Dominican Republic ... Traditional and current data collection and classification treat race and Hispanic origin as two separate and distinct concepts.... People who are Hispanic may be of any race and people in each race group may be either Hispanic or Not Hispanic. (2011, p. 5)

According to the census, of those classifying themselves as Hispanic, 65.4 percent are of Mexican heritage, 8.9 percent Puerto Rican, 3.5 percent Cuban, and 16 percent Central or South American (U.S. Census Bureau, 2011). However, for any particular family, Goldenberg and Goldenberg (1998) caution: "Socioeconomic, regional, and demographic characteristics vary among Hispanic American groups, making cultural generalizations risky. Within groups, the counselor needs to be alert to the client's generation level, acculturation level, languages spoken, educational background, socioeconomic status, rural or urban residence, adherence to cultural values, and religiosity/spirituality" (p. 307).

Mark Burnett/Alamy

Hispanic nuclear and extended family members celebrate a child's birthday.

Keeping in mind that specific variations exist within the many subgroups, we will discuss some cultural themes important to Hispanic families in general. These include the significance of a common language, the importance of family relationships including extended family, and the traditional strictness of gender roles.

The first theme important in understanding the environment for children growing up in Hispanic families is the significance of a *common language* (Delgado-Romero, Nevels, & Capielo, 2013; Furman, Negi, & Loya, 2010). Everyday communication among Hispanic people is frequently in English. Almost 60 percent of Latinos speak only English, or at least speak it fluently, and almost 80 percent speak Spanish fluently; the uniting symbolic importance of the Spanish language should not be disregarded (Longres & Aisenberg, 2008). So many cultural activities and aspects of pride are associated with Spanish. Consider the cultural events and holidays (e.g., Cinco de Mayo for Mexican Americans, which celebrates the glorious day a small Mexican army defeated a French army battalion). Other cultural aspects may be celebrated and promoted, such as community murals reflecting important aspects of culture, art, or history, and traditional foods associated with a Hispanic heritage (Delgado, 2007).

A second theme involves the importance of both nuclear and extended *family relationships* (Diller, 2015; Longres & Aisenberg, 2008; Magana & Ybarra, 2010). Hispanic people generally place great value on maintaining the original two-parent family and its intensive involvement with the extended family. Commitment to the extended family group and upholding responsibilities to family members are emphasized. Note, however, that these family ideals are not always realized when families face the harsh realities of poverty, unemployment, and immigration difficulties (Longres & Aisenberg, 2008).

It is also important to be aware of the community support systems often available to Hispanic families. These include *botanicas, bodegas, clubs sociales, como familial, compadrazo,* and faith healers. "Botanicas are shops that sell herbs as well as records and novels in Spanish. *Bodegas* are grocery stores, but they also serve as information centers for the Hispanic community, providing such information as where folk healers can be found. [Mexican, Puerto Rican, and Cuban Hispanic cultures espouse folk healers who help people deal with physical, emotional, and spiritual difficulties.] *Club sociales* provide recreation as well as links to community resources, including employment and housing." There also are "special friends who furnish reciprocal support called *como familial*" and "the ritual kinship of *compadrazo*" people who "participate in baptisms, first communions, confirmations, and marriages, and often serve as parent substitutes" (Chilman, 1993, p. 160).

A third theme often characterizing Hispanic families is the traditional *strict division of gender roles* (Delgado-Romero et al., 2013; Dhooper & Moore, 2001; Sanchez & Jones, 2010; Weaver, 2005). Weaver (2005) reports that historically there have been "clear and distinct expectations for men and

women. Men are expected to be strong, and women are expected to be submissive to male authority" (Weaver, 2005, pp. 145–146). However, Santiago-Rivera, Arredondo, and Gallardo-Cooper (2002) caution that "considerable debate" exists

over the extent to which Latinos adhere to traditional gender roles in contemporary U.S. society. Although evidence suggests that gender roles are undergoing transformation, the complexities surrounding this phenomenon are far from clear-cut.... When examining gender role-based behaviors among Latinos, one must consider a variety of influencing factors such as socioeconomic indicators (e.g., level of education, income), place of residency, migration experience, language, and family composition. These determinants significantly influence gender roles. (p. 51)

Many "Latinas now work outside the home and may wield decision-making power about family finances" (Weaver, 2005, p. 146). Additionally, "more Latinas are heading households and as a result must take on roles that were traditionally dominated by men. As single heads of households, women are responsible for making major decisions about the welfare of their families and for providing for and nurturing their children" (Santiago-Rivera et al., 2002, p. 51). In summary, "it is important to understand evolving gender roles within Latino families" (Weaver, 2005, p. 146).

Native American Families

We have stressed that there are hundreds of Native American groups with hundreds of languages and dialects. Sensitivity to differences among tribes and appreciation of these differences are vital to effective social work practice. However, as with Hispanic people, several themes characterize many Native American groups. These include the importance of extended family, cooperation, mutual respect, harmony with nature, the concept of time, spirituality, and noninterference.

As with Hispanic people, family ties, including those with *extended family*, are very important (Diller, 2015; Paniagua, 2005; Sue & Sue, 2008). Extended family members include parents, children, cousins, aunts, uncles, grandparents, and even other community members who are integrally involved with the family. Diller (2015) explains:

Although the specifics of power distribution, roles, and kinship definitions vary from tribe to tribe, the vast majority of Native Peoples live in an extended family system that is conceptually different from the Western notion of family. Some tribes are matrilineal, which means that property and status are passed down through the women of the tribe. When a Hopi man marries, for example, he moves in with his wife's family, and it is the wife's brothers, not the father, who have primary responsibility for educating the sons. Family ties define

(continued)

existence, and the very definition of being a Navaho or a Sioux resides not within the individual's personality, but rather in the intricacies of family and tribal responsibilities. When strangers meet, they identify themselves, not by occupation or residence but by who their relatives are. Individual family members feel a close and binding connection with a broad network of relatives (often including some who are not related by blood) that can extend as far as second cousins. (p. 270)

A second concept in Native American culture involves the emphasis on *cooperation* (Diller, 2015; Sue & Sue, 2008). The collective well-being of the family and tribe takes precedence over that of the individual (Paniagua, 2005). Weaver (2005) elaborates: "A sense of identity is rooted in group membership. Native people often refer to themselves as members of the Native community, regardless of their geographic location.... Social cooperation is often valued over independent decision making. The wishes and plans of individuals must be balanced along with the needs of family and community members.... This emphasis on the group leads to strong mutual support networks. The well-being of the group is paramount" (p. 90). Sue and Sue (2008) comment on how this emphasis on cooperation affects children: "Indian children tend to display sensitivity to the opinions and attitudes of their peers. They will actively avoid disagreements or contradictions. Most do not like to be singled out and made to perform in school unless the whole group would benefit" (p. 350).

A third theme that characterizes Native American culture is *mutual respect*, as Weaver (2005) explains: "Respect is emphasized in all social interactions. There are appropriate ways to communicate respectfully with others, including limiting eye contact and not interrupting someone who is speaking. People are accorded respect for the different roles they fulfill within a community. Elders are respected for their knowledge and wisdom, children are respected as the future of Native Nations, and leaders are respected for their willingness to sacrifice their own needs on behalf of First Nations [Native American] communities" (p. 91).

A fourth concept important in Native American culture is that of *harmony with nature*. Diller (2015) elaborates: "Native American cultures emphasize the interconnectedness and harmony of all living things and natural objects. This spiritual holism affirms the value and interdependence of all life forms. Nature is held in reverence, and Native People believe that it is their responsibility to live in harmony and safeguard the valuable resources we have been given" (p. 271).

A fifth theme of Native American life, related to harmony with nature, is the *concept of time* (Bearse, 2008; Diller, 2015). Time is considered an aspect of nature. Time flows along with life and, therefore, should not control or dictate how you live. Hence, other aspects of life, including interactions with other people, become more important than getting somewhere on

time. Sue and Sue (2008) further describe this orientation: "Indians are very much involved in the present rather than the future. Ideas of punctuality or planning for the future may be unimportant. Life is to be lived in the here and now" (p. 350).

A sixth theme of Native American values concerns the importance of *spirituality* (Bearse, 2008; Sue & Sue, 2008). "The spirit, mind, and body are all interconnected. Illness is a disharmony between these elements" (Sue & Sue, 2008, p. 351). Spirituality, involving both tribal religion and Christianity, plays a critical role in the lives of many Native Americans. Although religious beliefs vary from one tribe to another, "religion is incorporated into their being from the time of conception, when many tribes perform rites and rituals to ensure the delivery of a healthy baby, to the death ceremonies, where great care is taken to promote the return or the person's spirit to the life after this one" (Ho, 1987, p. 73).

A seventh important concept for Native Americans is *noninterference* (Sue & Sue, 2008, p. 350). "It is considered inappropriate in Native American culture to intrude or interfere in the affairs of others. Boundaries and the natural order of things are to be respected.... With regard to communication, a premium is placed on listening" (Diller, 2015, p. 270). It is generally considered better "to observe rather than react impulsively" (Sue & Sue, 2008, p. 350). Silence is often used as a means of conveying respect (Diller, 2015).

Asian American Families

People who are typically considered Asian Americans are composed of three basic groups that, in turn, consist of numerous subgroups. These are "Asian Americans (Japanese, Chinese, Filipinos, Asian Indians, and Koreans), Asian Pacific Islanders (Hawaiians, Samoans, and Guamanians), and Southeast Asian refugees (Vietnamese, Cambodians, and Laotians)" (Paniagua, 2005, p. 73). Obviously, there is great variation among these groups, even though they are clustered under the umbrella term *Asian Americans*. Here we discuss four themes that tend to characterize many Asian American families: the significance of family, interdependence, investment made in children, and patriarchal hierarchy.

Like Hispanic people and Native Americans, Asian Americans tend to consider the *family as the primary unit* and individual family members as secondary in importance (Balgopal, 2008; Diller, 2015; Leong, Lee, & Chang, 2008). Phillips (1996) elaborates: "The welfare and the integrity of the family are of great importance. The individual is expected to submerge or to repress emotions, desires, behaviors, and individual goals to further the welfare of family and maintain its reputation. The individual is obligated to save face, so as to not bring shame onto the family. Therefore, there is incentive to keep problems within the family so that the family will not 'lose face'" (p. 1).

⚜ **SPOTLIGHT ON DIVERSITY 4.3** *(continued)*

A second theme, related to the significance of the family, is *interdependence* (Balgopal, 2008; Diller, 2015; Leong et al., 2008; Sue, 2006). "Studies have found that for most Asian Americans, their immediate and extended family are important loci of identity formation, social learning, support, and role development" (Leong et al., 2008, p. 117). "Children are expected to strive for family goals and not to engage in behaviors that would bring dishonor to the family. Asian American parents tend to show little interest in the child's viewpoint regarding family matters. Instead, the emphasis is on family harmony, adapting to the needs of others, and adherence to 'correct' values (Rothbaum, Morelli, Pott, & Liu-Constant, 2000). Asian American adolescents appear to retain the expectation to assist, support, and respect their family even when exposed to a society that emphasizes adolescent autonomy and independence (Fuligni et al., 1999)" (Sue & Sue, 2008, pp. 362–363). An expectation that children will care for elderly parents is also important (Balgopal, 2008; Green, 1999).

A third theme characterizing many Asian American families *involves hierarchical* relationships (Balgopal, 2008; Sue, 2006; Sue & Sue, 2008). "Communication flows down from the parent to the child, who is expected to defer to the adults" (Sue & Sue, 2008, p. 363). Similarly, younger children are to defer to older children (Sue, 2006). Asian American families tend to have high expectations regarding children's behavior and tend to impose stricter discipline when misbehavior occurs (Balgopal, 2008; Sue, 2006; Sue & Sue, 2008).

"Problem behavior in children is thought to be due to a lack of discipline. However, differences in parenting style between Asian American groups have been found. Japanese and Filipino American families tend to have the most egalitarian relationships, while Korean, Chinese, and Southeast Asian Americans are more authoritarian (Blair & Qian, 1998)" (Sue & Sue, 2008, pp. 364–365).

A fourth theme involves *patriarchal hierarchy* (Balgopal, 2000, 2008; Sandhu & Madathil, 2013; Sue, 2006; Sue & Sue, 2008). Traditional values designate that men and older family members have greater status than other family members. Diller (2011) explains: "Family and gender roles and expectations are highly structured. Fathers are the breadwinners, protectors, and ultimate authorities. Mothers oversee the home, bear and care for children, and are under the authority of their fathers, husbands, inlaws, and at times even sons. Male children are highly prized.... Older daughters are expected to play a caretaking function with younger siblings" (p. 274).

A Note on Difference

Our discussion concerning cultural themes of values and behaviors is general and brief. Actual practices may vary dramatically from one ethnic group to another and from one family to another. The point here is to enhance your sensitivity to and appreciation of potential cultural differences so that you may better understand and serve your clients.

Rathus (2011a) describes sibling interaction:

In early childhood, siblings' interactions have positive aspects (cooperation, teaching, nurturance) and negative aspects (conflict, control, competition) (Parke & Buriel, 2006). Older siblings tend to be more caring but also more dominating than younger siblings. Younger siblings are more likely to imitate older siblings and accept their direction...

There is more conflict between siblings when the parents play favorites (Scharf et al., 2005). Conflict between siblings is also greater when the relationships between the parents or between the parents and children are troubled (Kim et al., 2006). (p. 167)

The Effects of Birth Order, Family Size, and Family Spacing

It is difficult to establish definite facts concerning birth order and development because so many

factors are involved (e.g., parenting style, cultural expectations, socioeconomic status, number of persons residing in the family). However, some personality differences have been linked to birth order. First-born children tend to be more achievement oriented (Kail & Cave-naugh, 2010; Latham & Budworth, 2007; Rathus, 2011a). They also tend to do better academically (Healy & Ellis, 2007; Rathus, 2011a). "Compared with later-born children, first-born children have also been described as more adult-oriented, helpful, conforming, and self-controlled," although such differences are usually small (Santrock, 2009, p. 434; 2012b). "On the negative side, firstborn children ... show greater anxiety and are less self-reliant than later-born children" (Rathus, 2011a, p. 167).

Rathus (2014c) reflects:

Later-born children may learn to act aggressively to compete for the attention of their parents and older siblings.... Their self-concepts tend to be lower than those of firstborn or only children, but the social skills later-born children acquire from dealing with their family position seem to translate into greater popularity with peers.... They also tend to be more rebellious and liberal than first-born children (Beck et al., 2006; Zweigenhaft & Von Ammon, 2000).

By and large, parents are more relaxed and flexible with later-born children. Many parents see that the firstborn child is turning out well and perhaps they assume that later-born children will also turn out well. (p. 161)

What about only children? Some research indicates that only children tend to be more achievement oriented and have more pleasant personalities than later-born children, especially those in large families (Jiao, Ji, & Jing, 1996; Kail & Cavanaugh, 2010; Santrock, 2012b). Please keep in mind, though, that no absolute predictors exist for how any child will turn out. Many other factors in the social environment can affect development.

Gender-Role Socialization

Infants are treated differently by virtue of their gender from the moment that they are born (Hyde & DeLamater, 2014; Yarber & Sayad, 2013). There is almost immediate segregation by pink or blue clothing. A basic question remains unresolved. To what extent are males and females inherently different, and in what ways?

This question is related to the nature-nurture argument regarding why people become the people they do. Supporters of the nature idea argue that people are innately programmed with inborn, genetic, or natural predispositions. According to the nurture perspective, people are the product of their environment. That is, people are affected by what happens to them from the day they're born; they learn from their environment and are shaped by it. Each side of the debate has evidence and research to support its perspective. Probably the answer lies somewhere in the middle. People are probably born with certain potentials and predispositions that are then shaped, strengthened, or suppressed by their environments. Gender roles will be discussed again later in this chapter, in regard to differences in play, and more extensively in Chapter 9.

LO 4-10 Assess Relevant Aspects of the Social Environment

EP 2.1.9a

The family does not provide the only means of socialization for children. They are also exposed to other children as they play and to other adults, especially in the school setting. The transactions children have with their peers and with adults in school directly affect both the children's behavior and their social development. Children learn how to relate to others socially. They learn what types of social behaviors others expect from them. They also are influenced by the amount of time they spend watching television. Issues to be addressed here include the social aspects of play, bullying, the influence of television and other media, and the role of the school. The impact of each will be related to the social development of children.

The Social Aspects of Play with Peers

Luther, who is 8, screamed at the top of his lungs, "Red light, green light, hope to see the ghosts tonight!" He spun around and peered through the darkness. He was playing his favorite game, and he was "it." That meant that he counted to 20 and then had to find the others and tag them. The first one tagged had to be "it" the next time.

"Where were those other kids anyway?" he said silently to himself. Randy usually hid in the garbage can. He thought that that made him smell so unappealing that no one would look for him there. Siggy, on the other hand, liked to hide in the bushes by the drainage ditch. However, a lot of mosquitoes were likely to consume anybody brave enough to venture over in that direction.

Horace was always an enigma. Luther never knew exactly where he was likely to hide. Once he had managed to squeeze into old Charlie's doghouse. Charlie was a miniature mongrel.

On serious consideration of which route to take, Luther decided that the garbage can was his fastest and easiest bet. Just as Luther could've sworn that he heard Randy sneeze inside the garbage can, he heard his mother's call. "Luther, you get in here this minute. I told you four times that you have to be home by 8:30 on weeknights. Come in right now, do you hear?"

"Aw, rats," mumbled Luther. Just when he started to have some fun, he always had to quit and go home. Along came the other guys. See, he was right. Randy was in the garbage can, and sure enough, Siggy popped out from behind the bushes by the drainage ditch. As usual, he was scratching. Randy's mother was really going to give it to him when he got home. He did smell awfully bad. Horace appeared suddenly out of nowhere. He wasn't about to waste a good secret hiding place for nothing.

All four boys dragged themselves home. They walked as slowly as they could and procrastinated appropriately. Another hard summer's day of play was done, but they were already thinking about tomorrow.

Children's play serves several purposes. It encourages children to use their muscles and develop physically. It allows them to fantasize and think creatively. Finally, play enables children to learn how to relate to peers. Play provides a format for learning how to communicate, compete, and share. It functions as a major avenue of socialization.

Garvey (1977) defines play as activity that involves the following five qualities: First, play must be something that is done purely for enjoyment and not for a reward or because it is considered appropriate. Second, play has no purpose other than to be an end in itself. Third, people who play choose to do it. No one can force a person to play. Fourth, play involves active participation in an activity. Either mentally or physically, the individual must be involved. Pure observation does not qualify as play. Fifth, play enhances socialization and creativity. Play provides a context in which to learn interaction and physical and mental skills.

Play and Interaction

There are at least two basic ways of looking at how children play. These include social play and fantasy play. *Social play* involves the extent to which children interact with other children as they play. *Fantasy play* involves what children think about and how they imagine their pretend games as they play.

Social Play

Parten (1932) conceptualized a model for how children progress in their development of social play. Her research, which was done in the 1920s, focused on children ages 2 to 5. Observations of the children

in action led to the proposition that there are actually six different levels of play. Theoretically, children progress through the following levels as they get older:

1. *Unoccupied behavior:* Unoccupied behavior involves little or no activity. A child might be sitting or standing quietly. Frequently, the child's attention is focused on observing something going on around him.
2. *Onlooker play:* A child involved in onlooker play is simply observing the playing behavior of other children. The child is mentally involved in what the other children are doing. However, the child is not physically participating in the play. Onlooker play differs from solitary play in that the child's attention is focused on the play of peers, instead of on simply anything that might be happening around him or her.
3. *Solitary play:* Solitary play involves the child playing independently. No attention is given to other children or what they might be doing.
4. *Parallel play:* A child involved in parallel play is playing independently but is playing in a similar manner or with similar toys as other children in the immediate vicinity. The child is playing essentially the same way as the other children, although no interaction occurs.
5. *Associative play:* Here children play together. There is some interaction, but the interaction is not organized. For example, children may share toys or activities and talk with each other. However, their play is very individualized. Each child plays independently from the others and focuses on individual activities.
6. *Cooperative play:* Cooperative play involves organized interaction. Children play with each other in order to attain a similar goal, make something together, or dramatize a situation together. Attention is focused on the group activity. Cooperation is necessary. Children clearly feel that they are a part of the group.

Parten proposed that different age levels are characterized by different types of play. Two-year-old children tend to play by themselves. By age 3, parallel play begins to be evident. Associative play is engaged in by more and more children as they reach the age of 4. By age 5, most children participate in cooperative play.

Parten's levels of play have been criticized on several fronts. For one thing, the model doesn't address the complexity of play; all children can be observed to participate in all levels of play (Papalia & Feldman, 2012; Rubin, Bukowski, & Parker, 1998). Another question involves how solitary play is viewed in Parten's model. Is solitary play really less mature than play occurring in groups? Much of children's solitary play is thoughtful, educational, and creative by nature, helping children to develop more advanced cognitive thinking. Where do such solitary activities such as drawing or building with blocks and Legos fit into Parten's conception of normal play development?

Parents need to be aware of the normal developmental aspects of play at different age levels. Expectations of parents and other caregivers need to be realistic. Children should be encouraged to play with other children in ways appropriate to their age level. Yet children should not be pushed into activities that are beyond them. Children who are isolated in their play activities at an age when they need to be more outgoing may need encouragement in that direction. Parents and other caregivers can help children develop their play and interactional skills.

Gender Differences in Play

EP 2.1.4c

Two gender-related differences in behavior appear early in life. One is a difference in aggressive behavior with respect to play (Hyde & DeLamater, 2014). Boys behave more aggressively than girls. The other early behavioral difference is in toy preference (Rathus, 2014b). By age 3 or 4 girls begin choosing to play with dolls and participate in housekeeping play. Boys are more oriented toward toys such as trucks and guns. The reasons for these differences are not clear. Perhaps children play with the toys they are given and encouraged to play with. Girls' rooms are filled with dolls and items devised for playing house. Boys' rooms display various action-oriented toys such as cars, trucks, guns, and sports equipment.

For example, when Aunt Karen took 3-year-old Andrea, her niece and the apple of her eye, to Kmart one day to buy her a toy, Andrea headed straight for the "girls' toys" not the "boys' toys." When Aunt Karen suggested Andrea look at some "fun" trucks and cars (Aunt Karen knew that it was good for girls to become oriented to cars and trucks, both because they'll have to use real ones someday and because such play aids in the development of spatial perception skills), Andrea screwed up her nose and said "No! Those are boys' toys!" Her response was interesting because Andrea's mother did most of the mechanical fixing and all of the outdoor work at their home. The impact of the media, especially television, and Andrea's observation of other people must have been very great.

Another reason for the differences in toy preference may be that children, who become conscious of gender by age 3 (Crooks & Baur, 2014), learn early how they should be playing. They watch television and observe Mommy and Daddy; they learn that girls and boys should like to do different things.

There are at least three logical reasons why girls' behavior is less aggressive than that of boys (Lott, 1987). These reasons all seem to relate to and reinforce each other. First, girls have fewer chances to "practice" aggressive behavior such as fighting, breaking, or hurting things. Second, girls' aggressive behavior is less likely to be encouraged by adults than is the aggressive behavior of boys.

For instance, Aunt Karen had an opportunity to observe 3-year-old Andrea in the company of her male and female nursery-school peers. They were on a field trip to a local pumpkin farm with the idea of picking some small pumpkins. All of the boys in Andrea's group were kicking, screaming, punching, bumping, running, and making b*rrrrrrrr* and g*rrrrrrrr* sounds. Several of the mothers calmly observed, smiled, and made proud comments like, "Isn't he a real boy?" Meanwhile the girls stood silently on the sidelines watching the boys have "fun." When one girl tried to get involved, her mother said, "Oh, no, Chrissy, you might get hurt. Those boys are so rough."

A third reason why girls are less aggressive, according to Lott, is that girls are less likely to "experience success" at being aggressive than are boys. Boys are encouraged by adults to be more practiced at aggression than girls. Girls, on the other hand, are reinforced for being gentler and more ladylike.

The Peer Group and Popularity

The *peer group* is made up of a child's equals. It can have an increasing impact on children as they get older, more independent, and more experienced. On a positive note, the peer group provides an arena for children to learn about themselves, build their self-concepts, and learn how to interact with others. On a negative note, the peer group can place pressure on children to do things they would never consider doing on their own.

Some children get along fabulously with peers; others are avoided, isolated, and withdrawn. What makes a child popular? Researchers have studied popular and unpopular children and concluded that popular children tend to display certain characteristics (Newcomb, Bukowski, & Pattee, 1993; Papalia & Feldman, 2012). They tend to be friendly with others and interact easily. They are neither too aggressive nor too passive. They tend to be trustworthy and able to supply emotional responsiveness and support to peers. They usually are bright and creative, yet don't act superior or arrogant.

On the other hand, children who are unpopular tend to be characterized by opposite traits. They are socially immature. They tend either to be too pushy and demanding, or very shy and withdrawn. They might not be the brightest children around or the most attractive. They may not have the listening skills and the ability to empathize with others that popular children seem to have.

A common technique for examining children's interaction is referred to as *sociometry*. This involves asking children questions about their relationships and feelings toward other people. The relationships can be illustrated on a diagram called a *sociogram*. Children in a group might be asked questions such as which three peers they like the best, which three they like the least, who they most admire, who would they like to sit next to, or who are they most afraid of. Each child can be represented by a circle. Arrows can then be drawn to the people they indicate in answer to each question.

Sociograms are shown in Figure 4.4. A sociogram can be created to illustrate the results of each question asked. Our example plots out two questions. The first reflects students' feelings about who they thought was the strongest leader in the group. The second illustrates which peer they most liked in the group.

Sociogram A clearly illustrates that Toby is thought to be the strongest leader in the group. He is bright, energetic, and very "street smart." However, Sociogram B clearly illustrates that he is not

Sociogram A

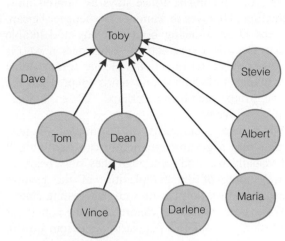

Students were asked who they felt was the strongest leader in the group. Arrows reflect their feelings. Toby clearly has that status.

Sociogram B

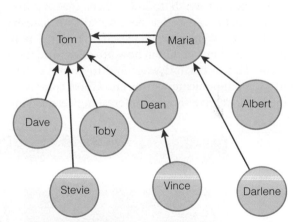

Here students were asked which person they liked the most in the group. Tom and Maria appear to be the most popular.

FIGURE 4.4 Sociograms of a Special Education Class

the most popular or best liked in the group. Both Tom and Maria shine there. They both are more mature than the other group members. They are assertive and fairly self-confident, yet don't impose their will on the others. They are among the brightest in the group. Toby, on the other hand, is more feared than respected. The others admire his apparent sophistication, yet don't trust him. He doesn't let anyone get close to him emotionally or physically. He keeps his distance.

Vince's opinions differ radically from those of other group members. Vince stays by himself most of the time. He loves to wander off whenever he can. He sees Dean as being both a strong and likable leader. Dean is a very active, verbal person who is always in the center of activity. He has some trouble controlling his behavior and tends to provoke the other group members. Perhaps Vince admires Dean's involvement.

These two sociograms are examples of how insights into a group's interaction can be obtained and visually pictured. Although they only begin to portray some of the complexities of the group's interaction, they do provide some interesting clues.

We've been speaking of children as being popular or unpopular. It is as if on a popularity scale from 1 to 10, each child is either a very unpopular 1 or a very popular 10. In real life, of course, most people lie somewhere in between. They may have some of the characteristics of the "popular person," but not others.

It appears that social skills provide a primary basis for popularity. It follows, then, that because skills in general can be learned, social skills can be learned and popularity increased. Training may focus on teaching children how to draw attention to themselves in positive ways and to improve their ability to communicate with peers. Good communication skills involve showing interest in peers, asking appropriate questions, and sharing information that might be interesting to other children. Sometimes role playing is employed to teach children more effective responses to make in various situations (e.g., when playing a game or trying to get in line for recess). Sometimes, DVDs are used to illustrate positive interaction, after which children can discuss what occurred and learn to apply this information to their own interpersonal situations (Ladd, Buhs, & Troop, 2002).

Bullying

"Nine-year-old Stephanie did not want to go to school…. She had gotten into a disagreement with Susan, and Susan had told her she would beat her mercilessly if she showed up at school again. To highlight her warning, Susan had shoved Stephanie across the hall" (Rathus, 2014c, p. 217).

In this example, Susan was the bully and Stephanie the bully-victim. Steinberg and his colleagues (2011b) describe bullying:

Bullying refers to aggression by an individual that is repeatedly directed toward particular peers (victims).… It may be physical (hitting, kicking, shoving, tripping), verbal (teasing, harassing, name-calling), or social (public humiliation or exclusion). Bullying differs from other forms of aggression in

Bullying involves aggressive, hurtful behavior by bullies toward targeted peer victims.

that it is characterized by specificity (bullies direct their acts to certain peers) and by an imbalance of power between the bully and the victim…. An older child bullies a younger one; a large child picks on a small, weaker one; a verbally assertive child torments a shy, quiet child. It is not bullying when equals have an occasional fight or disagreement. Bullies are more likely to use force unemotionally. (p. 318)

Although boys are more likely to bully, girls can also participate in such aggressive behavior (Perren & Alsaker, 2006). "In a national survey of more than 15,000 sixth- through tenth-grade students, nearly one of every three students said that they had experienced occasional or frequent involvement as a victim or perpetrator in bullying (Nansel & others, 2001)" (Santrock, 2009, p. 457; 2012b). Some research indicates that bullies and their victims are in regular contact with each other as 70 to 80 percent of them share the same classroom (Salmivalli & Peets, 2009). Therefore, it is a significant problem for many children.

The social environment and expectations about how peers should behave also can affect the occurrence of bullying (Salmivalli, Peets, & Hodges, 2011; Schwartz, Kelly, Duong, & Badaly, 2010). Peers are frequently aware of and observe bullying as it happens. Some bullies may even want observers so that they can feel important and powerful in front of witnesses.

Victims tend to fall into two categories (Rubin, Bukowski, & Parker, 2006). "The first are children who are shy, anxious, and socially withdrawn, which makes them easy prey. Often they do not have friends to protect them. But other victims are high in aggression themselves and engage in irritating behavior that elicits aggression. Other children see them as 'asking for it.'" (Steinberg et al., 2011b, p. 319).

What results from bullying? Some recent research indicates that when bullies and bully-victims become adolescents, they are more likely to become depressed, think about committing suicide, and actually commit suicide (Brunstein Klomek, Marrocco, Kleinman, Schonfeld, & Gould, 2007). Other research indicates that adolescents who had been either bullies or bully-victims "had more health problems (such as headaches, dizziness, sleep problems, and anxiety) than their counterparts who were not involved in bullying" (Santrock, 2009, p. 458, 2012b; Srabstein, McCarter, Shao, & Huang, 2006).

So what can be done about bullying? Dupper (2013) suggests nine steps that school personnel can take to discourage and stop bullying among students:

An essential first step is conducting an accurate assessment of the extent and nature of bullying in the school…. [This can be done by] administering an anonymous questionnaire to students about bullying…. Findings from this survey can be used to motivate adults to take action against bullying and to help administrators and other educators tailor a bullying prevention strategy to the particular needs of the school …

A second step involves garnering the widespread support and significant commitment of all key stakeholders (e.g., administrators, teachers, students, parents, auxiliary school staff, and community partners) in recognizing the importance of the problem and making a commitment to establish prevention and intervention programs and policies …

A third step is the formation of a school coordinating team. This team includes representatives from a number of groups, including a school administrator, a teacher from each grade, a member of the nonteaching staff, a school counselor or other school-based mental health professional (e.g., school social worker), a school nurse, and a parent. This team is involved in the development, implementation, maintenance, and evaluation of the program …

A fourth step involves the development and provision of ongoing in-service training for teachers and all adults in the school environment who interact with students …

A fifth strategy recognizes that antibullying efforts cannot be successful unless the language and needs of youth are taken into account…. [One study] found that many youths engaged in practices that adults label "bullying" but that the youths do not name them as such because admitting that they're being bullied (or worse, they are bullies) makes them feel weak and childish…. When teenagers acknowledge that they're being bullied, adults need to provide programs similar to those that help victims of abuse [that empower students and aid in] … emotional recovery …

A sixth strategy focuses on shifting group norms and dynamics in schools by targeting bystanders in antibullying interventions…. [In some schools bullying behavior is taken for granted and becomes the norm. Students must be educated about bullying and empowered to come forward, label such behavior, and help stop it when it occurs.]

The seventh strategy is the establishment and enforcement of a discipline policy that includes simple, clear rules about bullying as well as the development of appropriate positive and negative consequences that are consistently enforced….

An eighth strategy involves an increase in adult supervision in the areas of the school where bullying occurs with the greatest frequency (i.e., "hot spots")…. Once school personnel have identified these "hot spots," they should discuss and implement creative ways to increase adults' presence in these locations in order to reduce opportunities for bullying….

A ninth and final strategy is to direct prevention and intervention efforts at the transition from elementary to middle school and throughout the critical middle school years due to a documented increase in bullying during early adolescence. (pp. 73–81)

The Influence of Television and Other Media

Because television has become such a common aspect of a child's environment, it merits a few comments here. Children spend 20 to 25 hours a week watching television; if continued at that rate, a high school graduate would have spent a full 2 years watching television for 24 hours a day (Kail & Cavanaugh, 2013; Rathus, 2014c). Of course, this is only an average. Some children watch more television than others. For example, children from lower-income families watch more television than do their counterparts in families with higher economic status; "television is relatively cheap entertainment, and low-income families may not have the money to spend on other sources of entertainment" (Lemish, 2007; Martin & Fabes, 2009, p. 332). Also, the amount of time spent watching television varies with age. Martin and Fabes (2009) explain:

Children's television viewing time increases during the preschool years to an average of 2.5 hours each day and continues to increase through the elementary school years (Lemish, 2007). Viewing time

peaks at about 4 hours per day just before the start of adolescence, when competing activities reduce the number of hours spent in front of the television set (Pecora, Murray, & Wartella, 2007). When computers, DVDs, and video games are taken into account, children today spend an average of 5 hours a day in front of "video screens" (Woodward & Gridina, 2001). Similar patterns have been found in other countries (Lemish, 2007). (p. 332)

A major question raised about the impact of television is whether TV teaches children to be violent and aggressive. Research indicates that television does influence and increase children's violent behavior (Berk, 2008a; Newman & Newman, 2012; Rathus, 2011a; Wilson, 2008). Rathus (2011a) reflects:

Television is a fertile source of aggressive models (Villani, 2001). Children are routinely exposed to TV scenes of murder, beating, and sexual assault. Children who watch 2 to 4 hours a day of TV will see 8,000 murders and another 100,000 acts of violence by the time they have finished elementary school. (p. 172)

Even children's cartoons demonstrate extremely violent behavior. How many times have the Teenage Mutant Ninja Turtles battled "bad guys" with seriously lethal, sharp, and dangerous weapons? How many times has the Coyote been blown up with a stick of dynamite given to him by the Roadrunner? How many times has Donald Duck been smashed by a baseball bat or pushed off a steep cliff? When you think about it, the implications of the amount of violence depicted are scary.

Note that television isn't the only medium that can potentially teach and provoke aggressive behavior. Most video games provide a means not only to view, but also actually to practice, violent behavior. Many such games closely resemble reality. They provide a means to engage actively in violent pursuits, usually shooting down people or other figures. Even worse, they reinforce violent behavior by awarding points when targets are effectively annihilated.

At least three processes may operate to increase children's aggression in response to TV or video game violence (Newman & Newman, 2012; Rathus, 2014c). First, children may model the violent behavior they see. If Rambo and other famous movie and TV characters can do it, why can't they? Second, violence is arousing, so children are more likely to lose control and become more violent. TV violence can serve as a stimulus to trigger increased emotionality and aggression. Third, regular exposure to TV violence can influence a child's value system and beliefs about how the world really is. Children who see a lot of violence may take it for granted that violence happens everywhere much of the time. How many times might a child watch a young man get "blown away" in vivid blood-red color before that image becomes commonplace in that child's mind?

Other research establishes a relationship between the amount of violent television viewed in childhood and the amount of aggressiveness manifested by participants as adults (Huesmann & Miller, 1994; Johnson, Cohen, Smailes, Kasen, & Brook, 2002; Newman & Newman, 2012). In other words, children who watch more violent television may actually display more violent behavior themselves when they grow up. The link between TV violence and later aggression has been established even when other variables such as socioeconomic status and parents' level of education are taken into account (Johnson et al., 2002). A survey by *Time* found that 66 percent of respondents believed there was too much violence on television (Poniewozik, 2005). Playing violent video games has also been linked to increased aggression and decreased concern for others in children and teens (Anderson & Bushman, 2001; Anderson et al., 2003). Violence is enhanced when children play routinely and identify with violent characters used and displayed in the game (Konijn, Bijvank, & Bushman, 2007). Research also found that placing age restrictions on games or labeling them as being violent only increased their attractiveness to children of all age groups, including children ages 7 to 8 and girls (Bijvank, Konijn, Bushman, & Roelofsma, 2009).

Some young people commit extraordinarily violent acts as they grow into adults, possibly demonstrating a link with TV violence. Consider 20-year-old Adam Lanza who, after killing his mother, took three guns to Sandy Hook Elementary School in Newtown, Connecticut; after shooting his way into the security-locked building, he shot and killed twenty 6- and 7-year-old students and six adults (CNN.com, 2013). Remember 17-year-old senior Robert Butler, Jr., who on January 5, 2011, fatally shot one Omaha, Nebraska, school administrator and then seriously wounded another after Butler had been suspended; he later shot and killed himself (World-Herald News Service, 2011). Recall 23-year-old English major Cho Seung-Hui. Dressed in dark clothing resembling that portrayed in a popular video game, he suddenly opened fire on his fellow students at Virginia Tech, killing 31 of them, his instructor, and himself (ABC News, 2007; Romano, 2007). Recall former student Stephen Kazmierczak, who on February 15, 2008, abruptly opened fire on students at Northern Illinois University, killing 5 and wounding 16 before killing himself (NPR, 2008a, 2008b). Following the April 1999 massacre of 12 high school students and a teacher by two teens at Columbine High School in Littleton, Colorado, President Clinton made three pleas to the media (Harris, 1999). First, "he urged movie studios to stop showing guns in ads and previews that children can see" (p. A3). Second, "he asked theaters and video stores to more rigorously enforce rules barring unchaperoned children under age 17 from viewing R-rated movies" (p. A3). Third, "he called for re-evaluating the ratings system, 'especially the PG rating,' to decide whether the ratings are 'allowing too much gratuitous violence' in movies approved for children" (p. A3).

There is another side to television, however. According to Newman and Newman (2012), "Many programs, some developed for children and others intended for a broader viewing audience—convey positive ethical messages about the value of family life, the need to work hard and sacrifice in order to achieve important goals, the value of friendship, the importance of loyalty and commitment in relationships, and many other cultural values" (p. 261). For example, consider *Sesame Street*, which emphasizes the development of reading and arithmetic skills in addition to imparting such values as consideration for others' feelings. Television "can have a positive influence on children's development by presenting motivating educational programs, increasing their information about the world beyond their immediate environment, and providing models of prosocial behavior [interactions involving collaboration, support, and positive communication] (Wilson, 2008)" (Santrock, 2013, p. 317).

The American Academy of Pediatrics (AAP) (2007) suggests that parents scrutinize their children's viewing behavior by observing how their children act after watching TV and by watching the programs themselves. Limits should be set regarding what is appropriate and what is not. When violence does occur, parents should talk to children about it. Parents can emphasize that violence is a bad way to solve problems and that better, nonviolent ways are available. Finally, parents should seek out television programs, DVDs, and videos that provide high-quality, nonviolent content for children to watch.

Ethical Questions 4.6

EP 2.1.2

Is there too much violence on television? Should the amount of violence be monitored? Is so, who should be responsible for setting standards and scrutinizing content? Should children's viewing of television be limited? If so, in what ways?

The School Environment

School provides a major arena for socialization, where children are taught social customs, rules, and communication skills. Schools can influence children's dreams and aspirations about future careers. Schools help to mold the ways in which children think. Specific issues related to the school environment will be discussed here. They include the teacher's impact, the elements of an effective classroom, and the effects of social class and race.

The Teacher's Impact

Students frequently perform at the level of their teachers' expectations. This is sometimes referred to as a *self-fulfilling prophecy*—that is, students will perform to the level of expectation placed upon them. Higher expectations, therefore, can result in greater achievement.

There is some indication that low achievers are even more responsive to higher teacher expectations than are higher achievers (Madom, Jussim, & Eccles, 1997; Martin & Fabes, 2009; Smith, Jussim, & Eccles, 1999). Teachers should avoid categorizing students as poor performers, but rather should encourage them to work to the best of their ability.

Martin and Fabes (2009) reflect on how teachers can also influence children's social development (Pianta, 2006): "This influence can be quite positive, encouraging feelings of competence and well-being. For example, teachers have been found to enhance positive outcomes for students if they (1) reduce the tendency of students to compare themselves with one another, (2) use cooperative interaction strategies in the classroom, (3) promote beliefs about students' competencies rather than their deficiencies, (4) increase chances for students to be successful, and (5) are warm, encouraging, and supportive (Pianta & Stuhlman, 2004; Stipek, 1997)" (p. 437).

Effective School Environments

The school environment can be a warm, welcoming place that encourages learning and productivity. Or, it can be a scary, intimidating setting that discourages students from even being there. A substantial body of research has established that the following variables are related to an effective school environment (Rathus, 2014b; Shaffer & Kipp, 2010, pp. 624–625):

- *School Climate:* Students' positive perception of the school's climate is an important variable in encouraging learning. This includes both their feelings of safety and teachers' "support and encouragement" (Loukas & Robinson, 2004; Shaffer & Kipp, 2010, p. 624; Taylor & Lopez, 2005a). If students feel welcome and safe, it makes sense that they would experience greater freedom and have more energy to devote to making academic and social progress (Eccles & Roeser, 2005; Taylor & Lopez, 2005b).
- *Academic Emphasis:* Children perform best in schools that stress on academic work. Academic goals should be clearly specified. Homework that is explained, discussed, and evaluated should be required.
- *Challenging, Developmentally Appropriate Curricula:* Children can relate much better to content that focuses on their ethnicity, cultural background, customs, and history, and that involves the issues they're currently facing in life. Incorporating such content into the curriculum can motivate students to learn because what they're learning is interesting and relevant to them. Using such appropriate curricula enhances their achievement in areas such as "effort, attention, attendance, and appropriate classroom behavior"

(Jackson & Davis, 2000; Lee & Smith, 2001; Shaffer & Kipp, 2010, p. 624). On the other hand, content that "turns off" student interest can lead to lower achievement levels and distancing from the educational environment (Eccles & Roeser, 2005; Jackson & Davis, 2000).

- *Classroom Management:* Having organized, efficient classrooms with structured expectations can encourage a healthy learning environment. Time management skills can be used to keep activities and lessons proceeding on time. This provides students with both direction and encouragement to get things done. Students should be consistently given positive reinforcement and praise to encourage productivity and high-quality effort. "The most effective teachers ask questions, give personalized feedback, and provide opportunities for drill and practice, as opposed to straight lecturing" (Rathus, 2011a, p. 431).

- *Discipline:* Rules should be clearly stated and consequences for rule violations imposed immediately. Physical punishment should be avoided, as it can lead to uncontrolled results and further aggressive behavior. "Students do not do well when teachers rely heavily on criticism, ridicule, threats, or punishment" (Rathus, 2011b, p. 431).

At the same time, encouraging obedient, cooperative children to use their own discretion in making decisions where possible enhances their self-confidence and ability to achieve (Deci & Ryan, 2000; Grolnick, Gurland, Jacob, & Decourcey, 2002; Ryan & Deci, 2000a, 2000b).

- *Teamwork:* "Effective schools have faculties that work as a team, jointly planning curricular objectives and monitoring student progress, under the guidance of a principal who provides active, energetic leadership" (Shaffer & Kipp, 2010, p. 625).

Spotlight 4.4 discusses how an educational program was developed to emphasize cultural strengths and meet the educational needs of Hawaiian students.

● ● ● ● **Ethical Question 4.7**

What elements in the classroom environment do you believe are most effective, and why?

EP 2.1.2

An effective school environment can positively enhance students' ability to learn and thrive.

Jim Cummins/Getty Images

SPOTLIGHT ON DIVERSITY 4.4

Educational Programming That Responds to Cultural Values

**EP 2.1.4a,
2.1.4c**

The Kamehameha Early Education Program (KEEP) was developed to focus on the cultural values of Native Hawaiians and to enhance students' learning processes (KEEP, n.d.; Tharp et al., 2007; Tinzmann et al., 1990). Phenice (1999) describes some aspects of Hawaiian culture:

> Cooperating, not only within the family but also with others in the ethnic community as well as in society, is an expectation inculcated in children at a very young age. Values such as harmony with nature and humanity are fundamental in their cognitive expressions. When there is a conflict with another, there is a saying, ho oponopono, which means to have a frank discussion to set matters right in order to restore a good relationship with the other, whether within the family or within the community. This process includes praying together, respecting all view points, and forgiving. Historically strength as a group came from cooperating and not competing with one another. (p. 115)

Western thought and values emphasize individualism, competition, and winning. Children take achievement tests where they are ranked in competition with each other. A grade of C is considered average, whereas a grade of A is exceptional. Traditional classrooms emphasize individual accomplishments and success. Winners of sports and other competitive events are admired as heroes. Anything that involves winners, of course, also includes losers, who are looked down upon and often considered inferior.

KEEP is built on the principle of collaborative classroom work that complies well with Hawaiian cultural values.

Classrooms are broken down not into individuals, but small groups of students who work together to assess issues, develop projects, and solve problems. All participants' input is valued and encouraged as groups focus on sharing the knowledge of individual members. Teachers encourage student input into activities by providing options students can choose. For example, a teacher might address the topic of Hawaiian geography. Student groups then might be allowed to determine how they will study this topic—by developing maps and charts, creating a videotape, or writing a paper on the subject. Another example of teacher-student collaboration involves a teacher assigning the topic of "garbage" to student groups and asking them to develop their own goals for a project (Tinzmann et al., 1990). "In one group, a student wanted to find out if garbage is a problem, another wanted to know what happens to garbage, a third wanted to know what is being done to solve the problem of garbage. The fourth member could not think of a goal, but agreed that the first three were important and adopted them" (p. 5).

Another process used by KEEP teachers is the use of talk story, a manner of speaking that is common in Hawaiian communities, where a group of individuals all contribute to the reiteration or creation of a story by contributing small pieces (KEEP, n.d.). Together, the small student groups compose the final result.

Research suggests KEEP is effective in enhancing learning. When students like their schools and have programs tailoring learning to their needs and interests, they tend to do better (Papalia & Feldman, 2012). This simply makes sense. Programs using KEEP principles, adapting learning approaches to incorporate respective cultural values, have also been developed elsewhere, such as the Navajo Nation in Arizona.

Race, Ethnicity, and Schools

**EP 2.1.4a,
2.1.4c**

Gaps exist between the educational attainment of whites and some other ethnic groups, including Hispanics and African Americans. Whereas 87.6 percent of Caucasians graduate from high school, 84.2 percent of African Americans and only 62.9 percent of Hispanics do so (U.S. Census Bureau, 2011). About 30.3 percent of Caucasians have a college education or more, whereas only 19.8 percent of African Americans and 13.9 percent of Hispanics achieve this educational level (U.S. Census Bureau, 2009).

A number of reasons may account for the discrepancies in educational attainment among whites, African Americans, and Hispanics. Some educators have attributed these differences to external factors such as lower socioeconomic status (Duncan & Brooks-Gunn, 2000; Steinberg et al., 2011b) and poorer quality schools (McAdoo, 2007). Both African Americans and Hispanics are more likely to have lower socioeconomic status than whites. Are schools in poorer neighborhoods receiving necessary resources to provide students with a good education? Other reasons for the discrepancy in educational attainment may involve internal variables, such as a social atmosphere, that discourage students and obstruct their performance. Also, textbooks and instructional materials may not adequately reflect relevant cultural values and ethnicity. For example, to what extent are African American and Hispanic history, literature, and values emphasized? Are teachers' and educational administrators' expectation levels for their students of different cultures too low? Do teachers have biases about the capabilities of students in particular ethnic groups?

Ongoing research is needed to establish what is really happening in school environments. Perhaps greater resources are necessary to update materials and enhance the multicultural learning atmosphere. Other targets of change may include teacher attitudes and skills. Teachers may require special training to meet the special needs of people from various cultural backgrounds.

LO 4-11 Examine Child Maltreatment

EP 2.1.9a, 2.1.10a

Ralphie, age 8, came to school one day with his arm in a gigantic cast. His teacher asked him what had happened. He said he fell down the steps and broke his arm. He didn't seem to want to talk about it much. When pressed about why the cast was so large, he replied, "Oh, that's 'cause I busted it in a couple of places." The teacher thought to herself how strange it was that he suffered such a severe injury from a simple fall. Eight-year-olds are usually so resilient.

Angel, age 4, didn't want to sit down when one of her caregivers at the day-care center asked her to. It was almost as if she was in pain. The caretaker called the center's nurse to examine Angel. The nurse found a doughnut-shaped burn on her buttocks. When asked how it happened, Angel said she didn't remember. The nurse thought to herself how strange this situation was.

As the plumber left the porch of the last house he visited, he wondered to himself how people could possibly live that way. There were three filthy, unkempt small children eating Froot Loops and glued to a blaring television set. The toilet was filthy; he was glad he had extra-thick rubber gloves on as he worked on the pipes.

Then, as he was leaving the home, a small puppy leisurely urinated on the porch before his and the woman's eyes. She looked at the salesman, making no effort to clean up the mess, and said, "Well, at least he didn't do it inside the house." She then turned around and walked back into the house.

Tony thought Alicia, one of his classmates at school, was just beautiful, albeit a little shy. They were both 14. He finally mustered up the courage to go over, talk to her, and ask her if she would like to go to the school dance next Friday night. She shrunk back from him as if she was terrified and said, in a whisper, that she couldn't possibly go. She added apologetically that her mother worked Friday nights and her "Daddy" always took her to the movies. That struck Tony as odd. However, he wasn't up to fighting with parents. Alicia was cute, but she wasn't the only girl around.

Each of these vignettes illustrates children who are being maltreated. Children can be abused or neglected in a number of ways. The umbrella term that includes all of them is child *maltreatment*. *Maltreatment* includes physical abuse; being given inadequate care and nourishment; deprivation of adequate medical care; insufficient encouragement to attend school consistently; exploitation by being forced to work too hard or too long; "exposure to unwholesome or demoralizing circumstances"; sexual abuse; and emotional abuse and neglect (Kadushin & Martin, 1988, p. 226). Definitions used by legal and social service agencies vary from locality to locality and state to state. However, most definitions include these eight aspects of maltreatment.

Many books have been written about each form of maltreatment. It is beyond the scope of this book to address them all in great depth. Usually, however, all can be clustered under two headings: child abuse (which includes both physical and sexual abuse) and child neglect. Child maltreatment is a critical issue for social workers to understand. They need to be aware of the clues that maltreatment is occurring. They also need to understand the dynamics of how child victims and their abusers behave in order to assess a situation and make treatment plans. Here, we will discuss the incidence and demographics of child maltreatment; the definitions of physical abuse, neglect, psychological maltreatment, and sexual abuse; the characteristics of victims and abusers; and some basic treatment approaches. Because of its distinctive characteristics and problematic features, sexual abuse will be discussed separately.

Incidence of Child Maltreatment

The actual number of child abuse and neglect cases is difficult to determine. Definitions for who can and can't be included in specific categories vary. How cases are reported and how data are gathered also vary dramatically. One thing is certain: The chances are that any reported figures reflect a small percentage of actual cases. Indications are that vast numbers of cases remain unreported.

Some data indicate that in 2011 there were 6.2 million referrals of children to Child Protective Services, 3.7 million child maltreatment investigations, and almost 677,000 determinations that maltreatment had occurred (First Star, Inc., 2013). Of these, 78 percent were neglect, 18 percent were physical abuse, and 9 percent were sexual abuse (First Star, Inc., 2013). The reporting matter becomes even more complex as states vary in their definitions of what maltreatment involves, and not all states collect data on all types of maltreatment.

Physical Child Abuse

Physical abuse can be defined very generally as "non-accidental injury inflicted on a child," usually "by a caregiver, other adults, or sometimes, an older child" (Crosson-Tower, 2013, p. 180). Some definitions focus on whether the alleged abuser's purpose is to intentionally harm the child. Other definitions ignore the intent and instead emphasize the potential or actual harm done to the child. However, there often is a very fine line between physical abuse and parental discipline. Historically, parents have had the right to bring up their children as they see fit. This has included administering punishment to curb behavior when they thought it was necessary. Consider a father who beats his 13-year-old daughter on the buttocks with a belt because her math grade dropped over the course of a year from an A to a C. Is that his right, or is that child abuse?

Spotlight 4.5 raises some questions about what is considered appropriate parental discipline and what is considered abuse in diverse cultural contexts.

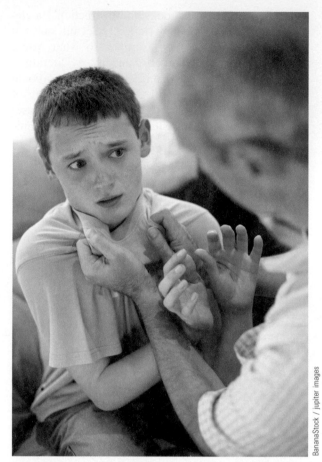

Angry outbursts and loss of emotional control on the part of parents can result in child abuse. Here, an angry father uses both hands to grab his son by his T-shirt.

BananaStock / jupiter images

Characteristics of Physically Abused Victims

Both physical indicators and behavioral indicators provide clues that a child is being physically abused. Physical indicators can be broken down into six basic categories.

1. *Bruises.* Bruises on any infant should be suspect. Infants are not yet mobile. Therefore, it's not likely that they can bruise themselves. Bruises in unusual places or forming unusual patterns may indicate physical abuse. Bruises that take a recognizable shape such as a hand mark or a belt mark should be noted. Finally, bruises that display a variety of colors may portray abuse. This may be an indication that a series of bruises have been received over time. On lighter-skinned people, bruises usually progress from an initial bright red to blue to blackish-purple within the first

SPOTLIGHT ON DIVERSITY 4.5

Diverse Cultural Contexts: Discipline or Abuse?

**EP 2.1.1e,
2.1.4c,
2.1.4d**

Crosson-Tower (2013) reflects on some of the issues concerning the cultural context of abuse versus parental discipline:

> Some cultures have customs or practices that child protection [agencies] would consider abusive. For example, some Vietnamese families, in a ritual called cao gio, rub their children with a coin heated to the point that it leaves burn marks. It is an intentional act, but designed, in that culture, to cure a variety of ills. Do the parents' good intentions exempt this practice from being considered abusive? Similarly, the use of corporal punishment is sanctioned in many Hispanic cultures, but is seen as abusive in this culture when it becomes excessive. Some child protection advocates adopt the "When in Rome do as the Romans do" attitude that says that minorities must abide by the laws of the culture in which they now reside. One Puerto Rican social worker, working in a predominantly Hispanic section of New York City, vehemently disagreed: "Yes, there are laws, but those laws were made by Anglos. Is it fair to deprive new immigrants of everything including their customs? Maybe the laws should be changed?"The reality is that if a child is reported as being harmed for whatever reason, a child protection agency will usually investigate. If the reason is one of culture, this will be considered. (p. 180)

Social workers should orient themselves to learning from their clients about clients' cultures. This is a career-long process, as the extent of variations in values and customs is infinite.

day; they become shaded with a dark green color after about 6 days and finally turn pale green or yellow after 5 to 10 days.

2. *Lacerations.* Cuts, scrapes, or scratches, especially if they occur frequently or their origin is poorly explained, may indicate physical abuse. Lacerations on the face and genitalia should be noted. Bite marks also may indicate abuse.

3. *Fractures.* Bone fractures and other skeletal injuries may indicate abuse. Strangely twisted fractures and multiple fractures are especially telltale signs. Infants' fractures may be the result of abuse. Additional indicators are joint dislocations and injuries in which the periosteum, the thin membrane covering the bone, is detached.

4. *Burns.* Burns, especially ones that take odd forms or are in patterns, may indicate abuse. Children have been burned by cigarettes and ropes (from being tied up and confined). Burns that occur on inaccessible portions of the body such as the stomach, genitals, or soles of the feet are clues to abuse. Patterned burns may indicate that the child has been burned with some hot utensil. Sac-like burns result when a hand or foot has been submerged into a hot liquid. A doughnut-shaped burn will occur on the buttocks if a child has been immersed in very hot water. The central unburned area results from where the child's skin touched the bottom of the receptacle holding the water.

5. *Head injuries.* Head injuries that can indicate abuse include skull fractures, loss of hair due to vigorous pulling, and subdural hematomas (blood collected beneath the outer covering of the brain after strenuous shaking or hitting). Black eyes should be suspect. Retinas may detach or hemorrhage if a child is shaken vigorously.

6. *Internal injuries.* Children have received injuries to their spleen, kidneys, and intestines due to hitting and kicking. The vena cava, the large vein by which blood is brought from the lower extremities to the heart, may be ruptured. Peritonitis, in which the lining of the abdominal cavity becomes inflamed, can be another indicator of abuse.

Some of the major questions to ask yourself if you think a child may have been physically abused include the following:

- Does this child get hurt too often for someone his or her age?
- Does the child have multiple injuries?
- Do the injuries occur in patterns, assume recognizable shapes, or look like some of the injuries described earlier?

- Are the injuries such that they don't seem possible for a child at that stage of development?
- Do the explanations given for the injuries make sense?

If something doesn't seem right to you, something may be wrong. If a little voice in the back of your mind is saying, "Oh-oh, that certainly is odd," pay attention. It might be a clue to abuse.

In addition to physical indicators, behavioral indicators provide a second major dimension of clues to physical abuse. A physically abused child tends to exhibit behavioral extremes. Virtually all children may display these extreme behaviors at one time or another. However, the frequency and severity of these behaviors in abused children are clearly notable. At least three categories, plus a variety of specific behavioral indicators, have been established (Crosson-Tower, 2013, 2014; Kolko, 2002; Runyon & Urquiza, 2011):

1. Extremely passive, accommodating, submissive behaviors aimed at preserving a low profile and avoiding potential conflict with parents that might lead to abuse. Abused children can be exceptionally calm and docile. They have learned this behavior in order to avoid any possible conflict with the abusive parent. If they are invisible, the parent may not be provoked. Many times abused children will even avoid playing because it draws too much attention to themselves. This behavioral pattern is sometimes called *hypervigilance*.
2. Notably aggressive behaviors and marked overt hostility toward others, caused by rage and frustration at not getting needs met. Some physically abused children assume an opposite approach to the overly passive manner identified earlier. These children are so desperately in need of attention that they will try almost anything to get it. Even if they can provoke only negative attention from their parents, their aggressive behavior is reinforced.
3. Developmental lags. Because abused children are forced to direct their attention and energy to coping with their abusive situation, they frequently show developmental delays. These may appear in the form of language delays, poorly developed social skills for their age level, or lags in motor development.

Characteristics of Abusers

The dynamics behind child physical abuse are complex and varied. However, the general characteristics of it tend to fall within six major domains (Crosson-Tower, 2013, 2014; Kolko, 2002; Miller-Perrin & Perrin, 2013; Runyon & Urquiza, 2011). Although no one person may have all the problems mentioned, a person will likely experience some.

Need for Personal Support and Nurturance A basic quality characterizing abusers is low self-esteem. Their emotional needs often remain unfulfilled from their own childhoods. Because their own needs were not met, they are unable to meet the needs of their children. They often invite rejection and hostility because they have little confidence in their own abilities. They don't know how to reach out for support. On the one hand, they often feel they are undeserving. On the other hand, they still have desperate needs for human support.

Social Isolation Perpetrators' own self-confidence may be low. They feel that no one will like them, so they isolate themselves. They reject attention, even though they need others for emotional support. They fear rejection, so they don't try to reach out to others. As a result, when normal everyday stresses build up, they have no one to help them cope.

Communication and Relationship Difficulties Relationships that abusers do have with family, a significant other, and others are often stormy. Communication may be difficult, hostile, and ineffective. Low self-esteem can also affect the relationship with a partner or a significant other. Abusers may not know how to get their needs met. They may allow their disappointments and anger to build up because they don't know how to express these feelings more appropriately to others. They may feel isolated and alone even within a marriage or partnership. Children may become easy targets for parents who can't communicate with each other. Children may provide a conduit for the expression of violence and anger that are really directed at a spouse or a significant other.

Poor Parenting Skills Many abusive people don't know how to raise their children in a nurturant family environment. Their own family of origin's environment may have been hostile and abusive. They may never have observed nurturant behavior on the part of their own parents and caregivers. They couldn't learn what they weren't taught.

Additionally, their expectations for what constitutes inappropriate behavior at the various development levels may be lacking. For instance, their demands on the child for behavioral submission and even perfection may be very inappropriate. Parenting behavior may be inconsistent, hostile, or lacking in positive interaction.

Poor General Coping Skills Perpetrators may be unable to cope with stress, lashing out at their children instead. They may lack anger management skills. In addition to not knowing how to meet their own emotional needs, they may not have learned to separate their feelings and emotions from their behavior. Therefore, if they get mad, they don't talk about it; they hit.

Another unlearned skill involves the appropriate delineation of responsibility. Perpetrators tend to blame others for their mistakes. For example, it's the child's fault that he got hit and broke his arm, because he was naughty.

They may also lack decision making or problem-solving skills. Abusers tend to have little confidence in their own ability, and so have little faith in their own judgment. They have difficulty articulating and evaluating the pros and cons of their alternatives, and are indecisive.

In addition, abusers often fail to learn how to delay their own gratification. The situation here and now becomes all-important. If a child misbehaves, a kick will take care of it immediately. If their stress level is too high, abusers need immediate relief. They focus on the moment and have trouble looking at what the consequences of their behavior will be in the future.

Extreme External Stress and Life Crises Child abuse is related to lower socioeconomic status.

Poverty causes stress. The abuser, who may lack coping strategies anyway, may feel isolated and incompetent. Additional life crises like job loss, illness, a marital or family dispute, or even a child's behavior problem may push people over the brink so that they cannot cope. They may take out their stress on the easiest, most available targets—their children.

Child Neglect

Because neglect involves the absence of resources instead of the presence of something that is negative, it is difficult to define. Every social environment is different. When does a family environment cease being adequate and instead display neglect?

Consider the following case examples:

- Mark, who is 8 years old, is left to care for his 3-year-old sister, Maria, while their parents go out.
- Margaret fails to provide medication for her 10-year-old daughter, who has a seizure disorder.
- Jonathan refuses to allow his 16-year-old son into the family's home and tells him not to return.
- Tyrone and Rachel live with their three children in a home that is thick with dirt and dust, smells of urine, and has nothing but rotting food in the refrigerator.
- Alicia leaves her 10-month-old infant unattended in a bathtub full of water. (Barnett, Miller-Perrin, & Perrin, 2011, p. 84)

Child neglect is a caregiver's "failure to meet a child's basic needs"; this may involve depriving a child of physical, emotional, medical, mental health, or educational necessities (Erickson & Egeland, 2011; Shireman, 2003, p. 32). Whereas child abuse involves harming a child through actions, child neglect causes a child harm by *not* doing what is necessary. Neglect occurs when children are not given what they need to survive and thrive.

Two of the most frequent aspects of neglect involve physical neglect and inadequate supervision. *Physical neglect* is the "failure to protect a child from harm or danger and provide for the child's basic necessities including adequate food, shelter, and clothing" (Erickson & Egeland, 2011, p. 105). *Inadequate supervision* "refers to situations in which children are without a caretaker or the caretaker is inattentive or unsuitable, and therefore the children are in danger of harming themselves or possibly others" (Downs, Moore, & McFadden, 2009, p. 209). Children need someone to direct them, care for them, support their daily activities, and give them emotional support. Inadequate supervision includes psychological neglect, discussed later in the chapter.

Sometimes neglect is related to poverty. Many neglectful parents don't have the resources to take care of themselves or their children. For instance, one woman who was charged with child neglect described her living conditions to a judge. She lived in a small, third-floor flat without hot water. She said, "It is an awful place to live. The wallpaper is in strips, the floor board is cracked. The baby is always getting splinters in his hands. The bathroom is on the floor above and two other families use it. The kitchen is on the first floor. I share it with another woman. I have no place to keep food. We buy for one meal at a time" (Hancock, 1963, p. 5).

A young social worker recounts a visit to a family suspected of child neglect:

It was my first visit to the Petersons' home, or should I say second floor flat. The house was in a very poor area in the inner city of Milwaukee. I was supposed to do an initial family assessment. Both parents and three small children were there. The house was filthy. Dirty laundry was heaped in piles on the living room floor. The walls were smeared with grease. Wads of dust rolled along the floor; if they had been at my apartment, I would've called them dinosaur dust bunnies.

The flat was small. The only furniture I could see included two double beds in the tiny living room, and a cheap, old dinette and appliances in the kitchen. The family asked me to sit at the old kitchen table. The chairs were black; I had to restrain myself from wiping one off with a Kleenex before I sat down. But I didn't want to offend my clients. I was clearly aware of my middle-class bias already. None of the children were wearing shoes, which might not be too unusual for summer. However, black dirt streaked all of the children's white arms, legs, feet, hands, and faces. Their hair was dirty and snarled.

As we talked, the parents asked me if I'd like a cup of coffee. The coffee maker in front of me was filthy as was the cup they gave me. It matched the dirty dishes heaped high in the sink. Again, not

wanting to offend my clients, I gratefully accepted the coffee. As we talked, I accepted the second cup of coffee and then a third. That was my mistake. Suddenly it occurred to me I desperately needed to use the bathroom. I wondered where it was. I asked if I could, and Mr. Peterson said, "Sure, just a minute." He stood up from the table, picked up a door that had been leaning against the wall around the corner, pointed to a literally open door out of my direct view around the refrigerator. Mortified as I was, I stepped into the bathroom. He laid the door in place (there were no hinges) and said he'd hold it until I was finished. Well, what else was there to do at that point? After I finished, I meekly said, "I'm through," at which point he picked up the door and put it back in its place leaning against the wall. We continued with the interview. One thing is for sure; my coffee drinking behavior on home visits will never be the same!

Characteristics of Neglected Children

Each of us has infinite needs. To define and categorize all that we need to maintain physical and emotional health would be an awesome task. This is why neglect is often difficult to define for any specific family situation. Nonetheless, we will present 12 general indicators of child neglect here (Barnett et al., 2011; Crosson-Tower, 2014; Erickson & Egeland, 2011; Miller-Perrin & Perrin, 2013; Zuravin & Taylor, 1987). They provide at least a basis for assessment of situations in which neglect may be involved. As with the characteristics of physically abused children, it should be noted that not all of these characteristics apply to all neglected children. However, any one of them might be an indicator of neglect.

1. *Physical health care.* Illnesses are not attended to, and proper dental care is not maintained.
2. *Mental health care.* Children's mental health problems are either ignored or left unattended. Sometimes caregivers refuse "to comply with recommended therapeutic interventions for a child with a serious emotional or behavioral disorder" (Erickson & Egeland, 2011, p. 105).
3. *Educational neglect.* "Parents fail to comply with laws that require children to attend school" (Erickson & Egeland, 2011, p. 104). Excessive

truancy and tardiness without adequate or appropriate excuses may indicate neglect. This often concerns a "parent [who] has been informed of the problem and does not take steps to remedy it"; educational neglect also involves "situations in which parents refuse to permit their children with special needs to receive the services they need" (Downs et al., 2009, p. 209).

4. *Supervision.* Children are often or almost always left alone without adequate supervision. Very young children or even infants may be left unattended. Another common situation is that very young children are left in the supervision of other children who themselves are too young to assume such responsibility. A third common situation occurs when unsupervised children get involved in activities in which they may harm themselves. For example, we periodically read in the newspaper that a young, unsupervised child plays with matches, starts a fire, and burns down the house or apartment building and usually dies in the fire. A fourth example involves children who don't receive adequate supervision to get them to school on time, or at all.

5. *Abandonment and substitute child care.* The most blatant form of neglect is abandonment, when parents leave children alone and unattended. A related scenario involves parents who fail to return when they're supposed to, thereby leaving designated care providers in the lurch, not knowing what to do with the children.

6. *Housing hazards.* Housing may have inadequate heat, ventilation, or safety features. Dangerous substances such as drugs or weapons may be left in children's easy reach. Electrical fixtures may not be up to code and therefore may be dangerous.

7. *Household sanitation.* Food may be spoiled. The home may be filled with garbage or excrement. Plumbing might not work or be backed up.

8. *Personal hygiene.* Children's clothing may be ripped, filthy, and threadbare. Their hair may be unkempt and dirty. They themselves may be unbathed and odorous. They may be plagued with head lice.

9. *Nutrition.* Children who frequently complain that they're hungry and search for food may be victims of neglect. Children receiving food that provides them with inadequate nutrition may be neglected. Significant delays in development resulting from malnutrition may also be a clue to neglect.

10. *"Social and attachment difficulties"* (Barnett et al., 2011, p. 96). Children may have problems interacting with parents, and they may fail to maintain secure attachment relationships (discussed in Chapter 3) in which they trust parents and respond positively and consistently to their parents' presence and interaction (Erickson & Egeland, 2011). Children may act "passive and withdrawn" with parents or the "parent exhibits low sensitivity to and involvement with [the] child" (Barnett et al., 2011, p. 96). Children may also display problems in peer relationships, including "deficits in prosocial behavior, social withdrawal, isolation, [and] few reciprocal friendships" (Barnett et al., 2011, p. 96).

11. *"Cognitive and academic deficits"* (Barnett et al., 2011, p. 96). Children may exhibit language deficits, poor academic achievement, low grades, deficits in intelligence, decreased creativity, and difficulties in problem solving (Barnett et al., 2011). One study found that neglected children tend to experience greater cognitive and academic problems than do physically abused children (Hildyard & Wolfe, 2002).

12. *"Emotional and behavioral problems"* (Barnett et al., 2011, p. 97). Neglected children may exhibit indifference, withdrawal and isolation, low self-esteem, behavioral and verbal aggression, difficulties in paying attention, and psychiatric symptoms such as those characterizing anxiety or depression (Barnett et al., 2011).

Two pronounced physical conditions that can result from extreme neglect are nonorganic failure-to-thrive syndrome and psychosocial dwarfism (Crosson-Tower, 2014). *Nonorganic failure-to-thrive syndrome* (NFTT) occurs in infancy. It is characterized by infants who are "below the fifth percentile in weight and often in height" (Crosson-Tower, 2014, p. 70). This means that 95 percent of all other infants that age weigh more. Additionally, the infant must have had normal health at one time. Lags in psychomotor development are also apparent.

Psychosocial dwarfism (PSD) can affect children age 18 months to 16 years. In these children, "emotional deprivation promotes abnormally low growth. PSD children are also below the fifth percentile in weight and height, exhibit retarded skeletal maturation, and a variety of behavioral problems" (Crosson-Tower, 2014, p. 71). Additionally, they tend to have speech difficulties and problems in their social interactions.

Characteristics of Neglectful Parents

Crosson-Tower (2013) explains: "Parents who neglect were often neglected themselves as children. For them, it is a learned way of life. Their childhoods have produced in them nothing but anger and indifference. Their adult lives are dedicated to meeting the needs that were not met for them as they were growing up" (p. 186).

Mothers who neglect their children can be divided into five basic types (Crosson-Tower, 2013; Polansky, Chalmers, Buttenwieser, & Williams, 1991; Polansky, Holly, & Polansky, 1975):

1. The indifferent, lethargic mother is best described as numb. She has little or no emotional response and has little energy to do anything.
2. The impulsive, irresponsible mother treats her children inconsistently and often inattentively. She has poor impulse control and lacks coping strategies.
3. The depressed mother is reacting to life's unhappy circumstances by giving up. Unlike the indifferent mother, she experiences extreme emotion by being depressed and miserable.
4. Mothers with intellectual disabilities neglect children because of their cognitive inabilities and a lack of the adequate support they need to help them assume their responsibilities. Note that not all women with intellectual disabilities neglect their children.
5. Mothers with serious mental illness, such as psychosis, are unable to function because of bizarre thought processes, delusions, or extreme anxiety.

•••• Ethical Questions 4.9

Should parents who neglect their children be punished or receive treatment? How should this be accomplished?

EP 2.1.2

Psychological Maltreatment

Psychological maltreatment is illustrated in the following case scenarios:

- *A mother locks her 3-year-old son in a dark closet as a method of punishment.*
- *A father shackles his 7-year-old son to his bed at night to prevent him from getting out of bed repeatedly.*
- *A mother says to her daughter, "You are the stupidest, laziest kid on earth. I can't believe you're my child. They must have switched babies on me at the hospital."*
- *A father tells his daughter that he will kill her new puppy if she or the puppy misbehaves.*
- *A mother and father provide alcohol to their 16-year-old son and his friends at a party.*
- *A mother refuses to look at or touch her child.*
- *A father repeatedly states to one of his children, "I don't love you." (Barnett et al., 2011, p. 106)*

Psychological (or emotional) maltreatment includes both psychological abuse and psychological neglect. *Psychological abuse*, like other abuse, is more aggressively active and negative. It is "belittling, humiliating, rejecting, undermining a child's self-esteem, and generally not [conducive to] creating a positive atmosphere for a child" (Cohen, 1992, p. 175). *Psychological neglect*, like other forms of neglect, involves passively failing to meet children's needs. It is the "passive or passive/aggressive inattention to the child's emotional needs, nurturing, or emotional well-being" (Brassard, Germaine, & Hart, 1987, p. 267). Parents may deprive an infant of needed holding and attention or may simply ignore children who are in desperate need of emotional involvement. Both emotional neglect and abuse focus on interfering with a child's psychological development and well-being.

At least five basic categories of behavior are involved in psychological maltreatment (Barnett et al., 2011; Crosson-Tower, 2014; Downs et al., 2009; Garbarino, Guttmann, & Seeley, 1986). They are summarized as follows:

1. *Rejection* includes "abandoning the child, failing to acknowledge the child, scapegoating the child [i.e., placing unjustified blame on a child for some behavior or problem or criticizing a child unfairly], and verbally humiliating the child." A parent might emphasize how stupid a child is in front of her friends or neighbors.

2. *Isolation* includes "keeping the child away from a variety of appropriate relationships." It might involve not allowing a child to play normally with peers or seeing other close family members. It might also involve locking a child in a closet for days, months, or years.
3. *Terrorizing* involves "threatening and scaring the child." A parent might threaten to kill a child's beloved pet if he doesn't do the dishes. Or a caregiver might hold a child outside a second-story window and threaten to drop her if she doesn't start "acting her age."
4. *Ignoring* involves failing to respond to a child or simply pretending that the child isn't there. Parents watching television might ignore children's pleas for help with homework or requests for food, thereby forcing children to take care of themselves.
5. *Corrupting* includes "encouraging or supporting illegal or deviant behaviors." A caregiver might force a child to shoplift or drink beer (Winton & Mara, 2001, pp. 90–91).

Characteristics of Psychologically Maltreated Children

Extensive research reveals that a multitude of problems in adulthood are related to psychological maltreatment during childhood. These potential effects include low self-esteem, anxiety, depression, a negative view of life, increased suicide potential, emotional instability, difficulties with impulse control, substance abuse, eating disorders, relationship difficulties, violence, criminal behavior, school problems, and poor performance on intelligence and achievement tests (Hart, Brassard, Binggeli, & Davidson, 2002; Hart et al., 2011).

Characteristics of Perpetrators

Like other parents and caregivers who abuse or neglect, those who psychologically maltreat their children usually suffer serious emotional problems or deficits themselves (Crosson-Tower, 2014; Shireman, 2003). They may find themselves in a marriage or a partnership that is disappointing or bland, and may seek easy targets (namely, children) for venting their anger and frustration. Like other people who maltreat children, perpetrators may lack coping skills to deal with their problems and emotional issues. Their own emotional needs may not have been met in childhood. Their own parents may have lacked nurturing

skills and, thus, failed to teach perpetrators how to be good parents. They may also be dealing with personal problems such as mental illness or substance disorders (Barnett et al., 2011).

Macro-System Responses to Child Maltreatment

Macro-system responses concern how society addresses a problem like child maltreatment. Such responses addressed here include Child Protective Services, the social work role in treatment, and treatment by the courts.

A Macro-System Response: Child Protective Services

EP 2.1.10h, 2.1.10i

An abused or neglected child is usually referred to a *Child Protective Services (CPS)* unit. CPS agencies are governmental units that (1) receive reports of suspected child maltreatment, (2) investigate these reports, (3) assess the extent that children are being harmed or are at risk of being harmed, (4) determine how safe the home environment is or if placement outside the home is necessary, and (5) provide or arrange for the provision of necessary and appropriate social, medical, legal, placement, and other services.

Although there is some variation from one local or state CPS program to another, the following themes reflect a common philosophy (Pecora et al., 2010):

- *A safe and permanent home is the best place for children to grow up....*
- *Most parents want to be good parents and have the strength and capacity, when adequately supported, to care for their children and keep them safe....*
- *Families who need assistance from CPS programs are diverse in terms of family structure, culture, race, religion, economic status, beliefs, values, and lifestyles....*
- *CPS efforts are most likely to succeed when clients are involved and actively participate as partners in the process....*
- *Services must be individualized and tailored....*
- *CPS approaches should be family centered. (p. 150)*

CPS workers are usually employed by state or county public agencies whose designated task it is to protect children from harm. During the intervention process, CPS workers help families establish treatment plans to address and remedy problems. In the event that problems cannot be resolved, CPS workers try to develop alternative long-term or permanent placement of the children. CPS staff may work with the courts to declare that children require protection and to determine appropriate safe placement for them.

Treatment of Physical Abuse, Neglect, and Psychological Maltreatment: Social Work Role

EP 2.1.1c, 2.1.10d, 2.1.10j

Treatment of physical abuse, neglect, and psychological maltreatment follows the same sequential steps used in other areas of social work intervention. These include receipt of the initial referral, gathering of information about the case through a social study, assessment of the situation (including safety, risk, and family assessment), case planning including goal setting, provision of treatment, evaluation of the effects of treatment, and termination of the case (Pecora et al., 2010). Assessment focuses on many of the dynamics of the case that we've already discussed. Questions a practitioner should address include:

EP 2.1.10e

1. "Is the child at risk from abuse or neglect and to what degree?
2. What is causing the problem?
3. What are the strengths or protective factors that could be built on with services to alleviate the problem?
4. Is the home a safe environment or must the child be placed?" (Crosson-Tower, 2014, p. 216)

Certain factors affect risk (Crosson-Tower, 2014). These include:

- *Child factors:* Children who are younger or have intellectual or other disabilities are at greater risk.
- *Caregiver factors:* "Initially, the worker notes the level of cooperation and capabilities shown by the caregivers, remembering to frame this within a cultural context. Parents who recognize there is a problem present a better prognosis and less risk to the children than those who demonstrate

hostility or refuse to cooperate. The physical, mental, and emotional capabilities of the parent—as evidenced by their expectations of the child, ability to protect the child, and the ability to control anger and other impulses—indicate the degree of risk to the victim. Parents who are unaware of children's needs or demonstrate poor judgment or concept of reality present a high risk to the dependent child" (Crosson-Tower, 2014, p. 220).

- *Abuser factors:* Perpetrators who have a history of irrational, abusive behavior and who harm the child intentionally increase risk. Perpetrators who have greater access to victims also increase the risk factor.
- *Environmental factors:* "The incident itself is weighed in the light of future potential harm to the child. The worker determines the likelihood of permanent harm, the location of the injury, the previous history of abuse or neglect, and the physical conditions of the home. Environmental factors provide additional information. Parents who do not use support systems place the child at higher risk, for example, than those who can reach out for help. The degree of stress in the home also affects the likelihood of abuse. Death, divorce, incarceration of a parent, unemployment, career change, residence change, and birth of a child can all place a child at greater risk. Again, all these factors must be evaluated within a cultural context" (Crosson-Tower, 2014, pp. 220–221).

General treatment goals include stopping the maltreatment and strengthening the family enough to keep it together and, hopefully, have it thrive. Specific treatment modalities may include family therapy, involvement in support groups (e.g., Parents Anonymous), couple's counseling, or individual counseling, depending on the family's and the individual family members' needs.

Parents may need to learn how to identify their feelings and express them appropriately. They may need to learn how to communicate their needs to others and, in two-parent homes, to each other. They might require building their self-concepts. They may also need to master effective child management techniques in order to gain control and avoid abusive situations. Being taught how to provide a nurturant family environment for their children and improve their parent-child relationships might also be necessary.

Many times outside resources are helpful. Day care for children can provide some respite for parents and time for themselves. Homemaker service provides training in household management and makes available to parents an individual to give support and nurturance. Parental aides can work in homes, form relationships with parents, and model how to nurture children as well as effective child management techniques.

Physically abused children also need treatment, including medical services for physical damage. Children suffering from developmental delays may need special therapy or remedial help. Exposure to appropriate adult role models through day care is often used. Organizations such as Big Brothers and Big Sisters provide another means of support.

Individual or group counseling may be needed for the maltreated child. At least three major categories of victims' needs should be addressed (Crosson-Tower, 2014). These categories relate directly to the characteristics of maltreated children that we've discussed. The first need involves improving the victim's relationships with other people, including both peers and adults. Their old behavior patterns most likely involved either defensive withdrawal or inappropriate aggression. New, more effective social interaction techniques need to be established. The second need involves helping victims learn how to express their feelings. Some maltreated children withhold and suppress their feelings to avoid confrontations; other abused children have never learned how to control their aggressive impulses. The third need concerns the maltreated child's self-concept. For the many reasons we've discussed, maltreated children have a poor opinion of themselves and have little confidence in their own abilities.

A Macro-System Response: Involvement of the Courts

Courts become involved in maltreatment cases "when the child is in imminent danger or the parents are unable or unwilling to cooperate with the social service agency in improving the care of their children"; court involvement also can occur when parents are incapacitated for some reason, abandon children, fail to provide adequate medical treatment for serious health issues, severely physically hurt or even kill the child, or sexually abuse children and are subject to legal prosecution (Crosson-Tower, 2014, p. 248). Court involvement is a very difficult and

scary process for both the family and victim. Juvenile court procedures vary from state to state. However, most involve three processes: the petition, adjudication, and disposition.

The *petition* is a written complaint submitted to the court that the alleged abuse or neglect has occurred. *Adjudication* is a hearing where the alleged abuse or neglect is proven or discounted. Both parents and victim are represented by separate legal counsel. The *disposition* involves a hearing in which the court determines what is to be done with the child. This is a separate hearing from the adjudication, where it is determined whether the abuse or neglect actually happened. The court process is complex and often lengthy. Many variations, including additional investigations and settlements, are possible. (See Crosson-Tower, 2014, for a detailed description of the process.) Protective service workers and other social workers are frequently called upon to provide input to aid in the court's decision. Such input often is very influential and can have a direct impact on what happens to a child.

Sexual Abuse

Sexual abuse is "any sexual activity with a child where consent is not or cannot be given…. This includes sexual contact that is accomplished by force or threat of force, regardless of the age of the participants, and all sexual contact between an adult and a child, regardless of whether there is deception or the child understands the sexual nature of the activity. Sexual contact between an older and a younger child also can be abusive if there is a significant disparity in age, development, or size, rendering the younger child incapable of giving informed consent. The sexually abusive acts may include sexual penetration, sexual touching, or noncontact sexual acts such as exposure or voyeurism" (the act of gaining sexual gratification from watching people who are naked or engaging in sexual activities) (Berliner & Elliott, 2002, p. 55). *Incest*, a special form of sexual abuse, involves "sexual activities between a child and a relative—a parent, stepparent, parent's live-in partner or lover, foster parent, sibling, cousin, uncle, aunt, or grandparent" (McAnulty & Burnette, 2003, p. 486). "Sexual activities" can include a wide variety of sexual behaviors, including "pornographic photography, sexual gestures, parental exposure of genitalia, fondling, petting, fellatio, cunnilingus, intercourse, and any and all varieties of sexual contact" (Crosson-Tower, 2014; Mayer, 1983, p. 4).

Specific statutes addressing definitions of and punishments for sexual abuse vary widely by state. Concerning the incidence of sexual abuse, it is very difficult to get accurate statistics for a number of reasons. For one thing, many experts believe that cases of sexual abuse are vastly underreported (Berliner, 2011; Berliner & Elliot, 2002; Crosson-Tower, 2014). It is also very difficult for children to report sexual abuse. Perpetrators emphasize secrecy and blame the victim. Often, if victims do try to tell someone, that person is uncomfortable talking about it and may avoid the subject altogether. Definitions of sexual abuse vary widely, so it's difficult to collect and congregate data. Research estimates indicate that from about 19 to 22 percent of all women and 7 to 9 percent of all men state that they were sexually abused as children (Crooks & Baur, 2014; Rathus et al., 2014).

The Dynamics of Child Sexual Abuse

A major myth involved in child sexual abuse is that children should be warned about strangers. They're told that they should not get into cars when strangers offer them lollipops and they should not talk to strange men who are hiding behind park bushes. The reality is that children are in much greater danger from people who are close to them, from people they trust.

Children are easy victims for sexual abuse. Because of the anxiety most people harbor about sexuality in general, children have little information about sex. They have limited life experience upon which to base judgments. Thus, they can easily be misled and tricked. They are small compared to adults and are easily intimidated. Adults, in some ways, are godlike to children. Adults tell them what to do, when to go to bed, when they can cross the street, and if they can go to McDonald's. Children are oriented toward obeying adults, and most children want to please them, especially those adults who control their access to being loved, having food and shelter, and feeling safe.

Some data indicate that the "vast majority of offenders are male, although boys are more likely than girls to be abused by women (20 percent vs. 5 percent)" (Berliner, 2011, p. 219). An estimated 60 to 70 percent of sexual abuse occurs within the family (Crosson-Tower, 2013). This does not mean that

the remaining 40 percent is perpetrated by strangers. Rather, much extra-familial abuse is done by others who are close to the family and trusted by the child. Only 5 to 15 percent of sexual abuse is committed by strangers (Berliner, 2011). When sexual abuse is perpetrated by someone outside the family, that person is usually called a *pedophile* (someone who prefers children for sexual gratification). Because of its prevalence, we focus on incest in the following discussion.

Progression of the incestuous relationship is usually gradual. It may appear innocent enough at first. For instance, the adult might appear nude or undress before a child. It then progresses to greater and greater intimacy. There are five basic phases to sexual abuse (Crosson-Tower, 2014, pp. 114–115). First comes the *engagement* phase. Here, the perpetrator will experiment with the child to see how close he can get and how the child will react. The second phase is the *sexual interaction* phase. Sexual activity in various degrees of intimacy occurs during this phase. Often the longer this phase lasts, the more intimate the abuser becomes with the victim. The third phase is one of *secrecy*. Sexual activity has already occurred, so the abuser will use some manipulations to hold the victim ensnared in the abuse. For instance, the perpetrator might say, "Don't you tell your mommy; she won't like you anymore," or "This is our special secret because I love you so very much," or "If you tell anybody, I'll punish you." Threats and guilt are used to maintain the secret. The fourth phase is the *disclosure*. For one reason or another, the victim reveals that abuse has occurred. It may be physically initiated if the child contracts a sexually transmitted disease or is damaged in some way. It may be the result of an accident if the sexual activity was observed or someone noted and reported the child's indicative behavior. It may be that the victim feels she must tell someone because she can't stand it anymore. Revealing abuse may or may not happen during childhood. The fifth and final phase is *suppression*. This is a time of high anxiety for both victim and family. Feelings may include denial on the part of the perpetrator, guilt and insecurity on the part of the victim, and anger on the part of other family members.

What factors increase the risk of child sexual abuse? Risk factors related to the child tend to differ depending on the source of the information (Berliner, 2011). Some research suggests that girls are more likely to be victimized than boys (Berliner, 2011). However, other data propose that "boys are almost equally as vulnerable" (Crosson-Tower, 2014, p. 122; Miller-Perrin & Perrin, 2013). Some research proposes that "the average age of those abused is between 4 and 6 years for boys and 11 and 14 years for girls (Berliner, 2011)" (Crosson-Tower, 2014, p. 122). In contrast, other sources suggest that "boys are older at onset of victimization" (Berliner, 2011, p. 219). Most studies reveal that children who have a disability are at greater risk of sexual abuse (Berliner, 2011; Crosson-Tower, 2014). These children are more vulnerable and less able to defend themselves. In essence, they offer easier targets for perpetrators.

There are also a number of risk factors characterizing families (Berliner, 2011; Crosson-Tower, 2014; Miller-Perrin & Perrin, 2013); these include:

- Absence of a biological parent from the home—stepfather or a mother's boyfriend may be present.
- Family conflict and communication problems—when communication is poor, roles may become blurred. For example, when husband and wife or partners are in conflict, the male partner may turn to a female child to fulfill his needs.
- Family isolation—because secrecy is necessary for abuse to occur, a family may intensify its isolation even more.
- Having a mother who is not readily available to children (e.g., being ill or employed outside the home)—if communication is poor between mothers and daughters, it becomes even more difficult for daughters to turn to their mothers for help.

Consider the unknown proportion of mothers who do not know that the incest is occurring. There may be many reasons for this. The marriage is conflictual. Communication is lacking between the woman and her husband and the woman and her daughter. She may see things that are strange, but she works hard to deny them. She has a lot to lose if the incest is brought out into the open. She may feel resentment toward a daughter who has taken her husband and lover away from her. She may feel shame that this taboo is occurring within her own family. She may feel guilt for being such a failure to her husband that he had to turn to another. She may desperately fear having her family ripped apart. It is a very difficult situation for a mother in the incest triangle. She is not the abuser. Yet no alternatives are available that offer her a happy solution.

In some ways, the mother in the incestuous triangle is also a victim. She has been raised in a patriarchal society where she has been taught to be dependent, unassertive, and passive. She has also been taught that she is supposed to be the caretaker of the emotional well-being of her family. She has not been given the skills needed to aggressively fight for herself and her daughter in this desperate situation.

The Internet and Sexual Abuse Predators

The Internet provides a readily accessible means for pedophiles to interact with each other, validate their thoughts and acts, and share pornographic materials (Crooks & Baur, 2014). It also provides fertile ground for pedophiles seeking victims to satisfy their pedophilic fantasies and needs. They can easily cruise bulletin boards and chat rooms intended for children and adolescents. Often, they adhere to the following process (Crooks & Baur, 2014). First, perpetrators converse with the intended victims online, trying to convince victims of genuine interest in victims' troubles and issues. Second, they seek contact information such as e-mail and home addresses. Third, perpetrators will send victims pornographic content, hoping to demonstrate that such behavior is proper and standard. Fourth, perpetrators will try to set up a meeting with intended victims.

EP 2.1.9a

Berliner (2011) reports on the incidence of Internet sexual abuse:

> Rates of unwanted Internet sexual solicitations declined from 19% to 13%, but harassment (6% to 9%) and unwanted exposure to pornography (25% to 34%) increased from 2000 to 2005 (Mitchell, Wolak, & Finkelhor, 2007). However, a 2005 survey found that youth were more likely to report aggressive solicitations, and the rates of different forms of online sexual victimization decreased or increased with variations by age, gender, race, and household. There is little data on voluntary participation in illegal sexual activities or involvement in child pornography. (p. 218)

Characteristics of Sexual Abuse Victims

Children who are sexually abused may display a variety of physical, psychological, and behavioral indicators. Physical indicators may include a variety of physical problems that are sexually related, such as sexually transmitted diseases, problems with the throat or mouth, difficulties with urination, penile or vaginal discharge, or bruises in the genital area. Pregnancy is also an indicator.

Psychological indicators include low self-esteem, emotional disturbance, anger, fear, anxiety, and depression, sometimes to the point of becoming suicidal (Berliner, 2011; Berliner & Elliott, 2002; Miller-Perrin & Perrin, 2013). Behavioral indicators include withdrawing from others and experiencing difficulties in peer interaction. Often, victims of either gender engage in excessive sexual activity and inappropriate sexual behavior (Berliner, 2011; Faller, 2003; Friedrich et al., 2001).

Behavior related to sex that strikes you as being odd may also be an indicator. This refers once again to your "gut reaction" that something's wrong. For example, a child may know sexual terms or display sexual gestures that strike you as being inappropriate for her age level. A child may touch herself or others inappropriately in a sexual manner. A child may express desperate fears about being touched, undressing and taking showers in gym class, or being alone with a certain gender or with certain people.

Specific things that children say may strike you as odd and may be indicative of sexual abuse. For instance, a child may say, "Daddy and I have a secret"; "My babysitter wears red underwear"; or "I don't like going to Aunt Shirley's house. She diddles me."

Long-Term Effects of Sexual Abuse

Although significant research indicates that sexual abuse victims can suffer long-term results, this is a very complex issue. Abuse can vary in intensity, duration, and extent of trauma to the survivor. Long-term effects vary dramatically from one person to another (Rathus et al., 2014). Receiving treatment can also help survivors deal with issues and effects.

Research has established that survivors, as compared with people who have not been sexually abused, are more likely to experience emotional problems such as depression, fear of relationships, interpersonal problems, sexual dysfunctions, sexual acting out, and symptoms of posttraumatic stress (Berliner, 2011; Miller-Perrin & Perrin, 2013). Sexual acting out may involve overt sexual behavior directed "toward adults or other children,

compulsive masturbation, excessive sexual curiosity, sexual promiscuity, and precocious sexual play and knowledge" (Miller-Perrin & Perrin, 2013, p. 123). *Posttraumatic stress disorder* is a condition in which a person continues to reexperience an excessively traumatic event such as a bloody battle experience or a sexual assault. Symptoms include extreme anxiety, nightmares, an inability to sleep or stay awake, an inability to concentrate, and explosive, angry emotional outbursts.

Note that because of the tremendous disparity in how sexual abuse affects individuals, no specific variables are consistently linked to long-term problems (Miller-Perrin & Perrin, 2013). Although they may contribute to the risk of having problems, sexual abuse experiences do not condemn a person to a miserable life. Effects depend on a number of factors. For example "the availability of social supports following the disclosure of abuse, such as maternal support or a supportive relationship with another adult, appears to mitigate negative effects and play a protective role" (Miller-Perrin & Perrin, 2013, p. 129; Pollio, Deblinger, & Runyon, 2011).

Research has established that the following five variables increase the risk of more serious problems in adulthood for survivors of sexual abuse (Berliner, 2011; Berliner & Elliott, 2002; Crosson-Tower, 2014; Miller-Perrin & Perrin, 2013):

1. *Closer relationship to the perpetrator.* Sexual abuse by a family member, or by another person the victim feels close to and trusts, is related to deeper trauma in adulthood.

2. *Duration of the abuse.* The longer the abuse continued, the greater the likelihood of long-term negative effects. However, even a single incident can cause severe trauma if extremely violent or sadistic behavior (the infliction of pain on the survivor for the offender's sexual gratification) occurred (Beitchman et al., 1992).

3. *Use of force and the intensity of abuse.* Using force or causing pain tends to result in more devastating effects. The occurrence of penile penetration is also related to greater trauma.

4. *Absence of parental and other support.* When a victim first reveals the abuse, lack of support from those close to her potentially results in greater long-term problems. If others criticize or blame her, she may suffer significant psychological distress. The victim may even decide to

HIGHLIGHT 4.3

Suggestions for Talking to Children Victimized by Sexual Assault

- Always believe the child. It takes courage to talk about such difficult things, and it's easy to turn the child off.
- Be warm and empathic. Encourage the child to talk freely to you. Reflecting the child's feelings back is useful.
- Don't react with shock or disgust no matter what the child tells you. That only communicates to the child that he or she is the one to blame.
- Encourage the child to share all feelings with you, including the negative ones. Even getting the angry feelings out helps the child overcome the feelings of victimization. Give the child the chance to ventilate his or her feelings so he or she can deal with them.
- Listen to the child. Don't disagree or argue. Interrupt only when you have to in order to understand what the child is saying.
- Talk to the child in a private place. The child may feel much more comfortable if others aren't around to hear.
- Tell the child that he or she is not the only child who has had this experience. Other children have, too.
- Allow the child to express feelings of guilt. Emphasize to the child that it was not his or her fault. The adult abuser is the one who has a problem and needs help.

- Talk in language that the child can understand. Give accurate information when it's needed. Let the child repeat things back to you to make certain he or she understands.
- Tell the child that you are very glad he or she told you about the incident(s). Emphasize that it was the right thing to do.
- Ask if the child would like to ask you any questions, and be sure to answer them honestly.
- Do not treat the child any differently after he or she has told you. This only communicates that you think he or she is to blame or did the wrong thing.
- If the child asks you to keep the abuse secret, answer honestly. Tell the child that you only want to help, that secrets that hurt people aren't good to keep, and that the secrets need to be brought out into the open in order to help the person who abused him or her.
- Finally, depending on your situation, don't let the issue drop. If you are the social worker involved, pursue the problem. Otherwise, tell the parents and/or the appropriate authorities so that the child can get help.

hide into adulthood what she may perceive as her "dirty secret." See Highlight 4.3 for suggestions about how to talk and positively relate to victims of sexual abuse.

5. *Inability of the survivor to cope.* Some individuals have a personality structure that naturally allows them to cope more effectively with crises and stress. Human personality is a complicated concept.

Treatment of Children Who Have Been Sexually Abused: Social Work Role

EP 2.1.1c,
2.1.10j

Because of its prevalence, we will focus on treatment of the incestuous family. Treatment usually progresses through three phases (Crosson-Tower, 2014, pp. 297–298). The first is the *disclosure-panic* phase. Strong feelings characterize this period of crisis. Family members display much anger and denial. The victim is often frightened about what will happen and eager to blame herself.

The second phase is the *assessment-awareness* phase. During this phase, the family acknowledges that the abuse has occurred and struggles to deal with its consequences. Family members learn about themselves and the dynamics involved in their family interaction. The social worker works to redefine and realign the boundaries of subsystems within the family. This phase tends to be characterized by conflicting feelings. On the one hand, they are angry that the abuse has occurred and eager to blame each other. On the other hand, they are struggling to realign their relationships and express the feelings of love they have for each other. The third phase is the *restructure* phase. Here the family regains emotional health. Boundaries are clearly established and family members learn how to function within them. Communication is greatly enhanced and members can use it to work out their differences. Parents take responsibility for their behavior, and the victim feels much better about herself.

Initial treatment has several major objectives. The first is to provide a safe environment where the incest survivor feels comfortable enough to talk

(Pollio et al., 2011). A survivor must learn how to identify, express, and share her feelings, even when they are negative and frightening. LeVine and Sallee (1999) explain:

> Although the child may not have experienced fear during an incestuous relationship, discovery may create anxiety. Children need assurances that no matter what has happened in the past, they are now safe. The end of abuse through the efforts of the police or the child welfare worker will begin to build trust in the child. The child must feel that it is all right for him or her to feel any suppressed guilt, hurt, anger, and confusion. The opportunity to express these feelings honestly, in an atmosphere of trust, begins a sense of security. (p. 329)

A second treatment goal involves having the survivor acknowledge that the abuse was not her fault (Crosson-Tower, 2014; LeVine & Sallee, 1999). Guilt may result from feelings of love for the perpetrator, appreciation of the special attention she received from the abuse, or worry about what the disclosure will do to the family (Crosson-Tower, 2014). Dwelling on inappropriate and unfair self-blame only hampers the recovery process.

A third treatment objective involves teaching survivors to identify and express their emotions in addition to getting control of their problematic behaviors.

Cognitive-behavioral therapy techniques, which reflect this objective, have been used effectively to help sexual abuse survivors (Miller-Perrin & Perrin, 2013; Pollio et al., 2011). These approaches embrace the conceptual framework espoused by behavioral (learning) theory (discussed earlier in the chapter). Additionally, they assume an educational perspective of providing information about sexual abuse and its effects, stress the use of homework, expect clients to become actively engaged in changing problematic behavior, and emphasize a strong role for the therapist (Corey, 2013). Cognitive-behavioral techniques "are time-limited, directive, transparent, evidence based, and active, and they focus on changing the factors thought to maintain psychological problems" (Wedding & Corsini, 2014, p. 195). Highlight 4.4 identifies a number of components that can be used in cognitive-behavioral therapy.

A fourth treatment goal involves enhancing family communication, support, functioning, and understanding of the abuse (Crosson-Tower, 2014). Individual concerns are dealt with in addition to family interaction issues. Miller-Perrin and Perrin (2013) explain:

> Typical themes addressed in family-oriented therapies include parents' failure to protect the victim from abuse, feelings of guilt and depression

---

◆ HIGHLIGHT 4.4

Use of Cognitive-Behavioral Techniques with Children Who Have Been Sexually Abused

Miller-Perrin and Perrin (2013) identify and describe the following components of cognitive-behavioral therapy that can be used to help children who have been sexually abused:

- *Psychoeducation:* Providing accurate information about the problem of sexual abuse and common reactions to this abuse. This component also includes teaching safety skills to help children feel empowered and to help them protect themselves from future victimization.
- *Anxiety Reduction Techniques:* Training and practice in various relaxation skills to reduce fear and anxiety.
- *Affective Expression*: Building various skills to help children express and manage their feelings effectively.

- *Exposure Therapy:* Gradual exposure to elements of the abuse experience in order to decondition negative emotional responses to memories of the abuse. This component involves verbal, written, and play activities to encourage children to share and process abuse-related experiences.
- *Cognitive Therapy Techniques:* Identifying negative attributions and distorted cognitions (e.g., irrational thinking and inaccurate perceptions) associated with the abuse and replacing them with more accurate thoughts and beliefs.
- *Parenting Skills:* Training parents in various management techniques to help them become more effective parents. (Emphasis added.) (p. 138)

resulting from the abuse, the inappropriateness of secrecy, the victims anger toward parents, the perpetrator's responsibility for the abuse, appropriate forms of touch, confusion about blurred role boundaries, poor communication patterns, and the effect the abuse has had on the child. (p. 142)

Prevention of Sexual Abuse: The Need for a Macro-System Response

EP 2.1.8a, 2.1.10i

The ideal way of dealing with sexual abuse is to prevent it from happening at all. Information and education are the keys to prevention. Parents need both education about how to raise children and knowledge that in the event they are in crisis resources are available to help. Parenting education could be made a required part of all high school curricula. Special programs could be made readily available in the community to help parents with these issues.

Educating Children About Sexual Abuse

Children need to be educated about sexual abuse. There are three basic preventative approaches. First, children should be taught that their bodies are their own and that they have private places where nobody can force them to be touched. What comes to mind are the parents who tell their 4-year-old son to go up to each relative at the culmination of an extended family event and "give them a kiss." The child obviously finds this distasteful. He frowns, looks down at his shoes, and hides behind his mother. He knows that old Aunt Hilda gives really slobbery, wet ones. And she hugs him like the Crusher in a wrestling match, too. He hates the very thought of it, even though his aunt is a kind person who loves him.

Children should have the right to say no if they don't want to have such intimacy. Parents and teachers can help children determine what are "good touches" and what are "bad touches." They can also help children develop the confidence to say no to adults in uncomfortable situations involving touching them in ways they don't like.

A second preventative measure for children is to learn correct sexual terminology right from the beginning. It's easy for parents, especially if they're uncomfortable with sexual terminology themselves, to sugarcoat words and refer to "ding-dongs" and

"bumps." One 3-year-old girl came out into the midst of a family gathering and told her mother, "My pooderpie hurts." She had her hand placed over her clothes on her genital area. Her mother, with a look of terror, desperation, and embarrassment, jumped up and dashed off with her to the bathroom. Apparently, the little girl had to urinate and didn't identify the feeling as such. A few months later, the same 3-year-old was chattering on about some topic that was desperately important to a 3-year-old, pointed to her buttocks, and interjected something about her pooderpie again. My reaction was, "Yikes, the pooderpie has moved. Where will it go next?"

The point is that if this little girl tells someone that a person touched her pooderpie, that someone might respond, "Oh, that's nice." Whomever she tells would have no idea what she was talking about. Inaccurate, childish terminology does not equip children with the communication skills they need if they encounter a sexually abusive situation. Children need to be able to specify what people are doing or have tried to do to them. Only then can their caregivers adequately protect them.

This leads to our third preventative suggestion. Lines of communication between caregivers and children should be encouraged and kept open. Children need to feel that they can share things with parents, including things that bother them. In the event that children are placed in a potentially abusive situation, they need to be encouraged and to be able to "tell someone."

Chapter Summary

The following summarizes this chapter's content as it relates to the learning objectives presented at the beginning of the chapter. Chapter content will help prepare students to:

LO 4-1 Explain the concept of socialization.

Socialization is the process through which individuals learn proper ways of acting in a society.

LO 4-2 Analyze the family environment (including variations in family structures, positive family functioning, macro systems and the pursuit of social and economic justice, and family system dynamics).

Wide variations in family structures exist. Important concepts include primary group, single-parent family, stepfamily, and blended family. Changes from traditional family patterns include marrying earlier or not at all, living together without marriage, being together but living separately, more births to single mothers, and higher levels of mothers' employment. Positive family functioning involves good communication.

Macro systems can affect families both positively and negatively. Families require resources such as adequate day care in order to function effectively.

LO 4-3 Apply systems theory concepts to families.

Systems theory concepts can be readily applied to families. Important concepts include systems, homeostasis, subsystems, boundaries, input, output, feedback, entropy, negative entropy, equifinality, and differentiation.

LO 4-4 Assess the family life cycle.

Formerly, it was thought that families progressed predictably through a six-stage family life cycle. Contemporary thought views families as passing through life-cycle stages in a less predictable, more diverse manner.

LO 4-5 Explain diverse perspectives on the family life cycle.

Family life cycles are dramatically affected by diverse variables, including class, culture, disability, ethnicity, gender, immigration status, race, religion, and sexual orientation. Diversity is also reflected in the context of single adults and immigration status.

LO 4-6 Describe learning theory.

Learning theory provides an exceptionally useful means of conceptualizing and understanding human behavior. It is a theoretical orientation that emphasizes behavior, its preceding event, and its subsequent consequences.

Behavior modification involves the therapeutic application of learning theory principles. Major approaches within learning theory include respondent conditioning, which focuses on stimuli and responses; modeling, which is based on observation; and operant conditioning, which emphasizes regulating the consequences of behavior. Major terms in operant conditioning are positive and negative reinforcement, punishment, and extinction.

LO 4-7 Apply learning theory concepts to practice (including positive reinforcement, punishment, issues related to the application of learning theory, and time-out from reinforcement).

Applications of learning theory to practice include the use of positive reinforcement, punishment, and time-out from reinforcement. When using positive reinforcement, quality, immediacy, and frequency are important. When using punishment, it's important to attend to potential negative consequences and use punishment only selectively.

Other significant issues in the application of learning theory include accidental training, using behaviorally specific terminology, measuring improvement, and the importance of parental attention. Timeout from reinforcement should be brief, boring, applied immediately and consistently, and used along with positive reinforcement for appropriate behavior.

LO 4-8 Examine common life events that affect children (including treatment of children in families, sibling subsystems, and gender-role socialization).

The family environment is of crucial importance to children's socialization and is characterized by various parenting styles. As members of family systems, children are affected by sibling subsystems (including the births of new siblings, sibling interaction, and the effects of birth order, family size, and family spacing) and gender-role socialization.

LO 4-9 Recognize ethnic and cultural differences in families.

The father's role in the family, availability and nature of support systems, and perspectives on disciplining children vary greatly among cultures. Themes in understanding Hispanic and Latino families include the significance of a common language, the importance of family relationships, and the strict division of gender roles. Concepts especially relevant to Native American families are the importance of extended family, cooperation, mutual respect, harmony with nature, treatment of time, spirituality, and noninterference. Themes that characterize Asian American families include the importance of family as the primary unit, interdependence among family members, investment in children, and patriarchal hierarchy.

LO 4-10 *Assess relevant aspects of the social environment (including the social aspects of play with peers, bullying, the influence of television and the media, and the school environment).*

Play is a significant aspect of children's interaction and development. Children may progress through developmental levels of play. Gender differences exist in terms of aggression and toy preference. Peer groups and popularity are very important to children.

Bullying is "aggression by an individual that is repeatedly directed toward particular peers (victims)" (Steinberg et al., 2011b, p. 318). Bullying has become a major problem for many children.

Children spend enormous amounts of time watching television and playing video games, resulting in concerns about the portrayal of violence, an unrealistic depiction of the world, and the teaching of aggressive, violent behavior. Suggestions for how school personnel can discourage and prevent bullying are provided.

The school environment provides a major arena for socialization. Effective teachers and school environments are important. Gaps in educational attainment exist among different racial groups and should be addressed.

LO 4-11 *Examine child maltreatment (including incidence, physical child abuse, child neglect, psychological maltreatment, Child Protective Services, treatment approaches for child maltreatment, and sexual abuse).*

Large numbers of children are physically abused, neglected, psychologically maltreated, or sexually abused.

Indications of physical abuse include bruises, lacerations, fractures, burns, head injuries, internal injuries, extremely passive or aggressive behavior, and lags in development.

Child neglect is often characterized by inadequate physical or mental health care, education, supervision, basic housing safety and sanitation, and personal hygiene in addition to abandonment. Victims may exhibit social and attachment difficulties, cognitive and academic deficits, and emotional and behavioral problems.

Psychological maltreatment involves active abuse such as rejecting, isolating, terrorizing, ignoring, or corrupting.

Child Protective Services (CPS) entail a macro-system response to child maltreatment. CPS agencies initiate investigations, conduct assessments, make custody determinations, and use various modalities to provide treatment that addresses child maltreatment. Social work practitioners can play significant roles as CPS workers and workers for other agencies in helping to address and stop child maltreatment. Another macro-system response concerns involvement of the courts.

Sexual abuse often occurs in a gradual process by someone a child knows and trusts. The Internet provides a readily accessible mechanism for pedophiles to prey on children and adolescents. Physical and behavioral indicators of sexual abuse may be evident. Sexual abuse may have long-term effects, with some variables increasing the risk of more serious problems. Treatment for sexual abuse involves providing child survivors with a safe environment, acknowledging that abuse is the perpetrator's fault, using cognitive-behavioral techniques, and enhancing family communication and interaction. Macro-system responses to child maltreatment may include enhancing programming for educating children about sexual abuse.

COMPETENCY NOTES

The entire chapter addresses competency Educational Policy (EP) EP 2.1.7 and its respective practice behaviors EP 2.1.7a and EP 2.1.7b (as cited below). (See p. 179.)

EP 2.1.7 Apply knowledge of human behavior and the social environment.

EP 2.1.7a Utilize conceptual frameworks to guide the processes of assessment, intervention, and evaluation. (Such conceptual frameworks will typically be identified by a "helping hands" icon.)

EP 2.1.7b Critique and apply knowledge to understand person and environment.
Other EP competencies and practice behaviors addressed in this chapter include the following:

EP 2.1.1c Attend to professional roles and boundaries.
(p. 242): Social work roles concerning intervention in physical abuse, neglect, and psychological maltreatment are discussed.
(p. 247): Social work roles with respect to treatment in sexual abuse cases are discussed.

EP 2.1.1e Engage in career-long learning.
(p. 217): Learning about cultural expectations for parenting with different client groups is a career-long process.
(p. 218): It is important for social workers to continue learning about other cultures throughout their careers.
(p. 235): Learning about clients' cultural values is a career-long process.

EP 2.1.2 Apply social work ethical principles to guide professional practice.
(pp. 184, 210, 215, 215, 216, 230, 231, 236, 240): Ethical questions are posed.

EP 2.1.3a Distinguish, appraise, and integrate multiple sources of knowledge, including research-based knowledge, and practice wisdom.
(p. 195): It is important to analyze the effectiveness of learning theory by evaluating its applications to and effectiveness in a wide range of specific situations.

EP 2.1.3c Demonstrate effective oral and written communication in working with individuals, families, groups, organizations, communities, and colleagues.
(p. 210): Implementing behavior modification techniques requires the use of specific behavioral terminology.

EP 2.1.4a Recognize the extent to which culture's structures and values may oppress, marginalize, alienate, or create or enhance privilege and power.
(p. 190): Spotlight 4.1 recognizes how cultural structures and values affect the family life cycles by focusing on class, culture, disability, ethnicity, gender, immigration status, race, religion, and sexual orientation.
(p. 232): Educational programming that responds to Hawaiian cultural values can enhance learning.
(p. 232): Race and ethnicity may result in alienation and lower achievement in a school setting.

EP 2.1.4c Recognize and communicate their understanding of the importance of difference in shaping life experiences.
(p. 190): Spotlight 4.1 focuses on how various dimensions of diversity shape life experiences during the family life cycle.
(p. 217): Cultural expectations affect parenting expectations and styles, as well as shape life experiences.

(p. 218): Cultural differences shape life experiences for families.
(p. 224): Gender is an aspect of difference that affects life experiences when it comes to children's play.
(p. 232): Educational programming that responds to Hawaiian cultural values can shape the school experience.
(p. 232): Race and ethnicity can shape children's life experiences in a school setting.
(p. 235): Cultural values shape people's expectations about children's behavior and treatment.

EP 2.1.4d View themselves as learners and engage those with whom they work as informants.
(p. 217): It is vital for social workers to learn from clients about their cultures.
(p. 218): Social workers can learn about other cultures from their clients.
(p. 235): Practitioners should learn from their clients about child-rearing expectations and values.

EP 2.1.5 Advance human rights and social and economic justice.
(p. 183): A democratic society is responsible for providing families with support in pursuit of social and economic justice.

EP 2.1.5a Understand the forms and mechanisms of oppression and discrimination.
(p. 190): Oppression is discussed concerning various dimensions of diversity (including class, race, and sexual orientation), and their effects on various stages of the family life cycle.

EP 2.1.6b Use research evidence to inform practice.
(p. 195): Social workers should utilize research on the effectiveness of specific behavioral techniques applied to particular practice scenarios to guide their interventions.
(p. 201): Practitioners should select evidence-based interventions to improve their practice effectiveness when applying learning theory.
(p. 214): Social workers should use evidence-based research to determine the most effective applications of time-outs when dealing with children's behavior.

EP 2.1.7 Apply knowledge of human behavior and the social environment.
(p. 190): Practitioners should be knowledgeable about human behavior across the life course, including the family life cycle.

(p. 215): Social workers must be knowledgeable about the range of social systems in which people live, including family systems and sibling subsystems.

EP 2.1.7a Utilize conceptual frameworks to guide the processes of assessment, intervention, and evaluation.

(p. 185): Systems theory provides a useful conceptual framework for understanding families.

(p. 190): Learning theory provides a helpful conceptual framework for understanding human behavior and effective child management techniques.

(p. 194): A seven-stage model for assessing the family life cycle is discussed.

EP 2.1.8a Analyze, formulate, and advocate for policies that advance social well-being.

(p. 183): Social workers should analyze the extent to which social policies maximize people's well-being.

(p. 249): Practitioners should advocate for policies and programs that prevent sexual abuse.

EP 2.1.9a Continuously discover, appraise, and attend to changing locales, populations, scientific and technological developments, and emerging societal trends to provide relevant services.

(p. 222): Practitioners must continuously keep abreast of issues and trends that are important for clients, such as peer relationships, effects of the media, and the school environment.

(p. 233): Social workers should attend to changing developments and trends in the area of child maltreatment in order to provide relevant, effective services.

(p. 245): Workers should continuously attend to changing technological developments and issues concerning the Internet.

EP 2.1.10a Substantively and affectively prepare for action with individuals, families, groups, organizations, and communities.

(p. 233): Social workers must understand the dynamics of child maltreatment, its assessment, and appropriate interventions to prepare for working with these issues in the field.

EP 2.1.10d Collect, organize, and interpret client data.

(p. 242): Questions to ask and risk factors to assess are summarized in preparation for work with families where child maltreatment is occurring.

EP 2.1.10e Assess clients' strengths and limitations.

(p. 218): Practitioners should identify the strengths inherent in families with diverse cultural backgrounds.

(p. 242): Social workers should strive to identify both strengths and limitations (risk factors) when working with families involved in child maltreatment.

EP 2.1.10g Select appropriate intervention strategies.

(p. 201): Appropriate intervention strategies should be selected from the wide range of learning-theory applications available.

EP 2.1.10h Initiate actions to achieve organizational goals.

(p. 241): Practitioners working in Child Protective Services (CPS) should seek to fulfill CPS goals.

EP 2.1.10i Implement prevention interventions that enhance client capacities.

(p. 241): Child Protective Services aim to strengthen families, if at all possible, in order to prevent removal of children from their own homes. A safe, permanent home environment is considered the best setting for children.

(p. 249): Social workers should support programs aimed at the prevention of sexual abuse. They should also educate children about sexual abuse in order to prevent it.

EP 2.1.10j Help clients resolve problems.

(p. 201): Applications of learning theory can help clients solve problems.

(p. 242): Practitioners should help clients solve problems involving child maltreatment.

(p. 247): Social workers should help clients solve problems involving sexual abuse.

EP 2.1.10m Critically analyze, monitor, and evaluate interventions.

(p. 211): Evaluation of intervention effectiveness involves the careful, conscientious observation of behavior and behavioral improvement.

WEB RESOURCES

See this text's companion website at *www.cengagebrain.com* for learning tools such as chapter quizzing, videos, and more.

ETHNOCENTRISM AND RACISM

McClatchy-Tribune Information Services / Alamy

Abraham Lincoln has the reputation of being the key person in ending slavery in our country. Yet it appears that Lincoln held racist beliefs, as indicated in the following excerpt from a speech he delivered in 1858:

> I will say, then, that I am not, nor ever have been in favor of bringing about in any way the social and political equality of the white and black races; that I am not, nor ever have been, in favor of making voters or jurors of Negroes, nor of qualifying them to hold office, nor to inter-marry with white people … and in as much as they cannot so live, while they do remain together there must be the position of superior and inferior, and I as much as any other man am in favor of having the superior position assigned to the white race.

Such a statement needs to be viewed in its historical context. Our country was more racist years ago than it is today. Lincoln, who was in the vanguard of moving for greater equality for African Americans, was also socialized by his culture to have racist attitudes. (The impact of culture on individuals was discussed in Chapter 1.)

A Perspective

Nearly every time we turn on the evening news, we see ethnic and racial conflict—riots, beatings, murders, and civil wars. In recent years we have seen clashes resulting in bloodshed in areas ranging from Afghanistan to Iraq, from Bosnia to Israel, and from the United States to South America. Practically every nation with more than one ethnic group has had to deal with ethnic conflict. The oppression and exploitation of one ethnic group by another is particularly ironic in democratic nations, considering these societies claim to cherish freedom, equality, and justice. In reality, the dominant group in all societies that controls the political and economic institutions rarely agrees to share equally its power and wealth with other ethnic groups. Ethnocentrism and racism are factors that can adversely affect the growth and development of minority group members.

Learning Objectives

This chapter will help prepare students to:

**EP 2.1.2a;
2.1.4a–d;
2.1.5a–c;
2.1.7a;
2.1.10e**

LO 5-1 *Define and describe ethnic groups, ethnocentrism, race, racism, prejudice, discrimination, oppression, and institutional discrimination*

LO 5-2 *Outline the sources of prejudice and discrimination*

LO 5-3 *Summarize the effects and costs of discrimination and oppression and describe effects of discrimination on human growth and development*

LO 5-4 *Suggest strategies for advancing social and economic justice*

LO 5-5 *Outline some guidelines for social work practice with racial and ethnic groups*

LO 5-6 *Forecast the pattern of race and ethnic relations in the United States in the future*

LO 5-1 Define and Describe Ethnic Groups, Ethnocentrism, Race, Racism, Prejudice, Discrimination, Oppression, and Institutional Discrimination

Ethnic Groups and Ethnocentrism

An ethnic group has a sense of togetherness, a conviction that its members form a special group, and a sense of common identity or "peoplehood." An *ethnic group* is a distinct group of people who share cultural characteristics, such as religion, language, dietary practices, national origin, and a common history, and who regard themselves as a distinct group.

Practically every ethnic group has a strong feeling of *ethnocentrism*, which is characterized or based on the belief that one's own group is superior. Ethnocentrism leads members of ethnic groups to view their culture as the best, as superior, as the one that other cultures should adopt. Ethnocentrism

Cheryl Koenig Morgan/MPI/Getty Images

A Native American woman creates jewelry that is revered in her culture—and is cherished by consumers. In general, it is important for ethnic groups to preserve their cultures.

In interactions between nations, ethnocentric beliefs sometimes lead to wars and serve as justifications for foreign conquests. At practically any point in the last several centuries, at least a few wars have occurred between nations in which one society has been seeking to force its culture on another or to eradicate another culture. For example, Israel has been involved in bitter struggles with Arab countries in the Middle East for more than four decades over territory ownership. Shiites, Sunnis, and Kurds are fighting for domination in Iraq.

Spotlight 5.1 details some of the violence against minorities that has taken place in U.S. history.

Race and Racism

Although a racial group is often also an ethnic group, the two groups are not necessarily the same. A *race* is believed to have a common set of physical characteristics. But the members of a racial group may or may not share the sense of togetherness or identity that holds an ethnic group together. A group that is both a racial group and an ethnic group is Japanese Americans, who have some common physical characteristics and also have a sense of peoplehood (Coleman & Cressey, 1984). On the other hand, white Americans and white Russians are of the same race, but they hardly have a sense of togetherness. In addition, some ethnic groups are composed of a variety of races. For example, a religious group (such as Roman Catholic) is sometimes considered an ethnic group and is composed of members from diverse racial groups.

In contrast to ethnocentrism, racism is more likely to be based on physical differences than on cultural differences. *Racism* is the belief that race is the primary determinant of human capacities and traits and that racial differences produce an inherent superiority of a particular race. Racism is frequently a basis of discrimination against members of other "racial" groups.

Similar to ethnocentric ideologies, most racist ideologists assert that members of other racial groups are inferior. Some white Americans in this country have gone to extreme and morally reprehensible limits in search of greater control and power over other racial groups.

also leads to prejudice against foreigners, who may be viewed as barbarians, uncultured people, or savages.

Feelings of ethnic superiority within a nation are usually accompanied by the belief that political and economic domination by one's own group is natural, is morally right, is in the best interest of the nation, and perhaps also is God's will. Ethnocentrism has been a factor leading to some of the worst atrocities in history, such as the American colonists' nearly successful attempt to exterminate Native Americans and Adolf Hitler's mass executions of more than 6 million European Jews, and millions more gypsies, people with disabilities, and other minority group members.

SPOTLIGHT ON DIVERSITY 5.1

Violence Against Minorities in the United States

Minorities have been subjected to extensive violence by whites in our society. (It has been a two-way street because a number of whites have been subjected to violence by nonwhites.)

During the second half of the 19th century, frequent massacres of Chinese mining and railroad workers occurred in the West. During one railroad strike in 1885, white workers stormed a Chinese community in Rock Springs, Wyoming, murdered 16 persons, and burned all the homes to the ground. No one was arrested. In 1871, a white mob raided the Chinese community in Los Angeles, killing 19 persons and hanging 15 to serve as a warning to survivors (Pinkney, 1972).

Pinkney (1972) comments on the treatment of African American slaves by their white owners:

Few adult slaves escaped some form of sadism at the hands of slaveholders. A female slaveholder was widely known to punish her slaves by beating them on the face. Another burned her slave girl on the neck with hot tongs. A drunken slaveholder dismembered his slave and threw him piece by piece into a fire. Another planter dragged his slave from bed and inflicted a thousand lashes on him. (p. 73)

Slaveowners often used a whip made of cowskin or rawhide to control their slaves. An elaborate punishment system was developed, linking the number of lashes to the seriousness of the offenses with which slaves were charged.

Shortly before the Civil War, roving bands of whites commonly descended on African American communities and terrorized and beat the inhabitants. Slaves sometimes struck back and killed their slaveowners or other whites. It has been estimated that during Reconstruction, more than 5,000 African Americans were killed in the South by white vigilante groups (Pinkney, 1972).

Following the Civil War, lynching of African Americans increased and continued into the 1950s. African Americans were lynched for such minor offenses as peeping into a window, attempting to vote, making offensive remarks, seeking employment in a restaurant, getting into a dispute with a white person, and expressing sympathy for another African American who had already been lynched. Arrests for lynching African Americans were rare. Lynch mobs included not only men but sometimes also women and children. Some lynchings were publicly announced, and the public was invited to participate. The public often appeared to enjoy the activities and urged the active lynchers on to greater brutality.

Race riots between whites and African Americans have also been common since the Civil War. During the summer of 1919, for example, 26 major race riots occurred, the most serious of which was in Chicago. In this riot, which lasted from July 27 to August 2, a total of 38 persons were killed,

537 were injured, and more than 1,000 were left homeless (Waskow, 1967).

Native Americans have been subjected to kidnapping, massacre, conquest, forced assimilation, and murder. Some tribes were completely exterminated. The treatment of Native Americans by whites in North America stands as one of the most revolting series of acts of violence in history.

The extermination of Native Americans began with the early Pilgrims. They were the first to establish a policy to massacre and exterminate Native Americans in this country. In 1636, the Massachusetts Bay Puritans sent a force to massacre the Pequot, a division of the Mohegan tribe. The dwellings were burned, and 600 inhabitants were slaughtered (Pinkney, 1972).

In 1642, the governor of New Netherlands began offering bounties for Native American scalps. A year later, this same governor ordered the massacre of the Wappinger tribe. Pinkney (1972) describes the massacre:

During the massacre infants were taken from their mother's breast, cut in pieces and thrown into a fire or into the river. Some children who were still alive were also thrown into the river, and when their parents attempted to save them they drowned along with their children. When the massacre was over, the members of the murder party were congratulated by the grateful governor. (p. 96)

A major motive for this violence was that the European settlers were land-hungry. The deliberate massacre and extermination of Native Americans continued from the 1660s throughout most of the 1800s. The whites frequently made and broke treaties with Native Americans during these years—and ended up taking most of their land and sharply reducing their population. For example, in a forced march on foot covering several states, an estimated 4,000 Cherokees died from cold and exhaustion in 1838 (Pinkney, 1972). During these years, Native Americans were considered savage beasts. Many whites felt, "The only good Indian is a dead one," and they exterminated Native Americans because it was felt they impeded economic progress.

Today, racial clashes between minority group members still occur, but on a smaller scale on the street and in some of our schools. In recent years, organizations that advocate white supremacy (such as the Ku Klux Klan and Skinheads) have continued to attract new members. Demonstrations by these organizations have led to several bloody clashes between supporters and those opposed to these racist groups.

Throughout U.S. history, there have also been incidents of police brutality by white officers against members of minority groups. For example, police brutality received national attention in 1991 when an African American motorist, Rodney King, was

(continued)

SPOTLIGHT ON DIVERSITY 5.1 *(continued)*

stopped after a lengthy car chase and beaten by four club-wielding white police officers in Los Angeles. The beatings were videotaped by a bystander. Mr. King received more than 50 blows from clubs and sustained 11 fractures in his skull, a broken ankle, and a number of other injuries. In April 1992, a jury (with no African American members) found the police officers "not guilty" on charges of using excessive force. The reaction of African Americans and others in Los Angeles has been described as the worst civil unrest in more than a century—nearly 60 people were killed and more than $800 million in damage resulted from rioting, looting, and destruction over a period of three days.

Aspects of Social and Economic Forces: Prejudice, Discrimination, and Oppression

Prejudice is a preconceived adverse opinion or judgment formed without just grounds or before sufficient knowledge. Prejudice, in regard to race and ethnic relations, is making negative prejudgments. Prejudiced people apply racial stereotypes to all or nearly all members of a group according to preconceived notions of what they believe the group to be like and how they think the group will behave. Racial prejudice results from the belief that people who have different skin color and other physical characteristics also have innate differences in behaviors, values, intellectual functioning, and attitudes.

The word *discrimination* has two very different meanings. It may have the positive meaning of the power of making fine distinctions between two or more ideas, objects, situations, or stimuli. However, in minority-group relations it is the unfair treatment of a person, racial group, or minority; it is an action based on prejudice.

Racial or ethnic discrimination involves denying to members of minority groups equal access to opportunities, residential housing areas, membership in religious and social organizations, involvement in political activities, access to community services, and so on.

Prejudice is a combination of stereotyped beliefs and negative attitudes, so that prejudiced individuals think about people in a predetermined, usually negative, categorical way. Discrimination involves physical actions—unequal treatment of people because they belong to a category. Discriminatory behavior often derives from prejudiced attitudes.

Robert Merton, however, notes that prejudice and discrimination can occur independently. In discussing discrimination in the United States, he describes four different "types" of people:

1. *The unprejudiced nondiscriminator*, in both belief and practice, upholds American ideals of freedom and equality. This person is not prejudiced against other groups and, on principle, will not discriminate against them.
2. *The unprejudiced discriminator* is not personally prejudiced but may sometimes, reluctantly, discriminate against other groups because it seems socially or financially convenient to do so.
3. *The prejudiced nondiscriminator* feels hostile to other groups but recognizes that law and social pressures are opposed to overt discrimination. Reluctantly, this person does not translate prejudice into action.
4. *The prejudiced discriminator* does not believe in the values of freedom and equality and consistently discriminates against other groups in both word and deed.

An example of an unprejudiced discriminator is the unprejudiced owner of a condominium complex in an all-white middle-class suburb who refuses to sell a condominium to an African American family because of fear (founded or unfounded) that the sale would reduce the sale value of the remaining units. An example of a prejudiced nondiscriminator is a personnel director of a fire department who believes Mexican Americans are unreliable and poor firefighters yet complies with affirmative action efforts to hire and train Mexican American firefighters.

It is very difficult to keep personal prejudices from eventually leading to some form of discrimination.

Strong laws and firm informal social norms are necessary to break the relationships between prejudice and discrimination.

Discrimination is of two types. *De jure discrimination* is legal discrimination. The so-called Jim Crow laws in the South (enacted shortly after the Civil War ended) gave force of law to many discriminatory practices against African Americans, including denial of the right to trial, prohibition against voting, and prohibition against interracial marriage. Today, in the United States, there is no de jure racial discrimination because such laws have been declared unconstitutional.

De facto discrimination refers to discrimination that actually exists, whether legal or not. Most acts of de facto discrimination abide by powerful informal norms that are discriminatory. Cummings (1977) gives an example of this type of discrimination and urges victims to confront it assertively:

> *Scene: department store. Incident: several people are waiting their turn at a counter. The person next to be served is a black woman; however, the clerk waits on several white customers who arrived later. The black woman finally demands service, after several polite gestures to call the clerk's attention to her. The clerk proceeds to wait on her after stating, "I did not see you." The clerk is very discourteous to the black customer, and the lack of courtesy is apparent, because the black customer had the opportunity to observe treatment of the other customers. De facto discrimination is most frustrating … ; [after all, say some] the customer was served. Most people would rather just forget the whole incident, but it is important to challenge the practice even though it will possibly put you through more agony. One of the best ways to deal with this type of discrimination is to report it to the manager of the business. If it is at all possible, it is important to involve the clerk in the discussion. (p. 200)*

Oppression is the unjust or cruel exercise of authority or power. Members of minority groups in our society are frequently victimized by oppression from segments of the White power structure. Oppression and discrimination are closely related, as all acts of oppression are also acts of discrimination. Oppression is the social act of placing severe restrictions on a group or institution.

Racial and Ethnic Stereotypes

Stereotypes are generalizations, or assumptions, that people make about the characteristics of all members of a group, based on an image (often wrong) about what people in a group are like.

Racial and ethnic stereotypes involve attributing a fixed and usually inaccurate or unfavorable conception to a racial or ethnic group. Stereotypes are closely related to the way we think, as we seek to perceive and understand things in categories. We need categories to group things that are similar in order to study them and to communicate about them. We have stereotypes about many categories, including mothers, fathers, teenagers, communists, Republicans, schoolteachers, farmers, construction workers, miners, politicians, Mormons, and Italians. These stereotypes may contain some useful and accurate information about a member in any category. Yet each member of any category will have many characteristics that are not suggested by the stereotypes and is apt to have some characteristics that run counter to some of the stereotypes.

Racial stereotypes involve differentiating people in terms of color or other physical characteristics. For example, historically there was the erroneous stereotype that Native Americans become easily intoxicated and irrational when using alcohol. This belief was then translated into laws that prohibited Native Americans from buying and consuming alcohol. A more recent stereotype is that African Americans have a natural ability to play basketball and certain other sports. Although at first glance, such a stereotype appears complimentary to African Americans, it has broader, negative implications. The danger is that if people believe the stereotype, they may also feel that other abilities and capacities (such as intelligence, morals, and work productivity) are also determined by race. In other words, believing this positive stereotype increases the probability that people will also believe negative stereotypes.

Racial and Ethnic Discrimination Is the Problem of Whites

Myrdal (1944) pointed out that minority problems are actually majority problems. The white majority determines the place of nonwhites and other ethnic groups in our society. The status of different minority groups varies in our society because whites apply different stereotypes to various groups. For example, African Americans are viewed and treated differently from Japanese Americans. E. H. Johnson (1973) noted, "Minority relationships become recognized by the majority as a social problem when the members of the majority disagree as to whether the subjugation of the minority is socially desirable or in the ultimate interest of the majority" (p. 344). Concern about discrimination and segregation has also received increasing national attention because of a rising level of aspiration among minority groups who demand (sometimes militantly) equal opportunities and equal rights.

Our country was founded on the principle of human equality. The Declaration of Independence and the Constitution assert equality, justice, and liberty for all. Yet in practice, our society has always discriminated against minorities.

The groups of people who have been singled out for unequal treatment in our society have changed somewhat over the years. In the late 1800s and early 1900s, people of Irish, Italian, and Polish descent were discriminated against, but that discrimination has been substantially reduced. In the 19th century, Americans of Chinese descent were severely discriminated against. However, such bias also has been declining for many decades. Because of 9/11, some Arab Americans are now being victimized by discrimination in the United States (see Spotlight 5.2).

White Privilege

An underexposed part of racism in the United States is that white people (and white men in particular) have privileges that other Americans do not have. Following is a list of some of these privileges (McIntosh, 1988):

- White people can go shopping alone and be pretty well assured that they will not be followed or harassed.
- White people have no problem finding housing to rent or purchase in an area they can afford and want to live in.
- White people can feel assured that their children will be given curricular materials in school that testify to the existence of their race.
- White people can go into any supermarket and find the staple foods that fit with their cultural traditions.

- When white people use checks, credit cards, or cash, they can be sure that their skin color is not being taken into account when their financial reliability is questioned.
- White people are never asked to speak for all white people.
- White people can go into a hairdresser's shop and find someone who can cut their hair.
- White people in affluent neighborhoods are generally confident that their neighbors will be neutral or pleasant to them.
- White people can assume that police officers will provide protection and assistance.
- White people can be sure that their race will not count against them if they need legal or medical help.

Hate Crimes

Hate crimes have been added to the penal codes in nearly every state in the United States. Hate crimes are violent acts aimed at individuals or groups of a particular race, ethnicity, religion, sexual orientation, or gender. The laws also make it a crime to vandalize religious buildings and cemeteries or to intimidate another person out of bias.

Examples of hate crimes include setting African American churches on fire, defacing a Jewish family's home with swastikas and anti-Semitic graffiti, assaulting a gay college student, burning a cross on the lawn of an African American family, and vandalism against Arab Americans. With hate crimes, judges can impose a higher sentence when they find that a crime was committed with a biased motive.

Race Is a Social Concept

Ashley Montague (1964) considered the concept of race to be one of the most dangerous and tragic myths in our society. Race is erroneously believed by many to be a biological classification of people. Yet, surprisingly to some, there are no clearly delineating characteristics of any race. Throughout history, the genes of different societies and racial groups have occasionally been intermingled. No racial group has any unique or distinctive genes. In addition, biological differentiations of racial groups have gradually been diluted through various sociocultural factors. These factors include changes in preferences of desirable characteristics in mates,

SPOTLIGHT ON DIVERSITY 5.2

Discrimination Against Arab Americans and American Muslims

Following the September 11, 2001, attacks on the World Trade Center and the Pentagon, there have been a number of hate crimes against Arab Americans and American Muslims. Emert (2007) gives some examples:

> In Texas, a Pakistani Muslim storeowner was murdered. In California, an Egyptian Christian was killed. In a Chicago suburb, hundreds of men and women chanting, "USA, USA" marched on a local mosque and were stopped by police. In Brooklyn, an Islamic school was pelted with rocks and bloody pork chops (Muslims are forbidden to eat pork). Fire-bombings of mosques and Islamic centers occurred in Chicago, Seattle, Texas and New York.

Mosques, Arab community centers, and Arab-owned businesses have been vandalized. Women and girls wearing the traditional Muslim head covering, the hijab, have been harassed and assaulted. As an example of this discrimination, Rev. Terry Jones, a Florida minister, announced in August 2010 that he was going to publicly burn a number of Qurans on the ninth anniversary of the attacks on the World Trade Center and the Pentagon. Rev. Jones said that he believes the Quran is evil because it espouses something other than biblical truth and because he (erroneously) believes it incites radical, violent behavior among Muslims. (After intense international opposition, Rev. Jones announced he was canceling the burning of Qurans.)

Stereotypes abound of Arab Americans, and they are mostly negative. The Western images of Arabs are of Ali Baba, Sinbad, the thief of Baghdad, white slaveowners, harem dwellers, and sheiks. The facts are that harems and polygamy have been abolished, for the most part, in the Arab world, and only a small number of Arab nations have "sheiks." Arabs are almost always portrayed on TV or in movies as evil or foolish. One *Sesame Street* character, always dressed like an Arab, is always the one that teaches negative words like "danger." In movies, they're often portrayed as villains or financial backers of espionage plots.

It is important for all of us to remember what happened to Japanese Americans after Pearl Harbor was attacked in 1941. Emert (2007) notes:

> After the unexpected attack on Pearl Harbor on December 7, 1941, distrust, fear and anger against the 130,000 Japanese-Americans living in the United States at that time intensified, especially in California where an enemy invasion was anticipated. About 115,000 Japanese lived on the West Coast, and their presence was considered a security threat. Americans questioned the loyalty of these Japanese people even though 80,000 of them were second-generation, natural-born U.S. citizens. There was fear that these Japanese-Americans would resort to sabotage or treason to aid America's enemies.

> Public leaders like the California Governor, Attorney General, and U.S. military commanders supported the idea of a mass evacuation of all Japanese from the West Coast. Beginning on March 22, 1942, approximately 110,000 Japanese were transported to 15 temporary assembly centers in California, Oregon, Washington and Arizona. Several months later, they were moved to 10 permanent relocation centres scattered throughout the country. These Japanese-Americans lost nearly everything they owned. They were forced to sell their homes and businesses at rock bottom prices.

In September 2001, after 9/11, the U.S. Senate passed a resolution calling for the protection of the "civil rights and civil liberties of all Americans, including Arab-Americans and American Muslims" (Emert, 2007). Virtually all major Arab American organizations and American Muslim organizations have condemned the actions of Osama bin Laden's militant fringe.

Some factual information about Arab Americans and American Muslims may be useful. There are about 6 million Arab Americans in the United States, which is about 2 percent of the American population. There are 22 separate Arab nations (Schaefer, 2010).

There's no simple definition of who an "Arab" is. The word refers to those who speak the Arabic language, but almost every country's version of Arabic is different from another's (e.g., Jordanian Arabic is quite different from Algerian Arabic), and to make matters more complicated, several Arab countries have internal ethnic groups who speak a totally different form of Arabic or some non-Arabic language.

American Muslims and Arab Americans are different groups in the United States. There is some overlap between these two groups, with some American Muslims being of Arab ancestry. Most Arab Americans are not Muslim, however, and most Muslim Americans are not of Arab background. Many Arab Americans are Christians, some are Hindu, and a few are agnostics or atheists. Arab Americans are an ethnic group, and Muslims are a religious group.

Islam, with approximately 1.3 billion followers worldwide, is second to Christianity among the world's religions (Schaefer, 2012). Schaefer notes that Christianity and Islam are faiths that are very similar:

> Both are monotheistic (i.e., based on a single deity) and indeed worship the same God. Allah is the Arabic word for God and refers to the God of Moses, Jesus, and Muhammad. Both Christianity and Islam include a belief in prophets, an afterlife, and a judgment day. In fact, Islam recognizes Jesus as a prophet, though not the son of God. Islam reveres both the Old and New Testaments as integral parts of its tradition. Both faiths

(continued)

SPOTLIGHT ON DIVERSITY 5.2 *(continued)*

impose a moral code on believers, which varies from fairly rigid proscriptions for fundamentalists to relatively relaxed guidelines for liberals. (p. 263)

(Christianity and Islam are described more fully in Chapter 15.)

As to the ethnic background of American Muslims in the United States, Schaefer (2012, p. 263) gives the following estimates:

Based on the most recent studies, there are at least 2.6 million and perhaps as many as 3 million Muslims

in the United States. About two-thirds are U.S.-born citizens. In terms of ethnic and racial background, the more acceptable estimates still vary widely. Estimates range as follows:

- *20–42 percent African American,*
- *24–33 percent South Asian (Afghan, Bangladeshi, Indian, and Pakistani),*
- *12–32 percent Arab, and*
- *15–22 percent "other" (Bosnian, Iranian, Turk, and White and Hispanic converts)*

---

effects of different diets on those who reproduce, and such variables as wars and diseases in selecting those who will live to reproduce (Johnson, 1973).

Despite definitional problems, it is necessary to use racial categories in the social sciences. Race has important (though not necessarily consistent) social meanings for people. In order to have a basis for racial classifications, social scientists have used a social, rather than a biological, definition. A social definition is based on the way in which members of a society classify each other by physical characteristics. For example, a frequently used social definition of an African American is anyone who either displays overt African American physical characteristics or is known to have an African American ancestor (Schaefer, 2008).

A social definitional approach to classifying races sometimes results in different societies' use of different definitions of *race*. For example, in the United States anyone who is known to have an African American ancestor is considered to be African American; in Brazil, anyone known to have a white ancestor is considered to be white (Schaefer, 2008).

Ethical Question 5.1

Do you believe that some ethnic groups are more intelligent than other ethnic groups?

EP 2.1.2

Race, according to Montague (1964), becomes a dangerous myth when people assume that physical traits are linked with mental traits and cultural achievements. Every few years, it seems, some noted scientist stirs the country by making this erroneous assumption. For example, Herrnstein and Murray (1994) assert that whites, on the average, are more intelligent, because IQ tests show that whites average scores of 10 to 15 points higher than African Americans. Herrnstein and Murray's findings have been sharply criticized by other authorities as falsely assuming that IQ is largely genetically determined (Lefrancois, 1996). These authorities contend that IQ is substantially influenced by environmental factors, and it is likely that the average achievement of African Americans, if given similar opportunities to realize their potentialities, would be the same as whites. Also, it has been charged that IQ tests are racially slanted. The tests ask the kinds of questions that whites are more familiar with and thereby more apt to answer correctly.

Johnson (1973) summarizes the need for an impartial, objective view of the capacity of different racial groups to achieve:

Race bigots contend that, the cultural achievements of different races being so obviously unlike, it follows that their genetic capacities for achievements must be just as different. Nobody can discover the cultural capacities of any population or race … until there is equality of opportunities to demonstrate the capacities. (p. 50)

Most scientists, both physical and social, now believe that in biological inheritance all races are alike in everything that really makes any difference (such as problem-solving capacities, altruistic tendencies, and communication capacities). With the exception of several very small, inbred, isolated, primitive tribes, all racial groups appear to show a wide distribution of every kind of ability. All important race differences that have been noted in personality, behavior, and achievement (e.g., high school graduation rates) appear to be due primarily to environmental factors.

Many Americans classify themselves as "mixed-race" or "multiracial," as they have parents of different races. Tiger Woods (a noted golfer), for example, has a multiracial background, with a Caucasian, African American, Native American, and Asian heritage.

Institutional Values and Racism: Discrimination in Systems

In the last four decades, institutional racism has become recognized as a major problem. *Institutional racism* refers to discriminatory acts and policies against a racial group that pervade the major macro systems of society, including the legal, political, economic, and educational systems. Some of these discriminatory acts and policies are illegal, whereas others are not.

Institutional racism can best be understood through a systems perspective on discrimination.

Institutional values form the foundation for macro-system policies. These policies are enacted in organizations and communities. Here, we refer to institutional racism as a prevailing orientation demonstrated in policies and procedures throughout our entire culture. It is an all-encompassing term that envelopes institutional values, communities, and organizational macro systems.

In contrast to institutional racism is *individual racism*, which Barker (2003) defines as "the negative attitudes one person has about all members of a racial or ethnic group, often resulting in overt acts such as name-calling, social exclusion, or violence" (p. 215). Carmichael and Hamilton (1967) make the following distinction between individual racism and institutional racism:

> *When white terrorists bomb a black church and kill five black children, that is an act of individual racism, widely deplored by most segments of society. But when in the same city ... five hundred black babies die each year because of the lack of proper food, shelter, and medical facilities, and thousands more are destroyed and maimed physically,*

> *emotionally, and intellectually because of conditions of poverty and discrimination in the black community, that is a function of institutional racism. (p. 4)*

Discrimination and Oppression in Organizational Macro Systems

Institutional discrimination is the unfair treatment of an individual that is due to the established operating procedures, policies, laws, or objectives of large organizations (such as governments, corporations, schools, police departments, and banks).

Discrimination is built, often unwittingly, into the very structure and form of our society. It is demonstrated by how organizational macro systems treat clients. The following examples reflect how agencies can engage in institutional discrimination:

- A family counseling agency with branch offices assigns its less skilled counselors and there by provides lower-quality services to an office located in a minority neighborhood.
- A human services agency encourages white applicants to request funds for special needs (e.g., clothing) or to use certain services (e.g., day-care and homemaker services), whereas nonwhite clients are not informed (or are less enthusiastically informed) of such services.
- A human services agency takes longer to process the requests of nonwhite for funds and services.
- A police department discriminates against nonwhite staff in terms of work assignments, hiring practices, promotion practices, and pay increases.
- A real estate agency has a pattern of showing white homebuyers houses in white neighborhoods and African American homebuyers houses in mixed or predominantly African American areas.
- A bank and an insurance company engage in red-lining which involves refusing to make loans or issue insurance in areas with large minority populations.
- A probation and parole agency tends to ignore minor rule violations by white clients but seeks to return nonwhite parolees to prison for similar infractions.
- A mental health agency tends to label nonwhite clients "psychotic" while ascribing a less serious disorder to white clients.
- White staff at a family counseling center are encouraged by the executive board to provide intensive services to clients with whom they have

a good relationship and are told to give less attention to clients "they aren't hitting it off well with," resulting in fewer services provided to nonwhite clients.

Whether these differences in treatment are undertaken consciously or not, they nevertheless represent institutional discrimination.

Discrimination and Oppression in Community Macro Systems

Institutional racism also pervades community life. It is a contributing factor to the following: The unemployment rate for nonwhites has consistently been more than twice that for whites. The infant mortality rate for nonwhites is nearly twice as high as for whites. The life expectancy for nonwhites is several years less than for whites. The average number of years of educational achievement for nonwhites is considerably less than for whites (Schaefer, 2012).

Many examples of institutional racism are found in the educational macro system. Schools in white neighborhoods generally have better facilities and more highly trained teachers than do those in minority neighborhoods. Minority families are, on the average, less able to provide the hidden costs of free education (higher property taxes, transportation, class trips, clothing, and supplies); as a result, their children become less involved in the educational process. History texts in the past concentrated on achievements of white people and gave scant attention to minorities. J. Henry (1967) wrote in the 1960s about the effects of such history on Native American children:

What is the effect upon the student, when he learns that one race, and one alone, is the most, the best, the greatest; when he learns that Indians were mere parts of the landscape and wilderness which had to be cleared out, to make way for the great "movement" of white population across the land; and when he learns that Indians were killed and forcibly removed from their ancient homelands to make way for adventurers (usually called "pioneering gold miners"), for land grabbers (usually called "settlers"), and for illegal squatters on Indian-owned land (usually called "frontiersmen")? What is the effect upon the young Indian child himself, who is also a student in the school system, when he is told that Columbus discovered America, that Coronado "brought civilization" to the Indian people, and that the Spanish missionaries

provided havens of refuge for the Indians? Is it reasonable to assume that the student, of whatever race, will not discover at some time in his life that Indians discovered America thousands of years before Columbus set out upon his voyage; that Coronado brought death and destruction to the native peoples; and that the Spanish missionaries, in all too many cases, forcibly dragged Indians to the missions? (p. 22)

Since the 1960s and the civil rights movement, the true story of minorities and their experiences are being better told.

Our criminal justice macro system also has elements of institutional racism. Our justice system is supposed to be fair and nondiscriminatory. The very name of the system, *justice*, implies fairness and quality. Yet, in practice, racism is evident. Although African Americans compose only about 12 percent of the population, they make up about 50 percent of the prison population (Schaefer, 2012). (There is considerable debate as to what extent this is due to racism as opposed to differential crime rates by race.) The average prison sentence for murder and kidnapping is longer for African Americans than for whites. Nearly half of those sentenced to death are African American (Schaefer, 2012). Police departments and district attorney's offices are more likely to enforce vigorously the kinds of laws broken by lower-income groups and minority groups than by middle- and upper-class white groups. Poor people are substantially less likely to be able to post bail. As a result, they are forced to remain in jail until their trial, which often takes months or sometimes more than a year. Unable to afford a well-financed defense (including the fees charged by the most successful criminal defense teams), they are more likely to be found guilty.

LO 5-2 Outline the Sources of Prejudice and Discrimination

Sources of Prejudice and Discrimination

No single theory provides a complete picture of why racial and ethnic discrimination occur. By being exposed to a variety of theories, social workers should at least be better sensitized to the nature and sources of discrimination. The sources of discrimination come from inside and outside a person.

Projection

Projection is a psychological defense mechanism in which one attributes to others characteristics that one is unwilling to recognize in oneself. Many people have personal traits they dislike in themselves. They desire to get rid of such traits, but this is not always possible. Such people may project some of these traits onto others (often to some other group in society), thus displacing the negative feelings they would otherwise direct at themselves. In the process, they then condemn those onto whom they have projected the traits.

For example, a minority group may serve as a projection of a prejudiced person's fears and lusts. People who view African Americans as lazy or preoccupied with sex may be projecting onto African Americans their own internal concerns about their industriousness or their sexual fantasies. While some whites view African Americans as promiscuous, historically it has generally been white men who forced African American women (particularly slaves) into sexual encounters. It appears many white males felt guilty about these sexual desires and adventures and dealt with their guilt by projecting their own lusts and sexual conduct onto African Americans.

Frustration-Aggression

Another psychological need satisfied by discrimination is the release of tension and frustration. All of us at times become frustrated when we are unable to achieve or obtain something we desire. Sometimes we strike back at the source of frustration, but many times direct retaliation is not possible. For example, we are reluctant to tell our employers what we think of them when we feel we are being treated unfairly because we fear repercussions.

Some frustrated people displace their anger and aggression onto a *scapegoat*. The scapegoat may be a particular person or it may be a group of people. Similar to people who take out their job frustrations at home on their spouses or family pets, some prejudiced people vent their frustrations on minority groups. (The term *scapegoat* derives from an ancient Hebrew ritual in which the goat was symbolically laden with the sins of the entire community and then chased into the wilderness. It "escaped," hence the term *scapegoat*. The term was gradually broadened to apply to anyone who bears the blame for others.)

Countering Insecurity and Inferiority

Still another psychological need that may be satisfied through discrimination is the desire to counter feelings of insecurity or inferiority. Some insecure people seek to feel better about themselves by putting down another group. They then can tell themselves that they are better than these people.

Authoritarianism

A classic work on the causes of prejudice is *The Authoritarian Personality* by Adorno, Frenkel-Brunswik, Levinson, and Sanford (1950). Shortly after World War II, these researchers studied the psychological causes of the development of European fascism and concluded that a distinct type of personality was associated with prejudice and intolerance. The *authoritarian personality* is inflexible and rigid and has a low tolerance for uncertainty. This type of personality has a great respect for authority figures and quickly submits to their will. Such a person highly values conventional behavior and feels threatened by unconventional behavior of others. In order to reduce this threat, such a personality labels unconventional people as being immature, inferior, or degenerate and thereby avoids any need to question his or her own beliefs and values. The authoritarian personality views members of minority groups as being unconventional, degrades them, and tends to express authoritarianism through prejudice and discrimination.

History

Historical explanations can also be given for prejudice. Kornblum and Julian (2012) note that the groups now viewed by white prejudiced persons as being second class are groups that have been either conquered, enslaved, or admitted into our society on a subordinate basis. For example, African Americans were imported as slaves during our colonial period and stripped of human dignity. Native Americans were conquered, and their culture was viewed as inferior. Mexican Americans were allowed to enter this country primarily to do seasonal, low-paid farmwork.

Competition and Exploitation

Our society is highly competitive and materialistic. Individuals and groups compete daily with one another to acquire more of the available goods.

These attempts to secure economic goods usually result in a struggle for resources and power. In our society, once whites achieved dominance, they then used (and still are using) their power to exploit nonwhites through cheap labor—for example, as sweatshop factory laborers, migrant farmhands, maids, janitors, and bellhops.

Members of the dominant group know they are treating the subordinate group as inferior and unequal. To justify such discrimination, they develop an ideology (set of beliefs) that their group is superior, and therefore that it is right and proper that they have more rights, goods, and so on. Sometimes they assert that God selected their group to be dominant. At the same time, they assign inferior traits to the subordinate group and conclude that the minority needs and deserves less because it is biologically inferior. Throughout history in most societies, the dominant group (which has greater power and wealth) has sought to maintain the status quo by keeping those who have the least in an inferior position.

Socialization Patterns

Prejudice is also a learned phenomenon and is transmitted from generation to generation through socialization processes. Our culture has stereotypes of what different minority group members "ought to be" and the ways they "ought to behave" in relationships with members of the majority group. These stereotypes provide norms against which a child learns to judge persons, things, and ideas. Prejudice, to some extent, is developed through the same processes by which we learn to be religious or patriotic, to appreciate and enjoy art, or to develop our value system. Prejudice, at least in certain segments in our society, is thus a facet of the normative system of our culture.

Belief in the One True Religion

Some people are raised to believe that their religion is the one true religion—that they will go to heaven, while everyone who believes in a different religion is a heathen who will be eternally damned. A person with such a belief system comes to the conclusion that he or she is one of "God's chosen few." Feeling superior to others often leads a person to devalue them as "heathens" and then to treat them in an inferior way. Belief in the "one true religion" has led to numerous wars between societies, each of which thought its religion was superior. Such societies thought they were justified in spreading their chosen

religion by any possible means, including by physical force. This belief may be one of the most crucial determinants in developing an attitudinal system of racial prejudice. (It should be noted, as elaborated on later in this chapter and in Chapter 15, that religion has a number of beneficial components for many people.)

White Supremacy

White supremacy is the belief, and promotion of the belief, that white people are superior to people of other racial backgrounds. The term is sometimes used to describe a political ideology that advocates the social and political dominance of whites. The belief in white supremacy has frequently been a factor that has led whites to discriminate against people of color.

White supremacy was a dominant belief in the United States before the American Civil War and for decades after Reconstruction. In some parts of the United States, many people who were considered nonwhite were disenfranchised, and barred from holding most government jobs well into the second half of the 20th century. Many U.S. states banned interracial marriage through anti-miscegenation laws until 1967, when these laws were declared unconstitutional. White lenders often viewed Native Americans, Chinese Americans, and other people of color as inferior. Bradley (2009) notes that most U.S. presidents who were in office prior to the 20th century (and in the early 20th century) believed in white supremacy—one of those presidents was Abraham Lincoln. Lincoln believed that whites and blacks could not coexist in the same nation. He promoted his idea of colonization—that is, resettling blacks in foreign countries. He urged blacks be resettled in Central America, because of the similarity of climate conditions to Africa (Magness & Page, 2011).

White supremacy was also a dominant belief in many other countries, as in South African under apartheid. The Ku Klux Klan still advocates and asserts white supremacy.

Evaluation of Discrimination Theories

No single theory explains all causes of prejudices because prejudices have many origins. Taken together, however, they identify a number of causative factors. All theories assert that the causative factors of prejudice are in the personality and experiences of the person holding the prejudice, and not in the character of the group against whom the prejudice is directed.

A novel experiment documenting that prejudice does not stem from contact with the people toward whom prejudice is directed was conducted by Eugene Hartley (1946). Hartley gave his subjects a list of prejudiced responses to Jews and African Americans and to three groups that did not even exist: Wallonians, Pireneans, and Danireans. Prejudiced responses included such statements as, "All Wallonians living here should be expelled." The respondents were asked to state their agreement or disagreement with these prejudiced statements. The experiment showed that most of those who were prejudiced against Jews and African Americans were also prejudiced against people whom they had never met or heard about.

Closely related to the theories about the sources of racial and ethnic prejudice and discrimination is the conceptualization that compares racist thinking to criminal thinking. Spotlight 5.3 explores the question "Is racial discrimination based on criminal thinking?"

LO 5-3 Summarize the Effects and Costs of Discrimination and Oppression and Describe the Effects of Discrimination on Human Growth and Development

Impacts of Social and Economic Forces: The Effects and Costs of Discrimination and Oppression

Racial discrimination is a barrier in our competitive society to obtaining the necessary resources to lead a contented and comfortable life. Being discriminated against due to race makes it more difficult to obtain adequate housing, financial resources, a quality education, employment, adequate health care and other services, equal justice in civil and criminal cases, and so on.

Discrimination also has heavy psychological costs. All of us have to develop a sense of identity—who we are and how we fit into a complex, swiftly changing world. Ideally, it is important that we form a positive self-concept and strive to obtain worthy goals. Yet, according to Cooley's (1902) "looking-glass self," our idea of who we are and what we are is largely determined by the way others relate to us. When members of a minority group are treated by the majority group as if they are inferior, second-class citizens, it is substantially more difficult for such members to develop a positive identity. Thus, people who are the objects of discrimination encounter barriers to developing their full potential as human beings.

Young children of groups who are the victims of discrimination are likely to develop low self-esteem at an early age. African American children who have been subjected to discrimination even display a preference for white dolls and white playmates over black (Schaefer, 2012).

Pinderhughes (1982) has noted that the history of oppression of African Americans, combined with racism and exclusion, has produced a "victim system."

A victim system is a circular feedback process that exhibits properties such as stability, predictability, and identity that are common to all systems. This particular system threatens self-esteem and reinforces problematic responses in communities, families, and individuals. The feedback works as follows: Barriers to opportunity and education limit the chance for achievement, employment, and attainment of skills. This limitation can, in turn, lead to poverty or stress in relationships, which interferes with adequate performance of family roles. Strains in family roles cause problems in individual growth and development and limit the opportunities of families to meet their own needs or to organize to improve their communities. Communities limited in resources (jobs, education, housing, etc.) are unable to support families properly and the community all too often becomes an active disorganizing influence, a breeder of crime and other pathology, and a cause of even more powerlessness. (p. 109)

Is Racial Discrimination Based on Criminal Thinking?

Why do people discriminate on the basis of racial differences? Why do these people believe that it is proper to do so? One way of analyzing the problem of racial discrimination is to look at the thought processes that lead to racism. Benjamin's (1991) theory that racism is "a process of justification for the domination, exploitation, and control of one racial group by another" supports the idea that specific thought processes are involved. One such set of thoughts that has been used to justify racism provides the basis for *Social Darwinism*, the belief that the "superior race" must dominate all other races in order to ensure survival.

Benjamin's definition links the thought processes behind racism to widely accepted theories of *criminal thinking*. These theories attribute to the criminal personality certain thinking patterns that differ significantly from the thought processes of noncriminals—and that the criminal uses to justify criminal activities (Ellis, 1957; Freyhan, 1955; Keniston, 1965; Yochelson & Samenow, 1976). If we accept the American ideals of human dignity, freedom, and justice for all, then the idea that one group should dominate, exploit, and control another group is maladaptive. Thus, we can theorize that the thinking patterns that enable the racist to justify these coercive acts must be flawed. Not only do such patterns constitute "errors" in thinking from the "perspective of responsibility" (Yochelson & Samenow, 1976, p. 251), they also are used to strip others of their personal dignity and freedom and cause these victims to receive unequal treatment.

An Overview of Criminal Thinking

The concept of criminal thinking (Yochelson & Samenow, 1976) derives from the theory of rational therapy (self-talk) developed by Albert Ellis (1957). It posits that persons who commit crimes hold certain irrational beliefs that allow them to tell themselves that their behavior is acceptable. For example, an accountant who embezzles from her employer may rationalize her crime by telling herself that she deserves the money because she has been underpaid for the last seven years; or that it is a temporary loan that she expects to repay once she has become financially stable again; or that the employer is so wealthy that the small amount she is taking will never be missed.

Treatment programs to rehabilitate juvenile delinquents, sex offenders, domestic abuse perpetrators, and others who make excuses for their maladaptive behaviors use various terms for this type of rationalization. For the purposes of this discussion, they can be thought to be synonymous: errors in thinking, criminal thinking, faulty thinking, and deviant thinking. During a decade of study of the criminal personality, Dr. Samuel Yochelson defined and conceptualized a number of errors in thinking that he found to be common among the criminal population (Yochelson & Samenow, 1976). Yochelson's definitions and later variations (Bays & Freeman-Longo, 1989) are paraphrased and summarized as follows:

Power thrust: The criminal inflates low self-esteem by viewing himself or herself as an all-powerful, unique individual whose needs must come first and who can force others to meet those needs. The criminal rejects legitimate authority.

Ownership: An extreme form of control over others based on the criminal's attitude that his or her rights are unlimited; allows the criminal to disregard all personal and social boundaries.

Failure to consider injury to others: The criminal minimizes or denies injuring victims by an immediate criminal act or its far-reaching effects on the victims and others in society in order to maintain his or her self-image.

Lack of empathy: The criminal can maintain feelings of uniqueness only by refusing to consider the experiences or feelings of others.

Good-person self-image: The criminal has a distorted view of self as a good person who can do no wrong and may offer examples of "goodness" as evidence.

Closed-channel thinking: The secretiveness, closed-minded, and self-righteous attitude of the criminal do not allow for an open channel of communication or for being receptive to other points of view. Criminals acknowledge the faults of others but are not self-critical.

Victim stance: The criminal avoids taking responsibility for behavior by blaming others and by viewing himself or herself as a victim of others; often includes blaming the victim.

Disregard for responsible performance: The criminal's energy and motivation are directed toward self-serving goals rather than socially responsible activities. The criminal avoids and disregards personal obligations in order to maintain a power position.

Lack of a time perspective: Refers to several aberrations in time concepts, including the failure to make positive changes based on past experiences and the tendency to live for the moment (instant gratification) rather than anticipate future benefits or outcomes.

Fear of fear: Fear reactions are not used as a guide to responsible living, but are taken as threats to the criminal's self-esteem. Criminals often have irrational fears.

Lack of trust: Trust of others is seen as a weakness and interferes with the criminal's need for power and control.

SPOTLIGHT ON DIVERSITY 5.3 *(continued)*

Thinking Errors Common to Racist Beliefs

In the following discussion of racist thinking, the term *racist* will not be limited to bigots and white supremacists who hold extreme beliefs. The term will include everyone whose beliefs and thoughts contain elements of racial or ethnic prejudice and/or who have supported racial or ethnic discrimination to any degree. We will use the set of "thinking errors" that were just described as the standard by which we can test our theory of the racist's flawed, or criminal, thinking.

Three of these thinking errors account for many of the severest forms of domination, exploitation, and control of minority populations. They are the power thrust, ownership, and a failure to consider injury to others. Everything we know about racial discrimination allows us to acknowledge that it is based on a power thrust—control of one person over others and a resulting sense of power or triumph (Yochelson & Samenow, 1976). Slaveholding is ownership by definition, and it is human control carried to the extreme. White ownership of black populations did not end with emancipation; white society's sustained attitude of control over African Americans continued well into the 1960s. Yochelson and Samenow (1976) referred to the criminal's view of people as "pawns or checkers waiting for me to deal with them as I wish" (p. 381), and this aptly describes the real-life effect of institutional discrimination—especially as it is experienced by people of color in the lower socioeconomic levels. Whenever people of color are forced to suffer (by comparison to their white counterparts) from lower grades of service, fewer opportunities for advancement, higher rates of infant mortality, longer periods of incarceration, and fewer options for neighborhoods in which they may live, then a racist society has met the criteria for the type of criminal thinking referred to as failure to consider *injury* to others.

Oppression of people of color continues because of two additional errors in thinking on the part of the racist: a lack of empathy and a distorted self-image. If we believe that others are inferior to us, it reduces our motivation to empathically consider how they might feel or otherwise be affected by unequal treatment. Racists, like criminals, put considerable effort into building a good-person self-image. The good-person self-image was held by slaveowners who asserted that they treated their slaves well. This self-image is reclaimed by white society every time it adopts a benevolent social policy, such as affirmative action. We would all like to view ourselves as good people. In fact, social work counselors are taught specific skills that allow them to help individuals strengthen their sense of self-worth. The error in thinking occurs when individuals hold this belief on the basis of a few good deeds and do not acknowledge their other destructive behaviors.

Is the white racist guilty of closed-channel thinking? We don't have to belong to a white supremacist group to be self-righteous and closed-minded. Many of us are guilty of not being particularly open in either our thinking or our communication with others, particularly when we feel that our viewpoint is justified. Anyone who has tried to reason with a bigoted relative or colleague is aware of the impossibility of finding a receptive listener. Closed-channel thinkers tend to overgeneralize and to see the world in absolute terms: good and bad, right and wrong, black and white.

Racists also justify their narrow ethnocentric viewpoint by adopting a victim stance. This can be done by assuming an attitude of being victimized by "heavy tax burdens that force us to support people who are taking advantage of us—and who are undeserving." Racists blame the politicians and government for making people of color dependent on social welfare programs. They blame the victim by classifying people of color as lazy, illiterate, and irresponsible; and they point to high rates of school failure, unemployment, illegitimate births, and crime in the inner cities to support this characterization. Society has created a no-win situation for oppressed people of color, because many whites also believe themselves to be victimized by people of color who compete for their jobs, their educational scholarships, and their tax dollars to upgrade housing and public services in the inner cities. The victim perspective is all-encompassing and self-serving. It is used by the racist to justify discrimination and promotes a disregard for responsible performance. After all, if we can convince ourselves that people of color are already taking advantage of a too-benevolent society, then there is no need to support social welfare programs or to make any effort toward improving their opportunities for success.

Racists demonstrate a lack of time perspective in their failure, or refusal, to consider the long-term benefits of providing all people with equal opportunities to be successful, contributing members of society. Again, this is a self-serving attitude that places the present needs of a few above the future outcomes of many. Prejudice, racism, and racial discrimination are based on a fear of fear. In this case, there is an irrational fear that equality, shared power, integrated living, and racial blending (intermarriage) somehow threaten the worth and well-being of white society. A lack of trust, which is implicit in all areas of racism, fosters the desire of many in the dominant mainstream society to retain their power position.

From these comparisons, it appears that racist thinking shares many common elements with criminal thinking. In addition, it seems likely that racist thinking is not limited to the "prejudiced discriminators" (Merton, 1949) who openly embrace white supremacy. It is employed as well by those of us who fall into the less obvious categories of "prejudiced nondiscriminators" and "unprejudiced discriminators" (Merton, 1949). In many regions of the United States, a pervasive atmosphere of distrust fed by irrational fears has fostered a racist mentality among the general population. The same errors in thinking that are attributed to the criminal personality are used by racists to justify the domination, exploitation, and control of people of color by the mainstream white society.

Source: Patricia Danielson, social worker, Jefferson County Human Services Dept., Jefferson, WI, 1995.

Discrimination also has high costs for the majority group. It impairs intergroup cooperation and communication. Discrimination is also a factor in contributing to social problems among minorities—for example, high crime rates, emotional problems, alcoholism, drug abuse—all of which have cost billions of dollars in social programs. It has been argued that discrimination is a barrier to collective action (e.g., unionization) among whites and nonwhites (particularly people in the lower income classes), and therefore is a factor in perpetuating low-paying jobs and poverty. Less affluent whites who could benefit from collective action are hurt.

The effects of discrimination are even reflected in life expectancy. The life expectancy of nonwhites is six years less than that of whites in the United States (Schaefer, 2012). The fact is that nonwhites tend to die earlier than whites because they tend to receive inferior health care and because they generally earn less money, which results in a higher probability of a less nutritions diet and of living in deteriorating housing.

Finally, discrimination in the United States undermines some of our nation's political goals. Many other nations view us as hypocritical when we advocate human rights and equality. In order to make an effective argument for human rights on a worldwide scale, we must first put our own house in order by eliminating racial and ethnic discrimination. Few Americans realize the extent to which racial discrimination damages our international reputation. Nonwhite foreign diplomats to America often complain about being victims of discrimination because they are mistaken for being members of American minority groups. With most of the nations of the world being nonwhite, our racist practices severely damage our influence and prestige.

Stereotyping and Multiculturalism: A Perspective

The National Association of Social Worker's *Code of Ethics* (1996, p. 27) states:

> *Social workers should act to prevent and eliminate domination of, exploitation of, and discrimination against any person, group, or class on the basis of race, ethnicity, national origin, color, sex, sexual orientation, age, marital status, political belief, religion, or mental or physical disability.*

Similar to most other social work texts, this text presents descriptive information about these groups. It has traditionally been thought that presenting such descriptive information will increase social worker's capacities to be culturally competent with these groups.

It is important to note that some social work authorities are now raising questions about whether presenting descriptive information about groups leads to stereotypes and prejudices against these groups (Mor Barak, 2005). For example, if we describe women as being more emotional than men, and men as being more rational than women, such a perception and categorization may steer expectations for an individual or a group. Such perceptions and categorizations are often inaccurate when applied to an individual member of a group, as well as to the group as a whole.

Another example may help further clarify this perspective. There is a perception that Asian Americans are a "model minority" because they are viewed as an "overachieving, supersuccessful ethnic group without significant problems" (*Chicago Tribune*, 1998). If we perceive Asian Americans as overachieving and supersuccessful, it raises a number of questions that may negatively affect those labeled as Asian Americans. A few of these questions are the following: Will it lead Asian American children to feel undue pressure to be super-successful? Will it lead those Asian Americans who are not supersuccessful to view themselves as "failures"? Will social service agencies and policy makers tend to ignore developing human service programs for Asian Americans because they are already perceived to be "supersuccesful"? Will providers of services (such as dentists, car dealers, plumbers, electricians) tend to charge Asian Americans more because they are apt to be perceived as "wealthy"?

The stereotyping of Asian Americans as being overachieving and supersuccessful misrepresents the diverse experiences of Asian Americans by glossing over huge differences within a group of people who come from more than two dozen countries, most of which have their own distinct language and culture. In this regard, Ziaddlin Sardar (2001, pp. 14–16) notes:

> *White people … look at me and exclaim: "Surely, you're Asian." However, there is no such thing as an Asian. Asia is not a race or identity: it is a continent.*

Even in Asia, where more than half of the world's population lives, no one calls him or herself "Asian." … In the U.S., the Asian label is attached to Koreans, Filipinos, and Chinese. In Britain, we do not use the term Asian *to describe our substantial communities of Turks, Iranians, or Indonesians, even though these countries are in Asia.*

There is a danger that presenting descriptive information about a group may lead to negative stereotyping and then overt discrimination. For example, descriptive information indicates African Americans tend to have higher rates (compared with whites) of poverty, homelessness, births outside of marriage, dropping out of school, criminal arrests, and criminal convictions (Schaefer, 2012). Does such information lead to the expectation by non–African Americans that African American individuals they meet are apt to "fit" such descriptive information? For example, the poverty rate for African Americans is about 20 percent, whereas for whites it is 10 percent (Schaefer, 2012). Will this lead non–African Americans to expect that African American individuals they encounter are apt to be "poor"? What may be ignored by the non–African American is that most African Americans (80 percent) are not living in poverty.

This text will continue to use the traditional approach of presenting descriptive information about the diverse categories identified in the Educational Policy and Accreditation Standards (EPAS) for two reasons. First, most social work educators deduce that the EPAS was written with the expectation that descriptive information will be presented in the social work curriculum on these categories. Second, the social work authorities who are concerned about the presentation of descriptive information have not arrived at a new definition of diversity that enables us to develop a knowledge base of information about the diverse groups identified in the EPAS who have been victimized in the past (and during the present time) by discrimination. The authors of this text, however, urge readers to be aware of the dangers of stereotypes being generated by descriptive information about the diverse groups identified in this text.

An additional caveat about diversity will be mentioned. Everyone has multicultural diversity. We differ from one another in such variables as age, economic status, education, family type, gender, personality type, ethnicity, religion, geographic origin, sexual orientation, communication types, native-born or immigrant status, attire, language, political views, physical abilities, lifestyle, and so forth. Therefore, when we meet someone who, for example, is Japanese American, it is essential to recognize that there are many other facets to that individual in addition to his or her ethnicity.

It is impossible in this text to present information on all the types and forms of diversity. If we consider ethnicity alone, there are literally thousands of different populations. For example, there are about 500 different Native American tribes in the United States, each with its distinctive culture. Therefore, we will present descriptive information on only a few illustrative groups.

Intersectionality of Multiple Factors

The EPAS (2008) states:

The dimensions of diversity are understood as the intersectionality of multiple factors including age, class, color, culture, disability, ethnicity, gender, gender identity and expression, immigration status, political ideology, race, religion, sex, and sexual orientation.

Intersectionality holds that the classical models of oppression within society (such as those based on race, ethnicity, religion, gender, class, age, or disability) do not act independently of one another; instead, these forms of oppression interrelate, creating a system of oppression that reflects the "intersection" of multiple forms of discrimination. Intersectionality is a theory to analyze how social and cultural categories interwine. For example, intersectionality asserts there are vast differences in the life experiences of an African American male, 57 years old, upper class, and healthy, as compared to an African American female, 75 years old, indigent, and legally blind.

In working with clients, social workers need to view individuals in terms of "intersectionality."

The Effects of Discrimination on Human Growth and Development

The effects of discrimination will be illustrated by examining the research conducted on African Americans, the largest racial minority group, composing about 12 percent of the population in the

United States. We begin by examining some background material on the history and culture of African Americans in our society.

History and Culture of African Americans

The United States has always been a racist country. Although our country's founders talked about freedom, dignity, equality, and human rights, our economy before the Civil War depended heavily on slavery.

Many slaves came from cultures that had well-developed art forms, political systems, family patterns, religious beliefs, and economic systems. However, their home culture was not European, and therefore, slaveowners viewed their cultural patterns as being of no consequence. They prohibited slaves from practicing and developing their art, language, religion, and family life. For want of practice, their former culture soon died in America.

The life of a slave was harsh. Slaves were viewed not as human beings but as chattel to be bought and sold. Long, hard days were spent working in the fields, with the profits of their labor going to their white owners. Whippings, mutilations, and hangings were commonly accepted control practices. The impetus to enslave African Americans was not simply racism because many whites believed that it was to their economic advantage to have a cheap supply of labor. Cotton growing, in particular, was thought to require a large labor force that was also cheap and docile. Marriages among slaves were not recognized by law, and slaves were often sold with little regard to the effects on marital and family ties. Throughout the slavery period and even after it, African Americans were discouraged from demonstrating intelligence, initiative, or ambition. For a period of time, it was illegal to teach African Americans to read or write.

Some authorities (Henderson & Kim, 1980) have noted that opposition to the spread of slavery preceding the Civil War was primarily due to northern fears of competition from slave labor and the rapidly increasing migration of African Americans to the North and West, rather than to moral concern for human rights and equality. Few whites at the time understood or believed in the principle of racial equality—not even Abraham Lincoln, who believed that African Americans were inferior to whites.

Following the Civil War, the federal government failed to develop a comprehensive program of economic and educational aid to African Americans. As a result, most African Americans returned to being economically dependent on the same planters in the South who had held them in bondage. Within a few years, laws were passed in the southern states prohibiting interracial marriages and requiring racial segregation in schools and public places.

A rigid caste system in the South hardened into a system of oppression known as Jim Crow laws. The system prescribed how African Americans were supposed to act in the presence of whites, asserted white supremacy, embraced racial segregation, and denied political and legal rights to African Americans. African Americans who opposed Jim Crow laws were subjected to burnings, beatings, and lynchings. Jim Crow laws were used to teach African Americans to view themselves as inferior and to be servile and passive in interactions with whites.

World War II opened up new employment opportunities for African Americans. A large migration of African Americans from the South began. Greater mobility afforded by wartime conditions led to upheavals in the traditional caste system. Many African Americans served in the armed forces during this war, fought and died for their country, and yet their country maintained segregated facilities. Awareness of the disparity between the ideal and reality led many people to try to improve race relations, not only for domestic justice and peace, but to answer criticism from abroad. With each gain in race relations, more African Americans were encouraged to press for their rights.

A major turning point in African American history was the U.S. Supreme Court decision in *Brown v. Board of Education* in 1954, which ruled that racial segregation in public schools was unconstitutional. Since 1954, numerous organized efforts have been made by both African Americans and certain segments of the white population to secure equal rights and opportunities for African Americans. Attempts to change deeply entrenched racist attitudes and practices have produced much turmoil: the burning of many inner cities in the late 1960s, the assassination of Martin Luther King Jr. in 1968, and clashes between African American militant groups and the police. There have also been significant advances. Wide-ranging civil rights legislation protecting rights in areas such as housing, voting, employment, and use of public transportation and facilities has been passed. During the riots in

1968, the National Advisory Commission on Civil Disorders (Gelman, 1988) warned that our society was careening "toward two societies, one black, one white—separate and unequal" (p. 19).

The United States today is not the bitterly segregated society that the riot commission envisioned. African Americans and whites now more often work together and lunch together—yet few really count the other as friends.

We, as a nation, have come a long way since the U.S. Supreme Court's decision in 1954. The election of Barack Obama as president in 2008 is a clear example of increased respect that African Americans are receiving in the United States. But we still have a long way to go before we eliminate African American poverty and oppression. Living conditions in some African American communities remain as bleak as they were when our inner cities erupted in the late 1960s.

Two developments have characterized the socioeconomic circumstances of African Americans in recent years. A middle class has emerged that is better educated, better paid, and better housed than any group of African Americans that has gone before it. However, as middle-class African Americans move to better neighborhoods, they leave behind those who are living in poverty. The group that has been left behind generates a disproportionate share of the social pathology that is associated with a deteriorating urban neighborhood—including high rates of crime, unemployment, drug abuse, school dropouts, births outside of marriage, and families receiving public assistance.

More than half of all African American children are being raised in single-parent families (Schaefer, 2012). However, many of the children living in single-parent families are living in family structures composed of some variation of the extended family. Many single-parent families move in with relatives during adversity, including economic adversity. In addition, African American families of all levels rely on relatives to care for their children while they work.

Schaefer (2012) summarizes five strengths identified by the National Urban League that allow African American families to function effectively in a racist society:

1. *Strong kinship bonds.* Blacks are more likely than whites to care for children and the elderly in an extended family network.

2. *A strong work orientation.* Poor blacks are more likely to be working, and poor black families often include more than one wage earner.
3. *Adaptability of family roles.* In two-parent families, the egalitarian pattern of decision making is the most common. The self-reliance of black women who are the primary wage earners best illustrates this adaptability.
4. *Strong achievement orientation.* Working-class blacks indicate a greater desire for their children to attend college than working-class whites. Even a majority of low-income African Americans desire to attend college.
5. *A strong religious orientation.* Black churches since the time of slavery have been the source of many significant grassroots organizations.

While it is a reality that many African American families are headed by single mothers, it would be a serious error to view such family structures as inherently pathological. A single parent with good parenting skills, along with a supportive extended family, can lead to healthy family functioning.

Many African Americans have had the historical experience of being subjected to negative evaluations by school systems, social welfare agencies, health-care institutions, and the justice system. Because of their past experiences, African Americans are likely to view such institutions with apprehension. Schools, for example, have erroneously perceived African Americans as being less capable of developing cognitive skills. Such perceptions about school failure are often a self fulfilling prophecy. If African American children are expected to fail in school systems, teachers are likely to put forth less effort in challenging them to learn, and African American children may then put forth less effort to learn, resulting in a lower level of achievement.

Some of the attitudes and behaviors exhibited by African Americans who seek services from white social agencies are often labeled resistant. However, the attitudes and behaviors are better viewed as attempts at coping with powerlessness and racism. For example, if there are delays in the provision of services, African Americans may convey apathy or disparage the agency because they interpret the delay as being due to racism; they then respond in ways they have learned in the past to handle discrimination.

Effects of Discrimination on Development of Self-Concept

The term *self-concept* refers to the positive and negative thoughts and feelings that one has toward oneself. It is often used interchangeably with such terms as *self-image*, *sense of self*, *self-esteem*, and *identity*. A positive self-concept is a key element in school achievement, in positive social interactions with others, and in emotional, social, and intellectual growth (Santrock, 2008).

Solomon (1983) notes that if African American adults accept society's label of inferiority, they are likely to convey such thoughts and feelings to their children. The children are likely not only to develop a negative self-concept but also to put less effort into developing cognitive skills and school achievement. Because of low self-esteem and underdeveloped cognitive skills they are less likely to develop interpersonal and technical skills, which then results in having difficulties in social interactions and to being restricted in adulthood to low-paying, low-skill jobs. The vicious circle is then completed when such difficulties confirm and reinforce feelings of inferiority and of negative value, feelings that are then passed on to their children.

Numerous studies have been conducted on the extent to which discrimination adversely affects self-concept development in African American children. Very significantly, these studies indicate that the African American child's concept of self does not necessarily have to be impaired by racism. Concludes Powell (1983):

> *Afro-Americans have survived a harsh system of slavery, repression, and racism. Although there have been casualties, there have been many more survivors, achievers, and victors. The cultural heritage of coping with adversity and overcoming has been passed on from generation to generation, laced with stories of those with remarkable courage and fortitude. (p. 73)*

Given the pervasiveness of racism and discrimination in our society, why is it that many African American children overcome these obstacles to self-concept development and develop a fairly positive sense of self-esteem? The reason appears to be that every person is embedded simultaneously in at least two systems: One is the larger society, and the other is one's immediate social and physical environment.

The latter environment includes family members, other relatives, peers, friends, and neighbors. One's immediate environment appears to be the predominant system in shaping one's self-concept. It appears that the child who is loved, accepted, and supported in his or her immediate environment comes to love and respect himself or herself as someone worthy of love.

African American children, as they grow older, learn of the larger society's devaluation. Practically all African American children are aware by age 7 or 8 of the social devaluation placed on their racial group (Schaefer, 2012). But awareness of this devaluation does not necessarily extend to the African American child's self-evaluation. The sense of self developed in the immediate environment acts as a buffer against the potential devaluation by the larger society.

Certainly, racism has the potential for adverse effects on self-esteem development in African American children. Despite racism in our economic, political, and social structures, however, African American families have not only survived but have also interacted with their children in ways that foster the development of a positive identity. Celebrations such as Kwanzaa (see Spotlight 5.4) are ways of promoting pride for African Americans in their racial identity.

The Afrocentric Perspective and Worldview

African American culture has numerous components: elements from traditional African culture; elements from slavery, Reconstruction, and subsequent exposure to racism and discrimination; and elements from mainstream white culture. An emerging perspective is the *Afrocentric perspective* (Devore & Schlesinger, 1996), which acknowledges African culture and expressions of African beliefs, values, institutions, and behaviors. It recognizes that African Americans have retained to some degree a number of elements of African life and values.

The Afrocentric perspective asserts that the use of Eurocentric theories of human behavior to explain the behavior and ethos of African Americans is often inappropriate. Eurocentric theories of human behavior were developed in European and Anglo-American cultures. Eurocentric theorists have historically vilified people of African descent and other people of color. Such theorists have explicitly or implicitly claimed that people of African descent were pathological or inferior in their social,

Kwanzaa

Parents help their child light the candles at the beginning of Kwanzaa.

Kwanzaa means "first fruits of the harvest" in Swahili. Kwanzaa is a seven-day festival observed by some African Americans in late December and early January. It is not a substitute for Christmas, and it is a nonreligious celebration. Many people who celebrate Kwanzaa also celebrate Christmas. Inspired by a traditional African harvest festival, it was originated in 1966 by M. Ron Karenga, a Los Angeles–based activist, to increase awareness of African heritage and encourage the following seven qualities, which are stated in Swahili and English:

Umoja (unity). African Americans strive for unity within family, community, and the world as a whole.

Kujichagulia (self-determination). African Americans define themselves and have the determination not to accept or internalize negative definitions.

Ujima (collective work and responsibility). African Americans live, work, and are responsible for harmonizing personal wants and needs with the collective wants and needs of the race.

Ujamaa (cooperative economics). African Americans become their own economic bosses through owning and supporting African American businesses.

Nia (purpose). African Americans contribute distinct gifts to the world, and they propose to develop those gifts and talents.

Kuumba (creativity). African Americans are creative, and all that they touch is made more beautiful through the contact.

Imani (faith). African Americans remain alive, giving, and compassionate people because of their faith that, though African Americans suffer in their todays, they will succeed in their tomorrows.

Kwanzaa is a time to rededicate efforts to putting these principles into daily practice. Each day during the festival in the homes of many celebrants, a family member discusses one of the principles. The festival seeks to unite and empower African Americans in joyous testimony that they are a distinct people with a specific culture and perspective. Celebrants light a candle each night of their festival. On the last day, family members tend to exchange small gifts—generally gifts that have cultural significance.

Mark Adams/Getty Images

personality, or moral development (Schiele, 1996). The origins of this denigration can be found in the slave trade, as slave traders and slaveowners were pressed to justify the enslavement of Africans. The fallout of Eurocentric theories is the portrayal of the culture of people of African descent as having contributed little of value to world development and human history.

The Afrocentric perspective also seeks to dispel the negative distortions about people of African ancestry by legitimizing and disseminating a *worldview* that goes back thousands of years and that exists in the hearts and minds of many people of African descent today. Worldview involves one's perceptions of oneself in relation to other people, objects, institutions, and nature. The worldviews of African Americans are shaped by unique and important experiences, such as racism and discrimination, an African heritage, traditional attributes of the African American family and community life, and a strong religious orientation.

The Afrocentric perspective also seeks to promote a worldview that will facilitate human and societal transformation toward moral, spiritual, and humanistic ends. It seeks to persuade people of different cultural and ethnic groups that they share a mutual interest in this regard. The Afrocentric perspective rejects the idea that the individual can be understood separately from others in his or her social group. It emphasizes a collective identity that encourages sharing, cooperation, and social responsibility.

The Afrocentric perspective also emphasizes the importance of spirituality, which includes moral development and attaining meaning and identity in life. It views the major sources of human problems in the United States as being oppression and alienation. Oppression and alienation are generated not only by prejudice and discrimination, but also by a worldview that teaches people to see themselves primarily as material, physical beings seeking immediate pleasure. It further asserts that this worldview discourages spiritual and moral development.

The Afrocentric perspective has been used to provide explanations of the origins of specific social problems. For example, violent crimes by youths are thought to be a result of the limited options and choices they have to advance themselves economically. Youths seek a life of street crime as a logical means to cope with, and protest against, a society that practices pervasive employment discrimination. These youths mentally calculate that they can make more money from street crime than from attending college or starting a legitimate business. Turning to a life of crime is also thought more likely to occur in a society with a worldview that deemphasizes spiritual and moral development.

The Afrocentric perspective values a more holistic, spiritual, and optimistic view of human beings. It supports the strengths perspective and empowerment concepts of social work practice, which are described later in this chapter.

LO 5-4 Suggest Strategies for Advancing Social and Economic Justice

Community Strategies to Promote Social and Economic Justice

Widely ranging strategies have been developed to reduce racial and ethnic discrimination and oppression. These strategies include mass media appeals, strategies to increase interaction among racial and ethnic groups, civil rights laws, activism, affirmative action programs, confrontation of racist and ethnic remarks and actions, minority-owned businesses, confrontation of the problems in inner cities, and asset-based community development. Because racism is a more serious problem in our society than ethnocentrism, most of the strategies against discrimination primarily focus on curtailing racial discrimination and oppression.

Mass Media Appeals: Striving to Change Institutional Values

The mass media are able to reach large numbers of people simultaneously. By expanding public awareness of the existence of discrimination and its consequences, the media may strengthen control over racial and ethnic extremists. But newspapers, radio, and television have limitations in changing prejudiced attitudes and behaviors; they are primarily providers of information and seldom have a lasting effect in changing deep-seated prejudices through propaganda. Highly prejudiced persons are often unaware of their own prejudices. Even if they are aware of their prejudices, they generally ignore mass media appeals as irrelevant to them or dismiss the appeals as propaganda.

However, the media probably have had a significant impact in reducing discrimination through showing nonwhites and whites harmoniously working together in commercials, on news teams, and on TV shows. These settings provide at least one avenue for changing institutional values rooted in racism and discrimination.

Greater Interaction Between Minority Groups and the Majority Group

Increased contact between minority groups and the majority group is not in itself sufficient to alleviate prejudice. In fact, increased contact may, in some instances, highlight the differences between groups and increase suspicions and fear. Prejudice is likely to be increased when contacts are tension-laden or involuntary (Schaefer, 2012). Prejudice is likely to subside when individuals are placed in situations in which they share characteristics in nonracial and nonethnic matters—for example, as coworkers, fellow soldiers, or classmates. Equal-status contacts, rather than inferior-superior status contacts, are also more apt to reduce prejudices (Schaefer, 2012).

Civil Rights Laws: Changing the Legal Macro System

In the past 60 years, equal rights have been legislated in areas of employment, voting, housing, public accommodation, and education. A key question is, how effective are laws in changing prejudice?

Proponents of civil rights legislation make certain assumptions. The first is that new laws will reduce discriminatory behavior patterns. The laws define what was once normal behavior (discrimination) as now being deviant behavior. Through time, it is expected that attitudes will change and become more consistent with the forced nondiscriminatory behavior patterns.

A second assumption is that the laws will be used. Civil rights laws were enacted after the Civil War but were seldom enforced and gradually were eroded. It is also unfortunately true that some officials will find ways of evading the intent of the law by eliminating only the extreme, overt symbols of discrimination, without changing other practices. Thus, the enactment of a law is only the first step in the process of changing prejudiced attitudes and practices. However, as Martin Luther King Jr. noted, "The law may not make a man love me, but it can restrain him from lynching me, and I think that's pretty important."

Activism

The strategy of activism attempts to change the structure of race relations through direct confrontations of discrimination and segregation policies. Activism has three types of politics: the politics of creative disorder, the politics of disorder, and the politics of escape.

The *politics of creative disorder* operates on the edge of the dominant social system and includes school boycotts, rent strikes, job blockades, sit-ins (e.g., at businesses that are alleged to discriminate), public marches, and product boycotts. This type of activism is based on the concept of nonviolent resistance. A dramatic illustration of nonviolent resistance began on December 1, 1955, in Montgomery, Alabama, when Rosa Parks refused to give up her seat on a bus to a white person. Spotlight 5.5 describes Rosa Parks's act of courage.

The *politics of disorder* reflects alienation from the dominant culture and disillusionment with the political system. Those being discriminated against resort to mob uprisings, riots, and other forms of violence.

In 1969, the National Commission on Causes and Prevention of Violence reported that 200 riots had occurred in the previous five years when inner cities erupted (Sullivan, Thompson, Wright, Gross, & Spady, 1980). In 1992, as discussed previously, there was a devastating riot in the inner city of Los Angeles following the not-guilty verdict by a jury to charges that four white police officers had used excessive force in arresting Rodney King, an African American. The focus of most of these riots has been minority group aggression against white-owned property. In 2001, rioting occurred in Cincinnati after an African American had been shot and killed by a white police officer.

The *politics of escape* engages in rhetoric about minority victimization. But because the focus is not on solutions, the rhetoric has not been productive, except perhaps in providing an emotional release.

The principal value of social protest seems to be the stimulation of public awareness of certain problems. The civil rights protests in the 1960s made practically all Americans aware of the discrimination to which nonwhite groups were being subjected.

Rosa Parks's Act of Courage Sparked the Civil Rights Movement

Rosa Parks became a national hero for her actions, courage, and persistance.

On December 1, 1955, Rosa Parks was in a hurry. She had a lot of things to do. When the bus came to the boarding area where she was standing in Montgomery, Alabama, she got on without paying attention to the driver. She rode the bus often and was aware of Montgomery's segregated seating laws, which required blacks to sit at the back of the bus.

In those days in the South, black people were expected to board at the front of the bus, pay their fare, then get off and walk outside the bus to reboard at the back. But Rosa Parks noted that the back was already crowded, standing room only, with black passengers even standing on the back steps of the bus. It was apparent to Rosa that it would be all but impossible to reboard at the back. Besides, bus drivers sometimes drove off and left black passengers behind, even after accepting their fares. Rosa Parks spontaneously decided to take her chances. She paid her fare in the front of the bus, then walked down the aisle and took a seat toward the back of the bus that was still in the area reserved for whites. At the second stop after she boarded, a white man got on and had to stand.

The bus driver saw the white man standing, and ordered Rosa Parks to move to the back. She refused, thinking, "I want to be treated like a human being." Two police officers were called, and they arrested Rosa. She was taken to city hall, booked, fingerprinted, jailed, and fined. Her arrest and subsequent appeal all the way to the U.S. Supreme Court were the catalyst for a year-long boycott of the city buses by blacks, who composed 70 percent of the bus riders. The boycott inspired Martin Luther King Jr. to become involved. The boycott ended when the Supreme Court declared Montgomery's segregated seating laws unconstitutional. Rosa Parks's unplanned defiance of the segregated seating law sparked the civil rights movement. This movement has not only promoted social and economic justice for African Americans, but has also served to inspire other groups to organize to advocate for their civil rights. These groups include other racial and ethnic groups, women, the elderly, persons with disabilities, and gays and lesbians.

Bob Adelman/Corbis

With this awareness, at least some of the discrimination has ceased, and race relations have improved. Continued protest beyond a certain (although indeterminate) point, however, appears to have little additional value (Schaefer, 2012).

Affirmative Action: A Macro-System Response

Affirmative action programs require that employers demonstrate that they are actively employing minority applicants. Employers can no longer defend themselves by claiming that a decision not to hire a minority group member was based on some criterion other than ethnic group membership. If the percentage of minority group members in their employ is significantly lower than the percentage in the workforce, employers must accept a goal for minority employment and set up timetables stating when these goals are likely to be met.

Affirmative action programs provide for preferential hiring and admission requirements (e.g., admission to medical schools) for minority applicants.

Affirmative action programs cover all minority groups, including women. These programs also require that employers make active efforts to locate and recruit qualified minority applicants and, in certain circumstances, have hard quotas under which specific numbers of minority members must be accepted to fill vacant positions. For example, a university with a high proportion of white male faculty may be required to fill half of its faculty vacancies with women and members of other minority groups. Affirmative action programs require that employers must demonstrate according to a checklist of positive measures that they are not guilty of discrimination.

A major dilemma with affirmative action programs is that preferential hiring and quota programs involve *reverse discrimination*, in which qualified majority group members are sometimes arbitrarily excluded. Numerous lawsuits have been filed over the years in which complainants have alleged they have been victimized by reverse discrimination. The best-known case to date has been that of Alan Bakke, who was initially denied admission to the medical school at the University of California at Davis in 1973. He alleged reverse discrimination because he had higher grades and higher scores on the Medical College Admissions Tests than several minority applicants who were admitted under the university's minorities quota policy. In 1978, his claim was upheld by the U.S. Supreme Court in a precedent-setting decision (Sindler, 1978). The Court ruled that strict racial quotas were unconstitutional, but did not rule out using race as one among many criteria in making admissions decisions.

Supporters of affirmative action programs note that the majority group expressed little concern about discrimination when its members were the beneficiaries instead of the victims of discrimination. They also assert there is no other way to make up rapidly for past discrimination against minorities— many of whom may presently score slightly lower on qualification tests because they have not had the opportunities and the quality of training that the majority group members have had.

With affirmative action programs, some minority group members are given preferential treatment, which results in some whites being discriminated against. But minority group members still face more employment discrimination than whites do.

Supporters of affirmative action contend that as long as businesses rely on personal recommendations, informal social networks, and family ties, white men will have a distinct advantage (in filling job/position vacancies) built on generations of being in positions of power.

Affirmative action programs raise delicate and complex questions about achieving equality through giving preferences in hiring and admissions to minorities. Yet no other means has been found to end subtle discrimination in hiring and admissions.

Admission to educational programs and well-paying jobs is a crucial element in working toward integration. The history of immigrant groups who have "made it" (such as the Irish, Japanese, and Italians) suggests equality will be achieved only when minority group members gain middle- and upper-class status. Once such status is achieved, the minority group members become an economic and political force to be reckoned with. The dominant groups are pressured into modifying their norms, values, and stereotypes. For this reason, a number of authorities have noted that the elimination of economic discrimination is a prerequisite for achieving equality and harmonious race relations (Kornblum et al., 2012). Achieving educational equality between races is also crucial because lower educational attainments lead to less prestigious jobs, lower incomes, lower living standards, and the perpetuation of racial inequalities from one generation to the next.

Critics of affirmative action assert that it is a highly politicized and painful remedy that has stigmatized many of those it was meant to help. Affirmative action is now perceived by many in our society as a system of preferences for the unqualified. Critics further assert that while affirmative action may have been necessary 50 years ago to make sure that minority candidates received fair treatment to counter the social barriers to hiring and admission that stemmed from centuries of unequal treatment, such programs are no longer needed. They assert that it is wrong to discriminate against white males for the sole purpose of making up for an injustice that somebody's great-grandfather may have done to somebody else's great-grandfather. They assert that it is wrong for the daughter of a wealthy African American couple, for example, to be given preference in employment over the son of a homeless alcoholic who happens to be white.

In 1996, voters in California passed Proposition 209, which explicitly rejects the idea that women and other minority group members could get special consideration when applying for jobs, government contracts, or university admission. This affirmative action ban became law in California in August 1997. In addition, numerous lawsuits have been filed objecting to reverse discrimination. If the courts rule in favor of those filing the lawsuits, the power of affirmative action programs will be sharply reduced. In November 1997, the U.S. Supreme Court rejected a challenge to the California law that ended racial and gender preferences in that state. This Supreme Court action clears the way for other states and cities to ban affirmative action. Michigan is another state that has banned affirmative action programs.

Supporters of affirmative action believe that if we abandon affirmative action, we return to the "old-boy" network. They assert that affirmative action has helped many women and people of color to attain a good education and higher-paying positions, and thereby to remove themselves from the ranks of the poor. They assert that in a society in which racist and sexist attitudes remain, it is necessary to have affirmative action in order to give women and people of color a fair opportunity at attaining a quality education and well-paying jobs.

A number of authorities are now proposing race-blind policies that will not create reverse discrimination but will address past patterns of racism and the inequalities engendered by racism. Such policies would deal with the needs of people on a class basis rather than in terms of race of ethnic status. An example of a race-blind social policy in the interests of increasing equality of opportunity is the practice recently established by Harvard University and other private universities of awarding full scholarships to accepted students whose families earn less than $50,000 per year (Kornblum & Julian, p. 255).

Ethical Question 5.3

EP 2.1.2

Do you believe affirmative action programs should be (1) expanded to give greater preferential treatment to minorities, (2) reduced to give less preferential treatment to minorities, or (3) eliminated?

AP Images/Hadi Mizban

A truck bomb struck a Shiite mosque in central Baghdad, killing 75 people and wounding more than 200.

Confronting Racist Remarks and Actions

Racist jokes and sarcastic remarks help shape and perpetuate stereotypes and prejudices. Whites and nonwhites need to tactfully but assertively indicate they do not view such remarks as humorous or appropriate. It is also important that people tactfully and assertively point out the inappropriateness of racist actions by others. Such confrontations make explicit that subtle racist remarks and actions are discriminatory and harmful, which has a consciousness-raising effect. It is expected that such confrontations gradually will reduce racial prejudices and actions.

Ethical Question 5.4

Are you aware that if you listen to (and laugh at) racist jokes, you are involved in perpetuating stereotypes and prejudices?

EP 2.1.2

Noted 19th-century author, lecturer, and abolitionist Frederick Douglass stated:

> *Power concedes nothing without a demand—it never did, and it never will. Find out just what people will submit to, and you've found out the exact amount of injustice and wrong which will be imposed upon them. This will continue until they resist, either with words, blows, or both. The limits of tyrants are prescribed by the endurance of those whom they oppress. (quoted in Cummings, 1977, p. 201)*

Minority-Owned Businesses

Many people aspire to run their own business. Running a business is particularly attractive to many members of minority groups. It means an opportunity to increase one's income and wealth. It is also a way to avoid some of the racial and ethnic discrimination that occurs in the work world, such as the "glass ceilings" that block the promotion of qualified minority workers in corporations.

Since the 1970s, federal, state, and local governments have attempted to assist minority-owned businesses in a variety of ways. Programs have provided low-interest loans to minority-owned businesses. There are set-aside programs that stipulate that government contracts must be awarded to a minimum proportion, usually 10 to 30 percent, of minority-owned businesses. Some large urban areas have created enterprise zones, encouraging employment and investment in blighted neighborhoods through tax breaks. Minority-owned businesses have slowly been increasing in number. Yet only a small fraction of the total number of people classified as being a member of a minority group has benefited from government support of minority-owned businesses (Schaefer, 2012).

An ethical dilemma is described in "Are Native American Casinos a Benefit or a Detriment?"

Asset-Based Community Development

Many American (and foreign) cities have pockets of deeply troubled communities. These pockets have high rates of: crime, violence, unemployment, welfare dependency, gangs, drug involvement, homelessness, and vacant and abandoned land and buildings.

There are two paths for seeking to find solutions for deteriorated communities: the deficiency-oriented model and the asset-based approach. Both of these approaches will be briefly described.

The deficiency model focuses attention on what is "wrong" with a community. A key instrument used in the deficiency model is a "needs" survey, which focuses on the deficits in a community. The deficiency model often leads to the creation of "client neighborhoods." The creation of a client neighborhood is often accelerated by the mass media with its focus on emphasizing the spectacularly problematic components of a client neighborhood. It is apt to lead residents in these neighborhoods to view themselves as deficient victims who are incapable of taking charge of their lives and of their community's future. Targeting resources based on a "needs map" directs funding to service providers rather than directly to the residents. The service providers, with the deficiency approach, then relate to the residents as "clients." This approach furthers the perception that only outside experts can provide "real help." Such an approach hinders the development of the leadership capacities of the residents.

ETHICAL DILEMMA

Are Native American Casinos a Benefit or a Detriment?

In 1988, Congress passed the Indian Gaming Regulatory Act, which recognized the right of Native American tribes in the United States to establish gambling and gaming facilities on their reservations as long as the states in which they are located have some form of legalized gambling. A majority of states have now made arrangements with Native American tribes to have casinos. Gambling operations vary, but may include offtrack betting, casino tables such as blackjack and roulette, sports betting, video games of chance, telephone betting, slot machines, and high-stakes bingo. The vast majority of gamblers are non–Native Americans. The actual casinos are a form of tribal government enterprises as opposed to private business operations.

The economic impact on some reservations has been enormous. Many casinos take in millions of dollars in profits annually. Schaefer (2010, pp. 160–161) notes that about one-third of the recognized Native American tribes have casinos. Tribes that have opened casinos have greatly reduced their rate of unemployment, as the casinos tend to hire a number of members of the tribe. (They also employ non–Native Americans.) The revenues generated have helped spur economic development on land owned by the tribes. Welfare rates on reservations with casinos have dropped. Tribes are using their profits for the betterment of the reservation and its people. They are building schools and colleges and community centers, setting up education trust funds and scholarships, investing in alcohol and drug treatment programs, financing new business enterprises (entrepreneurships), and

putting in water and sewer systems on the reservations. The national prominence of tribal casinos has also given Native American leaders potential political clout with federal, state, and local governments.

There are also some drawbacks. One negative effect is gambling addiction. Many communities where casinos have been built have seen dramatic increases in the number of people addicted to gambling. Such an addiction may lead to higher rates of domestic violence and alcoholism. Another negative aspect of gambling is that those who can least afford to gamble usually are the most affected. The poor spend a greater percentage of their income on gambling than the wealthy, giving gambling the same effect on income as regressive taxes, with the poor being hit the hardest.

Opposition to gambling on reservations has arisen from both Native Americans and non–Native Americans. Some Native Americans fear losing their traditional values to corruption and organized crime. Others fear that as more and more casinos are built, the gambling market will become saturated with casinos competing with one another "for the same dollar." As a result, the tribes may be left with empty casinos and high unemployment rates. Some tribal members feel that casinos trivialize and cheapen their heritage. The issue of who shares in gambling profits has led in some tribal communities to heated conflicts over who is a member of the tribe.

Non–Native American critics sharply question the special economic status given to Native Americans in operating casinos and demand an even playing field.

Furthermore, service providers are under funding pressure to provide annual evidence that problems continue to intensify—in order for funding to be renewed. All of these factors tend to lead to the deepening of the cycle of dependence.

The asset-based model focuses on the development of policies and activities based on the assets, skills, and capacities of lower income people and their neighborhoods (Kretzmann & McKnight, 1993). The asset-based approach believes that significant community development only occurs when local community people are committed to investing themselves and their resources in improving the community. This approach believes sustainable development of a community must start from within the community—rather than waiting for significant help to arrive from outside the community. Instead of viewing the residents of a deteriorated neighborhood as being "clients," this model views

residents as being "citizens"—who have untapped resources, assets, capabilities, and potential. The focus is on the community's assets, capacities, and abilities. In addition, every community has a number of citizen's associations—where the citizens assemble to share common interests and activities, and to solve problems. (Every community has associations with religious, athletic, cultural, and recreational purposes.) These associations are key instruments in having the potential for community development.

Additional assets in a community are: private businesses; public institutions such as police and fire stations, parks, schools and libraries; social service agencies; hospitals; and medical clinics.

The key to asset-based community development is mobilizing the assets of individuals, associations, businesses, and public institutions to build a community from inside out.

How can this mobilization be accomplished? Mathie and Cunningham (2008) edited a text that summarizes a number of successful efforts in many countries—in Egypt, Brazil, the United States, Ecuador, Vietnam, Canada, Morocco, India, South Africa, Kenya, and the Philippines. The mobilization of one of these efforts, Building the Mercado Central in Minneapolis, will be summarized (Sheehan, 2008).

The Mercado Central is located on Minneapolis's Lake Street. Historically this area was a commerce center. However, in the 1960s, the area experienced serious deterioration. Established businesses began to close their doors. Homeowners fled this area. City services no longer were sufficient to upgrade the aging infrastructure. By 1970, this area was a "seedy" district with pawn shops, liquor stores, bars, and adult sex businesses.

Today, the Mercado Central is a thriving retail business cooperative that was developed by the Latino immigrant community in Minneapolis. More than 40 established businesses are located in this area. It is the hub of this community. It is a place of pride and culture for Latinos, and for non-Latinos.

The Mercado Central is a central market place where people gather to socialize, shop, celebrate, share news, and share concerns. Traditional *mercados* in Latin American cities are in the center of a city and are designed to be an informal place for families to shop, socialize, and dine.

What led to the transformation of this "seedy area" in the 1970s to a thriving central market area that Latinos and non-Latinos now cherish?

According to Sheehan (2008), it began in 1990 when five Salvadoran immigrants asked Juan Linares, a social worker for Catholic Charities, to make St. Stephen's (the local Catholic church) available to community access during the week. The immigrants wanted a place to pray, and gather, during the week. (The church had been locked during the week.) Juan Linares had moved to the United States from Mexico City. Juan Linares's request that this church be opened during the week was granted. The Salvadoran immigrants then requested some church masses be held in Spanish. With the assistance of *Isaiah* (a multi-denominational, congregation-based community organizing coalition in Minneapolis) the first Spanish mass was conducted at St. Stephen's in 1991. The deacon, Carl Valdez, in this area (at the request of Juan Linares) then arranged for 12 bilingual priests to commit to a weekly rotation at St. Stephen's.

(From the 1970s to the 1990s, this area of the city increasingly saw Latino immigrants settle in this neighborhood. These Latino immigrants were from Mexico, Central and South America, Cuba, and Puerto Rico.)

The deacon, Carl Valdez, then visited over 200 families in the neighborhood to discuss their desire to build a spiritual community in this area. He also asked them whether they were willing to help build such a spiritual community. In 1995, a church was established in St. Stephen's Parish called Sagrado Corazon, which resulted in over 750 Latino families regularly attending this new Spanish-focused church. This church eventually became the center from which Latino residents would mobilize to build their local economy and to address community concerns.

From these church families, a "sponsoring team" of community members was formed to develop an action plan that addressed the community's concerns about what the community believed were unfair immigration practices of the Immigration and Naturalization Service (INS). This team wanted the INS to transform its interactions with Latino residents in ways that respected language barriers and other concerns.

Juan Linares and Salvador Miranda (one of *Isaiah's* community organizers) then began working with congregation members to develop a "Community Talent Inventory" (CTI) that was focused on developing entrepreneurial skills within the community and building relationships among community members. This CTI identified a desire for targeted entrepreneurial training.

Since an entrepreneurial training program in Spanish was already offered in the neighboring city of St. Paul, the provider of this training, Neighbourhood Development Center, agreed to offer this training to this geographic area in Minneapolis.

During this 16-week entrepreneurial training, the participants began to discuss how they could develop individual businesses that would be profitable, without competing with one another. The participants agreed to develop a "cooperative" that would allow each business owner to make a profit, while working together and supporting each other's efforts.

Reflecting on their assets and cultures, this cooperative decided to build the Mercado Central, which is a central marketplace for people to gather, shop, and socialize.

The plan that emerged from the coordinating committee was fairly complex. A plan was developed for the Mercado Central. Land was purchased. A business development plan was formulated for the business start-ups. In addition, financing for the Mercado Central was obtained from about 25 sources—including banks, the city of Minneapolis, foundations, local corporations, nonprofit development organizations, and the Catholic Campaign for Human Development.

Many residents of this geographic area contributed their time, talents, capabilities, and assets to transform this geographic area from a "seedy district" into a thriving community that is a source of pride and a cultural treasure.

An asset-based community development has the potential to turn other deteriorated neighborhoods into communities that will prosper and flourish.

Human Rights and Social Justice

In recent years, the Council on Social Work Education has placed increased emphasis on human rights. Its 2008 Educational Policy and Accreditation Standards (EPAS) declare:

> Service, social justice, the dignity and worth of the person, human rights, the importance of human relationships, integrity, competence, and scientific inquiry are the core values of social work....
>
> Each person, regardless of position in society, has basic human rights, such as freedom, safety, privacy, an adequate standard of living, health care, and education. Social workers recognize the global interconnections of oppression and are knowledgeable about theories of justice and strategies to promote human and civil rights. (Council on Social Work Education, 2008)

Reichert (2007), however, points out that "human rights" has received very limited attention in social work curriculum, course materials, and lectures. Often, a human rights focus is "invisible" in social work curriculum. Social work literature continually prefers the term "social justice" in analyzing core values relevant to the social work profession.

Social justice is an "ideal" in which all members of a society have the same opportunities, basic rights, obligations, and social benefits. Integral to this value, social workers have an obligation to engage in advocacy to confront institutional inequities, prejudice, discrimination, and oppression.

Human rights are conceived to be fundamental rights to which a person is inherently entitled simply because she or he is a human being. Human rights are thus universal (applicable everywhere) and egalitarian (the same for everyone).

Reichert (2007, p. 4) compares the concepts of "human rights" and "social justice":

> Human rights provide the social work profession with a global and contemporary set of guidelines, whereas social justice tends to be defined in vague terminology such as fairness versus unfairness of equality versus inequality.... This distinction gives human rights an authority that social justice lacks. Human rights can elicit discussion of common issues by people from all walks of life and every corner of the world.

What are basic "human rights"? A clear specification of basic human rights has not been agreed upon. A key starting point in articulating such rights is the Universal Declaration of Human Rights (UNDR; United Nations, 1948). The rights identified in this document are:

- All humans are born free and equal in dignity and rights
- Everyone is entitled to all of the rights in the UNDR, regardless of any distinction
- The right to life, liberty, and the security of the person
- Prohibition of slavery
- Prohibition of torture
- Right to recognition as a person before the law
- All must be treated equally under the law
- Right to a remedy of any violation of these rights
- Prohibition of arbitrary arrest, detention, or exile
- Right to a fair trial
- People shall be presumed innocent until proven guilty
- Right to freedom from arbitrary interference with private life
- Right to freedom of movement
- Right to seek asylum
- Right to a nationality
- Right to marry; marriage must be consented to by both parties; the family is entitled to protection from the state
- Right to property
- Right to freedom of thought, conscience, and religion
- Right to freedom of opinion and expression
- Right to freedom of assembly and association

- Right to participate in the government of one's country
- Right to economic, social, and cultural rights necessary for dignity and free development of personality
- Right to work and equitable compensation
- Right to rest and leisure from work
- Right to an adequate standard of living, including food, clothing, housing, and medical care
- Right to education
- Right to participate in cultural activities and to share in scientific achievements
- Right to a world order in which these rights can be realized
- Each has duties to their community; rights shall be limited only in regard to respecting the rights of others
- None of the rights may be interpreted as allowing any action to destroy these rights

Every member nation of the United Nations has approved this Declaration. Yet it is not legally binding on any nation. Because this Declaration articulates human rights in somewhat vague terms, it is sometimes difficult to determine when (or if) a country/government is violating basic human rights.

Most countries now recognize that safeguarding human rights has evolved into a major, worldwide goal. Yet identifying violations is currently an imprecise science. It is common for a government to accuse other governments of violating human rights while at the same time "overlooking" its own violations. Reichert (2007, p. 8) states:

> The United States, compared to many other countries, fails to fulfill its obligation to promote human rights for all…. The infant mortality rate is higher in the United States than in any other industrialized nation … and, within the U.S. itself, infant mortality rates are disparate among racial groups, with African-American infants suffering a mortality rate more than twice that of non-Hispanic whites.

It is hoped that greater attention to articulating basic human rights will lead countries to initiate programs that safeguard such rights for all citizens. Increased attention to articulating and protecting basic human rights has the promise of being a key countervailing force in curbing discrimination against people of color, women, persons with a disabilities, gays and lesbians, and other groups that are currently victimized by discrimination.

LO 5-5 Outline Some Guidelines for Social Work Practice with Racial and Ethnic Groups

Social Work Practice with Racial and Ethnic Groups

Social workers and other helping persons have many of the prejudices, stereotypes, and misperceptions of the general society. There is a danger that a social worker will use her or his own cultural, social, or economic values in assessing and providing services to clients.

The problematic nature of cross-cultural social work does not preclude its effectiveness. While many white practitioners can establish productive working relationships with minority clients, others cannot. In other instances, minority practitioners are sometimes effective and sometimes not with others of the same race or ethnic group.

Ethnic-Sensitive Practice

Traditionally, professional social work practice has used the medical model for the delivery of services. The medical model is a deficit model that focuses on identifying problems or deficits within a person. The medical model largely ignores environmental factors that impact the person-in-situation. A major shortcoming of a deficit model is that it focuses on the deficits of a person or a group while ignoring strengths and resources. Emphasizing people's shortcomings is apt to have a severe negative effect on their self-esteem—they may define themselves in terms of shortcomings and, in the process, overlook strengths and resources.

A better model is ethnic-sensitive practice, which seeks to incorporate understanding of diverse ethnic, cultural, and minority groups into the theories and principles that guide social work practice (Devore & Schlesinger, 1996). Ethnic-sensitive practice is based on the view that practice must be attuned to the values and dispositions related to clients' ethnic group membership and social-class position. Ethnic-sensitive practice requires that social workers have an in-depth understanding of the effects of oppression on racial and ethnic groups.

Another important aspect of the conceptual framework is the "dual perspective" mentioned in Chapter 3 (Beckett & Johnson, 1995; Norton, 1978). This concept is derived from the view that all people are a part of two systems: (1) the dominant or sustaining system (the society that one lives in), which is the source of power and economic resources; and (2) the nurturing system, composed of the physical and social environment of family and community. The dual perspective asserts that the adverse consequences of an oppressive society on the self-concept of a person of color or of any minority group can be partially offset by the nurturing system.

Ethnic-sensitive practice holds that social workers have a special obligation to be aware of and to seek to redress the oppression experienced by ethnic groups. Ethnic-sensitive practice assumes that each ethnic group's members have a history that has a bearing on the members' perceptions of current problems. For example, the individual and collective history of many African Americans leads to the expectation that family resources will be available in times of trouble (Devore & Schlesinger, 1996). Ethnic-sensitive practice, however, also assumes that the present is most important. For example, many Mexican American and Puerto Rican women currently feel tension as they attempt to move beyond traditionally defined gender roles into the mainstream as students and paid employees (Devore & Schlesinger, 1996).

Ethnic-sensitive practice introduces no new practice principles or approaches. Instead, it urges the adaptation of prevailing therapies, social work principles, and skills to take account of ethnic reality. Regardless of which practice approach is used, three concepts and perspectives that are emphasized are empowerment, the strengths perspective, and culturally competent practice.

Empowerment

People who work with ethnic or racial groups can help empower members of those groups by countering negative images (established through a long history of discrimination) with positive values or images and an emphasis on the ability of each group member to influence the conditions of his or her life. Empowerment counters hopelessness and powerlessness with the belief that each person is able to address problems competently, beginning with a positive view of the self. Empowerment counters oppression and poverty by helping members of ethnic groups increase their ability to make and implement basic life decisions.

Strengths Perspective

The strengths perspective is closely related to empowerment (see Chapter 1). It emphasizes people's

abilities, interests, aspirations, resources, beliefs, and accomplishments. For example, strengths of African Americans in the United States include more than 100 predominantly African American colleges and universities, fraternal and women's organizations, and numerous social, political, and professional organizations. Many of the schools, businesses, churches, and organizations that are predominantly African American have developed social service programs—such as family support services, mentoring programs, food and shelter services, transportation services, and educational and scholarship programs. Through individual and organized efforts, self-help approaches and mutual aid traditions continue among African Americans. African Americans tend to have strong ties to immediate and extended family. They tend to have a strong religious orientation, a strong work and achievement orientation, and egalitarian role sharing (Billingsley, 1993).

Culturally Competent Practice

Current projections indicate that by the middle of the 21st century, more than half the population of the United States will be composed of people of color (Dhooper & Moore, 2001). Increasingly, social workers will be dealing with people who are more diverse, politically more active, and more aware of their rights. It is therefore incumbent on social workers to become increasingly culturally competent. In order to become culturally competent, social workers need to (1) become aware of culture and its pervasive influence; (2) learn about their own culture; (3) recognize their own ethnocentricity; (4) learn about other cultures; (5) acquire cultural knowledge about the clients they are working with; and (6) adapt social work skills and intervention approaches to the needs and styles of the cultures of these clients (Dhooper & Moore, 2001).

●●●● **Ethical Question 5.5**

How culturally competent are you?

EP 2.1.2

Professional therapist providing services during counseling session.

In 2001, the National Association of Social Workers (NASW, 2001) approved the following 10 standards for cultural competence in social work practice:

Standard 1. **Ethics and Values**—*Social workers shall function in accordance with the values, ethics, and standards of the profession, recognizing how personal and professional values may conflict with or accommodate the needs of diverse clients.*

Standard 2. **Self-Awareness**—*Social workers shall seek to develop an understanding of their own personal cultural values and beliefs as one way of appreciating the importance of multicultural identities in the lives of people.*

Standard 3. **Cross-Cultural Knowledge**—*Social workers shall have and continue to develop specialized knowledge and understanding about the history, traditions, values, family systems, and artistic expressions of major client groups that they serve.*

Standard 4. **Cross-Cultural Skills**—*Social workers shall use appropriate methodological approaches, skills, and techniques that reflect the workers' understanding of the role of culture in the helping process.*

Standard 5. **Service Delivery**—*Social workers shall be knowledgeable about and skillful in the use of services available in the community and broader society and be able to make appropriate referrals for their diverse clients.*

Standard 6. **Empowerment and Advocacy**—*Social workers shall be aware of the effect of social policies and programs on diverse client populations, advocating for and with clients whenever appropriate.*

Standard 7. **Diverse Workforce**—*Social workers shall support and advocate for recruitment, admissions and hiring, and retention efforts in social work programs and agencies that ensure diversity within the profession.*

Standard 8. **Professional Education**—*Social workers shall advocate for and participate in educational and training programs that help advance cultural competence within the profession.*

Standard 9. **Language Diversity**—*Social workers shall seek to provide or advocate for the provision of information, referrals, and services in the language appropriate to the client, which may include use of interpreters.*

Standard 10. **Cross-Cultural Leadership**—*Social workers shall be able to communicate information about diverse client groups to other professionals.*[1]

---

[1]Copyrighted material reprinted with permission from the National Association of Social Workers, Inc.

Learning the Culture of the Group

In working with a diverse culture, the following questions are crucial: How are the members likely to view someone from a different culture? What kinds of communications and actions are likely to lead to the development of a constructive relationship? How do members view asking for help from a social agency? If the agency is viewed as being part of the dominant white society that has devalued this group in the past, how are the members likely to view the social agency? What are the values of the group? When the members of this group need help, who are they most likely to turn to—relatives, friends, neighbors, churches, social agencies, the school system, or the local government? What are culturally acceptable ways of providing help to people in need?

As a corollary of becoming accepted by clients of diverse racial or ethnic groups, the social worker must live his or her personal life in a manner that will not offend important values and mores of those groups.

There are an *immense* number and variety of racial and ethnic groups in our society. It is beyond the scope of this chapter to describe the unique characteristics of these diverse groups. Instead, a few characteristics of some minority groups will be summarized to illustrate the importance of learning about the minority group of a client. For example, when working with Native Americans, it is considered rude—an attempt to intimidate, in fact—to maintain direct eye contact (Hull, 2010).

Chicano men, as contrasted to Anglo men, have been described as exhibiting greater pride in their maleness (Schaefer, 2012). *Machismo*—a strong sense of masculine pride—is highly valued among Chicano men and is displayed by males to express dominance and superiority. *Machismo* is demonstrated differently by different people. Some may seek to be irresistible to women and to have a number of sexual partners. Some resort to weapons or fighting. Some interpret *machismo* to mean pride in one's manhood, honor, and ability to provide for one's family. Others boast of their achievements, even those that never occurred. Recent writers have noted that the feminist movement, urbanization, upward mobility, and acculturation are contributing to the decline of *machismo* (Shaefer, 2012). Chicanos also tend to be more "familistic" than Anglos. *Familism* is the belief that the family takes precedence over the individual. Familism has a number of components, including the following. Family members believe in the benefits of financially taking care of one another. Comadrazgo (the godparent-godchild relationship) is valued, seeking and receiving advice from relatives is valued. The active involvement of older persons in the family is valued. Close family ties help maintain the mental and social well-being of older persons in the family. The extended family approach provides emotional strength in times of crisis.

On the negative side, familism may discourage youth from pursuing opportunities that will take them away from the family. It should be noted that differences between Chicanos and Anglos with regard to *machismo* and familism are ones of degree, not of kind.

Hull (2010) suggests that natural support systems are a useful resource in providing assistance to Chicanos. These support systems include extended family, folk healers, religious institutions, and merchant and social clubs. The extended family includes the family of origin, nuclear family members, other relatives, godparents, and those considered to be like family. Folk healers are prominent in Chicano communities. Some use treatments that blend natural healing methods with religious or spiritual beliefs. Religious institutions (especially the Roman Catholic church) provide such services as pastoral counseling, emergency money, job-locating and housing assistance, and some specialized programs, such as drug abuse treatment and prevention. Merchant and social clubs can provide such items as native foods, herbs, referral to other resources, credit and information, prayer books, recreation, and the services of healers. The reluctance of Chicano clients to seek help from a social welfare agency can be reduced by use of these natural support systems. Out reach can be done through churches and community groups. If a social welfare agency gains a reputation of utilizing such natural support systems in the intervention process, Chicanos will have greater trust in the agency and be much more apt to seek help. Utilizing such natural support systems also increases the effectiveness of the intervention process.

Religious organizations that are predominantly African American usually have a social and spiritual mission. They are apt to be highly active in efforts to combat racial discrimination. Many prominent African American leaders, such as the late Martin Luther King Jr. and Jesse Jackson, have been members of the clergy. African American churches have served to develop leadership skills. They have also served as social welfare organizations to meet such basic needs as food, clothing, and shelter. African American churches are natural support systems that workers need to utilize to serve troubled African American individuals and families.

Self-Awareness of Values, Prejudices, and Stereotypes

Because social workers live in a society in which racial and ethnic prejudices abound, they also have prejudices and stereotypes. Think about these questions: In the past year, have you listened to racial or ethnic jokes? Did you laugh? If you did laugh, do you think your laughter, in a small way, was perpetuating some racial or ethnic stereotypes? Have you told in the past year some racial or ethnic jokes? If yes, was the content derogatory? By telling such jokes, are you demonstrating some of your prejudices and stereotypes? By telling such jokes, are you not, in some way, reinforcing some of the harmful stereotypes and prejudices that exist in our society?

Racial and ethnic prejudices can be demonstrated by the following exercise:

Assume you are single; place a check mark beside the ethnic and racial groups that you would be hesitant or reluctant to marry a member of:

___Iranian	___White American
___Chinese	___Egyptian
___Japanese	___Irish
___Samoan	___Cuban
___Filipino	___Puerto Rican
___African American	___German
___Native American	___Vietnamese
___Italian	___French
___Mexican	___Russian

If you have checked some of these (most people check several), analyze your thoughts as to why you would be hesitant to marry those you have checked. There is a fair chance that such an analysis will help you identify some of your prejudices.

A helping professional needs to be aware of his or her racial and ethnic stereotypes and prejudices in order to remain objective in working with clients. When working with a client of a group that you have negative perceptions about, you should continually be asking the following questions: Am I individualizing this person as a unique person with worth, or am I making the mistake of viewing this person in terms of my prejudices and stereotypes? Am I working up to my full capacities with this individual? Or am I seeking to cut corners by probing less deeply, by not fully informing this person of the services he or she is eligible for, or by wanting to end the interview before fully exploring all the client's problems and all possible alternatives? When we have negative stereotypes about someone, there is a strong likelihood that we will discriminate against that person in providing services. Being aware of our stereotypes is the first step in preventing such discrimination.

Application of Theory to Practice: Techniques of Intervention

Along with cultural knowledge and self-awareness, the social worker needs to learn which intervention approaches are likely to be effective, and which are likely to be ineffective, with the ethnic or racial group he or she is working with. Several guidelines will be presented for illustrative purposes.

Social workers should seek to use their own patterns of communication and avoid the temptation to adopt the client's accent, vocabulary, or speech (Hull, 2010). The worker who seeks to speak like the client is apt to make mistakes in enunciations, and thereby come across as a phony, or may offend the client if the client interprets the worker's communication to be mimicry.

A social worker with an urban background who has a job in a small rural community needs to live his personal life in a way that is consistent with community values and standards. A worker who gains a reputation as being a violator of community norms will not be effective in a small community. Neither the power structure nor a majority of clients is likely to give such a worker credibility. A worker in a small community needs to identify community values in areas such as religious beliefs and patterns of expression, dating and marriage patterns, values toward domestic and wild animals (e.g., opposing deer hunting in many communities may run counter to strong local values), drug usage, political beliefs and values, and sexual mores. Once such values are identified, the social worker needs to seek to achieve a balance between the kind of lifestyle he wants and the kind of lifestyle the community expects he will live.

Hull (2007) recommends using all of the formalities in initial meetings with adult clients of diverse racial and ethnic groups. Such usage should include the formal title (Mr., Miss, Mrs., Ms.), the client's proper full name, greeting with a handshake, and the other courtesies usually extended. In initial contacts, workers should also usually show their agency identification and state reasons for the meeting.

Agencies and social workers should establish working hours that coincide with the needs of the groups being served. Doing so may mean having evening and weekend hours to avoid forcing clients, already with financial difficulties, to lose time from their jobs.

In the area of group services to racially diverse clients, Hull (2010) recommends that membership be selected in such a manner that no one race vastly outnumbers the others. Sometimes it is necessary to educate clients about the processes of individual or group counseling. Using words common to general conversation is much better than using technical and sophisticated jargon that clients are not likely to comprehend.

In working with adult clients who are not fluent in the English language, it is generally a mistake to use bilingual children of the clients as interpreters (Hull, 2010). Having children as interpreters is embarrassing to the parents because it places them in a position of being partially dependent on their children and erroneously suggests the parents are deficient in learning essential communication mechanisms. In addition, children often lack an adult's knowledge, which reduces their value as interpreters. Also, when using interpreters, the worker should direct his or her conversation to the client and not to the interpreter. Talking to the interpreter diverts attention from the client and places the client in the position of bystander rather than the central figure in the relationship.

Native Americans place a high value on the principle of self-determination (Hull, 2010). This sometimes provides a perplexing dilemma for a social worker who wonders, How can I help if I can't intervene? Native Americans will request intervention only infrequently, and the non–Native American worker needs to have patience and wait for the request. How long this will take varies. During the waiting period, the non–Native American worker should be available and may offer assistance as long as there is no hint of coercion. Once help is accepted, the worker will be tested. If the client believes the worker has been helpful, the word will spread, and the worker is likely to have more requests for help. If the client concludes the worker is lacking in helpful capacities, this assessment will also spread, and the worker will be less apt to be sought out by potential clients.

In establishing rapport with African American, Hispanic, or Native American clients, or members of other groups that have suffered from racial oppression, a peer relationship should be sought in which there is mutual respect and mutual sharing of information. A white-superiority type of relationship should be totally rejected because it is likely to be interpreted by racially diverse clients as being offensive—which it is.

For clients who have emotional or behavioral issues, there are over a hundred intervention approaches that have been developed—some of which are much more effective than others. In seeking to select an intervention approach, social workers should be guided by "evidence-based practice" (EBP). EBP urges social workers to use the best available scientific knowledge from existing outcome studies to select which intervention approach to use. Ideally (although studies may not be available) the intervention approach that is selected should have evidence of being effective with the racial or ethnic group that the client is a member of.

Social Work Roles for Countering Discrimination

Social workers have an obligation to work vigorously to end racial discrimination as well as other forms of discrimination. The major professional social work organizations have, over the years, taken strong positions aimed at ending racial discrimination. The National Association of Social Workers, for example, has lobbied for the passage of civil rights legislation. The NASW *Code of Ethics* (1999) has the following explicit statement about discrimination:

> *Social workers should act to prevent and eliminate domination of, exploitation of, and discrimination against any person, group, or class on the basis of race, ethnicity, national origin, color, sex, sexual orientation, age, marital status, political belief, religion, or mental or physical disability. (p. 24)*

The Council on Social Work Education (CSWE), in its Educational Policy and Accreditation Standards (EPAS) (2008), requires that baccalaureate and master's programs in social work include content on racism in the social work curriculum. The EPAS also requires that accredited programs provide considerable content on diversity and on the promotion of social and economic justice. Professional social work education is committed to preparing social work students to understand and appreciate cultural and social diversity. Students are taught to understand the dynamics and consequences of oppression, and they learn to use intervention strategies to combat social injustice, oppression, and their effects. There is an Association of Black Social Workers that has been very active in combating racial prejudice and discrimination.

In working to end racial and other forms of discrimination, social workers can take on a variety of roles. They can be *advocates* for equal treatment for those who are being oppressed or discriminated against. They can be *analysts* of societal conditions that result in institutional racism and then be *advocates* for the development of programs to counter such racism. They can be *initiators* of action by seeking to inform social service systems and the political systems of social injustices and then advocating for changes in policies and programs. At times, they can fulfill an *educator* role by giving information on options to counter oppression and by conveying information on how to organize and advocate for change. If several organizations are working somewhat independently to counter related forms of discrimination and oppression, social workers can serve as *integrators/coordinators* by seeking to have these organizations form a coalition in which they work together in some organized manner to effect change. At times, social workers may, in the role of *counselor*, work with oppressed individuals and small groups to problem-solve personal concerns related to being victimized by oppression and discrimination. Social workers may also be *brokers*, by linking oppressed client systems with needed resources.

LO 5-6 Forecast the Pattern of Race and Ethnic Relations in the United States in the Future

The Future of U.S. Race and Ethnic Relations

It is clear that minorities such as African Americans, Hispanics, Asian Americans, and Native Americans will assertively, and sometimes aggressively, pursue a variety of strategies to change racist prejudices and actions. Counteractions by certain segments of the white dominant group are also likely to occur. (Even in the social sciences, every action elicits a reaction.) For example, organizations that advocate white supremacy, such as the Ku Klux Klan, continue to attract new members.

Minorities have been given hope of achieving equality of opportunity and justice. Their hope has been kindled, and they will no longer submit to a subordinate status. Struggles to achieve racial equality will continue.

The past few decades have been a struggle for minorities as they have tried to hold onto past gains in the face of reactions against minority rights. Vowing to take "big government" off the back of the American people and to strengthen the economy by giving businesses the incentive to grow and produce, the Reagan administration (1980–1988) largely removed the federal government from its traditional role as initiator and enforcer of programs to guarantee minority rights. The George Bush administration (1988–1992) continued to follow a similar strategy. The federal government under the Reagan and George Bush administrations asserted that private businesses were in the best position to correct the problems of poverty and discrimination. (Because businesses generally profit from paying low wages, most companies in the 1980s and early 1990s did not aggressively seek to improve the financial circumstances and living conditions of minorities.) Perhaps because of the federal government's shift in policies, minorities were less active in the 1980s and 1990s (as compared to the 1960s and 1970s) in using the strategy of activism. In the 1980s and 1990s, minority groups were experiencing difficulties in maintaining the gains they had achieved two decades earlier in the job market through affirmative action and Equal Employment Opportunity programs. Bill Clinton, elected president in 1992, ran on a platform that promised a more active role by the federal government in promoting social and economic justice for all racial and ethnic groups in this country.

Bill Clinton's views on resolving social problems were consistent with a moderate (middle-of-the-road) to liberal orientation. His liberal proposals that would have benefited populations-at-risk included a health insurance program for all Americans and significantly expanded educational and training programs for individuals on welfare to help them become self-supporting.

The move toward liberalism in the early 1990s was, however, short-lived. In the congressional elections of

1994, the Republicans won majority control of both the Senate and the House of Representatives. (This was the first time in 40 years that Republicans held a majority in the House.) Most of these Republicans had a conservative political agenda that included shifting spending from crime prevention to prison construction, eliminating affirmative action programs, reducing spending for many social welfare programs, and reducing the amount of taxes paid by high-income individuals. Such proposals were not, in the Clinton administration, enacted into law.

George W. Bush was elected president in 2000 in a very close election. He ran on a largely conservative agenda. His top priority was cutting taxes, and both houses of Congress passed tax cuts in 2001. (These tax cuts widened further the income gap between the rich and the poor.) George W. Bush had few proposals that were specifically directed at benefiting people of color. He advocated for increased funding for historically black colleges. In addition, he appointed African Americans and Latinos to some high-level positions in his administration.

Barack Obama was elected president in 2008. The election of an African American as president demonstrates our country has made significant progress in white Americans having respect for African Americans and for other people of color.

What will be the pattern of race relations in the future? M. Gordon (1961) outlined three possible patterns of intergroup relations: Anglo-conformity, melting pot, and cultural pluralism.

Anglo-conformity *assumes the desirability of maintaining modified English institutions, language, and culture as the dominant standard in American life. In practice, "assimilation" in America has always meant Anglo-conformity, and the groups that have been most readily assimilated have been those that are ethnically and culturally most similar to the Anglo-Saxon group [early British colonists].*

The melting pot *is, strictly speaking, a rather different concept, which views the future American society not as a modified England but rather as a totally new blend, both culturally and biologically, of all the various groups that inhabit the United States. In practice, the melting pot has been of only limited significance in the American experience.*

Cultural pluralism *implies a series of coexisting groups, each preserving its own tradition and culture but each loyal to an overarching American nation.*

Although the cultural enclaves of some immigrant groups, such as the Germans, have declined in importance in the past, many other groups, such as the Italians, have retained a strong sense of ethnic identity and have resisted both Anglo-conformity and inclusion in the melting pot. (pp. 363–365)

Members of some European ethnic groups such as the British, French, and Dutch formed the dominant culture of the United States. Other European ethnic groups such as the Irish, Italians, Polish, Germans, Scandinavians, Greeks, and Hungarians are now nearly fully assimilated and integrated.

Cultural pluralism appears to be the form that race and ethnic relations are presently taking. Renewed interest on the part of a number of ethnic European Americans in expressing their pride in their own customs, religions, and linguistic and cultural traditions is evident. Slogans on buttons and signs say, "Kiss me, I'm Italian," "Irish Power," and "Polish and Proud." African Americans, Native Americans, Hispanics, and Asian Americans are demanding entry into mainstream America but are not demanding assimilation. They want coexistence in a pluralistic society while seeking to preserve their own traditions and cultures. They are finding a source of identity and pride in their own cultural backgrounds and histories.

Some progress has been made toward ending discrimination since the *Brown v. Board of Education* decision in 1954. Yet equal opportunity for all people in the United States is still only a dream.

Chapter Summary

The following summarizes this chapter's content as it relates to the learning objectives presented at the beginning of the chapter. Chapter content will help prepare students to:

LO 5-1 Define and describe ethnic groups, ethnocentrism, race, racism, prejudice, discrimination, oppression, and institutional discrimination.

An ethnic group is a distinct group of people who share a common language, set of customs, history, culture, race, religion, or origin.

Ethnocentrism is an orientation or set of beliefs that views one's own culture, ethnic or racial group, or nation as superior to others.

Race is a social concept; it is the way in which members of a society classify each other by physical characteristics.

Racism is stereotyping and generalizing about people, usually negatively, because of their race; it is commonly a basis of discrimination against members of racial minority groups.

Prejudice is a negative opinion about an individual, group, or phenomenon that is developed without proof or systematic evidence.

Discrimination is the negative treatment of people based on identifiable characteristics such as race, gender, religion, or ethnicity.

Oppression is the social act of placing severe restrictions on a group or institution.

Institutional discrimination is prejudicial treatment in organizations based on official policies, overt behaviors, or behaviors that may be covert but approved by those with power.

LO 5-2 Outline the sources of prejudice and discrimination.

Theories about the sources of prejudice and discrimination include projection, frustration-aggression, countering insecurity and inferiority, the authoritarian personality, historical explanations, competition and exploitation, socialization processes, the belief in only one true religion, and white supremacy.

LO 5-3 Summarize the effects and costs of discrimination and oppression and describe the effects of discrimination on human growth and development.

Being discriminated against makes it more difficult to obtain adequate housing, financial resources, a quality education, employment, adequate health care and other services, equal justice in civil and criminal cases, and so on. It has heavy psychological costs, as it makes it more difficult to develop a positive identity. It impairs intergroup cooperation and communication. It is a factor contributing to social problems among minorities. It lowers life expectancy among minorities. It undermines some of our nation's political goals, such as being an advocate for human rights and equality.

LO 5-4 Suggest strategies for advancing social and economic justice.

Strategies against discrimination include mass media appeals, increased interaction between minority groups and the majority group, civil rights legislation, protests and activism, affirmative action, minority-owned businesses, confronting racist and ethnic remarks and actions, confronting problems in inner cities, and asset-based community development.

LO 5-5 Outline some guidelines for social work practice with racial and ethnic groups.

Guidelines include ethnic-sensitive practice, empowerment, the strengths perspective, and culturally competent practice.

LO 5-6 Forecast the pattern of race and ethnic relations in the United States in the future.

Three possible patterns of inter group ethnic and race relations in the future are Anglo-conformity, melting pot, and cultural pluralism. Cultural pluralism is the form that race and ethnic relations are presently taking, and may well take in the future.

COMPETENCY NOTES

The following identifies where Educational Policy (EP) competencies and practice behaviors are discussed in the chapter.

EP 2.1.2a *(All of this chapter)* Recognize and manage personal values in a way that allows professional values to guide practice.

EP 2.1.4a *(All of this chapter)* Recognize the extent to which a culture's structures and values may oppress, marginalize, alienate, or create or enhance privilege and power.

EP 2.1.4b *(All of this chapter)* Gain sufficient self-awareness to eliminate the influence of personal biases and values in working with diverse groups.

EP 2.1.4c *(All of this chapter)* Recognize and communicate their understanding of the importance of difference in shaping life experiences.

EP 2.1.4d *(All of this chapter)* View themselves as learners and engage those with whom they work as informants.

EP 2.1.5a *(All of this chapter)* Understand forms and mechanisms of oppression and discrimination.

EP 2.1.5b *(All of this chapter)* Advocate for human rights and social and economic justice.

EP 2.1.5c *(All of this chapter)* Engage in practices that advance social and economic justice.

EP 2.1.7a *(All of this chapter)* Utilize conceptual frameworks to guide the process of assessment, intervention, and evaluation.

EP 2.1.10e *(All of this chapter)* Assess client strengths and limitations.
The content of the chapter is focused on students acquiring all of these practice behaviors.

EP 2.1.2 Apply social work ethical principles to guide professional practice. *(pp.* 262, 266, 280, 281, 286) Ethical questions are posed.

WEB RESOURCES

See this text's companion website at *www.cengage brain.com* for learning tools such as chapter quizzing, videos, and more.

BIOLOGICAL DEVELOPMENT IN ADOLESCENCE

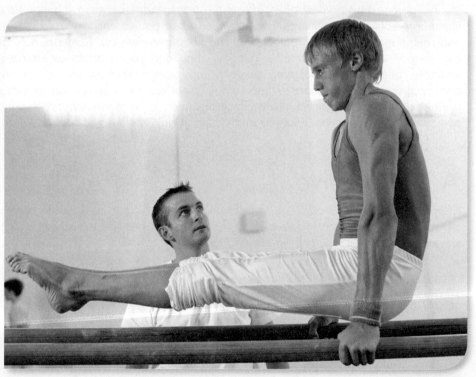

Alistair Berg/Stone/Getty Images

Roger sat in study hall gazing out the window. He had an intense, pained expression on his face. Roger was 15 years old, and not one thing was going right for him. His arms were too long for the rest of his body. He felt like he couldn't walk from the desk to the door without tripping at least once. Homecoming was coming up soon, and his face suddenly looked like a pepperoni pizza. Amanda, the light of his life, wouldn't even acknowledge his existence. To top it all off, even if he managed to get Amanda to go to homecoming with him, he'd still either have to scrounge up another older couple to drive or else have his father drive them to the dance. How humiliating. Roger continued to gaze out the study hall window. The primary theme in his thoughts was, Life is hard.

Change and adjustment characterize adolescence. Roger is not unique. Like other people his age, he is trying to cope with drastic physical changes, increasing sexual awareness, desires to fit in with the peer group, and the desperate need to develop a personal identity.

We have established that the attainment of developmental milestones is directly related to human behavior. We have also established that within any individual, the biological, psychological, and social aspects of development mutually affect each other. Together, they interact and significantly impact growth, change, and ultimately, well-being.

Biological development and maturation affect both how adolescents perceive themselves and how they behave. Rapid and uneven physical growth may cause awkwardness, which may result in feeling self-conscious and consequently uncomfortable in social interactions. For example, some psychological and behavioral differences exist between males who develop earlier or later and those who develop at an average rate.

Biological development often affects the transactions between individuals and their immediate social environments. For instance, when adolescents begin to attain physical and sexual maturity, sexual relationships may begin to develop. Likewise, new and different alternatives become available to adolescents and young adults as they mature. For example, alternatives concerning sexuality may range from no sexual activity to avid and frequent sexual relations. These new alternatives merit evaluation in terms of their positive and negative consequences. Decisions need to be made about such critical issues as whether to have sexual relations and which, if any, methods of contraception to use.

A Perspective

Chapters 6, 7, and 8 address, respectively, the biological, psychological, and social-environmental aspects of adolescence. The goal is to provide a framework for a better understanding of this difficult yet exciting time of life.

Learning Objectives

This chapter will help prepare students to:

**EP 2.1.7,
2.1.7a,
2.1.7b**

LO 6-1 *Define adolescence*

LO 6-2 *Describe major physical changes during adolescence (including puberty, the growth spurt, the secular trend, and primary and secondary sex characteristics)*

LO 6-3 *Explain psychological reactions to physical changes*

LO 6-4 *Describe sexual activity in adolescence*

LO 6-5 *Assess sex education and empowerment*

LO 6-6 *Identify sexually transmitted diseases*

LO 6-7 *Explain major methods of contraception*

LO 6-1 Define Adolescence

EP 2.1.7

Adolescence is the transitional period between childhood and adulthood during which young people mature physically and sexually. The word is derived from the Latin verb *adolescere*, which means "to grow into maturity."

There is no precise time when adolescence begins or ends, although it usually extends from about age 11 or 12 to the late teens or early 20s. Adolescence should be differentiated from puberty, which is more specific. Adolescence might be considered a cultural concept that refers to a general time during life. *Puberty*, on the other hand, is a physical concept that refers to the specific time during which people mature sexually and become capable of reproduction. The word *puberty* is derived from a Latin word meaning "to grow hairy" (Nairne, 2014, p. 97).

Some societies have specific rites of passage or events to mark the transition from childhood into adulthood. For example, among the Mangaia of the South Pacific (Hyde & DeLamater, 2008; Marshall, 1980), when a boy reached the age of 12 or 13 years, he participated in a ceremony where a superincision was made on his penis. The cut was made along the entire length of the top of the penis. After the completion of this extremely painful ceremony, the boy ran out into the ocean or a stream to ease the pain. He then typically exclaimed, "Now I am really a man."

Our society has no such distinct entry point into adulthood. Although we might breathe a sigh of relief at not having such a painful custom, we're still left with the problem of the vague transitional period we call adolescence. There are no clear-cut guidelines for how adolescents are supposed to behave. On the one hand, they are children, but on the other hand, they are adults.

Some occurrences tend to contribute to becoming an adult. These include getting a driver's license, graduating from high school, graduating from college, and perhaps getting married. However, not all individuals do these things. Some young people drop out of high school, and many high school graduates don't go on to college. Substantial numbers of young people choose not to marry or to marry much later in life. Even people who do go through these rites do so with varying levels of maturity and ability to handle responsibility. At any rate, becoming an adult still remains a confusing concept.

The gradual, but major, physical changes do not help to clarify the issue. Adolescents must strive to cope with drastic changes in size and form, in addition to waves of new hormones sweeping through their bodies. Resulting emotions are often unexpected and difficult to control. Within this perspective of change and adjustment, we will look more closely at specific physical changes and at the effects of these changes on the developing personality.

LO 6-2 Describe Major Physical Changes During Adolescence

A range of physical changes occur during adolescence. These include puberty, a growth spurt, results of the secular trend, and the development of primary and secondary sex characteristics.

Puberty

Puberty is marked by the sudden enlargement of the reproductive organs and sexual genitalia, and the development of secondary sex characteristics (features that distinguish the genders but are not directly involved in reproduction). Most girls begin puberty at about age 12 or 13, whereas boys enter puberty a bit later by age 13 or 14 (Nairne, 2014). Girls tend to attain their full height by about age 16, whereas boys may continue to grow until age 18 to 20 (Sigelman & Rider, 2012).

The two-year age difference in beginning puberty causes more than its share of problems for adolescents. Girls tend to become interested in boys before boys begin noticing girls. One dating option for girls involves older boys of the middle or late teens. This can serve to substantially raise parental anxiety. An option for boys is to date girls who tower over them.

There is a wide age span for both boys and girls when puberty begins. Although in general, there is a two-year difference, substantial individual differences also must be taken into account. In other words, one boy may begin puberty four years earlier than another.

What causes the abrupt and extraordinary changes brought on by puberty? Acting as a catalyst for all of these changes is an increase in the production of hormones. *Hormones* are chemical substances secreted by the endocrine glands. Among other things, they stimulate growth of sexual organs and characteristics. Each hormone targets specific areas and stimulates growth. For example, testosterone directly affects growth of the penis, facial hair, areas in the brain, and even cartilage in the shoulder joints. In women, the uterus and vagina respond to the female hormones of estrogen and progesterone.

The Growth Spurt

The initial entrance into puberty is typically characterized by a sharp increase in height. During this spurt, boys and girls may grow between 2 and 5 inches. Before the growth spurt, boys tend to be 2 percent taller than girls. However, because girls start the spurt earlier, they tend to be taller, to weigh more, and to be stronger than boys during ages 11 to 13. By the time both sexes have completed the spurt, boys once again are usually larger than girls.

The adolescent growth spurt affects virtually the entire body, including most aspects of the skeletal and muscular structure. However, boys and girls grow differently during this period. Boys' shoulders get relatively wider, and their legs and forearms relatively longer, than those of girls. Girls, on the other hand, grow wider in the pelvic area and hips. This is to enhance childbearing capability. Girls also tend to develop a layer of fat over the abdomen, hips, and buttocks during puberty. This eventually will give a young woman a more shapely, rounded physique. However, the initial chubby appearance can cause the adolescent a substantial amount of emotional stress. Crash and starvation diets can create a physical health hazard during this period.

Adolescents tend to have unequal and disproportionate growth. Most adolescents have some features that look disproportionate. The head, hands, and feet reach adult size and form first, followed by the legs and arms. Finally, the body's trunk reaches its full size. A typical result of this unequal growth is motor awkwardness and clumsiness. Until the growth of bones and muscles stabilizes, and the brain adjusts to an essentially new body, awkward bursts of motion and misjudgments of muscular control will result.

The Secular Trend

People generally grow taller and bigger than they did a century ago. They also reach sexual maturity and their adult height faster than in the past. This tendency toward increasing size and earlier achievement of sexual maturity is referred to as the *secular trend*.

The trend apparently has occurred on a worldwide basis, especially in industrialized nations such as those of Western Europe and Japan. This suggests that an increased standard of living, along with better health care and nutrition, is related to the trend.

This secular trend seems to have reached its peak and stopped. A 14-year-old boy of today is approximately 5 inches taller than a boy of the same age in 1880.

Primary and Secondary Sex Characteristics

A major manifestation of puberty is the development of primary and secondary sex characteristics.

Primary sex characteristics are those directly related to the sex organs and reproduction. The key is that they have a direct role in reproduction. For females, these include development of the uterus, vagina, and ovaries. The ovaries are the major sex glands in a female, which both manufacture sex hormones and produce eggs that are ready for fertilization.

For males, primary sex characteristics include growth of the penis and development of the prostate gland and the testes. The prostate gland, which is located below the bladder, is responsible for a significant portion of the ejaculate or whitish alkaline substance that makes up semen, which carries the sperm. The testes are the male sex glands that both manufacture sex hormones and produce sperm.

We have already defined *secondary sex characteristics* to include those traits that distinguish the genders from each other but play no direct role in reproduction. These include menstruation, hair growth, development of breasts, growth of reproductive organs, voice changes, skin changes, and nocturnal emissions.

Proof of Puberty

One of the most notable indications that a female has achieved the climax of puberty is her first menstruation, also called *menarche. Menstruation* is the monthly discharge of blood and tissue debris from the uterus when fertilization has not taken place.

Girls today are experiencing first menstruation at earlier ages than girls growing up three or four decades ago. The average age for first menstruation, menarche (pronounced "men-ar-key") in the United States is now 12½ years. That means that many girls have their first period before the end of seventh grade, and many begin as early as fourth or fifth grade. It also means that many girls will at least be in the eighth grade before their first period, and some may be seniors in high school before they get a period. All of these situations are normal. (Greenberg, Bruess, & Oswalt, 2014, p. 417)

Note that frequently young females begin to menstruate before they begin to ovulate, so they might not be capable of becoming pregnant for two or more years after menarche (Hyde & DeLamater, 2014). During puberty, females also experience an increased blood supply to the *clitoris* (a small structure at the entrance to the vagina that's highly sensitive to stimulation and gives sexual pleasure), a thickening of the vaginal walls, and significant growth of the uterus, which doubles in size from the beginning of puberty to age 18 (Hyde & DeLamater, 2011).

A wide variation in the age for first menstruation is found from one female to another. A Peruvian girl of age 5 is the youngest mother ever recorded to have a healthy baby. This occurred in 1939. The baby was born by cesarean section. At the time, physicians found that the mother was mature sexually, and that she apparently had begun menstruation at the age of 1 month. The youngest parents known are an 8-year-old mother and 9-year-old father. This Chinese couple had a son in 1910 (Hyde, 1982). Spotlight 6.1 reviews some recent research on the differences in the age of menarche for various ethnic groups in the United States.

It is somewhat more difficult to establish that a boy has entered the full throes of puberty. In males, hormones cause the testes to increase in size and to begin producing sperm by age 14 on average (Rathus, Nevid, & Fichner-Rathus, 2014). Increased testosterone production also initiates a growth in penis size, first in thickness and then in length.

Hair Growth

Hair begins to grow in the pubic area during puberty. After a period of months and sometimes years, this hair changes in texture. It becomes curlier, coarser, and darker. About two years after the appearance of pubic hair, axillary hair begins to grow in the armpits. However, the growth of axillary hair varies so much from one person to another that in some people axillary hair appears before pubic hair. Boys' facial hair also begins to grow on the upper lip and gradually spreads to the chin and cheeks. Chest hair appears relatively late in adolescence.

Development of Breasts

Breast development is usually one of the first signs of sexual maturity in girls. The nipples and areola, the darkened areas surrounding the nipples, enlarge. Breasts initially tend to be cone-shaped and eventually assume a more rounded appearance.

Some women in our culture tend to be preoccupied with breast size and feel that breasts come in one of two sizes—too small or too large. However, all breasts are functionally equipped with 15 to 20 clusters of mammary or milk-producing glands. Each gland has an individual opening to the nipple or tip of the breast into which the milk ducts open. The glands themselves are surrounded by various amounts of fatty and fibrous tissue. The nipples are also richly supplied with sensitive nerve endings, which are important in erotic stimulation. There is no indication that breast size is related to a woman's ability to experience pleasurable sensation (Masters, Johnson, & Kolodny, 1995).

✳ SPOTLIGHT ON DIVERSITY 6.1

Diversity and Menarche

EP 2.1.4c

Some research has found differences in the age of menarche among white Americans, African Americans, and Hispanic Americans (Chumlea et al., 2003). The sample included 2,500 girls aged 8 to 20. African Americans began menstruating significantly earlier than the other two groups in the study. Hispanic girls also began menstruating earlier than white girls, but not as early as African American girls. Between ages 13½ and 14, a total of 90 percent of girls in all three groups had begun menarche.

Some adolescent boys also undergo temporary breast development. Although this may cause them some anxiety concerning their masculinity, this enlargement is not abnormal. Hyde and DeLamater (2014) indicate that this occurs in approximately 80 percent of boys in puberty. The probable cause is small amounts of female sex hormones produced by the testes. The condition usually disappears within about a year.

Voice Changes

Boys undergo a noticeable lowering in the tone of their voices, usually fairly late in puberty. The process involves a significant enlargement of the larynx or Adam's apple and a doubling in the length of the vocal cords. Many times it takes two years or more for boys to gain control over their new voices.

Girls also experience a slight voice change during adolescence, although it's not nearly as extreme as the change undergone in boys. Girls' voices achieve a less high-pitched, more mature tone due to a slight growth of the larynx.

Skin Changes

Adolescence brings about increased activity of the sebaceous glands, which manufacture oils for the skin. Skin pores also become coarser and increase in size during adolescence. The result is frequently a rapid production of blackheads and pimples, commonly referred to as acne, on the face and sometimes on the back. Unfortunately, a poor complexion is considered unappealing in many cultures (Hyde & DeLamater, 2014). Acne adds to the stress of adolescence. It tends to make young people feel even more self-conscious about their bodies and physical appearance.

Nocturnal Emissions

Most males have nocturnal emissions at one time or another (Yarber & Sayad, 2013). A nocturnal emission, also referred to as a wet dream, is the ejaculation or emission of semen while a male is asleep. The highest frequency of approximately once a month tends to occur during the late teens. The number then tapers off during the 20s, and finally stops after age 30.

Nocturnal emissions are a natural means of relieving sexual tension. Often, but not always, they are accompanied by sexual dreams. It's important that adolescents understand that this is a normal occurrence and that there's nothing physically or mentally wrong with them.

Females also have orgasms during sleep (Yarber & Sayad, 2013). However, these apparently don't occur as frequently or as early as males' nocturnal emissions.

LO 6-3 Explain Psychological Reactions to Physical Changes

One thing that marks adolescence is self-criticism. Physical imperfections are sought out, emphasized, and dwelled on. It may be a large lump on a nose. Or it may be an awesome derriere. Or it may even be a dreadful terror of braces locking unromantically during a goodnight kiss. Adolescents seek to conform to their peers. Any aspect that remains imperfect or too noticeable becomes the object of criticism. Perhaps it's because the age is filled with change and mandatory adjustment to that change that adolescents strive to conform. Perhaps before an individual personality can develop, a person needs some predictability and security.

A substantial amount of research focuses on adolescents' perceptions of themselves. Special areas of intense interest include body image, self-concept, weight level, weight worries, and eating disorders.

Body Image and Self-Concept

Perception of one's body image and attractiveness is related to adolescents' level of self-esteem, especially for girls (Bearman, Presnall, Martinez, & Vaughn, 2006; Moore & Rosenthal, 2006; Newman & Newman, 2012). People who consider themselves attractive tend to be more self-confident and satisfied with themselves.

Girls generally tend to be more critical of and dissatisfied with their physical appearance than are boys (Newman & Newman, 2012). This is especially true concerning weight. One national survey of adolescents explored their thoughts about weight control; 85 percent of respondents thought that girls emphasized weight control, but only 30 percent thought that boys did (Newman & Newman, 2009). This is probably due to the extreme importance placed on females' appearance in this culture. For example, a girl might think, "My thighs are too fat, and my butt sticks out too much. I'd really like to fit into size 7 jeans, but can't get under a size 9. Can girls my age have cellulite?" Chapter 8 discusses eating disorders, which are problems directly related to weight control and self-perception.

Although before puberty levels of depression among girls and boys are similar, during adolescence girls are more likely to experience depression; this is true for white, African American, and Hispanic adolescents (Leadbeater, Kuperminc, Blatt, & Hertzog, 1999; Newman & Newman, 2012). This may be due to at least four factors (Newman & Newman, 2012). First, the estrogen cycle is linked to emotional variations and low self-esteem. Second, girls tend to criticize their appearance and weight when they reach puberty. This may set the stage for long-term displeasure with themselves, eventually resulting in depression. Third, girls tend to blame themselves for their problems and issues. They are more introspectively self-critical. Boys, on the other hand, tend to blame others and things outside of themselves as causes for their problems. Fourth, girls tend to be more perceptive of and upset by experiences their friends, family, and others are having. Such sensitivity and deep concern may lead to depression.

Ethical Questions 6.1

EP 2.1.2 *Is it right or fair to place so much importance on external physical appearance, especially when this emphasis concerns weight? Is it equitable that the burden of weight control rests more heavily on women than on men? How have these concerns about weight and physical appearance affected you and aspects of your own biological, psychological, and social development?*

Early and Late Maturation in Boys

Rathus (2014b) summarizes the research on early- and late-maturing boys:

> *Research findings about boys who mature early are mixed, but most of the evidence suggests that the effects of early maturation are generally positive (Teunissen et al., 2011). Late-maturing boys may feel conspicuous because they are among the last of their peers to lose their childhood appearance….*

> *Early-maturing boys tend to be more popular than their late-maturing peers and more likely to be leaders in school (Graber et al., 2004; Windle et al., 2008). Early-maturing boys in general are also more poised, relaxed, and good-natured. Their edge in sports and the admiration of their peers heighten their sense of self-worth….*

> *On the negative side, early maturation is associated with greater risks of aggression and delinquency (Lynn et al., 2007) as well as abuse of alcohol and other drugs (Costello et al., 2007; Engels, 2009). (p. 467)*

What are the reasons for such negative effects of early maturation in boys? Possibly, early-maturing males may not yet have gained the emotional and intellectual maturity that ongoing development and simple life experience can provide them. Because such boys look older and more mature, other people might attribute to them greater decision-making skills, perceptiveness, and leadership ability than they actually possess (Ge, Conger, & Elder, 2001; Newman & Newman, 2012). They might be thrown into situations they can't handle because they're not yet ready. Because they look older, they might get involved with older peers and be exposed to situations they're emotionally and intellectually unable to handle. They might be unprepared to make responsible decisions regarding involvement in antisocial behavior.

In comparison to early-maturing boys, prior studies viewed boys who matured late as feeling inferior because of their smaller size and younger appearance. This, in turn, led to lower levels of self-esteem and more adjustment problems (Sigelman & Rider, 2012). It is still thought that late-maturing boys perceive themselves more negatively and feel less popular than their early-maturing counterparts (Santrock, 2008). Late-maturing boys may be denied the respect and attention given to more mature-looking boys.

However, one earlier study found that when boys who matured late reached their 30s, they established a stronger and more robust sense of identity than did those in other maturation groups (Peskin, 1967). Perhaps, dealing with earlier stress made late maturers more resilient and, as a result, stronger. Possibly having more time to mature gave them more opportunities to focus on exploring educational and career options. Or maybe they tended to focus on achievement and personality development instead of relying on their advanced physical prowess. What comes to mind is a character in a movie who was an unpopular, "geeky nerd" in high school. However, at his 20-year high school reunion, he was admired by all because he had invented and patented a number of high-tech innovations, thus becoming a multimillionaire.

**EP 2.1.1e,
2.1.3a,
2.1.9a**

By adulthood, the differences between early and late maturers become much less clear (Kail & Cavanaugh, 2014; Santrock, 2012b). So many other elements are involved in a person's development, including those that are cognitive and social, that it is difficult to predict the effects of any one variable, such as maturation rate. This illustrates an area where practitioners should continue to review and evaluate the research in a pattern of career-long learning in order to understand the dynamics involved in and effecting adolescence.

Early and Late Maturation in Girls

A number of studies report that early-maturing girls are disadvantaged in various areas. Santrock (2012a) explains:

> In recent years, an increasing number of researchers have found that early maturation increases girls' vulnerability to a number of problems … Early-maturing girls are more likely to smoke, drink, be depressed, have an eating disorder, engage in delinquency, struggle for earlier independence from their parents, and have older friends; and their bodies are likely to elicit responses from males that lead to earlier dating and earlier sexual experiences…. And early-maturing girls are less likely to graduate from high school and more likely to cohabit and marry earlier. (p. 61)

Maybe, as with early-maturing boys, their lack of life experience, level of cognitive development, and naivete put them at risk of problems. They may have to make "adult" choices before they are ready to accept the consequences of behavior or even acknowledge such consequences.

Sigelman and Rider (2012) explain the situation for late-maturing girls:

> Late-maturing girls (like late-maturing boys) may experience some anxiety as they wait to mature, but they do not seem to be as disadvantaged as late-maturing boys. Indeed, whereas later-developing boys tend to perform poorly on school achievement tests, later-developing girls outperform other students (Dubas, Graber, & Petersen, 1991). Perhaps late-developing girls focus on academic skills when other girls have shifted some of their focus to extracurricular activities. (p. 159)

The differences between early- and late-maturing girls in adulthood are complex and tentative (Sigelman & Rider, 2012). As with boys, the picture is much more complicated than simply focusing on the life results caused by one specific variable, such as early maturation.

Brain Development During Adolescence

An adolescent's brain also undergoes physical changes in response to new hormonal production. Such changes can result in behavioral and emotional consequences. Consider that

> the hormonal changes that characterize puberty also influence brain function. The adrenal glands—located near the kidneys—release testosterone-like hormones that attach themselves to receptor sites throughout the brain and directly influence the neurotransmitters serotonin and dopamine, which play an important role in regulating mood and excitability (Blakemore & Choudhury, 2006; Spear, 2003[b]). Two results of this hormone-induced chain of events are that adolescents' emotions easily reach a flash point, and they are now more motivated to seek out intense experiences that will thrill, scare, and generally excite them (Paus, 2005; Steinberg, [2006]…). Unfortunately, the brain regions that inhibit risky, impulsive behavior are still maturing, so there often is an insufficient internal brake on teenagers' sensation-seeking desires and roller-coaster emotions (Steinberg, 2004). Where in the brain does this internal brake reside? The primary area is the prefrontal lobes of the cerebral cortex, which are responsible for complicated cognitive activities, such as planning, decision making, [and] goal setting…. However, while the adolescent brain is undergoing hormonal assault, the prefrontal cortex is not quite ready to rein in or redirect the resulting emotions and thrill-seeking desires. Precisely at this time, the prefrontal cortex is experiencing a new phase of brain cell elimination and rewiring based on the use-it-or-lose-it principle. This pruning of unnecessary neuronal connections

eventually results in much more efficient and more focused information-processing, and a prefrontal cortex that can serve as a reliable internal brake on runaway emotions and impulsive actions. In the meantime, developmental psychologists recommend that parents serve as the external brake while the adolescent brain is in this new phase of development. (Bjorklund & Blasi, 2012; Franzoi, 2008, p. 111)

During adolescence, boys experience greater changes in their brains than girls (Goldstein et al., 2001; Segovia et al., 2006). This "may account for the increased aggressiveness and irritability often associated with adolescence" (Martin & Fabes, 2009, p. 448).

Adolescent Health, and Substance Use and Abuse

During any time of life, including adolescence, lifestyle directly impacts health and the ability to function effectively. Discussed here is the use of mind-altering drugs, alcohol, and tobacco.

Use of Mind-Altering Substances

Berk (2012b) summarizes the current situation:

Teenage alcohol and drug use is pervasive in industrialized nations. According to the most recent, nationally representative survey of U.S. high school students, by tenth grade, 33 percent of U.S. young people have tried smoking, 59 percent drinking and 38 percent at least one illegal drug (usually marijuana). At the end of high school, 15 percent smoke cigarettes regularly, and 16 percent have engaged in heavy drinking during the past month. About 24 percent have tried at least one highly addictive and toxic substance, such as amphetamines, cocaine, phencyclidine (PCP), Ecstasy (MDMA), inhalants, heroin, sedatives (including barbiturates), or OxyContin (a narcotic painkiller) (Johnston et al., 2010).

These figures represent a substantial decline since the mid-1990s, probably resulting from greater parent, school, and media focus on the hazards of drug taking. But use of some substances—marijuana, inhalants, sedatives, and Oxy-Contin—has risen slightly in recent years (Johnson et al., 2010). Other drugs, such as LSD, PCP, and Ecstasy, have made a comeback as adolescents' knowledge of their risks faded. (p. 560)

Use of Alcohol

We have established that many young people drink alcohol. Small amounts of alcohol may have a calming effect. However, immediate dangers from alcohol consumption include potential death when used with other drugs and accidents while driving. A scary finding of recent research is that extensive

Tomas Rodriguez/Fancy/Corbis

Use of mind-altering substances by adolescents can have devastating effects.

alcohol use as a teenager can cause impairment of mental functioning later on in life (Berk, 2012b; Newman & Newman, 2012).

Variables putting adolescents at risk for alcohol and other substance abuse can be clustered into four categories: environmental factors, peer influences, family influences, and personal characteristics (McWhirter, McWhirter, McWhirter, & McWhirter, 2012). *Environmental* factors including poverty, inadequate education, high unemployment, lack of positive role models, and absence of opportunity can place pressure on young people to escape through mind-altering substances. *Peer pressure* is a second major influence (Lewis, Neighbors, Lindgren, Buckingham, & Hoang, 2010). If "everybody's doing it," it may be more tempting. *Parental* factors related to drug use include lack of involvement with children and parents' failure to monitor adequately their children's behavior (Dishion, Kavanagh, Schneiger, Nelson, & Kaufman, 2002). If parents appear not to care or don't provide support or direction, it's easier for adolescents to succumb to temptation. Another parental factor is the use of alcohol and other substances by the parents themselves. Parents can provide role models for abuse. *Personal characteristics* of adolescents that increase risk of alcohol and other substance abuse include poor coping skills in response to the powerful emotional pain often experienced in adolescence, relationship and achievement problems at school, and a desire for excitement and self-gratification.

McWhirter, McWhirter, McWhirter, and McWhirter (2013) describe a case scenario portraying the reflections of a counselor who worked with one at-risk adolescent.

One of us worked with a 13-year-old boy named Joe for two months after Joe's mother requested that he receive counseling. She and her husband, Joe's stepfather, were concerned about his poor school performance, his acting out, his group of "delinquent" friends, and his alternately hostile and completely withdrawn behavior at home.

Joe's stepfather was a machine operator who provided severe yet inconsistent discipline. Joe disliked his stepfather, and he reported that the dislike was mutual. He described his mother as "nicer," but complained that she did not permit him to do what he wanted. His mother was primarily a *homemaker, but occasionally she did temporary office work. She frequently placated her husband so that he would not get angry with Joe. She felt Joe needed to change, however, and believed that counseling might "fix" him. Joe's parents refused to come in for counseling as a family because Joe was the problem.*

Joe spent a great deal of time with his friends both during and after school. He reported smoking marijuana and cigarettes fairly regularly. Shortly after our first counseling session, he was arrested for possession of drug paraphernalia. His parents refused to let him see any of his friends after the arrest.

Joe's school performance and effort were poor. Joe probably had a mild learning disability, but a recent psycho-educational evaluation had been inconclusive. Joe's primary problem at school was his acting out. Unfortunately, when Joe got into trouble with a teacher, he was inadvertently rewarded for his disruption. He could effectively avoid the schoolwork that he found so difficult and distasteful by sitting in the assistant principal's office "listening to stupid stories." Joe was doing so poorly at school and misbehaving with such frequency that his stepfather threatened to send him to a strict boarding school unless his behavior improved. Joe said that would be fine with him because he had heard that the work was easier there. His stepfather's threat to cut his hair short was the only consequence he seemed concerned about.

Joe primarily used marijuana, which did not change during the two months he was in counseling. We don't know whether Joe experimented with more powerful substances because he showed a great deal of resistance to coming to counseling and seemed very disinterested in changing himself, although he did want his stepfather to move out. Joe was a frustrated and angry adolescent who resented his parents and received little direction or consistent structure from them. He was unsure of their expectations, hated school, felt isolated from his friends, and could see no solution to his problems. He directed his anxiety and poor self-esteem inward and acted out by skipping school, talking back to his teachers, or roaming the streets with his friends. (pp. 181–182)

Joe's situation resembles that of many young people at risk for alcohol and other substance abuse. He received little support and no steady, coherent discipline from his parents. He was in constant conflict with his stepfather, whom he disliked intensely. He experienced serious difficulties in school and was rapidly falling behind. It was easy to turn to peers who probably experienced similar problems. Peer pressure then could reinforce problem behaviors and his substance abuse. Joe felt abused, isolated, and neglected by parents and school. He avoided responsibility for his behavior by escaping through drugs. His parents failed to see problems from a family system perspective and refused to participate in treatment. They eventually removed Joe from counseling. What do you think happened to him?

• • • • / Ethical Questions 6.2

EP 2.1.2

To what extent should efforts be made to make Joe a productive member of society? Whose responsibility is it to help Joe? His parents'? The community's? His school's? To what extent is a 13-year-old like Joe responsible for improving his own behavior?

Use of Tobacco

Subject to extreme peer pressure, adolescents find it easy to begin smoking, but very hard to quit. As with alcohol and other substance use, the positive news is that adolescent cigarette smoking, although still a serious problem, continues to be on the decline after peaking in 1996 and 1997 (Johnston, O'Malley, Bachman, & Schulenberg, 2012). Santrock (2012a) reports:

> *Following peak use in 1996, smoking rates for U.S. eighth-graders have fallen by 50 percent. In 2010, the percentages of adolescents who said they smoked cigarettes in the last 30 days were 19 percent (twelfth grade), 14 percent (tenth grade), and 7 percent (eighth grade). (p. 439)*

Smoking is related to heart disease. Cigarette smoke contains nicotine, which acts as a stimulant. As nicotine enters the lungs, it is quickly absorbed by the small blood vessels in the lungs and immediately transported throughout the body. As a stimulant, it causes both an increased heart rate and increased blood pressure. Over time, the heart will be overworked and eventually be damaged.

Lung cancer is another possible consequence of smoking. Cigarette tars and other particles in the smoke gradually accumulate in the tubes and air sacs of the lungs. This causes a gradual change in the lung tissue's normal cells. Eventually these affected cells may reproduce new cells that are different from the original ones. The new, cancerous cells produce more cancerous cells that eventually kill off the normal cell tissue. The result is the growth of a malignant tumor that invades the lung and spreads to other parts of the body.

Risk factors for adolescents becoming addicted to smoking include lack of parental attention and support, having friends who smoke, and disinterest in education and school (Tucker, Ellickson, & Klein, 2003).

Significant Issues and Life Events

Certain significant experiences and life events tend to characterize adolescence and young adulthood. Some issues are of special concern to people in this age group. Several of these issues have been selected for discussion here. They were chosen on the basis of their relevance to and impact on the physical well-being of young people. Because adolescence is a period of sexual development, sexuality will be emphasized. The issues include sexual activity in adolescence, unplanned pregnancy, teenage fatherhood, motivation for pregnancy, sex education, sexually transmitted infections, and contraception. Highlight 6.1 discusses young people's experience with masturbation.

LO 6-4 Describe Sexual Activity in Adolescence

A major trend characterizing adolescent sexual activity from the 1950s to the 1970s was a dramatic increase in teenagers having intercourse (Crooks & Baur, 2014). This was more true for boys than girls. Today, 25 percent of males and 26 percent of females have had sexual intercourse by age 15; 69 percent of males and 77 percent of females have had sexual intercourse by age 19 (Kinsey Institute, 2010).

HIGHLIGHT 6.1

Masturbation

Masturbation refers to self-stimulation of the genitals that causes sexual arousal. It appears that masturbation begins fairly early. By the time they reach age 19, the end of adolescence, 86 percent of all males and about two-thirds of all females have masturbated (Crooks & Baur, 2014). Some data indicate that adolescents are beginning to masturbate earlier than they have in the past (Bancroft, Herbenick, & Reynolds, 2003; Hyde & DeLamater, 2014). However, African American and Latino youths are less likely to masturbate than are white teens (Laumann, Gagnon, Michael, & Michaels, 1994; Yarber & Sayad, 2013).

Boys are more likely to masturbate than girls (Crooks & Baur, 2014; Laumann et al., 1994; Yarber & Sayad, 2013). Such gender differences may be related to sex roles and sexual expectations of men and women. Our society expects men to be sexual—and sexual athletes at that. Additionally, it may be possible that many women take longer to become comfortable with their own sexuality.

Greenberg et al. (2014) describe the masturbation process:

Males masturbate by stroking the shaft of the penis, often stimulated by erotic literature, films, or the Internet. Some men use gadgets to assist them. Artificial vaginas, furlike clothes, inflatable dolls, and other devices have been reported as masturbatory aids by some men.

Women masturbate by rubbing the vulva [the female's external genitals]—in particular, the clitoris—or inserting an object (a finger, a dildo, a banana, or a similarly shaped object) into the vagina. There are, of course, many variations on this theme, and the use of a vibrator to stimulate the vulva, cream to decrease friction on the area rubbed, pillows or other soft objects to rub the genitals against, and squeezing together of the thighs are all common adjuncts to the standard masturbatory techniques. (pp. 505–506)

Kelly (2008) describes how adolescents talk about masturbation:

Adolescent boys have tended to discuss masturbation among themselves—often in a joking way—more than adolescent girls. Consequently, more slang terms have evolved to describe male masturbation (jerk off, jack off, whack off, beat off, beat the meat) than for female masturbation (rubbing off, rolling the pill, fingering). (p. 153)

Other terms for female masturbation include "flick your Bic" and "itch the ditch." Additional terms for male masturbation are "bop your bologna," "wax the cucumber," "burp the worm," "play the piccolo solo," "choke the chicken," and "tickle the pickle."

It's important to address the issue of masturbation. As we've already established, it is very common among adolescents. However, it is also looked down on. The numerous slang terms used to describe it are very uncomplimentary. Perhaps the traditional negative attitude about masturbation can best be expressed by the statements of H. R. Stout in the 1885 edition of *Our Family Physician:*

When the evil has been pursued for several years, there will be an irritable condition of the system; sudden flushes of heat over the face; the countenance becomes pale and clammy; the eyes have a dull, sheepish look; the hair becomes dry and split at the ends; sometimes there is pain over the region of the heart; shortness of breath; palpitation of the heart (symptoms of dyspepsia show themselves); the sleep is disturbed; there is constipation; cough; irritation of the throat; finally the whole man becomes a wreck, physically, morally, and mentally. (p. 333)

After such a tirade, it would be a wonder if a person would dare to masturbate. This presents quite a contradiction and a source of confusion for adolescents. They are actually participating in the activity of masturbation. Yet there is some tendency for it to be considered an unappealing and even disgusting behavior. Although attitudes are more positive than they have been historically, negative feelings can include anxiety, defensiveness, embarrassment, and guilt (Greenberg et al., 2014; Hyde & DeLamater, 2014).

Adolescents need to understand that masturbation is not abnormal or harmful. In a period of their lives when they are coping with many physical changes and new life situations, they do not need to be burdened with unnecessary confusion and even guilt. Masturbation is a normal means of relieving sexual tension and other stress, allowing a means of self-discovery, learning to control sexual needs and impulses, and fighting isolation and loneliness. Masturbation is even a prescribed means of treatment for sexual dysfunction. Women with orgasmic dysfunctions (i.e., the inability to experience orgasms) are counseled to use masturbation. This helps them overcome anxiety and understand their sexual responses. This information can later be transferred to a partner.

Another trend from the 1950s to 1970s was having sexual intercourse at younger and younger ages across many ethnic groups (Crooks & Baur, 2014). Today, the average age for first intercourse for females is 16.9 and for males 17.4 (Kinsey Institute, 2010).

There are a range of reasons why adolescents have sexual intercourse (Rathus et al., 2014).

Racial and Other Differences in Adolescent Sexual Activity

EP 2.1.4c

In the United States, significantly different patterns of adolescent sexual intercourse exist among various racial groups. For example, African American teenagers are more likely to have sexual intercourse than are their white and Hispanic counterparts (Carroll, 2013; Crooks & Baur, 2014). The average age for African American youths to have sexual intercourse is 15.8, for whites 16.6, for Hispanics 17, and for Asian Americans 18.1 (Kinsey Institute, 2010).

Differences in rates of sexual activity may relate more to poverty than to race or ethnicity (Crooks & Baur, 2014).

African American and Hispanic youth often live in less affluent environments than their white counterparts. It's been found that African American adolescents raised in affluent homes are more likely to abstain from sexual relationships than those raised in poorer environments (Crooks & Baur, 2014; Kissinger, Trim, Williams, Mielke, Koporc, & Brosn, 1997; Murry, 1996). Other variables associated with earlier intercourse include lack of closeness with parents and lack of parental supervision and involvement (Crooks & Baur, 2014; Hyde & DeLamater, 2014; Rathus et al., 2014; Welch, 2011).

Many adolescents, especially young men, are responding to the surge of hormones their bodies are experiencing. Many men and women say they have intercourse because they're curious about it or because they're simply ready for it. Showing love and affection is yet another reason for sexual intercourse.

Spotlight 6.2 discusses some racial and other differences in adolescent sexual activity.

Ethical Questions 6.3

At what age do people have the right to have sexual intercourse? What are the reasons for your answer?

EP 2.1.2

Unplanned Pregnancy in Adolescence

The United States has one of the highest, if not the highest, rates of teenage pregnancy among Western industrialized nations (Akers, Holland, & Bost, 2011; Crooks & Baur, 2014). For example, "the U.S. birth rate for female teens was 42.5 births per 1,000" while in Canada it was 13, Germany 10, and Italy 7 per 1,000 (Carroll, 2013, p. 194). In one year, 750,000 teenagers, or about 7 percent of young women under age 20, become pregnant (Guttmacher Institute, 2013d). Most of these pregnancies are

unintended (Downs, Moore, & McFadden, 2009; Guttmacher Institute, 2013d). About 26 percent of all pregnancies for young women age 15 to 19 are terminated by abortion; about 59 percent end in live births (with the remaining pregnancies resulting in miscarriages) (Guttmacher Institute, 2013d).

About 5 percent of children born to teenage mothers are placed for adoption (Downs et al., 2009). The birth rate for teens has been declining almost continuously over the last 20 years, although, as we have established, it remains higher than that of most other developed nations (Office of Adolescent Health, 2013). Its decline probably is a result of such factors as more effective and varied types of contraception and enhanced caution in avoiding sexually transmitted infections, especially HIV (Crosson-Tower, 2009, 2013). About 80 percent of teen mothers are single (Pfeiffer, 2009).

As few babies are placed for formal adoption, the vast majority of babies born to single teens remain at home with their young mothers. This places these young women in a very different situation than that of most of their peers. Adolescence and young adulthood are the usual time of life for meeting and socializing with friends, dating, possibly selecting a mate, obtaining an education, and making a career choice. The additional responsibility of motherhood poses serious restrictions on the amount of freedom and time available to do these other things. Additionally, such young women are most often ill-prepared for motherhood. They are usually in the midst of establishing their own identities and learning to care for themselves.

Teen pregnancy has a number of other strikingly negative consequences. First, such pregnancies are marked by increased physical risks, both to the child and to the mother (Crooks & Baur, 2014; Klein and the Committee on Adolescence, 2005). Such problems include prolonged labor, anemia, toxemia, hemorrhaging, miscarriage, and, in the extreme, the pregnant teen's death. The babies have a much greater chance either of being premature or of having a lower-than-normal birth weight (March of Dimes Foundation, 2009). A related finding concerning maternal and child health is that many teenage mothers are poverty-stricken and receive very little prenatal health care (Hyde & DeLamater, 2014; Yarber & Sayad, 2013). This contributes to the health risks of the mothers and their babies.

Other, longer-term research indicates that negative effects continue long after the baby's birth. Teen mothers are much less likely to finish high school than their peers who are not mothers (Downs et al., 2009). Adolescent mothers are often poor and dependent on social services (Crooks & Baur, 2014; Klein and the Committee on Adolescence, 2005). Later in life, they are more likely than their peers without children to be unemployed or underemployed (Crooks & Baur, 2014). Teen mothers also may have poorer parenting skills (Crooks & Baur, 2011; Klein and the Committee on Adolescence, 2005). Thus, the added stress and responsibility of motherhood tend to take a toll on teen mothers. Raising a child demands time, energy, and attention. Time taken to care for a baby must be subtracted from the time available for school and recreational activities. There are potentially serious impacts on the mental health and daily functioning of young mothers.

The children themselves are more likely not only to have a low birth weight, but also a higher mortality rate (March of Dimes Foundation, 2009). Long-term studies also reveal negative effects on the children of teen mothers. As these children mature, they tend to have more emotional, intellectual, and physical problems than do their counterparts born to adult mothers (Crooks & Baur, 2011; Downs et al., 2009; Rathus, Nevid, & Fichner-Rathus, 2011).

The consequences of teenage parenthood are emphasized here to provide a realistic perspective on teen pregnancy. Teenagers need to be at least intellectually aware of the impacts of motherhood. They need this information in order to make more realistic decisions for themselves concerning their sexual activity and their use of contraception.

The other reason to focus on the consequences of teenage pregnancy concerns helping young mothers who have already had their babies. Social workers need to understand the problems of teenage parenthood. This is needed to help young mothers realistically appraise their situations, make decisions about what to do for themselves, and get involved with the supportive services they need.

On a more positive note, Klein and the Committee on Adolescence (2005) report:

> Research suggests that long-term negative social outcomes are not inevitable. Several long-term follow-up studies indicate that two decades after giving birth, most former adolescent mothers are not welfare-dependent; many have completed high school, have secured regular employment, and do not have large families. Comprehensive adolescent pregnancy programs seem to contribute to good outcomes, as do home-visitation programs designed to promote good child health outcomes. (p. 6)

Teenage Fathers

Variables making a person more likely to become a teen father include living in an inner city, doing poorly in school, being poor, and being involved in delinquent acts (Klein and the Committee on Adolescence, 2005; Yarber & Sayad, 2013). Yarber and Sayad (2013) comment on the situation facing adolescent fathers:

> Adolescent fathers typically remain physically or psychologically involved throughout the pregnancy and for at least some time after the birth. It is usually difficult for teenage fathers to contribute much to the support of their children, although most express the intention of doing so during the pregnancy. Most have a lower income, less education, and more children than men who postpone having children until age 20 or older. They may feel overwhelmed by the responsibility and may doubt their ability to be good providers. Though many teenage fathers are the sons of absent fathers, most do want to learn to be fathers. Teen fathers are a seriously neglected group who face many hardships. Policies and interventions directed at reducing teen fatherhood will have to take into consideration the many factors that influence it and focus efforts throughout the life cycle. (pp. 180–181)

Highlight 6.2 illustrates the potential effects of teenage fatherhood.

HIGHLIGHT 6.2

Portrait of a Single Father

Gary didn't know what to do. Linda had just ruined his day and probably his life. She had just told him that she was pregnant. How could this happen? What could he do?

Gary, a 17-year-old high school sophomore, had never done very well in school and had even flunked sixth grade once. Ever since then, he'd been taking special ed classes and was just barely squeaking by.

He had always considered himself a freak. He liked to do a lot of drugs—that is, whenever he had the money to get them. He also liked to listen to booming hip-hop and was intimately familiar with radio station WROK's top-10 hits. His uniform included well-patched blue jeans, construction-worker boots, and 18-inch-long, somewhat scraggly, greasy hair.

Beneath this exterior, Gary was an extremely sensitive person. He really cared about other people, although sometimes he had trouble showing it. This thing about Linda and a baby had really shaken him up. He really loved Linda. In fact, she was the best thing that had ever happened to him. She actually cared about him. It seemed like nobody had ever done that before. Gary really didn't have much self-confidence. The fact that Linda cared simply amazed him.

Gary lived in Chicago with his mother and younger sister, Hillary, age 11. He cared about Hillary, but they really didn't have much in common. There was too much of an age difference. Sometimes they stuck up for each other, though, when their mother went out with some new boyfriend and came home drunk. That happened pretty often. His mother was really something else. It seemed like she loved him, but she had always had a horrible problem accepting responsibility. A lot of times he felt like he had to take care of her, instead of vice versa. No, she wasn't one to depend on much.

Another problem was that they were dirt poor. He could never remember having a lot of things. For years he had wanted to learn how to play the guitar. He picked one up two years ago at a sleazy neighborhood auction, but it never really sounded like much. The other problem, of course, was that he felt he had absolutely no talent. He often thought the guitar looked good, though, sitting on an old peach crate in his basement room, his place of retreat.

Sometimes Gary thought about his father out in Utah. Although he had only seen him once in the last 10 years, he talked to him sometimes on the phone on holidays. His big dream was to go out and live with his dad and his dad's new family. Gary liked nature and camping. He thought that Utah would be the perfect place to go to and get away. In his more somber moments, he realized this was only a dream. His dad was pleasant enough on the phone, but he knew he really didn't care. It was fun to think about sometimes though. Sometimes when he got a better batch of drugs, he'd just sit in his room and think. He dreamed of all the wonderful things he'd do in Utah. That's what it was, though, just a dream.

Gary dreamed a lot. He didn't have much hope for the future. He thought that was pretty hopeless. One of his teachers asked him once if he ever thought about going to college. College, hah! How could he ever afford to go to college? He couldn't even afford a Super Big Kmart guitar. The other problem was how poorly he always did in school. He stopped really studying years ago. Now he was so far behind he knew he'd never catch up. He didn't like to think much about the future. There was no future in it.

But now Gary's problem was Linda—Linda and the baby. It's funny how he already thought of it as a baby even though it wasn't born yet. He liked the thought of having something that was really his. He liked Linda, too, and he didn't want to lose her. She was crying when she told him she was pregnant. He bet she'd like it if they lived together, or maybe even got married. Then he could move out of his mother's apartment. He could be free and on his own. He could drop out of school. School wasn't much anyhow. Maybe he could get that second-shift job slinging burgers at the local hamburger shack. That wouldn't be too bad. He could see his friends there. They could have a good time.

Yeah, that's what he'd do. He'd do a good thing for once in his life. He'd marry Linda and be a father. Maybe everything would be all right then. Maybe they'd all live happily ever after.

Epilogue

Gary and Linda did get married 10 months later. By then, Linda had given birth to a 6-pound, 8-ounce baby boy whom they named Billy. The problem was that things really didn't get any better. They didn't change much at all. Gary was still poor. Now, however, he was poor but with adult responsibilities. He still couldn't afford a guitar. He had to go to work at the hamburger shack every day at 5:00 p.m. just like he used to have to go to school every morning. There wasn't much money for him and Linda to have any fun with. As a matter of fact, there wasn't much money to do anything much at all. Their small apartment was pretty cramped. Sometimes the baby's crying drove him almost crazy. He and Linda weren't doing too well either. When they weren't fighting, they weren't talking. Things hadn't changed much at all; he still didn't have much hope for the future.

Commentary

This case example isn't meant to portray the thoughts of a typical teenage father. For example, Gary was very poor. In reality, teenage parents originate in all socioeconomic levels.

(continued)

HIGHLIGHT 6.2 (continued)

However, this example is intended to illustrate the lack of experience and information adolescents often have available to them. Without information, it's difficult to make insightful, well-founded decisions. A major job of a social worker is to help young people in a situation like this rationally think through the alternatives available to them. Potential services need to be talked about, and plans need to be made. Young people often need both support and suggestions regarding how to proceed. They need to examine their expectations about the future and make certain that they're being realistic.

Why Do Teens Get Pregnant?

An adolescent who is sexually active has a 90 percent chance of becoming pregnant in one year of unprotected intercourse (Guttmacher Institute, 2011). Adolescents often do not use contraception conscientiously and frequently don't use it at all (Crooks & Baur, 2014; Rathus et al., 2014). Many adolescents fail to use contraception the first few times they have sex (Crooks & Baur, 2014; Guttmacher Institute, 2011). This is especially true for younger adolescents (Rathus et al., 2014). Note that contraceptive use by adolescents has improved over the past decades. In 1985, only 56 percent of adolescents used contraception during their first sexual intercourse experience; this rose to 76 percent in 2000 to 2004, and to 84 percent in 2005 to 2008 (Guttmacher Institute, 2011). From 2006 to 2010, 86 percent of female teens and 93 percent of males indicated they used some type of contraceptive method the last time they had sex (Guttmacher Institute, 2013d). Still, that leaves a significant percentage of teens who use no contraceptive method during sexual intercourse. Why do many teens fail to use adequate contraception?

Some teens are embarrassed to find and purchase contraceptive apparatus or are concerned about confidentiality (Crooks & Baur, 2014). Others may feel uncomfortable talking to partners about sexual matters or lack assertiveness to do so. For instance, a young woman may find it difficult to talk to a partner about such intimate issues as putting on a condom or placing a diaphragm in her vagina. Depending on the information to which they've had access, adolescents may not have adequate knowledge about contraceptive methodology and its effectiveness (Crooks & Baur, 2014).

Other adolescents adhere to erroneous myths (Crooks & Baur, 2011; Rathus et al., 2011). For instance, many teens inaccurately believe that they are not old enough to conceive, that "the first time" doesn't count, that they must have intercourse much more frequently than they do in order to conceive, that it is perfectly safe to have sex during certain times of the month, and that withdrawal before ejaculation is an effective birth control method. Some young women may illogically feel that if they ignore the issue of potential pregnancy, it will cease to exist. If they don't think about their own sexual activity, then they don't have to worry about it.

There are yet other reasons why teens may not use birth control. They might not like the bother of using contraception. They might feel sexual activity is more pleasurable without it. They may worry that parents will find out. They may feel invulnerable to pregnancy, that it's something that only happens to other people. Finally, they may simply think that they want to get pregnant.

LO 6-5 Assess Sex Education and Empowerment

A heated controversy often develops over the issue of providing teens with information about sex. The fear is that giving adolescents information about sexuality will encourage them to start experimenting sexually. An underlying assumption is that adolescents won't think about sex or be interested in it unless someone around them brings up the subject.

Two fallacies can be pointed out in this approach. First, it assumes that adolescents have little or no access to sexual information other than that which adults choose to give. In reality, most teenagers say they've learned the most about sex from the media and their friends (Hyde & DeLamater, 2014).

Obviously, adolescents are functioning within a complex environment that exposes them to many new ideas. They are not locked up in a sterile cage. The media place tremendous emphasis on sexuality and sexual behavior. Television, the Internet, magazines, newspapers, and books are filled with sexual episodes and anecdotes. Adolescents indeed have numerous exposures to the concept of sex.

A second fallacy is that adolescents will automatically try anything they hear about. If a parent tells a young person that some people are murderers, will the young person go out and try murdering someone? Of course not. Although adults, especially parents, might wish they had such control over adolescents, they do not.

Perhaps an analogy concerning sex education could be made to the situation of buying a used Ford SUV. An analogous assumption would be that it would be better to have no information about how the van works before buying it and hope for the best. This is ludicrous. In this situation, you would want as much information as possible to make the best decision about whether or not to buy the van. It would be wise to take the van to a mechanic to have it thoroughly evaluated. You would both need and want information. People, including adolescents, need as much information as possible in order to make responsible decisions about their own sexual behavior and avoid ignorant mistakes. It is illogical to deprive them of information and have them act on the basis of hearsay and chance.

One primary source of information about sex is friends; yet friends probably don't know much more about sex than they do. Information that is available from friends is likely to be vague and inaccurate. Just because adolescents use sexual terms does not mean they are very knowledgeable about sexuality.

Over half (55 percent) of teens in grades 7 to 12 have researched sexual information online when they had a question related to themselves or to their friends; however, in one survey of relevant websites, 46 percent of those providing information about contraception and 35 percent of those dealing with abortion were inaccurate (Guttmacher Institute, 2012a).

Sex Education by Parents

Another aspect of the sex education controversy is the idea that sex education should be provided by parents in the home. Among teenagers, 70 percent of males and 79 percent of females do talk to parents about sex; however, questions tend to fall within at least

one of six categories (Guttmacher Institute, 2012a). These categories include saying no to sex, methods of contraception, how to get contraception, how to use a condom, sexually transmitted infections (STIs), and how to avoid contracting an HIV infection. However, consider the potential effectiveness of such sex education provided by parents (Guttmacher Institute, 2012a). First, teens may only talk to their parents about one of these issues, not all. Second, more girls talk to parents about sex than boys. Third, girls tend to focus on ways to "say no" and types of contraception. Fourth, parents may often provide "inaccurate" or "incomplete" information.

Consider also the many remaining children who receive no sex education in the home (Hyde & DeLamater, 2014). There may be several reasons for this. Adolescents may feel uncomfortable talking about such intimacy with parents, and vice versa. Many young people have extreme difficulty envisioning their parents and grandparents being involved in sexual scenarios. Similarly, parents often don't relish the picture of their children involved in such acts either. Parents may fear that by talking about it, they will encourage children to have sex, a fallacy we have already discussed. Parents may also fear their own ignorance. What if their children ask them questions they can't answer? An implication of these concerns is that it is probably easier to avoid the issue altogether.

Public surveys in the United States and Canada consistently find that parents support sex education in the schools (Greenberg et al., 2014; Hyde & DeLamater, 2014). For example, one opinion poll conducted in the United States and Canada found that 93 percent of parents of junior high–age students and 91 percent of parents of high school–age students indicate that "it is very or somewhat important to have sexuality education as part of the school curriculum" (Kaiser Family Foundation, 2004; SIECUS, 2007a; Weaver et al., 2002). This contrasts starkly with the 4 percent of parents of junior high students and the 6 percent of parents of high school students who think sexuality education should not be part of the school curriculum (*Sex Education in America*, 2004; SIECUS, 2007a). It is interesting to note that when parents were asked about the sexual behavior of their own teenager, 83 percent believed that the teen had gone no further sexually than kissing (SIECUS, 2005i). To what extent do you think this is accurate?

Sex educators do not want to take the parents' place in this sphere. Rather, they want to ensure that children have adequate and accurate information about sex. Many times parents are uncomfortable or embarrassed talking about sex with their children. One student shared her 8-year-old son's reaction to her own discomfort in talking to him about sex. As she was trying to explain to him some of the basics of human reproduction, he put his hand on her arm and said, "It's okay, Mom, I get the general idea."

Current Policy and Sex Education Programs

The major focus of the current sex education debate is on the type of program that should be offered in schools. Most sex educators promote a comprehensive program providing a wide range of information to students. The opposite approach involves abstinence-only-until-marriage programs.

Abstinence-Only-Before-Marriage Sex Education Programs

Abstinence-only programs discourage young people from engaging in any sexual behavior, exaggerate the negative effects of sexual involvement, and frequently omit information on contraception or prevention of STIs (Carroll, 2013). Supporters often say that this approach drives home the point to young people that there is no choice when it comes to nonmarital sexual activity—they simply should not do it.

The Bush administration strongly supported the development and operation of such programs (Stein, 2010). More than $1.5 billion in state and federal support was made available for these programs over the past 30 years (Greenberg et al., 2014). The current Obama administration still made $55 million available in 2012 (Kiff, 2012). As of November 2013, 37 states require that information about abstinence be included; 25 of these states mandate that abstinence be emphasized (Guttmacher Institute, 2013h). Nineteen states mandate that sex education programs stress the significance of engaging in sexual activity only within the context of marriage (Guttmacher Institute, 2013h). (Note that the terms "abstinence-only" and "abstinence-only-before-marriage" are used interchangeably here.)

Do abstinence-only programs work? A range of studies indicate that they do not work. Research indicates that abstinence-only-before-marriage programs failed to fulfill their sole purpose—namely, increasing the rates of sexual abstinence (Carroll, 2013; Kirby, 2007; SIECUS, 2007b, 2008; Week, 2008). One analysis studied the effects of involvement in abstinence-only programs on teenagers who took virginity pledges compared with matched teens who took no such pledges (Rosenbaum, 2009). She found that teenagers who took the pledge did not delay sexual involvement any more than did their nonpledging peers, were less likely to use contraception, were less likely to get tested for STIs, and were more likely to go untreated for such a disease for longer periods if they did contract one (Rosenbaum, 2009). Other research found that participants in abstinence-only-before-marriage programs had the same rate of STIs as their peers who did not participate in these programs (Bearman & Bruckner, 2005; SIECUS, 2005m, 2007b). Yet other research found that participation in abstinence-only programs produced no significant effects in sexual behavior generally (Kirby, 2007; Trenholm, Devaney, Fortson, Quay, Wheeler, & Clark, 2007).

The following is an example of a virginity pledge:

I, _____, promise to abstain from sex until my wedding night. I want to reserve my sexual powers to give life and love for my future spouse and marriage. I will respect my gift of sexuality by keeping my mind and thoughts pure as I prepare for my true love. (Sex Respect, Parent Guide, p. 13, cited in SIECUS, 2005d)

According to a report sponsored by the U.S. House of Representatives, there are at least five criticisms of abstinence-only programs (Waxman, 2004):

1. *Abstinence-only curricula contain false information about the effectiveness of contraceptives. Many curricula misrepresent the effectiveness of condoms in preventing sexually transmitted diseases and pregnancy. One curriculum says that "the popular claim that 'condoms help prevent the spread of STDs,' is not supported by the data"; another states that "in heterosexual sex, condoms fail to prevent HIV approximately 31% of the time"; and another teaches that a pregnancy occurs one out of every seven times that couples use condoms. These erroneous statements are presented as proven scientific facts. (p. i)*

2. *Abstinence-only curricula contain false information about the risks of abortion. One curriculum states that 5% to 10% of women who have legal abortions will become sterile; that "premature birth, a major cause of mental retardation, is increased following the abortion of a first pregnancy"; and that "tubal and cervical pregnancies are increased following abortions." In fact, these risks do not rise after the procedure used in most abortions in the United States. (p. i)*

3. *Abstinence-only curricula blur religion and science. Many of the curricula present as scientific fact the religious view that life begins at conception. For example, one lesson states: "Conception, also known as fertilization, occurs when one sperm unites with one egg in the upper third of the fallopian tube. This is when life begins." Another curriculum calls a 43-day-old fetus a "thinking person." (pp. i–ii)*

4. *Abstinence-only curricula treat stereotypes about girls and boys as scientific fact. One curriculum teaches that women need "financial support," while men need "admiration." Another instructs: "Women gauge their happiness and judge their success on their relationships. Men's happiness and success hinge on their accomplishments." (p. ii)*

5. *Abstinence-only curricula contain scientific errors. In numerous instances, the abstinence-only curricula teach erroneous scientific information. One curriculum incorrectly lists exposure to sweat and tears as risk factors for HIV transmission. Another curriculum states that "twenty-four chromosomes from the mother and twenty-four chromosomes from the father join to create this new individual"; the correct number is 23. (p. ii)*

There is one additional criticism of abstinence-only curricula. Emphasizing how important it is to wait for sexual interaction until heterosexual marriage tends to alienate lesbian and gay youth even more than they already are (SIECUS, 2005j, 2008). Gay marriage remains a highly controversial issue. Lesbian and gay students are already at great risk of being threatened or harassed. More than twice as many lesbian and gay high school students (19 percent) as heterosexual students (8 percent) are threatened or harmed with a weapon (SIECUS, 2005j). Ninety-two percent of lesbian and gay students "in middle and high school report that they frequently

or often hear homophobic remarks, such as 'faggot,' 'dyke,' or the expression 'that's so gay' from their peers. Almost one in five of these students heard homophobic remarks from faculty or staff at their school" (SIECUS, 2005j).

Comprehensive Sex Education Programs

The Obama administration has treated the concept of sex education quite differently than the Bush administration. The Affordable Care Act of 2010 includes a program called the Personal Responsibility Education Program (PREP); PREP makes $75 million available annually for comprehensive sex education programs that ensure the provision of medically accurate information (Greenberg et al., 2014).

EP 2.1.8a, 2.1.10h, 2.1.10k

In contrast to abstinence-only programs, comprehensive sexuality education empowers young people by teaching them "about both abstinence and ways to protect themselves from STDs, HIV, and unintended pregnancy" (SIECUS, 2005e). Note that most Americans support the provision of sex education that includes content on abstinence in addition to information about contraception and STIs (Carroll, 2013). Thus, a range of concepts are included in comprehensive sex education programs. These include abstinence, having the right to say no to a sexual encounter, the value of good communication, and the importance of taking responsibility for one's own behavior. Some research found that teenagers who received information about both abstinence and contraception were more likely to use condoms, were more likely to delay their first experience with sexual intercourse, and established "healthier" relationships with partners (Guttmacher Institute, 2012a; Wind, 2012).

The Sex Information and Education Council of the United States (SIECUS) is an organization dedicated to providing comprehensive, effective sex education (it can be accessed at www.siecus.org). SIECUS (2004, 2011) recommends that a comprehensive sex education program should have the following four goals:

1. Information. *Sexuality education seeks to provide accurate information about human sexuality including growth and development, human*

reproduction, anatomy, physiology, masturbation, family life, pregnancy, childbirth, parenthood, sexual response, sexual orientation, gender identity, contraception, abortion, sexual abuse, HIV/AIDS, and other sexually transmitted diseases.

2. Attitudes, values, and insights. *Sexuality education seeks to provide an opportunity for young people to question, explore, and assess their own and their community's attitudes about society, gender, and sexuality. This can help young people understand their family's values, develop their own values, improve critical-thinking skills, increase self-esteem and self-efficacy [effectiveness], and develop insights concerning relationships with family members, individuals of all genders, sexual partners, and society at large. Sexuality education can help young people understand their obligations and responsibilities to their families and society.*

3. Relationships and interpersonal skills. *Sexuality education seeks to help young people develop interpersonal skills, including communication, decision-making, assertiveness, and peer refusal skills, as well as the ability to create reciprocal and satisfying relationships. Sexuality education programs should prepare students to understand*

sexuality effectively and creatively in adult roles. This includes helping young people develop the capacity for caring, supportive, non-coercive, and mutually pleasurable intimate and sexual relationships.

4. Responsibility. *Sexuality education seeks to help young people exercise responsibility regarding sexual relationships by addressing such issues as abstinence, how to resist pressures to become involved in unwanted or early sexual intercourse, and the use of contraception and other sexual health measures. (2004, p. 19)*

Research has determined that effective sex education programs that delay first intercourse, reduce the frequency of intercourse, decrease the number of sexual partners, and increase contraceptive use have seven characteristics (Kirby, 2001, 2007; Kirby et al., 1994; SIECUS, 2005c; United Nations Program on HIV/AIDS, 1997). First, they focus on decreasing specific risk-taking behavior that could potentially lead to pregnancy or STDs. Second, they're based on social learning theory that emphasizes assuming responsibility for behavior, recognizing consequences, and teaching effective strategies to protect oneself, thereby enhancing motivation to adopt those behaviors. Third, they provide vital,

© grafvision/Shutterstock.com

Comprehensive sex education programs help adolescents make responsible decisions about romantic involvement and sexual behavior.

practical, and accurate information about the risks of sexual behavior, how to avoid risks, and how to protect oneself from pregnancy and STDs. Fourth, they address how the media encourage young people to become involved in sexual behavior and help them think about how to respond. Fifth, they provide examples of and opportunities to practice "communication, negotiation, and refusal skills" (Greenberg et al., 2014, p. 423). Sixth, such programs reinforce values that address the worth of postponing sexual activity and avoiding risky sexual behavior. Seventh, they use interactive teaching approaches to engage participants and help them personalize what they learn (e.g., using small-group discussions and role-playing).

Comprehensive sex education programs employing these principles have been endorsed by the American Medical Association, the American Academy of Pediatrics, the American Psychological Association, the American Public Health Association, the Institute of Medicine, and the American Foundation for AIDS Research (Guttmacher Institute, 2012a; SIECUS, 2010).

Ethical Questions 6.4

What type of sex education do you support? What specific content should and should not be taught?

EP 2.1.2

Spotlight 6.3 discusses empowerment through sex education for Native Americans.

SPOTLIGHT ON DIVERSITY 6.3

Empowerment Through Sex Education for Native Americans

EP 2.1.4c

Goodman (1998) cautions that most sex education curricula espouse a limited, unilateral view of the world, thereby failing to adequately serve people of color. She describes a case study focusing on a small community in the Cherokee Nation where an empowerment model proposed by Freire (1970, 1985) was used to develop sex education curricula.

Freire suggests that any teaching should occur within a context where community members are active participants in developing and approving content. The process involves three phases. First, developers of curricula should explore the community's needs by actively communicating with residents and observing interaction, expectations, and activities. Second, developers should talk with community members about what principles and values preside over community customs and behavior, thereby identifying recommendations for change. During this phase, community members should be actively recruited to lead discussions and provide input. Third, Freire proposes taking action to solve identified problems.

This model was applied to developing a sex education curriculum in a small Cherokee community of about 200 families in Oklahoma. Goodman (1998) describes the community as consisting of families living in subsidized housing "built on both sides of a state highway" in addition to "two small gas stations/convenience stores, a school, and a church. The community has a reputation for being violent and is located in a county that rumor says has the most unsolved murders of any county in the United States. The county is poor and has one of the highest teen pregnancy rates" in the state (p. 137).

The participatory research process included conducting discussion groups, interviews, and surveys throughout the Cherokee Nation in addition to holding various meetings and seminars. Identified issues during phase 1 were the huge gap between the community's needs for education about healthy sexual decision making and what was actually being done to meet these needs; school issues including prejudice and discrimination; teen pregnancy; the absence of men in many families' lives; and the influence of drugs on sexual behavior. Phase 2 involved focusing discussion on each issue and reviewing alternatives to address it.

Phase 3 entailed putting community recommendations into action. After-school sex education training sessions were held for teachers. Sex education programs and content can be adapted to meet the special requirements for information and respond to cultural issues relevant to young Native Americans (Planned Parenthood, 2007). A special Saturday program was provided for male Cherokee youth aged 9 to 13 stressing topics such as "talking about tough issues, making good sexual decisions, AIDS, and feeling proud to be Indian" (Goodman, 1998, p. 140). Other project results included improving community members' knowledge about the access to the appropriate social services, developing a video, initiating an Alateen program,* and acquiring access to a tribal substance abuse counselor for individual assessments.

Alateen is an organization providing support for teenage children living in a family with an alcoholic. As in Al-Anon, members meet regularly to discuss the facts about alcoholism, provide mutual support and coping suggestions, improve personal attitudes, and reduce family tension.

LO 6-6 Identify Sexually Transmitted Infections

EP 2.1.9a

Sexually transmitted infections (STIs), or *sexually transmitted diseases (STDs)*, are infections that people can contract through sexual relations. They include some conditions that can also be transmitted in other ways not involving sexual contact. In the past, STIs were referred to as *venereal diseases (VD)*.

We've already established that young people are choosing to become sexually active earlier than ever. The Centers for Disease Control (CDC) (2013f) estimates that 20 million new cases of STIs develop every year. Half of these involve people aged 15–24; it is estimated that 110 million people nationally are living with an STI (CDC, 2013f). It's critical that people have as much information as possible to make responsible decisions both for themselves and for their partners, even when they're very young. People need information about what the common STIs are, how they are transmitted, their effects, if and how they can be cured, and, perhaps most important, how they can be prevented. Discussion here will focus on information about some of the most common STIs. Bacterial infections include chlamydia, gonorrhea, and syphilis. Infections caused by other organisms include pubic lice, scabies, and trichomoniasis. Viral infections include genital herpes (herpes simplex viruses 1 [HSV-1] and 2 [HSV-2]), and human papillomavirus (HPV) (sometimes resulting in "genital warts"). HIV/AIDS will be mentioned briefly here, but discussed in greater detail in Chapter 10.

Chlamydia

Chlamydia is the most commonly reported bacterial STI in the United States (CDC, 2011b; Crooks & Baur, 2014). It is estimated that 2,291,000 "non-institutionalized civilians" in the United States have chlamydia, which is caused by a bacterium called *Chlamydia trachomatis* (CDC, 2011b). This bacterium causing chlamydia in women can cause *nongonococcal urethritis (NGU)*, also called *nonspecific urethritis (NSU)*, in men. NGU is "any inflammation of the urethra that is not caused by gonorrhea" (Crooks & Baur, 2014, p. 441). (NGU can also be caused by other microscopic organisms.)

Chlamydia trachomatis is transmitted via vaginal, oral, or anal sexual contact.

A majority of women and about 50 percent of men experience no symptoms after infection by *Chlamydia trachomatis* (CDC, 2008a; Crooks & Baur, 2014). In the event women do have symptoms, the most common involve one of two conditions. First, there may be an infection of the lower reproductive tract—specifically, irritation of the urethra or a cervical infection that results in vaginal discharge or burning sensations during urination. Second, women may get *pelvic inflammatory disease (PID)*, an infection in the uterus, the fallopian tubes, and possibly the ovaries that result in a buildup of scar tissue. Untreated or consecutive cases of PID can result in pelvic pain and possibly sterility. PID occurs in 10 to 15 percent of women with untreated chlamydia (CDC, 2011b).

A male's symptoms may include a discharge from his penis or burning sensations during urination. Men may also develop *epididymitis*, an infection of the *epididymis* ("the structure along the back of each testis in which sperm maturation occurs") (Crooks & Baur, 2014, p. G-3). If a man or woman contracts chlamydia in the throat or rectum, he or she may experience pain in those areas.

Diagnosis of a chlamydial infection includes laboratory tests examining urine or a specimen of infected cells. Treatment comprises antibiotics, usually azithromycin or doxycycline (CDC, 2011b). Chlamydial infections can easily be passed back and forth between sexual partners even when one of the partners has been cured. Therefore, infected people should avoid sexual intercourse until they're sure they're cured. People contracting chlamydial infections are supposed to refer all previous sexual partners for treatment.

Gonorrhea

It is estimated that in the United States more than 700,000 people contract gonorrhea each year (CDC, 2011b). Gonorrhea (also called "the clap" and "drip") is caused by a bacterium "that can grow and multiply easily in the warm, moist areas of the reproductive tract" and other mucous membranes (CDC, 2011b). The infection is easily transmitted by various sexual contacts, including intercourse, oral stimulation of the genitals, and possibly even kissing. Gonorrhea can infect the vagina, uterus, or fallopian tubes in women, and the urethra, mouth, throat, eyes, and anus in both men and women, causing pain, discharge, or itching.

A woman has a 50 to 70 percent and a man a 20 percent chance of contracting gonorrhea by having intercourse with a contagious person just one time; however, a male's chance of contracting gonorrhea increases sharply to 60 to 80 percent if he has vaginal intercourse four or more times with an infected partner (Greenberg et al., 2014). A man's symptoms include a yellowish, pus-like discharge secreted from the opening at the tip of the penis. Urination is usually quite painful. Only about 5 to 10 percent of men experience no symptoms (Greenberg et al., 2014). Symptoms may first appear as early as two days or as late as a month after infection.

Most women, on the other hand—as many as 80 percent—have no symptoms early on after contracting the disease (Hyde & DeLamater, 2014; Rathus et al., 2014). This is due to the fact that the infection most frequently invades the *cervix* (the lower end of an opening to the uterus). Thus, a woman is not as likely as a man either to notice the discharge or to experience pain. Unfortunately, without symptoms, a woman won't know she has gonorrhea. If she doesn't know she has it, she won't seek treatment and therefore will continue to be contagious.

If unchecked, gonorrhea usually spreads from the cervix, up the uterus, and into the fallopian tubes. It then can cause pelvic inflammatory disease and possibly sterility. Because men feel pain as a symptom, they are much more likely to seek treatment. Otherwise, for both genders, the organisms can move into other sexually related organs, causing pain and possibly fever. Sterility in men is possible, although it occurs infrequently. Other possible results of gonorrhea include infection and the resulting inflammation of organs such as the heart, brain, or joints.

Diagnosis of gonorrhea involves obtaining a sample of the discharge and conducting laboratory tests. Treatment entails administering antibiotics. Note that increasingly resistant strains of gonorrhea are evolving throughout the world, making treatment increasingly more difficult (CDC, 2008a). People remain contagious to others until they are cured.

Syphilis

There are approximately 36,000 cases of syphilis annually in the United States (CDC, 2011b). Although it is not as common as either gonorrhea or chlamydial infections, syphilis is much more deadly.

Syphilis is transmitted during sexual intercourse through a mucous membrane, usually by means of the genitals, vagina, anus, rectum, mouth, or lips. Also, a fetus may become infected by its mother; results include being stillborn, experiencing developmental delays, having seizures, or dying soon after birth (CDC, 2011b).

The symptoms of syphilis progress through four phases. The first is the *primary* stage. Most notable during this phase is the appearance of a round, crater-like sore, which, despite its very unpleasant appearance, is painless. The *chancre*, as this lesion is called, marks the spot where the bacteria initially penetrated the body. Most frequently, syphilis enters the body through a mucous membrane, around the tip of the penis, in the vagina, or at the cervix. Syphilis can, however, also be contracted through a cut anywhere on the skin. The chancre usually appears from 10 to 90 days (an average of 21 days) after infection and disappears after three to six weeks (CDC, 2011b).

The *secondary stage* begins with lesions in mucous membranes and a rash that may occur almost any place on the body. The rash neither itches nor hurts. This stage usually begins as the chancre is healing or a few weeks after it vanishes (CDC, 2011b). By this time, the bacteria have spread throughout the body. A number of other symptoms may characterize the secondary stage, including sore throat, hair loss, headaches, weight loss, nausea, joint pains, and fever. Most of these symptoms could also characterize a number of other illnesses, masking the fact that a person has syphilis. The individual might not seek treatment at all or seek it for some other illness.

Another aspect of the disease makes it difficult to pin down and diagnose. The time periods during which these generalized symptoms occur vary greatly and can be long. It's difficult to relate the symptoms of a disease like syphilis to a time perhaps six months earlier when it was contracted.

The *latent stage* begins sometime after all secondary stage symptoms have disappeared. No symptoms occur during this stage. The bacteria concentrate in some organ of the body such as the brain, spinal cord, or bones. After about one year in the latent stage, they are no longer contagious (Carroll, 2013). One exception is a pregnant woman, who may still pass the disease on to her child.

About 15 percent of the people who progress to the latent stage and remain untreated enter the final *late stage* of syphilis (CDC, 2011b). During this phase, the bacteria viciously attack the organs where they've concentrated. The disease may cause serious damage to the heart, eyes, brain, spinal cord, digestive organs, liver, or endocrine glands. Even death may result.

For diagnosis, laboratory tests examining a specimen of the chancre or blood tests are used. People with syphilis significantly increase their risk of contracting HIV. Penicillin or other antibiotics are common treatments that can be very effective if administered within a year after becoming infected. People who have had the disease longer require greater doses of drugs for a cure. Note that drugs when administered will kill the disease, but can't repair organs that syphilis has already damaged.

Pubic Lice

Pubic lice or "crabs" are tiny insects that cling to pubic hair and feed off the blood vessels in the skin of the pubic area. People become infected through direct contact. The primary symptom is itching, which can range from slight to extreme. A case of pubic lice can be diagnosed by visual observation of them and their eggs. Treatment involves applying Kwell, a prescription ointment or shampoo, to the affected areas for a period of 12 hours. Because pubic lice are highly contagious, all clothing, towels, and bedsheets coming into contact with the lice should be boiled or washed in very hot water.

Scabies

The mite *Sarcoptes scabiei* causes scabies. People become infected through direct contact with the organism. Symptoms include a red skin rash and severe itching. Diagnosis is through visual observation of the rash. Various creams are available for treatment. Like pubic lice, scabies are highly contagious, so all clothing, towels, and bedsheets coming into contact with them should be thoroughly cleaned.

Trichomoniasis

About 7.4 million new cases of trichomoniasis occur in the United States each year (CDC, 2011b). Caused by a single-celled protozoan parasite, it can be contracted through sexual intercourse or by genital-to-genital area contact. After infection, women usually experience a vaginal discharge that is yellow-green in color. Men experience either no symptoms or mild burning in the urethra after urination.

Diagnosis requires a laboratory test. Trichomoniasis is readily treated by prescription drugs such as metronidazole or tinidazole taken by mouth in a single dose. It is recommended that all sexual partners of the person with the disease be treated at the same time. Sexual intercourse should not resume until all symptoms have vanished. Trichomoniasis also makes people more susceptible to HIV infection (CDC, 2008a; Hyde & DeLamater, 2014).

Genital Herpes

Across the nation, one out of six people aged 14 to 49, or 16.2 percent of the entire U.S. population, has genital herpes (CDC, 2011b). Genital herpes is caused by *herpes simplex viruses type 1* (HSV-1) and *type 2* (HSV-2). Most cases of genital herpes are of the HSV-2 type, which causes outbreaks of painful blisters that break open and become sores. HSV-1, traditionally causing fever blisters or cold sores often found in and around the mouth, has only minor differences in its genetic code from HSV-2. Because of the increase in oral sex, HSV-1 has also often infected genital areas by mouth-genital contact. Either HSV-1 or HSV-2 infecting the genitals is considered genital herpes. Genital herpes can also occur by touching fingers to infected areas and subsequently touching other receptive mucous membranes such as those in the genital area or in the mouth. We used to think that people were only contagious when they were broken out in sores. However, now we know that infected people can also transmit the disease to others when sores aren't evident.

The first genital herpes outbreak usually occurs within two weeks of infection, although it may not happen for years (CDC, 2011b). This occurrence may last for two to four weeks before healing. Most people experience four to five outbreaks within the first year and then outbreaks tend to decrease in frequency over time (CDC, 2011b). After the first outbreak, subsequent ones tend to be less severe. In addition to the sores, other symptoms may resemble the flu, including headache, fever, and muscular aches. One of the most serious consequences of herpes is that it may be passed on to a developing fetus through the placenta. Often, a cesarean section is performed at birth.

Diagnosis is performed by visual observation, testing tissue specimens, or administering blood tests. Because it's a virus, genital herpes can't be cured; at this point, no virus can. However, oral antiviral medications can shorten episodes, decrease their severity, or prevent them from occurring while the medication is being taken. Psychological stress may also be related to outbreaks (Carroll, 2013).

Human Papillomavirus (HPV)

It is estimated that over 79 million people in the United States currently have *human papillomavirus* (HPV); most sexually active people will contract it at some time during their lives (CDC, 2013f). It is the most common STI (CDC, 2011b). Often, people experience no symptoms, although the virus may live in their tissues and continue to be contagious. In about 90 percent of cases, the body's immune system will clear up the virus within about two years (CDC, 2013f). Although there is no treatment for the virus itself, there are treatments available for the various diseases HPV can cause (CDC, 2013f). Some people develop "genital warts," "soft, moist, pink, or flesh-colored swellings" usually occurring somewhere on the genitals; they can be "single or multiple, small or large, and sometimes cauliflower shaped" (CDC, 2008a). They are transmitted through sexual contact with the infected area. Genital warts can be treated with chemicals that are applied directly to the affected area. They can also be eliminated by applying liquid nitrogen, burning them off with electrodes, employing laser surgery, or removing them surgically (Rathus et al., 2014).

HPV can cause cervical and other cancers (e.g., cancer of the penis or throat) (CDC, 2013f). Due to the prevalence of cervical cancer, it is recommended that women have regular PAP smears for early detection and treatment.

Because most sexually active people will contract HPV at some time, the Centers for Disease Control (2013f) urge use of the HPV vaccine:

> *HPV vaccines are routinely recommended for 11 or 12 year old boys and girls, and protect against some of the most common types of HPV that can lead to disease and cancer, including most cervical cancers. CDC recommends that all teen girls and women through age 26 get vaccinated, as well as all teen boys and men through age 21 (and through*

> *age 26 for gay, bisexual, and other men who have sex with men). HPV vaccines are most effective if they are provided before an individual ever has sex.*

HIV (Human Immunodeficiency Virus)

AIDS (acquired immunodeficiency syndrome) is a disease caused by HIV (*human immunodeficiency virus*) that breaks down the body's immune system, leaving it vulnerable to numerous diseases that could not successfully attack a normal immune system. Sometimes its progression can be slowed down, but it cannot be cured and eventually usually leads to death. HIV can be transmitted in a variety of ways involving bodily fluids, including sexual intercourse. Chapter 10 examines AIDS and HIV in much greater depth. HIV is briefly mentioned here, however, because of its significant transmission during adolescence (Crooks & Baur, 2014). Although many teens are informed about AIDS and high-risk behaviors, they don't view themselves as vulnerable and fail to alter their sexual behavior to prevent infection; for instance, they may have multiple partners and fail to use condoms (Crooks & Baur, 2014).

It should also be emphasized that having another STI increases one's vulnerability to HIV (CDC, 2011b). Genital sores or lesions such as those present in syphilis or herpes result in breaks in the skin where HIV can readily enter the bloodstream if it's exposed. Additionally, it has been discovered that HIV becomes more concentrated in bodily fluids of people with an STI, "The higher the concentration of HIV in semen or genital fluids, the more likely it is that HIV will be transmitted to a sex partner" (CDC, 2011b).

Preventing STIs

Suggestions for preventing STIs include using condoms because they prevent contact between the penile tissues and a woman's genital tissues or a partner's anal tissues. A condom or a *dental dam* (a small sheet of latex that can be placed over a woman's genitalia during oral sex) can help prevent STI transmission between mouth and genitalia. Spermicides have also been found to help kill some STIs. Washing the genital areas with soap and water before sexual contact can

EP 2.1.10i

help. Urinating both before and after intercourse can also help clear the urethra of bacteria.

These are specific behaviors that people can follow to help prevent contracting an STI. However, perhaps suggestions concerning thought and choice are the most effective. There are at least six suggestions for preventing the transmission of STIs (Carroll, 2013; Crooks & Baur, 2014; Hyde & DeLamater, 2014). First, each person should be knowledgeable about STIs. Know what STIs are and how they can be contracted. Second, each individual should be attentive and careful. This doesn't necessarily mean one should say, "Well, excuse me, dear, but may I please take a moment to examine your genitals for symptoms of STIs?" However, it does mean that being aware and watching for symptoms may help a person avoid contracting a disease. Third, choose a sexual partner carefully. A partner who has had several other sexual partners recently is at significant risk of having an STI. Of course, being in a truly monogamous relationship prevents STIs. Fourth, be truthful and straightforward. That means if a person has an STI, he or she should tell a prospective partner about it. It also means that if someone is worried about a potential partner having an STI, that person should ask about it. Fifth, be responsible. If a person thinks he or she might have an STI, that person should immediately seek diagnosis and treatment. Sixth, use condoms, which decrease the chances of getting an STI.

LO 6-7 Explain Major Methods of Contraception

EP 2.1.6b, 2.1.10g, 2.1.10i

Anyone who is considering becoming sexually active and who is not intentionally trying to conceive a child needs accurate and specific information about contraceptive methods.[1] This includes adolescents; without adequate information, they cannot make responsible decisions. Information helps to prevent people from taking unnecessary risks. We've already established the importance of sex education. Information concerning contraception is especially important.

---

[1]An excellent source of information on contraception is Planned Parenthood at http://www.plannedparenthood.org.

The risk of unplanned pregnancy and the resulting impact on the lives of adolescents are too important to ignore. Over 99 percent of American women aged 15 to 44 who have been sexually active have used at least one type of contraceptive method (Guttmacher Institute, 2013b).

Major methods of contraception are described in the following sections. Hormonal methods of contraception include the contraceptive pill, the birth control patch, the vaginal ring, Depo-Provera injections, hormonal implants, and emergency contraception. Spermicides are chemical contraceptives. Barrier methods of contraception include condoms for men, the female condom, the diaphragm, and the cervical cap (FemCap). The birth control sponge (Today Sponge) serves as both a chemical and barrier method. The intrauterine device (IUD), including the ParaGard IUD and hormonal IUDs (Mirena and Skyla), is inserted inside the uterus. Other means of contraception include withdrawal, fertility awareness methods (FAMs), and sterilization.

Each method's level of effectiveness is indicated, and the advantages and disadvantages of each method are explored. No one best method of birth control exists for everybody. Each individual must select a method according to how it fits with his or her lifestyle. Some methods are easier to use than others. Some methods require responsible adherence to a schedule. Other methods are best suited for persons who have only occasional sexual contacts.

The Pill

Birth control pills or oral contraceptives are one of the most effective forms of contraception other than sterilization. There are two major types of birth control pills. Various companies produce numerous brands of these two types of pills. The most commonly used type combines a synthetic *estrogen* (a female hormone that helps regulate the menstrual cycle) and *progestin* (a synthetic version of *progesterone*, a female hormone that makes the lining of the uterus thicken). The *combined pill* targets a 28-day menstrual cycle and is distributed in monthly packs.

Combined pills are taken in one of three ways. The most commonly used brands of combined pills are sold in packages of 21 pills, which should be taken daily until they are used up. A woman then refrains from starting her next monthly pack of pills for seven days. During this time she will have her menstrual period. Other brands of combined pills come in packs of 28 pills. These include placebos or ineffective sugar pills for the last seven days of the cycle. This serves to reinforce a woman's habit of taking one pill each day. A third way of taking birth control pills involves pills (called Seasonale) that are taken daily "for three straight months, followed by one week of inactive pills"; "a woman gets her period about four times a year, during the 13th month of her cycle" (National Institutes of Health [NIH], 2011). Combined pills prevent the ovaries from ovulating, or releasing a ripened egg ready for fertilization. In a sense, they trick the body into thinking that the woman is pregnant. A pregnant woman temporarily stops ovulating in order to prevent multiple pregnancies. Combined pills also contain progestin, which makes the cervical mucus thicker and more acidic, thereby making it more difficult for sperm to infiltrate. Progestin also alters the lining of the uterus, making it more difficult for egg implantation. Progestin can also hamper ovulation.

Combined pills are *theoretically* more than 99 percent effective, which is considered excellent (Hyde & DeLamater, 2014; Planned Parenthood, 2014). Theoretical effectiveness rates refer to the number of women out of 100 in whom pregnancy is prevented. A theoretical effectiveness rate of 100 percent means that for every 100 women, none should become pregnant.

However, the combined pill's *actual* effectiveness rate is approximately 91 percent (Planned Parenthood, 2014). Actual effectiveness refers to how effective the method is in actual daily use. The differences between the two rates can probably be explained by human error. For example, forgetting to take a pill one day increases the chance of pregnancy as hormonal levels may change enough to allow a woman to ovulate.

In addition to the combined pill, so named because it combines some amount of estrogen with progestin, there are other pills. These include triphasic pills and the progestin-only pill.

The progestin-only pill or *minipill* contains only progestin, as its name implies (NIH, 2011). We have established that progestin affects the consistency of cervical mucus and alters the uterine lining. The progestin-only pill's effectiveness rate is somewhat less than that of combined pills (Hyde & DeLamater, 2014; NIH, 2011). About half of women taking progestin-only pills fail to ovulate at all; progestin also inhibits implantation in the uterus should fertilization take place (Greenberg et al., 2014). Progestin-only pills can provide a useful alternative for women who are breast-feeding, as combined pills sometimes interfere with that process (Hyde & DeLamater, 2014). Progestin-only pills are also a better possibility for women who, for some reason, cannot use estrogen (Greenberg et al., 2014).

The *triphasic pill* involves three stages, where the dosage of hormones is increased for each of the three weeks they are taken (instead of maintaining a constant dose over the three-week period as is the case with the combined pill (Carroll, 2013). The idea is to decrease the total amount of hormones consumed (Hyde & DeLamater, 2014).

Contraceptive pills should be taken regularly at approximately the same time each day. Today's birth control pills have lower dosages of hormones than they did three decades ago. This is to minimize unpleasant side effects. However, their low dosage makes it more important that they be taken at approximately the same time each day. Otherwise, there is a chance that their pregnancy-inhibiting abilities will be decreased to the point that they will not work. With combination pills, it is important that the hormonal levels maintained by the pill do not drop to a level that makes ovulation possible. Once ovulation occurs, pregnancy is risked. With progestin-only pills, if the internal reproductive environment is not kept hostile enough to prevent fertilization and implantation, pregnancy may occur.

Even the most organized, conscientious woman may occasionally forget to take her contraceptive pill. Should you miss taking a pill, you should take it as soon as possible and then resume taking your next pill at the regular time; should you miss taking more than one pill, you should consult a health-care professional and also use an alternate form of contraception for backup during the rest of your cycle (Crooks & Baur, 2014).

Advantages of taking either form of birth control pill are numerous. They are very effective. They are fairly easy to use, in that they must simply be swallowed daily. Nothing needs to be inserted into the vagina. No complicated process is involved. Nothing interferes with the spontaneity of a sexual encounter. Those who are frequently sexually active are always prepared. The method is readily reversible. Both combination and progestin-only birth control pills can decrease menstrual cramping, produce lighter menstrual periods, and provide some defense against PID (Planned Parenthood, 2014). Combination birth control pills can also provide some protection against endometrial (the *endometrium* is the lining of the uterus) and ovarian cancers, ovarian cysts, *benign* (not cancerous) breast growths, iron deficiency anemia, acne, *ectopic pregnancy* (a pregnancy that develops outside of the uterus that is very dangerous for the mother), uncomfortable symptoms occurring prior to menstruation such as headaches and depression, and vaginal dryness linked to menopause (Planned Parenthood, 2014).

Disadvantages to taking birth control pills include undesirable side effects such as nausea, vomiting, bleeding between menstrual periods, and breast tenderness (Planned Parenthood, 2014). These side effects resemble those of the first trimester of pregnancy; they are due to similar changes in hormonal levels. These symptoms usually disappear after two to three months, as they do in pregnancy. Changing brands of birth control pills sometimes helps because different brands often have minor variations in hormonal dosages. Such variations affect various women differently. Another disadvantage of birth control pills is that they provide no help in preventing STIs.

Birth control pills also have interactive effects with some other drugs, such as insulin, blood-thinning medications, and some tranquilizers. Some medications such as antibiotics and some tranquilizers can decrease the pill's effectiveness. Thus, any woman taking birth control pills should check with her physician regarding possible interactive effects with any other drugs she may be taking.

Note that after discontinuing pill use, menstrual periods may not resume until a month or two later; sometimes, a woman will remain irregular for up to six months (Planned Parenthood, 2011). Although it appears that after stopping the pill, women may take from 0 to 26 weeks to resume ovulation (with an average of 2 weeks), no long-term effects on fertility have been found (Hatcher & Nelson, 2004).

Serious problems resulting from the contraceptive pill are very rare. They include cardiovascular problems such as a "heart attack, stroke, having a blood clot in the legs, lungs, heart, or brain, or developing high blood pressure" as well as "liver tumors, gallstones, or yellowing of the skin or eyes (*jaundice*)" (Planned Parenthood, 2014). Variables

that can increase risk include being age 35 or older, being overweight, smoking, and suffering from a number of specified health problems such as high cholesterol, high blood pressure, or diabetes (Planned Parenthood, 2014).

One important factor to consider before using the pill as a means of contraception is a person's general approach to life. In other words, a person must be notably responsible and conscientious in order to take the pill regularly every day. Many people, despite their good intentions, find it difficult to follow a regimented procedure. Women who are only occasionally sexually active might also find it unappealing to take the pill every day.

The Birth Control Patch and Vaginal Ring

Both introduced in 2003, the birth control patch (with the brand name Ortho Evra) and the vaginal ring (with the brand name NuvaRing) use the same hormones—estrogen and progestin—as the combination birth control pill. *Ortho Evra* consists of a thin patch of material that sticks to the skin and releases hormones into the body to prevent pregnancy. Patches are applied to the skin once a week for three weeks; then a week passes without a patch application. They can be placed "on the buttock, abdomen, upper outer arm, or upper torso" (Crooks & Baur, 2014, p. 291).

The *NuvaRing* is a "2-inch-diameter soft and transparent" flexible ring that's inserted into the vagina "between day 1 and day 5 of a menstrual period" and left in place for three weeks (Crooks & Baur, 2014, p. 291). After insertion, vaginal "moisture and body heat activate the release of hormones" (Carroll, 2013, p. 353). The ring is then removed for a week, and a week later replaced with a new ring.

The actual effectiveness and most of the advantages and disadvantages of both the patch and the vaginal ring are the same as for combination birth control pills. They have the additional advantage of being somewhat easier to use, as a woman doesn't have to remember to take a pill at the same time every day. She must, however, remember to change the patch after seven days and the ring after three weeks. A disadvantage of both is that they don't help prevent STIs.

The patch has the potential disadvantages that a woman must take care not to dislodge it and that it may cause skin irritation.

Many women using the vaginal ring indicate that they "have more regular, lighter, and shorter periods" (Planned Parenthood, 2014). However, sometimes the vaginal ring can cause "increased vaginal discharge, vaginal irritation, or infection" (Planned Parenthood, 2014).

Depo-Provera Injections

Depo-Provera is the most commonly used hormonal injection method for contraception. It is a progestin-only method like the progestin-only birth control pill. A shot is administered once every 12 weeks. Theoretical effectiveness is over 99 percent, and actual effectiveness is 94 percent (Planned Parenthood, 2014). Actual effectiveness is better than that of the contraceptive pill, patch, or vaginal ring, probably because there is less room for human error.

Advantages of Depo-Provera include avoiding the use of estrogen (thus evading potential negative effects such as cardiovascular problems); a high actual effectiveness rate; convenient, easy use; and decreased risk of endometrial cancer (Planned Parenthood, 2014). As with other hormonal methods, one disadvantage is the lack of protection against STIs. Other potential disadvantages include disturbances in the menstrual cycle (e.g., fewer, lighter periods; longer, heavier periods; or increased spotting between periods), weight gain, breast tenderness, headache, nausea, and depression (Planned Parenthood, 2014).

Negative symptoms may continue until all chemicals are cleared from the body, which usually takes 12 to 14 weeks (Planned Parenthood, 2014). It may take from 6 to 10 months or more for the shot to wear off enough to become pregnant (Planned Parenthood, 2014).

Hormonal Implants

A hormonal implant with the brand names *Implanon* or *Nexplanon* consists of a "thin, flexible plastic implant about the size of a cardboard matchstick" (Planned Parenthood, 2014). A health-care provider places it under the skin of the upper arm, where it can remain effective for up to three years. Although not yet readily available everywhere, increasing numbers of health-care providers are being trained in the insertion procedure.

Implanon and Nexplanan involve a progestin-only hormonal method of contraception, so their functioning and effects resemble those of other progestin-only approaches. Their actual effectiveness rate is over 99 percent (Planned Parenthood, 2014).

A hormonal implant has several advantages (Planned Parenthood, 2014). It's easy to use because it is long lasting and requires no direct action by the woman using it. It is an appropriate option for women who can't use estrogen or who are breastfeeding. Women can become pregnant relatively soon after removing the implant. A woman can choose to have the implant removed by a health-care provider at any time.

There are also disadvantages (Planned Parenthood, 2014). The most common complaint is irregular bleeding, including spotting between periods. Menstrual periods may be longer and heavier, fewer and lighter, or may stop altogether. Hormonal implants provide no protection against STIs. Less common consequences include changes in sex drive, headache, nausea, pain or discoloration at the insertion site, and sore breasts (Planned Parenthood, 2014). Warning signs of rare but potentially serious side effects include bleeding or pus at the insertion site, development of a breast lump, movement or expulsion of the implant, stoppage of menstruation after having had regular periods, or unusually heavy vaginal bleeding (Planned Parenthood, 2014).

Emergency Contraception (EC)

Despite the controversy over newer chemical methods of abortion, several types of emergency contraception have been approved and are available in the United States (NIH, 2011; Planned Parenthood, 2014). *Emergency contraception* (EC) is typically used when unplanned, unprotected intercourse has occurred; when another method of contraception fails (e.g., a condom breaks); when a woman forgets to take birth control pills; or after a sexual assault. EC is intended for emergency use only. EC is different than the "abortion pill" in that it is meant to be taken after sexual intercourse to prevent pregnancy rather than after pregnancy has already occurred (NIH, 2011).

Three types of EC are approved for use in the United States; two of them are pills containing synthetic hormones and one an IUD (Planned Parenthood, 2014). One type of pill contains levonorgestrel (a synthetic progestin hormone). There are two brands marketed under the names Plan B One-Step and Next Choice. Both brands involve taking a single tablet as soon as possible after unprotected intercourse occurs.

Means of access to EC vary depending on the type of EC (Planned Parenthood, 2014). Any woman regardless of age can acquire Plan B One-Step over the counter without having to obtain a medical prescription. It is available at drugstores, Planned Parenthood clinics, and other family planning centers. To obtain Next Choice, a prescription from a health-care professional is needed for women age 16 or younger.

The second type of EC pill contains ulipristal acetate (another type of synthetic progestin hormone) marketed under the name Ella (CenterWatch, 2013). One pill is taken orally within five days of unprotected intercourse or failure of a contraceptive method (CenterWatch, 2013). A prescription is needed to obtain Ella regardless of age, although prescriptions are available online at http://www .ella-kwikmed.com/ (Planned Parenthood, 2014).

EC pills potentially prevent pregnancy by suppressing or delaying ovulation so that the sperm cannot make contact with an egg to fertilize it. Note, therefore, they do not cause an abortion because there is no fertilized egg to abort.

Although EC pills can be taken up to five days after intercourse has occurred, the earlier the pill is taken, the better (NIH, 2011). Levonorgestrel pills (Plan B One-Step and Next Choice One Dose) are "up to 89 percent effective when taken up to 72 hours (three days) after unprotected sex"; the pills "continue to reduce the risk of pregnancy up to 120 hours (five days) after unprotected sex," but their effectiveness decreases as time passes after that (Planned Parenthood, 2014). Levonorgestrel is less effective in preventing pregnancy in women who are overweight. Ella's effectiveness rate is 85 percent if the pill is taken within five days of unprotected intercourse (Planned Parenthood, 2014). It is more effective in women with higher weight levels than the levonorgestrel pills. Costs of EC pills vary considerably by area and type of available insurance, usually ranging from $30 to $65 (Planned Parenthood, 2014).

No severe difficulties have been reported by the millions of women who have taken EC pills;

disagreeable side effects may include menstrual periods that occur "earlier or later, or are heavier or lighter than usual," headaches, breast tenderness, or nausea and vomiting (Planned Parenthood, 2014). It is strongly recommended that EC pills not be used as an ongoing means of contraception, because such a practice may affect the predictability of menstrual periods and cycles (Planned Parenthood, 2014).

The third type of EC involves insertion of the ParaGard IUD (intrauterine device, which is discussed more thoroughly in a later section) (Planned Parenthood, 2014). If it is put in place by a health-care professional within five days (120 hours) of unprotected sexual intercourse, it is 99.9 percent effective in preventing pregnancy. Although initial insertion is expensive ($550 to $900), it can subsequently be used as a form of contraception for as long as 12 years (Planned Parenthood, 2014). In the long run, this is very cost effective. See the subsequent section on "The IUD" for a discussion of the benefits and risks of using IUDs. To be used as EC it requires a prescription for all women age 16 or younger (Planned Parenthood, 2014).

Vaginal Spermicides

Spermicides are chemical contraceptives that function in two ways. First, the chemicals act to kill sperm. Second, the substance itself acts as a barrier that inhibits sperm from entering the uterus. Spermicides are available in creams, gels, or foams that are squeezed or thrust into a tube, which in turn is inserted into the vagina. Other spermicides include suppositories and thin, tissue-like sheets of spermicide, which are placed directly into the vagina. It is important to read the instructions carefully to be effective. Some condoms are lubricated with a spermicide.

Advantages of spermicides include relative ease of use, ready availability, low cost, and their use only when needed. Despite these advantages, when used alone the theoretical effectiveness rate is only 85 percent, with an actual effectiveness rate of 71 percent (Planned Parenthood, 2014). However, effectiveness increases significantly when used in conjunction with another form of contraception such as a diaphragm, a male condom, or a female condom. Other disadvantages of spermicides are that they must be used "exactly as directed" or they may be less effective and some women complain that they are "messy" (Planned Parenthood, 2014). One other important note is that most spermicides contain an agent called nonoxynol-9 (NIH, 2011; Planned Parenthood, 2014). If this substance is used too frequently, it can cause irritation and make tissues more vulnerable to HIV and other STIs.

Condoms for Men

A *condom*, also called a *prophylactic* or *rubber*, is a thin sheath made of latex or plastic that fits over the penis and serves as a barrier form of contraception. This means that the device acts as a barrier to keep sperm from reaching and fertilizing the egg. The condom is initially rolled up into a little circular packet. This packet must be placed and unrolled on an erect penis. Because it fits rather snugly, it acts as a barrier method of birth control. After ejaculation, sperm are contained in the rubber sheath. They are never allowed to enter the vagina.

Many condoms have a small bulge at the tip to allow room for semen. Otherwise, some empty space must purposefully be left at the tip of the condom so that there is a place to hold the semen.

Condoms are available with a number of variations. Many are lubricated. They come with slightly different textures and a variety of colors and even flavors. (Note that novelty condoms are also available that do not provide contraceptive protection. You can use your imagination about what they might be like. Users should read labels carefully to make certain that they're getting the protection they need.) The condom's theoretical effectiveness is 98 percent, and the actual effectiveness 82 percent (Planned Parenthood, 2014). Once again, this decrease in effectiveness from theoretical to actual can be attributed to human error. Effectiveness is significantly increased if used together with a spermicide or if the penis is withdrawn from the vagina prior to ejaculation (Planned Parenthood, 2014).

After ejaculation in the vagina, the condom must be held at the base of the penis as the penis is withdrawn from the vagina. This is to make sure that none of the sperm is spilled and can enter the vagina. Condoms should not be reused.

A major advantage of condom use is protection from STIs. It is recommended that condoms be used for disease prevention even in conjunction with other contraceptive methods; this is especially important for women, who are 10 to 20 times more likely to contract an STI than men because of the shape and location of their sexual organs (Planned Parenthood, 2014). Condoms may also be used to prevent the spread of STIs during oral sex.

There are other advantages as well. Condoms provide the only nonsurgical means of giving the male some direct responsibility for contraception. They are readily available at a relatively low cost. They don't require a prior physical examination or a medical prescription. They are small and easy to carry for use at any time. They help some men maintain a longer erection. Some people incorporate their use into their sex play prior to intercourse. Condoms cause no adverse side effects, except for people who are allergic to latex. Such people, who comprise up to 6 percent of the population, should use plastic condoms instead (Planned Parenthood, 2014).

Other than an allergic reaction, there are some other potential psychological disadvantages (Planned Parenthood, 2014). Some couples feel that condoms interfere with the spontaneity of lovemaking. Other men and women feel it reduces sensation during sexual intercourse. Some men feel embarrassed about putting them on or pressured to maintain an erection once they are on. Such feelings are unfortunate. Ideally, it is best to develop a perspective that focuses on the usefulness and purpose of condoms instead of on negative psychological issues.

The Female Condom

The *female condom*, available since 1994, provides one of several vaginal barrier forms of contraception. It consists of two rings connected by latex. One ring fits over the cervix; the latex protects the cervix from contact with either the penis or semen. The other ring rests outside the vagina; here the latex forms a pouch for the penetrating penis, thus protecting the penis from vaginal contact. A lubricant or spermicide should be put outside of the closed end to facilitate insertion (Planned Parenthood, 2014). After use, the female condom should be discarded (not in a toilet). They should never be reused. A female condom should never be used together with a male condom because they might stick together, "causing slippage or displacement of one or both devices" (Cates & Stewart, 2004, p. 366). It is also useful during anal intercourse where it is inserted into the anus instead of the vagina (Planned Parenthood, 2014).

The female condom's theoretical effectiveness rate is 95 percent, although the actual rate is 79 percent (Planned Parenthood, 2014). As with the male condom, a major advantage is protection from STIs. Another advantage is that the female condom enables a woman to take responsibility for both contraception and protection from STIs. Other advantages include not requiring a prescription and not affecting a woman's natural hormones.

Disadvantages may involve reactions such as rashes resulting from a latex allergy or minor problems like skin irritation (Cates & Stewart, 2004; NIH, 2011). Other disadvantages include the possibility of slippage during intercourse and the potential reduction of sensation (Planned Parenthood, 2014).

The Diaphragm and Cervical Cap

In addition to male and female condoms, two other barrier methods of contraception are the diaphragm and the cervical cap (brand name FemCap). Each is currently available in the United States with a prescription from a health-care provider. Each is inserted through the vagina and fits around the cervix. Because of their similarities, they will be discussed together.

The *diaphragm* is a thin circular piece of rubber stretched over a flexible ring of wire. It is shaped like a dome. A woman inserts it by pushing it with her fingers up into the vagina to cover the cervix. Because a cervix will vary in size from one woman to another, a woman must be fitted for the correct size diaphragm.

FemCap is "a silicone cup shaped like a sailor's hat" that snugly covers the cervix with the rim of the hat conforming to the contours of the vagina (Planned Parenthood, 2014). FemCap comes in three sizes. Small is for women who have never experienced a pregnancy, medium for women who have been pregnant and subsequently had an abortion or a cesarean delivery, and large for women who have given birth through the cervix and vagina.

Each of the devices should be used with spermicidal cream or jelly that is placed inside the bottom of the cup or dome and spread around the edges. The diaphragm can be inserted up to 6 hours before intercourse and left in place for no more than 24; FemCap can be inserted up to 8 hours prior to

sexual intercourse and remain in place for no more than 48 hours (Crooks & Baur, 2014). Leaving any of these devices inside the vagina for a longer time poses the danger of *toxic shock syndrome* (TSS), a potentially fatal bacterial infection. When using the diaphragm, more spermicide should be injected into the vagina if intercourse occurs more than six hours after insertion or before each subsequent act of intercourse. When wearing FemCap, the device should be checked to be sure it is in place before subsequent acts of intercourse, and more spermicide may be applied.

The diaphragm has a theoretical effectiveness rate of 94 percent and an actual rate of 88 percent (Planned Parenthood, 2014). FemCap has an actual effectiveness rate of 86 percent for women who have never been pregnant and 71 percent for women who have given birth vaginally (Planned Parenthood, 2014). Effectiveness for both methods can be enhanced by using spermicide as recommended, using a latex condom in addition to the diaphragm or cervical cap, and making certain that the device is snugly in place over the cervix (Planned Parenthood, 2014). Cates and Stewart (2004) caution that the "contraceptive effectiveness of vaginal barriers is influenced by the characteristics of the individuals using them. The most important fact in determining effectiveness is correct and consistent use" (p. 370).

Neither method should be used by women who have allergies to the substances involved, find the device difficult or uncomfortable to insert, have experienced some trauma to the uterus, have an infection in the area, or have vaginal obstructions (Planned Parenthood, 2014).

There are a number of advantages to using the diaphragm or FemCap (Planned Parenthood, 2014). They are easy to carry with you. They can be used only when you need them. They don't interfere with normal hormones. They're effective right away. They can be inserted hours before intercourse occurs, so they don't have to interfere with spontaneity.

Both methods also have disadvantages (Planned Parenthood, 2014). They may be pushed out of position during some sexual positions or behaviors. They are not effective unless they're in place every single time intercourse occurs. As with many other contraceptive methods, these devices don't help prevent STIs. Both diaphragms and FemCap may necessitate being refit for another size. Women may be allergic to the materials they're made of or to the spermicide used. Some women experience recurrent bladder infections when using the diaphragm or a cervical cap. Some women experience pain when using a cervical cap. FemCap should not be used while menstruating.

The Birth Control Sponge

The *contraceptive sponge* that goes by the brand name of Today Sponge, currently available over the Internet and possibly in some stores, is a soft, cuplike sponge device that can be inserted into the vagina and covers the cervix. It is saturated with a spermicide to provide additional protection. Before insertion, it should be moistened with tap water. It can be inserted up to 24 hours before sexual intercourse occurs; the sponge should be left in the vagina for at least 6 hours after sexual intercourse, but no longer than 30 hours because of the potential of TSS (Planned Parenthood, 2014).

The sponge's effectiveness is based on three principles. First, it acts as a barrier to prevent sperm from entering the cervix. Second, the chemical spermicide it contains acts to kill sperm. Third, its potential for absorbing sperm is also thought to be beneficial. Like the cervical cap, it is significantly more effective for women who have never had children than for those who have had children. Its theoretical and actual effectiveness for women who have not had children are 91 and 88 percent, respectively; the respective rates for women who have borne children are 80 and 76 percent (Planned Parenthood, 2014).

Most advantages resemble those of other barrier methods in that the sponge is easy to use, it's used only when needed, it has no effect on natural hormones, and partners usually remain unaware of its presence. Disadvantages are that some women find insertion difficult, some notice vaginal irritation, and some find it messy because liquid must be added prior to insertion.

The IUD (Intrauterine Device)

The *intrauterine device (IUD)* is a plastic device that is placed in a woman's uterus. IUDs, which are made in various shapes, need to be inserted by a physician or trained health professional. Today IUDs are widely used around the world (Crooks & Baur, 2014). Two types of IUDs are available in the United States (Planned Parenthood, 2014). One goes by the brand name ParaGard, introduced here in 1988 as the Copper T. The ParaGard has fine copper wire wrapped around the base of the T which releases a tiny amount of copper into the uterine environment. Once inserted, it is effective for up to 12 years (Planned Parenthood, 2014).

The second type of IUD, available in the United States since 2000, is hormonal. Such IUDs also assume a T shape and go by the brand names Mirena or Skyla. Hormonal IUDs release a small amount of progestin into the system and remain effective for up to five years (Planned Parenthood, 2014).

Both types of IUDs work in two ways (Planned Parenthood, 2014). First, they alter how sperm move and prevent sperm from fertilizing the egg. There is no pregnancy without a fertilized egg. Second, they change the interior lining of the uterus, the endometrium. It is thought that this prevents a fertilized egg (in the event that one does become fertilized) from attaching itself to the endometrium, although no factual evidence for this exists.

Hormonal IUDs also produce effects because of their progestin. As we know, progestin prevents ovaries from releasing eggs for fertilization. Additionally, it thickens cervical mucus, making it more difficult for sperm to enter the uterus.

A range of contraceptive methods have been developed, having various rates of effectiveness.

Charles Thatcher/The Image Bank/Getty Images

Either type of IUD is attached to a string that hangs out of the cervix. A woman should check the IUD regularly, especially for the first few months after initial insertion because that's the time it's most likely to slip out. She can check by inserting her finger into the vagina and feeling if the string is still there. (The cervix feels like the tip of your nose.)

The IUD is one of the most effective contraceptive methods available, with an actual effectiveness rate over 99 percent. There are other advantages as well (Planned Parenthood, 2014). An IUD provides long-term contraception, requiring no effort other than occasionally checking the string. Using an IUD places no restrictions on spontaneity in lovemaking. Shortly after removal of the IUD, a woman can become pregnant. ParaGard IUD does not affect a woman's natural hormones. Hormonal IUDs may decrease menstrual cramping and diminish menstrual flow by an average of 90 percent (Planned Parenthood, 2014).

IUDs also have disadvantages (Planned Parenthood, 2014). Many women experience spotting between menstrual periods. Some women have more severe cramping. ParaGard may cause increased menstrual flow in addition to worse menstrual cramps (Planned Parenthood, 2014). Of course, IUDs don't help prevent STIs. Very rarely, women may experience pelvic inflammatory disease or IUD perforation of the uterine wall. Infrequently, an IUD may slip out unnoticed, especially in women who have never been pregnant.

Withdrawal

Withdrawal, or *coitus interruptus*, refers to withdrawing the penis before ejaculating into the vagina. Although it has often been considered a relatively ineffective method of birth control, in actuality its effectiveness resembles that of the barrier methods of contraception.

Theoretical or perfect effectiveness is 96 percent and actual effectiveness 73 percent (Planned Parenthood, 2014). One problem with this method is that a few drops of semen are expelled by a pair of glands called Cowper's glands before the full ejaculation. Both urine and semen pass through the urethra. Urine is acidic. An acidic environment is not conducive for sperm. It is thought that these few drops of semen are discharged before ejaculation in order to clear the urethra of some of its acidic

quality and better prepare it for sperm (Crooks & Baur, 2014). However, sometimes live sperm remain in the urethra. It is possible, although not probable, that these sperm can be transported out through the tip of the penis by the Cowper's glands' secretion and still impregnate a woman.

Major advantages of withdrawal are that no extraneous devices or substances are needed and it's free. A primary disadvantage is that its effectiveness depends mainly on the man's ability to withdraw in time. In the heat of emotion, it may be difficult for some men to exercise great control over ejaculation.

Fertility Awareness Methods

Fertility awareness methods (FAMs) (formerly sometimes referred to as the rhythm method) involve monitoring a woman's ovulation cycle and initiating sexual relations only during the safe times of her cycle. Because so many variables are involved, it's difficult to calculate theoretical effectiveness. These methods are much more effective when the couple can accurately identify the woman's window of fertility and the couple is capable of following clearly specified procedures in monitoring the menstrual cycle (Jennings, Arevalo, & Kowal, 2004).

There are at least four types of FAMs (Planned Parenthood, 2014). Due to their complicated procedures, we will not address them in detail here. The *calendar method* is the simplest of the three. It involves counting the days of the menstrual cycle and trying to determine when ovulation occurs. The idea is to have intercourse only when it is certain that the woman is not ovulating.

A second method is the *basal body temperature method*. A woman's body temperature undergoes minor predictable variations depending on where she is in her ovulatory cycle. Using this method involves taking her temperature every morning as soon as she wakes up. A problem with this method is that the major temperature differential occurs only after ovulation has taken place. By this time pregnancy prevention could be too late.

A third type of FAM is the *cervical mucus* (or *ovulation*) *method*. It necessitates that a woman examine her cervical mucus throughout her menstrual cycle. The consistency, amount, and clarity of the mucus tend to change predictably depending on where she is in her ovulatory cycle.

Using any two or all of the methods together is referred to as the *symptothermal method*. This tends to be more effective than when one method is used alone, because information from one data-gathering method can provide input useful in monitoring another method. It can enhance accuracy.

The actual effectiveness rate for using these methods is 76 percent; effectiveness can be enhanced when the methods are used correctly and consistently (Planned Parenthood, 2014).

Advantage of using a FAM or FAMs is that there is no manipulation of hormones and that nothing must be done directly prior to sexual intercourse. A major disadvantage is that using any of the FAM methods requires conscientious attention to gathering data every day. FAMs do not help prevent STIs.

Sterilization

Sterilization is "rendering a person incapable of conceiving with surgical procedures that interrupt the passage of the egg or sperm" (Kelly, 2008, p. 314). It is one of the most common family planning methods used in the world; it is also common for couples who are of fertile age in the United States (Carroll, 2013). The procedures are considered to be permanent, although they can be reversed in some cases.

Sterilization for women involves a *tubal ligation*, in which the fallopian tubes leading from the ovaries to the uterus are severed. Hence, sperm are unable to reach the egg. Sterilization for men entails a *vasectomy*; a small section of the vas deferens is removed near the place where the scrotum is attached to the body. The *vas deferens* is the tube that transports sperm from the testicles to the urethra. Thus, sperm are not ejaculated.

Many young people ask whether sterilization interferes with sexual responsiveness. They wonder if having a vasectomy means that a man will not be able to ejaculate or have an orgasm. Neither concern, of course, is valid. Most of the milky liquid contained in semen is produced by the seminal vesicles and the prostate gland, other organs that feed into the vas deferens later in the ejaculation process. This liquid is still ejaculated, but without any sperm in it. Because sperm are so tiny, the volume of semen ejaculated is virtually unaffected. Sterilization has no effect on either men's or women's ability to respond sexually or enjoy sexual activity.

An advantage of sterilization is that it is considered permanent. No more attention need be given to contraceptive methods. A disadvantage is that a person may change his or her mind about having children. Sterilization allows little room for that choice. Another disadvantage is that sterilization has nothing to do with preventing STIs.

Ethical Questions 6.5

EP 2.1.2

To what extent should contraception be made readily available to anyone who wants it? What kinds of contraception should be offered, if any? Who should pay for contraception (e.g., individuals using it or the government)?

Contraceptive Methods of the Future

A number of contraceptive methods are being investigated for future use:

EP 2.1.9a

1. *Hormones to suppress sperm production.* Research has focused on injecting males with hormones linked to decreased sperm production or to inhibiting the ability of sperm to fertilize an egg effectively (Greenberg et al., 2014). Hormonal implants that inhibit sperm production are also being investigated (Carroll, 2013).

2. *Contraceptive vaccines (immunocontraceptives) for men.* Such vaccines would cause infertility by inducing the man's immune system to inhibit a phase in sperm or testosterone production (Carroll, 2013; Crooks & Baur, 2014; Hyde & DeLamater, 2014).

3. *Contraceptive vaccines (immunocontraceptives) for women.* A vaccine is being investigated that would immunize women against the hormonal changes necessary to make the uterus hospitable for implantation of a fertilized egg (Carroll, 2013; Crooks & Baur, 2014).

4. *Microbicides.* These are chemicals that potentially kill bacteria and viruses causing STIs as well as sperm (Carroll, 2013; Crooks & Baur, 2014; Hyde & DeLamater, 2014). Microbicides might

be used alone or in conjunction with a condom or diaphragm (Hyde & DeLamater, 2014).

5. *Spray-on contraception.* Nesterone, a progestin that can be sprayed on the skin daily, is being studied; it is almost immediately absorbed by the skin and then slowly diffused into the bloodstream (Crooks & Baur, 2014; Greenberg et al., 2014; Hyde & DeLamater, 2014).

6. *New sterilization methods.* New procedures are being investigated that would be more readily reversible than current methods (Guha, 2007). "One involves injecting a blocking gel into the vas deferens [the tube that carries sperm from the testes to the urethra]; to reverse the procedure, the gel can be dissolved" (Crooks & Baur, 2014, p. 307; Hyde & DeLamater, 2014).

7. *New IUDs.* A number of new IUD designs are being studied (Crooks & Baur, 2014; Hyde & DeLamater, 2014). One, with an anticipated minimal effectiveness period of five years, is frameless, composed only of a string attached to copper tubes (Hyde & DeLamater, 2014).

8. *A new vaginal ring.* Rings being investigated involve releasing some combination of hormones that prevent both conception and STIs (Greenberg et al., 2014; Hyde & DeLamater, 2014).

9. *Natural factors.* Some research is investigating whether women might monitor their saliva or urine in order to determine when they are ovulating (Carroll, 2013).

10. *Fertility computers.* Computers are being studied regarding their potential ability to identify when a women is fertile (Carroll, 2013).

Chapter Summary

The following summarizes this chapter's content as it relates to the learning objectives presented at the beginning of the chapter. Chapter content will help prepare students to:

LO 6-1 *Define adolescence.*

Adolescence is the transitional period between childhood and adulthood during which young people mature physically and sexually.

LO 6-2 *Describe major physical changes during adolescence (including puberty, the growth spurt, the secular trend, and primary and secondary sex characteristics).*

Puberty is marked by the sudden enlargement of the reproductive organs and sexual genitalia, and the development of secondary sex characteristics (features that distinguish the genders but are not directly involved in reproduction). The initial entrance into puberty is typically characterized by a sharp increase in height, referred to as a growth spurt. People generally grow taller and bigger than they did a century ago, which is referred to as the secular trend. The development of primary and secondary sex characteristics reflect the proof of puberty.

LO 6-3 *Explain psychological reactions to physical changes.*

Adolescents have strong psychological reactions to their physical changes. It is important for adolescents to feel that they are physically attractive.

Adolescents mature at different rates. Research reveals mixed results regarding early-maturing boys. Early maturers tend to be more popular and to become leaders. However, they also have a greater tendency to be aggressive and delinquent. Late maturers tend to have lower self-esteem. Because of the many variables involved in human development, differences between early- and late-maturing boys become much less clear by adulthood. Early-maturing girls have an increased vulnerability to a range of problems. As with boys, in adulthood, differences between early and late maturers become much less clear.

An adolescent's brain undergoes physical changes in response to new hormonal production.

Environmental factors, peer influences, family influences, and personal characteristics may place adolescents at risk for using mind-altering substances.

LO 6-4 *Describe sexual activity in adolescence.*

Sexual activity during adolescence can result in unplanned pregnancy and various other consequences for adolescent parents and their children. Research suggests that comprehensive adolescent pregnancy programs and other supports can improve the futures of adolescent mothers and their children. Teenage fathers are often neglected and could benefit from greater understanding and support.

LO 6-5 *Assess sex education and empowerment.*

Comprehensive sex education programs can help prepare adolescents to make responsible decisions by providing information; addressing attitudes, values, and insights; discussing relationships and teaching interpersonal skills; and emphasizing taking responsibility for one's own behavior. Sex education curricula should be responsive to the needs and values of diverse racial and ethnic groups.

LO 6-6 *Identify sexually transmitted diseases.*

Each year, millions of young people contract sexually transmitted infections (STIs), including chlamydia, gonorrhea, syphilis, pubic lice, scabies, trichomoniasis, genital herpes, human papillomavirus (HPV), and human immunodeficiency virus (HIV).

LO 6-7 *Explain major methods of contraception.*

Anyone considering becoming sexually active requires accurate and specific information about contraception. There is no one best method of contraception for everyone. Hormonal methods of contraception include the contraceptive pill, the birth control patch, the vaginal ring, Depo-Provera injections, hormonal implants, and emergency contraception. Spermicides are chemical contraceptives. Barrier methods of contraception include condoms for men, the female condom, the diaphragm, and the cervical cap (FemCap). The birth control sponge (Today Sponge) serves as both a chemical and barrier method. Intrauterine devices (IUDs), including the ParaGard IUD and hormonal IUDs (Mirena or Skyla), are inserted inside the uterus. Other means of contraception include withdrawal, fertility awareness methods (FAMs), and sterilization. Each individual should evaluate the effectiveness, advantages, and disadvantages of each method in order to determine the most effective method for him or her.

COMPETENCY NOTES

The entire chapter addresses competency Educational Policy (EP) EP 2.1.7 and its respective practice behaviors EP 2.1.7a and EP 2.1.7b (as cited below). (See *p. 296*.)

EP 2.1.7 Apply knowledge of human behavior and the social environment.

EP 2.1.7a Utilize conceptual frameworks to guide the processes of assessment, intervention, and evaluation.
(Such conceptual frameworks will typically be identified by a "helping hands" icon.)

EP 2.1.7b Critique and apply knowledge to understand person and environment.
Other EP competencies and practice behaviors addressed in this chapter include the following:

EP 2.1.1e Engage in career-long learning.
(p. 302): The effects of early and late maturation provide an example of how ongoing research reflects changes in so-called "facts," requiring social workers to engage in career-long learning concerning the issue.

EP 2.1.2 Apply social work ethical principles to guide professional practice.
(pp. 301, 305, 307, 315, 329): Ethical questions are posed.

EP 2.1.3a Distinguish, appraise, and integrate multiple sources of knowledge, including research-based knowledge, and practice wisdom.
(p. 302): Practitioners should utilize multiple sources of research and knowledge to understand human development and guide their practice.

EP 2.1.4c Recognize and communicate their understanding of the importance of difference in shaping life experiences.
(p. 299): Race is related to the age of menarche.
(p. 307): Race and factors related to race affect life experiences such as time of first intercourse.
(p. 315): Social workers should strive to understand how cultural structures and values can affect diverse populations. Appropriate sex education programs and procedures for Native American adolescents are explored.

EP 2.1.6b Use research evidence to inform practice.
(p. 320): Social workers should utilize research on the effectiveness of various contraceptive methods to help clients make informed decisions.

EP 2.1.7 Apply knowledge of human behavior and the social environment.
(p. 297): Social workers must be knowledgeable about human behavior across the life course, including adolescence.

EP 2.1.8a Analyze, formulate, and advocate for policies that advance social well-being.
(p. 313): Practitioners should advocate for policies and programs that provide effective sex education that enhance responsible behavior and advance social well-being.

EP 2.1.9a Continuously discover, appraise, and attend to changing locales, populations, scientific and technological developments, and emerging societal trends to provide relevant services.
(p. 302): Practitioners must keep abreast of current research to understand the context of human development and provide relevant services.
(p. 316): Social workers should attend to changing trends in STIs and their treatments to help clients make informed decisions about prevention and treatment.
(p. 329): Practitioners addressing the issue of contraception with clients should keep abreast of current technological developments and trends in effectiveness.

EP 2.1.10g Select appropriate intervention strategies.
(p. 320): Practitioners should be knowledgeable about the major methods of contraception to help clients choose the most appropriate alternatives.

EP 2.1.10h Initiate actions to achieve organizational goals.
(p. 313): Practitioners should encourage communities and schools to implement effective sex education programs to empower students for making responsible decisions.

EP 2.1.10i Implement prevention interventions that enhance client capacities.
(p. 319): Strategies for preventing STIs are provided.
(p. 320): Social workers can help clients prevent unwanted pregnancies by helping them make informed decisions about contraceptive methods.

EP 2.1.10k Negotiate, mediate, and advocate for clients.
(p. 313): Social workers can advocate on their clients' behalf for effective sex education programs.

WEB RESOURCES

See this text's companion website at *www.cengage brain.com* for learning tools such as chapter quizzing, videos, and more.

PSYCHOLOGICAL DEVELOPMENT IN ADOLESCENCE

Banana Stock/Jupiter Images

"Teen Alcoholism Shows Dramatic Increase"
"Twenty-Two-Year-Old Hangs Self in Kenosha Jail"
"$600,000 Worth of Cocaine Found in College Drug Bust"
"Teen Mother Shoots Infant Daughter, Husband, and Self"
"Four Killed by Drunk Teen Driver"

These statements might all be seen in newspaper headlines. They refer to tragedies that involve adolescents and young adults. Although the media often address sensationalist and tragic events, the fact that such things are occurring merits our attention. What psychological variables operate to help cause such happenings?

A Perspective

This chapter will focus on some of the major psychological growth tasks and pitfalls confronting adolescents and young adults. Psychological systems involve such aspects of growth and development as forming an identity and developing a personal morality. An individual's psychological system interacts with biological and social systems to affect behavior.

We have already addressed some of the interactions between biological and psychological systems. For example, maturation rate and body weight (which relate to an individual's biological system) can affect body image and self-concept (which relate to the psychological system). Knowledge of psychological milestones normally negotiated during adolescence and young adulthood is important for the overall assessment of behavior and functioning. Additionally, this chapter will discuss two categories of critical issues that affect many individuals in this age group: assertiveness and suicide.

Learning Objectives

This chapter will help prepare students to:

EP 2.1.7, 2.1.7a, 2.1.7b

LO 7-1 *Explore identity formation in adolescence (including Erikson's psychosocial theory and Marcia's categories of identity)*

LO 7-2 *Examine race, culture, ethnicity, and identity development*

LO 7-3 *Explore moral development (including Kohlberg's theory, Gilligan's approach, and a social learning perspective)*

LO 7-4 *Review Fowler's theory of faith development*

LO 7-5 *Assess empowerment through assertiveness and assertiveness training*

LO 7-6 *Explore suicide in adolescence*

LO 7-1 Explore Identity Formation in Adolescence

EP 2.1.7a

Personal identities crystallize during adolescence. Through experimentation and evaluation of experience and ideas, the adolescent should establish some sense of who he or she really is. In other words, people get to know themselves during adolescence. Explored here are Erikson's psychosocial theory and Marcia's categories of identity.

Erikson's Psychosocial Theory

Erik Erikson (1950, 1968) proposed a theory of psychological development comprising eight stages. This theory focuses on how personalities evolve throughout life as a result of the interaction between biologically based maturation and the demands of society. The emphasis is on the role of the social environment in personality development. The eight stages are based partly on the stages proposed by Freud and partly on Erikson's studies in a wide variety of cultures. Erikson writes that the society in which one lives makes certain psychic demands at

SW Productions/Getty Images

Forming your identity is a process of serious reflection about who you are and who you want to become.

each stage of development. Erikson calls these demands *crises*. During each psychosocial stage, the individual must seek to adjust to the stresses and conflicts involved in these crises. The search for identity is a crisis that confronts people during adolescence.

Although Erikson's psychosocial theory addresses development throughout the life span, it is included here because of the importance of identity formation during adolescence. After the entire theory is discussed, its application to adolescence will be explored in greater depth.

Each stage of human development presents its characteristic crises. Coping well with each crisis makes an individual better prepared to cope with the next. Although specific crises are most critical during particular stages, related issues continue to arise throughout a person's life. For example, the

conflict of trust versus mistrust is especially important in infancy. Yet children and adults continue to struggle with whether or not to trust others.

Resolution of each crisis is an ideal, not necessarily a reality. The degree to which crises in earlier stages are resolved will affect a person's ability to resolve crises in later stages. If an individual doesn't learn how to trust in stage 1, that person will find it very difficult to attain intimacy in stage 6.

Stage 1: Basic Trust Versus Basic Mistrust

For infants up to 18 months of age, learning to trust others is the overriding crisis. To develop trust, one must understand that some people and some things can be depended on. Parents provide a major variable for such learning. For instance, infants who consistently receive warm, loving care and nourishment learn to trust that these things will be provided to them. Later in life, people may apply this concept of trust to friends, an intimate partner, or their government.

Stage 2: Autonomy Versus Shame and Doubt

The crisis of autonomy versus shame and doubt characterizes early childhood, from 18 months to 3 years. Children strive to accomplish things independently. They learn to feed themselves and to use the toilet. Accomplishing various tasks provides children with feelings of self-worth and self-confidence. On the other hand, if children of this age are constantly downtrodden, restricted, or punished, shame and doubt will emerge instead. Self-doubt will replace the self-confidence that should have developed during this period.

Stage 3: Initiative Versus Guilt

Preschoolers aged 3 to 6 years must face the crisis of taking their own initiative. Children at this age are extremely active physically; the world fascinates them and beckons them to explore it. They have active imaginations and are eager to learn. Preschoolers who are encouraged to take initiative to explore and learn are likely to assimilate this concept for use later in life. They will be more likely to feel confident in initiating relationships, pursuing career objectives, and developing recreational interests. Preschoolers who are consistently restricted, punished, or treated harshly are more likely to experience the emotion of guilt. They want to explore and experience, but they are not allowed to. Instead of learning initiative, they are likely to feel guilty about their tremendous desires to do so many things.

In reaction, they may become passive observers who follow the lead of others instead of initiating their own activities and ideas.

Stage 4: Industry Versus Inferiority

School-age children 6 to 12 years old must address the crisis of industry versus inferiority. Children in this age group need to be productive and succeed in their activities. In addition to play, a major focus of their lives is school. Therefore, mastering academic skills and material is important. Those who do learn to be industrious master activities. Comparison with peers becomes exceptionally important. Children who experience failure in school, or even in peer relations, may develop a sense of inferiority.

Stage 5: Identity Versus Role Confusion

Adolescence is a time when young people explore who they are and establish their identity. It is the transition period from childhood to adulthood when people examine the various roles they play (e.g., child, sibling, student, Catholic, Native American, basketball star) and integrate these roles into a perception of self, an identity. Some people are unable to integrate their many roles and have difficulty coping with conflicting roles; they are said to suffer from *role confusion*. Such persons feel confused and uncertain about their identity.

Stage 6: Intimacy Versus Isolation

Young adulthood is characterized by a quest for intimacy, which involves more than the establishment of a sexual relationship. Intimacy includes the ability to share with and give to another person without being afraid of sacrificing one's own identity. People who do not attain intimacy are likely to suffer isolation. These people have often been unable to resolve some of the crises of earlier psychosocial development. Various types of intimate relationships and how people experience them will be discussed in more detail in Chapter 8.

Stage 7: Generativity Versus Stagnation

Mature adulthood is characterized by the crisis of generativity versus stagnation. During this time of life, people become concerned with helping, producing for, or guiding the following generation. Generativity involves a genuine concern for the future beyond one's own life track, although it does not necessarily involve procreating one's own children. Rather, it concerns a drive to be creative and productive in a way that will aid people in the future. Adults who lack generativity become self-absorbed. They tend to focus primarily on their own concerns and needs rather than on those of others. The result is stagnation—a fixed, discouraging lack of progress and productivity.

Stage 8: Ego Integrity Versus Despair

The crisis of ego integrity versus despair characterizes old age. During this time of life, people tend to look back over their years and reflect on them. If they appreciate their life and are content with their accomplishments, they are said to have *ego integrity*—the ultimate form of identity integration. Such people enjoy a sense of peace and accept the fact that life will soon be over. Others who have failed to cope successfully with past life crises and have many regrets experience despair.

CONCEPT SUMMARY

Erikson's Eight Stages of Development

Stage	Crisis	Age	Important Event
1.	Basic trust versus basic mistrust	Birth to 18 months	Feeding
2.	Autonomy versus shame and doubt	18 months to 3 years	Toileting
3.	Initiative versus guilt	3 to 6 years	Locomoting
4.	Industry versus inferiority	6 to 12 years	School
5.	Identity versus role confusion	Adolescence	Peer relationship
6.	Intimacy versus isolation	Young adulthood	Love relationship
7.	Generativity versus stagnation	Maturity	Parenting and creating
8.	Ego integrity versus despair	Old age	Reflecting on and accepting one's life

Implications of Identity Formation in Adolescence

Achieving genital maturity and rapid body growth signals young people that they will soon be adults. They therefore begin to question their future roles as adults.

The most important task of adolescence is to develop a sense of identity, a sense of "who I am." Highlight 7.1 poses some questions to help you explore and articulate your sense of identity. Making a career choice is an important part of this search for identity.

HIGHLIGHT 7.1

How to Determine Who You Are

**EP 2.1.1b,
2.1.2a,
2.1.10b**

Forming an identity essentially involves *thinking* about, and arriving at, answers to the following questions: (1) What do I want out of life? (2) What kind of person do I want to be? (3) Who am I? The most important decisions you make in your life may well be in arriving at answers to these questions.

Answers to these questions are not easy to arrive at. They require considerable contemplation and trial and error. But if you are to lead a fulfilling life, it is imperative to find answers to give direction and meaning to your life. Without answers, you are apt to muddle through life by being a passive responder to situations that arise, rather than a continual achiever of your life's goals.

Knowing who you are and where you are going are important both for clients and for you as a practitioner. The following questions may be a useful tool in pursuing that quest:

1. What do I find satisfying, meaningful, and enjoyable? (Only after you identify what is meaningful and gratifying will you be able to consciously seek involvement in activities that will make your life fulfilling, and avoid those activities that are meaningless or stifling.)
2. What is my moral code? (One possible code is to seek to fulfill your needs and to seek to do what you find enjoyable, doing so in a way that does not deprive others of the ability to fulfill their needs.)
3. What are my spiritual beliefs?
4. What are my employment goals? (Ideally, you should seek employment that you find stimulating and satisfying, that you are skilled at, and that provides you with enough money to support your lifestyle.)
5. What are my sexual morals? (All of us should develop a consistent code that we are comfortable with and that helps us to meet our needs without exploiting others. There is no one right code—what works for one may not work for another, due to differences in lifestyles, life goals, and personal values.)
6. Do I want to have a committed relationship? (If yes, with what type of person and when? How consistent are your answers here with your other life goals?)
7. Do I want to have children? (If yes, how many and when? How consistent are your answers here with your other life goals?)

8. What area of the country or world do I want to live in? (Variables to be considered are climate, geography, type of dwelling, rural or urban setting, closeness to relatives or friends, and characteristics of the neighborhood.)
9. What do I enjoy doing with my leisure time?
10. What kind of image do I want to project to others? (Your image will be composed of your dressing style and grooming habits, your emotions, personality, assertiveness, capacity to communicate, material possessions, moral code, physical features, and voice patterns. You need to assess your strengths and shortcomings honestly in this area, and seek to make needed improvements.)
11. What type of people do I enjoy being with, and why?
12. Do I want to improve the quality of my life and that of others? (If yes, in what ways, and how do you hope to achieve these goals?)
13. What types of relationships do I want to have with relatives, friends, neighbors, and people I meet for the first time?
14. What are my thoughts about death and dying?
15. What do I hope to be doing in 5 years, 10 years, 20 years?

To have a fairly well-developed sense of identity, you need to have answers to most, but not all, of these questions. Very few people are able to arrive at rational, consistent answers to all the questions. Having answers to most of them will provide a reference for developing your views in the yet unanswered areas.

Honest, well-thought-out answers to these questions will go a long way toward defining who you are. Again, what you want out of life, along with your motivation to achieve these goals, will primarily determine your identity. These questions are simple to state, but arriving at answers is a complicated, ongoing process. In addition, expect some changes in your life goals as time goes on. Environmental influences change (e.g., changes in working conditions). Also, as personal growth occurs, changes are apt to occur in activities that you find enjoyable and also in your beliefs, attitudes, and values. Accept such changes. If you have a fairly good idea of who you are, you will be prepared to make changes in your life goals, which will give continued direction to your life. Your life is shaped by events that are the results of decisions you make and decisions that are made for you. Without a sense of identity, you will not know what decisions are best for you. With a sense of identity, you will be able to direct your life toward goals you select and find personally meaningful.

The primary danger during the identity development process, according to Erikson, is *identity confusion*. This confusion can be expressed in a variety of ways. One is to delay acting like a responsible adult. Another is to commit oneself to poorly thought-out courses of action. Still another way is to regress into childishness to avoid assuming the responsibilities of adulthood. Erikson views the cliquishness of adolescence and its intolerance of differences as defenses against identity confusion. Falling in love is viewed as an attempt to define identity. Through self-disclosing intimate thoughts and feelings with another, the adolescent is articulating and seeking to better understand his or her identity. Through seeing the reactions of a loved one to one's intimate thoughts and feelings, the adolescent is testing out values and beliefs and is better able to clarify a sense of self.

Adolescents and young adults experiment with roles that represent the many possibilities for their future identity. For instance, students take certain courses to test out their future career interests. They also experiment with a variety of part-time jobs to test occupational interests. They date and go steady to test relationships with the opposite sex. Dating also allows for different self-presentations with each new date. Adolescents and young adults may also experiment with drugs—alcohol, tobacco, marijuana, cocaine, and so on. Many are confused about their religious beliefs and seek in a variety of ways to develop a set of religious and moral beliefs with which they can be comfortable. They also tend to join, participate in, and then quit a variety of organizations. They experiment with a variety of interests and hobbies. As long as no laws are broken (and health is not seriously affected) in the process of experimenting, our culture gives teenagers and young adults the freedom to experiment in a variety of ways in order to develop a sense of identity.

Erikson (1959) uses the term *psychosocial moratorium* to describe a period of free experimentation before a final sense of identity is achieved. Generally, our society allows adolescents and young adults freedom from the daily expectations of role performance. Ideally, this moratorium allows young people the freedom to experiment with values, beliefs, and roles so that they can find a role in society that maximizes their personal strengths and affords positive recognition from the community.

The crisis of identity versus role confusion is best resolved through integrating earlier identifications, present values, and future goals into a consistent self-concept. A sense of identity is achieved only after a period of questioning, reevaluation, and experimentation. Efforts to resolve questions of identity may take the young person down paths of emotional involvement, overzealous commitment, alienation, rebellion, or playful wandering.

Many adolescents are idealistic. They see the evils and negatives in our society and in the world. They cannot understand why injustice and imperfection exist. They yearn for a much better life for themselves and for others and have little understanding of the resources and hard work it takes for advancements. They often try to change the world, and their efforts are genuine. If society can channel their energies constructively, adolescents can make meaningful contributions. Unfortunately, some become disenchanted and apathetic after being continually frustrated with obstacles.

Importance of Achieving Identity

Adolescents and young adults struggle with developing a sense of who they are, what they want out of life, and what kind of people they want to be. Arriving at answers to such questions is among the most important tasks people face in life. Without answers, a person will not be prepared to make such major decisions as which career to select; deciding whether, when, or whom to marry; deciding where to live; and deciding what to do with leisure time. Unfortunately, many people muddle through life and never arrive at well-thought-out answers to these questions. Those who do not arrive at answers are apt to be depressed, anxious, indecisive, and unfulfilled.

The Formation of Identity

Identity development is a lifelong process. During the early years, one's sense of identity is largely determined by the reactions of others. A long time ago, Cooley (1902) coined this labeling process as resulting in the *looking-glass self*—that is, people develop their self-concept in terms of how others relate to them. For example, if a neighborhood identifies a teenage male as being a troublemaker or delinquent, neighbors are then apt to distrust him, accuse him of delinquent acts, and label his behavior as such. This labeling process, the youth begins to realize, also results in a type of prestige and status, at least from his peers. In the absence of objective ways to gauge whether he is in fact a delinquent, the youth will rely on the subjective evaluations of others. Thus, he is apt to begin to gradually perceive himself as a delinquent, and to begin to enact the delinquent role.

Labels have a major impact on our lives. If a child is frequently called stupid by his or her parents, that child is apt to develop a low self-concept, anticipate failure in many areas (particularly academic), put forth little effort in school and in competitive interactions with others, and end up failing.

Because identity development is a lifelong process, positive changes are probably possible even for those who view themselves as failures. In identity formation, it is important to remember that what we want out of the future is more important than past experience in determining what the future will be. The past is fixed and cannot be changed, but the present and the future can be. Although the past may have been painful and traumatic, it does not follow that the present and the future must be so. We are in control of our lives, and we largely determine what our future will be.

Marcia's Categories of Identity

James Marcia (1980, 1991, 2002; Marcia & Carpendale, 2004) has done a substantial amount of research on the Eriksonian theory of psychosocial development. He identifies four major ways in which people cope with identity crises: (1) identity achievement, (2) foreclosure, (3) identity diffusion, and (4) moratorium. People may be classified into these categories on the basis of three primary criteria: First, whether the individual experiences a major crisis during identity development; second, whether the person expresses a commitment to some type of occupation; and third, whether there is commitment to some set of values or beliefs.

Identity Achievement

To reach the stage of *identity achievement*, people undergo a period of intense decision making. After much effort, they develop a personalized set of values and make their career decisions. The attainment of identity is usually thought of as the most beneficial of the four status categories.

Foreclosure

People who fall into the *foreclosure* category are the only ones who never experience an identity crisis as such. They glide into adulthood without experiencing much turbulence or anxiety. Decisions concerning both career and values are made relatively early in life. These decisions are often based on their parents'

values and ideas rather than their own. For example, a woman might become a mother and a part-time waitress as her own mother had done, not because she makes a conscious choice, but because she assumes it's what she is expected to do. Likewise, a man might become an auto mechanic or an accountant just because his father was an auto mechanic or an accountant, and it seemed a good way of life.

It's interesting that the term *foreclosure* is used to label this category. Foreclosure involves shutting someone out from involvement, as one would foreclose a mortgage and bar a person who mortgaged his or her property from reclaiming it. To foreclose one's identity implies shutting off various other opportunities to grow and change.

Identity Diffusion

People who experience *identity diffusion* suffer from a serious lack of decision and direction. Although they go through an identity crisis, they never resolve it. They are not able to make clear decisions concerning either their personal ideology or their career choice. These people tend to be characterized by low self-esteem and lack of resolution. For example, such a person might be a drifter who never stays more than a few months in any one place and defies any serious commitments.

Moratorium

The *moratorium* category includes people who experience intense anxiety during their identity crisis, yet have not made decisions regarding either personal values or a career choice. However, moratorium people experience a more continuous, intense struggle to resolve these issues. Instead of avoiding the decision-making issue, they address it almost constantly. They are characterized by strong, conflicting feelings about what they should believe and do. For example, a moratorium person might struggle intensely with a religious issue, such as whether there is a God. Moratorium people tend to have many critical, but as yet unresolved, issues.

•••• Ethical Questions 7.1

EP 2.1.2 *To what extent is there an ideal identity everyone should strive to acquire? How much individuality should be allowed or encouraged in identity formation?*

Critical Thinking: The Evaluation of Theory and Application to Client Situations

EP 2.1.3

Both Erikson's and Marcia's theories provide interesting insights into people's behavior and their interaction with others. Both provide a framework for better understanding "normal" life crises and events. For example, stage 2 of Erikson's psychosocial theory focuses on ages 18 months to 3 years. Most of this period is frequently referred to as the "terrible twos." Understanding that children in this age group are striving to achieve some autonomy and control over their environment during this time helps us also understand that their behavior is full of action and exploration. Children should not be reprimanded for the types of behavior that are normal and natural during this stage of development. Such insight can better prepare social workers for helping parents develop age-appropriate expectations and behavior management techniques.

Marcia's emphasis on the acquisition of coping skills also provides insights for work with clients. Those people who are trapped in foreclosure, identity diffusion, or moratorium identity crises may benefit from help in the resolution of these crises. Social workers can give feedback in addition to helping people formulate and evaluate new alternatives. Acknowledgment of the existence of such crises and understanding their dynamics are the first steps toward resolution.

Both Marcia's and Erikson's theories emphasize the importance of identity formation. Looking at adolescence and young adulthood with some understanding of the forces at work can help social workers better understand the dynamics of human behavior within the social environment. For instance, strife between parents and children is common during adolescence. It is also understandable. Parents try to maintain some control with their leadership roles. Adolescents struggle to define themselves as individuals and to become independent. Knowing that these are natural occurrences provides clues to insights social workers can give to clients regarding their feelings and behaviors. The struggle for control can be identified and discussed. Parental restrictiveness and adolescent rebelliousness can be examined. New behavioral options for interaction can be explored.

Traditional theories of identity development such as Erickson's and Marcia's have limitations due to their Westernized perspective on how people *should* develop. For example, traditional Asian and Native American cultures generally emphasize interdependence instead of stressing the development of an independent identity. A subsequent section explores some of the issues concerning cultural background and identity development. Spotlight 7.1 addresses the special issues involved in identity development for lesbian and gay adolescents.

We established in an earlier chapter that social workers need to evaluate theory and determine for themselves what theoretical concepts and frameworks are most suited for their own practice with clients. Questions to keep in mind while doing this include the following:

EP 2.1.2b, 2.1.3b

1. How does the theory apply to client situations?
2. What research supports the theory?
3. To what extent does the theory coincide with social work values and ethics?
4. Are other theoretical frameworks or concepts available that are more relevant to practice situations?

LO 7-2 Examine Race, Culture, Ethnicity, and Identity Development

EP 2.1.4c

Questions might be raised regarding the extent to which Erikson's and Marcia's theories apply to all people. This includes various racial and ethnic groups. For instance, some cultures emphasize respect for and deference to older family members. Young people are expected to conform until they too become older and "wiser." To what extent, then, is it important for each individual to struggle to achieve a strikingly unique and independent personality? Must this particular aspect of behavior be stressed to a great extent? Or should the ability to assume a strong identification with the family and cultural group be given precedence?

SPOTLIGHT ON DIVERSITY 7.1

Lesbian and Gay Adolescents: The Need for Empowerment

**EP 2.1.2a,
2.1.3a,
2.1.4,
2.1.4a,
2.1.4c,
2.1.5a,
2.1.9a**

Lesbian and gay adolescents in this culture suffer even more extreme obstacles to identity development than do their heterosexual peers. Perhaps their biggest obstruction is the constant oppression of homophobia. *Homophobia* is an extreme and irrational fear and hatred for lesbian and gay people simply because they are lesbian and gay. (Chapter 13 addresses sexual orientation and homophobia in much greater detail.) Homophobia and the oppressive reactions of others to homosexuality isolate lesbian and gay youth. On the one hand, lesbian and gay adolescents are trying to establish individual identities, just as heterosexual adolescents are. On the other hand, lesbian and gay youth are severely discouraged from expressing and establishing their sexual identities. The question that should be raised is, To what extent do Erikson's and Marcia's theories concerning identity development apply to these young people? Do these theories go far enough to explain the serious crises lesbian and gay people go through?

Lesbian and gay youth often experience extreme isolation (Miller, 2008; Morrow, 2006, 2008; Papalia & Feldman, 2012; Santrock, 2012b). "Alienation from the traditional church's teachings, lack of access to gay-friendly counseling services, being privy to a barrage of hostile comments about 'fags' and 'bull-dykes,' feeling displeasure from one's family—all combine to close the avenues to much needed social support" (van Wormer, Wells, & Boes, 2000, p. 48). *Coming out* is the process of a person's acknowledging publicly that he or she is gay or lesbian. If a young person comes out, he or she is often ostracized and demeaned. On the other hand, if young people cautiously hide their true feelings and identity, they risk depression, avoidance behaviors such as drug or alcohol abuse, and rebellious acting out, such as running away or truancy.

**EP 2.1.1b;
2.1.4d;
2.1.5b&c;
2.1.10a, b,
g, j&k**

Social work practitioners should be especially sensitive to the issues facing lesbian and gay adolescents. There are at least 10 suggestions for helping and empowering lesbian and gay youth (Barret & Logan, 2002):

1. Evaluate your own homophobic attitudes. Strive to develop a caring, empathic, nonjudgmental perspective that can be communicated to lesbian and gay clients. What stereotypes do you harbor? What do you personally feel about sexuality and sexual identity?

How comfortable do you feel with people who have a sexual orientation other than your own?
2. Become knowledgeable about the needs and issues of lesbian and gay adolescents.
3. Understand that adolescence is a time for exploration of one's sexual identity. "Many sexual minority youth don't crystallize their sexual identity until late adolescence, and same-sex sexual behavior does not necessarily cement sexual orientation. For example, boys may engage in group masturbation, competing to see who can have an orgasm first, and girls may be very affectionate with each other, holding hands, walking with their arms around each other, and even kissing. This does not necessarily mean they are gay or lesbian" (p. 138).
4. Confront insulting, offensive, and belittling comments. Challenge adolescent peers when they use name-calling and make comments that reflect stereotypes. Educate people about facts, and help them understand what cruel effects myths and homophobic treatment can have on lesbian and gay people.
5. Provide accurate information about sexuality, sexual orientation, and safe sexual behavior.
6. Never assume that a person is heterosexual. A young woman's significant other just might be a girlfriend, not a boyfriend.
7. Advocate for the rights of lesbian and gay people when they are being violated.
8. Have resources about sexual orientation on hand, or advocate for schools to make them available. These may include books, articles, DVDs, CDs, or websites.
9. Help lesbian and gay youth become connected with others of their own sexual orientation. Many cities have helplines, support groups, speakers' bureaus, and activities available for lesbian and gay young people.
10. As a social worker, you can help lesbian and gay youth navigate through the coming-out process. Such youth may need help answering a variety of questions: Should they come out or not? What should they say? Whom should they tell? How will people react?

In summary, it appears that Erikson's and Marcia's theories have only limited relevance for lesbian and gay identity development. The theories can be applied to a certain extent; they indicate that all young people go through an identity crisis. However, they do little to focus on the special issues of lesbian and gay young people.

It is up to you as a social worker to scrutinize theories closely and use what you can from them. However, it is just as important to recognize limitations of theories.

Approximately one-third of adolescents in the United States belong to an ethnic group that is a racial or ethnic "minority," which, of course, includes such groups as African Americans, Native Americans, Hispanics, and Asian Americans (Kail & Cavanaugh, 2013). It is very important that these young people establish an ethnic identity along with their individual identity (Hendricks, 2005; Kail & Cavanaugh, 2014; Phinney, 2005). This involves identifying with their ethnic group, feeling that they belong, and appreciating their cultural heritage. Older adolescents are more likely to have established an ethnic identity than are younger ones (French, Seidman, Allen, & Aber, 2006). The former apparently have had more time to explore aspects of their culture, develop their cognitive ability, and think about who they are.

Phinney (1989) suggests a parallel development for children from diverse ethnic groups that coincides with Marcia's four coping strategies for identity development. A person with a *diffused identity* demonstrates little or no involvement with his or her ethnic and cultural heritage and may be unaware of or disinterested in cultural issues. A person with *foreclosed identity* has explored his or her cultural background to a minor extent. However, feelings about ethnic identity are vague. He or she most likely simply adopts the ideas of parents or other relatives without giving them much thought. Someone with a *moratorium identity* displays an active pursuit of ethnic identity. This state reflects an ethnic identity crisis. Finally, a person who has *achieved an ethnic identity* has struggled with its meaning and come to conclusions regarding how this ethnic identity is an integral part of his or her life. Cross and Fhagen-Smith (1996) summarize how Phinney's model relates to ethnic identity development:

> The … model states that ethnic and racial minorities enter adolescence with poorly developed ethnic identities (diffusion) or with an identity "given" to them by their parents (foreclosure). They may sink into an identity crisis, during which the conflicts and challenges associated with their minority status are sorted out (moratorium), and should all go well, they achieve an ethnic identity that is positive and gives high salience to ethnicity (achieved ethnicity). (p. 111)

Moratorium is reflected in the thoughtful words of a Mexican American adolescent who stated, "I want

Paul Chesley/Getty Images

It is very important that young people establish an ethnic and cultural identity along with their individual identity. This involves identifying with their racial and ethnic group, feeling that they belong, and appreciating their cultural heritage. Here, Native American Blackfoot children participate in cultural events.

to know what we do and how our culture is different from others. Going to festivals and cultural events helps me to learn more about my own culture and about myself" (Phinney, 1989, p. 44). Likewise, an Asian American teen describes his feelings about his ethnic identity achievement: "I have been born Filipino and am born to be Filipino.... I'm here in America, and people of many different cultures are here, too. So I don't consider myself only Filipino, but also American" (Phinney, 1989, p. 44).

An Alternative Model of Racial and Cultural Identity Development

As an alternative approach to understanding racial and cultural identity development, Howard-Hamilton and Frazier (2005) describe the five-phase Racial/Cultural Identity Development Model (R/CID) initially developed by Sue and Sue (1990). To some degree, this model parallels the stages proposed by Marcia, but it centers on racial and cultural identity development. Stages range from having little or no development of ethnic and cultural identity to having complete integration of such identity. The model asks: "(a) who do you identify with and why; (b) what minority cultural attitudes and beliefs do you accept or reject and why; (c) what dominant cultural attitudes and beliefs do you accept or reject and why; and (d) how do your current attitudes and beliefs affect your interaction with other minorities and people of the dominant culture?" (Howard-Hamilton & Frazier, 2005, p. 78). R/CID proposes that people progress through the following five stages to establish an integrated racial or cultural identity (Howard-Hamilton & Frazier, 2005, pp. 78–82; Sue & Sue, 2008, pp. 242–252):

1. *Conformity stage.* During this stage, people identify closely with the dominant white society. "Physical and cultural characteristics that are common to the individual's racial or cultural group are perceived negatively and as something to be avoided, denied, or changed. In this stage, the person may attempt to mimic 'White' speech patterns, dress, and goals. A person at this stage has low internal self-esteem" (Howard-Hamilton & Frazier, 2005, p. 79).
2. *Dissonance stage.* Usually initiated by some crisis or negative experience, the person during this stage "becomes aware that racism does exist,

and that not all aspects of minority or majority culture are good or bad. For the first time, the individual begins to entertain thoughts of possible positive attributes" of his or her own culture and "a sense of pride in self" (p. 79). Suspicion about the values inherent in the dominant culture grows.
3. *Resistance and immersion stage.* "Movement into this stage is characterized by the resolution of the conflicts and confusions that occurred in the previous stage" (p. 79). The person's awareness of social issues grows along with a growing appreciation of his or her own culture. "A large amount of anger and hostility is also directed toward White society. There in turn is a feeling of dislike and distrust for all members of the dominant group" (p. 80).
4. *Introspection stage.* During this stage, the individual "discovers that this level of intensity of feelings is psychologically draining and does not allow time to devote energy into understanding one's racial/cultural group; the individual senses the need for positive self-definition and a proactive sense of awareness. A feeling of disconnection emerges with minority group views that may be rigid. Group views may start to conflict with individual views.... The person experiences conflict because she or he discovers there are many aspects of American culture that are desirable and functional, yet the confusion lies in how to incorporate these elements into the minority culture" (pp. 80–81).
5. *Integrative awareness stage.* Persons of color in this stage "have developed an inner sense of security and can appreciate various aspects of their culture that make them unique. Conflicts and discomforts experienced in the previous stage are not resolved, hence greater control and flexibility are attained. Individuals in this stage recognize there are acceptable and unacceptable aspects of all cultures and that it is important for them to accept or reject aspects of a culture that are not considered desirable to them. Attitudes and beliefs toward self are self-appreciating. A positive self-image and a feeling of self-worth emerge. An integrated concept of racial pride in identity and culture also develops. The individual sees himself or herself as a unique person who belongs to a specific minority group, a member of a larger society, and a member of the human race" (p. 81).

The person begins to view those in the dominant culture in a selective manner, allowing trust and relationships to develop with those who denounce the oppression of minority groups.

Communities and Schools Can Strengthen Racial and Cultural Identity Development for Adolescents

EP 2.1.8a, 2.1.10e

A positive social environment that celebrates cultural strengths can enhance the development of a positive racial and cultural identity and pride (Delgado, 1998a, 1998b, 2000b, 2007). Both schools and the community-at-large can stress cultural strengths of resident groups. School curricula can have relevant historical and cultural content integrated throughout. Assignments can focus on learning and appreciating cultural strengths. "A social studies teacher, for example, might assign a student to interview an elder member of his or her family or community about life in his or her place of origin as part of a lesson on ethnic origins" (Delgado, 1998a, p. 210). Schools and recreational facilities can develop programs that emphasize cultural pride and help adolescents "come to terms with their newly developing [racial and cultural] identities as individuals and as participants in an increasingly multicultural society while preserving essential links to their history, families, and culture" (Delgado, 1998b, p. 213).

For example, one such program, called Nuevo Puente (New Bridge), was designed initially to address substance abuse by Puerto Rican youth. Staff developed an educational curriculum

that involved obtaining input from all sectors of the Puerto Rican community. Major content areas were identified through…. [a survey,]…. interviews, focus groups, meetings, and discussions with community leaders, parents, and educators. [A focus group (discussed in Chapter 8) is a specially assembled collection of people who respond through a semi-structured or structured discussion to the concerns and interests of the person, group, or organization that invited the participants.]

The curriculum included knowledge development and skills building that were culturally relevant for Puerto Rican youths. Participants received 72 hours

of training over a seven-month period in cultural pride (Puerto Rican history, values, culture, arts, and traditions); group leadership skills (recruiting and leading groups); self-sufficiency and self-determination; communication and relationship skills (conflict resolution and identifying situations that lead to violence and other risk-taking behaviors); [and] strategies to deal with substance abuse (increased awareness of alcohol and other drugs)….

As a whole, the curriculum had a significant impact on the participants. However, the greatest effect was achieved by the module on identity and culture, which was measured by the participants' interest and pride in speaking Spanish; awareness of Puerto Rican cuisine, history, geography, and folklore; willingness to participate in Puerto Rican folk dancing; interest in and willingness to celebrate Puerto Rican holidays; interest in learning the lyrics to the Puerto Rican anthem; and eagerness to learn about their ancestors. (Delgado, 1998b, p. 217)

Community festivals such as African American Fest or German Fest can provide other avenues through which community residents of all ages can learn about and appreciate various facets of their and others' cultures. Such events can celebrate history, arts, crafts, music, and food.

The following explains how murals in urban settings can portray cultural symbols and honor ethnic traditions:

A mural is an art form that is expressed on a building's walls as opposed to a canvas…. Murals represent a community effort to utilize cultural symbols as a way of creating an impact internally and externally. Murals should not be confused with graffiti. A mural represents an artistic impression that is not only sanctioned by a community, but often commissioned by it … and invariably involve a team of artists. Graffiti, on the other hand, represent an artistic impression … that is individual centered and manifested on subway trains, doors, mailboxes, buses, public settings, and other less significant locations. Their content generally focuses on the trials and tribulations associated with urban living, issues of oppression, or simply a "signature" of the artist….

Murals represent a much higher level of organization, and the community often participates in their design and painting; their location within the community also reflects the degree of community sanctioning—those that are prominently located enjoy a high degree of community acceptance, whereas those in less prominent locations do not…. Murals provide communities of color with an important outlet for expressing their cultural pride….

Among Latino groups, for example, murals allow subgroups to express the uniqueness of their history and culture. (Delgado, 2000a, pp. 78–80)

"Pre-Columbian themes, intended to remind Chicanos of their noble origins, are common. There are motifs from the Aztec … [ancient manuscripts], gods from the Aztec [temples and mythology,] … allusions to the Spanish conquest and images of the Virgin of Guadalupe, a cherished Mexican icon" (Treguer, 1992, p. 23, cited in Delgado, 1998b, p. 80).

LO 7-3 Explore Moral Development

EP 2.1.3a, 2.1.3b, 2.1.7a

Young adulthood is filled with avid quests for intimate relationships and other major commitments involving career and life goals. A parallel pursuit is the formulation of a personal set of moral values. *Morality* involves a set of principles regarding what is right and what is wrong. Many times these principles are not clearly defined in black or white, but involve various shades of gray. There is no one absolute answer. For example, is the death penalty right or wrong? Is it good or bad to have sexual intercourse before marriage?

Moral issues range from very major to minor day-to-day decisions. Although moral development can take place throughout life, it is especially critical during adolescence and young adulthood. These are the times when people gain the right to make independent decisions and choices. Often the values developed during this stage remain operative for life. Explored here are theoretical perspectives proposed by Kohlberg and by Gilligan, in addition to a social learning outlook on moral development.

Ethical Questions 7.2

EP 2.1.2

What are the major principles in your personal code of morality? How would you answer the following moral questions regarding what is right and what is wrong: Should there be a death penalty for monstrous crimes and, if so, how monstrous? Why or why not? Should there be national health insurance under which all people receive medical services regardless of their level of wealth? If so, who should pay for it? Should corporal punishment be allowed in schools? Why or why not? Should prayer be allowed in schools? Why or why not?

Moral Development: Kohlberg's Theory

Lawrence Kohlberg (1963, 1968, 1969, 1981a, 1981b) has proposed a series of three levels, and six stages, through which people progress as they develop their moral framework. These six stages are clustered within three distinct levels, as shown in the Concept Summary box on page 346.

Level 1: The Preconventional or Premoral Level

The first level, the *preconventional* or *premoral* level, is characterized by giving precedence to self-interest. People usually experience this level from ages 4 to 10. Moral decisions are based on external standards. Behavior is governed by whether a child will receive a reward or punishment. The first stage in this level is based on avoiding punishment. Children do what they are told in order to avoid negative consequences. The second stage focuses on rewards instead of punishment. In other words, children do the "right" thing in order to receive a reward or compensation. Sometimes this involves an exchange of favors: "I'll scratch your back if you'll scratch mine."

Level 2: The Conventional Level

Level 2 of Kohlberg's theory is the *conventional* level, in which moral thought is based on conforming to conventional roles. Frequently, this level occurs from ages 10 to 13. There is a strong desire

CONCEPT SUMMARY

Kohlberg's Three Levels and Six Stages of Moral Development

Level/Stage	Description
Level 1: Preconventional (Self-Interest)	Controls are external. Behavior is governed by receiving rewards or punishments.
Stage 1: Punishment and obedience orientation	Decisions concerning what is good or bad are made in order to avoid receiving punishment.
Stage 2: Naive instrumental hedonism	Rules are obeyed in order to receive rewards. Often favors are exchanged.
Level 2: Conventional (Role Conformity)	The opinions of others become important. Behavior is governed by conforming to social expectations.
Stage 3: "Good boy/girl morality"	Good behavior is considered to be what pleases others. There is a strong desire to please and gain the approval of others.
Stage 4: Authority-maintaining morality	The belief in law and order is strong. Behavior conforms to law and higher authority. Social order is important.
Level 3: Postconventional (Self-Accepted Moral Principles)	Moral decisions are finally internally controlled. Morality involves higher-level principles beyond law and even beyond self-interest.
Stage 5: Morality of contract, of individual rights, and of democratically accepted law	Laws are considered necessary. However, they are subject to rational thought and interpretation. Community welfare is important.
Stage 6: Morality of individual principles and Conscience	Behavior is based on internal ethical principles. Decisions are made according to what is right rather than what is written into law.

Source: Adapted from Kohlberg (1968, 1981a, 1981b).

to please others and to receive social approval. Although moral standards have begun to be internalized, they are still based on what others dictate, rather than on what is personally decided.

Within Level 2, stage 3 focuses on gaining the approval of others. Good relationships become very important. Stage 4, "authority-maintaining morality," emphasizes the need to adhere to law. Higher authorities are generally respected. "Law and order" are considered necessary in order to maintain the social order.

Level 3: The Postconventional Level

Level 3, the *postconventional* level, involves developing a moral conscience that goes beyond what others say. At this level, people contemplate laws and expectations and decide on their own what is right and what is wrong. They become autonomous, independent thinkers. Behavior is based on principles instead of laws. This level progresses beyond selfish concerns. The needs and well-being of others become very important. At this level, true morality is achieved.

Within Level 3, stage 5 involves adhering to socially accepted laws and principles. Law is considered good for the general public welfare. However,

laws are subject to interpretation and change. Stage 6 is the ultimate attainment. During this stage, one becomes free of the thoughts and opinions expressed by others. Morality is completely internalized. Decisions are based on one's personal conscience, transcending laws and regulations. Examples of people who attained this level include Martin Luther King Jr. and Gandhi.

Critical Thinking: Evaluation of Kohlberg's Theory

Many questions have been raised concerning the validity and application of Kohlberg's theory (Helwig & Turiel, 2011; Killin & Smetana, 2008; Santrock, 2012a; Walker & Frimer, 2011). For one thing, Kohlberg places primary emphasis on how people think, not what they do. Presidents and kings talk about the loftiest moral standards, but what they do is often another matter. Richard Nixon espoused high moral standards but was forced to resign after his cover-up of the Watergate break-in and theft of

EP 2.1.3, 2.1.3a, 2.1.3b, 2.1.4c

Democratic Party documents was brought to light. Many times, difficult moral decisions must be made in crisis situations. If you find yourself in a burning building with a crowd of people, how much effort will you expend to save others before yourself? What is the discrepancy between what you think is right and what you would really do in such a situation?

A second criticism of Kohlberg's theory is that it is culturally biased (Kail & Cavanaugh, 2013; Santrock, 2012a). Even Kohlberg (1978) himself has conceded that stage 6 may not apply across all cultures, societies, and situations. Snarey (1987) studied research on moral development in 27 countries and found that Kohlberg's schema does not incorporate the higher moral ideals that some cultures embrace. Examples of higher moral reasoning that would not be considered such within Kohlberg's framework include "principles of communal equity and collective happiness in Israel, the unity and sacredness of all life forms in India, and the relation of the individual to the community in New Guinea" (Santrock, 2008, p. 361).

Moral Development and Women: Gilligan's Approach

A major criticism of Kohlberg's theory is that virtually all of the research on which it is based used only men as subjects. Gilligan (1982; Gilligan & Attanucci, 1988; Gilligan, Brown, & Rogers, 1990) maintains that women fare less well according to Kohlberg's levels of moral development because they tend to view moral dilemmas differently than men do. Kohlberg's theory centers on *a justice perspective*, in which each person functions independently and makes moral decisions on an individual basis (Hyde & Else-Quest, 2013; Newman & Newman, 2012; Santrock, 2012a, p. 231). In contrast, Gilligan maintains that women are more likely to adopt a *"care perspective*, which views people in terms of their connectedness with others and emphasizes interpersonal communication, relationships with others, and concern for others" (Santrock, 2012a, p. 231). In other words, women tend to view morality in terms of personal situations.

Women often have trouble moving from a very personalized interpretation of morality to a focus on law and order. This bridge involves a generalization from the more personal aspects of what is right and wrong (how individual moral decisions affect one's own personal life) to morality within the larger, more impersonal society (how moral decisions, such as those instilled in law, affect virtually everyone). Kohlberg has been criticized because he has not taken into account the different orientation and life circumstances common to women.

Gilligan and her associates (Gilligan, 1982, 1996; Gilligan & Attanucci, 1988; Gilligan et al., 1990) reason that women's moral development is often based on their personal interest and commitment to the good of others close to them. Frequently, this involves giving up or sacrificing one's own well-being for others. Goodness and kindness are emphasized. This contrasts with a common male focus on assertively making decisions and exercising more rigid moral judgments.

Gilligan maintains that females' sense of morality emphasizes personal relationships and the assumption of responsibility for the care and well-being of those close to them. Here, two close friends enjoy sweet treats together.

Thinkstock/Jupiter Images

Gilligan initially targeted 29 women who were receiving pregnancy and abortion counseling. She postulated that pregnancy was an area in women's lives in which they could emphasize choice, yet it still was an intimate area to which they could relate. Gilligan interviewed the women concerning their pregnancies. She arrived at a sequence of moral levels that relate specifically to women. She found that women tend to view morality "based on an *ethics of caring* rather than a *morality of justice*" (Dacey, Travers, & Fiore, 2009, p. 248). She maintains that women's perspective on right and wrong emphasizes interpersonal relationships and the assumption of responsibility for the care and well-being of others close to them. This contrasts with Kohlberg's more abstract view of morality as the determination of what is fair and right in a much more general sense.

Gilligan describes the following levels and transitions of moral development for women.

Level 1: Orientation to Personal Survival

This level focuses purely on the woman's self-interest. The needs and well-being of others are not really considered. At this level, a woman focuses first on personal survival. What is practical and best for her is most important.

Transition 1: Transition from Personal Selfishness to Responsibility

This first transition involves a movement in moral thought from consideration only of self to some consideration of the others involved. During this transition, a woman comes to acknowledge the fact that she is responsible not only for herself but also for others, including the unborn. In other words, she begins to acknowledge that her choice will affect others.

Level 2: Goodness as Self-Sacrifice

Level 2 involves putting aside one's own needs and wishes. The well-being of other people becomes important. The "good" thing to do is to sacrifice herself so that others may benefit. A woman at this level feels dependent on what other people think. Often a conflict occurs between taking responsibility for her own actions and feeling pressure from others to make her decisions.

Transition 2: From Goodness to Reality

During this transitional period, women begin to examine their situations more objectively. They draw away from depending on others to tell them what they should do. Instead, they begin to take into account the well-being of everyone concerned, including themselves. Some of the concern for personal survival apparent in level 1 returns, but in a more objective manner.

Level 3: The Morality of Nonviolent Responsibility

Level 3 involves women thinking in terms of the repercussions of their decisions and actions. At this level, a woman's thinking has progressed beyond mere concern for what others will think about what she does. Rather, it involves accepting responsibility for making her own decisions. She places herself on an equal plane with others, weighs the various consequences of her potential actions, and accepts that she will be responsible for these consequences. The important principle operating here is that of minimizing hurt, both to herself and to others.

Gilligan's sequence of moral development provides a good example of how morality can be viewed from different perspectives. It is especially beneficial in emphasizing the different strengths manifested by men and women. The emphasis on feelings, such as direct concern for others, is just as important as the ability to decisively make moral judgments.

Critical Thinking: Evaluation of Gilligan's Theory

Some research has established support for Gilligan's proposed gender-based differences in moral reasoning. For example, some studies have found that females consider moral dilemmas concerning caring aspects of social relationships more important and a greater moral dilemma than males do (Eisenberg & Morris, 2004; Wark & Krebs, 2000). Another study found that girls were more likely than boys to use Gilligan's caring-based approaches when addressing dating predicaments (Weisz & Black, 2002). However, yet another study found "that girls' moral orientations are 'somewhat more likely to focus on care for others than on abstract principles of justice, but they can use both moral orientations when needed (as can boys …)' " (Blakemore, Berenbaum, & Liben, 2009, p. 132; cited in Santrock, 2012a, p. 231).

EP 2.1.3, 2.1.3a, 2.1.3b

Other research has found that little if any difference exists between the moral reasoning of men and women (Blakemore et al., 2009; Glover, 2001;

CONCEPT SUMMARY

Gilligan's Theory of Moral Development for Women

Level 1: Orientation to personal survival

Transition 1: *Transition from personal selfishness to responsibility*

Level 2: Goodness as self-sacrifice

Transition 2: *From goodness to reality*

Level 3: The morality of nonviolent responsibility

Hyde & Else-Quest, 2013; Walker, 1995; Wilson, 1995). One mega-analysis involved examining the results of 113 studies focusing on moral decision-making. Results question the accuracy of Gilligan's belief in significant gender differences concerning moral development (Hyde, 2007; Hyde & Else-Quest, 2013; Jaffee & Hyde, 2000). This study found that the overall picture revealed only small differences in how females and males made moral decisions. Although females were slightly more likely than males to use Gilligan's caring-based approach instead of Kohlberg's justice-based perspective, this disparity was larger in adolescence than adulthood. Whether caring- or justice-based approaches were used depended more on the situation being evaluated. For example, both females and males were more likely to emphasize caring when addressing interpersonal issues and justice when assessing more global social issues.

Coon and Mitterer (2013) comment:

> *Indeed, both men and women may use caring and justice to make moral decisions. The moral yardstick they use appears to depend on the situation they face (Wark & Krebs, 1996). Just the same, Gilligan deserves credit for identifying a second major way in which moral choices are made. It can be argued that our best moral choices combine justice and caring, reason and emotion—which may be what we mean by wisdom. (Pasupathi & Staudinger, 2001, pp. 110–111)*

Ethical Applications of Gilligan's Theory to Client Situations

EP 2.1.2b

Social work has a sound foundation of professional values expressed in the National Association of Social Workers (NASW) *Code of Ethics.* Ethics involve making decisions about what is right and what is wrong. Ethics provide social workers with guidelines for practice with clients.

Gilligan emphasizes the relationship between responsibility and morality. People develop morally as they gradually become more capable and willing to assume responsibility. Morality provides the basis for making ethical decisions. Gilligan "bases the highest stage of decision making on care for and sensitivity to the needs of others, on responsibility for others, and on nurturance" (Rhodes, 1985, p. 101). This principle is central to the NASW *Code of Ethics.* Gilligan's theory can provide some general ethical guidelines to which we can aspire in our day-to-day practice with clients. Social workers should strive to be sensitive to the needs of their clients. They should assume responsibility for effective practice with clients. Finally, they should provide help and nurturance to meet their clients' needs.

Moral Development: A Social Learning Theory Perspective

Social learning theorists including Albert Bandura (1991, 2002; Bandura, Caprara, Barbaranelli, Pastorelli, & Regalia, 2001) apply many of the principles of learning theory (discussed in Chapter 4) to moral actions. They

> *have been primarily interested in the behavioral component of morality—in what we actually do when faced with temptation or with an opportunity to behave prosocially. These theorists say that moral behavior is learned in the same way that other social behaviors are learned: through observational learning and reinforcement and punishment principles. They also consider moral behavior to be strongly influenced by situational factors—for example, by how closely a professor watches exam takers, by whether jewelry items are on the counter or behind glass in a department store. (Sigelman & Rider, 2012, p. 428)*

The social learning perspective, then, indicates that we gradually learn how to behave morally. Early on, young children receive reinforcement for behaving correctly and punishment for behaving incorrectly. They also see their parents and others as models for doing what is right or wrong. As children grow older, they gradually internalize these expectations and standards of conduct. Then as they encounter situations in which they must make moral decisions on how to behave, they use these internalized values. Additionally, as learning theory also predicts, they respond to the circumstances of the moment and the potential consequences they might encounter.

For example, the following example illustrates how social learning theory principles might be used to predict whether a teenager, arbitrarily called Waldo, will cheat on his upcoming math test. Social learning theory would focus on

> the moral habits Waldo has learned, the expectations he has formed about the probable consequences of his actions, his ability to self-regulate his behavior, and his ultimate behavior [choice]. If Waldo's parents have consistently reinforced him when he has behaved morally and punished him when he has misbehaved; if he has been exposed to models of morally acceptable behavior rather than brought up in the company of liars, cheaters, and thieves; and if he has well-developed self-regulatory mechanisms that cause him to take responsibility for his actions rather than to disengage morally, he is likely to behave in morally acceptable ways. Yet Bandura and other social learning theorists believe in the power of situational influences and predict that Waldo may still cheat on the math test if he sees his classmates cheating and getting away with it or if he is under pressure to get a B in math. (Sigelman & Rider, 2006, pp. 364–365)

Ethical Questions 7.3

EP 2.1.2

What do you think is the moral thing for Waldo to do concerning his upcoming math test? What do you think Waldo would do? If you were Waldo, to what extent would you be tempted to cheat on the math test? What aspects in your upbringing would influence your decision?

LO 7-4 Review Fowler's Theory of Faith Development

Chapter 3 defined *spirituality* as "one's values, beliefs, mission, awareness, subjectivity, experience, sense of purpose and direction, and a kind of striving toward something greater than oneself. It may or may not include a deity.... *Religion*, on the other hand,... refers to a set of beliefs and practices of an organized religious institution" (e.g., organized churches under Roman Catholic, Muslim, or Methodist denominations) (Frame, 2003, p. 3).

EP 2.1.4, 2.1.7a

Spirituality and religion are two separate concepts. Frame (2003) explains:

> Many followers of religion find that its organization, doctrine, rituals, programs, and community are means through which their spirituality is supported and enhanced. Likewise, many persons who think of themselves as spiritual, rather than religious, find that the institutions of religion interfere with their private experiences of spirituality. It is possible, therefore, for these two constructs to be related in a variety of ways and played out differently in individual lives. For example, a person may care very deeply about the meaning of life, may be very committed to her purpose and direction, may even engage in spiritual practices such as meditation, and yet not be involved in a religious organization. Thus, one may be spiritual without being religious. Another person may be a member of a synagogue, keep a kosher kitchen, be faithful to Torah, and never really take these Jewish practices to heart. He may go through the motions of being religious without being spiritual. Yet another person may be an active member of a church, attend worship regularly, read the Bible, and pray, finding great inspiration in these activities and support through the institutional church. Therefore, one may be religious and spiritual simultaneously. (p. 4)

(Chapter 15 discusses several predominant religions, including Judaism, Christianity, Islam, and Buddhism, more thoroughly.)

Spirituality is an important aspect of human diversity. It shapes major dimensions of many people's lives and can provide a significant source of strength. As a later section explains, spirituality can serve as a major source of empowerment that social workers must address.

James Fowler (1981) proposed a theory of faith development in which people progress through seven stages that focus "on the formation and transformation of faith throughout the life cycle.... [B]y faith Fowler meant 'the pattern of our relatedness to self, others, and our world in light of our relatedness to ultimacy' (1996, p. 21). 'Ultimacy' refers to that which a person gives a sense of first importance and greatest profundity in orienting his or her life with fundamental values, beliefs, and meanings.... [F]aith may take religious or nonreligious forms. Fowler depicted faith as a universal aspect of human nature that gives coherence and meaning to life, connects individuals together in shared concerns, relates people to a larger cosmic frame of reference, and enables us to deal with suffering and mortality" (Canda & Furman, 2010, p. 256; Fowler, 1981, 1996). During each faith stage, an individual grows closer to a higher power and becomes more concerned about the welfare of other people.

Fowler's Seven Stages of Faith Development

Fowler based his seven-stage theory on "a study conducted from 1972 to 1981 to determine how people viewed their personal history, how they worked through problems to solutions, and how they formed moral and religious commitments. He and his collaborators conducted 359 in-depth interviews with mostly White men and women, primarily Christian and Jewish, ranging in age from early childhood to past age 61" (Robbins, Chatterjee, & Canda, 2012, p. 283).

The following explains each of the seven stages.

Stage 1: Primal or Undifferentiated Faith (Birth to 2 Years)

All people begin to develop their views of faith and the world from scratch. Infants learn early on whether their environment is safe or not, whether they can trust or not. Are they being cared for in warm, safe, secure family environments? Or are they being hurt, neglected, and abused? People begin to develop their use of language to express thought and distinguish between themselves and others. They start to develop relationships and ideas about what those relationships mean.

Stage 2: Intuitive-Projective Faith (Ages 2 to 6)

Children aged 2 to 6 continue developing their ability to glean meaning from their environments. What children are exposed to in terms of spiritual language and experiences is what they conceptualize on their faith. During stage 2, children are egocentric and manifest preoperational thought patterns. Their view of faith and religion lacks in-depth conceptualization and application to life experiences. Their view of faith is that it is out there someplace; it is whatever they're exposed to. For instance, to Herman, whose parents adhere to strict Wisconsin Synod Lutheran Church beliefs, faith is going to church, singing hymns, attending Sunday school, and saying bedtime prayers every night. If asked where God is, he says, "Everywhere," because that's what he's been told.

Stage 3: Mythic-Literal Faith (Ages 6 to 12)

Development of conceptual thought continues over this period. Stories are especially important as ways to help children develop their thinking about life and relationships. Individuals can be deeply moved by dramatic representations and spiritual symbolism such as religious ceremonies. The concrete operations period helps children distinguish between what is real and what is not. During this stage, children think more seriously about aspects related to faith, although their "beliefs are literal and one dimensional"; Frame (2003) explains:

> *People in this stage often develop a concept of God in as a cosmic ruler who acts with fairness and moral reciprocity (Fowler, 1987). Persons in the mythic-literal stage often assume that God rewards goodness and punishes evil. They might exhibit a kind of perfectionism in their efforts to be rewarded for their goodness. On the other hand, they could be self-abasing, assuming that because they have been abused or neglected by significant others, they are inherently bad and will be punished. (p. 41)*

Stage 4: Synthetic-Conventional Faith (Ages 12 and Older)

During this stage, individuals develop their ability to conceptualize and apply information in new ways. They are exposed to much more of the world through social, school, and media experiences. They no longer perceive the world as literally as they did in stage 3. On the one hand, people begin to think more abstractly and, in some ways, view the world from new perspectives. On the other hand, they strive to conform. They have not yet critically evaluated the fundamental basis of their faith. Rather, they adhere to conventional ideology. Duffey (2005) reflects on stage 4:

> *Faith is seen as that which brings people together and provides a unifying concept and sense of belonging for family, congregation, and society. For many, this is the terminal stage of development. In this stage, individuals do not acknowledge differences in faith practices of others and view their faith as the "one right, true, only way." An example of this stage can be seen in adolescents who form groups based on fitting in: if you wear these clothes, listen to this type of music, like these people, etc., then you are part of the group. At this stage, any image of deity is seen as a companion and ally. Faith is rule bound and hierarchical with no questioning of the group's norms and beliefs. (pp. 323–324)*

Stage 5: Individuative-Reflective Faith (Early Adulthood and Beyond)

Critical thinking about the meaning of life characterizes stage 5. "The focus of faith moves away from being viewed as the unifying concept of the group and more as making sense of the individual" (Duffey, 2005, p. 324). People confront conflicts in values and ideas, and they strive to establish their individualized belief system. For example, a young woman will seriously consider the extent to which her own personal beliefs coincide with conventional religious practices and beliefs. If her church condemns abortion, does she agree or not? If her church denies membership to lesbian and gay people, does she support this or not? Stage 5 marks the construction of a more detailed internal spiritual belief system that reflects an individual's critical evaluation of the physical and spiritual world. "This stage may occur in those who stay within organized religious practice, as well as in those who leave" (Duffey, 2005, p. 324).

Stage 6: Conjunctive Faith (Midlife and Beyond)

Only one-sixth of all respondents in Fowler's study reached stage 6, conjunctive faith, and then never before age 30. The concept that characterizes this phase is integration. Individuals have confronted the conflicts between their own views and conventional ones and have accepted that such conflicts exist. They have integrated their own beliefs into their perception of the physical and spiritual universe. They have accepted that diversity and opposites characterize life. Good exists along with evil. Happiness dwells beside sadness. Strength subsists alongside weakness. Spiritual beliefs assume a deeper perspective. Duffey (2005) explains: "The individual becomes more open to religious and spiritual traditions different from one's own. An example of someone at this stage is a person willing to respect the validity of another's 'truth' even when it contradicts one's own, while simultaneously being able to communicate one's own authentic 'truth' " (p. 324). Frame (2003) notes that people "develop a passion for justice that is beyond the claims of race, class, culture, nation, or religious community. These convictions enable people in the conjunctive stage to lay down their defenses and to tolerate differences in belief while staying firmly grounded in their own personal faith systems" (pp. 42–43).

Stage 7: Universalizing Faith (Midlife and Beyond)

Universalizing faith is characterized by selfless commitment to justice on behalf of others. In stage 6, people confront discrepancies and unfairness, integrating them into their perception of how the world operates. However, the self remains the primary reference point. An individual accepts and appreciates his own vulnerability, and seeks his own continued existence and salvation. Stage 7, however, reflects a deeply spiritual concern for the greater good, the benefit of the masses, above oneself. Such commitment may involve becoming a martyr on behalf of or devoting one's life to some great cause at the expense of personal pleasure and well-being. Only a tiny minority of people may reach this point. Martin Luther King Jr., Mother Teresa, and Joan of Arc are examples.

Critical Thinking: Evaluation of Fowler's Theory

Fowler provides a logically organized theory concerning the development of faith. It follows Piaget's proposed levels of cognitive development, advancing from the more concrete to the more abstract. It makes sense that people increase their ability to think critically, integrate more difficult concepts, and develop deeper, more committed ideas and beliefs as their lives and thinking progress.

EP 2.1.3,
2.1.5a,
2.1.9a

However, at least three criticisms of the theory come to mind. First, the sample on which it was based is very limited in terms of race and religious orientation. Questions can be raised regarding the extent to which it can be applied universally to non-Christian faiths worldwide.

Second, concepts of human diversity, oppression, and discrimination are not taken into account. There is an inherent assumption that all people start out with a clean slate. In reality, some are born richer, some poorer, some in high-tech societies, others in third-world environments. To what extent do people's exposure to more ideas and greater access to the world's activities and resources affect the development of faith? Are all people provided an equal opportunity to develop faith? Do oppression and discrimination affect one's spirituality and the evolution of faith?

A third criticism is the difficulty of applying Fowler's theory to macro situations. How does the development of faith from an individual perspective fit into the overall scheme of the macro environment? How does faith development potentially affect organizational, community, and political life?

•••• / Ethical Questions 7.4

EP 2.1.2

What are your personal beliefs about spirituality and religion? To what extent do you believe all people should also hold your views?

Social Work Practice and Empowerment Through Spiritual Development

EP 2.1.4b,
2.1.4d
2.1.10e

Spirituality rises above concern over worldly things such as possessions and expands consciousness to a realm beyond the physical environment. It is a "universal aspect of human culture" (Canda, 1989; Cowley & Derezotes, 1994) that concerns "developing a sense of meaning, purpose, and morality" (Canda, 1989, p. 39). It can provide people with strength to withstand pain and guidance to determine what life paths to take.

Determining a client's spiritual beliefs and possible membership in an organized religion can lead to various means of empowerment. "Religious and spiritual organizations can be the source of support for clients . . . because they can provide a sense of belonging, safety, purpose, structure, and opportunities for giving and receiving service" (Frame, 2003, p. 94).

Boyle, Hull, Mather, Smith, and Farley (2009) expand upon the significance of spirituality for social workers:

Social work and other helping professions have begun to recognize the immense power these beliefs can have over the ability of clients to withstand trauma and tragedy when things look the darkest…. Spirituality helps some people make sense out of a sometimes senseless world. For others, it is part of an attempt to better understand themselves and to answer the question, "What is my purpose?" …

Spirituality and religious beliefs tend to play even more crucial roles in the lives of clients who are coping with critical events such as a terminal illness, a bereavement, or serious health issues. In these and similar situations, social workers should be comfortable raising the topic of religion or spirituality with clients. Likewise, social workers have come to recognize the importance of these issues for many ethnic and minority groups. For many such groups, the church and religion play a major role in their everyday lives and in efforts to bring about institutional and environmental change….

Social workers should be alert to the fact that their clients may have significant religious or spiritual beliefs and values and be familiar with the commonalities across various religious doctrines. At the very least, the practitioner should ask clients about this area and listen carefully when clients identify their religion or other spiritual beliefs as a coping resource. Failure to explore this area prevents social workers from understanding a major area of strength for many clients and a potential area for some others. (pp. 297–298)

However, as important as it is to consider spirituality as a potential strength, it is just as important for social workers not to impose their own values and spiritual beliefs on clients. Van Hook, Hugen, and Aguilar (2001) explain:

> Incorporating spiritual and religious diversity into social work practice raises a challenging question for each social worker of faith: How do I hold my truth to be The Truth, when everyone perceives the truth differently? The professional challenge is to learn to listen intently to another person's explanation of reality, even when that worldview differs significantly from one's own. As practitioners, we need not share a client's view of reality, nor even agree with it. But if we are willing to listen, we will come away knowing clients in new ways—and this knowledge and awareness will not only increase our own cultural sensitivity but also help us demonstrate a genuine respect for clients by truly honoring their religious and spiritual perspective. (p. 6)

Social workers may encounter a wide range of situations involving clients' spirituality that require careful thought regarding how to proceed ethically. For instance, Roeder (2002) cites the following practice situation:

> You work for a faith-based organization that offers services to teens who are pregnant, in hopes of preparing them for motherhood. You are the first social worker ever to be hired onto the staff, which is composed mostly of religiously trained persons and committed volunteers. During your first staff meeting in this organization, you find that staff are reviewing a policy that suggest "all who work with clients should pray with them to develop their relationship with God." During the meeting you are asked for your input on this policy. What would you say in response? (p. 11)

Spotlight 7.2 discusses the current outlook concerning research on practice effectiveness and spirituality.

 SPOTLIGHT ON DIVERSITY 7.2

Evidence-Based Practice and Spirituality

EP 2.1.6a, 2.1.6b

The social work profession and its accreditation standards emphasize the importance of employing evidence-based interventions, evaluating practice effectiveness, and using research results to improve service delivery (CSWE, 2008). Rubin and Babbie (2014) explain:

> Evidence-based practice (EBP) is a process in which practitioners make practice decisions in light of the best research evidence available. But rather than rigidly constrict practitioner options, the EBP model encourages practitioners to integrate scientific evidence with their practice expertise and knowledge of the idiosyncratic circumstances bearing on specific practice decisions. (p. 28)

There has not been much empirical research in social work regarding the effectiveness of practices involving spirituality; however, research conducted in other helping professions is establishing positive relationships "between religious participation and well-being" (Canda, 2008, p. 416; Canda & Furman, 2010). Canda and Furman (2010) conclude that "empirical research is showing through hundreds of studies in several disciplines that positive sense of spiritual meaning and religious participation are related to reduced levels of depression, anxiety, substance abuse, and risk behaviors along with an increased sense of well-being and mutual support.... Specific spiritually based practices, such as forgiveness, meditation, and spiritually oriented cognitive-behavioral therapy are also showing promise" (p. 22). Other research results indicate that spiritual well-being is related to people's ability to respond resiliently to sickness and other crises, and to lower incidences of family violence (Canda, 2008).

Canda and Furman (2010) reflect that

> The concept of spirituality includes certain quantifiable and measurable aspects (such as frequency of church attendance or level of self-assessed sense of meaning) [and] ... various processes, experiences, and systems that are best explored through qualitative methods of observation (such as the subjective experience of meditation or the communal patterns of mutual support in religious groups) ... While we recognize the utility of the scientific method as it has derived from European and American cultures, we also respect the forms of knowledge and wisdom found among the elders, mentors, and adepts of religious traditions and culturally specific healing systems around the world. We value understanding that comes from a convergence of sensory, rational, emotional, and intuitive ways of knowing. For a truly integral approach we need to combine inquiry approaches that address both the subjective and objective dimensions of individual and collective phenomena of spirituality (Wilber, 2006). (p. 23)

Significant Issues and Life Events: Assertiveness and Suicide

EP 2.1.10g, 2.1.10j

Each phase of life tends to be characterized by issues that receive considerable attention and concern. Two issues that command special attention as they relate to adolescence and youth are assertiveness and suicide. Although these issues continue to elicit concern with respect to any age group, they have an especially critical quality for those whose lives are just beginning. Lives marked by either docile meekness and nonassertiveness, on the one hand, or pushy, self-serving aggression, on the other, can be damaging and nonproductive. Young lives terminated at an early age represent tragic and regrettable losses of potential.

Each of these issues may be viewed from either a psychological or a social perspective. They will arbitrarily be addressed in this chapter, which focuses on the psychological aspects of adolescence.

LO 7-5 Assess Empowerment Through Assertiveness and Assertiveness Training

Assertiveness involves behavior that is straightforward, yet not offensive. The behavior can be either verbal or nonverbal. Assertiveness involves taking into account both your own rights and the rights of others. It sounds simple, but for many people appropriate assertiveness is difficult to master. For instance, consider the two people sitting in front of you in a movie theater who are talking loudly. How should you react? Should you ignore them even though it's the scariest portion of the latest horror film? Should you scream, "Shut up!"? Or should you tap one of them gently on the shoulder and politely ask the person to please be quiet?

Your best friend asks to borrow your car. Your friend emphasizes it'll only be for one time and it's needed for *such an important reason.* You happen to know that your friend is not a very good driver, has gotten two speeding tickets in the past six months, and sometimes drives after drinking. Should you say, "No way! You know what a horrible driver

you are"? Should you say, "Sure"? Should you say, "Well, okay, I guess so"? Or should you say, "No. You know I don't let other people drive my car. Would it help if I drive you somewhere?"

Many times it's difficult to look at a situation objectively and take the feelings and needs of all concerned into account. Often, it's especially difficult for adolescents and young people. On the one hand, they are still getting to know themselves and establishing their own identities. On the other hand, they want to fit in socially and respond to the feelings of others.

Assertiveness involves specific skills that can be taught. This, of course, is referred to as *assertiveness training.* Adolescents and young people may find assertiveness skills especially valuable as they decide how to react in new situations, especially when under social pressure. For example, they might struggle regarding how to respond in sexual situations: *What do I want to do versus what does my partner want to do?* Or they might wonder about taking drugs: *Everyone is doing it; what should I do?* Here we will discuss, in more depth, the meaning of assertiveness and some concepts involved in assertiveness training.

Most people remember occasions when they wish they had been more assertive. Yet at those moments, they felt very uncomfortable doing so. Many people have also experienced situations in which they "lost it," and exploded in a loud burst of anger. An example is a newly married 22-year-old woman who is "at her wits' end" with her husband's best friend. He continues to make derogatory racial slurs against almost anyone who is not white, of a certain religious group, and of European heritage. The young woman, a newly graduated social worker, tries everything she can think of to turn the friend's comments off. She tries ignoring him. She tries to change the subject. Yet she doesn't want to offend the man. After all, he is her husband's best friend. Finally, something snaps and she screams, "I can't stand it anymore. I think you're a disgusting bigot. Just shut up!" This outburst does little for their relationship.

The Relevance of Assertiveness

Assertiveness and assertiveness training are included here for three reasons. First, appropriate assertiveness is an important skill to be acquired in adolescence. When someone uses an assertive approach, that person values both his or her own rights and the rights of others. Assertiveness is a critical aspect of establishing both a personal identity and a moral perspective toward other people.

A second reason for including assertiveness is its importance in working with clients. As a social work practitioner, you must recognize your own professional and personal rights in order to communicate effectively with clients and get your job done. On the other hand, you must also recognize, respect, and appreciate your clients' rights and needs. An assertive approach enables you to take both your rights and your clients' rights into consideration. (These rights are discussed in Highlight 7.2.) In assessing human behavior, you must seek to understand why people behave the way they do. Observing human behavior from an assertiveness perspective helps you focus on who is getting their needs met and who is not. It allows you to identify who is pushing others around inappropriately and who is being pushed.

The third reason for including assertiveness here is its significance for clients. Not only must you assess human behavior as part of the intervention process, you must also work with clients to plan and achieve positive changes. Many clients may benefit from using an assertiveness perspective to understand their own actions and the effects of these actions on others. In your role as educator, you can teach your clients assertiveness principles to enhance their own interpersonal effectiveness.

Nonassertive, Assertive, and Aggressive Communication

On an assertiveness continuum, communication can be rated as nonassertive, assertive, or aggressive. Assertive communication involves verbal and nonverbal behavior that permits speakers to make points clearly and straightforwardly. *Assertive* speakers take into consideration both their own value system and the values of whoever is receiving their message. They consider their own points to be important; yet they also consider the points and reactions of the communication's receiver important.

For example, the president of the Student Social Work Club asks Maria to take notes at a meeting three meetings in a row. The club's secretary, who is supposed to take notes, is absent all three times. Maria is willing to serve, but feels it's unfair to ask her to do the work every time instead of letting others help, too. Maria assertively states to the

---

HIGHLIGHT 7.2

Each of Us Has Certain Assertive Rights

EP 2.1.5

Part of becoming assertive involves believing that we are worthwhile people. It's easy to criticize ourselves for our mistakes and imperfections. And it's easy to hold our feelings in because we're afraid that we will hurt someone else's feelings or that someone will reject us. Sometimes feelings that are held in too long will burst out in an aggressive tirade. This applies to anyone, including our clients.

A basic principle in social work is that each individual is a valuable human being. Everyone, therefore, has certain basic rights.

The following are eight of your, and your clients', assertive rights:

1. You have the right to express your ideas and opinions openly and honestly.
2. You have the right to be wrong. Everyone makes mistakes.

3. You have the right to direct and govern your own life. In other words, you have the right to be responsible for yourself.
4. You have the right to stand up for yourself without unwarranted anxiety and make choices that are good for you.
5. You have the right *not* to be liked by everyone. (Do you like everyone you know?)
6. You have the right to make requests and to refuse them without feeling guilty.
7. You have the right to ask for information if you need it.
8. Finally, you have the right to decide not to exercise your assertive rights. In other words, you have the right to choose not to be assertive.

Source: Most of these rights are adapted from Lynn Z. Bloom, Karen Coburn, and Joan Pearlman, *The New Assertive Woman* (New York: Dell, 1976), and from Kathryn Apgar and Betsy Nicholson Callahan, *Four One-Day Workshops* (Boston: Resource Communications, Inc., and Family Service Association of Greater Boston, 1980).

club president, "This is the third meeting in a row that you've asked me to take notes. I'm happy to help out, but I feel that it's fair to share this task with other club members. Why don't you ask someone else to take notes this time?"

Aggressive communication involves bold and dominant verbal and nonverbal behavior in which a speaker presses his or her point of view as taking precedence over all others. Aggressive speakers consider only their views as important and devalue what the receiver has to say. Aggressive behaviors are demanding and most often annoying. Consider, for example, the man who barges in at the return desk in front of 17 other people standing in line and demands *service*!

Nonassertive communication is the opposite of aggressive. Speakers devalue themselves. They feel that what the other person involved thinks is much more important than their own thoughts. For example, for lunch, one day Cassie orders a hamburger well done. The waitress brings her a burger that's practically dripping blood. However, Cassie is afraid of what the waitress will think if she complains. She doesn't want to be seen as a "bitch." So, instead of assertively telling the waitress that the hamburger is much too rare, Cassie douses it in ketchup and forces herself to eat half of it.

There is no perfect recipe for what to say to be assertive in any particular situation. The important thing is to take into consideration both your own rights and the rights of the person you are talking to. Following are a few examples.

Situation 1

A 16-year-old girl is on her first date with a young man she likes. After a movie and pizza, they drive around a bit and find a secluded spot in the country where he pulls over and parks. The girl does not want to get sexually involved with the young man. She thinks this is too soon in their relationship. What will he think of her? She doesn't know him well enough yet to become intimate. What can she say?

Nonassertive response: She says nothing and lets him make his sexual advances.
Aggressive response: "Get your slimy hands off me, you pervert!"
Assertive response: "I like you, Harry, but I don't think we know each other well enough yet to get involved this way. Would you please take me home now?"

Aggressive behavior reflects the dominance of the aggressor and devalues the rights and needs of others.

Situation 2

Biff, Clay's supervisor at Stop 'n' Shop, tells Clay that he needs him to work several extra hours during the upcoming weekend. Biff has often asked Clay to work extra time on weekends. However, he doesn't ask any of the other workers to do so. Clay thinks this is unfair. He needs his job, but he hates to work extra hours on weekends. What can he say?

Nonassertive response: "Okay."
Aggressive response: "No way, Jose! Get off my butt, Biff!"
Assertive response: "You know I like my job here, Biff. However, I'm sorry, but I can't work extra hours next weekend. I've already made other plans."

Situation 3

Dinah Lee and Hannah, both 18, hang around with the same group of friends. However, they don't like each other very much. Dinah Lee approaches Hannah one day and says, "It's too bad you're gaining so much weight." What can Hannah say?

> *Nonassertive response*: "Yes, you're right. I'm trying to go on a diet."
>
> *Aggressive response*: "I'm not nearly as fat or ugly as you are, Buzzard Breath!"
>
> *Assertive response*: "No, I haven't gained any weight. I think that was a very inappropriate thing to say. It sounded as if you were just trying to hurt my feelings."

The Advantages of Assertiveness

Developing assertiveness skills has many benefits. For one thing, you can gain more control over your interpersonal environment. Assertiveness may help you avoid uncomfortable or hostile interactions with others. You will probably feel that other people understand you better than they did before. Your self-concept can be enhanced as the result of your gain in control and interpersonal effectiveness. Appropriate assertiveness helps to alleviate building up undue tension and stress and diminish such psychosomatic reactions as headaches or stomach upsets. Finally, other people may gain respect for you, your strength, and your own demonstration of respect for others. People may even begin to use you as a role model for their own development of assertive behavior.

Assertiveness Training

EP 2.1.10j

Assertiveness training leads people to realize, feel, and act on the assumption that they have the right to be themselves and express their feelings freely. Assertive responses generally are not aggressive responses. The distinction between these two types of interactions is important. For example, a woman has an excessively critical father-in-law. Intentionally doing things that will bother him (bringing up topics that she knows will upset him, forgetting Father's Day and his birthday, not visiting) and getting into loud arguments with him would be considered aggressive behavior.

An effectively assertive response, however, would be to counter criticism by saying, "Dad, your criticism deeply hurts me. I know you're trying to help

when you give advice, but I feel that you're criticizing me. I'm an adult, and I have the right to make my own decisions and mistakes. The type of relationship that I'd like to have with you is a close adult relationship and not a father–child relationship."

As we know, social work is practical. Therefore, you can use the suggestions provided to enhance both your client's assertiveness and your own. Alberti and Emmons (1976a, 1976b, 2001, 2008) developed the following 13 steps to help establish assertive behavior:

1. Examine your own actions. How do you behave in situations requiring assertiveness? Do you think you tend to be nonassertive, assertive, or aggressive in most of your communications?
2. Make a record of those situations in which you felt you could have behaved more effectively, either more assertively or less aggressively.
3. Select and focus on some specific instance when you felt you could have been more appropriately assertive. Visualize the specific details. What exactly was said? How did you feel?
4. Analyze how you reacted. Examine closely your verbal and nonverbal behavior. Alberti and Emmons (2008, pp. 71–81) cite the following seven aspects of behavior that are important to monitor:
   a. *Eye contact*. Did you look the person in the eye? Or did you find yourself avoiding eye contact when you were uncomfortable?
   b. *Body posture*. Were you standing up straight, or were you slouching? Were you leaning away from the person sheepishly? Were you holding your head up straight as you looked the person in the eye?
   c. *Gestures*. Were your hand gestures fitting for the situation? Did you feel at ease? Or were you tapping your feet or cracking your knuckles? In the beginning of his term, people often criticized President George H. W. Bush for moving his arms and hands around during his public speeches. This tended to give the public the impression that he was frantic. Professional coaches helped him gain control of this behavior and present a calmer public image.
   d. *Facial expressions*. Did you have a serious expression on your face? Were you smiling or

giggling uncomfortably, thereby giving the impression that you were not really serious?

e. *Voice tone, inflection, volume*. Did you speak in a normal voice tone? Did you whisper timidly? Did you raise your voice to the point of stressful screeching? Did you sound as if you were whining?

f. *Timing*. It is best to make an appropriately assertive response just after a remark is made or an incident happens. It's also important to consider whether a particular situation requires assertiveness. At times it might be best to remain silent and just "let it go." For example, it might not be wise to criticize your professor for being a "dreary bore" in a class presentation you are giving and that your professor is simultaneously grading.

g. *Content*. What you say in your assertive response is obviously important. Did you choose your words carefully? Did your response have the impact you wanted it to have? Why or why not?

5. Identify a role model, and examine how he or she handled a situation requiring assertiveness. What exactly happened during the incident? What words did your model use that were particularly effective? What aspects of his or her nonverbal behavior helped to get points across?

6. Identify a range of other assertive responses that could address the original problem situation you targeted. What other words could you have used? What nonverbal behaviors might have been more effective?

7. Picture yourself in the identified problematic situation. It often helps to close your eyes and concentrate. Step by step, imagine how you could handle the situation more assertively.

8. Practice the way you envisioned yourself being more assertive. You could target a real-life situation that remains unresolved. For example, perhaps the person you live with always leaves dirty socks lying around the living room or drinks all your soda and forgets to tell you the refrigerator is bare. Or you can ask a friend, teacher, or counselor to help you role-play the situation. Role playing provides an effective mechanism for practicing responses before you have to use them spontaneously in real life.

9. Once again, review your new assertive responses. Emphasize your strong points, and try to remedy your flaws.

10. Continue practicing steps 7, 8, and 9 until your newly developed assertive approach feels comfortable and natural to you.

11. Try out your assertiveness in a real-life situation.

12. Continue to expand your assertive behavior repertoire until assertiveness becomes part of your personal interactive style. You can review the earlier steps and try them out in an increasingly wider range of situations.

13. Give yourself a pat on the back when you succeed in becoming more assertive. It's not easy changing long-standing patterns of behavior. Focus on and revel in the good feelings you experience as a result of your successes.

Application of Assertiveness Approaches to Social Work Practice

Helping clients learn to be more assertive is appropriate in a wide range of practice situations. For example, teenagers may need to develop assertiveness skills to ward off the massive peer pressure engulfing them. This means more than "just saying no" to drugs, sex, or any other activity they feel pressured to participate in. Assertiveness training involves helping people identify alternative types of responses in uncomfortable situations. Finally, assertiveness training involves working out and practicing these alternative responses ahead of time so that they become easier and more natural.

Another example of a client needing assertiveness training is a shy, reserved client who needs to ask his landlord to do some repairs needed in the client's apartment. Still another client might need help becoming more assertive in preparation for a job interview.

Workers themselves need to develop assertiveness skills in order to advocate for services on behalf of their clients. Good communication skills and a respect for others are basic necessities for social work practice. You can lead your clients through each step in assertiveness training to become more competent and effective communicators.

EP 2.1.1b, 2.1.10k

LO 7-6 Explore Suicide in Adolescence

Why do people decide to terminate their lives? Is it because life is unbearable, painful, hopeless, or useless? Suicide can occur during almost any time of life. However, it might be considered especially critical in the years of adolescence and youth. This is the time of life when people could enjoy being young and fresh and looking forward to life's wide variety of exciting experiences. Instead, many young people decide to take their own lives.

Incidence of Suicide

Suicide is one of the most critical health problems in the United States today. Consider these frightening facts: About 34,600 deaths are due to suicide in the United States each year (U.S. Census Bureau, 2011). The number of adolescent suicides in the United States "tripled between the mid-1960s and mid-1990s," with a subsequent small decline since then (Berk, 2012b, p. 631). Suicide is the third leading cause of death for people age 15 through 24 in the United States (surpassed only by accidents and homicides) (U.S. Census Bureau, 2011). It is the second leading cause of Canadian adolescents' deaths, exceeded only by motor vehicle collisions (Canadian Mental Health Association, 2013). No one knows how many of those accidents were really suicides. The suicide rate is lowest in childhood and highest in old age, although it increases "sharply during adolescence" (Berk, 2012b, p. 631). Tremendous variation exists among industrialized nations in adolescent suicide rates (Bridge, Goldstein, & Brent, 2006). Singapore, New Zealand, and Finland have high rates. The United States, Canada, Japan, and Australia have intermediate rates. Spain, Italy, Greece, and the Netherlands have low rates. The reasons for this are not clear.

Far more adolescents think about committing suicide or make an unsuccessful attempt than those who actually succeed (CDC, 2012, 2014). One national survey found that 16 percent of adolescents in U.S. high schools had thought seriously about suicide within the past year, 13 percent had established a plan for how to do it, and 8 percent actually attempted suicide (CDC, 2014). One in 10,000 adolescents actually succeeds in committing suicide (Kail & Cavanaugh, 2013). White adolescents are more likely to commit suicide than their African American counterparts; Native American and Alaskan Native adolescents are the most likely to commit suicide of any ethnic group in the United States (Anderson & Smith, 2005; Kail & Cavanaugh, 2013). Hispanic female adolescents are more likely to attempt suicide than their non-Hispanic Caucasian or African American counterparts (CDC, 2014) (Spotlight 7.3 will address this issue later in the chapter).

Causes of Adolescent Suicide

No specific recipe of variables contributes to any individual adolescent's suicide probability. However, adolescents who threaten or try to commit suicide tend to experience problems in three main arenas: increased stress, family issues, and psychological variables (particularly depression) (Berk, 2012b; CDC, 2014; Sigelman & Rider, 2012; Steinberg, Vandell, & Bornstein, 2011b).

EP 2.1.7,
2.1.7b,
2.1.10d,
2.1.10e

Increased Stress

Many teenagers today express concern over the multiple pressures they have to bear. To some extent, these pressures might be related to current social and economic conditions. Many families are breaking up. Pressures to succeed are great. Many young people are worried about what kind of job they will find when they get out school. Peer pressure to conform and to be accepted socially is constantly operating. Suicidal adolescents may lose any coping powers they may have had and simply give up.

A range of significant events might increase stress and jar adolescents into suicidal thinking. Unwanted pregnancy or even fear of unwanted pregnancy is an example. Other stressful events include losses such as the death of someone close, divorce, family relocation, or even national disasters (Nairne, 2014; Sigelman & Rider, 2012). Even the stress resulting from declining grades in school might contribute to suicide.

Problems in peer relationships can contribute to stress. An adolescent may feel unwanted or isolated, that he or she simply does not fit in. Or an adolescent might experience devastating trauma after being "dumped" by a girlfriend or boyfriend.

Adolescents' lack of experience in coping with such situations may make it seem as though life is over after losing "the one and only person" they love. Many adolescents have not yet had time to work through such experiences and learn that they can survive emotional turmoil.

Evidence suggests that teenagers who are over-achievers experience greater stress and therefore are more likely to commit suicide (Kurpius, Kerr, & Harkins, 2005; McWhirter, McWhirter, McWhirter, & McWhirter, 2013). Overachievers may expect too much of themselves and respond to pressure from parents, school, and friends in an overly zealous manner. One teenager comes to mind. Terri was a popular high school cheerleader. She had been homecoming queen one fall. She was an A student and editor of the yearbook. When she killed herself, everyone was surprised. Most of the people around her felt that she had everything and wondered why she threw it all away. They said it was such a shame. Apparently, she had hidden her inner turmoil very well. Perhaps she was just tired of working (and playing) so hard. Or maybe, no matter how she seemed to others, she never measured up to her own expectations for herself. At any rate, no one will ever know. We all probably know of someone like Terri. (Chapter 14 will discuss stress and stress management in greater detail.)

Family Issues

Turbulence and disruption at home contribute to the profile of an adolescent suicide (Coon & Mitterer, 2014; McWhirter et al., 2013; Sigelman & Rider, 2012). There might be serious communication problems, parental substance abuse, parental mental health problems, or physical or sexual abuse (McWhirter et al., 2013; National Institute of Mental Health [NIMH], 2010). Lack of a stable home environment contributes to the sense of loneliness and isolation for both boys and girls. Highlight 7.3 describes a young woman who struggled to cope with family and other issues, but failed.

Psychological Variables

Psychological variables, usually relating to depression, make up the third arena for problems leading to suicidal thoughts. One such factor is low self-esteem (Coon & Mitterer, 2014; McWhirter et al., 2013). When people don't feel strong internally, they find it very difficult to muster the support necessary to cope with outside pressures.

 HIGHLIGHT 7.3

Joany: A Victim of Suicide

Joany, age 15, was one of the "fries." People said that she used a lot of drugs and was wild. She did poorly in school, when she did manage to attend. Her appearance was striking. Her hair was cropped short, somewhat unevenly, and was characterized by a different color of the rainbow every day, including purple, green, and hot pink. Short leather miniskirts, multiple piercings, and dark, exaggerated makeup were also part of her style. Black appeared to be her favorite color, as it was about all she wore. She hung around with a group who looked and behaved much like herself. More studious, upper-middle-class, college-bound peers couldn't understand why she behaved that way. It was easy for them to point and snicker at her as she walked down the high school halls.

One day she came to school looking almost normal, noted Karen, one of her more scholarly classmates. Karen had at times felt sorry for Joany when people made fun of her. But this day Joany was wearing an unobtrusive skirt and sweater.

More noticeably, her hair was combed in a much more traditional manner than usual. Joany finally looked like she fit in with her classmates. Karen called out a compliment to Joany as she was walking down the hall, laughing with some of her other weird-looking friends. Joany turned, smiled, gave a hurried thanks, and returned to her conversation.

The next day the word spread like wildfire throughout the student population. Joany, it seemed, had hanged herself in her parents' basement. The rumor was that she was terribly upset because her parents were getting a divorce. No one really knew why she had killed herself. People didn't understand the sense of hopelessness and desolation she felt. Nor did anyone know why she did not turn to friends or family or school counselors for help. There seemed to be so many unanswered questions.

All that remained of Joany several months later was an oversized picture of her on the last page of the high school yearbook. It was labeled "In Memoriam."

Adolescents experience many pressures and anxieties. Young people are not sure that they will find a job with which they can support themselves when they get out of school.

Feelings of helplessness and hopelessness may also contribute to suicide potential (Coon & Mitterer, 2014; McWhirter et al., 2013; Sue, Sue, Sue, & Sue, 2013). As adolescents struggle to establish an identity and function independently of their parents, it's no wonder that many feel helpless. They must abide by the rules of their parents and schools. They suffer from peer pressure to conform to the norms of their age group. They are seeking acceptance by society and a place where they will fit in. At the same time, an adolescent must strive to develop a unique personality, a sense of self that is valuable for its own sake. At times such a struggle may indeed seem hopeless.

Impulsivity, or a sudden decision to act without giving much thought to the action, is yet another variable related to adolescent suicide (McWhirter et al., 2013). Confusion, isolation, and feelings of despair may contribute to an impulsive decision to end it all.

Adolescents today face a hard transition into adulthood. Social values are shifting. Peer pressure is immense. Adolescents have not had time to gain life experience and so tend to behave impulsively. Any trivial incident may become a crisis. Every moment of the day can feel like the end of the world if something goes wrong.

Lesbian and Gay Adolescents and Suicide

There has been concern that lesbian and gay adolescents are more likely to commit suicide than are their heterosexual peers (Alderson, 2013; Berk, 2012b; Hunter & Hickerson, 2003; McWhirter et al., 2013). It makes sense that a quest for identity

EP 2.1.4

in a heterosexual world may result in isolation, low self-esteem, and other problems potentially related to suicide. In September 2010 the nation was "shocked" by three gay youth who killed themselves after extensive bullying by peers; the methods used were gunshot, hanging, and jumping off a bridge, respectively (Dotinga & Mundell, 2010). Another 2013 incident involved a gay 15-year-old sophomore named Jadin Bell in La Grande, Oregon; after extensive bullying both on a one-to-one basis and online, he couldn't take it anymore and hung himself on playground equipment at a local elementary school (Williams, 2013). These incidents may reflect how "adolescence renders young people especially vulnerable to harassment, and the difficulties of grappling with sexuality can complicate that further" (Dotinga, 2013; Dotinga & Mundell, 2010). Additionally, suicide attempts by gay and lesbian youth may be related to "sexual milestones such as self-identification as homosexual, coming out to others, or resulting loss of friendship" (McWhirter et al., 2013, p. 261). However, from a strengths perspective, remember that the majority of "lesbian and gay youth cope with the stressors of their lives well and most of them do not attempt suicide" (Hunter & Hickerson, 2003, p. 331).

Suicidal Symptoms

W.M. Patterson and his associates (Patterson, Dohn, Bird, & Patterson, 1983) cite various risk

EP 2.1.7a,
2.1.10a,
d & e

factors that are related to a person's potential for carrying through with a suicide. They propose a mechanism for evaluating suicide potential, the SAD PERSONS scale. Each letter in the acronym corresponds to one of the high-risk factors.

It should be emphasized that any of the many available guidelines to assess suicide potential are just that—guidelines. People who threaten to commit suicide should be believed. The fact that they are talking about it means that they are thinking about doing it. However, the following variables are useful as guidelines for determining risk— that is, how high the probability is that they will attempt and succeed at suicide. Highlight 7.4 cites

a number of suicide notes that reflect these symptoms.

Sex

Among adolescents, females are much more likely to try to kill themselves than males (CDC, 2014; Nairne, 2014). However, males are four times more likely to succeed in their attempts (CDC, 2012). Adolescents of either gender may have serious suicide potential. However, greater danger exists if the person threatening suicide is a male. One reason for this is that males are more likely to choose a more deadly means of committing suicide, such as firearms or hanging, whereas women tend to use less lethal methods such as a drug overdose; unfortunately, however, women increasingly are using deadlier, more effective methods (Coon & Mitterer, 2014; NIMH, 2010).

◆ HIGHLIGHT 7.4

Suicide Notes

The following are suicide notes written by people of various ages shortly before they successfully committed suicide.

Whomever—I wrote this sober, so it is what I planned, sober or drunk. I love you all and please don't feel guilty because it is what I planned drunk or sober. Life still happens whether it is today or tomorrow. But after 23 years I would think that I could have met a person that I would mean more than personal advantage. If only I meant something. People just don't seem to care. Is it that I give the impression that I don't care? I wish and want to know. I feel so unimportant to everyone. As though my presence does not mean anything to anybody. I wish so much to be something to someone. But I feel the harder I try the worse I do. Maybe I just have not run into the right person. I am still 6 feet underground. My mind just didn't want any of it obviously. Make sure _____ goes to mom. No matter what I do, in my life, I still am going to die. By someone else's hands OR MY OWN.
(Female, age 23, died of a gunshot wound.)

I can't put up with this shit. I'm sorry I have to do this, but I have nothing left.
P.S. Closed casket please.
Give my guns to_____
(Male, age 25, died of a gunshot wound.)

Mom and Dad
don't feel bad—I have problems—don't feel the blame for this on you _____
(Male, age 18, died of a gunshot wound.)

Please forgive me for leaving you. I love you very much, but could not cope with my health problems plus financial worries etc. Try to understand and pray for me.
I wish you all the best and that you will be able to find the happiness in life I could not.
Love and Kisses Mom
Good Bye and God bless oxoxoxox
(Female, age 47, died of carbon monoxide poisoning.)

I can't take the abuse, the hurt, the rejection, the isolation, the loneliness. I can't deal with all of it. I can't try anymore. The tears are endless. I've fallen into a bottomless pit of despair. I know eternal pain and tears....
No one knows I'm alive or seems to care if I die. I'm a terrible, worthless person and it would be better if I'd never been born. Tabby was my only friend in the world, and now she's dead. There's no reason for me to live anymore....
Mom and Dad, I hate you!
Love Tommy

SOURCE: Recorded in "A Cry for Help: Teen Suicide," prepared and presented by Tom Skinner, Edison Junior High School, Janesville, WI. Reprinted by permission of the Rock County Coroner's Office, Beloit, WI.

Age

Although a person of almost any age may attempt and succeed at suicide, the risks are greater for some age groups than for others. Statistics indicate that people ages 15 to 24, or 65 or older, are in the high-risk groups (Coon & Mitterer, 2014). Older white males are especially at risk (Coon & Mitterer, 2014). Suicide accounts for 20 percent of all deaths for people ages 15 to 24 (CDC, 2012). However, the number of suicides among middle-aged Americans has recently risen significantly, which may affect the assessment of suicidal potential in the future (Jaslow, 2013).

Depression

Depression contributes to a person's potential to commit suicide (Coon & Mitterer, 2014; McWhirter et al., 2013; Steinberg et al., 2011b). *Depression*, technically referred to as *depressive disorder*, is

Depression, characterized by a disheartened mood, unhappiness, and pessimism, can contribute to an adolescent's suicide potential.

a psychiatric condition characterized by a disheartened mood; unhappiness; a lack of interest in daily activities; an inability to experience pleasure; pessimism; significant weight loss not related to dieting, or weight gain; insomnia; an extremely low energy level; feelings of hopelessness and worthlessness; a decreased capacity to focus and make decisions; and a preoccupation with thoughts about suicide and one's own death. Being depressed doesn't involve simply feeling bad. Rather, it involves a collection of characteristics, feelings, and behaviors that tend to occur in conjunction with each other.

Previous Attempts

People who have tried to kill themselves before are more likely to succeed than people who are trying to commit suicide for the first time (Coon & Mitterer, 2014; Nairne, 2014; NIMH, 2010).

Ethanol and Other Drug Abuse

People who abuse alcohol and other drugs are much more likely to commit suicide than people who do not (CDC, 2014; Coon & Mitterer, 2014; Nevid, 2013; Rathus, 2014d). Mind-altering substances may affect logical thinking, causing emotional distress to escalate.

Rational Thinking Loss

People who suffer from mental or emotional disorders, such as depression or psychosis, are more likely to kill themselves than those who do not (McWhirter et al., 2013; Nairne, 2014; NIMH, 2010). Hallucinations, delusions, extreme confusion, and anxiety all contribute to an individual's risk factors. If a person is not thinking realistically and objectively, emotions and impulsivity are more likely to take over.

Social Supports Lacking

Loneliness and isolation have already been discussed as primary contributing factors (Coon & Mitterer, 2014; McWhirter et al., 2013). People who feel that no one cares about them may feel useless and hopeless. Suicide potential may be especially high in cases in which a loved one has recently died or deserted the individual who's threatening suicide.

Organized Plan

The more specific and organized an individual's plan regarding when and how the suicide will be undertaken, the greater the risk (Coon & Mitterer, 2013; McWhirter et al., 2013; Sheafor & Horejsi, 2012; Sue et al., 2013). Additionally, the more dangerous the method, the greater the risk. For instance, the presence of a firearm increases suicide risk (CDC, 2014; Coon & Mitterer, 2014; NIMH, 2010). A plan to use the loaded rifle you have hidden in the basement tomorrow evening at 7:00 p.m. is more lethal than a plan of somehow getting some drugs and overdosing sometime. Several questions might be asked when evaluating this risk factor. How much detail is involved in the plan? Has the individual put a lot of thought into the specific details regarding how the suicide is to occur? Has the plan been thought over before? How dangerous is the chosen method? Is the method or weapon readily available to the individual? Has the specific time been chosen for when the suicide is to take place?

No Spouse

As adults, single people are much more likely to commit suicide than married people (Coon & Mitterer, 2014; Sue et al., 2013). "The highest suicide rates are found among the divorced, the next highest rates occur among the widowed, lower rates are recorded for [never married] single persons, and married individuals have the lowest rates of all" (Coon, 2006, p. 521). Generally, people without partners have a greater chance of feeling lonely and isolated.

Sickness

People who are ill are more likely to commit suicide than those who are healthy (Coon & Mitterer, 2014). This is especially true for those who have long-term illnesses that place substantial limitations on their lives. Perhaps in some of these instances, their inability to cope with the additional stress of sickness and pain eats away at their overall coping ability.

Other Symptoms

Other characteristics operate as warning signals for suicide. For example, rapid changes in mood, behavior, or general attitude are other indicators that a person is in danger of committing suicide (Coon & Mitterer, 2013; James & Gilliland, 2013; Kail & Cavanaugh, 2013; McWhirter et al., 2013). A potentially suicidal person may be one who has suddenly become severely depressed and withdrawn. But a person who has been depressed for a long time and suddenly becomes strikingly cheerful may also be in danger. Sometimes in the latter instance, the individual has already made up his or her mind to commit suicide. In those instances, the cheerfulness may

stem from relief that the desperate decision has finally been made. Suddenly giving away personal possessions that are especially important or meaningful is another warning signal of suicide potential (Kail & Cavanaugh, 2013; McWhirter et al., 2013; Rathus, 2014b). It is as if once the decision has been made to commit suicide, giving things away to selected others is a way of finalizing the decision. Perhaps it's a way of tying up loose ends, or of making certain that the final details are taken care of.

Note that other variables can also contribute to suicide potential. These include a family history of suicide, a recent traumatic event or significant loss, and finding out about other people's suicides (CDC, 2014).

We have already established that there are racial and ethnic disparities in suicide. Spotlight 7.3 explores the relatively high rate of suicide attempts by Hispanic females, compared to their non-Hispanic Caucasian and African American female counterparts.

How to Use the SAD PERSONS Scale

Patterson et al. (1983, p. 348) suggest a framework for using the SAD PERSONS scale when evaluating suicide potential. The scale itself is presented in Highlight 7.5. One point is assigned to each condition that applies to the suicidal person. For example, if a person is depressed, he or she would automatically receive a score of 1. Depression in addition to alcoholism would result in a score of 2, and so on. Although the SAD PERSONS scale was developed specifically to teach medical students how to evaluate suicide potential, social workers can use it in a similar manner. It may be helpful in assessing the intensity of treatment an individual might need. The following decision-making guidelines are recommended:

Total	Points Proposed Clinical Actions
0 to 2	Send home with a follow-up.
3 to 4	Close the follow-up; consider hospitalization.
5 to 6	Strongly consider hospitalization, depending on confidence in the follow-up arrangement.
7 to 10	Hospitalize or commit.

Zero to 2 points indicate a mild potential that still merits some follow-up and attention. At the other extreme, a score of 7 to 10 indicates

SPOTLIGHT ON DIVERSITY 7.3

Suicide and Adolescent Hispanic Females

**EP 2.1.4a,
2.1.4c**

We have established the importance of understanding and focusing on the many aspects of cultural, racial, and ethnic diversity to better understand people's behavior. This is also true when evaluating suicide potential. The rate of suicide attempts by adolescent Hispanic females is higher than for their Caucasian or African American non-Hispanic peers (CDC, 2012, 2014; Zayas, 2011). Zayas, Kaplan, Turner, Romano, and Gonzalez-Ramos (2000) propose an "integrative model" for understanding suicide attempts by adolescent Hispanic females that reflects their cultural context and immediate environment (p. 53).

One of the integrative model's dimensions is *sociocultural*. One aspect of this concerns the degree to which the adolescents' families are acculturated—that is, have accepted and adopted the cultural patterns and behaviors manifested by the dominant cultural group. Discrepancies in acculturation between daughters and parents are apparent in Hispanic families with suicidal female adolescents (Zayas et al., 2000). Daughters strive to adopt customs and values evident in the overriding non-Hispanic culture, whereas parents maintain their allegiance to values, beliefs, and behavior characterizing their original cultural heritage. The result may be high levels of family stress and conflict, contributing to the adolescent's anguish and suicide potential.

A second dimension involved in the integrative model is *family domain*. Regardless of racial and ethnic background, family discord, including "low cohesiveness, familial and marital conflict and violence, low parental support and warmth, [and] parent-adolescent conflict," contributes to suicide potential (Zayas et al., 2000). With respect to female Hispanic adolescents, Zayas and associates explain that "traditionally structured (i.e., patriarchal and male-dominated) Hispanic families tend to emphasize restrictive, authoritarian parenting, especially with regard to girls. This traditionalism may affect a family's capacity to respond flexibly to a daughter during a developmental move toward autonomy and individualism, even when the father is absent" (p. 57). As daughters strive for independence and are faced with inflexibility, conflict may result. This, in turn, may contribute to young women's distress and suicide potential.

Still another dimension stressed in the integrative model involves a *psychological domain*. We have established that depression is one factor contributing to suicidal potential. Zayas and his associates (2000) explain that "among adolescents who attempt suicide, a key factor in coping is how they manage anger. Because of the cultural prohibitions on women's direct expressions of anger, the adolescent Hispanic female also may be socialized by her own more tradition-bound parents to suppress her anger…. [As a result] having limited abilities to cope with anger and lacking appropriate problem-solving skills may interact to trigger the suicide attempt" (p. 59).

HIGHLIGHT 7.5

The SAD PERSONS Scale

S   (Sex)
A   (Age)
D   (Depression)
P   (Previous Attempt)
E   (Ethanol Abuse)
R   (Rational Thinking Loss)
S   (Social Supports Lacking)
O   (Organized Plan)
N   (No Spouse)
S   (Sickness)

Source: This article was published in *Psychosomatics* 24(4), W. M. Patterson, H. H. Dohn, J. Bird, and G. A. Patterson, "Evaluation of Suicidal Patients: The SAD PERSONS Scale," pp. 343–349. Copyright Elsevier 1983.

severe suicide potential. These cases would merit immediate attention and action. Hospitalization or commitment are among available options. Scores ranging from 3 to 6 represent a range of serious suicide potential. Although people with these scores need help and attention, the immediacy and intensity of that attention may vary. In each case, professional discretion would be involved.

We have indicated that the SAD PERSONS scale was developed to aid physicians in training. It is most likely that such physicians will not be proficient in addressing mental health problems themselves. Thus, there is an emphasis on referral to someone else and on hospitalization. Social workers, on the other hand, may often be called upon to work directly with suicidal people. Some guidelines are described next.

Guidelines for Helping Suicidal People

Two levels of intervention are possible for dealing with a potentially suicidal person. The first involves addressing the immediate crisis. The person threatening to commit suicide needs immediate help and support literally to keep him or her alive. The second level would address the other issues that worked to escalate his or her stress. This second level of intervention might involve longer-term treatment to address issues of longer duration that were not necessarily directly related to the suicide crisis.

For example, consider a 15-year-old male who is deeply troubled over the serious problems his parents are experiencing in their marriage. This preoccupation, in addition to his normally shy personality, has alienated him from virtually any social contacts with his peers. The result is a serious consideration regarding whether life is worth it. The first priority is to prevent the suicide. However, this young man also needs to address and resolve the problems that caused the stress in the first place—his parents' conflicts and his lack of friends. Longer-term counseling or treatment might be necessary.

Reactions to a Suicide Threat

**EP 2.1.10b,
e, g, i, & j**

You get a phone call in the middle of the night from an old friend you haven't heard from in a while who says she cannot stand living anymore. Or a client calls you late Friday afternoon and says that he is planning to shoot himself. What do you do? Specific suggestions for how to treat the potentially suicidal person include the following.

- *Remain calm and objective* (Kail & Cavanaugh, 2013; Smith, Segal, & Robinson, 2013). Don't allow the emotional distress being experienced by the other person to contaminate your own judgment. The individual needs help in becoming more rational and objective. The person does not need someone else who is drawn into the emotional crisis.
- *Be supportive* (McWhirter et al., 2013; Smith et al., 2013). Jobes, Berman, and Martin (2005) suggest that "connecting with the pain can be achieved through careful and thoughtful listening, emotional availability, and warmth; it may be shown by eye contact, posture, and nonverbal

cues that communicate genuine interest, concern, and caring" (p. 407). They note further that it is vital to "respect the depth and degree of pain reported by a youth. Self-reports of extreme emotional pain and trauma should not be dismissed as adolescent melodrama. The experience of pain is acute and real to adolescents and potentially life-threatening.... [Y]oung people tend to be present oriented and lack the years of life experience that may provide the perspective needed to endure a painful period" (p. 408).

- *Identify the immediate problem* (Jobes et al., 2005; Sue et al., 2013). Help the person clearly identify what is causing the excessive stress. The problem needs to be recognized before it can be examined. The individual may be viewing an event way out of perspective. For example, a 16-year-old girl was crushed after her steady boyfriend of 18 months dropped her. In this instance, the loss of her boyfriend overshadowed all of the other things in her life—her family, her friends, her membership in the National Honor Society, and her favorite activity, running. She needed help focusing on exactly what had caused her stress—the loss of her boyfriend. To her, it felt like she had lost her whole life, which was a gross distortion of reality.
- *Identify strengths* (Jobes et al., 2005; Sue et al., 2013). It is helpful to identify and emphasize the person's positive qualities. For example, the individual might be pleasant, unselfish, hardworking, conscientious, bright, attractive, and so on. People who are feeling suicidal are most likely focusing on the "bad things" they perceive about themselves. They forget their positive characteristics.
- *Decrease isolation* (Jobes et al., 2005; McWhirter et al., 2013). Another source of strength lies in people close to the suicidal person. Who can that person turn to for emotional support and help? These people may include family, friends, a religious leader, a guidance counselor, or a physician—people the person trusts and can communicate with.
- *Explore past coping mechanisms* (Jobes et al., 2005; Roberts, 2005). When the person has hit rough spots before, how has he or she dealt with them? You can emphasize how the person has survived such tough times before. Suicidal people may be in a rut of negative, depressing thoughts. They may be blind to anything but their immediate crisis. Sometimes, people in this suicidal rut

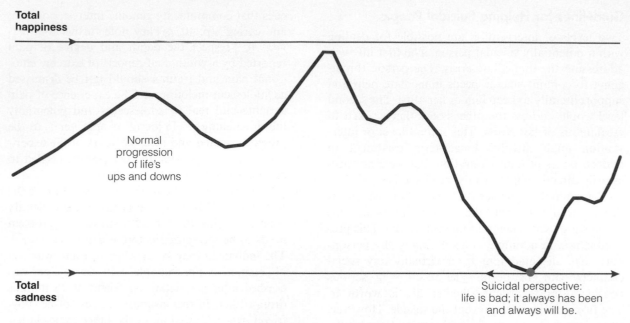

Total happiness

Normal progression of life's ups and downs

Total sadness

Suicidal perspective:
life is bad; it always has been
and always will be.

FIGURE 7.1 Life's Ups and Downs

have hit their lowest emotional point. Their perspective is such that they feel that life has always been as bad as this, and that it always will be as bad as this (see Figure 7.1). A suicidal person has probably been "up" before and probably will be "up" again. Many times this historical perspective can be pointed out and used beneficially. If possible, help the person understand that suicide is a permanent, fatal option in response to a temporary crisis (Sheafor & Horejsi, 2012).

- *Avoid clichés.* Don't argue with the suicidal person about the philosophical values of life versus death (James & Gilliland, 2013; Santrock, 2012b). Don't use clichés like "There's so much that life has to offer you," or "Your life is just beginning." This type of approach only makes people feel like you're on a different wavelength and don't understand how they feel. People who threaten suicide have real suicidal feelings. They're not likely to be exaggerating them or making them up. What they need is objective, empathic support (McWhirter et al., 2013).

- *Examine potential options* (Jobes et al., 2005; Sheafor & Horejsi, 2012). One of the most useful and concrete things that can be done for suicidal people is to help them get the help they need. Because suicidal people tend to be isolated, this help often involves referring them to the various

resources—both personal and professional—that are available. Referrals to police or a hospital emergency room can be helpful when an emergency situation arises. Finally, professionals in mental health are available to provide long-term help to people in need.

Professional Counseling of Suicidal People

Jobes and his associates (2005) suggest at least five steps for social workers or counselors to consider when working with, and establishing a plan of action with, suicidal clients:

1. Make the environment safe. Take away, or make minimally available, the means by which the person was contemplating suicide. Depending on the plan, this might include removing pills or guns. It might also include making certain supportive people remain with the client.

2. "Negotiating safety." Jobes and his associates (2005) explain: "Generally, the concrete goal of these negotiations is to ensure the patient's physical safety by establishing that the patient will not hurt him- or herself for a specific period of time. The more concrete and specific the understanding, the better. Typically, the patient will agree to maintain his or her safety until the next clinical contact, at which point a new understanding can

be negotiated" (p. 410). Although such an agreement does not guarantee safety, it serves as one means of bolstering support.

3. Plan for future support. The suicidal client should have continuity of social and professional support. This includes scheduling future counseling sessions, making follow-up calls to ensure that the client is all right, and planning meetings and events the client can look forward to.

4. Minimize loneliness and seclusion. Jobes and his associates (2005) reflect: "The patient must not be left alone in the midst of a suicidal crisis. It is critical that a trustworthy friend or family member remain with the patient through the crisis phase. Efforts must be made to mobilize friends, family, and neighbors, making them aware of the importance of ongoing contact with the suicidal youth" (pp. 410–411).

5. Provide more intensive care via hospitalization. If it's not possible to stabilize the client and his or her environment to keep the client safe, hospitalization may be necessary.

A Cautionary Note

It's important to realize that suicide prevention may not always be possible. All you can do is your very best to help a suicidal person hold on to life. The ultimate decision whether to continue living or not lies with the individual.

Community Empowerment: Suicide Prevention and Crisis Intervention

EP 2.1.8a & b; 2.1.10i & k

Community resources are critical for successful suicide prevention. You cannot refer people for help if the appropriate services don't exist. If resources are not available, you as a social worker may need to advocate for new programs or to expand services within your own or other agencies. A community system can address suicide prevention in many ways. Four are discussed here: task forces for suicide prevention, crisis lines, peer-helping programs in schools, and training programs for community professionals.

Creation of a *suicide prevention task force* provides a potentially effective means to evaluate the need for services and decide what types of services to offer. A *task force* is a group established for a specific purpose, usually within the context of an organization or community, that pursues designated goals and disbands when these goals have been achieved (Kirst-Ashman & Hull, 2012a). A task force can be made up of interested individuals within an organization or a cross section of professionals and citizens within a community. The task force can then make decisions regarding how the agency or community can best meet the community's need for suicide prevention services. It can answer a number of questions and decide on a plan of action. Who are the potential clients? Are there services already existing within the community that can best meet the suicide prevention need? If not, what types of programs should be initiated? What resources are available to develop such programs?

For example, the Task Force on Suicide in Canada was established to evaluate extensively suicide in Canada and report its findings and recommendations (Health Canada, Health Programs and Services Branch, 1994). The group addressed the needs of the entire country instead of smaller community systems. The report's intent was to

deal with the nature and extent of suicide and suicide-related problems, discuss demographic and sociological parameters, and identify the Canadian groups at greatest risk …; it also summarized knowledge of etiological processes [reasons and causes of the behavior] and gathered information on programs of suicide prevention, intervention, and postvention….

Prevention *refers to the implementation of measures to prevent the onset of suicidal crises by eliminating or mitigating particular … situations of heightened risk …, by promoting life-enhancing conditions, and by reducing negative societal conditions. Several such measures … [included] improved approaches to media coverage, broader-based public education programs (disseminating information about how to recognize a potentially suicidal person, what to do and where to go for help), and a reduction in the availability and lethality of means.*

Intervention *refers to the actions aimed at the immediate management of the suicidal crisis and the longer-term care, treatment and support of persons at risk. Actions involved include identification of potential sources of referral, crisis recognition, risk assessment, reducing the intensity of the crisis, and treatment and support of the person at risk…. [The task force recommended] education and training for health care professions and gate-keepers, especially in areas such as "first-aid" interventions and methods of treatment for those who are in acute and chronic suicidal crises.*

Postvention refers to activity undertaken to deal with the aftermath of a suicide. The purpose of such actions is twofold: to provide social support and counseling to bereaved persons, and to collect psychological autopsy information for the purpose of reconstructing the social and psychological circumstances associated with the suicide. (Health Canada, Health Programs and Services Branch, 1994, pp. xi–xiii)

Recommendations were also made concerning the ways the legal system could address the suicide problem (e.g., by decriminalizing attempted suicide). The task force emphasized the need for research regarding the reasons for suicide, the most effective treatment approaches, and the evaluation of suicide prevention programs.

Another example of an ongoing task force addressing suicide is the Task Force for Child Survival and Development. Although its base is in Georgia, it focuses on both domestic and international health issues. Its purpose initially was "to help public and private organizations achieve their mission in promoting health and human development by building coalitions, forging consensus, and leveraging scarce resources" in the prevention of suicide (Task Force for Child Survival and Development [TFCSD], 2004a). In recent years, its focus has expanded "to include other aspects of child health and development" (TFCSD, 2004a, 2011, 2014). Its goals have included the promotion of public awareness about suicide, the creation of suicide prevention programs, the provision of training programs concerning suicide assessment and treatment, and the promotion of research (TFCSD, 2004b).

Crisis telephone lines are another approach to suicide prevention. Such crisis lines can be for a specific type of crisis (such as domestic violence or suicidal potential) or can provide crisis intervention and referral information for virtually any type of crisis. An advantage of either type of crisis line is that people thinking about suicide can call anonymously for help at the time they need such help the most. People

working on crisis lines need thorough training in suicide prevention. Additionally, such lines should have staff available at all hours of the day. Imagine the reaction of the person contemplating suicide who is told to leave a message at the sound of the beep. Finally, crisis lines should be well publicized. People must know about them to use them.

Another example of a community system's approach to suicide prevention is the establishment of a *peer-helping program*, such as Teen Lifeline (2013) in Arizona. The "heart" of the program is its Peer Counseling Hotline that provides daily access to a Peer Counselor. Troubled teens often want to talk to other teens about their problems. Volunteer Peer Counselors "can empathize and understand the problems of the callers because, in many cases, they have or are going through the same things themselves." The program receives more than 11,000 calls annually, many from teens who are depressed or suicidal. Participant volunteers receive 70 hours of Life Skills training that focuses on "listening skills, communication skills, self-esteem, problem solving and relevant teen issues." The hotline is supervised by a master's-level mental health clinician. The program also provides opportunities to schools for community education on suicide and a variety of other issues including "depression, grief, dying, stress/anxiety, and substance abuse."

The fourth example of a community system's response to the suicide problem is the development and provision of *suicide prevention training programs for community professionals and other caregivers*. Caregivers include professionals such as social workers, psychologists, psychiatrists, and counselors. Caregivers may also include any others that potentially suicidal people may turn to for help. These include clergy, family members, nurses, teachers, and friends. Training as many caregivers as possible significantly increases the chance for a potentially suicidal person to make contact with someone who can help.

• • • • Ethical Questions 7.5

EP 2.1.2 *Does a person have the right to take his or her own life? What if the person is terminally ill or in chronic, severe pain?*

Chapter Summary

The following summarizes this chapter's content as it relates to the learning objectives presented at the beginning of the chapter. Chapter content will help prepare students to:

LO 7-1 Explore identity formation in adolescence (including Erikson's psychosocial theory and Marcia's categories of identity).

Erikson proposed eight stages of psychosexual development: basic trust versus basic mistrust, autonomy versus shame and doubt, initiative versus guilt, industry versus inferiority, identity versus role confusion (which occurs during adolescence), intimacy versus isolation, generativity versus stagnation, and ego integrity versus despair.

Marcia's four categories of identity are identity achievement, foreclosure, identity diffusion, and moratorium.

There are questions regarding the applicability of Erikson's and Marcia's theories to people of all racial, cultural, and ethnic backgrounds.

LO 7-2 Examine race, culture, ethnicity, and identity development.

The Racial/Cultural Identity Development Model describes a five-stage process: conformity, dissonance, resistance and immersion, introspection, and integrative awareness. Communities and schools can strengthen racial and cultural identity development for adolescents.

LO 7-3 Explore moral development (including Kohlberg's theory, Gilligan's approach, and a social learning perspective).

Kohlberg's theory of moral development has three levels: preconventional, conventional, and postconventional. Gilligan's theory on moral development, which is more relevant to women, establishes three levels: orientation to personal survival, goodness as self-sacrifice, and the morality of nonviolent responsibility, in addition to the two transitions involved. A social learning theory perspective on moral development applies learning theory principles to the development of moral behavior.

LO 7-4 Review Fowler's theory of faith development.

Fowler proposes a seven-stage theory of faith development in spirituality that parallels Piaget's stages of intellectual growth; the stages are primal or undifferentiated faith, intuitive-projective faith, mythic-literal faith, synthetic-conventional faith, individuative-reflective faith, conjunctive faith, and universalizing faith.

LO 7-5 Assess empowerment through assertiveness and assertiveness training.

People need to distinguish between nonassertive, aggressive, and assertive styles of interaction. Both social workers and their clients have specific assertive rights, which are based on a feeling of self-worth. Social workers and clients can learn and use assertiveness by practicing the 13 steps of assertiveness training.

LO 7-6 Explore suicide in adolescence.

Potential causes of suicide include increased stress, family issues, and psychological variables. The SAD PERSONS scale evaluates 10 factors: sex, age, depression, previous attempts, ethanol abuse, rational thinking loss, social supports lacking, organized plan, no spouse, and sickness. Other warning signs of suicide include a sudden change of mood and the giving away of precious possessions.

Reactions to a suicide threat include remaining calm, being supportive, identifying the immediate problem, identifying strengths, decreasing isolation, exploring past coping mechanisms, avoiding clichés, and examining potential options. Examples of community empowerment include the creation of task forces to address the issue of suicide prevention, crisis intervention telephone lines, peer-helping programs, and training programs for community professionals and other caregivers.

COMPETENCY NOTES

The entire chapter addresses competency Educational Policy (EP) EP 2.1.7 and its respective practice behaviors EP 2.1.7a and EP 2.1.7b (as cited following). (See *p. 334*)

EP 2.1.7 Apply knowledge of human behavior and the social environment.

EP 2.1.7a Utilize conceptual frameworks to guide the processes of assessment, intervention, and evaluation.
(Such conceptual frameworks will typically be identified by a "helping hands" icon.)

EP 2.1.7b Critique and apply knowledge to understand person and environment.
Other EP competencies and practice behaviors addressed in this chapter include the following:

EP 2.1.1b Practice personal reflection and self-correction to assure continual professional development.
(p. 337): Practitioners must practice personal reflection about their own identity to function effectively.
(p. 341): Social workers should practice self-reflection to correct homophobic attitudes.
(p. 359): Practitioners should practice personal reflection regarding their own assertiveness skills so that they may work effectively with clients.

EP 2.1.2 Apply social work ethical principles to guide professional practice.
(pp. 339, 345, 350, 353, 370): Ethical questions are posed.

EP 2.1.2a Recognize and manage personal values in a way that allows professional values to guide practice.
(p. 337): Reflection about personal values allows practitioners to manage these values so that they don't interfere with professional values and ethics.
(p. 341): Social workers should recognize and manage their own values concerning sexual orientation so that professional values may guide practice.

EP 2.1.2b Make ethical decisions by applying standards of the National Association of Social Workers (NASW) Code of Ethics and, as applicable, of the International Federation of Social Workers/International Association of Schools of Social Work Ethics in Social Work, Statement of Principles.
(p. 340): Practitioners should evaluate the extent to which theories coincide with ethical practice.
(p. 349): Aspects of Gilligan's theory coincide with principles in the NASW *Code of Ethics*.

EP 2.1.3 Apply critical thinking to inform and communicate professional judgments.
(p. 340): Practitioners should think critically about which theories are most effective in their application to understanding human behavior.
(p. 346): Social workers should critically evaluate the extent to which Kohlberg's theory applies to social work practice.

(p. 348): Practitioners should critically appraise the extent to which Gilligan's theory applies to social work practice.
(p. 353): Social workers should use critical thinking to evaluate Fowler's theory.

EP 2.1.3a Distinguish, appraise, and integrate multiple sources of knowledge, including research-based knowledge, and practice wisdom.
(p. 341): Practitioners should evaluate and integrate multiple sources of knowledge to understand and work effectively with lesbian and gay adolescents.
(p. 345): The following sections appraise two theories of moral development regarding their value and appropriateness with respect to social work practice.
(p. 346): Social workers should integrate multiple sources of knowledge, such as Kohlberg's theory, to understand human behavior.
(p. 348): Practitioners should incorporate research-based knowledge when evaluating a theory such as Gilligan's.

EP 2.1.3b Analyze models of assessment, prevention, intervention, and evaluation.
(p. 340): Social workers should think critically about which theories are most effective in their application to human behavior.
(p. 345): Three models for assessing moral development—Kohlberg's, Gilligan's, and social learning—are discussed in the following sections.
(p. 346): Practitioners should analyze Kohlberg's model of assessing moral development.
(p. 348): Social workers should analyze Gilligan's model of assessing moral development.

EP 2.1.4 Engage diversity and difference in practice.
(p. 341): Sexual orientation is a dimension of diversity.
(p. 350): Religion and spirituality are aspects of diversity.
(p. 362): Sexual orientation is an important aspect of human diversity.

EP 2.1.4a Recognize the extent to which culture's structures and values may oppress, marginalize, alienate, or create or enhance privilege and power.
(p. 341): Social workers should recognize the extent to which gay and lesbian people are oppressed and alienated.

(p. 366): Cultural, racial, and ethnic diversity may affect suicidal potential.

EP 2.1.4b Gain sufficient self-awareness to eliminate the influence of personal biases and values in working with diverse groups.

(p. 353): Social workers should gain sufficient self-awareness concerning their own values and spiritual beliefs so that they don't impose those beliefs on their clients.

EP 2.1.4c Recognize and communicate their understanding of the importance of difference in shaping life experiences.

(p. 340): Practitioners should recognize the extent to which sexual orientation shapes life experiences.

(p. 341): Social workers must recognize how race, culture, and ethnicity affect identity development.

(p. 346): Social workers should recognize that moral development in different cultures may not conform well to Kohlberg's theory.

(p. 347): Gilligan maintains that gender shapes life experiences in terms of moral development.

(p. 366): Practitioners must recognize the importance of difference, including cultural, racial, and ethnic diversity, in shaping life experiences and influencing suicidal potential.

EP 2.1.4d View themselves as learners and engage those with whom they work as informants.

(p. 341): Social workers should view themselves as learners and engage gay and lesbian adolescents as informants.

(p. 353): Practitioners must learn about their clients' spiritual and religious beliefs from their clients without imposing personal beliefs on clients.

EP 2.1.5 Advance human rights and social and economic justice.

(p. 356): It's important that people understand that each individual has basic human rights concerning assertiveness.

EP 2.1.5a Understand the forms and mechanisms of oppression and discrimination.

(p. 341): Social workers should strive to understand the oppressed circumstances often experienced by nonheterosexual adolescents.

(p. 353): Fowler's theory does not take concepts such as oppression and discrimination into account.

EP 2.1.5b Advocate for human rights and social and economic justice.

(p. 341): Practitioners should advocate on the behalf of lesbian and gay adolescents.

EP 2.1.5c Engage in practices that advance social and economic justice.

(p. 341): Social workers should engage in practices that advance social and economic justice for gay and lesbian adolescents.

EP 2.1.6a Use practice experience to inform scientific inquiry.

(p. 354): More social work research needs to be conducted concerning spirituality and practice.

EP 2.1.6b Use research evidence to inform practice.

(p. 354): Social workers should utilize research on the effectiveness of approaches involving spirituality to improve their practice effectiveness.

EP 2.1.7 Apply knowledge of human behavior and the social environment.

(p. 360): Social workers must understand how the social systems in which adolescents live affect suicidal potential.

EP 2.1.7a Utilize conceptual frameworks to guide the processes of assessment, intervention, and evaluation.

(p. 334): Social workers can use conceptual frameworks such as Erikson's psychosocial theory and Marcia's categories of identity to understand identity formation.

(p. 345): Practitioners should use conceptual frameworks such as Kohlberg's theory of moral development, Gilligan's approach to the moral development of women, and the social learning perspective on moral development to guide the processes of assessment, intervention, and evaluation.

(p. 350): Social workers should use conceptual frameworks such as Fowler's theory of faith development to guide the processes of assessment, intervention, and evaluation.

(p. 363): The SAD PERSONS scale provides a useful conceptual framework for assessing suicidal potential.

EP 2.1.7b Critique and apply knowledge to understand person and environment.

(p. 360): Practitioners must understand and apply knowledge about factors contributing to adolescent

suicide in order to understand the dynamics involved.

EP 2.1.8a Analyze, formulate, and advocate for policies that advance social well-being.

(p. 344): Social workers should strive to establish policies and programs that are culturally sensitive and appropriate in order to advance social well-being.

(p. 369): Practitioners should advocate for policies and services that prevent suicide and advance social well-being.

EP 2.1.8b Collaborate with colleagues and clients for effective policy action.

(p. 369): Social workers scan collaborate with colleagues and clients to develop resources for suicide prevention such as suicide prevention task forces, crisis telephone lines, peer-helping programs, and suicide prevention training programs for community professionals.

EP 2.1.9a Continuously discover, appraise, and attend to changing locales, populations, scientific and technological developments, and emerging societal trends to provide relevant services.

(p. 341): Practitioners should continuously respond to the changing issues and conditions affecting lesbian and gay adolescents.

(p. 353): It's important for social workers to appraise continuously the extent to which the immediate social and political environment may affect people's ability to function, including in the area of faith development.

EP 2.1.10a Substantively and affectively prepare for action with individuals, families, groups, organizations, and communities.

(p. 341): Social workers should prepare for action with gay and lesbian adolescents.

(p. 363): The SAD PERSONS scale helps practitioners prepare for action with potentially suicidal people.

EP 2.1.10b Use empathy and other interpersonal skills.

(p. 337): Self-reflection about their own identity helps social workers better empathize with and understand the identity development of others.

(p. 341): Practitioners should develop empathy with lesbian and gay adolescents in terms of the issues they face. Workers should use their interpersonal skills to help lesbian and gay adolescents navigate through the coming-out process.

(p. 367): Social workers should use interpersonal skills when helping potentially suicidal clients.

EP 2.1.10d Collect, organize, and interpret client data.

(p. 360): Social workers must collect, organize, and interpret appropriate client data in order to assess suicidal potential effectively.

(p. 363): The SAD PERSONS scale provides a means of collecting and interpreting client data when assessing suicidal potential.

EP 2.1.10e Assess clients' strengths and limitations.

(p. 344): Practitioners should assess and strive to strengthen the racial and cultural identity development of adolescents through school and community programs.

(p. 353): Social workers should assess their clients' spirituality as a potential strength.

(p. 360): The assessment of both client strengths and limitations is essential in understanding suicidal potential.

(p. 363): The SAD PERSONS scale focuses on assessing limitations people experience that may contribute to suicidal potential.

(p. 367): Practitioners should identify and focus on client strengths and past coping mechanisms to help clients deal with current crises.

EP 2.1.10g Select appropriate intervention strategies.

(p. 341): Social workers should select the appropriate intervention strategies when working with gay and lesbian adolescents.

(p. 355): Approaches involved in assertiveness training and suicide prevention may provide practitioners with appropriate intervention strategies.

(p. 367): Appropriate intervention strategies for working with potentially suicidal clients are identified here.

EP 2.1.10i Implement prevention interventions that enhance client capacities.

(p. 367): Suicide prevention approaches aim to eliminate the suicidal threat and enhance clients' capacities to survive and thrive.

(p. 369): Widely ranging community suicide prevention initiatives are identified.

EP 2.1.10j Help clients resolve problems.

(p. 341): Practitioners should assist lesbian and gay adolescents in addressing the problems they encounter.

(p. 355): Assertiveness training and approaches used in suicide prevention may help clients address and solve problems.

(p. 358): Teaching clients assertiveness skills may help them resolve problems.

(p. 367): Implementing approaches and strategies for suicide prevention aims to help clients address and solve their problems.

EP 2.1.10k Negotiate, mediate, and advocate for clients.

(p. 341): Social workers should mediate and help resolve the issues of gay and lesbian adolescents on the one hand, and heterosexual adolescents on the other. Workers should advocate on the behalf of gay and lesbian clients.

(p. 359): Practitioners may require appropriate assertiveness skills to advocate effectively on their clients' behalf.

(p. 369): Social workers should advocate for community services to prevent suicide.

WEB RESOURCES

See this text's companion website at *www.cengage brain.com* for learning tools such as chapter quizzing, videos, and more.

SOCIAL DEVELOPMENT IN ADOLESCENCE

Clayton Sharrard / Photo Edit

Laura Sardina is 19 years old and is wondering what the future holds for her. She lives with her parents and has a job as a hotel maid, for which she receives the minimum hourly wage. She has frequent arguments with her mother, and both of her parents have encouraged her to get a better-paying job so that she can become self-supporting and move out of the house. She realizes that a minimum-wage job will not enable her to live in an apartment, buy a car, buy clothes and food, and have sufficient money for entertainment.

Laura was raised in a middle-class family. Her brother is attending college to become a minister. Religion has always been an important aspect of Laura's parents' lives, but not of Laura's. She detests going to church. Her parents have often called her "stupid" and negatively compared her to her brother, who they believe can do no wrong. This disparagement of Laura has in many ways become a self-fulfilling prophecy. She repeated a grade in elementary school, seldom studied, and often received failing grades.

In school, she saw herself as a failure and hung out with other students who viewed themselves as failures. In high school, she frequently skipped school and partied. Eight weeks before graduation, she was expelled for skipping too much school. Her parents and the school system had tried numerous times to motivate Laura to apply herself in school; she even had a number of individual sessions with three different social workers and a psychiatrist.

Laura's parents are especially irate when she leaves home for three or four days at a time and parties in an abandoned house in the inner city of Milwaukee. She has lied to her parents about her sexual activities, when the truth is she has a variety of partners. Fortunately, she is taking birth control pills. Some of Laura's male friends are putting pressure on her to become a prostitute so that there will be more money to buy drugs and party. Laura and her friends have had several encounters with the police for shoplifting, running away from home, drinking liquor under age, kicking police officers while being arrested, and driving in high-speed auto chases after radar detected they were speeding.

Laura is asking herself a number of questions: Should she prostitute herself? Or should she stop associating with her friends and try to make peace with her parents by getting a high school education and a better-paying job? Whenever she has tried to achieve the middle-class goals of her parents, they have criticized her as being a failure. She wonders what her chances are of heading in a better direction this time. The one thing she has found enjoyable in life is partying with her friends, but she realizes her friends are getting her in trouble with the police. She is worried that cutting ties with her friends will result in living a life in which she will be continually rejected and put down by others. She wants a better-paying job but realizes her chances are not good, especially because she hasn't completed high school. She wants a one-to-one relationship with a caring male, but because she has a low self-concept, the only thing she feels that males will find attractive about her is sexual intercourse. This is one reason she has had multiple sex partners. She is increasingly concerned that being so sexually active is not right and may result in her acquiring a sexually transmitted disease (such as AIDS). What should she do about all of these concerns? She is deeply perplexed and confused.

A Perspective

This chapter will focus primarily on the social changes and some social problems encountered by adolescents. The social growth from puberty to age 19 involves a number of passages: from being dependent on parents to becoming more independent, from adjusting to puberty to establishing a sexual identity, from beginning to date to serious dating and perhaps marrying, from being a child with parents to sometimes parenting children, from earning money from babysitting to having a full-time job or attending college, from buying baseball gloves and playing ball to buying a car, and from drinking soda to drinking beer and hard liquor and experimenting with drugs. The pressures and stresses of this time period produce many casualties who suffer from a variety of problems.

Learning Objectives

This chapter will help prepare students to:

EP 2.1.7a, 2.1.7b

LO 8-1 *Describe the social development changes that adolescents undergo*

LO 8-2 *Describe some major problems encountered by this age group: emotional and behavior problems, crime and delinquency, delinquent gangs, and eating disorders*

LO 8-3 *Understand theoretical material on the causes and treatments of these problems*

LO 8-4 *Understand material on social work with groups, including theories about group development and theories about group leadership*

LO 8-1 Describe the Social Development Changes That Adolescents Undergo

Social Development Changes in Adolescence

During adolescence, people move from dependence on parents to becoming more independent and establishing peer relationships and perhaps intimate relationships.

Movement from Dependence to Independence

Young people often are in a conflict between wanting to be independent of their parents but on another level realizing their parents are providing for many of their wants and needs: food, shelter, clothes, emotional support, spending money, and so on. Many young people see their parents as having shortcomings and conclude that they know more than their parents. Yet when their car breaks down and they have no idea of how to fix it, mom or dad almost always knows what to do to get it fixed.

In the pursuit of independence, adolescents often rebel against their parents' attempts to guide them and reject their views as being out-of-date and stupid. They sometimes do things to shock their parents, as if to say "See, I'm my own person, and I'm going to live my life my way!" Interestingly,

once young people become more independent in their 20s and have to pay their own bills, they tend to have a greater appreciation for their parents' knowledge. Mark Twain noted (as quoted in Papalia & Olds, 1981, p. 375), "When I was fourteen my father knew nothing, but when I was twenty-one, I was amazed at how much the old man had learned in those seven years."

Children who are raised in families in which the parents have provided opportunities to learn self-reliance, responsibility, and self-respect tend to make a smoother transition from dependency to adulthood interdependence. Children who are raised in families where the parents are overly permissive or take little interest in their children's behavior tend to have greater difficulty making the transition to adulthood. These young people lack structure or a system of standards and values to gauge whether their behavior is suitable and their decisions are appropriate. Children who have overly protective parents also have difficulty making this transition; they usually do not learn how to assume responsibilities or make important decisions.

Some parents are wary about their children growing up. In particular, some fathers and mothers become alarmed and uncomfortable when their "little girl" starts dating. Many parents worry that their daughter may become sexually involved and pregnant, which they believe will interfere with their dreams and hopes for her having a good life. When teenagers assert their right to becoming more independent, it changes the components of the family system.

Any change in the components of the system will create tension within the family. This tension is expressed by teens with such statements as "You don't understand me," "Get off my back," "I know what I'm doing—don't treat me like a baby," and "Chill out."

Parents may feel hurt by what they perceive as a lack of appreciation or gratitude. Common areas of conflict between parents and adolescents are home chores, use of time, attitude toward studies, expenditures of money, morals and manners, choice of friends, clothes selection, use of phone, dating practices, and use of car.

How should parents seek to cope with thrusts of independence from their teenagers? A key is keeping the lines of communication open. All teenagers need help, even if they sometimes do not recognize this need or seem ungrateful for help that is given. Teenagers need to feel that their parents are a resource they can turn to. If communication is severed, teenagers have only their peers to turn to—and suggestions and advice from another teenager are apt to be less constructive (and potentially more destructive) in resolving a dilemma than suggestions from a responsible adult. Keeping the lines of communications open is admittedly easier said than done. It requires work! Highlight 8.1 offers some techniques for effective communication between adults and young people.

The task of becoming independent involves attaining emotional, social, and economic independence. Emotional independence involves progressing from emotional dependence on parents or others to increased independence while still being able to maintain close emotional ties, it involves moving from a parent-child relationship to an adult-adult relationship. Emotional independence involves becoming self-reliant with the knowledge that "I am put together well enough emotionally that I can fend for myself, but I am willing to share my feelings with others and let them become part of me." Emotional independence involves receiving, sharing, and being interdependent, without being emotionally dominated or overwhelmed.

Social independence involves becoming self-directed rather than other-directed. Many adolescents are *other-directed* because they are so strongly motivated by the need for social acceptance that much of what the group says is what adolescents think and do. *Self-directed* people think things out for themselves and make decisions based on their personal interests. Becoming socially independent does not mean becoming selfish. Socially independent people realize that their best interests are served by becoming involved in political, civic, educational, religious, social, and community affairs.

Economic independence involves earning sufficient money to meet one's financial needs. Many older teenagers do not have special skills, so that obtaining well-paying jobs to meet their financial needs is very difficult. Economic independence also involves learning to limit one's desires and purchases to one's ability to pay. To become economically independent, it is necessary to develop at least one marketable set of skills that one can offer an employer in exchange for a job. Interestingly, the more money that people earn, the more material items they usually desire; from their improved financial position, they see a whole new set of material items that they "just have to have."

Is Adolescent Rebellion a Myth?

The teenage years have been called a time of adolescent rebellion. The rebellion is believed to include: the adolescent being in conflict with parents, being alienated from adult society, engaging in dangerous and reckless behavior, being in emotional turmoil, and rejecting adult values.

A few adolescents do rebel, and fit this stereotype. However, Margaret Mead (1935), who studied teenagers in Samoa and other South Pacific islands, found that when a culture provides a gradual serene transition from childhood to adulthood, rebellion is not typical. Papalia and Feldman (2012) note that in the United States (and in most other countries), most teenagers feel close to their parents and value their parents' approval. Although family conflict and engaging in risky behavior are more common during adolescence than during other parts of the life span, in most families, the difficulties do not cross the line to open rebellion.

Interaction in Peer Group Systems

Adolescents have a strong *herd* drive and desire to be accepted by their peers. Peers are an important influence on adolescents. Some studies indicate that peers are more of a factor than parents in determining whether a youth will become involved in serious juvenile delinquency (Papalia et al., 2012).

HIGHLIGHT 8.1

Interaction in Families: Effective Communication Between Parents and Children

Thomas Gordon (1970), in his book *Parent Effectiveness Training*, identified the following four communication techniques designed to improve relationships between parents and their children.

Active Listening

This technique is recommended for use when a child indicates that he or she has a problem—for example, when a 16-year-old daughter looks in a mirror and states, "I'm fat and ugly—everyone but me has a boyfriend." For such situations, Gordon recommends that the parent use *active listening*.

The steps involved in active listening are these: The receiver of a message tries to understand what the sender's message means or what the sender is feeling. The receiver then puts this understanding into his or her own words and returns this understanding for the sender's verification. In using this approach, the receiver does *not* send a message of his or her own, such as asking a question, giving advice, expressing feelings, or giving an opinion. The aim is to feed back only what he or she feels the sender's message meant. An active listening response to the 16-year-old girl in the previous example might be, "You want very much to have a boyfriend and think the reason you don't is related to your physical appearance." An active listening response involves either *reflecting feelings* or *restating content*.

Dr. Gordon lists a number of advantages to using active listening. It facilitates problem solving by young people, which fosters the development of responsibility. By talking a problem through, a person is more apt to identify the root of the problem and arrive at a solution than by merely thinking about a problem. When a teenager feels his or her parents are listening, a by-product is that he or she will be more apt to listen to the parents' point of view. In addition, the relationship between parent and youth is apt to be improved because children feel they are being heard and understood. Finally, the approach helps a teen to explore, recognize, and express his or her feelings.

Certain parental attitudes are required to use this technique. The parent must view the young person as being a separate person with his or her own feelings. The parent must be able to accept the youth's feelings, whatever they may be. The parent should genuinely want to be helpful and must want to hear what the child has to say. Additionally, the parent must have trust in the child's capacities to handle problems and feelings.

"I"-Messages

Many occasions arise when a young person causes a problem for the parent. For example, a son may turn up the stereo so high that the music is irritating, or he may stay out after curfew hours, or he may recklessly drive an auto. Confronted with such situations, many parents send either a solution message (they order, direct, command, warn, threaten, preach, moralize, or advise), or a put-down message (they blame, judge, criticize, ridicule, or name-call). Solution and put-down messages can have devastating effects on a child's self-concept and are generally counterproductive in helping a child become responsible.

Solution and put-down messages are primarily *you-messages*: "You do what I say," "Don't you do that," "Why don't you be good," "You're lazy," "You should know better."

Dr. Gordon advocates that parents should instead send *I-messages* for those occasions when a teenager is causing a problem for the parent. For example, consider a parent who is riding in a car with the son driving and exceeding the speed limit. Instead of the parent saying, "Slow down, you idiot, before you get us killed," Dr. Gordon urges the parent to use an I-message: "I feel frightened when driving this fast."

I-messages, in essence, are nonblaming messages that communicate only how the sender of the message believes the receiver is adversely affecting the sender. I-messages do not provide a solution, nor are they put-down messages. It is possible to send an I-message without using the word I ("Driving this fast really frightens me"). The essence of an I-message involves sending a nonblaming message of how the parent feels the child's behavior is affecting the parent.

You-messages are generally put-downs that either convey to youths that they should do something or that convey to them how bad they are. In contrast, I-messages communicate to young people much more honestly the effect of the behavior on the parent. I-messages are also more effective because they help teenagers learn to assume responsibility for their own behavior. An I-message tells a teenager that the parent is trusting the teen to respect the parent's needs and that the parent is trusting him or her to handle the situation constructively.

You-messages frequently lead to an argument between parent and youth; I-messages are much less likely to do so. I-messages lead to honesty and openness in a relationship, and generally foster intimacy. Teenagers, as well as adults, often do not know how their behavior affects others. I-messages produce startling results; parents frequently report that their teenagers express surprise upon learning how their parents really feel.

Note that I-messages will work only if the youth does not want his actions to adversely affect his parent. If the youth does not want to cause discomfort in his parent, he will seek to change his adverse behavior when informed by an I-message of how he is adversely affecting his parent. However, if the youth enjoys causing discomfort in his parent, then the use of an I-message by the parent is apt to result in an *increase* in the youth's adverse behavior because he is now more fully aware of how to cause discomfort in the parent.

No-Lose Problem Solving

In every parent-teenager relationship, there are inevitably situations in which the youth continues to behave in a way that interferes with the needs of the parent. Conflict is part of life and is not necessarily bad. Conflict is bound to occur because people are different and have different needs and wants, which at times do not match. What is important is not how frequently conflict arises, but how the conflicts get resolved. Generally in a conflict between parent and youth, a power struggle is created.

In many families, the power struggle is typically resolved by one of two win-lose approaches. Most parents try to resolve the conflict by having the parent win and the young person lose. Psychologically, parents almost always are recognized as having greater authority. The outcome of the parents' winning is that it creates resentment in the teenager toward his or her parents, leads to low motivation for the teenager to carry out the solution, and does not provide an opportunity for him or her to develop self-discipline and self-responsibility. Such teenagers are likely to react by becoming either hostile, rebellious, and aggressive, or submissive, dependent, and withdrawing.

In other families, fewer in number, the win-lose conflict is resolved by the parents' giving in to their teenagers out of fear of frustrating them or fear of conflict. In such families, teenagers come to believe that their needs are more important than anyone else's. They generally become self-centered, selfish, demanding, impulsive, and uncontrollable. They are viewed as being spoiled, have difficulty in interacting with peers, and lack respect for the property or feelings of others.

Of course, few parents use either approach exclusively. Oscillating between the two approaches is common. There is evidence that both approaches lead to the development of emotional problems in children (Gordon, 1970).

Gordon seriously questions whether power is necessary or justified in a parent-teenager relationship. For one reason, as teenagers grow older, they become less dependent, and parents gradually lose their power. Rewards and punishments that worked in young years become less effective as youths grow older. Teenagers resent those who have power over them, and parents frequently feel guilty after using power. Gordon believes that parents continue to use power because they have had little experience in using nonpower methods of influence.

Gordon suggests a new approach, the *no-lose* approach to solving conflicts. In this approach, parents and youth solve their conflicts by finding their own unique solutions acceptable to both.

The no-lose approach is simple to state: Each person in the conflict treats the other with respect, neither person tries to win the conflict by the use of power, and a creative solution acceptable to both parties is sought. The two basic premises are (1) that all people have the right to have their needs met and (2) that what is in conflict between the two parties involved is not their *needs* but their *solutions* to those needs.

Gordon (1970, p. 237) lists the following six steps in the no-lose method:

1. Identifying and defining the needs of each person
2. Generating possible alternative solutions
3. Evaluating the alternative solutions
4. Deciding on the best acceptable solution
5. Working out ways of implementing the solution
6. Following up to evaluate how it worked

This approach motivates youths to carry out the solution because they have participated in the decision. It develops their thinking skills and a sense of responsibility. It requires less enforcement, eliminates the need for power, and improves relationships between parents and teenagers. It also develops their problem-solving skills. Conflict resolution strategies are more fully described in Chapter 12.

Collisions of Values

Collisions of values are common between parents and their children, particularly as the children become adolescents and young adults. Likely areas of conflict include values about sexual behavior, clothing, religion, choice of friends, education, plans for the future, use of drugs, hairstyles, and eating habits. In these areas, emotions run strong, and parents generally seek to influence their offspring to follow the values the parents hold as important. Teenagers, on the other hand, often think their parents' values are old-fashioned and declare that they want to make their own decisions about these matters.

Gordon identifies three constructive ways in which parents and teenagers can seek to resolve these conflicts. (For the sake of simplicity, we will use the term *mother* in describing what should be done—a father or a teenager can also use these same techniques.)

The first way a mother can influence her offspring's values is to model the values she holds as important. If she values honesty, she should be honest. If she values responsible use of alcohol, she should exhibit a responsible model. If she values openness, she should be open. She needs to ask herself if she is living according to the values she professes. If her values and behavior are incongruent in certain areas, she needs to change

(continued)

HIGHLIGHT 8.1 *(continued)*

either her values or her behavior in the direction of congruency. Congruence between behavior and values is important if she wants to be an effective model.

The second way she can influence her teenagers' values is to act as a consultant to them. There are some do's and don'ts of a good consultant. First of all, a good consultant finds out whether the other person would like her consultation. If the answer is yes, she then makes sure she has all the available pertinent facts. She then shares these facts—once—so that the young person understands them. She then leaves him or her the responsibility for deciding whether to follow the advice. A good consultant is neither uninformed nor a nag; otherwise she is not apt to be used as a consultant again.

The third way for a mother to reduce tensions over values issues is to modify her values. By examining the values held by her teenagers, she may realize their values have merit, and she may move toward their values or at least toward an understanding of why they hold them.

Note that all of these techniques for more effective communication can be used to improve communication and relationships in practically all interactions, such as adult-adult and counselor-client. The techniques are much broader in application than just a parent-teenager interaction.

SOURCE: Adapted from Charles Zastrow, *The Practice of Social Work*, 2nd ed. (Homewood, IL: Dorsey, 1985). © 1985 The Dorsey Press.

However, a study by Patterson, DeBaryshe, and Ramsey (1989) indicates that the strongest predictor of delinquency is the family's supervision and discipline of children. The process of becoming delinquent, this study found, starts out in childhood and has its roots in troubled parent-child interactions. Children get certain payoffs for antisocial behavior: They get attention or their own way by acting up, and they avoid punishment by lying or by cheating on school tests. Children's antisocial behavior interferes with their schoolwork and their ability to get along with their classmates. As a result, these children—unpopular and nonachieving—seek out other antisocial children. These children influence each other and learn new forms of problem behavior from one another.

The particular kind of peer group that an adolescent selects depends on a variety of factors: socioeconomic status (most peer groups are bound by social class); values derived from parents; the neighborhood one lives in; the nature of the school; special talents and abilities; and the personality of the adolescent. Once an adolescent becomes a member of a peer group, the members of that subgroup influence each other in their social activities, study habits, dress, sexual behavior, use or nonuse of drugs, vocational pursuits, and hobbies.

Not all adolescents join cliques. Some prefer to be loners. Some are already pursuing what they believe will be their life goals. Some may be busy babysitting for younger children in the family. Some prefer having only one or two close friends.

Some are excluded from the cliques that exist in their area.

Adolescents tend to identify with other teenagers, rather than with adults or younger children. This identification may be due to the belief that most other teens share their personal values and interests, whereas younger and older people have more divergent interests and values. Compared to people in their 40s and 50s, adolescents view themselves as being less materialistic, more idealistic, healthier sexually, and better able to understand friendships and what is important in life.

Friends and peer groups help adolescents make the transition from parental dependence to independence. Friends give each other emotional support and serve as important points of reference for young people to compare their beliefs, values, attitudes, and abilities. In a number of cases, friendships forged during adolescence endure throughout life.

Empowerment of Homeless Youth

Youth in poverty often experience a special sense of powerlessness and hopelessness; this is even more intensified for those who are homeless. Although no one knows exactly how many young people are homeless in the United States, homelessness among teenagers is a significant problem (Mooney, Knox, & Schacht, 2013). Homeless youth tend to experience many serious difficulties, including those that are health-related and those involving the mental health, substance abuse, and unemployment of other family members, especially parents (Mooney et al., 2013). Few resources and supports exist for such young people in their immediate social environments.

Rees (1998) proposes that social workers can help homeless youth become more empowered by helping them progress through four stages. The stages are based on the ability of youth to express themselves and their experiences through biographical storytelling. Stage 1 involves "understanding powerlessness" (p. 137). Young people must be allowed to express their despair, disappointment, fear, and hurt before social workers and others rush in to help them. They must get their feelings out before they can begin to focus on positive change.

Stage 2 is "awareness and mutual education" (p. 138). After expressing feelings, homeless youth should be encouraged to talk about their experiences, as painful as they have been. Articulating and sharing experiences can help young people organize their thoughts and identify themes characterizing their lives. Rees (1998) comments that "this stage of dawning awareness gives practitioners a chance to encourage young people to construct their stories so they can begin to think of different choices in their lives. Usually their stories reconstruct experiences of Powerlessness.... Such spelling out is a crucial part of empowerment" (p. 139).

Stage 3 is "dialogue and solidarity" (p. 140). After telling their stories, continuing to exchange information and share feelings with others provides opportunities to learn from and support each other. Such discourse can involve their rights to education, services, income, housing, and legal assistance. They can help each other begin to formulate plans for empowering themselves and demanding access to resources. Together, homeless youth can establish solidarity, supporting each other in their quest for empowerment.

Stage 4 is "action and political identity" (p. 141). This involves a sense of self-confidence in one's ability to make progress, seek changes in conditions, and improve one's overall quality of life. Political identity is the sense that one has the right and power to seek improvements in life. Effects can include an improved self-concept, more effective communication skills, better relationships with professionals and family, and more productive interactions with resource providers and legal system representatives. Rees (1998) furnishes two example

of homeless youth experiencing empowerment. Sean's empowerment involved seeing that his future could become more than an early, violent death. He gained confidence in his ability to advocate for himself with healthcare professionals, the police, and resource providers. The second youth, Dean, indicated that for the first time he had hope that someday he would get a job and even live in a home of his own, things he never thought were possible before. He began to like himself more and eagerly participated in a job-training program.

LO 8-2 Describe Some Major Problems Encountered by This Age Group: Eating Disorders

Social Problems

In addition to the normal phases of social development, such as becoming more independent, a number of situations and life crises tend to occur in adolescence (or in the years following adolescence). The following pages will focus on certain social problems: eating disorders, emotional and behavioral problems, crime and delinquency, and delinquent gangs. The latter two can be viewed as macrosystem problems because large systems are often involved in the planning and carrying out of criminal activity, and large systems are involved in investigating, prosecuting, preventing, and curbing criminal activity.

Eating Disorders

Eating disorders are occurring in epidemic proportions. Although they have existed for a long time, the dramatic increase in the number of individuals affected is now a major concern for mental health professionals. The majority of people who have eating disorders are female. The three primary eating disorders are anorexia nervosa, bulimia nervosa, and compulsive overeating. All three are serious disorders that create life-threatening health problems.

Anorexia Nervosa

Anorexia nervosa means "loss of appetite due to nerves." This definition is inaccurate, because people with anorexia do not actually lose their appetite until the late stages of their starvation. Until then, they do feel hungry; they just do not eat. Anorexia nervosa is a disorder characterized by the excessive pursuit of thinness through voluntary starvation. The predominant features of this disorder include excessive thinness, intense fear of gaining weight or becoming fat, a distorted body image in which anorexics view themselves as being overweight, and amenorrhea (cessation of menses) in females.

Anorexics refuse to accept that they are too thin. They eat very little, even when experiencing intense hunger. They insist they need to lose even more weight. They erroneously believe that an ultrathin body is a perfect body, and that achieving such a body will bring happiness and success. As they lose weight, their health deteriorates and they tend to become increasingly depressed. Symptoms of physical deterioration include reduced heart rate, lowered blood pressure, lowered body temperature, increased retention of water, fine hair growth on many parts of the body, amenorrhea in females, and a variety of metabolic changes (Koch, Dotson, Troast, & Curtis, 2006). Even while their health is deteriorating, anorexics stubbornly cling to the belief that through controlling their body weight, they can gain control of their lives.

On the surface, someone who is prone to develop anorexia appears to be a model child. She is eager to please, well-behaved, a good student, and someone who appears to get along well with her peers. She rarely asks for help, and she is unlikely to indicate that anything is wrong. Behind this mask is an insecure, self-critical perfectionist who feels she is unworthy of any praise that she receives. She is also apt to be concerned about whether other people like her.

The development of this disorder usually proceeds according to the following pattern:

1. It begins with a diet. Dieting for these individuals usually begins just before or just after a major change occurs—such as entering puberty, breaking up with a boyfriend, or leaving home for college.
2. Dieting creates a feeling of control. At first the person feels better about herself because dieting is something she can do successfully. Soon, however, food and the fear of becoming fat become the major concerns in life.
3. Exhausting exercise is added. The anorexic exercises excessively, such as running 10 miles before eating.

4. Health begins to fail. Weight loss and malnutrition begin, leading to mental and physical deterioration. Although the person may sense something is wrong, she refuses to conclude that she needs to start eating more. Anorexia can lead to the shrinking of internal organs, including the brain, heart, and kidneys. As the heart muscle weakens, the chances of irregular heart rhythm and congestive heart failure increase. Other complications include muscle aches and cramps, swelling of joints, constipation, difficulty urinating, inability to concentrate, digestive problems, and injuries to nerves and tendons. In addition, loss of fat and muscle tissue makes it difficult for the body to keep itself warm, which leads to the sensation of feeling cold. The unusual growth of fine body hair (especially on the arms and legs) may be the body's response in seeking to make up for heat loss.

A large number of anorexics engage in excessive exercise for prolonged periods of time in an attempt to lose more weight. They prefer solitary activities (such as running and exercise machines) over team sports. At mealtimes, to avoid conflicts with others over eating so little, they are apt to say that they have already eaten, or if they are forced to be at the table with others, they may dispose of their food by slipping it into a container under the table. Because they are always hungry, anorexics are preoccupied with food, grocery shopping, nutritional information, and cooking. They may collect cookbooks and memorize calorie charts.

Anorexics, even in warm weather, tend to wear several layers of bulky clothing, or sweaters and baggy pants, to warm their cold bodies and to conceal their thinness. (Their thinness often brings questions or criticisms from relatives and friends, so wearing bulky clothing is a way to avoid being questioned.) Anorexics usually deny that they need help with their eating patterns; they insist their bodies are normal and attractive.

Anorexics tend to maintain rigid control over nearly all aspects of their lives. To avoid criticism, they often withdraw from others and are introverted. They often develop compulsive rituals involving exercise, food, housekeeping, studying, and other aspects of their lives. A favorite ritual is to weigh themselves several times a day. They may cut their

Sadly, some movie stars, by being ultrathin, promote anorexia nervosa among their fans.

wrong, successes or failures, beautiful or ugly, fat or thin. They do not deal well with complexity or shades of gray. Anorexics seek to be perfectionists in all aspects of their lives, including relationships, school or job responsibilities, and personal appearance.

Ninety-five percent of those affected with anorexia nervosa are females (Koch et al., 2006). Onset usually occurs during adolescence, although the onset can occur from prepuberty to the early 30s. Estimates of the number of teenage females affected by this disorder range from 1 in 100 to 1 in 800 (Koch et al., 2006). Although this disorder is found in all ethnic and socioeconomic groups, especially vulnerable are overly perfectionistic "model" children from upper-middle-class and upper-class backgrounds.

To prevent death by starvation, anorexics frequently need hospitalization. Studies estimate mortality rates of between 5 and 18 percent from a variety of medical complications, including heart attack, kidney damage, liver impairment, malnutrition, and starvation. Starvation weakens the body's immune system, which leaves the anorexic vulnerable to pneumonia and other infections. Suicide following severe depression is also a danger. The mortality rate for anorexia nervosa is thought to be higher than for any other psychiatric disorder (Koch et al., 2006).

Bulimia Nervosa

The term *bulimia* is derived from a Greek word meaning "ox-like hunger." But the binge-purge cycle that is characteristic of bulimics is triggered not by physical hunger but by emotional upset. Binge eating is the rapid, uncontrolled consumption of large amounts of food. A binge may last from a few minutes to several hours. Purging is the process of getting rid of the food eaten during a binge. The most frequent method of purging is self-induced vomiting. Other methods of purging include strict dieting or fasting, vigorous exercise, diet pills, and abuse of diuretics and laxatives. Some bulimics chew food to enjoy the taste and then spit it out to avoid calories and weight gain. Estimates of the incidence of bulimia nervosa among high school and college-age females range between 4.5 and 18 percent (Koch et al., 2006).

small morsels of food into tiny pieces and then spend extended time eating each piece. They find security in discipline and order. To achieve greater control of their lives, they tend to avoid social activities, sexual relationships, parties, and friends.

Some anorexics occasionally yield to their hunger pangs and eat—and perhaps even binge. After eating and binging, they are apt to feel guilty because they failed in their efforts to always follow a restricted diet.

Anorexics tend to think in black-and-white terms. They view themselves, and others, as being right or

The development of bulimia tends to proceed according to the following pattern:

1. A diet is started. The person wants to lose weight and improve self-esteem. However, dieting increases hunger and leads to a craving for sweet, high-calorie food.
2. Overeating begins. The overeating is often triggered by stress such as anger, depression, loneliness, frustration, and boredom. Food helps to relieve hunger and also is a comfort for emotional pain.
3. Guilt develops. The person feels guilty about gaining weight in a society where "thin is in."
4. Purging is discovered. The person discovers that self-induced vomiting or other forms of purging will allow her to binge but not gain weight.
5. A binge-purge habit takes hold. Binge eating and purging become a way of coping with life and emotional pain. Bulimics tend to fear that others will discover their habit and view it as disgusting.

The average bulimic binge involves between 1,000 and 5,500 calories, although daylong binges of more than 50,000 calories occur in some bulimics. (The average American's food intake is about 3,000 calories a day.) Bulimics tend to binge on high-calorie junk foods, such as sweets and fried foods. Bulimics generally feel considerable shame about their binging and purging, but continue to resort to the binge-purge cycle as a way to relieve the pain of their daily problems.

Most bulimics are within a normal weight range, although some are somewhat overweight or underweight. Obesity in adolescence may be a contributing factor in the development of the disorder in some bulimics. The parents of bulimics are often overweight, and close relatives of bulimics have a higher-than-chance frequency of alcoholism and depression (Koch et al., 2006).

The usual age of onset for bulimia nervosa is late adolescence or early adulthood. Alcohol and other substance abuse is fairly common among bulimics. This is because the psychological dynamics that lead a person to abuse alcohol or drugs are similar to the dynamics that lead a person to be bulimic. Substance abuse may be easier to treat than bulimia, however, because a substance abuser can completely abstain from using alcohol or drugs, but a bulimic needs to continue to eat (which acts as a trigger to binging) in order to survive.

Because bulimia nervosa is seldom incapacitating, the disorder can go undetected by family and friends for years. Physical complications, however, begin to develop. Chronic vomiting can lead to gum disease and innumerable cavities, because of the hydrochloric acid content of vomit. Vomiting can also lead to severe tearing and bleeding in the esophagus. Chronic vomiting may result in a potassium deficiency, which then may lead to muscle fatigue, weakness, numbness, erratic heartbeat, kidney damage, and, in severe instances, paralysis or death. Digestive problems range from stomach cramps, nausea, ulcers, and colitis to a fatal rupturing of the stomach. Sore throats are also common. Bulimia can also lead to diabetes.

Dehydration and electrolyte imbalance can occur and in some cases cause cardiac arrhythmias and even death. Psychotropic drugs (such as tranquilizers and antidepressant drugs) may affect the body differently because of changes in body metabolism. For bulimics who are substantially below normal weight, physical complications associated with anorexia nervosa may also occur.

Both anorexia and bulimia lead to serious health problems. Stating the obvious, nutritious meals are needed for good health and survival. Anorexics risk starvation, and both bulimics and anorexics risk serious health problems. Fat synthesis and accumulation are necessary for survival. Fatty acids are a major source of energy. When fat levels are depleted, the body must draw on carbohydrates (sugar). When sugar supplies dwindle, body metabolism decreases, which often leads to drowsiness, inactivity, pessimism, depression, dizziness, and fatigue.

Although a few bulimics at times binge with friends, usually bulimics binge alone and secretly. Because binging leads to guilt, anxiety, and fear of weight gain, the process of purging serves as a reinforcer for binging because purging often results in a sense of again being in control with a flat stomach. However, many bulimics feel shame and personal disgust about their binging-purging cycle.

Bulimics tend to be people pleasers who crave affection, attention, and approval from others. Unlike anorexics, they usually have active social lives with a number of friends and acquaintances. However, they are often filled with self-doubt and insecurity. Although they want close personal relationships, they also tend to fear such relationships, partly because they fear their eating disorder is more apt to be discovered. Many bulimics are sexually promiscuous, partly because they want affection and have low self-esteem. Some bulimics may shoplift and steal food. Most bulimics feel they do not have control of their lives, and feel especially out of control around food. They worry that once they begin to eat, they will be unable to refrain from binging. Bulimics are more likely than anorexics to seek help for their eating disorder.

Compulsive Overeating and Obesity

Compulsive overeating is the irresistible urge to consume excessive amounts of food for no nutritional reason. In most cases, compulsive overeating is a response to a combination of familial, psychological, cultural, and environmental factors. Compulsive overeating results in excessive accumulation of body fat. Compulsive eaters are overweight. Estimates are that three out of five Americans are overweight (Mooney et al., 2013).

Treatment is recommended for persons whose body weight is more than 20 percent over ideal body weight (Koch et al., 2006). The more overweight a compulsive overeater is, the greater the health risks. Being overweight is correlated with such health problems as hypertension, elevated cholesterol levels, and diabetes. People who are overweight are also prone to heart attacks and other heart diseases.

Compulsive overeaters have many of the characteristics that are commonly found in bulimics. A key distinguishing factor between the two disorders is that bulimics frequently engage in purging, whereas compulsive overeaters seldom, if ever, do. Similar to bulimics, compulsive overeaters tend to binge in an effort to temporarily escape painful problems in their lives. Compulsive overeaters generally feel considerable shame and embarrassment about their eating patterns and their weight. Alcohol and other substance abuse are common. Like bulimics, compulsive overeaters tend to be people pleasers who crave attention and approval from others and who are often filled with self-doubt and insecurity. Overeaters have a high incidence of depression and are apt to have low self-esteem. Age of onset of the disorder is usually during adolescence.

Compulsive overeaters are apt to display one or more of the following:

1. Frequent diet plan failures. Overeaters attempt and fail at numerous diet plans. They are apt to try nearly every new diet fad briefly, believing that their latest effort will be the one that achieves permanent weight loss. No diet fad really works for them. Repeated diet failures result in a sense of hopelessness and self-deprecation.

2. Avoidance of health warning signs. Being excessively overweight eventually leads to health problems, such as diabetes and hypertension. Compulsive overeaters tend to ignore early warning signs of health problems, choosing instead to continue binging rather than making a commitment to developing healthier eating patterns.

3. Social isolation. Overeaters often feel shame and guilt about being overweight; as a result, they may seek to reduce interpersonal contact. For some, avoiding interactions with others becomes a dominant behavioral pattern.

4. Nutritional ignorance. Compulsive overeaters often lack adequate knowledge of basic nutrition. Many have a distorted view of what constitutes a well-balanced and healthy diet.

5. Selective eating amnesia. Compulsive overeaters are unlikely to conscientiously count their calorie intake. They are also apt to binge several times a day without keeping track of the frequency of their binging.

6. Overeating as a response to unwanted emotions. When overeaters feel unwanted emotions such as loneliness, frustration, insecurity, anger, and depression, they are apt to ease the pain of these emotions through binging. Binging temporarily takes their mind off their concerns, so it does work—but only during the short time while they are eating. After binging, overeaters are not only apt to feel the pain of their original unwanted emotions, which now return, but also to feel shame and guilt over their excessive eating.

Obesity is a medical condition in which excess body fat has accumulated to the extent that it may have an adverse impact on health, leading to increased health problems and/or reduced life expectancy. Obesity increases the likelihood of various diseases, including heart disease, certain types of cancer, breathing difficulties during sleep, type 2 diabetes, and osteoarthritis. Obesity is a leading preventable cause of death worldwide, with increasing prevalence in adults and children. Authorities view it as one of the most serious public health problems of the 21st century. Alarmingly, two-thirds of U.S. adults are either obese or overweight (Mooney et al., 2013).

Obesity is most commonly caused by compulsive overeating, lack of physical activity, and genetic susceptibility. (More rarely, obesity may be caused by endocrine disorders and by certain medications—such as steroids, some antidepressants, and some medications for seizure disorders.)

The primary treatments for obesity are dieting and physical exercise. In case these two treatments do not work, antiobesity drugs may be taken to reduce appetite or inhibit fat absorption. In severe cases, surgery may be performed to reduce stomach volume and/or bowel length—thereby reducing the person's ability to absorb nutrients from food.

Interrelationships Among Eating Disorders

As noted previously, there are a number of differences among the three eating disorders, but there are also interrelationships. Some people have symptoms of both anorexia and bulimia, and are identified as having the disorder *anorexia bulimia*. Many of those who have anorexia bulimia occasionally move back and forth between being anorexic and bulimic. In addition, some overeaters occasionally have episodes of purging, and at times fit the criteria for being bulimic. Koch and his associates (2006) indicate that it is important to conceptualize these three eating disorders as forming a continuum, ranging from being overly thin to being excessively overweight:

> *Eating disorder symptoms and behaviors seem to exist on a continuum. On the extreme left are those struggling with anorexia, who achieve drastic weight loss by severely restricting food intake. Moving to the right toward the center are individuals with anorexic bulimia who eat and binge on occasion, but primarily maintain a much lower than normal weight by strict dieting and purging In the center are normal-weight bulimics who repeatedly binge and purge thousands of calories per episode, yet are neither significantly under or over normal weight. Although overly preoccupied with body shape and body image, it is not unusual for normal-weight bulimics to experience rapid weight fluctuations of ten or more pounds because*

of intense cycles of bingeing and purging. At the other end of the continuum, the binge eater will repeatedly eat excess amounts of food, gaining significant amounts of weight without engaging in any of the purging behavior associated with anorexia or bulimia nervosa. Individuals may move back and forth along this continuum, alternatively restricting or bingeing, depending on their circumstances and the progression of their disorder. (p. 28)

LO 8-3 Understand Theoretical Material on the Causes and Treatments of These Problems

Causes

Many factors contribute to the development of an eating disorder. The factors differ from one individual to another. Some bulimics and compulsive over-eaters may be genetically predisposed to these disorders. Depression or alcoholism tends to be present in parents or other family members. People with an eating disorder tend to feel inadequate and worthless. Their low self-esteem combined with their quest for perfectionism leads them to be intolerant of any flaws. They tend to compare themselves to others, and usually conclude "I'm not good enough." A significant number of anorexics and bulimics have been victimized by molestation, rape, or incest (Koch et al., 2006).

Anorexics and bulimics have some similarities. Both are likely to have been brought up in middle-class, upwardly mobile families, where their mothers are overinvolved in their lives and their fathers are preoccupied with work outside the home. For the most part, bulimics and anorexics were good children, eager to comply and eager to achieve in order to obtain the love and approval of others. Both tend to have a distorted body image in which they view themselves as being fatter than others view them. Both have an obsessive concern with food. Their parents tended to be overprotective and did not allow them to become more independent and learn from their mistakes. Their parents still treat them as if they were young children rather than teenagers and young adults. A smaller number of anorexics and bulimics come from nonsupportive and non-nourishing families that were demanding, critical, and rejecting. Others with eating disorders were raised by parents who combined obsessive concern with criticism and rejection, which places the children in a double bind of wanting to protest but feeling guilty because their parents are so "caring." Still others were raised by parents who have good parenting skills and show love and act appropriately with their children. In such families, other factors lead to the development of an eating disorder.

Bulimics are often overachievers, and in college tend to attain high academic averages. Purging for bulimics often becomes a purification rite because it is frequently viewed as a way to overcome self-loathing. They tend to believe they are unlovable and inadequate. Through purging, they feel completely fresh and clean again. These feelings of self-worth are only temporary. They are extremely sensitive to minor insults and frustrations, which are often used as excuses to initiate another food binge.

Ethical Questions 8.1

EP 2.1.2

Do you know someone who has an eating disorder? If so, what might you do or say that would be helpful to this person?

Impacts of Social Forces

One reason for the increased incidence of anorexia and bulimia may be the increasing value that our society places on being slim and trim. Why are bulimics and anorexics primarily women? Koch and his associates (2006) make a strong case that there are many more pressures on women to be thin than on men. Our socialization practices also overemphasize the importance of women being slender.

Eating disorders have become epidemic in the United States in the past 50 years. Before that time, society allowed all people, and especially women, to be rounder and heavier. Weight-gain products and breast enhancers were popular products that were purchased by thin women who wanted to look like Marilyn Monroe. However, norms for what is attractive have changed.

Some authorities assert that our body size is partially genetically determined by "set point." Koch and his associates (2006) note:

Researchers believe an eating disorder may develop after prolonged dieting when individuals try to achieve or maintain a body size that is in direct conflict with their biology. They maintain that one's weight is genetically predetermined. This weight is referred to as the body's set point, and family history is the best indication of what a person's set point weight should be. According to the set point theory, efforts to reduce body weight below set point [are] resisted by an increase in appetite and lethargic behavior, and a reduction in basic metabolic rate, all designed to increase body weight. (p. 30)

Treatment

Because eating disorders are complex and serious, professional intervention is generally needed. Treatment for an eating disorder usually has the following three goals: (1) resolution of the psychosocial and family dynamics that led to the development of the eating disorder; (2) provision of med-

EP 2.1.10g & j

ical services to correct any medical problems that resulted from starving, binging and purging, or being obese; and (3) reestablishment of normal weight and healthy eating behavior.

Many anorexics and bulimics who enter treatment for eating disorders want to be treated for their unhealthy eating habits, but still want to be very thin. These two objectives are incompatible. Unless anorexics and bulimics truly comprehend that ultra-thinness is unhealthy, they will soon return to their old behaviors. Treatments must be comprehensive and multifaceted because eating disorders are complex and multidimensional. Each person's unique circumstances need to be carefully assessed so that the specific needs of each client can be treated.

The client may be treated on an inpatient or outpatient basis. Hospitalization of a person with an eating disorder is sometimes needed. Inpatient care should be considered for anorexics when weight loss continues or when there is an absence of weight gain after a reasonable length of time in outpatient treatment. It should be considered for bulimics who are unable to break the binge-purge cycle after a reasonable period of time in outpatient treatment. If a client with an eating disorder indicates suicidal thoughts or severe self-destructive behavior, in-patient care should be seriously considered. Hospitalization is usually necessary when physical complications require close medical supervision (e.g., when an anorexic is in danger of severe heart dysfunction, or when a bulimic needs treatment for dehydration and electrolyte imbalance). A compulsive overeater may occasionally need to be hospitalized for medical conditions such as heart disease or problems associated with diabetes. Because hospitalization severely disrupts a person's life, it should be used only when necessary.

Individual psychotherapy plays a prominent part in practically all comprehensive treatment of people who have an eating disorder. Goals of individual therapy include the establishment of healthy eating patterns, increased self-esteem, increased sense of power and control over one's life, resolution of negative and unwanted emotions such as guilt and depression, and resolution of internal conflicts and personal problems. Individual psychotherapy may also have the goals of reducing stress, increasing assertiveness, and exploring relationship issues and career options.

Because family dynamics are usually contributing factors to an eating disorder, family therapy is also important, particularly if the affected person is living at home. Other family members are always affected, and sometimes victimized, by the turmoil experienced by the individual with the eating disorder. Through therapy, family members are better able to understand the dynamics of the eating disorder and can make changes that provide increased support for the affected person. The family therapist seeks to improve family functioning, which facilitates the recovery of the individual. Family sessions are also helpful to eating-disordered individuals who are struggling with issues of separation from their primary family.

Group therapy is also an important intervention. It may be provided in a variety of forms, including self-help, psycho-educational, and behavioral therapy. Through group interaction, members are able to put their problems in perspective because they see that others have problems as serious as theirs. Groups also enable members to test out more appropriate interaction patterns. Members can also share their unwanted emotions and problematic behaviors, and discover ways to think and act in more realistic ways. Groups also provide interpersonal support. Groups are useful in confronting members about the health hazards of their eating patterns. Group

treatment provides an arena for diminishing feelings of isolation and secrecy, sharing successful techniques for better coping with common problems, demystifying eating disorders, expressing feelings, obtaining feedback from other members, and facilitating realistic goal setting.

Nutritional counseling is an essential component of any treatment plan. A registered dietician can provide information about proper nutrition and the body's need for nutritious food. The dietician can provide information on the physiology of dieting and weight management, and can help the affected person to establish healthier eating patterns as well.

Because some persons with eating disorders are depressed, antidepressant medication is sometimes beneficial. Such medication is prescribed by a psychiatrist or physician. Couples therapy is sometimes needed when there is significant conflict in a couple's relationship. Some elementary, secondary, and higher education school systems are now developing prevention programs that seek to inform students about the risks of eating disorders and to identify services for students who are beginning to develop an eating disorder.

LO 8-2 Describe Some Major Problems Encountered by This Age Group: Emotional and Behavioral Problems

Emotional and Behavioral Problems

Emotional problems (involving unwanted feelings) and behavioral problems (involving irresponsible actions) are two comprehensive labels covering an array of problems. Emotional difficulties include depression, feelings of inferiority or isolation, feeling guilty, shyness, having a low self-concept, having a phobia, and excessive anxiety. Behavioral difficulties include being sadistic or masochistic, being hyperactive, committing unusual or bizarre acts, being overly critical, being overly aggressive, abusing one's child or spouse, being compulsive, committing sexual deviations, showing violent displays of temper, attempting suicide, and being vindictive.

Everyone, at one time or another, will experience emotional and/or behavioral problems. Severe emotional or behavioral problems have been labeled as mental illnesses by certain members of the helping professions. The two general approaches to viewing and diagnosing people who display severe emotional disturbances and abnormal behaviors are the *medical model* and the *interactional model.*

Medical Model

The medical model views emotional and behavioral problems as a mental illness, comparable to a physical illness. The medical model applies medical labels (schizophrenia, paranoia, psychosis, insanity) to emotional problems. Adherents of the medical approach believe the disturbed person's mind is affected by some generally unknown, internal condition. That condition, they assert, might be due to genetics, metabolic disorders, infectious disease, internal conflicts, unconscious use of defense mechanisms, or traumatic early experiences that cause emotional fixations and hamper psychological growth.

The medical model has a lengthy classification of mental disorders that are defined by the American Psychiatric Association in the DSM-5 (2013) (see Highlight 8.2).

The medical model arose in reaction to the historical notion that the emotionally disturbed were possessed by demons, were mad, and were to blame for their disturbances. These people were "treated" by being beaten, locked up, or killed. The medical model led to viewing the disturbed as in need of help; it stimulated research into the nature of emotional problems and promoted the development of therapeutic approaches.

The major evidence for the validity of the medical model comes from studies that suggest that some mental disorders, such as schizophrenia, may be influenced by genetics (heredity). The bulk of the evidence for the significance of heredity comes from studies of twins. For example, studies have found identical twins to have a *concordance* rate (i.e., if one has it, both have it) for schizophrenia of about 50 percent (Comer, 2010). The rate of schizophrenia in the general population is about 1 percent (Comer, 2010). So when one identical twin is schizophrenic, the other is 50 times more likely than the average to be schizophrenic. This suggests a causal influence of genes, but not genetic determination, because concordance for identical twins is only 50 percent, not 100 percent.

Interactional Model

Critics of the medical (mental illness) model assert that such medical labels have no diagnostic or treatment value and frequently have an adverse labeling effect.

Thomas Szasz (1961a) was one of the first authorities to assert that mental illness is a myth—that it does not exist. Szasz's theory is an *interactional model* that

focuses on the processes of everyday social interaction and the effects of labeling on people. Beginning with the assumption that the term *mental illness* implies a "disease of the mind," he categorized all of the so-called mental illnesses into three types of emotional disorders and discussed the inappropriateness of calling such human difficulties mental illnesses.

1. *Personal disabilities*, such as excessive anxiety, depression, fears, and feelings of inadequacy. Szasz said that such so-called mental illnesses may appropriately be considered mental (in the sense that thinking and feeling are considered mental activities), but they are not diseases.
2. *Antisocial acts*, such as bizarre homicides and other social deviations. Homosexuality used to be in this category, but was removed from the American Psychiatric Association's list of mental illnesses in 1974. Szasz said antisocial acts are social deviations and are neither mental nor diseases.
3. *Deterioration of the brain with associated personality changes.* This category includes the disorders labeled as mental illnesses in which personality changes result following brain deterioration from such causes as arteriosclerosis, chronic alcoholism, general paresis, or serious brain damage following an accident. Common symptoms are loss of memory, listlessness, apathy, and deterioration of personal grooming habits. Szasz said these disorders can appropriately be considered diseases, but are diseases of the brain (i.e., brain deterioration that specifies the nature of the problem) rather than diseases of the mind.

Szasz (1961b) asserted that the notion that people with emotional problems are mentally ill is as absurd as the belief that the emotionally disturbed are possessed by demons:

> *The belief in mental illness as something other than man's trouble in getting along with his fellow man, is the proper heir to the belief in demonology and witchcraft. Mental illness exists or is "real" in exactly the same sense in which witches existed or were "real." (p. 87)*

The point that Szasz and many others are striving to make is that people do have emotional problems, but they do not have mystical, mental illnesses. Terms that describe behavior, they believe, are very useful. For example, depression, anxiety, obsession, compulsion, excessive fear, hallucinations, or feelings of being failures describe personal problems

Major Mental Disorders According to the American Psychiatric Association

NEURODEVELOPMENTAL DISORDERS include, but are not limited to intellectual disabilities (sometimes called cognitive disabilities), communication disorders (such as language disorder), autism spectrum disorder, attention-deficit/hyperactivity disorder, specific learning disorder (such as impairment in reading), and motor disorders (such as developmental coordination disorder, stereotypic movement disorder, and Tourette's disorder).

SCHIZOPHRENIA SPECTRUM AND OTHER PSYCHOTIC DISORDERS include, but are not limited to schizotypal (personality) disorder, delusional disorder, schizophrenia, schizoaffective disorder, and catatonic disorder.

BIPOLAR AND RELATED DISORDERS include, but are not limited to bipolar I disorder, bipolar II disorder, and cyclothymic disorder.

DEPRESSIVE DISORDERS include, but are not limited to disruptive mood dysregulation disorder (such as major depressive disorder), persistent depressive disorder, and premenstrual dysphoric disorder.

ANXIETY DISORDERS include separation anxiety disorder, specific phobia (such as fear of injections and transfusions), social anxiety disorder, panic disorder, and agoraphobia.

OBSESSIVE-COMPULSIVE AND RELATED DISORDERS include obsessive-compulsive disorder, hoarding disorder, trichotillomania (hair-pulling disorder), and excoriation (skin-picking) disorder.

TRAUMA- AND STRESSOR-RELATED DISORDERS include reactive attachment disorder, posttraumatic stress disorder, and acute stress disorder.

DISSOCIATIVE DISORDERS include dissociative identity disorder and dissociative amnesia.

SOMATIC SYMPTOM AND RELATED DISORDERS include somatic symptom disorder, illness anxiety disorder, and factitious disorder (includes factitious disorder imposed on self, and factitious disorder imposed on another).

FEEDING AND EATING DISORDERS include pica, rumination disorder, avoidant/restrictive food intake disorder, anorexia nervosa, bulimia nervosa, and binge-eating disorder.

ELIMINATION DISORDERS include enuresis, and encopresis.

SLEEP-WAKE DISORDERS include insomnia disorder, hypersomnolence disorder, narcolepsy, breathing-related sleep disorders (such as central sleep apnea), and parasomnias (such as sleepwalking type, sleep terror type, nightmare disorder, rapid eye movement sleep behavior disorder, restless legs syndrome, and substance/medication-induced sleep disorder).

SEXUAL DYSFUNCTIONS include delayed ejaculation, erectile disorder, female orgasmic disorder, female sexual interest/arousal disorder, genito-pelvic pain/penetration disorder, male hypoactive sexual desire disorder, and premature (early) ejaculation.

GENDER DYSPHORIA includes gender dysphoria.

DISRUPTIVE, IMPULSE-CONTROL, AND CONDUCT DISORDERS include oppositional defiant disorder, intermittent explosive disorder, conduct disorder, antisocial personality disorder, pyromania, and kleptomania.

SUBSTANCE-RELATED AND ADDICTIVE DISORDERS include alcohol-related disorders (such as alcohol use disorder, and alcohol intoxication); caffeine-related disorders (such as caffeine intoxication); cannabis-related disorder (such as cannabis use disorder cannabis intoxication); hallucinogen-related disorders; inhalant-related disorders; opioid-related disorders; sedative-, hypnotic-, or anxiolytic-related disorders; stimulant-related disorders (such as cocaine abuse); tobacco-related disorders; and non-substance-related disorders (such as gambling disorders).

NEUROCOGNITIVE DISORDERS include delirium, major and mild neurocognitive disorders (such as Alzheimer's disease, vascular disease, traumatic brain injury, substance/medication use, HIV infection, Parkinson's disease, and Huntington's disease).

PERSONALITY DISORDERS include paranoid personality disorder, schizoid personality disorder, schizotypal personality disorder, antisocial personality disorder, borderline personality disorder, histrionic personality disorder, narcissistic personality disorder, avoidant personality disorder, dependent personality disorder, and obsessive-compulsive personality disorder.

HIGHLIGHT 8.2 *(continued)*

PARAPHILIC DISORDERS include voyeuristic disorder, exhibitionistic disorder, frotteuristic disorder (such as recurrent sexual arousal from touching or rubbing against a nonconsenting person), sexual masochism disorder, sexual sadism disorder, fetishistic disorder, and transvestic disorder.

OTHER MENTAL DISORDERS include mental disorders due to another medical condition.

MEDICATION-INDUCED MOVEMENT DISORDERS AND OTHER ADVERSE EFFECTS OF MEDICATION include neuroleptic-induced Parkinsonism and medication-induced acute dystonia.

OTHER CONDITIONS THAT MAY BE A FOCUS OF CLINICAL ATTENTION include relational problems (such as parent-child relational problems), abuse and neglect (such as child abuse and neglect, child sexual abuse, child psychological abuse, spouse or partner violence or neglect, and adult abuse by nonspouse), educational and occupational problems, housing and economic problems (such as homelessness), problems related to crime or interaction with the legal system, religious or spiritual problems, victim of terrorism or torture, personal history of military deployment, and overweight or obesity.

SOURCE: *Diagnostic and Statistical Manual of Mental Disorders-5*, Fifth Edition by the American Psychiatric Association, 2013, Washington, DC: American Psychiatric Association.

---

that people have. But they assert that medical terms (such as schizophrenia and psychosis) are not useful because there is no distinguishing symptom that would indicate whether a person has, or does not have, the illness. In addition, Caplan (1995) points out that there is considerable variation between cultures regarding what is defined as a mental illness, and even within a given culture, psychiatrists frequently disagree on the medical diagnosis to be assigned to those who are disturbed.

In a dramatic study, psychologist David Rosenhan (1973) demonstrated that professional staff in mental hospitals could not distinguish insane patients from sane patients. Rosenhan and seven normal associates went to 12 mental hospitals in five different states claiming they were hearing voices, all eight were admitted to these hospitals. After admission, these pseudopatients stated they had stopped hearing voices and acted normally. The hospitals were unable to distinguish their sane status from the insane status of other patients. The hospitals kept these pseudopatients hospitalized for an average of 19 days, and all were then discharged with a diagnosis of "schizophrenia in remission."

The use of medical labels has severe adverse effects (Comer, 2010). The person labeled mentally ill believes that he or she has a disease for which, unfortunately, there is no known cure. (Frequently the therapist believes this as well.) The label gives the labeled person an excuse for not taking responsibility for his or her actions (e.g., a defendant pleads innocent by reason of insanity). Because no cure is known, the disturbed frequently idle away their time waiting for someone to discover a cure, rather than assuming responsibility for their behavior, examining the reasons why there are problems, and making efforts to improve. Being labeled mentally ill has other undesirable consequences. The labeled persons may lose some of their legal rights; they may be stigmatized in their social interactions as being dangerous, unpredictable, untrustworthy, or of weak character; and they may find it more difficult to secure employment or receive a promotion (Comer, 2010).

The question of whether mental illness exists is important. The assignment of mental illness labels to disturbed people has substantial implications for how they will be treated, for how others will view them, and for how they will view themselves. Cooley's "looking-glass self-concept" (1902) applies here. The looking glass says we develop our self-concept in terms of how other people react to us. If a man is labeled mentally ill, other people are apt to react to him as if he were mentally ill, and that person may well define himself as being different and crazy, and begin playing that role. Authorities who adhere to the interactional model raise a key question: If we relate to people with emotional problems

Ethical Questions 8.2

EP 2.1.2

Do you believe it is useful to society to label some people as mentally ill? Do you believe labeling someone as mentally ill may lead that person to continue to act irresponsibly?

as if they were mentally ill, how can we expect them to act in emotionally healthy and responsible ways?

Adherents of the interactional approach believe that people get labeled mentally ill for two reasons: They may have an intense unwanted emotion, or they may be engaged in dysfunctional (or deviant) behavior. Assigning a mental illness label to unwanted emotions or dysfunctional behaviors does not tell us how the emotions or behaviors originated nor how to treat such emotions and behaviors. The rest of this section, based on a rational therapy approach, does both. It gives us an approach for identifying the sources of unwanted emotions and dysfunctional behaviors, and it provides strategies for changing them.

LO 8-3 Understand Theoretical Material on the Causes and Treatments of These Problems

Assessing and Treating Unwanted Emotions: Application of Theory to Client Situations

EP 2.1.10g & j

A variety of theoretical frameworks can be used for assessing and treating emotional problems. (A summary of these frameworks is in Zastrow, 1999.) The rational therapy approach, described here, is one of the more useful approaches. The primary developer of rational therapy is Albert Ellis (1962).

Many people erroneously believe that emotions are primarily determined by experiences (i.e., by events that happen to them). Rational therapy has demonstrated that the primary cause of our emotions is what we tell ourselves about events that happen to us.

All emotions occur according to the following format:

Events
(Our experiences)

↓

Self-Talk
(The set of evaluating thoughts we give ourselves about facts and events that happen to us)

↓

Emotions
(May include remaining calm)

This basic principle is not new. The stoic philosopher Epictetus wrote in the Enchiridion in the first century. A.D.: "Men are disturbed not by things, but by the view which they take of them" (quoted in Ellis, 1979, p. 190). An example will illustrate this process:

Event
Jane Lewis studies extensively for her first human behavior exam, takes the exam, and receives a C.

Jane's Self-Talk

"Gee, this is awful. I studied so hard for this exam, and bombed out. It sure looks like I'm going to fail this course. Human behavior is not for me. I'm simply dumber than other students. Since this is a required course in the social work major, it looks like I'll never make it as a social worker. I'm a failure. Maybe I should drop out of college right now, rather than continuing to waste my money, when I'll never graduate anyway."

↓

Jane's Emotions
Jane feels depressed, feels like a failure, is disgusted with herself.

If on the other hand, Jane tells herself the following about receiving a C, her emotions will be very different:

Event
Jane Lewis studies extensively for her first human behavior exam, takes the exam, and receives a C.

↓

Jane's Self-Talk

"Wow—I just got by on this exam. Nearly half the class got a C or lower on the exam, so it looks like I'm doing about as well as the others. All I need is a grade of C in this course to pass and fulfill the requirement. I see where I made some mistakes that I shouldn't have made, so I think I will be able to do better on the next exam. I'll also talk with the instructor to get some ideas on how I can improve in this course. I feared I had flunked this exam, and I wound up doing better than I expected. I'm progressing satisfactorily in the social work major, but I think I can do better."

↓

Jane's Emotions

Jane feels mildly anxious about receiving a C, relief that she hadn't flunked the exam, optimistic about improving her grade on the next exam, and optimistic about passing the course and continuing in the social work major.

The most important point about this process is that our self-talk determines how we feel, and by changing our self-talk we can change any unwanted emotion. An unwanted emotion can be defined as either an emotion we want to change or an emotion we have that others have become significantly concerned about—for example, excessive depression that has continued since a loved one died several years earlier. It is possible that an emotion that is generally viewed as being positive can be an unwanted emotion. For example, if you find you are feeling happy at a funeral, you may want to change that emotion. Similarly, an emotion that is generally viewed as negative can be a wanted emotion in certain situations, such as feeling sadness at a funeral.

Changing Unwanted Emotion

There are only five ways to change an unwanted emotion, and only three of them are constructive: getting involved in meaningful activity; changing the negative and irrational thinking that underlies the unwanted emotion; and changing the distressing event.

Meaningful Activity The first constructive way to change an unwanted emotion is to get involved in some meaningful or enjoyable activity. When we become involved in activity that is meaningful, it provides satisfaction and structures and fills time, thereby taking our mind off a distressing event.

Practically all of us encounter day-to-day frustrations and irritations—having a class or two that are not going too well, having a job with irritations, or having a blah social life. If we go home in the evening and continue to dwell on the irritations, we will develop such unwanted emotions as depression, anger, frustration, despair, or feeling of being a failure. (Which of these emotions we will have will depend directly on what we tell ourselves.)

By having an escape list of things we enjoy doing, we can nip unwanted emotions in the bud. Everyone should develop an escape list of things that he or she enjoys doing: taking a walk, golfing, going to a movie, shopping, doing needlework, visiting friends, exercising, and so on. By getting involved in things we enjoy, we take our minds off our day-to-day concerns and irritations. The positive emotions we experience instead will stem directly from what we tell ourselves about the enjoyable things we are doing.

In urging people to use an escape list, we are not suggesting that people should avoid trying to change unpleasant events. If something can be done to change an unpleasant event, all constructive efforts should be tried. However, we often do not have control over unpleasant events and cannot change them. Yet we always have the capacity to control and change what we tell ourselves about unpleasant events. It is this latter focus that is often helpful in learning to change our unwanted emotions.

Changing Self-Talk A second approach to changing unwanted emotions is to identify and then change the negative and irrational thinking that leads to unwanted emotions. Maultsby (1975) developed an approach, called *rational self-analysis (RSA)*, that is very useful for learning to challenge and change irrational thinking. An RSA has six parts, as shown in Highlight 8.3.

The goal in doing an RSA is to change an unwanted emotion (anger, love, guilt, depression, hate, and so on). An RSA is done by recording the event and self-talk on paper. Under Part A (facts and events), simply state the facts or events that occurred. Under Part B (self-talk), write all of your thoughts about A. Number each statement in order (1, 2, 3, 4, and so on). Also write either good, bad, or neutral after each self-talk statement to show yourself how you believed each statement reflected on you as a person. (The RSA example presented in Highlight 8.4 illustrates the mechanics of doing an RSA.)

Under Part C (emotional consequences), write simple statements describing your gut reactions/emotions stemming from your self-talk in B. Part D(a) is to be written only *after* you have written sections A, B, and C. Part D(a) is a "camera check" of the A section. Reread the A section and ask yourself, If I had taken a moving picture of what I wrote was happening, would the camera verify what I have written as facts? A moving picture would probably have recorded the facts, but not personal beliefs or opinions. Personal beliefs or opinions belong in the B section. A common example of a personal opinion mistaken as a fact is: "Marty made me look like a fool when he laughed at me while I was trying to make a serious point." Under D(a), correct the opinion part of this statement by writing only the factual part: "I was attempting to make a serious point when Marty began laughing at what I was saying." Then add the personal opinion part of the statement to B ("Marty made me look like a fool").

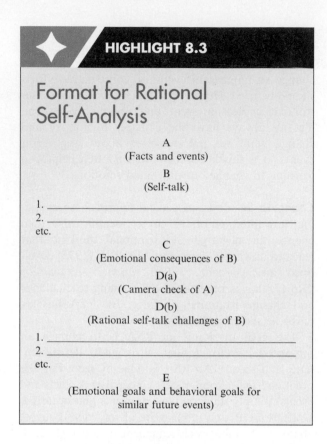

HIGHLIGHT 8.3

Format for Rational Self-Analysis

A
(Facts and events)

B
(Self-talk)

1. _____
2. _____
etc.

C
(Emotional consequences of B)

D(a)
(Camera check of A)

D(b)
(Rational self-talk challenges of B)

1. _____
2. _____
etc.

E
(Emotional goals and behavioral goals for
similar future events)

Part D(b) is the section designed to challenge and change negative and irrational thinking. Take each B statement separately. Read B-1 first, and ask yourself if it is inconsistent with any of the five questions for rational thinking. It will be *irrational* if it does one or more of the following:

1. **Does not fit the facts.** For example, you tell yourself no one loves you after someone has ended a romantic relationship—and you still have several close friends and relatives who love you.

2. **Hampers you in protecting your life.** For example, if you decide you can drive 30 miles home when you are intoxicated.

3. **Hampers you in achieving your short- and long-term goals.** For example, you want to do well in college and you have two exams tomorrow, which you haven't studied for, but instead you decide to go out and party.

4. **Causes significant trouble with other people.** For example, you think you have a right to challenge anyone to a fight whenever you interpret a remark as being an insult.

5. **Leads you to feel emotions that you do not want to feel.**

If the self-talk statement is rational, merely write, "That's rational." If, on the other hand, the self-talk statement meets one or more of the guidelines for irrational thinking, then think of an alternative self-talk to that B statement. This new self-talk statement is of crucial importance in changing your undesirable emotion. It needs to be rational and to be a self-talk statement you are willing to accept as a new opinion for yourself. After writing down this D(b-1) self-talk in the D (b) section, then consider B-2, B-3, and so on in the same way.

Under Part E, write down the new emotions you want to have in similar future A situations. In writing these new emotions, keep in mind that they will follow from your self-talk statements in D(b). This section may also contain a description of certain actions you intend to take to help you achieve your emotional goals when you encounter future A situations.

In order to make a rational self-analysis work, you have to put effort into challenging the negative and irrational thinking with your rational debates whenever you start thinking negatively. With effort, you can learn to change any unwanted emotion. This capacity is one of the most important abilities you have. (Once you gain skill in writing out an RSA, you will be able to do the process in your head without having to write it out.) An illustration of writing an RSA is displayed in Highlight 8.4.

This process of challenging negative and irrational thinking *will* work to change unwanted emotions if you put the needed effort into it. Just as dieting is guaranteed to assist someone who is overweight to lose some pounds, so is this approach guaranteed to change unwanted emotions. Both, however, require an effort and commitment to use the process in order to make it work.

Changing the Distressing Event A third way to change unwanted emotions is to change the distressing event. Some distressing events can be changed by directly confronting the events and taking constructive action to change them. For example, if we are let go from a job, we can seek another; when we find one, we will feel better. Or if we are receiving failing grades, we can meet individually with our instructors to obtain their suggestions on how to do better. If we receive suggestions that are practical and have merit, we will feel better.

HIGHLIGHT 8.4

A Rational Self-Analysis to Combat Unwanted Emotions Following the Ending of a Romantic Relationship

A. Facts and Events

I dated a guy steadily for two months that I really thought I liked. I knew something was not quite right with our relationship. I was unable to figure out what it was until he finally said that he had been dating another girl for two years and was still seeing her. However, he promised that they would break up soon and urged me to "hang on" for a little while. Three weeks passed, and then I saw them speaking to each other one night. When she left, I went over to talk to him, and he seemed to be in a bad mood. I tried to get out of him what was the matter. Then, we began to talk about the other girl, and he said he could not break up with her for a while and we were not going to see each other at all for a while. Then, I started to yell at him for various things, and the crying began.

D(a). Camera Check of A

All of this is factual.

B. Self-Talk

1. I hate him! (bad)

2. How could I have been such a sucker for the last two months? (bad)
3. All guys are jerks. (bad)

4. I'll never date anyone else again. (bad)

5. I'm glad I know now where I stand for sure. (good)
6. What did I ever do to him to be treated like this? (bad)

7. No one loves me. (bad)

8. I'm a failure. (bad)

9. I'll never find anyone I love as much as him. My life is ruined. (bad)

D(b). My Rational Debates of B

1. I don't really hate him. He was good to me, and we did enjoy the times we had together.
2. I should not feel as if I was a sucker because I did not know about the other girl until he finally told me.
3. Guys are not all jerks. I have many male friends who are far from being jerks. In fact, I do not even know what a jerk is. I've never seen a jerk. Guys are humans, not jerks. It is irrational to label someone a jerk and then to relate to that person as if the label were real.
4. I know I will date again, because I always have after other breakups.
5. That's rational.
6. He told me I never did anything to have this happen. It was just a situation he got himself into, and now he needs time to work things out.
7. How can I say that! I have a lot of close friends and relatives, and I know several guys who think highly of me.
8. I'm not a failure. I'm doing well in college and at my part-time job.
9. My life is certainly not ruined. I'm accomplishing many of my goals in life. With two million eligible guys in the world, there are certainly many other worthy guys to form a relationship with. I told myself the same erroneous things a few years ago when I broke up with someone else. I will eventually get involved in another relationship with someone else I love. I need to think positively and dwell on the positive things I've learned in this relationship.

(continued)

◆ **HIGHLIGHT 8.4** (continued)

10. This guy just used me and took what he could get. (bad)

11. My life is over. I'll never find happiness again. (bad)

12. This is awful! This is the worst thing that could happen to me. (bad)

C. My Emotions

Outward emotions were crying and yelling. Inner emotions consisted of feeling angry, hurt, depressed, embarrassed, a failure, and unloved.

10. Neither of us used the other. I'm even uncertain what "used" means. We enjoyed being together and had a lot of good times. He told me he has a lot of positive feelings toward me. He was forced to make a choice between two people, both of whom he enjoyed being with.

11. My life is certainly not over. I have many positive things happening to me right now, and there are many things I enjoy doing. I also have a number of close relatives and friends who'll be there when I need them.

12. Life is full of ups and downs. It is a mistake to "awfulize" and to exaggerate how this breakup will affect my future. There are many other more dreadful things that could happen—such as a terminal illness.

E. My Emotional and Behavioral Goals

I want to be able to change my unwanted emotions so that I no longer am angry, depressed, and hurt about this breakup. Also, I would like to talk to him in private and apologize for my behavior. After I become more comfortable with this breakup, I will gradually be interested in dating someone else in the future.

Not all distressing events can be changed. For example, you may have a job that you like but be forced to interact with an employee who displays behaviors you dislike. If you cannot change the behaviors, the only other constructive option is to bite the bullet and seek to adapt to the circumstances. However, when it is feasible and practical to change distressing events, we should seek to do so. If we are successful, we are apt to feel better because we will then give ourselves more positive self-talk about the changed events.

Destructive Ways to Change Unwanted Emotions

Unfortunately, some people turn to two other ways to change unwanted emotions. One of these ways is seeking to temporarily relieve intense unwanted emotions through the use of alcohol, other drugs, or food. Unfortunately, many people seek to relieve unwanted emotions through the use of such mind altering drugs as alcohol, cocaine, or tranquilizers. When the effects of the drug wear off, the problems and unwanted emotions still remain, and there is a danger that through repeated use a person will become dependent on the drug. Some people overeat for the same reasons. Such people are apt to become overweight or bulimic—or both.

The only other way to relieve unwanted emotions is suicide. This is the ultimate destructive approach to changing unwanted emotions.

Assessing and Changing Deviant Behavior: Application of Theory to Practice

Our thinking determines both our emotions and our actions, as depicted in the following diagram:

Events

↓

Self-Talk

↓

Emotions

↓

Actions

To demonstrate this principle, reflect on the last time you did something bizarre or unusual. What self-talk statements were you giving yourself (i.e., what were you thinking) prior to and during the time you did what you did?

Thinking processes determine behavior. The reasons behind unusual or dysfunctional behavior can always be identified by determining what the perpetrator was thinking prior to and during the time the act was being committed. Following are some examples of cognitions leading to dysfunctional behavior.

Cognition: A 17-year-old boy sees an unlocked Mustang and thinks, "Hey, this is really a neat car to take a ride in. Let me cross the starting wires, and take it for a drive."

Behavior: car theft

Cognition: A 27-year-old man is on his second date, is in his date's apartment, and thinks, "She is really sexy. Since I've now wined and dined her twice, it's now time for her to show her appreciation to me. She wants it as much as I do. I'll show her what a great lover I am. She may protest a little, but I'll overcome that with force. Once we get involved sexually, she'll be emotionally attracted to me."

Behavior: date rape

Cognition: A 31-year-old bartender thinks, "Cocaine gives me such a great high. Unfortunately I don't make the kind of money to buy as much as I need. I have no other choice but to buy more than I use, and then sell some of it for a profit."

Behavior: drug trafficking

Cognition: A 16-year-old girl who has run away from home thinks, "Now what am I going to do? Where am I going to stay? Where will I get enough money to eat? Maybe I can find some guys on the street who will give me a place to stay and some money. They'll probably want to jump on me—but that's OK. That's better than going back home and being beaten by my father when he's drunk."

Behavior: prostitution

Cognition: A 48-year-old bookkeeper of a retail computer firm thinks, "This is an awful financial mess I'm in. I've got so many bills: mortgage payments, gambling debts, and tuition payments for two kids in college. Hopefully I can win at the next poker game. But I need a stake. The only way to get it is to take a couple grand from this company and pay the money back in a few weeks. With me handling the books, no one will ever miss it."

Behavior: embezzlement

• • • •   Ethical Question 8.3

Do you sometimes engage in unethical or dysfunctional behavior because of your negative and irrational self-talk?

EP 2.1.2

The cognitions underlying each dysfunctional behavior may vary considerably among perpetrators.

For example, possible cognitions for shoplifting a shirt might be: "This shirt would look really nice for the wedding I'm going to on Saturday. Since I'm buying a number of other items from this store, they will still make a profit from me even if I take this without paying for it." Another may be: "This will be a challenge to see if I can get away with taking this shirt. I'll put it on in the fitting room and put my own shirt and coat on over it, and no one will see me walk out of the store with it. I'll act real casual as I walk out of the store." Or "My son really needs a decent shirt. He doesn't have any nice ones to wear. I don't get enough money from being on public assistance to buy my children what they need. I know my son is embarrassed to wear the rags that he has. I'll just stick this shirt under my coat and walk out with it."

Assessing human behavior is largely a process of identifying the cognitions that underlie unwanted emotions or dysfunctional behavior. The stages of this process are as follows:

1. Identify as precisely as possible the unwanted emotions and/or dysfunctional behavior that a client has.
2. Identify the cognitions or thinking patterns that the client has during the time when he or she is having unwanted emotions or is displaying dys-functional behavior. There are two primary ways of identifying these cognitions. One is to ask the client what he was thinking prior to and during the time when he or she was having unwanted emotions or displaying dysfunctional behavior. If this does not work (perhaps because the client refuses to divulge what he or she was thinking), a second approach is to obtain information about the client's life circumstances at that time. Once these life circumstances are identified, the professional conducting the assessment needs to place himself or herself mentally into the life circumstances of the perpetrator, and then reflect on the kinds of cognitions that would lead to specific unwanted emotions or dysfunctional behavior. For example, if the client is a 16-year-old female who has run away from home and is unemployed, it is fairly easy to identify (to some extent) the kinds of cognitions that would lead her to turn to prostitution.

A deduction from the principle that thinking processes determine dysfunctional behaviors and unwanted emotions is that in order to change these outcomes, the affected person needs to change his or her thinking patterns. These concepts are illustrated in Highlight 8.5.

HIGHLIGHT 8.5

Our Thinking Determines Our Behavior and Our Emotions

One of the authors was describing to a class the concept that our thinking primarily causes our emotions and our actions. A male student voluntarily self-disclosed the following:

What you're saying makes a lot of sense. It really applies to something that happened to me. I was living with a female student who I really cared about. I thought though that she was going out on me. When I confronted her about it, she always said I was paranoid and denied it.

Then one night I walked into a bar in this town and I saw her in a corner hugging and kissing some other guy. I told myself things like, "She really is cheating on me. Both of them are playing me for a fool." Such thinking led me to be angry.

I also told myself, "I'm going to set this straight. I'm going to get even with them. I'll break the bottoms off these two empty beer bottles and then jab each of them with the jagged edges." I proceeded to knock off the bottoms on the bar, and then started walking toward them. I got to within 8 feet of them and they were still arm in arm and didn't see me. I began though to change my thinking. I thought that if I jabbed them, the end result would be that I would get 8 to 10 years in prison, and I concluded she isn't worth that. Based on this thinking I decided to drop the beer bottles, walk out, and end my relationship with her—which is what I did.

LO 8-2 Describe Some Major Problems Encountered by This Age Group: Crime and Delinquency

Macro-System Problems: Crime and Delinquency

A life event or social problem frequently experienced during adolescence is crime or delinquency. A crime is a violation of the criminal law. Practically everyone occasionally breaks the law. For example, if a person drives a car, it is likely that person has intentionally or unintentionally broken such laws as speeding, driving the wrong way on a one-way street, or making an illegal turn. Many people have also committed such offenses as jaywalking, taking something of value from work, and perhaps some liquor violations. If a criminal is defined as someone who has violated the law, then in a broad sense we are all criminals.

Ethical Question 8.4

Is it better to use a treatment approach or a punitive approach with criminal offenders?

EP 2.1.2

The people who tend to get arrested and spend time in jail or prison are generally those who commit more serious crimes—such as armed robbery, burglary, or rape. On rare occasions, a person may be arrested, charged, and convicted of a crime he or she did not commit. This has adverse effects on the person's emotional well-being, trust in the justice system, reputation, and finances.

Adolescents (and young adults) commit the bulk of crimes and are by far the most arrested age group in our society (Mooney et al., 2013). Juveniles can be arrested for committing all of the same crimes as adults. However, they can also be arrested for violating an additional set of laws involving *status offenses*—acts that are defined as illegal if committed by juveniles but not if committed by adults. Status offenses include running away from home, being truant from school, violating curfew, having sexual relations, being ungovernable, and being beyond the control of parents.

When arrested, juveniles are generally treated differently than adults. The juvenile court tries to act in the best interests of the child, as parents should act. Juvenile courts (in theory) have a *treatment orientation*. In adult criminal proceedings, the focus is on charging the defendant with a specific crime, holding a public trial to determine if the defendant is guilty as charged, and, if found guilty, punishing the wrong-doer via a sentence. In contrast, the focus in juvenile courts is on the current physical, emotional, psychological, and educational needs of the children as opposed to punishment for their past misdeeds. Reform or treatment of the juvenile is the goal, even though the juvenile or his or her family may not agree that the court's decision is in the juvenile's best interest.

Of course, not all juvenile court judges live up to these principles. In practice, some juvenile judges focus more on punishing, rather than treating, juvenile offenders. Court appearances by children can have adverse labeling effects, such as youths viewing themselves as delinquent and then continuing to break the law.

LO 8-3 Understand Theoretical Material on the Causes and Treatments of These Problems

Causes

Why do people violate the law? There are many theories about crime causation. (For a review of these theories, see Mooney et al., 2013.) Crime is a comprehensive label covering a wide range of offenses, such as drunkenness, possession of narcotics, rape, auto theft, arson, shoplifting, attempted suicide, purse snatching, incest, gambling, prostitution, fraud, false advertising, homicide, and kidnapping. Obviously, since the nature of these crimes varies widely, the motives or causes underlying them must also vary widely.

According to the self-talk theory described by Zastrow and Navaile (1979), the reasons for any criminal act can be identified by discovering what the offender was thinking prior to and during the time when the crime was being committed. This theory derived from rational therapy, is described earlier in this chapter. (A case example of this theory is presented in Highlight 8.6.) The motive for committing any crime is precisely the reasons why the perpetrator thinks he/she should commit the crime.

How does society stop a perpetrator from continuing to commit a specific crime? In a nutshell, the perpetrator has to come to the conclusion that the adverse consequences of committing that crime outweigh the benefits. Any society has a variety of tools/strategies to assist the perpetrator in arriving at the conclusion that he/she would be better off to no longer engage in committing that crime. A few of these strategies will be mentioned. Parents, school systems, and religious organizations can seek to instill in children and adults that it is morally wrong to commit crimes. Self-help groups (such as gamblers anonymous) can provide support and guidance to those who are addicted to committing certain types of crime. Individual counseling, group counseling, and family counseling can be used to dissuade a perpetrator from continuing to engage in committing a crime. The criminal justice system has a variety of penalties to assit a perpetrator in concluding the consequences outweigh the benefits of committing a crime, these penalties include: release with a warning, fines, jail time, prison time, restitution to the victims, probation, parole following incarceration, and death penalty.

What crime deterrent/prevention strategies are most effective? This is a difficult question to answer. What is effective for one perpetrator may not be effective for another perpetrator.

It should be noted that dissauding a perpetrator from committing another crime is extremely difficult. Recidivism rates are very high for most crimes; recidivism rates are measurements of the rates at which offenders commit additional crimes—as indicated by arrest or conviction baselines. Recidivism rates of former prisoners indicate approximately 50% of males and 40% of females are reincarcerated (Cole, Smith, & De Jong, 2013).

LO 8-2 Describe Some Major Problems Encountered by This Age Group: Delinquent Gangs

Macro-System Problems: Delinquent Gangs

Juvenile gangs have existed for many decades in the United States and in other countries. In recent years in the United States, there have been increases in the number of gangs, the number of youths belonging to gangs, gang youth drug involvement, and gang violence. Violent, delinquent urban gang activity has become a major social problem. The scientific knowledge base about delinquent gangs is very limited. There is no universal agreement on a definition of "gang" or on the types of groups that should be labeled as gangs (Regulus, 1995). In addition, no agreed-upon recording system exists, and no data on

HIGHLIGHT 8.6

Self-Talk Explanation for Columbine Massacre

On April 20, 1999, Columbine High School in Colorado, near Denver, was under attack by two of the students. The school had 1,945 students enrolled. During lunch hour, in less than 15 minutes, two students, Eric Harris, age 18, and Dylan Klebold, age 17, shot and killed 12 students and one teacher. The two gunmen also wounded 21 other people. The two apparently wanted to kill as many people as they possibly could. The massacre could have been much worse because the gunmen had also placed over 30 bombs in the school. However, they were not able to detonate the bombs, as the police quickly arrived. When the police arrived, Eric Harris fired a shotgun into his mouth, and died. Dylan Klebold apparently killed himself by shooting himself in the right temple. This massacre was the most devastating school shooting in U.S. history.

Why did Harris and Klebold commit these horrendous crimes? We will never fully know. However, Eric Harris left a diary, as well as notes on his computer, that provide us with substantial clues to his thought processes and those of Dylan Klebold. (The two gunmen had linked their personal computers on a network.)

The diary indicated the two teenagers planned to kill upward of 500 students in their school using guns and home-made bombs. They also planned on attacking other schools. They then planned to run into the surrounding neighborhood and the downtown area, and kill neighbors on the street and in apartment buildings. Finally, they planned to either escape the United States and go live on an island or to hijack an airplane and crash it into the heart of New York City. They planned the attack on Columbine High for about a year.

Some of the thought processes of Eric Harris follow:

I hate the f——world.... If you recall your history, the Nazis came up with a "final solution" to the Jewish problem: kill them all. Well, in case you haven't figured it out yet, I say, kill mankind: No one should survive.... I live in Denver, and dammit, I would love to kill almost all of its residents.

Harris railed against every conceivable person of color. He stated his hate in very negative, extremely derogatory terms. John Kiekbusch, one of the officers who read the diary, stated that Harris had a nondiscriminating hate against practically everyone else, including rich people, poor people, martial arts experts, *Star Wars* fans, people who mispronounce words, people who drive slow in the fast lane, and so on.

The diary indicated the two gunmen planned to take their lives if cornered by the police, which they did. It also indicated they just wanted to achieve notoriety, which they did, by hurting and killing as many people as they could. The diary also noted the two gunmen thought they were being teased, abused, and mistreated by other students at Columbine High. Harris and Klebold admired Hitler, Nazism, and Nazism's "Final Solution." Harris and Klebold viewed themselves as being above everyone else, as being superior to others, to the extent that they thought they constituted a two-man master race.

SOURCE: Dave Cullen, URL: http://www.salon.com/news/feature/1999/09/23/journal.

---

gang offenses are collected in systematic ways by governmental agencies.

The inadequacy of the knowledge base about delinquent gangs is a major obstacle to developing effective intervention strategies. The lack of consensus among investigators is indicated by the numerous and diverse categories that have been used by different investigators to classify gangs: corner group, social club, conflict group, pathological group, athletic club, industrial association, predatory organization, drug addict group, racket organization, fighting-focused group, defensive group, unconventional group, criminal organization, turf group, heavy metal group, punk rock group, satanic organization, skinheads, ethnic or racial group, motorcycle club, and scavenger group (Goldstein, 1991).

Four Types of Gangs

An illustration of one categorization of gangs is provided by Morales, Sheafor, and Scott (2010), who classified youth gangs into four types: criminal, conflict, retreatist, and cult/occult.

The primary goal of *criminal gangs* is material gain through criminal activities. Criminal activities include theft of property from persons or premises, extortion, fencing, and obtaining and selling illegal substances (particularly drugs). Drug trafficking of rock cocaine is presently a major source of income for criminal gangs.

Conflict gangs are turf-oriented and will engage in violent conflict with individuals or rival groups that invade their neighborhood or that commit acts that they consider degrading or insulting. Respect is highly valued and defended. Hispanic gangs are heavily represented among conflict gangs. The Code of the Barrio mandates that gang members watch out for their neighborhood and be willing to die for it.

Retreatist gangs focus on getting "high" or "loaded" on alcohol, cocaine, marijuana, heroin, or other drugs. Individuals tend to join this type of gang in order to secure continued access to drugs. In contrast to criminal gangs that become involved with drugs for financial profit, retreatist gangs become involved with drugs for consumption.

The fourth type of gang is the *cult/occult gang.* Morales et al. (2010) describe this type as:

> *The word cult, as used here, pertains to a system of worshiping the devil or evil. Occult means something hidden or secret, or a belief in mysterious or supernatural powers. Not all cult/occult devil or evil worship groups are involved in criminal activity or ritualistic crime. The Ku Klux Klan, for example, may be seen as a cult group, and some KKK chapters, in spite of their hate rhetoric, are law abiding, whereas other chapters have committed criminal acts. The majority of occult groups are composed of adults, although some juvenile groups*

> *are becoming interested in satanic and black magic practices and are using them for their own gratification of sadistic, sexual, and antisocial impulses. They are not turf-oriented like conflict gangs but are typically found in middle-class locations. For example, a neo-Nazi subtype of white cult/occult gang groups are the Skinheads, whose racist, anti-Semitic, homophobic "gay bashing," and other violent behavior has appeared in the South, Midwest, and West Coast. Their group structure and behavior comply with the gang pattern, including use of colors, tattoos, common dress and hairstyle, name, drug use, and criminal behavior (usually "hate" crimes). (p. 196)*

Contradictions in Conceptualizing Gangs

Contradictions abound in conceptualizing delinquent gangs. Gangs are believed to be composed largely of ethnically homogeneous minority youths (African American, Hispanic, or Asian); yet some gangs composed of white youths exist. Most gang members are believed to be between the ages of 12 and 18, yet evidence indicates some gangs include and may be controlled by adults (Mooney et al., 2013). Gangs are believed to be composed of males; yet some gangs have female members, and a few gangs consist exclusively of females (Regulus, 1995). Gangs are

A retreatist gang.

A. Ramey/PhotoEdit

believed to be primarily involved in drug trafficking; yet some delinquent gangs have other illegal foci, such as burglary, robbery, larceny, or illegal drug consumption. Gang activity is thought to be primarily located in large, inner-city, urban areas; yet gang activity is flourishing in many smaller cities and in some suburbs (Regulus, 1995).

At the present time, there are inadequate statistical data on the number of gangs, the number and characteristics of members, and their criminal activities. No uniform definition of a gang-related offense exists across police jurisdictions (even within the same state or city).

LO 8-3 Understand Theoretical Material on the Causes and Treatments of These Problems

Sociological Theories: Applications of Theories to Gangs

Numerous attempts have been made to explain why youths join gangs and why gangs engage in delinquent or criminal activities. These explanations include biological, psychological, and sociological theories (see Goldstein, 1991, for a review). No consensus exists as to which theories are most useful, and insufficient research has been conducted to ascertain their validity. In order to illustrate the existing theories, we will summarize four of them: differential association theory, anomie theory, deviant subcultures theory, and control theory.

Edwin Sutherland (Sutherland & Cressey, 1970) advanced his famous *theory of differential association* in 1939. This theory asserts that criminal behavior is the result of a learning process that stems primarily from small, intimate groups—family, neighborhood peer groups, and friends. In essence, the theory states, "A person becomes delinquent because of the excess of definitions favorable to violation of law over definitions unfavorable to violation of law" (p. 76). People internalize the values of the surrounding culture. When the environment includes frequent contact with criminal elements and infrequent contact with noncriminal elements, a person is apt to engage in delinquent or criminal activity. Past and present learning experiences in intimate personal groups define whether a person should violate laws; for those deciding to commit

crimes, the learning experiences also include which crimes to commit, the techniques of committing these crimes, and the attitudes and rationalizations for committing them. Thus, a youth whose most admired person is a member of a gang involved in committing burglaries or in drug trafficking will seek to emulate this model, will receive instruction from gang members in committing these crimes, and will also receive approval from the gang for successfully committing these crimes.

Robert Merton (1968) applied *anomie theory* to delinquency and crime. This approach views delinquent behavior as resulting when an individual or a gang is prevented from achieving high-status goals in a society. Merton begins by noting that every society has both approved goals (for example, wealth and material possessions) and approved means for attaining these goals (going to college, getting a job). When certain members of society want these goals but have insufficient access to the approved means for attaining them, a state of anomie results. (*Anomie* is a condition in which the acceptance of the approved standards of conduct is weakened.) Unable to achieve the goals through society's legitimately defined channels, the individuals' and gangs' respect for these channels is weakened, and they seek to achieve the desired goals through illegal means. Merton asserts that higher crime rates are apt to occur among those groups discriminated against (i.e., those groups facing additional barriers to achieving the high-status goals). These groups include the poor and racial minorities. Societies with high crime rates (such as the United States) differ from those with low crime rates because, according to Merton, they tell all their citizens that they can achieve, but in fact they block achievement for some of them.

Deviant subcultures theory offers another explanation for delinquent gang behavior. This theory asserts that some groups have developed their own attitudes, values, and perspectives that support criminal activity. Walter Miller (1958), for example, argues that American lower-class culture is more conducive to crime than middle-class culture. He asserts that lower-class culture is organized around six values—trouble, toughness, excitement, fate, smartness (ability to con others), and autonomy—and allegiance to these values produces delinquency. Miller concludes that the entire lower-class subculture is deviant in the sense that any male growing up in it will accept these values and almost certainly violate the law.

Albert Cohen (1955) advanced another subculture theory. He contends that gangs develop a delinquent subculture that represents solutions to the problems of young male gang members. A gang gives them a chance to belong, to amount to something, to develop their masculinity, and to fight middle-class society. In particular, the delinquent subculture, according to Cohen, can effectively solve the status problems of working-class boys, especially those who are rejected by middle-class society. Cohen contends that the main problems of working-class boys revolve around status.

Control theories (Hirschi, 1969) ask the question, Why do people not commit crimes? Theories in this category assume that all people would naturally commit crimes and therefore must be constrained and controlled by society from breaking the law. Control theorists have identified three factors for preventing crime. One is the internal controls through the socialization process that society builds up in an individual; it is believed that developing a strong conscience and a sense of personal morality will prevent most people from breaking the law. A second factor is thought to be a strong attachment to small social groups, such as the family, which prevents individuals from breaking the law, because they fear rejection and disapproval from the people who are important to them. A third factor is that people do not break the law because they fear arrest and incarceration. Control theories assume that the basic nature of humans is asocial or evil. Such an assumption has never been proved.

Hirschi (1969) suggests that the prospects of delinquent behavior decline if the adolescent is controlled by social bonds such as affective ties to parents, involvement in school activities, success in school, high educational and occupational aspirations, and belief in the moral rightness of conventional norms. The weaker the social bonding, the greater the likelihood that an adolescent will become involved in delinquent gang activities. Social bonding is weakened by such factors as parental criminality, parental difficulties such as excessive drinking and extensive unemployment, inadequate parental supervision and monitoring, parental rewarding of deviant behavior, parental modeling of aggressive behavior, and inadequate parental warmth.

Social Work Roles and Intervention Programs

Various programs have attempted to reduce delinquent gang activities. These have included detached worker programs, in which workers join gangs and seek to transform antisocial into prosocial attitudes and behaviors; formal supervision of those gang members adjudicated delinquent through juvenile probation departments; placement of delinquent gang members in group homes, residential treatment facilities, or reform schools; drug treatment of gang members who have a chemical addiction; programs to support and strengthen families, particularly single-parent families in urban areas; and programs to prevent dropping out of school and to provide academic support (Goldstein & Huff, 1993).

The outcomes of such interventions have not been sufficiently researched. The factors that lead adolescents to join delinquent gangs and then to engage in delinquent activities are multifaceted and highly complex. It is clear that delinquent gang activities are on the increase in our society. The reasons for this increase are largely unknown. Also unknown are the most effective programs to reduce delinquent gang activities.

Of all the helping professions, it would appear that social work is best suited from the perspective of knowledge, values, and skills to develop intervention strategies to use with gangs. Gangs as a focus for practice find the social worker intervening with individuals, groups, families, organizations, and the community (i.e., micro-, mezzo-, and macro-level intervention).

Social workers intervene on a one-to-one level with a delinquent gang member in a variety of settings—as a juvenile probation officer, as a counselor at a group home or residential treatment facility, as a school social worker in a school setting, and as an alcohol and drug counselor in a chemical dependency treatment program. On a one-to-one level, social workers may assume the following roles: *counselor*, *educator*, *case manager*, and *broker*.

Social workers intervene on a mezzo level with a delinquent gang with a group approach; the worker is viewed as a "detached worker" or "gang group worker." Working with gangs requires that the social worker spend a considerable amount of time in the gang's immediate environment rather than in the agency—hence the term "detached worker" or "street worker." Spergel (1995) found that most gangs are receptive to a worker engaging the gang as a group within the purposes of social work practice, and that a social worker can help urban gangs to change from being a destructive force to being a constructive contributor to the community while maintaining the gang's right to self-determination. In working with gangs, a worker can function in the roles of *group facilitator*, *educator*, *enabler*, and *advocate* in helping the gang obtain needed resources. The worker can also function as a *negotiator* or a *mediator* when there is intragang conflict or when there is a conflict between rival gangs. At a mezzo level, a worker may also work with the families of gang members to assist them in being constructive forces in curbing their children's delinquent behavior.

Spergel (1995) presents documentation that gangs develop primarily in local communities that are socially disorganized and/or impoverished. Gang members typically come from communities in which parents lack effective parenting skills, school systems give little attention to students who are falling behind in their studies, youths are exposed to adult crime groups, and youths feel there is practically no opportunity to succeed through the legitimate avenues of education and a good job. Spergel (1995) asserts that youths join gangs for many reasons—security, power, money, status, excitement, and new experiences—particularly under conditions of social deprivation or community instability. In essence, he presents a community disorganization approach to understanding the attraction of joining a gang.

In a very real sense, a delinquent gang is created because the needs of youths are not being met by the family, neighborhood, or traditional community institutions (such as the schools, police, and recreational and religious institutions). A social worker can function as an *analyst* and *evaluator* of community conditions that are conducive to the formation of gangs. A worker can also function as an *initiator* and an *advocate* for social policy changes. Some useful changes suggested by Spergel (1995) are reduced access to handguns; improved educational resources; access to recreation, job training, jobs, family counseling, and drug rehabilitation; and mobilization of community groups and organizations to restrain gang violence (such as neighborhood watch groups). Social policy changes are also needed at state and national levels to funnel more resources to urban centers. Funds are needed to improve the quality of life for city residents, including youths, so that the needs of youths are met in ways other than through gang involvement. Social workers have an obligation to advocate for such local, state, and national changes in social policy.

Regulus (1995) asserts that community mobilization appears to be the most effective strategy to reduce gang problems.

> *Community mobilization is a strategy that attempts to integrate and coordinate the collective resources of citizens and organizations in gang control. In the broadest sense, community mobilization attempts to harness the combined efforts of governmental agencies, schools, police and criminal justice agencies, youth agencies, indigenous grass-roots organizations, churches, and so on within a community. (p. 1052)*

LO 8-4 Understand Material on Social Work with Groups, Including Theories About Group Development and Theories About Group Leadership

Empowerment Through Social Work with Groups

Today it is not uncommon to find social workers as both group leaders and participants in a myriad of settings, helping solve or ameliorate human or social problems and planning for and creating change. We have established that empowerment is the "process of increasing personal, interpersonal, or political power so that individuals can take action to improve their life situations" (Gutierrez, 1990, p. 149). Groups can provide forceful and effective means to accomplish these ends. Johnson and Johnson (1997) define a *group* as: "two or more individuals in face-to-face interaction, each aware of his or her membership in the group, each aware of the others who belong to the group, and each aware of their positive interdependence as they strive to achieve mutual goals" (p. 12).

From this description, we can see that the members of a group relate to one another within a context of sensing that they form a distinct entity, that they share a common goal or purpose, and that they have confidence that together they can accomplish as much as or more than would be possible working separately. This commonality is characteristic of a wide variety of groups dealing with a multitude of societal problems. The beginning social worker is likely to be surprised at the diversity of groups in existence and excited by the challenge of practicing social work in groups. This section gives an introduction to social work with groups—including types of groups, theories about group development, and theories about group leadership.

Types of Groups

The following types of groups are frequently encountered in social work practice: recreation, recreation-skill, educational, task, problem-solving and decision-making, focus, self-help, socialization, therapy, and encounter groups. This list is not an exhaustive one.

Recreation Groups

The objective of recreation groups is to provide activities for enjoyment and exercise. Often such activities are spontaneous and the groups are practically leaderless. The group service agency (such as the YMCA or neighborhood center) may offer little more than physical space and the use of some equipment. Spontaneous playground activities, informal athletic games, and an open game room are examples. Some group agencies providing such physical space claim that recreation and interaction with others help build character and prevent delinquency among youth by providing an alternative to the street.

Recreation-Skill Groups

The objective of a recreation-skill group is to improve a set of skills while providing enjoyment. In contrast to recreational groups, this group has an adviser, coach, or instructor; also there is more of a task orientation. Examples of activities include golf, basketball, needlework, arts and crafts, and swimming. Competitive team sports and leagues may emerge. Frequently such groups are led by professionals with recreational training rather than social work training. Social service agencies providing such services include the YMCA, YWCA, Boy Scouts, Girl Scouts, neighborhood centers, and school recreation departments.

Educational Groups

The focus of educational groups is to help members acquire knowledge and learn more complex skills. The leader generally is a professional person with considerable training and expertise in the subject area. Examples of topics include child-rearing practices, assertiveness training, techniques for becoming a more effective parent, preparing to be an adoptive parent, and training volunteers to perform a specialized task for a social service agency. Educational group leaders often function in a more didactic manner and frequently are social workers. These groups may resemble a class, with considerable group interaction and discussion being encouraged.

Task Groups

Task groups are formed to achieve a specific set of tasks or objectives. The following are examples of task groups that social workers are apt to interact with or become involved in. A *board of directors* is an administrative group charged with responsibility for setting the policy governing agency programs. A *task force* is a group established for a special purpose and is usually disbanded after the task is completed. A *committee* of an agency or organization is a group that is formed to deal with specific tasks or matters. An *ad hoc committee*, like a task force, is set up for one purpose and usually ceases functioning after completion of its task.

Problem-Solving and Decision-Making Groups

Both providers and consumers of social services may become involved in groups concerned with problem solving and decision making. There is considerable overlap between task groups and these groups; in fact, problem-solving and decision-making groups can be considered a subcategory of task groups.

Providers of services use group meetings for objectives such as developing a treatment plan for a client or a group of clients, deciding how to best allocate scarce resources, deciding how to improve the delivery of services to clients, arriving at policy decisions for the agency, and deciding how to improve coordination efforts with other agencies.

Potential consumers of services may form a group to study an unmet need in the community and to advocate for the development of new programs to meet the need. Data on the need may be gathered, and the group may be used as a vehicle either to develop a program or to influence existing agencies to provide services. Social workers may function as stimulators and organizers of such group efforts as well as participants.

In problem-solving and decision-making groups, each participant normally has some interest or stake in the process and may gain or lose, depending on the outcome. Usually, there is a formal leader, although other leaders sometimes emerge during the process.

Focus Groups

Closely related to task groups and problem-solving and decision-making groups are focus groups. Focus groups are formed for a variety of purposes: to identify needs or issues, to generate proposals to resolve an identified issue, to test reactions to alternative approaches to an issue, and so forth. A *focus group* is a specially assembled collection of people who respond through a semistructured or structured discussion to the concerns and interests of the person, group, or organization that invited the participants. Members of the group are invited and encouraged to bring up their own ideas and views.

A *representative group* is a version of the focus group. Its strength is that its members have been selected specifically to represent different perspectives and points of view in a community. At its best, a representative group is a focus group that reflects the diversity in the community and seeks to bring these diverse views to the table. At its worst, it is a front group manipulated by schemers to make the community think that it has been involved.

Self-Help Groups

Self-help groups are becoming increasingly popular in our society and are often successful in helping individuals with certain social or personal problems. Katz and Bender (1976) provide a comprehensive definition of *self-help groups*:

> *Self-help groups are voluntary, small group structures for mutual aid and the accomplishment of a special purpose. They are usually formed by peers who have come together for mutual assistance in satisfying a common need, overcoming a common handicap or life-disrupting problem, and bringing about desired social and/or personal change. The initiators and members of such groups perceive that their needs are not, or cannot be, met by or through existing social institutions. Self-help groups emphasize face-to-face social interactions*

> *and the assumption of personal responsibility by members. They often provide material assistance as well as emotional support; they are frequently cause-oriented, and promulgate an ideology or values through which members may attain an enhanced sense of personal identity. (p. 9)*

Powell's (1987) classification of self-help groups conveys the variety and focuses of these groups:

1. *Habit disturbance organizations.* These organizations focus on a problem that is specific and concrete. Examples include Alcoholics Anonymous, Smoke Stoppers, Overeaters Anonymous, Gamblers Anonymous, Take Off Pounds Sensibly (TOPS), Women for Sobriety, Narcotics Anonymous, and Weight Watchers.

2. *General-purpose organizations.* These organizations address a wide range of problems and predicaments. Examples are Parents Anonymous (for parents of abused children); Emotions Anonymous (for persons with emotional problems); the Compassionate Friends (for persons who have experienced a loss through death); and GROW, an organization that works to prevent the hospitalization of mental patients through a comprehensive program of mutual aid.

3. *Lifestyle organizations.* These organizations seek to provide support for, and advocate for, the lifestyles of people whose members are viewed by society as being different (and the dominant groups in society are generally indifferent or hostile to that difference). Examples include Widow-to-Widow Programs, Parents Without Partners, ALMA (Adoptees' Liberty Movement Association), PFLAG (Parents and Friends of Lesbians and Gays), the National Gay and Lesbian Task Force, and the Gray Panthers (an intergenerational group that advocates for the elderly).

4. *Physical handicap organizations.* These organizations focus on major chronic diseases and conditions. Some are for people with conditions that are relatively stable, some for conditions that are likely to get worse, and some for terminal illnesses. Examples of this category include Make Today Count (for the terminally ill and their families), Emphysema Anonymous, Lost Chord clubs (for those who have had laryngectomies), stroke clubs, Mended Hearts, the Spina

Bifida Association, and Self-Help for Hard of Hearing People.

5. *Significant-other organizations.* The members of these organizations are parents, spouses, and close relatives of troubled and troubling persons. Very often, members of significant-other groups are last-resort caregivers contending with dysfunctional behavior. Through sharing their feelings, they obtain a measure of relief. In the course of sharing, they may also learn about new resources or new approaches. Examples of such organizations include Al-Anon, Gam-Anon, Toughlove, and the National Alliance for the Mentally Ill.

The American Self-Help Group Clearinghouse is a web-based database of more than 1,100 national and international self-help support groups for health, mental health, addictions, abuse, disabilities, parenting, caregiver concerns, and other stressful life situations. It is compiled and edited by Barbara J. White and Edward J. Madara, with the web version updated by Anita M. Broderick and Paul Riddleberger, Ph.D. Any self-help group contained in the database can be accessed by typing a keyword on the website. The website can be easily accessed by going to the Internet and typing in "American Self-Help Group Clearinghouse."

Many self-help groups stress (1) a confession by members to the group that they have a problem, (2) a testimony by members to the group recounting their past experiences with the problem and their plans for handling the problem in the future, and (3) support. That is, when a member feels an intense urge of a recurrence (such as to drink or to abuse a child), he or she calls a member of the group, and that member comes over to stay with the person until the urge subsides.

Such self-help groups are successful for several reasons. The members have an internal understanding of the problem, which helps them help others. Having experienced the consequences of the problem, they are highly motivated to find ways to help themselves and their fellow sufferers. The participants also benefit from the *helper therapy principle*: the helper gains psychological rewards by helping others (Riessman, 1965). Helping others makes a person feel good and worthwhile; it also enables the helpers to put their own problems into perspective as they see that others' problems may be as serious as or even more serious than their own.

When people help each other in self-help groups, they tend to feel empowered and in control of important aspects of their lives. When help is received from the outside (from an expert or a professional), there is a danger of dependency, which is the opposite of empowerment. Empowerment increases motivation, energy, personal growth, and an ability to help that goes beyond helping oneself or receiving help.

Some self-help groups advocate for the rights and lifestyles of people whose members are viewed by society as being different. One such group is the National Gay and Lesbian Task Force. Some self-help groups (such as The Arc of the United States) raise funds and operate community programs. Many people with a personal problem use self-help groups in the same way others use social agencies. An additional advantage is that self-help groups generally are able to operate with a minimal budget. Hundreds of these groups are now in existence. Social workers often act as brokers in linking clients to appropriate self-help groups.

Socialization Groups

The objective of socialization groups generally is to develop or change attitudes and behaviors of group members to become more socially acceptable. Social-skill development, increasing self-confidence, and planning for the future are other goals. Illustrations include working with predelinquent youth in group activities to prevent delinquency, with a youth group of diverse racial backgrounds to reduce racial tensions, with pregnant young females at a maternity home to make plans for the future, with elderly residents at a nursing home to remotivate them and get them involved in various activities, and with boys at a correctional school to help them make plans for returning to their home community. Leadership of such groups requires considerable skill and knowledge in using the group to foster individual growth and change. These leadership roles are frequently filled by social workers. (The RAP framework, which can be used for leading multiracial groups, is presented in Spotlight 8.1.)

Therapy Groups

Therapy groups are generally composed of members with rather severe emotional or personal problems. Similar to one-to-one counseling, the goal of therapy groups is to have members explore their problems in depth and then to develop one or more strategies for resolving them.

SPOTLIGHT ON DIVERSITY 8.1

The RAP Framework for Leading Multiracial Groups

Whenever people of different races interact in a group, the leader should assume that race is an issue, but not necessarily a problem. Race is an issue in a multiracial group because it is a very apparent difference among participants and one that is laden with considerable social meaning. The leader of a multiracial group should not attempt to be color-blind, because being color-blind leads to ignoring important dynamics related to race.

In leading a multiracial group, Davis, Galinsky, and Schopler (1995) urge that the leader use the RAP framework. RAP stands for *recognize*, *anticipate*, and *problem-solve*. Each element will be briefly described in the sections that follow.

Recognize

Recognizing crucial ethnic, cultural, and racial differences in any group requires the leader to be both self-aware and aware of the racial dynamics of the group. A leader of a multiracial group needs to:

- Be aware of personal values and stereotypes.
- Recognize racial, ethnic, and cultural differences among the members.
- Respect the norms, customs, and cultures of the populations represented in the group.
- Become familiar with resources (community leaders, professionals, agencies) in the community that are responsive to the needs of the racial components of the group. These resources can be used as consultants by the leader when racial issues arise and may also be used as referral resources for special needs of particular members.
- Be aware of various forms of institutional discrimination in the community and of their impact on various population groups.
- Be aware of racial tensions in the community that may concern members of the group. Such tensions may directly impact interactions among members of different races in the group.

Anticipate

Anticipating how individual members will be affected by racial issues prepares the leader to respond preventively and interventively when racial issues arise. The leader should anticipate potential sources of racial tension in the group when the members formulate their group goals, and when the leader structures the group's work. Because relationships between members and race-laden outside issues (i.e., outside the group) change over time, anticipating racial tensions is an ongoing leadership responsibility. To anticipate tensions and help members deal effectively with them, the leader should:

- Seek to include more than one member of any given race. If the group has a solo member, the leader should acknowledge the difficulty of this situation for that member and should make it clear that that member is not expected to serve as the representative of his or her race.
- Develop a leadership style that is culturally appropriate to the group's specific racial configuration. This requires that the leader become knowledgeable about the beliefs, values, and cultures of the various racial components of the group.
- Treat all members with respect and equality in both verbal and nonverbal communications.
- Help the group formulate goals responsive to the concerns and needs expressed by all the members.
- Seek to empower members to obtain their rights, particularly if they are being victimized by institutional discrimination or other forms of racism in the community.
- Acknowledge in initial contacts with members and in initial sessions that racial and ethnic differences do exist in the group and that any issues that arise in the group regarding race must be openly discussed—even if discussing such issues and differences is uncomfortable.
- Encourage the development of norms of mutual respect and appreciation of diversity.
- Announce in initial sessions that at times people do and say things that are racially inappropriate. When this occurs, these comments and actions will be thoroughly discussed in order to resolve the issues and to work toward an appreciation of differences.

Problem-Solve

When incidents related to racial issues do arise, the leader must intervene to resolve the issues. The leader should:

- Use a problem-solving approach. Briefly, this approach involves identifying the issues and needs of each party, generating alternatives to meet those needs, evaluating the merits of each of these alternatives, and selecting and implementing the most promising alternative.
- Use conflict-resolution approaches (described in Chapter 12). These approaches include role reversal, empathy, inquiry, I-messages, disarming, stroking, and mediation.
- Use interventions and goals that are culturally acceptable and appropriate for all members of the group.
- Provide some rules when involving members in problem solving and conflict resolution (for example, no name calling).
- Assist members in being assertive in confronting and dealing with problems related to race.
- Be prepared to advocate outside the group on a member's behalf when that member is being victimized by discrimination and oppression in the community.

Leadership of therapy groups requires considerable skill, perceptiveness, knowledge of human behavior and group dynamics, group counseling capacities, and ability to use the group to bring about behavioral changes. Among other skills, the group leader needs to be highly perceptive about how each member is being affected by what is being communicated. Considerable competence is needed to develop and maintain a constructive atmosphere within the group. The group therapist generally uses one or more therapy approaches as a guide for changing attitudes and behaviors; these approaches include psychoanalysis, reality therapy, learning theory, rational therapy, transactional analysis, client-centered therapy, and psychodrama.

Group therapy is being used increasingly in social work. It has several advantages over one-to-one therapy. The *helper therapy* principle (in which members interchange roles and sometimes become the helper for someone else's problems) is generally operative. In such roles, members receive psychological rewards for helping others. Groups also help members put their problems into perspective as they realize others have equally serious problems. Groups also help members who are having interaction problems test out new interaction approaches. Research has shown that it is generally easier to change the attitudes of an individual in a group than in one-to-one counseling, and that group pressure can have a substantial effect on changing attitudes and beliefs (Johnson & Johnson, 1997). Furthermore, group therapy permits the social worker to help more than one person at a time, with potential savings in the use of professional effort. (See Highlight 8.7, "Case Example: Therapy Group for Spouses of Adults with Cancer.")

Encounter Groups

Encounter groups and sensitivity-training groups (these terms are used more or less synonymously) refer to a group experience in which people relate to each other in a close interpersonal manner and self-disclosure is required. The goal is to improve interpersonal awareness.

An encounter group may meet for a few hours or for as long as a few days. Once increased interpersonal awareness is achieved, it is anticipated that attitudes and behaviors will change.

In the encounter group, the leader usually does not act like a leader. He or she frequently starts with a brief statement encouraging the group members to participate, to be open and honest, and to expect things to be different. Group members may begin by taking off their shoes, sitting in a circle on the floor, and holding hands with their eyes closed. The leader then encourages them to feel intensely the sensations they are experiencing, the size and texture of the hands they are holding, and so forth.

Other structured exercises or experiences may be planned to help the group focus on the here and now. For example, pairs may go for "trust walks" in which each person alternatively is led around with his eyes closed.

The goal of sensitivity groups provides an interesting contrast to that of most therapy groups. In therapy, the goal is to have all members explore personal or emotional problems and then develop a strategy to resolve the problems. In comparison, sensitivity groups seek to foster increased personal and interpersonal awareness and then develop more effective interaction patterns. Sensitivity groups generally do not attempt to identify and change specific emotional or personal problems (such as drinking problems, feelings of depression, or sexual dysfunction). The philosophy behind sensitivity groups is that with increased personal and interpersonal awareness, people will be better able to cope with specific personal problems that arise.

In our society, sensitivity groups are used for a variety of purposes: to train professional counselors to be more perceptive and effective in interpersonal interactions with clients and with other professionals; to train people in management positions to be more effective in their business interactions; to help clients with overt relationship problems become more aware of how they affect others and to help them develop more effective interaction patterns; and to train interested citizens in becoming more aware and effective in their interactions.

Models of Group Development over Time

Groups change over time. Numerous models or frameworks have been developed to describe the changes that occur in groups over time. Here we will describe the following models of group development: (1) the Garland, Jones, and Kolodny model; (2) the Tuckman model; (3) the Schiller model; and (4) the Bales model.

HIGHLIGHT 8.7

Case Example: Therapy Group for Spouses of Adults with Cancer

Eight years ago, Linda Sonsthagen's husband was diagnosed with cancer. Linda was a social worker, and her husband was a successful life insurance agent. They had two sons in grade school. Mr. Sonsthagen died 4½ years ago, after having gone through a variety of treatment programs and through considerable pain. He lost weight and his hair fell out. These years were extremely difficult for the Sonsthagens. Linda had to take a larger role in raising the children and was the primary caregiver to both her husband and the children. During these years, the Sonsthagens found that relatives and friends shied away from them—it took several months before they became aware that the reason was that friends and relatives saw cancer as something they didn't understand and wanted to avoid. Even more difficult was dealing emotionally with not knowing the course of the disorder, going through cycles of hope and then disappointment as different treatment approaches were tried. As her husband became more incapacitated, Linda found she had to assume more of his tasks—for example, home repairs, maintaining their two cars, disciplining the children, and other daily household tasks.

After her husband's death, Linda and the two children went through several months of mourning and grief. Linda also discovered it was somewhat awkward to go to social functions alone. Fortunately, she had two single female friends with whom she increasingly socialized. These were very difficult years for Linda. She needed more than two years after her husband's death to rebuild her life in such a way that she was again comfortable.

During these years, she received some financial help from the local chapter of the American Cancer Society. Through this society, she also met another woman whose husband was dying of cancer. They gave each other emotional support and shared useful ideas of handling problems.

Eighteen months ago, Linda proposed to the local chapter of the American Cancer Society that she was willing to volunteer her time to start a group for spouses of people with cancer, and for spouses adjusting to a recent cancer death. The Cancer Society gave its approval and endorsement.

Linda started with nine members. The objectives were to give emotional support, to help members handle the new responsibilities they had to take on, and to help them deal with their emotional reactions. Linda used primarily a combination of choice theory and rational therapy (choice theory is described in Chapter 11 and rational therapy is summarized earlier in this chapter). Reality therapy helped the group members better understand and make decisions and plans for the problems they faced. For example, for the members whose spouses had cancer, one focus was how to inform and handle their friends' and relatives' reactions to illness. Survivors focused on rebuilding their lives. Rational therapy countered unwanted emotions. Common emotions included depression, guilt, anxiety, the feeling of being overwhelmed, and anger (particularly resulting from "Why does this have to happen to me?"). Members were instructed on how to do a Rational Self-Analysis (described earlier in this chapter) on their unwanted emotions, and members often shared and discussed their RSAs at group meetings.

Group members stated on several occasions that the group was very helpful. They mentioned that knowing others faced similar plights was beneficial in and of itself. Seeing how others handled difficult decisions inspired them and gave them useful ideas on how to handle crises they faced. When a member suffered a serious crisis (e.g., a spouse hospitalized for a serious operation), other members were available for telephone contact and to lend physical assistance.

After eight months, the local chapter of the American Cancer Society was so encouraged by the results that it offered Linda a full-time position to run additional groups and to be available for individual counseling for people with cancer and their relatives. Linda gave up her part-time job as a counselor at the YWCA and took this position. Her first effort was to divide her group, which was growing, into two groups. The definition of eligible membership was also expanded: One group was for adults who have a family member with cancer, and the other for survivors. At this time, Linda is leading one group of the first type and two groups of the second type.

Garland, Jones, and Kolodny Model

Garland, Jones, and Kolodny (1965) developed a model that identifies five stages of development in social work groups. This model seeks to describe the kinds of problems that commonly arise as groups begin to form and continue to develop. Understanding these problems, it is theorized, enables the designated leader to anticipate and respond more effectively to the reactions of group members. The conceptualization of Garland and his colleagues (1965) appears particularly applicable to socialization groups, therapy groups, and encounter groups. To a lesser extent, the model is also applicable to self-help groups, problem-solving and decision-making groups, educational groups, recreation-skill groups, and task groups.

Closeness (i.e., the question of how near group members will allow themselves to become to one another emotionally) is the central focus of the model. The question of closeness is reflected in *struggles* that occur at five levels of growth of the group: preaffiliation, power and control, intimacy, differentiation, and separation.

In the first stage, *preaffiliation*, members are ambivalent about joining the group. Interaction is guarded. Members test out, often through approach and avoidance behavior, whether they really want to belong to the group. New situations are often frightening, and the members try to protect themselves from being hurt or taken advantage of in such new situations. They attempt to maintain a certain amount of distance and get what they can from the group without risking much of themselves. Individuals are aware that group involvement will make demands that may be frustrating or even painful. At the same time, members are attracted to the group because they generally have had satisfying experiences in other groups, and this group offers the hope of similar rewards. In the first stage, the leader should seek to increase the attractions toward the group "by allowing and supporting distance, gently inviting trust, facilitating exploration of the physical and psychological milieu, and by providing activities if necessary and initiating group structure" (Garland & Frey, 1973, p. 3). The first stage gradually ends when members come to feel fairly safe and comfortable with the group and view the rewards as being worth a tentative emotional commitment.

The second stage, *power and control*, emerges as the characteristics of the group begin to develop. Patterns of communication within the group emerge, alliances and subgroups begin to appear, members begin to take on certain roles and responsibilities, norms and methods for handling group tasks develop, and membership questions arise. Such processes are necessary for the group to conduct its business. However, these processes lead to a struggle as the members establish their places within the group. Each member seeks power, partly for self-protection and partly to attempt to gain greater control over the rewards to be received from the group. In this struggle, the group leader is a major source of gratification. The leader is perceived as having the greatest power to influence the direction of the group and to give or withhold emotional and material rewards. At this point, members realize that the group is becoming important to them.

The second stage is a transitional stage, with certain basic issues needing to be resolved: Does the group or the leader have primary control over the group's affairs? What are the limits of the power of the leader and of the group? To what extent will the leader use his or her power?

This uncertainty results in anxiety among group members and considerable testing by them to gauge the limits and establish norms for the power of both the group and the group leader. Rebellion is not uncommon; the dropout rate in groups is often highest at this stage. During this struggle, the leader should (1) seek to help the members understand the nature of the power struggle, (2) give emotional support to weather the discomfort of uncertainty, and (3) help the group establish norms to resolve the uncertainty. It is important that group members develop trust in the leader so he or she will maintain a safe balance of shared power and control. When this trust is achieved, group members make a major commitment to become involved in the group.

In the third stage, *intimacy*, the likes and dislikes of intimate relationships are expressed. The group becomes more like a family, with sibling rivalry arising between members and the leader sometimes even being referred to as a parent. Feelings about the group at this stage are more openly expressed and discussed. The group is now viewed as a place where growth and change take place. Individuals feel free to examine and make efforts to change personal attitudes, concerns, and problems. Group tasks are also worked on, and there is a feeling of "oneness" or cohesiveness within the group. Struggle or turmoil during this stage leads the members to explore and make changes in their personal lives and to examine "what this group is all about."

During the fourth stage, *differentiation*, there is increased freedom for members to experiment with new and alternative behavior patterns. There is a recognition of individual rights and needs and a high level of communication among members. At this stage, the group is able to organize itself more efficiently. Leadership is more evenly shared, and roles are more functional. Power problems are now minimal, and decisions are made and carried out on a less emotional and more objective basis. Garland and Frey (1973) note:

> *This kind of individualized therapeutic cohesion has been achieved because the group experience has all along valued and nurtured individual integrity....*

The worker assists in this stage by helping the group to run itself and by encouraging it to act as a unit with other groups or in the wider community. During this time the worker exploits opportunities for evaluation by the group of its activities, feelings, and behavior. (p. 5)

The differentiation stage is analogous to a healthy functioning family in which the children have reached adulthood and are now becoming successful in pursuing their own lives; relationships are more between equals, members are mutually supportive, and members are able to relate to each other in ways that are more rational and objective.

The final stage is *separation*. The purposes of the group have been achieved, and members have learned new behavioral patterns to enable them to move on to other social experiences. Termination is not always easily accomplished. Members may be reluctant to move on and may even display regressive behavior in an effort to prolong the safety of the group. Members may also express anger over ending the group or even psychologically deny the end is near. Garland and Frey (1973) suggested the leader's role should be the following:

To facilitate separation the worker must be willing to let go. Concentration upon group and individual mobility, evaluation of the experience, help with the expression of the ambivalence about termination, and recognition of the progress which has been made are his major tasks. Acceptance of termination is facilitated by active guidance of members as individuals to other ongoing sources of support and assistance. (p. 6)

Tuckman Model

Tuckman (1965) reviewed more than 50 studies of mostly therapy and sensitivity groups, of a limited duration, and concluded that these groups go through five predictable developmental stages: forming, storming, norming, performing, and adjourning.

1. *Forming.* In this stage, members become oriented toward each other, work on being accepted, and learn more about the group. During this stage, there is a period of uncertainty in which members try to determine their place in the group and the rules and procedures of the group.
2. *Storming.* In this stage, conflicts begin to arise as members resist the influence of the group and rebel against accomplishing the task. During this stage, members often confront their various differences, and the management of conflict becomes the focus of attention.
3. *Norming.* In this stage, the group establishes cohesiveness and commitment, and in the process discovers new ways to work together. Norms are also set for appropriate behavior.
4. *Performing.* In this stage, the group works as a unit to achieve its goals. The group develops proficiency in achieving its goals and becomes more flexible in its patterns of working together.
5. *Adjourning.* In this stage, the group disbands. The feelings that members experience are similar to those in the separation stage of the Garland, Jones, and Kolodny model.

Schiller Model

Schiller (1995) has advanced a relational model of group development that is most applicable to women's groups. The model has the following five stages:

1. *Preaffiliation.* In women's groups, the same dynamics occur as in the preaffiliation stage of the Garland, Jones, and Kolodny model.
2. *Establishing a relational base.* In contrast to most models of group development that focus on power and control, in this second stage, women in groups focus on establishing common ground and a sense of connection with each other and with the facilitator. Members find similarities in their experiences and seek approval from the facilitator and from other group members.
3. *Mutuality and interpersonal empathy.* During this stage, members move beyond making connections and recognize their similarities. They have increased trust in one another and feel free to disclose their thoughts and feelings. Members also respect differences and display empathy for one another.
4. *Challenge and change.* Members challenge themselves and each other during this stage, which facilitates growth and change among members. During this stage, members have a sense of community with one another, which facilitates challenging one another, taking risks, and expressing disagreements without fearing the loss of valued connections made with one another.

5. *Separation.* In women's groups, the members experience the same dynamics in this final stage as suggested in the separation stage of the Garland, Jones, and Kolodny model.

Bales Model

Both the Garland, Jones, and Kolodny model and the Tuckman model are sequential-stage models; both models specify sequential stages of group development. In contrast, Bales (1965) developed a *recurring-phase* model. Bales asserted that groups continue to seek an equilibrium between task-oriented work and emotional expressions to build better relationships among group members. (Task roles and social/emotional roles performed by members in a group are discussed in the next section.) Bales asserts that a group tends to oscillate between these two concerns. Sometimes it focuses on identifying and performing the work tasks that must be conducted in order for the group to achieve its goals. At other times, the group focuses on building morale and improving its social-emotional atmosphere.

Note that the sequential-stage perspective and the recurring-phase perspective are not necessarily contradictory. Both are useful for understanding group development. The sequential-stage perspective assumes that a group is apt to move through various phases while dealing with basic themes that surface as they become relevant to the group's work. The recurring-phase perspective assumes that the issues underlying the basic themes are never completely resolved but tend to recur later.

Task and Maintenance Roles

All groups, whether organized for therapeutic reasons, for problem solving, or for other objectives, rely on the performance of a variety of roles by their members. The group's needs generally require that both task roles and group-building roles be performed satisfactorily. *Task roles* are those that are needed to accomplish the specific goals set by the group; *maintenance roles* are those that serve to strengthen the social/emotional aspects of group life.

Johnson and Johnson (1975) summarized task roles as follows:

- *Information and opinion giver:* Offers facts, opinions, ideas, suggestions, and relevant information to help group discussion.

- *Information and opinion seeker:* Asks for facts, information, opinions, ideas, and feelings from other members to help group discussion.
- *Starter:* Proposes goals and tasks to initiate action within the group.
- *Direction giver:* Develops plans on how to proceed and focuses attention on the task to be done.
- *Summarizer:* Pulls together related ideas or suggestions and restates and summarizes major points discussed.
- *Coordinator:* Shows relationships among various ideas and harmonizes activities of various subgroups and members.
- *Diagnoser:* Figures out sources of difficulties the group has in working effectively and the blocks to progress in accomplishing the group's goals.
- *Energizer:* Stimulates a higher quality of work from the group.
- *Reality tester:* Examines the practicality of ideas, evaluates alternative solutions, and applies them to real situations to see how they will work.
- *Evaluator:* Compares group decisions and accomplishments with group standards and goals.

Johnson and Johnson (1975) also identified the group maintenance roles, which strengthen social/emotional bonds within the group:

- *Encourager of participation:* Warmly encourages everyone to participate, giving recognition for contributions and demonstrating openness to ideas of others; is friendly and responsive to group members.
- *Harmonizer and compromiser:* Persuades members to analyze constructively their differences in opinions, searches for common elements in conflicts, and tries to reconcile disagreements.
- *Tension reliever:* Eases tensions and increases the enjoyment of group members by joking, suggesting breaks, and proposing fun approaches to group work.
- *Communication helper:* Shows good communication skills and makes sure that each group member understands what other members are saying.
- *Evaluator of emotional climate:* Asks members how they feel about the way in which the group is working and about each other, and shares own feelings about both.
- *Process observer:* Watches the process by which the group is working and uses the observations to help examine group effectiveness.

- *Standard setter:* Expresses group standards and goals to make members aware of the direction of the work and the progress being made toward the goal and to get open acceptance of group norms and procedures.
- *Active listener:* Listens and serves as an interested audience for other members, is receptive to others' ideas, goes along with the group when not in disagreement.
- *Trust builder:* Accepts and supports the openness of other group members; reinforces risk taking and encourages individuality.
- *Interpersonal problem solver:* Promotes open discussion of conflicts between group members in order to resolve conflicts and increase group togetherness.

Hersey and Blanchard (1977) developed a situational theory of leadership that serves as a guideline for when effective leaders should focus on task behaviors, when they should focus on maintenance behaviors, and when they should focus on both. In essence, the theory asserts that when members have low maturity in terms of accomplishing a specific task, the leader should engage in high-task and low-maintenance behaviors. Hersey and Blanchard refer to this situation as *telling*, because the leader's behavior is most effective when he or she defines the members' roles and tells them how, when, and where to do needed tasks. The task maturity of members increases as their experience and understanding of the task increases. For moderately mature members, the leader should engage in high-task and high-maintenance behaviors. This combination of behaviors is referred to as *selling*, because the leader should not only provide clear direction as to role and task responsibilities, but should also use maintenance behaviors to get the members to psychologically buy into the decisions that have to be made.

Also, according to Hersey and Blanchard, when group members' commitment to the task increases, so does their maturity. When members are committed to accomplishing the task and have the ability and knowledge to complete the task, the leader should engage in low-task and high-maintenance behaviors, referred to as *participating*. Finally, for groups in which members are both willing and able to take responsibility for directing their own task behavior, the leader should engage in low-task and low-maintenance behaviors, referred to as

delegating. Delegating allows members considerable autonomy in completing the task.

Leadership Theories

There are at least five major approaches to leadership theory: trait, position, style, distributed functions, and servant leadership.

The Trait Approach

Aristotle observed, "From the hour of their birth some are marked for subjugation, and others for command" (quoted in Johnson & Johnson, 1987, p. 39). As implied by this comment, this approach to leadership has been in existence for centuries. The *trait approach* assumes that leaders have personal characteristics or traits that make them different from followers. It also implies that leaders are born, not made, and that leaders emerge naturally rather than being trained. The trait approach has also been called the *great person theory* of leadership.

Two postulated leadership traits that have received considerable attention are charisma and Machiavellianism.

Charisma Johnson and Johnson (1987, p. 43) define charisma as "an extraordinary power, as of working miracles." They give the following definition of a charismatic leader:

> *The charismatic leader must have a sense of mission, a belief in the social-change movement he or she leads, and confidence in oneself as the chosen instrument to lead the movement to its destination. The leader must appear extremely self-confident in order to inspire others with the faith that the movement he or she leads will, without fail, prevail and ultimately reduce their distress. (p. 44)*

Some charismatic leaders appear to inspire their followers to adore and be fully committed to them. Other charismatic leaders offer their members the hope and promise of deliverance from distress.

Charisma has not been precisely defined, and its components have not been fully identified. The qualities and characteristics that any charismatic leader has will differ somewhat from those of other charismatic leaders. The following leaders have all been referred to as charismatic, yet they differed substantially in personality characteristics: John F. Kennedy, Martin Luther King Jr., Julius Caesar, General

George Patton, Confucius, Gandhi, and Winston Churchill.

One difficulty with the charisma approach to leadership is that people who are viewed as charismatic tend to express this quality in a variety of ways. A second difficulty is that many leaders do well as leaders without being viewed as having charisma. For example, many group therapists are very effective in leading groups, even though they are not viewed as charismatic.

Machiavellianism Niccolò Machiavelli (1469–1527) was an Italian statesman who advocated that rulers use cunning, craft, deceit, and duplicity as political methods for increasing their power and control. Machiavelli was not the originator of his approach; some earlier theorists had conceptualized leadership in terms of manipulation for self-enhancement. However, the term *Machiavellianism* has become associated with the notion that politics is amoral and that any unscrupulous means can justifiably be used in achieving political power. Machiavellian leadership is based on the concepts that followers (1) are basically fallible, gullible, untrustworthy, and weak; (2) are impersonal objects; and (3) should be manipulated in order for the leader to achieve his or her goals.

Christie and Geis (1970) concluded that Machiavellian leaders have four characteristics:

1. They have little emotional involvement in interpersonal relationships, because it is emotionally easier to manipulate others when viewing them as impersonal objects.
2. They are not concerned about conventional morality and take a utilitarian (what they can get out of it) rather than a moral view of their interactions with others.
3. They have a fairly accurate perception of the needs of their followers, which facilitates their capacity to manipulate them.
4. They have a low degree of ideological commitment; they focus on manipulating others for personal benefit rather than to achieve long-term ideological goals.

Although a few leaders may have Machiavellian characteristics, most do not. Few groups would function effectively or efficiently with Machiavellian leaders.

In recent years, the trait theory of leadership has declined in popularity, partly because research results have raised questions about its validity. For example, different leadership positions often require different leadership traits. The characteristics of a good leader in the military differ markedly from those of a good group therapy leader. Moreover, traits found in leaders have also been found in followers. Though qualities such as high intelligence and a well-adjusted personality may have some correlation with leadership, many highly intelligent people never get top leadership positions, and some highly intelligent leaders (e.g., Adolf Hitler) have been emotionally unstable. The best rule for leader selection involves choosing individuals with the necessary skills, qualities, and motivation to help a group accomplish its goals.

The Position Approach

Most large organizations have several levels of leadership, such as president, vice-president, manager, and supervisor. The *position approach* defines leadership in terms of the authority of a particular position and has focused on studying the behavior of people in high-level positions. At times, the training and personal background of leaders have also been examined.

Studies using the position approach, however, have revealed little consistency in how people assume leadership positions. Obviously, some individuals become leaders with little related training (in family businesses, for example), whereas others spend years developing their skills. Also, what is viewed as "desirable" leadership behavior in one position may be considered "undesirable" behavior in a different type of position. For example, a drill sergeant in basic military training is not expected to be empathetic, but a sensitivity group leader is. It is difficult to compile a list of leadership traits using this approach. Not surprisingly, the position approach has shown that what constitutes leadership behavior depends on the particular requirements of the position.

It is also difficult to define which behaviors of a designated leader are leadership behaviors and which are not. Certainly not all of the behaviors of a designated authority figure are leadership behaviors. For instance, an inexperienced individual in a position of authority can mask incompetence with an authoritarian attitude. Also, leadership behavior among group members who are not designated leaders is difficult to conceptualize with the position approach, because the position approach focuses only on the behaviors of designated leaders.

The Style Approach

Because research on the *trait approach* was turning out contradictory results, Lewin, Lippitt, and White (1939) took a *leadership style approach*. These researchers described and studied three leadership styles: authoritarian, democratic, and laissez-faire.

Authoritarian leaders have more absolute power than democratic leaders. They alone set goals and policies, dictate the activities of the members, and set major plans. They hand out rewards and punishments, and they alone know the succession of future steps in the group's activities. In contrast, democratic leaders seek maximum involvement and participation of every member in all decisions affecting the group. They seek to spread responsibility rather than to concentrate it.

Authoritarian leadership is generally efficient and decisive. One of the hazards, however, is that group members may do what they are told out of necessity and not because of any commitment to group goals. The authoritarian leader who anticipates approval from subordinates for accomplishments achieved may be surprised to find backbiting and bickering common in the group. Unsuccessful authoritarian leadership is apt to generate factionalism and behind-the-scenes jockeying and maneuvering for position among members, and lead to a decline in morale.

Democratic leadership, in contrast, is slow in decision making and sometimes confusing, but frequently proves to be more effective because of strong cooperation that generally emerges with participation in decision making. With democratic leadership, interpersonal hostilities between members, dissatisfactions with the leader, and concern for personal advancement all become issues that are discussed and acted on. The danger is that the private, behind-the-scenes complaining of the authoritarian approach becomes public conflict in a democratic approach. Once this public conflict has been resolved in a democratic group, however, a strong personal commitment develops that motivates members to implement group decisions rather than to subvert them. The potential for sabotage in an authoritarian group is high, and therein lies the advantage of the democratic style.

The democratic leader knows that some mistakes are inevitable, and that the group will suffer from them. Yet such mistakes require the leader's ability to stand by without interfering because to do otherwise might harm the democratic process and impede the progress of the group in developing the capacity to make decisions as a group.

In some situations, authoritarian leadership is more effective, whereas in others democratic leadership is more effective (Hare, 1962). As in any situation, the group will be more effective when members' expectations about the behavior appropriate for that situation are met. When group members anticipate a democratic style, as they do in educational settings, classrooms, or discussion groups, the democratic style usually produces the most effective group. When members anticipate forceful leadership from their superiors, as in industry or military service, a more authoritarian form of leadership results in a more effective group.

In the *laissez-faire* style, there is little participation by the leader. The group members are left to function (or flounder) with little input from the designated leader. There are a few conditions in which group members function best under laissez-faire style: when the members are committed to a course of action, have the resources to implement it, and need a minimum of designated leader influence to work effectively.

Because different leadership styles are required in different situations (even with the same group), research interest in recent years has switched to the distributed functions approach.

The Distributed-Functions Approach

With this approach, leadership is defined as the performance of acts that help the group reach its goals and maintain itself in good working order (Johnson & Johnson, 1997). The functional approach to leadership seeks to discover what tasks are essential to achieve group goals under various circumstances and how different group members should take part in these actions.

The *distributed-functions approach* disagrees with the great person theory of leadership. It asserts that *any member* of a group will at times be a leader by taking actions that serve group functions. With this approach, leadership is viewed as being specific to a particular group in a particular situation. For example, telling a joke may be a useful leadership function in certain situations if it relieves tension, but telling a joke when other members are revealing intense personal feelings in a therapy group may be counterproductive and therefore not a leadership function.

The functional approach defines leadership as occurring whenever one member in a group influences other members to help the group reach its goals. Because at times all group members influence other group members, each member in a group exerts leadership. A difference exists in most groups between being a designated leader (such as a president or chairperson) and engaging in leadership behavior. A *designated leader* has certain responsibilities (such as calling meetings and leading the discussion), whereas *leadership* means that one member is influencing other group members to help the group reach its goals.

The functional approach asserts that leadership is a learned set of skills that anyone with certain minimal requirements can acquire. Responsible membership is the same thing as responsible leadership; both involve doing what needs to be done to help the group maintain itself and accomplish its goals. This approach asserts that people can be taught the skills and behaviors that help the group accomplish its tasks.

Like any member of a group, the designated leader may be called on or may be forced to adopt one or more of the task or maintenance roles discussed earlier in this chapter. Indeed, the leader has a special obligation to be alert for such occasions and to assume, or to assist others to assume, whichever roles are timely and appropriate. The leader's contribution to the group is not limited, however, to the assumption of specified roles. Each leader is responsible for a variety of functions. The needs and developmental stage of a group may at different times require a leader who can assume any of the previously described roles as well as those that follow:

- *Executive:* being the top coordinator of the activities of a group.
- *Policymaker:* establishing group goals and policies.
- *Planner:* deciding the means by which the group will achieve its goals.
- *Expert:* serving as the source of readily available information and skills.
- *External group representative:* being the official spokesperson for the group.
- *Controller of internal relations:* controlling the structure as a way to control in-group relations.
- *Purveyor of rewards and punishments:* determining promotions, or demotions, and assigning pleasant or unpleasant tasks.
- *Arbitrator and mediator:* acting as both judge and conciliator with the power to reduce or to increase factionalism within the group.
- *Exemplar:* serving as a model of behavior to show what the members should be and do.
- *Ideologist:* serving as the source of the beliefs and values of the members.
- *Scapegoat:* serving as the target for ventilating members' frustrations and disappointments.

The Servant Leadership Approach

Servant leadership is an approach to leadership that was initially developed by Robert K. Greenleaf (1982). A servant leader is someone who looks to the needs of the group she is working with, and asks herself how she can help the members solve problems and promote personal development among the members. She places her main focus on the members, as she believes that content and motivated members are best able to reach their goals. In contrast to an autocratic style of leadership in which the autocratic leader makes most of the decisions, decision-making responsibilities are shared with the members in the servant leadership style. The highest priority of a servant leader is to support, encourage, and enable members to unfold their full potential and abilities. (A highly competent teacher probably uses many of the concepts of a servant leader.)

Larry C. Spears and Michele Lawrence (2004) have identified the following 10 concepts that characterize a servant leader:

- Listening: A servant leader is motivated to listen to members and is supportive of their opinions, and validates their concerns. The servant leader not only attends to verbalized concerns, but also to what is "unspoken."
- Empathy: A servant leader seeks to understand and empathize with the members. The members are viewed as people who need respect and appreciation in order to facilitate personal development; and the more that members develop, the more successful and productive they are apt to become.

- Healing: A servant leader seeks to help members solve their issues and conflicts in relationships, as she wants to encourage and support the personal development of each member. Such "healing" is postulated to lead to a working environment in the group that is dynamic, fun, and free of the fear of failure.
- Awareness: A servant leader seeks to have a high level of self-awareness, and to be perceptive of what the members are thinking and feeling. She also seeks to be aware of their interpersonal relationships in the group.
- Persuasion: A servant leader does not try to coerce members into compliance with what she wants, but instead seeks to convince members to share decision-making responsibilities.
- Conceptualization: A servant leader thinks beyond day-to-day realities. She also conceptualizes long-term goals and strategies for reaching those goals. She has a personal vision that incorporates what is in the best interests of all members of the group.
- Foresight: A servant leader has the capacity to foresee the likely outcome of possible implementation strategies. (This characteristic is closely related to conceptualization.)
- Stewardship: A servant leader not only seeks to facilitate the personal development and productivity of the group, but also realizes she has an obligation to do what is best for the greater society. Openness and persuasion are more important than control.
- Commitment to the growth of people. A servant leader focuses on nurturing the professional, personal, and spiritual growth of members. She seeks to validate the ideas of all the members, and involves them in decision making.
- Building Community: A servant leader not only seeks to develop a productive and contented group, but also seeks to build a strong community. It is postulated that members will have considerable growth with this style of leadership, which will lead these members to add to the development of the communities in which they live.

Servant leadership is a lifelong journey that includes self-discovery, a desire to serve others, and a commitment to developing the group members that one works with. Servant leaders are humble, caring, visionary, empowering, relational, competent, good stewards, and community builders. They put others first, are skilled communicators, are compassionate collaborators, are systems thinkers, and are ethical. Instead of a top-down hierarchical style, servant leaders emphasize trust, collaboration, empathy, and ethical use of power. Servant leaders do not seek to increase their own power, but seek to lead by better serving others.

Servant leadership not only facilitates the personal development of group members, but has the potential to influence the broader society in a positive way. Group members tend to be attracted to this style of leadership, and tend to be happier and more productive. (Servant leadership is not only an effective approach to leading a group, but is also an effective management style for a supervisor to use in supervising employees. Managers who empower and respect their staff tend to get better performance in return.)

Will servant leadership work well in all groups? Undoubtedly not! Certain settings probably require a more forceful form of leadership—such as in the military or in a prison setting.

Chapter Summary

The following summarizes this chapter's content as it relates to the learning objectives presented at the beginning of the chapter. Chapter content will help prepare students to:

LO 8-1 Describe the social development changes that adolescents undergo.

Young people during this time period face the social developmental tasks of moving from parental dependence to becoming more independent, establishing peer relationships, and perhaps forming intimate relationships with others.

LO 8-2 Describe some major problems encountered by this age group: eating disorders, emotional and behavior problems, crime and delinquency, and delinquent gangs.

Eating disorders (anorexia nervosa, bulimia nervosa, and compulsive overeating) have recently been recognized as a serious problem. Anorexics eat very little food, bulimics binge and purge, and overeaters binge.

Adolescents encounter a wide variety of emotional and behavioral problems. Two models for conceptualizing such problems are the medical model, which views emotional and behavioral problems as mental illnesses, and an interactional model, which holds that mental illness does not exist.

Adolescents (and young adults) commit the bulk of crimes. Juvenile courts have more of a treatment orientation than the adult criminal justice system. Delinquent gang activity has become a major social problem in the United States, but the scientific knowledge base about delinquent gangs is limited.

LO 8-3 Understand theoretical material on the causes and treatments of these problems.

Because eating disorders are complex and serious, professional intervention is generally needed. Treatment for an eating disorder usually has the following three goals: (1) resolution of the psychosocial and family dynamics that led to the development of the eating disorder; (2) provision of medical services to correct any medical problems that resulted from starving, binging and purging, or being obese; and (3) reestablishment of normal weight and healthy eating behavior.

The rational therapy approach provides a useful way to assess and treat unwanted emotions and dysfunctional behaviors. This approach asserts that thinking patterns primarily determine all emotions and behaviors, and that assessing human behavior is largely a process of identifying the cognitions that underlie unwanted emotions or dysfunctional behaviors. Furthermore, the approach asserts that in order to change dysfunctional behaviors or unwanted emotions, the affected person needs to change his or her thinking patterns.

There are many theories about the causes of crime and delinquency. Our society uses two different approaches to perpetrators of crime and delinquent actions. One is a punishment approach, such as fines and incarceration. The other is a treatment approach, which seeks to reform the perpetrator.

The motive for committing any crime is precisely the reasons why the perpetrator thinks he/she should commit the crime. How does society stop a perpetrator from continuing to commit a specific crime? In a nutshell, the perpetrator has to come to the conclusion that the adverse consequences of committing that crime outweigh the benefits.

LO 8-4 Understand material on social work with groups, including theories about group development and theories about group leadership.

Doing social work with groups is a typical activity for today's social workers. Types of groups frequently encountered in practice include recreation, recreation-skill, educational, task, problem-solving and decision-making, focus, self-help, socialization, therapy, and encounter groups.

Four models of group development explain how groups change over time. The Garland, Jones, and Kolodny model hypothesizes five stages: preaffiliation, power and control, intimacy, differentiation, and separation. The Tuckman model conceptualizes groups as having the following stages: forming, storming, norming, performing, and adjourning. Schiller developed a relational model that is applicable to women's groups. Bales developed a recurring-phase model in which he asserted that groups continue to seek an equilibrium between task-oriented work and emotional expressions to build better relationships among group members.

All groups have task roles and maintenance roles that need to be performed by members. Task roles are needed to accomplish the specific goals set by the group; maintenance roles strengthen the social or emotional aspects of group life.

The theory of leadership highlighted in this chapter is distributed functions. With this approach, leadership is defined as the performance of acts that help the group reach its goals and maintain itself in good working order. Leadership occurs when one member influences other members to help the group reach its goals. Because all group members at times influence other group members, each member in a group exerts leadership. Four other approaches to leadership theory are the trait approach, the position approach, the style approach, and the servant leadership approach

COMPETENCY NOTES

The following identifies where Educational Policy (EP) competencies and practice behaviors are discussed in the chapter.

EP 2.1.7a Utilize conceptual frameworks to guide the process of assessment, intervention, and evaluation.
(*All of this chapter*) and

EP 2.1.7b Critique and apply knowledge to understand person and environment.
(*All of this chapter*): The content of this chapter is focused on students' acquisition of both of these practice behaviors in working with adolescents.

EP 2.1.10g Select appropriate intervention strategies.
(*pp. 389–390*) and

EP 2.1.10j Help clients resolve problems.
(pp. 389–390): With clients with eating disorders, select appropriate intervention strategies, and help them resolve problems.

EP 2.1.10g Select appropriate intervention strategies.
(pp. 394–399) and

EP 2.1.10j Help clients resolve problems.
(pp. 394–399): With clients who have emotional problems or behavioral dysfunctions, select appropriate

intervention strategies, and help them resolve problems.

EP 2.1.2 Apply social work ethical principles to guide professional practice.
(pp. 389, 393, 399, 400): Ethical questions are posed.

WEB RESOURCES

See this text's companion website at *www.cengage brain.com* for learning tools such as chapter quizzing, videos, and more.

GENDER, GENDER IDENTITY, GENDER EXPRESSION, AND SEXISM

AP Images/J. ScottApplewhite

Girls are pretty. Boys are strong.
Girls are emotional. Boys are brave.
Girls are soft. Boys are tough.
Girls are submissive. Boys are dominant.

These statements express some of the traditional stereotypes about men and women.
*   Stereotypes are "fixed mental images of members belonging to a group based on assumed attributes that portray an overly simplified opinion about that group"*

(Kirst-Ashman & Hull, 2012b, p. 25). The problem with such fixed images is that they allow no room for individual differences within the group. One of the major values adhered to in social work is that each individual has the right to self-determination. Clinging to stereotypes violates this basic value.

Stereotypes about men and women are especially dangerous because they affect every one of us. To expect all men to be successful, strong, athletic, brave leaders places an impractical burden on them. To expect all women to be sweet, submissive, pretty, and born with a natural love of housekeeping places tremendous pressure on them to conform.

A Perspective

EP 2.1.5a

Sexism is "prejudice or discrimination based on sex, especially discrimination against women," that involves "behavior, conditions, or attitudes that foster stereotypes of social roles based on sex" (Mish, 2008, p. 1141). *Prejudice* involves negative attitudes and prejudgments about a group. *Discrimination* is the actual treatment of that group's members in a negative or unfair manner. Aspects of diversity directly affect how individuals function and interact with other systems in the social environment.

The aspect of diversity addressed here is gender. First, the concepts of gender, gender identity, and gender expression will be addressed. Then, because men in our society have traditionally held the majority of positions of power, a large portion of this chapter will focus on the state and status of women as victims of sexism.

Learning Objectives

This chapter will help prepare students to:

**EP 2.1.7,
2.1.7a,
2.1.7b**

LO 9-1 *Define gender, gender identity, gender expression, and gender roles*

LO 9-2 *Discuss the social construction of gender*

LO 9-3 *Examine the complexities of gender, gender identity, and gender expression.*

LO 9-4 *Evaluate traditional gender-role stereotypes over the life span*

LO 9-5 *Assess some differences between men and women (including abilities and communication styles)*

LO 9-6 *Discuss economic inequality between men and women*

LO 9-7 *Examine sexual harassment*

LO 9-8 *Review sexist language*

LO 9-9 *Examine rape and sexual assault*

LO 9-10 *Explore domestic violence and battered women*

LO 9-11 *Identify means of empowering women*

LO 9-1 Define Gender, Gender Identity, Gender Expression, and Gender Roles

EP 2.1.4

This chapter will explore various aspects of what it's like to be male or female. It will also address differential and sometimes discriminatory treatment based on gender. In an overly simplistic view of the world, one might think that a person is either a male or a female—period. As you will see, the concept of gender is much more complex than you might initially think. First, let's define our basic terms.

Gender *"refers to the social and psychological characteristics associated with being female or male. Characteristics typically associated with the female gender include being gentle, emotional, and cooperative; characteristics typically associated with the male gender include being aggressive, rational, and competitive. In popular usage, gender is dichotomized as an either/or concept (feminine or masculine), but gender may also be viewed as existing along a continuum of femininity and masculinity"* [as a later section of this chapter will explore]. (McCammon & Knox, 2007, p. 112)

The title of this chapter includes gender identity and gender expression. *Gender identity* is a person's internal psychological self-concept of being either male or female, or possibly some combination of both (Gilbert, 2008). *Gender expression* concerns how we express ourselves to others in ways related to gender that include both behavior and personality. *Gender roles* are the "attitudes, behaviors, rights, and responsibilities that society associates with" being male or being female (Yarber & Sayad, 2013, p. G-5). *Gender-role socialization* is the process of conveying what is considered appropriate behavior and perspectives for males and females in a particular culture.

We will differentiate the concepts of gender and sex. *Sex* "refers to the biological distinction between being female and being male, usually categorized on the basis of the reproductive organs and genetic makeup" (McCammon & Knox, 2007, p. 606). Sex, then, focuses on the biological qualities of being male or female; gender emphasizes social and psychological aspects of femaleness or maleness. The following section will explore how we can think theoretically about gender and its implications.

LO 9-2 Discuss the Social Construction of Gender

EP 2.1.7a

We can look at the concept of gender in many ways. One conceptual framework that fits well with a social work perspective is the *social constructionist* approach (Bay-Cheng, 2008; Kondrat, 2008). Social construction is "the process by which people's perception of reality is shaped largely by the subjective meaning that they give to an experience.... From this perspective, little shared reality exists beyond that which people socially create. It is, however, this social construction of reality that influences people's beliefs and actions" (Kendall, 2013, p. 14). In other words, how people *think* about situations as they interact with others becomes what is *real* to them. It's easy to view the world around us as a physical fact. However, social construction reveals that "we also apply subjective meanings to our existence and experience. In other words, our experiences don't just happen to us. Good, bad, positive, or negative—we attach meanings to our reality" (Leon-Guerrero, 2011, p. 9).

A positive aspect of the social constructionist approach is that it incorporates the concept of human diversity, a major focus in social work. People learn how they're expected to behave through their interactions with others around them. People's behavior will differ depending on the vast range of circumstances in which they find themselves. Therefore, human diversity should be accepted and appreciated.

Lorber and Moore (2011) note that gender is one's "legal status as a woman or man, usually based on sex assigned at birth, but may be legally changed. Gender status produces patterns of social expectations for bodies, behavior, emotions, family and work roles. Gendered expectations can change over time both on individual and social levels" (p. 5). At least three major points are stressed in these comments. First, gender is a legal status, usually determined at birth, that can be changed. Second, gender status results from social expectations. Therefore, the makeup of gender is determined by the social context in which a person lives. Third, expectations for how people of each gender are supposed to act can change over time, depending on the expectations of people around them.

The *social construction of gender* "looks at the structure of the gendered social order as a whole and at the processes that construct and maintain it" (Lorber, 2010, p. 244). It assumes that traditional gender expectations are not facts carved in stone, but rather perceptions and expectations that can be changed. Perhaps gender is a dynamic, developing concept that allows for great flexibility in roles and behavior. A more inclusive approach might be to stop dividing humanity up into males and females and, instead, appreciate a continuum of gender expression. According to Kramer (2005), the *social construction of gender* stresses that

> the differences between females and males are not based in some biologically determined truth. For example, in the nineteenth century, affluent white women in the United States were expected to stay at home once their pregnancies were apparent (a period called "confinement") and to be treated as infirm for weeks after delivery. Enslaved women, in contrast, worked until going into labor and resumed work shortly afterward. The impact of pregnancy and childbirth on a woman's physical capacities was constructed differently depending on social categories other than her sex....
>
> But social construction ... refers to the social practice of perceiving and defining aspects of people and situations inconsistently, to force our observations to fit our social beliefs. Thus, before the women's movement (which started in the late 1960s), the scoring of vocational tests, taken by people to determine what careers they might best follow, was done with two answer keys—one for females and one for males. Even if your answers were identical to those of someone of the other sex, the vocational advice was different.
>
> For a more dramatic example, the very notion that all humans can be clearly and without argument categorized as female or male is a social construction. Some people have chromosomal patterns associated with one sex, and they have primary (genital) sex characteristics or secondary (e.g., facial hair) sex characteristics, or both, associated with the other [as a later section addresses]. Some

> people have genitalia that are not clearly what our culture labels either "male" or "female." These variations in people's biological characteristics are more common than our cultural beliefs suggest....
>
> Because so many social statuses have gendered expectations attached to them, people may often find themselves, one way or another, feeling marginal to some sphere of their social lives. This affects the way that they perform their roles and the ways that others interact with them, affecting how they are able to perform their roles. They will have to put more energy into establishing their credentials in each position to be treated as a legitimate occupant of it by others. If the veteran is a woman returning to military service, in some ways she will be marginalized; both male veterans and nonveteran females feel that she is somehow not a "regular" member of their own category. If you have read the last sentence believing that times have changed, go to your local post office and look at the forms for registering for the Selective Service. Men must register, and women cannot. (pp. 3–5)

LO 9-3 Examine the Complexities of Gender, Gender Identity, and Gender Expression

Do you still think gender is a simple concept? Consider the following story (Colapinto, 2007).

Frank and Linda, both raised in religious families on farms, met in their mid-teens and married when they were ages 20 and 18, respectively. Making a move to an urban area, Frank got what he regarded as a great job. The couple soon joyfully discovered they were expecting twins. Much to their delight, identical twins John and Kevin were born to them on August 22, 1965.

"But when the twins were 7 months old, Linda noticed that their foreskins were closing, making it hard for them to urinate. Their pediatrician explained that the condition, called phimosis, was not rare and was easily remedied by circumcision. Linda and Frank then sought to remedy the condition through surgery.

But early the next morning [after surgery], they were jarred from sleep by a ringing phone. It was the hospital. "There's been a slight accident," a nurse told Linda. "The doctor needs to see you right away."

In the children's ward, they were met by the surgeon. Grim-faced, businesslike, he told them that John had suffered a burn to his penis. Linda remembers being shocked into numbness by the news.... The doctor seemed reluctant to give a full explanation—and it would, in fact, be months before [the couple] ... would learn that the injury had been caused by an electro-cautery needle, a device sometimes used in circumcisions to seal blood vessels as it cuts. Through mechanical malfunction or doctor error, or both, a surge of intense heat had engulfed John's penis. 'It was blackened,' Linda says, recalling her first glimpse of his injury. 'It was like a little string. And it went right up to the base, up to his body.' Over the next few days, the burnt tissue dried and broke away in pieces" (p. 3).

Appalled and frantically worried, Frank and Linda visited a range of specialists. They were told that it might be possible to construct a structure from skin grafts, but that this *penis* would neither look like nor function like a normal penis. Its only useful purpose would be urination. Frank and Linda foresaw a bleak and dismal future for John who would always be very *different* and would never really experience a *normal* life.

Finally, Frank and Linda came into contact with a charismatic famous physician who was just beginning to conduct transsexual surgery. Remember that the state of practice was unfamiliar and primitive compared to what can be accomplished medically and surgically today. This physician urged the couple to undertake corrective surgery to change John's *gender* to female as soon as possible. He stressed that gender identity becomes firmly established by age 30 months. Frank and Linda, who only had sixth-grade educations, reflect later on their lack of understanding. They didn't comprehend that this procedure had never really been performed on an otherwise normal baby before and that such surgery was indeed experimental. Friends and family raised serious questions. But, constantly faced with the poor baby's deformity, they hoped for the best and decided to proceed.

In 1967 at age 22 months, John "underwent surgical castration" (p. 10). Medical records indicate that the operating physician "slit open the baby's scrotum along the midline and removed the testes, then enclosed the scrotal tissue so that it resembled labia. The urethra was lowered to approximate the position of the female genitalia, and a cosmetic vaginal cleft was made by forming the skin around a rolled rub of gauze during healing" (p. 10).

Over the next years, Frank and Linda desperately tried to make John, now called Joan, act like a female and develop a female gender identity. The famous physician who persuaded them to have the surgery done in the first place advised them neither to talk about it nor to inform Joan about her real biological gender. Joan's parents tried to make her wear feminine clothing and play with girls' toys. However, Joan persistently remained a tomboy, clearly preferring the masculine dress and behavior demonstrated by her brother Kevin. By kindergarten Joan, her peers, and her teacher know that she was "different." Joan couldn't identify exactly what this difference was, but she knew she didn't feel like a girl. She continued to experience interpersonal difficulties throughout grade school.

Joan was given female hormones beginning at age 12. By age 14, "the drugs were in competition with her male endocrine system, which, despite the absence of testicles, was now in the full flood of puberty—a fact readily apparent not only in her loping walk and the angular manliness of her gestures, but also in the dramatic deepening of her voice, which, after a period of breaking and cracking, had dropped into its current rumbling register. Physically, her condition was such that strangers turned to stare at her" (p. 18).

At this point, Joan decided that she would henceforth live life the way she chose. She wore masculine clothing, refused to fuss with her hair, and urinated standing up. She "transferred to a technical high school, where she enrolled in an appliance-repair course. There she was quickly dubbed Cave-woman and Sasquatch and was openly told, 'You're a boy' " (p. 18).

Frank finally explained to Joan/John, at age 14, what had happened and about really being a biological male. After the initial shock, Joan/John's reaction was pure relief. Suddenly, his life, feelings, and behavior all began to make sense to him.

Joan's decision to undergo a sex change was immediate. She changed her name to John and demanded male-hormone treatments and surgery to complete her metamorphosis back from girl to boy. That fall, he had his breasts surgically excised; the following summer, a rudimentary penis was constructed. The operation was completed one month prior to his 16th birthday. (p. 19)

Male peers tended to accept John immediately. It was his relationships with females that bred complications. Although he was strikingly handsome and attractive to women, his lack of a functioning penis remained quite a challenge and embarrassment for him.

When John was 21, he had another operation that provided him with a penis that appeared much more realistic. Nerve transplants provided some sensation.

At 23, John met a woman three years older than himself who already had three children. They married when John was 25, and he adopted her children.

Eventually, John came forward and spoke out against sex reassignment surgery on young children. He shared how devastatingly difficult it had made many years of his life. His hope was to prevent the procedure from being performed on other unknowing innocents.

Very unfortunately, John killed himself in 2004 when he was 38.

EP 2.1.3a, 2.1.10d

Money (1987) proposed that gender is a complex concept involving six physical and two psychological variables:

1. Gender designated by chromosomes, XX for females and XY for males
2. Presence of testes or ovaries
3. Prenatal response in gender and brain development to the presence of testosterone for males and to the lack of it for females
4. Presence of internal organs related to reproduction, including the uterus, fallopian tubes, and vagina in females, and the seminal vesicles and prostate in males
5. Appearance of the external genitals
6. Hormones evident during puberty (estrogen and progesterone in the female, testosterone in the male)
7. Gender assigned at birth ("It's a boy!" or "It's a girl!")
8. Gender identity, a person's internal psychological self-concept of being either a male or a female

It is estimated that 1 out of every 1,500 to 2,000 babies born has some combination of physical characteristics demonstrated by both sexes (Crooks & Baur, 2014; Intersex Society of North America [ISNA], 2008a; National Institutes of Health [NIH],

2013a). Reasons include having "an atypical combination of sex chromosomes or as a result of prenatal hormonal irregularities" (Crooks & Baur, 2014, p. 120). For example, Klinefelter's syndrome is a sex chromosome disorder in which males are born with an extra X chromosome, resulting in an XXY designation; "the Y chromosome triggers the development of male genitalia, but the extra X prevents them from developing fully" (Carroll, 2013b, p. 86). Results include a feminized body appearance, low testosterone levels, small testicles, and, possibly, infertility (Lee, Cheng, Ahmed, Shaw, & Hughes, 2007). Treatment may involve testosterone therapy.

Another example of contradiction in physical gender is a genetic female who as a fetus is exposed to excessive androgens (a class of male hormones); as a result she develops external genitals that resemble a male's (Crooks & Baur, 2014). Her clitoris is enlarged enough to resemble a penis and the labia (folds of tissue around the vaginal entrance) may converge and resemble a scrotum (the pouch that holds the male testes) (Carroll, 2013b; Crooks & Baur, 2014). When diagnosed at birth, cosmetic surgery can often be performed to "feminize" the person's genitalia.

There are many other examples of people who have some mixture of male and female predisposition and configuration of reproductive structures. Such a person is referred to as *pseudohermaphrodite* or *intersex*. A true *hermaphrodite* is a person "born with fully formed ovaries and fully formed testes, which is exceptionally rare" (Carroll, 2013b, p. 86). Intersex is much more common.

The Intersex Society of North America (ISNA) (2008c) and the National Institutes of Health (2013a) raise serious questions regarding the right of parents and physicians to make arbitrary decisions about surgically altering a child without that child's knowledge and consent. Such procedures apparently are undertaken theoretically in the best interests of the child, possibly without parental consent (ISNA, 2008b). The ISNA (2008c) makes several recommendations regarding how intersexed children and their families should be treated. First, these children and their parents should be treated with respect; physicians and medical staff should address the condition and issues openly and honestly without shame. Second, families with intersexed children should be referred to social workers or other mental health professionals to address issues and potential decisions. Third, these families should also be connected with other families who have intersexed children for peer support and deeper insight into the issues involved. Fourth, after careful consideration, an intersexed child should be assigned a gender "as boy or girl, depending on which of those genders the child is more likely to feel as she or he grows up." Such gender assignment should not involve surgery, because surgery may destroy tissue that the child may want later on in life. Fifth, the child should receive medical treatment "to sustain physical health" (e.g., "surgery to provide a urinary drainage opening when a child is born without one"). Sixth, surgeries to make the child "look 'more normal' " should be avoided until the child is old enough to decide for him- or herself.

Spotlight 9.1 reviews other avenues of gender expression. The next sections will address gender roles and the social expectations traditionally and currently attached to them. These include gender-role stereotypes in childhood, adolescence, and adulthood, in addition to more general differences in males and females.

• • • • / Ethical Questions 9.1

EP 2.1.2

When infants are born with an ambiguous or unclear gender, should they be assigned to one gender or the other? At that time, should they be physically altered to more closely resemble the assigned gender? If so, who should be responsible for making this decision? To what extent might children with ambiguous genitals (even after being given an assigned gender as the ISNA suggests) fit in with their peers and be able to function well socially? Would it be better to wait until children reach adulthood to determine gender and/or to do any relevant surgery? Why or why not? Should society become more open-minded and expand its views of sex and gender to include more variations of male and female (a proposal that the ISNA does not support)?

LO 9-4 Evaluate Traditional Gender-Role Stereotypes over the Life Span

EP 2.1.1b, 2.1.2a, 2.1.4a-c

From the moment they're born, boys and girls are treated very differently. Girls are wrapped in pink blankets, and parents are told that they now have "a beautiful little girl." Boys, on the other hand, are wrapped in blue blankets, and parents are told that they now are the proud parents of "a bouncing baby boy." The process of gender stereotyping continues through childhood, adolescence, and adulthood. Gender stereotyping involves expectations about how people should behave based on their gender. Female stereotypes include being "nurturant, supportive, intuitive, emotional, ... needful, dependent, tender, timid, fragile, ... childlike, ... passive, ... obedient, ... [and] ... submissive"; in stark contrast, male stereotypes include being "powerful, creative, intelligent, rational, independent, self-reliant, strong, courageous, daring, responsible, ... forceful, ... authoritative, ... [and] successful" (see also Richardson, 2007; Ruth, 1998, p. 153; Yarber & Sayad, 2013). These stereotypes have nothing to do with an individual's personality, personal strengths and weaknesses, or likes and dislikes. Note, however, that gender stereotypes held by many in this culture do not apply equally to all racial and ethnic groups. For example, the traditional gender role for African American women includes both strength and independence (McCammon & Knox, 2007; Yarber & Sayad, 2013).

A major problem with gender-based stereotypes is that they often limit people's alternatives. Pressure is exerted from many sources for people to conform to gender-based expectations. This pressure affects the individual and the alternatives available to him or her.

For example, until 1920, when women finally were allowed to vote in national elections, concrete political input was not available to them. Before that time, the political macro system (the U.S. government) dictated that women could not vote. Gender-based stereotypes about women that helped maintain that law may have included the following: Women were not bright enough to participate in decision making; women belonged in the home,

SPOTLIGHT ON DIVERSITY 9.1

Other Forms of Gender Expression

EP 2.1.4

There are a number of other means by which people express their gender. Carroll (2013a) reflects:

In Western culture, when babies are born, the genital anatomy is used to determine biological sex. If there is a penis, the child is a boy; if there is no penis, the child is a girl. Today we know that gender is much more complicated than that. Our biology, gender identity, and gender expression all intersect, creating a multidimensional gender spectrum. One person can be born female ([with] XX [chromosomes]), identify as a woman, act feminine, and have sex with a man, whereas another can be born female (XX), identify as a woman, act masculine, and have sex with both men and women. (p. 79)

A number of terms have been used to characterize people who have various traits and demonstrate various behaviors along the gender spectrum. *Transgenderism* includes people "whose appearance and/or behaviors do not conform to traditional gender roles" (Crooks & Baur, 2014, p. 129). In other words, "people whose sex and gender differ are known as transgender" (Greenberg, Bruess, & Oswalt, 2014, p. 325). *Transsexuals* are people who feel they are imprisoned in the physical body of the wrong gender. Because their gender identity and sense of self are at odds with their biological inclination, they often seek to adjust their physical appearance closer to that of their gender identity through surgery and hormonal treatment. Many transsexual people prefer to be referred to as *transgender people*. The word *transsexual* emphasizes sex, whereas *transgender* emphasizes gender, which they say is the real issue. *Transwoman* "may be used by male-to-female transsexuals to signify they are female with a male history"; *transman* is a term "that may be used by female-to-male transsexuals to signify they are male with a female history" (Carroll, 2013a, p. 80; Rosenthal, 2013). *Transyouth* may "be used to describe youths who are experiencing issues related to gender identity or expression" (Carroll, 2013a, p. 80).

Many other groups of people are often identified along the gender spectrum. *Transvestites* are those who derive sexual gratification from dressing in the clothing of the opposite gender. In our society, almost all transvestites are heterosexual males (Carroll, 2013b; Wheeler, Newring, & Draper, 2008), perhaps because women have much greater freedom and flexibility in how they dress. *Drag queens* are gay men who dress up as women. Lesbians who dress up in traditionally masculine clothing may be referred to as *drag kings*. *Female impersonators* are men who dress up as women, usually for the purpose of providing entertainment. They may be heterosexual or gay. A common performance involves mimicking the dress and style of famous female performers, often lip-synching (moving their lips to a song and music without producing any sound) their greatest hits.

Other Cultures and Diversity Concerning the Gender Spectrum

Carroll (2013a) comments on cultural diversity concerning the gender spectrum:

Some cultures challenge our notions of gender and even have a gender category that encompasses both aspects of gender. Two-spirits (or berdache) have been found in many cultures throughout the world, including American Indian, Indian, and Filipino cultures. A two-spirit was usually (but not always) a biological male who was effeminate or androgynous in behavior and who took on the social role of female (Blackwood, 1994; Jacobs et al., 1997; W. L. Williams, 1986). Being a two-spirit was considered a vocation, like being a hunter or warrior … In all social functions, the two-spirit was treated as a female. They held a respected, sacred position in society and were believed to have special powers.

Biologically female two-spirits began showing interest in boys' activities and games during childhood (Blackwood, 1984; Jacobs et al., 1997). Adults, recognizing this desire, would teach the girls the same skills the boys were learning. (In one tribe, a family with all girl children might select one daughter to be their "son," tying dried bear ovaries to her belt to prevent conception!)

Other cultures have similar roles. The Persian Gulf country of Oman has a class of biological males called the xani-th (Wikan, 1977). The xani-th are exempt from the strict Islamic rules that restrict men's interaction with women because they are not considered men. They sit with females at weddings and may see the bride's face; they may not sit with men in public or do tasks reserved for men. Yet, the xani-th are not considered females either; for example, they retain men's names.

Another important example is the hijra of India. The hijra are men who undergo ritual castration in which all or part of their genitals are removed, and they are believed to have special powers to curse or bless male children. Hijra dress as women, although they do not really try to "pass" as women; their mannerisms are exaggerated, and some even sport facial hair. In India, the hijra are considered neither men nor women but inhabit a unique third social gender (Nanda, 2001). (pp. 82–83)

Gender-role stereotypes persist despite the complexity of gender.

caring for husband and children, not in the hectic world of politics; women were destined to be the virtuous upholders of purity and human dignity (Rothman, 1978)—qualities not to be muddied in the political arena. Whatever the reasons, women were simply not allowed to vote.

In order to understand and assess human behavior, one must be aware of the pressures that gender-based stereotypes have on people. Social workers need to understand how human diversity affects behavior. Gender is one critical type of diversity. Gender-based differences and stereotypes will be examined within the contexts of childhood, adolescence, and adulthood.

Childhood

We established in Chapter 4 that females and males are treated differently from the moment they are born. Even parents who state that they consciously try to avoid imposing gender stereotypes on their children nevertheless do treat girls and boys differently (Bernstein, Penner, Clarke-Stewart, & Roy, 2003; Crooks & Baur, 2014). Thus, it's difficult to separate out any inborn differences from those that are learned.

Parents generally treat boys in a more physical manner than they treat girls. Parents also tend to communicate to male and female children differently (Yarber & Sayad, 2013). For example, they tend to respond positively to boys who behave actively and to girls who talk calmly or touch gently.

Boys are discouraged from emotional expression such as crying (Carroll, 2013b; Yarber & Sayad, 2013). If 6-year-old Susie falls, skins her knee, and comes into the house crying, her mother might respond, "You poor thing. Did you hurt yourself? It's okay now. Let me kiss it and make it better." If 6-year-old Bill falls, skins his knee, and runs into the house, his mother might respond, "Now, now, Bill, big boys don't cry. It'll be okay. Let me put a Band-Aid on it." Even very little boys are often encouraged to be strong, brave, and bereft of outward emotion. A tragic result of this is that as adults, males often maintain this facade. This sometimes creates problems in adult love and sexual relationships in which men are expected to express their feelings and communicate openly.

Gender differences are demonstrated in how children play (Crooks & Baur, 2014; Papalia & Feldman, 2012; Renzetti, Curran, & Maier, 2012). Boys are more aggressive than girls. Additionally, children tend to choose gender-related toys. Boys are drawn to "masculine" toys such as guns and trucks, whereas girls tend to prefer "feminine" playthings like Barbies.

Adolescence

Because it is a time of change, adolescence can be difficult. Bodies change drastically, sexual desires emerge, peers exert tremendous pressure to conform, personal identities are struggling to surface, and conflicts with parents are rampant. In addition to these other issues, adolescents may have to deal with powerful pressures to conform to gender stereotypes exerted by parents, peers, teachers, and the media (Carroll, 2013b; Crooks & Bauer, 2014). This process has been called *gender intensification*, a period of "increased pressures for gender-role conformity" (Hyde & Else-Quest, 2013, p. 152). Hyde and Else-Quest (2013) reflect:

The pressure, then, is for girls to become more feminine and less masculine, beginning around 11 or 12 years of age. A recent study of youth who entered adolescence in the 21st century, however, questioned whether gender intensification is as strong as it once was (Priess et al., 2009). Girls did not increase in femininity scores from age 11 to 15, and girls actually scored as high as boys on masculinity. Pressures for gender conformity may not be as strong today as they once were, or perhaps they have simply become more subtle, like modern sexism. (pp. 152–153)

Carroll (2013b) comments:

What is masculine? What is feminine? Not too long ago, the answers would have seemed quite obvious: men naturally have masculine traits, meaning they are strong, stable, aggressive, competitive, self-reliant, and emotionally undemonstrative; women are naturally feminine, meaning they are intuitive, loving, nurturing, emotionally expressive, and gentle. Even today, many would agree that such traits describe the differences between the sexes. These gender stereotypes, however, are becoming less acceptable as our culture changes. **Masculinity** *and* **femininity** *refer to the ideal cluster of traits that society attributes to each gender. (p. 90)*

Who do you feel best embody ideal masculine and feminine traits today? As an adolescent, whom did you look up to and why? To what extent did these people serve as role models? How did you alter your behavior in response to them and their behavior? To what extent do you feel that improving insight into yourself and your own behavior can provide better understanding of other people's behavior?

Spotlight 9.2 describes the importance of cross-cultural influences on gender-role development.

Adulthood

Women are often taught that they should be fulfilled by becoming wives and mothers (Geller, 2004; Shaw & Lee, 2012). Men, on the other hand, are often taught that their main source of self-satisfaction should come from their jobs (Shaw & Lee, 2012). The pressures and expectations resulting from both of these stereotypes often create serious problems. A woman who devotes herself entirely to being a wife and homemaker makes herself entirely dependent on her husband. If her husband dies, becomes ill, or leaves her, such a woman is in a vulnerable position. Almost one out of two marriages in the United States ends in divorce (American Psychological Association, 2014).

Traditional gender-role socialization and stereotypes are associated with at least three disadvantages for women. First, women are encouraged to enter fields segregated by gender where they earn significantly less money than men do (Kendall, 2013; U.S. Census Bureau, 2011). Kendall comments that even though many people "are optimistic about the gains U.S. women have made in employment, it should be noted that women's position as a social category in the labor force is lower than men's in terms of status, opportunities, and salaries" (p. 86). A later section of the chapter will discuss this in greater depth.

A second disadvantage for women is that even when they work outside the home, which most do, they are still expected to do the majority of the housework and provide most of the child care (Hyde & Else-Quest, 2013; Kirk & Okazawa-Rey, 2013). This is true regardless of social class, the status of the woman's job, or rural or urban residence. When more time and energy are devoted to home and family, less time and energy are left to contribute to outside work and career. Often this expectation can create marital stress as the wife pressures the husband to share household and child-care tasks equally; even when husbands participate significantly in household tasks, it still primarily remains the wives' *responsibility* to get things done (Hyde & Else-Quest, 2013; Kirk & Okazawa-Rey, 2013).

For example, Sharon and Dick, who were both professionals in their late 30s, married late and chose to have no children. They lived in a tiny duplex for several years to save money so that they might buy a new home. Finally, they made it. They had saved enough, and it was moving day. They asked Dick's parents to help them move. That was a big mistake. For years, Sharon and Dick had both worked long hours outside the home. They had divided the housework up by room. Sharon had the kitchen, the extra bedroom, which was her office, and the bathroom to keep clean; Dick had their bedroom and the living room as his domain. When the large pieces of furniture were moved out, Sharon made the mistake of walking into the bedroom, Dick's domain, as Dick's father was sweeping large dust balls around the floor. He barked abrasively at Sharon, "You better not let your new house get this dirty! This is disgusting!" Sharon's father-in-law, and the world at large, made housecleaning Sharon's responsibility and burden because she was the wife. Any uncleanliness was clearly considered her fault, even though she had never been the least bit domestically oriented. Housework had always bored her to tears.

SPOTLIGHT ON DIVERSITY 9.2

Cross-Cultural Perspectives on Gender-Role Development

EP 2.1.4c

Gender-role socialization, of course, varies depending on one's cultural background. Differences in roles between men and women are exaggerated in some cultures and diminished in others.

Traditional Asian American families are patriarchal, with status and power determined by age, generation, and gender (Balgopal, 2008; Brammer, 2012; Lu, 2008). Huang and Ying (1998) describe the values associated with a Chinese heritage:

Gender and birth position were … associated with certain duties and privileges. Sons were more highly valued than daughters; family lineage was passed through the male, while females were absorbed into the families of their husbands. The first-born son, the most valued child, received preferential treatment as well as more familial responsibilities. The prescriptive roles for daughters were less rewarding; females often did not come into positions of authority or respect until they assumed the role of mother-in-law. (p. 38)

A son's primary responsibility is to be a "good son" throughout life, including caring for aging parents (Balgopal, 2008, p. 156; Lu, 2008). This does not apply to daughters.

Note that China continues to enforce the policy that most couples may have only one child. Because male infants are valued much more highly than females, many parents choose to give their infant girl up for adoption and try again for a boy.

Although gender roles are changing somewhat for Mexican Americans, as they are for Americans in general, traditional Mexican American families adhere to strict separation of gender roles; men are to be heads of the household and women should submit themselves to their husbands, devoting their attention to caring for the family (Crooks & Baur, 2014; Diller, 2015; Longres & Aisenberg, 2008). Ramirez (1998) describes the gender-role socialization of many Mexican Americans:

Differences in sex-role socialization are clearly evident in this culture and become especially prominent at adolescence. The adolescent female is likely to remain much closer to the home than the male and to be protected and guarded in her contacts with others beyond the family, so as to preserve her femininity and innocence. The adolescent male, following the model of his father, is given much more freedom to come and go as he chooses and is encouraged to gain worldly knowledge outside the home in preparation for the time when he will assume the role of husband and father. (p. 220)

Diller (2015) explains gender-role differences between Arab and Muslim American men and women within the family context:

The Arab family has been described as patriarchal and authoritarian, hierarchical, and extended…. Men and women are expected to follow specific codes of family and honor, maintain the family, and rear the children. Communication within the family tends to be vertical rather than horizontal—top-down…. Boys and girls are treated differently, with an eye to instilling traditional sex role expectations in both…. They are expected to obey the authority of the father and family, as opposed to having and acting upon their own ideas. They spend more time with and are emotionally attached to the mother, who often acts as a go-between in communication with the father. (p. 319)

However, Hakim-Larson, Nassar-McMillan, and Paterson (2013) remark:

While Arab American women have had their share of difficulties in negotiating between American values and ideals and those of their Middle Eastern heritage, they have been resilient and resourceful in developing individualized solutions to conflicts about issues such as modesty in clothing, dating, chastity, and rebellion against husband or spousal authority. For example, some Middle Eastern women have developed strategies to flexibly adapt their clothing and social behavior according to the social situation…. Some also maintain a high motivation to assimilate to North American life by voluntarily participating in community organizations and by adopting American cultural traditions. They perceive fewer restrictions on their freedom if they are successful in doing so. (p. 275)

In contrast to cultures with highly differentiated gender roles, African Americans are often taught to assume more egalitarian roles (Diller, 2015; Moore, 2008). Evans (2013) explains:

African American families have historically promoted egalitarian gender-role socialization. Both boys and girls are trained to be assertive and are usually required to learn all household tasks rather than the tasks being split according to gender (e.g., girls wash dishes, boys take out garbage[)]…. Interestingly, these nonspecific gender roles may be a throwback to African roots (Hill, 1999). In West Africa, "women were expected to be economically productive and had some power and authority in sociopolitical matters" (Hill, 1999, p. 109). This socialization is said to account for the leadership roles of black females, in that they have benefited from developing

(continued)

SPOTLIGHT ON DIVERSITY 9.2 (continued)

traditionally "masculine" traits of assertiveness and independence while keeping traditional female traits of nurturing and relationship building. Black males are hurt more for the feminine traits that they acquire, in that U.S. society already values masculine traits more than feminine ones. (p. 142)

Remember, however, not to make automatic assumptions. Just because an individual belongs to a particular ethnic or racial group, that individual does not automatically conform to the gender-role traits that often characterize that group. Instead, be sensitive to differences and appreciative of diverse strengths. Any individual may experience some degree of *acculturation*: "an ethnic person's adoption of the dominant culture in which he or she is immersed. There are several degrees of acculturation; a person can maintain his or her own traditional cultural beliefs, values, and customs from the country of origin [or cultural heritage] to a greater or a lesser extent" (Lum, 2000, p. 201).

A third disadvantage that women may experience based on gender-role stereotypes is the potential stress generated from the demands of being beautiful and attractive (Yarber & Sayad, 2013). Bartky (2007) explains:

There is something obsessional in the preoccupation of many women with their bodies, although the magnitude of the obsession will vary somewhat with the presence or absence in a woman's life of other sources of self-esteem and with her capacity to gain a living independent of her looks. Surrounded on all sides by images of perfect female beauty … in modern advertising … of course we fall short.… Whose nose is not the wrong shape, whose hips are not too wide or too narrow? …

It is a fact that women in our society are regarded as having a virtual duty "to make the most of what we have".… [I]t is within our power to make ourselves look better—not just neater and cleaner, but prettier, and more attractive. What is presupposed by this is that we don't look good enough already, that attention to the ordinary standards of hygiene would be insufficient, that there is something wrong with us as we are. Here, the "intimations of inferiority" are clear: Not only must we continue to produce ourselves as beautiful bodies, but the bodies we have to work with are deficient to begin with. (p. 56)

Men, too, experience lack of freedom and negative consequences from gender-role stereotyping. At least three repercussions result. First, men are expected to be doers who are competent, aggressive, and successful (Shaw & Lee, 2012; Yarber & Sayad, 2013). As a result, they are pressured to succeed in a career, be it engineering, crime scene investigation, real estate sales, dentistry, or some other avenue of achievement. A man holding a job with lesser status is often thought to be a lesser person.

A second negative impact on men of gender-role stereotyping is the pressure not to express emotions (Crooks & Baur, 2014; Yarber & Sayad, 2013). Men are taught that they should not cry, and that they should be strong and decisive. They should especially withhold any emotional demonstrations associated with weakness, such as depression, fear, and sadness (Crooks & Baur, 2014). Intimacy may be more difficult for men than women, perhaps because of how they were socialized. This may relate to the idea that displaying emotion shows weakness. Therefore, revealing true intimate feelings may be seen as a sign of weakness to be avoided.

A third negative consequence of gender-role stereotyping for men involves the fact that their average life span is significantly less than that of women. For instance, white females live an average of almost five years longer than white males, and African American females almost seven years longer than their male counterparts (U.S. Census Bureau, 2011). Biology, of course, is involved. In addition, however, the "traditional male role emphasizes achievement, competition, and suppression of feelings, all of which may produce stress. Not only is stress itself harmful to physical health, it also may lead to compensatory behaviors, such as smoking, alcohol and drug abuse, and dangerous risk taking" (McCammon, Knox, & Schacht, 1993, p. 302).

The ongoing problem for both men and women is that gender stereotypes pressure people to conform.

HIGHLIGHT 9.1

The Special Issues and Needs of Men

From a social constructionist perspective, Kosberg and Adams (2008) emphasize that there are many "masculinities" that differ according to the social context in which men function; they cite the following as special issues experienced by men:

1. Society attempts to socialize men to conform to male gender-role stereotypes. Men should be tough, strong, vital, definitive, and unemotional. They should be as unfeminine as possible. These demands place great pressure on men to refrain from expressing emotion. This, in turn, negatively affects their ability to gain insight into their emotions and behavior. It also hampers their ability to communicate freely even in their most intimate and important relationships. Such pressures may prevent them from seeking the human support and love they need.

2. Men risk greater health problems than women. They don't live as long. They have higher death rates than women in all of the 15 leading categories of death, with the exception of Alzheimer's disease (Courtenay, 2003). They are more likely than females to be murdered, to successfully complete suicide attempts, to be homeless, to die in car accidents, to abuse mind-altering substances, and to experience injuries related to their work.

3. Men who experience major disturbances or losses in their lives such as divorce or death of a loved one may have difficulty turning to others for emotional support and help. They may experience difficulties in undertaking domestic tasks for which they've never learned the skills. Inability to cope may have harmful effects on their

self-concepts. Providing care to children or aging partners may be exceptionally difficult when they were not socialized into those roles.

4. Men of color experience even greater difficulty. They are more likely to be poor, uneducated, and incarcerated. They are also more likely to experience health problems and die earlier than white men.

5. Men are more likely to use detrimental coping mechanisms such as turning to substance abuse and denial. Because of the pressures on them to be strong and independent, they often under use community services, especially those involving mental health.

Blundo (2008) makes a number of recommendations regarding social work practice with men. Note that the majority of social workers are women. First, practitioners should strive to be aware of any gender-role stereotypes and expectations they harbor toward men, just as with any other diverse group. Biases might affect practitioners' objectivity and effective practice. Second, it's important to be aware of the wide range of diversity and "masculinities" among men. It's essential to understand how gender-role stereotypes and expectations affect men's behavior and emotions in order to develop appropriate goals when working with men. It's also crucial to be aware of and attend to the special issues faced by men of color. Third, as traditional treatment has focused on repairing the deficits inherent in masculinity (such as helping a man to become better at expressing emotion and seeking help when needed), it's important to focus on strengths. The extent to which a man is an active problem-solver and doer should be used to his advantage instead of disadvantage.

They don't allow much room for individuality and creativity. If we become more flexible and gender stereotypes dissolve, maybe people will be more objective in assessing themselves and not feel pressured to be something they're not. Abolishing gender stereotypes may give us all the freedom to develop more realistic expectations and to live the way we choose.

Much of this chapter is devoted to women's social and economic issues and the social injustices they face. However, we have established that men also suffer from oppressive demands based on gender-role stereotypes and expectations. Highlight 9.1 speaks to this issue.

LO 9-5 Assess Some Differences Between Men and Women

Some differences do emerge between males and females. To what extent they are due to biological predisposition or to environmental influences is unknown. Some of these differences are evident in abilities and in communication styles.

Ability Level

Although there are no differences between male and females in terms of intellectual ability or IQ, there has been heated debate for many years regarding the differences in males' and females' verbal ability. Males have traditionally been thought to have better mathematical ability and females better verbal ability. However, later research has raised some serious questions about the extent of these differences and even whether significant differences exist at all.

Sigelman and Rider (2012) summarize a number of current findings:

- Sometimes females display better verbal skills than males in some areas at some ages, but differences are so small they often don't matter (Arden & Plomin, 2006; Galsworthy, Dionne, Dale, & Plomin, 2000; Hyde & Else-Quest, 2013).
- Males display a better grasp of spatial manipulation and understanding ("for example, arranging blocks in patterns or identifying the same figure from different angles") (Hyde & Else-Quest, 2013; Sigelman & Rider, 2012, p. 384). Differences in some areas surface in childhood, and some discrepancies continue into adulthood (Johnson & Bouchard, 2007; Kaufman, 2007). Note that training can enhance spatial manipulation skills for both women and men (Hyde & Else-Quest, 2013).
- In the past, males scored higher than females on standardized math tests. However, currently males and females perform similarly on such tests, although girls get better grades in math classes (Hyde & Else-Quest, 2013; Kenney-Benson, Pomerantz, Ryan, & Patrick, 2006; Lachance & Mazzocco, 2006; U.S. Department of Education, 2005).
- Some studies indicate that females are better at remembering things than their male counterparts, although possibly only in some areas, such as recalling where items are placed (Johnson & Bouchard, 2007; Voyer, Postma, Brake, & Imperato-McGinley, 2007).

So, what really is true? The debate continues. At its core is the nature-nurture controversy. To what extent are such abilities innate, and to what extent are they the result of the differential treatment of boys and girls? The important thing is not to make assumptions regarding an individual's ability on the basis of gender.

Communication Styles

Another area in which differences between males and females are evident is in verbal and nonverbal communication style (Sapiro, 2003; Shaw & Lee, 2012). Shaw and Lee (2012) explain:

Feminine speech differs from masculine speech in that the latter involves more direct interruptions of other speakers. Listening to real people talking, we find that although men and women interrupt at about the same rate in same-sex conversations (women interrupting women, and men interrupting men), in mixed groups men interrupt other speakers more than women do, and men are more likely to change the subject in the process, whereas women tend to interrupt to add to the story with their own experiences and thoughts. Although there are cultural differences around interruptions, it is clear that who interrupts and who gets interrupted is about power....

[F]eminine speech and masculine speech fulfill different functions. Feminine speech tends to work toward maintaining relationships, developing rapport, avoiding conflict, and maintaining cooperation. Masculine speech, on the other hand, is more likely oriented toward attracting and maintaining an audience, asserting power and dominance, and giving information. (pp. 179–180)

Women tend to be better than men at understanding nonverbal cues and reading other people's emotions (Hall, 1998; Hyde & DeLamater, 2014). In general, women are in better touch with their emotions and the feelings of others.

Although many of these differences in communication styles are subtle and minor, in combination they mean a lot. Many of women's most salient issues involve unfairness and victimization due to sexism. To begin to examine the issues and to initiate change, some of the foundations of sexism need to be understood. Changes in these behaviors, when they're all considered together, may bring about significant adjustments in gender-role expectations and the distribution of power.

● ● ● ● / **Ethical Questions 9.2**

EP 2.1.2 *What, if any, qualities do you think are biologically innate for females and males? To what extent are the gender-related behavior and traits of females and males due to influences in the environment as they're growing up?*

People as Individuals

Men and women are more similar than dissimilar. The differences we refer to are differences in treatment and differences in what people have learned. Sexism needs to be addressed because it's unfair. It causes people to be treated differently because of their gender when there are no objective reasons for differential treatment.

Each individual, whether male or female, has the right to make choices. Cutting through and obliterating gender stereotypes and sexism will give people as individuals more freedom. Each individual will then have a better chance of being the way he or she is comfortable being. The idea is to confront the hidden rules that pressure people to conform on the basis of gender. Women can then be assertive without being pushy. Men won't have to be strong all the time and will be freer to express their feelings. Tasks and the burdens of leadership can then be shared or divided on the basis of mutual decision making. The best of each individual's personality traits can then blossom and be nurtured.

Significant Issues and Events in the Lives of Women

Women have been the victims of sexism in many striking and concrete ways. Historically, they have had fewer rights and have been financially less well off to a significant degree. They are victims of life events (rape and domestic violence) that rarely touch the lives of men.

The issues addressed here were selected on the basis of prevalence, severity, and current relevance. These issues are economic inequality, sexual harassment, sexist language, sexual assault, battered women, and the empowerment of women.

LO 9-6 Discuss Economic Inequality Between Men and Women

It is well known that women generally earn less than men. Today, the median income of women who work full-time is about 77 percent of what men earn (American Association of University Women [AAUW], 2013; Kirk & Okazawa-Rey, 2013; National Committee on Pay Equity [NCPE], 2014; Shaw & Lee, 2012). The wage gap between women and men becomes even worse when race is taken into account. That is, women of color are significantly more disadvantaged than are white women. Spotlight 9.3 indicates that Hispanic women earn less than African American women, and both groups earn less than white women. Also, consider that for all races women earn significantly less than men do at

EP 2.1.4a, 2.1.5a

🔆 SPOTLIGHT ON DIVERSITY 9.3

Gender/Racial Comparison of Median* Annual Earnings

	All Races	White	African American	Hispanic**
Females	$20,957	$21,118	$19,470	$16,210
Males	$32,184	$33,748	$23,738	$22,256

SOURCE: U.S. Census Bureau. (2011). "Median Income of People in Constant (2009) Dollars by Sex, Race, and Hispanic Origin: 1999–2009." *Statistical Abstract of the United States: 2012* (131st ed., p. 447). Washington, DC: Government Printing Office.

*The *median* is "the middle number in a given sequence of numbers" (Nichols, 1999, p. 822).
**Persons of Hispanic or Latino origin may be of any race.

Women of color are gradually moving into positions of power, although many barriers still remain.

every educational level. The median income for women with a bachelor's degree or more is 64 percent of what men with a college education or more earn; similarly, the average annual income for women with a high school education is approximately 74 percent of what correspondingly educated men earn (U.S. Census Bureau, 2011).

Almost 60 percent of all women age 25 and over work outside the home (U.S. Census Bureau, 2011). This work is critical to their livelihood and, in many cases, to their self-concept. As noted earlier, women earn 77 percent of what men earn. A number of reasons have been given for gender-based salary differences. For one thing, women tend to be clustered in low-paying, supportive occupations. "Many women and people of color are still segregated into a small number of jobs such as clerical, service workers [e.g., waitresses, maids, and dental assistants], nurses, and teachers" (NCPE, 2007, p. 185). Men tend to be found in higher-paying occupations. For example, they are more likely to become doctors, dentists, or lawyers (U.S. Census Bureau, 2011) (see Table 9.1). Men also dominate professions involving science, technology,

engineering, and math. Hill, Corbett, and St. Rose (2010) report for the American Association of University Women (AAUW):

The number of women in science and engineering is growing, yet men continue to outnumber women, especially at the upper levels of these professions. In elementary, middle, and high school, girls and boys take math and science courses in roughly equal numbers, and about as many girls as boys leave high school prepared to pursue science and engineering majors in college. Yet fewer women than men pursue these majors. Among first-year college students, women are much less likely than men to say that they intend to major in science, technology, engineering, or math (STEM). By graduation, men outnumber women in nearly every science and engineering field, and in some, such as physics, engineering, and computer science, the difference is dramatic, with women earning only 20 percent of bachelor's degrees. Women's representation in science and engineering declines further at the graduate level and yet again in the transition to the workplace. (p. xiv)

TABLE 9.1	EMPLOYMENT POSITIONS HELD BY WOMEN		
FEMALE-DOMINATED PROFESSIONS	**PERCENT FEMALE**	**MALE-DOMINATED PROFESSIONS**	**PERCENT FEMALE**
Preschool and kindergarten teachers	97.8	Brickmasons, blockmasons, and stonemasons	0.1
Secretaries and administrative assistants	96.8	Roofers	0.5
Dental hygienists	96.6	Aircraft pilots and flight engineers	1.3
Speech language pathologists	95.8	Carpenters	1.6
Child-care workers	95.0	Automotive service technicians and mechanics	1.8
Word processors and typists	92.2	Electricians	2.2
Bookkeeping, accounting, and auditing clerks	92.2	Construction laborers	2.7
Registered nurses	92.0	Firefighters	3.4
Receptionists and information clerks	91.5	Installation, maintenance, and repair occupations	4.2
Teacher assistants	91.5	Truck drivers	5.2
Medical assistants and other healthcare support occupations	90.7	Grounds maintenance workers	5.3
Hairdressers, hair stylists, and cosmetologists	90.4	Machinists	5.4
Billing and postal clerks and machine operators	89.9	Mechanical engineers	5.9
Maids and housekeeping cleaners	89.8	Surveying and mapping technicians	7.8
Occupational therapists	87.0	Engineering managers	8.1
Paralegals and assistants	85.9	Architecture and engineering occupations	13.8
Massage therapists	85.7	Police and sheriff's patrol officers	15.5
Personal and home care aides	85.2	Dentists	30.2
Librarians	81.8	Physicians and surgeons	32.2
Social workers	80.7	Lawyers	32.4

SOURCE: U.S. Census Bureau. (2011). *Statistical Abstract of the United States* (130th ed., pp. 393–396, No. 615). Washington, DC: Government Printing Office.

Perhaps an even more striking finding is that women earn less than men even when they're in the same occupation. Census data reinforce the gender gap in earnings (U.S. Census Bureau, 2010). Women in management, business, and financial occupations earn a median full-time, year-round salary of 72 percent of what their male counterparts earn. Similarly, women in professional and related occupations earn less than 70 percent of what men earn. Female physicians "are still overwhelmingly found in certain specialties as pediatrics, dermatology, and public health work, and less likely to be found in surgical specialties, orthopedics, and more entrepreneurial positions.... Female physicians on the average earned approximately 36 percent less than what male physicians made.... Similarly, female lawyers are less likely to be in criminal law and are more likely to practice family law and make

about 80 percent of male lawyers' salaries" (Shaw & Lee, 2012, pp. 409–410).

With "equivalent work experience and skills, professional women are far less likely to get to the top of their professions or corporations. They are halted by unseen barriers, such as men's negative attitudes to senior women and low perceptions of their leadership abilities and styles, their motivation, training, and skills. This barrier has been called a *glass ceiling*" (a concept introduced in Chapter 3) (Kirk & Okazawa-Rey, 2013, p. 316).

The same picture of wage inequity is found in social work. Research conducted since 1961 reflects a significant, consistent wage differential between men and women in social work (Gibelman, 2003). Some recent research focusing on people with master's degrees in social work found that women earned an average of $12,000 less than men; even when various factors were controlled, women earned 14 percent less than men (Brandwein, 2008; Center for Workforce Studies, 2006). Another recent national survey by the National Association of Social Workers found that median salaries for female social workers were $11,000, or 17.2 percent, less than those for male social workers (Pace, 2010).

Academia is another area characterized by gender discrepancies in status and earnings. The *Annual Report of the Economic Status of the Profession* (concerning university professors and instructors) presented by the American Association of University Professors (2013) found that the "breakdown by gender indicates that men generally earn higher salaries, except in baccalaureate colleges. (Women are more likely than men to hold non-tenure-track appointments, and more women than men responded to the survey. According to US Department of Education national data for fall 2009, 44 percent of women in full-time faculty positions were off the tenure track, compared with 33 percent of men.)"

Women also have less direct political power in terms of the actual number of political offices they hold. As of this writing, 99 women are serving in the U.S. Congress, making up 18.5 percent (Center for American Women and Politics [CAWP], 2014). (This reflects an increase of 11 positions or 2.5 percent since 2010.) Of these 99 women, 20 are U.S. senators, making up 20 percent of the 100 senators. The remaining 79 serve in the House of Representatives, making up 18.2 percent of the 435 U.S. representatives. Note that Congresswoman Nancy Pelosi, a Democrat from California, became the first woman Speaker of the House, and is currently minority leader. Even though the number of women holding national public office does not approach their proportion of the total population (almost 51 percent) (U.S. Census Bureau, 2011), women have made some progress over past decades.

Women tend to do a bit better in state governments. For example, although in early 2014 only 5 of the 50 state governors, or 10 percent, were women, women made up 22.6 (or 72) percent of the 318 statewide elective executive offices (including governors, lieutenant governors, attorney generals, various commissioners, and other such officials) (Center for American Women in Politics, 2014).

The statistics reflect ways in which women are disadvantaged and undervalued in our society.

People who hold important political positions have significant power and control over other people's lives.

LO 9-7 Examine Sexual Harassment

Ann's male boss states that if she doesn't have sex with him, she won't make it through her 6-month probationary period. She really needs the job. She doesn't know what to do.

EP 2.1.5a

Barbara's male supervisor likes to sneak up behind her and surprise her by putting his arms around her. This makes her feel very uncomfortable. However, he's responsible for scheduling her hours, evaluating her, and giving her raises. She is terrified of confronting him.

Harry really needs to get a good grade in his course with Dr. Getsom, a female professor, in order to keep his scholarship and stay in school. So far he has a D in the course. When he goes to see Dr. Getsom, she likes to touch him a lot and acts very friendly. Last Thursday she said she would "see what could be done about helping him with his grade" if they'd start dating. He feels trapped. He doesn't know what to do.

One of the other financial assistance workers in the county social services department really annoys Buella. The man is constantly telling dirty jokes about women. Additionally, he whistles at any woman under 25 who passes his desk.

Sexual harassment is a serious form of sex discrimination that affects business, industrial, academic, and public work environments. According to available data, the highest number of sexual harassment complaints filed with the federal Equal Employment Opportunity Commission (EEOC) was 15,889 in 1997; in 2011, the figure was 11,364 (EEOC, 2014b).

Sexual harassment is illegal. Title VII of the Civil Rights Act of 1964 outlaws discrimination on the basis of sex as well as race. Legal precedents have been established that include sexual harassment as a form of sex discrimination (EEOC, 2010a). In 1991, the Civil Rights Act "was amended to allow juries to award compensatory and punitive damages" to people seeking legal action concerning sexual harassment in employment-related civil cases[1] (Ahmad, 1998, p. 61). Additionally, individual state laws can prohibit sexual harassment and provide legal recourse to victims.[2] Title IX of the Higher Educational Amendments of 1972 specifically prohibits sex discrimination on university campuses. Finally, individual agencies, organizations, or universities may have established policies prohibiting sexual harassment.[3]

The Definition of Sexual Harassment

The EEOC (2014a) defines *sexual harassment* as follows: "Unwelcome sexual advances, requests for sexual favors, and other verbal and physical conduct of a sexual nature constitute sexual harassment when this conduct explicitly or implicitly affects an individual's employment, unreasonably interferes with an individual's work performance, or creates an intimidating, hostile, or offensive work environment."

Sexual harassment occurs when a female employee is made to tolerate the regular touching of her arms, waist, neck, or buttocks by her male supervisor in order to ensure that she gets good supervisory reviews. Sexual harassment exists when a female administrative assistant is pressured to become sexually involved with the vice-president she works for if she wants to keep her job. Sexual harassment also is evident when a male college professor likes to touch young male students in suggestive ways and refers to them as "pretty boys."

Sexual harassment almost always involves elements of unequal power and coercion. Sometimes it involves promising a victim a reward or threatening a punishment on the basis of the victim's sexual cooperation. Other times it involves becoming overly and inappropriately personal with a victim, either by sharing intimacies or prying into the victim's personal life.

Although most victims are women, sexual harassment can be directed at either males or females. In 2011, some 16.3 percent of complaints filed with the EEOC were filed by males (EEOC, 2014b). Therefore, sexual harassment can be considered a human rights issue. A member of either gender may be the victim of harassing, offensive behavior of a sexual nature. For example, consider the case of Joseph Oncale, who filed a sexual harassment suit against Sundowner Offshore Services, a Houston firm that drills for oil in the Gulf of Mexico. The following describes the situation:

Oncale had worked on offshore rigs before (and does today), but says he never encountered such abusive treatment as when he signed on with Sundowner in 1991. He claims, for instance, that three male coworkers held him down in a shower and shoved a bar of soap between his buttocks. One of them threatened rape, he says. He quit and later was found to have posttraumatic stress. (Cloud, 1998, p. 55)

After the case was thrown out by an appeals court, the U.S. Supreme Court later ruled unanimously that "men who sexually harass other men (and women who harass women) are discriminating against them and thus breaking the law" (Cloud, 1998, p. 55). A key is that the harassment must involve dissimilar treatment of men and women.

One example of same-gender harassment involves harassment of gay and lesbian people. They can be targets of inappropriate sexual advances, threats, and promises whether such overtures involve someone of their same gender or the opposite gender.

Sexual harassment can also take place when verbal remarks make the work or academic atmosphere offensive or stifling. Sexual remarks that are not related to the work at hand can interfere with productivity and performance. For example, female students might be forced to endure derogatory remarks from a male instructor that focus on women's anatomy or on their inferior ability. Or female employees might force themselves to tolerate a male supervisor's annoying behaviors. These might include his constant reference to women as "girls," his comments that "it must be that time of month" whenever a woman is moody, his remarks about how he likes "his girls" to wear short skirts, and his placing of pictures of naked women on the office bulletin board. Any of these behaviors disrupts a positive, productive working environment.

---

[1] *Civil court cases* "relate to private rights and to remedies [such as cash awards] sought by action or suit distinct from criminal proceedings" (Mish, 2008, p. 226)

[2] For example, the state of Wisconsin's Fair Employment Act, as amended in 1978, prohibits sexual harassment.

[3] For example, the University of Wisconsin Board of Regents has stated, in its Resolution 2384 of May 8, 1981, that sexual harassment "is unacceptable and impermissible conduct which will not be tolerated."

Strengthening the Definition: A Macro-System Response

EP 2.1.8a

A U.S. Supreme Court decision in late 1993 reinforced the seriousness of a hostile and offensive working environment as one aspect of sexual harassment (Kaplan, 1993; Sachs, 1993). Teresa Harris waited six years for the Supreme Court to hear her case after filing a sexual harassment case against her former employer, Charles Hardy, president of a Nashville truck rental company. Harris had been a rental manager in Hardy's employ. She accused Hardy of asking her and other female employees to retrieve coins out of his front pants pocket, suggesting that Harris "accompany him to the local Holiday Inn to negotiate her raise," and "regularly [responding] to her with remarks like, 'You're a woman; what do you know?' " (Sachs, 1993, p. 44). He also "called her a 'dumb ass woman' " and "suggested she won an account by having sex with a client" (Kaplan, 1993, p. 34).

Although lower courts found that Hardy's behavior toward Harris "was not so severe as to be expected to seriously affect her psychological well-being," the Supreme Court unanimously ruled in her favor (Sachs, 1993, p. 44). Justice Sandra Day O'Connor wrote on behalf of the Court that it rejected the former "psychological injury" standard courts typically upheld. In prior cases, people filing charges had to prove that they had suffered severe psychological injury in order to win cases and collect damages (Kaplan, 1993). This standard makes that unnecessary. Now "an employer has broken the law if a 'reasonable person' would find the workplace so filled with sexual improprieties that it had become a hostile and abusive environment" (Sachs, 1993, p. 44).

The U.S. Supreme Court has made other rulings that determine appropriate "parameters of behavior in the school or workplace" (Lavelle, 1998, p. 30). The three relevant cases involved "a lifeguard who was threatened and assaulted with vulgarities by her supervisors; a sales agent who was urged to submit to the sexual demands of a boss who could make life 'very hard or very easy' for her; and a 14-year-old student accosted by a teacher who visited her home on the pretext of returning a book" (Lavelle, 1998, p. 30). The three rules established by these cases both facilitate a complainant's ability to file and win a sexual harassment lawsuit and provide some protection for companies that develop strong prevention and disciplinary programs.

The first rule is that an employee can successfully claim sexual harassment even though she has been treated well on the job. This contrasts with the old rule that dictated that "to prove harassment, a worker has to show that because she resisted sexual advances she was punished in terms of salary, assignments or promotions" (Lavelle, 1998, p. 30).

The second established principle is that a manager can be held accountable for a harasser's action if the company does not have a strong system of handling harassment issues. This deviates from the prior rule that a manager is probably not held responsible for a harasser's behavior if he "isn't informed that one of his employees is harassing other workers" (Lavelle, 1998, p. 31). In short, it is now management's job to know about and handle harassment problems.

The third standard is that a victim of harassment must tell someone "with decision-making power" if she is being harassed (Lavelle, 1998, p. 31). This deviates from the old rule that she should inform some other person (a friend or colleague, for example).

The Extent of Sexual Harassment

An accurate profile of when, where, how, and to whom sexual harassment occurs does not exist. However, some surveys suggest that it is quite prevalent in a variety of venues including the workplace and educational settings (Rathus, Nevid, & Fichner-Rathus, 2014; Renzetti et al., 2012).

Sexual Harassment in the Workplace

There is some indication that up to 70 percent of all working women have experienced sexual harassment (Shaw & Lee, 2012). Renzetti and her colleagues (2012) reflect:

Women in all types of occupations, from mining … to law enforcement…, experience sexual harassment on the job. Some researchers maintain that sexual harassment is especially pervasive in male-dominated jobs, regardless of whether the jobs are white-collar or blue-collar, because harassment may serve as a means for male workers to assert dominance and control over women who otherwise would be their equals …, although women in these fields may remain silent about the pervasive sexual harassment they experience in order to keep peace with their coworkers …

Temporary workers appear to be at high risk of sexual harassment … Immigrant women who hold low-wage factory and agricultural jobs are also frequent victims of sexual harassment.… These women are particularly vulnerable because they often do not understand U.S. employment laws or their rights as workers, they may speak little or no English, and they have little or no job mobility. (pp. 229–230)

Sexual Harassment in Educational Settings

One survey of 1,965 students published by the American Association of University Women found that almost half (48 percent) of students in grades 7 through 12 had experienced sexual harassment; a majority of students (87 percent) indicated that sexual harassment experiences affected them negatively (Hill & Kearl, 2011). Hill and Kearl (2011) elaborate:

Sexual harassment is part of everyday life in middle and high schools.… Verbal harassment (unwelcome sexual comments, jokes, or gestures) made up the bulk of the incidents, but physical harassment was far too common. Sexual harassment by text, e-mail, Facebook, or other electronic means affected nearly one-third (30 percent) of students. Interestingly, many of the students who were sexually harassed through cyberspace were also sexually harassed in person. Girls were more likely than boys to be sexually harassed by a significant margin (56 percent versus 40 percent).

Girls were more likely than boys to be sexually harassed both in person (52 percent versus 35 percent) and via text, e-mail, Facebook, or other electronic means (36 percent versus 24 percent). This finding confirms previous research showing that girls are sexually harassed more frequently than boys … and that girls' experiences tend to be more physical and intrusive than boys' experiences … Being called gay or lesbian in a negative way is sexual harassment that girls and boys reported in equal numbers (18 percent of students).

Witnessing sexual harassment at school was also common. One-third of girls (33 percent) and

about one-quarter (24 percent) of boys said that they observed sexual harassment at their school in the 2010-11 school year. More than one-half (56 percent) of these students witnessed sexual harassment more than once during the school year. While seeing sexual harassment is unlikely to be as devastating as being the target of sexual harassment, it can have negative effects such as reducing students' sense of safety. Witnessing sexual harassment at school may also "normalize" the behavior by bystanders.

College students also experience sexual harassment. Hill and Silva (2005) report on a "nationally representative survey of undergraduate college students commissioned by the American Association of University Women":

Sexual harassment is widespread among college students across the country. A majority of college students experience sexual harassment. More than one-third encounter sexual harassment during their first year. A majority of students experience noncontact forms of harassment—from sexual remarks to electronic messages—and nearly one-third experience some form of physical harassment, such as being touched, grabbed, or forced to do something sexual. Sexual harassment occurs nearly everywhere on campus, including student housing and classrooms. It happens on large and small campuses, at public and private colleges and university, and at two-year and four-year institutions. It is most common at large universities, four-year institutions, and private colleges.…

Male and female students are nearly equally likely to be sexually harassed on campus. Female student are more likely to be the target of sexual jokes, comments, gestures, or looks. Male students are more likely to be called gay or a homophobic name.

Sexual harassment is a serious problem. Despite the lack of a definitive profile of its occurrence, sexual harassment occurs frequently in a variety of employment and educational settings.

Effects of Sexual Harassment

Negative psychological effects of sexual harassment include "fear of retaliation, fear of not being believed, feelings of shame and humiliation, a belief

Erin Patrice O'Brien/The Image Bank/Getty Images

Sexual harassment can result in victim humiliation and fear.

that nothing can or will be done, and a reluctance to cause problems for the harasser. In many ways, a woman who reports sexual harassment is viewed as a troublemaker or whistle-blower and is treated accordingly" (Renzetti et al., 2012; Stout & McPhail, 1998, p. 196). Harassed women may become "nervous, irritable, depressed, and exhibit other symptoms of posttraumatic stress" (Renzetti et al., 2012, p. 230).

Hill and Silva (2005) comment on the effects of sexual harassment for women in college:

> *Female students are more likely [than their male counterparts] to be upset by sexual harassment and to feel embarrassed, angry, less confident, afraid, worried about whether they can have a happy relationship confused or conflicted about who they are, or disappointed in their college experience. Female students are also more likely to change their behavior in some way as a result of the experience. For example, more than half of female victims avoid the person who harassed them or avoid a particular building or place on campus. Female victims are more likely to find it hard to pay attention in class or have trouble sleeping as a result of sexual harassment.*

Women also report various physical reactions to sexual harassment. These include "chronic neck and back pain, upset stomach, colitis and other gastrointestinal disorders, and eating and sleeping disorders" (Renzetti et al., 2012, p. 230).

Because of its distressing effects, many women try to ignore sexual harassment. In reality, the vast majority of sexually harassed women do not file a complaint (Kirk & Okazawa-Rey, 2013; Renzetti et al., 2012; Stout & McPhail, 1998).

Sexual harassment incurs financial costs as well. Over the past decade, many millions of dollars have been awarded in federal sexual harassment suits (EEOC, 2010b). Additional costs for the federal government include job turnover costs such as hiring and training new employees, costs due to absenteeism and increased health problems, and reduced worker productivity due to emotional stress. The personal and emotional costs placed on the victims themselves cannot even be measured.

Highlight 9.2 provides some suggestions for confronting sexual harassment.

●●●● **Ethical Question 9.3**

Why do people sexually harass other people?

EP 2.1.2

LO 9-8 Review Sexist Language

One form of sexual harassment involves making verbal remarks that establish an offensive or stifling work or educational environment. Such language can include jokes with inappropriate sexual connotations. It can also include derogatory comments about ability based on gender. For example, a male professor might say to his students, "Girls don't usually do very well in this major. They're usually not as bright as men. They just run off and get married anyway." Such a comment is discriminatory. The professor is making an unfounded, unfair prediction. He is not attending to each student's ability to perform on an individual basis.

EP 2.1.5a

HIGHLIGHT 9.2

Confronting Sexual Harassment

**EP 2.1.5c,
2.1.10j**

Victims of sexual harassment have several routes available to them. Alternatives include ignoring the harassing behavior, avoiding the harasser, or asking the harasser to stop (Martin, 1995; Rogers & Henson, 2007). The most common approach women choose is to ignore the harasser, which has limited effect in the long run; asking the harasser to stop, although more difficult, may be more effective (EEOC, 2010a; Rogers & Henson, 2007).

Avoiding the harasser is another option. A severe short-coming of this approach is that the victim is the one who must expend the effort. The ultimate avoidance measure is quitting the job or dropping the class in order to avoid contact with a sexual harasser. This is the least fair (and potentially most damaging) alternative for the victim. Further, it does nothing to reeducate the harasser, prevent harassment from recurring, or prepare the victim to deal with it in subsequent incidents.

There are several other ways to help victims confront sexual harassment. In many cases, using these strategies will stop harassment. First, a victim needs to know his or her rights. A call to the Equal Employment Opportunity Commission (EEOC), the federal agency designated to address the issue of sexual harassment, is helpful. The EEOC will provide necessary information about the individual's rights and the appropriate procedures to follow for filing a formal complaint.

Many states have laws that make sexual harassment illegal. Such states often have agencies or offices that victims may call for help and information. Organizations and agencies also have specific policies against sexual harassment. Filing a formal complaint through established procedures is often an option.

As mentioned previously, most victims choose not to pursue the formal complaint route. Some victims fear reprisal or retaliation; others don't want to be labeled troublemakers. Still others don't choose to expend the time and effort necessary in carrying out a formal process. Most victims simply want the harassment to end so that they can work peacefully and productively.

In addition to knowing your rights, the following suggestions can be applied to most situations in which sexual harassment is occurring (New Media Learning, 2007; Rathus et al., 2014; Sandler, 2008).

1. *Confront your harasser.* Tell the harasser which specific behaviors are unwanted and unacceptable. If you feel you cannot handle a direct confrontation, write the harasser a letter. It is helpful to criticize the harasser's behavior rather than the harasser as a person. The intent is to stop the harassment and maintain a pleasant, productive work environment. There is also the chance that the harasser is not aware that his or her behavior is offensive. In this case, giving specific feedback is frequently effective.

2. *Be assertive.* When giving the harasser feedback, look him or her directly in the eye. Look as though you mean what you're saying. Don't smile. Rather, look the harasser directly in the eye, stand up straight, adopt a serious expression, and calmly state, "Please stop touching me by putting your arms around me and rubbing my neck. I don't like it." This is a serious matter. You need to get a serious point across.

3. *Document your situation.* Record every incident that occurs. Note when, where, who, and what was said or done, what you were wearing, and any available witnesses. Be as accurate as possible. Documentation does not have to be elaborate. Simple handwritten notes that state the facts will suffice. It is also a good idea to keep copies of your notes in another location.

4. *Talk to other people about the problem.* Get support from friends and colleagues. Sexual harassment often erodes self-confidence. Victims do not feel they are in control of the situation. Emotional support from others can bolster self-confidence and give victims the strength needed to confront sexual harassment. Frequently, sharing these problems with others will also allow victims to discover they're not alone. Corroboration from other victims will not only provide emotional support, but will also strengthen a formal complaint if that option needs to be taken sometime in the future. We have already established that telling someone with decision-making power is important in the event a suit is filed.

5. *Get witnesses.* Look around when the sexual harassment is occurring and note who can observe it. Talk to these people and solicit their support. Try to make arrangements for others to be around you when you anticipate that sexual harassment is likely to occur.

6. *Follow the established complaint procedure.* Ultimately, you have the right to work or be educated in a harassment-free environment. You have the options of using the complaint procedure established by the organization or filing a sexual harassment complaint with the EEOC. It is "unlawful to retaliate against an individual for opposing employment practices that discriminate based on sex or for filing a discrimination charge" (EEOC, 2008a).

HIGHLIGHT 9.3

Using Nonsexist Language

EP 2.1.1b, 2.1.3c

There are ways to minimize the use of sexist language. Frequently, all it takes is becoming accustomed to a different way of phrasing words and sentences. The following are some suggestions aimed at maximizing fairness and objectivity through language.

1. Replace the word *man* with other, more inclusive terms such as *human* or *person*. For example, *mankind* can become *humankind, chairman* can become *chairperson* or *chair*, and the *nature of man* can become *human nature*.
2. Use the term *Ms.* instead of *Miss* or *Mrs. Ms.* and *Mr.* are equivalent terms.
3. Try to phrase sentences so that the masculine pronouns *he, him,* and *his* can be avoided when referring to both sexes. This can be done in several ways. First, pronouns can be eliminated altogether. For example, "The average

American likes to drink *his* coffee black" can be changed to: "The average American likes black coffee." Second, statements can frequently be rephrased into the plural: "Average Americans like their coffee black."
4. Third, masculine pronouns can be replaced with *one, you,* or *his or her.* For example: "The average American likes to drink his or her coffee black." Avoid using patronizing and derogatory stereotypes. These include phrases such as *sweet young thing, the little lady, bubble-brained blonde, hen-pecked husband, frustrated spinster, nagging mother-in-law, dirty old man,* and *dumb jock.*

Many good suggestions can be found for using nonsexist language. However, the main idea is for a person to be sensitive to what he or she is saying. Subtle implications need to be examined in order to communicate accurately and objectively. This is especially true for social workers and is pertinent to what they say and write.

Many times English words themselves reflect an aura of sexism and unfairness. For instance, the word *man* seems to occur everywhere. Consider such words and phrases as *mankind, chairman, salesman, congressman,* and the *best man for the job.* Such terms often imply that women are included, but in a subsidiary way.

Another example of how sexism has infiltrated the English language is in the proper titles for men and women. On reaching adulthood, a man becomes a "Mr." for the remainder of his life. This is a polite term that makes no reference to the status of a man's personal life. A woman, however, traditionally starts as a "Miss." Following that tradition she becomes a "Mrs." upon marriage, which clearly establishes her marital status. At least it establishes the fact that at one time or another she has been married.

Highlight 9.3 offers some suggestions for replacing sexist language in everyday conversation.

LO 9-9 Examine Rape and Sexual Assault

The most intimate violation of a person's privacy and dignity is rape. According to the Bureau of Justice Statistics (BJS) (2013), *rape* is "forced sexual intercourse including both psychological coercion as

well as physical force." "This can include forced oral sexual activity, penile-vaginal sexual activity, and anal sexual activity. Penetration may be made by a body part [such as a penis or a finger] or an object. If a person is forced to do any of these things when he or she does not want to, that is rape" (Greenberg et al., 2014, p. 551). "*Attempted rape* includes [not only physical attempts, but also] verbal threats of rape" (Emphasis added) (BJS, 2013).

A *sexual assault* involves "a wide range of victimizations, separate from rape or attempted rape. These include attacks or attempted attacks generally involving unwanted sexual contact between victim and offender" (BJS, 2013). A sexual assault may entail the use of force or the verbal threat of force. Unwanted "grabbing or fondling" are sexual assaults (BJS, 2013).

Throughout their lives, the fear of assault and rape lingers in the minds of women. It is an act of violence over which they may feel they have neither control nor protection. Several aspects of sexual assault and rape will be addressed here to give an understanding of the effects on women and how women might best cope with the fact that rape exists. Note that we will refer to people who have survived sexual assault as *survivors*, not *victims*. Instead of focusing on a woman's weakness, which the word *victim* implies, we will use the term *survivor* to emphasize a woman's survival strengths.

A social worker counsels a rape survivor.

Incidence of Rape

The Federal Bureau of Investigation (FBI) (2014) reported 83,425 rapes in 2011; 93 percent of these were completed and 7 percent attempted. One study found that 20 percent of female college students said "they had been forced to have sexual intercourse, most often by someone known to them" (Brener, McMahon, Warren, & Douglas, 1999; Kelly, 2008, p. 458). Another long-term study found that almost 70 percent of college women reported having experienced some type of forced sexual interaction since age 14 (McCammon & Knox, 2007; O'Sullivan, 2005). A range of studies indicate that a woman has a 14 to 25 percent chance of being raped sometime during her life (Hyde & DeLamater, 2014; Koss, 1993). It is estimated that the number of rapes being reported is only 12 to 28 percent of those actually committed (Crooks & Baur, 2014).

Women fail to report being raped for many reasons. Survivors whose bodies have been brutally violated often desperately want to forget that the horror ever happened. To report it means dwelling on the details and going over the event again and again in their minds. Other survivors fear retribution from the rapist. If they call public attention to him, he might do it again to punish them. No police officer will be available all of the time for protection. Other survivors feel that people around them will think less of them because they've been raped. It's almost as if a part of them has been spoiled, a part that they would prefer to hide from other people. Rape is an ugly crisis that takes a great amount of courage to face.

Theoretical Views of Rape

EP 2.1.7a & b

There are at least three theoretical perspectives on why rape occurs (Albin, 1977; Baron & Straus, 1989; Hyde & DeLamater, 2014; Ward, 1995; Zurbriggen, 2010): victim precipitation of rape, the psychopathology of rapists, and the feminist perspective. The intent is not to state which one is the best theory but to present three different ways of conceptualizing rape.

Victim-Precipitated Rape

This perspective assumes that the survivor is actually to blame for the rape—that the woman "asked for it." Perhaps she was wearing provocative clothing or subconsciously desired to be raped.

An unfortunate example of how destructive this perspective can be is provided by a young female student who came to her instructor seeking help for her friend. Her friend, age 18, had attended a local festival the previous summer. The woman somehow got separated from her friends and found herself talking and flirting with two men about age 20. Because it was a hot July day, the woman was wearing a halter top and jeans. Suddenly, before she realized what had happened, the men shoved her into a car and swept her away to a city apartment. There they raped her throughout the night.

The next morning the men put her into the car and dropped her off at the festival entrance. In terror and tears, she called her father and, sobbing, explained what had happened. His response was, "I told you not to ask for it. Why do you have to dress like that?" The woman was crushed.

This father had adopted the victim-precipitated view of rape. He immediately assumed it was his daughter's fault. Unfortunately, the young woman did not recover very well. What she needed from her father was support and help. What she got was blame. Six months later, the young woman found herself terrified of men. Her reaction was so extreme that on the following New Year's Eve at midnight, she could not bear to watch people give each other New Year's kisses. She rushed from the room crying.

The instructor listening to the story strongly suggested that the young rape survivor get counseling help. She needed to work through her feelings and put the blame where it belonged, on her attackers.

Many male students have also found the victim-precipitated view offensive. The implication is that men are animalistic and cannot control their own impulses. Various men have indicated that they find this you-know-how-men-are point of view as degrading as women might find the you-know-how-women-are perspective. Neither perspective takes into account individual differences or personal morals and values.

Rapist Psychopathology

A second theoretical perspective concerns rapist psychopathology. This view proposes that the rapist is emotionally disturbed or mentally unbalanced. He rapes because he is sick. This view places virtually none of the blame on society or on social attitudes.

The Feminist Perspective on Rape

The feminist perspective emphasizes that rape is the logical reaction of men who are socialized to dominate women (Rosenthal, 2013). Rape is seen as a manifestation of men's need to aggressively maintain power over women. It has little to do with sexuality. Sexuality only provides a clear-cut means for exercising power. Rape is seen as a consequence of attitudes toward women that are intimately intertwined throughout the culture. The feminist perspective sees rape as a societal problem, rather than only an individual one.

Both aggressors and survivors are brought up to believe that sexual aggression is natural (Crooks & Baur, 2014; Herman, 1984). As a result, survivors often blame themselves. The rationale is that they should have expected to be raped. They should have been prepared or have done something to prevent it.

An analogous situation concerning self-blame is the example of a woman who has her purse snatched while shopping on a Saturday afternoon. If the self-blame concept were applied, it would follow that the woman would blame herself for the incident. She would chastise herself by saying that she never should have taken her purse with her to shop in the first place. Maybe she should shop only through the home-shopping channel from now on. Of course, taking that course of action would be absurd. It was not the woman's fault. It was the purse snatcher who broke the law. He is the one who should be held responsible.

The feminist view holds that society is wrong for socializing people to assume that male sexual aggression is natural. Socializing women to consider themselves weak and nurturant also contributes to the problem. It fosters a victim mentality—that is, an expectation that it's natural for women to be victims. The feminist perspective emphasizes that these attitudes need to be changed. Only then can rape as a social problem disappear.

Common Myths About Rape

Various myths about rape need to be examined and corrected. Women need accurate information in order to make responsible decisions. They need to learn what types of conditions and circumstances prompt rape so that they can be avoided.

One myth is that rapes tend to occur in dark alleys. Although some circumstances such as hitchhiking or walking home alone in the dark tend to increase the chances of being raped, many rapes occur in a woman's own residence (Kirk & Okazawa-Rey, 2013; Yarber & Sayad, 2013).

In cases occurring indoors, especially in their own homes, survivors are very likely to know the rapist. This presents a problem because people tend to feel safe when they're in their own homes with a person they know. However, knowledge of this fact is important if it helps people be more cautious.

One incident emphasizes the importance of caution. A 20-year-old female student sheepishly approached her instructor and finally blurted out that she had been raped at a party the past Saturday night. Although it was not in her home, it was in the home of a good friend. Apparently, people attending the party were drinking and not concerning themselves with the noise level. The student found herself talking with a young male lawyer while sitting on the bed in one of the bedrooms. Suddenly, the lawyer closed and locked the door. He pinned her to the bed and began to rape her. She was awestruck that this could be happening. Although he was not a good friend, he was an acquaintance. They shared several mutual friends. After all, he was even a lawyer. She resisted to the best of her ability. She was too ashamed to scream.

As she was talking about the incident several days later, her main concern was what her friends would think about her if they ever found out. Although she dreamed about getting revenge, she didn't want to jeopardize her reputation. As she continued to relate her story, her instructor discussed her feelings, the potential physical ramifications, and possible legal alternatives. Her instructor also helped the student gain a more objective perception of the incident. It was especially important for this survivor to place the blame where it belonged—on the rapist. Finally, her instructor referred her to counseling to give her a chance to work out and deal with the feelings about such a horrible experience.

Another myth is that only strangers are potential rapists (Greenberg et al., 2014; Rosenthal, 2013; Yarber & Sayad, 2013). According to the Bureau of Justice Statistics, 57 percent of sexual assaults and rapes were committed by someone the survivor knew, and 20 percent of perpetrators were intimate partners (Catalano, Smith, Snyder, & Rand, 2009). Acquaintance or date rapes have become common occurrences, particularly on college campuses.

Of special note are so-called date-rape drugs that are used to spike a woman's drink, cause her to lose consciousness, and make her vulnerable to rape. One such drug is Rohypnol (row-HIP-nawl), or "roofie." Another drug implicated in rapes is ketamine hydrochloride (Special K) (Crooks & Baur, 2014). Another drug, gamma hydroxybutyrate (GHB), poses an even greater threat because it can be lethal (Crooks & Baur, 2014). (Chapter 11 discusses these drugs further.) Women are encouraged to watch their drinks carefully from the time they're made to the time they finish them.

Still another rape myth is that women really "want to be raped" (Crooks & Baur, 2014, p. 510; Yarber & Sayad, 2013, p. 574). "This myth supports the misconception that a woman enjoys being raped because she sexually 'surrenders,' and it perpetuates the belief that rape is a sexual act rather than a violent one" (Yarber & Sayad, 2013, p. 575).

A woman always has the right to say no, and should be believed when she does. If you're a woman, are you looking forward to being raped? Or is your mother or sister secretly desiring to be raped? Of course not. That's how ridiculous this myth is.

One final myth that requires debunking is that "women ask for it" because of their behavior and the way they dress (Yarber & Sayad, 2013, p. 575). This myth places the responsibility for the violent and aggressive act on the victim, not the perpetrator. There is tremendous pressure on women in our culture to be attractive. Styles of clothing currently emphasize women's physical assets. A woman has the right to dress the way she wants and be attractive. "No one, female or male, ever deserves to be raped, and regardless of what a person says, does, or wears, she or he does not cause the rape. Actually, most rapes are premeditated and planned by the perpetrator. Opportunity is the critical factor in determining when a rapist will rape" (Yarber & Sayad, 2013, p. 575).

Highlight 9.4 proposes suggestions for rape prevention.

Profile of a Rapist

There is no clearly defined profile of a rapist in terms of occupation, educational level, marital status, prior criminal history, or even reasons for committing rape (Crooks & Baur, 2014; Hyde & DeLamater, 2014). However, a number of variables can predispose men to rape (Crooks & Baur, 2014;

HIGHLIGHT 9.4

Suggestions for Rape Prevention

EP 2.1.10i

Rape is not the survivor's fault. Women do not have control over being attacked. However, women can take some measures to minimize their chances of being assaulted. Most of these suggestions are simply matters of common sense. It is unfortunate that women must be extra cautious, must plan ahead, and sometimes must change patterns of behavior in minor ways. However, it is necessary.

The following four rape prevention suggestions are from: Women Organized Against Rape (WOAR, 2014):*

1. Be aware of the things around you. Notice the people and cars in your immediate surroundings. Think ahead about what areas might be especially dangerous in your usual walking routes. If you have to travel through such areas, think ahead about what you would do if you were attacked. Try to stay in well-lighted areas and walk in the middle of the sidewalk. Walking in the middle of the street when there is little traffic is also a possibility. If you can, use different routes to get where you are going, especially at night. Avoid establishing a predictable pattern for a potential assailant.

2. Be aware of your own behavior. Notice how you're standing or walking, and how you might appear to other people. Always walk with an air of confidence and strength. Try not to appear confused, vulnerable, or preoccupied, because attackers often look for such people. Walking with others or taking public transportation are other options.

    If you think someone is following you, don't be afraid to look behind you. You might want to cross the street or travel in another direction. If you continue to have the feeling that someone is following you, it's best to go to the nearest lighted store or house and call a friend or the police for help. Don't hesitate to scream for help if you feel you are in danger. Screaming "fire" or "police" is usually better than screaming words like "help" or "rape."

3. Trust yourself and your gut reactions. If you're feeling unsure about a dating situation or being at a certain party, change your circumstances. Leave or go to a public place with lots of people. Don't doubt yourself if you're being pressured to do something sexually that you don't want to do. Say, "NO."

4. Be vigilant about the whereabouts of your drinks. Keep a beverage in sight or take it with you. Don't give a potential perpetrator the opportunity to drug you and take advantage of you.

Some additional specific suggestions can also be followed for avoiding sexual assault when driving your car. First of all, try to park in well-lighted areas and have your car keys ready to use. Check the backseat before getting in. While driving, keep your car doors locked and your windows partly rolled up. If approached by someone while at a stoplight, put your hand on your horn and be ready to blow it. It's also a good idea to keep at least a quarter tank of gas in the car whenever you drive to avoid running out of gas in potentially dangerous situations.

If you should have car trouble, pull over to the side of the road and stay in the car with doors locked and windows raised. When no one is around, get out and raise the car's hood to alert others to your distress. It's best to wait until police come to assist you. In the event that a man should stop and volunteer help, roll your window down only slightly and ask that he call for police help. Although such persons offering assistance may have only the best intentions, there is no way to know for sure.

Hitchhiking is very dangerous and should be avoided. The best way to prevent sexual assault when hitchhiking is simply not to hitchhike at all.

There are also ways to maintain your safety at home. Outside entrances and hallways should all be well lighted. Doors should have good dead-bolt locks instead of simple key locks, which offer virtually no protection. Windows should also have locks so that potential assailants cannot enter that way. Women who live by themselves or with other women should use only their first initials on the mailboxes, which helps prevent potential assailants from targeting women. It's also very helpful to know your neighbors even if you live in a large, relatively impersonal apartment complex. You should know where you can go for help if you need it. Don't allow strangers into your home. If a man knocks on your door and says he's a serviceman, ask for identification and have him slide it under the door, or call his company for identification.

In the event of an attack, there are some guidelines that may help to lessen the probability of being raped (Crooks & Baur, 2014). The first suggestion is simply to run. It's more advantageous to get angry instead of scared and to react immediately. Screaming loudly is also suggested.

Traditional weapons such as guns or knives usually do not provide an effective defense. It's too easy for the attacker to take them away and use them on the victim. Rather, carrying ordinary objects such as whistles, keys, rings, umbrellas, or hat pins is helpful. To fight back, aim for the face, including eyes, ears, nose, and mouth, which are more sensitive to pain. Pulling hair is another option, and loud screams in the attacker's ear will stun him. Biting or kicking is sometimes effective. A kick aimed at his knees may be more effective in order to knock an attacker off balance, because he will be most likely to protect his genitals first.

*WOAR's address, One Penn Center, 1617 John F Kennedy Blvd., Suite 1100, Philadelphia, PA 19130; office telephone (215) 985-3315; telephone hotline (215) 985–3333; e-mail http://www.woar.org/index.php

Hall et al., 2005, 2006; Malamuth, 1998; Malamuth, Sockloskie, Koss, & Tanaka, 1991; Rathus et al., 2014). First, rapists tend to come from hostile, violent family environments. Perhaps they learned to demonstrate anger violently after witnessing or experiencing battery or sexual abuse. Second, perpetrators are more likely to have a history of delinquency. It makes sense that a potential rapist might associate with peers who also harbor hostile feelings and reinforce the idea of behaving aggressively to get what you want. Delinquency, of course, is also associated with hostile home environments. A third factor characterizing perpetrators is sexual promiscuity. Rapists might perceive that the violent subjugation of women enhances their self-esteem and status, especially within an angry or violent delinquent peer group. A fourth variable often characterizing rapists is that they are hostile toward women, scorning traits that might be construed as feminine such as empathy or nurturance (Hyde & DeLamater, 2014).

McCammon and Knox (2007) point out that rapists tend to believe in rape myths that they can use as a rationale for their behavior. McCammon and Knox (2007, p. 528) summarize a number of personality traits that often characterize rapists:

In addition to believing in rape myths, men who rape may share these characteristics: They ignore personal space (e.g., hands all over you), abuse alcohol or other drugs (reduced judgment), sexualize conversations, are dominant/aggressive, have rigid gender roles, use threats in displays of anger, have a quick temper, are sadistic [getting satisfaction from hurting others]/narcissistic [harboring an exaggerated sense of self importance and lack of empathy for others], and are impersonal/aloof emotionally (Fouts & Knapp, 2001; Laufersweiler-Dwyer & Dwyer, 2005; Rozee & Koss, 2000).

Rapists often harbor anger toward women (Rathus et al., 2014), which can be behaviorally expressed in violent sexual behavior. They often maintain hardened attitudes toward women, viewing them as sexual objects (Crooks & Baur, 2014). Other research has supported the idea that men who rape adhere to traditional gender-role stereotypes (Ben-David & Schneider, 2005; Crooks & Baur, 2014; Rathus et al., 2014). Rapists "may view women as owing them sexual favors. Their lack of empathy for others would negate the impact of their

victims' discomfort or suffering. Finally, their exaggerated sense of self-importance may facilitate their ability to rationalize their behavior" by using rape myths such as the victim really wanted it or asked for it (Crooks & Baur, 2014, p. 513).

Some research has established at least three basic categories of rapists—the anger rapist, the power rapist, and the sadistic rapist (McCabe and Wauchope, 2005; Yarber & Sayad, 2013). As the name implies, the key concept distinguishing an *anger rapist* is anger. He "displays his anger in overt ways, such as by using a knife, using force, displaying overwhelming anger, and projecting a macho image" (McCabe & Wauchope, 2005). The anger rapist may inflict substantial injury on victims ranging from verbal abuse to brutal beatings to murder, although the last is rare. The rage does not appear to be related to sexual gratification or to the goal of carrying out any sexual fantasies. Such assaults may be "a displaced expression of rage and anger, with the victim representing the person or group of people that the offender hates.... [A]nger may also be expressed as a means to humiliate women and put them in their place" (McCabe & Wauchope, 2005).

Although there are several subtypes of this category, the *power rapist* demonstrates his power by exploiting his victims. He often has a sexual dysfunction or an obvious physical deformity for which he is trying to compensate. By "being demeaning towards his victim, using moderate force, and a blitz style attack," he rapes to assert his power and control over his victim and dominate her (McCabe & Wauchope, 2005).

The *sadistic rapist* is motivated to assault in order to live out his sexual and aggressive fantasies. He gains gratification from restraining, torturing, or humiliating the victim by focusing on where she is most vulnerable—her sexuality. The sadistic rapist may resemble the angry rapist except for three things. First, he often does considerably more planning to orchestrate an attack designed to live out a specific fantasy. Second, the sadistic rapist derives gratification from hurting the victim. Third, anger may or may not be involved. The category under which a perpetrator falls depends to some extent on the amount of sadism, on the one hand, and anger, on the other, that is expressed during the assault.

Note that there is considerable variation in individual rapists. People, their motivations, and their behaviors are complex. Often, the categories of rapists overlap (McCabe & Wauchope, 2005).

Date Rape

As previously mentioned, women are in danger of being raped by someone they know and in a place where they feel safe. On college campuses, approximately 80 percent of rapes are perpetrated by someone known to the victim (Greenberg et al., 2014). It seems that many men feel that it is appropriate, expected, or at least tolerable to try to force women to have sex with them. Dates provide the perfect opportunity. Unfortunately, the vast majority of date rapes go unreported.

"Alcohol and/or drugs are often involved in date rapes … Men who believe in rape myths are more likely to see alcohol consumption as a sign that females are sexually available" (Yarber & Sayad, 2013, p. 576).

Another dynamic of date rape involves the misconception that although her words say "No, no," her eyes say "Yes, yes" (Greenberg et al., 2014; Rosenthal, 2013; Yarber & Sayad, 2013). In other words, there is a mythical idea that women love being raped, that they "really want it." There's also the idea that "she shouldn't have started it or let it go so far if she wasn't ready to go all the way." These misconceptions trap women. Women can't win under these conditions. On the one hand, there's the idea that "all she needs is a good_____," which implies that all women really want to have their animal sexual drives released by sex with a "good" man. So, the man, of course, is expected to try to release these imprisoned sexual drives. Women, in return, are expected to respond and to participate in some kind of sexual interaction with men they really care about. However, date-rape dynamics lead men to think that once a woman becomes involved in the developing sexual interaction, she loses her right of choice to stop. She's expected to finish what she has allowed to start.

McCammon and Knox (2007) report one college student's experience:

Last spring, I met this guy and a relationship started which was great. One year later, he raped me. The term was almost over and we would not be able to spend much time together during the summer. Therefore, we planned to go out to eat and spend some time together.

After dinner we drove to a park. I did not mind or suspect anything for we had done this many times. Then he asked me into the back seat. I got into the back seat with him because I trusted him and he said he wanted to be close to me as we talked. He began talking. He told me that he was tired of always pleasing me and not getting a reward. Therefore, he was going to "make love to me" whether I wanted to or not. I thought he was joking, so I asked him to stop playing. He told me he was serious, and after looking at him closely, I knew he was serious. I began to plead with him not to have sex with me. He did not listen. He began to tear my clothes off and confine me so that I could not move. All this time I was fighting him. At one time, I managed to open the door, but he threw me back into the seat, hit me, then he got on me and raped me. After he was satisfied, he stopped, told me to get dressed and stop crying. He said he was sorry it had to happen that way.

He brought me back to the dorm and expected me to kiss him good night. He didn't think he had done anything wrong. Before this happened, I loved this man very much, but afterward I felt great hatred for him. (p. 529)

Since then the young woman's life has changed. She no longer trusts men as she used to. She avoids intimacy with her current boyfriend because her memories are too painful. The boyfriend wants to know what's wrong. She won't tell him because he knows the guy who did it.

The point is not that rapists are worthless scum. From a helping professional's perspective, they are people who have problems, cause damage, and need help. However, the trouble is that, in many instances, the act of rape is glamorized and associated with positive behaviors and results.

> • • • •   **Ethical Question 9.4**
>
> *Why do you think men rape?*
>
> **EP 2.1.2**

Survivors' Reactions to Rape

Women can experience serious psychological effects that can persist for a half year or more following a rape (Burgess & Holstorm, 1974a, 1974b, 1988; Greenberg et al., 2014; Hyde & DeLamater, 2014; Yarber & Sayad, 2013). They call these emotional changes the *rape trauma syndrome*, "now considered to be a specific aspect of posttraumatic stress disorder" (Greenberg et al., 2014; Menna, 2011). *Posttraumatic stress disorder* (PTSD) is "a psychological reaction occurring after a highly stressing event (as wartime combat, physical violence, or a natural disaster) that is usually characterized by depression, anxiety, flashbacks, recurrent nightmares, and avoidance of reminders of the event" (Mish, 2008, p. 970). The rape trauma syndrome has two basic phases. The first is the *acute phase*, which involves the woman's emotional reactions immediately following the rape and up to several weeks thereafter. The survivor reacts in one of two ways (Carroll, 2013b; Masters et al., 1995; Rathus et al., 2014). She may show her emotions by crying, expressing anger, or showing fear. On the other hand, she may try to control these intense emotions and keep them from view. Emotions experienced during the acute phase range from humiliation and guilt to shock to anger and desire for revenge (Lott, 1994).

Additionally, during this phase women will often experience physical problems including difficulties related directly to the rape, such as irritation of the genitals or rectal bleeding from an anal rape. Physical problems also include stress-related discomforts such as headaches, stomach difficulties, or inability to sleep.

The two primary emotions experienced during the acute phase are fear and self-blame. Fear results from the violence of the experience. Many rape survivors report that during the attack they felt their life had come to an end. They had no control over what the attacker would do to them and were terrified. Such fear can linger. Often survivors fear that rape can easily happen again. The second emotion, self-blame, results from society's tendency to blame the victim, as discussed in the theory of victim-precipitated rape and the feminist perspective on rape.

The second stage of the rape trauma syndrome is the *long-term reorganization and recovery phase* (Carroll, 2013b; Yarber & Sayad, 2013). The emotional changes and reactions of this phase may linger on for years. Most rape survivors feel that the rape has changed their lives in one way or another. Reported reactions include fear of being alone, depression, sleeplessness, and most frequently,

an attitude of suspicion toward other people. Other long-term changes that sometimes occur include avoiding involvement with men (Greenberg et al., 2014; Masters et al., 1995; Yarber & Sayad, 2013) and suffering various sexual dysfunctions such as lack of sexual desire, aversion to sexual contact, or difficulties in having orgasms (Masters et al., 1995; Yarber & Sayad, 2013).

It is very important for survivors of rape to deal with even the most negative feelings and get on with their lives. In some ways rape might be compared to accepting the death of a loved one. The fact that either event has occurred cannot be changed. Survivors must learn to cope. Life continues.

Suggestions for Counseling Rape Survivors: Keys to Empowerment

Three basic issues are involved in working with a survivor of rape. First, she is most likely in a state of emotional upheaval. Her self-concept is probably seriously shaken. Various suggestions for helping a rape survivor in such a traumatic emotional state will be provided. Second, the rape survivor must decide whether to call the police and press charges. Third, the rape survivor must assess her medical status following the rape—for example, injuries or potential pregnancy.

EP 2.1.10e, g & j

Emotional Issues

Counseling survivors of rape involves three major stages (Collier, 1982). First, the counselor or social worker needs to provide the survivor with immediate warmth and support (Hyde & DeLamater, 2014). The survivor needs to feel safe; she needs to feel free to talk. She needs to ventilate and acknowledge her feelings before she can begin to deal with them. To the extent possible, the survivor should be made to feel she is now in control of her situation. She should not be pressured to talk, but rather encouraged to share her feelings.

Although it is important for the survivor to talk freely, it is also important that she not be grilled with intimate, detailed questions. She will have to deal with enough of those if she reports the incident to the police.

Frequently, the survivor will dwell on what she could have or should have done. It is helpful to emphasize what she did right. After all, she is alive, safe, and physically not severely harmed. She managed to survive a terrifying and dangerous experience. It is also helpful to indicate that she reacted normally, as anyone else in her situation would most probably have reacted. This does not mean minimizing the incident. It does mean objectively talking about how traumatizing and potentially dangerous the incident was. One other helpful suggestion for dealing with a rape survivor is to help her place the blame where it belongs—on the rapist. He chose to rape her. It was not her doing.

The second stage of counseling involves eliciting support from others. This support may include that of professional resources such as local rape crisis centers as well as support from people who are emotionally close to the survivor. Doege (2002) tells the story of Alice, a survivor of an exceptionally brutal rape by two men, and explains how difficult it was for her to deal with her friends' negative reactions:

"Why are all my friends acting so weird?" Alice wondered in the weeks after the attack. "I need to talk about this, but they can't."

One close friend, a male coworker, went on a three-day drinking binge after learning what happened. Months later, he still was deeply troubled and prone to occasional sullen periods when they were together.

Another friend—one she had been planning to meet the night she had been abducted—learned about the rapes the next day, and didn't talk to Alice again for 10 months. (p. 3L)

Sometimes those close to the survivor need to be educated. They need to know that what the survivor needs is warmth and support, and to feel loved. They must understand that she needs to talk about her feelings when she's ready. Questions that emphasize her feelings of self-blame (such as why she didn't fight back or why she was wearing a low-cut blouse) should be completely avoided.

The third stage of counseling involves rebuilding the survivor's trust in herself, in the environment around her, and in her other personal relationships. Rape weakens a woman. It destroys her trust in herself and in others. This stage of counseling needs to focus on the survivor's objective evaluation of herself and her situation. Her strong points need to be clarified and emphasized so that she can gain confidence in herself.

The survivor also needs to look objectively at her surrounding environment. She cannot remain cooped up in her apartment for the rest of her life. It is impractical and unfair. She can take precautions against being raped, but needs to continue living a normal life.

Finally, the survivor needs to assess her other personal relationships objectively. Even though she was intimately violated by one aggressor, it has nothing to do with the other people in her life. She needs to concentrate on the positive aspects of her other relationships. She must not allow the fear and terror she experienced during that one horrible incident to color and taint other relationships. She must clearly distinguish the rape from her other relationships.

A raped woman may initially want to talk with another woman. However, it might also be beneficial to talk to men, including those close to her. It is important for the survivor to realize that not all men are rapists. Sometimes there is a male partner. His willingness to let the survivor express her feelings, and in return offer support and empathy, may be the most beneficial thing that can be done for her.

Reporting to the Police

The initial reaction to being raped might be to call the police and relate the incident. However, many survivors choose not to do this. There are numerous reasons why this is so, including fear that the rapist will try to get revenge, fear of public embarrassment and derogation, an attitude that it won't matter anyway because most rapists get off free, and fear of the legal process and questioning (Masters et al., 1995; Rosenthal, 2013). It's financially expensive and emotionally draining to take a rape case to court. In reality, even when they are persistent, women have found it difficult to have rapists prosecuted. In many cases, as we've already discussed, police determine that the case is unfounded.

A study conducted by the University of Kentucky Center for Research on Violence Against Women (2011) reported the following findings:

- A national study estimates only 37% of reported rapes are prosecuted.
- 18% of prosecuted rape cases end in a conviction....
- The criminal justice system can often deter women from continuing their cases due to secondary victimization. Women may be retraumatized by

having to repeatedly tell their story and detailed investigations by law enforcement may make survivors feel like they are not believed....

- Prosecutors often only take cases they can win, for rape cases many factors may be considered. Often cases are unwittingly approached with rape myths and stereotypes about race, class, gender, and the deservingness of rape victims.
- Research shows that even when charges are filed, the legal system often downgrades or drops felony rape charges for guilty pleas on other crimes. This often does not feel like justice for survivors since the offender never has to admit or acknowledge that his actions were rape.

Rape prosecution laws vary greatly from one state to another (Rosenthal, 2013). States can make progressive changes in their sexual assault prosecution laws to improve the situation for survivors (Greenberg et al., 2014). They can make the survivor's past sexual history inadmissible for presentation in court. When such information is introduced, it can serve to humiliate and discredit the survivor. More progressive laws can impose stricter penalties that focus on the amount of harm done to the survivor and the amount of force used in the assault, instead of how hard the survivor tried to fight off the assault. Additionally, laws should allow a wife to prosecute her husband for sexual assault when he forces sexual relations on her.

Despite the potential difficulties in reporting a rape, if the survivor does not report it, the rapist will not be held responsible for his actions. A rape survivor needs to think through the various alternatives that are open to her and weigh their respective positive and negative consequences in order to come to this often difficult decision.

In the event that a survivor decides to report, she should not take a shower. Washing will remove vital evidence. However, survivors often feel defiled and dirty, and it is a logical initial reaction for them to want to cleanse themselves and try to forget that the rape ever occurred. In counseling situations, it's important to emphasize the reason for not washing immediately.

Reporting a rape should be done within 48 hours at the absolute latest. The sooner the rape is reported and the evidence gathered, the better the chance of being able to get a conviction.

Medical Status of the Victim

A third major issue that rape survivors need to address is their medical status following the assault. At some point, the survivor needs to attend to the possibility of pregnancy. She should be asked about this issue at an appropriate time and in a gentle manner. She should be encouraged to seek medical help both for this possibility and for screening for sexually transmitted infections, including HIV. The negative possibilities should not be emphasized. However, the survivor needs to attend to these issues at some point. And the survivor should, of course, be urged to seek immediate medical care for any physical injury.

Ethical Question 9.5

What should be the consequences for men who rape?

EP 2.1.2

LO 9-10 Explore Domestic Violence and Battered Women

Terms associated with wife beating include *domestic violence*, *family violence*, *spouse abuse*, and *battered women*. *Battering* is a catchall term that includes, but is not limited to, physical abuse that may involve slapping, punching, knocking down, choking, kicking, hitting with objects, threatening with weapons, stabbing, and shooting, and emotional abuse that involves "the instillment of fear, oppression and control of the victim" (Barnett, Miller-Perrin, & Perrin, 2005, p. 252). The *battered woman syndrome* implies the systematic and repeated use of one or more of the above against a woman by her husband or lover.

Some of the myths about battered women include the following (Barnett, Miller-Perrin, & Perrin, 2011):

- Battery is rare and infrequent.
- Battered women aren't really hurt that badly.
- Beatings and other abuses just happen; they aren't a regular occurrence.
- "Battered women 'ask for it' " (p. 34).
- Wife battering only occurs in lower-class families.

White, Donat, and Bondurant (2009) comment on the incidence of violence toward women in intimate relationships:

> The greatest threat to adult women is from their intimate partners; for men, the greatest threat is from other men. Women are more likely to be physically or sexually assaulted by an intimate partner than by a stranger. It is estimated that 2 to 3 million women are assaulted by male partners in the United States each year and that at least half of these women are severely assaulted.... As many as 21% to 34% of women will be assaulted by an intimate partner during adulthood. Further, it is estimated that 33% to 50% are also the victim of partner rape. Studies have shown that 22% to 40% of the women who seek health care at clinics or emergency rooms are victims of battering.
>
> Intimate violence may escalate resulting in homicide. Approximately 66% of family violence deaths are women killed by their male partners; over 50% of all murders of women are committed by current or former partners. In contrast, only 6% of male murder victims are killed by wives or girlfriends. (pp. 126–127)

The situation in Canada is also frightening with regard to both battering and sexual assault. Ann Jones (2008) reports:

> Statistics Canada attempted to find out by interviewing 12,300 women nationwide in the most comprehensive study of violence against women ever undertaken. The results were worse than expected. They showed violence against women to be far more common than earlier, smaller scale studies had indicated. They revealed that more than half of Canadian women (51 percent) have been physically or sexually assaulted at least once in their adult lives. And more than half of those women said they'd been attacked by dates, boyfriends, husbands, friends, family members, or other men familiar to them. One in ten Canadian women, or one million, had been attacked in the past year. (p. 483)

In the vast majority of heterosexual partner-abuse cases, men abuse women (Barnett et al., 2011; Hyde & Else-Quest, 2013; Papalia & Feldman, 2012). Although some women abuse their male partners, the dynamics in these cases are often different. Because women are generally smaller and weaker than men, they are much more likely to experience serious harm than men (Davis, 1995; Gibbs, 1998; Hyde & Else-Quest, 2013; Renzetti et al., 2012). Men are generally bigger and stronger than women and can thus expend greater force.

Renzetti and her colleagues (2012) propose that the motivations of men and women who participate in battering differ. Men tend to use violence as a means of control or when they feel their authority has been questioned. Women, on the other hand, tend to use violence in self-defense or when they fear being attacked (Barnett, Lee, & Thelan, 1997; Dobash, Dobash, Cavanagh, & Lewis, 1998; White et al., 2009).

Battered women don't like to be beaten. They may initially experience "shock, disbelief, and denial, followed by terror, then attempts to reestablish the level of safety previously believed to have existed, followed by depression with intermittent inner-directed rage and outbursts of anger" (Barnett et al., 2011; Harway, 1993, p. 38). Women go to domestic violence programs for help to stop the beatings and maintain their marriages.

Battering women is not limited to poor families or families of particular racial, ethnic, or cultural backgrounds, although it occurs more frequently in families with very low incomes and economic problems (Barnett et al., 2011; Brush, 2000; Kirk & Okazawa-Rey, 2013; Renzetti et al., 2012; Shaw & Lee, 2012; Tolman, 1999). Women of color are more likely to be abused, but this is complicated by the fact that they are over-represented in impoverished populations (Barnett et al., 2011; Kirk & Okazawa-Rey, 2013; Renzetti et al., 2012).

The Abusive Perpetrator

A series of traits tend to characterize men who batter their female partners. They are likely to adhere to common masculine gender-role stereotypes, such as not displaying emotion or sensitivity to others, because they perceive these as reflecting weakness (Shaw & Lee, 2012). Batterers likely feel it's important to maintain male dominance in society and to keep women under control; "gender-based violence against women is still widely considered normal, acceptable, and justifiable" (Barnett et al., 2011; Sapiro, 1999, p. 191; Shaw & Lee, 2012).

Batterers may be insecure and jealous, which results in their lashing out viciously when threatened and trying to isolate their partner (Carlson, 2008;

Hyde & Else-Quest, 2013). The consequence can be serious injury for a female partner, and even murder (Basile & Black, 2011).

Although battering occurs in all classes and at all socioeconomic levels, stress from job loss or poverty, or emotional distress such as depression, can contribute to the potential for violence (Basile & Black, 2011; Hyde & Else-Quest, 2013). Even family holidays such as Thanksgiving and Christmas can initiate enough stress to trigger abusive incidents (Bennett, 1995; Davis, 1995; Sapiro, 1999). It can also be "very stressful for some men to have wives with higher-status occupations because the men have learned that they are supposed to be superior to their wives" (Sapiro, 1999, p. 191). Alcohol use is linked to violent episodes (Basile & Black, 2011; Carlson, 2008; Mooney, Knox, & Schacht, 2013; Renzetti et al., 2012; Walker, 2009).

The Battering Cycle

Three basic phases tend to characterize battery in an intimate relationship (Barnett et al., 2011; Davis, 1995; Walker, 1979, 2009; Women's Resource Center, 2013). In the first phase, stress and tension build up. The woman tries to make things okay and

Battering usually occurs during the second phase of the battering cycle, the explosion. It is preceded by a phase of building tension and followed by a phase of making up.

James W. Porter/Cusp/Corbis

avoid confrontations. There may be a few minor abusive incidents.

The second phase in the battering cycle is the explosion. This is when the battering occurs. It is generally the shortest of the three phases, but it may last for up to several days.

The third phase involves making up. Once the man's tension has been released, he adamantly states that he is truly sorry for what he has done. He swears he will never do it again. The battered woman relents and believes him. He is forgiven and all seems well—until the cycle of violence begins again.

Why Does She Stay?

Women stay in the battering environment for many reasons. Many women who seek help from shelters, and even initiate separation through the courts, eventually return to their abusive home situations as the cycle of violence progresses. The reasons

EP 2.1.7b

why they remain or return include economic dependence, lack of self-confidence, lack of power, fear of the abuser, guilt, feeling isolated with nowhere to go, fear for their children, and love.

Economic Dependence

Many battered women stay with the perpetrator for economic reasons (Basile & Black, 2011; Hyde & Else-Qquest, 2013; Shaw & Lee, 2012). Many are financially dependent on the abuser as the primary wage earner for themselves and their children. Although battering occurs at all socioeconomic levels, it is more likely to happen in families with fewer resources.

Lack of Self-Confidence

Domestic violence involves not only physical abuse but also sexual abuse and psychological abuse (Papalia & Feldman, 2012; Shaw & Lee, 2012). Psychological abuse may entail regular tirades by battering men who criticize and blast survivors with derogatory remarks. Bit by bit, such treatment eats away at women's self-esteem and shrinks self-confidence. Perpetrators tend to claim that their female partners couldn't survive without them, and after an extended period of time, many of these women start to believe them. In some ways, psychological abuse is similar to the brainwashing of war prisoners (Davis, 1995).

It takes initiative and courage to muster the self-confidence required to leave a painful situation and strike out for the unknown. The unknown is frightening. At least if the domestic violence survivor remains in the home, she knows she has a place to stay. Often, it takes five to seven attempts at leaving an abuser before a survivor permanently succeeds (Doege, 2002).

Lack of Power

A battered woman views herself as having significantly less power in her relationship with an abusive man than does a woman with a partner who is nonviolent (Kirk & Okazawa-Rey, 2013; Walker, 2009). Battered women see their relationships as almost completely dominated by the perpetrator. Batterers' systematic regimen of intimidation, criticism, and violence places women in a vulnerable and difficult position. However, it should be noted that even in the face of such adversity, which for many is daily torture, these woman utilize their strengths; Burstow (1992) explains:

> They are not simply submitting, even where submission is key and even though submission is expectable and blameless. They are also making active and critical decisions about how to cope and survive on a moment-to-moment basis. They are deciding to hide certain things. They are deciding to duck. They are deciding not to duck. They are each in her own way also resisting. They are actively and passively resisting violation, whether that resistance takes the form of numbing themselves so that they will not feel the pain, finding ways of avoiding the abuser's ire, or saying no. (p. 153)

Fear of the Abuser

It is logical for a battered woman to fear brutal retaliation by the perpetrator if she leaves him (Barnett et al., 2011; Basile & Black, 2011; Hyde & Else-Quest, 2013; Papalia & Feldman, 2012; Shaw & Lee, 2012). A man who has dealt with stress by physical brutality might do so again if his female partner leaves him. The battered woman might even fear death at the hands of an abandoned male partner. One myth is that battered women stay in their relationships because they *like* being beaten. This is not true. For reasons discussed here, they tolerate their circumstances in order to survive.

The following excerpt from a novel titled *The Woman Who Walked into Doors* describes what it's like to be under an abusive partner's thumb:

> *For seventeen years. There wasn't one minute when I wasn't afraid, when I wasn't waiting. Waiting for him to go, waiting for him to come. Waiting for the fist, waiting for the smile. I was brainwashed and brain dead, a zombie for hours, afraid to think, afraid to stop, completely alone. I sat at home and waited. I mopped up my own blood. I lost all my friends, and most of my teeth. He gave me a choice, left or right; I chose left and he broke the little finger on my left hand. Because I scorched one of his shirts. Because his egg was too hard. Because the toilet seat was wet. Because because because. He demolished me. He destroyed me. (Doyle, 1996, pp. 176–177, cited in Chornesky, 2000, pp. 491–492)*

Guilt

Many battered women feel it is their own fault that they are abused (Barnett et al., 2011; Shaw & Lee, 2012). They tend to believe in men being the dominant decision makers and leaders of the family, and that women should be submissive and obedient. To some extent this guilt may be due to their husbands telling them that they're to blame for causing trouble. Perhaps because of their low self-esteem, it's easy for them to be critical of themselves. Their beliefs in traditional gender-role stereotypes may cause them to wonder how they have failed in their nurturant role of wife.

Feeling Isolated with Nowhere to Go

Battered women often try to keep the facts of their battering a secret. They may feel isolated from friends and family (Papalia & Feldman, 2012; Renzetti et al., 2012; Shaw & Lee, 2012). Frequently, the perpetrator strongly discourages his female partner's interactions with friends and family. He criticizes them. He makes it as difficult as possible for her to communicate with them. He gradually gets her to cut others off. When the abuser becomes everything to the survivor, losing him means that she will be all alone.

Fear for Her Children

A battered woman usually fears for her children's safety. First, she might be worried about her ability to support them financially on her own (Basile & Black, 2011; Hyde & Else-Quest, 2013; Renzetti et al., 2012). Second, she may firmly adhere to the belief that children need a father. She may think that a father who abuses his wife is better than no father at all. Third, she may even fear losing custody of her children. The abuser may threaten to take them away from her. She may have little knowledge of the complicated legal system and may believe that he can and will do it.

Love

Many battered women still feel love or emotional attachment to their abusive husbands (Barnett et al., 2011; Basile & Black, 2011). Many who seek help would prefer to remain in their relationships if the battering could be stopped (Chornesky, 2000; Hyde & Else-Quest, 2013). Walker (1979) cited one older woman's reactions to the death of her husband, who had battered her throughout their 53-year marriage. The woman stated, "We did everything together.... I loved him; you know, even when he was brutal and mean.... I'm sorry he's dead, although there were days when I wished he would die.... He was my best friend.... He beat me right up to the end.... It was a good life and I really do miss him."

Note that battering does not occur only in heterosexual relationships. It may also occur in lesbian and gay relationships. Spotlight 9.4 introduces the issue of battering in such relationships.

Community Responses to Empower Battered Women: Their Alternatives

Despite the difficulties in dealing with domestic violence, definite intervention strategies can be undertaken. They involve police departments, shelters, and specific counseling approaches.

EP 2.1.5b, 2.1.8a

The Police, Social Policy, and Battered Women

Police officers are usually the first outside means of intervention in episodes of domestic abuse. Historically, police have often tried to avoid intervention in domestic struggles, feeling that people should take care of their own problems privately at home (Barnett et al., 2011). In the past, police have generally been lenient to batterers (Erez & Belknap, 1998). Domestic violence was trivialized as domestic spats (Berk, Fenstermaker, & Newton, 1988; Kirk & Okazawa-Rey, 2013). "Blaming or humiliating

---

SPOTLIGHT ON DIVERSITY 9.4

Battering in Gay and Lesbian Relationships

EP 2.1.4

White and her colleagues (2009) explain how battering can occur in gay and lesbian relationships:

Relationship abuse is not limited to heterosexual relationships. Although there have been no prevalence studies, research with convenience samples indicates that partner abuse is a significant problem for lesbian women and gay men. Gay male couples report slightly less sexual abuse than lesbian couples, but more severe physical violence. Apparently, violence in committed relationships is not simply a gender issue. Issues of power and control arise in all relationships, and provide the basis for abuse. Partner abuse has been associated with issues of power and dependency in both lesbian and heterosexual couples. For lesbians and gay men, the internalization of societal homophobic

attitudes may, in part, lead to aggression against partners and reduce reporting due to threats that they may be "outed" by their partner. For gay men, the fear of AIDS or the stress of having AIDS or caring for a partner with AIDS may be associated with abuse. Fortunately, shelters and organizations are slowly beginning to assimilate information on the issue. For gay men, there are still few resources. (pp. 127–128)

Note that lesbian and gay people experience additional stress because of the homophobia and discrimination to which they are subjected; the additional potential threat of exposing a partner's sexual orientation to unaware work colleagues, family, or friends can escalate this stress (Carlson, 2008). Furthermore, social services are usually directed at and more readily available to the heterosexual population; revealing one's non-heterosexual orientation in order to receive services can be threatening in itself (Carlson, 2008).

comments" to survivors "such as, 'It's your own fault. You shouldn't have married him' " (Barnett et al., 2005, p. 275) or "Why didn't you just leave?" should never be made.

Some recommend that it is crucial for police to take such situations seriously and follow through on existing laws (Lemon, 2002). One group of experts on domestic violence recommends that police "comply with four major strategies: (a) identify the primary aggressor, (b) execute a proarrest or mandatory arrest policy, (c) gather evidence at the scene for use in prosecutions, and (d) arrange for a temporary restraining or no-contact order" (Barnett et al., 2005, p. 274, 2011; Healey, Smith, & O'Sullivan, 1998).

Jones (2008) expresses a negative view of how many battering situations are handled:

In the short run, the most effective way to protect women and children, save lives, and cut down violence is to treat assault as the crime it is: to arrest batterers and send them to jail.

Usually, that's not what happens. Right now, most batterers suffer no social or legal consequences at all for their criminal behavior. Although police in most states and localities are now authorized to arrest batterers, many police departments still don't enforce the law. If police do make arrests, prosecutors commonly fail to prosecute. And if batterers are convicted, judges often release them—or worse, order them into marital counseling with the women they've assaulted. Many men are required to attend a few weekly sessions of a therapeutic support group where they shoot the breeze with other batterers, after which their crime is erased from the record books.... The average batterer taken into custody by police is held less than two hours. He walks away laughing at his victim and at the police as well. (p. 486)

On the other hand, many police departments, despite their previous reluctance, are taking an increasingly active interest in addressing family violence (Barnett et al., 2005; Kirk & Okazawa-Rey, 2013). Because of the seriousness of the issue and the high potential for fatality and injury, they are acknowledging that something must be done. For example, training programs targeting domestic violence are being developed for police and other personnel working with battered women (Renzetti

et al., 2012). One thrust of these programs is the development of specialized interpersonal skills for dealing with such situations. Some police departments have made significant progress by developing *"specialized police units"* to address such domestic violence situations (Barnett et al., 2011, p. 394).

Kirk and Okazawa-Rey (2013) reflect on the current state of policy initiatives:

Forty years ago there were no U.S. laws concerning domestic violence. Now there is a growing, if uneven, body of law, mainly at the state level, including protection orders that prohibit the abuser from coming near or contacting the woman and her children. (p. 271)

Some states have implemented mandatory arrest laws under which police must remove people who have been violent. Such laws allow "judges to exert some control over perpetrators. Judges may, for example, compel offenders to seek treatment, place them under probation, or take other actions," such as removing the batterer from the home in order to avoid harm to the partner and children (Barnett et al., 2005, p. 276). The effectiveness of such laws is currently under debate. Others have raised concerns over inappropriate judicial behavior, lack of judicial training, and judges' failure to follow sentencing guidelines (Barnett et al., 2011).

The federal Violence Against Women Act (VAWA) of 1994 "includes increased funding for battered women's shelters and programs, a mandate for harsher penalties for batterers, and a provision that makes crossing state lines in pursuit of a fleeing partner a federal offense" (Renzetti et al., 2012, p. 208). Additionally, VAWA "prohibits the purchase and possession of firearms by defendants who have a PO [protection order or civil restraining order] issued against them. VAWA also requires states to honor protective orders issued by other states, tribes, or nations and to encourage or mandate arrests for violations of POs" (Miller, Iovanni, & Kelley, 2011, p. 274). "Research has found that VAWA has resulted in more aggressive criminal justice responses to violence against women and more contact between victims and criminal justice and legal authorizes" (Renzetti et al., 2012, p. 208).

Numerous other suggestions have been made for improving policy and empowering battered women (Barnett et al., 2005, 2011). First, legislatures should require training about domestic violence for everyone involved in the criminal justice system. Second, laws prohibiting the carrying of weapons by perpetrators should be established and upheld. Survivors should be made to feel as safe as possible. Third, communities should develop and fund legal services, with attorneys having an expertise in domestic violence issues, to help survivors negotiate the complex legal system. Fourth, in potentially violent and dangerous situations, restraining orders should not only be issued, but should also be enforced to enhance a survivor's safety. Fifth, schools, communities, and society in general should "change the lingering patriarchal practices that undermine female … victims' opportunities to lead violence-free lives" (Barnett et al., 2005, p. 280).

Epstein (1999) discusses a case in which the criminal justice system failed.

> *Over a year's time, two different police departments responded to 22 calls from Karen and Richard Graves's residence. None of the police officers involved was aware of any of the previous calls. Although Richard seriously injured Karen by hitting her with the baby's car seat, stomping on her ear, and assaulting her, several different judges set aside six different warrants for Richard's arrest. Karen and Richard appeared before 10 different judges (none of whom had any notification of previous cases and rulings) at 16 hearings in the local family and criminal courts.*
>
> *Three different judicial officers at eight separate hearings heard Karen's petitions for divorce, custody, and child support. Richard participated in three separate court-ordered counseling programs for alcohol and drug abuse and anger management. Advocates from four different agencies (e.g., child protective services) addressed various problems the couple had, but none of the agencies communicated with any of the others.*
>
> *When Karen started seeing a new boyfriend, Richard fired a gun near Karen and made repeated death threats that Karen reported. Eventually, Karen wrote a letter to the court begging the court to read the entire file of her case, to force Richard to follow the court's directives, and to protect her and her children. Six months later, Richard killed Karen with a shotgun and then killed himself. (p. 3)*

Ethical Question 9.6

What could and should have been done to protect Karen Graves?

EP 2.1.2

Shelters for Battered Women

The most immediate need of a battered woman who seeks to flee her situation is a place to go. For this purpose, shelters have been developed around the country. Late 1973 marked the opening of the first U.S. shelter for battered women, Rainbow Retreat, in Phoenix, Arizona (Hutchins & Baxter, 1980).

Such shelters and domestic violence programs provide a safe place where battered women can obtain *temporary shelter*. "The typical maximum stay at a domestic violence shelter is 30 days, although most programs offer extensions as needed" (Sullivan & Gillum, 2001, p. 249). The following describes a woman's initial involvement with a shelter:

> *Although domestic violence shelter programs are not all alike, most share certain commonalities. Most shelter stays begin with a telephone call from a woman who has either just been assaulted or who knows she is in imminent danger of being assaulted. The staff person or volunteer who answers the call is trained to assess the immediacy of the situation, to provide emotional support and understanding, and to arrange for the woman to come directly to the shelter, to receive medical attention at a local hospital, or to go to the home of a friend or relative.*
>
> *If the shelter volunteer determines with the woman that the best option is for the survivor to enter the shelter, arrangements are made for her to get there safely. Most shelters have a policy that they will not pick women up from their homes, as doing so could result in danger to the woman and/or shelter volunteer if the perpetrator is still present. Not picking women up at their homes also minimizes the risk of perpetrators following the car to the shelter, which is generally in a confidential location. Some shelters allow their*

volunteers to pick women up from hospitals, hotels, or other locations deemed safe to both the volunteer and the family. Some women can arrange their own transportation to the shelter, either driving their own cars or taking public transportation.

It is important to understand that most women choose to enter shelter programs only as a last resort. The woman has likely just experienced a traumatic event, she is in both physical and emotional pain, and, if she has children, she is trying to comfort them and think of their needs as well. Entering a brand new environment that involves living collectively with many other women and children, having little to no privacy, and abiding by numerous rules that come with such a living situation is not something most women look forward to doing. If they can stay with friends or relatives, if they can secure their homes to feel safe living there, or if they can afford to move either temporarily or permanently, these choices are generally deemed more desirable and less traumatic for women and their children. Unfortunately, many women lack the social and economic resources to choose any of these options, and for them, a shelter is the best alternative. (Sullivan & Gillum, 2001, p. 248)

EP 2.1.10k

Domestic violence shelters and programs often provide a range of other services in addition to temporary shelter (Association for the Prevention of Family Violence (APFV), 2014). *Crisis phone lines* can provide immediate assistance when women are in the midst of or have just experienced domestic violence and sexual assault crises. *Counseling* is often provided to offer support, help women look objectively at their situations, develop safety plans in the event a crisis occurs, talk about potential alternatives, and help women make their own decisions about what they feel is best for them. *Advocacy* can involve offering assistance to victims in obtaining outside community resources or services (such as health or housing) and networking with agencies in the community (APFV, 2014). *Public education* presented to a range of audiences can teach community residents about domestic violence and sexual assault. *Legal advocacy* can help domestic violence survivors negotiate the legal system, obtain restraining orders, and address divorce and custody issues. *Children's services* may include

individual counseling, support groups, and public education (APFV, 2014). Information and referral services can link battered women and their families to the resources they need. *Support groups* for domestic violence survivors can provide not only mutual support, but also suggestions from others regarding how to handle situations group members have commonly encountered. *Batterer's intervention programs* can work with people who batter to educate them about the dynamics involved in domestic violence, teach anger management techniques, enhance self-esteem to decrease the need to control, and develop alternatives to abusive behavior.

There are endless possibilities for innovative types of services that domestic violence programs can provide. "Transitional housing programs are designed to help survivors and their children as they make the transition from a domestic violence shelter to a more permanent residence. Such housing often is provided in apartment units where women can live for a set period of time or until they can obtain permanent housing" (Sullivan & Gillum, 2001, p. 253). Other innovative resources include "intervention services to abused pregnant teens and their children; a comprehensive program of age-appropriate activities for preschool children; services to meet the educational needs and goals of teenage residents; … bilingual English/Spanish services; … employment assistance; … and substance abuse prevention and education" (Sullivan & Gillum, 2001, p. 253).

Counseling Strategies for Empowerment

The following are some basic suggestions gathered from a range of sources regarding how social workers and counselors can help battered women (Burstow, 1992; DePorto, 2003; Petretic-Jackson & Jackson, 1996; Register, 1993; Walker, 2009).

EP 2.1.10b, e, g & j

The Initial Interview A battered woman is probably very anxious during her initial meeting with a social worker or counselor. She may be worried about what to say. The counselor should try to make the survivor as comfortable as possible and emphasize that she doesn't have to talk about anything she doesn't want to.

The survivor may also feel that the counselor will be judgmental and critical. It is important that the counselor put personal feelings aside and not pressure the battered woman into any particular course of action. This may be especially difficult when the counselor has strong feelings that the survivor should leave the abusive situation. A basic principle is that it is the woman's decision as to what she will choose to do. In those cases in which the survivor chooses to return home, it may be useful for the counselor to help her clarify the reasons behind that decision.

Confidentiality may also be an issue for the battered woman. She may be fearful of the abuser's finding out that she is seeking help and of his possible retaliation. The counselor needs to assure her that no information will be given to anyone without her consent. In the event that the survivor does need a place to go, it should be made clear to her that shelter is available.

The survivor may show some embarrassment at being a "battered woman." The label may make her feel uncomfortable. The counselor should make an effort to downplay any embarrassment by emphasizing that the woman is a survivor of victimization and that her situation has nothing to do with her character or with her intrinsic human value.

Offer Support
A battered woman has probably been weakened both physically and emotionally. She needs someone to empathize with her and express genuine concern. She needs some time to sit back, experience some relief, and think.

Encourage Expression of Feelings
Many battered women will display a range of emotional reactions, including helplessness, fear, anger, guilt, embarrassment, and even doubts about their sanity. The counselor needs to encourage the survivor to get all of these emotions out in the open. Only then will she be able to deal with them. The counselor can then help the survivor to look objectively at various aspects of her situation and help get control of her own life.

Focus on Strengths
One aspect of counseling that is easy to forget is focusing on the survivor's strengths. A battered woman will probably be suffering from low self-esteem. She probably needs help in identifying her positive characteristics.

Furnish Information
Most survivors probably don't have much information about how they can be helped. Information about available legal, medical, and social services may open up alternatives to them to better enable them to help themselves.

Review Alternatives
A battered woman may feel trapped. She may be so overwhelmed that alternatives other than surviving in her abusive situation may not even have occurred to her. Her alternatives may include returning to the marriage, getting counseling for both herself and her partner, temporarily separating from him, establishing other means of financial support and independent living conditions for herself, or filing for divorce.

A battered woman is often overwhelmed and confused. One of the most helpful things a counselor can do is to help her sort through her various problems. A survivor cannot do everything at once. However, she can begin getting control of her life by addressing one issue at a time and making decisions step by step.

Establish a Safety Plan
One other important counseling technique is helping the survivor establish a safe plan of action. She needs to clearly understand and define what she chooses to do. This choice may include formulating major goals such as divorcing her husband. It may involve setting smaller subgoals such as developing a list of existing day-care centers she can call to find out about available child-care options.

Advocate
An advocate can seek out information for a survivor of domestic violence and provide her with encouragement. An advocate can also help the survivor get in touch with legal, medical, and social service resources and find her way

EP 2.1.10k

through bureaucratic processes. Perhaps, an even more critical aspect of advocacy involves changing legal macro systems, as discussed earlier.

LO 9-11 Identify Means of Empowering Women

Social workers can help women regain their sense of having power and of being in control of their lives. The "personal traits that have clearly been shown to relate positively to measures of self-esteem or

EP 2.1.10l

subjective well-being are the same for women as for men; and include assertiveness, independence, self-responsibility, and efficacy, characteristics typically included in the stereotype of masculinity" (Lott, 1987, p. 277). Social workers can help women build up their self-confidence and self-esteem. Positive qualities can be identified and emphasized. Social workers can help women recognize the various alternatives available to them and evaluate the pros and cons of each. Decision-making and problem-solving skills can be taught. Success at using such skills breeds more success. Once women have learned the process of making their own decisions and solving their own problems, they can apply these skills to more decisions and more problems. This can help to build their feelings of being in control.

Social workers can teach women about assertiveness and how to develop assertiveness skills. They can provide practice situations and guide their female clients through more effective ways of handling difficult or uncomfortable situations. Assertiveness improves personal interactions, which in turn builds confidence.

Social workers can also encourage women to express their anger instead of holding it in. The real causes and targets of their anger can be identified. Once causes are recognized, social workers can "help the client learn to deal with anger directly through verbal and nonverbal communications styles, negotiation, confrontation, alliances and networks, compromises and resoluteness" (Collier, 1982, p. 277). Women can be helped to address the situations that cause their anger. If a woman is angry with her spouse, she can be taught how to express her feelings effectively so that whatever is happening to cause the anger can be changed.

Finally, social workers can encourage women to take care of themselves. The qualities they like about themselves can be nurtured. Women can learn that they have the right to their own time for themselves and to participate in activities they enjoy.

All of these suggestions are related to each other. Each one enhances the accomplishments of the others. Becoming more assertive enhances one's sense of control. An increased sense of control improves self-esteem. Greater self-esteem increases one's confidence in being assertive. The overall

intent is to establish a confident, competent sense of self, which is every person's right. Spotlight 9.5 offers some basic suggestions for combating sexism in terms of changing cultural values in the macro social environment.

Chapter Summary

The following summarizes this chapter's content as it relates to the learning objectives presented at the beginning of the chapter. Chapter content will help prepare students to:

LO 9-1 Define gender, gender identity, gender expression, and gender roles.

Gender refers to the social and psychological characteristics associated with being female or male (McCammon & Knox, 2007, p. 112). Gender identity is a person's internal psychological self-concept of being either a male or a female, or possibly some combination of both. Gender expression concerns how we express ourselves to others in ways related to gender that include behavior and personality. Gender roles are the "attitudes, behaviors, rights, and responsibilities that society associates with" being male or being female (Yarber & Strong, 2013, p. G-5). Gender-role socialization is the process of conveying what is considered appropriate behavior and perspectives for males and females in a particular culture.

LO 9-2 Discuss the social construction of gender.

Social constructionism is the theoretical approach that social reality is constructed by how people think about situations as they interact with others. The social construction of gender "looks at the structure of the gendered social order as a whole and at the processes that construct and maintain it" (Lorber, 2010, p. 244).

LO 9-3 Examine the complexities of gender, gender identity, and gender expression.

Eight variables contribute to gender, of which six are physical and two psychological. An intersex or pseudohermaphrodite is a person who has some mixture of male and female predisposition and configuration of reproductive structures. Transgenderism includes people "whose appearance and/or behaviors do not conform to traditional gender roles" (Crooks & Baur, 2014, p. 129).

SPOTLIGHT ON DIVERSITY 9.5

Strategies for Empowering Women and Achieving Sexual Equality

**EP 2.1.1b,
2.1.2a,
2.1.4b**

In many ways, problems discussed in this chapter are simply manifestations of the core problem of sexism. Sexism involves misinformation and attitudes that result in discrimination based on sex. Some basic suggestions for combating sexism involve supplying accurate information, revising attitudes, and changing behavior.

- Become conscious of the gender-role stereotypes affecting people from birth on. Don't force boys to be little men who must be actively aggressive and never dare cry when they're sad or hurting. Likewise, don't force girls to be little ladies who must wear frilly pink dresses, play with dolls, and be passive and submissive. The concept of androgyny may be helpful here. *Androgyny* refers to the capacity to have both traditionally feminine and masculine characteristics and qualities at the same time. It does not mean that men should be like women, or that women should be like men. Instead, androgyny implies that each individual, regardless of gender, should be allowed to develop positive personal qualities. It means that males could be freer to express their emotional feelings and develop their communication skills. It also means that women could be freer to be assertive and have a greater share in leadership and decision making.
- Throughout life, place less emphasis on the need to conform with gender-based stereotypes. If less pressure were placed on men to be dominant, successful leaders, perhaps the midlife crisis would no longer exist for most men. (A *midlife crisis* is the internal discord and, sometimes,

changed behaviors experienced by people in middle age as they reassess their perspective on life, which is different from that of a younger person. It involves examining goals and facing mortality.) Likewise, if less pressure were placed on women to be beautiful, docile homemakers, perhaps they would be happier, more self-satisfied, and more comfortable in their relationships with men.

- To combat the discriminatory effects of sexism on women, encourage women to develop their assertiveness skills, enhance their self-confidence, and learn to develop and appreciate analytical and spatial manipulation skills. (Lack of these skills seems to be barring women from many of the more profitable career alternatives.) Encourage both males and females to pursue whatever interest they have from early on. Females should be encouraged to develop their mathematical ability. Males should be equally encouraged to develop their domestic skills.
- Encourage more freedom in adult domestic relationships. Allow couples to negotiate both household tasks and outside work career goals without external pressure and criticism. Encourage men and women to share in child-care tasks. Doing so would allow children to know their fathers better and fathers to know their children. Don't criticize men who opt to stay home and manage the house or women who choose to work outside the home. Allow people the freedom to live their lives the way they want.
- Confront laws and regulations that are discriminatory and restrictive on the basis of gender. Raise questions about them if you feel they're unfair. Vote for legislators and support administrators who adopt nonsexist stances. If necessary, fight for your own rights and advocate for the rights of your clients.

Transgender groups include transsexuals, transvestites, drag queens, drag kings, and female impersonators.

LO 9-4 Evaluate traditional gender-role stereotypes over the life span.

Parents treat boys and girls differently from the moment they're born. Early gender-related differences between boys and girls include emotional expression and aggression.

Adolescence may be a time of gender intensification, a period of "increased pressures for gender-role conformity" (Hyde & Else-Quest, 2013,

p. 152). Masculinity and femininity "refer to the ideal cluster of traits that society attributes to each gender" (Carroll, 2013b, p. 90).

There are disadvantages for both women and men who adhere strictly to gender-role stereotypes. Women enter fields of work where they earn less, continue to do most of the work at home, and experience the stress of demands to be beautiful. Men experience performance demands, pressure not to express emotions, and shorter life spans.

Practitioners working with men should understand their special issues and pressures. Social workers should strive to identify the gender-role stereotypes that men maintain, understand the diversity of "masculinities," and emphasize men's strengths.

Gender-role socialization varies depending on one's cultural background.

LO 9-5 Assess some differences between men and women (including abilities and communication styles).

Debate continues concerning differences in male and female ability levels, especially in the areas of verbal, mathematical, and spatial skills. Women and men demonstrate different patterns of interruption when communicating. Women are better at understanding nonverbal cues. It is important to remember that men and women are more similar than dissimilar and to appreciate individual differences.

LO 9-6 Discuss economic inequality between men and women.

Women generally earn less than men in virtually every job category. Hispanic and African American women commonly earn less than white women. Women tend to be clustered in lower-paying, female-dominated occupations. Men generally earn more than women in work as professionals, in social work, and in academia. Women hold significantly fewer political offices.

LO 9-7 Examine sexual harassment.

"Unwelcome sexual advances, requests for sexual favors, and other verbal and physical conduct of a sexual nature constitute sexual harassment when this conduct explicitly or implicitly affects an individual's employment, unreasonably interferes with an individual's work performance, or creates an intimidating, hostile, or offensive work environment" (EEOC, 2014a).

Sexual harassment is common in many venues including the workplace and educational settings. It results in many negative effects on victims.

Suggestions for confronting sexual harassment include confronting your harasser, being assertive, documenting occurrences, talking to others about the problem, getting witnesses, and following the established complaint process.

LO 9-8 Review sexist language.

Sexist language generally differentiates women from men in a negative or unfair manner. Sexist language should be avoided. More gender-neutral concepts and terms should be used.

LO 9-9 Examine rape and sexual assault.

A sexual assault involves any unwanted sexual contact where physical force is used. Theoretical views of sexual assault include the victim-precipitated, rapist psychopathology, and the feminist perspectives. Various myths about rape should be examined and corrected.

Certain characteristics tend to characterize rapists, although they come from virtually all walks of life. Rapist types include anger, power, and sadistic.

Date rape is very common. Rape survivors tend to experience a rape trauma syndrome, a dimension of posttraumatic stress disorder that involves both an acute phase and a long-term reorganization phase.

Empowering rape survivors involves addressing emotional issues, reporting to the police, and exploring medical status. Suggestions for rape prevention are provided.

LO 9-10 Explore domestic violence and battered women.

The battering of women by significant others is very common in the United States and Canada. *Battering* is a catchall term reflecting various types of physical and emotional abuse. Battering involves power and control, and can be linked to poverty-related stress. The battering cycle involves stress escalation, the abusive explosion, and making up. Women tend to stay in battering relationships because of economic dependence, lack of self-confidence, lack of power, fear of the abuser, guilt, feeling isolated with nowhere to go, fear for her children, and love. Battering also occurs in gay and lesbian relationships.

Domestic violence shelters and programs can provide a wide range of services to help battered women. Empowering a battered woman involves making her feel safe, offering support, encouraging expression of feelings, focusing on strengths, furnishing information, reviewing alternatives, establishing a safety plan, and advocating for rights and services.

LO 9-11 Identify means of empowering women.

You can combat sexism and achieve sexual equality by identifying gender-role stereotypes, placing less emphasis on the need to conform to stereotypes, enhancing assertiveness, encouraging freedom in adult domestic relationships, and confronting discriminatory laws and regulations.

COMPETENCY NOTES

The entire chapter addresses competency Educational Policy (EP) EP 2.1.7 and its respective practice behaviors EP 2.1.7a and EP 2.1.7b (as cited below). (See *p. 424*).

EP 2.1.7 Apply knowledge of human behavior and the social environment.

EP 2.1.7a Utilize conceptual frameworks to guide the processes of assessment, intervention, and evaluation.
(Such conceptual frameworks will typically be identified by a "helping hands" icon.)

EP 2.1.7b Critique and apply knowledge to understand person and environment.
Other EP competencies and practice behaviors addressed in this chapter include the following:

EP 2.1.1b Practice personal reflection and self-correction to assure continual professional development.
(p. 429): Social workers should practice self-reflection to avoid clinging to traditional gender-role stereotypes. Such reflection and self-correction is a continuous process.
(p. 446): Practitioners should practice personal reflection so that they avoid using sexist language.
(p. 465): Personal reflection to combat gender-role stereotypes is an ongoing process in professional development.

EP 2.1.2 Apply social work ethical principles to guide professional practice.
(pp. 429, 436, 444, 452, 455, 461): Ethical questions are posed.

EP 2.1.2a Recognize and manage personal values in a way that allows professional values to guide practice.
(p. 429): Practitioners should recognize and manage personal values about gender-role stereotypes so that such values don't interfere with professional values and practice.
(p. 465): Social workers should recognize and manage their own values concerning potentially sexist stereotypes so that professional values may guide practice.

EP 2.1.3a Distinguish, appraise, and integrate multiple sources of knowledge, including research-based knowledge, and practice wisdom.
(p. 428): Practitioners should distinguish and integrate multiple sources of knowledge, including research-based knowledge, when considering the concept of gender.

EP 2.1.3c Demonstrate effective oral and written communication in working with individuals, families, groups, organizations, communities, and colleagues.
(p. 446): Social workers should communicate using nonsexist language.

EP 2.1.4 Engage diversity and difference in practice.
(p. 425): Gender, gender identity, and gender expression are important aspects of human diversity.
(p. 430): The gender spectrum reflects intersectionality as it applies to gender, gender identity, gender expression, sex, and sexual orientation.
(p. 459): Sexual orientation is an important aspect of human diversity in the context of battering.

EP 2.1.4a Recognize the extent to which culture's structures and values may oppress, marginalize, alienate, or create or enhance privilege and power.
(p. 429): Gender-role stereotypes may oppress both genders and limit potential and opportunities.
(p. 437): Economic inequality is a form of oppression for women.

EP 2.1.4b Gain sufficient self-awareness to eliminate the influence of personal biases and values in working with diverse groups.
(p. 429): Practitioners must work hard at developing self-awareness regarding any gender-role stereotypes and prejudices they may harbor.
(p. 465): Social workers should develop self-awareness concerning any of their own sexist biases in order to prevent them from interfering with effective intervention.

EP 2.1.4c Recognize and communicate their understanding of the importance of difference in shaping life experiences.
(p. 429): Social workers should recognize that gender-role stereotypes may shape and limit life experiences.
(p. 433): Practitioners should recognize how cultural differences shape life experiences in terms of gender-role development.

EP 2.1.5a Understand the forms and mechanisms of oppression and discrimination.
(p. 424): Sexism is a mechanism of oppression and discrimination.
(p. 437): Economic inequality is a form of oppression for women.
(p. 440): Sexual harassment is a means of oppression.
(p. 444): Sexist language can marginalize and oppress women.

EP 2.1.5b Advocate for human rights and social and economic justice.
(p. 459): Practitioners should advocate for legislation, policies, and services that help battered women.

EP 2.1.5c Engage in practices that advance social and economic justice.
(p. 445): Confronting sexual harassment serves to advance social justice.

EP 2.1.7a Utilize conceptual frameworks to guide the processes of assessment, intervention, and evaluation.
(p. 425): The social constructionist approach provides a useful conceptual framework for understanding the concept of gender.
(p. 447): Practitioners can utilize conceptual frameworks concerning sexual assault to understand and assess the dynamics involved.

EP 2.1.7b Critique and apply knowledge to understand person and environment.
(p. 447): Practitioners should critique the various theoretical perspectives concerning rape and apply them to assessment.
(p. 457): Social workers should apply their knowledge about why women remain in abusive relationships to understand the dynamics involved in individual clients' situations.

EP 2.1.8a Analyze, formulate, and advocate for policies that advance social well-being.
(p. 442): Supreme Court decisions that affect policies concerning sexual harassment are discussed.
(p. 459): Practitioners should advocate for policies and services that provide effective intervention on the behalf of battered women.

EP 2.1.10b Use empathy and other interpersonal skills.
(p. 462): Social workers should use empathy and other interpersonal skills when helping battered women.

EP 2.1.10d Collect, organize, and interpret client data.
(p. 428): Social workers should address and interpret multiple variables to understand gender.

EP 2.1.10e Assess clients' strengths and limitations.
(p. 453): Social workers counseling rape survivors should focus on client strengths, especially since their actions allowed them to survive the rape.
(p. 462): Practitioners should assess and focus on clients' strengths when working with battered women.

EP 2.1.10g Select appropriate intervention strategies.
(p. 453): Appropriate intervention strategies for working with survivors of rape are discussed.
(p. 462): Social workers should select the appropriate intervention strategies when working with battered women.

EP 2.1.20i Implement prevention interventions that enhance client capacities.
(p. 450): Social workers can make suggestions to clients regarding how they might prevent rape.

EP 2.1.10j Help clients resolve problems.
(p. 445): Social workers can help clients resolve sexual harassment problems by providing recommendations for how to confront it.
(p. 453): Practitioners can address emotional issues, reporting to the police, and medical status to help rape survivors address their problems.
(p. 462): Suggestions are provided for how to help battered women resolve their problems.

EP 2.1.10k Negotiate, mediate, and advocate for clients.
(p. 462): Social workers should advocate for survivors of domestic violence to obtain the services they need.
(p. 463): Practitioners should advocate on the behalf of clients who are battered women.

EP 2.1.10l Facilitate transitions and endings.
(p. 463): Social workers can empower clients by helping them plan and prepare for taking control of their lives after treatment has ended.

WEB RESOURCES

See this text's companion website at *www.cengagebrain.com* for learning tools such as chapter quizzing, videos, and more.

BIOLOGICAL ASPECTS OF YOUNG AND MIDDLE ADULTHOOD

Roy Morsch/Flirt/Corbis

Shannon Bailey, age 22, is a senior in college, majoring in English. She is nearing gradu-ation and is seeking a career focus. She realizes that a degree in English will indicate to potential employers that she probably writes well. Yet she also knows that an English major is not linked to professional positions the way a degree in engineering, for example, is linked to engineering positions. She is confused about what kind of career she wants, and also what kind of career she is qualified for. To add to her confusion, Eric Kim, whom she has been dating for three years and who is two years older than she, proposed to her a week ago. He wants to get married in a year or two.

At first, Shannon was flattered by the proposal and accepted the ring. But now she is having second thoughts, as she does not know if she wants to be in a committed relationship with Eric for the rest of her life. Shannon realizes that the decisions she makes in young adulthood will have a major impact on the rest of her life—including her health, well-being, and happiness.

Shannon's parents, Patrick and Laura Bailey, are in the middle adulthood phase of their lives. They have been married for 23 years and have had relatively few serious conflicts. Shannon is their only living child; another child died of sudden infant death syndrome when he was 8 months old. This was very traumatic for them for several years. Patrick, who is 50, has been a bus driver for the city of Milwaukee for the past 11 years. Laura, age 48, has been a carrier for Federal Express for the past 13 years. They have a family income in excess of $85,000 a year. Their early years together were a financial struggle; the past 10 years, however, have been better. Except for the monthly mortgage payment on their small house, they have no major outstanding debts. They are active in church activities and enjoy taking walks, gardening, playing softball, and bowling. For the past five summers, they have been spending their vacations traveling to various places in the United States in their Buick Enclave SUV.

A Perspective

Young adulthood is both an exciting and a challenging time of life. Growth and decline go on throughout life, in a balance that differs for each individual. In young adulthood, human beings build a foundation for much of their later development. This is when young people typically leave their parents' homes, start careers, get married, start to raise children, and begin to contribute to their communities.

Middle adulthood has been referred to as the prime time of life. Patrick and Laura Bailey illustrate this. Most people at this age are in fairly good health, both physically and psychologically. They are also apt to be earning more money than at any other age and have acquired considerable wisdom through experiences in a variety of areas. However, middle adulthood also has developmental tasks and life crises. This chapter will examine human biological subsystems in young and middle adulthood and discuss how they affect people's lives.

Learning Objectives

This chapter will help prepare students to:

**EP 2.1.7a,
2.1.7b**

LO 10-1 *Recognize the contributions of physical development, health status, and other factors to health during young adulthood*

LO 10-2 *Describe the physical changes in middle adulthood, including those affecting physical appearance, sense organs, physical strength and reaction time, and intellectual functioning*

LO 10-3 *Describe the midlife crises associated with female menopause and male climacteric*

LO 10-4 *Summarize sexual functioning in middle age*

LO 10-5 *Describe AIDS—its causes and effects; how it is contracted; how its spread can be prevented; and understand AIDS discrimination*

LO 10-1 Recognize the Contributions of Physical Development, Health Status, and Other Factors to Health During Young Adulthood

Young Adulthood

It is difficult to pinpoint the exact time of life we are referring to when we talk about young adulthood. The transition into adulthood is not a clear-cut dividing line. People become voting adults by age 18. However, in most states, they are not considered adult enough to drink alcoholic beverages until 21. A person cannot become a U.S. senator until age 30 or president until age 35. All this presents a confusing picture of what we mean by adulthood.

Various theorists have tried to define young adulthood. Buhler (1933) clustered adolescence and young adulthood together to include the ages from 15 to 25. During this time, people focus on establishing their identities and on idealistically trying to make their dreams come true. Buhler saw the next phase as young and middle adulthood. This period lasts from approximately ages 23 to 45 or 50. This group focuses on attaining realistic, concrete goals and on setting up a work and family structure for life.

Levinson, Darrow, Klein, Levinson, and McKee (1974) broke up young adulthood into smaller slices. They believed that in the process of developing a life structure, people go through stable periods separated by shorter transitional periods. The stage from ages 17 to 22 is characterized by leaving the family and becoming independent. This is followed by a transitional phase from ages 22 to 28, which involves entering the adult world. The age-30 transition focuses on making a decision about how to structure the remainder of life. A settling-down period then occurs from about ages 32 to 40.

For our purposes, we will consider young adulthood as including the ages from 18 to 30. This is the time following the achievement of full physical growth when people are establishing themselves in the adult world. Specific aspects of young adulthood addressed in this chapter include physical development, health status, and the effects of lifestyle on health.

Physical Development

Young adults are in their physical prime. Maximum muscular strength is attained between the ages of 25 and 30, and generally begins a gradual decline after that. After age 30, decreases in strength occur mostly in the leg and back muscles. Some weakening also occurs in the arm muscles.

Top performance speed in terms of how fast tasks can be accomplished is reached at about age 30. Young adulthood is also characterized by the highest levels of manual agility. Hand and finger dexterity decrease after the mid-30s (Papalia, & Feldman, 2012).

Sight, hearing, and the other senses are their keenest during young adulthood. Eyesight is the sharpest at about age 20. A decline in visual acuity isn't significant until age 40 or 45, when there is some tendency toward *presbyopia* (farsightedness). At that point, you start to see people read their newspapers by holding them 3 feet in front of them.

Hearing is also sharpest at age 20. After this, there is a gradual decline in auditory acuity, especially in sensitivity to higher tones. This deficiency is referred to as *presbycusis.* Most of the other senses—touch, smell, and taste—tend to remain stable until approximately age 45 or 50.

Health Status

Young adulthood can be considered the healthiest time of life. Young adults are generally healthier than when they were children, and they have not yet begun to suffer the illnesses and health declines that develop in middle age. More than 93 percent of people aged 15 to 44 perceive their health as being either good or excellent (Papalia et al., 2012). Many people in all socioeconomic classes show a significant interest in measures that promote health. For example, running and other forms of exercising, health foods, and weight control have become very popular.

> •••• **Ethical Question 10.1**
>
> *Are you taking good physical care of yourself?*
>
> **EP 2.1.2**

Even though young adulthood is generally a healthy time of life, health differences can be seen between men and women. For example, women of all ages tend to report more illnesses than do men (Lefrancois, 1999). However, these health issues may be related to gender (such as contraception, pregnancy, or an annual Pap test), rather than more general health problems. Perhaps women are also more conscientious about preventive health care in general. The following section discusses the important health issue of breast cancer.

Of all the acute or temporary pressing health problems occurring during young adulthood, approximately half are caused by respiratory problems. An additional 20 percent are due to injuries. The most frequent chronic health problems of young adulthood are spinal or back difficulties, hearing problems, arthritis, and hypertension. These chronic problems occur even more frequently in families of lower socioeconomic status. For example, young African Americans experience hypertension more frequently than their white counterparts (Papalia et al., 2012).

Alarmingly, about 50 percent of all U.S. adults have had a sexually transmitted infection by age 29 (Papalia et al., 2012).

Breast Cancer

Within the context of health status, an extremely important issue confronting women is the incidence of breast cancer. According to the American Cancer Society (ACS, 2013d), breast cancer is the most common form of cancer among women, except for lung cancer. Approximately 1 out of 8 women will develop breast cancer during their lifetimes and almost 40,000 women will die from it in one year (ACS, 2013d). Although older adult women are much more likely to get breast cancer than their younger counterparts, because of its general prevalence, it will be discussed here.

Being knowledgeable about the issue of breast cancer is especially important in helping your female clients become aware of risks, prevention, and treatment. If you are a woman, it's important for your own health. If you are a man, it's important for the women who are close to you.

Benign Lumps

To begin with, it's important to note that 80 percent of all breast lumps are benign (not cancerous) (WebbMD, 2013). These usually take one of two forms (Crooks & Baur, 2014). First, there are *cysts*, which are pouches of fluid. The other form of lump is a *fibroadenoma*, which is a more solid, rounded growth of cells resembling scar tissue (Crooks & Baur, 2014, p. 81).

Symptoms

A number of symptoms other than identification of a lump or tumor can indicate malignancy. Tumors can assume a number of shapes and forms. Generally, any change in the external appearance of the breasts should make one suspicious. For instance, one breast becoming significantly larger or hanging significantly lower than the other is a potential warning sign. Discharges from the nipple or nipple discoloration are additional indications, as is any pain in the breast. Dimpling or puckering of the nipple or skin of the breast should be noted. Nipple retraction (where the nipple turns inward) is also a potential sign of cancer. Finally, any swelling of the upper arm or lymph nodes under the arm should be investigated.

Risk Factors

Numerous risk factors are involved in getting breast cancer (ACS, 2013e). Some are variables that can't be changed. *Gender* is obviously involved, as women are 100 times more likely to get breast cancer than men (ACS, 2013e). We have already established that advancing *age* also increases risk. About two-thirds of women with breast cancer are age 55 or older by the time the cancer is discovered.

Between 5 and 10 percent of breast cancers are related to *genetic mutations*, most frequently in the genes labeled BRCA1 and BRCA2 (ASC, 2013e). Women with mutations in these specific genes may increase their likelihood of breast cancer by as much as 80 percent. Note that mutations in other genes may also be linked to increased risk.

Family history is another relevant variable in assessing breast cancer risk. Having close female relatives on either side of the family with breast cancer increases a woman's chances. Risk doubles for women who have a mother, sister, or daughter who has breast cancer and triples for women with two such relatives. (However, note that over 85 percent of all women with breast cancer do not have it in their family history.) Having a *prior history* of breast cancer increases the chances of developing a new cancer in the same or the other breast.

Race affects risk. "White women are slightly more likely to get breast cancer than are African-American women but African-American women are more likely to die of this cancer. However, in women under 45 years of age, breast cancer is more common in African-American women. Asian, Hispanic, and American Indian women have a lower risk of developing and dying from breast cancer" (ACS, 2013e).

Women who have been exposed to *radiation* treatment in the chest area at some earlier time have greater risk. Risk may also be related to *menstruation*. It increases a bit for women who started menstruating before age 12 or who went through *menopause* (the normal change of life occurring in middle age when a woman stops menstruating and can no longer bear children) after age 55. Having dense breast tissue (the fatty, fibrous, and glandular tissue making up breasts) increases the risk of developing breast cancer. Additionally, having been diagnosed with certain benign breast conditions (e.g., certain benign breast tumors) also increases breast cancer risk, although the level of risk varies with the particular condition.

Some risk factors for breast cancer are linked to lifestyle and life choices. Risk increases slightly for *childless women* and for women *having their first child after age 30*. Conversely, having numerous pregnancies and bearing children at a young age reduces a woman's chance of getting breast cancer. The risk posed by taking *oral contraception (birth control pills)* is not yet understood. Studies have found that women now using birth control pills have a slightly greater risk of breast cancer than women who have never used them. Women who stopped using the pill more than 10 years ago do not seem to have any increased risk. Women should address issues such as this with a physician. Long-term use of *combined hormone therapy (HT)* with estrogen and progesterone to diminish the negative symptoms of menopause increases the risk of breast cancer and of dying from the disease. The use and effects of hormone therapy are complex and should be carefully discussed with a physician. Since combined HT also "appears to increase the risk of heart disease, blood clots, and strokes," "there appear to be few strong reasons to use post-menopausal hormone therapy" (ACS, 2013e). *Alcohol consumption*, especially in greater quantities on a regular basis, increases risk, as does *being overweight*.

Several other factors that may contribute to the risk of breast cancer are under investigation. However, research results aren't clear at this time. These factors include high-fat diets, chemicals in the environment, tobacco smoke, and working at night. In contrast, exercise appears to reduce risk, as does having breast-fed a child, especially if the practice lasted for one-and-a-half to two years.

Remember that the factors discussed here do not condemn a woman to getting breast cancer. Such discussion should only alert women to be careful and aware.

Suspicion of Breast Cancer

In the event that a suspicious lump is detected, numerous options can be pursued. First, a *mammogram* (X-ray of the breast) can be used to detect a tumor. (Note that mammograms are also used for regular screenings described later.) Improvements in mammogram technology have resulted in decreased amounts of radiation, so there is little if any risk of negative consequences. *Diagnostic mammograms* "are used to diagnose breast disease in women who have breast symptoms (like a lump or nipple discharge) or an abnormal result on a screening mammogram" (ACS, 2013c). They involve taking more images and images depicting greater detail of the suspicious area in the breast.

Second, *magnetic resonance imaging (MRI)* scans "use radio waves and strong magnets instead of x-rays" (ACS, 2013c). A dye is injected into the bloodstream to accentuate effects. Healthy and diseased bodily tissues absorb the energy in different ways so that a computer can interpret results and discover abnormalities. Some research has found that MRIs can discover more and smaller cancers than can mammograms. However, MRIs are more expensive, may take up to an hour, and involve being confined in a tube (which makes some people quite uncomfortable). In current practice, MRIs are usually used along with mammograms to screen women in high-risk groups, to investigate suspicious tissue, to determine the mass of a cancer that has already been detected, or to check for the existence of cancer in the opposite breast. New imaging tests are also being studied.

Third, an *ultrasound* (picture of an internal area by the use of sound waves) may also be employed. Ultrasound has become a valuable tool to use along with mammography because it is widely available and less expensive than other options such as MRI. The use of ultrasound instead of mammograms for breast cancer screening is not recommended. Usually, breast ultrasound is used to target a specific area of concern found on the mammogram. Ultrasound helps distinguish between cysts (fluid-filled sacs) and solid masses and sometimes can help tell the difference between benign and cancerous tumors.

Ultrasounds can be beneficial in assessing breasts with exceptionally dense tissue, as tumors may be more difficult to see in mammograms. Research is currently being done to determine the value, pros, and cons "of adding breast ultrasound to screening mammograms in women with dense breasts and a higher risk of breast cancer" (ACS, 2013c).

Fourth, for women with nipple discharge, a *ductogram* (or *galactogram*) can be performed. This involves inserting "a very thin plastic tube into the opening of the duct in the nipple" producing the discharge and injecting a very small quantity of a liquid into the duct (ACS, 2013c). This provides a contrast between the injected liquid and breast tissue, thus delineating the structure of the duct. An X-ray can then determine if a mass exists within the duct.

Fifth, a *biopsy* involves extracting some amount of tissue to examine for cancerous cells. In a *fine needle aspiration biopsy (FNAB)*, an extremely fine needle extracts fluid from the lump for evaluation. In a *core needle biopsy,* a larger needle is used to remove several cores of tissue from a potentially problematic area discovered during an ultrasound or mammogram. "Because it removes larger pieces of tissue, a core needle biopsy is more likely than an FNAB to provide a clear diagnosis, although it may still miss some cancers" (ACS, 2013c). *Vaccuum-assisted biopsies* such as Mammotome® or ATEC® (Automated Tissue Excision and Collection) (trade names) are outpatient procedures that involve the suctioning of tissue using a hollow probe through a small incision. A *surgical biopsy* entails a removal by incision of a larger section of the identified mass or abnormal area in addition to some of the surrounding tissue. This more complex procedure, used because of the tissue's location or because the results of a core biopsy are unclear, is usually performed in a hospital's outpatient unit and requires anesthesia. The type of biopsy selected depends on a woman's specific circumstances. "Some of the factors your doctor will consider include how suspicious the lesion appears, how large it is, where in the breast it is located, how many lesions are present, other medical problems you may have, and your personal preferences" (ACS, 2013c).

Treatment of Breast Cancer

If it is established that the lesion is cancerous, several alternative treatments are available (National Cancer Institute [NCI], 2013). Some of the most common will be mentioned here. First, there are surgeries of varying complexity and severity. The simplest surgical procedure is *lumpectomy*, in which only the tumor and a small portion of the surrounding tissue are removed. Radiation therapy usually follows. This allows for the least disruption of the breast's external appearance. A *partial mastectomy* involves surgery to remove a portion or the breast containing the tumor and "some normal tissue around it. The lining over the chest muscles below the cancer may also be removed" (NCI, 2013). The next option is a *simple* or total *mastectomy*. Here, the entire breast is removed and possibly some of the lymph nodes under the arm. Although some of us find it offensive to use the term *simple* in this context ("It's simple for you to say my breast should be removed"), the term refers to the fact that the musculature in the chest remains pretty much intact after this procedure.

Lymph nodes may be removed because they are the first structures to receive drainage from the tumor (NCI, 2013). The *sentinel lymph node* is the lymph node to receive such drainage first. A radioactive material or a dye is injected close to the tumor in order to determine which node is the sentinel lymph node. The sentinel lymph node is then removed to be evaluated for cancer cells. If no cancer cells are found, removal of more lymph nodes may be unnecessary.

For some women anticipating immediate reconstructive surgery, *a skin-sparing mastectomy* is an alternative (Mayo Clinic, 2013). Here the same amount of internal breast tissue is removed as with a simple mastectomy, but the breast's skin remains intact in preparation for the reconstruction. The next more extensive alternative to a partial mastectomy is a *modified radical mastectomy*, in which the breast "many of the underarm lymph nodes, the lining over the chest muscles, and sometimes, part of the chest wall muscles" are removed (NCI, 2013).

The surgical procedure chosen depends on a number of factors. One, of course, is how far the cancer has progressed. All cancerous cells must be removed. In the past, the most common procedure by far was the most severe—the *radical mastectomy*, where the entire breast, underarm lymph nodes, and chest wall muscles are removed. Now, less extreme options are available and often effective. It should be emphasized that breasts are given tremendous significance in this society. Additionally, external appearance and physical shape are highly acclaimed. A woman's perception of herself, of how others perceive her, and of the effects on her sexual relationships all can be severely affected by breast removal.

After a mastectomy, reconstructive surgery to make the breast look as natural as possible is an option. In 2012, 91,655 breast reconstruction procedures were performed in the United States (American Society of Plastic Surgeons, 2012). This involves two general plastic surgery approaches. First, tissue from another part of the body (e.g., the stomach or upper back) can be used to reconstruct the breast. Second, an artificial breast implant filled with a saline or silicone solution may be inserted. Reconstruction may be performed during the initial surgery or at a later time. If reconstruction is being performed during the initial surgery, the woman should plan this with her physician ahead of time and involve a plastic surgeon. The extent of reconstructive surgery required depends on how much of the breast and other tissue remain after removing cancerous tissue. On the one hand, reconstructive surgery can boost a woman's self-image and adjustment. On the other, it can be a disappointment when the resulting breast reconstruction is imperfect in one or more ways (e.g., breast size or shape, or nipple appearance).

Radiation therapy involves using "high-powered beams of energy, such as X-rays" to destroy cancer cells" (Mayo Clinic, 2013). It can be administered either by a machine outside the body or by placing radioactive substances inside the body next to the cancer's location. Treatment schedules vary. Most commonly, radiation therapy is administered five days a week for several weeks (NCI, 2013). Various approaches to and schedules of radiation therapy are being studied. Each radiation treatment lasts only a few minutes and is painless. Side effects of radiation therapy include fatigue, redness of the skin that resembles sunburn, and sometimes swelling or increased firmness of breast tissue (Mayo Clinic, 2013).

Chemotherapy involves administering cancer-fighting drugs either by injecting them into a vein or ingesting them in pill or liquid form. They're intended to fight and eliminate cancer cells that may have split off from the tumor and migrated to other parts of the body. Chemotherapy is administered "in cycles, with each period of treatment followed by a recovery period. Treatment usually lasts for several months" (ACS, 2013a). Sometimes it's used before surgery to shrink a tumor, thereby facilitating the tumor's removal. Side effects may include extreme tiredness, nausea, hair loss, appetite loss, mouth sores, and greater vulnerability to infections and diseases because of a decreased supply of white blood cells.

Hormone therapy involves administration of drugs that block or decrease the effects of the female hormone estrogen in those women in whom estrogen encourages the development of breast cancer. One example of hormone therapy is *tamoxifen*, a drug in pill form that is usually administered for five years after breast cancer surgery. Side effects can include "fatigue, hot flashes, vaginal dryness or discharge, and mood swings" in addition to, more rarely, uterine cancer or blood clots (ACS, 2013b). Among other drugs used are *aromatase inhibitors* that can be prescribed for women past menopause whose cancers have been found to respond positively to estrogen. Side effects include joint stiffness and calcium depletion in bones, potentially resulting in fractures. This effect is due to the elimination of estrogen, which helps to maintain bone density.

Many procedures and therapies exist to combat breast cancer. However, early detection is key to effective treatment. Highlight 10.1 describes what women can do to facilitate detection as soon as possible.

A Final Note

Breast cancer is a critically important issue. In summary, there are two important principles for women to remember. First, women should become experts on their own bodies. The earlier a lump is found, the smaller it will probably be and the easier it will be to treat. Second, in the event that a lump is found, women should seek help immediately and become knowledgeable about alternative remedies. They should seriously consider the pros and cons of each available option.

Early Detection of Breast Cancer

There are three primary recommendations for early detection of breast cancer. First, the American Cancer Society strongly recommends that women should have an annual mammogram beginning at age 40. Women with a high risk of breast cancer should discuss the issue of having mammograms or other screening tests conducted at an earlier age. Some high-risk women should perhaps have an annual MRI in addition to their mammogram.

Second, beginning in their 20s or 30s, women should begin having a clinical breast exam (CBE) performed by a health-care practitioner at least every three years. Note that many cancers cannot currently be detected by mammography. CBE exams involve the practitioner examining your breasts for abnormalities or changes. The practitioner will also use the pads of her fingers to search for lumps in the breast and under the arms.

The third means of early detection involves conducting a breast self-exam (BSE) beginning in your 20s. The idea is that getting to know the contours and structure of your own breasts can help you detect any changes or abnormalities. You can develop much greater expertise in checking yourself than can a physician or other health professional who checks you only once a year or less. It has been suggested that women conduct a BSE monthly, or at least occasionally. The following describes how to do a BSE:

1. Lie down and put your left arm over your head (when checking your left breast with your right hand). This position spreads out the breast tissue more uniformly and allows you to explore the breast more thoroughly.
2. Use the pads on your three middle fingers to feel for lumps by using circular motions about the size of a dime.
3. Use three levels of pressure—mild, medium, and deep—in order to explore the depth of the entire breast.
4. Move in an up-and-down pattern, illustrated in Figure 10.1 (ACS, 2010a). You should start under your arm and make certain you check all areas of the breast down to the bottom of the rib cage and up to the collarbone.

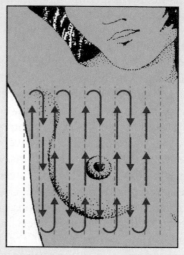

FIGURE 10.1 Breast Self-Exam

5. Duplicate the procedure using the three middle fingers of your left hand to check your right breast. Don't forget to put your right arm over your head.
6. Now get up and look at yourself in the mirror. Push your hands down tightly on your hips, as this tends to emphasize any changes in your breasts. Examine your breasts carefully for any differences or abnormalities.
7. Either standing or sitting in a chair, elevate your left arm slightly (do not raise it too high, as this tenses the muscles too much and makes it more difficult to detect lumps or abnormalities). Carefully inspect your left underarm with your right hand's three middle finger pads.
8. Using the same approach, examine your right underarm with your left hand.

Lifestyle and Good Health

Good health doesn't just happen. It is related to specific practices and to a person's individual lifestyle. People begin developing either beneficial or harmful health habits at an early age. Several simple, basic habits have been found to prolong life. People who follow all of them tend to live longer than people who follow only some of them. In fact, a clear relationship exists between the number of the suggested habits followed and the state of overall health.

These positive health habits include eating breakfast and other meals regularly. Snacking on high-fat and high-sugar foods should be avoided. Moderate eating in order to maintain a normal, healthy weight is important. Smoking and heavy alcohol consumption are dangerous to health and should be avoided. Moderate exercise and adequate sleep also contribute to good health.

Excessive consumption of alcohol has a very negative effect on health. Alcoholics are people who have a continual and compulsive need for alcohol. Physical dependence occurs when body tissues become dependent on the continuous presence of alcohol. Approximately three-quarters of all alcoholics show some impaired liver function. About 8 percent of alcoholics eventually develop cirrhosis of the liver. Cirrhosis involves gradual deterioration of the liver tissue until it no longer can adequately perform its normal functions. These functions include converting food to usable energy. Other effects of alcoholism include cancer, heart problems and heart failure, a variety of gastrointestinal disorders including ulcers, damage to the nervous system, and psychosis.

Stress is another variable related to health problems (seaward, 2012). The more stress a person is experiencing, the greater is his or her chance of becoming ill. Interestingly, stress is caused not only by negative occurrences, such as the death of a close relative, but also by new positive occurrences, such as an outstanding personal achievement or even a vacation. Apparently, change in general causes stress. Adjustment to new situations requires expending energy. This additional energy is apparently related to stress regardless of whether the adjustment is to a happy or a sad occasion.

Poor people are likely to suffer stress related to their lack of resources. They may be worrying about what to feed their kids near the end of the month when money has run out. Maybe they're worried about having their phone disconnected or their electricity turned off because they couldn't pay the bills.

Some behaviors have been found to be positively related to good health. For example, physical exercise helps to prevent heart disease, reduce stress and anxiety, enhance mental health, strengthen muscles, maintain a healthy bone structure, lower blood pressure, and extend life (Seaward, 2012).

Diet also affects health. Being overweight increases the risk of heart disease, high blood pressure, and other health problems. On the other hand, choosing a well-balanced diet, limiting food intake, and avoiding foods infused with salt and fat can promote good health, especially in conjunction with exercise. For instance, limiting cholesterol intake decreases the risks of heart disease (Seaward, 2012). Cholesterol is "a soft, fat-like substance found among the fats in the bloodstream" (American Heart Association, 1984, p. 1). It can collect in arteries, thereby stalling blood flow. Extreme blockages can arrest the blood flow into the heart and ultimately cause a heart attack.

Eating foods low or lacking in cholesterol can significantly decrease these risks.

Health is obviously related to the incidence of death. Spotlight 10.1 discusses the differential death rates and causes of death experienced by different groups.

LO 10-2 Describe the Physical Changes in Middle Adulthood, Including Those Affecting Physical Appearance, Sense Organs, Physical Strength and Reaction Time, and Intellectual Functioning

Middle Adulthood

Middle age has no distinct biological markers. Different writers identify the beginning of middle adulthood as ranging from 30 to 40 and the end of this age period as ranging from 60 to 70. Somewhat arbitrarily, this text will view middle adulthood as ranging from ages 30 to 65. This period indeed covers a large number of years.

Physical Changes in Middle Age
Changes in Physical Functioning
Most middle-aged people are in good health and have substantial energy. Small declines in physical functioning are barely perceptible. At age 48, for example, Althea Lawrence, who jogs, may notice it takes her a little longer to run the course. These decreases in physical functioning may be sufficient to make people feel they are aging.

People age at different rates, and the decline of the body systems is gradual. A major change is a reduction in reserve capacity, which serves as a backup in times of stress and during a dysfunction of one of the body's systems. Common physiological changes in middle age include diminished ability of the heart to pump blood. The gastrointestinal tract secretes fewer enzymes, which increases the chances of constipation and indigestion. The diaphragm weakens, which results in an increase in the size of the chest. Kidney function is reduced. In some males, the prostate gland (the organ surrounding the neck of the urinary bladder) enlarges, which can cause urinary and sexual problems.

SPOTLIGHT ON DIVERSITY 10.1

Differential Incidence of Death

The leading causes of death among all young adults in the United States ages 15 to 24 are accidents, homicide and legal intervention, suicide, and cancer, respectively; among people 25 to 44, the leading causes of death are accidents, cancer, heart disease, and suicide (U.S. Census Bureau, 2012).

When gender and racial groups are looked at separately, some differences emerge. Death rates for men 15 to 24 are almost three times higher than those for women (U.S. Census Bureau, 2012).

As for racial differences, the death rate for African American males 15 to 24 is almost double that of their white counterparts (U.S. Census Bureau, 2012). The incidence of violent death in the two groups contributes to this difference. Murder is the number one cause of death for young African American men. Recent census data report that African American men ages 15 to 19 are seven times more likely to die from a homicide than are their white peers, and those 20 to 24 are almost nine times more likely. The U.S. homicide rate is six times the rate in Holland, five times the rate in Canada, and eight times the overall rate in Europe (Mooney, Knox, & Schacht, 2013). You might ask yourself why you live in such a violent society.

The death rate for people of color between the ages of 15 and 44 is about twice as high as that for whites (U.S. Census Bureau, 2012).

The difference in the death rates of people of color and whites reflects a significant difference in environment. Of course, there are people of virtually every ethnic and racial background who are poor. However, in the United States, if you are African American or a member of a number of other minority groups, including Latinos/Latinas and Native Americans, you are more likely to be poor than if you are white. This is a complicated issue. However, much of the difference in circumstances is due to a long history of prejudice and discrimination. If you're poor, you're more likely to be living in the crowded urban center of a city than in the suburbs. If you're poor and live in the inner city where the crime rate is higher, you are more likely to be a homicide victim. Inner cities also have higher rates of air pollution, which (similar to smoking cigarettes) causes lung and heart disease.

If you are poor, you are also more likely not to have employment that provides adequate health insurance. You're more likely to find yourself in a position where you can't go to a doctor when you're sick because you have no money and no insurance. Young adulthood is supposed to be the healthiest time of life, and it is for most people. However, overall health status varies drastically depending on environment and living conditions. It's important for social workers to be aware of the impact that poor environments can have on people.

Poverty is often linked to minority status. Many minorities have been physically abused, burdened by the abuse of others' power, and treated unfairly. The result is the likelihood of a poor standard of living, including a poor health status with more health problems. Instead of asking what people can do to get out of poor environments, social workers need to ask how these environments can be changed to improve the living conditions of the oppressed people.

Despite changes in physical functioning, it is important for people to remain physically active as they age.

kali9/E+/Getty Images

In addition to gradual reductions in energy levels, middle-aged adults also have less capacity to do physical work. A longer time is needed to recoup strength after an extended period of strenuous activity. Working full-time at a job and then socializing into the wee hours of the morning is harder. Recovering from colds and other common ailments generally takes longer. It takes longer for pain in joints and muscles to subside after extensive physical exercise. Middle-aged adults are best at tasks that require endurance rather than rapid bursts of energy; they need to make adjustments in their physical activities to compensate for these changes in energy level.

Health Changes

In the early 40s, a general slowing down in metabolism usually begins. Individuals who reach this age either begin to gain weight or have to compensate by eating less and exercising more.

Health problems are more apt to arise. Signs of diabetes may occur, and the incidence of gallstones and kidney stones increases. Hypertension, heart problems, and cancer also occur at higher rates during the middle adult years than in the younger years. Back problems, asthma, arthritis, and rheumatism are also more common. Because nearly all these ailments can be treated, middle-aged adults need to have periodic physical examinations in order to detect and treat these illnesses in their early stages.

One major health problem during middle age is hypertension, or high blood pressure. The disorder predisposes people to heart attacks and strokes. The disorder affects about 40 percent of adults in the United States, and is more prevalent among African Americans and poor people (Papalia et al., 2012). Fortunately, the disorder is now often detected by blood pressure screening, and can generally be effectively treated with medication.

The typical middle-aged American is quite healthy. The three leading causes of death for those between the ages of 35 and 54 are, in order, cancer, heart disease, and accidents. Between ages 55 and 64 the leading causes are cancer, heart disease, and strokes (Papalia et al., 2012).

Changes in Physical Appearance

Gradual changes in appearance take place. Some people become alarmed when they discover these changes. Gray hairs begin to appear. The hair may thin. Wrinkles gradually appear. The skin may become dry and lose some of its elasticity. There is a redistribution of fatty tissue; males are apt to develop a "tire" around their waist, and the breasts of women may decrease in size. Minor ailments develop that cause a variety of twinges.

Some studies with interesting results have been conducted on personal appearance. Knapp and Hall (2010) reviewed studies in which slides of both women and men were shown to subjects. The studies found that those judged to be physically attractive were also judged to be brighter, richer, and more successful in their social lives and career.

Having a physically attractive body has become an obsession in our society. Americans spend thousands of hours and millions of dollars on grooming themselves, exercising, and dieting. The "body beautiful" cult leads those who judge themselves to be attractive to believe that they are superior to those they judge to be less attractive.

The Double Standard of Aging

Gray hair, coarsened skin, and crow's-feet are considered attractive in men; they are viewed as signs of distinction, experience, and mastery. Yet the same physical changes in women are viewed as unattractive indicators that they are "over the hill." Many men in our society view older women as having less value as sexual and romantic partners and even as business associates or prospective employees (Knapp & Hall, 2010). For example, some middle-aged television anchorwomen allege they have been discharged from their positions because normal changes in their physical features are considered unattractive.

Today, the double standard of aging is waning (Papalia et al., 2012). Men too are suffering from the premium placed on youth. Both men and women age 50 and older encounter age discrimination (although it's illegal) in looking for a job.

In the area of career advancement, men are more apt than women to feel old before their time if they have not achieved career or financial success. Our society places more pressure on men than on women to have a successful career.

•••• / Ethical Question 10.2

If you were an employer, would you be reluctant to hire someone who was 50 or older?

EP 2.1.2

Changes in Sense Organs

A gradual deterioration occurs in the sense organs during middle adulthood. Middle-aged adults are apt to develop problems with their vision that may force them to wear bifocals, reading glasses, or contact lenses. As the lens of the eye becomes less elastic with age, its focus does not adjust as readily. As a result, many people develop *presbyopia*—which means they become farsighted. They are unable to focus sharply for near vision and thus need reading glasses. The psychological impact of having to wear glasses may be minor or can be fairly serious if the person is fearful about growing older.

During middle age, there is also a gradual hardening and deterioration of the auditory nerve cells. The most common deterioration in middle adulthood is *presbycusis*, which is a reduction in hearing acuity for high-frequency tones. Middle-aged men generally have significantly greater losses of high-frequency tones than middle-aged women. Sometimes the hearing loss is enough so that a hearing aid is needed. There are generally some minor changes in taste, touch, and smell as a person grows older. Most of these changes are so gradual that a person makes adjustments without recognizing that changes are occurring.

Changes in Physical Strength and Reaction Time

Physical strength and coordination are at their maximum in the 20s and then decline gradually in middle adulthood. Generally these declines are minor. Manual laborers and competitive athletes (boxers, football players, weight lifters, wrestlers, ice skaters) are most apt to be affected by these gradual declines. As Highlight 10.2 illustrates, some sports figures who have been applauded and worshipped by fans may experience an identity crisis in middle adulthood when they are no longer as competitive. Their lifestyle and identity have been based on excelling with athletic skills; as those skills fade, they need to find new interests and another livelihood.

 HIGHLIGHT 10.2

An Identity Crisis: When the Applause Stops

Chuck Walters excelled in sports in grade school and high school. In high school, he lettered in basketball, football, and baseball. In his senior year, he was 6′ 1″ tall and weighed about 220 pounds. He was a halfback on the football team and scored 10 touchdowns in eight games. He was an outfielder on the baseball team and batted .467, hitting 13 home runs. Especially good at basketball, he was quick and averaged 23.4 points a game.

He was recruited by a number of universities for both his football and basketball skills. He chose to accept a basketball scholarship at a major midwestern university. As a bonus for accepting a scholarship, an alumnus bought him a Hummer. The purchase was hidden, as it violated NCAA rules for athletes. Another alumnus gave him a summer job as a construction worker, which paid well and didn't require much work. Chuck had concentrated on sports and partying in high school and college. In college, he chose the easiest major he could find (physical education) and only occasionally went to class. By taking the minimum number of credits needed to maintain his basketball eligibility and by having a tutor, he managed to make his grades and play varsity basketball. He loved college. He had plenty of money, a new vehicle, many dates, and was worshipped on campus as a hero. He thought this was the way to live. In his junior year, he averaged 16.7 points as a guard, and in his senior year, he was an all-conference selection and averaged 22.3 points a game.

He also began experimenting with cocaine. He loved being applauded and adulated. He thought the merry-go-round would keep whirling around. To his surprise, he wasn't drafted by the pros. So he went to Europe to play basketball, hoping to excel so that some professional team would give him a tryout. He played in Europe for five years and was traded several times. At age 30, he was finally cut.

This cut led to a major identity crisis. Chuck realized the applause and adulation were now coming to a screeching halt. He drank and used cocaine to excess to try to numb the pain of his loss. He had failed to graduate from college, having only junior standing when his scholarship eligibility ran out. He had been carried in college by his tutor because his reading and writing skills were at the 10th-grade level. He now fears he has no saleable skills and is worried his money may soon run out. He can no longer support his extravagant lifestyle. At the present time, he is considering trying to get some fast money by smuggling cocaine into the United States. His cocaine habit is costing him $100 per day. What should he do? He doesn't know, but he's dulling the pain with cocaine.

Simple reaction time reaches its optimum at around age 25 and is maintained until around age 60, when the reflexes gradually slow down. As people grow older, they learn more and are generally better at a number of physical tasks in middle adulthood than they were in their 20s. Such tasks include driving ability, hunting, fishing, and golf. The improvement that comes from experience outweighs minor declines in physical abilities. The same is true in other areas. Skilled industrial workers are most productive in their 40s and 50s, partly because they are more careful and conscientious than younger workers. Middle-aged workers are less likely to have disabling injuries on the job—which is probably due to learning to be careful and to use good judgment. Another factor in reduced accident rates for this age group may be a reduction in the abuse of mind-altering substances among middle-aged workers.

Changes in Intellectual Functioning
Contrary to the notion that you can't teach an old dog new tricks, mental functions are at a peak in middle age. Middle-aged adults can continue to learn new skills, new facts, and can remember those they already know well. Unfortunately, many middle-aged people do not fully use their intellectual capacities. Many settle into a job and family life and are less active in using their intellectual capacities than they were in their younger years, when they were attending school or when they were learning their profession or trade. Some middle-aged adults are unfortunately trapped by the erroneous belief that they can't learn anything new.

If a person is mentally active, that person will continue to learn well into later adulthood. Practically all cognitive capacities show no noticeable declines in middle adulthood. Adults who mistakenly believe that they completed their education in their 20s are apt to show declines in their intellectual functioning in middle adulthood. There is truth in the adage, "What you do not use, you will begin to lose."

There are variations in regard to specific intellectual capacities. People in middle adulthood who use their verbal abilities regularly (either on the job or through some other mental stimulation such as reading) further develop their vocabulary and verbal abilities. There is some evidence that middle-aged adults may be slightly less adept at

tests of short-term memory, but this is usually compensated by wisdom gained from a variety of past experiences (Papalia et al., 2012). If middle-aged adults are mentally active, their IQ scores on tests are apt to show slight increases.

Creative productivity is at its optimum point in middle age. Scientists, scholars, and artists have their highest rate of output generally in their 40s—and their productivity tends to remain high in their 60s and 70s (Papalia et al., 2012). There are different age peaks for different types of creative production. In general, the more unique, original, and inventive the production, the more likely it is to have been created in the 20s and 30s rather than later in life. The more a creative act depends on accumulated development, however, the more likely it is to occur in the later years of life.

Middle-aged adults tend to think in an integrative way. That is, they tend to interpret what they see, read, or hear in terms of its personal and psychological meaning. For example, instead of accepting what they read at face value (as younger people are apt to do), middle-aged adults filter information through their own learning and experience. This ability to interpret events in an integrative way has a number of benefits. It enables a person to better identify scams and "con games," because an integrative thinker is less naive. It enables many adults to come to terms with childhood events that once disturbed them. It enables middle-aged people to create inspirational legends and myths by putting truths about the human condition into symbols that younger generations can turn to for guidelines in leading their lives. Papalia and her associates (2012) note that people need to be capable of integrative thought before they can become spiritual and moral leaders.

Integrative thinking also enables people in their 40s and 50s to be at the peak of their *practical problem-solving capacities.* People in this age group are best able to arrive at quality solutions for everyday problems and crises, such as what is wrong with an automobile that fails to start, how to repair a hole in drywall in a house, and what types of injuries require medical attention.

In the past few decades, an increasing proportion of middle-aged adults have been returning to college. Some want an additional degree to move up a career ladder. Some seek training that will help them to perform their present jobs better. Some are preparing to seek a new career. Some are taking courses to fill leisure time and to learn about subjects they find challenging. Some want to expand their knowledge in special-interest areas, such as photography or sculpting. Some want to expand their interests in preparation for retirement years. Professionals in rapidly expanding fields (such as computer science, law, health care, gerontological social work, engineering, and teaching) need to keep up with new developments. Social work practitioners often take workshops and continuing education courses to keep abreast of new treatment techniques, new programs, and changes in social welfare legislation. In our modern, complex society, it is essential that learning continue throughout one's life span.

Life is more meaningful if one's intellectual capacities are being challenged and used. College instructors are generally delighted to have returning students in their classes, because such students have a wealth of experiences to share and are usually highly committed to learning. Compared to younger students, they are less apt to major in "having a good time."

When middle-aged adults return to college, they often need a few weeks to get used to the routine of taking notes in classes, writing papers, and studying for exams. A few courses, such as mathematics and algebra, tend to be particularly difficult because returning students have forgotten some of the basic concepts they learned years ago. Because people at age 50 learn at nearly the same rate and in the same way as they did at age 20, most returning students do well in their courses.

Colleges are not the only places that offer adult education courses. Courses are also provided by vocational and technical centers, businesses, labor unions, professional societies, community organizations, and government agencies. The concept of lifelong education has been a boon for many colleges and universities.

In middle adulthood, there is generally only a small amount of deterioration in physical capacities, and almost no deterioration in potential for mental functioning. Cognitive functioning may actually increase well into later adulthood (Lefrancois, 1999). The sad fact is that many people are not sufficiently active, both mentally and physically. As a result, their actual performance, physical and mental, falls far short of their potential performance.

LO 10-3 Describe the Midlife Crises Associated with Female Menopause and Male Climacteric

Female Menopause

Menopause is the event in every woman's life when she stops menstruating and can no longer bear children. The median age when menopause occurs is 51 years, although it may occur in women as young as 36, or may not occur until a woman is in her mid-50s. The time span ranging from two to five years during which a woman's body undergoes the physiological changes that bring on menopause is called the *climacteric.* There is some evidence of a hereditary pattern for the onset of menopause, because daughters generally begin and end menopause at about the same age and in the same manner as their mothers.

Menopause is caused by a decrease in the production of estrogen, which leads to a cessation of ovulation. Menopause begins with a change in a woman's menstrual pattern. This pattern varies between women. Periods may be skipped and become irregular. There may be a general slowing down of flow of blood during menstruation. There may be irregularity in the amount of blood flow and in the timing of periods. Or there may be an abrupt cessation of menstruation. The usual pattern is skipped periods, with the periods occurring further and further apart.

During menopause, a number of biological changes occur. The ovaries become smaller and no longer secrete eggs regularly. The fallopian tubes, having no more eggs to transport, become shorter and smaller. The vagina loses some of its elasticity and becomes shorter. The uterus shrinks and hardens. The hormone content of urine changes. All of these changes are biologically related to cessation of functioning of the reproductive system.

The reduction of activity of the ovaries affects other glands and may produce disturbing symptoms in some women. A majority of women undergoing menopause encounter few, if any, disturbing symptoms. As Spotlight 10.2 indicates, the symptoms of menopause may even vary among cultures.

The most common symptom of menopause is the hot flash, which affects approximately 50 percent of menopausal women (Hyde & DeLamater, 2011). A hot flash generally occurs quite rapidly, involves

---

✳ / **SPOTLIGHT ON DIVERSITY 10.2**

Cultural Differences in Women's Experience of Menopause

The importance of doing cross-cultural research on widely held beliefs is indicated in a study by Lock (1991) that compares Japanese women's experience of menopause to that of Canadian women. Vast differences were found. Only 12.6 percent of Japanese women who were beginning to experience irregular menstruation reported experiencing hot flashes in a two-week period compared to 47.4 percent of Canadian women. Fewer than 20 percent of Japanese women had ever had a hot flash, compared to almost 65 percent of Canadian women.

There is no specific Japanese word for a hot flash, which is surprising, because the Japanese language makes many subtle distinctions about all kinds of body states. This lack of a word for a hot flash supports the finding of a low incidence of what most Western women report as the most troubling symptom of menopause.

Chornesky (1998) notes that Mayan women in Mexico do not report having any symptoms related to menopause.

Chornesky also reports that symptoms of menopause are uncommon among Native American women. Interestingly, in Native American cultures menopause is viewed as an important rite of passage, signifying entrance into the highly respected state of elderhood and opening up the opportunity to assume important new social roles. For example, in the Lakota Sioux tribe, only after menopause can a Lakota woman become a midwife or a medicine woman and assume roles that are equal to those of men in tribal affairs (Chornesky, 1998).

What does this research tell us? It emphasizes the importance of conducting cross-cultural studies on biological phenomena. The findings also mean that it would be a mistake to use a list of menopausal symptoms drawn up in one country to assess women in another country. The findings also suggest the possibility of biological interpopulation variations in physical symptoms, such as hot flashes. Finally, the research suggests that different cultures view events (such as menopause) differently.

---

a feeling of warmth over the upper part of the body (very similar to generalized blushing), and is usually accompanied by perspiring, reddening, and perhaps dizziness. Some women have hot flashes infrequently (once a week or less), whereas others may have them every few hours. A hot flash may last just a few seconds and be fairly mild, or it may last for 15 minutes or more. It tends to occur more often during sleep than during waking hours. A hot flash while sleeping tends to awaken the woman, which contributes to insomnia.

Hot flashes appear to be due to a malfunction of temperature control mechanisms in the hypothalamus (Hyde & DeLamater, 2011). Estrogen deficiency contributes to this malfunction. Hot flashes generally disappear spontaneously after a few years.

Other changes may occur during menopause, most of which are due to reduced estrogen. The hair on the scalp and external genitalia may become thinner. The labia may lose their firmness. The breasts may lose some of their firmness and become smaller. There is a tendency to gain weight, and the body contour may change, though some women lose weight. Itchiness, particularly after showering, may occur. Headaches may increase, and insomnia may

occur. Some muscles, particularly in the upper legs and arms, may lose some of their elasticity and strength. Growth of hair on the upper lip and at the corners of the mouth may appear. Many of these symptoms can be minimized by regular exercise. In approximately one of four women who are postmenopausal, the decrease in estrogen leads to osteoporosis (see Highlight 10.3).

A variety of psychological reactions also accompany menopause, but certainly not every woman encounters psychological difficulties at this time. If a woman is well adjusted emotionally before menopause, she is unlikely to experience psychological problems during it (Hyde & DeLamater, 2011).

The psychological reactions a woman has to menopause are partly determined by her interpretations of this life change. If a woman sees this change as simply being one of many life changes, she is not apt to have any adverse reactions. She may even view menopause as a positive event, for she no longer has to bother with menstruation or worry about getting pregnant.

On the other hand, if a woman views menopause negatively, she is apt to develop such emotions as anxiety, depression, feelings of low self-worth, and lack of fulfillment. Some women believe menopause

Osteoporosis

Osteoporosis is a thinning and weakening of the bones. As a result of a drop in blood calcium level, bones become thin and brittle, with a consequent reduction in bone mass. Osteoporosis is a major factor leading to broken bones in later life. Women are much more susceptible to osteoporosis, particularly women who are white, thin, and smokers, and those who do not get enough exercise or calcium. Women who have had their ovaries surgically removed in middle age are also more susceptible to osteoporosis.

One of the dangers of osteoporosis is fractures of the vertebrae, which can lead to those affected becoming stooped from the waist up, with a height loss of 4 inches or more. Osteoporosis also often leads to hip fractures in older women.

Osteoporosis is preventable. The most important preventive measures include exercising, getting more calcium, and avoiding smoking. Exercise appears to stimulate new bone growth. It should become part of the daily routine early in life, and continue at moderate levels throughout life. Weight-bearing exercises (such as jogging, aerobic dancing, walking, bicycling, and jumping rope) are particularly beneficial in increasing bone density.

Most women in the United States drink too little milk and eat few foods rich in calcium. It is recommended that women should get between 1,000 and 1,500 milligrams (or more) of calcium daily, beginning in their youth (Papalia et al., 2012). Dairy foods are calcium-rich. To avoid high-cholesterol dairy products, low-fat milk and low-fat yogurt are recommended. Other foods rich in calcium include canned sardines and salmon (if eaten with the bones still present), oysters, and certain vegetables, such as broccoli, turnips, and mustard greens. Also useful is taking recommended daily amounts of vitamin D, which helps the body absorb calcium.

An alternative treatment that used to be recommended is hormone replacement therapy (HRT), which involves the administration of estrogen to women at high risk for developing osteoporosis, such as those who have had their ovaries removed at a fairly young age. HRT is now seldom recommended for preventing osteoporosis, as a major study in 2002 found that women who received HRT, rather than a placebo, suffered more strokes, more heart attacks, and more blood clots, and had higher rates of invasive breast cancer (Spake, 2002).

---

is a signal they are losing their physical attractiveness, which they further erroneously interpret as meaning the end of their sex life. Some no longer feel needed, especially if their children have left the nest and they have a low-paying, boring job—or no job at all. Some are widowed, separated, or divorced, and regret still having to "scrimp and save to make ends meet." For many women, this is a time of reexamining the past; if the past is interpreted as having been something other than what they had desired, they feel unfulfilled and cheated. Even worse, if they believe the chances for a better life to be nil, they are apt to be depressed and have a low sense of self-worth. If they viewed their main role in life as being a mother and raising children, they now may feel a sense of rolelessness; and if their children fall far short of meeting their hopes and expectations, they are apt to view themselves as a failure. Some women seek to relieve their problems through alcohol. Others seek out understanding lovers. Some isolate themselves, while others cry much of the time and are depressed.

There is no clear-cut way to identify the exact time when menopause ends. Most authorities agree

that the climacteric can be considered as ending when there has been no menstrual period for one year. Physical symptoms of menopause usually end when ovulation ceases.

Some doctors urge that some type of birth control be continued for two years after the last period in order to prevent pregnancy. "Change-of-life" babies are rare because conception, although possible, is unlikely to occur. Middle-aged pregnancies do present increased health risks. The child has a higher chance of having a birth defect. For example, the risk of Down syndrome is greatest with older parents; the chances rise from 1 in 2,000 among 25-year-old mothers to 1 in 40 for women over 45 (Papalia et al., 2012). Spontaneous abortions are more common in women who become pregnant after the age of 40. In addition, older women are more apt to have a prolonged labor due to the loss of elasticity of the vagina and the cervix.

Since the most troublesome physical symptoms of menopause are linked to reduced levels of estrogen, hormone replacement therapy (HRT) in the form of artificial estrogen is sometimes prescribed by physicians. Because estrogen taken alone increases the risk of uterine cancer, women who still have a uterus are usually given estrogen in combination with progestin, a form of the female hormone progesterone. The use of HRT has become highly controversial, as it has been found that HRT increases the risk of strokes, heart attacks, invasive breast cancer, and blood clots (Spake, 2002). The medical profession is now studying using alternative approaches to treating menopause.

Male Climacteric

In recent years, there has been considerable discussion about "male menopause." In a technical sense, the term is a misnomer, as menopause means the cessation of the menses. The term *male climacteric* is more accurate. It should be noted that men who have gone through male climacteric still retain the potential to reproduce.

Sometime between the ages of 35 and 60 men reach an uncertain period in their lives that has been termed a *midlife crisis*. It is a time of high risk for divorce, for extramarital affairs, for career changes, for accidents, and even for suicide attempts. All men experience it to some degree and emerge a bit changed, for better or for worse. It is a time of questions: "Is what I'm doing with my life really satisfying and meaningful? Would I be better off if I had pursued a different vocation or career? Do I really want to be married to my wife?"

Male climacteric is a time when a man reevaluates his marriage and his family life. This period of reassessment is often characterized by nervousness, decrease in sexual activity, depression, decreased memory and concentration, decreased sexual interests, fatigue, sleep disturbances, irritability, loss of interest or self-confidence, indecisiveness, numbness and tingling, fear of impending danger, and/or excitability. Other possible symptoms are headaches, vertigo, constipation, crying, hot flashes, chilly sensations, itching, sweating, and/or cold hands and feet.

A man going through male climacteric usually encounters some event that forces him to examine who he is and what he wants out of life. During this crisis, he looks back, as well as ahead, on his successes and failures, his degree of dependency on others, the outcomes of his dreams, and his capabilities for what lies ahead. Depending on what he sees and how he deals with it, this experience can be either exhilarating or demoralizing. He sees the disparity between youth and age, between hope and reality.

Male climacteric is caused by a combination of biological and psychological factors. As a male grows older, his hair thins and begins to turn gray. He develops more wrinkles and tends to develop a "tire" around his waist. His physical energy gradually decreases, and he can no longer run as fast as he once did. There are changes in his heart, his prostate, his sexual capacity, his chest size, his kidneys, his hearing, and his gastrointestinal tract.

The production of testosterone gradually decreases. Testosterone is an androgen that is the most potent naturally occurring male hormone. It stimulates the activity of male secondary sex characteristics, such as hair growth and voice depth, and helps to prevent deterioration in the sex organs in later life. The male sex glands are essential for the vitality of youth. These glands are the first glands to suffer when aging occurs. Two of the more subtle changes (as compared to hair loss, wrinkles, slowing blood circulation, and more sluggish digestion) are a decline in the number of sperm in an ejaculation and a reduction of testosterone present in the plasma and urine. The testes lose their earlier vigorous functioning and produce decreasing amounts of hormones. Older men generally take a longer time to achieve an erection. It also takes a longer time before an erection can be regained after an orgasm.

Some men do have greater hormonal fluctuations at climacteric. Hyde and DeLamater (2011) summarize studies that have found evidence of monthly cycles in some men with hormonal fluctuations in a 30-day rhythm.

While biological changes (including the diminishing production of sex hormones) play an important part in male climacteric, perhaps even more important is the problem of being middle-aged in a culture that worships youth. Many of the problems associated with male climacteric are due to psychological factors.

There is the fear of aging, which is intensified by the awareness that mental and physical capacities are declining, including sexual capacities. Also involved is the fear of failure, either in a job or in the man's personal life. Fear of women may be a part of this. A man may think that his sexual prowess is waning, and then may fear women's greater sexual capacities. He may also have a fear of failing in his sexual activities. The man with self-doubts is especially susceptible to the fear of rejection. He is very sensitive to derogatory comments about his age, his physique, or his thinning hair. A fear of death may be apparent as he realizes he has probably lived at least half of his life. All of these fears are apt to have an adverse impact on his emotional and sexual functioning.

A significant part of male climacteric is due to depression, which is often brought on when a man fears aging and recognizes that his sexual powers are waning (Hyde & DeLamater, 2011). He also realizes that he will never achieve the successes that he envisioned for himself years earlier. His bouts with depression may be so profound that he may contemplate suicide. Depression during this midlife crisis may also be triggered by a reevaluation of childhood dreams, conflicts in need of resolution, new erotic longings and fantasies, sadness over opportunities lost, and a new questioning of values. All of this is coupled with a search for new meaning in life. He realizes half of his life may be gone, and time becomes more precious. He worries about things undone, and there does not seem to be enough time for everything. He has the feeling of missing out on a big chunk of life. The man who is engaged in activities outside his daily job is a less likely candidate for depression. It is unbalanced to be so busy with getting ahead that the pleasures of life are missed. To recapture some of his former enthusiasm and perhaps to shake some of his unsettling doubts and fears, he may drive himself to work harder, to exercise more, or to seek younger women.

A man at midlife is also apt to experience a growing dissatisfaction with his job. He feels a sense of entrapment as the pressure to pay bills forces him to continue working at a job that he finds increasingly boring and unfulfilling. At the same time, his personal identity is deeply entwined with his work roles. His job has provided him with an opportunity to further develop his identity, to enter into a stable set of relationships with colleagues and/or clients, and to explain his place in the world. Now he questions that place. Occupational aspirations may change several times during this period. The emphasis may shift from measuring success in terms of achievement to measuring it in terms of economic security. Also at this time, movement up the occupational ladder is largely completed. If a man has not achieved his work goals by age 40 or 50, he may realize he may never achieve them; he may even be demoted one or two steps down the occupational ladder.

Midlife Crisis: True or False?

The ease or panic with which a man faces his middle years will depend on how he has accepted his faults and his strengths throughout life. The man who has developed a strong affective bond with his family will fare better than the man who has followed a more isolated and career-oriented course. To age gracefully is to realize that he has done the best he could with his life.

Many physicians will prescribe antidepressant therapy and counseling, and recommend the support and understanding of family and close friends (Hyde & DeLamater, 2011). Men who undergo a midlife crisis need to realize that there is still a great deal of pleasure and satisfaction to be gotten out of life. This is not the end; there are still things left for them to do.

Women go through similar psychological worries (for example, the empty-nest syndrome). Recent research indicates that a declining proportion of women are affected by the empty-nest syndrome because more women are emphasizing careers. Midlife is a time of reassessment for both sexes as people in this age group look over their lives. It is a time of reprioritizing one's life. With the right attitude, this period can become a time of reappraisal, renewed commitment, and growth.

But the realization of slow deterioration in one's physical capacities and of a disparity between one's earlier dreams and present reality is apt to be a crisis for many people.

Some health evidence shows that midlife is a time of crisis for many people. Hypertension, peptic ulcers, and heart disease are most often diagnosed in middle-aged patients. The rate of first admissions for alcoholism treatment is higher for middle-aged individuals than for younger adults (U.S. Census Bureau, 2012). These statistics suggest that middle adulthood can be a period of stress and turmoil.

Thus, it appears that midlife is a time of transition and change. It is a crisis for some, but not for others (Hyde & DeLamater, 2011). For some women, menopause is a precipitating factor that sets off a midlife crisis; for other women, some of the symptoms may be uncomfortable, but an identity crisis is not precipitated. For some men and women, their children leaving home precipitates an identity crisis; other men and women delight in seeing their children grow and develop, and experience a new sense of freedom in being able to travel more and to pursue more vigorously special interests and hobbies. Most men and women look forward to the departure of the youngest child.

Men who undergo a midlife crisis are apt to have had adjustment problems for a long time. Kaluger and Kaluger (1984, p. 541) conclude: "Midlife crises may be the result of unadjusted adolescents and young adults who grow up to be unadjusted middle-aged adults rather than the result of a universal crisis confined to midlife."

Stage theorists (such as Daniel Levinson; see Chapter 11) view midlife as a crisis, believing that the middle-aged adult is suspended between the past and the future, trying to cope with this gap that threatens life's continuity. Adult development experts are virtually unanimous in their belief that midlife crises have been exaggerated (Santrock, 2013). There is often considerable variation in the way people experience the stages of life.

In contrast to stage theories, the *contemporary life events approach* asserts that such events as divorce, remarriage, death of a spouse, and being terminated from employment involve varying degrees of stress, and therefore vary in their influence on an individual's development (Lorenz, Wickrama, Conger, & Elder, 2006). This approach asserts that how life events influence an individual's development depends not only on the life event itself but also on a variety of other factors, including physical health, family supports, the individual's coping skills, and the sociohistorical context. (For example, an individual may be better able to cope more effectively with divorce today than in the 1960s because divorce has become more commonplace and accepted in today's society.)

LO 10-4 Summarize Sexual Functioning in Middle Age

Sexual Functioning in Middle Age

Sexual expression is an important part of life for practically all age groups. In this section, we will focus on sexual functioning during middle adulthood—in marriage, in extramarital relationships, for those who are divorced or widowed, and for people who have never married.

Sex in Marriage

A close relationship exists between overall marital satisfaction and sexual satisfaction, particularly for men (Hyde & DeLamater, 2011). These two factors probably influence each other. Marital satisfaction probably increases the pleasure derived from sexual intercourse, and a satisfying sexual relationship probably increases the satisfaction derived from a marriage. Women are much more likely to be orgasmic in very happy marriages than in less happy marriages (Hyde & DeLamater, 2011).

Generally speaking, marriage partners report satisfaction with marital sex. For men, satisfaction is highest in the 18–24 age group and decreases slightly as men grow older. For women, satisfaction is highest in the 35–44 age group. These findings are consistent with studies that have found that a man's sex drive reaches its peak at a relatively young age, whereas a woman's tends to peak in her late 30s or early 40s (Hyde & DeLamater, 2011).

The percentage of people engaging in sexual intercourse by age groups is presented in Table 10.1. The frequency of coitus is highest when the individuals are in their 20s and 30s, and then gradually declines as people grow older.

Hyde and DeLamater (2011) note that for women there is a strong correlation between the frequency of intercourse and satisfaction with marital sex. There is also a strong correlation between a wife's ability to communicate her sexual desires and feelings to her husband and the quality of marital sex.

After the birth of their first child, couples report less sexual satisfaction on the average than do childless couples (Hyde & DeLamater, 2011). The presence of children in a family generally functions as an inhibition to sexual relations. Contrary to popular belief, the highest frequency of sexual intercourse occurs in childless couples. Many adjustments, pressures, and problems can be associated with parenthood.

For some couples, the birth of the first child produces difficulties, particularly if the pregnancy was unplanned. Wives usually experience the most stress after the birth of the first child. They are apt to be concerned about their physical appearance, have increased responsibilities that lead to fatigue, and sometimes feel neglected by their husbands as the husband-wife interactions and social activities tend to decline. The arrival of more children tends to further lessen sexual satisfaction in the marriage.

TABLE 10.1	PERCENTAGE ENGAGING IN SEXUAL INTERCOURSE				
AGE GROUPS	NOT AT ALL	A FEW TIMES PER YEAR	A FEW TIMES PER MONTH	2–3 TIMES A WEEK	4 OR MORE TIMES A WEEK
Men					
18–24	15	21	24	28	12
25–29	7	15	31	36	11
30–39	8	15	37	23	6
40–49	9	18	40	27	6
50–59	11	22	43	20	3
Women					
18–24	11	16	2	9	12
25–29	5	10	38	37	10
30–39	9	16	6	33	6
40–49	15	16	44	20	5
50–59	30	22	35	12	2

SOURCE: Santrock (2013, p. 493.)

The frequency of sexual intercourse appears to be negatively related to the number of children in a family (Hyde & DeLamater, 2011). To some extent, the reduction of sexual activity and sexual gratification with parenthood is offset by the increased gratifications that most parents receive from being parents—watching and helping their children grow and develop, and feeling pride in performing parental roles.

Married couples now use a greater variety of sexual techniques than couples in earlier generations did. The female-on-top position is increasingly being used, because it gives the female greater control over stimulation of the clitoris than the man-on-top position. Oral sex has also become more popular. Couples today also spend a longer time making love than couples did decades ago. Most couples now spend between 15 minutes and an hour having sex (Hyde & DeLamater, 2011). This change may reflect a greater awareness by married men and women that women are more likely to enjoy sex more and to be orgasmic if intercourse is unhurried.

Crooks and Baur (2011) summarize information on masturbation:

Most men and women, both married and unmarried, masturbate on occasion. Woman tend to masturbate more after they reach their 20s than they did in their teens. Kinsey hypothesized that this was due to increased erotic responsiveness, opportunities for learning about the possibility of self-stimulation through sex play with a partner, and a reduction in sexual inhibitions. Masturbation is often considered inappropriate when a person has a sexual partner or is married. Some people believe that they should not engage in a sexual activity that excludes their partners, or that experiencing sexual pleasure by masturbation deprives their partners of pleasure. Others mistakenly interpret their partner's desire to masturbate as a sign that something is wrong with their relationship. But unless it interferes with mutually enjoyable sexual intimacy in the relationship, masturbation can be considered a normal part of each partner's sexual repertoire. It is common for people to continue masturbation after they marry. In fact, individuals who engage in sexual activity with their partners more frequently than other individuals also masturbate more often. (p. 233)

See Highlight 10.4—Five languages of love.

Extramarital Sexual Relationships

Different studies have found a wide variation in the percentage of men and women who report having had an affair while they were married: 10 to 25 percent of husbands, and 5 to 15 percent of wives

HIGHLIGHT 10.4

Five Languages of Love

Some people mistakenly believe that being a great sex partner is the best way to communicate love to one's mate. A good sex life is indeed important, but there are five other more important ways to express love to ones mate, according to Gary Chapman (1992). These five emotional love languages are: (1) Words of affirmation, (2) Quality time, (3) Gifts, (4) Acts of service, and (5) Physical touch. We fall in love because of the way we feel about ourselves when we are with that person. In a nutshell, if we want a certain person to love us, we need to make that person feel special. What is the secret to making someone feel special? Chapman indicates it is through the above five emotional love languages. It is important to recognize that there is considerable variation in how each person prioritizes these love languages; examples, one person may assign the highest value to physical touch, and the lowest to gifts—while another person may assign the highest value to quality time, and the lowest to words of affirmation. If we want our mate to feel special, it is critical for each of us to determine the values that our mate assigns to each of these love languages. Before we discuss how we determine our mate's priorities about these five languages of love, each of these love languages will be briefly describe.

(1) Words of Affirmation: Words of appreciation, or verbal compliments, are powerful communicators of love. Examples include the following: "You look great in that outfit;" "The dinner you just made is the best I've eaten in a long time;" "I truly appreciate you doing the laundry this evening," and "I love how you can talk with anyone." Words of affirmation have an additional benefit of building your mate's self image and confidence. (The focus of love should not be on getting something you want, but on doing something for the well-being of the one you love.)

(2) Quality Time: Some mates believe that doing things together, being together, and focusing in on one another is the best way to show love. "Quality time" involves giving your mate your undivided attention. If your mate highly values quality time, you need turn off the TV and focus on attending to what your mate is desiring. Quality time is not being in close proximity, but being together with focused attention. One way to learn to better communicate focused attention with your mate is to establish a daily sharing time in which each of you talks about some significant things that happened to you that day and how you feel about them.

(3) Gifts: In every culture, members give gifts to one another. A gift is something your mate can hold in his or her hand and conclude "Look he is thinking of me" or "She values me." If your mate's primary love language is receiving gifts, you should become a proficient gift giver. Giving gifts may be the easiest love language to learn. Gifts do not necessarily have to always be material in nature; for example, if your mate is encountering a crisis, your most powerful gift may be physical presence. Gifts do not need to be expensive to send a powerful message of love. Mates who forget a special day of their mate's (such as a birthday) will soon discover that their mate feels neglected and unloved.

(4) Acts of Service: There are an infinite number of acts of service—vacuuming, cooking a meal, doing the dishes, washing your mate's car, painting a room, making the bed, taking out the trash, fixing a broken appliance, going to the grocery store to purchase products your mate wants, volunteering to visit your mate' parents, and so on. Discovering what your mate most wants you to do in regard to acts of service requires observation and trial and error. (You can let your mate know what you most desire in regards to acts of service by highlighting what you most cherish—while remembering that demands stop the flow of love.)

(5) Physical Touch: Physical touch is a way to communicate emotional love. Everyone needs to be held and hugged. Rene Spitz (1945) demonstrated that even young children need physical contact, such as being cuddled and held. Without such direct physical contact, the social, intellectual, emotional, and physical development of children will be severely stunted. Everyone needs to observe what their mate cherishes in regard to physical touch—sometimes hugging your mate, stroking your mate's back, holding hands, or a kiss on the cheek will fulfill this need. The right physical touch can improve a relationship, while the wrong physical touch (such as hitting) can break a relationship. If your mate's primary love language is physical touch, holding him or her when he or she is in crisis may be the most important thing you can do. Physical touch includes learning and doing what your mate cherishes in your sexual relationship.

Each of us has a primary love language—odds are that your mate's primary love language is not the same as yours. All of us need to observe and learn (often through trial and error) what our mate's primary love language is. And then we need to seek to fulfill our mate's love language—if we want him or her to feel special and be in love with us.

Interestingly, each person can learn his or her love language preferences by taking a 30-question quiz at: www.5lovelanguages.com/profile/ If you want to know the love language preferences of your mate, you can ask him or her to take the quiz, and then share the results with you.

reported having affairs (Hyde & DeLamater, 2011). For males, the frequency of extramarital coitus decreases with age, whereas with females, there is a gradual increase up to around age 40. These sex differences may reflect differences in the peaking of the sex drive. Wives with full-time jobs outside the home are more apt to have extramarital affairs than are wives who do not have jobs. Wives with full-time jobs have an increased opportunity to become acquainted with a variety of men who are not known by the husband.

EP 2.1.2

Do you believe an extramarital affair is sometimes justifiable? If you were married and your spouse had an extramarital affair, would you seek a divorce?

Spouses become involved in extramarital coitus for a variety of reasons. In some cases, marital sex may not be satisfying. The spouse's partner may have a long-term illness or a sexual dysfunction, or the couple may be separated. The extramarital affair may represent an attempt to obtain what is missing in the marriage. Some seek extramarital involvements to obtain affection, to satisfy curiosity, to find excitement, or to add to their list of sexual conquests. Some become involved in extramarital affairs to get revenge for feeling wronged by their spouse. Some want to punish their spouse for not being more affectionate or appreciative. In many cases, there is a combination of reasons for an extramarital affair.

Some surveys have examined why a high percentage of married couples do not have extramarital affairs. The most mentioned reason is that it would be a betrayal of trust in the love relationship. Other stated reasons are that it would damage the marital relationship, that it would hurt the spouse, and that the probable benefits of an affair are not worth the consequences (Hyde & DeLamater, 2011).

In most cases, extramarital affairs are carried out in secret. Sometimes the spouse later discovers the affair. Typical reactions to the affair are summarized by Maier (1984) through his experiences as a marriage counselor:

> *Among the most common feelings expressed by a spouse after such a discovery are anger and a sense of being deceived and betrayed. In addition, the affair is often seen as a symbolic insult to the spouse's affection and sexual adequacy. Certain subcultures consider it appropriate to seek some type of revenge or retribution.*
>
> *Generally speaking, isolated sexual experiences are less disturbing to spouses than prolonged*

extramarital affairs. Brief sexual encounters can sometimes be written off as temporary reactions to sexual frustration; however, longer affairs are seen as greater threats to the marital love relationship. (p. 322)

The discovery of an extramarital affair may lead to a divorce, but not always. Sometimes the discovery of an affair is a crisis that forces a couple to recognize that problems (sexual or nonsexual) exist in their marriage, and the couple then seek to work on these to improve the marriage. Some spouses reluctantly accept and adjust to the affair without saying much. They may be financially dependent on their partner, or they may have a low sense of self-worth and have made adjustments to being emotionally abused by their spouse in the past. Others show little reaction because they realize a divorce is expensive, socially degrading, and may result in loneliness. In such marriages, the relationship may become devitalized, with the partners having little emotional attachment to each other.

A few spouses react to an extramarital affair by gradually entering into a consensual extramarital relationship. In such a relationship, extramarital sexual relationships are permitted and even encouraged by both partners. One type of consensual extramarital sex arrangement is *mate swapping*. In this arrangement, two or more couples get together and exchange partners, either retiring to a separate place to have sexual relations or having sex in the same room with various combinations of partners.

EP 2.1.2

Do you view mate swapping as being unethical?

Sex Following Divorce

A great majority of formerly married persons become sexually active within a year after divorce. When matched for age, divorced men have a slightly higher frequency of coitus than do married men. Divorced men also tend to have a variety of partners (Hyde & DeLamater, 2011). Divorced women also generally have a fairly active sex life, although the incidence of postmarital sex tends to be lower than when they were married. They also tend to have a smaller number of partners than do divorced men (Hyde & DeLamater, 2011). Divorced women report a higher frequency of orgasm than they experienced in marital sex (Hyde & DeLamater, 2011). Divorced men also report that sexual relationships are satisfying.

These results do not mean that sex following a divorce is more satisfying than marital sex. People who have a satisfying sexual relationship may be less likely to get a divorce. People who get divorced are probably not as likely to give high ratings to their sexual relationship when they were married.

Divorced people today are less concerned about hiding their sexual relationships from their children than were divorced people a generation ago. Divorced people apparently now have more liberal views on sex than in the past.

Sex in Widowhood

Ending a marriage by divorce can be traumatic, but a marriage ended by the death of one's spouse is usually more traumatic. In a divorce, a spouse has input into the decision to part, but most widows and widowers have no input and wish their partner were still alive. They have to adjust not only to being single, but also to the death of a loved one.

Widowers are more likely than widows to establish a new sexual relationship. In middle and later adulthood, there are substantially more single women than single men. There is greater cultural acceptance of older men dating younger women than vice versa. Cultural patterns also encourage widowers to establish new sexual relationships, whereas widows feel pressure to be sexually loyal to their deceased spouse. Widows also tend to receive more emotional support from friends and family, and therefore they may feel less need to form a new sexual relationship.

Sex Among the Never Married

Very little research has been conducted on the sexual lifestyles of never-married adults. The attitudes of singles about their status vary widely. Some plan never to marry. Some want to marry, but haven't found the right partner; others have found someone they want to marry but that person refuses to marry. Some desperately seek a partner.

The lifestyles of the never-married vary tremendously. Some contently become celibate. Others are highly involved in the singles scene—living in apartments for single people, going to singles bars, and joining singles clubs. Some singles have numerous sexual partners. Some singles, on the other hand, become involved in their careers or hobbies, and though they may date occasionally, they do not want the restrictions of marriage. Some singles are content to date someone steadily for a few years and, when that relationship sours, move on to another. Some cohabit with an opposite-sex or same-sex partner. Some become addicted to alcohol or to some other drug, and spend relatively little time in romantic relationships.

Celibacy

A small minority of people choose to abstain from sexual intercourse. Certain religious leaders (such as Buddhist monks and Roman Catholic nuns and priests) are required to remain celibate. In other cases, individuals choose to abstain for a variety of reasons. They may not want the entanglements of sexual relationships. They may have a low sex drive. They may enjoy other ways, such as masturbation, of expressing their sexuality. They may fear acquiring a sexually transmitted disease, or they may have a sexually transmitted disease and do not want to risk passing it on to someone else. They may be in conflictive relationships with partners and therefore may not desire to become sexually intimate. They may have partners who have low sex drives or who are physically incapable of intercourse.

Although some people find abstinence to be very difficult, others experience it as satisfying. Periods of celibacy may be important for self-exploration and recovery from broken romances.

LO 10-5 Describe AIDS—Its Causes and Effects; How It Is Contracted; How Its Spread Can Be Prevented; and Understand AIDS Discrimination

People Living with AIDS: A Population-at-Risk

The remainder of this chapter will focus on AIDS (acquired immunodeficiency syndrome). AIDS is a devastating disease that has the potential to kill more people than any other. It is a contagious, incurable disease that targets the body's immune system and greatly reduces the body's capacity to defend itself against disease.

What Causes AIDS?

AIDS is caused by a type of virus called HIV, an abbreviation for human immunodeficiency virus. A virus is a protein-coated package of genes that invades a healthy body cell and alters the normal genetic apparatus of the cell, causing the cell to reproduce the virus. In the process, the invaded cell is often killed. The HIV virus falls within a special category of viruses called *retroviruses*, so named because they reverse the usual order of reproduction within the cells they infect.

HIV invades cells involved in the body's normal process of protecting itself from disease and causes these cells to produce more of the virus. Apparently, HIV destroys normal white blood cells, which are supposed to fight off diseases invading the body. As a result, the body is left defenseless and can fall prey to other infections. The virus devastates the body's immune, or defense, system so that other diseases occur and eventually cause death. Without a functioning immune system to combat germs, the affected person becomes vulnerable to bacteria, fungi, malignancies, and other viruses that may cause life-threatening illnesses, such as cancer, pneumonia, and meningitis.

How Is AIDS Contracted?

Documented ways in which the AIDS virus can be transmitted are by sexual intercourse with someone who has HIV, by using hypodermic needles that were also used by someone who has the virus, and by receiving contaminated blood transfusions or other products derived from contaminated blood. Babies can also contract the AIDS virus before or at birth from their infected mothers and through breast milk.

HIV has been isolated in semen, blood, vaginal secretions, saliva, tears, breast milk, and urine. Only blood, semen, vaginal secretions, and to a much lesser extent, breast milk have been identified as capable of transmitting the AIDS virus. Many experts doubt whether there is enough of the virus present in tears and saliva to be transmitted in these fluids. Experts rule out casual kissing or swimming in pools as a means of contracting AIDS. Sneezing, coughing, crying, or handshakes also have not proven to be dangerous. Only the exchange of body fluids (for example, through anal, oral, or genital intercourse)

permits infection. The virus is very fragile and cannot survive long without a suitable environment, nor is it able to penetrate the skin. In summary, evidence has not been found to show that AIDS can be spread through any type of casual contact. You cannot get AIDS from doorknobs, toilets, or telephones.

Few lesbians have contracted AIDS. Lesbians are at low risk unless they use intravenous drugs or have unsafe sexual contact with people in high-risk groups. Female-to-female transmission *is* possible, however, through vaginal secretions or blood.

Women who use sperm for artificial insemination from an infected donor are also at risk of infection. Donors should be screened by licensed sperm banks as a preventive measure.

Blood that is used in blood transfusions is now tested for the presence of antibodies to the AIDS virus; therefore, it is unlikely that the virus will be transmitted by transfusions. But because antibodies do not form immediately after exposure to the virus, a newly infected person may unknowingly donate blood after becoming infected but before his or her antibody test becomes positive. As an added precaution, donated blood is heat-treated to inactivate HIV. There is no risk of contracting the AIDS virus by being a blood donor.

Many people infected by HIV will eventually develop AIDS. The length of time between initial infection of HIV and the appearance of AIDS symptoms is called the incubation period for the virus. The average incubation period (before the development of drugs used to treat the disease) was estimated to be 7 to 11 years (Lloyd, 1995). There is considerable variation in this incubation period, ranging from a few months (particularly for babies who are HIV-positive) to 20 years or more.

Another major health problem involves people who are HIV-positive but have no symptoms of AIDS. Most of these individuals have not been tested for the AIDS virus and therefore are unaware they have the virus. These people can infect others even though they experience no life-threatening symptoms themselves. The following are high-risk factors in contracting AIDS:

- Having multiple sex partners without using safe sex practices (such as using condoms). The risk of infection increases according to the number of sexual partners one has, male or female. In considering the risks of acquiring AIDS, a person should heed this warning: When you have sex with a new partner, you are having sex not only with this person but also with all of this person's previous sexual partners.

- Sharing intravenous needles, because HIV can be transmitted by reusing contaminated needles and syringes.
- Having anal intercourse with an infected person.
- Having sex with prostitutes. Prostitutes are at high risk because they have multiple sex partners and are more apt to be intravenous drug users.

Although some people believe any contact with someone who is HIV-positive guarantees illness and death, such fears are not justified. Body fluids (such as fresh blood, semen, urine, and vaginal secretions) infected with the virus must enter the bloodstream in order for the virus to be transmitted from one person to another. Gay men account for so many AIDS cases because they are apt to engage in anal intercourse. Anal intercourse often results in tearing the lining of the rectum, which allows infected semen to get into the bloodstream. Sharing a needle (during mainlining a drug) with someone who is carrying the virus is also dangerous because a small amount of the previous user's blood is often drawn into the needle and then injected directly into the bloodstream of the next user.

Transmission of the virus from mother to child can occur in utero during the last weeks of pregnancy or at childbirth. If the mother has access to antiretroviral therapy and gives birth by cesarean section, the rate of transmission to the child is very low. Transmission of the virus to a child can also occur during breast-feeding. HIV-infected mothers are generally urged not to breast-feed their infants.

Diagnosis

Several tests have been developed to determine if a person has been exposed to the AIDS virus. These tests do not directly detect the virus, but rather the antibodies a person's immune system develops to fight the virus. For a person who has been infected with HIV, it generally takes two to three months before enough antibodies are produced to be detected by the test. The tests only establish the presence of antibodies that indicate exposure to the virus.

The Effects of HIV

Once a person is infected with HIV, several years are apt to go by before symptoms of AIDS appear.

Initial symptoms include dry cough, abdominal discomfort, headaches, oral thrush, loss of appetite, fever, night sweats, weight loss, diarrhea, skin rashes, tiredness, swollen lymph nodes, and lack of resistance to infection. (Many other illnesses have similar symptoms, so it is irrational for people to conclude they are developing AIDS if they have some of these symptoms.) As AIDS progresses, the immune system is less and less capable of fighting off "opportunist" diseases, making the infected person vulnerable to a variety of cancers, nervous system degeneration, and infections caused by other viruses, bacteria, parasites, and fungi. Ordinarily, opportunistic infections are not life-threatening to people with healthy immune systems, but they are frequently fatal to people with AIDS, whose immunological functioning has been severely compromised.

The serious diseases that afflict people with AIDS include Kaposi's sarcoma (an otherwise rare form of cancer that accounts for many AIDS deaths), pneumocystic carinii pneumonia (a lung disease that is also a major cause of AIDS deaths), and a variety of other generalized opportunistic infections, such as shingles (herpes zoster), encephalitis, severe fungal infections that cause a type of meningitis, yeast infections of the throat and esophagus, and infections of the lungs, intestines, and central nervous system.

AIDS is a syndrome, not one specific disease. AIDS simply makes those infected by the virus increasingly more vulnerable to any disease that might come along. The disease process of AIDS involves a continuum whereby those affected become more and more vulnerable to devastating diseases.

In some patients, AIDS may attack the nervous system and cause damage to the brain. The deterioration, called AIDS-dementia complex, occurs gradually over a period of time (sometimes a few years). Several specific intellectual functions may be affected by AIDS, resulting in inability to concentrate, forgetfulness, inability to think quickly and efficiently, visuospatial problems that make it difficult to get from place to place or to perform complex and simultaneous tasks, and slowed motor ability. It is interesting that language capacity and the ability to learn, which people with Alzheimer's disease may have difficulty with, do not seem to be affected.

A. Ramey/Photo Edit

A person with AIDS receives medical attention.

Treatment and Prevention of AIDS

At this time, there is no cure for AIDS. There are a multitude of hurdles to overcome in combating the disease. AIDS is caused by a form of virus, and even with modern technology, we don't know how to cure a virus. The common cold is caused by a virus; despite millions of dollars spent on research in the hopes of finding an effective cure, such a treatment has not yet been found for this common ailment. Currently, serious research is being undertaken to understand, prevent, and fight AIDS.

Prevention can be pursued in two major ways. First, people can abstain from activities and behaviors that put them at risk for contracting the disease. Second, scientists can work on developing a vaccine to prevent contracting the disease, similar to vaccines that prevent polio or measles. A vaccine might either block the virus from attacking a person's immune system or bolster the immune system so that HIV is unable to invade it.

Ethical Questions 10.5

EP 2.1.2 *If you knew someone who was HIV positive, would you be hesitant to interact with that person? If you had children, would you be hesitant to have them interact with children who are HIV-positive?*

Current treatment for HIV infection consists of *highly active antiretroviral therapy* (HAART). This has been very beneficial to many HIV-infected individuals since its introduction in 1996 when HAART initially became available. Current optimal HAART options consist of combinations (or "cocktails") consisting of at least three drugs belonging to at least two types of antiretroviral agents.

Standard goals of HAART include improvement in the patient's quality of life, reduction in complications, extension of life, and delaying the onset of AIDS symptoms. HAART does not cure the patient of HIV. For some patients, HAART achieves far less than optimal results, due to medication side effects/intolerance or infection with a drug-resistant strain of HIV. Antiretroviral drugs are expensive, and the majority of the world's infected individuals do not have access to medications and treatments for HIV and AIDS.

The U.S. government and health organizations endorse the ABC approach to lower the risk of acquiring AIDS during sex:

- Abstinence or delay of sexual activity, especially for youth.
- Being faithful, especially for those in committed relationships.
- Condom use, for those who engage in risky behavior. It is advisable to use a condom when having sexual intercourse with a new partner until it is certain that the person does not test positive for HIV.

Impacts of Social and Economic Forces: AIDS Discrimination and Oppression

People who test positive for HIV or who have AIDS are often victimized by discrimination. Many Americans have a "them and us" mentality about those who test positive for HIV or who have AIDS. They want to have no contact with anyone who has HIV. They erroneously think that casual social contact may put them at risk. As a result, people who have the

AIDS: A Global Epidemic

In the United States, the number of deaths from AIDS has been dropping since 1995 (Hyde & DeLamater, 2011). This drop has largely been due to expensive drug treatments, which are mainly available in more affluent nations. More than 33 million people worldwide are now infected with AIDS (Mooney, 2013), most of them in the developing nations of Asia and Africa. Rates of infection are increasing most rapidly in the world's poorest regions, especially in Africa, India, and China. More than 25 million people have died of AIDS since 1981 (Avert, 2010).

Sub-Saharan Africa (southern Africa) is more heavily affected by AIDS and HIV than any other region of the world. This area is estimated to have around two-thirds of the global total infected by HIV. There are nearly 17 million AIDS, orphans, whose parents have died of AIDS (Mooney, et al., 2013).

Prospects for coping with the AIDS epidemic in poor nations are gloomy, because of the high cost of drugs that delay the onset of AIDS.

AIDS virus are apt to be shunned, risk losing their jobs, and often are abandoned by family, spouses, lovers, and friends. In some communities, when it becomes public knowledge that a child has the AIDS virus, parents of other children have reacted by not allowing their children to attend the same school and by prohibiting their children from having any contact with the child who is HIV-positive.

Spotlight 10.3 summarizes material on the social and economic impact of AIDS worldwide.

Professional Values and AIDS

Social work has traditionally supported and advocated for oppressed and disenfranchised groups in our country—African Americans, Hispanics, the poor, older people, gays and lesbians, and women. Social workers have an ethical obligation to combat the numerous injustices connected with AIDS. AIDS is not a gay disease nor an intravenous drug user's disease. It is a human disease.

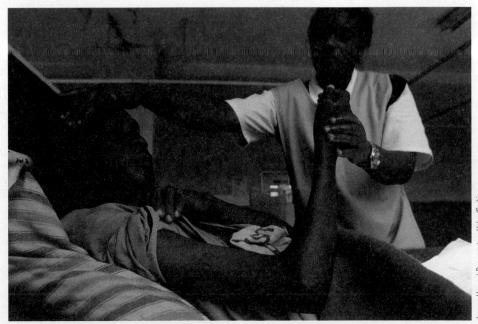

Medical care for a person with AIDS in Africa.

Jeremy Horner/ Documentary Value/Corbis

Ethical Question 10.6

EP 2.1.2

Do you believe the United States and other developed countries have a moral obligation to provide assistance to developing countries to empower them to more effectively prevent the transmission of HIV and to treat those who are HIV-positive?

It should be noted that in June 1998 the U.S. Supreme Court ruled that people infected with HIV (including those who have AIDS) are covered by the 1990 Americans with Disabilities Act, which protects those with a disability against discrimination in jobs, housing, and public accommodations.

Chapter Summary

The following summarizes this chapter's content as it relates to the learning objectives presented at the beginning of the chapter. Chapter content will help prepare students to:

LO 10-1 Recognize the contributions of physical development, health status, and other factors to health during young adulthood.

Young adulthood, from ages 18 through 30, is the healthiest time of life. Some lifestyles contribute to good health, whereas others, such as alcohol abuse

---

ETHICAL DILEMMA

Do You Have a Duty to Inform a Person Who Is at Risk of Acquiring HIV?

Assume you are a social worker and one of your clients informs you that he recently tested positive for HIV. You begin to assist him with his feelings and concerns, and you give him the name of a physician who has expertise in medically treating HIV-positive individuals. The client also tells you that he has a female sexual partner who is unaware of his HIV status. You urge him to tell her, so that they can take precautions to prevent her from being infected with the HIV virus. You also suggest that she be tested to determine her HIV status. He refuses to inform her, saying she'll leave him if she finds out about his HIV status.

Clients who are HIV-positive may be reluctant to inform their sexual partners for a variety of reasons. They may be concerned about the possibility of being abandoned. They may be angry that their partners may, in fact, have infected them. They may fear that their partners might tell others that they are HIV-positive.

When an HIV-positive client refuses to inform his or her partner, the social worker is confronted with two opposing values: the client's right to privacy versus the duty to warn a potential victim. The "duty to warn" principle was established by the 1974 case *Tarasoff* v. *Regents of the University of California.* In this precedent-setting case, the California Supreme Court ruled that psychotherapists have a duty to warn a potential victim when the professional believes there is a clear danger, even if this means breaching confidentiality. The court concluded, "The protective privilege ends where the public peril begins." Whether *Tarasoff* applies to AIDS cases has not been tested. All *Tarasoff* cases tested in court have involved threats with weapons or arson, not sexually transmitted diseases.

If you are a social worker in an agency that does not have a policy statement on this issue (and most agencies do not), what do you do?

Dickson (1998) advises the following:

For social workers—and other professionals—disclosure of a patient's or client's HIV/AIDS status to others presents significant ethical and perhaps legal problems Ethically, a strong argument can be made that if the patient or client refuses to tell a spouse, sexual partner, or other who is in danger of exposure, the social worker should take steps to protect that individual.... However, there is often a conflicting state confidentiality statute, with penalties for unauthorized disclosure of HIV or AIDS. Until the case and statutory law are better harmonized, the best course for the social worker is to work with the patient or client to get him or her to notify those at risk or, failing that, to gain an informed consent for notification. If this is unsuccessful, a court-ordered release of the confidential information is possible. As always, consultation and careful documentation are called for. (p. 212)

If you had a male client who was HIV-positive and refused to inform his girlfriend, would you seek a court-ordered release of confidential information? If the court order could not be obtained in a week, would you contact the girlfriend? Would you violate confidentiality by revealing her partner's HIV status, which in the long run may lengthen her life and improve her quality of life? What other options do you have?

and cigarette smoking, have a negative effect on health. Early detection of breast cancer is important because one in eight women will get it sometime in their lines.

LO 10-2 Describe the physical changes in middle adulthood, including those affecting physical appearance, sense organs, physical strength and reaction time, and intellectual functioning.

For many people, middle adulthood is the prime of life. Most middle-aged adults are in good health (both physically and psychologically), and they tend to earn more money than at any other age. Middle adulthood covers a range of years; somewhat arbitrarily, the authors consider middle adulthood to range from age 30 to age 65.

Some decline in physical capacities occurs in middle adulthood. There is also a higher incidence of health problems than in younger years. Cognitive functioning may actually increase during middle adulthood. Unfortunately, many people fail to be sufficiently active both mentally and physically, so their actual performance falls short of their potential performance.

LO 10-3 Describe the midlife crises associated with female menopause and male climacteric.

Female menopause is the time when a woman stops menstruating and can no longer bear children. For a few women, menopause is a serious crisis, but for many it is just another of life's developmental changes.

Many males reach an uncertain period in their lives, which is referred to as a midlife crisis. The ease or panic with which a man faces his middle years will depend on how he has accepted his weaknesses and strengths throughout life.

LO 10-4 Summarize sexual functioning in middle age.

A man's sex drive reaches its peak in his early 20s, while that of a woman tends to peak in her 30s or early 40s. There appears to be a close relationship between overall marital satisfaction and sexual satisfaction.

LO 10-5 Describe AIDS—its causes and effects; how it is contracted; how its spread can be prevented; and understand AIDS discrimination.

AIDS is a contagious and incurable disease that destroys the body's immune system. AIDS is caused by the HIV virus.

The two primary ways in which AIDS is spread are by sexual intercourse with someone who is HIV-positive and by using hypodermic needles that were also used by someone who is HIV-positive. Presently, the best way to stop the spread of AIDS is through educating people to avoid exposing themselves to known risks.

People who test positive for HIV or who have AIDS are often discriminated against.

COMPETENCY NOTES

The following identifies where Educational Policy (EP) competencies and practice behaviors are discussed in this chapter.

EP 2.1.2 Apply social work ethical principles to guide professional practice.
(pp. 471, 479, 490, 494, 496): Ethical questions are posed.

EP 2.1.7a Utilize conceptual frameworks to guide the process of assessment, intervention, and evaluation.
(All of this chapter)

EP 2.1.7b Critique and apply knowledge to understand person and environment.
(All of this chapter): The content of this chapter is focused on acquiring both of these practice behaviors in working with young and middle-age adults.

WEB RESOURCES

See this text's companion website at *www.cengage brain.com* for learning tools such as chapter quizzing, videos, and more.

PSYCHOLOGICAL ASPECTS OF YOUNG AND MIDDLE ADULTHOOD

It is Saturday night on Michigan Avenue in Chicago, and Doug and Debbie Peepers are engaged in a favorite activity on a warm summer evening: strolling down this "Gold Coast" street and watching the thousands of other people who are also strolling and people watching. While strolling, Doug and Debbie enjoy discussing why people do what they do. For example, they look at the elderly bag lady dressed in a moth-eaten red plaid overcoat, knee-high nylon hose, and ancient blue sneakers. They wonder what happened in her past that resulted in her now living on the street. Is she the victim of some tragic story? Where is her family, or doesn't she have any? Likewise, Doug and Debbie look at the *sleek, jet-set millionaire pulling up to the curb in his Maserati Biturbo so that a fastidious, uniformed doorman can help him out of the car. The millionaire is striking with his fashionable haircut, glowing gold jewelry, and well-cut clothes. Doug and Debbie wonder if he is a self-made computer magnate displaced from Silicon Valley, or if he's the product of generations of wealth.*

A Perspective

Figuring out the underlying reasons that cause others' actions often has substantial payoffs. If a salesperson knows what motivates people to buy a certain product, he or she can then structure the sales pitch around this focus. If a social worker knows why a father is abusing his child, the worker then knows what has to be changed to stop the abuse. If a mother knows what discipline techniques will be effective with her children, she is then better prepared to curb their unwanted behavior. The primary focus of this human behavior and social environment text is to provide theoretical frameworks that will help the reader to observe and assess human behavior.

Debbie Peepers is a computer programmer; her husband, Doug, is a mechanical engineer. Although they have had little formal training in assessing human behavior, playing amateur psychologist is one of their favorite leisure activities. As with anything else, assessments of human behavior are apt to be more accurate when one has greater knowledge and awareness of the significant cues to attend to. Professional social workers who will be planning interventions with people and organizations have a special need to develop their assessment skills. Young and middle adulthood provides another developmental stage to examine some of the psychological dynamics of human behavior. Because there is a paucity of psychological theories specifically directed at young and middle adulthood, the primary focus of this chapter will be on describing contemporary theories and models for assessing human behavior throughout the life span.

Learning Objectives

This chapter will help prepare students to:

LO 11-1 *Describe Erikson's theories of psychological development during young and middle adulthood*

LO 11-2 *Describe Peck's theory of psychological development during middle adulthood*

EP 2.1.7a,   **LO 11-3** *Describe Levinson's theories of life structure, life eras, and*
2.1.7b   *transitions during adulthood*

LO 11-4 *Summarize Maslow's theory on hierarchy of needs*

LO 11-5 *Describe emotional intelligence and social intelligence*

LO 11-6 *Describe nonverbal communication cues*

LO 11-7 *Summarize Glasser's choice theory of human behavior*

LO 11-8 *Describe Gawain's theories about intuition and how human behavior is affected by it*

LO 11-9 *Understand the issue of substance abuse*

LO 11-1 Describe Erickson's Theories of Psychological Development During Young and Middle Adulthood

Intimacy Versus Isolation

Erikson (1950) theorized that after young people develop a sense of identity, they next face the psychosocial crisis of intimacy versus isolation, which generally occurs in young adulthood (roughly during the 20s). *Intimacy* is the capacity to experience an open, tender, supportive relationship with another person, without fear of losing one's own identity in the process of growing close. In such a relationship, the partners are able to understand, cognitively and emotionally, each other's points of view. An intimate relationship permits the sharing of personal feelings as well as the disclosure of ideas and plans that are not fully developed. There is respect for each other and mutual enrichment in the interactions. Each person perceives an enhancement of his or her well-being through the stimulating interactions with the other.

Intimacy involves being empathetic and able to give and receive pleasure within the relationship. Although intimacy is often established within the context of a marital relationship, marriage itself does not produce intimacy. In some marriages, there is considerable intimacy (including sharing and mutual respect). However, in empty-shell marriages and in marriages with considerable conflict, there is very little intimacy. There are additional contexts where intimacy is apt to develop. The work setting is one of these, where close friendships are often formed. Close friendships are also apt to develop through membership in social and religious organizations.

Traditional socialization patterns in our society create different problems for males and females in the establishment of intimacy. Many boys are taught to be restrained in expressing their feelings and personal thoughts. They are also socialized to be competitive and self-reliant. They are raised to believe that they should be sexually aggressive and seek to "go as far as possible" in order to demonstrate their virility to their male friends. Males are thus often unprepared for intimate heterosexual relationships—which require that they express their feelings, be supportive rather than competitive, and have a commitment to continuing the relationship rather than piling up sexual trophies.

Traditionally, girls are socialized to be better prepared for the emotional demands of intimacy. They are socialized to express their feelings and personal thoughts and to be nurturant. They may, however, enter an intimate relationship with inappropriate expectations based on traditional gender-role stereotypes. For example, they may expect their partner to be stronger or more resourceful than he is. (The women's movement has changed gender-role expectations and socialization practices for males and females; hopefully, the difficulties that men and women experience in forming intimate relationships will be reduced in future years.)

The negative pole of the crisis of young adulthood is isolation. People who resist intimacy continually erect barriers between themselves and others. Some people view intimacy as a blurring of the boundaries of their own identity and therefore are reluctant to become involved in intimate relationships. Some people are so busy seeking or maintaining their identity that they cannot share and express themselves in an intimate relationship.

Isolation may also result from situational factors. A young person may be so involved in studying to get into medical school that he or she may not have the time for an intimate relationship. Or a teenage girl may become pregnant, deliver and start raising the child, and then have few opportunities to become involved in a close relationship with an adult.

Isolation may also result from diverging spheres of activity and interest. An example of how isolation may develop in a traditional marriage involves Bill and Mary Ramsey. They married while in their early 20s, after dating for four years and enjoying doing many activities together. They were very much in love. They both wanted a traditional marriage. In their early years of marriage, they had two children, and Mary was content to stay at home to raise them. In her leisure time, she interacted with the other wives in the neighborhood. Bill worked as an insurance agent and spent his leisure hours hunting, fishing, and attending sporting events with male friends. As the years passed, Mary and Bill had less and less in common. Isolation became increasingly evident in their lack of mutual understanding and their lack of support for each other's needs and life goals.

Generativity Versus Stagnation

Erikson's (1963) seventh life-stage developmental crisis is generativity versus stagnation. Generativity involves a concern with and interest in establishing and guiding the next generation. The crisis of generativity versus stagnation is perceived by a middle-aged adult to involve a commitment to improve the life conditions of future generations. The achievement of generativity involves a willingness to care about the people and the things that one has produced. It also involves a commitment to protecting and enhancing the conditions of one's society.

The achievement of generativity is important for the survival and development of any society. It involves the adult members' dedicating themselves to contributing their skills, resources, and creativity to improve the quality of life for the young.

The contributions may be monumental, as were Martin Luther King Jr.'s and Gandhi's to equality and human rights. For most people, however, the contributions are less well known—for example, the work done by volunteers for human service organizations. Adults serve on school boards, are active members of parent–teacher associations, serve on local government boards, are active in church activities, and so on. In each of these roles, adults have opportunities to positively influence the quality of life for others. To some extent, it is a reciprocity situation—when these adults were younger they were recipients of such services from other adults; now they are providers of such services. (See Highlight 11.1 The Key to Success in Work, and in Life—Be Focused)

The opposite of generativity is stagnation. Stagnation indicates a lack of psychological movement or growth. Some adults are self-centered and seek to maximize their pleasures at the expense of others; such people are stagnated because they have difficulty looking beyond their own needs or experiencing satisfaction in taking care of others. Having children does not necessarily guarantee generativity; adults who are unable to cope with raising children or with maintaining a household are likely to feel a sense of stagnation. Burnout has been identified as being one of the signs of stagnation (Davis, McKay, & Eshelmen, 2000).

Different individuals manifest stagnation in different ways. A narcissistic individual who generally relates to others in terms of how others can serve him may be fairly happy until the physical and psychological consequences of aging begin to occur. Such individuals often then experience an identity crisis when they realize their beautiful bodies and other physical attributes are waning. Many of these individuals experience a conversion to finding other meanings in living. For example, they coach Little League teams or become active in church activities.

On the other hand, a depressed person is likely to perceive himself or herself as having insufficient resources to make any contribution to society. Such a person is apt to have low self-esteem, to be pessimistic about opportunities for improvement in the future, and therefore to be unwilling to invest effort in self-improvement or in seeking to help others.

LO 11-2 Describe Peck's Theory of Psychological Development During Middle Adulthood

Peck's Theories of Psychological Development

Peck (1968) asserted that there are four psychological advances critical to successful adjustment in middle adulthood:

1. *Socializing versus sexualizing in human relationships.* Peck suggests it is psychologically healthy for middle-aged adults to redefine the men and women in their lives so that they value them as individuals, friends, and companions, rather than primarily as sex objects.
2. *Valuing wisdom versus valuing physical powers.* Peck views wisdom as the capacity to make wise choices in life. He suggests that well-adjusted middle-aged adults are aware that the wisdom they now have more than compensates for decreases in stamina, physical strength, and youthful attractiveness.
3. *Emotional flexibility versus emotional impoverishment.* Emotional flexibility is the capacity to shift emotional investments from one activity to another, and from one person to another. Middle-aged adults are apt to experience breaking of relationships due to the deaths of friends, parents, and other relatives and the growing independence of children and their moving out

HIGHLIGHT 11.1

The Key to Success in Work, and in Life—Be Focused

Daniel Goleman (2013) makes a strong case that the key to being successful in work, in love, and in life is to have the right focus. Doing a job well requires applying concentration. Creative insights flow best when we have an open mind, carefully exploring and analyzing all options. Having a good love life involves having a focus on doing what will lead our partner to feel that he or she is special.

Goleman (2013) asserts that there are three types of focuses: inner, other, and outer. The successful person becomes skilled at all three.

"Inner focus" involves having a high level of self-awareness and self-management. It involves knowing our strengths and limits. It involves having a set of values that involves a respect for ourselves and for others. It involves the ability to handle our distressing emotions so that those emotions do not interfere with getting things done. It involves marshaling our positive emotions to stay motivated in working toward our goals. It involves being able to bounce back from setbacks.

"Other focus" involves our ability to empathize with other people. It includes being able to understand how others perceive things, to connect with their feelings, and to figure out how we can help them to face their life challenges and to improve their lives. Being skilled at "other focus" leads to teamwork and collaboration. It leads others to respect us, to want to resolve interpersonal conflicts, and to attend to what we say.

"Outer focus" involves our abilities to sense the larger forces that shape our world. It involves having the capacity to engage in critical thinking, including the ability to formulate constructive and winning strategies.

Goleman (2013) asserts that the capacity to focus constructively can be enhanced in a variety of ways. A few will be summarized. When we are studying a subject (such as statistics) we should give that subject our full attention—tune out external distractions, such as a TV playing in the background or thinking about how our social life is going. It is very useful to receive expert feedback on how we can improve our capacities in reaching the goals we set. That expert might be a mentor, a life coach, a teacher, or someone who has excelled in an area involving a goal that we have set. Another suggestion is the necessity to put in the needed time to develop our

capacities to achieve our goals; the more we engage in focused practice, the more our brain circuitry establishes the habits we need to be successful.

An example of someone who excelled at all three of the above focuses was Susan Butcher. Butcher won the Iditarod four times. The Iditarod Trail Dog Race is the biggest sporting event in Alaska. It is an annual long-distance dog race in early March from Anchorage to Nome, Alaska. Mushers and a team of 16 dogs, of which at least 6 must be in harness at the finish line, cover the 1,000-mile distance in 9–15 days. Teams frequently race through blizzards causing whiteout conditions, subzero temperatures and gale-force wind which can cause wind chills to reach –100°F. This race has typically been won by macho men who race their dogs all day and rest at night, or go all night with rest during the day. Butcher observed her dogs closely (other focus) and concluded they performed much better by running and resting alternately in four- to six-hour chunks throughout the night and day instead of twelve hours on and twelve off. She took the risk of using this strategy (outer focus) to run the Iditaroid, while the macho men used the 12-hour on-and-off strategy. She also sensed (inner focus) that she had the internal fortitude to survive and thrive with this new strategy. She won four times!!!

An example of a leader who was not focused was Tony Howard, who was the CEO of BP in 2010 when the BP oil disaster occurred in the Gulf of Mexico. In the spring of 2010 the *Deepwater Horizon* oil rig exploded and sank in the Gulf. An estimated 210 million gallons of oil were discharged. Eleven persons died from the disaster. The oil spill was the largest oil spill in the history of the petroleum industry. Countless sea animals and birds were killed. The coasts of the Gulf were severely impaired environmentally. BP, the owner of the oil rig, has paid over $42 billion to settle criminal and civil suits. Tony Howard showed little concern for the spill's victims. He seemed annoyed by this "inconvenience" to his company and to his personal life. He claimed the disaster was not BP's fault but the subcontractor's fault. He took no responsibility. In fact, at the peak of the crisis he took a vacation and had a number of photos taken of him sailing on his yacht. A few months later BP discharged him as CEO. His actions during this crisis indicate he had extremely low levels of inner, other, and outer focuses.

of the home. Physical limitations may also necessitate a change in activities.

4. *Mental flexibility versus mental rigidity.* By middle age, most people have completed their formal education and have been sufficiently trained for their jobs or careers. They have also arrived at a

set of beliefs about an afterlife, religion, politics, desirable forms of entertainment, and so on. Some middle-aged adults stop seeking new information and ideas and become set in their ways and closed to new ideas. Such people are apt to be stymied in their intellectual growth and are apt to view life as mundane, unfulfilling, and unrewarding. Others are apt to continue to seek new experiences and be challenged by additional learning opportunities. They use their prior experiences and answers they've already arrived at as provisional guides to the solution of new issues. Such people are likely to view life as being meaningful, rewarding, and challenging.

LO 11-3 Describe Levinson's Theories of Life Structure, Life Eras, and Transitions During Adulthood

Levinson's Theories of Life Structure, Life Eras, and Transitions for Men

Levinson and his colleagues (Levinson, Darrow, Klein, Levinson, & McKee, 1974; Levinson & Levinson, 1978) studied 40 men ages 35 to 45, including business executives, academic biologists, novelists, and hourly workers in industry. These men were interviewed and given personality tests. From these data, Levinson constructed some developmental theories of life changes in adulthood.

At the heart of Levinson's theory is the concept of *life structure*. This term is defined as "the underlying pattern or design of a person's life at a given time" (Levinson, 1986, p. 6). A person's life structure shapes and is shaped by the person's interactions with the environment. Components of the life structure include the people, institutions, things, places, and causes that a person decides are most important, as well as the dreams, values, and emotions that make them so. Most people build their life structures around their work and their families. Other important aspects of one's life structure may include religion, racial identification, ethnic heritage, societal events (such as wars and economic depressions), and hobbies.

According to Levinson, life involves a number of passages: from the freedom of childhood to entering school; from school to the work world; from not dating to dating; from dating to breaking up or marrying; from marrying to divorce; and so on. Levinson sees some structure to these series of life passages. He asserts that people shape their life

structures during the following four overlapping eras (each of which is 20 to 30 years in length):

1. *Preadulthood* (birth to age 22) is the formative time from conception to the end of adolescence.
2. *Early adulthood* (age 17 to age 45) is the era in which people make choices that significantly influence their lives, and the era in which people display the greatest energy and experience the most stress.
3. *Middle adulthood* (age 40 to age 65) is the era in which people tend to have reduced biological capacities but increased social responsibilities.
4. *Late adulthood* (age 60 and beyond) is the final phase of life.

There are transitional periods within some of these eras, and there are also transitional periods of about five years each that connect these eras. These transitional periods are displayed in Table 11.1, which shows the approximate ages when these transitions occur. (The transitions do not consume all the time in these periods because there are times of stability within each transitional period.)

During these transitional periods, men review the life structures they have built and explore options for restructuring their lives. According to Levinson, people spend nearly half their adult lives in transition. These transitional periods are described in the following paragraphs.

Early adult transition (ages 17 to 22). During this transition (which may take three to five years), men move from preadulthood into adulthood. A person moves out of his or her parents' home and becomes more financially and emotionally independent. Going to college or joining the military service serves as a transitional institutional situation between being a child in a family and reaching full adult status.

Entry life structure for early adulthood (ages 22 to 28). This phase has been called "entering the adult world." During this phase, a young person becomes an adult and builds the entry life structure for early adulthood. Aspects of this phase often include: involvement with work, which may lead to a career choice; intimate relationships with others, which may lead to marriage and children; choosing a home; involvement with social and civic groups; and relationships with family and friends.

Two important features of this phase are a *dream* and a *mentor*. During this phase, men often have a

TABLE 11.1	ERAS AND TRANSITIONAL PERIODS IN LEVINSON'S THEORIES OF ADULT DEVELOPMENT (MALES)
ERAS	**TRANSITIONS**
1. Preadulthood (ages 0 to 22)	Early adult transition (ages 17 to 22)
2. Early adulthood (ages 17 to 45)	Entry life structure for early adulthood (ages 22 to 28)
	Age-30 transition (ages 28 to 33)
	Culminating life structure for early adulthood (ages 33 to 40)
	Midlife transition (ages 40 to 45)
3. Middle adulthood (ages 40 to 65)	Entry life structure for middle adulthood (ages 45 to 50)
	Age-50 transition (ages 50 to 55)
	Culminating life structure for middle adulthood (ages 55 to 60)
	Late adult transition (ages 60 to 65)
4. Late adulthood (age 60 and beyond)	

dream of their future, which is usually viewed in terms of a career. The vision of becoming a highly successful corporate president or a famous writer spurs them on and energizes their work activities. A man's success during these apprenticeship years is strongly influenced by finding a mentor. A mentor is older (usually by about 8 to 15 years). The relationship with the mentor is a friendship with adult equality, but the mentor also performs the fatherly tasks of teaching, caring, criticizing, helping, and offering constructive suggestions in both career and personal matters.

Ethical Question 11.1

Our dream of our future often becomes a self-fulfilling prophecy. What is your dream of your future?

EP 2.1.2

Age-30 transition (ages 28 to 33). During this phase, men take another look at their lives. They may review whether the commitments made during the previous decade were premature, or they may consider making strong commitments for the first time. Some men move fairly effortlessly through this transition. Others experience crises in which they decide their present life structures are intolerable, yet they have grave difficulty in formulating better ones. Marriage conflicts may erupt during this phase, and divorce is common. Work responsibilities may shift as the man is promoted, changes jobs, or settles into his job after a period of uncertainty. Some men seek counseling to help clarify their goals.

Culminating life structure for early adulthood (ages 33 to 40). This phase is ushered in by a period of "settling down." The person makes a concerted effort to realize youthful dreams. The apprenticeship is over. During this phase, men make deeper commitments to family, work, and other important aspects of their lives. They set specific goals for themselves (such as a certain level of income and moving into their own house) with a set timetable. They work at finding a niche in society by anchoring their lives in terms of career, family, and community involvement. They also work on advancing themselves to build a better life, become more creative, improve their skills, and so on. In the middle to late 30s, toward the end of the settling-down period, comes a phase called "becoming one's own man" (BOOM). During BOOM, a man often becomes independent of his mentor and may be at odds with his wife, boss, children, friends, lover, or coworkers. During this phase, a man chafes under the authority of those who have power and influence over him, and seeks to break away and speak with his own voice. However, he also fears a loss of respect from significant others during this period.

Midlife transition (ages 40 to 45). This transition is focused on completing the work of early adulthood while learning the ropes of middle adulthood. Similar to all other transitional periods, this transition is both an ending and a beginning. During this period, men (now more acutely aware of their mortality) question nearly every aspect of their lives. Many men find this as a time of moderate or severe crisis. People in this stage undergo a midlife reappraisal that often involves emotional turmoil. Previous values are reviewed. Such a review is often healthy; through examining the choices that they made early in life, they have the opportunity to focus on aspects of themselves that may have been neglected. Those who successfully negotiate this phase come to terms with the dreams of their youth and emerge with a more realistic view of themselves. Many men at this stage experience a midlife crisis (described in Chapter 10).

A man at midlife feels older than the younger generation, but is not yet ready to call himself middle-aged. A person at this age needs to integrate his need for separateness and his need for attachment to others. People at this age need to become "more compassionate, more reflective and judicious, less tyrannized by inner conflicts and external demands, and more genuinely loving of themselves and others" (Levinson, 1986, p. 5). People who fail in this task lead lives that become increasingly stagnant and trivial.

Entry life structure for middle adulthood (ages 45 to 50). During this transition, a man in his mid-40s begins a life structure that may involve new choices: perhaps a new wife or a different way of relating to his wife, or perhaps a new career or a restructuring of his present work. The most successful people often find middle age to be the most gratifying and creative time of life as they use opportunities that arise to allow new facets of their personalities to flower. Those who are unsuccessful in resolving the tasks of midlife lead a constricted life, or they keep busy in an organized but unfulfilling lifestyle.

Age-50 transition (ages 50 to 55). This transition is likely to be an especially difficult time for men whose midlife transition has been relatively smooth. Most men experience a moderate crisis at this time. It is another time at which men review where they have come from, and make plans for where they are heading.

Culminating life structure for middle adulthood (ages 55 to 60). This phase is generally a stable transition in which men finish the framework of their life structure for middle adulthood. During this phase, those who are able to rejuvenate themselves enrich their lives and generally find the 50s a time period of great fulfillment.

Late adult transition (ages 60 to 65). This is a major transitional turning point, as it is a time for ending middle age and preparing for late adulthood.

Note that Levinson primarily studied middle-aged men. As a result, he has only limited and speculative information of the transitions and adjustments that occur in late adulthood. However, an important finding of Levinson is that life is a series of passages—from periods of stability to periods of instability. This cycle continues throughout life.

Various researchers have applied Levinson's theories to women's lives, as discussed in Spotlight 11.1.

LO 11-4 Summarize Maslow's Theory on Hierarchy of Needs

Maslow's Hierarchy of Needs

Abraham Maslow (1954, 1968, 1971) viewed humans as having tremendous potential for personal development. He believed it was human nature for people to seek to know more about themselves and to strive to develop their capacities to the fullest. He viewed human nature as basically good and saw the striving for *self-actualization* as a positive process because it leads people to identify their abilities, to strive to develop them, to feel good as they become themselves, and to be beneficial to society. Yet he believed that very few people fully attain a state of self-actualization. Rather, Maslow saw most people as being in a constant state of striving to satisfy their needs.

Maslow identified a hierarchy of needs that motivate human behavior. When people fulfill the most elemental needs, they strive to meet those on the next level, and so forth, until the highest order of needs is reached. In ascending order, these needs are:

1. *Physiological:* Food, water, oxygen, rest, and so on.
2. *Safety:* Security, stability, and freedom from fear, anxiety, threats, and chaos. A social structure of laws and limits assists in meeting these needs.
3. *Belongingness and love:* Intimacy and affection provided by friends, family, and lover.

Application of Levinson's Theories to Women: An Evaluation

Papalia and Olds (1992) reviewed four unpublished dissertations describing studies that used female subjects and Levinson's research design. The four investigators interviewed a total of 39 women from 28 to 53 years old. The women were primarily white, although eight were African American. Most respondents were employed, but some were not. The studies included a mix of married and unmarried respondents, with and without children.

These studies tend, in general, to support the idea that women undergo similar kinds of age-linked changes as men, but they also found some important differences.

The Mentor: Women were substantially less likely to have a mentor. Many of the women identified role models during their 20s, but only four had a true mentor relationship. If these women's patterns are typical, many women may be hampered in their careers by lack of a mentor.

The Love Relationship: Levinson found that men want a "special woman" who helps them pursue their dreams. In the studies on women, all 39 respondents sought a "special man," but these women mostly saw themselves as supporting their special man's dreams, rather than wanting a special man who would support them in achieving their goals.

The Dream: Most respondents had dreams (goals they wanted to achieve in life). But their dreams were vaguer, more complex, more tentative and temporary, and less career-oriented than those of men. Most women's dreams were split between achievement and relationships. Women were more likely to define themselves in relation to others—husbands, children, parents, or colleagues. Whereas men tend to "find themselves" by separating from their families of origin and pursuing their own interests, women tend to develop their identity through the responsibilities and attachments of relationships.

Whereas men dream of achievements in occupations or careers, women dream of a mix of family and career interests. Although many female respondents sought to help their "special man" achieve his goals, others began at about age 30 making greater demands on their husbands to accommodate their interests and goals in regard to career, marriage, and raising children.

Levinson and Levinson (1996) completed a study in which 45 women were intensively interviewed. The women ranged in age from 35 to 45 years. The study was designed to focus on three subgroups: (1) 15 homemakers drawn randomly from the city directory of New Haven, Connecticut, (2) 15 women who had careers in major corporate financial organizations in New York City, and (3) 15 female faculty members in colleges and universities. The latter two groups were struggling to combine career and family.

A major finding of the study was that women, similar to men, go through a predictable, age-linked series of developmental stages, moving from one period to the next via transitions that are often painful and turbulent. Levinson concludes that his conception of life cycle, eras, and periods in life structure development provides a framework for the study of both men and women.

Yet Levinson found a number of profound differences between how men and women develop throughout their lives. Many of these differences relate to the phenomenon he calls *gender splitting*—the rigid division between male and female. Gender splitting includes such dimensions as differences in traditional gender-role expectations between men and women, the splitting between the female homemaker and the male provisioner, and the splitting of the personal qualities identified as "feminine" and "masculine." (Levinson notes that the evolution of society in the past few centuries has been gradually reducing the splitting.)

The women in the homemaker sample sought, at a young age, to lead predominantly traditional, family-centered lives. They entered marriage with the belief that their primary role was to continue the traditional family; the wife's role was to be the homemaker, have children, and do most of the domestic tasks. They viewed the husband's role as occupying the dominant family position and being the provisioner—devoting himself to outside work and bringing back the resources needed to sustain the family. These women were in for a shock. By midlife, only 1 homemaker of the 15 was not working outside the home. Fifty percent were legally divorced, and most of the rest were psychologically divorced. Most of these women were currently in the workforce, and several of those who had legally divorced were in a second marriage. At midlife, motherhood was becoming a less central component of their life structure. Many of these women, as they developed in their 30s and 40s, became more independent and sought to exist on more equal terms with men. Thus, young women who actively sought at a young age to have a traditional, family-centered life eventually sought to establish a more modern lifestyle, which Levinson called the "anti-traditional figure." Levinson concludes that a traditional marriage is no longer viable in our culture.

The women who had careers, in contrast, attempted even at a young age to modify the traditional pattern. A recurrent theme in their lives was the intense conflict between the "traditional homemaker figure" and the "internal anti-traditional figure." These women struggled with being everything to everyone and seeking to have everything. They spoke of excitement and joy and playfulness and challenge. But they were constantly plagued by exhaustion, worries about their children, and exasperation with their spouses who failed to do their fair share in helping with the household responsibilities and raising the children.

The study reveals considerable hardships for both the homemakers and the "career women"—anguish, stressful and traumatic experiences, marital difficulties, problems in raising their children, problems at work, and difficulties in personal relationships. The difficulties and anguish reported by these female subjects appear more pronounced than do those reported by Levinson in his earlier study of men.

4. *Self-esteem:* Self-respect, respect of others, achievement, attention, and appreciation.

5. *Self-actualization:* The sense that one is fulfilling one's potential and is doing what one is suited for and capable of. This need results in efforts to create and to learn. A fully developed, self-actualized person displays high levels of all of the following characteristics: accepts self, others, and nature; seeks justice, truth, order, unity, and beauty; has problem-solving abilities; is self-directed; has freshness of appreciation; has a richness of emotional responses; has satisfying and changing relationships with other people; is creative; and has a high sense of moral values.

Maslow's hierarchy of needs is illustrated in Figure 11.1. The needs at each level must be fairly well satisfied before the needs at the next level become important. Thus, physiological needs must be fairly well satisfied before safety needs become important, and so on. As applied to social work practice, Maslow's theory indicates that social workers must first help clients meet basic needs (e.g., physiological needs). Once clients' basic needs are met, higher-level needs can be dealt with.

Maslow did not offer an age-stage approach to development. Striving for self-actualization is seen as a universal process that can be observed at nearly all ages. However, it is likely that there is some progression among age groups. Infants probably have a strong emphasis on physiological needs. As a person gradually grows older, safety needs are emphasized, and then belongingness and love needs, and so on. Because middle-aged adults have had a variety of

learning experiences and tend to be at the peak of their earning potential, they tend to have a greater opportunity to focus on meeting self-actualization needs. However, such crises as unemployment, prolonged illness, and broken relationships can switch the emphasis to a lower level of need.

LO 11-5 Describe Emotional Intelligence and Social Intelligence

Emotional Intelligence

Psychologists Peter Salovey and John Mayer coined the term *emotional intelligence (EI)* in 1990 (Papalia et al., 2012). It refers to the ability to recognize and deal with one's own feelings as well as the feelings of others. Daniel Goleman (1995) popularized the EI concept and expanded it to include such qualities as empathy, motivation, social competence, optimism, and conscientiousness.

McClelland had done some earlier work on factors related to emotional intelligence (Papalia et al., 2012). In the 1960s, the U.S. State Department concluded that a test of general knowledge was a poor predictor of how well those applying to be foreign service officers would perform. In addition, the test tended to screen out women and people of color. McClelland devised a selection process that had nothing to do with general knowledge. He found that the best foreign service officers had positive expectations of others, were perceptive of the needs of others, and were skillful in forming social networks. His selection process emphasized these characteristics, and led to the appointment of effective foreign service officers. It also ended the discrimination against women and people of color.

Goleman (1995) developed an EI test. Studying nearly 500 corporations, Goleman found that those who rose to the top of the corporate ladder tended to score highest on EI. Goleman (1998, 2001) found the following competencies to be most closely associated with effective work performance:

- Self-awareness (accurate self-assessment, emotional self-awareness, and self-confidence)
- Self-management (trustworthiness, achievement drive, initiative, adaptability, and self-control)
- Social awareness (empathy, organizational awareness, and service orientation)

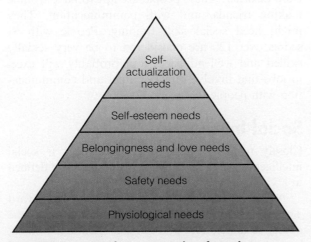

FIGURE 11.1 Maslow's Hierarchy of Needs

According to Maslow, we have a basic need to "belong" and a basic need to be "loved."

- Relationship management (exerting influence, conflict management, leadership, communication, building bonds, teamwork and collaboration, being a catalyst for change, and developing others)

Goleman (1998) found that excelling in at least one competency in each of these four areas appears to be a key to success in almost any job.

Emotional intelligence is not the opposite of cognitive intelligence. Some very bright people score high in EI, whereas others score lower. Some less-than-average scorers on IQ tests score high on EI, whereas others score lower.

Emotional intelligence is not easy to measure.

There are many emotions. How do we rate someone who can handle fear, but not guilt? The usefulness of a certain emotion may also depend on the circumstances; for example, it may not be functional for a person to be happy at a funeral when everyone else is sad.

Daniel Goleman (2006) has drawn on social neuroscience research to propose that social intelligence is made up of social awareness (including social cognition, empathy, attunement, and empathic accuracy) and social facility (including self-presentation, influence, concern, and synchrony).

There are various types of intelligence, including intellectual competencies, emotional intelligence, and social intelligence. Counseling/psychotherapy often involves helping people to modify their patterns of social intelligence, particularly those that cause clients to have problems in their interpersonal relationships.

Some tests have been developed to measure SI (Goleman, 2006). Like IQ tests, SI tests are usually based on a 100-point scale in which 100 is the average score. Most people score between 85 and 115. Scores of 140 are considered to be very high. People with SI scores below 80 may have an autism spectrum disorder. These people are apt to have trouble making friends, and with communication. They might need social skill training. People with SI scores over 120 are considered to be very socially skilled and well adjusted, and probably will excel in jobs that involve direct contact and communication with people.

Social Intelligence

Closely related to emotional intelligence is social intelligence. *Social Intelligence (SI)* has been defined in a variety of ways.

According to the original definition of Edward Thorndike (1920, p. 228), social intelligence is "the ability to understand and manage men and women, boys and girls, to act wisely in human relations."

According to this definition, it is equivalent to *interpersonal intelligence*.

Some authors have restricted the definition of SI to deal only with knowledge of social situations. With this perspective, SI is synonymous with social cognition or social marketing intelligence.

A common, contemporary definition of SI is the capacity to effectively negotiate complex social relationships and environments. People with high SIs are considered socially skilled, and generally work well in jobs that involve direct contact and communication with other people. People with low SIs are best suited to work in positions with low customer contact because they are apt not to have the required interpersonal communication and social skills for success with customers/clients.

LO 11-6 Describe Nonverbal Communication Cues

Mezzo-System Interactions: Nonverbal Communication

In seeking to assess human behavior, it is also important to attend to nonverbal communication. Sigmund Freud (quoted in Knapp & Hall, 1992) noted, "He that has eyes to see and ears to hear may convince himself that no mortal can keep a secret. If his lips are silent, he chatters with his finger tips; betrayal oozes out of him at every pore" (p. 391).

It is impossible not to communicate. No matter what we do, we transmit information about ourselves. Even an expressionless face communicates messages. As you are reading this, stop for a minute and analyze what nonverbal messages you would be sending if someone were observing you. Are your eyes wide open or half closed? Is your posture relaxed or tense? What are your facial expressions communicating? Are you occasionally gesturing? Do you occasionally roll your eyes? What would an observer deduce from these nonverbal cues about what you are feeling at the moment?

At times, nonverbal cues (such as sweating, stammering, blushing, and frowning) convey information about feelings that we desire to hide. By developing skill in reading nonverbal communication, we can be more aware of what others are feeling and better able to interact effectively. Because feelings stem from thoughts, nonverbal cues such as blushing also transmit information about what people are thinking.

The Functions of Nonverbal Communication

Nonverbal communication interacts with verbal communication. Nonverbal communication has the following functions in relation to verbal communication:

1. Nonverbal messages may *repeat* what is said verbally. A husband may say he is really looking forward to becoming a father and repeat this happy anticipation with glowing facial expressions.
2. Nonverbal messages may *substitute* for verbal ones. If a close friend has just failed an important exam, you can get a fairly good idea what he or she is thinking and feeling by looking at your friend's facial expressions.
3. Nonverbal messages may *accent* verbal messages. If someone you are dating says he or she is angry and upset with something you did, the depth of these feelings may be emphasized by pounding a fist and pointing an accusing finger.
4. Nonverbal messages may serve to *regulate* verbal behavior. Looking away from someone who is talking to you is a way of sending a message that you are not interested in talking.
5. Nonverbal messages may *contradict* verbal messages. An example of such a double message is someone with a red face, bulging veins, and a frown on the face, yelling, "Me—angry? Hell no, what makes you think I'm upset?" When nonverbal messages contradict verbal messages, the nonverbal messages are often more accurate. When receivers perceive a contradiction between nonverbal and verbal messages, they usually believe the nonverbal (Adler & Towne, 1981, p. 257).

Although nonverbal messages can be revealing, they can also be unintentionally misleading. Think of the times when people have misinterpreted your nonverbal messages. Perhaps you tend to say little when you first wake up, and others have interpreted this as meaning that you are preoccupied with a personal concern. Perhaps you have been quiet on a date because you are tired or because you're thinking about something that has recently happened. Has your date at times misinterpreted such quietness to mean you are bored or unhappy with the relationship? When you have been thinking deeply about a subject, have you had an expression on your face that others have interpreted as a frown? Nonverbal behavior is often difficult to interpret. A frown, for example, may represent a variety of feelings: being tired or angry; feeling rejected, confused, unhappy, irritated, disgusted, or bored; or simply being lost in thought. Nonverbal messages should not be interpreted as facts, but as clues that need to be checked out verbally to determine what the sender is thinking and feeling.

The remainder of this section will examine some examples of how we communicate nonverbally. Many of the examples are taken from white, middle-class American nonverbal communication. Nonverbal communication is strongly culture-based. In other words, the identical nonverbal behavior may be interpreted differently depending on the cultural/ethnic/racial background of the observer. For example, a comfortable interpersonal distance may be six inches in some cultures and six feet in others. Awareness of these differences is especially critical when communicating with clients of different cultural/ethnic/racial backgrounds. Such awareness is the only thing that makes accurate understanding possible. To illustrate, direct eye contact by a social worker is usually considered desirable by white clients but is considered rude and intimidating by many Native Americans. Kissing between adult males is usually interpreted as indicating a gay relationship in our culture, but such kissing is a greeting custom in some European cultures. Adult males who wear skirts in our culture are viewed as weird, but kilts (knee-length pleated skirts) are commonly worn by men in Scotland and by Scottish regiments in the British army. (An example of the importance of nonverbal communication is presented in Highlight 11.2.)

Posture

In picking up nonverbal cues from posture, one needs to note the overall posture of a person and the changes in posture. We tend to take relaxed postures in nonthreatening situations and to tighten up when under stress. Some people never relax, and their rigid posture shows it.

Watching the degree of tenseness has been found to be a way of detecting status differences. In interactions between a higher-status person and a lower-status person, the higher-status person is usually more relaxed, while the lower-status person is usually more rigid and tense (Knapp & Hall, 2010). For example, note the positions that are usually assumed when a faculty member and a student are conversing in the faculty member's office.

Teachers and public speakers often watch the posture of listeners to gauge how the presentation is going. If members in the audience are leaning forward in their chairs, it is a sign that the presentation is going over well. The audience slumping in their chairs is a cue that the presentation is beginning to bomb.

Body Orientation

Body orientation is the extent to which we face toward or away from someone with our head, body, and feet. Facing directly toward someone signals an interest in starting or continuing a conversation; facing away signals a desire to end or avoid conversation. The phrase "turning your back" on someone concisely summarizes the message that is sent when you turn away from someone. Can you remember the last time someone signaled that he or she wanted to end a conversation with you by turning away from you?

Gestures

Most of us are aware that our facial expressions convey our feelings. When we want to hide our true feelings, we concentrate on controlling our facial expressions. We are less aware that our gestures also reveal our feelings, and we put less effort into controlling our gestures when we want to cover up our feelings. As a result, gestures are sometimes better indicators of how we really feel.

People who are nervous tend to fidget. They may bite their fingernails, tap their fingers, rub their eyes or other parts of their body, bend paper clips, or tap a pencil. They may cross and uncross their legs. They may rhythmically swing one leg or move one foot back and forth.

Many gestures provide cues to a person's thoughts and feelings. Clenched fists, whitened knuckles, and pointing fingers signal anger. When

HIGHLIGHT 11.2

Eye-Accessing Cues

Neuro-linguistic programming (NLP) focuses on better understanding verbal and nonverbal communication (Lankton, 1980). Everyone has, at most, five sensory systems through which we connect with physical reality: the eyes (visual), ears (auditory), skin (kinesthetic), nose (smell), and tongue (taste). For each situation, your memories involved only one or two senses. For example, what do you remember most about the last grocery store that you were in? Perhaps you recalled an *image* of fresh fruits and vegetables, or *heard* the hustle and bustle of the activity, or *smelled* the fresh flowers.

Whenever we interact with the external world, we do so through sensory representations. Your sensory connection with a grocery store is apt to be quite different from your friend's. The same applies for everyone. Your most enjoyable sexual experience may be a visual one; your partner's may be auditory or kinesthetic.

We operate out of our sensory representations of the world, and not in "reality" itself. Our sensory representations provide us with a *map* of the territory. But the map is *not* the territory.

According to NLP, to assess another's actions accurately, it is important to identify the sensory representational system used by that person. If we are able to identify the other's representational system and "join with" that system in our interactions with the person, communication is apt to flow much more smoothly and rapport is enhanced. Conversely, if two people are unable to "join" together with the same representational system, communication may be tangential, and rapport will be adversely affected. The implications of this point are immense. Successful salespersons, educators, and therapists identify and "join" with the representational systems of the people they seek to influence. Once a person (customer, student, or client) has joined with the influencer, the influencer is able to lead the person in the direction she or he chooses. To a large extent the process of therapy, education, and sales can be defined as involving two steps: (1) the influencer's finding a way to join with the person to be influenced, and (2) the influencer then leading the person in a new (and, one hopes, positive) direction.

In our culture, people primarily use the visual, auditory, and kinesthetic (touch) systems. (A few other cultures place greater emphasis on smell and taste.) Unless the listener is aware of the sensory representational system the speaker is using, the listener may misinterpret what the speaker is intending. For example, when a client says "I understand you," the intended message depends on the representational system he or she is in:

Visual: "That looks really good to me."
Auditory: "I hear you clearly."
Kinesthetic: "What you are saying feels right to me."

In the course of growing up, people learn to favor particular representational systems for particular events. We are not only visual or auditory or kinesthetic. The sense in use depends on the situation, the context. It appears, though, that we tend to have a primary mode, in that we use more of one mode.

Eye-accessing cues are a fairly reliable way to determine which representational system is dominant at a given time. The following chart shows the eye-accessing cues for the three representational systems used in our culture: visual, auditory, and kinesthetic.

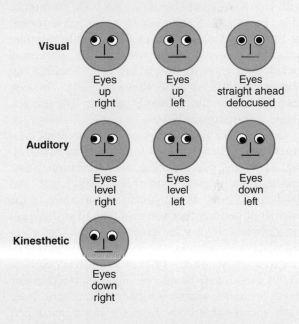

A simple example illustrates the importance of recognizing eye-accessing cues. In our society, when parents scold their children, they often become additionally angry when the children look down. Such parents erroneously assume their children are ignoring what they are saying. They may even yell, "Look at me when I'm talking to you!" In actuality, the eyes being down signals that the children feel bad about their misbehavior.

people want to express friendship or attraction, they tend to move closer. Hugs can represent a variety of feelings: physical attraction, good to see you, best wishes in the future, and friendship. Shaking hands is a signal of friendship and a way of saying, "Hello" or "Good-bye."

Albert Scheflen (1974) notes that a person's sexual feelings can be signaled through gestures.

He describes preening behavior, which is designed to send a message that the sender is attracted to the receiver. Preening behavior includes rearranging one's clothing, combing or stroking one's hair, and glancing in a mirror. Scheflen cites a number of invitational preening gestures that are specific to women: exposing or stroking a thigh, protruding the breast, placing a hand on the hip, and exhibiting a wrist or palm. Naturally, these gestures do not always suggest sexual interest; they may occur for a variety of other reasons.

There are also invitational preening gestures for men. As a woman talks, a man may gaze into her eyes intently. As conversation continues, he may lean in farther and farther toward the woman until he starts to close the gap between them. A man may stand with his pelvis thrust forward or sit or stand with legs wide apart. He may also stick his thumbs in his belt hoops, fingers aiming at his pelvic region; or thrust his hands in his pocket, thumbs pointing toward his pelvis. Male preening behaviors may include straightening his jacket or tie, rolling, up sleeves or cuffs, or smoothing his hair. He may tend to mimic the woman's gestures (Renninger, Wade, & Grammar, 2004).

Gestures are also used in relation to verbal messages for a variety of purposes: repeating, substituting, accenting, contradicting, and regulating. Some people literally speak with their hands, arms, and head movements. Many people are unaware of the number of gestures they use, and then (if videotaped) are surprised to view the extent to which they communicate with gestures.

Psychologists Michael Kraus and Dacher Keltner (2009) found that people of higher socioeconomic status are ruder when conversing with others. Their study showed that body language can signal a person's socioeconomic status. The researchers videotaped pairs of undergraduate students, who were strangers to one another, during one-on-one interviews. The researchers then observed certain gestures that indicate level of interest in the other person during one-minute slices of each conversation. They found that students whose parents were from backgrounds of higher socioeconomic status (SES) engaged in more "impolite" gestures such as doodling, grooming, and fidgeting. Lower-SES students engaged in more "I'm interested" gestures, such as laughter and raising of the eyebrows. Like a peacock's tail, the seemingly snooty gestures of higher-SES students indicate modern society's version of "I don't need you." Lower-SES individuals cannot afford to brush off others. They have fewer resources, and tend to be more dependent on others.

Touching

Rene Spitz (1945) demonstrated that young children need direct physical contact, such as being cuddled, held, and soothed. Without such direct physical contact, the emotional, social, intellectual, and physical development of children will be severely stunted. Spitz observed that in the 19th century high proportions of children died in some orphanages and other child-care institutions. The deaths were not found to be due to poor nutrition or inadequate medical care, but instead to lack of physical contact with parents or nurses. From this research came the practice of nurturing children in institutions—picking them up, holding them close, playing with them, and carrying them around several times a day. With this physical contact, the infant mortality rate in institutions dropped sharply.

Knapp and Hall (2010) describe findings that suggest that eczema, allergies, and certain other medical problems are in part caused by a person's lack of physical contact with a parent during infancy. Physical stimulation of children facilitates their intellectual, social, emotional, and physical development.

Adults also need physical contact. People need to know that they are loved, recognized, and appreciated. Touching through holding hands, hugging, and pats on the back are ways of communicating warmth and caring. Unfortunately, we have been socialized to refrain from touching, except in sexual contacts.

Touching someone is in fact an excellent way of conveying a variety of messages, depending on the context. A hug at a funeral will connote caring, while a hug when meeting someone connotes "It's good to see you." A hug between parent and child conveys "I love you," whereas a hug on a date may have sexual meanings. Numerous therapists have noted that communication and human relationships would be vastly improved if people reached out and touched others more—with hugs, squeezes of the hand, kisses, and pats on the back. Touch is crucial for the survival and development of children, and touch is just as crucial for adults, to assure them that they are worthwhile and loved.

Clothing

Clothes keep us warm and cover certain areas of our body so we are not arrested for indecency. But clothes have many other functions. Certain uniforms tell us what a person does and who we can receive services from: for example, uniforms of police officers, firefighters, nurses, physicians, and waiters. People intentionally and unintentionally send messages about themselves by what they wear. Clothes give messages about our occupations, personality, interests, sexuality, groups we identify with, social philosophies, religious beliefs, status, values, mood, age, nationality, and personal attitudes. For example, the way an instructor dresses sends messages to the class as to the kind of atmosphere he or she is seeking to create.

Any given item of clothing can convey several different meanings. For example, the tie a man selects to wear may reflect sophistication or nonconformity. In addition, the way the tie is worn (loosened, tightly knotted, thrown over one's shoulder, soiled and wrinkled) may provide additional information about the wearer.

A problem often encountered by women is that they lack a socially dictated business uniform. Men wear ties and suits in bland, dark colors. Women interested in developing professional and business careers are still seeking clothing that will convey the best impression. Often they must choose between "masculine-looking," unattractive, bland clothing and clothing that is more colorful and aesthetically attractive but considered unprofessional in some settings.

Clothes also affect our self-image. If we feel we are well dressed in a situation, we are apt to be more self-confident, assertive, and outgoing. If we feel we are poorly dressed in a situation, we are apt to feel more reserved, feel less confident, and be less assertive. When we're feeling at a low tide, dressing up can make us feel better about ourselves and raise our spirits.

There is a real danger of misreading nonverbal messages. We often stereotype others on skimpy information, and frequently our interpretations are in error—which may lead to serious adverse consequences. One of the authors remembers a client he interviewed in a correctional facility who for the previous four years had lived in an elegant fashion, traveled all over Europe and North America, and stayed in the finest hotels. He financed this lifestyle by writing bad checks. He stated that whenever he needed money, he would carefully dress in an expensive suit and would have no trouble cashing his bogus checks.

Personal Space

Each of us carries around a kind of invisible bubble of personal space wherever we go. The area inside this bubble is perceived as our private territory. The only people we are comfortable in allowing to enter our private territory are those we are emotionally close to. We feel we are being invaded when strangers and people we are not emotionally close to enter our private territory.

Edward Hall (1969) identified four distances or zones that we set in our daily interactions. We use these distances to guide us in setting the type of interactions we want to have with others. The particular zone we choose depends on the context of the conversation, how we feel toward the other person, and what our interpersonal goals are. These zones include the intimate zone, the personal zone, the social zone, and the public zone.

Intimate Zone

The *intimate zone* begins with skin surface and goes out about 18 inches. We generally let only people we are emotionally very close to enter this boundary, and then mostly in private situations—comforting, conveying caring, making love, and showing love and affection. When we voluntarily let and want someone to enter this zone, it is a sign of trust. We lower our defenses. Think about the dates you have. If the person moves within this zone and sits tight against you, it is a signal that he or she is comfortable with the relationship and may want it to progress further. On the other hand, if the person seeks to maintain a safe distance of two or more feet, the person is still sorting out the relationship or wants a more distant relationship.

When someone moves into this intimate zone without our wanting them to, we feel invaded and threatened. Our posture becomes more upright, and our muscles tense. We may move back and avoid eye contact as a way of signaling we want a more distant relationship. When we are forced to get close to strangers (on crowded buses and elevators), we tend to avoid eye contact and try not to touch

When two people are romantically involved, they love to be as close as possible to each other.

others, probably as a way of conveying, "I'm sorry I'm forced to invade your territory. I'll try not to bother you."

Personal Zone

The *personal zone* ranges from about 18 inches to approximately four feet. This is the distance at which couples stand in public. Interestingly, if someone of the opposite sex at a party stands this close to someone we are dating or are married to, we tend to become suspicious of that person's intentions. If we see our spouse or date move this close to someone of the opposite sex at a party, we may become suspicious and sometimes jealous.

The far range of the personal zone (from about two-and-a-half to four feet) is the distance at which we convey that we are seeking to keep the other person at arm's length. It is the distance just beyond the other person's reach. Interactions at this distance may still be reasonably close, but they are much less personal than the ones that occur at a closer distance. Sometimes in communication at arm's length people are testing whether they want the relationship to become emotionally closer.

Social Zone

The *social zone* ranges from about 4 feet to about 12 feet. Business communications are frequently

exchanged in this zone. The closer part of this zone (from four to about seven feet) is the distance at which people who work together usually converse, and it is the distance at which salespeople and customers usually interact.

The 7- to 12-foot range is the distance for more impersonal and formal situations. For example, this is the distance at which our boss talks to us from behind his or her desk. If we were to pull our chair around to the boss's side of the desk in order to sit closer, a different kind of relationship would be signaled. Furniture arrangement in an office also conveys signals about the type of relationship the officeholder wants to have. For example, an office in which there is a desk between the officeholder and the customer/client/student suggests that a formal and impersonal interaction is being sought. An office in which a desk is not used as a barrier suggests that a warmer, less formal interaction is allowed.

Public Zone

The *public zone* runs outward from 12 feet. Teachers and public speakers often use a distance of 12 to 18 feet from their audience. In the farther distances of public space (beyond 25 feet), two-way communication is difficult. Any speaker who voluntarily chooses to have considerable distance from the audience is not interested in having a dialogue.

Territoriality

Territoriality is behavior characterized by identification with an area in such a way as to indicate ownership and defense of this territory against those who may invade it (Knapp & Hall, 2010). Many animals will strike back against much larger organisms if they feel their territory is being invaded.

Territoriality also exists in humans. There are even things we feel we own that we really do not own. Students tend in each class to select a certain seat to sit in. If someone else should happen to sit in your chosen seat, do you feel your territory is being invaded?

What we acquire as property is a strong indicator of our interests and values. The things we acquire are often topics of conversation—cars, homes, leisure-time equipment, plants, clothes. These material things also communicate messages about our status. Wealthy people acquire more property. Interestingly, we generally grant more personal space and greater privacy to people of higher status. For example, we will knock at the boss's office and wait for an invitation to walk in before entering. With people of a status similar to ours or of a lower status, we frequently walk right in.

Facial Expressions

For most people, the face and eyes are the primary sources of nonverbal communication. Facial expressions often mirror our thoughts and feelings. Yet facial expressions are a complex source of information for several reasons. First, they can change rapidly. Slow-motion films have shown that a fleeting expression can come and go in as short a time as a fifth of a second (Knapp & Hall, 2010). In addition, researchers have found that there are at least 8 distinguishable positions of the eyes and lids, at least 8 positions for the eyebrows and forehead, and at least 10 for the lower face (Knapp & Hall, 2010). As a result, we have several hundred different possible expressions, and compiling a directory of them and their corresponding emotions is almost impossible.

Ekman and Friesen (1975) identified six basic emotions that facial expressions reflect: fear, surprise, anger, happiness, disgust, and sadness. These expressions appear to be recognizable in all cultures. People seeing photos of these expressions are quite accurate in identifying these emotions. Therefore, although facial expressions are complex, these six emotions can fairly accurately be identified (Knapp & Hall, 2010).

A word of caution should be noted about reading facial expressions. Because people are generally aware that their facial expressions reflect what they are feeling and thinking, they may seek to mask their facial expressions for a variety of reasons. For example, a person who is angry, but doesn't want others to see the anger, may seek to hide this feeling by smiling. Therefore, in reading facial expressions we should be aware that the sender may be seeking to conceal his or her real thoughts and feelings.

The eyes are also great communicators. When we want to end a conversation or avoid a conversation, we look away from the other person's eyes. When we want to start a conversation, we often seek out the other's eyes. We may wait until the receiver looks at us as a signal to begin. The eyes also communicate dominance and submission. When a high-status person and a low-status person are looking at each other, the low-status person tends to look away first. Downcast eyes signal submission or giving in. (Downcast eyes may also signal sadness, boredom, or fatigue.)

Good salespeople are aware that eyes are a sign of involvement. When they know they have caught our eye, they begin their pitch and seek to maintain eye contact. They know there are social norms in our society, such as the courtesy of hearing what a person has to say once we allow the person to begin speaking. These social norms trap us into hearing the sales pitch once eye contact has been made. Good salespeople watch eyes in a store in another way. They observe what items we are looking at and then seek to emphasize those items in their sales pitch.

Eye expressions suggest a wide range of human emotions. Wide-open eyes suggest wonder, terror, frankness, or naivete. Raised upper eyelids may mean displeasure. A constant stare connotes coldness. Eyes rolled upward suggest another's behavior is unusual or weird.

When we become emotionally aroused or interested in something, the pupils of our eyes dilate. Some counselors are so skilled in reading pupil dilation that they can tell when they touch on a subject that a client is sensitive about.

Voice

The tone of one's voice often has more influence than do the actual words spoken. The same word or phrase may have many meanings. Therefore, the way we say the word is the meaning we give to the word. For example, Knapp and Hall (2010, p. 367) show how the meaning of the following sentence is changed by the word that is emphasized.

1. *He's* giving this money to Herbie. (*He* is the one giving the money, nobody else.)
2. He's *giving* this money to Herbie. (He is *giving*, not lending the money.)
3. He's giving *this* money to Herbie. (The money being exchanged is not from another fund or source; it is *this* money.)
4. He's giving this *money* to Herbie. (Money is the unit of exchange, not a check.)
5. He's giving this money to *Herbie*. (The recipient is Herbie, not Eric or Bill or Rod.)

When we ask a question, we usually raise our voice at the end of the sentence. When we make a declarative statement, we usually lower our voice at the end of the sentence. Sometimes we intentionally manipulate our voice to contradict the verbal message.

In addition to emphasizing certain words in a sentence, one's voice can communicate in many other ways. These ways include length of pauses, tone, pitch, speed, volume, and disfluencies (such as stammering or saying, "uh," "um," and "er"). All of these factors together have been called *paralanguage.* Paralanguage deals with how something is said and not with what is said (Knapp & Hall, 2010).

Paralanguage can communicate the exact opposite of what the verbal message is. You might practice through changing your voice how you would seek to convey literally, and then sarcastically, messages such as:

"I really like you."

"I'm having a perfectly wonderful time."

"You're really terrific."

When paralanguage and the verbal message are contradictory, the former will carry more meaning. When there is a contradiction between words and the way something is said, subjects usually interpret the message in terms of the way it is said (Knapp & Hall, 2010).

An excellent way to learn more about the way you are using paralanguage is to videotape one of your conversations or speeches and then watch the replay. Such a process will also give you valuable feedback about your other forms of nonverbal communication.

Physical Appearance

Although it is common to hear people say that only inner beauty really counts, research shows that outer beauty (physical attractiveness) plays an influential role in a broad range of interpersonal interactions. Male college professors tend to give higher grades to females who are physically attractive than to those who are less attractive. In one study, attractive females were more effective in modifying the attitudes of male students on national issues than were less attractive females. Attractive persons, regardless of sex, are rated high on credibility, which greatly increases their ultimate persuasiveness in a variety of areas, including sales, public speaking, and counseling (Knapp & Hall, 2010). Conversely, unattractive defendants are more likely to be judged guilty in courtrooms and more likely to receive longer sentences (Knapp & Hall, 2010). The evidence is clear that *initially* we respond much more favorably to those perceived as physically attractive than to those seen as less attractive. Attractiveness serves to open doors and create greater opportunities.

Physically attractive people have been found to outstrip less attractive people on a wide range of socially desirable evaluations, including personality, popularity, success, sociability, persuasiveness, sexuality, and often happiness (Knapp & Hall, 2010). For example, attractive women are more apt to be helped and less likely to be the objects of aggressive (nonsexual) acts.

Less attractive people are at a disadvantage from early childhood on. Teachers, for example, interact less (and less positively) with unattractive children. Physical attractiveness is also a crucial factor in determining who we decide to date and who we decide to marry. In many situations, practically everyone prefers the most attractive date regardless of her or his own attractiveness and regardless of being rejected by the most attractive date (Knapp & Hall, 2010).

 Ethical Questions 11.2

EP 2.1.2 *Do you sometimes discriminate against people who are less attractive? For example, do you seek to date only people who are physically attractive?*

Unattractive men who are seen with attractive women are judged higher in a number of areas than are attractive men who are seen with attractive partners (Bar-Tal & Saxe, 1976). They are judged as making more money, as being more successful in their occupation, and as being more intelligent. Apparently, the evaluators reason that unattractive males must have to offset this imbalance by succeeding in other areas to be able to obtain dates with attractive women.

Being physically attractive does *not* mean that a person will *be* more intelligent, more successful, better adjusted, and happier than less attractive people. Attractiveness *initially* opens more opportunities to be successful, but after a door is opened, it is performance that determines outcome.

The shape of one's body suggests certain stereotypes that may or may not be accurate. People who are overweight are judged to be older, more old-fashioned, less strong physically, more talkative, less good-looking, more agreeable and good-natured, more trusting of others, more dependent on others, and more warmhearted and sympathetic. People who are muscular are rated as being stronger, better looking, younger, more adventurous, more self-reliant, more mature in behavior, and more masculine.

People with a thin physique are rated as younger, more suspicious of others, more tense and nervous, less masculine, more pessimistic, quieter, more stubborn, and more inclined to be difficult. Both overweight people and very thin people have been found to be discriminated against when seeking to obtain jobs, buy life insurance, adopt children, and be accepted into college. Being tall is a strong advantage in the business world for men but not for women. Shorter men are shortchanged on salaries and job opportunities (Knapp & Hall, 2010).

We have considerable capacity to improve our physical appearance. Eating well, exercising, learning to manage stress, learning to be assertive, getting adequate sleep, improving grooming habits, and improving choice of clothes will substantially improve physical appearance. Improving physical appearance will open more doors and create more opportunities.

The Environment

Most of us have been in immaculate homes that have "un-living rooms" with plastic furniture coverings, lampshade covers, and spotless bare tables that send off-putting nonverbal messages: Do not get me dirty, do not touch, do not put your feet up. In such homes, we are not able to relax; their owners wonder why guests don't relax and have a good time. They are unaware that the environment is communicating messages that lead guests to feel uncomfortable.

The attractiveness of a room shapes the kind of communication that takes place and also influences the happiness and energy of people working in it. When people are in an unattractive room, they tend to become tired and bored and take longer to complete assigned work than when in an attractive room. When people are in a pleasant room, they display a greater desire to work, and they communicate many more feelings of comfort, importance, and enjoyment. Workers do a better job and generally feel better in an attractive environment (Knapp & Hall, 2010).

The color of rooms apparently affects mood and productivity. In one study, children who were given an IQ test scored about 12 points higher in rooms they described as beautiful than they did in rooms they described as having ugly colors (Knapp & Hall, 2010). The beautiful rooms appeared to stimulate alertness and creativity. Friendly words and smiles increased in the beautiful rooms, and irritability and hostility decreased. The most arousing colors are, in order, red, orange, yellow, violet, blue, and green. The pastel colors of pink, baby blue, and peach are thought to have a calming effect. Some prison and jail administrators are now painting cells in pastel colors, hoping that it will have a calming and relaxing effect on inmates.

Businesses have found that they can control the rate of customer turnover through environmental design. Dim lighting, comfortable seats, and subdued noise levels will encourage customers to talk more and spend more time in a bar or restaurant (Knapp & Hall, 2010). If the goal is to run a high-volume business (as in a fast-food place), businesses can encourage customer turnover with bright lights, uncomfortable seats, and high noise levels (for example, by having poor soundproofing). Chairs can be constructed to be comfortable, or they can be made uncomfortable by putting pressure on the sitter's back. Airports seek to get travelers into the restaurants and bars where they will spend money by having comfortable chairs, tables where people can converse, and dim lighting. They discourage travelers from sitting in waiting areas by using bright lighting and by having uncomfortable chairs bolted shoulder to shoulder in rows facing outward, which makes conversation and relaxation more difficult.

Casino owners in Las Vegas build their facilities without windows or clocks so that customers will be less aware of how long they have been gambling. The aim is to keep people gambling as long as possible. Without windows, some customers are unaware that they are gambling into the next day.

The shape and design of buildings affect interaction patterns in many ways. In apartment buildings, people who live near stairways and mailboxes have more contact with neighbors than do those who live in less heavily traveled parts of the building. Access to neighbors increases communication. Fences, rows of trees, and long driveways increase privacy.

As indicated earlier, types and placement of furniture in offices convey messages about whether the officeholder wants informal, relaxed communication or formal, to-the-point communication. A round table, for example, suggests the officeholder is seeking to have the communication seen as egalitarian, whereas a rectangular table suggests the communication should recognize status and power differentials. With a rectangular table, the high-status people generally sit at one end of the table. If the meeting is between parties of equal strength, one contingent tends to sit on one side, and the other on the other side, rather than intermingling the members. A classroom in which the chairs are in a circle suggests the instructor wants to create an informal discussion atmosphere. A classroom with the chairs in rows suggests the instructor wants to create a formal, lecture-type atmosphere.

LO 11-7 Summarize Glasser's Choice Theory of Human Behavior

Choice Theory

William Glasser (1998) developed a *choice theory* explanation of human behavior. A major thrust of choice theory is that we carry around pictures in our heads, both of what reality is like and of how we would like it to be. Glasser (1984, p. 32) asserts, "All our behavior is our constant attempt to reduce the difference between what we want (the pictures in our heads) and what we have (the way we see situations in the world)."

Some examples will illustrate this idea. Each of us has a detailed idea of the type of person we would like to date; when we find someone who closely matches our idea, we seek to form a relationship. Each of us carries around a picture album of our favorite foods; when we're hungry, we select an item and go about obtaining that food.

How do we develop the pictures/albums/ideas that we believe will satisfy our needs? According to Glasser, we begin to create them at an early age (perhaps even before birth) and we spend our whole lives enlarging them. Essentially, whenever what we do gets us something that satisfies a need, we store the picture of it in our personal albums. Glasser (1984) gives an example of this process by describing how a hungry child added chocolate chip cookies to his picture album:

Suppose you had a grandson and your daughter left you in charge while he was taking a nap She said she would be right back, because he would be ravenous when he awoke and she knew you had no idea what to feed an eleven-month-old child. She was right. As soon as she left, he awoke screaming his head off, obviously starved. You tried a bottle, but he rejected it—he had something more substantial in mind. But what? Being unused to a howling baby, and desperate, you tried a chocolate chip cookie and it worked wonders. At first, he did not seem to know what it was, but he was a quick learner. He quickly polished off three cookies. [Your daughter] returned and almost polished you off for being so stupid as to give a baby chocolate. "Now," she said, "he will be yelling all day for those cookies." She was right. If he is like most of us, he will probably have chocolate on his mind for the rest of his life. (p. 19)

When this child learned how satisfying chocolate chip cookies are, he placed the picture of these cookies in his personal picture album.

By *pictures*, Glasser means *perceptions* from our five senses of sight, hearing, touch, smell, and taste. The pictures in our albums do not have to be rational. Anorexics picture themselves as too fat and starve themselves to come closer to their irrational picture of thinness. Rapists have pictures of satisfying their power needs and perhaps sexual needs through sexual assault. To change a picture, we must replace it with one that will at least reasonably satisfy the need in question. People who are unable to replace a picture may endure a lifetime of misery. Some battered women, for example, endure brutal beatings and humiliations in marriage because they cannot picture themselves as worthy of a loving relationship.

Glasser notes that whenever the picture we see and the one we want to see differ, a *signal* generated by this difference leads us to behave in a way that will obtain the picture we want. We examine our behavior and select one or more desired pictures that we believe will help us reduce this difference. These behaviors include not only straightforward problem-solving efforts but also manipulative strategies such as anger, pouting, and guilt. People who act irresponsibly or ineffectually have either failed to select responsible behaviors from their repertoires or have not yet learned responsible courses of action.

Glasser believes we are driven by five basic, innate needs. As soon as one need is satisfied, another need (or perhaps two or more acting together) pushes for satisfaction. Our first need is *survival*. This includes such vital functions as breathing, digesting food, sweating, regulating blood pressure, and meeting the demands of hunger, thirst, and sex.

Our second need is *love and belonging*. We generally meet this need through family, friends, pets, plants, and material possessions.

Our third need is *power*. According to Glasser, this need involves getting others to obey us and then receiving the esteem and recognition that accompany power. Our drive for power sometimes conflicts with our need to belong. Two people in a relationship may struggle to control it rather than create an egalitarian relationship.

Our fourth need is *freedom*. People want the freedom to choose how they live their lives, to express themselves, to read and write what they choose, to associate with whom they want, and to worship or not worship as they believe.

Our fifth need *is fun*. Glasser believes learning is often fun; this gives us a great incentive to assimilate what we need to satisfy our needs. Classes that are grim and boring are major failings of our educational system. Laughter and humor help fulfill our need for fun. Fun is such a vital part of living that most of us have trouble conceiving of life without it.

Choice theory explains why and how we make the choices that determine the course of our lives. It is an *internal control psychology;* Glasser (1998) asserts that we choose everything we do. Following are the major axioms of choice theory:

1. The only behavior we can control is our own. No one can make us do anything we do not want to do, as long as we are willing to endure the consequences (i.e., punishment for not doing what others want us to do). If we choose to do what others want us to do under the threat of severe punishment, we tend to be passive-aggressive by not performing well. When we try to force others to do what they do not want to do, they may choose not to do it—or choose to also be passive-aggressive by not performing well.

2. All we can give or get from other people is information. How we deal with that information is our choice or theirs. A teacher, for example, can assign readings to students, but he is not responsible if some students choose not to read them. The teacher therefore should not feel responsible for those students who choose not to do the readings. The teacher can choose, of course, to give consequences to those students who fail to follow the reading instructions—such as giving them a lower grade.

3. All we can do from birth to death is "behave." Glasser indicates all behavior is "total behavior" and is made up of four inseparable components: acting, thinking, feeling, and physiology. Each of these components interacts and affects the three other components. (The next two axioms elaborate on this interaction.)

4. All long-lasting psychological problems are relationship problems. Relationship problems are also a partial cause of many other problems, such as fatigue, pain, weakness, and autoimmune diseases (such as fibromyalgia and rheumatoid arthritis). Glasser (1998) states:

Most doctors believe that adult rheumatoid is caused by the victims' immune systems attacking their own joints as if these joints were foreign bodies. Another way of putting it is that their own creative systems are trying to protect these people from a perceived harm. If we could figure out a way to stop this misguided creativity, millions of people who suffer from this disease and a host of other relentless diseases, called autoimmune diseases, could be helped. (pp. 137–138)

Our usual way of dealing with an important relationship that is not working out the way we want it to is to choose misery—emotional misery and physical misery.

5. Human brains are very creative. A woman who has been sexually abused as a child may develop a dissociative identity disorder to psychologically shield herself from the emotional pain of the abuse. According to Glasser, almost all medical problems for which physicians are unable to identify the cause are partially created by the ill person's brain to deal with unhappiness that she or he is experiencing. Unhappiness is the force that inspires the creativity inherent in the brain to be a partial cause of symptoms described in the *DSM-5* (American Psychiatric Association, 2013a)—aches and pains (such as migraine headaches) and physical illnesses (such as heart disease, cancer, adult asthma, and eczema).

In regard to the brain creating the symptoms in the *DSM-5*, Glasser (2003) describes how unhappiness may lead the brain to create hallucinations:

Suppose, instead of your creativity presenting an idea to you as a thought, it created a voice uttering a threat or any other message directly into the auditory cortex of your brain. You would hear an actual voice or voices; it could be a stranger or you might recognize whose voice it was. It would be impossible, just by hearing it, for you to tell it from an actual voice or voices. (p. 114)

Since we can hear voices, our brain's can create voices that we hear when no one else is around. Since we can see, it can create visual hallucinations. Since we can feel pain, it can create pain—perhaps in greater severity and duration than what we experience from an injury or illness. Since we are able to fear, the brain can and does create disabling phobias.

Our thoughts also have an impact on our physiological functioning. Highlight 11.3 provides some examples of healing thoughts versus disease-producing thoughts.

6. Barring untreatable physical illnesses or severe poverty, unsatisfying relationships are the primary source of crimes, addictions, and emotional and behavioral disorders.

7. It is a serious mistake (from which it is irrational to expect positive results) to seek to control others by nagging, preaching, punishing, or threatening to punish them. As indicated earlier, the only person one can effectively control is oneself. In order to progress in improving human relationships, we need to give up seeking to control others through nagging, preaching, putting down, or threatening punishment.

Ethical Questions 11.3

Is it unethical to seek to control others by nagging, preaching to, or punishing them? Do parents sometimes need to nag, preach to, and punish their children?

EP 2.1.2

8. The unsatisfying (problematic) relationship is always a current one. We cannot live happily without at least one satisfying relationship. In a quality relationship, each person seeks to meet his or her needs and wants, and those of the other person.

9. The solving circle is a good strategy for two people who know choice theory to use in redefining their freedom and improving their relationship. Glasser advocates its use in marital and dating relationships. Each person pictures the relationship inside a large circle, called the solving circle. An imaginary circle is drawn on the floor. The two people sit on two chairs within the circle. They are told there are three entities in the solving circle: the two of them and the relationship. They are asked to agree that maintaining the relationship takes precedence over what each person wants. In the circle, each person tells the other what he or she will agree to do to help the relationship. Within those limits, the two must reach a compromise on their conflicts.

10. Painful events that happened in the past greatly influence what we are today, but dwelling on the past can contribute little or nothing to what we need to do now—which is to improve an important present relationship.

11. It is not necessary to know our past before we can deal with the present. It is good to revisit the parts of our past that were satisfying, but it is even better to leave what was unhappy alone.

HIGHLIGHT 11.3

The Impact of Thoughts on Physiological Functioning

Diseases and medical conditions are caused by a variety of factors: what we eat; exposure to germs, viruses, and bacteria; genetics; too much or too little sun; lack of exercise; lack of sleep; and thoughts. The following are examples of how our thoughts impact our physiological functioning.

1. Under hypnosis: "I will feel no pain" → painless surgery without anesthesia.
2. Under hypnosis: " Something hot is burning my arm" → blister.
3. Deep breathing relaxation: "I am relaxing: → painless dental drilling without anesthesia.
4. "I no longer want to live" → death in a few years.
5. "I don't want to die yet" → ravaged by cancer, person continues to live.
6. When having a cold: "I must get all these things done" → cold lingers for weeks. When having a cold: "I will take time off to rest and relax" → cold ends after a few days.
7. Hangover: "This pain is killing me" → intense pain Hangover: "I will relax and ignore the pain" → pain soon subsides (the same is true for most other headaches).
8. "I am worried about such and such," or "I have *so* much to do tomorrow" → inability to fall asleep.
9. "I will have serious complications if I have this surgery" → greater likehood of complications.
10. "This plane I'm going to fly on is going to crash" → anxiety, panic attacks. (Panic attacks, if frequent, can lead to a variety of illnesses, including hypertension and heart problems.)
11. A woman thinking she's pregnant, when she isn't → morning sickness and enlarged stomach.
12. Thinking relaxing thoughts → immune system functions well, fights off illnesses, and facilitates healing.
13. Thinking alarming thoughts (such as "I miss——*so* much!") → high stress level → a variety of illnesses,

including heart problems, colitis, stomach problems, skin rashes, ulcers, aches and pains, headaches, cancer, colds, and flus. (Immune system is suppressed when a person is under high levels of stress.)

14. "I will do well today in this sport, by focusing on" → being good at tennis, golf, bowling, baseball, or other sport.
15. "I am too fat; by controlling my eating, I can control part of my life" → anorexia and a variety of health problems.
16. "By throwing up after eating, I can maintain my weight and figure and also enjoy the good taste of food" → bulimia and a variety of health problems.
17. "I need several drinks to get through the day and numb my pain" → alcoholism.
18. "I love food so much, I don't care what happens to me" → compulsive overeating, obesity, diabetes, and a variety of other health problems.
19. Are certain thought processes involved in autoimmune diseases, such as multiple sclerosis, rheumatoid arthritis, fibromyalgia?
20. "I need to get more work done, in a shorter time, for the next 10 years" → Type A personality, hypertension, heart problems, and strokes.
21. "I will never forgive——for what s/he did." Or "I'll get even with her/him if it's the last thing I do in life" → hostility, heart problems, and strokes.
22. "Sex is disgusting," or "My partner stinks," or "My partner is inept at lovemaking" → lack of sexual arousal and other sexual dysfunctions.

Note: Rational therapy (see Chapter 8) assumes that our emotions and our actions/behaviors are largely determined by our thoughts. Choice theory suggests that our thoughts affect our physiological functioning. It appears that our thoughts have a major impact on our lives!

12. We can satisfy our basic needs only by satisfying one or more pictures in our quality world. Our quality world consists of three kinds of need-satisfying pictures: people (such as parents), things (such as a car and clothes), and beliefs (such as religious and political beliefs). The most freedom we ever experience is when we are able to satisfy one or more pictures in our quality world. We are giving up part of our freedom when we put pictures that we cannot satisfy into our quality world.

13. When we have difficulty getting along with other people, we usually make the mistake of

choosing to employ *external control psychology*, attempting to coerce or control others by nagging, preaching, moralizing, criticizing, or using put-down messages.

14. Because relationships are central to human happiness, improving our emotional and physical well-being involves exploring how we relate to others, and looking for ways to improve how we relate to others (particularly those we feel closest to).

15. It is therapeutic to view our behavior in terms of verbs. For example, it is more accurate to say to oneself, "I am choosing to depress," or "I am

depressing," instead of thinking, "I am suffering from depression," or "I am depressed." When we say, "I am depressing," we are immediately aware that we are choosing to depress, and have the choice to do and feel something else (such as "I will go golfing and enjoy the day"). People who instead say, "I am depressed," mistakenly tend to believe the depressing is beyond their control. In addition, they are apt to mistakenly believe the depressing has been caused by what someone else has done to them. To recognize that we have the power to choose to stop depressing (or to stop angering or frustrating) is a wonderful freedom that people who adhere to the view that they are largely controlled by others will never have.

16. All behavior (thinking, feeling, acting, and physiology) is chosen, but we have direct control over only the acting and thinking components. We do, however, control our physiology and our feelings through how we choose to act and think. It is not easy to change our actions and thoughts, but it is all we can do. When we succeed in coming up with more satisfying actions and thoughts, we gain a great deal of personal freedom.

17. Whenever you feel as if you don't have the freedom you want in a relationship, it is because you, your partner, or both of you are unwilling to accept a key axiom of choice theory: *You can only control your own behavior.* The more you and your partner learn choice theory, the better you will get along with one another. Choice theory supports the Golden Rule.

18. People choose (although some are unaware of doing so) to play the mentally ill roles described in the *DSM-5* (American Psychiatric Association, 2013). These people have the symptoms described in the *DSM-5*, but they are not mentally ill (if mental illness is defined as a disease of the mind). These people do not have an untreatable or incurable mental illness. The symptoms only indicate that these people are not as healthy as they could learn to be. (For additional information on this topic, see "Interactional Model" in Chapter 8.)

19. A mentally healthy person enjoys being with most of the people he or she knows—especially the important people, such as family and friends. A mentally healthy person likes people

and is more than willing to help an unhappy friend, colleague, or family member to feel better. A mentally healthy person laughs a lot and leads a mostly tension-free life. He or she enjoys life and has no trouble accepting others who are different. He or she does not focus on criticizing others nor on trying to change them. He or she is creative. When unhappy (no one can be happy all the time), a mentally healthy person knows why he or she is unhappy and will attempt to do something about it.

Glasser's views are controversial. Thoughts are not the only determinants of physiological illnesses (as Glasser suggests). Many other factors contribute to the formation of physiological illnesses. For example, substances such as tomatoes, milk, and chocolate can cause eczema in certain people. Some illnesses, such as Huntington's disease, are caused by genetic inheritance.

LO 11-8 Describe Gawain's Theories About Intuition and How Human Behavior Is Affected by It

Intuition

The cerebrum (the area of conscious mental processes of the brain) is composed of two cerebral hemispheres. The right hemisphere has been called the *right brain*, and the left hemisphere has been called the *left brain*. Anatomically, the two hemispheres appear to be quite similar, but there is abundant evidence that their functions are by no means identical (Gleitman, 1986). Movements of the left side of the body are under the control of the right hemisphere; movements of the right side of the body are controlled by the left hemisphere.

The left hemisphere of the brain ordinarily controls language and speech functions. It appears the left hemisphere is also more centrally involved in rational thought processes, logic, deduction, and mathematical skills. In contrast, the right hemisphere may be more centrally involved in creativity, musical abilities, intuition, and feelings. (It should be noted that research on the location of different functions is somewhat speculative and, further, that there is considerable overlap in functions across the two hemispheres.)

The self-talk approach, described in Chapter 8, demonstrates that humans, by thinking rationally, can learn to better control their emotions and their actions, and obtain better control of their lives. However, Gawain (1986) theorizes that it is also important for humans to develop and use their intuition. "A strong body/personality structure is not created by eating certain foods, doing certain exercises, or following anybody's rules or good ideas. It is created by trusting your intuition and learning to follow its direction" (p. 18).

Gawain asserts that it is important for all of us to learn to trust our intuitive knowledge. "Most of us have been taught from childhood not to trust our feelings, not to express ourselves truthfully and honestly, not to recognize that at the core of our being lies a loving, powerful, and creative nature" (1986, p. 69). Through reeducating ourselves to listen to and trust our intuition, Gawain asserts, we will gain integrity, creativity, and wholeness. Learning to trust this inner voice may feel risky at first, because we are no longer playing it safe, doing what we "should" do, pleasing others, deferring to outside authority, or following rules.

An important step toward identifying and following your intuition is simply taking time (perhaps several times a day) to relax and listen to your "gut feelings." The inner voice of intuition will present itself in a variety of ways, including images, feelings, and words. When you have an important decision to make, your true feelings can more easily be identified if you are relaxed. When you are relaxed (perhaps through using meditation or some other relaxation technique), your intuition will inform you which alternative is in your best interest. Frequently, your intuition will inform you of creative alternatives that you were previously unaware of.

Human intuition is similar (and perhaps identical) to the instinct in geese that guides them to fly south in fall and north in spring. It is similar to the instinct in dogs that makes them wary upon seeing a bear in the wild—even when they have never seen a bear before.

Your intuition can assist you in making such major decisions as whether to stay in college, choosing a career, whether to end a romantic relationship, what kind of automobile to purchase, and what hobbies to pursue. Your intuition can also lead you to be a more creative, productive, contented, and fulfilled person.

LO 11-9 Understand the Issue of Substance Abuse

Chemical Substance Use and Abuse

The remainder of this chapter will focus on a critical issue affecting, in one way or another, nearly every person in our society—chemical substance use and abuse. Nearly everyone has one or more relatives or friends who are abusing alcohol or some other drug. Some of the readers of this text may be personally struggling with this issue.

We begin our discussion with some examples. There was going to be a big party at Evelyn's on Saturday night. Georgia, a high school junior, couldn't wait to go. Everybody was going to be there. Evelyn said she had some great hash. Georgia didn't like to smoke all that much. However, people would think there was something wrong with her if she didn't, and that was the last thing she wanted.

Marty, age 15, liked to drink a couple of six packs on the weekend. After all, his father did, and Marty was almost an adult.

Virgil, age 18, liked to get high because then he could forget about all his problems. He wouldn't have to think about his alcoholic mother and all the problems she and his father were having. He wouldn't have to worry about all the pressures he had in school. He wouldn't even have to think about how his girlfriend recently dumped him. He just couldn't wait until the next chance he had to get high.

Drugs have become part of our daily lives. We use drugs to relax, to increase our pleasure, to feel less inhibited, to get rid of unwanted emotions, to keep awake, and to fall asleep. Practically all Americans use drugs of one kind or another. People have coffee in the morning, soda (which has caffeine) during the day, cocktails before dinner, and aspirin to relieve pain.

When the Pilgrims set sail for America, they loaded on their ships 14 tons of water—plus 10,000 gallons of wine and 42 tons of beer (Robertson, 1980). Ever since, Americans have been widely using and abusing drugs.

Pharmacologically, a drug is any substance that chemically alters the function or structure of a living organism. Such a definition includes food, insecticides, air pollutants, water pollutants, acids, vitamins, toxic chemicals, soaps, and soft drinks. Obviously, this definition is too broad to be useful. For our purposes, a definition based on context is more useful. In medicine, for example, a drug is any substance that is manufactured specifically to relieve pain or to treat and prevent diseases and other medical conditions.

Here drugs will be addressed within the context most useful for social workers. We will focus on drugs that can dramatically affect human behavior and have serious consequences on people's lives. For our purposes, then, a *drug* is any habit-forming substance that directly affects the brain and the nervous system; it is a chemical substance that affects moods, perceptions, bodily functions, or consciousness and that has the potential for misuse as it may be harmful to the user.

Drug abuse is the regular or excessive use of a drug when, as defined by a group, the consequences endanger relationships with other people, are detrimental to a person's health, or jeopardize society itself. All of the drugs mentioned earlier are types of chemicals. Another way of referring to drug abuse is *chemical substance abuse*. Drug or chemical substance intake becomes abusive when an individual's mind and/or body are affected in negative or harmful ways.

Both legal drugs, such as alcohol and tobacco, and prescription drugs are frequently abused. Among the most abused prescription drugs are sedatives, tranquilizers, painkillers, and stimulants. Many prescribed drugs have the potential to be psychologically and physiologically addicting. Drug companies spend millions in advertising to convince customers that they are too tense and too irritable, take too long to fall asleep, should lose weight, and so on. These companies then assert that their medications will relieve these problems. Unfortunately, many customers accept this easy symptom-relief approach and end up dependent on pills, rather than making the necessary changes in their lives to be healthy. Such changes include exercise, stress management techniques, positive thinking, and a healthy diet.

Illegal drugs such as cocaine and heroin are also frequently abused. People use them to distort their own realities. They can be used to attain unrealistic "highs" or to escape unpleasant life situations. However, as we will see, heavy drug use can often result in serious physical deterioration and slave-like psychological and physical dependence.

This section will describe a variety of over-the-counter, prescription, and illegal drugs and will examine various issues of drug use and treatment. Finally, the relationship between knowledge about drug use and assessment in social work practice will be proposed.

Specific Drugs: What They Are and What They Do

Knowing what a specific drug is and what it does to a person is important both in treatment and in considering its use and abuse. Specific drugs discussed here include depressants, stimulants, narcotics, hallucinogens, marijuana, tobacco, and anabolic steroids. Highlight 11.4 summarizes information about these drugs.

Depressant Drugs

Depressant drugs are those that slow down bodily functioning and activity. Alcohol, barbiturates, tranquilizers, and Quaalude all fall within this category.

Alcohol *Alcohol* is a colorless liquid found in beer, wine, brandy, whiskey, vodka, rum, and other intoxicating beverages. The type of alcohol found in beverages is ethyl alcohol; it is also called grain alcohol because most of it is made from fermenting grain.

Who Drinks? The American adult consumes an average of 21.7 gallons of beer, 2.0 gallons of wine, and 1.3 gallons of distilled spirits a year (Kornblum & Julian, 2012). The vast majority of teenagers and adults in our society drink.

Several factors are related to whether an individual will drink and, if so, how much. These variables include biological factors, socioeconomic factors, gender, age, religion, urban/rural residence, and cultural influences (Kornblum & Julian, 2012):

- *Biological factors*: Close relatives of an alcoholic are four times more likely than nonrelatives to become alcoholics themselves. This tendency holds true even for children who were adopted away from their biological families at birth and raised in a nonalcoholic family. Such findings clearly suggest that drinking and alcoholism are due in part to biological factors. Some Asian populations have highly negative reactions to alcohol, which tends to diminish their risk of

HIGHLIGHT 11.4

Drugs of Abuse: Facts and Effects

| Drug | Dependence Potential | | | Duration of Effects (hours) | Usual Methods of Administration | Possible Effects | Effects of Overdose | Withdrawal Symptoms |
	Physical	Psychological	Tolerance					
Narcotics								
Opium	High	High	Yes	3 to 6	Oral, smoked	Euphoria, drowsiness, respiratory depression, constricted pupils, nausea	Slow and shallow breathing, clammy skin, convulsions, coma, possible death	Watery eyes, runny nose, yawning, loss of appetite, irritability, tremors, panic, chills and sweating, cramps, nausea
Morphine	High	High	Yes	3 to 6	Injected, smoked			
Heroin	High	High	Yes	3 to 6	Injected, sniffed			
Depressants								
Alcohol	High	High	Yes	1 to 12	Oral	Slurred speech, disorientation, drunken behavior, loss of coordination, impaired reactions	Shallow respiration, cold and clammy skin, dilated pupils, weak and rapid pulse, coma, possible death	Anxiety, insomnia, tremors, delirium, convulsions, possible death
Barbiturates	High	High	Yes	1 to 16	Oral, injected			
Tranquilizers	Moderate	Moderate	Yes	4 to 8	Oral			
Quaalude	High	High	Yes	4 to 8	Oral			
Stimulants								
Caffeine	High	High	Yes	2 to 4	Oral	Increased alertness, excitation, euphoria, dilated pupils, increased pulse rate and blood pressure, insomnia, loss of appetite	Agitation, increase in pulse rate and blood pressure, loss of appetite, insomnia	
Cocaine	Possible	High	Yes	2	Injected, sniffed		Agitation, increase in body temperature, hallucinations, convulsions, tremors, possible death	Apathy, long periods of sleep, irritability, depression, disorientation
Crack	Possible	High	Yes	2	Smoked			
Amphetamines	Possible	High	Yes	2 to 4	Oral, injected			
Butyl nitrate	Possible	Unknown	Probable	Up to 5	Inhaled	Excitement, euphoria, giddiness, loss of inhibitions, aggressiveness, delusions, depression, drowsiness, headache, nausea	Loss of memory, confusion, unsteady gait, erratic heartbeat and pulse, possible death	Insomnia, decreased appetite, depression, irritability, headache
Amyl nitrate	Possible	Unknown	Probable	Up to 5	Inhaled			
Hallucinogens								
LSD	None	Degree	Yes	Variable	Oral	Illusions and hallucinations, poor perception of time psychosis, and distance	Longer and more intense "trip" episodes, possible death	Unknown
Mescaline and Peyote		Unknown			Oral, injected			
Psilocybin psilocin					Oral			
PCP					Oral, injected			
MDMA (Ecstasy)					Oral, injected, smoked			
Cannabis								
Marijuana Hashish	Degree unknown	Moderate	Yes	2 to 4	Oral, smoked	Euphoria, relaxed inhibitions, increased appetite, disoriented behavior, increased heart and pulse rate	Fatigue, paranoia, possible psychosis, time disorientation, slowed movements	Insomnia, hyperactivity, decreased appetite
Nicotine (Tobacco)	High	High	Yes	2 to 4	Smoked, chewed	Increased alertness, excitation, euphoria, dilated pupils, increased pulse rate and blood pressure, insomnia, loss of appetite	Agitation, increase in pulse rate and blood pressure, loss of appetite, insomnia	Apathy, long periods of sleep, irritability, depression
Anabolic steroids	None	High	Unknown	Unknown	Oral	Moodiness, depression, irritability	Virilization, edema, testicular atrophy, gynecomastia, acne, aggressive behavior	Possible depression

becoming alcoholics. On the other hand, some ethnic groups (such as Native Americans) have a lower tolerance for alcohol than other groups do, which places them at a greater risk for alcoholism.

- *Socioeconomic factors*: Drinking is more frequent among younger men who are positioned at higher socioeconomic levels, and less frequent among older women at lower levels.
- *Gender*: Men are more likely to use and abuse alcohol than are women. Still, recent decades have seen a dramatic increase in alcoholism among adult women. Why? One explanation is that cultural taboos against heavy drinking among women have weakened. Another explanation is that increased drinking is related to the changing roles of women in our society.
- *Age*: Older people are less likely to drink than younger people, even if they were drinkers in their youth. Heavy drinking is most common at ages 21 to 30 for men and ages 31 to 50 for women.
- *Religion*: Nonchurchgoers drink more than regular churchgoers. Heavy drinking is more common among Episcopalians and Catholics, whereas conservative and fundamentalist Protestants are more often nondrinkers or light drinkers. Fewer Jews are heavy drinkers.
- *Urban/rural residence*: Urban residents are more likely to drink than rural residents.

In the 1980s and 1990s, the federal government put considerable financial pressure on states to raise the drinking age to 21; if a state did not raise the age, federal highway funds were withheld. All states have now raised the drinking age to 21. Many secondary schools, colleges, and universities have initiated alcohol awareness programs. Many businesses and employers have developed Employee Assistance Programs designed to provide treatment services to alcoholics and problem drinkers. Many states have passed stricter drunk-driving laws, and police departments and the courts are more vigorously enforcing such laws. Organizations such as Mothers Against Drunk Driving and Students Against Drunk Driving have been fairly successful in creating greater public awareness of the hazards of drinking and driving. A cultural norm is emerging in many segments that it is stylish not to have too much to drink. Despite these promising trends, rates of alcohol use and abuse in the United States remain extremely high.

What Alcohol Does Many drinkers believe alcohol is a stimulant, because it relaxes tensions, lessens sexual and aggressive inhibitions, and seems to facilitate interpersonal relationships. However, it acts as a depressant to the central nervous system, reducing functional activity of this system. Its chemical composition and effects are very similar to those of ether (an anesthetic used in medicine to induce unconsciousness).

Alcohol slows down mental activity, reasoning ability, speech ability, and muscle reactions. It distorts perceptions, slurs speech, lessens coordination, and slows down memory functioning and respiration. In increasing quantities, it leads to stupor, sleep, coma, and finally death. A hangover (the aftereffects of too much alcohol) includes headache, thirst, muscle aches, stomach discomfort, diarrhea, and nausea. Alcohol can seriously affect how one drives an automobile. Behavior resulting from excessive alcohol intake can also have negative effects on family, friend, and work relationships.

The effects of alcohol vary with the percentage of alcohol in the bloodstream as it passes through the brain. Generally, the effects are observable when the concentration of alcohol in the blood reaches one tenth of a percent. Five drinks (a drink is defined as 1 ounce of 86-proof alcohol or 12 ounces of beer or 3 ounces of wine) in 2 hours for a 120-pound person will result in a blood alcohol concentration of one tenth of a percent, which exceeds the legal criterion in all states for being intoxicated.

Alcohol also has long-term effects on a person's health. Alcoholics have a life expectancy that is 10 to 12 years less than that of nonalcoholics (Kornblum & Julian, 2012). The life span is shorter for several reasons. One is that alcohol, over an extended period of time, gradually destroys liver cells and replaces the cells with scar tissue. When the scar tissue is extensive, a medical condition occurs called *cirrhosis*. Continued drinking by people impacted by cirrhosis often results in death. Also, although it has no nutritional value, alcohol contains a high number of calories. As a result, heavy drinkers have a reduced appetite for nutritious food and thus frequently suffer from vitamin deficiencies and are more susceptible to infectious diseases. Heavy drinking also causes kidney problems, contributes to a variety of heart ailments, is a factor in diabetes, and appears to contribute to cancer. In addition, heavy drinking is associated with thousands of suicides annually (Kornblum & Julian, 2012).

However, for some as yet unknown reason, the life expectancy for light-to-moderate drinkers exceeds that for nondrinkers. Perhaps an occasional drink helps people to relax and thereby reduces the likelihood of developing life-threatening stress-related illnesses.

Alcohol also can seriously affect sexual response. The effects of alcohol vary considerably. A small amount of alcohol may reduce inhibitions and anxiety, thereby improving responsiveness. A large amount of alcohol, however, acts as a depressant and reduces sexual arousal, thereby causing sexual dysfunction (Hyde & DeLameter, 2011). Male alcoholics who are exposed to repeated high doses of alcohol frequently have sexual dysfunctions, including erectile dysfunction and loss of sexual desire. Women who have consumed small amounts of alcohol (compared with controls who have consumed none) report greater sexual arousal and more pleasurable orgasms, although their orgasms are slightly delayed. However, when a large amount of alcohol is consumed (and the state of being intoxicated is approached), an orgasm takes significantly longer to occur, and women report that the orgasm is less intense. Although a high proportion of recovering alcoholics still experience some form of sexual dysfunction, the majority of alcohol-related sexual problems will disappear after a few months of abstinence.

Combining alcohol with other drugs can have disastrous, and sometimes fatal, effects. Two drugs taken together may have a *synergistic interaction*— that is, they interact to produce an effect much greater than either would cause alone. For example, sedatives such as barbiturates (often found in sleeping pills) or Quaaludes taken with alcohol can so depress the central nervous system that a coma or even death may result.

Other drugs tend to create an *antagonistic response* to alcohol—one drug negates the effects of the other. Many doctors now caution patients not to drink while taking certain prescribed drugs because the alcohol will reduce, and even totally negate, the beneficial effects of those drugs.

Whether drugs will interact synergistically or antagonistically depends on a wide range of factors: the

properties of the drugs, the amounts taken, the amount of sleep of the user, the kind and amount of food that has been eaten, and the user's overall health and tolerance. The interactive effects may be minimal one day and extensive the next.

When used by pregnant women, alcohol may gravely affect the unborn child by causing mental retardation, deformities, stunting of growth, and other abnormalities. This effect has been termed *fetal alcohol syndrome.*

Withdrawal from alcohol, once the body is physically addicted, may lead to the DTs (delirium tremens) and other unpleasant reactions. The DTs include rapid heartbeat, uncontrollable trembling, severe nausea, and profuse sweating.

Barbiturates *Barbiturates,* another type of depressant, are derived from barbituric acid, and depress the central nervous system. Barbiturates were first synthesized in the early 1900s, and there are now more than 2,500 different barbiturates. They are commonly used to relieve insomnia and anxiety. Some are prescribed as sleeping pills, and others are used during the daytime by tense and anxious persons. They are also used to treat epilepsy and high blood pressure, and to relax patients before or after surgery. Barbiturates are illegal unless obtained by a physician's prescription.

Taken in sufficient doses, barbiturates have effects similar to alcohol. Users experience relief from inhibitions, have a feeling of euphoria, feel "high" or in good humor, and are passively content. However, these moods can change rapidly to gloom, agitation, and aggressiveness. Physiological effects include slurred speech, disorientation, staggering, appearance of being confused, drowsiness, and reduced coordination.

Prolonged heavy use of barbiturates can cause physical dependence, with withdrawal symptoms similar to those of heroin addiction. Withdrawal is accompanied by body tremors, cramps, anxiety, fever, nausea, profuse sweating, and hallucinations. Many authorities believe barbiturate addiction is more dangerous than heroin addiction, and it is considered to be more resistant to treatment than heroin addiction. Abrupt withdrawal (*cold turkey*, the sudden and complete halting of drug use) can cause fatal convulsions.

Barbiturate overdose may cause convulsions, coma, poisoning, and sometimes death. Barbiturates are particularly dangerous when taken with alcohol, because alcohol acts synergistically to magnify the potency of the barbiturates. Accidental deaths due to excessive doses are frequent. Barbiturates are also the number one drug used for suicide. A number of famous people have fatally overdosed on barbiturates.

Barbiturates are generally taken orally, although some users inject them intravenously. Use of barbiturates, like alcohol, may also lead to traffic fatalities. See Highlight 11.5, Drug-Related Deaths of Famous People.

Tranquilizers Yet another type of depressant is the group of drugs classified as tranquilizers. Common brand names are: Librium, Miltown, Serax, Tranxene, and Valium. Tranquilizers reduce anxiety, relax muscles, and are sedatives. Users have

moderate potential of becoming physically and psychologically dependent. The drugs are usually taken orally, and the effects last for four to eight hours. Side effects include slurred speech, disorientation, and behavior resembling being intoxicated. Overdoses are possible, with the effects including cold and clammy skin, shallow respiration, dilated pupils, weak and rapid pulse, coma, and possibly death. Withdrawal symptoms are similar to those from alcohol and barbiturates and include anxiety, tremors, convulsions, delirium, and possibly death. Highlight 11.6 discusses depressants that are used as so-called date-rape drugs.

Quaalude Methaqualone (better known by its patent name Quaalude) has effects similar to barbiturates and alcohol, although it is chemically different. It has a reputation as a love drug, as

---

Drug-Related Deaths of Famous People

There are hundreds of famous people whose deaths were drug related. The following are a few examples. Their ages at death are in parentheses ( ).

John Belushi (33), actor and comedian; heroin and cocaine overdose

Len Bias (22), basketball star; died of cocaine overdose before ever playing in the NBA

Lenny Bruce (40), comedian; morphine overdose

Richard Burton (59), actor; alcohol-related causes

Truman Capote (59), writer; liver disease complicated by phebitis and multiple drug intoxication

Kurt Cobain (27), musician; heroin overdose and a shotgun wound in head

Tommy Dorsey (51), jazz musician and band leader; choked to death while sleeping with the aid of drugs

Chris Farley (33), comedian; cocaine and morphine overdose

W. C. Fields (67), performer and actor; complications of alcoholism

Sigmund Freud (83), psychoanalyst; long-term cocaine use; physician-assisted morphine overdose

Judy Garland (47), singer and actress; disputed drug overdose as cause of death

Andy Gibb (30), singer; cardiac damage strongly exacerbated by cocaine and alcohol abuse

Bobby Hatfield (63), singer and musician; heart attack triggered by cocaine overdose

Billie Holiday (44), jazz singer; cirrhosis of the liver attributed to longtime alcohol and heroin abuse

Whitney Houston (48), pop singer; overdose of cocaine, alcohol, and other drugs

Howard Hughes (70), aviator, engineer, industrialist, movie producer; liver failure—autopsy showed lethal amount of codeine and Valium in body

Michael Jackson (41), pop singer; personal physician gave lethal dose of propofol

Janis Joplin (27), singer and musician; heroin overdose

Alan Ladd (50), actor; acute overdose of alcohol and barbiturates (probable suicide)

Heath Ledger (28), actor; combined drug intoxication of various prescription drugs, including oxycodone

Billy Martin (61), baseball player and manager; alcohol-related auto accident

Marilyn Monroe (36), actress; overdose of barbiturate-based sleeping pills

River Phoenix (23), actor; overdose of heroin and cocaine

Elvis Presley (42), singer; heart attack brought on by overdose of barbiturates

Freddie Prinze (22), comedian, actor; self-inflicted gunshot wound while under the influence of Quaaludes

Anna Nicole Smith (39), actress, reality show star; lethal combination of chloral hydrate and various benzodiazepines

Sid Vicious (21), musician; heroin overdose, disputed suicide

Keith Whitley (33), country singer; alcohol poisoning

Hank Williams (29), country singer; drugs and probably alcohol

Amy Winehouse (28), singer; alcohol poisoning

Natalie Wood (43), actress; drowned while intoxicated

Date-Rape Drugs

In the mid-1990s, Rohypnol became known as the date-rape drug. A number of women were sexually assaulted after the drug was slipped into their drinks (both alcoholic and nonalcoholic). Rohypnol often causes blackouts, with complete loss of memory. Female victims who were slipped the drug and then raped often cannot remember any details of the crime.

Rohypnol is a sedative that is related to Valium, but 10 times stronger. Rohypnol is legally available in more than 60 countries for severe insomnia. It is illegal in the United States. Much of the Rohypnol in the United States is smuggled in from Mexico and Colombia. It should be noted that Rohypnol is also addictive, and there is a potential for lethal overdosing.

Rohypnol is popular with teens and young adults who like to combine it with alcohol for a quick punch-drunk hit. Another reason for its popularity is that it's relatively inexpensive—often being purchased on the street for $1 to $5 per pill. In some jurisdictions, drivers are now tested for Rohypnol when they appear drunk but register a low alcohol level. Rohypnol can be lethal when mixed with alcohol and/or other depressants.

Because of the ease through which Rohypnol can be slipped into a drink, rape crisis centers are urging women to *never* take their eyes off their drinks. In 1997, the marketer of Rohypnol, Hoffman-LaRoche, announced it intended to sell only a new version of Rohypnol—one that would cause any liquid that it is put into to turn blue. Even with this change, however, people (particularly women) need to beware—other sedatives have similar effects. In addition, people who intend to commit a sexual assault facilitated by Rohypnol are now offering blue tropical drinks and punches to their intended victim so the blue dye can be disguised.

Gamma hydroxybutyrate (GHB) is another drug that is increasingly being used as a date-rape drug. GHB is a central nervous system depressant that is approved as an anesthetic in some countries. It can be readily made at home from a mixture of chemicals normally used for cleaning, such as lye. Just one gram of this liquid home brew provides an intoxicating experience equivalent to 26 ounces of whisky. Similar to Rohypnol, GHB is put into the drink of the intended victim.

Alcohol is also classified as a date-rape drug.

---

users believe it makes them more eager for sex and enhances sexual pleasure. These effects are probably due to the fact that it lessens inhibitions. Quaalude also reduces anxiety and gives a feeling of euphoria.

Users can become both physically and psychologically dependent on Quaalude. Overdose can result in convulsions, coma, delirium, and even death— most deaths occur when the drug is taken together with alcohol, which vastly magnifies the drug's effects. Withdrawal symptoms are severe and unpleasant. Abuse of the drug may also cause hangovers, fatigue, liver damage, and temporary paralysis of the limbs.

Stimulants

Stimulants are substances that produce a temporary increase in a person's activity level or efficiency. They include caffeine, amphetamines, cocaine, crack, amyl nitrate, and butyl nitrate.

Caffeine   *Caffeine* is a stimulant to the central nervous system. It is present in coffee, tea, cocoa, and many soft drinks. It is also available in tablet form (e.g., No-Doz). Caffeine is widely used— practically all Americans use it daily. It reduces hunger, fatigue,

and boredom, and improves alertness and motor activity. The drug appears addictive, as many users develop a tolerance for it. A further sign that it is addictive is that heavy users (e.g., habitual coffee drinkers) will experience withdrawal symptoms of mild irritability, headaches, and depression.

Excessive amounts of caffeine cause insomnia, restlessness, and gastrointestinal irritation. Surprisingly, excessive doses can even cause death.

Because caffeine has the status of a "nondrug" in our society, users are not labeled criminals, there is no black market for it, and no subculture is formed to give support in obtaining and using the drug. Because caffeine is legal, its price is low compared to that of other drugs. Users are not tempted to resort to crime to support their habit. Some authorities assert that our approach to caffeine should serve as a model for the way we react to other illegal drugs (such as marijuana) that they feel are no more harmful than caffeine (Kornblum & Julian, 2012).

Amphetamines   Another type of stimulant, amphetamines, are often called "uppers" because of their stimulating effect. When prescribed by a physician, they are legal. Some truck drivers have obtained prescriptions in order to stay awake and more alert while making a long haul. Dieters have received prescriptions to help them lose weight, and they often find that the pills tend to give them more self-confidence and buoyance. Others who have used amphetamines to increase alertness and performance for relatively short periods of time include college students, athletes, astronauts, and executives. Additional nicknames for this drug are speed, ups, pep pills, black beauties, and bennies.

Ethical Question 11.4

Is it unethical to drink excessively and to abuse other drugs?

EP 2.1.2

Amphetamines are synthetic drugs that are similar to adrenalin, a hormone from the adrenal gland that stimulates the central nervous system. The better known amphetamines include dexedrine, benzedrine, and methedrine. Physical reactions to amphetamines are extensive: consumption of fat stored in body tissues is accelerated, heartbeat is increased, respiratory processes are stimulated, appetite is reduced, and insomnia is common. Users feel euphoric, stronger, and have an increased capacity to concentrate and to express themselves verbally. Prolonged use can lead to irritability, deep anxiety, and an irrational persecution complex that can lead to sudden acts of violence.

Amphetamines are usually taken orally in tablet, powder, or capsule form. They can also be sniffed or injected. "Speeding" (injecting the drug into a vein) produces the most powerful effects and can also cause the greatest harm. An overdose may cause a coma, with possible brain damage and, in rare cases, death. Speeders may also develop hepatitis, abscesses, convulsions, hallucinations, delusions, and severe emotional disturbances. Another danger is that, when sold on the street, the substance may contain impurities that are health hazards.

An amphetamine high is often followed by mental depression and fatigue. Continued amphetamine use leads to psychological dependence. It is unclear whether amphetamines are physically addictive, as the withdrawal symptoms are uncharacteristic of withdrawal from other drugs. Amphetamine withdrawal symptoms include sleep disturbances, apathy, decreased activity, disorientation, irritability, exhaustion, and depression. Some authorities believe such withdrawal symptoms indicate that amphetamines may be physically addicting.

One of the legal uses of certain amphetamines is in the treatment of *hyperactivity* in children. Hyperactivity (also called *hyperkinesis*) is characterized by a short attention span, extensive motor activity, restlessness, and mood shifts. Little is known about the causes of this condition. As children become older, even without treatment, the symptoms tend to disappear. Interestingly, some amphetamines (Ritalin is a popular one) have a calming and soothing effect on hyperactive children—the exact opposite effect occurs when Ritalin is taken by adults. It should be noted that treating uncontrollable children with amphetamines has sometimes been abused. Some of the children for whom Ritalin was prescribed were not really hyperactive. They were normal children who simply refused to submit to what their teachers and parents considered appropriate childhood behavior. As a result, these children were labeled as troublemakers and were introduced to the world of taking a mood-altering drug on a daily basis.

One amphetamine that has had increasing illegal use in recent years is methamphetamine hydrochloride, known on the street as "meth" or "ice." In liquid form, it is often referred to as "speed." Under experimental conditions, cocaine users often have difficulty distinguishing cocaine from methamphetamine hydrochloride. Use of this drug has spread, as the "high" lasts longer than that from cocaine and the drug can be manufactured relatively easily in laboratories from products that are sold legally in the United States. As a "last resort," methamphetamine hydrochloride (Desoxyn) is legally used to treat obesity as one component of a weight-reduction regimen. However, this drug has a serious side effect when used for weight reduction: The user's appetite returns with greater intensity after withdrawal from the drug.

Cocaine and Crack Cocaine is obtained from the leaves of the South American coca plant. Although legally classified as a narcotic, it is in fact not related to the opiates from which narcotic drugs are derived. It is a powerful stimulant and antifatigue agent.

In the United States, cocaine is generally sniffed and then absorbed through the nasal membranes.

Someone snorting cocaine.

The most common method is "snorting," sniffing up through a straw or a rolled-up banknote. It may also be injected intravenously, and in South America the natives chew the coca leaf. It may be added in small quantities to a cigarette and smoked. Cocaine has been used medically in the past as a local anesthetic, but other drugs have largely replaced it for this purpose.

Cocaine constricts the blood vessels and tissues, and thereby leads to increased strength and endurance. It also is thought by users to increase creative and intellectual powers. Other effects include a feeling of euphoria, excitement, restlessness, and a lessened sense of fatigue.

Larger doses, or extended use, may result in hallucinations and delusions. A peculiar effect of cocaine abuse is "formication," the illusion that ants, snakes, or bugs are crawling on or into the skin. Some abusers have such intense illusions that they literally scratch, slap, and wound themselves trying to kill these imaginary creatures.

Physical effects of cocaine include increased blood pressure and pulse rate, insomnia, and loss of appetite. Heavy users may experience weight loss or malnutrition due to appetite suppression. Physical dependence on cocaine is considered to be a low-to-medium risk. However, the drug appears to be psychologically habituating. Termination of use usually results in intense depression and despair, which drives the person back to taking the drug. Additional effects of withdrawal include apathy, long periods of sleep, extreme fatigue, irritability, and disorientation. Serious tissue damage to the nose can occur when large quantities of cocaine are sniffed over a prolonged period of time. Regular use may result in habitual sniffing and sometimes leads to an anorexic condition. High doses can lead to agitation, increased body temperature, and convulsions. A few people who overdose may die if their breathing and heart functions become too depressed.

Crack, also called "rock," is obtained by separating the adulterants from the cocaine by mixing it with water and ammonium hydroxide. The water is then removed from the cocaine base by means of a fast-drying solvent, usually ether. The resultant mixture resembles large crystals, similar to rock sugar. Crack is highly addictive. Some authorities claim that one use is enough to lead to addiction. Users generally claim that after they have finished one dose, they crave for another.

Crack is generally smoked, either in a specially made glass pipe or mixed with tobacco or marijuana in a cigarette. The effects are similar to those of cocaine, but the "rush" is more immediate, and the drug gives an intensified high.

An overdose is more common when crack is injected than when it is smoked. Withdrawal effects include an irresistible compulsion to have the drug, as well as apathy, long periods of sleep, irritability, extreme fatigue, depression, and disorientation.

Communal use of needles spreads AIDS. Cocaine and crack can have serious effects on the heart, straining it with high blood pressure, with interrupted heart rhythm, and with raised pulse rates. Cocaine and crack may also damage the liver. Severe convulsions can cause brain damage, emotional problems, and sometimes death. Smoking crack may also damage the lungs. The effects on babies who are born to crack users are described in Highlight 11.7.

Amyl Nitrate and Butyl Nitrate Amyl nitrate (poppers) is prescribed for patients who aren't in risk of certain forms of heart failure. It is a volatile liquid that is sold in capsules or small bottles. When the container is opened, the chemical begins to evaporate (similar to gasoline). If the vapor is sniffed, the user's blood vessels are immediately dilated and the heart rate increases. These physical changes create feelings of mental excitation (head rush) and physical excitation (body rush). The drug is supposedly sold only by prescription, but (as with many other drugs) the illicit drug market distributes it.

Butyl nitrate is legally available in some states without a prescription and has an effect similar to amyl nitrate's. Trade names under which it is sold are Rush and Locker Room. Similar to amyl nitrate, butyl nitrate vapor is sniffed. It is available at some sexual aid and novelty stores.

Both of these drugs have been used as aphrodisiacs and as stimulants while dancing. The drugs have some short-term, unpleasant side effects that

---

HIGHLIGHT 11.7

Babies Who Are Crack Exposed

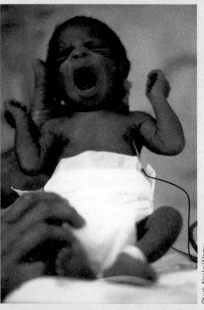

Chuck Nacke/Alamy

Cocaine use during pregnancy can increase the risk of miscarriage or preterm labor. A baby who has been exposed to crack is more likely to have low birth weight, which can make the baby more susceptible to health problems.

In the 1980s, a flurry of media reports suggested a link between women's cocaine use during pregnancy and a range of damaging effects on babies. Some media articles stated these babies would have permanent brain damage, suggesting they would have severe cognitive disabilities for the remainder of their lives. A *Washington Post* column by Charles Krauthammer (7/30/89), for example, stated, "The inner-city crack epidemic is now giving birth to the newest horror: a bio-underclass, a generation of physically damaged cocaine babies whose biological inferiority is stamped at birth."

Now, however, researchers who have followed these children who were exposed to cocaine before birth have concluded that the long-term effects of such exposure on children's brain development and behavior appear to be relatively small. Cocaine is undoubtedly bad for the fetus. But experts say its effects are less severe than those of alcohol and are comparable to those of tobacco. (Sometimes the media seizes on supposed medical phenomenon and hypes it beyond recognition, distorting facts irresponsibly or simply getting the "facts" wrong.) It appears the lack of good prenatal care, use of tobacco and alcohol, and poverty are more serious factors in poor fetal development among pregnant cocaine users than cocaine itself.

SOURCE: http://www.fair.org/index.php?page=3702.

may include fainting, headaches, and dizziness. A few deaths have been reported due to overdoses. Both drugs are classified as stimulants.

Narcotics The most commonly used narcotic drugs in the United States are the opiates, such as opium, heroin, and morphine. The term *narcotic* means sleep-inducing. In actuality, drugs classified as narcotics are more accurately called *analgesics,* or painkillers. The principal effect produced by narcotic drugs is a feeling of euphoria.

The opiates are all derived from the opium poppy, which grows in many parts of the world: Turkey, Southeast Asia, and Colombia have, in the recent past, been major sources of the opiates. The drug opium is the dried form of a milky substance that oozes from the seed pods after the petals fall from the flowers. It has been used for centuries.

Morphine is the main active ingredient of opium. It was first identified early in the 1800s and has been used extensively as a painkiller. Heroin was first synthesized from morphine in 1874. It was once thought to be a cure for morphine addiction, but later was also found to be addictive. Heroin is a more potent drug than morphine.

Opium is usually smoked, although it can be taken orally. Morphine and heroin are either snorted or injected into a muscle or into a vein (called "mainlining"), which maximizes the drugs' effects.

Opiates affect the central nervous system and produce feelings of tranquility, drowsiness, or euphoria. They produce a sense of well-being that makes pain, anxiety, or depression seem unimportant. Blaze-Gosden (1987) notes that opiates

> have been described as giving an orgasmlike rush or flash that lasts briefly but memorably. At the peak of the euphoria, the user has a feeling of exaggerated physical and mental comfort and well-being, a heightened feeling of buoyancy and bodily health, and a heightened feeling of being competent, in control, capable of any achievement, and being able to cope. (p. 95)

Overdoses can cause convulsions and coma and, in rare cases, death by respiratory failure. All opiates are now recognized as highly addictive.

Opiate addiction occurs when the user takes the drug regularly for a period of time. Whether addiction will occur depends on the opiate drug taken, the strength of the dosage, the regularity of use, the characteristics of the user, and the length of time taken—sometimes as short as a few weeks. Users rapidly develop a tolerance, and may eventually need a dose that is up to 100 times stronger than a dose that would have been fatal during the initiation to the drug (Abadinsky, 2011).

The withdrawal process is very unpleasant. Symptoms include chills, cramps, sweating, nervousness, anxiety, running eyes and nose, dilated pupils, muscle aches, increased blood pressure, severe cramps, sometimes extreme nausea, and fever. Most addicts are obsessed with securing a fix to avoid these severe withdrawal symptoms.

Addiction to opiates is extremely difficult to break, partly because an intense craving for the drug may recur periodically for several months afterward. Most opiate addicts are under age 30, of low socioeconomic status, and poorly educated. A disproportionate number are African Americans. Distribution of and addiction to narcotic drugs occur primarily in large urban centers.

Heroin is the most widely abused opiate. In addition to the above mentioned effects, heroin slows the functioning parts of the brain. The user's appetite and sex drive tend to be dulled. After an initial feeling of euphoria, the user generally becomes lethargic and stuporous. Contrary to popular belief, most heroin users take the drug infrequently and do not, as a rule, become addicted (Abadinsky, 2011), although frequent use is highly addictive.

When heroin was first discovered in the late 1880s, it was initially used as a painkiller, as a substitute for morphine, and as a drug taken by many to experience euphoria. A fair number of people became addicted, and in the early 1900s, laws were passed to prohibit its sale, possession, and distribution.

Heroin abuse continues to be regarded by some Americans as our most serious drug problem. This stereotype does not appear warranted because only a tiny fraction of the U.S. population has ever tried heroin. In fact, such drugs as alcohol and barbiturates contribute to many more deaths.

One reason heroin has the reputation it does is because users are thought to be "dope fiends" who commit violent crimes and reject the values of contemporary society. Addicts, however, are unlikely to commit violent crimes such as rape or aggravated assault. They are more apt to commit crimes against property (shoplifting, burglary, pickpocketing, larceny, and robbery) in order to support their habit

©ejwhite/shutterstock.com

A user injects heroin.

(Kornblum & Julian, 2012). Prostitution among female addicts is also common. Because the severe withdrawal symptoms begin about 18 hours after the last fix, addicts who have experienced these symptoms will do almost anything to avoid them.

Unsanitary injections of heroin may cause hepatitis and other infections. Communal use of needles can spread AIDS. Also, the high cost of maintaining a heroin habit—often more than $100 daily—may create huge financial problems for the user.

Because the price of illicit narcotic drugs is so high, organized crime has made huge profits in the smuggling and distribution of these drugs. Often, such drugs are diluted with dangerous impurities, which pose serious health hazards for the users. And unfortunately, addicts often participate in illegal activities in order to pay for their daily supply and avoid the withdrawal symptoms.

Hallucinogens

Hallucinogens were popular as psychedelic drugs in the late 1960s. These drugs distort the user's perceptions, creating hallucinations consisting of sensory impressions of sights and sounds that do not exist. The six hallucinogens most commonly used in this country are mescaline (peyote), psilocybin, psilocin, LSD, PCP, and ecstasy. All are taken orally—in capsule form, on a sugar cube, or licked from the back of a stamp.

Peyote is derived from a cactus plant. Mescaline is the synthetic form of peyote. Psilocybin and psilocin are found in approximately 90 different species of mushrooms. They are sometimes called "magic mushrooms." Both peyote and psilocybin have had a long history of use by certain Native American tribes. Members of the Native American Church, a religious organization, have won the legal right to use peyote on ceremonial occasions (Robertson, 1980).

One of the most popular hallucinogens is LSD (lysergic acid diethylamide). LSD is a synthetic material derived from a fungus (ergot) that grows on rye and other plants. It is one of the most potent drugs known; a single ounce will make up to 300,000 doses.

The effects of LSD vary a great deal, depending on the expectations and psychological state of the user and the context in which it is taken. A given person may experience differing reactions on different occasions. The effects that may be experienced include the apparent "seeing" of sounds; "hearing" of color; colors seeming unusually bright and shifting kaleidoscopically; exaggerations of color and sound; and objects appearing to expand and contract. Users become highly suggestible and easily manipulated.

Bizarre hallucinations are also common. The experience may be peaceful or may result in panic. Some users have developed severe emotional disturbances that resulted in long-term hospitalization. Usually a "trip" will last 6 to 16 hours. Physical reactions include increased heartbeat, goose bumps, dilated pupils, hyperactivity, tremors, and increased sweating. Aftereffects include acute anxiety and depression. Flashbacks sometimes occur after the actual drug experience. Flashbacks may happen at any time and place, with no advance warning. If the user is driving a car when a flashback occurs, a life-threatening condition is present for the user and for others in the vicinity.

There is no evidence of physical or psychological dependence on LSD. Users do develop tolerance to the drug very rapidly as the effects can only be achieved in the future by larger doses. Cessation of use, even for a few days, will restore sensitivity to the drug, enabling the user to take smaller quantities to experience the effects.

Phencyclidine (better known as PCP) was developed in the 1950s as an anesthetic. This medical use was soon terminated because patients displayed symptoms of severe emotional disturbance after receiving the drug. PCP is used legally today to tranquilize elephants and monkeys, as they apparently do not experience the adverse side effects.

PCP is primarily used by young people who are often unaware of its hazards. It is usually smoked, often after being sprinkled on a marijuana joint. It may also be sniffed, swallowed, or injected.

PCP is a very dangerous drug. It distorts the senses, disrupts balance, and leads to an inability to think clearly. Effects produced are similar to those of hallucinogens. Larger amounts of PCP may cause a person to become paranoid, lead to aggressive behavior, and may cause the user to display temporary symptoms of severe emotional disturbance. Continued use can lead to prolonged emotional disturbance. Overdose can result in coma or even death. Research has not yet concluded whether PCP induces physical and/or psychological dependence. The drug has the potential to be used (and abused) extensively, as it is relatively easy to prepare in a home laboratory from ingredients and recipes that are widely available. An additional danger of PCP is that even one-time users sometimes have flashbacks in which the hallucinations are reexperienced, even long after use has ceased.

The effects and dangers of mescaline, psilocybin, and psilocin are similar to those of LSD and PCP. The latter two, however, are the most potent of these hallucinogens.

Ecstasy was developed and patented in the early 1900s as a chemical forerunner in the synthesis of pharmaceuticals. Chemically, ecstasy is similar to a stimulant (amphetamine) and to a hallucinogen (mescaline), as it can produce both stimulant and psychedelic effects. Effects last for approximately three to six hours, although confusion, depression, sleep problems, anxiety, and paranoia have been reported to occur even weeks after the drug is taken. Ecstasy is sometimes used by young adults at all-night dance parties, such as "raves." The stimulant effects of ecstasy enable users to dance for extended periods.

Ecstasy use in high doses can be extremely dangerous. It can lead to dehydration, hypertension, and heart or kidney failure. It can cause a marked increase in body temperature. Chronic use of ecstasy can produce long-lasting, perhaps permanent damage to the neurons that release serotonin, and consequent memory impairment.

Tobacco

The use of tobacco has now become recognized as one of the most damaging drug habits in the United States. Smoking can cause emphysema, cancer of the mouth, ulcers, and lung cancer, and it reduces life expectancy. It significantly increases the risk of strokes and heart disease, particularly in women who use birth control pills. Smoking by a pregnant woman can lead to miscarriage, premature birth, and underweight birth. Yet despite these widely publicized hazards, about 20 percent of the adult population continues to smoke (Abadinsky, 2011).

Tobacco is the number one killer drug. It contributes to far more deaths than all other drugs combined (Kornblum & Julian, 2012). Tobacco is estimated to contribute to more than 400,000 deaths per year in the United States. This is more than double the number of deaths attributed to alcohol abuse and hundreds of times the number of deaths due to cocaine. Most of the tobacco-related deaths are the results of diseases such as heart disease and lung cancer. However, more than 2,000 deaths per year result from fires caused by careless smoking (Kornblum & Julian, 2012). There is also substantial evidence that "passive smoking" (breathing the smoke from others' cigarettes, cigars, or pipes) is also hazardous to health. One source of evidence for this is that young children whose parents smoke have a higher incidence of pneumonia and other respiratory disorders than young children whose parents do not smoke (Kornblum & Julian, 2012).

In 1988, the surgeon general of the United States, C. Everett Koop, declared that tobacco is as addictive as heroin or cocaine (Rosellini, 1988). Koop noted that people addicted to tobacco are drug addicts. The attitudes of Americans toward tobacco use are gradually becoming more negative. In the past two decades, a movement has developed that is increasingly viewing tobacco as a dangerous drug, and nonsmokers are increasingly considering smokers to be pariahs. Some authorities now predict that cigarettes will someday be outlawed in many countries.

Tobacco is highly habit-forming. Nicotine is the primary drug in tobacco. Nicotine has remarkable capacities—it can act as a depressant, a stimulant, or a tranquilizer. Smokers quickly develop a tolerance for nicotine and often gradually increase consumption to one or two packs or more a day.

Special clinics and a variety of other educational and therapeutic programs help people quit smoking. Users undergoing withdrawal become restless, irritable, depressed, and have an intense craving to smoke. Studies show that only a minority of smokers who make determined efforts to quit actually succeed (Kornblum & Julian, 2012).

At the same time that the government is widely publicizing the hazards of drugs, the Department of Agriculture is subsidizing tobacco farmers. While educational programs urge people not to smoke, tobacco companies are permitted to advertise that cigarette smoking is "cool" and "sexy," connoting rugged manliness in men and social sophistication in women.

In the biggest civil settlement in U.S. history, tobacco companies agreed in 1998 to pay more than $240 billion to the 50 states to settle claims against the industry for health-care costs blamed on tobacco-related illnesses. The payments to the states, which began in 2000, will be distributed over 25 years. A portion of the funds will go to a foundation to study how to reduce teen smoking. A major objective of the deal is to discourage children from smoking by imposing restrictions on advertising and sharp limits on the ways cigarettes are marketed.

Marijuana

Marijuana, or "grass" or "pot," comes from a variety of the hemp plant, *Cannabis sativa.* This hemp plant grows throughout the world, and its fibers are legally used to produce rope, twine, paper, and clothing.

The main use of the plant now, however, centers on its dried leaves—marijuana—and on its dried resin—hashish. Both may be taken orally, but are usually smoked. Hashish is several times more potent than marijuana.

The effects of marijuana (and hashish) vary, as with any other drug, according to the mood and personality of the user, circumstances, and the quality of the drug. The effects are rather complicated and may induce a variety of emotions.

Many of the effects are produced because marijuana has sedative properties and creates in the user a sense of relaxed well-being and freedom from inhibition. There may also be mild hallucinations that create a dreamy state in which the user may experience fantasies. Smokers become highly suggestible and may engage in actions (such as sexual activities) in which they would not otherwise be involved. The drug may induce feelings of joyousness, hilarity, and sociability. It may lead to talkativeness, disconnected ideas, a feeling of floating, and laughter. It may also intensify sensory stimulation, create feelings of enhanced awareness and creativity, and increase self-confidence. A person may gradually experience some of these emotions, followed by others.

The threat of physical dependence is rated low, while the threat of psychological dependence is rated as moderate. Withdrawal, however, may be very unpleasant for the user, who may suffer from insomnia, hyperactivity, and loss of appetite.

The short-term physical effects of marijuana are minor: a reddening of the eyes, dryness of the throat and the mouth, and a slight rise in heart rate. There is some evidence that continued use by young teenagers can result in these users becoming apathetic, noncompetitive, and uninterested in school and other activities.

Frequent users may have impairments of short-term memory and concentration, and of judgment and coordination. They may find it difficult to read, to understand what they read, and to follow moving objects with their eyes. Users may feel confident that their coordination, reactions, and perceptions are quite normal while they are still experiencing the effects of the drug; under these conditions, such activities as driving a vehicle may have tragic consequences for them and for others.

An overdose of the active ingredients of cannabis can lead to panic, fear, confusion, suspiciousness, fatigue, and sometimes aggressive acts. One of the most frequently voiced concerns about marijuana is that it will be a stepping-stone to using other drugs. About 60 percent of marijuana users progress to using other drugs (Kornblum & Julian, 2009). However, other factors, such as peer pressure, are probably more crucial determinants of what mind-altering drugs people will progress to. In addition, those who experiment with one drug are more likely to experiment with another.

The attempt to restrict the use of marijuana through legislation has been described as a "second prohibition," which has had results similar to those of the first, because a large number of people are using the drug and disregarding the law. The unfortunate effect of laws that outlaw the use of marijuana is that they criminalize the private acts of many people who are otherwise law-abiding. Such laws also foster the development of organized crime and the illicit drug market.

For years, debates have raged about the hazards of long-term marijuana use. Some studies claim it causes brain damage, chromosome damage, irritation of the bronchial tract and lungs, and a reduction in male hormone levels. These findings have not been confirmed by other studies, and so the controversy rages on.

One of the reversible, short-term health effects of marijuana use is impairment of motor coordination, which adversely affects driving or machine-operating skills. The drug also impairs short-term memory, slows learning abilities, and may cause periods of confusion and anxiety. Smoking marijuana may affect the lungs and respiratory system in much the same way that tobacco smoke does, and may be a factor in causing bronchitis and precancerous changes.

Marijuana may be useful in treating glaucoma, asthma, certain seizure disorders and spastic conditions, and in controlling severe nausea caused by cancer chemotherapy. In 1996, voters in California and Arizona approved the medical use of marijuana—for example, for treating symptoms of AIDS, cancer, and other diseases. At the time of this writing, 18 states and the District of Columbia had approved laws that legalize medical use of marijuana.

In 2001, the U.S. Supreme Court ruled that federal law definitely classifies the use of marijuana as illegal, and that marijuana has no medical benefits worthy of an exception. The high court did not strike down state laws allowing medical use of marijuana, but it left those distributing the drug for that purpose open to prosecution. In 2005, the Court upheld the power of Congress to legislate to prohibit the possession and use of marijuana for medical purposes, even in the 18 states that permit it. Again, this ruling does not invalidate laws in the 18 states that have approved medical marijuana, but it does deflate these states' power to protect users and doctors who prescribe the drug. The controversy over the medical use of marijuana continues to be an issue.

Ethical Questions 11.5

Do you know someone who is abusing one or more drugs? If yes, what might you do or say to help this person?

EP 2.1.2

Anabolic Steroids

Anabolic steroids are synthetic male hormones, derivatives of testosterone. Although steroids have been banned for use by athletes in organized sports competition, steroids are still being used by some athletes, bodybuilders, and teenagers who want to look more muscular and brawny.

From early childhood, many boys have been socialized to believe that the ideal man looks something like Mr. Universe. Many adolescents who use steroids want to be sports champions. Some young male bodybuilders who use steroids to promote tissue growth and to endure arduous workouts routinely flood their bodies with 100 times the testosterone they produce naturally (Abadinsky, 2011). Most steroid users are middle class and white.

Steroid-enhanced physiques are a hazardous prize. Steroids can cause temporary acne and balding, upset hormonal production, and damage the heart and kidneys. Doctors suspect they may contribute to liver cancer and atherosclerosis (Toufexis, 1989). In teens, the drugs can stunt growth by accelerating bone maturation. Male steroid users have also experienced a shrinking of the testicles, impotence, a yellowing of the skin and eyes, and the development of female-type breasts. In young boys, steroids can have the effect of painfully enlarging the sex organs. In female users, the voice deepens permanently, breasts shrink, periods become irregular, the clitoris swells in size, and hair is lost from the head but grows on the face and body.

Steroid users are prone to moodiness, depression, and irritability. Users are apt to experience difficulty in tolerating stress. After prolonged use, some formerly easygoing males experience raging hostility, which may be displayed in a variety of ways—ranging from being obnoxious to continually provoking physical fights. Some users become so depressed that they commit suicide.

HIGHLIGHT 11.8

Use of Performance-Enhancing Drugs in Baseball

On March 30, 2006, baseball commissioner Bud Selig asked former senator George Mitchell to investigate steroid use in baseball. On December 13, 2007, Mitchell released his report. The report found steroid use to be rampant among former and current players.

Eighty-six former and current players were named in the report. (It is thought that there are many other users among baseball players who have not yet been identified.) Steroids have been on baseball's banned substance list since 1991; however, testing of Major League players did not begin until 2003.

Seven Most Valuable Player Award winners were named in the report, along with 31 All-Stars—at least one for every position. Some of the biggest names in baseball are alleged to have been users, including Barry Bonds, Roger Clemens, Mark McGwire, David Justice, Jason Giambi, Gary Sheffield, Miguel Tejada, Lenny Dykstra, Rafael Palmeiro, Andy Pettitte, Chuck Knoblauch, and Alex Rodriguez. (Some of these players have denied, under oath, that they used steroids.)

To avoid testing positive for steroids, many athletes looking for an edge have now turned to human growth hormone (HGH) to build muscle. It is difficult to detect, and the best test available has a window of detection of only 48–72 hours. Like steroids, HGH is a performance-enhancing drug (PED).

In 2013 there was an investigation by Major League Baseball of Biogenesis of America, a clinic in Florida. Evidence was obtained that this health clinic provided performance-enhancing drugs to a number of baseball players. In the summer of 2013, Ryan Braun was suspended for 65 games, and Alex Rodriguez was suspended for the entire 2014 season for using PEDs. Twelve other players were given 50-game suspensions. The only player appealing these suspensions was Alex Rodriguez.

Steroid users generally experience considerable difficulty in terminating steroids after prolonged use. One reason is that bulging biceps and hamhock thighs soon fade when steroid use is discontinued. Concurrent with the decline in muscle mass is the psychological feeling of being less powerful and less manly. Most users who try to quit wind up back on the drug. A self-image that relies on a steroid-enhanced physique is difficult to change. (See Highlight 11.8 on the use of performance-enhancing drugs in baseball.)

Dependence on Alcohol and Other Drugs

Habit-forming drugs can lead to *dependence*, which is a tendency or craving for the repeated use or compulsive use (not necessarily abuse) of a chemical. This dependence may be physical, psychological, or both. When physical dependence occurs, the user will generally experience bodily withdrawal symptoms when drug use is discontinued. Withdrawal may take many forms and range in severity from slight tremblings to fatal convulsions.

When psychological dependence occurs, the user feels psychological discomfort if use is terminated. Dependent users tend to believe that they will use the chemical for the rest of their lives as a regular part of social or recreational activities. They question whether the desired emotional state can be achieved without the use of the chemical, and they have a preoccupation with thinking and talking about the chemical and activities associated with using it.

Users also generally develop a *tolerance* for some drugs, which means they have to take increasing amounts over time to achieve a given level of effect. Tolerance depends partly on the type of drug, because some drugs (such as aspirin) do not create tolerance.

Drug addiction is difficult to define. In a broad sense, addiction refers to an intense craving for a particular substance. The problem is that this definition could be applied to an intense craving for a variety of substances—pickles, ice cream, potato chips, strawberry shortcake. To avoid this problem, we will define *addiction* as an intense craving for a drug that develops after a period of heavy use.

Why Do People Use and Abuse Alcohol and Other Drugs?

The effects of using drugs are numerous, ranging from feeling light-headed to death through overdosing. Drug abuse may lead to deterioration in health, relationship problems, automobile accidents, child abuse, spouse abuse, loss of job, low self-esteem, loss of social status, financial disaster, divorce, and arrests and convictions.

A distinction needs to be made between responsible drug use and drug abuse. Many drugs do have beneficial effects when used responsibly; aspirin relieves pain, alcohol helps people relax, tranquilizers reduce anxiety, antidepressant drugs reduce depression, amphetamines increase alertness, morphine is a painkiller, and marijuana is useful in treating glaucoma. Irresponsible drug use is abuse, which was defined earlier in this chapter.

Why do people abuse drugs? The reasons are numerous. Drug companies widely advertise the beneficial effects of their products. The media (such as television and movies) glamorize the mind-altering effects. Many popular songs highlight drinking. Bars and cocktail lounges have become centers for socializing, and promote drinking. Through such channels, Americans have become socialized to accept drug usage as a part of daily living. Socialization patterns lead many people to use drugs, and for some the use is a stepping-stone to abuse.

Attitudes toward drug use also encourage abuse. For example, some college students believe they should get blitzed or stoned after a tough exam. Ryne Duren (1985), former pitcher for the New York Yankees, asked this question: "I started becoming an alcoholic at age four, even though I had my first drink at age nine—how can this be?" Duren went on to explain that at a very young age he became socialized to believe that a real man was "someone who could drink others under the table," and that the way to have fun was to get high on alcohol.

People abuse drugs for a variety of reasons. Some people build up a tolerance to a drug and then increase the dosage to obtain a high. Physical and psychological dependence usually leads to abuse. People with intense unwanted emotions (such as loneliness, anxiety, feelings of inadequacy, guilt, depression, insecurity, and resentment) may turn to drugs. For many abusers, their drug of choice becomes their best friend because they tend to personalize it and value it more highly than they value their friends. The drug is something that they can always count on to relieve pain or give them the kind of high they desire. Many abusers become so highly attached to their drug that they choose to continue using it even though it leads to deterioration of health, divorce, discharges from jobs, automobile accidents, alienation from children, loss of friends, depletion of financial resources, and court

appearances. Drug abusers usually feel they need their drug as a crutch to make it through the day.

Abusers develop an intimate relationship with their drug of choice. Even though this relationship is unhealthy, the drug plays a primary role in the abuser's life, dictates a certain lifestyle, fills a psychological need, and more often than not takes precedence over family, friends, and work. Most abusers *deny* their drug usage is creating problems for them, because they know that admitting they have a drug problem means they will have to end their relationship with their best friend, and they deeply believe they need their drug to handle their daily concerns and pressures. Drug abusers are apt to use a number of defense mechanisms in order to continue using drugs. They *rationalize* adverse consequences of drug abuse (such as the loss of a job) by twisting or distorting reality to explain the consequences of their behavior while under the influence. They *minimize* the adverse consequences of their drug use. They use *projection* to place the blame for their problems on others; for example, "If you had a wife like mine, you'd drink too."

Theories About Drug Use

A variety of theories have been offered as to why people use drugs. *Biological theories* assert that physiological changes produced by the drugs eventually generate an irresistible craving for the drug. Some biological theories also postulate that some people are predisposed by their genetic structure to abuse certain types of drugs. For example, some authorities believe that genes play a role in predisposing some people to alcoholism. *Behavioral theories* hold that people use drugs because they find them pleasurable and continue to use them because doing so prevents withdrawal distress. *Interactionist theories* maintain that drug use is learned from interaction with others in our culture. For example, people drink alcohol because drinking is widely accepted. Interactionist theories assert that those who use illegal drugs such as marijuana or cocaine have contact with a drug subculture that encourages them to experiment with illegal drugs.

Interaction in Family Systems: A Theoretical Approach to Drug Abuse

Wegscheider (1981) maintains that chemical dependency is a family disease that involves and affects each family member. Although she focuses on the families of alcoholics, much of what she says may also apply to the families of other types of chemical substance abusers.

She cites several rules that tend to characterize the families of drug abusers. First, the dependent person's alcohol use becomes "the most important thing in the family's life" (Wegscheider, 1981, p. 81). The abuser's top priority is getting enough alcohol, and the family's top priorities are the abuser, the abuser's behavior, and keeping the abuser away from alcohol. The goals of the abuser and of the rest of the family are at completely opposite poles.

A second rule in an alcoholic family is that alcohol is not the cause of the problem. Denial is paramount. A third family rule maintains that the dependent person is not responsible for his or her behavior and that the alcohol causes the behavior. There is always someone or something else to blame. Another rule dictates that no one should rock the boat, no matter what. Family members strive to protect the family's status quo, even when the family is miserable. Yet other rules concern forbidding discussion of the family problem either within or outside of the family, and consistently avoiding stating one's true feelings. Wegscheider (1981) maintains that these rules protect the dependent person from taking responsibility for his or her behavior, and that the rules serve to maintain the drinking problem.

Wegscheider (1981) goes on to identify several roles that family members typically play. In addition to the chemically dependent person, there is the chief enabler, the family hero, the scapegoat, the lost child, and the mascot.

The chief enabler's main purpose is to assume the primary responsibility for family functioning. The abuser typically continues to lose control and relinquishes responsibility. The chief enabler takes on more and more responsibility and begins making more and more of the family's decisions. A chief enabler is often the parent or spouse of the chemically dependent person.

Conditions often continue to deteriorate as the chemically dependent person loses control. A positive influence is needed to offset the negative. The family hero fulfills this role. The family hero is often the person who does well at everything he or she tries. The hero works hard at making the family look as though it is functioning better than it is. In

this way, the family hero provides the family with self-worth.

Another role typically played by someone in the family is that of scapegoat. Although the alcohol abuse is the real problem, a family rule mandates that this fact must be denied. Therefore, the blame must be placed elsewhere. Frequently, another family member is blamed for the problem. The scapegoat often behaves in negative ways that draw attention to him or her (e.g., the person gets caught stealing, runs away, or becomes extremely withdrawn). The scapegoat's role is to distract attention away from the chemically dependent person and onto something else. This role helps the family avoid addressing the problem of chemical dependency.

Often, someone plays the role of lost child. This is a person who seems relatively uninvolved with the rest of the family and never causes any trouble. The lost child's purpose is to provide relief from some of the pain the family is suffering. At least there is someone in the family who neither requires much attention nor causes any stress. The lost child is simply there.

Finally, chemically dependent families often have someone playing the role of mascot. The mascot is someone who has a good sense of humor and appears not to take anything seriously. Despite how much the mascot might be suffering inside, he or she provides a little fun for the family.

In summary, chemical dependency is a problem affecting the entire family. Each family member suffers from the chemical dependency, yet each assumes a role in order to maintain the family's status quo and help the family survive. Family members are driven to maintain these roles no matter what happens. The roles eventually become associated with survival.

The Application of Theory to Client Situations: Treatment for the Chemically Dependent Person and His or Her Family

EP 2.1.3b, 2.1.6b, 2.1.10a, d, e, g, & j

One of the first tasks in treatment is for the chemically dependent person to take responsibility for his or her own behavior. The abuser must acknowledge that he or she has a problem before beginning to solve it. Several concepts are critical in working with the family (Wegscheider, 1981). Family members must first come to realize the extent of the problem. They need to identify the chemical abuse as their major problem. Additionally, they need to learn about and evaluate their family dynamics. They need to evaluate their own behavior and break out of the roles that have been maintaining the chemical abuse. The chief enabler, in particular, must stop making excuses and assuming the chemically dependent person's responsibilities. If the chemically dependent person is sick from a hangover and cannot make it to school or work the next day, it must be that person's responsibility, not a parent's or spouse's, to call in sick.

Family members eventually learn to confront the chemically dependent person and give him or her honest information about his or her behavior. For instance, they are encouraged to tell the dependent exactly how he or she behaved while having a blackout. If the dependent person hit another family member while drunk, this fact needs to be confronted. The confrontation should occur not in an emotional manner but rather in a factual one.

The family also needs to learn about the progression of the disease. We've already discussed some characteristics of drug dependence. There is a typical progression of an alcoholic's feelings and behavior. At first, only occasional relief drinking occurs. Drinking becomes more constant. The dependent person then begins to drink in secret and to feel guilty about drinking. Memory blackouts begin to occur and gradually increase in frequency. The dependent person feels worse and worse about his or her drinking behavior, but seems to have less and less control over it. Finally, the drinking begins to seriously affect the person's work, family, and social relationships. A job may be lost or all school classes flunked. Perhaps family members leave or throw the dependent person out. The dependent person's thinking becomes more and more impaired.

Eventually, the dependent person hits rock bottom. Nothing seems to be left but despair and failure, and the dependent person admits complete defeat. It is at this point that the dependent person may make one of two choices. He or she will either continue on the downward spiral to a probable death related to alcohol or may desperately struggle. Typically during this period, the dependent one will make some progress only to slip back again. Vicious cycles of drinking and stopping are often apparent.

Finally, the dependent person may express an honest desire for help. A dependent person on the path to recovery will stop drinking. Meeting with other people who are also alcoholics or addicts is very helpful. Support from others is especially critical at this time in the process of recovery.

Alcoholics Anonymous (AA) is a self-help organization that has provided the support, information, and guidance necessary for many dependent people to continue on in their recovery. The nationwide group is made up of recovering alcoholics. The organization's success seems to rest on several principles. First, other people who really understand are available to give the recovering dependent person friendship and warmth. Each new member is given a sponsor who can be called for support at any time during the day or night. Whenever the dependent person feels depressed or tempted, there is always the sponsor to turn to.

AA provides the recovering alcoholic with a new social group and activities. The recovering alcoholic can no longer participate in the drinking activity. Old friends with well-established drinking patterns usually become difficult to associate with; often social pressure is applied to drink again. AA provides a respite from such pressure and the opportunity to meet new people, if such an opportunity is needed. For more on AA, see Highlight 11.9.

AA also helps the recovering person to understand that alcoholism is a disease. This means that the alcoholic cannot cure himself or herself. He or she need no longer feel guilty about being an alcoholic. What must be done is to stop drinking. AA also encourages introspection. Members are encouraged to look inside themselves and face whatever they see. They are urged to acknowledge that they have flaws and will never be perfect. This perspective often helps people to stop fleeing from the pain of reality and hiding in alcohol or drugs. It helps them to redefine expectations for themselves and to gain control. Within this context, people often can also acknowledge their strengths. They can learn that they do have some control over their own behavior and that they can accomplish things for themselves and for others.

Organizations are also available to provide support for other family members and to give them information and suggestions. For example, AA is an organization for the families of alcoholics, and Alateen is specifically for teenagers within these families. Likewise, self-help organizations similar to AA, such as Narcotics Anonymous, exist to help other types of chemical substance abusers.

HIGHLIGHT 11.9

An AA Meeting

Alcoholics Anonymous (AA) is a remarkable human organization. Its chapters now cover every part of the United States and most of the world. There is more caring and concern among the members for one another than in most other organizations. Group members work together to save each other's lives and to restore their self-respect and sense of worth. AA has helped more people overcome their drinking problems than all other therapies and methods combined.

AA is supported entirely by voluntary donations from the members at meetings. There are no dues or fees. Each chapter is autonomous, and free of any outside control by the AA headquarters in New York City or by any other body. There is no hierarchy in the chapters. The only office is that of the group secretary. This person chooses a chairperson for each meeting, makes the arrangements for meetings, and sees that the building is open, the chairs are set up, and the tea and coffee put on. The group secretary holds office for only a limited time period; after a month or two the secretary's responsibilities are transferred to another member.

The only requirement for membership in AA is a desire to stop drinking. All other variables (such as economic status, social status, race, religion) do not count. Members can even attend meetings while drunk, as long as they do not disturb the meeting.

AA meetings are held in a variety of physical locations—churches, temples, private homes, business offices, schools, libraries, or banquet rooms of restaurants. The physical location is unimportant.

When a newcomer first arrives, he or she will usually find people setting up chairs, placing ashtrays, putting free literature on a table, and making coffee. Other members will be socializing in small groups. Someone is apt to introduce himself or herself and other members to the newcomer. If someone is shy about attending the first meeting alone, he or she can call AA and someone will take the person to the meeting and introduce him or her to the other members.

When the meeting starts, everyone sits down around tables or in rows of chairs. The secretary and/or chairperson, and one or more speakers, sit at the head of the table or on a platform if the meeting is in a hall.

The chairperson opens with a moment of silence, which is followed by a group recitation of a nondenominational prayer. The chairperson then reads or gives a brief description of Alcoholics Anonymous and may read or refer to a section of the book *Alcoholics Anonymous* (a book that describes the principles of AA and gives a number of case examples).

Then the chairperson usually asks if anyone is attending for the first, second, or third time. The new people are asked to introduce themselves according to the following: "Hello, my name is [first name], and this is my first [second, third] meeting." Those who do not want to introduce themselves are not pressured to do so. New members are the lifeblood of AA, and are the most important people at the meeting in the members' eyes. (All the longer-term members remember their first meeting and how frightened and inhibited they felt.)

If the group is small, the chairperson usually then asks the longer-term members to introduce themselves and say a few words. If the group is large, the chairperson asks volunteers among the longer-term members to introduce themselves by saying a few words. Each member usually begins by saying, "My name is [first name]; I am an alcoholic," and then discloses a few thoughts or feelings. (The members do not have to say they are alcoholic, unless they choose to do so. Each member sooner or later generally chooses to say this, to remind himself or herself that he or she is an addictive drinker who is recovering and that alcoholism is a lifelong disease that must be battled daily.) Those who introduce themselves usually say whatever they feel will be most helpful to the newcomers. They may talk about their first meeting, or their first week without drinking, or something designed to make the newcomers more comfortable. Common advice for the newcomers is to get the phone numbers of other members after the meeting so that they can call a member when they feel a strong urge to drink. AA considers such help as vital in recovering. The organization believes members can remain sober only through receiving the help of people who care about them and who understand what they are struggling with.

AA members want newcomers to call when they have the urge to drink, at any time day or night. The members sincerely believe that by helping others they are helping themselves to stay sober and grow. Members indicate that such calling is the newcomer's ace in the hole against the first drink, if everything else fails. They also inform newcomers that it is good to call others when lonely, just to chat.

In his own words, a newcomer explains how AA began to help him:

Here's what happened to me. When I finally hit bottom and called AA for help, a U.S. Air Force officer came to tell me about AA. For the first time in my life, I was talking to someone who obviously really understood my problem, as four psychiatrists had not, and he took me to my first meeting, sober but none too steady. It was amazing. I went home afterward and didn't have a drink. I went again the next night, still dry, and the miracle happened a second time. The third morning my wife went off to work, my boys to school, and I was alone. Suddenly I wanted a drink more than I had ever wanted one in my life. I tried walking for a while. No good. The feeling was getting worse. I tried reading. Couldn't concentrate. Then I became really desperate, and although I wasn't used

HIGHLIGHT 11.9 *(continued)*

to calling strangers for help, I called Fred, an AAer who had said that he was retired and would welcome a call at any time. We talked a bit; he could see that talking on the phone wasn't going to be enough. He said, "Look, I've got an idea. Let me make a phone call, and I'll call you back in ten minutes. Can you hold on that long?" I said I could. He called back in eight, asking me to come over to his house. We talked endlessly, went out for a sandwich together, and finally my craving for a drink went away. We went to a meeting. Next morning I was fine again and now I had gone four days without a drink.*

After such discussion, speakers may describe their life of drinking, how drinking almost destroyed their life, how they were introduced to AA, their struggles to remain sober one day at a time, how AA has helped them, and what their life is like now.

At the end of a meeting, the chairperson may ask the newcomers if they wish to say anything. If they do not wish to say much, that is okay. No one is pressured to self-disclose what they do not want to reveal.

Meetings usually end after the chairperson makes announcements. (The collection basket for donations is also passed around. New members are not expected, and frequently not allowed, to donate any money until after the third meeting. If someone cannot afford to make a donation, none is expected.) The group then stands, usually holding hands, and repeats in unison the Lord's Prayer. Those who do not want to join in this prayer are not pressured to do so. After a meeting, the members socialize. This is a time for newcomers to meet new friends and to get phone numbers.

AA is a cross section of people from all walks of life. Anonymity is emphasized. It is the duty of every member to respect the anonymity of every person who attends. Concern for anonymity is a major reason for two kinds of meetings in AA, open and closed. Anyone is welcome at open meetings. Only people with drinking problems are allowed at closed meetings. Therefore, if a person feels uncomfortable going to an open meeting and has a drinking problem, then closed meetings are an alternative.

Members do not have to believe in God to get help from AA. Many members have lost, or never had, a faith in God. AA does, however, assert that faith in some higher power is a

tremendous help in recovery because such a belief offers a source of limitless power, hope, and support whenever one feels one has come to the end of one's resources.

How does AA help? New members, after years of feelings of rejection, loneliness, misunderstanding, guilt, and embarrassment, find they are not alone. They feel understood by others who are in similar predicaments. Instead of being rejected, they are welcomed. They see that others who had serious drinking problems are now sober, apparently happy that way, and are in the process of recovering. It gives them hope that they do not need alcohol to get through the day and that they can learn to enjoy life without alcohol. They find that others sincerely care about them, want to help them, and have the knowledge to do so.

At meetings, they see every sort of personal problem brought up and discussed openly, with suggestions for solutions being offered from others who have encountered similar problems. They can observe that group members bring up "unspeakable" problems without apparent embarrassment, and that others listen and treat them with respect and consideration. Such acceptance gradually leads newcomers to share their personal problems and to receive constructive suggestions for solutions. Such disclosure leads individuals to look more deeply into themselves and to ventilate deep personal feelings. With the support of other members, newcomers gradually learn how to counter strong desires to drink, through such processes as calling other members.

Newcomers learn that AA is the means of staying away from that first drink. AA also serves to reduce the stress that compels people to drink by providing a comfortable and relaxed environment and by having members help each other to find ways to reduce the stresses encountered in daily living. AA meetings and members become a safe port that is always there when storms start raging. AA helps members to be programmed from negative thinking to positive thinking. The more positive a member's thinking becomes, the more stress is relieved, the better he or she begins to feel about himself or herself, the more the compulsion to drink decreases, and the more often and more effectively the person begins to take positive actions to solve his or her problems.

*Clark Vaughan, *Addictive Drinking* (New York, Penguin, 1984), pp. 75–76.

Today may treatment approaches are available to chemical substance abusers. Types of facilities and treatment include inpatient and outpatient treatment programs at community mental health centers, chemical abuse rehabilitation centers and medical hospitals, halfway houses, and chemical treatment programs such as Antabuse. When Antabuse is taken, a person who then drinks an alcoholic

beverage will soon become flushed, experience a rapid pulse, and feel nauseated, often to the point of regurgitation.

Treatment programs almost always advocate that abusers abstain totally from their drug of choice in the future, because research indicates that even one use will return the abuser to drug abuse. It should also be noted that when abusers complete a treatment program they are urged to view themselves as *recovering*, rather than being cured, because they must continually work on abstaining in order to avoid the temptations of using.

It is important that those receiving treatment also make lifestyle changes. The social activities of users almost always revolve around using the drug of choice; to successfully abstain, recovering abusers need to form new friendships and establish drug-free social activities and interests. Making such lifestyle changes is extremely difficult. Many recovering addicts fail in making these changes and then return to using their drug of choice.

Roles assumed by social workers in treating addicts and family members include counselor, group facilitator, broker, program initiator, and educator. The role of a social worker in confronting denial is described in Highlight 11.10.

 HIGHLIGHT 11.10

Motivational Interviewing with Alcoholic Clients Who Are in Denial*

Admitting the existence of a problem is difficult because clients often (erroneously) perceive themselves as weak, sinful, or irresponsible. Also recognition brings with it an acknowledgment that change is inevitable. Clients often mourn the loss of that which must be changed. Alcoholics thus mourn the loss of their drinking because their social activities are centered around it. Alcohol has become their "best friend," which they do not want to give up. Denial of a drinking problem helps them to "keep their best friend." Constructive changes are not apt to occur for people in denial, unless counselors find a way to convince them that the problem exists.

Researchers have found that people go through a process when they make positive changes, and this process can be conceptualized in a series of steps or stages. The Stages of Change Model, part of the Transtheoretical Model of Change, outlines the process of change that individuals go through when they successfully make changes in their lives (Prochaska & Diclemente, 1982).

Brief Definition of Each Stage of Change

Stage	Basic Definition
1. PRECONTEMPLATION	A person is not seeing a need for a lifestyle change
2. CONTEMPLATION	A person is considering making a change but has not decided yet
3. PREPARATION	A person has decided to make changes and is considering how to make them
4. ACTION	A person is actively doing something to change
5. MAINTENANCE	A person is working to maintain the change or new lifestyle. There may be some temptations to return to the former behavior or even small relapses.

Motivational interviewing is designed to help clients in stages 1, 2, or 3 to move toward stages 4 and 5. The Stages of Change are dynamic—a person may move through them once or recycle through them several times before reaching success and maintaining a behavior change over time. Individuals may move back and forth between stages on any single issue or may simultaneously be in different stages of change for two or more behaviors.

Motivational interviewing is not a technique but rather a style, a facilitative way of being with people. This facilitative style encourages self-motivation for positive change within individuals. The development of motivational interviewing in the early 1980s by William R. Miller and Stephen Rollnick (1981) was out of response to substance abusers in treatment who had high dropout rates, high relapse rates, and poor outcomes overall in treatment. This lack of progress in treatment cast the individuals as resistant and unmotivated to change. The question of why people *do* change became the foundation of developing motivational interviewing. Instead of dismissing challenging clients as unmotivated and unable to change, motivational interviewing skills allow social workers to become equipped with the skills to enhance motivation and to help clients become active in the change process.

The principles of motivational interviewing include the following:

● **Express Empathy:** Empathy involves seeing the world through the client's eyes, thinking about things as the client thinks about things, feeling things as the client feels them, and sharing in the client's experiences. Expression of empathy is critical to the motivational interviewing process. When clients feel that they are understood, they are more apt to open up and share their own experiences. Having clients share experiences in depth allows the social worker to assess when and where they need support and what barriers there may be to the change-planning process. When clients perceive the social worker as empathetic, they become more open to gentle challenges by the social worker about lifestyle changes. Clients become more comfortable openly examining their ambivalence about change and less likely to defend their ideas of possible denial. The social worker's accurate understanding of the client's experience facilitates change. The following is an example of an empathic statement to a client who acknowledges he has a challenge, at times, of getting into trouble associated with his drinking: "I applaud you for looking at whether you need to make some changes about your drinking patterns. Looking at how much one drinks can be very scary."

- **Roll with Resistance:** In motivational interviewing, the social worker does not fight resistance but "rolls with it." Statements made by the client demonstrating resistance are not challenged. Instead the social worker uses the client's momentum to further explore the client's views. Using this approach, resistance tends to be decreased rather than increased, as the client is not being reinforced for being argumentative to the social worker's statement. Motivational interviewing encourages clients to develop their own solutions to problems that they themselves have defined. Thus, there is no real power in the client–social worker relationship for the client to challenge. In exploring client concerns, social workers invite new ways of thinking about things, but do not impose their ways of thinking on clients.

  A useful technique when a client is resisting change is using a reflection, where the social worker is responding to resistance with nonresistance by repeating the client's statement in a neutral form. An example of this would be if a social worker says to a client "I would like to talk to you about when you spent a night in jail after receiving a citation for driving while intoxicated." The client responds: "What's to talk about? The police and you have already made your minds up that it was my fault." Instead of responding with a statement reflecting the facts documented in the police report, the social worker would respond with the reflection "so you feel like your opinion doesn't matter?" Rolling with resistance avoids confrontations with clients on issues they have.

- **Develop Discrepancy:** Motivation for change occurs when people perceive a discrepancy between where they are and where they want to be, social workers help clients examine the discrepancies between where their current behavior is at and what they have identified as their goals. When clients perceive that their current behaviors are not leading toward some important future goal, they become more motivated to make life changes. Social workers respectfully and gently help clients gain insight that some of their current ways of living may lead them away from, instead of toward, their goals.

  If a client states he has a problem with drinking alcoholic beverages but is uncertain if he is ready to commit to no longer drinking, the social worker can create a gap between where he is currently at and where he wants to be by the following types of statements/questions:

  "What will your life be like 10 years from now if you continue to use?

  "How do you believe your life will improve if you stop drinking?"
  "Tell me some of the good things, and less good things, about your drinking."
  "What was your life like before you started having problems with drinking?"

- **Support Self-Efficacy:** Self-efficacy is the belief that one is capable of performing in a certain manner to attain certain goals. A client's belief that change is possible is an important motivator to succeeding in making a change. As clients are held responsible for choosing and carrying out actions to change in the motivational interviewing approach, the social worker focuses his or her efforts on helping the clients stay motivated. Supporting client's sense of self-efficacy is a great way of helping individuals stay motivated. The belief that there is no right way to change can help develop a belief within an individual that he or she can make a change. The social worker wants the client to develop the argument for change. Change should be derived from within the individual not from outside the individual. One technique for helping a client assess his or her willingness to change is the following "Readiness to Change Ruler":

On the following scale (show client) from 1 to 5, what number best reflects how ready you are *at the present time* to change your (the behavior)? CIRCLE ONE

Not Ready to Change	Thinking of Changing	Undecided/ Uncertain	Somewhat Ready	Very Ready to Change
1	2	3	4	5

The social worker needs to operate at the same level of change where the client is, in order to minimize resistance and gain cooperation.

For example, if a client states he is "somewhat ready" to give up drinking alcoholic beverages, the social worker may gently inquire, "What will it take for you to be ready to give up drinking?"

- **Conveying Hope:** Finding and nurturing hope with a client is a key to recovering. Conveying hope includes not just optimism, but also conveying the belief that the client has the capacity to conquer his or her drinking challenges.

- **Supportive Relationships:** A common component of recovery is the presence of others who believe in the person's potential to recover. Therefore, the social worker seeks to foster supportive relationships for the client with friends, family, and others in the community, for many alcoholics AA assists in being a critical source of support. AA members have experienced similar difficulties, and are on a similar journey of recovery. Reciprocal relationships and mutual support networks enhance the alcoholic's self-esteem and recovery journey.

(continued)

HIGHLIGHT 11.10 *(continued)*

● **Empowerment:** The social worker seeks to convey to the client that he or she has the resources (internal strengths and social support networks) to conquer his or her drinking demons.

● **Coping Strategies:** The social worker facilitates the client developing coping and problem-solving skills to resolve other personal and family challenges that the client is facing.

● **Meaning in Life:** Developing a sense of meaning and overall purpose is important for sustaining the recovery process. The social worker facilitates the client setting

(and achieving) short- and long-term goals that are personally meaningful and gratifying to him or her.

Interestingly, these principles of motivational interviewing can also be used by family members and friends of an alcoholic who is in denial.

*This Highlight was coauthored by Charles Zastrow and Katherine Drechsler, doctoral student in social work at George Williams College of Aurora 4.

Understanding and Treating Codependency

Codependent people are so trapped by a loved one's addiction that they lose their own identity in the process of obsessively managing the day-to-day trauma created by the addict. Codependency is unhealthy behavior learned amid chaos. Some codependent people are as dysfunctional as the addict, if not more so. Living with addiction triggers excessive caretaking, suppression of one's own needs, a feeling of low self-worth, and strained relationships. The life and identity of a codependent person becomes enmeshed with the everyday problems of living with an addict.

Many codependent people have grown up in dysfunctional families. Some are adult children of alcoholics. They marry or become romantically involved with people who abuse alcohol or some other drug. To some extent, the addict fills the needs of the codependent—needs such as caretaking, loneliness, and addiction to destructive behavior such as excessive partying and thrill seeking. Codependency can be viewed as a normal reaction to abnormal stress.

If the addict terminates the use of his or her drug of choice, the codependent's dysfunctional behaviors generally continue, unless he or she receives treatment. There are a variety of treatment approaches for codependent people—individual psychotherapy, self-help groups (such as Al-Anon and Adult Children of Alcoholics), and codependency therapeutic groups. For many codependent people, treatment involves recognition that they have lives and identities separate from the addict; that the addict alone is responsible for his or her drug abuse; and that their lives and the addict's will improve by terminating

their caretaking and enabling behaviors. Through treatment, many codependent people regain (or gain for the first time) their own identity. Treatment is designed to banish the self-destructive habits that sabotage codependent people's happiness.

Roles assumed by social workers in treating codependent people include counselor, educator (conveying information about addiction and codependency), facilitator (leading treatment groups), broker (linking codependent people to self-help groups and to other human service resources), and program initiator (developing programs to serve codependent people in communities where such treatment programs are scarce or nonexistent).

The Relationship Between Knowledge and Assessment

Considerable attention has been given to the issue of chemical substance abuse. This problem was selected because it is especially critical and widespread. To be able to intervene and help facilitate people's recovery from chemical dependency, social workers need a base of knowledge. Social workers need to know some of the dynamics involved in the behavior of chemically dependent individuals and families, and they need to understand the concept of enabling. Only then can they assess a family accurately and know at what point intervention is needed. With this base of knowledge, they can apply skills to help family members stop their enabling and their maintenance of false rules. Social work skills can also be used to encourage the family to realign responsibility and relinquish it to the chemically

ETHICAL DILEMMA

Punishing or Treating Users of Prohibited Drugs?

The United States primarily uses a punitive approach with anyone found guilty of possessing or using prohibited drugs. Some advocates of a treatment approach to the drug problem point to the Netherlands as a model.

Coleman and Kerbo (2002, p. 412) describe the Dutch approach:

> Dutch drug policy is an interesting combination of four elements. The first is the official tolerance of "soft drugs" (marijuana and hashish—a condensed form of marijuana). Although sale is technically illegal, many cafes openly sell marijuana without fear of arrests or fines. The second is a tough enforcement effort aimed at the dealers of hard drugs, such as heroin and cocaine, that are often smuggled into Rotterdam, the world's largest port. The third element of Dutch policy is the decriminalization of all users. No one is jailed for merely using or possessing small amounts of any drug. Finally, the Dutch have made treatment and maintenance programs easily available to all addicts.

What have been the effects of this approach? The Netherlands, since the program's inception a number of years ago, has seen a sharp decline in the number of heroin addicts and an increase in their average age (indicating that fewer younger people are becoming addicted). In addition, the Netherlands did not experience the cocaine epidemic that happened in the United States (Abadinsky, 2011).

Abadinsky (2011, p. 411) notes:

> Dutch policy is based on the idea that drug use is a fact of life and needs to be discouraged in as practical a manner as possible ... the Dutch have implemented a pragmatic and nonmoralistic approach whose main objective is to minimize the risks associated with drug use, both for users themselves and for those around them. The Dutch distinguish between "soft" drugs such as marijuana and "hard" drugs such as heroin, cocaine, and ecstasy. The idea is to separate the marker so that users of soft drugs are less likely to come into contact with hard drugs and will not suffer the negative consequences of labeling.

Critics of this approach are skeptical that it would work in the United States. They claim the Netherlands is less susceptible to drug abuse because it has less of a poverty problem (the country has a much more generous welfare system), and it does not have large and deteriorating urban areas (Coleman & Kerbo, 2002). Critics also note that the Netherlands has the additional problem of "drug tourism"—an increasing number of travelers are going to the Netherlands specifically to buy marijuana.

---

dependent person. In summary, the examination of such a major life issue should provide social workers with a starting point on which to begin problem assessment. The intent is to provide a map or guide to begin the process of intervention.

Chapter Summary

The following summarizes this chapter's content as it relates to the learning objectives presented at the beginning of the chapter. Chapter content will help prepare students to:

LO 11-1 Describe Erikson's theories of psychological development during young and middle adulthood.

Erikson asserted that young adults face the developmental crisis of intimacy versus isolation, and that middle-aged adults face the developmental crisis of generativity versus stagnation.

LO 11-2 Describe Peck's theory of psychological development during middle adulthood.

Peck theorized that four psychological advances are critical to successful adjustment in middle adulthood: (1) emphasizing socializing rather than sexualizing in human relationships, (2) valuing wisdom rather than physical power, (3) having emotional flexibility rather than emotional impoverishment, and (4) having mental flexibility rather than mental rigidity.

LO 11-3 Describe Levinson's theories of life structure, life eras, and transitions during adulthood.

Levinson theorized that people shape their life structures during four overlapping eras: preadulthood, early adulthood, middle adulthood, and late adulthood. There are transitional periods within some of these eras, and there are also transitional periods that connect these eras. According to Levinson, people spend nearly half their adult lives in transition.

LO 11-4 Summarize Maslow's theory on hierarchy of needs.

Maslow proposed a hierarchy of needs that people seek to fulfill in ascending order: physiological, safety, belongingness and love, self-esteem, and self-actualization.

LO 11-5 Describe emotional intelligence and social intelligence.

Emotional intelligence is the ability to recognize and deal with one's own feelings as well as the feelings of others.

Social intelligence has been defined in diverse ways. Goleman (2006) defines it as social awareness and social facility.

LO 11-6 Describe nonverbal communication cues.

Nonverbal cues include posture, body orientation, gestures, touching, clothing, personal space, territoriality, facial expressions, tone of voice, physical appearance, and environment.

LO 11-7 Summarize Glasser's choice theory of human behavior.

Glasser's choice theory asserts that all human behavior is an attempt to reduce the differences between the pictures of what we want and the way we perceive situations in the world. This theory asserts that our thoughts are the primary determinants not only of our emotions and our actions but also of our physiological functioning.

LO 11-8 Describe Gawain's theories about intuition and how human behavior is affected by it.

Gawain asserts that it is important for all of us to learn to trust our intuitive knowingness.

LO 11-9 Understand the issue of substance abuse.

Chemical substances include alcohol, barbiturates, tranquilizers, Quaalude, amphetamines, cocaine and crack, amyl and butyl nitrate, narcotics, hallucinogens, tobacco, marijuana, and anabolic steroids. As part of the treatment process, chemically dependent people need to assume responsibility for their behavior.

COMPETENCY NOTES

The following identifies where Educational Policy (EP) competencies and practice behaviors are discussed in this chapter.

EP 2.1.7a Utilize conceptual frameworks to guide the process of assessment, intervention, and evaluation; and

EP 2.1.7b Critique and apply knowledge to understand person and environment.
(All of this chapter): The content of this chapter is focused on acquiring both of these practice behaviors in working with young and middle-age adults.

EP 2.1.3b Analyze models of assessment, prevention, intervention, and evaluation;

EP 2.1.6b Use research evidence to inform practice;

EP 2.1.10a Substantively and affectively prepare for action with individuals, families, groups, organizations, and communities;

EP 2.1.10d Collect, organize, and interpret client data;

EP 2.1.10e Assess client strengths and limitations;

EP 2.1.10g Select appropriate intervention strategies; and

EP 2.1.10j Help clients resolve problems.
(pp. 540–547): This material introduces readers to assessing and treating the chemically dependent person and his or her family. Material is provided on the other practice behaviors.

EP 2.1.2 Apply social work ethical principles to guide professional practice.
(pp. 504, 516, 520, 530, 537): Ethical questions are posed.

WEB RESOURCES

See this text's companion website at *www.cengagebrain.com* for learning tools such as chapter quizzing, videos, and more.

SOCIOLOGICAL ASPECTS OF YOUNG AND MIDDLE ADULTHOOD

Jose Luis Pelaez Inc/Getty Images

George Andrus is spending 55 hours a week getting his insurance business going and uses his leisure time working around his house. Jenny Savano recently got a divorce, is trying to raise her three children on a meager monthly public assistance grant, and is attending a vocational school to train as a secretary. Tom and Eleanor Townsend have their careers well established, their two children have grown and left home, and they enjoy traveling to such exotic places as the Greek Isles. Joan Sarauer spends much of her day caring for her husband, who is dying of emphysema. Carmen and Carlos Garcia attend church every Sunday and take leadership roles in church activities during the week. Ben Katz and Julie Immel are seniors in college and are planning their wedding.

A Perspective

There is obviously considerable variation in the major social interests of young and middle-aged adults. However, there are some fairly common themes: choosing a personal lifestyle and perhaps marrying; settling into a career; raising children and maintaining a household; participating in hobbies; becoming grandparents; adjusting to relationship changes with a spouse and children after the children leave home; and socializing with friends.

Learning Objectives

This chapter will help prepare students to:

**EP 2.1.7a,
2.1.7b**

LO 12-1 *Describe the following lifestyles and family forms that young adults may enter into: marriage, cohabitation, single life, parenthood, and the life of a childless couple*

LO 12-2 *Describe three major sociological theories about human behavior: functionalism, conflict theory, and interactionism. These are macro-system theories*

LO 12-3 *Understand three social problems that young and middle-aged adults may encounter: poverty, empty-shell marriages, and divorce. One-parent families, blended families, and mothers working outside the home will also be discussed*

LO 12-4 *Understand material on assessing and intervening in family systems*

LO 12-5 *Summarize material on social work with organizations, including several theories of organizational behavior*

LO 12-6 *Describe liberal, conservative, and developmental perspectives on human service organizations*

LO 12-1 Describe the Following Lifestyles and Family Forms That Young Adults May Enter Into: Marriage, Cohabitation, Single Life, Parenthood, and the Life of a Childless Couple

Interaction in Family Systems: Choosing a Personal Lifestyle

Most people make decisions during their young adult years about how they want to live their adult years. Decisions about lifestyles include whether to marry or stay single; whether to have children; what kind of career to pursue; what area of the country to live in; whether to live in an apartment, duplex, or house. (As time goes on, it is important to remember that a person has a right to make changes in these decisions.) In choosing a lifestyle, what many people experience is not a matter of ideal choice, but rather a result of opportunities. In other words, financial resources, personal deficiencies, discrimination, and so on may greatly limit or modify free choice. In addition, unexpected life events—such as unplanned pregnancy, divorce, or death of a spouse—can dramatically alter a person's lifestyle and family living arrangements. In regard to lifestyles and family forms, we will take a brief look at marriage, cohabitation, single life, parenthood, and the life of a childless couple.

Marriage

Marriage is defined as a legally and socially sanctioned union between two people, resulting in mutual obligations and rights. Throughout recorded history, regardless of the simplicity or sophistication of the society, the family has been the basic biological and social unit in which most adults and children live. In addition, all past and present societies sanction the family through the institution of marriage. Clayton (1975) suggests that one of the primary reasons for instituting the custom of marriage was to enable the two partners to enjoy sexuality as fully as possible with a minimum of anxieties and hazards. The natural sex drive of men and women needs to be satisfied, yet control needs to be exercised over the spread of sexually transmitted diseases. Children that result from sexual relationships need to be raised and cared for.

Close to 92 percent of all adults in our society will get married. More than 90 percent of all married couples will have children (Papalia et al., 2012). People marry for a variety of reasons, including desire for children, economic security, social position, love, parents' wishes, escape, pregnancy, companionship, sexual attraction, common interests, and adventure. Other reasons for marrying include societal expectations and the psychological need to feel wanted more than anyone else by someone and to be of value to another person. Highlight 12.1 presents some

HIGHLIGHT 12.1

Theories About Why People Choose Each Other as Mates

The reasons why people choose each other as partners are complex and vary greatly. Certainly such factors as religion, age, race, ethnic group, social class, and parental pressure influence the choice of mates. In addition, many theories suggest additional factors. Some of these theories are summarized here. No theory fully identifies all of the factors involved in mate selection, and mate selection may involve aspects of more than one theory.

- *Propinquity theory* asserts that being in close proximity is a major factor in mate selection. This theory suggests we are apt to select a mate with whom we are in close association, such as at school or at work, or whom we meet through neighborhood, church, or recreational activities (Rubin, 1973).
- *Ideal mate theory* suggests we choose a mate who has the characteristics and traits we desire in a partner. This

theory is symbolized by the statement, "He's everything I've ever wanted."
- *Congruence in values theory* holds that our value system consciously and unconsciously guides us in selecting a mate who has similar values (Grush & Yehl, 1979).
- *Homogamy theory* suggests that we select a mate who has similar racial, economic, and social characteristics.
- *Complementary needs theory* holds that we either select a partner who has the characteristics we wish we had ourselves or someone who can help us be the kind of person we want to be.
- *Compatibility theory* asserts that we select a mate with whom we can enjoy a variety of activities. This is someone who will understand us, accept us, and with whom we feel comfortable in communicating because that person has a similar philosophy of life.

ETHICAL DILEMMA

Should You Marry Someone You Are Not in Love With?

EP 2.1.2

If you are a woman, assume you are four months pregnant. You once were in love with the father of your unborn child, but no longer are. He is in love with you and wants to marry you. What do you do? How would you go about arriving at a decision?

If you are a man, assume the woman you have been dating for the past few years is four months pregnant. You once were in love with her, but no longer are. She is in love with you and wants to marry you. What do you do? How would you go about arriving at a decision?

What ethical values are involved in such a decision?

theories as to why people choose each other as mates. In our impersonal and materialistic society, marriage helps meet the need to belong because it helps to provide emotional support and security, affection, love, and companionship.

Predictors of Marital Success

A number of studies have sought to identify factors associated with marital happiness and unhappiness (Kail & Cavanaugh, 2010; Kornblum & Julian, 2012; Papalia et al., 2012; Santrock, 2013). Some factors can help predict whether a future marriage will be happy or not. Other factors are related to whether an already existing marriage is happy or

not. The findings of these studies are summarized in Highlight 12.2.

Benefits of Marriage

Marriage leads to the formation of a family, and the family unit is recognized as the primary unit in which children are to be produced and raised. The marriage bond thus provides for an orderly replacement of the population. The family is the primary institution for the rearing and socializing of children.

Marriage also provides an available and regulated outlet for sexual activity. Failure to regulate sexual behavior would result in clashes between

HIGHLIGHT 12.2

Predictive Factors Leading to Marital Happiness/Unhappiness

Factors for Marital Happiness

Premarital Factors
  Parents' marriage is happy
  Personal happiness in childhood
  Mild but firm discipline by parents
  Harmonious relationship with parents
  Gets along well with the opposite sex
  Acquainted for more than one year before marriage
  Parental approval of the marriage
  Similarity of age
  Satisfaction with affection of partner
  Love
  Common interests
  Optimistic outlook on life
  Emotional stability
  Sympathetic attitude
  Similarity of cultural backgrounds
  Compatible religious beliefs
  Satisfying occupation and working conditions
  A love relationship growing out of companionship
    rather than infatuation

Self-insight and self-acceptance
Awareness of the needs of one's partner
Coping ability
Interpersonal social skills
Positive self-identity
Holding common values

Factors During Marriage
  Good communication skills
  Egalitarian relationship
  Good relationship with in-laws
  Desire for children
  Similar interests
  Responsible love, respect, and friendship
  Sexual compatibility
  Enjoying leisure-time activities together
  Companionship and an affectional relationship
  Capacity to receive as well as give

Factors for Marital Unhappiness

Premarital Factors
  Parents divorced
  Parent or parents deceased
  Incongruity of main personality traits with partner
  Acquainted less than one year before marriage
  Loneliness as a major reason for marriage
  Escape from one's own family as major reason for marriage
  Marriage at a young age, particularly under age 20
  Predisposition to unhappiness in one or both spouses
  Intense personal problems

Factors During Marriage
  Husband more dominant
  Wife more dominant
  Jealous of spouse
  Feeling of superiority to spouse
  Feeling of being more intelligent than spouse
  Living with in-laws
  Whining, acting defensively, being stubborn, and
    withdrawing by walking away or not talking to spouse
  Domestic violence

individuals due to jealousy and exploitation. Every society has rules that regulate sexual behavior within family units (e.g., incest taboos).

A marriage is also an arrangement to meet the emotional needs of the partners, such as affection, companionship, approval, encouragement, and reinforcement for accomplishments. (Interestingly, Highlight 12.3 indicates that emotional needs are better satisfied over the long term by rational love than by romantic love.) If people do not have such affective needs met, emotional, intellectual, physical, and social growth will be stunted. (Our high divorce rate indicates that this ideal of achieving an emotionally satisfying relationship is not easily attained.) Married people of all ages tend to report somewhat higher rates of satisfaction about their lives than do people who are single, divorced, or widowed (Papalia & Feldman, 2012). Two alternative factors may be operating here—either a number of people do find happiness in marriage, or else happy people are more apt to be married.

Marriage also correlates with good health. Married people live longer, particularly men (Papalia et al., 2012). But we cannot conclude that marriage *confers* health. Healthy people may be more interested in getting married, may be better marriage partners, and may attract mates more easily. Or married people may lead safer, healthier lives than single people.

Widowed and divorced men have shorter life expectancies than do single men, whose life expectancy is closest to the rate of married men (Santrock, 2013). Perhaps widowed and divorced men have shorter life expectancies because they feel they have less to live for.

The marriage relationship encourages personal growth; it provides a setting for the partners to share their innermost thoughts. In a marriage, a lot of decisions need to be made. Should the husband and wife both pursue careers? Do they want children? How will the domestic tasks be divided? How much time will be spent with relatives? Should they buy a new car or a house? Should a vacation be taken this year; if so, where? Problems in these areas can erupt into crises that, if resolved constructively, can lead to personal growth. Through successful resolution, people often learn more about themselves and are better able to handle future crises. However, if the problems remain unresolved, conflict may fester and considerable discord result.

Highlight 12.4 summarizes some useful guidelines for building and maintaining a successful marriage. (This chapter focuses on heterosexual marriages. Chapter 13 provides some material on gay and lesbian marriages.)

Cohabitation

Cohabitation is the open living together of an unmarried couple. Most such couples live together for a relatively short time (less than two years) before they either marry or separate (Papalia et al., 2012). For some, cohabitation serves as a trial marriage. For others it offers a temporary or permanent alternative to marriage. And for many young people, it has become the modern equivalent of dating and going steady.

People who cohabitated before marriage do not have better marriages than those who did not. In fact, some research shows that couples who lived together before getting married report lower-quality marriages, a lower commitment to the institution of marriage, and a greater likelihood of divorce than do noncohabiting couples (Papalia et al., 2012).

Why do couples decide to live together without a marriage ceremony? The reasons are not fully clear. Many people want close intimate and sexual arrangements but are not ready for the financial and long-term commitments of a marriage. With our society being more accepting of cohabitation than in the past, some couples appear to be choosing this living arrangement. To some extent, they can have friendship, companionship, and a sexual relationship without the long-term commitment of marriage. Living with someone helps many young adults to learn more about themselves, to better understand what is involved in an intimate relationship, and to grow as a person. Cohabitating may also help some people clarify what they want in a mate and in a marriage.

Cohabitating also has its problems, some of which are similar to those encountered by newlyweds: adjusting to an intimate relationship, working out a sexual relationship, overdependency on the partner, missing what one did when living alone, and seeing friends less. Other problems are unique to cohabitation, such as explaining the relationship to parents and relatives, discomfort about the ambiguity of the future, and a desire for a long-term commitment from one's partner.

HIGHLIGHT 12.3

Romantic Love Versus Rational Love

Achieving a gratifying, long-lasting love relationship is one of our paramount goals. The experience of feeling in love is exciting, adds meaning to living, and psychologically gives us a good feeling about ourselves. Unfortunately, few people are able to maintain a long-term love relationship. Instead, many people encounter problems with love relationships, including falling in love with someone who does not love them; falling out of love with someone after an initial stage of infatuation; being highly possessive of someone they love; and having substantial conflicts with the loved one because of differing sets of expectations about the relationship. Failures in love relationships are more often the rule than the exception.

The emotion of love, in particular, is often erroneously viewed as a feeling over which we have no control. A number of common expressions connote or imply this: "I fell in love," "It was love at first sight," "I just couldn't help it," and "He swept me off my feet." It is more useful to think of the emotion of love as being primarily based on our self-talk (i.e., what we tell ourselves) about a person we meet.

Romantic love can be diagrammed as follows:

Event
Meeting or becoming acquainted with a person who has some of the overt characteristics you want in a lover.

Self-Talk

"This person is attractive, personable; has all of the qualities I admire in a lover/mate."

Emotion
Intense infatuation, being romantically in love; a feeling of being in ecstasy.

Romantic love is often based on self-talk that stems from intense unsatisfied desires and frustrations, rather than on reason or rational thinking. Unsatisfied desires and frustrations include extreme sexual frustration, intense loneliness, parental and personal problems, and strong desires for security and protection.

A primary characteristic of romantic love is to idealize the person with whom we are infatuated; that is, we notice this person has some overt characteristics we desire in a lover and then conclude that this person has *all* the desired characteristics.

A second characteristic is that romantic love thrives on a certain amount of distance. The more forbidden the love, the stronger it becomes. The more social mores are threatened, the stronger the feeling. (For example, couples who live together and then later marry often report living together was more exciting and romantic.) The greater the effort necessary to be with each other (e.g., traveling long distances), the more intense the romance. The greater the frustration (e.g., loneliness or sexual needs), the more intense the romance.

The irony of romantic love is that if an ongoing relationship is achieved, the romance usually withers. Through sustained contact, the person in love gradually comes to realize what the idealized loved one is really like—simply another human being with certain strengths and limitations. When this occurs, the romantic love relationship either turns into a rational love relationship, or the relationship is found to have significant conflicts and dissatisfactions and ends in a broken romance. For people with intense unmet desires, the latter occurs more frequently.

Romantic love thus tends to be of temporary duration and based on make-believe. A person experiencing romantic love never loves the real person—only an idealized image of the person.

Rational love, in contrast, can be diagrammed in the following way:

Event
While being aware of and comfortable about your own needs, goals, identity, and desires, you become well acquainted with someone who fulfills, to a fair extent, the characteristics you desire in a lover or spouse.

Self-Talk
"This person has many of the qualities and attributes I seek in a lover or spouse. I admire this person's strengths, and I am aware and accepting of his or her shortcomings."

Emotion
Rational love

The following are ingredients of a rational love relationship: You are clear and comfortable about your desires, identity, and goals in life. You know the other person well. You have accurately and objectively assessed the loved one's strengths and shortcomings and are generally accepting of the shortcomings. Your self-talk about this person is consistent with your short- and long-term goals. Your self-talk is realistic and rational, so that your feelings are not based on fantasy, excessive desires, or pity. You and this person are able to communicate openly and honestly, so that problems can be dealt with when they arise and so that the relationship can continue to grow and develop. Rational love also involves giving and receiving; it involves being kind, showing affection, knowing and doing what pleases the other person, communicating openly and warmly, and so on.

Because love is based on self-talk that causes feelings, it is we who create love. *Theoretically*, it is possible to love anyone by making changes in our self-talk. On the other hand, if we are in love with someone, we can gauge the quality of the relationship by analyzing our self-talk to determine the nature of our attraction and to determine the extent to which our self-talk is rational and in our best interests.

SOURCE: Charles Zastrow, *You Are What You Think: A Guide to Self-Realization*. Chicago: Nelson-Hall, 1993.

HIGHLIGHT 12.4

Guidelines for Building and Maintaining a Happy Marriage

A successful and satisfying marriage requires ongoing work by each partner. The following are some useful guidelines on how to achieve and maintain a successful marriage:

1. Make your spouse feel special. We fall in love because of the way we feel about ourselves when we are with that person. If we fall out of love, it is because that person no longer makes us feel good about ourselves.
2. Seek to foster the happiness, personal growth, and well-being of your spouse as much as you seek to foster your own happiness and personal growth.
3. Seek to use the no-lose problem-solving approach (described in Highlight 12.7), rather than the win-lose technique to settle conflicts with partners. Be tolerant and accepting of trivial shortcomings and annoyances.
4. Do not try to possess, stifle, or control your partner. Also, do not seek to mold your partner into a carbon copy of

your opinions, values, beliefs, or your personal likes and dislikes.
5. Be aware that everyone has up-and-down mood swings. When your partner is in a down cycle, be considerate and understanding.
6. When arguments occur—and they will—try to fight fair. Limit the discussion to the issue at hand, and keep past events and personality traits out of the fight.
7. Be affectionate, share pleasant events, and be a friend and a good listener.
8. Keep the lines of communication open. Learn to bite the bullet on minor or unimportant issues. Voice the concerns that are important to you, but in a way that does not attack, blame, or threaten the other person. Try to use I-messages (described in Highlight 12.7).

Closely related to cohabitating is a relationship in which the man and woman maintain separate addresses and domiciles, but live together for several days a month (perhaps on weekends). This latter form is more of a trial honeymoon than a trial marriage. When people live together for only a few days a month, they are apt to seek to put their best foot forward.

In some recent instances, courts have decided that cohabitating couples who dissolve their nonmarital living arrangements have certain legal obligations to one another. For example, under certain circumstances, such as an oral agreement between two individuals to pool their earnings, some courts view assets acquired during the time the couple was living together as "marital property," which then is divided (sometimes not equally) between the two individuals after the relationship is dissolved.

EP 2.1.2

If you are currently involved in a love relationship with someone, do you seek to make that person feel special? Does your partner seek to lead you to feel good about yourself?

Common-law marriage is an irregular form of marriage that can be legally contracted in a limited number of jurisdictions. The original concept of a common-law marriage is a marriage that is considered valid by both partners, but has not been formally registered with a state or church registry. Common-law marriages can be contracted in nine states in the United States (Alabama, Colorado, Iowa, Kansas, Montana, Rhode Island, South Carolina, Texas, and Utah). It is also a legal contract in the District of Columbia. The requirements for a common-law marriage to be validly contracted differ from state to state. Despite much belief to the contrary, the length of time a man and a woman live together does not by itself determine whether a common-law marriage exists. All states in the United States recognize common-law marriages lawfully contracted in those jurisdictions that permit it.

Single Life

Some people choose to remain single; they like being alone and prefer not being with others much of the time. Others end up being single because they do not find a partner they want to marry or because they are in a relationship with a partner who chooses not to marry. Historically, there was a greater expectation that people would marry than at the present time. Now, people are freer to make decisions about whether to marry and what kind of lifestyle to seek.

Single people have fewer emotional and financial obligations. They do not need to consider how their decisions and actions will affect a spouse and children. They are freer to take economic, physical, and social risks. They can devote more time to the pursuit of their individual interests.

Studies reviewed by Papalia and her associates (2012) reported the following advantages of being single as listed by respondents who were not married: satisfaction of being self-sufficient, increased career opportunities, an exciting lifestyle, mobility, sexual availability, the freedom to change, opportunities to have a variety of experiences, opportunities to play a variety of roles, and opportunities to have friendships with a variety of people. Reported disadvantages of being single include wondering how single people fit into the social world of mostly married people, lack of companionship, concerns about how well friends and family accept unmarried adults, and concerns about how being single affects self-esteem.

Parenthood

The birth of a baby is a major life event. (See Highlight 12.5 for information on parental gender preferences.) Caring for a baby changes lifestyles of parents and also changes the marriage. For some, having a child (who is totally dependent) is a troublesome crisis. For others, caring for a baby is viewed as a fulfillment and an enhancement of life.

For many couples, parenthood has troublesome aspects while also enhancing their lives.

What are some of the problem areas of parenthood? The birth of a baby signals to parents that they are now adults and no longer children; they now have responsibilities not only to themselves, but also in caring for someone who needs 24-hour care. A baby demands a huge amount of time and attention.

Women generally assume the majority of both household and child-care responsibilities. Levinson and Levinson (1996) found that the more the division of labor in a marriage changes from egalitarian to traditional, the more marital happiness declines, especially for nontraditional wives.

Thompson and Walker (1989) found that one-third of mothers view mothering as both enjoyable and meaningful, a third find it unpleasant and not meaningful, and another third report mixed experiences. Fathers tend to treasure and to be emotionally committed to their children, but they generally report less enjoyment in looking after them than mothers do.

Why do people have children? Historically, in agricultural and preindustrial societies, children were an economic asset; their labor was important in planting and harvesting crops and in tending domestic animals. Parents wanted large families to help with the work. When parents grew old children tended to provide much of the care. Because children were an economic asset, values were gradually established that it was natural and desirable for married couples to want to have children. Motherhood became invested with a unique emotional aura.

 HIGHLIGHT 12.5

Parental Gender Preferences

In most countries, boys are generally preferred to girls. Although it is the male's sperm that determines the gender of the child,* in many developing countries and countries where the status of women is low, a woman's capacity to remain married may depend on her producing sons. In some of these countries, boys are fed better, given better medical care, and receive more schooling. The death rate for female children is significantly higher than for male children because female children are more apt to be neglected.

In the United States, couples who want only one child usually desire a boy. Those who want two generally desire one of each; and those who prefer three usually want two boys and one girl. Men, in particular, tend to have a strong preference for a boy. The reasons a couple desire a boy or a girl vary. Those couples desiring a boy generally prefer someone to carry on the family name and bring honor to the family; those who prefer a girl want someone who is easier to raise, is lovable, is fun to dress, and is able to help with the housework (Santrock, 2013).

*Sperm carrying the X chromosome will produce a female; sperm carrying the Y chromosome will produce a male.

Some psychological theories reflected this aura by asserting that women (interestingly, not men) had a nurturing instinct that could only be fulfilled by having and caring for children. (It now appears the supposed nurturing instinct was in reality a value that was largely learned by women through socialization.)

Today, children are an economic liability rather than an economic asset. In our society, there is an expectation that Social Security and other retirement programs will care for older parents, rather than this being a responsibility of their children. Children can have negative, as well as positive, effects on lifestyles and on marital relationships. For these and other reasons, married couples in our society over the years have gradually decided to have fewer children. Now most couples usually want zero to three children. Contraception now makes such wishes a reality.

Parenthood has many rewards and many joyful moments. Some of the rewards include having someone to love and return that love, the joy of playing and interacting with a child, watching and helping a child grow and develop, and socializing with other parents.

Parenthood also has many demands and stresses, including discipline problems, increased responsibilities, financial demands, interference with previous lifestyles, cleaning up messes, trying to accomplish some task while stepping over a child, running time-consuming errands, planning a schedule around a child's needs, listening to a crying or whining child, changing diapers, interrupted rest and sleep, fatigue, and concerns about being able to give less attention to personal appearance.

Children are less likely to lower marital satisfaction in families where the parents wanted to have children, and where the parents have outside resources for helping to care for the children. In marriages that deteriorate after parenthood, one or both partners tend to have low self-esteem, and the husbands are likely to be less sensitive (Belsky & Rovine, 1988). The partners in deteriorating marriages are also more likely to be younger and less educated, to earn less money, and to have been married for fewer years.

Even when parenting has a negative influence on marital satisfaction, it often has a positive effect on the self-concepts of the parents and on their work roles. Thus, parenting appears to contribute to the personal development of an individual.

The Group for the Advancement of Psychiatry (1973) views parenting as a developmental process and has identified the following four stages:

1. *Anticipation*: This stage occurs during pregnancy when the expectant parents think about how they will raise their children, how their lives will change, and the meaning of parenthood. Some expectant parents have ambivalent feelings about what lies ahead. During this stage, the expectant parents begin the process of viewing themselves as their children's parents, instead of being their parents' children.
2. *Honeymoon*: This stage occurs after the birth of the first child and lasts for a few months. Parents are often very happy about having and holding a baby. It is also a time of adjustment and learning, as attachments are formed between parents and child, and family members learn new roles in relation to one another.
3. *Plateau*: This stage occurs from infancy through the teenage years. Parents must make frequent adjustments as they adapt their parenting behavior to the level of the child.
4. *Disengagement*: This stage occurs when the child disengages (e.g., when the child marries). Because the child disengages, the parents should also change their behavior and disengage from the child. Relationships change from parent–child to adult–adult.

These stages illustrate that children have a great effect on parents. The Group for the Advancement of Psychiatry (1973) also notes that parents often judge their parenting on how well their children turn out. When children fulfill their expectations, the parents usually pat themselves on the back for a job well done. The danger of this approach is that if the children fall short of meeting parental expectations (which sometimes are unrealistic), parents are apt to conclude that they have failed. Parents need to realize that the final product is not entirely under their control because children are influenced by many other factors that are external to the family.

Childless Couples

Having children is recognized legally and religiously as one of the central components of a marriage. Our society still considers that something is wrong with a couple if they decide not to have children.

Ken Seet/CORBIS

Fathers generally report less enjoyment in looking after children than mothers do, but fathers who enjoy parenting usually see it as one of their most important life roles.

However, this value is no longer as strongly held as it once was. Perhaps in the future this value will disappear in the face of overpopulation and the high cost of raising children. CNN Money (2013) notes that a middle-income family can expect to spend a quarter-million dollars to raise a child from birth through age 17.

Ethical Question 12.2

Given the high cost of raising a child, how many children do you want to have?

EP 2.1.2

Married couples may decide not to have children. Some feel they do not have what it takes to be good parents. Some have heavy commitments to their careers or to their hobbies and do not want to take time away from them to raise a family. Others feel that having children would be an intrusion into their marital relationship. Still others enjoy the freedom to travel and to make spur-of-the-moment plans, and do not want their lifestyle changed. Some feel that choosing not to have children is desirable in order to avoid contributing to overpopulation.

Unwanted children are adversely affected in a variety of ways; they are more apt to be abused, have more frequent illnesses, receive poorer school grades, and have more behavior problems than children whose births are desired (Kail & Cavanaugh, 2010). Such findings suggest that if couples do not want to have children, it is probably in their best interest and that of society for them not to do so.

LO 12-2 Describe Three Major Sociological Theories About Human Behavior: Functionalism, Conflict Theory, and Interactionism

Macro-Social-System Theories

People interact with various-sized systems within their social environments. These interactions have major impacts on human behavior. We have defined a macro system as one that is larger than a small group. We have established that culture, communities, institutions, and organizations are examples of macro systems. To maximize their effectiveness, social workers must understand and assess the impacts of macro systems on their clients.

Micro-system theories, on the other hand, seek to make sense of the effects of group life on individuals. Prominent theories of this type include Erikson's theory, which was summarized in Chapter 7, and learning theory, summarized in Chapter 4.

This chapter will first describe three theories addressing macro social systems. These theories explore how macro systems function and propose explanations for how these systems influence human behavior. Macro-system theories seek to make sense of the behavior of large groups of people and the workings of entire societies. We begin by looking at the three most prominent macro-system theories in sociology: functionalism, conflict theory, and interactionism. (Note that these theories are applicable to all age groups, not only middle-aged adults.)

Advocates of these various theories often disagree with one another, and each theory has certain merits and shortcomings. The theories vary in their usefulness for analyzing any particular issue or problem individuals encounter within their social environments. Having a knowledge of a range of contemporary theories enables the social worker to select the theory or theories that are most useful in understanding a particular human behavior, problem, or issue. Often, the greatest understanding results from combining and critically thinking about a combination of these theories.

The Functionalist Perspective

In recent years, *functionalism* has been one of the most influential sociological theories. The theory was originally developed by Emile Durkheim, a French sociologist, and was refined by Robert K. Merton, Talcott Parsons, and many others. The theory views society as a well-organized system in which most members agree on common values and norms. Institutions, groups, and roles fit together in a unified whole. Members of society do what is necessary to maintain a stable society because they accept its regulations and rules.

Society is viewed as a system composed of interdependent and interrelated parts. Each part makes a contribution to the operation of the entire system.

The various parts are involved in a delicate balance, and a change in one part affects the other parts.

A simple way to picture this approach is to use the analogy of a human body. A well-functioning person has thousands of parts, each having a specific function. The heart pumps blood, the lungs draw oxygen into the body and expel carbon dioxide, the stomach digests food for energy, the muscles move bodily parts to perform a variety of functions, and the brain coordinates the activities of the various parts. Each of these parts is interrelated in complex ways to the others and is also dependent on them. Each performs a vital function, without which the entire system might collapse, as in the case of heart failure.

Functionalism asserts that the components of a society, similar to the parts of the human body, do not always work the way they are supposed to work. Things get out of whack. When a component of a society interferes with efforts to carry out essential social tasks, that part is said to be *dysfunctional*. Often, changes in society introduced to correct a particular imbalance may produce other imbalances, even when things are going well. For example, developing effective contraceptives and making them readily available is quite effective in preventing unwanted pregnancies. However, contraceptives may also be a factor leading to increased premarital and extramarital sexual relationships—which is viewed as a problem by some groups.

According to the functionalist perspective, all social systems have a tendency toward equilibrium—maintenance of a steady state or particular balance, in which the parts of the system remain in the same relationship to one another. The approach asserts that systems have a tendency to resist social change; change is seen as disruptive unless it occurs at a slow pace. Because society is composed of interconnected parts, a change in one part of the system will lead to changes in at least some of the other parts. The introduction of the automobile into our society, for example, led to drastic changes: people being able to commute long distances to work; vacation travel to distant parts of the country; the opening of many new businesses (service stations, car dealerships, etc.); and sharp increases in air pollution and traffic fatalities.

Some of the functions and dysfunctions of a social system are *manifest*—that is, obvious to everyone. For example, a manifest function of police departments is to keep crime rates low. Other functions and dysfunctions are *latent*—hidden and unintended. Sociologists have discovered that when police departments label people they arrest with such stigmatizing labels as "criminal," "outlaw," and "delinquent," a hidden consequence is that those who are so labeled may commit more crimes over the long run than they would have if they had never been arrested in the first place. Thus, in trying to curb crime, police departments may sometimes unintentionally contribute to an increase in crime.

According to functionalists, social problems occur when society, or some part of it, becomes disorganized. *Social disorganization* occurs when a large organization or an entire society is imperfectly organized to achieve its goals and maintain its stability. When disorganization occurs, the organization loses control over its parts.

Functionalists see thousands of potential causes of social disorganization. However, underlying all these causes is rapid *social change*, which disrupts the balance of society. In recent years, more technological advances (such as the development of telephones, computers, television, robots, heart transplants, the Internet) have occurred in less time than at any other time in human history. These advances have led basic institutions (such as the family and the educational system) to undergo drastic changes. Technological advances have occurred at such a pace that other parts of the culture have failed to keep pace. This *cultural lag* between technological changes and our adaptation to them is viewed as one of the major sources of social disorganization.

Examples of such social disorganization abound. The development of nuclear weapons has the potential to destroy civilization. Advances in sanitation and medical technology have lengthened life expectancy but have also contributed to a worldwide population explosion. Advances in artificial insemination have led to surrogate motherhood, which our society has not yet decided whether to encourage or discourage. The development of technological advances in performing abortions has led to the capacity to terminate pregnancies quite safely on request, but has also led to a national controversy about the desirability of legalized abortions.

Critics of functionalism assert that it is a politically conservative philosophy, as it takes for granted the idea that society as it is (the status quo) should be preserved. As a result, basic social injustices are ignored. Critics also argue that the approach is value-laden, because one person's disorganization is another person's organization. For example, some people view divorce as being functional, because it is a legal way to terminate a relationship that is no longer working.

Functionalism has also been criticized as being a philosophy that works for the benefit of the privileged social classes, while perpetuating the misery of the poor and those who are being victimized by discrimination.

The Conflict Perspective

The *conflict theory* views society as a struggle for power among various social groups. Conflict is thought to be inevitable and in many cases actually beneficial to society. For example, most Americans would view the struggle of the "freedom fighters" during the Revolutionary War as being highly beneficial to our society. (England, however, viewed them as ungrateful insurgents.)

The conflict perspective rests on an important assumption: members of society highly value certain things (such as power, wealth, and prestige), and most of these valued resources are in scarce supply. Because of their scarcity, conflict theory asserts that people—either individually or in groups—struggle with one another to attain them. Society is thus viewed as an arena for the struggle over scarce resources.

Struggle and conflict may take many forms: competition, disagreements, court battles, physical fights and violence, and war. If the struggles usually involved violence, then nearly everyone would be involved in violent activities, and society would be impossible. As a result, norms have emerged that determine what types of conflict are allowable for which groups. For example, participating in a labor strike or acquiring a higher education is an approved way of competing for the limited money available in our society, whereas robbery is not an acceptable way.

From the conflict perspective, social change mainly involves reordering the distribution of scarce goods among groups. Unlike functionalism, which views change as potentially destructive, the conflict approach views change as potentially beneficial. Conflict can lead to improvements, advancements, the reduction of discrimination against oppressed groups, and the emergence of new groups as dominant forces in society. Without conflict, society would become stagnant.

Functionalism and conflict theory differ in another way. Functionalists assert that most people obey the law because they believe the law is fair and just. Conflict theorists assert that social order is maintained by authority backed by the use of force. They assert that the privileged classes hold legal power and use the legal system to make others obey their will. They conclude that most people obey the law because they are afraid of being arrested, imprisoned, or even killed if they do not obey.

Functionalists assert that most people in society share the same set of values and norms. In contrast, conflict theorists assert that modern societies are composed of many different groups with divergent values, attitudes, and norms—and therefore conflicts are bound to occur. The abortion issue illustrates such a value conflict. Pro-life groups and traditional Roman Catholics believe that the human fetus at any stage after conception is a living human being, and therefore aborting a pregnancy is murder. In contrast, pro-choice advocates assert that an embryo for the first few months after conception is not yet a human being because it is unable to survive outside the womb. They also assert that if the state were to forbid a woman to obtain an abortion, the state would be violating her right to control her own life.

Not all conflicts stem from disagreements over values. Some conflicts arise in part *because* people share the same values. In our society, for example, wealth and power are highly valued. The wealthy spend considerable effort and resources to maintain their position, whereas the poor and oppressed groups vehemently advocate for equal rights and a more equitable distribution of income and wealth. Labor unions and owners in many businesses are in a continual battle over wages and fringe benefits. Republicans and Democrats continually struggle with one another in the hopes of gaining increased political power.

Whereas functionalism has been criticized as too conservative, conflict theory has been criticized as too radical. Critics say that if there were as much conflict as these theorists claim, society would have disintegrated long ago. Conflict theory has also been criticized as encouraging oppressed groups to revolt

against the existing power structure, rather than seeking to work within the existing system to address their concerns.

Ethical Question 12.3

EP 2.1.2 *Do you believe it is better for oppressed groups to revolt against the existing power structure, rather than work within the existing system to address their concerns?*

The Interactionist Perspective

The *interactionist approach* focuses on individuals and the processes of everyday social interaction between them rather than on larger structures of society, such as the educational system, the economy, or religion. Interactionist theory views behavior as a product of each individual's social relationships. Cartwright (1951) noted:

How aggressive or cooperative a person is, how much self-respect or self-confidence he has, how energetic and productive his work is, what he aspires to, what he believes to be true and good, whom he loves or hates, and what beliefs or prejudices he holds—all these characteristics are highly determined by the individual's group memberships. In a real sense, they are products of groups and of the relationships between people. (p. 383)

The interactionist theory asserts that human beings interpret or define each other's actions instead of merely reacting. This interpretation is mediated by the use of symbols (particularly words and language).

Interactionists study the socialization process in detail because it forms the foundation for human interaction. The approach asserts that people are the products of the culture and social relationships in which they participate. Coleman and Cressey (1984) summarize this approach:

People develop their outlook on life from participation in the symbolic universe that is their culture. They develop their conceptions of themselves, learn to talk, and even learn how to think as they interact early in life, with family and friends. But unlike the

Freudians, interactionists believe that an individual's personality continues to change throughout life in response to changing social environments.

The work of the American philosopher George Herbert Mead has been the driving force behind the interactionists' theories of social psychology. Mead noted that the ability to communicate in symbols (principally words and combinations of words) is the key feature that distinguishes humans from other animals. Individuals develop the ability to think and to use symbols in the process of socialization. Young children blindly imitate the behavior of their parents, but eventually they learn to "take the role of the other," pretending to be "Mommy" or "Daddy." And from such role taking children learn to understand the interrelationships among different roles and to see themselves as they imagine others see them. Eventually, Mead said, children begin to take the role of a generalized *other. In doing so, they adopt a system of values and standards that reflect the expectations of people in general, not just those in the immediate present. In this way* reference groups *as well as actual* membership groups *come to determine how the individual behaves. (p. 21)*

Cooley (1902) observed that it is impossible to make objective measurements of most aspects of our self-concept—such as how brave, likable, generous, attractive, or honest we are. Instead, in order to gauge the extent to which we have these qualities, we have to rely on the subjective judgments of the people we interact with. In essence, Cooley asserted, we learn what kind of person we are by seeing and hearing how others react to us; in effect, the reactions of others become a mirror or "looking glass" that we use to judge our own qualities.

Another important concept is that social reality is what a particular group agrees it is. Social reality is not a purely objective phenomenon.

The interactionist theory views human behavior as resulting from the *interaction* of a person's unique, distinctive personality and the groups he or she participates in. Groups are a factor in shaping one's personality, but the personality is also shaped by the person's unique qualities.

The reality we construct is mediated through symbols. We respond to symbolic reality, not physical reality. Sullivan, Thompson, Wright, Gross, and Spady (1980) describe the importance of symbols in shaping our reality:

Symbols are the principal vehicles through which expectations are conveyed from one person to another. A symbol is any object, word, or event that stands for, represents, or takes the place of something else. Symbols have certain characteristics. First, the meaning of symbols derives from social consensus—the group's agreement that one thing will represent something else. A flag represents love of country or patriotism; a green light means go, not stop; a frown stands for displeasure. Second, the relationship between the symbol and what it represents is arbitrary—there is no inherent connection. There is nothing about the color green that compels us to use that, rather than red, as a symbol for go; a flag is in reality a piece of cloth for which we could substitute anything, as long as we agreed that it stood for country. Finally, symbols need not be tied to physical reality. We can use symbols to represent things with no physical existence, such as justice, mercy, or God, or to stand for things that do not exist at all, such as unicorns.

A direct offshoot of the interactionist perspective is the labeling theory. This theory holds that the labels assigned to a person have a major impact on that person's life. Labels often become self-fulfilling prophecies. If a child is continually called "stupid" by his or her parents, that child is apt to develop a low self-concept, anticipate failure in many areas (particularly academic), put forth little effort in school and in competitive interactions with others, and end up failing. If a teenage girl gets a reputation as being promiscuous, adults and peers may label her as such, with other girls then shunning her, teenage boys ridiculing her, and perhaps some boys seeking to date her for a one-night stand. If a person is labeled an ex-con for spending time in prison, that person is likely to be viewed with suspicion, have trouble finding employment, and be stigmatized as dangerous and untrustworthy, even though the person may be conscientious and hardworking. Scheff (1966) has developed a labeling theory to explain why some people develop a career of being mentally ill. He asserts that the act of labeling people as mentally ill is the major determinant for their acting as if they were mentally ill. Once they have been labeled, others interact with them as if they were mentally ill, which leads them to view themselves as being mentally ill, and they then enact this role.

The most common criticism of the interactionist theory is that it is so abstract and vaguely worded that it is nearly impossible either to prove or disprove it (Coleman & Cressey, 1984).

LO 12-3 Understand Three Social Problems That Young and Middle-Aged Adults May Encounter: Poverty, Empty-Shell Marriages, and Divorce. One-Parent Families, Blended Families, and Mothers Working Outside the Home Will Also Be Discussed.

Poverty: Impacts of Social and Economic Forces

The functionalist, conflict, and interactionist perspectives are further illustrated by discussing how each of these theories explains poverty. Poverty is a problem of major macro-system consequence. It dramatically affects a majority of social welfare resource recipients.

The Rich and the Poor

Poverty and wealth are closely related. In most countries of the world, wealth is concentrated in a small percentage of the population. Abundance for a few is created by depriving others.

There are two ways of measuring the extent of economic inequality. *Income* refers to the amount of money a person makes in a given period. *Wealth* is a person's total assets—real estate holdings, cash, stocks, bonds, and so forth.

The distribution of wealth and income is highly unequal in our society. Similar to most countries, the United States is characterized by *social stratification*—that is, it has social classes, with the upper classes having by far the greatest access to the pleasures that money can buy. As Spotlight 12.1 indicates, the income disparities between the very rich and very poor are astounding. Although this chapter focuses on poverty in the United States, it is important to note that there is a growing gap between the rich and the poor throughout the world (Mooney, Knox, & Schacht, 2013).

These growing disparities between rich and poor throughout the world have a direct bearing on the situation of the poor in the United States, as some of their job opportunities are being "outsourced" to areas where extremely poor people are willing to accept work at almost any wage. In addition, the huge gap between the "haves" and the "have-nots" is a major factor leading to political instability in some countries, and to some of the "have-nots"

 SPOTLIGHT ON DIVERSITY 12.1

Personal Income Disparities Are Astounding

In some countries in the world, the average per capita income is less than $500 per year. In the United States, more than 46 million people (about 15 percent of the population) are living in poverty. In 2010, the poverty threshold for a family of four was $22,050. Most Americans (58 percent) will spend at least one year below the poverty line at some point between ages 25 and 75.

In the fall of 2007, Alex Rodriguez signed a 10-year deal for $275 million with the New York Yankees (a professional baseball team). This deal of $27.5 million per year is now one of the richest long-term sports contracts.

In one year (June 1998 to June 1999), the personal worth of Bill Gates (chairman of the Microsoft Corporation) rose $39 billion, from $51 billion to $90 billion. During this one-year period, he made an astounding average of $750 million per week, or more than $100 million per day! Globally, more than 1.2 billion people—1 in 5 on this planet—survive on an income of less than $1 per day.

SOURCE: L.A. Mooney, D. Knox, & C. Schacht, 2013, *Understanding Social Problems* (8th ed.). Belmont, CA: Brooks/Cole.

resorting to terrorism and violence in an effort to improve their financial circumstances.

In the United States, the wealthiest 1 percent of all households hold more than one-third of all personal wealth (Kornblum & Julian, 2012). *Net worth* refers to the value of all assets minus debts; assets include savings and checking accounts, automobiles, real estate, and stocks and bonds. The distribution of income is also unequal. The wealthiest 20 percent of households in the United States receive almost 50 percent of all income, whereas the poorest 20 percent receive less than 5 percent of all income (Kornblum & Julian, 2012).

In the words of a pastoral letter issued by a committee of Roman Catholic bishops, "The level of inequality in income and wealth in our society... must be judged morally unacceptable" (quoted in Kornblum & Julian, 2001, p. 225). Paul Samuelson (1980), an economist, provides a dramatic metaphor of the disparity between the very rich and most people in the United States:

> *If we made an income pyramid out of a child's blocks, with each layer portraying $1,000 of income, the peak would be far higher than the Eiffel Tower, but almost all of us would be within a yard of the ground. (p. 34)*

Given the huge wealth of the richest 20 percent, it is clear that a simple redistribution of some of the wealth from the top one-fifth to the lowest one-fifth could easily wipe out poverty. Of course, that is not politically acceptable to members of the top fifth, who have the greatest control of the government.

In contrast, millions of Americans regularly do not get enough to eat because they are poor. The brain of a child grows to 80 percent of its adult size within the first three years of life. If supplies of protein are inadequate during this period, the brain stops growing, the damage is irreversible, and the child will be permanently retarded (Robertson, 1980).

Coleman and Cressey (1990) describe the effects of having, and not having, wealth:

> *The poor lack the freedom and autonomy so prized in our society. They are trapped by their surroundings, living in rundown, crime-ridden neighborhoods that they cannot afford to leave. They are constantly confronted with things they desire but*

have little chance to own. On the other hand, wealth provides power, freedom, and the ability to direct one's own fate. The wealthy live where they choose and do as they please, with few economic constraints. Because the poor lack education and money for travel, their horizons seldom extend beyond the confines of their neighborhood. In contrast, the world of the wealthy offers the best education, together with the opportunity to visit places that the poor haven't even heard of.

> *The children of the wealthy receive the best that society has to offer, as well as the assurance that they are valuable and important individuals. Because the children of the poor lack so many of the things everyone is "supposed" to have, it is much harder for them to develop the cool confidence of the rich. In our materialistic society people are judged as much by what they have as by who they are. The poor cannot help but feel inferior and inadequate in such a context. (p. 161)*

The Problem

About 15 percent of the population in the United States is living below the poverty line (Mooney et al., 2013). *The poverty line* is the level of income that the federal government considers sufficient to meet basic requirements of food, shelter, and clothing. In 2010, the poverty line for a family of four in the United States was $23,550 (Mooney et al., 2013). One of the alarming elements about poverty is that the rate of poverty in recent years has been increasing. In addition, many people who do not fall under the government's poverty line still have very limited incomes and a living standard that is similar to those below the poverty line.

Poverty does not simply mean that poor people in the United States are living less well than people of average income. It means eating diets largely of beans, macaroni, and cheese, or, in severe cases, even dog and cat food. It may mean not having running water, living in substandard housing, and being exposed to rats, cockroaches, and other vermin. It means not having sufficient heat in the winter and being unable to sleep because the walls are too thin to deaden the sounds from the neighbors living next door. It means being embarrassed about the few ragged clothes that one has to wear. It means high susceptibility to emotional disturbances, alcoholism,

The financial and housing crises in recent years have led to an increase in the number of homeless individuals and families.

and victimization by criminals, as well as a shorter life expectancy. It means few opportunities to advance oneself socially, economically, or educationally. It often means slum housing, unstable marriages, and little opportunity to enjoy the finer things in life—traveling, dining out, movies, plays, concerts, sports events.

The infant mortality rate among the poor is almost double the rate among the affluent (Kornblum & Julian, 2012). The poor have less access to medical services and receive lower-quality care from health-care professionals. The poor are exposed to higher levels of air pollution, water pollution, and unsanitary conditions. They have higher rates of malnutrition and disease. Schools in poor areas are of lower quality and have fewer resources. As a result, the poor achieve less academically and are more apt to drop out of school. They are more apt to be arrested, indicted, imprisoned, and given longer sentences. They are less likely to receive probation, parole, or suspended sentences (Kornblum & Julian, 2012).

Poverty also often leads to despair, low self-esteem, and stunting of physical, social, emotional, and intellectual growth. A second level of damage from poverty occurs from the *feeling* that lack of financial resources is preventing one from having equal opportunities and the *feeling* that one is a second-class citizen. Poverty hurts deeply when it leads to viewing oneself as inferior or second-class.

We like to think that America is a land of equal opportunity and that there is considerable upward mobility for those who put forth the effort (see Highlight 12.6). The reality is the opposite of the dream. Extensive research has shown that poverty is almost inescapable. Children raised in poor families are themselves apt to live in poverty in their adult years. Most people have much the same social status as their parents had. Movement to a higher social status is unusual in practically all societies—including the United States (Kornblum & Julian, 2012).

Who Are the Poor?

Before the 20th century, a majority of the population lived in poverty. President Franklin D. Roosevelt (1937) stated, "I see one-third of a nation ill-housed, ill-clad, ill-nourished." In 1962, one-fifth of the population lived in poverty (U.S. Census Bureau, 1982). Now about 15 percent of the people are estimated to be below the poverty line. Since 1978, the

HIGHLIGHT 12.6

The Ideology of Individualism

Wealth is generally inherited in this country. There are few individuals who actually move up the social status ladder. Having wealth opens many doors (through education and contacts) for children of the wealthy to make large sums of money when they become adults. For children living in poverty, there is little chance to escape when they become older.

Yet there is the myth of individualism, held by many Americans. It states that the rich are personally responsible for their success, and that the poor are to blame for their failure. The main points of this myth are:

1. Each individual should work hard and strive to succeed in competition with others.

2. Those who work hard should be rewarded with success (seen as wealth, property, prestige, and power).
3. Because of widespread and equal opportunity, those who work hard will, in fact, be rewarded with success.
4. Economic failure is an individual's own fault and reveals lack of effort and other character defects.

The poor are blamed for their circumstances in our society. Blaming the poor has led to a stigma on poverty, particularly on those who receive public assistance.

---

proportion of the population who are poor has increased slightly.

Poverty is concentrated among certain population categories, including one-parent families, children, older adults, large-size families, people of color, and the homeless. Attainment of less than a ninth-grade education is a good predictor of poverty. Completing high school, however, is not a guarantee that one will earn wages adequate to avoid poverty, as many of the poor have graduated from high school. A college degree is an excellent predictor of avoiding poverty, as only a small proportion of those with a college degree live in poverty (Kornblum & Julian, 2012).

Being unemployed is also associated with poverty. People who live in rural areas have a higher incidence of poverty than people who live in urban areas. In rural areas, there is high unemployment, work tends to be seasonal, and wages are low. The Ozarks, Appalachia, and the South have pockets of rural poverty with high rates of unemployment (Kornblum & Julian, 2012).

People who live in deteriorated urban areas constitute the largest geographical group in terms of numbers of poor people. The decaying cities of the Northeast and Midwest have particularly large deteriorated areas. Poverty is also extensive on Native American reservations and among seasonal migrant workers. Spotlight 12.2 tells a tragic story of urban poverty.

The concept of "marginalization" appears in the EPAS (Council on Social Work Education, 2008). A marginalized group refers to a group of people who have been relegated to the lower echelons, outer edges, or "margins" of society based on such characteristics as gender, economic status, education, culture, race, religion, ethnicity, or political affiliation. The group is seen as being of little importance by the dominant cultural group. In our society the poor are a relatively powerless group, and hence marginalized.

What Causes Poverty?

There are a number of possible causes of poverty, including unemployment, poor physical health, emotional problems, drug addiction, low education level, racial and sexual discrimination, budgeting problems and mismanagement of resources, and mental retardation.

This list is not exhaustive. However, it serves to show that (1) poverty has many causes; (2) eliminating the causes of poverty would require a wide range of social programs; and (3) poverty interacts with almost all other social problems—emotional problems, alcoholism, unemployment, racial and sexual discrimination, medical problems, crime, gambling, and cognitive disabilities. The interaction between poverty and these other social problems is complicated. These social problems are contributing causes

SPOTLIGHT ON DIVERSITY 12.2

Poverty Perpetuates Poverty

The following summary of Marcee Calvello's life describes how poverty and dismal living conditions lead to despair, hopelessness, and failure.

Marcee Carvel was born and raised in New York City. Her father had trouble holding a job because he was addicted to cocaine, and her mother was an alcoholic who divorced her husband when Marcee was 3 years old. Marcee's mother at first sought to provide a better home for Marcee and her three brothers. She worked part-time and also went on public assistance. However, her addiction to alcohol consumed most of her time and money. Neighbors reported that the children were living in abject neglect, and Protective Services removed Marcee and her brothers to foster care. Marcee was placed in a series of foster homes—a total of 17 different homes. In one of these homes her foster father sexually assaulted her, and in another a foster brother assaulted her. Being moved from foster home to foster home resulted in frequent school changes. Marcee grew distrustful of the welfare system, schoolteachers and administrators, males, and anyone else who sought to get close to her.

When she turned 18, the state no longer paid for her care in foster care. She got a small efficiency apartment that cost her several hundred dollars a month. Because she had dropped out of school at age 16, she had few marketable job skills. She worked for a while at some fast-food restaurants. The minimum wages she received were insufficient to pay her bills. Eight months after she moved into her apartment she was evicted. Unable to afford another place, she started living in the subway system of New York City. She soon lost her job at McDonald's because of poor hygiene and an unkempt appearance.

Unable to shower and improve her appearance, she has not been able to secure another job. For the past two years she has been homeless, living on the street and in the subway. She has given up hope of improving her situation. She now occasionally shares IV needles and has been sexually assaulted periodically by men at night in the subway. She realizes she is at high risk for acquiring the AIDS virus but no longer cares very much. Death, to her, appears to be the final escape from a life filled with victimization and misery.

of poverty. Yet, for some social problems, poverty is also a contributing *cause* of those problems (such as emotional problems, alcoholism, and unemployment). And being poor intensifies the effects (the hurt) of all social problems.

To some extent, poverty is passed on from generation to generation. This cycle of poverty is diagrammed in Figure 12.1.

In 2007, a very serious global recession began, which continued for several years. A short summary of the causes of this recession follows.

Through the mid-1990s and early years of the 21st century, the number of subprime mortgage loans rose significantly. Partly due to increased competition among mortgage lenders, many lenders began to focus almost exclusively on subprime mortgages. Their mortgage loans to subprime borrowers usually had much higher interest rates. Although the loans extended home ownership, many Americans could not really afford the high mortgage payments. From 2007 through 2013, there were huge increases in home foreclosures because people fell behind on their mortgage payments.

Soon, additional and related problems arose. With so many homes on the real estate market, the market value of homes dropped substantially. Lenders experienced sharp losses because many subprime borrowers did not make mortgage payments. A financial crisis ensued, with many large financial institutions experiencing financial instability themselves. This crisis extended to many foreign investors who had put money in U.S. markets, and to foreign markets. Stock markets around the world experienced meltdowns, and a worldwide recession developed. This worldwide financial crisis was exacerbated by additional factors, such as the sharp increase in the price of oil. As a result of the turmoil in stock markets, many investors lost substantial portions of their financial portfolios. People spent less. Companies had difficulties. So there were more problems—the number of homeless rose, workers were laid off or terminated, the unemployed were forced to take low-paying jobs that they were overqualified for, the unemployment rate in the United States rose to nearly 10 percent, and so on.

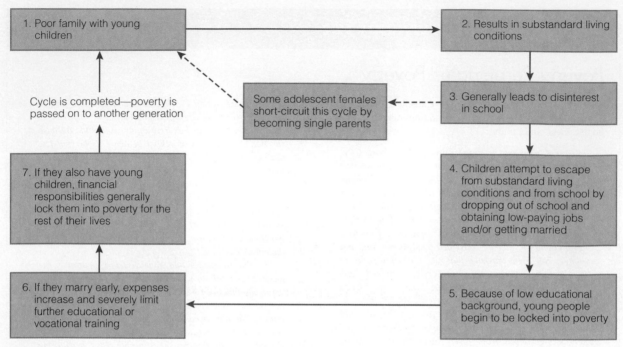

FIGURE 12.1 A Macro-System Problem: The Cycle of Poverty

The Culture of Poverty: Evaluation of the Theory and Its Application to Client Situations

Why is poverty passed on from one generation to another? Some authorities argue that the explanation is due to a "culture of poverty." Oscar Lewis (1966), an anthropologist, was a chief proponent of the cultural explanation. Lewis examined poor neighborhoods in various parts of the world and concluded that the poor are poor because they have a distinct culture or lifestyle. The key elements of Lewis's cultural explanation follow.

The culture of poverty arises after extended periods of economic deprivation in highly stratified capitalistic societies. Such deprivation is brought about by high rates of unemployment and low wages for those who are employed. Economic deprivation leads to the development of attitudes and values of despair and hopelessness. Lewis (1966) described these attitudes and values as follows: "The individual who grows up in this culture has a strong feeling of fatalism, helplessness, dependence and inferiority; a strong present-time orientation with relatively little disposition to defer gratification and plan for the future, and a high tolerance for psychological pathology of all kinds" (p. 23).

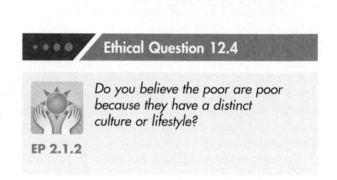

Ethical Question 12.4

Do you believe the poor are poor because they have a distinct culture or lifestyle?

EP 2.1.2

Once developed, this culture continues to exist, even though the economic factors that created it (e.g., lack of employment opportunities) no longer exist. These attitudes, norms, and expectations of the poor serve to limit their opportunities and prevent their escape. A major reason they remain locked into their culture is that they are socially isolated. They have few contacts with groups outside their own culture and are hostile to the institutions (e.g., social services and education) that might be able to help them escape poverty. They reject such institutions because they perceive them as belonging to the dominant class. Furthermore, because they view their financial circumstances as private matters and hopeless, and because they lack political and

Homeless people are often forgotten in the shadow of surrounding luxury.

organizational skills, they do not take collective action to try to resolve their problems.

The culture-of-poverty theory is controversial and has been widely criticized. Leacock (1971) argued that the distinctive culture of the poor is not the cause but the result of their continuing poverty. She agreed that the poor tend to emphasize instant gratification, which involves spending and enjoying one's money while it lasts. But she argued that instant gratification is a result of being poor rather than the cause, because it makes no sense to defer gratification when a person is pessimistic about the future. Deferred gratification is a rational response only when one is optimistic that postponing pleasure today by saving the money will reap greater benefits in the future. Studies have found that when inner-city residents are able to obtain a stable, good-paying job, they display the middle-class value of deferred gratification (Farley, 1992). Poverty, Leacock argues, forces the poor to abandon middle-class attitudes and values, because such values are irrelevant to their circumstances. If they had stable, well-paying jobs, they would likely take on the values of the middle class.

In an even stronger indictment, Ryan (1976) criticized the culture-of-poverty theory as a classic example of *blaming the victim*. Blaming the poor

for their circumstances is a convenient excuse, according to Ryan, for avoiding developing the programs and policies thought necessary to eradicate poverty. The real culprit is the social system that allows poverty to exist. Ryan said bluntly that the poor are not poor because of their culture, but because they do not have enough money.

Pro and con arguments for the culture of poverty theory continue to persist. There are many reasons, both external and internal, why a person may be poor. External reasons include high rates of unemployment, racial discrimination, automation or outsourcing of jobs, lack of job training programs, sex discrimination, a shortage of programs to eradicate poverty, and inflation. Internal reasons include having a physical or mental disability, being alcoholic, having obsolete job skills, becoming a parent at an early age, dropping out of school, and being uninterested in taking available jobs.

Poverty Is Functional

Obviously, poverty causes many problems, mainly for the poor themselves, but also for the affluent. However, realizing that poverty also has some functions can help us understand why some decision makers are not actively seeking to eradicate poverty.

Sullivan and his colleagues (1980, p. 390) listed 11 functions that the poor provide for the affluent:

1. They are available to do the unpleasant jobs that no one else wants to do.
2. By their activities, they subsidize the more affluent. (An example of such an activity is domestic service for low pay.)
3. Jobs are established for those people, such as social workers, who provide services to the poor.
4. The poor purchase goods, such as those of poor quality, that otherwise could not be sold.
5. They serve as examples of deviance that are frowned on by the majority and that thereby support dominant norms.
6. They provide an opportunity for others to practice their "Christian duty" of helping the less fortunate.
7. They make mobility more likely for others because they are removed from the competition for a good education and good jobs.
8. They contribute to cultural activities by providing, for example, cheap labor for the construction of monuments and works of art.
9. They create cultural forms (e.g., jazz and the blues) that are often adopted by the affluent.
10. They serve as symbolic opponents for some political groups and as constituents for others.
11. They often absorb the costs of change (e.g., by being the victims of unemployment that results from technological advances).

Also, denigrating the poor has the psychological function, for some Americans, of making them feel better about themselves.

Ethical Question 12.5

Is it functional for a society to have a segment of the population that is poor?

EP 2.1.2

Partly because poverty is functional, our society makes only a halfhearted effort to eradicate or at least reduce it. To eliminate poverty would mean a redistribution of income from the rich to the poor.

Because the rich control the political power, they have generally been opposed to proposals that would eliminate poverty, such as guaranteed annual income programs.

Our country has the resources to eliminate poverty—but not the will. We can find billions of dollars in resources within a few months to pay for a war, but we are not willing to allocate similar funds to improve living conditions for the homeless and millions of other Americans who are living in poverty.

Application of Functionalism to Poverty

Functionalists view poverty as being due to dysfunctions in the economy. A wide range of dysfunctions have been identified, some of which will be mentioned here. Rapid industrialization has caused disruption in the economic system. For example, people who lack job skills are forced into menial work at low wages. Then when automation comes, they are discharged, without having work, money, or marketable job skills. Some products produced by industry also become outdated—such as steam engines, milk bottles, and horse-drawn carriages. When such products become obsolete, workers lose their jobs. In addition, work training centers and apprenticeship programs may continue to produce graduates whose skills are no longer in demand. For example, there no longer is a job market for people who are trained to repair adding machines and manual typewriters, and direct telephone calling is sharply reducing the number of people needed as telephone operators.

Functionalists also note that the welfare system, which is intended to solve the problem of poverty, has a number of dysfunctions. Social welfare programs are sometimes established without sufficient funds to meet the needs of potential clients. Some bureaucrats are reluctant to bend the rules to help a deserving family that is technically ineligible for assistance. Social welfare programs at times have design dysfunctions in meeting the needs of recipients. For example, in the past, mothers of young children in some states were eligible for public assistance only if the fathers were out of the home. Consequently, some unemployed men were forced to desert their families so their children could be fed and sheltered.

Other problems in the welfare system are caused by inadequate information systems that fail to inform the poor about benefits to which they are entitled (in addition to the deliberate withholding of information due to prejudice). Job training and educational programs sometimes train people for positions in which there are no employment openings.

According to functionalists, the best way to deal with poverty is to make adjustments to correct these dysfunctions.

Many functionalists view some economic inequality (i.e., poverty) as being functional. Because the poor are at the bottom of the stratification system, they receive few of the material and social rewards in the society. Functionalists view the threat of being at the bottom of the heap as an important mechanism for motivating people to perform. According to functionalists, poverty becomes a social problem when it no longer performs the function of motivating people to make productive contributions to society. Poverty is also functional because the poor do the demeaning, difficult, and low-paying jobs that are essential but that no one else wants to do.

Application of Conflict Theory to Poverty

Conflict theorists assume that, because there is such enormous wealth in modern societies, no one in such societies should go without their essential needs being met. These theorists assert that poverty exists because the power structure wants it to exist. They assert that the working poor are being exploited, being paid poverty-level wages so that their employers can reap higher profits. The unemployed are also seen as victims of the power structure. Wealthy employers oppose programs to reduce unemployment (such as educational and job training programs) because they do not want to pay the taxes to support them.

Wealthy people are apt to cling to the ideology of individualism, viewing unemployment and poverty as stemming from a lack of effort rather than from social injustice or from circumstances beyond the control of the individual. As a result, the wealthy ignore the economic and political foundations of poverty and instead get involved in charitable efforts for the poor, which leaves them feeling they have done good deeds. Conflict theorists see charity and government welfare programs as perpetuating poverty and economic inequality, because such programs quell political protests and social unrest that

threaten the status quo. Conflict theorists also assert that many poor people eventually come to accept the judgments passed on them by the rest of society and adjust their aspirations and self-esteem downward.

Conflict theorists do not see poverty as either essential or functional. They see poverty as arising because some groups benefit from the poverty of others. From the conflict perspective, poverty becomes a social problem when some group feels that the existing distribution of resources is unjust and that something should be done about it.

Conflict theorists believe that poverty can best be dealt with by the poor becoming politically aware and organizing to reduce inequality through government action. These theorists view poor people's adjustments to poverty as being a set of chains that must be broken. Most conflict theorists believe poverty can be significantly reduced only through political action that receives at least some support from concerned members of the power structure.

Application of Interactionist Theory to Poverty

Interactionists emphasize the subjective nature of poverty. Poverty is viewed as being relative, because it depends on what it is compared to. Most poor people in the United States today have a higher standard of living than middle-class people did 200 years ago. Poor people in this country are also substantially better off than poor people in third-world countries.

The main reference for poor people in this country is their poor neighbors. A successful person in some neighborhoods is someone who knows where the next meal is coming from, and a big success may be someone who gets a job on an assembly line. People with such attitudes become trapped in their own beliefs. Another value that traps them is instant gratification, in which they are not inclined to defer immediate rewards for the sake of long-range goals, such as a college education.

Interactionists view poverty as a matter of shared expectations. The poor are judged negatively by influential groups. Those who are the objects of such labeling are stigmatized and may begin to behave in accordance with those expectations. Interactionists emphasize that poverty is not just a matter of economic deprivation, but involves the person's self-concept. For example, a third-generation welfare recipient is apt to view himself or herself much more negatively than a person working his or her way through college, even if both have the same income.

To resolve the poverty problem, interactionists urge that the stigma associated with poverty be eliminated. Positive changes in the poverty problem will not occur until the poor are convinced that they are no longer doomed to live in poverty. The poverty trap can be sprung with improved public assistance programs that bring the poor up to an adequate standard of living, *combined* with programs that provide opportunities to move up the socioeconomic ladder and programs that encourage the poor to redefine their social environment.

Family Mezzo-System Problems

The first part of this chapter has emphasized the importance of understanding macro social systems when assessing human behavior. It is equally important to understand people's interactions with mezzo systems—small groups, including families. This section will examine problems and living arrangements in families.

Empty-Shell Marriages

In empty-shell marriages, the spouses feel no strong attachments to each other. Outside pressures keep the marriage together. Such outside pressures include business reasons (e.g., an elected official wanting to convey a stable family image), investment reasons (e.g., husband and wife may have a luxurious home and other property that they do not want to lose by parting), and outward appearances (e.g., a couple living in a small community may remain together to avoid the reactions of relatives and friends to a divorce). In addition, a couple may believe that ending the marriage would harm the children or may believe that getting a divorce would be morally wrong.

Cuber and Harroff (1971) identified three types of empty-shell marriages. In a *devitalized relationship*, husband and wife lack any real interest in each other or their marriage. Boredom and apathy characterize this marriage. Serious arguments are rare.

In a *conflict-habituated relationship*, husband and wife frequently quarrel in private. They may also quarrel in public, or they may put up a facade of

being compatible. The relationship is characterized by considerable conflict, tension, and bitterness. Highlight 12.7 provides strategies for couples—and people in general—to resolve interpersonal conflicts.

In a *passive-congenial relationship*, the partners are not happy, but are content with their lives and generally feel adequate. They may have some interests in common, but these interests are generally insignificant. The spouses contribute little to each other's real satisfactions. This type of relationship generally has little overt conflict.

•••• / Ethical Question 12.6

Is it better to get a divorce than live in an empty-shell marriage?

EP 2.1.2

The number of empty-shell marriages is unknown—it may be as high as the number of happily married couples. The atmosphere in empty-shell marriages is without much fun or laughter. Members do not share and discuss their problems or experiences with each other. Communication is kept to a minimum. There is seldom any spontaneous expression of affection or sharing of a personal experience. Children in such families are usually starved for love and reluctant to have friends over because they are embarrassed about having their friends see their parents interacting.

The couples in these marriages engage in few activities together and display no pleasure in being in one another's company. Sexual relations between the partners, as might be expected, are rare and generally unsatisfying. Visitors will note that the partners (and often the children) appear insensitive, cold, and callous to each other. Closer observation will reveal that the family members are highly aware of each other's weaknesses and sensitive areas, and manage to frequently mention these areas in order to hurt one another.

Both spouses have to put considerable effort into making a marriage work in order to prevent an empty-shell marriage from gradually developing. The number of empty-shell marriages ending in divorce is unknown. It is likely that many eventually do.

HIGHLIGHT 12.7

Conflict Resolution Strategies

Conflict, an antagonistic state or action involving divergent ideas or interests, is inevitable in interpersonal relationships. There is an erroneous belief in our society that conflicts always produce negative results and therefore should be avoided. But since people have divergent interests, beliefs, values, and goals, it is inevitable that conflicts will occur in our work settings and in our private lives. Conflicts are not only a natural component of any interpersonal relationship, but often desirable, because they have a number of potential payoffs. Conflicts produce lively discussions. When constructively handled, conflicts motivate the people involved to define issues more sharply, to search harder for resolution strategies, and to work harder in implementing solutions. Conflict, when handled effectively, can also lead to greater commitment to the relationship of the people involved, raise morale, and increase communication and cooperation. Successful resolution of conflict can lead to personal growth and facilitate innovation and creativity.

However, ineffective management of conflict can lead to deterioration of rapport between the people involved, distrust, and perhaps alienation and burnout. Unfortunately, some organizations have norms that urge frontline service providers to suppress their suggestions for changes. Such norms are often communicated informally by agency management taking adverse actions (such as dismissal, demotion, assignment to onerous tasks, and no salary raises) against those who press for changes. Efforts to suppress suggestions for change by agency management usually result in lower morale, lower productivity, and less commitment to the agency's mission by the staff.

Following are a variety of strategies for resolving conflicts: the win-lose approach, the problem-solving approach, role reversal, empathy, inquiry, being assertive, I-messages, disarming, stroking, letting go or forgiving, and mediation. This section ends with a discussion of what to do if none of these strategies works.

Win-Lose Approach

With the win-lose approach, the two sides engaged in the conflict attempt to sell their own solution without really listening to the other side. Each side denies the legitimacy of the other's interests and concerns. Sometimes each side seeks to form a power bloc of supporters.

In win-lose situations, both sides usually end up losing. The losing side is not motivated to carry out the winning decision. The losing side is apt to resent the winning side, and then search for subtle ways to get even. In a win-lose situation, distrust increases between the two opposing sides, communication becomes more limited and inaccurate, and rapport deteriorates.

Problem-Solving Approach

The problem-solving approach asserts that it is almost always possible for both sides to have their needs met in a conflict situation. This approach is based on two basic premises: both sides have the right to have their needs met; and what is in conflict between the two sides is almost never their needs but their solutions to those needs.

The six steps in the problem-solving approach are:

1. Identify and define the needs of each opposing side.
2. Generate possible alternative solutions.
3. Evaluate the merits and shortcomings of the alternative solutions.
4. Decide on the best acceptable solution.
5. Work out ways of implementing the solution.
6. At a later date, evaluate how well the solution is working.

The advantages of this approach are numerous. Both sides fulfill their needs. The resentment, hostility, and subversive actions of a win-lose situation are avoided. Open communication is increased, and trust between the parties is enhanced. Both sides are more prepared to handle conflicts constructively in the future, as they have now had experience in doing so. A cooperative, problem-solving approach also promotes creativity. The problem-solving approach often generates new perspectives on a problem and innovative alternatives for resolving it.

Role Reversal

A useful strategy in resolving conflict is role reversal. The basic rule for role reversal is: *Each person expresses his or her opinions or views only after restating the ideas and feelings of the opposing person.* These ideas and feelings should be restated in one's own words rather than parroted or mimicked in the exact words of the other person. It is advisable to begin the restatement with words such as "Your position is ... ," "You seem to be saying ... ," or "You apparently feel...." Approval or disapproval, blaming, giving advice, interpreting, or persuading should be avoided.

In addition, nonverbal messages should be consistent with the verbal paraphrasing and should convey interest, openness, and attentiveness to the opposition's ideas and feelings. Above all, role reversal should be the expression of a sincere interest in understanding the other person's feelings, ideas, and position.

Role reversal can result in a reevaluation and a change of attitude concerning the issue by both parties. The approach has also been found to increase cooperative behavior between role reversers, to clarify misunderstandings, to change win-lose situations into problem-solving situations, and, most important, to allow the issue to be perceived from the other person's frame of reference.

Empathy

A closely related technique to role reversal is the expression of empathy. *Empathy* involves putting yourself in the shoes of the

(continued)

person you are in conflict with, and expressing your understanding of what the other person is thinking and saying. Some phrases that may help you get started in expressing empathy are "What you seem to be saying is … ," "I take it that you think … ," and "I sense you feel … about this issue."

When expressing empathy, it is essential to mirror what was said in a nonjudgmental way, to grasp the essence of what the other person is thinking or feeling. Similar to role reversal, the use of empathy facilitates open communication, assists in clarifying misunderstandings, increases cooperative behavior, and facilitates the process of no-lose problem solving.

Inquiry

If you are in conflict with someone and you are confused regarding his or her thoughts and feelings, the inquiry technique is often useful. This technique involves using gentle, probing questions to learn more about what the other person is thinking and feeling. Tone of voice is very crucial in the inquiry technique, as asking a question sarcastically or defensively is apt to result in defensive responses from the other person.

Being Assertive

There are three basic styles of interacting with others: nonassertive, aggressive, and assertive. (See Chapter 7 for an expanded discussion of these terms.) Simply stated, assertive behavior is being able to express yourself in a confident, nonaggressive manner. The assertive approach in discussing issues with someone you are in conflict with is almost always more effective than the nonassertive approach or the aggressive approach. With the nonassertive approach you fail to express your thoughts and concerns. An aggressive approach usually results in escalation of the conflict.

I-Messages

When conflicts arise, most people respond with you-messages. There are two types of you-messages: a solution message and a put-down message. A solution message orders, directs, commands, warns, threatens, preaches, moralizes, or advises. A put-down message blames, judges, criticizes, ridicules, or name-calls. Examples of you-messages include: "You stop that," "Don't do that," "I hate you," and "You should know better." You-messages tend to inhibit open communication.

I-messages, in contrast, tend to foster open communication. I-messages are nonblaming messages that simply communicate how the sender of the message believes the receiver is affecting the sender. I-messages do not provide a solution, and they do not criticize. It is possible to send an I-message without using the word *I*. For example, when the driver is speeding at a reckless rate, an I-message that does not use *I* is, "Driving this fast really frightens me." The essence of I-messages involves sending a nonblaming message of how the sender feels the receiver is affecting him or her.

You-messages are generally counterproductive because people do not like to be ordered or criticized. You-messages

frequently result in an ongoing struggle between the two people involved.

In contrast, I-messages communicate much more honestly the effect of behavior. I-messages tend to be more effective because they help the other person to assume responsibility for his or her behavior. An I-message conveys to the person with whom you are in conflict that you are trusting him or her to respect your needs and that you are trusting him or her to handle the conflict constructively. I-messages are much less likely to produce an argument. They tend to facilitate honesty, openness, and more cordial relationships. (See Chapter 8 for an expanded discussion of I-messages.)

Disarming

When you are in conflict with someone, a frequently effective strategy in moving toward resolving the conflict is the disarming technique. This technique involves finding some truth in what the other person (or side) is saying and then expressing this "agreement"—even if you feel that what the other person is saying is largely wrong, unreasonable, irrational, or unfair. There is always a grain of truth in what the other person is saying, even if it sounds obnoxious and insulting. In response to disarming, the other person won't feel so dogmatic and will have less of an urge to insist that he or she is right and you are wrong. As a result, he or she is apt to be more willing to examine the merits of your point of view. If you want respect, you first have to give respect. This technique helps you to listen to the other person first and facilitates more open (rather than defensive) communication thereafter.

In using the disarming technique, it is important that you be genuine in what you say and express your agreement in a sincere way.

Stroking

A closely related technique to disarming is stroking. *Stroking* is saying something genuinely positive to the person (or side) you are in conflict with, even in the heat of battle. Stroking tells the other person that you respect him or her, even though both of you may be angry with each other. During an argument or conflict, we have a tendency to feel the need to reject the other person before we get rejected (so we can save face). Often we overreact, and differences of opinion become blown out of proportion. To prevent this rejection, all we need to do is let the other person know that, although we are at odds, we still think highly of him or her. This makes it easier for the other person to open up and to listen, as he or she feels less threatened.

Letting Go or Forgiving

If we hold a long-term grudge against someone, we are primarily hurting (both emotionally and health wise) ourselves. Emotionally we hurt ourselves by being in a state of periodic anger (which occurs when we think about the perceived "wrong"). By holding a grudge, we also raise our level of stress, which (as described in Chapter 14) often leads to a variety of stress-related illnesses. Mentally nursing a grudge puts your body through the same strains as a major stressful event, muscles tense, blood pressure rises, and sweating increases.

Two strategies to get rid of holding a long-term grudge are "letting go" and forgiving. With the "letting go" strategy, we reframe our thinking so that we no longer dwell on the perceived wrong. One way of reframing our thinking is to do a rational self-analysis (described in Chapter 8). If there is no way to change a perceived "wrong," the best thing we can do for our mental and physical well-being is to "let go" of it.

Forgiveness is actually another strategy for "letting go." When you forgive someone who has hurt you, you make yourself—rather than the person who hurt you—responsible for your happiness.

Mediation

In the past two decades, mediation has increasingly been used to resolve conflicts. *Mediation* involves the intervention of a mutually acceptable, impartial, neutral third party who has no authoritative decision-making power but who can assist contending parties in voluntarily reaching their own settlement of the issues in dispute. Mediation leaves the decision-making power in the hands of the people in conflict. Mediation is a voluntary process in that the participants must be willing to accept the assistance of the intervenor if the dispute is to be resolved. Mediation is usually initiated when the partners no longer believe that they can handle the conflict on their own and feel the need of impartial third-party assistance.

One of the major techniques a mediator uses is a caucus. At times a mediator, or either party, may stop the mediation and request a caucus. In a caucus, the two parties are physically separated and there is no direct communication between them. The mediator meets with one of the parties or with each party individually. There are many reasons for calling a caucus: to vent intense emotions privately, to clarify misperceptions, to reduce unproductive or repetitive negative behavior, to clarify a party's interests, to provide a pause for each party to consider an alternative, to convince an uncompromising party that the mediation process is better than going to court, to uncover confidential information, to educate an inexperienced disputant about the processes of mediation, or to design alternatives that will later be brought to a joint session.

In a caucus, one party may be willing to express possible concessions privately. Usually such concessions are conditional on the other party's making certain concessions. Through the use of caucuses, a mediator can go back and forth, relaying information from one party to the other, and seek to develop a consensus.

What if These Strategies Don't Work?

If used appropriately, these strategies can help resolve interpersonal conflicts in the vast majority of cases. When these strategies fail to work, you can probably correctly conclude that the person you are in conflict with does not really want to resolve the conflict. Perhaps the other person is a very hostile person who wants to generate conflicts to meet his or her personal needs by venting anger and hostility. Or perhaps the other person wants to be in conflict with you in order to make your life uncomfortable.

What can you do when you become aware that the other person really wants to sustain the conflict with you? Using the "law of requisite variety" is an option. This law states that if you continue to creatively come up with new ways of responding to the "daggers being thrown" at you, eventually the other person will grow tired of the turmoil and will finally decide to "bury the hatchet." Here are two examples:

Janice and Pete Palmer were married about a year ago. Unknown to Janice, Pete was having lunch about once a month with a former partner (Paula), whom he had dated over a three-year period. Seven months ago Janice walked into a restaurant at noon and saw her husband with Paula. In a fit of rage, Janice stomped out. That evening she and Pete had a major uproar about this. Pete claimed Paula was just a friend and that nothing romantic was occurring. Janice yelled and screamed. Pete indicated he would stop having lunch with Paula. But he didn't keep his promise. About once a month he continued to see Paula, and when Janice found out, there was a major argument. Janice suggested a number of resolution options, including marriage counseling. Pete refused to go to counseling and also indicated he had decided that he was going to continue having lunch with Paula (the win-lose approach).

Then one day Janice ran into one of her former partners—Dave. Dave invited Janice for lunch or dinner. A lightbulb went on for Janice—she accepted the invitation and made plans for dinner. She went home and gleefully told Pete she ran into Dave (who Pete knew had dated Janice in the past). Pete became very jealous and tried to talk Janice out of having dinner with Dave. Janice said, "No way." Pete was in anguish during the time Janice and Dave were having dinner. When Janice came home, Dave politely said he had called Paula that evening to cancel their next scheduled lunch and to tell her he felt it was best that they no longer meet for lunch. Pete then asked Janice if she also would no longer get together with Dave, and she agreed. Through this experience, Pete and Janice learned to respect and appreciate each other to a greater extent.

Vicki Stewart was a secretary for an attorney, Randy Fuller, who frequently criticized her and never complimented her. The harder she sought to perform well, the more it seemed she was criticized. She tried a variety of resolution strategies—discussing the conflict with him, discussing it with his supervisor, and making a point of complimenting him to set a good example. Nothing worked. Finally, she decided on a new approach. Mr. Fuller's grammar and spelling were atrocious. Ms. Stewart always improved the spelling and grammar when given rough drafts from Mr. Fuller and

(continued)

HIGHLIGHT 12.7 *(continued)*

the other attorneys in the office. When Mr. Fuller gave her a rough draft of a legal brief for the state supreme court, Ms. Stewart typed it as is and sent it after Mr. Fuller signed it (he frequently signed such documents without proofreading them). When Mr. Fuller finally read the brief three weeks later, he was first angry, and then discussed the matter with

his supervisor. His supervisor at first laughed, and then informed Mr. Fuller that in order to avoid a similar situation in the future, he needed to show appreciation to Ms. Stewart. After a few more days of reflecting about it, Mr. Fuller decided it was in his personal interest to display more respect and appreciation to Ms. Stewart.

Divorce

Our society places a higher value on romantic love than most other societies do. In societies where marriages are arranged by parents, being in love generally has no role in mate selection. In our society, however, romantic love is a key factor in forming a marriage.

Children in this country are socialized from an early age to believe in the glories of romantic love. Magazines, films, TV programs, and books portray "happy-ending" romantic adventures. All of these romantic stories suggest that every normal person falls in love with that one special person, gets married, and lives happily ever after. This happily-ever-after ideal rarely happens.

About one of two marriages ends in divorce (Kornblum & Julian, 2012). This high rate has gradually been increasing. Before World War I, divorce was comparatively rare.

Divorce usually leads to a number of difficulties for those involved. First, those who are divorcing face emotional concerns, such as concerns that they have failed, over whether they are able to give and receive love, about a sense of loneliness, over the stigma attached to divorce, about the reactions of friends and relatives, over whether they are doing the right thing by parting, and over whether they will be able to make it on their own. Many people feel trapped because they believe they cannot live with their spouse and cannot live without him or her. Dividing up the personal property is another area that frequently leads to bitter differences of opinions. If there are children, there are concerns about how the divorce will affect them.

Other issues also need to be decided. Who will get custody of the children? Joint custody is now an alternative. With joint custody, both parents have responsibility for decision making involving the children, and they may (or may not) share equally in the physical custody of the children. If one parent is

awarded custody, controversies are apt to arise over visiting rights, and how much (if any) child support should be paid. Both spouses often face the difficulties of finding new places to live, making new friends, doing things alone in our couple-oriented society, trying to make it on their own financially, and thinking about the hassles of dating.

Studies show that going through a divorce is very difficult for the spouses (Papalia et al., 2012). People are less likely to perform their jobs well and more likely to be fired during this period. Divorced people have a shorter life expectancy. Suicide rates are higher for divorced men.

Divorce per se is no longer automatically assumed to be a social problem. In some marriages where there is considerable tension, bitterness, and dissatisfaction, divorce is sometimes a solution. It may be a concrete step that some people take to end the unhappiness and to begin leading a more productive and gratifying life. It is also increasingly being recognized that a divorce may be better for the children, as they are no longer subjected to the tension and unhappiness in a marriage that has gone sour.

The rising rate of divorce does not necessarily mean that more marriages are failing. It may simply mean that more people are dissolving empty-shell marriages rather than continuing to live unhappily.

Reasons for Divorce

The reason people decide to divorce may have nothing to do with specific "bad" qualities of the marriage partners. Rather, a major reason people divorce is disappointment with each other. In other words, partners simply do not measure up to their spouse's expectations. Over time such disappointment and disillusionment lead to the decision to divorce. (Highlight 12.8 provides a framework for people to analyze their love relationships.)

HIGHLIGHT 12.8

Analyzing Love Relationships

Cameron-Bandler (1985) developed the following framework for understanding the various stages of a love relationship. Cameron-Bandler also gave suggestions for improving love relationships. Knowing when to get out of a destructive relationship is as important as knowing how to improve a healthy relationship.

1. *Attraction/Infatuation*: All of us have in mind a picture of our ideal date or mate. This picture may include a variety of characteristics about such items as physical appearance, color of hair, color of eyes, age, height, weight, personality, hobbies, personal interests, religion, musical interests, sports, education, career interests, family background, financial security, and sexual values and interests. Such pictures vary from person to person. When we meet someone who comes close to having the characteristics we desire, we tell ourselves that this is an ideal potential partner. We feel strongly attracted to the person and are in a stage of infatuation. After a few dates, the infatuation may intensify. Cameron-Bandler notes that this is "a fun time, full of intensity and excitement and romance" (p. 119).

2. *Appreciation*: In this stage the two persons are a couple who are seriously dating, living together, or even married. They are delighted to be together. They focus on each other's positive qualities. They appreciate each other, rather than taking one another for granted. Cameron-Bandler says, "This phase can be based on a wide range of illusions or varying degrees of knowledgeable understanding of each other's wants and needs. The extent to which it is based on knowledgeable understanding is the extent to which it can be depended upon to last" (p. 120).

   There are three basic elements for achieving and maintaining appreciation in a relationship. First, each partner has to know what he or she needs and wants in a relationship. Second, each partner must know what specifically fulfills these needs and wants. Third, each person must be able to elicit these fulfilling behaviors, lovingly, from his or her partner.

3. *Habituation*: Habituation is the stage of becoming accustomed to something. It involves being comfortable and secure with dependability and familiarity. For people who seek security, habituation is viewed as equaling safety and commitment. However, for people seeking adventure, habituation can be viewed as equaling boredom. Cameron-Bandler notes, "The phase of habituation can be a very positive one, provided it cycles back to appreciation and includes an occasional trip back to attraction" (p. 121).

   Partners in this state of a relationship are advised to engage in old and new activities that they enjoy. One suggestion is for the partners to commit two weekends each year for enhancing the relationship. The partners first agree on how much money will be spent for each weekend. Then one of the partners arranges the activities that are designed to meet his or her fantasies of how he or she wants to spend time with the partner. A few weeks later the other partner similarly arranges for his or her fantasy weekend. Among other benefits, these weekends serve as a learning experience for each partner as to the other's previously unexpressed or newly formed desires.

4. *Expectation*: Cameron-Bandler writes, "The difference between duty and pleasure often rears its ugly head in the phase of expectation" (p. 122). Many of the things that one did and were appreciated by one's partner now become an expectation. For example, at first A expressed intense appreciation when B shopped for groceries and cooked on certain evenings. Now these tasks have become expected duties, and B receives frowns and criticisms when they aren't done. This stage in a relationship is usually signaled by more complaints than compliments. Each partner focuses on what the other is not doing, rather than on what he or she is doing to benefit the relationship. One way of seeking to halt further deterioration in a relationship when this stage is reached is an intervention in which each partner is encouraged to once again treat the other as a lover instead of as a spouse.

5. *Disappointment/Disillusionment*: Unless the couple works on their relationship, disappointment and disillusionment soon follow expectation. In this stage the partners become increasingly disappointed because each is failing to fulfill the other's expectations. In this stage partners are apt to say their mate has started some bad habits; however, closer investigation usually shows the mate has been engaging in the undesirable behavior all along. In this stage the partners still remember the past as being wonderful and want things to be "the way they used to be." A relationship at this stage can be improved by a mutual commitment from each partner to put forth efforts to elicit those fulfilling behaviors, lovingly, from his or her partner.

6. *Threshold/Perceptual Reorientation*: The threshold is reached when one or both partners decide the relationship is over. The partner reaching this stage has a memory change—from remembering past pleasurable experiences to remembering primarily past unpleasant memories. Such partners are no longer able to *feel* the good times, even when they think about earlier good times. Sometimes the threshold is reached by the occurrence of a minor event that, like the straw that broke the camel's back, leads a partner to conclude the relationship is over. The partner reaching this threshold has a perceptual reorientation of discounting the partner's positive qualities and instead seeks to find evidence in the partner's behaviors that warrant terminating the relationship.

7. *Verification*: In this stage the partner who has decided to end the relationship focuses on observing the other's

(continued)

behaviors and qualities to find evidence that warrants termination. Sometimes during this phase, one or both partners experience the feeling that "I can't live with him/her and I can't live without him/her." Considerable emotional energy is generated by anyone with this feeling, because he or she is under intense stress.

Usually one of the partners reaches this stage sooner than the other. One wants out, and the other seeks to maintain the relationship. The person seeking to maintain it may engage in a variety of behaviors, such as seeking to please the partner, attempting to make the other partner feel guilty, seeking to have a child in order to "lock" the partner into the relationship, flirting with others to make the partner jealous, or threatening suicide. Relationships at this stage are not fun. The partner who wants out has the most power, as he or she decides whether the relationship continues or ends.

8. *Termination*: At this stage one or both partners decide to end the relationship. This stage is usually a painful experience for both. Property must be divided. Goodbyes are said—sometimes with considerable anger and animosity. If children are involved, custody and child support arrangements need to be worked out. If the couple is married, the legal divorce process must be gone through. In addition, each person has to work on forming a new life without the former partner.

We often tend to treat strangers with more respect than we give the people close to us. If a stranger does something we dislike, we usually ignore it or politely express our concerns. But if someone we love does something we dislike, we are apt to criticize and attempt to train the partner to meet our expectations. A major suggestion for improving intimate relationships is to seek to treat a partner with the same kind of respect given to strangers.

It is interesting to note that the same individual might be considered horrendous by one spouse but wonderful by the next, depending on the expectations of each spouse. Take Nick, for instance. His first wife, Judy, found him to be cold, noncommunicative, and unaffectionate. She lamented that he refused to sit with her on the couch, hold hands, and watch television as they relaxed in the evening. She once indicated that the purchase of a reclining chair caused the demise of their marriage because they could no longer sit together. After the divorce, however, his second wife, Karen, felt that Nick was very, very affectionate, even though he demonstrated the same or at least very similar behavior toward her. She loved having her independence in the evenings and having television sets in separate rooms. To Karen, with her love of horror movies and Nick's love of *Wall Street Week in Review*, living in this more independent manner was appealing.

There are many sources of marital breakdown, including alcoholism, economic strife caused by unemployment or other financial problems, incompatibility of interests, infidelity, jealousy, verbal or physical abuse of spouse, and interference in the marriage by relatives and friends.

As noted earlier, many people marry because they believe they are romantically in love. If this romantic love does not grow into rational love, the marriage is apt to fail. Unfortunately, young people are socialized in our society to believe that marriage will bring them continual romance, resolve all their problems, be sexually exciting, be full of adventure, and always be as wonderful as the courtship. (Most young people only need to look at their parents' marriage to realize such romantic ideals are seldom attained.) Unfortunately, living with someone in a marriage involves carrying out the garbage, washing dishes and clothes, being weary from work, putting up with the partner's distasteful habits, changing diapers, dealing with conflicts over such things as how to spend a vacation, and differences in sexual interests. Making a marriage work requires that each spouse put considerable effort into making it successful.

Another factor that is contributing to an increasing divorce rate is the unwillingness of some men to accept the changing status of women. Many men still prefer a traditional marriage in which the husband is dominant and the wife plays a supportive (subordinate) role as child rearer, housekeeper, and emotional supporter of her husband. Many women no longer accept such a status and demand an egalitarian marriage in which making major decisions, doing the domestic tasks, raising the children, and bringing home paychecks are shared responsibilities.

About 70 percent of women ages 16 to 65 years in the United States are now in the labor force (Mooney et al., 2013). As a result, women are no longer as dependent financially on their husbands. Women who are able to support themselves are more likely to seek a divorce if their marriage goes sour.

Another factor contributing to the increasing divorce rate is the growth of individualism. Individualism involves the belief that people should seek to develop their interests and capacities to the fullest, to fulfill their own needs and desires. The interests of the individual take precedence over the interests of the family. People in our society have increasingly come to accept individualism as a way of life. In contrast, people in more traditional societies and in extended families are socialized to put the interests of the group first, with their own individual interests being viewed as less important. In extended families, people view themselves as members of a group first and as individuals second. With the growing belief in individualism, people who conclude that they are unhappily married are much more apt to dissolve the marriage and seek a new life.

Another reason for the rising divorce rate is the growing acceptance of divorce in our society. With less stigma attached to divorce, more people who are unhappily married are now ending the marriage.

In addition, modern families do not have as many functions as traditional families did. Education, food production, entertainment, and other functions once centered in the family are now largely provided by outside agencies. In earlier times, the end of a marriage was far more likely to deprive both spouses of much more than each other's company. Because family members performed so many functions for one another, divorce in the past meant a father being without a wife as a partner in educating the children and doing the farm work, and meant a mother being without a husband to plow the fields and raise crops to feed their children. Today, when emotional satisfaction is the bond that holds marriage together, the waning of love and the failure to meet one another's expectations leave few reasons for a marriage to continue. (Highlight 12.9 provides some facts about divorce.)

Consequences of Divorce

Both members of the couple, even the person who initiated the divorce, experience grief at the loss. Familiar patterns of behavior must be changed. Even the loss of negative behavior patterns causes stress, because new ways of interacting must be established. The old ways, even when they were bad, were at least predictable. The unknown is scary to many people, making any kind of change more difficult.

Feelings are often strong and varied after a divorce. People may feel anger and anxiety. Things

---

◆ HIGHLIGHT 12.9

Facts About Divorce

- *Age of spouses*: Divorce is most likely to occur when the partners are in their 20s.
- *Length of engagement*: Divorce rates are higher for those whose engagement was brief.
- *Age at marriage*: People who marry at a very young age (particularly teenagers) are more apt to divorce.
- *Length of marriage*: Most divorces occur within three years after marriage. There is also an increase in divorce shortly after the children are grown; it seems that some couples wait until the children are ready to leave the nest before dissolving an unhappy marriage.
- *Social class*: Divorce occurs more frequently at the lower socioeconomic levels.
- *Education*: Divorce rates are higher for those with fewer years of schooling. Interestingly, divorce occurs more frequently when the wife's educational level is higher than the husband's.
- *Residence*: Divorce rates are higher in urban areas than in rural areas.
- *Second marriages*: The more often individuals have divorced, the more likely they are to divorce again.
- *Religion*: The more religious individuals are the less apt they are to divorce. Divorce rates are higher for Protestants than for Catholics or Jews. Divorce rates are also higher for interfaith marriages than for single-faith marriages.

SOURCES: William Kornblum and Joseph Julian, 2012, *Social Problems* (14th ed.). Upper Saddle River, NJ: Prentice Hall; L. A. Mooney, D. Knox, and C. Schacht, 2013, *Understanding Social Problems* (7th ed.). Belmont, CA: Brooks/Cole.

didn't work out as they had planned. It's easy to think of how unfair it all is and to blame the other partner for the failure. People may also feel self-blame and guilt.

In most divorce cases, mothers are awarded custody of the children (Papalia et al., 2012). Fathers are usually court-ordered to pay child support. But the amounts awarded are often insufficient to meet the financial needs of the children. In addition, many divorced fathers fail to pay the full amount of child support, and some do not make any payments. As a result, the income for the divorced mother and her children often plunges below the poverty level. In many cases, taxpayers wind up supporting the mother and her children through the welfare system.

The current trend is toward joint custody in divorce cases. When custody is shared, both parents are more apt to be closely involved with the children.

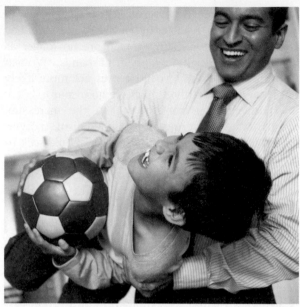

In general, children who have a good relationship with one parent are more well adjusted than children who grow up in a two-parent home where there is discord and discontent.

• • • • Ethical Questions 12.7

EP 2.1.2 *Is it desirable for mothers to be awarded custody of the children when divorce occurs? Does this tradition discriminate against fathers?*

Children of Divorce

Annually, more than 1 million children in the United States under the age of 18 are affected by a divorce (Mooney et al., 2013). These children must confront many unknowns. For instance, there is often a change of home environment, frequently to a home that is not as nice as the old one. Another issue is custody. *Legal custody* refers to whether one or both parents maintain all rights and responsibilities regarding the children.

Kaluger and Kaluger (1984) note that society places two conflicting demands on parents who are contemplating a divorce:

> One is that the couple's first concern should be with their parental roles and that they should try to put aside their marital problems, which imply that marriage roles are secondary to parental roles.

> Yet, in a society that places great emphasis on personal ego-need satisfaction in marriage, the placing of marriage in a secondary position may be difficult for the married person to accept. (p. 298)

A basic question that parents contemplating divorce ask themselves is, "Which would be better for the children—that we remain unhappily married or we end the marriage and thereby end the conflict and tension?" A key to answering this question depends on what life will be like after the divorce. In general, children grow up and become better adjusted when they have a good relationship with one parent than when they grow up in a two-parent home with discord and discontent. An inaccessible, rejecting, or hostile parent is worse than an absent one (Papalia et al., 2012).

Within five years after a divorce, three-quarters of all divorced people are remarried (Papalia et al., 2012). Therefore, most children of divorce eventually return to living in a family having an adult male and female.

The breakup of a marriage is traumatic not only for the parents but also for the children. Children appear to react more severely to a divorce than they do to the death of a parent, as children of divorce are more likely to get into trouble with the

Simon Jarratt/CORBIS

law than are those whose parent has died (Mooney et al., 2013). This delinquent behavior appears to be a reaction more to the discontent in the home that caused the divorce than to the separation and divorce itself, because children from intact homes where there is considerable conflict are also more likely to commit delinquent acts.

When parents end a marriage, the children are apt to be fearful of the future, to feel guilty for their own (usually fantasized) role in causing the breakup, to be angry at both parents, and to feel rejected by the parent who moves out. They may become irritable, accident-prone, depressed, bitter, hostile, disruptive, or even suicidal. They may suffer from skin disorders, inability to concentrate, fatigue, loss of appetite, and insomnia. They may also show less interest in their schoolwork and their social lives (Papalia et al., 2012).

Immediately after a breakup, there is considerable disruption and disorganization in family life. The parents have a variety of stresses to deal with, including economic pressures (partly the result of now maintaining two households), restrictions on recreational and social activities (more so for the custodial parent, especially if she or he is unemployed), and the need for affectionate and intimate relationships. A number of changes also occur in parent–child interactions. Divorced parents make fewer demands on the children, are less consistent in discipline, communicate less effectively with them, and have less control over them. These differences are greatest during the first year after the breakup. The first two years after a breakup tend to be stressful for everyone in the family.

A child's reaction to a divorce depends on a variety of factors, including the age and sex of the child, the length of time of severe discord in the marriage, and the length of time between the first separation and the formal divorce. A key factor in how traumatic the divorce will be for the child is how well the parents deal with the child's concerns, fears, questions, and anxieties. It is much more traumatic when parents do not explain that the breakup is not the child's fault and if the divorce and custody arrangements are hotly contested.

The trauma of divorce is exacerbated when one or both parents seek to turn the child against the other parent. Transferring anger and bitterness about the breakup to the child also increases the child's trauma. The many feelings children of divorce may experience include pain, confusion, anger, hate, bitter disappointment, a sense of failure, and self-doubt.

Children need to work through at least six major issues in order to maintain positive emotional adjustment. First, children need to accept that their parents' marriage is over. They need to understand that their parents will no longer be together and that their access to one or both parents will be changed. Second, children need to withdraw from any conflicts their parents might be having and get on with their own lives and activities. Third, children need to cope with their loss. This might include their loss of contact with a parent, home situation, family rules, or family routines. Fourth, children need to acknowledge and cope with their strong feelings of anger at their parents and of self-blame. They need to forgive all involved, stop dwelling on what went wrong, and attend to the present and future. Fifth, children need to understand that the situation is permanent. They need to relinquish any dreams they might have that their parents will get together someday. Sixth, children need to maintain a realism about their own relationships with other people. They need to understand and accept that just because their parents' relationship failed, it does not mean their own close relationships will fail.

Although the period during and immediately following a divorce is traumatic for both parents and children, the negative effects appear to lessen after two years. The worst disturbance seems to occur during the first year after the divorce. It seems that after a while the single-parent family is able to make adjustments to the new financial and social situation and regain its homeostasis. Over time, fathers also tend to become less and less available to their children. Perhaps children learn to accept their mother as the primary, single family leader. They have to (and do) adjust to the fact that a father is not always available.

A critical variable affecting children's adjustment to a divorce is the way the parents handle both the divorce and their children's feelings. For example, children react more negatively if the divorce proceedings are drawn out and bitter. Children also suffer when parents use them as a buffer and a means of transmitting hostility, because this only fosters children's confusion and resentment. As Highlight 12.10 indicates, the effects of a divorce on children depend largely on what happens after the divorce.

HIGHLIGHT 12.10

The Effects of a Divorce on Children Depend on What Happens After the Divorce

The Haag Family

Mary Beth and Doug Haag obtained a divorce after nine years of marriage. They had two children, John, 8, and David, 4. The divorce process was filled with a fair amount of emotional trauma, because both partners were uncertain whether to end the marriage. But both partners were honest in answering their children's questions about the divorce and made crystal clear to them that they were in no way at fault for the marriage ending. Mary Beth and Doug decided to each take custody of a child, partly because John wanted to live with Doug. Doug took custody of John, and Mary Beth took custody of David. The reasons for separating the children were carefully explained to them. The children frequently visited each other on weekends, holidays, and during the summer. Telephone calls between the children were frequent and encouraged.

Mary Beth and Doug respected each other after the divorce and no longer fought. Doug was an accountant, and Mary Beth, an elementary-school teacher; both earned enough so that neither was in serious financial difficulty. Doug was married a year and a half later to a woman who understood the harmonious relationship that had developed between Doug and Mary Beth after the divorce.

Mary Beth occasionally dates, but largely concentrates her free time on attending college to obtain her master's degree and on spending time with David. The home environment is now much better for all the Haags than it was in the final years of a marriage that was filled with bitterness and hostility.

The Denny Family

Robert and Corine Denny divorced after 13 years of marriage. Robert, a dentist, asked for the divorce because he was involved with one of his dental assistants. Corine was furious when she found out. Because she had stayed home to raise the children for the last 12 years, she got the larger part of the divorce settlement. She received the house, the year-old Buick, custody of the three children, and $2000 per month in child support. The reasons for the divorce were never fully explained to the children, because the parents wanted to hide the fact that Robert had been dating someone else for two years prior to the divorce. As a result, the children assumed they were responsible for causing the tension and arguments before the divorce and felt guilty because they thought they were responsible for their parents' separation.

Corine became depressed after the divorce and sought to drown her misery in vodka. She also began going out with a woman friend who was also divorced. Frequently she brought men home to stay overnight. Her standard of living dropped sharply. She refused to look for a job or seek job training and sought to live off the child-support payments. When the children were with their father (which was infrequent, because Corine tended to sabotage such times), Robert sought to dazzle his children with how well his life was now going. Both Robert and Corine sought to use the children as pawns to get back at each other. Corine viewed Robert as someone who had destroyed her comfortable life. Robert viewed Corine as an irresponsible lush.

The children suffered greatly. Their grades dropped sharply in school. They were embarrassed about having friends over because their house was a mess and they never knew when their mother would be intoxicated. The oldest daughter, Jill, 12, began skipping school and is now sexually active without using birth control. Bob, 10, was recently caught for shoplifting and is on informal supervision at the juvenile probation department. Dennis, 8, has withdrawn. He spends most of his free time watching rock videos on TV. In school he makes practically no effort, has few friends, and is receiving Ds and Fs.

The best thing parents can do is be open with the children about the fact that the marriage has failed. Children should not be made to feel that it was their fault. Parents should clearly take responsibility for their decision to part. Finally, parents should continue to be supportive of their children and understand that the children are suffering pain and loss too. Children need to be heard; they need to be able to express their anger, unhappiness, and shock. Only then can all family members begin to accept the new situation and start moving forward.

Lefrancois (1999) reviewed a number of studies of the effects on children of parental separation and divorce. One large body of research (conducted 30 to 50 years ago) found that divorce had significant negative effects on school achievement, behavior, adjustment, self-concept, and relations with both the remaining parent and the departed parent. Several explanations were offered, including the absence of one parent (the remaining parent has to struggle to raise the children alone), problems adjusting to the remaining parent (who may be in emotional turmoil over the breakup of the marriage), continuing conflict between the two parents, and economic hardship. Later investigations (Lefrancois, 1999), however, found fewer negative effects on children than did these earlier studies. Apparently, the impact of divorce was far stronger in the 1950s and 1960s than it is now. Why? Perhaps because divorces then were less culturally acceptable, both children and parents were more likely to encounter disapproval and less support from family members, the school system, and the community.

Social Work Roles: Marriage Counseling

The primary social service for people who are considering a divorce, or who have an empty-shell marriage, is marriage counseling. (Those who do divorce may also need counseling to work out adjustment problems—such as adjusting to a single person's life. Generally such counseling is one-on-one, but at times it may include the ex-spouse and the children, depending on the nature of the problem.)

Marriage counseling is provided by a variety of professionals, including social workers, psychologists, guidance counselors, psychiatrists, and members of the clergy. It is also provided by most direct social service agencies.

Marriage counselors generally use a problem-solving approach in which (1) problems are identified; (2) alternative solutions are generated; (3) the merits and shortcomings of the alternatives are examined; (4) the clients select one or more alternatives to implement; and (5) the extent to which the problems are being resolved by the alternatives are later assessed. Because the spouses own their problems, they are the primary problem solvers.

Married couples may encounter a wide range of problems. A partial list includes sexual problems, financial problems, communication problems, problems with relatives, interest conflicts, infidelity, conflicts over how to discipline and raise children, and drug or alcohol abuse problems. Marriage counselors seek to have spouses precisely identify their problems and then use the problem-solving format to resolve the issues. At times, some couples may rationally decide a divorce is in their best interests.

Marriage counselors try to see both spouses together during sessions. Practically all marital conflicts involve both partners, and therefore are best resolved when both partners work together to resolve them. (If the spouses are seen separately, each spouse is apt to become suspicious of what the other is telling the counselor.) By seeing both together, the counselor can facilitate communication between the partners and have them work together on resolving their concerns. Seeing both partners together allows each partner the opportunity to refute what the other is saying. Only in rare cases is it desirable to hold an individual session with a spouse. For example, if one partner wants to work on unwanted emotions dealing with an incestuous relationship in the past, meeting individually with that spouse might be desirable. When an individual session is held, the other spouse should be told why the session is being held and what will be discussed. If the other spouse is not informed, he or she might suspect that negative information is being related, which will increase his or her distrust of both the spouse and the counselor.

If some of the areas of conflict involve other family members (such as the children), it may be desirable to include them in some of the sessions. For example, if a father is irritated because his 14-year-old daughter is often disrespectful, the daughter may be invited to the next session to work on this subproblem.

The self-help organization Parents Without Partners serves divorced people, unwed mothers or fathers, and stepparents. It is partially a social organization, but it is also an organization to help members adjust to raising a family alone. Social workers may function as brokers in linking divorcing parents to this organization.

Divorce mediation helps spouses who have decided to obtain a divorce resolve such issues as dividing the personal property, resolving custody and child-support issues, and working out possible alimony arrangements. Some social workers are now receiving specialized training to provide divorce mediation services.

One-Parent Families

About one child in four in the United States lives in a home with only one parent present. Several reasons account for this: divorce, desertion, death of a spouse, and births outside marriage. About 90 percent of these families are headed by women. The rate of female-headed homes in African American families is nearly three times that in white families—more than 60 percent (Papalia et al., 2012). These rates have increased significantly over the past four decades. The traditional family configuration (two parents, one a

Because practically all marital conflicts involve both partners and therefore are best resolved when the partners work together on resolving their conflicts, marriage counselors try to see both spouses together.

mother who remains in the home to provide full-time child care) is becoming less and less common.

Just what effect does being raised in a one-parent home have on children? Obviously, a single parent must fulfill all the responsibilities of running a home, instead of being able to share them with a partner. A single parent wrestles with responsibilities and tasks equal to two full-time jobs in the traditional two-parent family. Research reviewed by Lefrancois (1999) parallels the findings, described earlier, regarding the effect of divorce: 30 to 50 years ago, children raised in one-parent families were found to be significantly more likely than those raised in two-parent families to experience behavioral, social, emotional, or academic problems.

It must be taken into consideration that this research was done during a time when a father's absence was considered an anomaly. Female-headed, one-parent families are much more common today. Possible negative influences on children, such as feeling different from other children or being stigmatized for their family situations, may no longer have as much adverse impact.

Poverty affects one-parent families significantly more than it does two-parent families. Differences in the average income levels of one-parent, female-headed families and two-parent families are striking.

Twenty-nine percent of female-headed families are living in poverty, compared to 7 percent of two-parent families (Mooney et al., 2013).

White mothers who live in poverty most likely have been married. Their current single status results from divorce, separation, or death of a spouse. African American mothers in poverty, however, are more likely to have borne their children without having been married (Mooney et al., 2013). See Highlight 12.11 for information on TANF, which is designed to assist one-parent families, as well as other low-income families.

Blended Families

As mentioned previously, one of two marriages in the United States ends in divorce (Papalia et al., 2012). Many people who divorce have children. Most people who divorce remarry within a few years. Some people who are marrying for the first time have parented a child while single. Some people cohabitat, and one or both partners may have children from a prior relationship. Thus, a variety of blended families are now being formed in our society.

As indicated in Chapter 4, a blended family is any nontraditional configuration of people who live together, are committed to each other, and perform

Temporary Assistance for Needy Families (TANF)

In 1996, President Bill Clinton and the Democrats and Republicans in Congress compromised on welfare reform and passed the Personal Responsibility and Work Opportunity Reconciliation Act. This act abolished the AFDC (Aid to Families with Dependent Children) program and replaced it with TANF. No longer is cash assistance to the poor an entitlement. It is now a short-term program and a variable one among the states. Key provisions of TANF are the following:

- The federal guarantee of cash assistance for poor families with children (under the AFDC program) is ended. Each state now receives a capped block grant (lump sum) to run its own welfare and work programs.
- The head of every family has to work within two years, or the family loses its benefits. After receiving welfare for two months, adults have to perform community service unless they have found regular jobs. (States can choose not to have a community service requirement.)
- Lifetime public welfare assistance is limited to five years. (States can establish stricter limits.) Hardship exemptions from this requirement are available for up to 20 percent of the recipients in a state.
- States can provide payments to unmarried teenage parents only if a mother under 18 is living at home, or in another adult-supervised setting, and attends high school or an alternative educational or training program as soon as the child is 12 weeks old.
- States are required to maintain their own spending on public welfare at 75 percent of their 1994 level, or 80 percent if they failed to put enough public welfare recipients to work.
- States cannot penalize a woman on public welfare who does not work because she cannot find day care for a child under 6 years old.
- States are required to deduct from the benefits of welfare mothers who refuse to help identify the fathers. States may deny Medicaid to adults who lose welfare benefits because of a failure to meet work requirements.
- A woman on public welfare who refuses to cooperate in identifying the father of her child must lose at least 25 percent of her benefits.
- Future legal immigrants who have not yet become citizens are ineligible for most federal welfare benefits and social services during their first five years in the United States. SSI benefits and food stamp eligibility ended in 1996 for noncitizens, including legal immigrants, receiving benefits.

Because each state has considerable leeway in designing its own version of TANF, it is accurate to say that there are 50 versions of TANF. Taking advantage of the flexibility allowed by the federal legislation, some states modified TANF services by setting stricter time limits on how long someone living in poverty could receive cash assistance. For example, Georgia and Florida set their limits at 48 months; Montana and Indiana, at 24 months; and Utah, at 36 months. Cash amounts given to TANF participants vary widely from one state to another, with Alabama and Mississippi on the low end, and California and New York on the high end.

Numerous studies have been conducted, and are continuing to be conducted, on the effects of Temporary Assistance to Needy Families. Supporters of the program tout several benefits. Critics cite a number of shortcomings.

Supporters of the program cite the following benefits:

- Employment of young single mothers (ages 18–24) has nearly doubled.
- Employment of never-married mothers has increased.
- The number of Americans on cash assistance (the AFDC program compared to TANF) has plummeted.
- Teenage birth rates have fallen since 1996. One motivation for the passage of the 1966 Welfare Reform Act was the desire to change policies that conservatives claim reward early childbearing by single mothers. The Welfare Reform Act denies public assistance payments to teenage mothers, except under the following conditions: States can provide payments to unmarried teenage parents only if a mother under 18 is living at home or in another adult-supervised setting and attends high school or an alternative educational or training program as soon as the child is 12 weeks old. The underlying reason behind denying welfare payments to most teenage mothers is to send a message to teenagers that having babies will not be financially rewarded.
- Almost all mothers (and fathers) who are working state they prefer work to welfare. Having a job may be more psychologically beneficial to the parents and to their children than being on a stigmatized welfare program. Some of these working parents may rise in socioeconomic status and have an increased sense of self-worth and a higher living status. Eventually these families will have more total income than when they received cash assistance. In such families, the children are apt to be proud of their working mothers (or parents), and such children are apt to follow their mothers' (or parents') example.

Critics of TANF cite the following shortcomings:

- Most mothers who leave the welfare rolls find jobs, but a large minority do not. Moreover, some of those who find jobs soon lose them and do not reappear on the welfare rolls.
- Some former welfare recipients are making successful transitions to work, often after many years of welfare dependency. Yet even the more successful job holders experience economic hardship and often must ask for

(continued)

⬥ **HIGHLIGHT 12.11** *(continued)*

help from family and friends. Incomes are rising at the top, but not at the bottom.

● The long-term impact of welfare reform on both single mothers and their children could well turn out to be similar to the long-term impact of deinstitutionalization on the mentally ill; good for some but terrible for others.

● There have been significant increases in the proportion of poor people, especially single mothers and their children, who are not covered by health insurance. Once people leave welfare to begin working, they may not be eligible for Medicaid, and their employers may not offer health insurance. (Implementation of Obama's Health Reform program, passed in 2010, may provide the needed health care.)

● Many working mothers report problems finding satisfactory child care. There is some evidence that young children are being left alone, sometimes for long periods. Will welfare reform end up helping parents but hurting their children?

● The people who have been kicked off the welfare rolls are pushing down wages for low-skilled workers in the United States. People desperate for food and shelter are being hired for lower wages than those currently employed, who may lose their jobs to former welfare recipients. Flooding the labor market with thousands of desperate workers has helped to lower labor costs for businesses. The welfare overhaul has depressed the median wage of all women workers. Increased competition for jobs makes it easier for employers to pay less, and harder for unions to negotiate good contracts.

● The group that has benefited most by welfare reform is employers—as this group now has a much larger pool of applicants for low-income jobs. Welfare reform has led to increased economic hardship for many low-income parents and their children.

● States now have much more choice in determining whom they will assist, what requirements they will impose upon those who receive aid, and what non-cash supports those families will receive. As a result, there is much more disparity between states than existed under AFDC. With this disparity between states, two children in identical situations in different states now live with very different realities. One may have household resources above the poverty level; stable, high-quality child care; and health insurance—the other may have none of these.

● Most of those who receive TANF do not make it above the poverty line, as TANF benefits are often below the poverty line. In addition, many of those who obtain a job often remain in poverty because the jobs are often minimum-wage (or slightly above) jobs that are below the poverty line.

● There is a serious danger that many TANF recipients will be trapped into long-term poverty. TANF programs provide almost no opportunities, via paid benefits, for TANF recipients to continue their education beyond high school. As a result TANF recipients are likely to obtain minimum-wage jobs and other "dead-end work" (work involving poor pay, scant fringe benefits, and little opportunity for advancement). The education offered to TANF recipients does not prepare or qualify them for higher-end work.

SOURCE: Alvin L. Schorr, *Welfare Reform: Failure and Remedies.* Westport, CT: Praeger Publishers, 2001; Kirk A. Johnson, Robert Rector, and Mimi Abramovitz, 2007, "Has Welfare Reform Worked?" in Howard Jacob Karger, James Midgley, Peter A. Kindle, and C. Brené Brown (eds.), *Controversial Issues in Social Policy* (3rd ed.). Boston: Pearson, pp. 200–216; William Kornblum and Joseph Julian, *Social Problems*, 14th ed. (Boston: Pearson, 2012), p. 217.

functions traditionally assumed by families. Such relationships may not involve biological or legal linkages. The important thing is that such groups *function* as families.

Many terms are used for two families that are joined together: stepfamily, blended family, reconstituted family, and nontraditional family. Regardless of which term is used, blended families involve complex situations. Variables include the number of children each member of the couple brings into the relationship and the existing relationships already established among members of the previously separate families.

In blended families, numerous adjustments have to be made. One or both partners have to adjust to raising children that are biologically parented by

someone else. The children in blended families have to form relationships with stepsiblings. The children in such families also often have to adjust to a prior divorce. Many children in blended families have to form new relationships with a biological parent who is absent from the home and with a stepparent. A man or woman who marries a divorced person who has children often has to form a relationship with the ex-spouse, as the ex-spouse is apt to have visitation rights and an impact on the family. If ex-spouses are still feuding, they are apt to use the children as pawns to create problems, thereby generating extensive strife and turmoil.

Blended families are increasing in number and proportion in our society. The family dynamics and relationships are much more complex than in the traditional nuclear family. Blended families are, in short, burdened by much more baggage than two childless adults who are forming a family for the first time. Blended families must deal with stress that arises from the losses (as a result of divorce or death) experienced by both adults and children, which can make them afraid to love and to trust. Previously established bonds between children and their biological parents may interfere with the formation of ties to the stepparent. If children go back and forth between two households, conflicts between stepchildren and stepparents may be intensified.

Some difficulties in adjustment can be anticipated (Lefrancois, 1999). Jealousies arise between new siblings. These jealousies may focus on the sharing of parental attention with the new partner and new siblings. Another issue for children is adjusting to a new parent, who may have different ideas, values, rules, and expectations. Yet another adjustment involves sharing space and property when children aren't used to sharing with these new people, or to sharing at all. Finally, if one member of the couple comes into the relationship with no child-rearing experience, an adjustment is apt to be necessary by all family members to allow time for the new parent to learn and adapt.

People come into a blended family with ideas and issues based on past experiences. Old relationships and ways of doing things still have their impacts. A blended family differs somewhat from a traditional family in that more people are involved—for example, ex-spouses, former in-laws, and an assortment of cousins, uncles, and aunts. The new couple can have both positive and negative interactions with this large supporting cast. If a prior marriage has ended bitterly, the unresolved emotions that remain will affect the present relationship.

The area of greatest stress for most stepparents is child rearing. A stepchild, used to being raised in a somewhat different way, may balk at having to conform to a new set of rules. The stepchild may also have difficulty accepting the stepparent as one who has the right to parent him or her. Such a difficulty is more likely to arise if the stepchild feels sad because the missing parent is not present. If the new couple disagree about how to raise children, the chances of conflict are substantially increased. Stepparents and stepchildren also face the problem of adjusting to each other's habits and personalities. Stepparents should not rush into establishing a relationship with stepchildren; a gradual approach is more likely to result in a trusting and positive relationship. Lefrancois (1999) notes that becoming a stepparent is usually more difficult for a woman

A blended family was created when this woman married a single dad.

because children tend to be emotionally closer to their biological mother and have spent more time with her than with the father.

Three myths about blended families can also be addressed. First, there is the myth of the wicked stepmother. This involves the idea that the stepmother is not really concerned about what is best for the children, but is more concerned about her own well-being. The story of Cinderella comes to mind. Here, the wicked stepmother cruelly keeps Cinderella from going to the ball in the hope that her own biological daughters will have a better chance at nabbing the handsome prince. In reality, stepmothers have been found to establish very positive and caring relationships with their stepchildren, provided that the stepmother has a strong self-concept and the support of her husband (Papalia et al., 2012).

A second myth about blended families is that "step is less." In other words, this myth asserts that stepchildren will never hold the same place in the hearts of parents that biological children do. This myth does not take into account the fact that people can learn to love each other and are motivated to bind members of their new family together.

The third myth about blended families is that the moment they become joined as one family, they will have instant love for each other. Relationships take time to develop and grow. The idea of instantly having strong love bonds for each other does not make sense. People involved in any relationship need time to get to know each other, test each other out, and grow to feel comfortable with each other. Kail and Cavanaugh (2010) reviewed the research literature on stepparenthood and concluded: (1) Integration tends to be easier in families that have been split by divorce than by death, perhaps because the children realize the first marriage was not working out. (2) Stepparents and stepchildren come to the blended family with unrealistic expectations that love and togetherness will rapidly occur. (3) Children tend to see a stepparent of the opposite sex as playing favorites with their own children. (4) Most children continue to miss and admire the absent biological parent. (5) Male children tend to more readily accept a stepparent, particularly if the new parent is also male. (6) Adolescents have greater difficulty accepting a stepparent than young children or adult children.

Stepfamilies need to pursue at least four tasks in order to achieve integration. The first task involves acknowledging that losses from old relationships do exist. In addition to the bad times suffered in these prior relationships, there are also memories of the good times. Recalling how good things used to be may elicit feelings of sadness that these times are gone and anger that they can be no more. As Janzen and Harris (1986) put it, "In this case, help is usually needed to assist stepfamily members in sorting out feelings, identifying sources of sadness and anger, and looking at the new family as an opportunity to develop and share meaningful relationships, without being disloyal to friends and relatives or desecrating pleasant memories from previous experiences" (p. 284).

A second task for stepfamilies is the creation of new customs and traditions. New ways of doing things need to be established to replace the old ways used in the old family structures. New traditions involve a combination of values and activities enjoyed by all new blended family members. For instance, one side of a newly blended family member celebrated at home on New Year's Eve and the other side celebrated the New Year on New Year's Day. A completely new tradition might be established where the family spends the New Year's holiday at a resort and celebrates both on New Year's Eve and New Year's Day.

The third task for blended families involves establishing new alliances within the family. Alliances may involve not only the new couple's relationship with each other, but also relationships among siblings and between parents and children. Spending time on activities together is one of several ways of working on alliances.

The fourth task for blended families is integration. Parents have the responsibility of providing organization for the family. Children need to have their limits defined and consistently upheld. One difficulty is that children are faced with a new stepparent attempting to gain control, when they have not yet enjoyed many supportive and positive experiences with this individual. It is important, therefore, for the new stepparent to provide nurturance and positive feedback to stepchildren, in addition to making rules and maintaining control.

Berman (1981) and Visher and Visher (1983) give the following suggestions to help parents in blended families increase the chances of positive relationships developing between adults and children:

1. **Understand the emotions of their children.** Although the new couple in a recently formed blended family may be fairly euphoric about their relationship, these adults need to be perceptive and responsive to the fears, concerns, and resentments of their children.

2. **Allow time for loving relationships to develop between stepparents and stepchildren.** Stepparents need to be aware that their stepchildren will probably have emotional ties to their absent biological parent, and that the stepchildren may resent the breakup of the former family. Some children may even feel they are responsible for the separation of their biological parents. Some may try to make life difficult for the stepparent so that he or she will leave, with the hope that the biological parents will then reunite. Stepparents need to be perceptive and understanding of such feelings, and patiently allow their stepchildren time to work out their concerns and to bond.

3. **New rituals, traditions, and ways of doing things** that seem right and enjoyable for all members of the blended family need to be developed. Sometimes it is helpful to move to a new house or a new apartment that does not hold memories of a past life. Leisure time should be given structure so that the children spend some time alone with the biological parent of the family, some time alone with the stepparent, some time with both of these parents together, and perhaps some time with the absent parent or parents. The new couple also need time to be alone. New rituals need to be developed for holidays, birthdays, and other special days.

4. **Seek social support.** Parents in blended families should seek to share their concerns, feelings, frustrations, experiences, coping strategies, and triumphs with other stepparents and stepchildren. Such sharing allows parents in blended families to view their own situations more realistically and to learn from the experiences of others.

Mothers Working Outside the Home

A major break with tradition has occurred with the surge of married women entering the workforce over the past several decades. Employment of married women with children under 18 has risen from 24 percent in 1950 to 40 percent in 1970 to 70 percent in 2013 (Mooney et al., 2013). Among female-headed one-parent families, 71 percent of the mothers were employed (Mooney et al., 2013). Most working mothers work full-time.

Many questions have been raised concerning the effects of working mothers (and single working custodial fathers) on the social and emotional development of children. The traditional view stressed the importance of a stable, supportive, caregiver being available consistently to meet the needs of children. In other words, it was important for a mother to remain in the home and coordinate the family's care and activities. However, research indicates that women do not have to remain home in order to maintain a well-adjusted family.

Reviews of the research on working mothers and their children conclude that if the mother is satisfied with her job and the provision for child care is reasonably good and suitable, there is no adverse effect on the child's development (Papalia et al., 2012). Many contemporary researchers emphasize the positive effects of a mother's employment on her entire family.

Some questions have been raised concerning the effects on children under age 3 when mothers work outside the home. These questions tend to revolve around the issue of maternal deprivation (i.e., that infants are emotionally deprived if they do not have enough contact with their mothers). Concerns were initially raised after some early research indicated that institutionalized infants suffered negative effects. This research related these negative effects to the fact that the mother was absent. However, could these effects have been due to the fact that the infants received inadequate care and very little attention from anyone? It may not necessarily be that they specifically missed their mothers.

There is no simple answer to the question about the effects on children of their mothers' working. Children need consistent nurturance, guidance, and care. Home conditions vary widely. Not all biological mothers provide adequate care and attention to their young children. Also, the conditions under which a mother works vary tremendously. Some mothers love their jobs; others hate having to work. The level of the mother's overall satisfaction with life must affect the child.

Indications are that good child care—that is, child care that provides the child with consistent attention and care—does not harm a child. Much of the research on the effects on children of mothers working was performed in good facilities with high-quality care. Many parents find it difficult to get good child care for a number of reasons, including cost, location, hours available, type of care, and age restrictions on children. Substantial concerns exist when the single mother works outside the home (or when both parents work outside the home) and the children receive poor child care or no care. It seems that the ideal solution is to make enough good alternative care available so that mothers can work with the knowledge that their children are well cared for.

Another issue is the role of the father in caring for children in those cases where a father is present in the home. Can't the father be a primary participant in child care? It's interesting that the term *maternal deprivation* is commonly used, whereas the parallel term *paternal deprivation* is not. In reality, mothers, whether they work outside the home or not, generally maintain the primary responsibility for child care in our society.

Child rearing is most often seen as the mother's responsibility. However, perhaps this idea was more credible when few women worked outside the home. Perhaps changing attitudes to encourage shared parenting would be in the best interest of families.

The "Sandwich" Generation

Many middle-aged adults are "sandwiched" between two generations—their parents and their children. This puts great demands and pressures on them. Because older adults are the fastest-growing age group in terms of numbers in our society, an increasing proportion of middle-aged adults will find themselves providing care for their parents as well as their children. Some middle-aged adults have their children and a parent or two living with them. People find it difficult to find the time and resources to respond to the needs and demands of their work, their children, and their parents.

Middle-aged adults who feel the obligations of caring for both their children and their aging parents may be torn between love and resentment. They love both their children and their parents—but may resent that caring for their parents may deprive them of any chance to fulfill their dreams of getting involved in more enjoyable activities.

For members of the sandwich generation who are working outside the home, flexible work schedules can help alleviate the stresses associated with both caregiving responsibilities and work responsibilities. The Family and Medical Leave Act, adopted in 1993, guarantees family caregivers some unpaid leave. In addition, some large corporations provide time off for caregiving.

LO 12-4 Understand Material on Assessing and Intervening in Family Systems

Assessing and Intervening in Family Systems

Families are characterized by multiple ongoing interactions. When social workers intervene with families, there is much to observe and understand. The dimensions of family interaction that will be discussed here include communication, family norms, and problems commonly faced by families. In addition, two prominent family-assessment instruments will be described: the ecomap and the genogram.

Verbal and Nonverbal Communication

Communication involves transmitting information from one person to another, using a common system of symbols, signs, or behaviors. Verbal communication involves the use of words and will be addressed first.

The first phase of verbal communication involves the translation of thoughts into words. The information sender must know the correct words and how to put them together. Only then will the information have the chance of being effectively received. The sender may be vague or inaccurate in forming the message, and interruptions and distractions may detract from the communication process.

The information receiver then must be receptive to the information. That is, he or she must be paying attention both to the sender and to the sender's words. The receiver must understand what the specific words mean. Inaccuracies or problems at any point in this process can stop the information from getting across to the receiver. At any point, distortions may interfere.

Verbal communication patterns inside the family include who talks a lot and who talks only rarely. They involve who talks to whom and who defers to whom. They also reflect the subtle and not so subtle qualities involved in family members' relationships.

The sender also transmits nonverbal messages along with the verbal messages. These include facial expressions, body posture, emotions displayed, and many other subtle aspects of communication. Somewhere between verbal and nonverbal aspects of communication are voice inflection, intonation, and loudness. All this gives the receiver additional information about the intent and specific meaning of the message that's being sent. Sometimes the receiver will attribute more value to the nonverbal aspects of the message than to the verbal.

For example, a 17-year-old son asks his father, "Dad, can I have the car next Saturday night?" Dad, who's in the middle of writing up his tax returns (which are due in two days), replies "No." Harry interprets this to mean that his father is an authoritarian tyrant who does not trust him with the family car. Harry stomps off in a huff. However, what Dad was really thinking was that he and Mom need the car this Saturday because they're taking their best friends, the Jamesons, out for their 20th wedding anniversary. Dad was also thinking that perhaps the Jamesons wouldn't mind driving. Or maybe he and Harry could work something out to share the car. At any rate, Dad really meant that he was much too involved with the tax forms to talk about it and would rather discuss it during dinner.

This is a good example of ineffective communication. The information was vague and incomplete, and neither person clarified his thoughts or gave feedback to the other. There are endless variations to the types of ineffective communication that can take place in families. Social workers can often help to clarify, untangle, and reconstruct communication patterns.

One especially important aspect of assessing messages is whether they are congruent or incongruent. Communication is *incongruent* when two or more messages contradict each other's meaning. In other words, the messages are confusing. Contradictory messages within families disturb effective family functioning.

Nonverbal messages can sometimes contradict verbal messages. For example, a recently widowed woman says, "I'm sorry Frank passed away," with a big grin on her face. The information expressed by the words indicates that she is sad. However, her accompanying physical expression shows that she is happy. Her words are considered socially appropriate for the situation. However, in this particular case, she seems relieved to get rid of "the old buzzard" and happy to be the beneficiary of a large life insurance policy.

The double message reflected by the widow's verbal and nonverbal behavior provides a relatively simple, clear-cut illustration of potential problem communication within families. However, congruence is certainly not the only important aspect of nonverbal communication. All of the principles of nonverbal communication discussed in Chapter 11 can be applied to communication within families.

Family Norms

Family *norms* are the rules that specify what is considered proper behavior within the family group. Many times the most powerful rules are those that are not clearly and verbally stated. Rather, these are implicit rules or repeated family transactions that all family members understand but never discuss. It's important for families to establish norms that allow both the entire family and each individual member to function effectively and productively.

Every family differs in its individual set of norms or rules. For example, the Myers family believes the husband's role is to earn enough money to support his wife and three children. Mr. Myers works as a bus driver for the city he lives in, and makes about $50,000 a year. He works 40 hours a week, and then is free to lie on the couch or pursue his hobbies of hunting and fishing. His wife is expected to stay at home, raise the children, and perform all the household tasks. She also home-schools the three school-age children. The Myers attend a fundamentalist church that urges the wife to play a supportive role to her husband. Mrs. Myers is unaware that she puts in more than 100 hours per week performing all her teaching and domestic tasks. The children are expected to concentrate on their studies, and are not asked to help out around the house. As a result, Mrs. Myers is becoming physically and emotionally exhausted, looks haggard, and her blood pressure is elevated.

The Woodbeck family has very different norms. Mr. and Mrs. Woodbeck value earning a lot of money so that the family can take exotic vacations and live a life of luxury. Mr. Woodbeck is an attorney, and Mrs. Woodbeck is a physician. They have a live-in housekeeper, Donna Maloney, who performs most of the domestic tasks. The Woodbecks send their two teenage children to a private high school and have urged them to aspire to attend prestigious colleges and eventually become high-paid professionals. Mr. and Mrs. Woodbeck cherish the values that the school is helping to instill in their children, as well as the socialization components of the school. Mr. and Mrs. Woodbeck have few hobbies, as both of them work an average of 70-plus hours per week. Their free time is spent primarily on family activities.

Social workers need to help families identify and understand that inappropriate, ineffective norms can be changed. For example, it simply is not in Mrs. Myers's best interest to be putting in more than 100 hours a week on home-schooling and domestic tasks. If a social worker became involved (perhaps after a referral from Mrs. Myers's physician, who is concerned about her blood pressure), that social worker could help Mrs. Myers (and probably eventually Mr. Myers) to examine the family norms that are adversely affecting her. Once such norms are identified, the social worker could help them clarify alternative solutions and help them assess which is the best solution for them.

Family System Assessment: The Ecomap

An *ecomap* is a paper-and-pencil assessment tool that practitioners use to assess specific troubles and plan interventions for clients. The ecomap is a drawing of the client/family in its social environment. An ecomap is usually drawn jointly by the social worker and the client. It helps both the worker and the client achieve a holistic or ecological view of the client's family life and the nature of the family's relationships with groups, associations, organizations, other families, and individuals. It has been used in a variety of situations, including marriage and family counseling, and adoption and foster-care home studies. The ecomap has also been used to supplement traditional social histories and case records. It is a shorthand method for recording basic social information. The technique helps users (clients and practitioners) gain insight into clients' problems and better sort out how to make constructive changes.

The technique provides a "snapshot view" of important interactions at a particular point in time. The primary developer of the technique is Ann Hartman (1978).

A typical ecomap consists of a family diagram surrounded by a set of circles and lines used to describe the family within an environmental context. The ecomap user can create her or his own abbreviations and symbols (see Figure 12.2).

To draw an ecomap, a circle (representing the client's family) is placed in the center of a large, blank sheet of paper (see Figure 12.3). The composition of the family is indicated within the family circle. A number of other circles are drawn in the area surrounding the family circle. These represent the other systems (i.e., the groups, other families, individuals, and organizations) with which the family ordinarily interacts.

Different kinds of lines are drawn to describe the nature of the relationships that the members of the client family have with the other systems. The directional flow of energy (indicating giving and/or receiving of resources and communication between the client family members and the significant

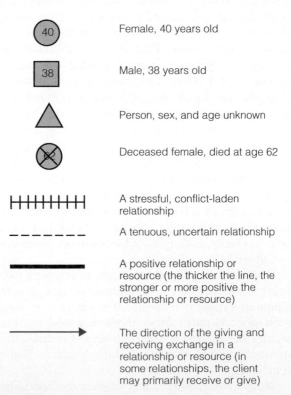

FIGURE 12.2 Commonly Used Symbols in an Ecomap

An ecomap is an assessment tool for depicting the relationships and interactions between a client family and its social environment. The largest circle in the center depicts the client family. The surrounding circles represent the significant groups, organizations, other families, and individuals that make up the family's social environment.

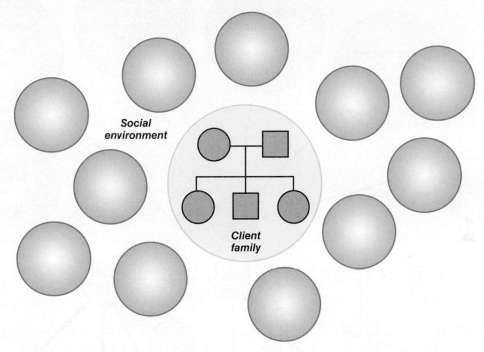

Social environment

Client family

FIGURE 12.3 Setting Up an Ecomap

systems) is expressed by the use of arrows. A case example of the use of an ecomap follows.

Barb and Mike Haynes are referred to the Adult Services Unit of the Greene County Human Services Department by Dean Medical Clinic. The clinic has been treating Mike's mother, Ruth Haynes, for Alzheimer's disease since she was diagnosed with the disorder four years ago. For the past three years she has been living with Barb and Mike. She now requires round-the-clock care, because during the evening hours she has trouble sleeping, wanders around the house, and starts screaming when she becomes lost and confused. Dean Medical Clinic has referred Barb and Mike Haynes to the Adult Services Unit to explore alternative caregiving arrangements.

Barb and Mike Haynes meet with Maria Garcia, Adult Services Worker. They indicate that they feel a moral obligation to continue caring for Ruth in their home, because Ruth spent most of her adult years caring for Mike and his brother and sister when they were children. Barb and Mike also indicate that they have a 2-year-old child, Erin, at home. This is a second marriage for both Barb and Mike, and they are paying for Mike's son, Brian, to attend the state university. With such expenses, both believe they need to continue to work. Mike's oldest sister, Mary Kruger, is a single parent who has two children in high school. Mary Kruger has a visual disability but has been able to be the primary care-giver for Ruth and Erin during the daylight hours when Mike and Barb are at work. Recently, Mary informed Mike and Barb that caring for Ruth is becoming too difficult and that some kind of alternative care is needed. Ms. Garcia suggests that adult day care for Ruth may be a useful resource.

Mike adds that it is emotionally devastating to see his mother slowly deteriorate. He indicates he is in a double bind; he feels an obligation to care for his mother, but doing so is causing major disruptions in his family life. The stress has resulted in marital discord with Barb, and he adds that both he and Barb have become increasingly short in temper and patience with Erin.

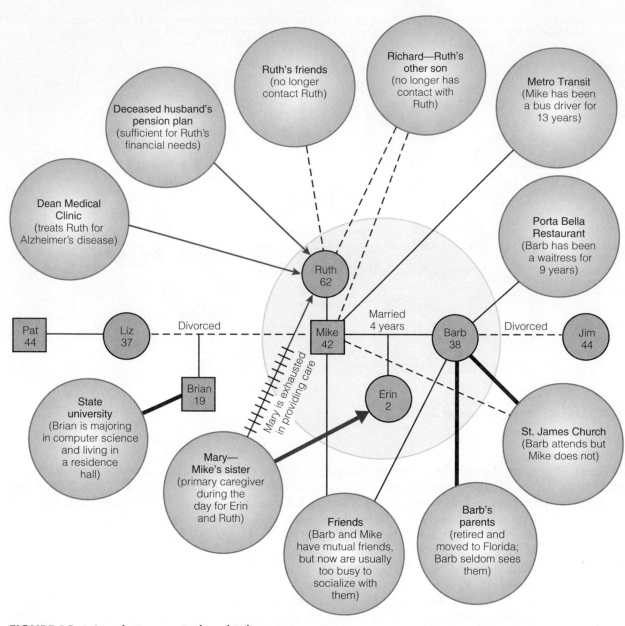

FIGURE 12.4 Sample Ecomap: Barb and Mike Haynes

At this point, Ms. Garcia suggests it may be helpful to graphically diagram their present dilemma. Together, the Hayneses and Ms. Garcia draw the ecomap shown in Figure 12.4. While drawing the map, Mike inquires whether Ruth's medical condition might soon stabilize. Ms. Garcia indicates that Ruth may occasionally appear to stabilize, but the long-term prognosis is gradual deterioration in mental functioning and in physical capabilities. The ecomap helps Mike and Barb see that even though they are working full-time during the day and spending the remainder of their waking hours caring for Erin and Ruth, they are becoming too emotionally and physically exhausted to continue doing so. During the past three years, they have ceased socializing with friends. Now they seldom have any time to spend even with Brian. Feeling helpless and hopeless, they inquire if some other care arrangement is available besides a nursing home. They indicate that Ruth has said on numerous occasions, "I'd rather die now than be placed in a nursing home." Ms. Garcia tells them of some high-quality adult group homes in the area and gives them the addresses.

After visiting a few of the care facilities, Barb and Mike ask Ruth to stay for a few days at one they particularly like. At first Ruth is opposed to going for a "visit." But after being there a few days, she adjusts fairly well and soon concludes (erroneously, but no one objects) that it is a home she bought and that the people on the staff are her "domestic employees." Ruth's adjustment eases the guilt that Barb and Mike feel in placing Ruth in a care facility, and this results in substantial improvements in their marital relationship and in their interactions with Erin, Brian, and their friends.

A major value of an ecomap is that it facilitates both the worker's and the client's view of the client's family from a systems and an ecological perspective. Sometimes, as happened in the case of the Hayneses, the drawing of the ecomap helps clients and practitioners gain greater insight into the social dynamics of a problematic situation.

Family System Assessment: The Genogram

A *genogram* is a graphic way of investigating the origins of a client's problem by diagramming the family over at least three generations. The client and the worker usually construct the family genogram jointly. The genogram is essentially a family tree. Murray Bowen is the primary developer of this technique (Kerr & Bowen, 1988). The genogram is a useful tool for the worker and family members to examine problematic emotional and behavioral patterns in an intergenerational context. Emotional and behavioral patterns in families tend to repeat themselves; what happens in one generation will often occur in the next. Genograms help family members to identify and understand family relationship patterns.

Figure 12.5 shows some of the commonly used symbols. Together, the symbols provide a visual representation of at least three generations of a family, including names, ages, genders, marital status, sibling positions, and so on. When relevant, additional items of information may be included, such as emotional difficulties, behavioral problems,

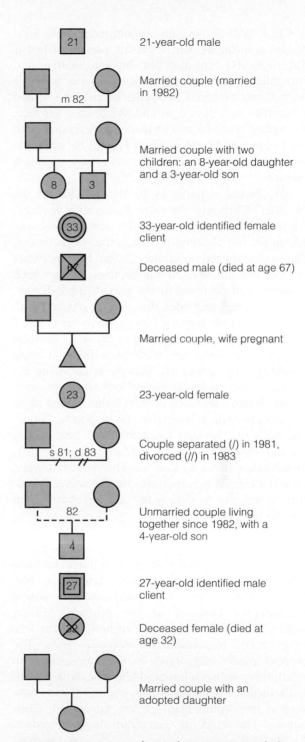

FIGURE 12.5 Commonly Used Genogram Symbols

religious affiliation, ethnic origins, geographic locations, occupations, socioeconomic status, and significant life events. The following case example illustrates the use of a genogram.

Chris Witt makes an appointment with Kyle Nolan, a social worker in private practice. Chris is distraught. He indicates that his wife, Karen, and two children are currently at Sister House, a shelter for battered women. Chris states he and his wife had a "scuffle" two days ago, and she bruised her face. Yesterday, when he was at work, she left home with the children and went to Sister House. He adds that she has contacted an attorney and is now seeking a divorce.

Mr. Nolan inquires as to the specifics of the "scuffle." Chris says he came home after having a few beers. His dinner was cold, and he "got on" Karen for not cleaning up the house. He adds that Karen then started mouthing off, and he slapped her to shut her up. Mr. Nolan inquires whether such incidents had occurred in the past. Chris indicates, "A few times," and adds that getting physical with Karen is the only way for him to "keep her in line." He says he works all day long in his small business as a concrete contractor, while his wife sits at home watching soap operas. He feels she is not doing her fair share and the house usually looks like a disaster.

Mr. Nolan asks Chris if he feels that getting physical with his wife is justifiable. He responds, "Sure," and adds that his dad frequently told him, "Spare the rod, and spoil both the wife and the kids." Mr. Nolan asks Chris if his dad was abusive to him when he was a child. Chris indicates that he was and adds that to this day he detests his dad for abusing him and his mother.

Mr. Nolan then suggests that together they draw a family tree, focusing on three areas: episodes of heavy drinking, episodes of physical abuse, and traditional versus modern gender stereotypes. Mr. Nolan explains that a *traditional gender stereotype* includes the husband as the primary decision maker, the wife as submissive to him, and the wife as primarily responsible for domestic tasks. The *modern gender stereotype* involves an egalitarian relationship between husband and wife. After an initial reluctance (Chris expresses confusion as to how such a tree would help get his wife back), Chris agrees. The resulting genogram is presented in Figure 12.6.

The genogram helps Chris to see that he and his wife are products of family systems that have strikingly different values and customs. In his family, the males tend to drink heavily, have a traditional view of marriage, and tend to use physical force in

interactions with their spouses and children. Upon questioning, Chris mentions that he has at times struck his own children. Mr. Nolan asks Chris how he feels about repeating the same patterns of abuse with his wife and children that he despised his father for using. Tears come to his eyes, and he says one word, "Guilty."

Mr. Nolan and Chris discuss what Chris might do to change his family interactions and how he might best approach his wife to request that she and the children return. Chris agrees to attend AA (Alcoholics Anonymous) meetings and a therapy group for batterers. After a month of attending these meetings, Chris contacts his wife and asks her to return. Karen agrees to return *if* Chris stops drinking (most of the abuse occurred when he was intoxicated) and *if he* agrees to continue to attend group therapy and AA meetings. Chris readily agrees. Karen's parents express their disapproval of her returning.

For the first few months, Chris Witt is on his best behavior, and there is considerable harmony in the Witt family. Then one day Chris has to fire one of his employees. Feeling bad, he stops afterward at a tavern and drinks until he is intoxicated. When he finally arrives home, he starts to verbally and physically abuse Karen and the children. This is the final straw for Karen. She takes the children to her parents' house, where they stay for several days until they are able to find and move into an apartment. She also files for divorce and follows through in obtaining one.

In many ways, this is not a success case (in reality, many cases are not). The genogram, however, was useful in helping Chris realize that he had acquired, and was acting out, certain dysfunctional family patterns. Unfortunately, he was not yet fully ready to make lasting changes. Perhaps sometime in the future he will be more committed to making changes. At the present time, he has returned to drinking heavily.

The ecomap and the genogram have a number of similarities. With both techniques, users gain insight into family dynamics. Some of the symbols used in the two approaches are identical. There are also differences. The ecomap focuses attention on a family's interactions with groups, resources, organizations, associations, other families, and other individuals. The genogram focuses attention on intergenerational family patterns, particularly those that are problematic or dysfunctional.

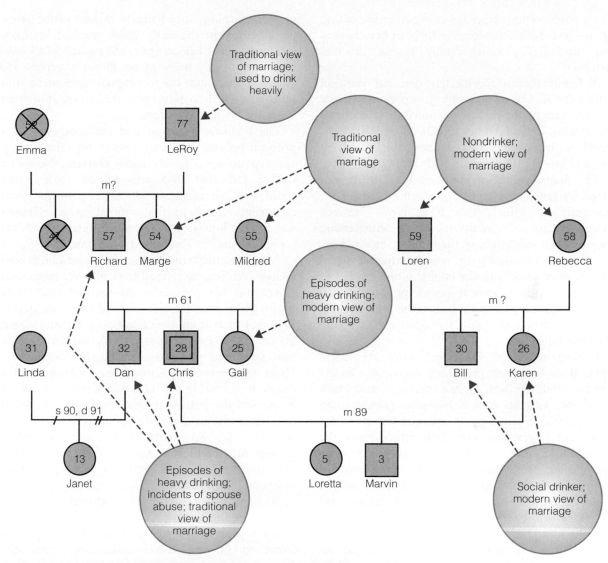

FIGURE 12.6 Sample Genogram: The Chris and Karen Witt Family

Family Problems and Social Work Roles

Thorman (1982) points out that although each family is unique, conflicts and problems within families tend to cluster in four major categories: (1) marital problems between the husband and wife; (2) difficulties between parents and children; (3) personal problems of individual family members; and (4) stresses imposed on the family by the external environment.

Family problems do not necessarily fall neatly into one or another of these categories. Frequently, families experience more than one category of problems. Nor are these problem categories mutually exclusive. Many times one problem will be closely related to another. Consider, for instance, the wife and mother of a family who is a department store manager and the primary breadwinner for her family. The store at which she has been working for the past 11 years suddenly goes out of business. Despite massive efforts, she is unable to find another job with similar responsibilities and salary. This can be considered a family problem caused by stresses in the environment. However, this is also a personal problem for the wife and mother. Her sense of self-worth is seriously diminished by her job loss and inability to find another position. She becomes cranky, short-tempered, and difficult to live with.

The environmental stress she is experiencing causes her to have difficulties relating to both her children and spouse. The entire family system becomes disturbed.

A family therapy perspective sees any problem within the family as a family group problem, not as a problem on the part of any one individual member (Okun & Rappaport, 1980). Social workers, therefore, need to assess the many dimensions of the problem and the effects on all family members.

The first category of problems typically experienced by families is marital problems between the husband and wife. Although problems between spouses affect all family members, intervention may target a subsystem of the family—in this case, the marital subsystem. In other words, a social worker may work with the couple alone instead of the entire family to solve a specific problem. When the marital pair gets along better, the entire family will be positively affected. A marital problem case example follows.

Gianna and Mark Di Franco were married in 1998. Both had been previously divorced. Gianna had two children from a prior marriage, and Mark had four. Gianna was a financial planner who owned her own company. Mark was vice president of a much larger company. Both earned about the same amount. On the night before they were married, Mark presented Gianna with a prenuptial agreement. It stated that the assets each brought into the marriage would be kept separate, and would be the property of the person bringing it into the marriage if a divorce occurred. The agreement also stated that each spouse would pay an equal share of the family expenses. Mark said he would not marry Gianna unless she signed the agreement. Gianna did not want to call off the wedding, so she signed the agreement.

After three years of marriage, Gianna had two major concerns. First, when Mark became angry with her, he would refuse to talk to her—often for as long as two weeks. Gianna often did not know "what she did wrong." Mark, after pouting for a while, would eventually start talking again. When she asked why he'd stopped communicating, he'd always respond, "If you can't figure it out, I'm not going to tell you."

Gianna's second concern was financial. Mark became president of his company and received a big increase in salary. Gianna, on the other hand, saw her earnings sliced nearly in half as the stock market drop in the early 2000s resulted in much less business for her company. She asked Mark several times to pay more of the family expenses. He always pulled out the prenuptial agreement and said he wanted to pay his extra money into trust funds for his four children.

The financial situation and the communication problem became such major issues for Gianna that she went to see a family social worker. The social worker indicated that progress on these issues could only be made if Mark came in for joint counseling. Mark at first refused to go. Gianna had to give him an ultimatum: "Either go with me for counseling, or I'm filing for divorce."

Mark relented and went for counseling with Gianna. At first, he refused to change the prenuptial agreement, but eventually he realized that if he didn't pay more of the household expenses, and if he didn't start communicating with Gianna about his concerns, she was going to file for divorce. He thus agreed to pay more of the family expenses. However, the communication issue was more of a hurdle for him. He was raised in a family in which he learned the pattern of not communicating from his father, who also would stop speaking for a week or two to his wife when he was angry with her. Gianna adopted the strategy of making a counseling appointment for Mark and her whenever Mark stopped talking to her for a day or two.

Richard B. Stuart (1983) developed a Couple's Pre-Counseling Inventory, which is used to assess a couple's problems. Each member of the couple is asked to fill out the questionnaire separately. Later, answers can be shared during counseling, and misconceptions each has about how the other person feels can be clarified. Areas that are evaluated include happiness with the relationship; caring behaviors liked, and perceptions of caring behaviors liked, by the partner; communication; how conflict is managed; how moods and other aspects of personal life are managed; sexual interaction; how children are managed; willingness to make changes; marital history; and specific goals each person wants to pursue.

Such an instrument provides an excellent mechanism for assessment because misconceptions between partners can be clearly pinpointed. For instance, under the topic of sexual interaction, members of the couple are asked to respond to a variety of statements, indicating their levels of satisfaction with the issue involved. The range is from 5, which means "very satisfied," to 1, which means "very dissatisfied." One statement concerns "the length of our foreplay." If one partner is very satisfied and the other very dissatisfied, this is clearly an area that needs to be addressed.

The second major type of family problem involves relationships between parents and children, including parents' difficulties controlling their children and, especially as children reach adolescence, communication problems.

There are many perspectives on child management and parent–child communication techniques. Two major approaches are the application of learning theory and Parent Effectiveness Training (PET), developed by Thomas Gordon (1970). Practitioners can help parents improve their control of children by assessing the individual family situations and teaching parents some basic behavior modification techniques. Behavior modification involves the application of learning theory principles to real-life situations. Practitioners can also teach the use of PET techniques. (The application of learning theory principles to positive parenting was discussed in Chapter 4, and PET was described in Chapter 8.)

Personal problems of individual family members make up the third category of problems typically experienced by families.

For example, John and Tara Altman brought their 12-year-old son, Terrell, into treatment because for two years he had shown decreasing interest in doing his schoolwork. His grades also slowly fell from a B average to one D (in physical education) and the rest Fs. The school system was considering recommending that Terrell repeat the seventh grade. John and Tara asked the social worker to "inspire" Terrell to become refocused on his schoolwork. The social worker asked Terrell why his grades had slid. He replied that his mom and dad used to help him with his schoolwork, but they had stopped showing much interest in him. In fact, it seemed that his parents had stopped talking to one another in the past two and a half years.

At this point, the social worker decided to meet at the next session with just John and Tara to explore what was happening between them. At that session, Tara revealed she had discovered two and a half years earlier that John had had a brief affair with one of her best friends shortly after they were married,

and she was unable to forgive him. At first, she was furious with John, but now she had become so depressed that she was on Prozac. She had given up talking to John, and they had not been intimate since her discovery. John acknowledged that he had had the affair, and said he was trying to do everything in his power to restore their former relationship. John added that he had thrown himself into his work as an electrician in order to escape his wife's wrath. He was also concerned that Tara was drinking too much. Tara said alcohol helped her escape the pain of knowing that John had had an affair. And she was seriously thinking about divorcing John once Terrell graduated from high school.

The social worker helped John and Tara see that Terrell's lack of interest in school was related to his parents' showing little interest in him; it was also his way of adapting to the animosity between John and Tara. The social worker helped Tara see that she needed to either divorce John now or let go of focusing on the pain she felt about the affair. After considerable reflection, Tara said she wanted to find a way to let go. The social worker helped her learn to tell herself "Stop" whenever she began to think about the affair, and to then think instead of positive attributes about John and her family. This process of learning to let go took Tara about three months to fully implement.

During this period, both Tara and John focused much more of their attention, in positive ways, on Terrell. He began refocusing on his schoolwork, his grades began to improve, and he also became more contented.

The Altman family provides a good illustration of a family-owned problem. All three family members were hurting emotionally. Terrell was the identified client, but all three family members needed to make changes in order for the family to function more effectively.

The fourth category of problems frequently found in families includes problems caused by factors outside the family. These problems may include inadequate income, unemployment, poor housing, inadequate access to means of transportation and places for recreation, and lack of job opportunities. Also included in the multitude of potential problems are poor health, inadequate schools, and dangerous neighborhoods.

To begin addressing these problems, social workers need effective brokering skills. That is, they need to know what services are available, and how to make a connection between families in need and these services.

Many times, appropriate services will be unavailable or nonexistent. Social workers will need to advocate, support, or even help to develop appropriate resources for their clients. Services that do not exist will need to be developed. Unresponsive agency administrations will need to be confronted. Legal assistance may be needed. There are no easy solutions to solving such nationwide problems as poverty or poor health care. This is an ongoing process, and political involvement may be necessary. Such environmental stresses pose serious problems for families, and social work practitioners cannot ignore them.

LO 12-5 Summarize Material on Social Work with Organizations, Including Several Theories of Organizational Behavior

When we first talk with students in classes about social work with organizations, they tend to "yawn," and show little interest. They tend to view such material as being irrelevant to their lives. Their interest, however, is usually accelerated when we note that most social workers are employed in agencies (which are organizations), and that it is critical that social work students learn "how to survive and thrive" in agencies/organizations.

Social Work with Organizations

As defined in Chapter 1, organizations are "(1) social entities that (2) are goal-directed, (3) are designed as deliberately structured and coordinated activity systems, and (4) are linked to the external environment" (Daft, 2007, p. 10). *Social entities* involve groups of people, all having their own strengths, needs, ideas, and quirks. Organizations are *goal-directed* in that they exist to accomplish some purpose or meet some need. As an *activity system*, an organization is made up of a coordinated series of units accomplishing different tasks yet working together to achieve some common end. Finally, organizations are in constant interaction with other people, decision makers, agencies, neighborhoods, and communities in the *external social environment* as they strive to achieve goals.

It is imperative that social workers have an extensive knowledge of organizations. As Chapter 1 indicates, working with organizations is one of the systems in which social workers are expected to have expertise. Highlight 12.12 expands on the importance of social workers being skilled in understanding and analyzing organizations. Several theories of organizational behavior are presented in this section. These different theories provide a variety of perspectives for viewing and analyzing organizations.

The Autocratic Model

The autocratic model has been in existence for thousands of years. During the Industrial Revolution, it was the predominant model for how an organization should function. This model depends on *power*. Those who are in power act autocratically. The message to employees is, "You do this—or else"; an employee who does not follow orders is penalized, often severely.

An autocratic model uses one-way communication—from the top to the workers. Management believes that it knows what is best. The employee's obligation is to follow orders. Employees have to be persuaded, directed, and pushed into performance, and this is management's task. Management does the thinking, and the workers obey the directives. Under autocratic conditions, the workers' role is *obedience* to management.

The autocratic model does work in some settings. Most military organizations throughout the world are formulated on this model. The model was also used successfully during the Industrial Revolution, for example, in building great railroad systems and in operating giant steel mills.

The autocratic model has a number of disadvantages. Workers are often in the best position to identify shortcomings in the structure and technology of the organizational system, but one-way communication prevents feedback to management. The model also fails to generate much of a commitment among the workers to accomplish organizational goals. Finally, the model fails to motivate workers to put forth an effort to further develop their skills (skills that often would be highly beneficial to the employer).

The Custodial Model

Many decades ago, when the autocratic model was the predominant model of organizational behavior,

HIGHLIGHT 12.12

Analyzing a Human Services Organization

It is essential that a social worker understand and analyze not only the agency or organization that she or he works for but also the other agencies and organizations that she or he interacts with. Some questions that are useful in analyzing an agency or organization are the following:

1. What is the mission statement of the organization?
2. What are the major problems of the organization's clients?
3. What services does the organization provide?
4. How are client needs determined?
5. What percentage of clients are people of color, women, gays or lesbians, older adults, or members of other at-risk populations?
6. What was the total cost of services of this organization in the past year?
7. How much money is spent on each program?
8. What are the organization's funding sources?
9. How much money and what percentage of funds does the organization receive from each source?
10. What types of clients does the organization refuse?
11. What other organizations provide the same services in the community?
12. What is the organizational structure? For example, does the organization have a formal chain of command?

13. Is there an informal decision-making process and structure at the organization? (That is, are there people who exert more influence than would be expected from their formal positions in the bureaucracy of the organization?)
14. How much input do the direct service providers at the organization have on major policy decisions?
15. Does the organization have a board that oversees its operations? If so, what are the backgrounds of the board members?
16. Do employees at every level feel valued?
17. What is the morale among employees?
18. What are the major unmet needs of the organization?
19. Does the organization have a handbook of personnel policies and procedures?
20. What is the public image of the organization in the community?
21. What has been the rate of turnover in recent years among the staff at the organization? What were departing staff members' major reasons for leaving?
22. Does the organization have a process for evaluating the outcomes of its services? If so, what is the process, and what are the outcome results?

some progressive managers began to study their employees. They found that the autocratic model often resulted in the employees' feeling insecure about their continued employment. Employees also had feelings of aggression toward management. Because the employees could not express their discontent directly, they expressed it indirectly. Some vented their anger on their families and neighbors, and the entire community suffered. Others sabotaged production. Davis and Newstrom (1989) described sabotage in a wood-processing plant:

> *Managers treated workers crudely, sometimes even to the point of physical abuse. Since employees could not strike back directly for fear of losing their jobs, they found another way to do it. They symbolically fed their supervisor to a log-shredding machine! They did this by purposely destroying good sheets of veneer, which made the supervisor look bad when monthly efficiency reports were prepared. (p. 31)*

In the 1890s and 1900s, some progressive employers thought that if these feelings could be alleviated, employees might feel more like working, which would increase productivity. To satisfy the employees' security needs, a number of companies began to provide welfare programs such as pension programs, child-care centers, health insurance, and life insurance.

The custodial approach leads to employee dependence on the organization. According to Davis and Newstrom (1989), "If employees have ten years of seniority under the union contract and a good pension program, they cannot afford to quit even if the grass looks greener somewhere else!" (p. 31).

Employees working under a custodial model tend to focus on their economic rewards and benefits. They are happier and more content than under the autocratic model, but they do not have a high commitment to helping the organization accomplish its goals. They tend to give *passive cooperation* to their employer. The model's most evident flaw is that most employees are producing substantially below their capacities. They are not motivated to advance to higher capacities. Most such employees do not feel fulfilled or motivated at their place of work. In summary, contented employees (which the custodial model is designed to ensure) are not necessarily the most productive.

The Scientific Management Model

One of the earliest and most important schools of thought on the management of functions and tasks in the workplace was based on the work of Frederick Taylor (1947). Taylor was a mechanical engineer, an American industrialist, and an educator. He focused primarily on management techniques that would lead to increased productivity. He asserted that many organizational problems in the workplace involved misunderstandings between managers and workers. Managers erroneously thought that workers were lazy and unemotional, and they mistakenly believed they understood workers' jobs. Workers mistakenly thought that managers cared most about exploiting them.

To solve these problems, Taylor developed the *scientific management model*, which focused on the need for managers to conduct a scientific analysis of the workplace. One of the first steps was to conduct a careful study of how each job could best be accomplished. An excellent way to do this, according to Taylor, was to identify the best worker at each job and then carefully study how he or she did the work. The goal of this analysis was to discover the optimal way of doing the job—in Taylor's words, the "one best way." Once this best way was identified, tools could be modified to better complete the work, workers' abilities and interests could be fitted to particular job assignments, and the level of production that the average worker could sustain could be gauged.

Once the level of production for the average worker was determined, Taylor indicated that the next step was to provide incentives to increase productivity. His favorite strategy was the piece-rate wage, in which workers were paid for each unit they produced. The goals were to produce more units, reduce unit cost, increase organizational productivity and profitability, and provide incentives for workers to produce more.

Taylor's work has been criticized as having a "technicist" bias, because it tends to treat workers as little more than cogs on a wheel. No two workers are exactly alike, so the "one best way" of doing a job is often unique to the person doing it. In fact, forcing the same work approach on different workers may actually decrease both productivity and worker satisfaction. In addition, Taylor's approach has limited application to human services providers. Because each client is unique, each situation has to be individualized, and therefore it is difficult (if not impossible) to specify the "one best way" to provide a service.

The Human Relations Model

In 1927, the Hawthorne Works of the Western Electric Company in Chicago began a series of experiments designed to discover ways to increase worker satisfaction and worker productivity (Roethlisberger & Dickson, 1939). Hawthorne Works manufactured telephones on an assembly line. Workers needed no special skills, and they performed simple, repetitive tasks. The workers were not unionized, and management sought to find ways to increase productivity. If job satisfaction could be increased, employees would work more efficiently, and productivity would then increase.

The company tested the effects on productivity of a number of factors: rest breaks, better lighting, changes in the number of work hours, changes in the wages paid, improved food facilities, and so on. The results were surprising. Productivity increased, as expected, with improved working conditions; but it also increased when working conditions worsened. This latter finding was unexpected and led to an additional study.

The investigators discovered that participation in these experiments was extremely attractive to the workers, who felt they had been selected by management for their individual abilities. As a result, they worked harder, even when working conditions became less favorable. In addition, the workers' morale and general attitude toward work improved, because they felt they were receiving special attention. Participating in a study enabled them to work in smaller groups and become involved in making decisions. Working in smaller groups allowed them to develop a stronger sense of solidarity with their fellow workers. Being involved in decision making decreased their feelings of meaninglessness and powerlessness about their work.

In sociological and psychological research, the results of this study have become known as the *Hawthorne effect.* In essence, when people know they are participants in a study, this awareness may lead them to behave differently and substantially influence the results.

The results of this study, and of other similar studies, led some researchers to conclude that the key variables affecting productivity are social factors. Etzioni (1964) summarized some of the basic tenets of the human relations approach:

- The level of production is set by social norms, not by physiological capacities.
- Noneconomic rewards and sanctions significantly affect the behavior of the workers and largely limit the effect of economic incentive plans.
- Workers do not act or react as individuals but as members of groups.
- The role of leadership is important in understanding social factors in organizations, and this leadership may be either formal or informal.

Numerous studies have provided evidence to support these tenets (Netting, Kettner, & McMurtry, 1993). Workers who are capable of greater productivity often will not excel because they are unwilling to exceed the "average" level set by the norms of the group, even if this means earning less. These studies have also found that attempts by management to influence workers' behavior are often more successful if targeted at the group as a whole, rather than at individuals. Finally, the studies have documented the importance of informal leadership in influencing workers' behavior in ways that can either amplify or negate formal leadership directives. This model asserts that managers who succeed in increasing productivity are most likely responsive to the workers' social needs.

One criticism of the human relations model is (surprisingly) that it tends to manipulate, dehumanize, oppress, and exploit workers. The model leads to the conclusion that management can increase productivity by helping workers become content, rather than by increasing economic rewards for higher productivity. The human relations model allows for concentrated power and decision making at the top. It is not intended to empower employees in the decision-making process or to assist them in acquiring genuine participation in the running of the organization. The practice of dealing with people on the basis of their perceived social relationships within the workplace may also be a factor in perpetuating the "good old boys" network; this network has disadvantaged women and people of color over the years. Another criticism of the human relations approach is that a happy workforce is not necessarily a productive workforce, because the norms for worker production may be set well below the workers' levels of capability.

Theory X and Theory Y

Douglas McGregor (1960) developed two theories of management. He theorized that management thinking and behavior are based on two different sets of assumptions, which he labeled Theory X and Theory Y.

Theory X managers view employees as being incapable of much growth. Employees are perceived as having an inherent dislike for work and attempting to evade work whenever possible. Therefore, X-type managers believe they must control, direct, force, or threaten employees to make them work. Employees are also viewed as having relatively little ambition, wishing to avoid responsibilities, and preferring to be directed. Theory X managers therefore spell out job responsibilities carefully, set work goals without employee input, use external rewards (such as money) to push employees to work, and punish those who deviate from established rules.

Because Theory X managers reduce responsibilities to a level at which few mistakes can be made, work usually becomes so structured that it is monotonous and distasteful. These Theory X assumptions, of course, are inconsistent with what behavioral scientists assert are effective principles for directing, influencing, and motivating people. Theory X managers are, in essence, adhering to an autocratic model of organizational behavior.

In contrast, *Theory Y managers* view employees as wanting to grow and develop by exerting physical and mental effort to accomplish work objectives to which they are committed. These managers believe that the promise of internal rewards, such as self-respect and personal improvement, are stronger motivators than external rewards (money) and punishment. They also believe that under proper conditions, employees will not only accept responsibility but seek it. Most employees are assumed to have considerable ingenuity, creativity, and imagination for problem solving. Therefore, they are given considerable responsibility to test the limits of their capabilities. Mistakes and errors are viewed as necessary phases of the learning process, and work is structured so that employees have a sense of accomplishment and growth.

Employees who work for Y-type managers are generally more creative and productive, experience greater work satisfaction, and are more highly motivated than employees who work for X-type managers. Under both management styles, expectations often become self-fulfilling prophecies.

The Collegial Model

A useful extension of Theory Y is the *collegial model*, which emphasizes the team concept. Employees work together closely and feel a commitment to achieving a common purpose. Some organizations—such as university departments, research laboratories, and most human services organizations—have a goal of creating a collegial atmosphere to facilitate achieving their purposes. (Sadly, many such organizations are unsuccessful in creating such an atmosphere.)

Creating a collegial atmosphere is highly dependent on management's building a feeling of partnership with employees. When such a partnership develops, employees feel needed and useful. Managers are then viewed as joint contributors rather than as bosses. Management is the *coach* that builds a better team. Davis and Newstrom (1989) described some of the approaches to developing a team concept:

> *The feeling of partnerships can be built in many ways. Some organizations have abolished the use of reserved parking spaces for executives, so every employee has an equal chance of finding one close to the workplace. Some firms have tried to eliminate the use of terms like "bosses" and "subordinates," feeling that those terms simply create perceptions of psychological distance between managers and nonmanagers. Other employers have removed time clocks, set up "fun committees," sponsored company canoe trips, or required managers to spend a week or two annually working in field or factory locations. All of these approaches are designed to build a spirit of mutuality, in which every person makes contributions and appreciates those of others. (p. 34)*

If the sense of partnership is developed, employees produce quality work and seek to cooperate with coworkers, not because management directs them to do so, but because they feel an internal obligation to produce high-quality work. The collegial approach thus leads to a sense of *self-discipline*. In this environment, employees are more apt to have a sense of fulfillment, to feel self-actualized, and to produce higher-quality work.

Theory Z

William Ouchi described the Japanese style of management in his 1981 best-seller *Theory Z*. In the late 1970s and early 1980s, attention in the U.S. business world became focused on the Japanese approach to management, as markets long dominated by U.S. firms (such as the automobile industry) were taken over by Japanese industries. Japanese industrial organizations had rapidly overcome their earlier reputation for poor-quality work and were setting worldwide standards for quality and durability.

Theory Z asserted that the theoretical principles underlying Japanese management went beyond Theory Y. According to Theory Z, a business organization in Japan is more than the profitability-oriented entity that it is in the United States. It is a way of life. It provides lifetime employment. It is enmeshed with the nation's political, social, and economic network. Furthermore, its influence spills over into many other organizations, such as nursery schools, elementary and secondary schools, and universities.

The basic philosophy of Theory Z is that involved and committed workers are the key to increased productivity. Ideas and suggestions about how to improve the organization are routinely solicited, and implemented where feasible. One strategy for accomplishing this is the *quality circle*, where employees and management routinely meet to brainstorm about ways to improve productivity and quality.

In contrast to American organizations, Japanese organizations tend not to have written objectives or organizational charts. Most work is done in teams, and decisions are made by a consensus. The teams tend to function without a designated leader. Cooperation within units, and between units, is emphasized. Loyalty to the organization is also emphasized, as is organizational loyalty to the employee.

Experiments designed to transplant Japanese-style management to the United States have resulted in mixed success. In most cases, American organizations have concluded that Theory Z probably works quite well in a homogeneous culture that has Japan's societal values, but some components do not fit well with the more heterogeneous and individualistic character of the United States. In addition, some firms in volatile industries (such as electronics) have difficulty balancing their desire to provide lifetime employment with the need to adjust their workforces to meet rapidly changing market demands.

Management by Objectives

Fundamental to the core of an organization is its purpose—that is, the commonly shared understanding of the reason for its existence.

Management theorist Peter Drucker (1954) proposed a strategy for making organizational goals and objectives the central construct around which organizational life is designed to function. In other words, instead of focusing on employee needs and wants, or on organizational structure, as the ways to increase efficiency and productivity, Drucker proposed beginning with the desired outcome and working backward. The strategy is first to identify the organizational objectives or goals and then to adapt the organizational tasks, resources, and structure to meet those objectives. This management by objectives (MBO) approach is designed to focus the organization's efforts on meeting these objectives. Success is determined, then, by the degree to which stated objectives are reached.

This approach can be applied to the organization as a whole, as well as to internal divisions or departments. When the MBO approach is applied to internal divisions, the objectives set for each division should be consistent with and supportive of the overall organizational objectives.

In many areas, including human services, the MBO approach can also be applied to the cases serviced by each employee. Goals are set with each client, tasks to meet these goals are then determined, and deadlines are set for the completion of these tasks. The degree of success of each case is then determined at a later date (often when a case is closed) by the extent to which stated goals were achieved.

An adaptation of the MBO approach, called strategic planning and budgeting (SPB), became popular in the 1990s and is still widely used. The process involves first specifying the overall vision or mission of an organization, then identifying a variety of more specific objectives or plans for achieving that vision, and, finally, adapting the resources to meet the specific high-priority objectives or plans. Organizations often hire outside consultants to assist in conducting the SPB process.

One major advantage of the MBO approach for an organization or its divisions is that it produces clear statements (made available to all employees) about the objectives and the tasks that are expected to be accomplished in specified time periods. This type of activity tends to improve cooperation and collaboration. The MBO approach is also useful because it provides a guide for allocating resources and a focus for monitoring and evaluating organizational efforts.

An additional benefit of the MBO approach is that it creates diversity in the workplace. Prior to this approach, those responsible for hiring failed to employ women and people of color in significant numbers. As affirmative action programs were developed within organizations, the MBO approach was widely used to set specific hiring goals and objectives. The result has been significant changes in recruitment approaches that have enabled more women and minorities to secure employment.

Total Quality Management

The theorist most closely associated with developing the concept of total quality management (TQM) is W. Edwards Deming (1986). Deming was a statistician who formed many of his theories during World War II, when he instructed industries on how to use statistical methods to improve the quality of military production. Following World War II, Deming taught the Japanese his theories of quality control and continuous improvement, and he is now recognized, along with J. Juran (1989) and others, as having laid the groundwork for Japan's industrial and economic boom.

Omachonu and Ross (1994) define total quality management as "the integration of all functions and processes within an organization in order to achieve continuous improvement of the quality of goods and services. The goal is customer satisfaction" (p. 1). TQM is based on a number of ideas. It means thinking about quality in terms of all functions of the enterprise and as a start-to-finish process that integrates interrelated functions at all levels. It is a systems approach that considers every interaction between the various elements of an organization.

TQM asserts that the management of many businesses and organizations makes the mistake of blaming what goes wrong in an organization on individuals rather than on the system. TQM, rather, believes in the "85/15 Rule," which asserts that 85 percent of the problems can be corrected by changing systems (structures, rules, practices, expectations, and traditions that are largely determined by management) and less than 15 percent of the problems can be solved by individual workers. When problems arise, TQM asserts, management should look for causes in the system and work to remove them before casting blame on workers.

TQM further maintains that customer satisfaction is the main purpose of the organization. Therefore, quality includes continuously improving all the organization's processes that lead to customer satisfaction. The customer is seen as part of the design and production process, as the customer's needs must be continually monitored.

In recent years, numerous organizations have adopted a TQM approach to improve their goods and services. One of the reasons that quality is being emphasized more is because consumers are increasingly shunning mass-produced, poorly made, disposable production. Companies are realizing that to remain competitive in global markets, quality of products and services is essential. Ford's motto, "Quality Is Job One," symbolizes this emphasis.

There are a variety of approaches to TQM, largely because numerous theoreticians (business gurus) have advanced somewhat diverse approaches. Hower (1994, p. 10) gives the following summary of the key principles of TQM:

- Employees asking their external and internal customers what they need, and providing more of it
- Instilling pride into every employee
- Concentrating on information and data (a common language) to solve problems, instead of concentrating on opinions and egos
- Developing leaders, not managers, and knowing the difference
- Improving every process (everyone is in a process), checking this improvement at predetermined times, then improving it again if necessary

- Helping every employee enjoy his or her work while the organization continues to become more productive
- Providing a forum or open atmosphere so that employees at all levels feel free to voice their opinions when they think they have good ideas
- Receiving a continuous increase in those suggestions, and accepting and implementing the best ones
- Utilizing the teamwork concept, because teams often make better decisions than individuals
- Empowering these teams to implement their recommended solutions and learn from their failures
- Reducing the number of layers of authority to enhance this empowerment
- Recognizing complaints as opportunities for improvement

These principles give the reader an idea of the "flavor" of TQM.

Summary Comments About Models of Organizational Behavior

Any of these models can be successfully applied in some situations. Which model to apply to obtain the highest productivity depends on the tasks to be completed and on employee needs and expectations. For example, the autocratic model will probably work well in military operations, where quick decisions are needed to respond to rapidly changing crises and where military personnel expect autocratic leadership. However, this model does not generally work well in human services organizations, in which employees are expecting the Theory Y style of managers.

Surviving and Thriving in a Bureaucracy

A bureaucracy is a subcategory (or type) of organization. A bureaucracy can be defined as a form of social organization whose distinctive characteristics include a vertical hierarchy with power centered at the top; a task-specific division of labor; clearly defined rules; formalized channels of communication; and selection, compensation, promotion, and retention based on technical competence.

There are basic structural conflicts between helping professionals and the bureaucratic systems in which they work. Helping professionals place a high value on creativeness and changing the system to serve clients. Bureaucracies resist change and are most efficient when no one is "rocking the boat." Helping professionals seek to personalize services by conveying to each client that "you count as a person." Bureaucracies are highly depersonalized, emotionally detached systems that view every employee and every client as a tiny component of a large system. In a large bureaucracy employees *don't* count as "people" but only as functional parts of a system. Additional conflicting value orientations between a helping professional and bureaucratic systems are listed in Highlight 12.13, "Value Conflicts Between a Helping Professional and Bureaucracies."

Any of these differences in value orientations can become an arena of conflict between helping professionals and the bureaucracies in which they work. Knopf (1979) summarized the potential areas of conflict between bureaucracies and helping professionals:

> *The trademarks of a BS (bureaucratic system) are power, hierarchy, and specialization; that is, rules and roles. In essence, the result is depersonalization. The system itself is neither "good" nor "bad"; it is a system. I believe it to be amoral. It is efficient and effective, but in order to be so it must be impersonal in all of its functionings. This then is the location of the stress. The hallmark of the helping professional is a highly individualized, democratic, humanized, relationship-oriented service aimed at self-motivation. The hallmark of a bureaucratic system is a highly impersonalized, valueless (amoral), emotionally detached, hierarchical structure of organization. The dilemma of the HP (helping person) is how to give a personalized service to a client through a delivery system that is not set up in any way to do that. (pp. 21–22)*

Numerous helping professionals respond to these orientation conflicts by erroneously projecting a "personality" onto the bureaucracy. The bureaucracy is viewed as being red tape, officialism, uncaring, cruel, the enemy. A negative personality is sometimes also projected onto the officials, who may be viewed as being paper shufflers, rigid, deadwood, inefficient, and unproductive. Knopf (1979) states:

> *The HP (helping person) ... may deal with the impersonal nature of the system by projecting values onto it and thereby give the BS (bureaucratic system) a "personality." In this way, we fool ourselves into thinking that we can deal with*

HIGHLIGHT 12.13

Value Conflicts Between a Helping Professional and Bureaucracies

Orientations of a Helping Professional	Orientations of Bureaucratic Systems
Desires democratic system for decision making.	Most decisions are made autocratically.
Desires that power be distributed equally among employees (horizontal structure).	Power is distributed vertically.
Desires that clients have considerable power in the system.	Power is held primarily by top executives.
Desires a flexible, changing system.	System is rigid and stable.
Desires that creativity and growth be emphasized.	Emphasis is on structure and the status quo.
Desires that focus be client-oriented.	System is organization-centered.
Desires that communication be on a personalized level from person to person.	Communication is from level to level.
Desires shared decision making and shared responsibility structure.	A hierarchical decision-making structure and a hierarchical responsibility structure are characteristic.
Desires that decisions be made by those having the most knowledge.	Decisions are made in terms of the decision-making authority assigned to each position in the hierarchy.
Desires shared leadership.	System uses autocratic leadership.
Believes feelings of clients and employees should be highly valued by the system.	Procedures and processes are highly valued.

it in a personal way. Unfortunately, projection is almost always negative and reflects the dark or negative aspects of ourselves. The BS then becomes a screen onto which we vent our anger, sadness, or fright, and while a lot of energy is generated, very little is accomplished. Since the BS is amoral, it is unproductive to place a personality on it. (p. 25)

A bureaucratic system is neither good nor bad. It has neither a personality nor a value system of its own. It is simply a structure developed to carry out various tasks.

A helping person may have various emotional reactions to these conflicts in orientation with bureaucratic systems. Common reactions are anger at the system, self-blame ("It's all my fault"), sadness and depression ("Poor me," "Nobody appreciates all I've done"), and fright and paranoia ("They're out to get me," "If I mess up I'm gone").

Knopf (1979) identified several types of behavior patterns that helping professionals choose in dealing with bureaucracies.

The *warrior* leads open campaigns to destroy and malign the system. A warrior discounts the value of the system and often enters into a win-lose conflict. The warrior generally loses and is dismissed.

The *gossip* is a covert warrior who complains to others (including clients, politicians, and the news media) how terrible the system is. A gossip frequently singles out a few officials for criticism. Bureaucratic systems often make life very difficult for the gossip by assigning distasteful tasks, refusing to promote, giving very low salary increases, and perhaps even dismissing.

The *complainer* resembles a gossip but confines complaints to other helping people, to in-house staff, and to family members. A complainer wants people to agree in order to find comfort in shared misery. Complainers desire to stay with the system, and generally do.

The *dancer* is skillful at ignoring rules and procedures. Dancers are frequently lonely, often reprimanded for incorrectly filling out forms, and have low investment in the system or in helping clients.

The *defender* is scared, dislikes conflict, and therefore defends the rules, the system, and bureaucratic officials. Defenders are often supervisors and are viewed by others as bureaucrats.

The *machine* is a bureaucrat who takes on the orientation of the bureaucracy. Often a machine has not been involved in providing direct services for years. Machines are frequently named to head study committees and policy groups and to chair boards.

The *executioner* attacks people within an organization with enthusiasm and vigor. An executioner usually has a high energy level and is impulsive. An executioner abuses power by indiscriminately attacking and dismissing not only employees but also services and programs. Executioners have power and are angry (although the anger is disguised, denied). They are not committed to either the value orientation of helping professionals or the bureaucracy.

Knopf (1979) listed 66 tips on how to survive in a bureaucracy. The most useful suggestions are summarized here:

1. Whenever your needs, or the needs of your clients, are not met by the bureaucracy, use the following problem-solving approach: (1) Precisely identify your needs (or the needs of clients) that are in conflict with the bureaucracy; this step is defining the problem. (2) Generate a list of possible solutions. Be creative in generating a wide range of solutions. (3) Evaluate the merits and shortcomings of the possible solutions. (4) Select a solution. (5) Implement the solution. (6) Evaluate the solution.

2. Obtain knowledge of how your bureaucracy is structured and how it functions. This knowledge will reduce fear of the unknown, make the system more predictable, and help in identifying rational ways to best meet your needs and those of your clients.

3. Remember that bureaucrats are people who have feelings. Communication gaps are often most effectively reduced if you treat them with as much respect and interest as you treat clients.

4. If you are at war with the bureaucracy, declare a truce. The system will find a way to dismiss you if you remain at war. With a truce, you can identify and use the strengths of the bureaucracy as an ally, rather than having the strengths be used against you as an enemy.

5. Know your work contract and job expectations. If the expectations are unclear, seek clarity.

6. Continue to develop your knowledge and awareness of specific helping skills. Take advantage of continuing education opportunities

(e.g., workshops, conferences, courses). Among other advantages, your continued professional development will assist you in being able to contract from a position of competency and skill.

7. Seek to identify your professional strengths and limitations. Knowing your limitations will increase your ability to avoid undertaking responsibilities that are beyond your competencies.

8. Be aware that you can't change everything, so stop trying. In a bureaucracy, focus your change efforts on those aspects that most need change and that you have a fair chance of changing. Stop thinking and complaining about those aspects you cannot change. It is irrational to complain about things that you cannot change or to complain about those things that you do not intend to make an effort to change.

9. Learn how to control your emotions in your interactions with the bureaucracy. Emotions that are counterproductive (such as most angry outbursts) particularly need to be controlled. Doing a rational self-analysis of unwanted emotions (see Chapter 8) is one way of gaining control of your unwanted emotions. Learning how to respond to stress in your personal life will also prepare you to handle stress at work better.

10. Develop and use a sense of humor. Humor takes the edge off adverse conditions and reduces negative feelings.

11. Learn to accept your mistakes and perhaps even to laugh at some of them. No one is perfect.

12. Take time to enjoy and develop a support system with your coworkers.

13. Acknowledge your mistakes and give in sometimes on minor matters. You may not be right, and giving in sometimes allows other people to do the same.

14. Keep yourself physically fit and mentally alert. Learn to use approaches that will reduce stress (see Chapter 14).

15. Leave your work at the office. If you have urgent unfinished bureaucratic business, do it before leaving work or don't leave.

16. Occasionally take your supervisor and other administrators to lunch. Socializing prevents isolation and facilitates your involvement with and understanding of the system.

17. Do not seek self-actualization or ego satisfaction from the bureaucracy. A depersonalized system is incapable of providing this. Only you can satisfy your ego and become self-actualized.

18. Make speeches to community groups that accentuate the positives about your agency. Do not hesitate to ask after speeches that a thank-you letter be sent to your supervisor or agency director.

19. If you have a problem involving the bureaucracy, discuss it with other employees; focus on problem solving rather than on complaining. Groups are much more powerful and productive than an individual working alone to make changes in a system.

20. No matter how high you rise in a hierarchy, maintain direct service contact. Direct contact keeps you abreast of changing client needs, prevents you from getting stale, and keeps you attuned to the concerns of employees in lower levels of the hierarchy.

21. Do not try to change everything in the system at once. Attacking too much will overextend you and lead to burnout. Start small and be selective and specific. Double-check your facts to make certain they accurately prove your position before confronting bureaucratic officials.

22. Identify your career goals and determine whether they can be met in this system. If the answer is no, then (1) change your goals, (2) change the bureaucracy, or (3) seek a position elsewhere in which your goals can be met.

Value Orientations in Organizational Decision Making

In theory, the task of making decisions about an organization's objectives and goals would follow a rational process. This process would include identifying the problems, specifying resource limitations, weighing the advantages and disadvantages of proposed solutions, and selecting the resolution strategy with the fewest risks and the greatest chance of success. In practice, however, subjective influences (particularly value orientations) can impede the rational process.

Most people tend to believe that decisions are made primarily on the basis of objective facts and figures. However, values and assumptions form the bases of most decisions, and facts and figures are used only in relation to these values and assumptions. Consider the following list of questions. What do they indicate about how we make our most important decisions?

- Should abortions be permitted or prohibited during the first weeks following conception?
- Should same-sex sexual behavior be viewed as a natural expression of sexuality?
- When does harsh discipline of a child become child abuse?
- Should the primary objective of imprisonment be rehabilitation or retribution?

Answers to these questions are usually not based on data uncovered after careful research; they are based on individual beliefs about the value of life, personal freedom, and protective social standards. Even everyday decisions are based largely on values.

Practically every decision is also based on certain assumptions. Without assumptions, nothing can be proved. Assumptions are made in every research study to test any hypothesis. For example, in a market research survey, analysts *assume* that the instruments they use (such as a questionnaire) will be valid and reliable. It cannot even be proved the sun will rise in the east tomorrow without *assuming* that its history provides that proof.

Every decision maker in an organization brings not only his or her objective knowledge and expertise to the decision-making process, but also his or her value orientations. *Value orientation* means an individual's own ideas about what is desirable and worthwhile. Most values are acquired through prior learning experiences in interactions with family, friends, educators, organizations such as a church, and anyone else who has made an impression on a person's thinking.

Philosopher Edward Spranger (1928) believed that most people eventually come to rely on one of six possible value orientations. Although it is possible for a person to hold values in all six orientations, each person tends to lean more heavily toward one type in the decision-making process. The six value orientations are as follows:

- *Theoretical.* A person with a theoretical orientation strives toward a rational, systematic ordering of knowledge. Personal preference does not count

as much as being able to classify, compare, contrast, and interrelate various pieces of information. The theoretical person places value on simply knowing what exists—and why.
- *Economic.* An economic orientation places primary value on the utility of things, and practical uses of knowledge are given foremost attention. Proposed plans of action are assessed in terms of their costs and benefits. If the costs outweigh the benefits, the economically oriented person is not likely to support the plan.
- *Aesthetic.* An aesthetic orientation is grounded in an appreciation of artistic values, and personal preferences for form, harmony, and beauty are influential in making decisions. Because the experience of single events is considered an important end in itself, reactions to aesthetic qualities will frequently be expressed.
- *Social.* A social orientation is an empathetic one that values other people as ends in themselves. Concern for the welfare of people pervades the behavior of the socially oriented decision maker, and primary consideration is given to the quality of human relationships.
- *Political.* A political orientation involves a concern for identifying where power lies. Conflict and competition are seen as normal elements of group activity. Decisions and their outcomes are assessed in terms of how much power is obtained, and by whom, because influence over others is a valued goal.
- *Religious.* A person with a religious orientation is directed by a desire to relate to the universe in some meaningful way. Personal beliefs about an "absolute good" or a "higher order" are employed to determine the value of things, and decisions and their outcomes are placed into the context of such beliefs.

●●●● **Ethical Question 12.8**

When you make major decisions, which of these value orientations do you tend to use?

EP 2.1.2

LO 12-6 Describe Liberal, Conservative, and Developmental Perspectives on Human Service Organizations

Liberal, Conservative, and Developmental Perspectives on Human Service Organizations

Three diverse views that have major impacts on human services organizations are the liberal, conservative, and developmental perspectives. Politicians and decision makers often make their decisions on human service issues in terms of whether they adhere to a liberal or a conservative philosophy. The Republican Party is considered to be relatively conservative, and the Democratic Party is considered to be relatively liberal. This discussion will focus on liberalism and conservatism in their pure forms. In reality, many people espouse a mixture of both views. For example, some Democrats are primarily conservative in ideology and some Republicans are primarily liberal in ideology.

Note that the three dimensions described in the following sections—conservative, liberal, and developmental—are portrayed in a purist fashion, implying that proponents rigidly adhere to the prescribed views. As with Democrats and Republicans, in real life, most people reflect a unique combination of these views.

Conservative Perspective

Conservatives (a term derived from the verb to *conserve*) tend to resist change. They emphasize tradition and believe rapid change usually results in more negative than positive consequences. In economic matters, conservatives feel that the government should not interfere with the workings of the marketplace. They encourage the government to support (e.g., through tax incentives) rather than regulate business and industry. A free market economy is thought to be the best way to ensure prosperity and fulfillment of individual needs. Conservatives embrace the old adage, "That government governs best which governs least." They believe that most government activities

constitute threats to individual liberty and to the smooth functioning of the free market.

Conservatives generally view individuals as being autonomous—that is, as being self-governing. Regardless of what a person's situation is, or what problems he or she has, each person is thought to be responsible for his or her own behavior. People are thought to choose whatever they are doing, and they therefore are viewed as being responsible for whatever gains or losses result from their choices. Conservatives view people as having free will, and thus as able to choose to engage in behaviors such as hard work that help them get ahead, or activities such as excessive leisure that contribute to failing (or being poor). Poverty and other problems are seen as being the result of laziness, irresponsibility, or lack of self-control. Conservatives believe that social welfare programs force hardworking, productive citizens to pay for the consequences of the irresponsible behavior of recipients of social welfare services.

Conservatives generally advocate the residual approach to social welfare programs (Wilensky & Lebeaux, 1965). The residual view holds that social welfare services should be provided only when an individual's needs are not properly met through other societal institutions, primarily the family and the market economy. Social services and financial aid should not be provided until all other measures or efforts have failed and the individual's or family's resources are fully used up. In addition, this view asserts that funds and services should be provided on a short-term basis (primarily during emergencies) and should be withdrawn when the individual or the family again becomes capable of being self-sufficient.

The residual view has been characterized as "charity for unfortunates." Funds and services are not seen as a right (something that one is entitled to) but as a gift, and the receiver has certain obligations; for example, in order to receive financial aid, recipients may be required to perform certain low-grade work assignments. Under the residual view, there is usually a stigma attached to receiving services or funds.

Conservatives believe that dependency is a result of personal failure, and they also believe it is natural for inequality to exist among humans. They assert that the family, religious organizations, and gainful employment should be the primary defenses against

ETHICAL DILEMMA

Are the Poor to Blame for Being Poor?

EP 2.1.2

The residual view of social welfare holds that people are poor as a result of their own malfunctioning. The following are illustrations of this view:

- Some are lazy.
- Some make bad decisions, such as buying too many useless items on credit cards.
- Some have more children than they can support.
- Some are unable to work because they are addicted to alcohol or other drugs.
- Some have a very low IQ.
- Some teenagers have children before they can finish their education, thus affecting job opportunities.

Since the poor are perceived as being to blame for their predicament, the residual view asserts that funds and social services to help them should be only minimally provided.

In contrast, the institutional view of social welfare holds that people are poor as a result of causes largely beyond their control. The following are illustrations of this view:

- Some are unemployed, or underemployed, because of a lack of employment opportunities.
- Racial discrimination and sexism prevent some people of color and some women from reaching their full economic potential.
- Economic recessions lead some to lose their jobs.
- Outsourcing of jobs to other countries results in some people in this country losing their jobs.
- Natural disasters, such as earthquakes, hurricanes, wildfires, and tornadoes, result in some people losing their homes and personal possessions.
- Low-quality school systems prevent some people from fulfilling their economic potential.
- Some lose most of their financial resources as a result of scams and corporate fraud.

With this institutional view, the poor are not perceived as being to blame for their predicament. They are viewed as being entitled to long-term assistance from society. Also, efforts should be made to improve economic opportunities for the poor.

Which view do you hold?

---

dependency. Social welfare, they believe, should be only a temporary function that is used sparingly. Prolonged social welfare assistance, they believe, will lead recipients to become permanently dependent.

Conservatives believe charity is a moral virtue and that the "fortunate" are obligated to help the "less fortunate" become productive, contributing citizens. If government funds are provided for health and social welfare services, conservatives advocate that such funding should go to private organizations, which are thought to be more effective and efficient than public agencies in providing services. Conservatives tend to believe that the federal government is not a solution to social problems but is part of the problem. They assert that federally funded social welfare programs tend to make recipients dependent on the government, rather than assisting recipients to become self-sufficient and productive.

Conservatives revere the traditional nuclear family and try to devise policies to preserve it. They see the family as a source of strength for individuals, and as the primary unit of society. Accordingly,

they oppose abortion, sex education in schools, rights for homosexuals, public funding of day-care centers, birth control counseling for minors, and other measures that might undermine parental authority or support alternative family forms such as single parenthood.

Liberal Perspective

In contrast, liberals believe that change is generally good as it brings progress; moderate change is best. They view society as needing regulation to ensure fair competition between various interests. In particular, the market economy is viewed as needing regulation to ensure fairness. Government programs, including social welfare programs, are viewed as necessary to help meet basic human needs. Liberals advocate government action to remedy social deficiencies and to improve human welfare. Liberals believe that government regulation and intervention are often necessary to safeguard human rights, to control the excesses of capitalism, and to provide equal chances for success. They emphasize egalitarianism and the rights of minorities.

Liberals generally adhere to an *institutional* view of social welfare. This view holds that social welfare programs are "accepted as a proper legitimate function of modern industrial society in helping individuals achieve self-fulfillment" (Wilensky & Lebeaux, 1965, p. 139). Under this view, there is no stigma attached to receiving funds or services; recipients are viewed as entitled to such help. Associated with this view is the belief that an individual's difficulties are due to causes largely beyond his or her control (e.g., a person may be unemployed because of a lack of employment opportunities). With this view, when difficulties arise, causes are sought in the environment (society) and efforts are focused on improving the social institutions within which the individual functions.

Liberals assert that because society has become so fragmented and complex, and because traditional institutions (such as the family) have been unable to meet human needs, few individuals can now function without the help of social services (including such services as work training, job location services, child care, health care, and counseling). Liberals believe that problems are often due to causes beyond the individual's control. Causes are generally sought in the person's environment. For example, a child with a learning disability is thought to be at risk only if that child is not receiving appropriate educational services to accommodate his or her disability.

In such a situation, liberals would seek to develop educational services to meet the child's learning needs.

Liberals view the family as an evolving institution, and therefore they are willing to support programs that assist emerging family forms—such as single-parent families and same-sex marriages.

Developmental Perspective

Liberals for years have criticized the residual approach to social welfare as being incongruent with society's obligation to provide long-term assistance to those who have long-term health, welfare, social, and recreational needs. Conservatives, on the other hand, have been highly critical of the institutional approach as they claim it creates a welfare state in which many recipients simply become dependent on the government to meet their health, welfare, social, and recreational needs without seeking to work and without contributing in other ways to the well-being of society. It is clear that conservatives will attempt to stop the creation of any major social program that moves the country in the direction of being a welfare society. They have the necessary legislative votes to stop the enactment of programs that are "marketed" to society as being consistent with the institutional approach.

Paul Conklin/PhotoEdit

A Peace Corps volunteer teaches a group of Costa Rican boys.

Is there a view of social welfare that can garner the support of both liberals and conservatives? Midgley (1995) contends that the *developmental view* (or perspective) offers an alternative approach that appears to appeal to liberals, conservatives, and to the general public. Midgley defines this approach as a "process of planned social change designed to promote the well-being of the population as a whole in conjunction with a dynamic process of economic development" (p. 25).

This perspective has appeal to liberals because it supports the development and expansion of needed social welfare programs. The perspective has appeal to conservatives because it asserts that the development of certain social welfare programs will have a positive impact on the economy. The general public also would be apt to support the developmental perspective. Many voters oppose welfarism, as they believe it causes economic problems (e.g., recipients living on the government dole, rather than contributing to society through working). Asserting and documenting that certain proposed social welfare programs will directly benefit the economy is attractive to voters.

Midgley and Livermore (1997) note that the developmental approach is, at this point, not very well defined. The approach has its roots in the promotion of social programs in developing (third-world) countries. Advocates for social welfare programs in developing countries have been successful in getting certain programs enacted by asserting and documenting that such programs will have a beneficial impact on the overall economy of the country. Midgley and Livermore note, "The developmental perspective's global relevance began in the Third World in the years of decolonization after World War II" (p. 576). The United Nations later used the developmental approach in its efforts to promote the growth of social programs in developing countries, asserting that such programs had the promise of improving the overall economies of these countries.

What are the characteristics of the developmental approach? It advocates social interventions that contribute positively to economic development, thus promoting harmony between economic and social institutions. The approach regards economic progress as a vital component of social progress, and it promotes the active role of government in economic and social planning (in direct opposition to the residual approach). Finally, the developmental approach focuses on integrating economic and social development for the *benefit of all* members of society.

The developmental approach can be used in advocating for the expansion of a wide range of social welfare programs. It can be argued that any social program that assists a person in becoming employable contributes to the economic well-being of a society. It can also be argued that any social program that assists a person in making significant contributions to his or her family, or to his or her community, contributes to the economic well-being of a society, as functional families and functional communities are good for businesses. Members of functional families tend to be better employees, and businesses desire to locate in communities that are prospering and that have low rates of crime and other social problems.

A few examples will illustrate how the developmental approach can be used to advocate for the expansion of social welfare programs. It can be argued that job training, quality child care, and adequate health insurance will all benefit the economy because they will help unemployed single parents obtain employment. All of these programs will facilitate the parents being able to work. It can be argued that providing mentoring programs and other social services will help at-risk children stay in school and eventually contributing to society as adults by obtaining employment and contributing to their families and to the communities in which they live. It can be argued that rehabilitative programs in the criminal justice system will help correctional clients become contributing members of society. It can be argued that alcohol and drug treatment programs, nutritional programs, eating disorder intervention programs, stress management programs, and grief management programs will help people with issues in these areas to handle them better, thereby increasing the likelihood that they will become contributors to the economy and to the well-being of society.

Chapter Summary

The following summarizes this chapter's content as it relates to the learning objectives presented at the beginning of the chapter. Chapter content will help prepare students to:

LO 12-1 *Describe the following lifestyles and family forms that young adults may enter into: marriage, cohabitation, single life, parenthood, and the life of a childless couple.*

In young adulthood, people choose a personal lifestyle. Choosing a personal lifestyle partly involves making career decisions. Young adults may also enter into a variety of family living arrangements, including marriage, cohabitation, single life, parenthood, and childless couples.

LO 12-2 *Describe three major sociological theories about human behavior: functionalism, conflict theory, and interactionism. These are macro-system theories.*

Three macro-system theories in sociology—functionalism, conflict theory, and interactionism—offer contrasting explanations of human behavior. Functionalism views society and other social systems as composed of interdependent and interrelated parts. Conflict theory is more radical, viewing society as a struggle for scarce resources among individuals and social groups. Interactionist theory views human behavior as resulting from the interaction of a person's unique, distinctive personality and the groups he or she participates in.

LO 12-3 *Understand three social problems that young and middle-aged adults may encounter: poverty, empty-shell marriages, and divorce. One-parent families, blended families, and mothers working outside the home will also be discussed.*

Those most vulnerable to being poor include one-parent families, children, older adults, large families, people of color, the homeless, those without a high school education, and those living in urban slums.

Three types of empty-shell marriages are devitalized relationships, conflict-habituated relationships, and passive-congenial relationships. About one of two marriages ends in divorce. Although a divorce is traumatic for everyone in the family, it appears that children become better adjusted when raised in a one-parent family in which they have a good relationship with that parent than in a two-parent family filled with discontent and tension.

Becoming more common in our society are one-parent families, blended families, and mothers working outside the home. Poverty affects one-parent families significantly more than it does two-parent families. The formation of a blended family requires substantial adjustments by a number of people, including the spouses, the children, the former spouses, and close relatives and friends. Because increasing numbers of mothers are working outside the home, our society needs to expand its effort to make good child-care arrangements available to the children in these families.

LO 12-4 *Understand material on assessing and intervening in family systems.*

Problems faced by families tend to be clustered in the following four categories: marital problems between the husband and the wife, conflicts between the parents and the children, personal problems of individual family members, and stresses imposed on the family by the external environment. Two family system assessment techniques are the ecomap and the genogram.

LO 12-5 *Summarize material on social work with organizations, including several theories of organizational behavior.*

Numerous theories provide a variety of perspectives for viewing and analyzing organizations. The theories covered include the autocratic model, the custodial model, the scientific management model, the human relations model, Theory X, Theory Y, the collegial model, Theory Z, management by objectives, and total quality management. Any of these models can be applied successfully in some situations. Material was also presented on Knopf's (1979) suggestions for social workers surviving and thriving while employed in a bureaucracy.

LO 12-6 *Describe liberal, conservative, and developmental perspectives on human service organizations.*

Values and assumptions (rather than facts and figures) form the bases of most decisions in organizations. Six value orientations frequently have an impact on decision making: theoretical, economic, aesthetic, social, political, and religious.

In regard to value orientations, three diverse views that have major impacts on human service organizations are the conservative, liberal, and developmental perspectives. Conservatives generally advocate the residual approach to social welfare programs, whereas liberals generally follow an institutional view of social welfare. The developmental perspective offers an alternative approach that appears to appeal to liberals, conservatives, and the general public. It advocates social interventions that contribute positively to economic development.

COMPETENCY NOTES

The following identifies where Educational Policy (EP) competencies and practice behaviors are discussed in this chapter.

EP 2.1.7a Utilize conceptual frameworks to guide the process of assessment, intervention, and evaluation.

EP 2.1.7b Critique and apply knowledge to understand person and environment.
(All of this chapter): The content of this chapter is focused on acquiring both of these practice behaviors in working with young and middle-age adults.

EP 2.1.2 Apply social work ethical principles to guide professional practice.
(pp. 551, 555, 558, 561, 568, 570, 572, 580, 610, 612): Ethical questions are posed.

WEB RESOURCES

See this text's companion website at *www.cengage brain.com* for learning tools such as chapter quizzing, videos, and more.

13

SEXUAL ORIENTATION

John had been attending the state university for more than a year. He didn't have a chance to visit his parents in their small Midwestern town very often. When he did get home, his visits were usually limited to holidays. So when Thanksgiving rolled around, he found himself hopping on the Greyhound bus headed for Slab City, Wisconsin, his home.

This trip home was a problem for him. No matter how often or how deeply he mulled it over in his mind, he couldn't find an answer. He had something to tell his parents that he didn't think they would like very much. Over the past year, John had come to realize something about himself. He had come out; he was gay.

As he watched the countryside roll by, he thought about his childhood, about his high school friends, and even about the girl he had gone steady with for two and a half years during high school. What would they think if they found out?

He had never really been interested in girls. Sure, he pretended to be. Once a guy got labeled a "fag," he might as well run off to a monastery. He had always been pretty bright. He had learned really fast how men were supposed to act. As all-conference fullback on the high school football team, he became quite adept at telling the appropriate locker room jokes and at exaggerating the previous weekend's conquests with women. He often wondered why he had to pretend so hard. The others seemed to really get into it. They seemed genuinely enthralled with the ideas of big-breasted women and sex. He never dared mention the fact that he'd rather spend time with Dan or Chuck. He certainly never came close to mentioning any of his secret fantasies.

He even asked Millie to go steady with him. She was a nice girl, in addition to being cute and extremely popular. With her, he didn't feel the pressure of constantly having to push for sex. Typically, every Saturday night they'd go to a movie or a basketball game or something like that. Then afterward they'd fool around in the driveway for just a bit. That couldn't last too long because Millie's parents were pretty strict and imposed a midnight curfew. She was in by midnight, or else. John always had to put a little bit of a move on her and try to get to second base. At that point, she always stopped him, told him she loved him, and firmly stated she was waiting for marriage. What a relief.

At college, things were different. John had chosen the state university for a variety of reasons. He found that a person could do a lot of hiding among 40,000 other students. He also found that there were other men who felt just like he did. There was an exceptionally active gay rights group that sponsored a spectrum of social and recreational activities for gay men. Through one of these activities, he had met Hank. Lately they had been spending a lot of time together. He had never felt so comfortable in a relationship before. He found he could talk to Hank about his most intimate thoughts. He also discovered how much he enjoyed expressing his affection for Hank both verbally and physically.

John was jolted from his reverie as the bus pulled up to the local bus stop. He could see his parents waiting to pick him up. There was his father with a big smile on his face, waving at the son he was so proud of. John smiled, waved back, and thought, "Oh, boy. Well, here goes." He stepped off the bus.

Although most people have a sexual orientation toward the opposite gender, many do not. Many are attracted to members of the same gender and some to both genders.

EP 2.1.2b

For whatever reasons, the idea of homosexuality, which involves having a sexual orientation for members of the same gender, frequently elicits a strong negative emotional response. As future professional social workers, you need to identify and address this negative response. The National Association of Social Workers' (NASW) Code of Ethics specifies that "social workers [should] respect and promote the right of clients to self-determination and assist clients in their efforts to identify and clarify their goals" (NASW, 1999, 1.02). Additionally, it specifies that "social workers should obtain education about and seek to understand the nature of social diversity and oppression with respect to race, ethnicity, national origin, color, sex, sexual orientation, age, marital status, political belief, religion, and mental or physical disability" (NASW, 1999, 1.04c). The NASW Policy Statement on "Lesbian, Gay, and Bisexual Issues" states that "NASW is committed to advancing policies and practices that will improve the status and well-being of all lesbian, gay, and bisexual people" (NASW, 2012, p. 221). Clearly, determination of one's sexual orientation is a person's right.

A Perspective

This chapter will provide information about various aspects of homosexuality. The intent is to encourage readers to examine their own feelings and reactions. Understanding the effects of diverse sexual orientations on human behavior is necessary for objective, professional social work practice. Assessing one's own values toward people's diverse sexual orientations is a major step in developing professional social work values.

Learning Objectives

This chapter will help prepare students to:

**EP 2.1.7,
2.1.7a,
2.1.7b**

LO 13-1 *Explain sexual orientation (including concepts such as homosexuality, bisexuality, and transgender people)*

LO 13-2 *Review stereotypes about lesbian and gay people*

LO 13-3 *Discuss conceptual frameworks concerning sexual orientation*

LO 13-4 *Address discrimination and the impacts of homophobia*

LO 13-5 *Describe lesbian and gay lifestyles (including lesbian and gay relationships, sexual interaction, gay pride, and empowerment and a sense of community)*

LO 13-6 *Explore significant issues and life events for lesbian and gay people (including legal empowerment, violence against them, coming out, ethnicity, adolescence, parenting, aging, and HIV/AIDS)*

LO 13-7 *Recognize gay and lesbian pride, empowerment, and a sense of community*

LO 13-1 Explain Sexual Orientation

Sexual orientation is "one's erotic, romantic, and affectional attraction to the same gender, to the opposite gender, or to both" (Greenberg, Bruess, & Oswalt, 2014, p. 370). Other aspects concerning sexual orientation addressed here include the meanings of homosexuality and bisexuality, related terms, and the numbers of lesbian and gay people.

Homosexuality and Bisexuality

A man is committed to prison and has sexual relations with other men. Is he a homosexual? A shy, lonely woman who has never dated any men is approached by a lesbian friend. The lonely woman decides to have an affair with her friend. Is she a homosexual? Two 14-year-old male adolescents experiment with each other by hand-stimulating each other to orgasm. Are they homosexuals? While having sexual intercourse with his wife, a man frequently fantasizes about having sexual relations with other men. He has never had any actual sexual contact with a man in his adult life. Is he a homosexual?

The answers to these questions are not so easy. Placing people in definite, distinct categories is difficult. It is not always easy to draw a clear distinction between a heterosexual and a homosexual. It may make us feel more secure and in control to cordon off the world into neat and predictable little boxes of black or white. However, in reality, the world is an endless series of shades of gray. People frequently like to polarize others as being either heterosexual or homosexual. Perhaps such labeling makes situations appear to be predictable. If a person is labeled a heterosexual, then many assume that they know a lot of things about that person. For example, if a woman is labeled a heterosexual, then she is probably unassertive, sweet, demure, and emotional. She will date men and probably marry and become a mother and homemaker. If a man is a homosexual, then he will probably frequently flick his wrists and become a hairdresser.

In reality, things are not so predictable and clear. Chapter 9 discussed the construction and complexity of gender.

The problem with these neat categories is that they foster stereotypes. As we know, a stereotype is a fixed mental image of a group that is frequently applied to all its members. Often the characteristics involved in the mental picture are unflattering. Stereotypes refuse to take into account individual differences. They negate the value and integrity of the individual. Highlight 13.1 identifies some of the stereotypes characterizing lesbian and gay people.

 HIGHLIGHT 13.1

LO 13-2 Review Stereotypes About Lesbian and Gay People

EP 2.1.4a, 2.1.5a

Lesbian and gay people are not only the victims of homophobia, but also the targets of derogatory, inaccurate stereotypes. Some of the more common ones are that gay and lesbian people like to assume either a male or female role, and that they are potential child molesters. These stereotypes are false.

The Queen and the Butch

A prevalent stereotype about gay and lesbian people is that gay men typically look extremely feminine and that lesbians appear very masculine. Words that are used to refer to effeminate gay males include *swish*, *nellie*, and *queen*. Words that are used to refer to masculine-looking lesbians include *dyke* and *butch*. In truth, these stereotypes are not accurate in most instances (Johnson, 2014; Nugent, 2014; Rathus, Nevid, & Fichner-Rathus, 2014; Tully, 2001). People are individuals with individual traits. With the breakdown of traditional gender roles, identifying lesbians and gay men by appearance is difficult.

The stereotypes about how gay and lesbian people look is the result of confusion between two central concepts—gender identity and sexual orientation. *Gender identity* refers to a person's internal psychological self-concept of being either male or female. We have indicated that *sexual orientation* refers to "one's erotic, romantic, and affectional attraction to the same gender, to the opposite gender, or to both" (Greenberg et al., 2014, p. 370).

These concepts should not be confused. For example, whether a man prefers to have sexual relations with another man has nothing to do with his own feeling that he is a man.

Most gay men think of themselves as being men. They do not think of themselves as being women, nor do they want to become women. Therefore, a gay man can look and act like any other man, yet still be attracted to men. Gender identity and sexual orientation should not be confused with respect to women either. A woman may feel like a woman and think of herself as a woman, yet still be attracted to women. The two concepts are separate and distinct.

Playing Male and Female Roles

Another common stereotype about gay and lesbian people is that in any particular pair, one will choose a "masculine," dominant role and the other a "feminine," submissive role. As with most heterosexual couples, this is usually not the case (Johnson, 2014; Morrow, 2006c; Rathus et al., 2014). Any individual, homosexual or heterosexual, may play a more dominant or more submissive role depending on his or her particular mood, activity, or the interaction involved. People are rarely totally submissive or totally dominant.

The Myth of Child Molesting

Another derogatory stereotype targeting gay and lesbian people is that they are inclined to molest children (Greenberg et al., 2014; Rathus et al., 2014; Tully, 2001). This stereotype is especially damaging for homosexual teachers in that it can cause them to lose their jobs. In reality, the majority of all child molesting is done to young girls by heterosexual men, usually people trusted and close to them (e.g., a father, stepfather, or brother) (McAnulty & Burnette, 2003). Heterosexual men are 11 times more likely to be child molesters than are gay men (McCammon & Knox, 2007; Moser, 1992).

Ethical Questions 13.1

Do you harbor any stereotypes about lesbian or gay people? If so, what are they? What, if anything, do you plan to do about them?

EP 2.1.2

What Does Being a Homosexual Mean?

The concept of homosexuality is complex. It is difficult to formulate a definition that reflects its many facets (Miller, 2008). A simplistic definition of a *homosexual* is a person who is attracted *primarily* to people of the same gender to satisfy sexual and emotional needs, which involves sexual orientation (Shernoff, 1995).

Many theories in the past have focused on how people develop their same-gender sexual orientation by passing through a number of stages. Numerous models have been proposed, all of which "tend to have several things in common. There is almost always a predictable progression from some sort of first awareness of same-gender attractions and feelings; to a stage of self-labeling as being gay, lesbian, or bisexual; through stages of becoming more

accepting of the new identity and sharing it with others; to a final stage of incorporating the identity into the total sense of self" (Crooks & Baur, 2014; Kelly, 2008, p. 375; Rathus et al., 2014).

However, such a perspective may be overly simplistic and ethnocentrically biased (taking account of only one's own cultural values and considering them superior over others) to North American and European groups (Martin, 2008; Messinger & Brooks, 2008; Miller, 2008). The concept of having a same-gender sexual orientation might be an ever-emerging social construction of reality that changes as social conditions and expectations change (Martin, 2008). There may be different perspectives depending on one's racial, ethnic, and cultural background. "For example, Latino immigrant men who have sex with other men may not consider themselves to be gay as long as they take a dominant role in sexual intercourse (Zea, Reisen, & Diaz, 2003)" (Martin, 2008, pp. 247–248). The important thing may be each person's self-identification of his or her own sexual orientation (Kelly, 2008; Martin, 2008).

An important aspect of any definition of "homosexual" is that above all else, a homosexual is a person. In the eyes of some heterosexuals, the sexuality of a lesbian or gay person often takes precedence over all other aspects of his or her personality, and the person becomes lost or invisible (see Figure 13.1).

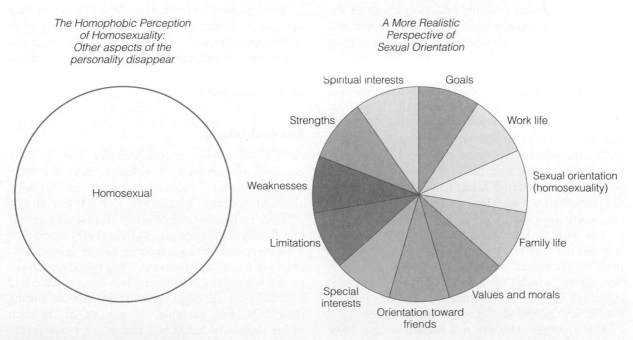

FIGURE 13.1 The Personality Pie

The homosexuality is seen as prominent, at the expense of all other aspects of the lesbian or gay person's personality. A more realistic view is one in which homosexuality is seen in context. The fact that a person is lesbian or gay is only one slice of a person's personality pie. A realistic perspective allows the many various aspects of the person's personality to be acknowledged and appreciated.

Many people are taught *homophobia*, the extreme and irrational fear and hatred of gay and lesbian people. These feelings warp their perception of homosexuals. Some people feel that being of the same-gender orientation is "pathological" (Bieschke, McClanahan, Tozer, Grzegorek, & Park, 2000, p. 311; Greenberg et al., 2014). Highlight 13.2 describes conversion therapy that attempts to change people to heterosexuals.

Another aspect of the definition of homosexual is that the homosexual is attracted *primarily* to people of the same gender to satisfy sexual and affectional needs. A gay male is attracted to and would choose to have an intimate sexual and affectional relationship with another male rather than a female. A lesbian would opt to have such an intimate involvement with another female instead of a male. This part of the definition excludes people who under certain circumstances engage in homosexual activities. For instance, prisoners and other institutionalized persons might establish homosexual relationships with others simply because persons of the opposite gender are unavailable. These people will typically return to heterosexuality when the opportunity arises.

The word *homosexual* is derived from the Greek root *homo*, meaning "same." The word *homosexual* itself, however, was not used until the late 1800s (Karlen, 1971). Terms used to refer to lesbian and gay people can be confusing. Both women and men with same-gender orientations have been labeled homosexuals. Gay men prefer the term *gay* instead of *homosexual* because it has neither the direct sexual connotations nor the demeaning implications frequently associated with the word *homosexual*.

The word *lesbian* refers to female homosexuals. Around the year 600 B.C., a woman named Sappho lived on the Greek island of Lesbos in the Aegean Sea (from which the term *lesbian* is derived). Although Sappho was married, she remains famous for the love poems she wrote to other women.

Many people who are not lesbian or gay have traditionally used the term *gay* to refer both to lesbians and gay men. However, many lesbians have expressed concern that men are given precedence over women when this term is used by itself to refer to both genders. There is some indication that the media now often use the phrase "gay men and lesbians" (American Association of Sex Educators, Counselors, and Therapists [AASECT], 2006, p. 17). Although we have established specific definitions of *lesbian*, *gay*, and *homosexual*, many who use these terms do not have a clear picture of what they mean. All three words may refer to a person with slight, moderate, or substantial interest in or sexual experience with persons of the same gender. Heterosexual people are often referred to as *straight*.

Note that sometimes the concepts of sexual orientation and gender identity are confused, although they are distinctly separate concepts. We have defined *gender identity* as a person's internal psychological self-concept of being either male or female, or possibly some combination of both. Some people assume that gay men really want to be women and that lesbians desire to be men. This is false. A gay man's gender identity is male. He identifies himself as a man and feels like a man. Similarly, a lesbian's gender identity is female, which is how she perceives herself. Gay men and lesbians are simply romantically attracted to (i.e., have a *sexual orientation* toward) their same gender instead of the opposite gender.

Some people, however, regardless of whether they are gay or heterosexual, feel that their biological gender identity is wrong. In a discussion about the complexity of gender, Chapter 9 introduced transgender and transsexual people. Spotlight 13.1 discusses this group further.

Bisexual People

A *bisexual* person is romantically and sexually attracted to members of either gender. We have already initiated the idea that homosexuality is not a clear-cut concept. Bisexuality is even less clearly defined. In the first major study of sexuality in our era, Kinsey, Pomeroy, and Martin (1948) found that it was very difficult to categorize people as homosexual, bisexual, or heterosexual. They found that many people who considered themselves heterosexual had had homosexual experiences at some time during their lives. For example, 37 percent of the men in his sample of 5,300 had had at least one sexual experience with another male, to the point of

HIGHLIGHT 13.2

The Ethical Problems of Conversion Therapy

EP 2.1.2b

Some people harbor the belief that "same-sex attraction represents a deviation from normal sexual and gender development" (Bieschke et al., 2000, p. 311). They support the idea of *conversion therapy* (also referred to as reparative or reorientation therapy) to convert people who are gay or lesbian to heterosexuals (Bieschke et al., 2000; Johnson, 2011b; Morrow, 2006b). The idea is that having a same-gender sexual orientation is simply wrong and should be changed. The implication is that external values (specifically, *heterosexism*, the intolerant attitude and discriminatory behavior against gay and lesbian people by heterosexuals) should be forcibly imposed upon people, thus denying their right to self-determination in this area.

In the past, such treatment included "techniques such as prayer, exorcism, religious-based guilt inducement, and punishment-oriented forms of behavior modification (Tozer & McClanahan, 1999; White, 1995)" (Morrow, 2006b, p. 185). Today's approaches tend to focus on "cognitive-behavioral techniques in an attempt to suppress an individual's attraction to others of the same sex" (Bieschke et al., 2000, p. 312). *Cognitive-behavioral therapy* "involves the modification of thoughts and actions by influencing an individual's conscious patterns of thought" (Boyle, Hull, Mather, Smith, & Farley, 2009, p. 363).

The American Psychological Association (APA) rejected the effectiveness of and ethics involved in conversion therapy after an APA panel reviewed "83 studies on sexual orientation change conducted since 1960" (Associated Press, 2009). The APA determined that no concrete support existed on the behalf of conversion therapy. If anything, it determined such "therapy" could be damaging by causing depression and suicidal inclinations.

Thirteen professional organizations of helping professionals and educators have published a pamphlet entitled "Just the Facts About Sexual Orientation and Youth" that is available online without charge (APA, 2008; Just the Facts Coalition, 2008). It concludes:

> Because of the aggressive promotion of efforts to change sexual orientation through therapy, a number of medical, health, and mental health professional organizations have issued public statements about the dangers of this approach. The American Academy of Pediatrics, the American Counseling Association, the American Psychiatric Association, the American Psychological Association, the American School Counselor Association, the National Association of School Psychologists, and the National Association of Social Workers, together representing more than 480,000 mental health professionals, have all taken the position that homosexuality is not a mental disorder and thus is not something that needs to or can be "cured."
> (Dively et al., 2008, p. 9)

Morrow (2006b) comments on conversion therapy for youth:

> Parents who are uncomfortable with having a gay or lesbian child may seek out conversion therapy practitioners

under the mistaken assumption that their child's sexual orientation can be changed through such therapy. There is no credible empirical support for the success of conversion therapy in actually changing sexual orientation…. Conversion therapy practice can cause psychological harm to GLBT [gay, lesbian, bisexual, and transgender] youth by reinforcing negative stereotypes and misinformation and inducing internalized homophobia. (pp. 185–186)

The *National Association of Social Workers Policy Statements* (NASW, 2012) state that conversion therapy is unethical. Specifically,

- *NASW supports the right of the individual to self-disclose, or to not disclose, sexual orientation and encourages the development of supportive practice environments for lesbian, gay, and bisexual clients and colleagues.*
- *NASW reaffirms its stance against reparative therapies and treatments designed to change sexual orientation or to refer to practitioners or programs that claim to do so.* (p. 222)

Morrow and Tyson (2006) suggest how social workers can help people who are seeking conversion therapy to better understand themselves and their sexual orientation:

> An initial response would be to assess the nature of the personal thoughts, feelings, and experiences that could have led the client to the point of seeking sexual orientation change. Affirmative practice would include helping the client understand the powerful forces of homophobia, internalized homophobia, and heterosexism—at the micro and macro levels of social power and influence—and the ways in which these forces create and perpetuate the internationalization of GLB-negative messages. Thus, initial intervention in such cases lies in helping clients understand the power of heterosexism in how they view sexual orientation in their own lives. Also, it would be appropriate to inform clients that conversion therapy is scientifically unproven and that its practice is considered unethical. (p. 396)

Ethical Question 13.2

What ethical issues do you think are involved in conversion therapy? Explain your reasons.

EP 2.1.2

SPOTLIGHT ON DIVERSITY 13.1

Transsexual and Transgender People

EP 2.1.4

Chapter 9 defined *transsexual* people as those whose gender identity is the opposite of their biological gender. It is frequently said that they "feel trapped in the body of the opposite gender." Often transsexual people prefer to be referred to as *transgender* people because the term *transsexual* emphasizes "sex," and gender identity involves so many more facets of an individual's personality and life circumstances. Technically, as Chapter 9 indicated, the term *transgender* can refer to a range of people, including transsexual people, transvestites, drag queens, drag kings, and female impersonators. Transsexual and transgender people involve complex concepts. Here we will use the term *transgender* to mean "transsexual" as defined above.

Many transgender people pursue surgery to enhance their physical appearance as people of the opposite gender—a process that usually involves four steps. First, they enter counseling to make certain that they are aware of their true feelings and that they understand the potential ramifications of changing genders. Second, they undergo a "real-life test" in which they actually live and undertake their daily activities as a person of the opposite gender. Third, they receive extensive hormone treatments to align their bodies with the opposite gender as much as possible—a process that they must continue for the rest of their lives. For example, female-to-male transgender people would take male hormones to encourage facial and body hair growth, while male-to-female transgender people would take female hormones to encourage the softening of body tissue and the redistribution of body fat. The fourth step involves undergoing surgery in which genitals and other areas of the body are surgically altered to more closely resemble the opposite gender. Of course, changes are primarily cosmetic because construction of internal organs is impossible. Genital tissue is used to create a penis-like organ and scrotum for female-to-male transgender people, and a vaginal canal and labia for male-to-female transgender people. Other physical alterations might include breast implants or breast removal, or decreasing the size of a biological male's Adam's apple.

Male-to-female operations have been more common than the reverse (Hyde & DeLamater, 2014). Female-to-male surgery is generally more complex. In view of the physical pain and discomfort, in addition to the high cost, many transgender people choose not to pursue surgery.

The NASW (2012) Policy Statement on "Transgender and Gender Identity Issues" reads as follows:

- *NASW reaffirms a commitment to human rights and freedom and opposes all public and private discrimination on the basis of gender identity and of gender expression, whether actual or perceived, and regardless of assigned sex at birth, including denial of access to employment, housing, education, appropriate treatment in gender segregated facilities, appropriate medical care and health care coverage, appropriate identity documents, and civil marriage and all its attendant benefits, rights, and privileges.*
- *NASW encourages the repeal of discriminatory legislation and the passage of legislation protecting the rights, legal benefits, and privileges of people of all gender identities and expressions. (p. 341)*

Ethical Questions 13.3

EP 2.1.2

Should transgender people have the right to physically alter themselves to better resemble their true gender identity? If so, who should pay for it? The individuals themselves? Insurance companies? The public?

orgasm, after reaching age 16. In a study of 5,940 women, Kinsey and his associates (1953) found that between 8 and 20 percent had had some type of homosexual contact between ages 20 and 35. A significantly smaller percentage of each group had exclusively homosexual experiences throughout their lifetimes.

Because Kinsey and his associates found it so difficult to place people into distinct categories of homosexual or heterosexual, they developed a six-point scale that placed people on a continuum concerning their sexual experiences (see Figure 13.2). A rating of zero on the scale meant that the individual was exclusively heterosexual—the person had never had any type of homosexual experience. Conversely, a score of 6 on the scale indicated exclusive homosexuality—this individual had never experienced any form of heterosexual behavior.

Those persons scoring 3 would have equal homosexual and heterosexual interest and experience.

More recent researchers have discovered similar difficulties in clearly categorizing people in terms of their sexual orientation. Storms (1980, 1981) suggests that the Kinsey scale still failed to provide an accurate description. He developed a two-dimensional scheme to reflect sexual orientation (see Figure 13.2). The two dimensions are homoeroticism (sexual interest in and/or experience with those of the same gender) and heteroeroticism (sexual interest in and/or experience with those of the opposite gender).

Additionally, Storms's scheme portrays level of sexual interest. Those individuals who express high interest in both sexes are placed in the upper right-hand corner. They are considered bisexuals. Those persons who have a very low sexual interest in either gender are placed in the lower left-hand corner.

They are considered asexual. Persons with primary sexual interest in the same gender, homosexuals, are placed in the upper left-hand corner. Similarly, people with primary sexual interest in the opposite gender, heterosexuals, are placed in the lower right-hand corner.

We've established that gender expression is complex. Terms used to refer to various groups depend on the issues involved. Lesbian, gay, bisexual, and transgender (LGBT) people may experience some of the same issues, such as homophobia and discrimination. In these contexts, the term LGBT or GLBT (gay, lesbian, bisexual, and transgender) might be used. However, each group also has its own special circumstances and issues, so sometimes only one or some of these groups (such as transgender people, or lesbians and gay men) will be the focus of reference.

The homophobic conceptualization: a "black-or-white," "all or nothing" perspective

Heterosexual   Homosexual

Kinsey's (1953) six-point scale

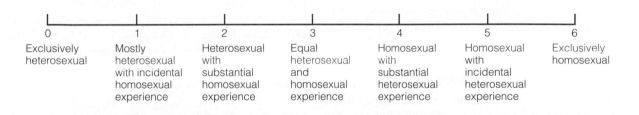

0	1	2	3	4	5	6
Exclusively heterosexual	Mostly heterosexual with incidental homosexual experience	Heterosexual with substantial homosexual experience	Equal heterosexual and homosexual experience	Homosexual with substantial heterosexual experience	Homosexual with incidental heterosexual experience	Exclusively homosexual

Storms's (1980) two-dimensional conceptualization

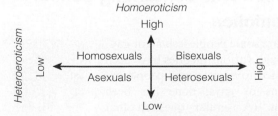

FIGURE 13.2 Conceptualizations of Homosexuality and Heterosexuality

Source: A. C. Kinsey, W. B. Pomeroy, and C. E. Martin (eds.). (1948). Sexual Behavior in the Human Male. Adapted by permission of the Kinsey Institute for Research in Sex, Gender & Reproduction, Inc., Bloomington, IN; Adapted from M. D. Storms, 1980, "Theories of Sexual Orientation," Journal of Personality and Social Psychology, 38, 783–792.

Note that a newer acronym sometimes being employed to refer to people whose sexual orientation is not strictly toward the opposite gender is LGBTQ. Here "Q" stands for "queer" or "questioning" (Carroll, 2013b, p. 270; Rosenthal, 2013, p. 234). Another term used is LGBTI (lesbian, gay, bisexual, transgender, and intersex) (Alderson, 2013). Chapter 9 discussed intersex people, individuals who have some mixture of male and female predisposition and configuration of reproductive structures.

However, Alderson (2013) cautions:

Terminology is often challenging when writing or talking about groups who have been historically oppressed and disenfranchised. Postmodern writers have become very sensitive to the labels used to describe individuals....

Identities [labels used to refer to some group of people] describe one aspect of a person. A lesbian woman, for example, is more than just her nonheterosexual identity—she is also someone's daughter, someone's neighbor, and someone's friend. She is a lover, a worker, and an inhabitor of earth. Similarly, referring to a transsexual individual as a "transsexual" diminishes this person's existence to this one aspect of self....

Identity labels—when chosen at all—are picked by individuals themselves to describe some aspect that defines their sense of self. Consequently, they can be transient labels, inaccurate labels, or oversimplified labels. Such is also the case with some LGBTI individuals—our sexuality and gender is so much more than the label we give it. (pp. 2–4)

Numbers of Lesbian and Gay People

It's difficult, if not impossible, to state exactly how many people are lesbian or gay. However, it may be useful to consider the numbers of people who have adopted a primarily lesbian or gay orientation over an extended period of time.

Based on Kinsey's work, "many authors have used 10 percent as the proportion of men who are gay" (Berger & Kelly, 1995, p. 1066; Mallon, 2008). Kinsey found that although more than one-third of American men had had homosexual experiences leading to orgasm during their adolescent or adult lives, only 10 percent of men were exclusively homosexual for a three-year period between ages 16 and 55, and only about 4 percent were gay throughout their lives.

Supposedly, two to three times as many men as women have a homosexual orientation. Although Kinsey found that 19 percent of American women had had homosexual experiences by the age of 40, only 2 to 3 percent of these remained lesbian throughout their lives.

The Kinsey research posed some methodological problems that make it difficult to compare it with more recent research. For example, Kinsey and his colleagues included a large number of prisoners and volunteers from gay organizations (Masters, Johnson, & Kolodny, 1995). They also "included feelings and fantasies in their definition of homosexuality, whereas some recent surveys focused exclusively on sexual behavior" (Berger & Kelly, 1995).

Many lesbian and gay organizations maintain that lesbians and gays make up 10 percent of the population; one such organization is called "The Ten Percent Society." However, the controversy regarding the actual number of lesbian and gay people continues (About.com, 2014; Berger & Kelly, 1995; Rogers, 1993; Tully, 1995), with various studies and polls producing different results. Somewhere between 2 and 10 percent of the population appears to be gay or lesbian (Johnson, 2011c; Kelly, 2008; Mallon, 2008). Other indications are that more than 5 percent of the total population over age 18 is probably gay or lesbian (Mallon, 2008). Yet other data indicate that about 2 percent of men and 1 percent of women have "a homosexual identity," which is quite different than having varying degrees of same gender sexual experiences (Hyde & DeLamater, 2014, p. 339). Regardless of whether lesbian and gay people make up 1 or 10 percent of the population, they are a sizable minority group.

LO 13-3 Discuss Conceptual Frameworks Concerning Sexual Orientation

Why are some people lesbian or gay? Although various theories have been proposed to explain why people are lesbians or gays, none has been proven. (A similar question that could be asked is, "Why are people heterosexual?") No one can give a

EP 2.1.3a

definitive answer concerning why some people are homosexual and others heterosexual. Some of the principal hypotheses will be reviewed here. They fall under the umbrellas of biological and psychosocial theories. Evaluation of theory, interactionist theory, ethical issues related to theory, and other research will also be discussed.

Biological Theories

The biological theories attempting to explain homosexuality can be clustered under three headings: genetic, anatomical (brain), and hormonal. They are based on the idea that homosexuality is caused by physiological factors over which individuals have no control.

Genetic Factors

The genetic explanation for homosexuality supports the idea that people's sexuality is programmed through their genes. Bailey and Pillard compared groups of identical twins, fraternal twins, and brothers who were adopted (1991). Identical twins develop from the splitting of a single fertilized egg. They are therefore genetically identical. Fraternal twins, on the other hand, develop concurrently from two separate eggs that were fertilized by two separate sperm. They are only as genetically similar as any brothers might be. Brothers who are adopted, unless they are family members, have no genetic commonality. The researchers found that when one identical twin was gay, 52 percent of their twin brothers were also gay. Among only 22 percent of fraternal twins and 11 percent of adoptive brothers were both brothers gay. The researchers concluded that this provides evidence for a genetic link. They indicated that the degree of genetic contribution to homosexuality could vary from 30 to 70 percent.

Another study looked at 108 lesbians who had either identical or fraternal twin sisters and another 32 lesbians who had adopted sisters (Bailey et al., 1993). They found that among almost half of the identical twins, both were lesbians. However, only 16 percent of fraternal twins and 6 percent of the unrelated sisters were both lesbians. These results further support the idea of a genetic component to homosexuality. Subsequent research using more refined methodology had similar findings that helped substantiate the results of this study (Kendler, Thornton, Gilman, & Kessler, 2000; Kirk et al., 2000).

"Gay men have more gay brothers than lesbian sisters, while lesbians have more lesbian sisters than gay brothers"; she also "found evidence of a 'gay' gene on the X chromosome but did not find a 'lesbian' gene" (Bogaert, 2005; Carroll, 2010, pp. 283–284).

Some research in Australia studied 1,538 pairs of twins (Bailey, Dunne, & Martin, 2000). The researchers used "a strict criterion for determining sexual orientation" and "found a concordance rate (the percentage of pairs in which both twins are homosexual) of 20% among identical male twins and 0% among pairs of male same-sex fraternal twins. The corresponding concordance rates for female identical and same-sex fraternal pairs were 24% and 10.5%, respectively" (Crooks & Baur, 2011, p. 255).

"There is a great deal of evidence that gay and lesbian sexual orientations run in families" (Bailey et al., 2000; Carroll, 2013b; Dawood, Pillard, Horvath, Revelle, & Bailey, 2000; Greenberg et al., 2014, p. 377; Kendler et al., 2000). However, "[s]exuality experts do caution that a specific gene linked to homosexuality has not been identified. Also, because of the complexity of sexual orientation, it is likely that a possible genetic link is only part of the picture" (Greenberg et al., 2014, p. 377).

Brain (Anatomical) Factors

LeVay (1991, 1996) studied the brains of 41 cadavers: 19 of gay men, 16 of supposedly heterosexual men, and 6 of supposedly heterosexual women. He found that the anterior hypothalamus (a marble-sized cluster of cells that regulates sexual activity in addition to appetite and body temperature) in gay men was only half the size of that in heterosexual men.

"More recent studies have also found brain differences—specifically in the cerebral hemispheres—of heterosexual and homosexual men and women" (Carroll, 2013b, p. 274). Yet, it is unknown whether such variations were present at birth or arose at some time after that; additionally, no evidence exists to confirm that such differences were directly related to sexual orientation (Carroll, 2013a Kinnunen, Moltz, Metz, & Cooper, 2004; Swaab, 2004). Therefore, at present, there are no clearly established brain differences related to sexual orientation (Carroll, 2013a; Gooren, 2006).

Hormonal Factors

Hormonal theories of heterosexuality suggest that hormonal type and level cause homosexuality. One subset of hormonal theories concerns differences in hormonal levels during adulthood. Another subset of the hormonal theories indicates that abnormal hormonal levels during the prenatal period may result in homosexuality (Berger & Kelly, 1995).

Research has established no relationship between hormonal levels and sexual orientation either during the prenatal period or in adulthood (Carroll, 2013b; Hyde & DeLamater, 2014). Hormone levels are related to sexual interest and activity in adulthood. However, as Hyde and DeLamater (2014) comment, "As a clinician friend of ours replied to an undergraduate male who was seeking testosterone therapy for his homosexual behavior, 'It won't make you heterosexual; it will only make you horny'" (p. 343).

Psychosocial Theories

Psychosocial or behavioral theories suggest that homosexual behavior is learned, just as any other type of behavior is learned. Early in life, homosexual behavior may be positively reinforced by pleasurable experiences and thereby strengthened. Or such behavior may be punished by negative, punitive experiences and, as a result, be weakened.

For instance, a child who has several positive sexual contacts with members of the same gender might be positively reinforced or encouraged to seek out more such contacts. Similarly, a child who has a negative experience with a member of the same gender might be discouraged from having more such encounters.

The Evaluation of Theory: What Is the Answer?

EP 2.1.7b

The answer to why people are gay is a multifaceted one. Genetic rationales have major shortcomings. For example, we discussed the research finding concerning identical twins. If, as some researchers postulate, genetic rationales explain some component or percentage of why people are gay, then what explains the remaining components or percentages? If people are gays or lesbians because of some hormonal impact (perhaps prenatally), why aren't all people lesbians or gays who experienced similar hormonal impacts?

At least two major shortcomings can be cited with respect to psychosocial theories of homosexuality that emphasize the learning process. First, there is a tremendous amount of negative feedback about homosexuality. Children learn early that being called a "fag" is not a compliment. How homosexual behavior would be reinforced and would increase in frequency, in view of such punitive circumstances, might be questioned.

Second, learning theory implies that a person must first have a homosexual experience. Then, if the experience was positively reinforcing or personally rewarding, the person would seek out more such experiences. However, might it not be the case that individuals who have homosexual desires seek out sexual experiences with the same gender in the first place? In other words, might not the desire for sexual contact with the same gender be there even before any actions ever occur?

Interactionist Theory

Storms (1981) has proposed a theory that focuses on the interaction of biological predisposition and the effects of the environment. He poses that the development of a homosexual orientation is related to the rate at which people mature during preadolescence. Children tend to play and interact with people of the same gender during preadolescence. This same-sex interaction reaches its peak at about age 12, after which heterosexual interactions begin to develop. Heterosexual dating may start around age 15. Storms suggests that the sex drive for some people emerges earlier than for others. If children who mature earlier are still in same-sex groupings, they may have positive sexual experiences with persons of the same gender during this time. They may develop a pattern whereby they remain oriented toward the same gender. They never become interested sexually in the opposite gender. This is where the environment plays a part. If these children happen to have positive sexual same-sex experiences, they may continue with that same sexual orientation. If early maturers do not have these experiences, they continue later to develop a heterosexual orientation as they begin interacting with people of the opposite gender.

Many experts agree that homosexuality probably results from some mixture of both biological and psychosocial variables. As yet we don't know what that mixture is. There is still no clearly established reason why people are lesbians or gays.

Ethical Issues Related to Theory

**EP 2.1.2,
2.1.2c**

Some lesbian and gay people have expressed ethical concerns regarding proving any theory about homosexuality involving a biological component. On the one hand, many express relief at the thought that others might consider their homosexuality not to be their "own fault." If there's a medical basis, the general public might become more accepting of lesbians and gay men. Gelman and his colleagues (Gelman, Foote, Barrett, & Talbot, 1992) found that people were generally more accepting of lesbian and gay people if they felt such people were "born that way" instead of *choosing* or *learning* that lifestyle.

On the other hand, if specific genetic or hormonal "ingredients" are found for homosexuality, lesbian and gay people might be considered defective by society at large. Taking this one step further, society at large might decide to make biological "corrections" prenatally. Might this mean changing what a person was meant to be into something else? Might potential parents be more likely to abort a fetus determined to be lesbian or gay if they learn about the homosexuality early in the gestational process? There are no easy answers to these questions in our technological age.

Other Research on the Origins of Homosexuality

Bell and his colleagues (Bell, Weinberg, Martin, & Hammersmith, 1981) undertook a massive investigation through the Alfred C. Kinsey Institute for Sex Research concerning the causes of homosexuality. They studied 979 lesbians and gay men, and compared them to 477 heterosexual women and men. Study participants were asked extensive questions about many aspects of their lives. A statistical method called *path analysis* allowed the researchers to explore possible causal relationships between a number of variables, such as prenatal characteristics and family relationships, and the development of sexual orientation.

Although the research offers some of the most extensive and methodologically sound findings available, none of the aforementioned theories to explain homosexuality was supported. If anything,

several of the variables proposed by these other theories were found not to be related to homosexuality. For instance, no relationship was found between being gay and having been seduced by a person of the same gender when young. The researchers found no ultimate answers, but they did identify some interesting aspects of being lesbian or gay. Three findings are of special significance.

First, sexual orientation appears to emerge by the time both males and females reach adolescence. This is the case even when people have little or no sexual experience. Sometimes people begin grasping that they're not heterosexual because of different feelings during childhood. "Many realize during adolescence that something is missing in their heterosexual involvements and that they find same-sex peers sexually attractive" (Crooks & Baur, 2014, p. 269).

Second, lesbian and gay people have similar amounts of heterosexual experience during childhood and adolescence when compared to heterosexual people. There is one basic difference, however. Although lesbian and gay people participate in heterosexual activity, they do not enjoy it very much.

The third major finding of the study involves the concept of gender nonconformity, which appears to begin in childhood for gay males and lesbians (Bailey & Zucker, 1995; Lippa, 2008; Rathus et al., 2014; Singh, Vidaurri, Zambarano, & Dabbs, 1999). Gender nonconformity refers to a child's preference for play and activities that our society generally considers appropriate for children of the opposite gender. For example, little girls usually choose to play with Barbie dolls and play dishes, whereas little boys generally prefer GI Joes and toy bulldozers. A little girl who only plays with tanks and footballs or a little boy who only plays with Barbie dolls would be examples of gender nonconformity. Gender nonconformity was a much stronger causal factor for gay men than for lesbians. Other factors such as family relationships have a stronger causal relationship with lesbianism.

This research indicates that sexual orientation develops very early in life. It also suggests that whether a person is gay or lesbian or heterosexual is not a matter of choice. Just as a heterosexual person may be sexually attracted to another heterosexual person, so is a lesbian or gay person sexually attracted to another of the same gender. It appears that it would be just as impossible for a lesbian or gay person to turn heterosexual as it would be for a heterosexual person to begin choosing sexual partners of the same gender.

The fact that many lesbian and gay people externally assume heterosexual roles for the sake of appearance is also logical. Numerous homophobic stigmas are placed on gay or lesbian people. They are often subjected to serious discrimination. In evaluating the consequences of the various alternatives open to them, some lesbian and gay people may decide that it is too difficult to survive openly as a gay or lesbian person (e.g., hold a job, relate to family members, participate in community activities). A lesbian or gay person with a heterosexual facade is burdened with pretending to be someone

she or he is not. Such pretense can violate individual dignity and freedom. Spotlight 13.2 discusses discrimination and the impact of homophobia on gay and lesbian people.

SPOTLIGHT ON DIVERSITY 13.2

LO 13-4 Address Discrimination and the Impacts of Homophobia

"Did you ever hear the one about the dyke who …"
"Harry sure has a 'swishy' way about him. You'd never catch me in the locker room alone with that guy."
"They're nothing but a bunch of lousy faggots."

EP 2.1.1b; 2.1.4b & d

Our common language is filled with derogatory terms referring to lesbian and gay people. Just as other diverse groups are subject to arbitrary stereotypes and to discrimination, so are gay and lesbian people. Because of negative attitudes and the resulting discriminatory behavior, alternatives for lesbian and gay people are often different and limited. There are often other negative consequences. Other, nonsexually related aspects of their lives are affected because of their sexual orientation.

For example, a male third-grade teacher may live in fear that the parents of his students will discover he's living with another man. He loves his job, which he's had for nine years. If parents put pressure on the school administration about his homosexuality, he may get fired. He may never get another teaching job again.

Another example is provided by a female college student who expends massive amounts of energy to disguise that she's a lesbian. She attends a state university in a small, Midwestern, rural town. She is terribly lonely. She keeps hoping that that special someone will walk into her life. However, she doesn't dare let her friends know she's lesbian or she really will be isolated. There wouldn't be anyone to talk to or to

go to dinner with. They would just never understand. People have committed suicide for less.

Lesbian and gay people are frequently the victims of homophobia. We have defined *homophobia* as the extreme and irrational fear and hatred of gay and lesbian people. People with same-gender sexual orientation have historically been discriminated against by the U.S. military, religious, mental health, medical, and various other institutions and systems.

Some feel that the term *homophobia* is too strong because the word *phobia* means "an intense and persistent fear of an object or situation" (Barker, 2014, p. 322). *Antihomosexual* or *antigay* stance, *prejudice*, or *discrimination* might be alternate terms. In reality, homophobia is likely a continuum. People probably vary markedly in the depth of their negative feelings about lesbian and gay people. Regardless of what it's called, many people harbor seriously negative perceptions and prejudice against lesbian and gay people (Carroll, 2013b; Kelly, 2008; LeVay & Valente, 2006; Messinger & Brooks, 2008).

It is not clear how homophobia originated. It may involve people's attempts to deny homosexual feelings in themselves (Maier, 1984). Perhaps the more strongly homophobic people are, the more they are working to deny such feelings in themselves. Regardless of the cause, the manifestations of homophobia are all around us. In the past, homosexuality was considered an illness. Not until 1974 did the American Psychiatric Association remove it from the list of mental illnesses.

SPOTLIGHT ON DIVERSITY 13.2 *(continued)*

Crooks and Baur (2011) potently describe how venomous homophobia can be:

Unfortunately, homophobia is still common and often plays a big role in the lives of many gay men, lesbians, and bisexuals (Symanski, 2009).... The homophobosphere, antigay postings on Internet blogs, both expresses and creates hate (Doig, 2008). Such expressions contribute to the ongoing daily harassment of and discrimination against anyone outside 'acceptable' heterosexual parameters, and they legitimize the mind-set of people who commit hate crimes directed at gays. Hate crimes include assault, robbery, and murder, and they are committed because the victim belongs to a certain race, religion, or ethnic group or has a certain sexual orientation (pp. 261–262).

Rathus and his colleagues (2014) relate that homophobia may assume "many forms, including the following:

- *use of derogatory names (such as queer, faggot, and dyke)*
- *telling disparaging "queer jokes"*
- *barring gay people from housing, employment, or social opportunities*
- *taunting (verbal abuse)*
- *gay bashing (physical, sometimes lethal, abuse) (p. 283)*

A potentially negative side effect would be to internalize such negative attitudes. In other words, a gay or lesbian person might think, "If being homosexual is bad, and I am homosexual, then that means that I am bad, too."

It is vitally important that social workers confront their own homophobia and learn more about the special issues of lesbian and gay clients. Social workers must explore and confront their own homophobia in order to understand and meet the needs of lesbian and gay clients and their families; not doing so raises grave questions about their ability to

undertake ethical social work practice (Alderson, 2013; Morales, 1995; Morrow, 2006c).

Social workers must:

1. *Develop a GLBT content knowledge base [including the recognition of current LGBT issues and an understanding of the LGBT lesbian and gay communities] ...*
2. *Challenge personal biases about sexual minority people and practice in accordance with social work values and ethics....*
3. *[N]ot presume the sexual orientation or gender identity of clients....*
4. *Use accurate and respectful language in all communication to and about clients....*
5. *Avoid assuming that the characteristics and needs of all sexual minority groups—gay, lesbian, bisexual, transgender—are the same....*
6. *Approach cases from an ecological systems perspective [It is important to appreciate the significance of the social environment and its effects on lesbian and gay people's lives. Practitioners should confront oppressive policies, laws, and treatment and advocate for change. Social workers should be aware of available resources and potential social supports.] ...*
7. *Honor diversity among GLBT people [Each lesbian or gay person is a distinct and unique individual, just as each heterosexual person is.]*
8. *Honor client self-determination regarding disclosure....*
9. *Honor clients' rights to privacy regarding their sexual orientation and gender identity....*
10. *Advocate for GLBT-affirmative work environments and GLBT-affirmation agency services. [Social workers should advocate for fair and equal treatment and for services designed to meet the needs of GLBT clients.]* (Morrow, 2006c, pp. 13–15)

LO 13-5 Describe Lesbian and Gay Lifestyles

What is it like to be a lesbian or gay person? How would life be different or similar if you awoke tomorrow morning and discovered that you were homosexual? What would happen to your relationships with family, friends, and colleagues?

No one typical lifestyle is practiced by all lesbians and gay people. Lesbians and gay men have lives that are just as varied as those of heterosexuals. Being a gay man in Dickeyville, Wisconsin, is different from being a gay man in a San Francisco

suburb. Being a white lesbian mother receiving public assistance in Utah is different from being an African American upper-class lesbian mother in Boston. However, some common patterns emerge in the lives of lesbian and gay people. Several issues reflected by these patterns are addressed here.

Lesbian and Gay Relationships

Individual relationships and lifestyles vary among lesbian and gay people just as they do among heterosexuals (Longres & Fredriksen, 2000; Mallon, 2008; Tully, 2001). As with heterosexuals, many lesbian

Gay people in a committed relationship differ little from their heterosexual counterparts.

and gay people live with a significant other as a couple. Others live by themselves or with a heterosexual partner, friends, children, or family. Additionally, many have children (Mallon, 2008; Messinger & Brooks, 2008). Same-sex couples face many of the same issues and hold many of the same values as their heterosexual counterparts (Crooks & Baur, 2014; Holmberg & Blair, 2009). The diversity characterizing heterosexual couples (e.g., socioeconomic status, educational level, racial and ethnic background, communication style) is also reflected in same-sex couples.

Rathus and his colleagues (2014) reflect on lesbian and gay relationships:

Most gay males and lesbians who share close relationships with their partners are satisfied with the overall quality of their relationships. Researchers find that heterosexual and gay couples report similar levels of satisfaction with their relationships (Henderson et al., 2009; Kurdek, 2005). Moreover, gay males and lesbians in enduring relationships generally report high levels of love, attachment, closeness, caring, and intimacy.

As with heterosexual people, not all the relationships of gay people are satisfying. Among both groups, satisfaction is higher when both partners feel that the benefits they receive from the relationship

outweigh the costs (Henderson et al., 2009). Like heterosexual people, gay men and lesbians are happier in relationships in which they share power and make joint decisions. (pp. 282–283)

Ossana (2000) elaborates:

The correlates of relationship quality are similar for all couples: appraisals that the relationship includes many rewards and few costs; personality characteristics such as high expressiveness; partner's placing higher value on security, permanence, shared activities, and togetherness; less belief that disagreement is destructive; higher mutual trust; better problem-solving and conflict resolution skills; more frequent shared or egalitarian decision making; and greater satisfaction with perceived social support. (p. 277)

Major social and legal obstacles do exist that prevent lesbian and gay people from establishing long-term relationships. For example, gay and lesbian marriages are a hotly debated issue and are illegal in most states (ProCon.org, 2014). Even if gays and lesbians are very much in love with each other and want to spend their lives together, social obstacles might exist, such as pressure from family and heterosexual friends to form heterosexual relationships, marry, and have children.

Sexual Interaction

Many people find it hard to imagine what lesbian and gay people do sexually. After all, they don't have the "necessary" ingredients of both penis and vagina. The fact is that lesbian and gay people engage in the same types of activities that heterosexuals also enjoy. These include hugging, kissing, touching, fondling of the genitals, and oral sex.

The physiological responses of gay and lesbian people are exactly the same as those of heterosexuals. They become aroused or excited, enter a plateau stage of high arousal, have an orgasm, and go through a period of resolution during which the body returns to its normal, unaroused state. The process is the same for all people, male or female, gay or heterosexual.

LO 13-6 Explore Significant Issues and Life Events for Lesbian and Gay People

EP 2.1.4a, 2.1.5a, 2.1.9b

As members of a diverse group, lesbian and gay people are victims of stereotypes and homophobia. Discrimination may frequently limit the alternatives available to them. Social workers and other human service professionals need to be aware of the special issues and life events confronting lesbian and gay people so that they might provide leadership in improving service delivery. In order to help clients define and evaluate the alternatives available to them, social workers must understand the effects of certain life events. Significant issues and life events of gay and lesbian people are examined here. Additionally, social work with gay and lesbian people is addressed.

The Impacts of Social and Economic Forces: Legal Empowerment and Social Justice

For hundreds of years, laws have existed to suppress homosexuality and ban *sodomy*, defined as anal or oral sex between same-gender or heterosexual people. Harper-Dorton and Lantz (2007) discuss the historical legal perspective:

> *Laws against homosexual behavior date back at least as far as Roman law. Colonists in early*

> *American history punished sodomists with floggings, hangings, and periods of confinement (Robinson, 2003). This history may seem ancient; however, as recently as 2002, sodomy laws continued to be enforceable in fourteen states in addition to Puerto Rico (Robinson, 2005). Legislation against homosexual acts in the United States and the prevailing homophobia in American culture have caused many gay and lesbian persons to fear revealing their sexual orientation. Perhaps for personal safety, many gay men and lesbian women remain covert about their sexual practices. Personal decisions about coming out and openness about sexual orientation are influenced by factors such as fear of hate crimes, discriminatory experiences in the workplace, and exclusion from institutional settings such as the military (Reicherzer, 2005; Tully & Nibao, 1979). (p. 162)*

In 2003, the U.S. Supreme Court in *Lawrence et al v. Texas* struck down a "Texas sodomy law that made private sexual contact between homosexuals illegal" (Crooks & Baur, 2014, p. 265). The Court found that such laws violated people's constitutional right to privacy. As a result, laws in several other states banning sex between homosexuals and prohibiting sodomy were also overturned (Crooks & Baur, 2014).

Four issues will be addressed in which lesbian and gay people are treated differently than heterosexual people under the law: employment, the military, personal relationships and finances, and child custody and visitation. In light of all these challenges, Spotlight 13.3 discusses the importance of a sense of community among gay and lesbian people.

Employment

LGBT people "suffer pervasive discrimination in employment, housing, public accommodation, education, medical care," and a host of other avenues in their everyday lives because they are not legally protected (American Civil Liberties Union [ACLU], 2014a; National Gay and Lesbian Task Force, 2008d). Not until 1976 was the federal government's personnel manual changed to forbid discrimination against lesbian and gay people in hiring or terminations unless the public agency involved could prove that homosexual behavior affected work completion (Dale, 1993). This means that most federal government agencies cannot discriminate against lesbian and gay people purely on the basis of their sexual

SPOTLIGHT ON DIVERSITY 13.3

LO 13-7 Recognize Gay and Lesbian Pride, Empowerment, and a Sense of Community

EP 2.1.10e

All people, gay, lesbian, and heterosexual, need places to socialize, to feel free to be themselves, and to feel that they belong. Gay and lesbian pride and the sense of community are important concepts (Greenberg et al., 2014; LeVay & Valente, 2006; van Wormer, Wells, & Boes, 2000). One young man summarized these concepts well by joyously stating:

As someone who has recently "come out," I have acquired a sense of pride in my homosexuality; a part of me I have run and hidden from for twenty of my twenty-five years. I owe much gratitude to many people in the gay community who have given me the courage to stand up for who I am. I am proud to call these people my gay brothers, the first real friends I have ever had. I'm not ashamed—I'm proud to be gay. My sense of gay pride has made me realize that I'm as good as any other person on this earth and deserving of the same basic human dignity and respect all human beings are entitled to. ("What Does Gay/Lesbian Pride Mean to You?" 1985, p. 2)

Heterosexual innuendos, expectations, values, and ideas saturate our society. One gay man said he always felt he had to be watchful and cautious in heterosexual groups. He carefully censored what he said to protect himself from homophobic attacks on himself and his lifestyle.

Within the lesbian and gay communities, lesbians and gay men can be themselves. They can let down their protective facades. They can be with other people who understand what it's like to be gay in a heterosexually oriented world. This is not to say that many lesbians and gay men have not openly and proudly proclaimed their sexual orientation. This is so even though it means they expose themselves to homophobic criticism, prejudice, and discrimination. In a way, by doing this, they are advocating for individual freedom and the end of discrimination.

In this homophobic world, there are a multitude of lesbian and gay activities and organizations. These range far beyond crisis lines and support groups. There are sports teams and organizations, choral groups, churches, bookstores, newspapers, magazines, advocacy groups, and computer dating services all oriented toward lesbians and gay men. The sense of community has developed and grown far beyond that of the gay bar.

People march in a gay pride parade. The rainbow flag is a common gay pride symbol.

©iStock.com/andipantz

orientation. However, these rules don't apply to state and local jobs. For example, police departments and public schools have often succeeded in driving out lesbian and gay employees (Dale, 1993). Discrimination occurs in a wide range of settings. One gay married man was recently offered a job as food services director at a Catholic girls' school; the school rescinded the offer two days later when an administrator noted that the man indicated on a form that his husband should be the emergency contact person (Valencia, 2014). The man allegedly was told that he couldn't be hired because the church did not recognize gay marriage.

Other than for federal government jobs, there are no federal statutes that prohibit employers from discriminating against lesbian and gay people in the private sector (Human Rights Campaign, 2014; NOLO, 2014b). They are not considered to be one of the groups, such as racial minorities, included under the equal protection clause of the U.S. Constitution. As of this writing the U.S. Congress is considering the Employment Non-Discrimination Act (ENDA), already passed by the U.S. Senate. The law would impart fundamental safeguards against discrimination in employment that is based on sexual orientation or gender identity (Human Rights Campaign, 2014). Prior attempts to pass similar legislation have failed, although such efforts solicit increasing support from members of Congress each year (NOLO, 2014b).

Twenty-one states and the District of Columbia have laws banning discrimination based on sexual orientation; another 17 states have banned discrimination based on gender identity (Human Rights Campaign, 2014). Numerous cities and counties have enacted nondiscrimination policies concerning sexual orientation (NOLO, 2014b). Nondiscrimination legislation might address such issues as hiring and employment, insurance eligibility, "housing, credit, and education" (Berger & Kelly, 1995, p. 1071).

Major progress has been made in implementing antidiscrimination policies in corporate America, although this progress is not reflected in many small businesses and organizations. Eighty-eight percent of Fortune 500 companies have nondiscrimination policies that include sexual orientation; 57 percent of these companies have policies that incorporate nondiscrimination involving gender identity (Human Rights Campaign, 2014).

Ethical Question 13.5

What, if anything, should be done to protect lesbian, gay, and bisexual people from discrimination in employment?

EP 2.1.2

The Military

Since gay and lesbian people historically have been prohibited from joining the CIA, the FBI, and the armed forces, it's important to view the current picture within a historical context (McCrary & Gutierrez, 1979/80; Tully, 1995). The following content discusses both the history of the treatment of lesbians and gay men in the military, and the current, much different scenario.

Leonard Matlovich provides one of the most publicized examples of discrimination against gay and lesbian people by the military. As the son of an air force sergeant, Matlovich was raised on air force bases. Upon his high school graduation, he immediately joined the air force. He received numerous decorations for his service, which included fighting in Vietnam. He was also labeled superior in his evaluations.

Years later, at age 30, Matlovich acknowledged that he was gay and became involved in gay activities. When he told this to his superiors, he was discharged with a general discharge, a type of discharge considered less than honorable. He eventually took his case to court. He "later collected $160,000 in back pay when the air force could not rebut his claim to an exemption from the no-gays policy."

In January 1993, President Clinton announced a plan to revoke the 50-year-old ban on gay and lesbian people in the military. However, Congress so eroded the plan that the final version entailed an uncomfortable "Don't ask, don't tell, don't pursue" guideline (Gelman, 1993, p. 28). This meant that military personnel were supposed to pretend, with an "out of sight, out of mind" approach, that homosexuality doesn't exist. Many questions were raised regarding this policy. Consider the following facts.

Under the so-called "Don't ask, don't tell" policy, 13,000 service members were fired or discharged (O'Keefe, 2011), many of them specialists who were critical to military operations. These included health-care specialists, sonar and radar specialists, combat engineers, law enforcement agents, security guards, and biological and chemical warfare specialists (Servicemembers Legal Defense Network [SLDN], 2005a). Many gay and military personal serving in Iraq and other places in the Middle East experienced serious difficulties because of their sexual orientation. Because they "couldn't tell" that they were gay or lesbian, they couldn't cite their partners as next of kin if something happened to them. And their partners were not beneficiaries of supportive services provided to heterosexual partners and families. At times, many partners were left hanging regarding whether their loved one was alive, hurt, or dead.

In December 2010, President Barack Obama repealed the "Don't Ask, Don't Tell" policy. The repeal finally went into effect on September 20, 2011; by that time almost "2 million service members had been trained in preparation" for the disclosure of sexual orientation by lesbian and gay military personnel in anticipation of potential issues (Bumiller, 2011).

Some estimate that at least 2 percent of service members (including active and reserve) are lesbian, gay, or bisexual (Bumiller, 2012). One survey found that 32 percent have divulged their nonheterosexual orientation; however, this estimate may be high due to a sample that may have used participants who are less guarded about their sexual orientation (Bumiller, 2012).

Bumiller (2012) makes several points concerning the new policy of military personnel being open about their gay or lesbian sexual orientation. The policy generally appears to be successful. Troops have not protested by quitting in droves, as some adversaries to the change had feared. Many gay and lesbian service members express relief that they may be open about their relationships without being discharged. However, many others remain fearful of negative repercussions if they come out to others in a military context. They feel that many heterosexual peers still think a nonheterosexual orientation is unacceptable. "[H]arassment and discrimination against gays in the military has not disappeared." There are derogatory comments and jokes. There have been incidents. For example, one female officer was dancing with her partner at a military ball. A senior officer commanded the women to stop dancing. When the women refused, the senior officer

"shoved" them off the floor. The female officer filed a complaint, the Pentagon investigated it, and the senior officer was removed from his position and compelled to retire.

A major positive aspect of the policy concerning openness is the fact that spouses of gays and lesbians in the military may now receive spousal benefits such as Social Security survivor benefits and family leave (Williams & McClam, 2013). Federal benefits for same-sex couples after new U.S. Supreme Court determinations will be discussed further in the next section.

Personal Relationships, Finances, and Same-Sex Marriage

The right of lesbian and gay people to marry legally in the United States has been a hotly debated issue. A major change occurred in June 2013 when the U.S. Supreme Court struck down major aspects of the federal 1996 Defense of Marriage Act (DOMA). DOMA had defined marriage as being between a man and a woman (Gacik, 2014). In 2013 the Court ruled that same-sex marriage must be accepted by the federal government and that such couples should receive all the federal benefits available to heterosexual couples. These benefits include "Social Security survivor benefits, immigration rights and family leave" (Williams & McClam, 2013). They also include federal tax benefits such as filing joint federal tax returns. Note, however, that federal agencies may determine which same-sex marriages are eligible for benefits; for example, some agencies such as the IRS will recognize all same-sex marriages, whereas the Social Security Administration takes into consideration the couple's state residence and whether that state recognizes same-sex marriage (NOLO, 2014a).

In its 2013 decision the Supreme Court did not force states to accept gay marriage, but rather left them to make their own determinations (Williams & McClam, 2013). Currently, 33 states ban same-sex marriage; 29 of them do so through their state constitutions, usually accompanied by other legislations concerning the issue (National Conference of State Legislatures [NCSL], 2014). It's generally easier to change laws than to change a state constitution, because the latter requires a popular vote (NCSL, 2014). Seventeen states and the District of Columbia allow same-sex marriage (NCSL, 2014). Several states are addressing challenges to bans on

Jim West/Alamy

The right of lesbian and gay people to legally marry is a hotly debated issue in the United States.

same-sex marriage laws through the courts (Eckholm, 2014; NCSL, 2014). States may or may not choose to accept gay marriages performed in other states (NOLO, 2014a).

Some people propose alternatives to same-sex marriage such as civil unions and domestic partnerships. A *civil union* is a legally recognized union that is similar to marriage in some or many respects. They carry essentially the same rights and responsibilities as heterosexual marriage (AASECT, April 2000, May 2000). Such rights include "child custody, probate court, workers' compensation, and family leave benefits" (AASECT, April 2000, p. 6). However, these civil union rights are not transferable to other states should a couple move. Factions criticizing the civil union legislation claim that it "undermine[s] traditional marriage," "goes against God's will," and reeks of "social rape" and "moral rot"

(AASECT, May 2000, p. 9). As of this writing, three states have legalized civil unions; five other states formerly recognizing civil unions now have same-sex marriage laws (NCSL, 2014).

Civil unions are not marriages, however. Depending on how these laws are drafted, they may not allow a number of privileges inherent in marriage, including Social Security survivor and spousal benefits, unlimited exemptions from federal gift and estate taxes on transfers to a spouse, the right not to testify against one's spouse in court, and unpaid leave to care for an ill spouse (National Gay and Lesbian Task Force, 2005).

Another proposed alternative to marriage is a *domestic partnership*, a legal agreement under which two people live together, establish a personal relationship intended to be permanent, and share a domestic life together without being in a marriage or a civil union. States determine the extent to which same-sex partners have spousal rights, so rights may vary widely (NCSL, 2014). Six states and the District of Columbia currently have domestic partnership legislation (NCSL, 2014).

How does the public feel about legalized same-sex relationships? Many polls report that a majority of Americans now support same-sex marriage; this percentage has gradually increased over recent years (PollingReport.com, 2014).

This controversial, heated debate over whether gay marriage is right or wrong continues to fume throughout the United States. The core of the debate focuses on a person's constitutional right to find happiness in an intimate relationship with another person versus the religious approach about the sanctity of marriage between a man and a woman. (Highlight 13.3 reviews an international perspective on same-sex marriage.)

Some people feel that the concept of marriage is clear and specific. However, Ballman (2004) cites the following:

● Mormons have practiced polygamy, primarily in Utah, and although illegal, some still do today.

● Marriages were not conducted by the Roman Catholic church (the sole Christian church then existing) until the 12th century anywhere, and not until the 18th century in England. Before the church or state regulated marriage, people "'married' through ceremonies in their community's tradition or simply by pairing up."

HIGHLIGHT 13.3

Same-Sex Marriage on a Global Basis*

Beginning with the Netherlands as the first country to legalize same-sex marriage, the following is a list of the 17 countries following suit since then (current as of February 5, 2014) (Pew Research Center, 2014):

The Netherlands (2000)
Belgium (2003)
Canada (2005)
Spain (2005)
South Africa (2006)
Norway (2009)
Sweden (2009)
Iceland (2010)
Portugal (2010)
Argentina (2010)
Denmark (2012)

Uruguay (2013)
New Zealand (2013)
France (2013)
Brazil (2013)
England and Wales (2013)
Scotland (2014)
Luxembourg (2014)

The following countries allow same-sex marriage in some jurisdictions (Pew Research Center, 2014):

United States (2003)
Mexico (2009)

*Please see http://www.pewforum.org/2013/12/19/gay-marriage-around-the-world-2013/ for greater detail.

- People in the United States and many other nations are allowed to marry, divorce, and remarry multiple times.
- Slaves were not permitted to marry in the United States until the Emancipation Proclamation (although they often did "marry" during "secret" ceremonies, usually presided over by religious leaders who were also slaves).
- Up to 40 states forbade marriage between whites and people of color until 1967, when the U.S. Supreme Court struck down such laws as violating essential personal rights. (p. 1J)

Heterosexual unions are characterized by, hopefully, much celebration and legal support. Families and friends hold wedding showers, give gifts, and make the wedding itself a major social event. Lesbian and gay people, however, do not always have this legal alternative. Without the sanction of marriage (and depending on the strength of a civil union or domestic partnership law in those few places that have them), same-sex couples denied legal marriage usually experience a number of disadvantages. Greenberg and his colleagues (2014) cite five of these:

1. Any potential *income tax benefits* applied to married partners do not apply to unmarried lesbian or gay partners.

2. Lesbian and gay couples have more difficulty *adopting children*. Sometimes, states forbid the practice.

3. "Married couples do not have to pay any *federal estate taxes* (and usually only a limited amount of state estate tax) on the death of a first spouse (Emphasis added). State law provides (for people without wills) that property moves directly to the spouse (or spouse and children, depending on the state)" (Greenberg et al., 2014, p. 393). In same-sex couples who live without the sanction of marriage, after a partner's death, his or her relatives can demand all of the deceased partner's assets. Wills may clearly specify what possessions will go to which people. Even with a will, however, relatives may still challenge it under the concept of "undue influence" (Peters, 1982). Lesbian and gay people are therefore encouraged to update their wills from time to time. Each time, they should ascertain that the will accurately reflects their current assets and is well documented.

4. Partners in same-sex couples are often denied *employment benefits* such as health or life insurance. Although many large companies provide benefits, many small companies do not.

5. Unmarried partners don't automatically have *decision-making rights* when partners are

seriously ill and unable to make decisions for themselves. Gay and lesbian partners have no legal rights under these circumstances because they do not fall under the legal definition of family. Lesbian and gay people are encouraged, therefore, to draw up a medical power of attorney; this may address "visitation rights, the right to be consulted, and to give or withhold consent about medical decisions, and in case of death, the right to personal effects and the right to dispose of the body" (Schwaber, 1985, p. 92).

One gay sex–advice columnist has a unique solution for those uncomfortable with gay sex: "if they really want to stop the gay sex, they should be behind gay adoption, because nothing put a stop to the sex in my house faster than adopting" (Crooks & Baur, 2002, p. 289).

Ethical Question 13.6

Should lesbian and gay people be given the right to marry?

EP 2.1.2

Child Custody and Visitation Rights

Lesbian and gay parents have experienced major difficulties in custody debates over their children because of their sexual orientation. Numerous courts have denied parents custody simply because they were lesbians or gays (ACLU, 2014b; Barusch, 2012; Carroll, 2013b; Hunter & Hickerson, 2003; Parks & Humphreys, 2006). For example, a Florida lesbian mother lost "custody of her 11-year-old daughter to the child's father, who was convicted of killing his first wife" (CNN, 1996). Further complicating the matter, the man's daughter with his first wife accused him of sexually abusing her when she was a teenager. In another case, an Alabama court refused custody to a lesbian mother; the chief justice condemned homosexuality as an "inherent evil and an act so heinous that it defies one's ability to describe it" (Kendell, 2003). Still another instance involves a grandmother who was awarded custody of her grandson because his mother was a lesbian living with a female partner; the Virginia judge

ruled that the mother's "conduct is immoral" and that her behavior "renders her an unfit parent" (Kendell, 2003). On the other hand, some state courts have ruled that child custody could not be denied purely on the basis of parental homosexuality unless it was proven that such sexual orientation would hurt the child (Berger & Kelly, 1995).

Judges presiding over custody disputes can make arbitrary judgments concerning what is in the child's best interests (Hyde & DeLamater, 2014; Kendell, 2003). Some judges may have homophobic ideas, which have the potential of influencing their decisions.

There are several myths about lesbian and gay parenthood that might influence people against lesbian and gay parents. First, there is the misconception that lesbian or gay parents will influence their children to become gays or lesbians. No verification exists for this myth or for the worry that children growing up in families with lesbian or gay parents are more likely to be lesbian or gay (Barusch, 2012; Carroll, 2013b; Hyde & DeLamater, 2014; Morales, 1995). Second, there is the idea that children will be damaged by growing up in lesbian or gay homes. All indications are that children growing up in such households flourish as well as those raised in heterosexual homes (Carroll, 2013b; Hyde & DeLamater, 2014). Third, some people mistakenly believe that gay and lesbian people's parenting skills are inadequate. No evidence bears this out (Barusch, 2012; Moses & Hawkins, 1982). Finally, research indicates that fears about children with lesbian or gay parents experiencing difficulties in peer relationships, having inadequate social skills, or enjoying less popularity than their peers with heterosexual parents are also unsupported (Hyde & DeLamater, 2014).

It's interesting that the American Association of Pediatrics "endorsed its support of gay and lesbian parents to adopt a partner's children" (AASECT, March 2002, p. 10). It maintained that it is in the best interest of children, and their security, that they live with legal parents.

Several suggestions can be made to human service professionals to help lesbian and gay people fight and win child custody battles (Moses & Hawkins, 1982). First of all, the parent must realize that although progress has been made, the odds for gaining custody may still not be good. The parent needs to realize that such cases usually take considerable time and energy. Court cases also frequently cause burdensome stress for both parent and children, and are expensive. Teaching the client such skills as assertiveness, stress management, and problem solving is frequently useful. In addition, he or she should get a highly competent attorney. Referring the lesbian or gay parent to support groups is also helpful. Finally, educating the parent by providing reading material is often beneficial.

The Future of Lesbian and Gay Rights

Although lesbian and gay people are not treated equally under the law, the great progress that has been made should be emphasized. Some states and localities are adopting equal housing and employment legislation for lesbian and gay people. Homosexuality is no longer considered a psychiatric illness. Federal government agencies should no longer be able to discriminate against gay and lesbian people. Lesbian and gay people, through their advocacy and hard work, have achieved a great deal.

Their struggle for equality is sometimes characterized by the expression "Remember Stonewall!" Stonewall was a gay bar in New York City's Greenwich Village. On June 28, 1969, police stormed and raided the bar, an incident not unusual in those times. How the gay men at the bar responded, though, was indeed unusual. They fought back. The struggle continued in the street for hours.

People involved in gay and lesbian liberation have provided much impetus to progress made in gay and lesbian legal rights. Such groups exist in many communities, especially in urban settings. Group meetings often provide opportunities to discuss issues, plan political interventions, and get help and support concerning personal difficulties such as employment discrimination. Additionally, they provide a means of becoming acquainted with other lesbian and gay people and with the gay and lesbian community in general.

EP 2.1.4a;
2.1.5a–c;
2.1.8a & b

Social workers need to attend to LGBT rights issues. Not only is an objective, open-minded attitude and belief in individual self-determination necessary, but an advocacy stance is also critical. Unfair, discriminatory rules in public and private agencies can be confronted. Attention can be called to any discrimination that does occur. Political candidates who encourage LGBT rights can be supported. Finally, others, including friends, family, and professional colleagues, can be educated about LGBT rights and encouraged to support them.

Community Responses: Violence Against LGBT People

A Phoenix gay bar explodes when it is attacked with a firebomb.

Two lesbians are thrown out of their apartment after their landlady spied on them through their apartment window and discovered their sexual orientation. Later, when the two women try to address the issue through court action, they are assaulted by the landlady's son and his friends. The group beats up and attacks one of the women with a knife, seriously injuring her.

A station wagon filled with five men passes by three gay teenagers. At first the men in the car only scream out verbal insults. However, as the situation intensifies, one of the men in the car hauls out a golf club and hits a gay teenager in the head, fracturing his skull.

"In October [1998] Matthew Shepard, a gay college student, was pistol whipped, beaten and left tied to a fence near Laramie, Wyoming, for 18 hours. Shepard died of his injuries four days later. Sources close to Russell Henderson, 21, and Aaron McKinney, 21, claimed that originally the two men had only intended to rob Shepard, but that awareness of his sexual orientation drove them to violence" (AASECT, 1998, p. 1).

Consider the following homophobic hate incidents against people of color. In May, 2013, Mark Carson, 32, was walking with a friend in Greenwich Village in New York City, when another man taunted him with insults and then shot him with one bullet directly in the face (Slattery, Badia, & Kemp, 2013). The gunman along with two companions had called Carson and his friend "f——s" and "gay wrestlers" prior to the shooting. RaShawn Brazell, 19, was allegedly on his way to meet a lover; he was found mutilated, chopped into pieces, and dumped in a Brooklyn, New York, subway tunnel (Burke & Lemire, 2005). Sakia Gunn, 15, an African American who was a lesbian, "was stabbed to death in Newark, NJ" by a man "after she and a friend refused his advances by declaring that they were lesbians" (LGBT Hate Crimes Project, 2010). Jose Sucuzhanay, 31, a Latino, died of injuries from being beaten over the head with a beer bottle, struck numerous times with a baseball bat, and kicked repeatedly (McFadden, 2008). He had been walking home with his brother after attending a church function and later stopping at a bar. "They may have been a bit tipsy as they walked home in the dead of night, arm-in arm, leaning close to each other, a common [practice] … of men in Latino cultures, but one easily misinterpreted by the biased mind" (McFadden, 2008). A car suddenly pulled up and three men jumped out shouting antigay and anti-Latino vulgar remarks. The beating ensued. Jose's brother managed to escape.

Carroll (2013b) describes the current context of violence against LGBT people:

> *Hate crimes* are those motivated by hatred of someone's religion, sex, race, sexual orientation, disability, or ethnic group. They are known as "message crimes" in that they send a message to the victim's affiliated group. (American Psychiatric Association, 1998). Typically, hate crimes involve strong feelings of anger (Parrott & Peterson, 2008). (p. 288)

Swigonski (2006) cites the following statistics, based on Mason's (2002) summary of surveys conducted in several English-speaking countries:

- 70 to 80 percent of lesbians and gay men reported experiencing verbal abuse in public because of their sexuality.
- 30 to 40 percent reported threats of violence.
- 20 percent of gay men reported physical violence.
- 10 to 12 percent of lesbians reported physical violence.

Swigonski concludes, "For people whose sexual orientation or gender expression is outside narrowly defined societal norms, violence is a normative part of life. That is a fact, but it is not a tolerable fact" (p. 366).

A total of 2,016 anti-LGBTQ and anti-HIV hate crimes were reported in 2012 (King, 2013; National Coalition of Anti-Violence Programs [NCAVP], 2013). NCAVP (2013) also cites the following facts for 2012:

- 25 documented anti-GLBTQ homicides were committed.
- LGBTQ people of color were 1.82 times more likely to be victims of physical violence than White LGBTQ people.

- Gay men were 3.04 times more likely to report being victims of hate violence compared to people who were not gay men.
- Gay men were 1.56 times more likely to require medical attention after hate violence incidents compared to other survivors of such violence.
- Transgender people, especially transgender people of color, experience special risk.

Seven types of victimization have been noted (Wertheimer, 1988): verbal harassment, which occurs most frequently; threatening behavior, such as being followed by harassers or being warned that attacks are forthcoming; physical attacks by groups of men, which can result in emotional and physical injury; assaults associated with AIDS and the resentment toward gay and lesbian people related to it; sexual assaults of women and men; assaults and discrimination by police; and even murder. Homophobia seems to form the foundation for these attacks.

What can be done to halt such victimization of lesbians and gay men? Wertheimer (1988) proposes four potential solutions. First, gay and lesbian civil rights legislation must be passed. Discrimination on the basis of sexual orientation must be clearly illegal. People must get the message that such behavior will not be tolerated. Victims need to feel safe in reporting abusive incidents.

Wertheimer's second suggestion involves the passage of laws that specifically address crimes committed because of hatred and prejudice toward specific groups. Such legislation would protect not only lesbian and gay people but also others subjected to prejudice because of their gender, race, ethnic status, religion, or beliefs.

The third proposal involves educating the police, and people working in the criminal justice system, about homophobia, gay and lesbian victimization, and the needs and rights of gay people. Education could include training employees to have greater empathy for lesbian and gay people, and to be more sensitive to their situations. This would encourage lesbian and gay victims to report crimes instead of fearing harassment and retribution from authorities.

Finally, Wertheimer's fourth suggestion for combating gay and lesbian victimization is to establish crisis centers for victims. Such resources would resemble the centers that have already been developed to help heterosexual victims of sexual assault and domestic violence.

●●●● **Ethical Question 13.7**

How can violence against lesbian, gay, bisexual, and transgender people be stopped?

EP 2.1.2

Coming Out

"Coming out of the closet," or "coming out," refers to the process of a person's acknowledging publicly that she or he is lesbian or gay. It is frequently a long and difficult process in view of the homophobia and stereotypes enveloping us (Crooks & Baur, 2014; Morrow, 2006a; Swigonski, 1995).

Lesbian and gay people today usually become aware that they are different from most others in terms of sexual orientation before the age of 20 (Martin, 2008; Moses & Hawkins, 1982). The process of coming out itself frequently takes one to two years. It should be noted, however, that there is great variation regarding how any specific individual comes out. For some people, it may take much longer, and they may come out much later in life. For many people, especially adolescents who do not have much independence and are subject to severe peer pressure, the coming-out period may be very difficult.

One way to describe coming out is to identify the four stages involved (Boston Women's Health Book Collective, 1984; Crooks & Baur, 2014). These stages are (1) coming out to oneself; (2) getting to know other people within the gay and lesbian community; (3) sharing with family and friends that one is lesbian or gay; and (4) coming out of the closet— that is, openly and publicly acknowledging one's sexual orientation.

The first stage of the process—namely, coming out to oneself—involves thinking about oneself as a person who is lesbian or gay instead of as one who is heterosexual (Crooks & Baur, 2014; Moses & Hawkins, 1982; Rathus, 2014b). This may involve a period of identity shifting, during which individuals experiment with the label. They may begin

conceptualizing themselves as lesbian or gay and begin thinking about what such a label will mean concerning their own lifestyle.

Part of the signification process involves accepting a label about which society has had so many negative things to say. Some people feel much better about themselves after applying a label of lesbian or gay. It seems that such a label helps in the process of establishing a self-identity. It also seems to give people permission to think and feel honestly about themselves. They then feel that they can pursue new thoughts and experiences they feared and avoided before.

Human service professionals can use several intervention strategies when helping lesbian and gay clients during their coming-out period. To begin with, it is important to provide the client with information about what being lesbian or gay is really like (Morrow, 2006a). Chances are that the client thinks in terms of some of the same stereotypes and has some of the same homophobic responses that many others in society do. A gay man who is coming out may need to be educated about the difference between gender identity and choice of sexual partner. He also needs to understand that homosexuality is not an illness.

EP 2.1.10j

The issue of self-concept may need to be addressed in counseling. Many times it is initially difficult for lesbian and gay people to distinguish between society's somewhat negative view of gay and lesbian people and their own views of themselves. They need to understand that they will not suddenly become different people with odd habits. Rather, they can be helped to see that different options are available to them, which may provide them with greater freedom to be themselves.

Another suggestion is the realistic identification and evaluation of the alternatives open to a lesbian or gay person (Chernin & Johnson, 2003). Signification may have advantages and disadvantages. Advantages might include the decreased fear and anxiety that result from pretending to be someone you're not. Another advantage might be the blossoming of new possibilities for social activities and support systems with other lesbian and gay people. Referrals to local organizations would be helpful here.

Disadvantages also need to be confronted. These might include the discrimination in employment and social settings sometimes suffered by lesbian and gay people. Another disadvantage might be the potential loss of some friends and family members. Any anxiety about potential risks in telling people needs to be explored.

The second phase of the coming-out process involves meeting and getting to know other lesbian and gay people. This involves searching for a sense of community where people can develop a feeling of belonging. The best way to curb fears and rid oneself of stereotypes is to meet other lesbian and gay people and find out that the horrible things one has heard simply are not true. It's important to establish a social support system made up of people who understand what it is like to come out and who can talk about it easily.

The third phase of coming out involves telling friends and family (Crooks & Baur, 2014; Morrow, 2006a). Most people come out to friends first, because it seems to be more difficult to tell family members (Boston Women's Health Book Collective, 1984). However, it's also difficult *not* to tell family members.

There are a number of specific suggestions for coming out to friends and family (Crooks & Baur, 2014; Morrow, 2006a; Moses & Hawkins, 1982). First, the potential consequences need to be realistically examined. It may not be necessary to tell all close friends, relatives, and colleagues if the consequences for the lesbian or gay person are likely to be negative.

For example, a young man, a junior in college, has recently come out. His relationship with his father has always been marginal in that they have never communicated well and do not feel close to each other. However, they do attend family functions together and participate in the family system with other family members. The father has often made derogatory statements about gay people for as long as the son can remember. In this case, it may serve no purpose to come out to the father, because the relationship will probably not be improved. On the contrary, coming out may cause the son much painful criticism and potential ostracism from the family unit.

The fourth phase of coming out involves publicly acknowledging that one is a lesbian or a gay man. As with friends and family, it's important to evaluate the potential positive and negative consequences of each alternative. That is, one must carefully consider if letting it be known that one is a lesbian or a gay man will be to one's advantage or disadvantage in any particular setting.

Many people choose not to come out of the closet. We've already discussed the criticism, rejection, and discrimination lesbian and gay people

Coming out can be a difficult process. Support from others is very important.

Kayte M. Deioma/PhotoEdit

experience. Perhaps each individual needs to consider what's best personally. Those on one side of the issue emphasize that discrimination victimizes people unfairly and that each individual must decide for herself or himself what is best. Some believe that this is a conservative approach. Those on the other side of the issue believe that one cannot be free to be oneself without honesty and openness to everyone. Spotlight 13.4 discusses some issues involving ethnicity and sexual orientation.

A reality-oriented approach entails looking at all available alternatives. The positive and negative consequences for each alternative must be evaluated. The idea is to assist clients in making decisions that are in their best interest. Highlight 13.4 addresses one woman's exploration of her self-identity and sexual orientation.

SPOTLIGHT ON DIVERSITY 13.4

Ethnicity and Sexual Orientation

EP 2.1.4c

It is critically important for social workers to assess "the impact of differences in class, ethnicity, health status, rural or urban background, and stage of gay identity formation, in addition to the individual's psychodynamics, ego strengths, and social supports" in order to help clients most effectively (Shernoff, 1995, p. 1077). Appreciation of people's individual strengths and differences is the key. For example, a 45-year-old Hispanic gay man living in a sparsely populated rural environment in Texas will experience very different life circumstances and issues than will an 18-year-old African American gay man living in a bustling urban Los Angeles neighborhood. Likewise, a 24-year-old Asian American lesbian living in uptown Manhattan will experience life very differently from a 78-year-old Native American lesbian living in northern Montana.

African American and Hispanic gay men may have difficulty experiencing a comfortable level of acceptance both in their ethnic communities and in the primarily white gay community (Alderson, 2013; Tully, 2000; van Wormer et al., 2000). This is also true for gay men who are Asian American and Native American (Alderson, 2013; Shernoff, 1995). On the one hand, white gay organizations may be racist or unresponsive to the needs of other ethnic groups despite reflecting the same sexual orientation. On the other hand, various ethnic and racial communities may be homophobic, resulting from a range of cultural traditions (Alderson, 2013; van Wormer et al., 2000).

Nonwhite gay men may see their racial and ethnic communities as safe havens from the oppressive white majority culture. Therefore, they may be less likely to divulge openly their sexual orientation for fear of losing that support (Morales, 1995). It can be very helpful for them to seek linkage and support from other gay men of similar racial and ethnic heritage who better understand the problems resulting from membership in two "minority" groups (Shernoff, 1995).

A special issue for gay Hispanic men involves their traditional religion and folk beliefs (Shernoff, 1995). Many Hispanic people are strongly influenced by "the impact of conservative Catholicism and its emphasis on traditional values (which strongly reject gay love or sexual expression)" (p. 1077). Additionally, many gay Hispanics place serious significance on the concept of *espiritismo*, or spiritualism (Shernoff, 1995). Social workers must be aware of such issues and explore the significance they have for clients.

Asian American gay men may see their sexual orientation as being incompatible with traditional values espoused by their culture. As a result, many may be pressured to adopt dual identities, one concerning their racial heritage and one their sexual orientation (Shernoff, 1995). Social workers may help them to think through their situations and make effective decisions regarding what choices and plans are best for them.

Tafoya and Rowell (1988) indicate that "Native American gay and lesbian clients often combine elements of common gay experiences with the uniqueness of their own ethnicity. To treat them only as gay and to ignore important cultural issues may bring ... [counseling] sessions to a quick end with little accomplished" (p. 63).

Lesbians of diverse ethnic and racial backgrounds experience pressures similar to those suffered by gay men of diverse ethnic and racial heritage; this is due to their membership in more than one diverse group (Alderson, 2013; Almquist, 1995; Hunter College Women's Studies Collective, 1995; Smith, 1995). Lesbians of nonwhite racial backgrounds confront a type of "triple jeopardy"; they suffer not only from racism and sexism but also from heterosexism (Greene, 1994). "Just as the experience of sexism is 'colored' by the lens of race and ethnicity for women of color, so is the experience of heterosexism similarly filtered for lesbian women of color" (p. 395). Furthermore, "for racially oppressed groups, lesbianism may seem like a betrayal of ... [their] ethnic community. Among African Americans and Native Americans, for example, reproductive sexuality may be viewed as contributing to the survival of a group subject to racist genocide attempts" (Hunter College Women's Studies Collective, 1995, p. 151). In other words, lesbianism may be viewed as a betrayal of one's racial heritage, because lesbians don't form traditional heterosexual pairs oriented toward reproduction and increasing racial numbers.

HIGHLIGHT 13.4

Cheryl's Exploration of Her Self-Identity and Sexual Orientation

Cheryl, age 19, worked as a sales clerk at Shopko, the local discount store. Although she still lived with her parents primarily for financial reasons, she was starting to make her own decisions. She debated moving into an apartment with several female friends, and whether she should attend the local technical school or college part-time. These were not the issues she addressed, however, as she came in for counseling.

Cheryl hesitantly explained that she was very anxious about the sexual feelings she was having. Although she was steadily dating her high school sweetheart, he did not interest her sexually. She was thinking more and more about her sexual attraction toward other women. She had had these feelings for as long as she could remember. Lately she was becoming obsessed about them. She was very worried that she might be a lesbian.

On further discussion, she expressed fears about what being a lesbian would be like. She was concerned about starting to look too masculine and about becoming sex-starved for other women. Cheryl's counselor provided some information about what being lesbian or gay is really like. They discussed and discarded some of Cheryl's negative stereotypes. The counselor referred Cheryl to some written material on lesbianism and to some local organizations so Cheryl could get more information.

As counseling progressed, Cheryl began to nurture her weakened self-image. Her years of anxiety and her efforts to hide her feelings had taken an emotional toll. Her counselor helped her to work through her confusion about all the negative things she'd heard about gays and her perception of herself. Cheryl began to look at herself more realistically. She began to focus on her personal strengths. These included her sense of humor, her pleasant disposition, and her desire to become more independent and establish a career for herself. She found that these attributes and her personal identity had nothing to do with the negative stereotypes she had previously heard about homosexuality.

Finally, her counselor helped her to define and evaluate the various alternatives open to her. For the first time, she explored the possibility of breaking up with her boyfriend. She considered the possibility of pursuing a sexual relationship with one of the women she had recently met at a gay and lesbian rights organization meeting. She was already beginning to develop friendships with other women she'd met in a lesbian support group.

After several months of counseling, Cheryl had made some decisions. She had gone through the signification process. She had moved out of her parents' home and into an apartment with several female friends, none of whom were lesbians. After much fear and trepidation, she had come out to them. To her relief, they indicated that although they were surprised, it made no difference concerning their friendship. She had broken off with her boyfriend and had started a sexual relationship with another woman. Not only did she have no regrets about her new romantic situation, but she felt extreme relief, satisfaction, and a new sense of freedom.

Cheryl still had not decided whether to come out to her parents. She was still working on that. Nor had she yet decided what career route would be best for her. However, her new sense of self-identity provided her with new confidence and strength. The future looked hopeful and exciting instead of dull and restrictive.

Lesbian and Gay Adolescents

Lesbian and gay adolescents have to deal with not only their identity development in general but also their identities as lesbians or gay males in a heterosexual world. This frequently occurs during adolescence when their sexual selves start to awaken. Social workers should pay particular attention to lesbian and gay adolescents during this time in their lives. (Chapter 7 addressed some of the issues facing adolescents concerning the special circumstances of their identity development.) Boes and van Wormer (2002), noting that adolescents "are sometimes treated as if they were less than human," go on to explain:

> Struggling to survive in environments (school, home, church) that are more often than not hostile to their very being, gay and lesbian youth have many intense personal issues to resolve. Among the most pressing issues … are:

- *The turmoil involved in coming out to yourself, discovering who you are and who you are not.*
- *Deciding who to tell, when, and how to tell it.*
- *Rebuilding relationships and grieving rejections when the truth is known.*
- *Developing new and caring support systems.*
- *Protecting oneself from a constant onslaught of attacks of one who is openly out or from the guilt feelings accompanying the secrecy and deception of being in the closet. (p. 621)*

Lesbian and gay adolescents are up to four times more likely to attempt suicide than are their heterosexual counterparts (Johnson, 2011a). A major suggestion

EP 2.1.4c & d; 2.1.5c

for working with lesbian and gay youth is to avoid minimizing or denying the young person's developing identity and sexual orientation. Rather, help to empower them by taking their thoughts and feelings seriously and providing them with the information and support they need.

Three principles should guide social workers when trying to help lesbian and gay youth (Woodman, 1995). First, acknowledge that some adolescents, perhaps many with whom you work and come into contact, are lesbian or gay. Second, increase your own awareness and that of your agency regarding how to provide accessible services to lesbian and gay youth. Third, do not allow antigay, homophobic sentiment to get in the way of providing lesbian and gay youth with the services they need. Such services may include "special advocacy efforts, peer support groups, recreational programs, and other resources to counter the isolation and despair that are all too common among gay and lesbian adolescents" (Alderson, 2013; Laird, 1995, p. 1611).

Empowering Lesbian and Gay Parents

Many lesbian and gay people have children (Carroll, 2013b; Mallon, 2008; Messinger & Brooks, 2008;

Rosenthal, 2013). It's impossible to give an exact number because no accurate numbers exist of how many people are homosexual. Many have them from prior marriages. Others choose new fertility methods such as sperm insemination or surrogacy. Still others seek to adopt children, but this is often unsuccessful because of prejudice against their sexual orientation (McCoy, 2006; Stone, 2006).

Even when a lesbian or gay parent gains custody of a child, there still may be problems to overcome. For instance, lesbian and gay parents must deal with the ongoing discrimination and social censure they face because of their sexual orientation. Losing a job or an apartment might have a much greater impact on lesbians with children than on lesbians who aren't parents. Much more may be at stake when the welfare, support, and living conditions of children must also be taken into consideration.

Several suggestions can be made to social workers and other human service professionals in their efforts to help lesbian and gay people cope with parenthood (Moses & Hawkins, 1982). First, social workers can help the lesbian or gay parent identify and appreciate the joys of parenthood. It may be all too easy to get lost in the

EP 2.1.10g & j

Many lesbian and gay people have children.

additional problems of being lesbian or gay and miss all of the normal pleasures of raising children.

Second, social workers can help lesbian and gay parents address the issue of coming out to children. Practitioners can help parents identify the various alternative ways of sharing information about their sexual orientation with children and evaluate the potential positive and negative consequences of each. Probably no perfect single approach exists for how parents should come out to their children (Morales, 1995). Lesbian and gay parents may use any of a number of tactics. Some hide their sexual orientation from their children because they fear custody battles or the effects such knowledge will have on children. Others encourage secrecy on the child's part, although such concealment can create quite a strain for the child (van Wormer et al., 2000).

Still other lesbian and gay parents feel it is important to come out to their children as soon as possible. Hunter and Hickerson (2003) recommend that parents adopt such an open attitude. There are some advantages to this approach. First, it may avoid family stresses and problems in communication that could result from the parents' hiding such an important aspect of their lives. Daily living is much more comfortable when the lesbian or gay parent can openly interact with and express affection toward a partner, without excluding the children. Finally, sharing the truth with children prevents them from finding out about it from someone else—which might cause them surprise and shock. Children would wonder why their parents hadn't told them, and this secrecy might convey a negative perspective about being lesbian or gay.

However, it should be remembered that every lesbian or gay family situation is unique. A social worker's role can be to help parents determine the best way to come out to children in their particular family system.

A third way social workers can assist lesbian or gay parents involves dealing with new partners. When a lesbian or gay parent finds a partner and decides to live with her or him, a social worker can help that parent address many of the same issues that need to be dealt with when a new heterosexual partner joins a household. Issues about child management need to be discussed. Expectations regarding how money will be shared or spent, how daily routines will be organized, and how the adults will act in front of the children need to be clarified openly.

Fourth, many lesbian and gay parents worry about the prejudice and discrimination their children might experience because of the parents' sexual orientation. Social workers can help such parents identify and evaluate ways to help children with these issues. Parents can learn to help their children think through situations and determine when to talk about their parents' sexual orientation and when not to (Laird, 1995).

One suggestion is to teach children situational ethics (Wolf, 1979). The idea here is for lesbian and gay parents to be open about their sexual orientation. Children then can learn about being lesbian or gay in a positive sense. However, at the same time, a lesbian or gay parent can teach a child that it is more appropriate to refer to and talk about sexual orientation in some situations than in others. For example, it is appropriate to be open about mother's female partner at home with the family. However, more discretion might be necessary when the child is giving a report before his or her class at school.

That children learn when certain behavior is appropriate or inappropriate is a normal part of growing up. One means of teaching the concept of appropriateness is to teach about individual differences (Moses & Hawkins, 1982). Children understand that each person is different. Every individual has his or her own ideas and beliefs. Each lives a distinctly unique life. Differences in sexual orientation are simply another type of human difference. Because people have divergent ideas about sexual orientation, they might be prejudiced. Therefore, it is not always wise to raise the issue.

Cohen, Padilla, and Aravena (2006) review how social workers can provide psychosocial support for families of LGBT people:

In sum, psychosocial intervention may include providing families with accurate information about gender identity and sexual orientation, helping families to deconstruct negative stereotypes about sexual orientation and gender identity, and assisting families of various cultural backgrounds in negotiating their values and beliefs regarding sexual and gender identity vis-a-vis the well-being of their GLBT [gay, lesbian, bisexual, and transgender] family member [or members]. Finally, intervention may also involve providing resources to family members, including information on how to access local agencies and other support organizations that offer services for families [that have GLBT members]. (p. 169)

As Lesbians and Gay Men Age

"The adage 'Nobody loves you when you're old and gray' has been modified by lesbian women and gay men to read, 'Nobody loves you when you're old and *gay*'" (Baron & Cramer, 2000, p. 207). Stereotypes further suggest that when older lesbians and gay men lose their youthful appearance, they are rejected by other lesbian and gay people as well as by homophobic heterosexuals. They become lonely, isolated, saddened human beings.

Contrary to this stereotype, some research indicates that what often happens is just the opposite. There are two basic summary statements about older lesbian and gay people based on their strengths (Alderson, 2013). First, most are relatively well adjusted (Lee, 1991; Longres & Fredriksen, 2000; Tully, 1992; van Wormer et al., 2000). Many have numerous gay and lesbian friends and a few heterosexual ones, have some ties with the gay and lesbian community and its support network, and have an age-appropriate sexual and emotional relationship with a longtime partner. The second major summary statement is that both the adjustment levels and the psychosocial needs of older lesbian and gay people are more similar to those of heterosexuals than dissimilar.

If anything, lesbian and gay people may adjust better to aging than do heterosexual people based on two principles: competence in being independent and experience in coping with stigma (Alderson, 2013; Berger, 1985; Fullmer, 2006; Moses & Hawkins, 1982). Establishing competence in independence means that being self-sufficient is nothing new to lesbian and gay people. Heterosexuals tend to be more involved with their traditional family systems and often have difficulties coping with the death of a spouse and other peers. In a sense, heterosexual people have been sheltered during their lives. Lesbian and gay people, however, often have had to fend for themselves and experience a lifetime of independence. Because their lifestyle did not fit with the traditional heterosexual one, they always had to reach out to others and forge new paths and relationships. Coping with the "aloneness" of old age theoretically might not be as great a shock to lesbian and gay people as it can be to heterosexuals.

The second concept that involves coping with stigma, suggests that lesbian and gay people are probably better at dealing with the stigma of old age because they already have experience dealing with stigma and rejection (Longres & Fredrikson, 2000). Coping with one stigma—namely, homosexuality—may help prepare them to cope with another, namely, aging. Note, however, that GLBT people continue to experience the effects of stigma and homophobia as they age, which is true even as they enter nursing homes (Carroll, 2013b; Rosenthal, 2013).

Both heterosexuals and lesbian and gay people face similar concerns as they get older, including health and financial security concerns. Consider, however, that because women generally earn less than men over the life span, older lesbians "are particularly vulnerable to financial woes.... Gay and lesbian seniors are also less likely to have a live-in partner or adult children to help care for them" (Rosenthal, 2013, p. 248). Additionally, lesbian and gay people have issues with institutional regulations, legal concerns, and emotional needs that heterosexual people don't necessarily face.

Institutional regulations often involve access to benefits and resources (National Gay and Lesbian Task Force, 2011). Until the recent Supreme Court ruling concerning federal benefits (discussed earlier), Social Security did not pay spousal benefits to same-sex partners. For example, it would pay survivor benefits to surviving heterosexual spouses, but not to the survivor in a same-sex relationship. There are still no guarantees at the state or private institutional levels that same-sex partners will receive the same benefits (e.g., tax, pension, leave, or insurance) that married heterosexual partners will.

Other institutional problems involve being placed in a nursing home or having to be hospitalized. A person's lover and closest friends may not be allowed input into whether and where the person is placed, nor even allowed admission to see the person. As was discussed under legal issues, the traditionally defined family can often take over and deny access to the lesbian or gay person's companion.

We have also already established that the legal system frequently ignores gay and lesbian relationships. If a will is not clearly written, well established, updated, and well documented, a lesbian or gay partner may lose much of what the couple has worked for. The biological, legal "family" may claim it all.

**EP 2.1.1c,
2.1.5b**

One of this chapter's themes is how important it is for social workers to advocate for improved rights, policies, and services for their LGBT clients. This is just as true for LGBT older adults as social workers address their special institutional and legal issues. Such advocacy is part of the social work role.

The emotional needs of older gay and lesbian people are much like the emotional needs of older heterosexuals. They need social contacts, human warmth, and self-respect. However, lesbian and gay people have the additional pressure of battling the biased assumptions of a heterosexual world. For instance, consider a social worker who can't understand why a client would want to take a leave from work and apply for public assistance in order to care for a very close "friend." Lesbians and gays must wage constant battle either to explain or defend themselves and their behavior.

McInnis-Dittrich (2014) reflects on the importance of social workers stressing and turning to an older person's support system, whomever that may include:

Effectively mobilizing support systems requires the practitioner to "think family." … Thinking family means seeing the older adult as part of a complex system of multigenerational relationships that have had a profound influence on his or her life and serve as the primary source of interaction and support. Family roles—such as spouse or partner, parent, grandparent, aunt, or uncle [or close friend]—are important parts of older adult's self-concepts, influencing older adults' thinking even when the specific functions associated with those roles [e.g., as a parent, raising children] have ceased. Human beings are born into various family constellations, create their own versions of family in adulthood, and turn to whatever they perceive to be family as they grow older. (p. 315)

Thus, it's important to view the lesbian or gay person's family configuration and support system however that individual defines it. Life partners and other significant people should be identified and be integrally involved in case planning and decision making for the older adult.

Gay and Lesbian People and AIDS

AIDS was discussed in depth in Chapter 10. Although initially many people labeled it a gay disease, it is now spreading among heterosexuals at a greater rate than among gays. Therefore, in Chapter 10, AIDS was discussed as a condition that could affect anyone, heterosexual or gay or lesbian. Because gay men were among the first to contract the disease in the United States, a few comments will be made here about its impact on them. (AIDS is virtually unknown among lesbians, except those who are IV drug users, a separate high-risk group.)

Before the existence of AIDS was acknowledged in the United States, many people had already been exposed to and had contracted it. Most of them were gay men. As a result, many gay people have seen dozens of their friends die of AIDS. The emotional impact on the gay community has been immense.

Little attention was initially given to AIDS. Many people saw it as something that happened to homosexuals, drug addicts, and other "bad" people. Homophobic responses by heterosexual people and the idea that AIDS is a punishment for bad behavior may have contributed to the relative inaction on the part of the government. Meanwhile, many gay men, along with their friends, families, and lovers, were suffering desperately from the disease.

Gay people can be thanked for much of the publicity about AIDS, the new resources directed to research for a cure, and the strong emphasis on prevention. Gay people were infuriated that the crisis was ignored by the government. The implication was that those contracting the disease weren't that important anyway and that they deserved it. As a result, people in the gay and lesbian community banded together, wrote letters to legislators, marched, advocated for people with the disease, and demanded that it be given some attention.

Gay people also took major steps to initiate a massive campaign aimed at prevention. They provided people with information in any way they could think of. For instance, brochures emphasizing the need for safer sex practices were distributed at gay bars. Gay people slowed the spread of the disease within their own communities.

Any social worker who works with a gay or lesbian client needs to be aware of the ramifications and emotional impacts AIDS has had. Those close to the client have likely dealt with many of the economic and social issues involved with AIDS. These include not only serious illness, but poverty when personal resources have been depleted, social isolation, insurance and public-assistance problems, and problems getting medication.

SPOTLIGHT ON DIVERSITY 13.5

Social Work with LGBT People: Promoting Optimal Well-Being

**EP 2.1.1b,
c & e;
2.1.2a;
2.1.4b &
d; 2.1.5b;
2.1.8a;
2.1.9b**

Social work has at least two important thrusts in working with LGBT people. One involves the individual practitioner's attitudes and skills. The other concerns agencies' provision of services to LGBT people.

Counseling

Josephine Stewart, who chaired the NASW National Committee on Lesbian and Gay Issues, has made several suggestions for social work practitioners working with LGBT clients (NASW, 1984). For one thing, we have established that it is very important to confront one's own homophobia. One of the worst things a practitioner can do is negatively label an LGBT client and criticize that client for her or his sexual orientation. This contradicts the basic social work value of the client's right to self-determination. A negatively biased practitioner can unknowingly work against a client's development and maintenance of a positive self-image. Alternatives involving an LGBT lifestyle and resources available in the LGBT communities might be ignored or even rejected.

Another suggestion for working with LGBT people is to become familiar both with the LGBT lifestyles and with the LGBT communities. This knowledge is necessary in order to help clients identify and evaluate the various alternatives available to them. Such learning is a career-long process. It's also helpful to know people within the LGBT community who can update a practitioner on new events and resources.

Agency Provision of Services

The other issue concerning social work with LGBT people involves agencies' provision of services. Social workers should provide leadership to improve and develop agency policies on the behalf of LGBT people and help initiate programs to serve them. LGBT people need various services that address specific aspects of lesbian and gay life. These might include lesbian support groups, groups for gay men who are in the process of coming out, legal advice for lesbian or gay parents seeking child custody, or couple counseling for same-sex partners. Such services can be provided by agencies focusing on and serving only LGBT people, or the services can be mainstreamed into traditional agencies.

Regardless of where services are provided for LGBT people, the fact is that they are needed. Social workers need to apply social work values to LGBT clients. They need to learn about resources available for LGBT people and make appropriate referrals. They also need to educate others about the special issues confronting LGBT people. Finally, many times social workers need to act as advocates for the rights of LGBT people. Sexual orientation needs to be addressed as simply another aspect of human diversity. Sexual orientation should be respected instead of denied. Political candidates in favor of LGBT rights need to be supported. Agencies that discriminate against LGBT people need to be confronted, educated, and pressured to provide needed services in a fair and unbiased manner.

Sensitivity to these issues can help social workers better serve their clients' needs. Spotlight 13.5 addresses the promotion of optimal well-being for all lesbian and gay people, not just those who are HIV-positive.

Chapter Summary

The following summarizes this chapter's content as it relates to the learning objectives presented at the beginning of the chapter. Chapter content will help prepare students to:

LO 13-1 Explain sexual orientation (including concepts such as homosexuality, bisexuality, and transgender people).

Sexual orientation is "one's erotic, romantic, and affectional attraction to the same gender, to the opposite gender, or to both" (Greenberg et al., 2014, p. 370). A homosexual person is someone who is attracted primarily to people of the same gender to satisfy sexual and emotional needs. A bisexual is a person who is sexually involved with or attracted to members of either gender. Transgender people are those whose gender identity is the opposite of their biological gender. It's difficult to determine exactly how many LGBT people there are. Gender identity and sexual orientation are two very different concepts. Sexual orientation appears to emerge early in life.

LO 13-2 Review stereotypes about lesbian and gay people.

Many people harbor untrue stereotypes about lesbian and gay people, including the queen and the butch, playing male and female roles, and the myth of child molesting.

LO 13-3 *Discuss conceptual frameworks concerning sexual orientation.*

Various theories, including biological (genetic, brain, and hormonal) and psychosocial, attempt to explain why people become lesbian, gay, or bisexual. However, no definite causes have been established. Most experts agree that homosexuality probably results from some interactionist mixture of biological and psychosocial variables.

LO 13-4 *Address discrimination and the impacts of homophobia.*

Homophobia is the extreme and irrational fear and hatred of gay and lesbian people. It can assume many forms and can have serious negative effects on its victims. Suggestions for how social workers can address homophobia are provided.

LO 13-5 *Describe lesbian and gay lifestyles (including lesbian and gay relationships, sexual interaction, gay pride, and empowerment and a sense of community).*

There is no one type of lifestyle adopted by all lesbian and gay people, just as there is no single lifestyle for all heterosexuals. Lesbian and gay relationships vary, as do heterosexual relationships. Many lesbian and gay people seek monogamous relationships. The physiological responses of lesbian and gay people are exactly the same as those of heterosexual people.

LO 13-6 *Explore significant issues and life events for lesbian and gay people (including legal empowerment, violence against them, coming out, ethnicity, adolescence, parenting, aging, and HIV/AIDS).*

Gay and lesbian people are impacted by social, political, and economic forces in many areas. These include employment, historically and informally in the military, personal relationships (including marriage and finances), and child custody and visitation rights.

Violence against gay and lesbian people is common and assumes many forms. Suggestions for confronting it include passing equal rights legislation on the part of LGBT people, passing laws specifically forbidding LGBT victimization, educating professionals in the criminal justice system about LGBT issues, and establishing crisis centers for victims.

Coming out usually involves (1) coming out to oneself, (2) getting to know other people within the gay and lesbian community, (3) sharing with family and friends that one is lesbian or gay, and (4) coming out publicly.

It is important for social workers to focus on the issues involved in racial and ethnic diversity when working with lesbian and gay people.

Various times of life can result in special concerns for lesbian and gay people. Adolescence can be an especially difficult time for lesbian and gay people. Many lesbian and gay people are parents and must address coming out to their children. Lesbian and gay people face many of the same issues as heterosexuals during the aging process. Additionally, they face institutional, legal, and emotional concerns. Although the gay and lesbian communities have made tremendous strides in curbing the spread of AIDS, the emotional and economic impacts on many gay people have been devastating.

To work with LGBT people, social workers need to confront their own homophobia, familiarize themselves with the LGBT communities, and advocate for policies and programs benefitting LGBT people.

LO 13-7 *Recognize gay and lesbian pride, empowerment, and a sense of community.*

Gay men and lesbians can be empowered by developing "gay and lesbian pride" and a sense of community. In this homophobic world, there are a multitude of lesbian and gay activities and organizations.

COMPETENCY NOTES

The entire chapter addresses competency Educational Policy (EP) EP 2.1.7 and its respective practice behaviors EP 2.1.7a and EP 2.1.7b (as cited below). (See *p. 620*.)

EP 2.1.7 Apply knowledge of human behavior and the social environment.

EP 2.1.7a Utilize conceptual frameworks to guide the processes of assessment, intervention, and evaluation. (Such conceptual frameworks will typically be identified by a "helping hands" icon.)

EP 2.1.7b Critique and apply knowledge to understand person and environment. Other EP competencies and practice behaviors addressed in this chapter include the following:

EP 2.1.1b Practice personal reflection and self-correction to assure continual professional development.

(p. 630): Practitioners should practice personal reflection about their own potential homophobic attitudes to pursue self-correction and practice effectively.

(p. 650): Social workers should practice self-reflection to address and correct homophobic attitudes.

EP 2.1.1c Attend to professional roles and boundaries.

(p. 649): The advocate role is very important in social work.

(p. 650): Professional roles include enabler, broker, and advocate.

EP 2.1.1e Engage in career-long learning.

(p. 650): Learning about LGBT issues and communities is a career-long process.

EP 2.1.2 Apply social work ethical principles to guide professional practice.

(pp. 621, 623, 624, 630 635, 639, 642): Ethical questions are posed.

(p. 629): Social workers should evaluate how theories coincide with ethical principles.

EP 2.1.2a Recognize and manage personal values in a way that allows professional values to guide practice.

(p. 650): Reflection about potentially homophobic personal views allows practitioners to manage and change these views so that they don't interfere with professional practice.

EP 2.1.2b Make ethical decisions by applying standards of the National Association of Social Workers (NASW) Code of Ethics and, as applicable, of the International Federation of Social Workers/International Association of Schools of Social Work Ethics in Social Work Statement of Principles.

(p. 618): The NASW *Code of Ethics* stresses self-determination concerning many aspects of diversity, including sexual orientation.

(p. 623): Conversion therapy violates NASW policy and ethical principles such as self-determination.

EP 2.1.2c Tolerate ambiguity in resolving ethical conflicts.

(p. 629): Social workers must tolerate ambiguity when assessing ethical issues related to theory.

EP 2.1.3a Distinguish, appraise, and integrate multiple sources of knowledge, including research-based knowledge, and practice wisdom.

(p. 626): The following sections review multiple sources of knowledge attempting to explain the reasons for people's sexual orientation.

EP 2.1.4 Engage diversity and difference in practice.

(p. 624): Transsexual and transgender people reflect some of the diversity inherent in gender identity and expression.

EP 2.1.4a Recognize the extent to which culture's structures and values may oppress, marginalize, alienate, or create or enhance privilege and power.

(p. 620): Stereotypes oppress lesbian and gay people.

(p. 633): The issues and life events discussed here explore how lesbian and gay people are oppressed and alienated.

(p. 640): Social workers should pay attention to and fight the oppression and discrimination of LGBT people.

EP 2.1.4b Gain sufficient self-awareness to eliminate the influence of personal biases and values in working with diverse groups.

(p. 630): Practitioners should strive for self-awareness regarding any homophobic prejudices and stereotypes they may harbor in order to eliminate them.

(p. 650): Self-awareness about potential homophobic biases is essential when working with LGBT people.

EP 2.1.4c Recognize and communicate their understanding of the importance of difference in shaping life experiences.

(p. 644): Practitioners should recognize the extent to which ethnicity, a dimension of diversity, shapes life experiences for lesbian and gay people.

(p. 646): Social workers should recognize the significance of sexual orientation in shaping adolescents' life experiences.

EP 2.1.4d View themselves as learners and engage those with whom they work as informants.

(p. 630): Social workers should view themselves as learners and engage gay and lesbian clients as sources of information about the gay and lesbian community.

(p. 646): Practitioners should learn from their lesbian and gay adolescent clients by taking these clients' thoughts and feelings seriously.

(p. 650): Social workers should view themselves as learners and their LGBT clients as informants about their issues and communities.

EP 2.1.5a Understand the forms and mechanisms of oppression and discrimination.

(p. 620): Stereotypes about lesbian and gay people promote oppression and discrimination.

(p. 633): Social workers should strive to understand the mechanisms of oppression and discrimination affecting lesbian and gay people.

(p. 640): Practitioners should work to understand discrimination against LGBT people.

EP 2.1.5b Advocate for human rights and social and economic justice.

(p. 640): Practitioners should advocate on the behalf of LGBT people.

(p. 649): As part of their professional role, social workers should advocate for the human rights of LGBT older adults.

(p. 650): Social workers should advocate for the human rights of LGBT people.

EP 2.1.5c Engage in practices that advance social and economic justice.

(p. 640): Social workers should engage in practices that advance social and economic justice for LGBT people.

(p. 646): Practitioners should engage in practices that advance social and economic justice for lesbian and gay adolescents.

EP 2.1.7b Critique and apply knowledge to understand person and environment.

(p. 628): Practitioners should critique and evaluate theories for understanding sexual orientation and human behavior.

EP 2.1.8a Analyze, formulate, and advocate for policies that advance social well-being.

(p. 640): Social workers should support political candidates who espouse proactive policies and legislation for LGBT people.

(p. 650): Practitioners should advocate for policies and services that serve LGBT people. They should also support political candidates who champion social and economic justice on the behalf of LGBT people.

EP 2.1.8b Collaborate with colleagues and clients for effective policy action.

(p. 640): Social workers can collaborate with colleagues to educate them about LGBT issues and urge them to support LGBT people.

EP 2.1.9b Provide leadership in promoting sustainable changes in service delivery and practice to improve the quality of social services.

(p. 633): Social workers must be aware of the issues and life events of gay and lesbian people so that they might provide leadership in improving service delivery.

(p. 650): Social workers should provide leadership to improve and develop agency policies on the behalf of LGBT people and help initiate programs to serve them.

EP 2.1.10e Assess clients' strengths and limitations.

(p. 634): Practitioners should assess and emphasize the strengths inherent in gay and lesbian pride and the sense of community.

EP 2.1.10g Select appropriate intervention strategies.

(p. 646): Social workers should select the appropriate intervention strategies when working with gay and lesbian parents.

EP 2.1.10j Help clients resolve problems.

(p. 642): Practitioners can help LGBT clients resolve the problems potentially involved in coming out.

(p. 646): Social workers can use the suggestions provided here to help lesbian and gay clients address the problems they face as parents.

WEB RESOURCES

See this text's companion website at *www.cengagebrain.com* for learning tools such as chapter quizzing, videos, and more.

BIOLOGICAL ASPECTS
OF LATER ADULTHOOD

©Bikeriderlondon/Shutterstock.com

LeRoy was a muscular, outgoing teenager. He was physically bigger than most of his classmates and starred in basketball, baseball, and football in high school. In football he was selected as an all-state linebacker in his senior year. At age16, he began drinking at least a six-pack of beer each day, and at 17 he began smoking. Because he was an athlete, he smoked and drank on the sly. Since LeRoy was good at conning others, he found it fairly easy to smoke, drink, party, and still play sports. That left little time for studying, but LeRoy was not interested in that, anyway. He had other priorities.

LeRoy received a football scholarship and went on to college. He did well in football and majored in partying. His grades suffered, and when his college eligibility in football was used up, he dropped out of college. Shortly after dropping out, he married

Rachel Rudow, a college sophomore. She soon became pregnant and also dropped out of college. LeRoy was devastated after leaving college. He had been a jock for 10 years, the envy of his classmates. Now he couldn't get a job with status. After a variety of odd jobs, he obtained work as a road construction worker. He liked working outdoors and also liked the macho-type guys with whom he worked, smoked, drank, and partied.

LeRoy and Rachel had three children, but he was not a good husband. He was seldom at home, and when he was, he was often drunk. After a stormy seven years of marriage that included numerous incidents of physical and verbal abuse, Rachel moved out and got a divorce. She and the children moved to Florida, along with her parents, so that LeRoy could not continue to harass her and the children. LeRoy's drinking and smoking increased. He was smoking more than two packs a day, and he sometimes also drank a quart of whiskey.

A few years later, he fathered a child for whom he was required to pay child support. At age 39, he married Jane, who was only 20. They had two children and stayed married for six years. Jane eventually left because she became fed up with being assaulted when LeRoy was drunk. LeRoy now had a total of six children to help support, but he seldom saw any of them. LeRoy continued to drink and also ate to excess. His weight went up to 285 pounds, and by age 48 he was no longer able to keep up with the other construction workers. The construction company discharged him.

The next several years saw LeRoy taking odd jobs as a carpenter. He didn't earn much, and he spent most of what he earned on alcohol. He was periodically embarrassed by being hauled into court for failure to pay child support. He was also dismayed because he no longer had friends who wanted to get drunk with him. When LeRoy was 61, the doctor discovered he had cirrhosis of the liver and told LeRoy he wouldn't live much longer if he continued to drink. Since LeRoy's whole life centered on drinking, he chose to continue to drink. LeRoy also noticed that he had less energy and frequently had trouble breathing. The doctor indicated that he probably had damaged his lungs by smoking and now had a form of emphysema. The doctor lectured LeRoy on the need to stop smoking, but LeRoy didn't heed that advice either. His health continued to deteriorate, and he lost 37 pounds. At age 64, while drunk, he fell over backward and fractured his skull. He was hospitalized for three and a half months. The injury permanently damaged his ability to walk and talk. He is now confined to a low-quality nursing home. He is no longer allowed to smoke or drink. He is frequently angry, impatient, and frustrated. He no longer has friends. The staff detests working with him; his hygiene habits are atrocious, and he frequently yells obscenities. LeRoy frequently expresses a wish to die to escape his misery.

Elroy Karas is 14 months younger than his brother LeRoy. Elroy's early years were in sharp contrast to LeRoy's. Elroy had a lean, almost puny, muscular structure and did not excel at sports. LeRoy was his parents' favorite, and also dazzled the young females in school and in the neighborhood. Elroy had practically no dates in high school and was viewed as a prude. He did well in math and the natural sciences. He spent much of his time studying and reading a variety of books, and he liked taking radios and electrical appliances apart. At first, he got into trouble because he was not skilled enough to put them back together. However, he soon became known in the neighborhood as someone who could fix radios and electrical appliances.

He went on to college and studied electrical engineering. He had no social life but graduated with good grades in his major. He went to graduate school and obtained a master's degree in electrical engineering. On graduating, he was hired as an engineer by Motorola in Chicago. He did well there and in four years was named manager of a division. Three years later, he was lured to RCA with an attractive salary offer. The group of engineers he worked with at RCA made some significant advances in television technology.

At RCA, Elroy began dating a secretary, Elvira McCann, and they were married when he was 36. Life became much smoother for Elroy after that. He was paid well and enjoyed annual vacations with Elvira to such places as Hawaii, Paris, and the Bahamas. Elroy and Elvira wanted to have children, but could not. When Elroy was in his early 40s, they adopted two children, both from South Korea. They bought a house in the suburbs and a sailboat. Elroy and Elvira occasionally had some marital disagreements but generally got along well. In their middle adult years, one of their adopted sons, Kim, was tragically killed by an intoxicated automobile driver. That death was a shock and very difficult for the whole family to come to terms with. But the intense grieving gradually lessened, and after a few years Elroy and Elvira put their lives back together.

Now, at age 67, Elroy is still working for RCA and loving it. In a few years, he plans to retire and move to the Hawaiian island of Maui. Elroy and Elvira have already purchased a condominium there. Their surviving son, Dae, has graduated from college and is working for a life insurance company. Elroy is looking forward to retiring so that he can move to Maui and spend more time on his hobbies—photography and making model railroad displays. His health is good, and he has a positive outlook on life. He occasionally thinks about his brother and sends him a card on his birthday. Since Elroy never had much in common with LeRoy, he seldom visits him.

A Perspective

Later adulthood is often the age of recompense (our return for the way we lived earlier). How we live in our younger years largely determines how we will live in our later years.

Learning Objectives

This chapter will help prepare students to:

EP 2.1.7a, 2.1.7b

LO 14-1 Define later adulthood

LO 14-2 Describe the physiological and mental changes that occur in later adulthood

LO 14-3 Understand contemporary theories on the causes of the aging process

LO 14-4 Describe common diseases and major causes of death among older adults

LO 14-5 Understand material on stress management and on other ways to maintain good physical and mental health throughout life

LO 14-1 Define Later Adulthood

What Is Later Adulthood?

Later adulthood is the last major segment of the life span. The age of 65 has usually been cited as the dividing line between middle age and old age (Santrock, 2013b). There is nothing magical or particularly scientific about 65. Wrinkles do not suddenly appear on the 65th birthday, nor does hair suddenly turn gray or fall out. In 1883, Germany set 65 as the criterion of aging for the world's first modern social security system (Sullivan, Thompson, Wright, Gross, & Spady, 1980). When our Social Security Act was passed in 1935, the United States followed the German model by selecting 65 as the age of eligibility for retirement benefits.

Older people are an extremely diverse group, spanning an age range of more than 30 years. Looking at this age span biologically, psychologically, and sociologically, we can see a number of differences, for example, between Sylvia Swanson, age 65, and her mother, Maureen Methuselah, age 86.

Sylvia owns and operates a boutique, making frequent buying trips to Paris, Mexico City, and San Francisco, while Maureen has been a resident of a nursing home since the death of her husband 13 years ago.

Gerontologists—doctors who specialize in medical care of older people—have attempted to deal with these age-related differences among older people by dividing later adulthood into two groups: *young-old*—ages 65 to 74 years; and *old-old*—ages 75 and above (Santrock, 2013b).

Our society tends to define old age mainly in terms of chronological age. In primitive societies, old age was generally determined by physical and mental condition rather than by chronological age. Such a definition is more accurate than ours. Everyone is not in the same mental and physical condition at age 65. Aging is an individual process that occurs at different rates in different people, and sociopsychological factors may retard or accelerate the physiological changes. As Spotlight 14.1 indicates, people can continue to live productive lives long past the age of 65.

 SPOTLIGHT ON DIVERSITY 14.1

Noted Individuals Prove That Age Need Not Be a Barrier to Productivity

At 100, Grandma Moses was still painting.

At 99, twin sisters Kin Narita and Gin Kanie recorded a hit CD single in Japan and starred in a television commercial.

At 94, Bertrand Russell was active in international peace drives.

At 93, George Bernard Shaw wrote the play *Farfetched Fables*.

At 93, Dame Judith Anderson gave a one-hour benefit performance.

At 91, Eamon De Valera served as president of Ireland.

At 91, Adolph Zukor was chairman of Paramount Pictures.

At 91, Hulda Crooks climbed Mount Whitney, the highest mountain in the continental United States.

At 90, Pablo Picasso was producing engravings and drawings.

At 89, Albert Schweitzer headed a hospital in Africa.

At 89, Arthur Rubinstein gave one of his greatest recitals in New York's Carnegie Hall.

At 88, Michelangelo drew architectural plans for the Church of Santa Maria degli Angeli.

At 88, Konrad Adenauer was chancellor of Germany.

At 87, Mary Baker Eddy founded the *Christian Science Monitor*.

At 85, Coco Chanel was the head of a fashion design firm.

At 84, W. Somerset Maugham wrote *Points of View*.

At 82, Leo Tolstoy wrote *I Cannot Be Silent*.

At 81, Benjamin Franklin effected the compromise that led to the adoption of the U.S. Constitution.

At 81, Johann Wolfgang von Goethe finished *Faust*.

At 80, George Burns won an Oscar for his role in *The Sunshine Boys*.

At 77, Ronald Reagan was finishing his second term as president of the United States.

These internationally noted individuals prove that age need not be a barrier to making major contributions in life. Unfortunately, the discrimination against older people in our society prevents many of them from having a meaningful and productive life.

A New View of Aging

It is a mistake to view later adulthood as a time of inevitable physical and mental decline. Stereotyping later adulthood as an "awful" life stage is erroneous, and sadly is a factor in older adults' being treated as "second-class citizens" by some people who are younger.

On the whole, people today are living longer and faring better than at any time in history. In Japan, old age is a mark of status. For example, travelers to Japan are often asked their age when checking into hotels—to ensure that if they are older adults they will receive proper deference (Papalia & Feldman, 2012).

In the United States, older adults as a group are healthier, more numerous, and younger at heart than ever before. Many 70-year-olds think, act, and feel as 50-year-olds did two decades ago. On television, older adults are less often portrayed as cranky and helpless, and more often as respected and wise.

LO 14-2 Describe the Physiological and Mental Changes That Occur in Later Adulthood

Senescence

The process of aging is called *senescence*. Senescence is the normal process of bodily change that accompanies aging. Senescence affects different people, and various parts of the body, at different rates. Some parts of the body resist aging more than others. In this section, we will look at the aging process in later adulthood.

Appearance

Changes in physical appearance include increased wrinkling, reduced agility and speed of motion, stooping shoulders, increasing unsteadiness of the hands and legs, increased difficulty in moving, thinning of hair, and the appearance of varicose veins. Wrinkling of the skin is caused by the partial loss of elastic tissue and of the fatty layer of the skin.

Senses

The acuity of the senses generally deteriorates in later years. The sense of touch declines with age due to drying, wrinkling, and toughening of the skin. The skin also has increased sensitivity to changes in temperature. Since the automatic regulation of bodily functions responds at a slower rate, older people often "feel the cold more." Exposure to cold and to poor living conditions may cause abnormally low body temperature, which is a serious problem for some older people. They cannot cope as well as younger people with heat either, and therefore cannot work as effectively in moderately high temperatures as younger people can.

The sense of hearing gradually deteriorates. The ability to hear very high tones is generally affected first. As time goes on, the level of auditory acuity becomes progressively lower. Many older people find it difficult to follow a conversation when there is a competing noise, as from a radio, television, or other people talking. An impairment in hearing is five times more likely in those age 65 to 79 than it is in individuals age 45 to 64 years. Men are more apt to experience hearing impairments than are women (Santrock, 2013b). People who have a hearing impairment are apt to feel lonely and isolated, as they cannot as readily join in conversations. Sometimes such an impairment and related feelings of isolation facilitate the development of personality quirks that make people harder to get along with, which further increases their loneliness. (We see once again how the physical and social environment can affect emotional development.)

Vision also declines. Most people over age 60 need glasses or contact lenses to see well. The decline in vision is usually caused by a deterioration of the lens, cornea, retina, iris, and optic nerve. The power of the eye to adjust to different levels of light and darkness is reduced, and color perception is also reduced. Older people are likely to have 20/70 vision or less, they are not as able to perceive depth as others are, and they cannot see as well in the dark, a problem that keeps many of them from driving at night. Half of the legally blind persons in the United States are over 65 (Papalia & Feldman, 2012).

In many older people, the eyes eventually appear sunken due to a gradual loss of orbital fat. The blink reflex is slower, and the eyelids hang loosely because of reduced muscle tone.

Cataracts are a common concern of older people. A cataract is a clouding of the lens of the eye, or of its capsule, that obstructs the passage of light. The consequences of a cataract for visual functioning depend on its location. The most common form of a cataract involves hardening of cell tissues in the lens. Cataracts prevent light from passing through and can thus cause blurred vision and blindness. In severe cases, double vision may result. Cataracts generally can be surgically removed and a substitute lens implanted. More than half of older adults develop cataracts (Papalia et al., 2012). Fortunately, with the development of corrective lenses and new surgical techniques for removing cataracts and implanting artificial lenses, many vision losses can be fully or partially restored.

A frequent cause of blindness among older people is glaucoma, which occurs when fluid pressure in the eye builds up. This pressure, if untreated, damages the eye internally. If this disease (which seldom has early symptoms) is detected through routine vision checkups, it can be treated and controlled with eyedrops, medication, surgery, or laser treatments.

Macular degeneration, which is age-related, is the leading cause of functional blindness in older people. This condition occurs when the center of the retina gradually loses the ability to sharply distinguish fine details. Smokers are about two-and-a-half times as likely to develop this condition (Papalia et al., 2012).

The senses of taste and smell have reduced functional capability during advancing years. Much of this reduced sensitivity appears to be related to illness and poor health rather than to a deterioration of sense organs due to age. Taste is often based on what people can smell. More than four out of five persons over 80 years of age have major impairments in smell, and more than half have practically no sense of smell at all (Papalia et al., 2012). Because food loses its taste for those who have serious impairments in smell and taste, those affected eat less and are often undernourished.

The vestibular senses, which function to maintain posture and balance, also lose some of their efficiency. As a result, older people are more prone to fall than younger adults. Older people are also more apt to suffer from dizziness, which increases the likelihood they will fall.

Teeth

As people grow older, their gums gradually recede, and the teeth increasingly take on a yellowish color. Periodontal disease (a disease of the gums) becomes an increasing problem. Many older people eventually lose many of their teeth; the problem is more severe for people from low income levels, who often have financial and transportation barriers to receiving dental care (Santrock, 2013b). Having teeth replaced with dentures takes several weeks of adjustment, and the person is not able to eat or sleep as well during this period. Poor teeth or the use of dentures may also be traumatic, as it indicates that the person is aging physically. A person's disposition can be adversely affected. On the other hand, for some people dentures improve their appearance and may lead to an improved self-concept. Many of the facial evidences of later adulthood can be prevented by proper dental care throughout life or by using dentures. Dental health is related to a combination of innate tooth structure and lifelong eating and dental health habits.

Voice

In later adulthood, the voice may become less powerful and more restricted in range. Public speaking and singing abilities generally deteriorate earlier than normal speaking skills. These changes are partly due to the hardening and decreasing elasticity of the laryngeal cartilages. Speech often becomes slower, and pauses become longer and more frequent. If there are pathological changes in the brain, slurring may occur.

Skin

The skin in many older people becomes somewhat splotchy, paler in color, and loses some of its elasticity. Some of the subcutaneous muscle and fat disappears, resulting in the skin hanging in folds and wrinkles.

Psychomotor Skills

Older people can do most of the same things that younger people can do, but they do them more slowly. A key factor in the high accident rates of older people is a slowdown in the processing of information by the central nervous system (Papalia, Olds, & Feldman, 2009). It takes older people longer to assess their environment, longer to make a decision after assessment, and then longer to implement the right action. This slowness in processing information shows up in many aspects of older people's lives. Their rate of learning new material is slowed, and the rate at which they retrieve information from memory is reduced.

Have you ever been irritated when an older person was driving a car slowly in front of you? Perhaps you even blasted your car horn in an attempt to hurry that person along. We need to remember that older people are probably functioning at the pace that is safe for them.

The slower processing times and reaction times have practical implications for drivers. Older people have higher accident rates than do middle-aged adults. Their rates are similar to those of teenagers (Papalia et al., 2012). However, the reasons for these relatively high accident rates differ. Teenagers frequently have accidents because they tend to be more reckless and often take risks. Older people tend to have accidents because they are slower in getting out of the way of potential problems and they have less efficient sensorimotor coordination. Older people have as great a need to drive as others. Being able to drive often means the difference between actively participating in society or facing a life of enforced isolation. Older drivers can compensate for any losses of ability by choosing easier routes, driving slower, driving shorter distances, and by only driving in daylight.

Physical exercise and mental activity appear to reduce losses in psychomotor skills, such as in the areas of speed, strength, and stamina. Regular exercise also helps to maintain the circulatory and respiratory systems and helps people be more resistant to physical ailments that might be fatal, such as heart attacks.

Intellectual Functioning

The notion that there is a general intellectual decline in old age is largely incorrect. Most intellectual abilities hold up well with age. Older people do tend to achieve somewhat lower scores on IQ tests than younger people, and the scores of older people gradually decline as the years pass (Santrock, 2013b). In explaining such differences, Papalia and associates (2012) note that a distinction needs to be made between *performance* and *competence*. While older people show a decline in performance on IQ tests, their actual intellectual competence may not be declining. Their lower performance on IQ tests could be due to a variety of factors. With their diminished capacities to see and hear, they have more difficulty perceiving instructions and executing tasks. Due to their reduced powers of coordination and agility, they may perform less well. They may be more fatigued, and fatigue has been found to suppress intellectual performance. Speed is a component of many IQ tests, and older people have a decline in speed because it takes them longer to perceive, longer to assess, and longer to respond (Santrock, 2013b). In addition, when older people know they are being timed, their anxiety increases, as they know that it takes them longer to do things than it

When older adults lose the capacity to drive a vehicle, it severely restricts their social interactions, is an assault on their mental well-being, and lessens their independence.

used to; such increased anxiety may actually lower performance (Papalia et al., 2012).

•••• / **Ethical Questions 14.1**

EP 2.1.2

Do you believe most older people will gradually become senile? If you answered yes, does this belief affect how you relate to an older person?

There are still other factors in older people's IQ test performance. IQ tests include items that are designed to test intelligence in younger people; as a result, some of the items may be less familiar to older people—which lowers their scores. Older people are consistently more cautious than the young; this may hinder their performance on IQ tests, which generally emphasize risk taking and speed. Older people are more apt to have self-defeating attitudes about their abilities to solve problems; such attitudes may become self-fulfilling prophecies on IQ tests.

The reduced performance by older people on IQ tests may also be partly due to a lessening of continuing intellectual activity in later adulthood. It appears that the reduced use of one's intellectual capacities results in a reduction of intellectual ability. Such a proposition underscores the need for older people to remain intellectually active.

A *terminal drop* in intelligence—that is, a sudden drop in intellectual performance—often occurs a few weeks or a few months before death from a terminal illness (Papalia et al., 2012). A terminal drop is not limited to older people; it is also found in younger people who have a terminal illness.

It is not possible at this time to draw definite conclusions as to whether intellectual functioning actually declines in later adulthood. IQ scores do go down, but that does not mean intellectual competence declines, for the reasons cited. Continuing intellectual activity serves to maintain intellectual capacities. Further information about myths surrounding intellectual and physical functioning of older people is presented in Highlight 14.1.

Height and Joints

A person's maximum height is reached by the late teens or early 20s. In future years, there is little or no change in the length of the individual bones. In older people, there may be a small reduction in overall height due to a progressive decline in the discs between the spinal vertebrae. The bones of the body also become less dense and more brittle due to changes in chemical composition. Such changes increase the risk of breakage. Joint movements also become stiffer and more restricted, and the incidence of disease (such as arthritis) affecting the joints increases with age. Older people need to stay physically active to exercise their joints, as the joints will increase in stiffness if there is little activity.

Homeostasis

Homeostasis becomes less efficient in later adulthood. The stabilizing mechanisms become sluggish, and the person's physiological adaptability is reduced. The heart and breathing rates take longer

---

✦ / HIGHLIGHT 14.1

Values and Aging: The Myth of Senility

Senility can be defined as an irreversible mental and physical deterioration associated with later adulthood. Many people erroneously believe that every older person will eventually become senile. This is simply not accurate. Although the physical condition of older people deteriorates somewhat, older people can be physically active until they are near death. Furthermore, the vast majority of older people show no signs of mental deterioration (Santrock, 2013b).

Senility is not a true medical diagnosis, but a wastebasket term for a range of symptoms that, minimally, include memory impairment or forgetfulness; difficulty in maintaining attention and concentration; a decline in general intellectual grasp and ability; and a reduction in emotional responsiveness to others.

Those older people who appear disoriented and confused are apt to be suffering from one or more of over 100 illnesses, many of which are treatable. Infections, an undiagnosed hardening of the blood vessels in the brain, Alzheimer's disease, anemia, brain tumors, and thyroid disorders—these are only a few of the medical conditions that can cause a person to have senile-like symptoms.

to return to normal. Wounds take longer to heal. The thyroid gland shrinks, resulting in a lower rate of basal metabolism. The pancreas loses part of its capacity to produce enzymes that are used in protein and sugar metabolism.

Muscular Structure

After age 30, there is a gradual reduction in the power and speed of muscular contractions, and the capacity for sustained muscular effort decreases. After the age of 50, the number of active muscle fibers gradually decreases, resulting in the older person's muscles being reduced in size. The handgrip strength of a 75-year-old man is only about 55 percent that of a 30-year-old man (Santrock, 2013b). The ligaments tend to harden and contract, sometimes resulting in a hunched-over body position. The reflexes respond more slowly, and incontinence (loss of bowel or bladder control) sometimes occurs. Involuntary smooth muscles that are part of the autonomic system show much less deterioration than do other muscle groups.

Nervous System

Although there is little functional change in the nerves with increasing age, some of the nerve tissue is gradually replaced by fibrous cells. Reflex and reaction times of an older person become slower. The total number of brain cells may decrease, but the brain continues to function normally unless its blood supply is blocked. The brain weight of an average 75-year-old person is similar to that of a middle-aged person (Santrock, 2013b). People with certain medical conditions (such as cerebral arteriosclerosis) will have progressive deterioration of brain tissue. If such deterioration takes place, the person may have a loss of recent and/or past memories; may become apathetic; may be less coordinated in body movements; may give less attention to grooming habits; and may have some personality changes (such as being more irritable, confused, and frustrated). In many older people, the cortical area of the brain that is responsible for organizing the perceptual processes gradually shows degenerative changes.

Digestive System

With increased age, there is a reduction in the amount of enzyme action, gastric juices, and saliva, which upsets the digestion process. Complaints about digestive disorders are among the most common complaints of older people. Since the digestive system is highly sensitive to stress, to emotional disturbances,

and to anxieties that accompany old age, many of the digestive disorders may be due to these factors rather than to age. The regularity of bowel movements is also more of a problem in later adulthood, resulting in diarrhea or constipation.

Respiration

As people age, their lungs decrease in size, resulting in a decrease of oxygen utilization. Some air sac membranes are replaced by fibrous tissue, which obstructs the normal exchange of gases within the lungs. The maximum breathing capacity and maximum oxygen intake in a 75-year-old are about 40 percent of those of a 30-year-old (Santrock, 2009). Moderate exercise throughout life is important for keeping oxygen intake and blood flow at their highest levels, thereby slowing down the aging process.

Heart

The heart and the blood vessels are the body parts in which aging produces the most destructive changes. The heart and arteries are the weakest link in the chain of life, as most of the other organs would probably last for 150 years if they received an adequate blood supply (Santrock, 2013b). The heart is affected by aging in a variety of ways. It shrinks in size, and the percentage of fat in the heart increases. The heart muscles tend to become stringy and dried out. Deposits of a brown pigment in the cells of the heart partly restrict the passage of blood and interfere with the absorption of oxygen through the heart walls. The elasticity in the valves of the heart is reduced, and deposits of cholesterol and calcium in heart valves also decrease valve efficiency.

The heart of an older person pumps only 70 percent as much blood as that of a younger person (Santrock, 2013b). The rhythm of the heart becomes slower and more irregular. Deposits of fat begin to accumulate around the heart and interfere with its functioning. Blood pressure also rises. These changes are not necessarily dangerous, provided the heart is properly treated. A nutritious diet, moderate exercise, adequate sleep, and a positive mental attitude will help keep the heart functioning properly.

In later life, the coronary artery has a tendency to harden and become narrow, which may lead to a partial blockage. The coronary artery is the site of many heart attacks that are brought on by increased emotional stress or physical effort. Hardening of the coronary artery may also increase blood pressure and may reduce the flow of blood to many parts of the body. Poor circulation of blood may cause a variety of problems. For example, poor circulation to the brain may lead to brain deterioration and to personality changes. Poor circulation to the kidneys may result in kidney problems and even kidney failure.

Reserve Capacity

Under ordinary circumstances, people do not use their body systems and organs to their limits. This backup capacity (which allows organs and body systems to respond at greater levels during times of stress) has been called *reserve capacity*. Younger adults have reserve capacities that put forth 4 to 10 times as much effort as usual (Papalia et al., 2012). Reserve capacity helps to preserve homeostasis.

As people age, their reserve capacities decrease. As a result, older people cannot respond to stressful demands as rapidly as younger adults. An older person who used to be able to mow the lawn, and then go waterskiing, may now exhaust the capacity of the heart by mowing the lawn. Young people usually recover fairly rapidly from the flu or pneumonia, while older people may succumb to these illnesses. Because older people no longer have fast reflexes, vigorous heart action, and quick-responding muscles, they are at a greater risk of being victims of certain accidents (e.g., traffic accidents that occur while crossing the street). As the reserve capacity continues to diminish, those affected become less able to care for themselves and more dependent on others.

Sexuality: Conceptualizing Sexual Response

Masters and Johnson (1966) identified four stages of sexual response in females and males: excitement, the plateau stage, orgasm, and resolution. There are many similarities in the physical responses of men and women. These include the two major body changes that result from individual stimulation—myotonia, or muscle tension; and vasocongestion, or blood engorgement.

• • • • / Ethical Question 14.2

Should older people be sexually active?

EP 2.1.2

In *excitement*, blood flows into the erectile tissue of the penis (vasocongestion), resulting in erection. The scrotum (the sac surrounding the testicle) becomes thicker, more wrinkled, and the testicles move up closer to the body.

Plateau response is characterized by the continuation of erection, although it often waxes and wanes during sex play with a partner. The testicles become fully elevated, rotate toward the front, and become blood-engorged, causing expansion in their size. The Cowper's gland secretes a small amount of clear fluid that comes out at the tip of the penis. The purpose of this fluid is generally thought to be to cleanse the urethra of urine, thereby neutralizing the chemical environment for the passage of sperm.

The *orgasm* stage in men consists of two phases. The first is ejaculatory inevitability, a short period during which the stimulation sufficient to trigger orgasm has occurred and the resulting ejaculation becomes inevitable. The second phase, ejaculation, results from rhythmic contractions (myotonia) forcing sperm and semen through the urethra. Simultaneous with this is the very pleasant physical sensation of orgasm.

The final stage, *resolution*, represents a return to the unstimulated state. In resolution, the penis loses its erection and the testicles lose their engorgement and elevation.

In women, the *excitement* stage of sexual response ushers in many changes. The process of vaginal lubrication begins. This response is analogous to the male erection; it is caused by sexual stimulation and is, physiologically, a blood-engorgement response. The uterus and cervix begin to move up and away from the vagina. The clitoris and labia minora (inner lips) enlarge and the labia majora (outer lips) spread. Breast size increases slightly and the nipples become erect.

In the *plateau* stage, the uterus continues in its movement up and back, the vagina lengthens and balloons at the rear, and the outer third of the vagina contracts, causing a gripping effect. The clitoris retracts under its hood, making it seem to disappear.

At *orgasm*, the uterus and vagina become involved in wavelike muscular contractions. This response, as well as the subjective pleasure of orgasm, is very similar to the experience of the male.

In *resolution*, the cervix and uterus drop to their normal position and the outer third of the vagina returns to normal, followed by the inner two-thirds. The clitoris and the breasts also return to normal.

There are many involuntary *extragenital* physical responses in men and women. These include muscle tension responses such as facial grimaces, spastic contractions of the hands and feet, and pelvic thrusting. Extragenital blood-engorgement responses include sex flush, blood pressure and heart-rate increases, and perspiration on the soles of the feet and the palms of the hands.

The effects of aging on sexual response are summarized in Figures 14.1 and 14.2.

Values and Sexuality

EP 2.1.4a

A common misconception is that older people lose their sexual drive. It is true that both sexual interest and sexual activity gradually decline among older adults (Hyde & DeLamater, 2011). However, many older people continue to engage in sexual activity.

Bodily processes slow down *but they do not stop.* A natural slowing down *does not* mean a loss of interest. *Regularity* of sexual release is most important in maintaining sexual response capability in later years.

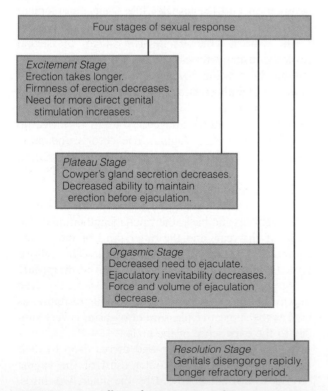

FIGURE 14.1 Effects of Aging on Sexual Response in Men

Bodily processes slow down *but they do not stop.* A natural slowing down *does not* mean a loss of interest. *Regularity* of sexual release is most important in maintaining sexual response capability in later years.

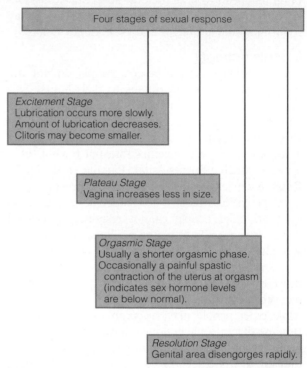

FIGURE 14.2 Effects of Aging on Sexual Response in Women

The scope of the sexual shifts launched by Viagra over a decade ago (perhaps as monumental as those triggered by the birth control pill) is now becoming apparent (Kotz, 2008, p. 50), considerably more 70-year-olds are enjoying sex regularly as compared to 30 years ago; 57 percent of men and 52 percent of women versus 40 percent and 35 percent before Viagra. In addition, about one-quarter of those ages 75 to 85 are now sexually active (Kotz, 2008, pp. 50–52).

Kotz (2008, p. 52) notes:

The merits of staying sexually active through the years are obvious and plentiful: joy and excitement, connectedness, and a host of health benefits. Scientists have shown that having sex regularly boosts the immune system and releases hormones that lower stress levels, improve sleep, and might even hold off wrinkles: A Scottish study found that people who enjoy sex every other day looked about seven to 12 years younger than their peers, on average.

Regarding sexuality in older years, there is truth to the saying, "If you don't use it, you'll lose it." Studies have found that those who were most active sexually during youth and middle age usually maintained sexual vigor and interest longer into old age.

If sexual behavior declines in later years, it probably is due to social rather than physical reasons. The most important deterrents to sexual activity, when one is older, are the lack of a partner; boredom with one's partner; overindulgence in drinking or eating; poor physical or mental health; fear of poor performance; negative attitudes toward menopause; and negative attitudes toward sex, such as the erroneous belief that sex is inappropriate for older persons (Hyde & DeLamater, 2011). Other factors that deter sexual activity include the lack of privacy in many living arrangements, such as in nursing homes. The fear of death from a stroke or a heart attack deters some older people from sexual activity. A variety of feelings—guilt, anxiety, depression, or hostility—also deter sexual activity. As a result, there is usually more interest in sex than there is sexual activity. (This is true, however, for almost all age groups.)

As noted in Figure 14.1, older men normally take longer to develop an erection and to ejaculate, may need more manual stimulation, and may experience longer intervals between erections. Erections may be smaller and less firm and may subside more quickly after ejaculation. Erectile dysfunction may increase, particularly in men with hypertension, heart disease, or diabetes (Papalia et al., 2012). Erectile dysfunction is often treatable; for example, drugs such as Viagra are now widely used by men affected by erectile dysfunction.

Attitudes of younger adults as to what is appropriate sexual behavior for older people commonly create problems. Many younger people believe that it is inappropriate for an unmarried older person to become romantically involved with someone. A widower or widow may face strong opposition to remarrying from family members. Negative views are often strongest when an older person becomes involved with someone younger who has the potential to become an heir if the older person dies.

Older people tend to feel less sexual tension, experience less physical intensity, and have less frequent sexual relations. The increased muscle tone and the sexual flush that accompany arousal are still present, but to a lesser degree. Both young and old people in

our society need to recognize that sexual expression among older people is normal and healthy. Older people need to accept their own sexuality without shame or embarrassment. Younger people need to avoid ridiculing or telling jokes about older persons who show signs of healthy sexuality.

Older people, like those in other age groups, have a right to sexual expression as long as they do not hurt anyone. Think about how angry you would feel if someone tried to control your sexual activity. Few efforts are made to control the sexual expressions of middle-aged people. It seems absurd for society to put restrictions on people as they move from middle to later adulthood. Being touched and receiving affection are something that everyone needs, at all ages, to promote feelings of self-worth and personal satisfaction.

Many of the current living arrangements for older people (group homes, assisted living facilities, nursing homes, and foster homes) overlook the need for privacy. Nursing homes, for example, often place two women or two men in a small room. Housing arrangements should give older men and women chances to socialize, with ample privacy. Physicians, when possible, should avoid prescribing drugs that interfere with sexual functioning. When such a drug needs to be prescribed, the patient should be told about its effects. Social workers and other health professionals should discuss sexual activity with older clients in a matter-of-fact way. For example, a person with heart problems may be too embarrassed to raise questions about the health risks of being sexually active. A social worker could initiate a conversation about this person's fears.

LO 14-3 Understand Contemporary Theories on the Causes of the Aging Process

What Causes Aging?

Everyone who lives to later adulthood will experience some of the physiological changes described in the preceding discussion. What causes these changes? No one knows all of the reasons. Numerous theories have been developed that involve biological, sociological, environmental, and psychological factors. Most of the theories involve biological factors.

Genetic Theories

These theories hypothesize that aging occurs as a result of damage or changes in the genetic information involved in the formation of cellular proteins. Such changes cause cells to die, which results in aging. The following theories have been classified as genetic theories.

An example of a genetic theory is the *running-out-of-program theory*, which asserts that there is a set amount of basic genetic material (DNA molecules) in each cell. As the cells age, the DNA is used up and the cells die. Research by Gerhard and Cristofalo (1992) supports this theory. Their findings showed that human cells will divide only a limited number of times, usually about 50. This limit controls the life span, which they estimate to be about 110 years for humans.

Nongenetic Cellular Theories

This category of theories postulates that changes take place in cellular proteins after they have been formed. Such changes cause some cells to die, which results in aging.

An example of this category of theories is the *accumulation theory*, which asserts that aging results from the accumulation of harmful substances in the cells of an organism. When the accumulation builds up, the cells eventually begin to die. The specific substances involved have not yet been identified.

Physiological Theories

These theories explain aging as being due to either the breakdown of an organ system or an impairment in physiological control mechanisms. An example of this category of theories is the *stress theory*, which asserts that aging is due to the accumulated effects of the stresses of living. Each stress encountered is thought to leave a small residual of accumulants and impairments, with the result that bodily systems age. This theory is consistent with clichés about how stressful events will turn a person's hair gray or cause one's hair to fall out.

Evaluation of Theories of Aging

Everyone grows old, so the conclusion is obvious that nature has a built-in mechanism that promotes aging. We still do not know what this mechanism is. As yet, sufficient evidence has not been presented to prove which (if any) theory is valid.

How Far Can the Life Span Be Extended?

Some people are now living beyond 100 years. Today, people over 100 are a fast-growing segment of the population. Is there a fixed limit on the life span? Experts disagree with one another (Papalia et al., 2012). Some assert there is no fixed limit on how long people may live, while others believe that genetics plays at least a partial role in human longevity, and therefore the idea of an exponential increase in the human life span is unrealistic.

One promising line of research to extend the life span centers on dietary restriction. Drastic caloric reduction (while still including all necessary nutrients) has been found to significantly extend the lifespan (Papalia et al., 2012).

LO 14-4 Describe Common Diseases and Major Causes of Death Among Older Adults

Diseases and Causes of Death Among Older People

Most older people have at least one chronic condition, and some have multiple conditions. The most frequently occurring chronic conditions are arthritis, hypertension, hearing impairments, heart disease, orthopedic impairments, cataracts, diabetes, visual impairments, and sinusitis (Papalia et al., 2012). Older people see their doctors more frequently, spend a higher proportion of their income on prescribed drugs, and once in the hospital, stay longer. As might be expected, the health status of the old-old (75 and over) is worse than that of the young-old.

The medical expenses of an older person average four times more than those of a young adult (Papalia et al., 2012). One of the reasons medical costs are high is that older adults suffer much more from long-term illnesses—such as cancer, heart problems, and diabetes.

An ethical dilemma associated with genetic testing for illnesses is described in Ethical Dilemma: Is Genetic Testing Desirable?

Factors That Influence the Aging Process

Aging is a complex process. There seem to be many variables that accelerate and decelerate the process. A person who has a serious long-term illness or a severe disability will often age much faster and earlier than someone who is healthy (Santrock, 2013b).

ETHICAL DILEMMA

Is Genetic Testing Desirable?

EP 2.1.2

Genetic testing involves ethical and political issues, including privacy and fair use of genetic information. It is now possible to undergo genetic testing to determine whether we carry genes that make it likely we will someday develop diseases that are partly genetically determined. Most diseases develop from a complex combination of genes interacting with lifestyle and other environmental factors. It is a misconception (identified as *genetic determinism*) that a person with a gene for a disease will definitely get the disease, as the actual development of a disease depends on the interaction of genes with environmental factors.

Many disorders arise from an inherited predisposition—that is, an abnormal variant of a normal gene interacting with environmental factors. Examples of these disorders are attention deficit disorder with hyperactivity; sickle-cell anemia, a blood disorder most common among African Americans; cystic fibrosis, a condition in which excess mucus accumulates in the lungs and digestive tracts; glaucoma, in which pressure builds up in the eye; Huntington's disease, a progressive degeneration of the nervous system; breast cancer; Alzheimer's disease; and alcoholism.

Scientists are increasingly identifying genes that predispose a person to developing a variety of illnesses. This process has been aided by the Human Genome Project, which has mapped the order of DNA base pairs in all the genes in the human body.

Genetic testing has a number of potential benefits. First, it will increase our ability to predict, control, prevent, and cure diseases, as well as to pinpoint specific drug treatments to specific individuals. For example, someone who is predisposed to alcoholism could be urged to reduce, or eliminate entirely, the intake of alcoholic beverages. Genetic testing can also help people decide whether to have children and with whom, and it can assist people with family histories of a disease to know the worst that is likely to happen.

On the other hand, there are a number of dangers associated with genetic testing. Job and health insurance discrimination may occur for those who are identified as at risk of developing a serious and costly genetic disorder. The adverse psychological impact of genetic testing results is another potential danger. A false positive result may cause needless anxiety (as predictions are imperfect). In addition, some genetic conditions are currently incurable. Thus there is little point in knowing you have the gene for such a condition if you cannot do anything about it. There are also adverse psychological consequences to knowing you might develop a life-threatening disease 20 or 30 years from now. Also chilling is the danger that genetic testing may result in urging people with "undesirable" genes to undergo sterilization.

Do the potential benefits of genetic testing outweigh the potential dangers? Considering the potential benefits and dangers, do you want to be tested to identify any illnesses that you are predisposed to develop? Should our government urge every person in this country to have genetic testing?

The precise reasons why such conditions accelerate the aging process are not known. More rapid aging in such individuals may be due to decreased exercise, to unknown biochemical changes, or to greater stress.

A large number of "biological insults" hastens the aging process. Such "insults" include accidents, broken bones, severe burns, severe psychological stress, and severe alcohol or drug abuse. Poor eating habits also accelerate aging (Santrock, 2013b).

Environmental factors influence the aging process. Being physically and mentally active tends to slow down the aging process. Inactivity speeds it up. A positive outlook (positive thinking) tends to slow down the aging process. Insecurity, the lack of someone to talk to, negative thinking, and being in a strange environment tend to accelerate the aging process (Santrock, 2013b). Prolonged exposure to excessive heat or cold will also speed up the aging process (Santrock, 2013b).

Genetic inheritance also plays a role. People whose parents lived a long time have a longer life expectancy than do people whose parents lived a shorter period of time (assuming that they died from natural causes). Our bodies apparently have a genetic time clock. Some individuals have a longer time than others. Within a family group, the rate of aging shows a high positive correlation with genetic factors for the different family members. It seems that some kind of timing device causes tissues and organ systems to break down at specific times. This timing device can be accelerated or decelerated by a variety of factors. Highlight 14.2 lists 10 health practices that are known to promote longevity.

The physical process of aging is one reason why older people have a higher rate of health problems.

HIGHLIGHT 14.2

Health Practices and Longevity

The following 10 health practices have been found to be positively related to good health and longevity:

1. Eating breakfast.
2. Eating regular meals and not snacking.
3. Eating moderately to maintain normal weight.
4. Exercising moderately.
5. Not smoking.

6. Drinking alcohol moderately or not at all.
7. Regularly sleeping seven to eight hours a night.
8. Avoiding the use of illegal drugs.
9. Learning to cope with stress.
10. Leading a healthy sexual life.

SOURCE: John W. Santrock, 2013b, *Life-Span Development* (13th ed.). New York: McGraw-Hill.

However, research has demonstrated that personal and social stresses also play major roles in causing disease. Older people face a wide range of stressful situations: death of family members and friends, retirement, loneliness, changes in living arrangements, reduced income, loss of social status, and a decline in physical capacities and physical energy. Medical conditions may also result from inadequate exercise, substandard diets, cigarette smoking, and excessive drinking of alcohol.

A special problem for older people is that when they become ill, their illness is often superimposed on an assortment of preexisting chronic illnesses and

on organ systems that are no longer functioning as well (because their reserve capacities are diminished). The health of older patients is thus more fragile, and even a relatively minor illness, such as the flu, can lead to major consequences or even death.

The most common conditions that limit the activities of older persons are high blood pressure, heart conditions, rheumatism, arthritis, orthopedic impairments, and emotional disorders. Some of these disorders, such as heart problems, high blood pressure, and arthritis, begin to appear among people in their 30s. Highlight 14.3 lists the leading causes of death among older adults.

HIGHLIGHT 14.3

Leading Causes of Death Among Older People

Cause of Death	Of Those Who Died, the Proportion Who Died of This Cause
1. Diseases of the heart	31.0
2. Malignant neoplasms (cancer)	19.4
3. Cerebrovascular diseases (stroke)	6.6
4. Chronic lower respiratory diseases (lung diseases)	6.2
5. Alzheimer's disease	4.0
6. Diabetes	2.9
7. Pneumonia and influenza	2.6
8. All other causes	27.3
Total	100.0%

SOURCE: U.S. Bureau of the Census, *Statistical Abstract of the United States*, 2012 (131st ed.). Washington, DC: Government Printing Office.

The discussion of these health problems needs to be put in context. Older people have higher rates of illnesses than younger people, but it needs to be emphasized that a majority of older people are reasonably healthy. People over 65 do have a health advantage over younger persons in a few areas—they have fewer flu infections, colds, and acute digestive problems. The reasons are unclear. They may be more immune to common germs, or they may go out less and therefore be exposed to fewer germs. (Information about Alzheimer's disease, an illness that affects many older people, is presented in Highlight 14.4.)

 HIGHLIGHT 14.4

Alzheimer's Disease

BSIP/Getty Images

This man, who has Alzheimer's disease, receives feeding assistance from his wife.

Tony Wiggleworth is 68 years old. Two years ago, his memory began to falter. As the months went by, he even forgot what the day of his wedding to Rose was like. His grandchildren's visits slipped from his memory in two or three days.

The most familiar surroundings have also become strange to him. Even his friends' homes seem like places he has never been before. When he walks down the streets in his neighborhood, he frequently becomes lost.

He is now quite confused. He has difficulty speaking and can no longer do such elementary tasks as balancing his checkbook. At times, Rose, who is taking care of him, is uncertain whether he knows who she is. All of this is very baffling for Tony. Until he retired three years ago, he had been an accountant and had excelled at remembering facts and details.

Tony has Alzheimer's disease. Although the disease sometimes strikes in middle age, most sufferers are over 65. About 5 million Americans have Alzheimer's; 5 to 10 percent of all people over 65 have it, but 47 percent of those 85 and over have it (Papalia et al., 2012).

Alzheimer's disease is named after Dr. Alois Alzheimer. In 1906, Dr. Alzheimer noticed changes in the brain tissue of a woman who had died having an unusual medical condition; her symptoms included memory loss, unpredictable behavior, and language problems. After she died, he examined her brain and found many abnormal clumps (now called amyloid plaques) and tangled bundles of fibers (now called tangles). Plaques and tangles in the brain are two of the main features of this disease.

Alzheimer's disease is a degenerative brain disorder that gradually causes deterioration in intelligence, memory, awareness, and ability to control bodily functions. In its final stages, Alzheimer's leads to progressive paralysis and breathing difficulties. The breathing problems often result in pneumonia, the

(continued)

most frequent cause of death for Alzheimer's victims. Other symptoms of Alzheimer's include irritability, restlessness, agitation, and impairment of judgment. Although most of those affected are over 65, the disease occasionally strikes people in middle age.

Over a period lasting from as few as 5 years to as many as 20, the disease destroys brain cells. The changes in behavior displayed by those afflicted may vary. Brownlee (1991) notes:

> *One sufferer refuses to bathe or change clothes, another eats fried eggs without utensils, a third walks naked down the street, a fourth has the family's beloved cats put to sleep, while yet another mistakes paint for juice and drinks it. The outlandish acts committed by Alzheimer's patients take as many forms as there are people who suffer the disease. Yet, in every case, the bizarre behavior serves as a sign that the sufferer is regressing towards unawareness, a second childishness. (p. 40)*

Researchers in recent years have made tremendous strides in identifying the causes of Alzheimer's disease. Several different genes have been identified as being linked to the disease, and there may be more genes involved. Yet having one or more of these genes does not necessarily mean one will develop this disorder. Therefore, researchers believe there must be some as yet unidentified triggers. Possible triggers are viral infections, biochemical deficiencies, high levels of stress, toxic substances, exposure to radiation, and nutritional deficiencies. Scientists are aware that genetic tendencies are a contributing factor because relatives of Alzheimer's patients have an increased risk of having the disease (Papalia et al., 2012).

Examination of the brains of victims has revealed a distinctive tangle of protein filaments in the cortex, the part of the brain responsible for intellectual functions. This research shows that the disease has biochemical causes and leads to the conclusion that aging does not automatically include senility.

Diagnosing Alzheimer's disease is difficult because the disorder has symptoms that are nearly identical to other forms of dementia. The only sure diagnosis at the present time is the observation of tissue deep within the brain, which can be done only by autopsy after death. Doctors usually diagnose the disease in a living person by ruling out other conditions that could account for the symptoms.

The most prominent early symptom of the disease is memory loss, particularly for recent events. Other early symptoms (which are often overlooked) are reduced ability to play a game of cards, reduced performance at sports, and sudden outbreaks of extravagance. More symptoms then develop—irritability, agitation, confusion, restlessness, and impairments of concentration, speech, and orientation. As the disease progresses, the symptoms become more disabling. The caregiver or caregivers eventually have to provide 24-hour care—which is a tremendous burden for caregivers. As the disease progresses in its final stages, a nursing home is often necessary. Near the end, the patient usually cannot recognize family members, cannot understand or use language, and cannot eat without help.

Brownlee (1991) briefly describes the mental and physical trauma that patients' caregivers and family members experience:

> *They live in a private hell, one that cannot be discussed with neighbors and friends in too much detail because the details are so devastating. They grieve even as their loved ones plunge them into a maelstrom of unreality, where mothers streak through the living room wearing nothing but a shower cap and garter belt and grandfathers try to punch their baby granddaughters. (p. 48)*

In addition, the patient's inability to reciprocate expressions of caring and affection robs relationships of intimacy.

Scientists are now investigating a number of hypotheses as to what triggers Alzheimer's. One intriguing finding is that victims of Down syndrome (a severe form of mental retardation due to a chromosome defect) who survive into their 30s frequently develop symptoms indistinguishable from Alzheimer's. Such a similarity may provide a clue as to what triggers Alzheimer's. A recent clue is the discovery of fragments of amyloid in brains of persons who have died from the disorder. Amyloid is a very tough protein that in normal amounts is necessary for cell growth throughout the body. Some researchers hypothesize that abnormal patches of this protein in the brain set up a chain reaction that progressively destroys brain cells. This amyloid protein is an abnormal product formed from a larger compound called the amyloid precursor protein, or APP.

Researchers are attempting to develop a test to detect Alzheimer's disease in its early stages. Detecting the disease early would enable people to plan for their future care and make arrangements for their families while they still retain control of their mental faculties. Furthermore, if in fact Alzheimer's disease results from an accumulation of the amyloid protein, and if the early accumulation of this protein can be detected, then it is likely that drugs can be developed to treat the disorder by blocking the formation of amyloid in the brain. There are high hopes that the causes of Alzheimer's can be found soon and new treatments developed.

Already, early diagnosis and treatment can slow the progress of the disease and improve the quality of life. Cholinesterase inhibitors (such as Aricept) can stabilize or slow symptoms for six months to a year in one-third to one-half of patients (Papalia et al., 2012). Behavioral therapies can improve communication, slow the deterioration in capabilities, and reduce disruptive behaviors. Certain drugs can lighten depression, relieve agitation, and assist patients in sleeping. Proper nourishment, appropriate exercise, physical therapy, and social interaction may slow the progression of the disease. Memory training and memory aids in the early stages may improve cognitive functioning. Especially helpful to patients and their families are emotional and social support provided by groups and professional counseling.

Life Expectancy

The average life expectancy in ancient Rome and during the Middle Ages was between 20 and 30 years. Some people lived to be 70 or 80, but infant mortality was very high, and famine, diseases, and wars took the lives of many more. The life expectancy for Americans has gradually been increasing due to better sanitation, nutrition, and disease control. In the middle of the 19th century, Americans lived for an average of 40 years. At the turn of the 20th century, the average was 49 years. The average life expectancy in 2013 was 79 years (Mooney, Knox, & Schacht, 2013). These gains have resulted from improvements in infant survival, medical care, diets, and sanitation. Two significant factors leading to these gains have been the immunization effort against many diseases that used to kill (such as whooping cough, polio, and diphtheria) and the development of antibiotics that reduce the severity of such illnesses as strep throat, bronchitis, and pneumonia.

···· Ethical Question 14.3

If it were possible, would you want to know the year in which you will die?

EP 2.1.2

Two life events are significant in predicting the death of an older person: death of a spouse and moving to a nursing home (Santrock, 2013b). A partial explanation for the effects of these life events is that those who lose a spouse or are moved to a nursing home may no longer have the will to live, which hastens their death. For those moved to a nursing home, an additional partial explanation for a higher death rate is that such individuals may be in poorer health and therefore more apt to die.

Significant sex differences are found in life expectancies. In 2009, females in the United States had a life expectancy at birth of 81 years, whereas males had a life expectancy of only 76 years (Papalia et al., 2012). There appear to be both environmental and biological reasons for the higher mortality rates among men. Environmental factors are demonstrated by the fact that men are more likely to die from suicide, accidents, and homicides (Santrock, 2013b).

Men are also more likely to die from lung cancer, heart disease, emphysema, and asthma, all of which have been linked to such environmental causes as smoking and alcohol abuse (Santrock, 2013b). A partial explanation for sex differences in mortality rates is that sex-role stereotypes allow women to be much more expressive of their feelings than men. It may be that the suppression of feelings leads to anger, frustration, and other unwanted emotions being bottled up inside, all of which increase stress, result in an increased number of stress-related disorders in men, and then shorten their life span.

Biological factors are probably also involved in leading to higher mortality rates among men. The higher mortality rate among males in the fetal stage and in infancy supports the notion of an inborn difference in resistance.

That there are many more women over age 65 than men means that women are much more apt to be widowed. In 2012, the sex ratio among those 65 and over was 136 women for every 100 men (Santrock, 2013b). Since there is a custom in our society for men to marry someone younger, husbands are even more likely to die before their wives. Women are thus much more likely than men to spend their later years alone.

A number of factors have been found to increase life expectancy (Santrock, 2013b):

1. Parents and grandparents lived to 80 or more.
2. Being married for most adult years.
3. Not being overweight.
4. Exercising regularly (such as jogging or walking briskly three times a week).
5. Light drinking (one or two drinks a day).
6. Not smoking.
7. Being basically happy and content with life.
8. Graduating from college.
9. Living in a rural environment.
10. Having regular medical checkups and regular dental care.
11. Routinely using stress management techniques.

···· Ethical Question 14.4

How many years would you like to live?

EP 2.1.2

Physical affection promotes self-worth and personal satisfaction for people of all ages.

Factors associated with a shorter life expectancy are:

1. Parents and grandparents died of an illness fairly early in their lives—such as a heart attack or a stroke before age 50.
2. Parents or grandparents had diabetes, thyroid disorders, breast cancer, cancer of the digestive system, asthma, or chronic bronchitis.
3. Being unmarried for most adult years.
4. Being overweight.
5. Not exercising regularly.
6. Having a sedentary job.
7. Drinking heavily (more than four drinks per day).
8. Smoking—cigarettes, pipe, or cigars.
9. Being aggressive, intense, and competitive.
10. Often being unhappy, or worried, or feeling guilty.
11. Not completing high school.
12. Living in an urban environment that has moderate to high levels of smog.
13. Experiencing frequent illness.
14. Experiencing high levels of stress without routinely using stress management techniques.
15. Engaging in activities that are high risk for the AIDS virus (Santrock, 2013b).

See Spotlight 14.2 for research on some reasons why people live to be 100.

LO 14-5 Understand Material on Stress Management and on Other Ways to Maintain Good Physical and Mental Health Throughout Life

Wellness: The Strengths Perspective

The preceding section echoes, over and over, a central theme: Older people are apt to experience little physical or mental deterioration (until near death) if they have a nutritious diet, are successful in managing stress, and stay mentally and physically active. A real key to good mental and physical health in later years is having a lifestyle throughout life that incorporates health-maintenance principles. Health is indeed one of our most important resources.

Traditionally, the health profession in this country has focused on treatment of disease rather than on prevention. The Chinese approach to medicine has focused on helping patients maintain good health. The holistic concept of treating the whole person is gaining ground in America. There is now greater emphasis on prevention, wellness, and treating a patient psychologically and socially as well as physically.

GoGo Images/Jupiter Images

SPOTLIGHT ON DIVERSITY 14.2

Longevity: Cross-Cultural Research on Centenarians

A centenarian is a person who is 100 years old, or even older. Why do some people live to be 100 or older? As yet, we do not know the answers. We do know that the number of centenarians in the world is increasing significantly. There are 55,000 centenarians in the United States (Santrock, 2013b). Research on the reasons why some people live to be centenarians is beginning.

One possibility involved in this trend is exceptional genes, which may offer protection against diseases such as Alzheimer's and cancer. There are undoubtedly also some environmental and cultural factors. We do know that some centenarians are vegetarians, and that others eat a lot of red meat. Some were athletes, and some engaged in little strenuous activity. One personality characteristic that appears to be shared by this group is the ability to manage stress (Perls, Hutter-Silver, & Lauerman, 1999).

Infusino and his associates (1996) studied 40 centenarians living in Calabria, a remote region of Italy. Most of these people continued to perform physical tasks and activities associated with daily life. They also had very low levels of depression, and were functioning well mentally. Significantly, they continued to feel important and valued in their culture.

Sadly, our society has tended to devalue the contributions of older adults. Lefrancois (1999) states that in our society: "Little is asked of the individual for the first twenty or so years of life, a contribution is expected during the middle thirty or thirty-five years, and after age sixty or sixty-five, little more is expected. This *discontinuity* between productive and nonproductive life, is, in effect, a clear social signal that differentiates between being useful and being useless, between being culturally valued and not being valued, between being wanted and not being wanted" (p. 496). Is the feeling of being valued one of the factors that increases one's life expectancy?

A 2008 study by Dr. Laurel Yates found that living past 90, and living well, may be more than a matter of good genes and good luck (Bakalar, 2008). Five behaviors in old-old men were found to be associated with living into extreme old age, and also with good health and independent living. These five behaviors are abstaining from smoking, weight management, blood pressure control, regular exercise, and avoiding diabetes.

Physical Exercise

For people who have had poor health-maintenance habits, it is nearly never too late to change. Many studies have shown that older people benefit from a variety of exercise programs that include walking, swimming, and weight lifting. There is also evidence that as people grow older, continued exercise reduces the degree of physical and mental slowness that occurs in many older people. However, before middle-aged and older adults embark on exercise programs (if they have been relatively inactive for a number of years), they should have physical examinations to identify heart conditions and other medical problems that may be aggravated by exercise.

Mental Activity

Just as physical exercise maintains the level of physiological functioning, mental exercise maintains good cognitive functioning. As mentioned, there are some age-related declines in cognitive functioning, but if a person is mentally active, the declines begin to appear at a later age and are less severe.

Our society needs to put more emphasis on ensuring that older people are exposed to intellectual stimulation. Some nursing homes and retirement communities now have daily programs that provide such stimulation; national issues or local issues are discussed, and guest speakers on a variety of subjects are sometimes brought in.

One innovative program is Road Scholar, which offers low-cost courses, often held on college campuses, for people over 55. People sign up for one-, two-, or three-week sessions to study a variety of topics at a relaxed pace. Some public universities also have provisions for those over 65 to attend regular classes with either reduced or no tuition. Older people have generally responded well to adult education courses. Some want to update earlier studies, and others want to pursue educational programs to enrich their lives. Still others want to acquire basic learning skills or obtain a high school or college diploma.

Traveling is yet another way for older people to stay mentally active. Some organizations, such as the AARP (formerly the American Association of Retired Persons) and Road Scholar, offer travel

The more mentally and physically active we are, the better our physical health, emotional well-being, and intellectual alertness.

tours within the United States and to other parts of the world.

Most authorities on aging now believe that intellectual decline in later adulthood is largely a myth. It thus appears that our society is wasting a precious resource—an older population with extensive experience, training, and intelligence. Our society needs to develop more educational programs to help older people maintain their intellectual functioning, and we must find additional ways to allow older people to be productive, contributing members of society.

Sleep Patterns

Many older people have one or more sleep disturbances, such as insomnia, difficulty in falling asleep, restless sleep, falling asleep when company is present, frequently awakening during the night, and feeling exhausted or tired after a night of fitful sleep.

What is a healthy sleep pattern for older people? The stereotype that older people need more sleep appears to be erroneous. It appears that older people in fairly good health require no more sleep than do those in middle adulthood (Santrock, 2013b).

Sleep disturbances that older people experience tend to be a result of anxiety, depression, worry, or illness. Restless sleep is common for those who are inactive, those who catnap too much, and those who have physical discomforts (such as arthritic pain).

Some normal changes occur in sleep patterns for older people. Deep sleep virtually disappears. Older people generally take a longer time to fall asleep and have more frequent awakenings. More important, older people distribute their sleep somewhat differently. They generally have several catnaps of 15 to 60 minutes during the day. Catnaps are normal, and caution should be used in attempting to use sleep medication to keep an older person asleep for eight hours throughout the night, as they need less sleep when they have catnaps. People develop their sleep patterns according to their physical needs and according to the responsibilities and activities they have.

Nutrition and Diet

The majority of older people have inadequate diets (Newman & Newman, 2009). Because of the relationship between diet and cardiac problems, physicians recommend that older adults eat a low-fat, high-protein diet.

Older people are the most undernourished group in our society (Papalia et al., 2012). Reasons for chronic malnutrition in older people include lack of money, transportation problems, little incentive to prepare a nutritious meal when one is living alone, inadequate cooking and storage facilities, decreased or altered sense of taste, poor teeth and lack of good dentures, and lack of knowledge about proper nutrition.

Some older people have a tendency to overeat. One way for people to occupy their free time is to eat, and most older people have a lot of free time. The caloric requirements decrease somewhat in the later years, and the excess calories turn into fat, increasing the risks of heart disease and other medical conditions.

Numerous programs have been developed to improve the nutritional health of older people.

Many communities, with the assistance of federal funds, now provide meals for older people at group eating sites. These meals, usually lunches, are generally provided four or five times a week. These programs not only improve the nutrition of older people but also offer opportunities for socialization. Meals on Wheels is a service that delivers hot and cold meals directly to housebound recipients who are unable to prepare their own meals, but who can feed themselves.

Stress and Stress Management

Learning how to manage stress is important for the physical and emotional health of all age groups. Because of its importance, we will discuss stress and techniques to manage stress in considerable detail.

Stress is a contributing factor in a wide variety of emotional and behavioral difficulties, including anxiety, child abuse, spouse abuse, temper tantrums, feelings of inadequacy, physical assaults, explosive expressions of anger, feelings of hostility, impatience, stuttering, suicide attempts, and depression (Seaward, 2012).

Stress is a contributing factor in most physical illnesses (Seaward, 2012), including hypertension, heart attacks, migraine headaches, tension headaches, colitis, ulcers, diarrhea, constipation, arrhythmia, angina, diabetes, hay fever, backaches, arthritis, cancer, colds, flu, insomnia, hyperthyroidism, dermatitis, emphysema, Raynaud's disease, alcoholism, bronchitis, infections, allergies, and enuresis. Stress-related disorders have been recognized as being our number-one health problem (Seaward, 2012).

Learning how to relax is important in treating and facilitating recovery from both emotional and physical disorders. The therapeutic value of learning how to manage stress has been dramatically demonstrated by Simonton and Matthews-Simonton (1978), who have had considerable success in treating terminal cancer patients by teaching them how to manage and reduce stress.

The increased recognition of stress management in treating physical and emotional disorders is gradually altering the traditional physician–patient relationship. Instead of being passive participants in the treatment process, patients are increasingly being taught (by social workers and other health professionals) how to prevent illness and how to speed up their recovery from illness by learning stress management strategies (Seaward, 2012).

People who are successful in managing stress have a life expectancy that is several years longer than those who are continually at high stress levels (Seaward, 2012). Effective stress management is a major factor in enabling people to live fulfilling, healthy, satisfying, and productive lives.

Conceptualizing Stress

Stress can be defined as the physiological and emotional reactions to stressors. A stressor is a demand, situation, or circumstance that disrupts a person's equilibrium (internal balance) and initiates the stress response. There are an infinite variety of possible stressors: loss of a job, a loud noise, toxic substances, retirement, arguments, the death of a spouse, a move to a nursing home, hot or cold weather, serious illness, a lack of a purpose in life, and so on. Every second we are alive, our bodies are responding to stressors that call for adaptation or adjustment. Our bodily reactions are continually striving for homeostasis, or balance.

Selye (1956), one of the pioneer researchers on stress, found that the body has a three-stage reaction to stress: (1) the alarm phase, (2) the resistance phase, and (3) the exhaustion phase. Selye called this three-phase response the *general adaptation syndrome (GAS)*.

In the alarm phase, the body recognizes the stressor and responds by preparing to fight or flee. The body's reactions are numerous and complex. Briefly, the body sends messages from the hypothalamus (a section of the brain) to the pituitary gland to release its hormones. These hormones trigger the adrenal glands to release adrenaline. The release of adrenaline and other hormones results in:

- Increased breathing and heartbeat rates
- A rise in blood pressure
- Increased coagulation of blood, which minimizes potential loss of blood in case of physical injury
- Diversion of blood from the skin to the brain, the heart, and contracting muscles
- A rise in serum cholesterol and blood fat
- Decreased mobility of the gastrointestinal tract
- Dilation of the pupils

These changes result in a huge burst of energy, better vision and hearing, and increased muscular strength—all changes that increase our capacity to fight or to flee.

A major problem of the fight-or-flight reaction is that we often cannot deal with a threat by fighting or by fleeing. In our complex, civilized society, fighting or fleeing generally runs counter to sophisticated codes of acceptable behavior. The fight-or-flight response was once functional for primitive humans, but now seldom is.

In the resistance phase, bodily processes seek to return to homeostasis. During this second phase, the body seeks to repair any damage caused by the stressors. In handling most stressors, the body generally goes through only the two phases of alarm and repair. In the course of a lifetime, a person goes through these two phases hundreds of thousands of times.

The third phase, exhaustion, occurs only when the body remains in a state of high stress for an extended period of time. If the body remains at a high level of stress, it is unable to repair damage that has occurred. If exhaustion continues, a person is apt to develop a stress-related illness.

A stressor has two components: the experiences or events we encounter, and our thoughts and

perceptions about these events (Seaward, 2012). (See Highlight 14.5.)

Stress is heavily dependent on what a person thinks about events. The following example shows how a person's thinking about a positive event can be a source of negative stress.

Stressor { Event: Glenda Wilcox (age 75) is informed by her granddaughter that her level of alertness is fantastic.

Ms. Wilcox's thinking about this event: "What a backhanded compliment! She expects me to become senile and is surprised I haven't yet. Young people are so inconsiderate. But I wonder if there is truth in what she's implying? Will I soon begin to lose my mind and have to leave my house and live my remaining years in confusion in a nursing home? It seems

---

◆ HIGHLIGHT 14.5

Conceptualizing Stressors, Stress, and Stress-Related Illnesses

Stressors { Events or experiences (e.g., being forced to retire from a job held for 27 years)

A certain kind of thinking (e.g., "What will I do now with all of my time? My work has been my life. Life is over for me now. All I have left to do is die. My income now will be sharply reduced—how will I pay my bills? The company has no right to force me to retire! This is unfair.")

Stress { Emotional reactions: Fear, anxiety, worry, alarm, depression, anger

Physiological reactions: The alarm stage of the general adaptation syndrome occurs, and the body prepares for fight or flight. Adrenaline and other hormones increase the heartbeat and rate of breathing, increase perspiration, raise blood sugar levels, dilate the pupils, and slow digestion. The process results in greater muscular strength, a huge burst of energy, and better vision and hearing.

Stress-related disorder: If the body remains at a high level of stress for a prolonged period, a stress-related disorder will develop.

there are things I'm starting to forget more frequently than I did in the past."

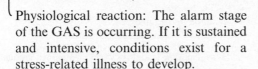

Stress { Emotion: Anger, anxiety, worry, alarm.

Physiological reaction: The alarm stage of the GAS is occurring. If it is sustained and intensive, conditions exist for a stress-related illness to develop.

(The relationship between traumas and stress disorders is discussed in Highlight 14.6.) Not all stress is bad. Life without stress would be boring. Selye (1974) notes that stress is often "the spice of life," and that it is impossible to be alive without experiencing stress. Dreaming even produces some stress. Stress is often beneficial, stimulating and preparing us to perform a wide variety of tasks. Students, for example, often find they need to feel a moderate level of stress before they can study for an exam—too little stress results in their being unable to concentrate and may even result in their falling asleep, while too high a level of stress results in too much anxiety and interferes with their concentration. High levels of the alarm phase of the GAS are very desirable during emergencies when physical strength is needed—such as in lifting a heavy object that has fallen on someone.

Selye (1974) calls the kind of stress that is harmful *distress*. Long-term distress occurs when we continue to think negatively about events that have happened to us. When unpleasant events occur, we always have a choice to think negatively or positively. If we continue to think negatively about the situation, our thinking keeps the body under a high level of stress, which can then lead to a stress-related illness. On the other hand, if we think positively about the situation, our thinking enables the body to relax and repair any damage that was done. In addition, when we are relaxed, the immune system is much more effective in combating potential illnesses. (In the alarm phase, the functioning of the immune system is sharply reduced, as bodily resources are primarily focused on facilitating the fight-or-flight response.)

A number of signals, presented in Table 14.1, can help us measure levels of stress. Most of us use these signals to judge whether our friends are under too much stress. But most of us fail to use these same signals to determine when our own stress level is too

high. For our emotional and physical health, we need to give more attention to monitoring these signals in ourselves.

Empowerment Approaches to Stress Management: Application of Theory

Of the five major categories of approaches to stress management, only three are constructive in terms of empowering a person and helping him or her gain greater control over life. The three constructive approaches are (1) changing the distressing event, (2) changing one's thinking about the distressing event, and (3) taking one's mind off the distressing event, usually by thinking about something else.

There are also two destructive ways that some people use to relieve stress. One involves resorting to alcohol, other drugs, or food. Perhaps the major reason for abusing alcohol and other drugs is to seek relief from stress and unwanted emotions. Drugs may provide temporary relief, but the next day a person's problems still remain, and there is a serious danger that drug abuse may become a destructive habit. Compulsive overeating is also an unhealthy way of temporarily relieving stress.

The second destructive way of escaping stress is suicide. We will focus here on constructive ways to relieving stress.

Changing a Distressing Event When distressing events occur, it is desirable to confront them directly to try to improve the situation. An older person concerned about what to do with his or her time after retiring needs to work on finding meaningful and enjoyable activities to become involved in. A person who is concerned about a deterioration in health should see a physician and receive medical treatment. Many distressing events can be improved by confronting them head on and taking constructive action to change them.

Changing One's Thinking About a Distressing Event Some events cannot be changed. For example, Juan Garcia (age 64) has experienced such a severe deterioration in his eyesight that he is no longer able to drive his truck (by which he earned a living) or even a car. Ophthalmologists have informed him that his eyesight will slowly continue to deteriorate and that the condition is not reversible. Since Juan cannot change the situation, the only constructive alternative is to accept it and find meaningful activities unrelated to driving. It is counterproductive to complain or get upset about something that cannot be changed. Acceptance of the situation will also improve Juan's disposition.

HIGHLIGHT 14.6

Traumas and Stress Disorders

Physical trauma is an injury to the body caused by violence or accident, such as a bruise or fracture. Psychological trauma is an emotional wound or shock, often having long-lasting effects. Physical traumas often lead to psychological traumas.

Traumatic experiences often involve a threat to life or safety, but any situation that leaves one feeling overwhelmed and alone can be traumatic, even if it does not involve physical harm. It's not the objective facts that determine whether an event is traumatic, but one's subjective emotional experience of the event.

A stressful event is most likely to be traumatic if:

- It happened unexpectedly.
- One is unprepared for it.
- It happened repeatedly.
- One felt powerless to prevent it.
- Someone was intentionally cruel.

Traumas can come in a huge variety of ways. The following is a short list: serving in combat in the military, being physically or sexually abused as a child, a sexual assault, an auto accident, the breakup of a significant relationship, a humiliating or deeply disappointing experience, and the discovery of a life-threatening illness or disabling condition.

People are more likely to be traumatized by a stressful experience if they are already under a heavy stress load or have recently suffered a series of losses. Not all potentially traumatic events lead to lasting psychological and emotional damage, some people rebound quickly from even the most shocking and tragic experiences, whereas others are devastated by experiences that appear on the surface to be "mildly upsetting."

Traumatic experiences in childhood can have a severe and long-lasting impact. Children who have been traumatized see the world as a dangerous and frightening place. When childhood trauma is unresolved, this sense of fear and helplessness carries over into adulthood, setting the stage for further trauma.

Emotional symptoms of trauma include:

- Denial, shock, or disbelief
- Anxiety and fear
- Withdrawing from others
- Feeling numb or disconnected
- Anger, irritability, mood swings
- Confusion, difficulty concentrating
- Guilt, self-blame, shame
- Feeling hopeless or sad

Physical symptoms of trauma include:

- Aches and pains
- Fatigue

- Muscle tension
- Being startled easily
- Racing heartbeat
- Agitation and edginess
- Difficulty concentrating

These emotional and physical symptoms gradually fade *if* the impacted person makes progress in coming to terms with the trauma. But even if the person is progressing in resolving the trauma, the person may be troubled from time to time by painful memories and emotions. Triggers for reliving the painful event include the anniversary of the event, or sounds and images of the situation that remind the traumatized individual of the traumatic experience.

There are two stress disorders associated with severe traumas: acute stress disorder and posttraumatic stress disorder–(PTSD). Acute stress disorder is an anxiety disorder in which fear and related symptoms are experienced soon after a traumatic event and last less than a month (American Psychiatric Association [APA], 2013a).

Posttraumatic stress disorder is an anxiety disorder in which fear and related symptoms continue to be experienced long after a traumatic event (APA, 2013a) Primary symptoms of PTSD include flashbacks or intrusive memories, living in a constant state of "red alert," and avoiding things that remind the impacted person of the traumatic event.

Working through trauma can be painful, scary, and potentially retraumatizing. The "healing" work is best done with a competent trauma expert. Trauma treatment involves:

- Processing the trauma memories and feelings
- Discharging the pent-up emotions/energy associated with the trauma
- Learning how to control strong emotions
- Rebuilding the capacity to trust other people

Treatment approaches for PTSD include the following:

- Cognitive-behavioral therapy, such as rational therapy (described in Chapter 8), in which the person learns to reframe the disturbing traumatic thoughts.
- Antianxiety drugs, which help control the anxieties and tensions associated with PTSD. Such medication provides some relief, but needs to be combined with a "talk" therapy approach.
- Eye movement desensitization and reprocessing (EMDR), which incorporates elements of cognitive-behavioral therapy; the impacted persons move their eyes in a rhythmic manner from side to side while flooding their minds with images of the objects and situations they try to avoid. These back-and-forth eye movements are thought to work by "unfreezing" traumatic memories, which then can be processed and resolved.

TABLE 14.1 / STRESS SIGNALS

A number of signals can be used to measure whether we are at a good level of stress or at too high a level of stress. Based on these signals, you have to use your own judgment to determine whether your stress is too high.

GOOD LEVEL	TOO HIGH
1. *Behaviors*	High-pitched, nervous laughter
Creative, makes good decisions	Lack of creativity
Friendly	Poor work quality
Generally successful	Overdrinks or overeats
Able to listen to others	Smokes to excess
Productive—gets a lot done	Stutters
Appreciates others, is perceptive of others, and recognizes	Inability to concentrate
contributions of others	Easily startled by small sounds
Smiles, laughs, jokes	Impatient
	Easily irritated
	Unpleasant to be around
	Puts others down
	Engages in wasted activity and motion
2. *Feelings*	Resentful, bitter, dissatisfied, angry
Feeling of confidence	Timid, tense, anxious, fearful
Feeling of being calm, relaxed	Paranoid
Feelings of pleasure and enjoyment	Weary, depressed, fed up
Feelings of excitement and exhilaration	Feelings of inadequacy or failure
	Confused, swamped, overwhelmed
	Feelings of powerlessness or helplessness
3. *Body Signals*	Loss of appetite; diarrhea or vomiting
Restfulness	Prone to accidents
Absence of aches and pains	Frequent need to urinate
Coordinated body reactions	Trembling, nervous tics
Unaware of body, which is functioning smoothly	Feelings of dizziness or weakness
Good health, absence of stress-related illnesses	Frequent colds and flu
	High blood pressure
	Tight or tense muscles
	Asthma or breathing irregularities
	Skin irritations, itches, and rashes
	Sleep problems
	Upset stomach and ulcers
	Various aches and pains—muscle aches, backaches, neck aches, headaches

One of the structured techniques for changing one's thinking about a distressing event is to challenge and change the negative and irrational thinking through a rational self-analysis, as described in Chapter 8.

When unpleasant events occur, we have a choice to take either a positive or a negative view. If we take a negative view, we are apt to experience more stress, and also apt to alienate friends and acquaintances.

Akin to *positive thinking* is having a philosophy of life that allows us to take crises in stride, to travel through life at a relaxed pace, to look at the scenery with enjoyment, to approach work in a relaxed fashion so as to permit greater creativity, to enjoy and use leisure time to develop more fully as a person, and to find enjoyment in each day.

HIGHLIGHT 14.7

Law of Attraction, and Becoming All That You Can Be

The Law of Attraction asserts that a person's thoughts (both conscious and unconscious) dictate the reality of that person's life, whether or not he or she is aware of it. The Law further asserts that if you really want something and truly believe it's possible, you'll get it. Furthermore, if you place a lot of attention and thought on something you don't want, you'll probably get that, too. For example, if you continue to worry and dwell on your belief that your romantic life "is in the pits," that belief system (along with the way you present yourself in accordance with this belief system) will lead you to have unhappy romantic relationships.

Think of the qualities you admire in others. A partial list might include honesty, a good listener, happy, contented, good sense of humor, charming, good problem solver, reliable, punctual, someone who helps you out when you need help, takes good care of her or his physical self, empathetic, perceptive, respectful of differences in others, usually has a smile, and focuses on the strengths of others.

The Law of Attraction asserts we are always sending out vibes/vibrations of what we are thinking/feeling. If we are thinking bad thoughts, we will have bad feelings and will be sending out negative vibes. It we are thinking good/positive thoughts, we will have good feelings and will be sending out good vibes.

We like to be with people who send out good vibes—and who have the qualities we admire. We generally do not like to associate with people who are sending out bad vibes.

In order for a salesperson to be successful, he or she needs to be sending out good vibes so that customers will want to converse with him or her. In order for a social worker to be effective with clients, he or she also needs to be sending out good vibes so that clients will want to converse with him or her. This rule applies to most professionals: physicians, attorneys, psychologists, psychiatrists, guidance counselors, teachers, and so on.

The Law of Attraction asserts that if you present yourself as exhibiting the positive qualities that are listed above, many doors will be opened up for you, and you will be successful, happy, contented, relaxed, and so on.

Are you willing to make a commitment to presenting yourself to others as having the positive characteristics you admire in others?

Every person needs someone to share good times with and to talk with about personal difficulties. *Sharing concerns with someone* helps to vent emotions. The listener may be a neighbor, friend, member of the clergy, or professional counselor. Talking a concern through often helps to reduce stress in two ways. It may lead to a new perspective on how to resolve the distressing event, or it may help by changing one's thinking about the distressing event to a more positive and rational attitude.

Closely related to discussing a distressing event with someone is having a social support group. Support groups allow people to share their lives, to have fun with others, to "let their hair down," and to be a resource for help when emergencies and crises arise. Possible support groups include friends in a retirement community, one's family, one's coworkers, a church group, or a community group.

Taking One's Mind Off the Distressing Event, Usually by Thinking About Something Else There are a variety of ways to stop thinking about a distressing event.

1. *Relaxation Techniques.* Deep-breathing relaxation, imagery relaxation, progressive muscle relaxation, meditation, and biofeedback are effective techniques for reducing stress and inducing the relaxation response (becoming relaxed). For each of these techniques, the relaxation response is facilitated by sitting in a comfortable position, in a quiet place, with closed eyes (Davis, McKay, & Eshelmen, 2000).

Deep-breathing relaxation helps you stop thinking about day-to-day concerns by concentrating on your breathing processes. For 5 to 10 minutes, slowly and gradually inhale deeply and exhale, while telling yourself something like, "I am relaxing, breathing more smoothly. This is soothing, and I'm feeling calmer, renewed, and refreshed." Continued practice on this technique will enable you to become more relaxed whenever you are in a tense situation—such as before giving a speech.

Imagery relaxation involves switching your thinking from your daily concerns to focusing (for 10 to 15 minutes) on your ideal relaxation place. It might be lying on a beach beside a scenic lake in the warm sun. It might be relaxing in warm water while you read a magazine. Savor all the pleasantness, the peacefulness—focus on everything that you find calming, soothing, relaxing. Sense your whole body becoming refreshed, revived, and rejuvenated.

©iStock.com/Christopher Futcher

Meditation is an excellent way to relax and reduce stress levels.

Progressive muscle relaxation is based on the principle that a person cannot be anxious if the muscles are relaxed (Jacobson, 1938). The approach is learned by having a person tighten and then relax a set of muscles. While relaxing the muscles, the person is advised to concentrate on the relaxed feeling while noting that the muscles are becoming less tense. Watson and Tharp (1973) give a brief description of the initial steps in this procedure:

Make a fist with your dominant hand (usually right). Make a fist and tense the muscle of your (right) hand and forearm: tense it until it trembles. Feel the muscles pull across your fingers and the lower part of your forearm…. Hold this position for five to seven seconds, then … relax…. Just let your hand go. Pay attention to the muscles of your (right) hand and forearm as they relax. Note how those muscles feel as relaxation flows through (twenty to thirty seconds). (pp. 182–183)

The procedure of tensing and then relaxing is continued for three or four times until the hand and forearm are relaxed. Next, other muscle groups are tensed and relaxed in the same manner, one group at a time. These groups might include left hand and forearm, right biceps, left biceps, forehead muscles, upper lip and cheek muscles, jaw muscles, chin and throat muscles, chest muscles, abdominal muscles, back muscles between the shoulder blades, right and left upper leg muscles, right and left calf muscles, and toes and arches of the feet. With practice, a person can develop the capacity to relax simply by visualizing the muscles.

A variety of meditative approaches are being used today. (Deep-breathing relaxation and imagery relaxation are two forms of meditation.) Benson (1975) has identified four basic components common to meditative approaches that induce the relaxation response: (1) being in a quiet environment free from external distractions; (2) being in a comfortable position; (3) having an object to dwell on, such as a word, sound, chant, phrase, or imagery of a painting (Benson suggests the word *one*); and (4) having a passive attitude in which you stop thinking about day-to-day concerns. This last component, Benson asserts, is the key element in inducing the relaxation response.

Biofeedback equipment provides mechanical feedback to a person about his or her level of stress. Such equipment informs people about levels of stress that they are usually unaware of until a markedly high level is reached. For example, a person's hand temperature may vary from 10 to 12 degrees in an hour's time, with an increase in temperature indicating an increase in calm and relaxation. Biofeedback equipment measures the levels of functioning of numerous physiological processes, such as blood pressure, hand temperature, muscle tension, heart rate, and brain waves. In biofeedback training, a person is first instructed in recognizing high levels of anxiety or tenseness. Then the person is instructed on how to reduce these levels, either by closing the eyes and adopting a passive, letting-go attitude or by thinking about something pleasant or calming. Often, relaxation approaches are combined with biofeedback to elicit the relaxation response. Biofeedback equipment provides immediate feedback to a person about the kind of thinking that is effective in reducing stress (Seaward, 2012).

2. *Exercise.* Since the alarm phase of the general adaptation syndrome automatically prepares us for large muscle activity, it makes sense to exercise. Through exercising, we use up fuel in the blood, reduce blood pressure and heart rate, and reverse the other physiological changes set off during the alarm state of the general adaptation syndrome. Exercising helps keep us physically fit so that we have more physical strength to handle stressful crises. Exercising also reduces stress and relieves tension, partly by switching our thinking from our daily concerns to the exercise we are involved in. For these reasons we need to have an exercise program. A key to making ourselves exercise daily is seeking a program we enjoy, whether walking,

 HIGHLIGHT 14.8

A Strategy to Improve Your Self-Concept

Having a positive self-concept is critical to having a happy, and gratifying life. When you have a low self-concept you are always worried how others are judging you. You are worried that you won't be able to succeed. You worry that you lack the abilities and skills to deal with the challenges that life may throw at you. You are scared of life and other people, and this fear holds you back from living life to the fullest.

If you have a positive self-concept, you will feel confident in yourself and your abilities. You will be willing to take more risks in life. You will sense that you have the ability to handle any challenges that life may throw at you. You will rarely worry what others think of you. This sense of confidence in yourself allows you to take full advantage of what life has to offer. Benefits of a positive self-concept include:

● You will be more ambitious as you have confidence you will achieve your goals.
● You will set higher goals, as you are optimistic you have the capacities to achieve high goals.
● You are more resilient to life's challenges as you are less likely to give in to defeat or despair.
● You will have a more gratifying social life, as you feel good about yourself and you seek out new people to talk with. Each new person may become a new friend, partner, customer, or romantic interest.
● You will probably have better physical health, as viewing oneself positively tends to lead to a healthier lifestyle.
● You are apt to treat others with more respect, as you do not perceive them as threats. When you treat others with respect, they are apt to reciprocate by treating you with respect.
● If you are confident in yourself, you are apt to attract and associate with confident, healthy, and successful people.

● Feeling confident in yourself, you will worry less, and have more energy and time to engage in creative and constructive activities.
● You will be more apt to utilize constructive feedback from others, as such feedback will not be viewed by you as being an emotionally crippling event.
● You will take more calculated risks. People who are willing to take more calculated risks tend to be more successful in their work and in their personal life.
● You will be happier, as having a positive outlook leads to looking forward to each new day.

How can you improve your self-concept? One strategy is to focus on establishing good mental habits by doing the following:

— List on a sheet of paper your good qualities, what you like about yourself.
— Then list what you dislike about yourself.
— Then list for each negative quality that you just mentioned, what positive things you will tell yourself whenever you start "awfulizing" about a negative quality. (The refuting positive quality may be a positive quality that you listed above about yourself.)
— Practice developing the habit of whenever you start awfulizing about negative characteristics about yourself that you refute them by focusing on your positive qualities.

Remember, a low self-concept stems from negative self-talk that you give yourself. One way to develop a positive self-concept is to identify the underlying negative self-talk and then challenge this self-talk with positive thoughts about yourself.

jogging, weight lifting, kick boxing, jumping rope, swimming, or any other physical activity.

3. *Pleasurable Goodies.* Pleasurable goodies relieve stress, change our pace of living, are enjoyable, make us feel good, and are, in reality, personal therapies. What is a "goody" (pleasurable experience) to one person may not be to another. Common goodies are being hugged, listening to music, going shopping, taking a bath, going to a movie, having a glass of wine, taking part in family and religious get-togethers, taking a vacation, and singing. Such goodies add spice to life and remind us we have worth.

Personal pleasures can also be used as payoffs to ourselves for jobs well done. Most of us would not seek to shortchange others for doing well, so we ought not to shortchange ourselves. Such rewards are a motivator to move on to new challenges.

Enjoyable activities beyond work and family responsibilities are also pleasurable goodies that relieve stress. Research has found that stress reduces stress—that is, an appropriate level of stressful activities in one area helps reduce excessive stress in others (Seaward, 2012). Getting involved in enjoyable outside activities switches our thinking from negative thoughts about our daily concerns to positive thoughts about the enjoyable activities. Therefore, it reduces stress if we become involved in activities we enjoy. Such activities may include golf, tennis, swimming, scuba diving, flying lessons, and traveling.

Application of Theory to Client Situations

Social workers are one of the groups of helping professionals, along with psychologists, psychiatrists, and guidance counselors, who are involved in developing and providing stress management programs. Social workers have a variety of roles in stress management. They can serve as *educators* in providing stress management educational programs to individuals and groups. Some physicians now refer patients who are experiencing high levels of stress, or those who have stress-related illnesses, to such programs. Social workers can incorporate relaxation training and biofeedback training in their *counseling* sessions with clients, particularly those experiencing high levels of stress; if highly stressed clients learn to relax, they are often more effective in solving their difficulties. Social workers can serve as *brokers* in referring highly stressed individuals to stress management programs, and they can serve as *group facilitators* in leading

therapeutic groups that emphasize stress management. Social workers can also serve as *initiators* and *consultants* in developing stress management programs in schools, businesses and industries, and in medical settings.

Chapter Summary

The following summarizes this chapter's content as it relates to the learning objectives presented at the beginning of the chapter. Chapter content will help prepare students to:

LO 14-1 Define later adulthood.

Later adulthood begins at around age 65. This grouping is an extremely diverse one, spanning an age range of more than 30 years.

LO 14-2 Describe the physiological and mental changes that occur in later adulthood.

Later adulthood is an age of recompense, a time when people reap the consequences of the kind of life they have lived. The process of aging affects different persons at different rates. Nature appears to have a built-in mechanism that promotes aging, but it is not known what this mechanism is.

LO 14-3 Understand contemporary theories on the causes of the aging process.

Theories on the causes of aging can be grouped into three categories: genetic theories, nongenetic cellular theories, and physiological theories.

Various factors accelerate the aging process: poor diet, overwork, alcohol or drug abuse, prolonged illnesses, severe disabilities, prolonged stress, negative thinking, exposure to prolonged hot or cold conditions, and serious emotional problems. Factors that slow down the aging process include a proper diet, skill in relaxing and managing stress, being physically and mentally active, a positive outlook on life, and learning how to control unwanted emotions.

LO 14-4 Describe common diseases and major causes of death among older adults.

Older people are much more susceptible to physical illnesses than are younger people, yet many older people are reasonably healthy. The two leading causes of death are diseases of the heart and cancer. Alzheimer's disease affects many older adults.

LO 14-5 *Understand material on stress management and on other ways to maintain good physical and mental health throughout life.*

Everyone needs physical exercise, mental activity, a healthy sleep pattern, proper nutrition and diet, and to use quality stress management strategies.

Three constructive stress management approaches are (1) changing the distressing event, (2) changing one's thinking about the distressing event, and (3) taking one's mind off the distressing event, usually by thinking about something else.

The chapter ends with a discussion of the effects of stress, and describes a variety of stress management techniques.

COMPETENCY NOTES

The following identifies where Educational Policy (EP) competencies and practice behaviors are discussed in the chapter.

EP 2.1.7a Utilize conceptual frameworks to guide the process of assessment, intervention, and evaluation.

EP 2.1.7b Critique and apply knowledge to understand person and environment.
(All of this chapter): The content of this chapter is focused on acquiring both of these practice behaviors in working with older persons.

EP 2.1.4a Recognize the extent to which a culture's structures and values may oppress, marginalize, alienate, or create or enhance privilege and power.
(pp. 664–665): Material is presented on the extent to which our culture's structures and values impact the sexual behavior of older persons.

EP 2.1.2 Apply social work ethical principles to guide professional practice.
(pp. 661, 663, 667, 671): Ethical questions are posed.

WEB RESOURCES

See this text's companion website at *www.cengagebrain.com* for learning tools such as chapter quizzing, videos, and more.

PSYCHOLOGICAL ASPECTS OF LATER ADULTHOOD

Mary Kate Denny/Alamy

Sandra Lombardino is 69 years old. Except for being overweight and having arthritis, she is in fairly good health. She is personable, well groomed, kind, and articulate. She retired two years ago from her job as an elementary school teacher; she was well liked by students and her fellow teachers in her 33 years of teaching. She raised four children, all of whom have started careers and families of their own.

Mrs. Lombardino would like to use her retirement years to travel and do volunteer work. She has worked hard for many years and has looked forward to enjoying her retirement.

She is increasingly frustrated because her husband's demands and offensive behavior are destroying her retirement dreams. Her husband, Benedito, has a number of health-care needs. Benedito used to be a carpenter and at one time was a good athlete. But he has been a heavy drinker for more than 40 years. When drunk, he has been physically and verbally abusive to his wife and to his children. His children left home to escape from him as soon as they were financially able to do so. The children love their mother but despise their father.

In many ways, Sandra Lombardino has been a martyr. She took a marriage vow to stay married for better or worse until death. She has fulfilled that vow, despite the urging of her friends and relatives to seek a divorce. Several years ago, Benedito was diagnosed with cirrhosis of the liver and had to stop working. He now receives a monthly disability check. Despite his illness, Benedito has continued to drink heavily and has developed high blood pressure and diabetes. He is grossly overweight and is often incontinent. The drinking and illnesses have caused brain deterioration; he now has difficulty walking, talking, and grooming himself, and he frequently hallucinates. His behavior has resulted in a loss of friends. Benedito has been pressured into attending a number of alcoholism treatment programs, including Alcoholics Anonymous, but he has always returned to drinking.

Sandra Lombardino is in a quandary about what she should do. She is angry that she has to spend most of her waking hours caring for someone who is obnoxious and verbally abusive. She resents not being able to travel and to leave home to do volunteer work. Sometimes she wishes her husband would die so that she could get on with her life. At other times, she feels guilty about wishing he would die.

She has contemplated getting a divorce, but such a process would mean her husband would get half of the property that she has worked so many years to acquire. She has also considered placing Benedito in a nursing home, but she feels an obligation to care for him herself and realizes that the expenses of a nursing home would deplete her life savings. Mrs. Lombardino feels that the cruelest injustice would be for her to die before her husband dies, so that she would be robbed of her chances to achieve her retirement dreams.

A Perspective

People need to make a number of psychological adjustments at all ages for their lives to be meaningful and fulfilling. Later adulthood is no exception.

Learning Objectives

This chapter will help prepare students to:

EP 2.1.7a, 2.1.7b

LO 15-1 *Describe the developmental tasks of later adulthood*

LO 15-2 *Understand theoretical concepts about developmental tasks in later adulthood*

LO 15-3 *Summarize theories of successful aging*

LO 15-4 *Understand the impact of key life events on older people*

LO 15-5 *Understand guidelines for positive psychological preparations for later adulthood*

LO 15-6 *Summarize material on grief management and death education*

LO 15-1 Describe the Developmental Tasks of Later Adulthood

Developmental Tasks of Later Adulthood

Most of the developmental tasks that older people encounter are psychological in nature. We will discuss a number of these tasks, using a couple, Douglas and Norma Polzer, as an example.

1. *Retirement and lower income.* In 1999, Douglas Polzer retired from his job as a road construction foreman in Dubuque, Iowa. Two years earlier, his wife, Norma, had retired from the post office. Retirement brought a number of changes to their lives. For several months after retiring, Douglas had difficulty finding things to do with his time. His work had been the center of his life. He seldom saw his former coworkers, and he had practically no hobbies or interests. When he was working, he always had stories to tell about unusual situations that happened. Now he no longer had much to talk about. Another problem for the Polzers was that they now had a lower standard of living. Their main sources of income were Social Security benefits and Norma's federal pension.

2. *Living with one's spouse in retirement.* Prior to retiring, Norma and Douglas did not see each other very much. Both worked during the week, and Norma worked on Saturdays. Each tended to socialize with his or her coworkers. Norma and Douglas tended to annoy each other if they were together a lot.

   After Douglas retired, both were generally at home. Since Norma had always done most of the domestic tasks, she kept busy. Finding things to do was not very difficult for her.

   For the first few months after Douglas retired, he followed Norma around the house telling her how she should do her work. That didn't go over very well. They got on each other's nerves and had a number of arguments. As time passed, Douglas became more interested in fishing, taking walks, and getting together with his retired friends. Gradually, with Douglas being gone more, the arguments faded.

3. *Affiliating with individuals of one's own age group or with associations for older people.* The Polzers joined the Senior Citizens Leisure Club in Dubuque. Norma participated more frequently than Douglas did. The club has a variety of activities: luncheons, speakers, bus tours, painting and craft sessions, bowling, and golf. The club also has a small library.

4. *Maintaining interest in friends and family ties.* Norma and Douglas formed a number of new friendships with people they met in the club. Through conversing with such friends, Norma and Douglas were able to gain new perspectives on the adjustments they had to make.

   Most of the Polzers' friends, prior to retiring, were coworkers. After retirement, they gradually saw less and less of these friends, because their interests were growing in different directions. These former friends still talked a great deal about what was happening at work, and both Norma and Douglas now found such conversations boring.

   The Polzers usually got together on Sunday with their son, Kirk, and his family, who lived in Dubuque. Their daughter, Devi, had left home at age 17 to marry. After she had three children, she obtained a divorce and was on public assistance for four years until she remarried. She moved to California and had two more children. The Polzers seldom saw her, but their relationship with her had improved since her adolescent years. Doug and Norma wished they could see Devi and her children more.

5. *Continuing social and civic responsibilities.* Douglas serves as a volunteer night watchman for the county fair that is held for four days during the summer. After they retired, Doug and Norma became more active in attending their church and participating in church activities; Doug became a church elder, and Norma became more active in the ladies' aid society.

6. *Coping with illness and the loss of a spouse and/ or friends.* After four years of retirement, life was going fairly smoothly for the Polzers. Then, in 2003, Doug had a stroke that left him partially paralyzed. Doug's and Norma's lives changed radically. Douglas almost never went outside the house. He became irritable, incontinent, and in need of constant attention. Visiting nurse services provided some help, and so did

the Polzers' son and daughter-in-law. But the major burden was Norma's. She was forced to drastically reduce her church and club activities. For the next two years, she spent most of her time caring for Douglas. He never said "Thank you," and he verbally abused her. At times, Norma wished he would die. Then, in 2005, he did.

Norma's world again changed. For the first time in many years, she was living alone. Douglas's death was very hard for her. She felt guilty because she had wished he would die. Initially, she was lonely. But as the months passed, she gradually started putting her life back together. She became active again in the church and in the seniors' leisure club. Sharing her grief with other club members helped. As the years passed, more of her friends died, and Norma found herself attending more funerals.

7. *Finding satisfactory living arrangements at the different stages of later adulthood.* After Douglas died, Norma became depressed and had less energy. Kirk helped, but he had his own family, career, and home to care for. Norma realized she was slowing down physically. After two years, Kirk began to encourage her to sell the house and move into an apartment complex that was especially built for older people. Norma resisted for more than a year. Then, in 2008, Norma slipped on the stairs and broke her leg. She had to crawl to the telephone. Kirk came and took her to the emergency room, where her leg was put in a cast. When she got out of the hospital, Kirk took her to his home. Norma's house was put up for sale.

Having to leave her house was almost as great a loss as when Douglas died. She spent two months with Kirk's family, but she did not get along with Kirk's wife. Each had different ways of doing things and different ideas on how children should be raised. When relationships became severely strained, Norma moved to an apartment for older people. The move meant that many cherished possessions had to be discarded. Norma began to realize that if her mental or physical condition deteriorated further, her next move would be to a nursing home; at times she thought she would rather die than enter a nursing home. The move also meant that Norma had to establish new relationships. Fortunately,

the move went more smoothly than Norma had hoped, and she was warmly welcomed by the staff and the residents.

8. *Adjusting to changing physical strength and health and overcoming bodily preoccupation.* For many years, Norma had struggled to get used to gray hair, wrinkles, and all the other physical changes of aging. Her arthritis often caused swelling and pain in her joints, and she no longer had as much energy and stamina as in the past.

9. *Reappraising personal values, self-concept, and personal worth in light of new life events.* A major adaptation task of older people is to conduct an evaluative life review. During this review, they reflect on their failures and accomplishments, their disappointments and satisfactions, and hopefully come to a reasonably positive view of their life's worth. The failure to arrive at a positive view can result in a case of overt psychopathology.

After Norma became settled in her apartment, she again had a lot of free time. She was now 76 years old, and her health was declining. She spent a lot of time thinking about the past. She had enjoyed the early years of retirement, but she acknowledged that the five years since Douglas's first stroke had been rocky.

10. *Accepting the prospect of death.* It is now 2014, and Norma has been living in her apartment for six years. Her arthritis is worse, and she has cataracts, but her last six years have been fairly uneventful. Kirk and his family visit almost every Sunday, and she has made a number of friends at her apartment complex. She has attended many funerals, and still occasionally mourns the death of Douglas, especially on holidays and on their wedding anniversary. Norma feels her life has been fairly full and meaningful. These assessments have also led her to think about her eventual death. She worries about the pain she may experience and is fearful about slowly deteriorating. To avoid being kept alive after her mental capacities have deteriorated, she has signed a living will, which declares that if she becomes unconscious for a prolonged period of time, she does not want heroic measures used to keep her alive. She is fully aware and accepting of the fact that she will die in the not-too-distant future. Since her life has been full and positive, she is prepared

for death. Her religion asserts there is a life after death; she is uncertain whether an afterlife exists, but if it does, she is hoping to be reunited with Douglas and to see many of her friends who have died.

LO 15-2 Understand Theoretical Concepts About Developmental Tasks in Later Adulthood

Theoretical Concepts About Developmental Tasks in Later Adulthood

In this section, we will examine various theoretical concepts relating to the developmental tasks of later adulthood.

Integrity Versus Despair

The final stage of life, according to Erikson (1963), involves the psychological crisis of *integrity versus despair*. The attainment of integrity comes only after considerable reflection about the meaning of one's life. *Integrity* refers to an ability to accept the facts of one's life and to face death without great fear. Older people who have achieved a sense of integrity view their past in an existential light. They have feelings of having achieved respected positions during their lifetimes and have inner senses of completion. They accept all of the events that have happened to them, without trying to deny some unpleasant facts or to overemphasize others. Integrity involves an integration of one's past history with one's present circumstances, and a feeling of being content with the outcome. In order to experience integrity, older people must incorporate lifelong sequences of failures, conflicts, and disappointments into their self-images. This process is made more difficult by the fact that the role of older people is devalued in our society. There are a lot of negative attitudes expressed in our society that (often erroneously) suggest older people are incompetent, dependent, and old-fashioned. The death of close friends and relatives and the gradual deterioration of physical health make it additionally difficult for older people to achieve integrity.

The opposite pole of integrity is despair. *Despair* is characterized by a feeling of regret about one's past and includes a continuously nagging desire to have done things differently. Despair makes an attitude of calm acceptance of death impossible, as those who despair view their lives as incomplete and unfulfilled. Either they seek death as a way of ending a miserable existence, or they desperately fear death because it makes any hope of compensating for past failures impossible. Some older people who despair commit suicide.

Men, particularly older men, are more apt to commit suicide than are women (Papalia & Feldman, 2012). The highest rate of suicide is found not among male adolescents or male young adults, but among older men (Papalia et al., 2012). One of the reasons the suicide rate among older men is so high is that men are more apt than women to view their chosen career as providing the primary source of meaning in life; when men with this perspective retire, they are more apt to despair and to select suicide as a way to end their misery.

Three Key Psychological Adjustments

Peck (1968) suggests that three primary psychological adjustments must be made in order to make later adulthood meaningful and gratifying. The first adjustment involves shifting from a work-role preoccupation to *self-differentiation*. Because retirement is a crucial shift in one's life, a new role must be acquired. The older person has to adjust to the fact that she or he will no longer go to work and needs to find a new identity and new interests. People who are in the process of making this adjustment must spend time assessing their personal worth. (A woman whose major work has been being a wife and a mother faces this adjustment when her children leave home or her husband dies.) A crucial question to resolve at this point is: "Am I a worthwhile person insofar as I can do a full-time job or can I be worthwhile in other different ways … ?" (Peck, 1968, p. 90). In making this adjustment, people need to recognize that they are richer and more diverse than the sum of their tasks at work.

A second adjustment involves shifting from body preoccupation to *body transcendence*. Health problems increase for older people, and energy levels decrease. One's physical appearance also shows signs of aging, such as graying and thinning of hair and increasing wrinkles. Many older people become preoccupied with their state of health and their appearance. Others, however, transcend these concerns and are able to enjoy life despite declining health. Those who accomplish this transcendence have generally learned to define comfort and happiness in terms of satisfying social relationships or creative mental activities.

The third adjustment involves shifting from self-preoccupation to *self-transcendence*. The inevitability of death must be dealt with. Although death is a depressing prospect, Peck (1968) indicates that a positive acceptance can be achieved by shifting one's concerns from "poor me" to "What can I do to make life more meaningful, secure, or happier for those who will survive me?"

Life Review

Most older persons conduct evaluative life reviews in which they assess their pasts and consider the future in terms of the inevitability of death. Frenkel-Brunswick (1970) referred to this life review as "drawing up the balance sheet of life." The two key elements in this review are (1) concluding that the past was meaningful and (2) learning to accept the inevitability of death. Those who psychologically achieve this are apt to be content and comfortable with their later years; those who conclude that life has been empty, and who do not as yet accept death, are apt to despair.

A life review involves a reconsideration of previous experiences and their meaning, and often includes a revision or an expanded understanding (Haight, 1991). This reorganization of the past may provide a more valid picture for the individual, providing a new and more significant meaning to his or her life.

Ethical Question 15.1

In a review of your life from birth to the present time, would you view your past as meaningful or meaningless?

EP 2.1.2

Self-Esteem

Self-esteem (the way people regard themselves) is a key factor in overall happiness and adjustment to life. According to Cooley's (1902) "looking-glass self" concept, people develop their sense of who they are in terms of the way others relate to them. If older people are treated by others as if they are old-fashioned, senile, dependent, and incompetent, they are apt to view themselves in the same way. With losses of friends and relatives through death, the loss of the work role, and a decline in physical appearance and in physical abilities, the elderly are vulnerable to a lowering of self-esteem.

For older persons to feel good about themselves, they need feedback from others indicating that they are worthwhile, competent, and respected. Like people in all other age groups, older people thrive by demonstrating their competence. People tend to feel competent when they exert control over their own lives. The more options they have, the more in control they are, and the higher their self-esteem will be.

Privacy is a factor in furthering competence and self-esteem. People who have a private place to go can decide when they want to be with other people and when they want to be alone. In a nursing home, those who have a private room can retreat to it whenever they find something distasteful, or too noisy, or whenever they want to rest. A private room gives them a way to control their environment.

Life Satisfaction

Life satisfaction is a sense of psychological well-being in general or of satisfaction with life as a whole. Life satisfaction is a widely used index of psychological well-being in older adults. Older adults who are in good health and have an adequate income are more likely to be content with their lives than those who have poor health and limited incomes (Santrock, 2013b). Older people who have extended social networks of friends and family are more satisfied than those who are socially isolated (Santrock, 2013b). An active lifestyle is also associated with psychological well-being in older adults. People who play golf, go out to dine, go to the theater, travel, exercise regularly, go to church, go to meetings, and are actively involved in the community are more content with their lives than are those who stay at home and lead sedentary lifestyles (Santrock, 2013b).

Low Status and Ageism

Older people suffer psychologically because our society has been generally unsuccessful in finding something important or satisfying for them to do. It is not older people but, rather, the younger age groups who determine the status and position of older people in a society. The young and the middle-aged not only determine the future for older people, they also determine their own future, as they will someday be old.

In most primitive and earlier societies, older people were respected and viewed as useful to the community to a much greater degree than is the case in our society. Industrialization and the growth of modern society have robbed older people of their high status. Prior to industrialization, older people were the primary owners of property. Land was the most important source of power; therefore, older people controlled much of the economic and political power. Now, people earn their living in the job market, and the vast majority of older people own little land and are viewed as having no salable labor. In earlier societies, older people were also valued because of the knowledge they possessed. Their experiences enabled them to supervise planting and harvesting and to pass on knowledge about hunting, housing, and crafts. Older people also played key roles in preserving and transmitting the culture. But the rapid advances of science and technology have tended to limit the value of the technological knowledge of older people, and books and other memory-storage devices have made older people less valuable as storehouses of culture and records.

Our society does not allow many older people to experience their later years positively. We don't respect their experience and wisdom, but instead dismiss their ideas as irrelevant and outdated.

The low status of older people is closely associated with ageism. The term *ageism* refers to having negative images of, and attitudes toward, people simply because they are old. Today, many people's reaction to older adults is a negative one. Ageism is similar to sexism or racism in that it involves discrimination and prejudice against all members of a particular social category. Children's books do not usually have older characters, and those that do usually portray older people unfavorably. The prejudice against older people is shown in everyday language by the use of such terms as "old biddy" and "old fogey." (The triple jeopardy of being female, African American, and old is discussed in Spotlight 15.1.)

Ageism is an additional burden for older people. Some older adults, particularly among the young-old, are able to refute ageism stereotypes by being productive and physically and mentally active. Unfortunately for others, ageism stereotypes become self-fulfilling prophecies. Older people are treated as if they were incompetent, dependent, and senile; such treatment lowers their self-esteem, and some end up playing the roles suggested by the stereotypes. Ageism adversely affects older people and restricts the roles and alternatives available to them.

Depression

The older person is often a lonely person. Most people 70 years of age or older are widowed, divorced, or single. When someone has been married for many years and his or her spouse dies, a deep sense of loneliness usually occurs that seems unbearable. The years ahead often seem full of emptiness. It is not surprising, then, that depression is the most common emotional problem of older people. It has been called the "common cold" of mental disorders for older persons. Symptoms of depression include feelings of uselessness, of being a burden, of being unneeded, of loneliness, and of hopelessness. Somatic symptoms of depression include a loss of weight and appetite, fatigue, insomnia, and constipation. It is often difficult to determine whether such somatic symptoms are due to depression or to an organic disorder.

Depression can alter the personality of an older person. Depressed people may become apathetic, withdrawn, and show a slowdown in behavioral actions. An older person's reluctance to respond to questions is apt to be due to depression rather than to the contrariness of old age (Papalia et al., 2012).

Those who have had unresolved emotional problems earlier in life will generally continue to have

Triple Jeopardy: Being Female, African American, and Old

Michael Ainsworth/Dallas Morning News/Corbis News/Corbis

Being female, African American, and old is a triple jeopardy. Many women in this category are among the financially poorest of all citizens.

The poverty rate for older females is almost double that of older males (Mooney, Knox, & Schacht, 2013). Despite their positive status in the African American family and culture, African American women over the age of 65 are one of the poorest population groups in the United States. Four out of every 10 African American women age 65 or older are living in poverty (Mooney et al., 2013).

Three out of five older African American women live alone; most of them are widowed (Mooney et al., 2013).

The poverty rate of this age group is related to ageism, sexism, and racism. When they were young, these women tended to hold very low-paying jobs—some were not even covered by Social Security. In the case of domestic service, their income was not apt to be reported by their employers.

Even though many of these women are struggling financially, socially, and physically, Schaefer (2012) notes they have shown remarkable adaptiveness, resilience, coping skills, and responsibility. Extensive family networks help them cope, providing them with the essentials of life and giving them a sense of being loved. African American churches have provided avenues for meaningful social participation, social welfare services, feelings of power, and a sense of internal satisfaction. These women also tend to live together in ethnic minority communities, which gives them a sense of belonging. They also tend to adhere to the American work ethic and view their religion as a source of strength and support. Nonetheless, the incomes and health of older African American women (as well as of other ethnic minority individuals) are important concerns in our aging society.

them when older. Often, these problems will be intensified by the added stresses of aging.

Two major barriers to good mental health in the later years are failure to bounce back from psychosocial losses (such as the death of a loved one) and failure to have meaningful life goals. Later adulthood is a time when drastic changes are thrust on

older people that may create emotional problems: loss of a spouse, loss of friends and relatives through death or moving to another place, poorer health, loss of accustomed income, and changing relationships with children and grandchildren.

Major depression can result not only in sadness, but also in suicidal ideation. Depression is a treatable condition for young adults, middle-age adults, and older adults. Combinations of psychotherapy and medications produce significant improvements in almost four out of five older adults who are depressed (Santrock, 2013b). Unfortunately, nearly 80 percent of depressed older adults receive no treatment (Santrock, 2013b).

Spirituality and Religion

Spirituality and religion are important components in the lives of older people—as they are in the lives of people in all age groups. In recent years, the social work profession has seen a renewal of interest in recognizing the importance of spirituality and religion.

Religion has been found to be an important factor that promotes emotional well-being in later life. Koenig, George, and Siegler (1988) asked 100 well-educated white women and men, ages 58 to 80, to describe the worst events in their lives and how they dealt with them. Heading the list of coping strategies were behaviors associated with religion—including praying, placing trust and faith in God, getting help and strength from God, having friends from church, participating in church activities, reading the Bible, and receiving help from a minister.

Koenig, Kvale, and Ferrel (1988), in a study of 836 older adults, found that people who were religious had

higher morale, had better attitudes toward aging, and were more satisfied and less lonely than those who were not affiliated with any religion. Women and people who were over 75 showed the highest correlations between religion and well-being in this study.

Ethical Question 15.3

Do you respect the religious beliefs of people who adhere to a different religion than yours?

EP 2.1.2

The church has always been important to most African Americans. Older African Americans who feel supported by their church tend to have high levels of emotional well-being and to report a higher level of life satisfaction (Schaefer, 2012).

As people grow older and reflect about death and the meaning of their lives, they are apt to focus more on spiritual matters. Many religious institutions have outreach programs to identify and to offer services to older persons. Spotlight 15.2 presents information on four prominent world religions, to help you work with clients from differing spiritual backgrounds.

Religious rituals, as long as they are not harmful, are legally protected in the United States.

Anders Ryman/Alamy

Spirituality and Religion

A major thrust of social work education is to prepare students for a culturally sensitive practice. Because religion and spirituality play important roles in all cultures, it is essential that social workers comprehend the influence of religion and spirituality in human lives. The Educational and Accreditation Standards (2008) of the Council on Social Work Education now require that accredited baccalaureate and master's programs provide practice content in this area, so that students will develop approaches and skills for working with clients with differing spiritual backgrounds.

Spirituality and religion are separate, though often related, dimensions. *Spirituality* can be defined as "the general human experience of developing a sense of meaning, purpose, and morality" (Miley, 1992, p. 2). Key components of spirituality are the personal search for meaning in life, having a sense of identity (discussed in Chapter 7), and having a value system. In contrast, the term *religion* is used to refer to formal institutional contexts of spiritual beliefs and practices.

Social work has its historical roots in religious organizations. Social work originated under the inspiration of the Judeo-Christian religious traditions of its philanthropic founders. Jewish scriptures and religious law requiring the emulation of God's caring have inspired social welfare activities for many centuries. Similarly, the Christian biblical command to love one's neighbor as oneself has been interpreted as a moral responsibility for social service and inspired the development of charity organizations and philanthropy in the United States during the 19th century.

Social workers need to train for an effective practice with religiously oriented clients, as many of the social issues today have religious dimensions—including abortion, use of contraceptives, acceptance of gays and lesbians, cloning, reproductive technology, roles of women, prayer in public schools, and physician-assisted suicide. Social workers need to have appreciation and respect for religious beliefs that differ from their own beliefs. There is a danger that those who believe that *their* religion is the "one true religion" will tend to view people with divergent religious beliefs as ill-guided, evil, mistaken, or in need of being "saved." More wars have been fought over religious differences than for any other cause.

Furman (1994) notes, "The goal of incorporating religious and spiritual beliefs in social work curricula should include a broad array of knowledge of many different religious and spiritual beliefs, primarily to expand students' understanding and sensitivity" (p. 10). As a beginning effort to move in this direction, this box summarizes information on four prominent world religions: Judaism, Christianity, Islam, and Buddhism. These religions were selected because of their prominence. You should be aware that there are hundreds of religions in the world. Practicing social workers need to have a knowledge and appreciation of the religious beliefs and value systems of their clients.

Judaism

Judaism is the religion of the Jewish people. Jews believe in one God, the creator of the world. The Hebrew Bible is the primary text of Judaism. (The Hebrew Bible was adopted by Christians as part of their sacred writings; they call it the Old Testament.) God is believed to have revealed his law (Torah) to the Jewish people; part of this law was the Ten Commandments, which were given to Moses by God. The Jews believe that God chose them to be a light to all humankind.

Next in importance to the Hebrew Bible is the Talmud, an influential compilation of rabbinic traditions and discussions about Jewish life and law. The Talmud consists of the Mishnah (the codification of the oral Torah) and a collection of early rabbinical commentaries. Various later commentaries and the standard code of Jewish law and ritual (Halakhah), produced in the later Middle Ages, have been important in shaping Jewish practice and thought.

Abraham (who lived roughly 2,000 years before Christ) is viewed as an ancestor or father of the Hebrew people. According to Genesis, he came from the Sumerian town of Ur (now part of modern Iraq) and migrated with his family and flocks via Haran (the ancient city of Nari on the Euphrates) to the "Promised Land" of Canaan, where he settled at Shechem (modern Nablus). After a sojourn in Egypt, he lived to be 175 years old and was buried with his first wife, Sarah. By Sarah, he was the father of Isaac (whom he was prepared to sacrifice at the behest of the Lord) and the grandfather of Jacob ("Israel"). By his second wife, Hagar (Sarah's Egyptian handmaiden), he was the father of Ishmael, the ancestor of 12 clans. By his third wife, Keturah, he had six sons who became the ancestors of the Arab tribes. He was also the uncle of Lot. Abraham is regarded by Judaism, Christianity, and Islam as an important ancestor or father of their religion.

All Jews see themselves as members of a community whose origins lie in the time in which Abraham lived. This past lives on in rituals. The family is the basic unit of Jewish ritual, although the synagogue has come to play an increasingly important role. The Sabbath, which begins at sunset on Friday and ends at sunset on Saturday, is the central time of religious worship. The synagogue is the center for community worship and study. Its main feature is the "ark" (a cupboard) containing the handwritten scrolls of the Pentateuch (the five books of Moses in the Hebrew Bible, comprising Genesis, Exodus, Leviticus, Numbers, and Deuteronomy). A rabbi is primarily a teacher and a spiritual guide.

There is an annual cycle of religious festivals and days of fasting. The first of these is Rosh Hashanah, the Jewish New Year, which falls in September or October. During this New Year's celebration, a ram's horn is blown as a call to repentance and spiritual renewal. The holiest day in the Jewish year is Yom Kippur, the Day of Atonement, which comes at the end of 10 days of penitence following Rosh Hashanah; Yom Kippur is a day devoted to fasting, prayer, and repentance for past sins. Another important festival is Hanukkah, held in December, commemorating the rededication of Jerusalem after the victory of Judas Maccabee over the Syrians. Pesach is the Passover festival, occurring in March or April, that commemorates the exodus of the Israelites from Egypt; the festival is named after God's passing over the house of Israelites when he killed the firstborn children of Egyptian families.

Christianity

Christianity is a religion practiced in numerous countries, centered on the life and work of Jesus of Nazareth, that developed out of Judaism. The earliest followers were Jews, who, after the death and resurrection of Jesus, believed him to be the Messiah, or Christ, as promised by the prophets in the Old Testament. He was declared to be the Son of God. During his life, he chose as disciples 12 men, who formed the nucleus of the church. This communion of followers believed that Jesus would come again to inaugurate the "Kingdom of God." God is believed to be one in essence but threefold in person, comprising the Father, the Son, and the Holy Spirit (known as the Trinity). Jesus Christ is also wholly human because of his birth to Mary. The Holy Spirit represents the touch or "breath" of God that inspires people to follow the Christian faith. The Bible is thought to have been written under the Holy Spirit's influence.

Jesus Christ was the son of Mary, yet also the Son of God, created by a miraculous conception by the spirit of God. He was born in Bethlehem (near Jerusalem), but began his ministry in Nazareth. The main records of his ministry are the New Testament Gospels, which show him proclaiming the coming of the Kingdom of God and, in particular, the acceptance of the oppressed and the poor into the kingdom. The duration of his public ministry is uncertain, but from John's Gospel, one gets the impression of a three-year period of teaching. Jesus was executed by crucifixion under the order of Pontius Pilate, a Roman ruler. The date of his death is uncertain, but is considered to be when Jesus was in his early 30s.

At the heart of the Christian faith is the conviction that through Jesus' death and resurrection, God has allowed humans to find salvation. Belief in Jesus as the Son of God, along with praying for forgiveness of sin, brings forgiveness of all sin. Many Christians believe that those who ask for forgiveness of their sins will join God in heaven, while nonbelievers who do not ask for forgiveness of their sins will be consigned to hell.

The Gospel of Jesus was proclaimed at first by word of mouth, but by the end of the first century A.D., it was written down and became accepted as the authoritative scripture of the New Testament. Through the witness of the 12 earliest leaders (apostles) and their successors, the Christian faith, despite sporadic persecution, spread through the Greek and Roman worlds, and in 315 A.D., Emperor Constantine declared it to be the official religion of the Roman Empire. It survived the breakup of the empire and the Dark Ages of Europe, largely through the work of groups of monks in monasteries in Europe and of the Eastern Christian church headquartered in Constantinople. The religion helped form the basis of civilization in medieval Europe. Since the Middle Ages, major divisions of Western Christianity have formed as a result of differences in doctrine and practice.

Islam

Islam is the Arabic word for "submission" to the will of God, or Allah. Islam is also the name of the religion originating in Arabia during the seventh century through the prophet Muhammad. Followers of Islam are known as Muslims, or Moslems.

Born in Mecca, Muhammad was the son of Abdallah, a poor merchant of the powerful tribe of Quaraysh, hereditary guardians of the shrine of Mecca. Muhammad was orphaned at 6 and raised by his grandfather and uncle. His uncle, Abu Talib, trained him to be a merchant. At the age of 24, he entered the service of a rich widow, Khadijah, whom he eventually married. They had six children. While continuing as a trader, Muhammad became increasingly drawn to religious contemplation. He began to receive revelations of the word of Allah, the one and only God. These revelations, given to Muhammad by the angel Gabriel over 20 years, were codified into the Quran (Koran). The Quran commanded that the numerous idols of the shrine should be destroyed and that the rich should give to the poor. This simple message attracted some support but provoked a great deal of hostility from those who felt their interests threatened. When his wife and uncle died, Muhammad was reduced to poverty, but he began making a few converts among the pilgrims to Mecca. Muhammad eventually migrated to Yathrib. The name of this town was changed to Medina, "the city of the prophet." This migration, known in Arabic as the *hijra*, marks the beginning of the Muslim lunar calendar. After a series of battles with warring enemies of Islam, Muhammad was able to take control of Mecca, which recognized him as the chief and prophet. By 360 A.D., he had control over all of Arabia. Two years later he fell ill and died in the home of one of his nine wives. His tomb in the mosque at Medina is venerated throughout Islam.

The religion of Islam embraces every aspect of life. Muslims believe that individuals, societies, and governments should all be obedient to the will of God as set forth in the Quran. The Quran teaches that there is one God who has no partners. He is the creator of all things and has absolute power over them. All persons should commit themselves to lives of praise-giving and grateful obedience to God, as everyone will be judged on the Day of Resurrection. Those who

(continued)

SPOTLIGHT ON DIVERSITY 15.2 (continued)

have obeyed God's commandments will dwell forever in paradise, whereas those who have sinned against God and have not repented will be condemned eternally to the fires of hell. Since the beginning of time, God has sent prophets (including Abraham, Moses, and Jesus) to provide the guidance necessary for the attainment of an eternal reward.

There are five essential religious duties, known as "the pillars of Islam":

1. The *Shahadah* (profession of faith) is the sincere recitation of the twofold creed: "There is no god but God" and "Muhammad is the Messenger of God."
2. The *Salat* (formal prayer) must be performed at fixed hours five times a day while facing toward the holy city of Mecca.
3. Almsgiving through the payment of *Zakat* ("purification") is regarded primarily as an act of worship and is the duty of sharing one's wealth out of gratitude for God's favor, according to the uses stated in the Quran.
4. There is a duty to fast (*Saum*) during Ramadan, the ninth month of the Muslim year; Muslims abstain from eating and drinking between sunrise and sunset.
5. The pilgrimage (*hajj*) to Mecca is to be performed if at all possible at least once during one's lifetime.

Shariah, the sacred law of Islam, applies to all aspects of life, not just religious practices. This sacred law is found in the Quran and the *Sunnah* (the sayings and acts of Muhammad).

Buddhism

Buddhism originated in India about 2,500 years ago. The religion derived from the teachings of Buddha (Siddhartha Gautama). Buddha is regarded as one of a continuing series of enlightened beings.

Buddha was born the son of the rajah of the Sakya tribe in Kapilavastu, north of Benares. His personal name was Gautama. At about age 30, he left the luxuries of the court, his beautiful wife, and all earthly ambitions. He became an ascetic, and he practiced strict self-denial as a measure of personal and spiritual discipline. After several years of severe austerities, he saw, in meditation and contemplation, the way to enlightenment. For the next four decades, he taught, gaining many followers and disciples. He died at Kusinagara in Oudh.

The teachings of Buddha are summarized in the Four Noble Truths, the last of which asserts the existence of a path leading to deliverance from the universal human experience of suffering. A central tenet of Buddhism is the law of karma, by which good and evil deeds result in appropriate rewards or punishments in this life or in a succession of rebirths. It is believed that the sum of a person's actions is carried forward from one life to the next, leading to an improvement or a deterioration in that person's fate. Through a proper understanding of the law of karma, and by obedience to the right path, humans can break the chain of karma.

The Buddha's path to deliverance is through morality (Sila), meditation (Samadhi), and wisdom (Panna). The goal is nirvana, which is the "blowing out" of the fires of all desires and the absorption of the self into the infinite. All Buddhas are greatly revered, with a place of special accordance being given to Gautama.

There are two main branches of Buddhism, dating from its earliest history. Theravada Buddhism adheres to the strict and narrow teachings of the early Buddhist writings; in this branch, salvation is possible for only the few who accept the severe discipline and the effort needed to achieve it. Mahayana Buddhism is more liberal and makes concessions to popular piety; it teaches that salvation is possible for everyone. It introduced the doctrine of the bodhisattva (or personal savior). A bodhisattva is one who has attained the enlightenment of a Buddha but chooses not to pass into nirvana and voluntarily remains in the world to help lesser beings attain enlightenment; this view emphasizes charity toward others. Mahayana Buddhism asserts that all living beings have the inner potential of the Buddha nature. The Buddha nature is a kind of a spiritual embryo that holds out the promise to all people that they can eventually become Buddhas because they all have the potential for Buddhahood.

LO 15-3 Summarize Theories of Successful Aging

Theories of Successful Aging: The Strengths Perspective

Three theories about how to age successfully are the activity theory, the disengagement theory, and the social reconstruction syndrome theory.

Activity Theory

The activity theory asserts that the more physically and mentally active people are, the more successfully they will age. Components of this theory were discussed at length in Chapter 14. One component of the theory asserts that the sexual response can be maintained in later adulthood by being sexually active. There is considerable evidence that being physically and mentally active helps to maintain the physiological, psychological, and intellectual functions of older people.

Some researchers assert that productive activity (paid or unpaid) is a key to aging well (Papalia et al., 2012). Older people who feel useful to others are more likely to remain healthy and alive. Adults in their 70s who do not feel useful to others are more likely than those who feel useful to experience increased disabilities and to have a shorter life expectancy (Papalia et al., 2012). Menec (2003) found that productive and social activities (such as housework, part-time jobs, gardening, and visiting family) were related to better physical functioning, self-rated happiness, and living longer.

Disengagement Theory

Cumming and Henry (1961) coined the term *disengagement* to refer to a process whereby people respond to aging by gradually withdrawing from the various roles and social relationships they occupied in middle age. Such a disengagement is claimed to be functional for older people, as they are thought to gradually lose the energy and vitality to sustain all the roles and social relationships they held in younger years.

Ethical Question 15.4

Is it functional for older people to gradually withdraw from the various roles and social relationships they occupied in middle age?

EP 2.1.2

Community Disengagement Theory

The disengagement theory refers not only to older people withdrawing from a community, but also to the community withdrawing from older people, or *community disengagement* (Atchley, 1983). It is claimed to be functional for our society (which values competition, efficiency, and individual achievement) to disengage from older people, who have the least physical stamina and the highest death rate. Community disengagement occurs in a variety of ways: employers may seek to force older people to retire; older people may not be sought out for leadership positions in organizations; their children may involve them less in making family decisions; and the government may be less responsive in meeting their needs as compared to people who are younger. Community disengagement is often unintended and unrecognized by employers, younger relatives, and other younger members of society. Disengagement theory also asserts that older people welcome this withdrawal and contribute to it.

Evaluation of the Disengagement Theory

The disengagement theory has generated considerable research over the years. There is controversy regarding whether disengagement is functional for older people and for our society. Research has found that some people do voluntarily disengage as they grow older (Papalia et al., 2012). However, critics assert that disengagement is related less to old age itself than to the factors associated with aging, such as retirement, poor health, death of a spouse and of close friends, and impoverishment. For example, when people are forced to retire, they tend to disengage from coworker friendships, union activities, professional friendships, and reading in their field. Once retired, they also have less money to spend on entertainment, so disengagement from some activities is forced on them.

Disengagement is neither universal nor inevitable. Contrary to the theory's predictions, most older persons maintain extensive associations with friends and active involvement in voluntary organizations (such as church groups and fraternal organizations). Also, after retiring, some older people develop new interests, expand their circle of friends, join clubs, and do volunteer work. Others rebel against society's stereotypes and refuse to be treated as if they had little to offer to society. Many of these people are marshaling political resources to force society to adapt to their needs and skills.

The disengagement theory at times advocates the exact opposite of the activity theory. The activity theory asserts it is beneficial for older people to be physically and mentally active, while the disengagement theory asserts it is beneficial to withdraw from a variety of activities.

Ethical Issues

A severe criticism of the disengagement theory is that it may be used to justify society's failure to help older people maintain meaningful roles. It may also be used to justify ageism. The disengagement theory may, at best, be merely a description of typical age–youth relationships (and reactions to them), which we should combat as we try to combat ageism.

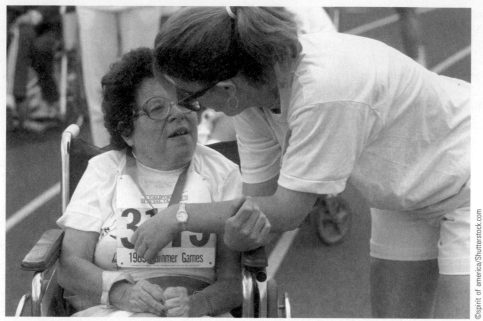

Here, an older adult volunteer advises a Special Olympics participant. The more physically and mentally active older adults are, the more successfully they will age. Volunteering provides a positive means of staying active. (Special Olympics was founded in 1968 in Chicago by Anne McGlone Burke, a special education teacher, with the support of Eunice Kennedy Shriver, the sister of President John F. Kennedy.)

Social Reconstruction Syndrome Theory

Social reconstruction syndrome theory was developed from the *social breakdown syndrome* conceptualized by Zusman (1966). According to Zusman, social breakdown occurs for older people because of the effects of labeling. Society has unrealistic expectations that all adults should work and be productive; younger people label older people as incompetent or lacking in some ways; older people accept the label and view themselves in terms of the label; they then learn behavior consistent with the label and downplay their previous skills. As a result, they become more dependent and incompetent, and feel inadequate.

Kuypers and Benston (1973) assert that this negative interaction between older people's environment and self-concept explains many of the problems of aging in our society. To break the vicious cycle of this labeling process, they recommend the *social reconstruction syndrome*, which includes three major recommendations. First, our society should liberate older people from unrealistic standards and expectations. The belief that self-worth depends on a person's productivity has adverse consequences for

those who are retired. Kuypers and Benston recommend that society be reeducated to change these unrealistic standards. Fischer (1977) specifies the direction such reeducation should take:

> *The values of our society rest upon a work ethic— an ethic of doing—that gives highest value to people in the prime of their productive years. We should encourage a plurality of ethics in its place—not merely an ethic of doing, but also an ethic of feeling, an ethic of sharing, an ethic of knowing, an ethic of enduring, and even an ethic of surviving. (p. 33)*

The second recommendation of Kuypers and Benston (1973) is to provide older people with the social services they need. Such services include transportation, medical care, housing, help with housekeeping, and programs that provide physical and mental activity.

The third recommendation is to find creative ways to give older people more control over their lives. For example, providing home health services, along with other services, may assist older people in living independently and thereby having a sense of control over their lives.

LO 15-4 Understand the Impact of Key Life Events on Older People

The Impact of Life Events on Older People

We will discuss a number of life events that affect life in later adulthood. These events directly affect the behavior of older people and often limit the alternatives available to them.

Marriage

Because people are living longer, many marriages are lasting longer as well. Today, 50th wedding anniversaries are much more common than they were in the past. But divorces are more common too.

Couples who are still married in their later years are less likely than younger couples to see their marriages as full of problems (Papalia et al., 2012). There could be a variety of reasons. They may well have worked out their major conflicts. Because divorce is now quite accessible, those marriages that survive many years may be the happier and more conflict-free ones. Or the difference may be one of development, as people learn to cope better with crises and conflicts.

Being in love is still important for successful marriage in late adulthood (Papalia et al., 2012). Spouses at this age also value open expression of feelings, companionship, respect from one another, and common interests.

Gilford (1986) found that people over age 70 tend to consider themselves less happily married than those aged 63 to 69; perhaps decline in physical health aggravates the strains on marriage. Gilford also found that older women tend to be less satisfied with marriage than are older men, partly because women generally expect more warmth and intimacy from marriage than men do.

Married older people are happier than the unmarried, and considerably happier than the widowed and the divorced. The extent to which older people, particularly women, are satisfied with their marriage influences their overall sense of well-being. Health and satisfaction with one's standard of living also positively correlate with an overall sense of well-being. Chronic illness has a negative impact on the morale of couples, even when only one member is ill.

The healthy partner may become depressed, angry, or frustrated with the responsibilities of taking care of the ill spouse and maintaining the household. The poor health of one spouse may also reduce the opportunities for enjoyable activities, may drain financial resources, and may reduce sexual involvement. Other crises and life events (such as retirement) can also generate considerable marital turmoil and conflict.

Poor health can also lead to role changes in the lives of older couples. The spouse who first develops a serious life-threatening illness is usually the husband—as women tend to be younger than their spouses and to live longer. If one spouse develops an illness (such as Alzheimer's disease) in which there is progressive deterioration of mental and physical capacities, the other spouse has to take on increasing decision-making and caregiving responsibilities. Gilford (1986) found that spouses (especially wives) who must care for mates with disabilities may experience anger, isolation, and frustration. They are also more apt to develop a chronic illness themselves.

Death of a Spouse

The death of a spouse is traumatic at any age. It is more apt to occur in later adulthood, as death rates are considerably higher in this age group. The surviving spouse faces a variety of emotional and practical problems. The survivor has lost a lover, a companion, a good friend, and a confidant. The more intertwined their lives have become, the deeper the loss is apt to be felt. In most marriages, household maintenance responsibilities are divided. The survivor now finds he or she has a lot more tasks to do, some of which were never learned.

The survivor's social life also changes. At first, relatives, friends, and neighbors usually rally to give the survivor sympathy and emotional support. But gradually they return to their own lives, leaving the widower or widow to form a new life. Friends and relatives are apt to grow tired of listening to the survivor talk about his or her loss and grief, and they may withdraw emotional and practical help. The survivor may have to make such decisions as moving to a smaller place that is easier to maintain and going to social events alone. Some survivors withdraw because they feel like fifth wheel, especially with other couples.

Widowhood

Because women tend to live longer than men and tend to be younger than their husbands, they are more likely to be widowed. The effects of widowhood are poignantly summarized by a 75-year-old widow: "As long as you have your husband, you're not old. But once you lose him, old age sets in fast" (quoted in Papalia & Olds, 1992, p. 514).

Widowed people of both sexes have higher rates of depression and mental illness than married people. Men are more likely to die within six months of a wife's death, and women are more apt to develop a chronic illness after a husband's death (Papalia et al., 2012).

People who adjust best to widowhood are those who keep busy, perhaps by taking on new, paying positions, doing volunteer work, or becoming more deeply involved in other activities (such as seeing friends or taking part in community programs). Participating in support groups for widowed people is also beneficial (Papalia et al., 2012).

Never Married

Only about 5 percent of older men and women have never been married. Papalia and her associates (2012) cite research indicating that those who have never been married tend to be more independent, have fewer social relationships, and express less concern about their age than do older people who have been married.

Remarriage

Our society has generally opposed the idea of older adults dating and remarrying. We think of younger people hugging and kissing each other, but such behavior by an older couple is often met with stares or crude remarks. Children of older people are sometimes opposed to their mother's or father's remarrying. (They may be concerned about inheritance, or they may believe that starting a new relationship is being unfaithful to or dishonoring the parent who has died.) Yet remarriage in later adulthood is increasing (Papalia et al., 2012).

For a variety of reasons, our society should change its negative attitude about remarriage in later adulthood. Married older people are happier than those who are living alone. They have companionship, can share interests, provide emotional support, and can assist each other with household tasks. It is also cost-effective for society to support single older people in remarrying as they are then less likely to need financial assistance and social services and are less likely to be placed in nursing homes (Papalia et al., 2012).

Gay and Lesbian Relationships

There is little research on gay and lesbian relationships in latter adulthood; this is largely because the current cohort of older persons grew up in an era when living openly in a gay-lesbian relationship was rare. (In 2004 Massachusetts became the first state to offer regular marriage licenses for gay and lesbian couples.)

Gradually, more and more states are legalizing same-sex marriages. As a result, more gay and lesbian couples will feel freer to participate in research on their experiences.

Gay and lesbian relationships in later life tend to be diverse, but generally strong and supportive. A number of these individuals have children from earlier marriages—some have adopted children. Those who have maintained close relationships with a gay and lesbian community tend to adapt to the later years with relative ease.

Some older gays and lesbians are impacted by discriminatory acts by some persons, strained relationships with family of origin, and insensitive policies of some social agencies. If a partner falls ill or dies, there are challenges in dealing with health-care providers, inheritance issues, and lack of access to a partner's social security benefits (Papalia et al., 2012).

Family System Relationships

There is a popular belief that older people disengage somewhat from their adult children and their grandchildren. There is also a belief that there is a generation gap (conflict in values) between older people and younger family members. These beliefs suggest that older people may have strained and somewhat unfavorable family relationships.

Research reviewed by Kail and Cavanaugh (2007), however, suggests that most older people's family relationships are generally quite positive. The findings suggest that family relationships with older people are substantially better than generally believed.

Gay men gather outside the John Snow pub in Soho to stage a group kiss.

In most instances, older people and their adult children do not live together for a variety of reasons. Many younger people live in small quarters that make it inconvenient to house another person. Older people are reluctant to move in, as they fear they will have little privacy. They may fear that there will be somebody else's rules to follow and that they may not have visitors when they wish. They may resent having to account to their children for how they spend their time. They may fear their children will put pressure on them to make lifestyle changes, such as giving up smoking, changing their eating habits, or reducing the intake of alcoholic beverages. They may also fear inconveniencing or becoming a burden to their children's families. And, many simply do not want to leave their own home, where they feel comfortable and have pleasant memories.

Although most older people do not live with their children, they tend to live close to them and to see them frequently. Most older people do not want to live with their children. Of the few who do, most are female and widowed (Santrock, 2013b).

As discussed earlier, our society's views about the contributions of older people are exactly opposite to those held by many other societies. In those societies, the advice and knowledge of older people are actively sought, and older people usually live with their children and receive needed care. In our society, middle-aged adults tend to feel that their first priorities are to meet their own needs and the needs of their children. The fact that many adults would rather see their parents cared for in a nursing home than living with them suggests that they do not feel as great an obligation to their parents as do members of many other societies. The question of whether to place one's partially incapacitated older parent in a nursing home or to provide care in one's own home is a question that many middle-aged adults struggle with.

Most older people see their children quite often— an average of once or twice a week. Most older persons feel emotionally closer to their children than they did when they were in their middle years. They tend to live near at least one adult child and to help their children in a number of ways. When they need help themselves, their children are usually the first people they ask for help (Papalia et al., 2012). Older people in good health report feeling close to family members and have frequent contact with them (Field, Minkler, Falk, & Leino, 1993).

Parenting Adult Children

Parents are usually the primary caregivers for adult children who have a mental illness, a moderate cognitive disability, or some other disability. Parents of divorced adults see their children more often after the divorce than they did before, and often take them into their homes.

In a study of 29 healthy, white, midwestern, middle-class and working-class married couples age 60 and over, Greenberg and Becker (1988) found that the subjects' children were a daily topic of conversation. "Although they had left home years ago, these children remained psychologically present in their parents' thoughts and conversations" (p. 789). These parents helped their children in a variety of ways—inviting divorced daughters to live with them, helping care for grandchildren, helping with household projects, paying for treatment for drug abuse, and lending or giving money for a variety of purposes.

Suitor and Pillemer (1988) found that when an adult moves into the home of his or her older parents, the parents report that they get along quite well. Such harmony may be explained in at least two ways. People who get along with others are those most likely to choose to live together. In addition, older parents may exaggerate the harmony in an effort to make reality match their wishes. When parents and children do *not* get along very well, the parents' marriage is sometimes adversely affected. Grandparents who are providing care to their grandchildren or to their adult children refute the societal myth that older adults are freed from active parenting and its stresses.

Grandparenthood

Neugarten and Weinstein (1964) identified five major styles of grandparenting in our society. The *fun seeker* is a playmate to the grandchildren in a mutual relationship that both enjoy. The *distant figure* has periodic contact with the grandchildren, generally on birthdays and holidays, but is quite uninvolved with their lives. The *surrogate parent* assumes considerable caretaking responsibilities, usually because the grandchildren's parents are working, or because the mother is single and working. The *formal figure* leaves all child-rearing responsibilities to the parents and limits his or her involvement with the grandchildren to providing special treats and occasional babysitting. The *reservoir of family wisdom* takes on an authoritarian role and dispenses special resources and skills.

The tacit "norm of noninterference" by grandparents tends to evaporate in times of trouble faced by their adult children and their grandchildren. Grandparents tend to perform the role of family "watchdogs." They stay on the fringes of the lives of their children and grandchildren, with varying degrees of involvement. During times of crisis (such as serious illness, money problems, or divorce), they tend to become much more involved by stepping in and playing more active roles. During good times, they are less involved, but they are still watching.

Some gender differences have been found in the degree of grandparenting. Cherlin and Furstenberg (1986) found that grandmothers tend to have closer and warmer relationships with their grandchildren and are more apt to serve as surrogate parents than are grandfathers. The same study also found that the mother's parents are likely to be closer to the grandchildren than the father's parents and are more apt to become involved during a crisis. Thomas (1986) found that grandmothers tend to be more satisfied with grandparenting than are grandfathers.

The typical profile of grandparents in the United States is changing. Increasing numbers of grandchildren live with their grandparents. Adolescent pregnancies, divorce, drug use by parents, and high unemployment rates are the main reasons grandparents return to the "parenting" role. Almost half of the grandchildren who move in with grandparents are raised by a single grandmother (Santrock, 2013b).

As divorce and remarriage become more common in the United States, a special concern of some grandparents is to have visitation rights with their grandchildren. In the past two decades, numerous states have passed laws giving the grandparents the right to petition a court for visitation rights, even when a parent objects.

Great-Grandparenthood

When grandchildren become parents, grandparents move into a new role: great-grandparenthood. Because of age, declining health, and the scattering of families, great-grandparents tend to be less involved than grandparents in a child's life. The great-grandparents who have the most intimate connections with their great-grandchildren are those who live nearby; such great-grandparents often help their grandchildren and great-grandchildren with gifts, loans, and babysitting.

Because older people are living longer, four and even five generations of families are becoming more common.

David Turnley/CORBIS

A great-grandparent assisting with raising a child.

LO 15-5 Understand Guidelines for Positive Psychological Preparations for Later Adulthood

Guidelines for Positive Psychological Preparation for Later Adulthood: The Strengths Perspective

Growing old is a lifelong process. Becoming 65 does not destroy the continuity of what a person has been, is now, and will be. Recognizing this should lessen the fear of growing old. For those who are financially secure and in good health and who have prepared thoughtfully, later adulthood can be a period of at least reasonable pleasure and comfort, if not luxury.

Some may be able to start small home businesses, based on their hobbies, or become involved in meaningful activities with churches and other organizations. Others may relax while fishing or traveling around the country. Still others may continue to pursue such interests as gardening, woodworking, reading, needlework, painting, weaving, and photography. Many older people have contributed as much (or more) to society as they did in their earlier years. One role model in this area is Jimmy Carter; see Highlight 15.1.

Our lives depend largely on our goals and our efforts to achieve those goals. How we live before retiring will largely determine whether later adulthood will be a nightmare or will be gratifying and fulfilling. The importance of being physically and mentally active throughout life was discussed in Chapter 14. Here are some factors that are closely related to satisfaction in later adulthood:

1. *Close personal relationships.* Having close relationships with others is important throughout life. Older people who have close friends are more satisfied with life. Practically everyone needs a person to whom one can confide one's private thoughts or feelings. Older people who have confidants are better able to handle the trials and tribulations of aging. Through sharing their deepest concerns, people are able to ventilate their feelings and to talk about their problems and possibly arrive at some strategies for handling them. Those who are married are more likely than the widowed to have confidants, and the widowed are more likely to have confidants than those who have never married. For those

Jimmy Carter: Stumbled as President, Excelled in Later Adulthood

Jimmy Carter (James Earl Carter Jr.) was born October 1, 1924, in the small rural community of Plains, Georgia. Carter graduated from the U.S. Naval Academy in Annapolis in 1946. After seven years as a naval officer, he returned to Plains, where he ran a peanut-producing business. In 1962, he entered state politics. Eight years later, he was elected governor of Georgia. In 1976, he was elected president of the United States. Although he had some noteworthy accomplishments as president, there were serious setbacks economically and in foreign affairs. Inflation, interest rates, and unemployment rates were at near-record highs. During Carter's four-year administration, the economy went into a recession. In 1979, more than 50 members of the U.S. Embassy staff in Iran were taken as hostages by militants. Despite 14 months of trying, the Carter administration was unable to secure release of the hostages. After a devastating defeat for reelection in 1980, Carter retired from political life—and left being very unpopular.

But the best was yet to come. He did not throw in the towel. Today he is a professor at Emory University in Georgia and a leading advocate for Habitat for Humanity, which helps build houses for low-income families. He established the Carter Center, which sponsors international programs in human rights, preventive health care, education, agricultural techniques, and conflict resolution. Carter and the Carter Center have secured the release of hundreds of political prisoners. He has become an elder statesman, a roving peacemaker, and a guardian of freedom. He oversaw the Nicaraguan elections that ousted the dictatorship of the Sandinistas. He brokered a cease-fire between the Serbs and the Bosnian Muslims. He has pressured China to release political prisoners. He was the first former U.S. president to visit Communist Cuba. He has helped set up fair elections in China, Mozambique, Nigeria, Indonesia, and several other developing countries. In addition, he has written 29 books. In 2002, at age 78, he was awarded the Nobel Peace Prize. Clearly, Carter's accomplishments in later adulthood surpass his accomplishments in his earlier years.

who are married, the spouse is apt to be the confidant, especially for men.

2. *Finances.* Health and income are two factors closely related to life satisfaction in later adulthood. When people feel good and have money, they can be more active. Those who are active—who go out to eat, go to meetings or museums, go to church, go on picnics, or travel—are happier than those who mostly stay at home. Saving money for later years is important, and so is learning to manage or budget money wisely.

3. *Interests and hobbies.* Psychologically, people who are traumatized most by retirement are those whose self-image and life interests center on their work. People who have meaningful hobbies and interests look forward to retirement in order to have sufficient time for these activities.

4. *Self-identity.* People who are comfortable and realistic about who they are and what they want from life are better prepared to deal with stresses and crises that arise.

5. *Looking toward the future.* A person who dwells on the past or rests on past achievements is apt to find the older years depressing. On the other hand, a person who looks to the future generally has interests that are alive and growing and is

therefore able to find new challenges and new satisfaction in later years. Looking toward the future involves planning for retirement, including deciding where one would like to live, in what type of housing and community, and what one looks forward to doing with his or her free time.

6. *Coping with crises.* If a person learns to cope effectively with crises in younger years, these coping skills will remain useful when a person is older. Effective coping is learning to approach problems realistically and constructively.

LO 15-6 Summarize Material on Grief Management and Death Education

Grief Management and Death Education

In the remainder of this chapter, we will discuss reactions to death in our society, including social work roles in grief management and guidelines for relating to a dying person and to survivors.

Death in Our Society: The Impact of Social Forces

People in primitive societies handle death better than we do. They are more apt to view death as a natural occurrence, partly because they have shorter life expectancies. They also frequently see friends and relatives die. Because they view death as a natural occurrence, they are better prepared to handle the death of loved ones. Spotlight 15.3 illustrates the cultural-historical context of death and bereavement.

In our society, we tend to shy away from thinking about death. The terminally ill generally die in institutions (hospitals and nursing homes), away from their homes. Therefore, we are seldom exposed to people dying. Many people in our society seek to avoid thinking about death. They avoid going to funerals and avoid conversations about death. Many people live as if they believe they will live indefinitely.

We need to become comfortable with the idea of our own eventual death. If we do that, we will be better prepared for the deaths of close friends and relatives. We will also then be better prepared to relate to the terminally ill and to help survivors who have experienced the death of a close friend or relative.

Funerals are needed for survivors. Funerals help initiate the grieving process so that people can work through their grief. (Delaying the grieving process may intensify the eventual grief.) For some, funerals also serve the function of demonstrating that the person is dead. If survivors do not actually see the dead body, some may mystically believe that the person is still alive. For example, John F. Kennedy was assassinated in 1963 and had a closed-casket funeral. Because the body was not shown, rumors abounded for many years that he was still alive.

The sudden death of a young person is more difficult to cope with, for three reasons. First, we do not have time to prepare for the death. Second, we feel the loss as more severe because we feel the person is missing out on many of the good things in life. Third, we do not have the opportunity to obtain a sense of closure in the relationship; we may feel we did not have the opportunity to tell the person how we felt about him or her, or we did not get the opportunity to resolve interpersonal conflicts. (Because the grieving process is intensified when closure does not occur, it is advisable to actively work toward closure in our relationships with others.)

 SPOTLIGHT ON DIVERSITY 15.3

The Cultural-Historical Context of Death and Bereavement

Cultural customs concerning the disposal and remembrance of the dead, the transfer of possessions, and even expressions of grief vary greatly from culture to culture. Often, religious or legal prescriptions about these topics reflect a society's view of what death is and what happens afterward.

In ancient Greece, bodies of heroes were publicly burned as a symbol of honor. Public cremation is still practiced by Hindus in India and Nepal. In contrast, cremation is prohibited under Orthodox Jewish law, as it is believed that the dead will rise again for a "last judgment" and the chance for eternal life. To this day, some Polynesians in the Tahitian Islands bury their parents in the front yard of their parents' home as a way of remembering them.

In ancient Romania, warriors went laughing to their graves, expecting to meet Zalmoxis, their supreme god.

In Mayan society, which prospered several centuries ago in Mexico and Central America, death was seen as a gradual transition. At first a body was given only a provisional burial. Survivors continued to perform mourning rites until the body decayed to the point where it was thought the soul had left it and transcended into the spiritual realm.

In Japan, religious rituals expect survivors to maintain contact with the deceased. Families keep an altar in their homes that is dedicated to their ancestors; they offer them cigars and food and talk to the altar as if they were talking to their deceased loved ones. In contrast, the Hopi (Native American tribe) fear the spirits of the deceased and try to forget, as quickly as possible, those who have died.

Some modern cultural customs have evolved from ancient ones. The current practice of embalming, for example, evolved from the *mummification* practice in ancient Egypt and China about 3,000 years ago that was designed to preserve a body so that the soul could eventually return to it.

Today, Muslims in Bali are encouraged to suppress sadness, and instead to laugh and be joyful at burials. In contrast, Muslims in Egypt are encouraged to express their grief with displays of deep sorrow.

Children should not be sheltered from death. They should be taken to funerals of relatives and friends and their questions answered honestly. It is a mistake to say, "Grandmother has gone on a trip and won't be back." The child will wonder if other significant people in his or her life will also go on a trip and not come back; or the child may be puzzled about why grandmother won't return from the trip. It is much better to explain to children that death is a natural process. It is desirable to state that death is unlikely to occur until a person is quite old, but that there are exceptions—such as an automobile accident. Parents who take their children to funerals almost always find the children handle the funeral better than they expected. Funerals help children learn that death is a natural process.

It is generally a mistake for survivors to seek to appear strong and emotionally calm following the death of a close friend or relative. Usually such people want to avoid dealing with their loss, and there is a danger that when they do start grieving they will experience more intense grief—partly because they will feel guilty about denying that they are hurting, and partly because they will feel guilty because they de-emphasized (by hiding their pain and feelings) the importance of the person who died.

Many health professionals (such as medical doctors) find death difficult to handle. Health professionals are committed to healing. When someone is found to have a terminal illness, health professionals are apt to experience a sense of failure. In some cases, they experience guilt because they cannot do more, or because they might have made mistakes that contributed to a terminal illness. Therefore, do not be too surprised if you find that some health professionals do not know what to say or do when confronted by terminal illness.

The Grieving Process

Nearly all of us are currently grieving about some loss that we have had. It might be the end of a romantic relationship, or moving away from friends and parents, or the death of a pet, or failing to get a grade we wanted, or the death of someone.

It is a mistake to believe that grieving over a loss should end in a set amount of time. The normal grieving process is often the life span of the griever. When we first become aware of a loss of great importance to us, we are apt to grieve intensively—by crying or

by being depressed. Gradually, we will have hours, then days, then weeks, then months when we will not think about the loss and will not grieve. However, there will always be something that reminds us of the loss (such as anniversaries), and we will again grieve. The intense grieving periods will, however, gradually become shorter, occur less frequently, and decrease in intensity.

Two models of the grieving process will be presented here: the Kübler-Ross (1969) model and the Westberg (1962) model. These models help us to understand the grief we feel from *any* loss.

The Kübler-Ross Model

This model posits five stages of grief:

1. *Stage One: Denial.* During this stage, we tell ourselves, "No, this can't be. There must be a mistake. This just isn't happening." Denial is often functional because it helps cushion the impact of the loss.
2. *Stage Two: Rage and Anger.* During this stage, we tell ourselves, "Why me? This just isn't fair!" For example, terminally ill patients resent that they will soon die while other people will remain healthy and alive. During this stage, God is sometimes a target of the anger. The terminally ill, for example, blame God as unfairly imposing a death sentence.
3. *Stage Three: Bargaining.* During this stage, people with losses attempt to strike bargains to regain all or part of the loss. For example, the terminally ill may bargain with God for more time. They promise to do something worthwhile or to be good in exchange for another month or year of life. Kübler-Ross indicates that even agnostics and atheists sometimes attempt to bargain with God during this stage.
4. *Stage Four: Depression.* During this stage, those having losses tell themselves, "The loss is true, and it's really sad. This is awful. How can I go on with life?"
5. *Stage Five: Acceptance.* During this stage, the person fully acknowledges the loss. Survivors accept the loss and begin working on alternatives to cope with the loss and to minimize its impact.

The Westberg Model

This model is represented graphically in Figure 15.1.

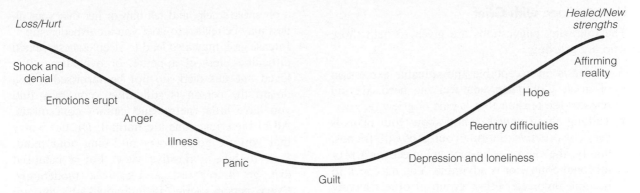

FIGURE 15.1 Westberg Model of the Grieving Process

- *Shock and Denial.* According to the Westberg model, many people, when informed of a tragic loss, are so numb, and in a state of such shock, that they are practically devoid of feelings. It could well be that when emotional pain is unusually intense, a person's response system experiences "overload" and temporarily "shuts down." The person feels hardly anything and acts as if nothing has happened. Such denial is a way of avoiding the impact of a tragic loss.

- *Emotions Erupt.* As the realization of the loss becomes evident, the person expresses the pain by crying, screaming, or sighing.

- *Anger.* At some point, a person usually experiences anger. The anger may be directed at God for causing the loss. The anger may be partly due to the unfairness of the loss. If the loss involves the death of a loved one, there is often anger at the dead person for what is termed "desertion."

- *Illness.* Because grief produces stress, stress-related illnesses are apt to develop, such as colds, flu, ulcers, tension headaches, diarrhea, rashes, and insomnia.

- *Panic.* Because the grieving person realizes he or she does not feel like the "old self," the person may panic and worry about going insane. Nightmares, unwanted emotions that appear uncontrollable, physical reactions, and difficulties in concentrating on day-to-day responsibilities all contribute to the panic.

- *Guilt.* The grieving person may blame himself or herself for having done something that contributed to the loss, or feel guilty for not doing something that might have prevented the loss.

- *Depression and Loneliness.* At times, the grieving person is apt to feel very sad about the loss and also to have feelings of isolation and loneliness. The grieving person may withdraw from others, who are viewed as not being supportive or understanding.

- *Reentry Difficulties.* When the grieving person makes efforts to put his or her life back together, reentry problems are apt to arise. The person may resist letting go of attachments to the past, and loyalties to memories may hamper the pursuit of new interests and activities.

- *Hope.* Gradually, hopes of putting one's life back together return and begin to grow.

- *Affirming Reality.* The grieving person puts his or her life back together again, and the old feeling of having control of one's life returns. The reconstructed life is not the same as the old, and memories of the loss remain. However, the reconstructed life is satisfactory. The grieving person resolves that life will go on.

Evaluation of Models of the Grieving Process

Kübler-Ross and Westberg note that some people continue grieving and never do reach the final stage (the acceptance stage in the Kübler-Ross model, or the affirming reality stage in the Westberg model). Kübler-Ross and Westberg also caution that it is a mistake to rigidly believe everyone will progress through these stages as diagrammed. There is often considerable movement back and forth among the stages. For example, in the Kübler-Ross model, a person may go from denial and depression to anger and rage, then back to denial, then to bargaining, then again to depression, back to anger and rage, and so on.

How to Cope with Grief

The following suggestions are given to help those who are grieving:

- Crying is an acceptable and valuable expression of grief. Cry when you feel the need. Crying releases the tension that is part of grieving.
- Talking about your loss and about your plans is very constructive. Sharing your grief with friends, family, the clergy, a hospice volunteer, or a professional counselor is advisable. You may seek to become involved with a group of others having similar experiences. Talking about your grief eases loneliness and allows you to ventilate your feelings. Talking with close friends gives you a sense of security and brings you closer to others you love. Talking with others who have similar losses helps put your problems into perspective. You will see you are not the only one with problems, and you will feel good about yourself when you assist others in handling their losses.
- Death often causes us to examine and question our faith or philosophy of life. Do not become concerned if you begin questioning your beliefs. Talk about them. For many, a religious faith provides help in accepting the loss.
- Writing out a rational self-analysis on your grief will help you to identify irrational thinking that is contributing to your grief (see Chapter 8). Once any irrational thinking is identified, you can relieve much of your grief through rational challenges to your irrational thinking.
- Try not to dwell on how unhappy you feel. Become involved and active in life around you. Do not waste your time and energy on self-pity.
- Seek to accept the inevitability of death—yours and that of others.
- If the loss is the death of a loved one, holidays and the anniversaries of your loved one's birth and death can be stressful. Seek to spend these days with family and friends who will give you support.
- You may feel that you have nothing to live for and may even think about suicide. Understand that many people who encounter severe losses feel this way. Seek to find assurance in the fact that a sense of purpose and meaning will return.
- Intense grief is very stressful. Stress is a factor that leads to a variety of illnesses, such as headaches, colitis, ulcers, colds, and flu. If you become ill, seek a physician's help, and tell him or her that your illness may be related to grief you are experiencing.
- Intense grief may also lead to sleeplessness, sexual difficulties, loss of appetite, or overeating. If a loved one has died, do not be surprised if you dream the person is still alive. You may find you have little energy and cannot concentrate. All of these reactions are normal. Do not worry that you are going crazy or losing your mind. Seek to take a positive view. Eat a balanced diet, get ample rest, and exercise moderately. Every person's grief is individual—if you are experiencing unusual physical reactions (such as nightmares), try not to become overly alarmed.
- Medication should be taken sparingly and only under the supervision of a physician. Avoid trying to relieve your grief with alcohol or other drugs. Many drugs are addictive and may stop or delay the necessary grieving process.
- Recognize that guilt, real or imagined, is a normal part of grief. Survivors often feel guilty about things they said or did, or feel guilty about things they think they should have said or done. If you are experiencing intense guilt, it is helpful to share it with friends or with a professional counselor. It might also be helpful to write a rational self-analysis of the guilt (see Chapter 8). Learn to forgive yourself. All humans make mistakes.
- You may find that friends and relatives appear to be shunning you. If this is happening, they probably are uncomfortable around you, as they do not know what to say or do. Take the initiative and talk with them about your loss. Inform them about ways in which you would like them to be supportive.
- If possible, put off making major decisions (changing jobs, moving) until you become more emotionally relaxed. When you're highly emotional, you're more apt to make undesirable decisions.

Application of Grief Management Theory to Client Situations

Most people are grieving about one or more losses—the end of a romantic relationship, the death of a pet, or the death of a loved one. Social workers may take on a variety of roles in the areas of grief management and death education: They can be *initiators* of educational programs in schools, churches, and elsewhere for the general public. They can be *counselors* in a variety of settings (including hospices, nursing

HIGHLIGHT 15.2

Celebration of Life Funerals

Traditional funeral services often leave attendees with sadness, emotional anguish, and grief. Such services have a focus on being mournful and on the tragedy of the loss of the deceased.

In contrast, increasingly funerals are now emphasizing including a component on "celebrating the life" of the deceased. Attendees of this type of service are finding this method of honoring a loved one as being more healing and uplifting. Instead of the focus of the funeral being on the loss of the deceased, the focus is on celebrating the deceased's life. Celebration of life services focus on the positive, encouraging, and some of the humorous aspects of the deceased's life. Shared laughter over the endearing qualities and idiosyncrasies of the deceased can offer a break from the tension, sadness, and stress of the loss—even if for a short time. In arranging a celebration of life service, the uniqueness, idiosyncrasies, humorous events, and admirable qualities need to be focused upon. Illustrations of possible elements include:

- Playing the deceased's favorite music or songs
- The attendees sharing stories of the deceased's memorable life moments
- Having a professional caterer bringing in and serving food
- Serving wine to toast the life of the deceased
- Showing a video of an interview with the deceased that was made a few years before the person died—highlighting the person's life, including accomplishments, brief history, challenges faced, positive thoughts about family members, humorous events that occurred, and how that person would like to be remembered
- Displaying important objects of the deceased's life: artwork, personal photos, handmade quilt, childhood memorabilia, awards received, and cherished objects (perhaps a motorcycle or fishing poles, musical instruments, and treasured purchases)

homes, and hospitals) in which they work on a one-to-one basis with the terminally ill and with survivors. They can be group *facilitators* and lead grief management groups (including bereavement groups for survivors) in settings such as hospitals, hospices, mental health clinics, and schools. They may also serve as *brokers* in linking individuals who are grieving, or who have unrealistic views about death and dying, with appropriate community resources.

In order for social workers to be effective in these roles, they need to become comfortable with the idea of their own eventual deaths. They also need to develop skills for relating to the terminally ill and to survivors. The following sections present some guidelines in these areas. The material is useful not only for social workers but also for anyone who has contact with a dying person or with survivors.

How to Relate to a Dying Person

First, you need to accept the idea of your own eventual death and view death as a normal process. If you cannot accept your own death, you will probably be uncomfortable talking to someone who is terminally ill and will not be able to discuss the concerns that the dying person has in an understanding and positive way. The questions in Highlight 15.3 will help you assess your attitudes toward the reality of death.

Second, tell the dying person that you are willing to talk about any concerns that he or she has. Let the person know that you are emotionally ready and supportive, that you care, and that you are available. Remember, the person has a right not to talk about concerns if he or she so chooses. Touching or hugging the dying person is also very helpful.

Third, answer the dying person's questions as honestly as you can. If you do not know an answer, find someone who can provide the requested information. Evasion or ambiguity in response to a dying person's questions only increases his or her concerns. If there is a chance for recovery, this should be mentioned. Even a small margin of hope can be a comfort. Do not, however, exaggerate the chances for recovery.

Fourth, a dying person should be allowed to accept the reality of the situation at his or her own pace. Relevant information should not be volunteered, nor should it be withheld. People who have terminal illnesses have rights to have access to all the relevant information. A useful question that may assist a dying person is, "Do you want to talk about it?"

Fifth, if people around the dying person are able to accept the death, the dying person is helped to accept the death. Therefore, it is therapeutic to help close family members and friends accept the

When a person's spouse dies, he or she is apt to feel sad, lonely, and isolated. Gradually, the grieving person reaches out to others.

Photodisc/Getty Images

death. Remember, they may have a number of concerns that they want to discuss, and they may need help to do this.

Sixth, if you have trouble with certain subjects involving death, inform the dying person of your limitations. This takes the guesswork out of the relationship.

Seventh, the religious or philosophical viewpoint of the dying person should be respected. Your own personal views should not be imposed.

How to Relate to Survivors

These suggestions are similar to the suggestions on relating to a dying person. It is very helpful to become accepting of the idea of your own death. If you are comfortable about your own death, you will be better able to calmly listen to the concerns being expressed by survivors.

It is helpful to initiate the first encounter with a survivor by saying something like, "I'm sorry," and then touching or hugging the person. Then convey that if he or she wants to talk or needs help, you're available. Take your lead from what the survivor expresses. You should seek to convey that you care, that you share his or her loss, and that you're available if he or she wants to talk.

It is helpful to use active listening with both survivors and persons who are terminally ill. In using active listening, the receiver of a message feeds back only what he or she feels was the intent of the sender's message. In using this approach, the receiver does *not* send a message of his or her own, such as asking a question, giving advice, expressing personal feelings, or offering an opinion.

It is frequently helpful to share with a survivor pleasant and positive memories you have about the person who has died. This conveys that you sincerely care about and miss the deceased person and also that the deceased person's life had positive meaning. Relating your memories will often focus the survivor's thoughts on pleasant and positive memories of his or her own.

Continue to visit the survivors if they show interest in such visits. It is also helpful to express your caring and support through a card, a little gift, or a favorite casserole. If a survivor is unable to resume the normal functions of living, or remains deeply depressed, suggest seeking professional help. Joining a survivor self-help group is another possible suggestion.

The religious or philosophical viewpoint of survivors should be respected. You should not seek to impose your views on the survivors.

How to Become Comfortable with the Idea of Your Own Eventual Death: The Strengths Perspective

Perhaps the main reason people are uncomfortable about death is that in our culture we are socialized to avoid seeing death as a natural process. We would be more comfortable with the idea of our own death if we could talk about it more openly and actively seek answers to our own questions and concerns. Comfort with the idea of our own death helps us be more supportive in relating to and understanding those who are dying. If you are uncomfortable about death, including

HIGHLIGHT 15.3

Questions About Grief, Death, and Dying

Arriving at answers to these questions is one way to work toward becoming more comfortable with your own eventual death.

1. Which of the following describe your present conception of death?
   a. Cessation of all mental and physical activity
   b. Death as sleep
   c. Heaven-and-hell concept
   d. A pleasant afterlife
   e. Death as being mysterious and unknown
   f. The end of all life for you
   g. A transition to a new beginning
   h. A joining of the spirit with an unknown cosmic force
   i. Termination of this physical life with survival of the spirit
   j. Something other than what is on this list
2. Which of the following aspects of your own death do you find distasteful?
   a. What might happen to your body after death
   b. What might happen to you if there is a life after death
   c. What might happen to your dependents
   d. The grief that it would cause to your friends and relatives
   e. The pain you may experience as you die
   f. The deterioration of your body before you die
   g. All your plans and projects coming to an end
   h. Something other than what is on this list
3. If you could choose, what age would you like to be when you die?
4. When you think of your own eventual death, how do you feel?
   a. Depressed
   b. Fearful
   c. Discouraged
   d. Purposeless
   e. Angry
   f. Pleasure in being alive
   g. Resolved as you realize death is a natural process of living
   h. Other (specify)
5. For what, or for whom, would you be willing to sacrifice your life?
   a. An idea or moral principle
   b. A loved one
   c. In combat
   d. An emergency where another life could be saved
   e. Not for any reason
6. If you could choose, how would you prefer to die?
   a. A sudden, violent death
   b. A sudden but nonviolent death
   c. A quiet and dignified death
   d. Death in the line of duty

   e. Suicide
   f. Homicide victim
   g. Death after you have achieved your life goals
   h. Other (specify)
7. If it were possible, would you want to know the exact date on which you would die?
8. Would you want to know if you had a terminal illness?
9. If you had six more months to live, how would you want to spend the time?
   a. Satisfying hedonistic desires such as sex
   b. Withdrawing
   c. Contemplating or praying
   d. Seeking to prepare loved ones for your death
   e. Completing projects and tying up loose ends
   f. Considering suicide
   g. Other (specify)
10. Have you seriously contemplated suicide? What are your moral views of suicide? Are there circumstances under which you would take your life?
11. If you had a serious illness and the quality of your life had substantially deteriorated, what measures do you believe should be taken to keep you alive?
    a. All possible heroic medical efforts should be taken.
    b. Medical efforts should be discontinued when there is practically no hope of returning to a life with quality.
    c. Other (specify).
12. If you are married, would you prefer to outlive your spouse? Why?
13. How important do you believe funerals and grief rituals are for survivors?
14. If it were up to you, how would you like to have your body disposed of after you die?
    a. Cremation
    b. Burial
    c. Donation of your body to a medical school or to science
    d. Other (specify)
15. What kind of funeral would you prefer?
    a. A church service
    b. As large as possible
    c. Small with only close friends and relatives present
    d. A lavish funeral
    e. A simple funeral
    f. Whatever your survivors want
    g. Other (specify)
16. Have you made a will? Why or why not?
17. Were you able to arrive at answers to most of these questions? Were you uncomfortable in answering these questions? If you were uncomfortable, what were you feeling, and what made you uncomfortable? For the questions you do not have answers to, how might you arrive at answers?

ETHICAL DILEMMA

Whether to Insert a Feeding Tube

EP 2.1.2

New technology has made it possible for patients with irreversible brain damage to be kept alive for decades. A key component of keeping someone alive is the insertion of a feeding tube. Once a feeding tube has been inserted, it is extremely difficult to obtain a court order to have it removed. Some patients have been kept alive in a chronic vegetative state for 10 to 15 years after a feeding tube has been inserted.

Assume the following: Your mother has a tragic automobile accident, and her brain is deprived of oxygen for 15 minutes. She is in a coma for 30 days, and medical tests indicate that she has suffered irreversible brain damage. It will take a miracle for your mother to ever regain consciousness. Your mother has not signed a living will, a document in which the signer asks to be allowed to die rather than be kept alive by artificial means if disabled and there is no reasonable expectation of recovery. The attending doctors ask you if you want to give permission for a feeding tube to be inserted. If a tube is not inserted, your mother will starve to death; however, she probably will experience little or no pain, as she is in a coma. If a tube is inserted, she will probably live in a vegetative state for many years.

What do you do?

This dilemma is obviously heartrending, but is included here to help prepare you for a decision you may someday have to make.

your own eventual death, here are some things you can do to become more comfortable.

• • • • Ethical Questions 15.5

EP 2.1.2

Are you comfortable with the fact that someday you will die? Most people are not. If you are not, what do you need to work on to become more comfortable?

Identify what your concerns are and then seek answers to these concerns. Numerous excellent books provide information on a wide range of subjects involving death and dying. Many colleges, universities, and organizations provide workshops and courses on death and dying. If you have intense fears about death and dying, consider talking to authorities in the field, such as professional counselors, or to clergy with experience and training in grief counseling.

Taboos against talking about death and dying need to be broken in our society. You may find that tactfully initiating discussions about death and dying with friends and relatives will be helpful to you, and to people close to you.

It is probably accurate that we will never become fully accepting of the idea of our own death, but we can learn a lot more about the subject and obtain answers to many of the questions and concerns we have. In talking about death, it is advisable to avoid using euphemisms such as "passed on," "gone to heaven," and "taken by the Lord." It is much better to be accurate and say the person has died. Using euphemisms gives an unrealistic impression of death and is part of an avoidance approach to facing death. Fortunately, an open communications approach about death is emerging in our society.

Additional ways to become more informed about death and dying are attending funerals; watching quality films and TV programs that cover aspects of dying; providing support to friends or relatives who are terminally ill; being supportive to survivors; talking to people who do grief counseling to learn about their approach; keeping a journal of your thoughts and concerns related to death and dying; and planning the details of your own funeral. Some persons move toward becoming more comfortable with their own death by studying the research that has been conducted on near-death experiences, as described in Highlight 15.4.

Mwalimu Imara (1975) views dying as having a potential for being the final stage of growth. Learning to accept death is similar to learning to accept other losses—such as the breakup of a romantic relationship or leaving a job we cherished. If we learn to accept and grow from the losses we encounter, such experiences will help us in facing the deaths of loved ones and our own eventual death.

Having a well-developed sense of identity (i.e., who we are and what we want out of life) is an important step in learning to become comfortable with our own eventual death. If we have well-developed

HIGHLIGHT 15.4

Life After Life

Several researchers have interviewed a number of people who have had near-death experiences (Papalia et al., 2012). The findings are remarkably similar. Those interviewed had been pronounced clinically dead, but then shortly after were revived. The following description of typical experiences is a composite summary of what has been found. (It is important to bear in mind that the following narrative is not a representation of any one person's experience; rather, it is a composite of the common elements found in many accounts.) The pronoun "he" will be used. The person reports he remembers physicians are trying to revive him. He realizes his "spirit" is leaving his body. His spirit watches the resuscitation attempt from "above." His spirit then moves away from the body, and goes through a tunnel. At the end of the tunnel a being of light appears. This being of light is interpreted as being his God. For Christians, it is interpreted as being Jesus Christ. This being of light is in front of his spirit, and there is a small border between him and the being of light. Other people then come to welcome him—many of these people are the spirits of friends and relatives who have preceded him in death. The being of light asks him a question, which leads him to have a panoramic review of major events in his life. He finds this whole experience to be enjoyable and peaceful.

He wants to cross the border, and enjoy his new existence. However, he finds he must return to his body, and he reluctantly returns. After he returns to his body, he becomes more peaceful, as he now believes there will be an afterlife when his death does occur.

No one is sure why such experiences are reported. Various explanations have been suggested (Siegel, 1981). One is that it suggests there may be a pleasant afterlife. This explanation gives comfort to those who dislike seeing death as an absolute end. Another explanation, however, is that these near-death experiences are nothing more than hallucinations triggered by chemicals released by the brain or induced by lack of oxygen to the brain. Scientists involved with near-death research acknowledge that so far there is no conclusive evidence that these near-death experiences prove there is life after death.

Nelson, Mattingly, and Schmitt (2007) suggest that some people may be biologically predisposed to near-death experiences. They interviewed 55 Europeans who said they had had such experiences. The researchers found that these research subjects also had these experiences in the transition between wakefulness and sleep. The researchers theorized that such people may have disturbances in the brain's arousal system that permit an intrusion of REM sleep elements when they are not quite asleep, bringing on temporary visual hallucinations.

blueprints of what will give meaning and direction to our lives, we are emotionally better prepared to accept that we will eventually die.

Chapter Summary

The following summarizes this chapter's content as it relates to the learning objectives presented at the beginning of the chapter. Chapter content will help prepare students to:

LO 15-1 Describe the developmental tasks of later adulthood.

Older adults must make a number of developmental psychological adjustments, such as adjusting to retirement and lower income and to changing physical strength and health.

LO 15-2 Understand theoretical concepts about developmental tasks in later adulthood.

Theoretical concepts about developmental tasks in later adulthood include integrity versus despair, shifting from work-role preoccupation to self-differentiation; shifting from body preoccupation to body transcendence; shifting from self-occupation to self-transcendence; conducting a life review; the importance of self-esteem; the significance of having a high level of life satisfaction; the negative effects of low status and ageism; the prevalence of depression and other emotional problems; and the significance of spirituality and religion.

LO 15-3 Summarize theories of successful aging.

Three theories of successful aging are the activity theory, the disengagement theory, and the social reconstruction syndrome theory.

LO 15-4 Understand the impact of key life events on older people.

Significant life events for older people may include marriage, death of a spouse, widowhood, remarriage, parenting adult children, grandparenthood, and great-grandparenthood.

LO 15-5 Understand guidelines for positive psychological preparations for later adulthood.

Suggestions for positive psychological preparations by younger adults for later adulthood include forming close personal relationships, preparing financially, having interests and hobbies, forming positive self-identities, looking toward the future, learning to cope with crises, and learning to cope with death.

LO 15-6 Summarize material on grief management and death education.

Guidelines are presented on grief management and death education, relating to a dying person, relating to survivors, and becoming more comfortable with the idea of one's own eventual death.

COMPETENCY NOTES

The following identifies where Educational Policy (EP) competencies and practice behaviors are discussed in the chapter.

EP 2.1.7a Utilize conceptual frameworks to guide the process of assessment, intervention, and evaluation.

EP 2.1.7b Critique and apply knowledge to understand person and environment.
(All of this chapter): The content of this chapter is focused on the students acquiring both of these practice behaviors in working with older persons.

EP 2.1.2 Apply social work ethical principles to guide professional practice.
(pp. 690, 691, 693, 697, 712): Ethical questions are posed.

WEB RESOURCES

See this text's companion website at *www.cengage brain.com* for learning tools such as chapter quizzing, videos, and more.

SOCIOLOGICAL ASPECTS OF LATER ADULTHOOD

Steve Petteway/UPI/Landov

On July 14, 2002, David Pearsall had his 70th birthday, and it was a day to remember. It was not only his birthday but also his last day of work at Quality Printers. That evening, the owners of Quality Printers gave a retirement party for Dave. He received a gold watch, and the owners and many of his fellow printers gave testimonial speeches about how much Dave had contributed to the morale and productivity of the company. Dave was deeply honored, and tears occasionally came to his eyes.

Dave felt strange waking up the next morning. He was used to getting up early to go to work. Work had become the center of his life. He even socialized with his fellow printers. Now he had nothing planned and nothing to do. He lay in bed thinking about what the *future would hold for him. Dave had generally muddled through life. His father had helped him obtain a position as a printer, and Dave seldom gave much attention to planning for the future. For example, while he thought it would be nice to retire, he had given little consideration to it.*

Dave got up, looked in a mirror, and noticed his thinning gray hair, the wrinkles on his face and hands, and the tire around his waist. In concluding that the best part of his life had passed by, he again wondered anxiously what the future would hold for him, and he contemplated what he should do with all of his time. He had no idea.

For the next few weeks, he followed his wife, Jeanette, around the house. Dave began giving Jeanette suggestions on how she could be more efficient and productive around the house. After a few weeks of such advice, Jeanette angrily told Dave to "get off her back." He visited the print shop where he used to work but soon realized everyone was too busy to spend time talking with him. He also stopped socializing with the printers, since they tended to talk about work. He felt useless. As the months went by, he spent most of his time sitting home and watching TV. Occasionally, he went to a neighborhood bar, where he drank to excess.

Dave and his wife had never given much attention to long-range financial planning. They both had worked for many years and tended to spend their paychecks shortly after they received them. When they bought their house in 1997, they gave little thought to how they would make their mortgage payments after retiring. Dave had hoped the Social Security system would take care of his bills.

Dave and Jeanette were in for a shock when they retired. The monthly Social Security checks were much less than they had anticipated. They stopped going out to eat, to movies, and to ball games. A few months after Dave retired, they realized they could no longer make the mortgage payments. They put the house up for sale and sold it four and a half months later, at a price lower than what the house was worth. Both were sad about leaving their home, but financially they had no other choice. They moved into a two-bedroom apartment. Both became even more inactive, as they no longer had yard work and now had fewer home maintenance tasks. One neighbor frequently played a stereo late into the night, and the Pearsalls had trouble sleeping.

In February 2004, Jeanette had a major heart attack. She was in the hospital for nearly two weeks and then was placed in a nursing home. Dave missed the companionship of his wife and became deeply depressed. He wished she could come home, but her medical needs wouldn't allow that, so he visited her every day. Dave had never learned to cook, and because he was depressed, his diet consisted mainly of cheese sandwiches and TV dinners. In November 2004, Jeanette suffered another heart attack and died.

Dave now became even more depressed. He no longer shaved or bathed. He no longer cleaned his apartment, and neighbors began to complain about the odor. Dave gave up the will to live. He seldom heard from his son, Donald, who was living in a distant city. Dave sought to drown his unhappiness in whiskey. One night in January 2011, he passed out in his apartment with a lighted cigarette in his hand, which set his couch on fire. Dave died of smoke inhalation.

Dave's later years raise some questions for our society. Have we abandoned elders to a meaningless existence? Is it a mistake for older people to count on Social Security to meet their financial needs when they retire? How can our society provide a more meaningful role for older people?

A Perspective

This chapter will focus on the social problems encountered by older people. The plight of older people has now become recognized as a major problem in the United States. Older people face a number of personal problems: high rates of physical illness and emotional difficulties, poverty, malnutrition, lack of access to transportation, low status, lack of a meaningful role in our society, elder abuse, and inadequate housing. To a large extent, older people are a minority group. Similar to other minority groups, older people are victims of job discrimination and are subjected to prejudice that is based on erroneous stereotypes.

Learning Objectives

This chapter will help prepare students to:

EP 2.1.7a, 2.1.7b

LO 16-1 *Summarize the specific problems faced by older people and the causes of these problems*

LO 16-2 *Describe the current services to meet these problems and identify gaps in these services*

LO 16-3 *Understand the emergence of older people as a significant political force in our society*

LO 16-4 *Describe a proposal to provide older people with a meaningful, productive social role in our society*

LO 16-1 Summarize the Specific Problems Faced by Older People and the Causes of These Problems

Older People: A Population-at-Risk

Human societies have different customs for dealing with incapacitated older people. In the past, some societies abandoned their enfeebled old. The Crow, Creek, and Hopi tribes, for example, built special huts away from the tribe where the old went to die. The Eskimos left incapacitated older people in snow banks, or sent them off in a kayak. The Siriono of the Bolivian forest simply left them behind when they moved on in search of food (Moss & Moss, 1975). Even today, the Ik of Uganda leave older people and the disabled to starve to death (Kornblum & Julian, 2012). Generally, the primary reason such societies have been forced to abandon older people is scarce resources.

Although we might consider such customs to be barbaric and shocking, have we not also abandoned older people? We urge them to retire when many are still productive. All too often, when a person is urged to retire, his or her status, power, and self-esteem are lost. Also, in a physical sense, we seldom have a place for large numbers of older people. Community facilities—parks, subways, libraries— are oriented to serving children and young people. Most housing is designed and priced for the young couple with one or two children and an annual income over $60,000. If older people are not able to care for themselves and if their families are unable or unwilling to care for them, we store them away from society in nursing homes. About one out of 10 older people is living in poverty (Mooney, Knox, & Schacht, 2013). (The poverty rate for older adults is lower than that of the total population.)

Beth A. Keiser/AP Images

Older people may face many problems, such as severe financial constraints, physical disabilities, and perceptual limitations.

Older people are subjected to various forms of discrimination—for example, job discrimination. Older workers are erroneously believed to be less productive. Unemployed workers in their 50s and 60s have greater difficulty finding new jobs and remain unemployed much longer than younger unemployed workers. Older people are given no meaningful role in our society, which is youth-oriented and deplores growing old (Santrock, 2013b). Our society glorifies physical attractiveness and thereby shortchanges older people. Older people are viewed as out of touch with what's happening, and their knowledge is seldom valued or sought. Intellectual ability is sometimes thought to decline with age, even though research shows that intellectual capacity, barring organic problems, remains essentially unchanged until very late in life (Santrock, 2013b).

Older people are erroneously thought to be senile, resistant to change, inflexible, incompetent workers, and a burden on the young. Given opportunities, older individuals usually prove such prejudicial concepts to be wrong. They generally react to prejudice against them in the same way that racial and ethnic minorities react—by displaying self-hatred and by being self-conscious, sensitive, and defensive about their social and cultural status (Santrock, 2013b). As we have mentioned previously, individuals who

frequently receive negative responses from others eventually tend to come to view themselves negatively.

Problems Faced by Older People

Individuals are dramatically affected by their interactions with other micro, mezzo, and macro systems. The following section will address a range of problems suffered by older people within the macro-system context. This involves two dimensions. The first concerns problems older people as individual micro systems suffer within the macro environment. These include poverty, malnutrition, health difficulties, elder abuse, and lack of transportation. The other dimension of problems affecting older people focuses on the macro systems providing them with support and services. Often, cost is of chief concern. For example, the general population might experience rapidly rising taxes to cover a range of services for older people, including medical care. Examining both perspectives can enhance your understanding of human behavior in preparation for assessment and practice.

A point to remember is that unlike other minorities, older people have problems that we all encounter eventually (assuming we do not die prematurely). By the time most of today's college students reach middle age (presumably their peak earning years), a larger proportion of the adult population will be retired, because older people are the fastest-growing segment of our population. Those who are retired depend heavily on Social Security, Medicare, and other government programs to assist in meeting their financial and medical needs. If we do not face and solve the financial problems of older people now, we will be in dire straits in the future.

Emphasis on Youth: The Impact of Social and Economic Forces

Our society fears aging more than most other societies do. Our emphasis on youth is illustrated by our dread of getting gray hair and wrinkles or becoming bald and by our being pleased when someone guesses our age to be younger than it actually is. We place a high value on youthful energy and action. We like to think we are doers. But why is there such an emphasis on youth in our society?

Industrialization resulted in a demand for laborers who are energetic, agile, and strong. Rapid advances in technology and science have made obsolete past knowledge and certain specialized work skills. Pioneer living and the gradual expansion of our nation to the west required brute strength, energy, and stamina. Competition has always been emphasized and

has been reinforced by a social interpretation of Darwin's theory of evolution, which highlighted survival of the fittest, though Darwin meant those that "fit" their environment, not those that were young and healthy. The cultural tradition of overvaluing youth in our society has resulted in our devaluation of older people. Spotlight 16.1 discusses the status of older people in China and Japan and lists factors associated with high status for older people.

The Increasing Older Population

There are now more than 10 times as many people age 65 and older as there were in 1900. Table 16.1 shows that the percentage of older people has been steadily increasing. As of 2010, there were about 38 million Americans age 65 and over. (U.S. Census Bureau, 2010).

By 2030, the number is projected to be 72 million—a 90 percent increase in 20 years, compared to a 30 percent growth in total population during the same period (Hooyman, 2007).

Several reasons can be given for the phenomenal growth of the older population. The improved care of expectant mothers and newborn infants has reduced the infant mortality rate. New drugs, better sanitation, and other medical advances have increased the life expectancy of Americans from

 SPOTLIGHT ON DIVERSITY 16.1

High Status for Older People in China, Japan, and Other Countries

For many generations, older people in Japan and China have experienced higher status than older people in the United States. In both of these countries, older people are integrated into their families much more than in the United States. In Japan, more than 75 percent of older people live with their children, whereas in the United States most older people live separately from their children (Santrock, 2009). Older people in Japan are accorded respect in a variety of ways. For example, the best seats in a home are apt to be reserved for older people, cooking tends to cater to the tastes of older people, and individuals bow to older people.

However, Americans' images of older people in Japan and China are somewhat idealized. Japan is becoming more urbanized and Westernized. As a consequence, the proportion of older people living with their children is decreasing, and

older people there are now often employed in lower-status jobs (Santrock, 2013b).

Five factors have been identified as predicting high status for older people in a culture (Santrock, 2013b):

1. Older persons are recognized as having valuable knowledge.
2. Older persons control key family and community resources.
3. The culture is more collectivistic than individualistic.
4. The extended family is a common family arrangement in the culture, and older persons are integrated into the extended family.
5. Older persons are permitted and encouraged to engage in useful and valued functions as long as possible.

TABLE 16.1	COMPOSITION OF U.S. POPULATION AGE 65 AND OLDER						
	YEAR						
	1900	1950	1970	1980	1990	2000	2010
Number of older persons (in millions)	3	12	20	25	31	35	40
Percent of total population	4	8	9.5	11	12	13	14

SOURCE: United States Bureau of the Census, *Statistical Abstract of the United States, 2012* (Washington, DC: U.S. Government Printing Office, 2011).

49 years in 1900 to 78 years in 2010 (U.S. Census Bureau, 2010).

Another reason for the increasing proportion of older people is that the birth rate is declining—fewer babies are being born, while more adults are reaching later adulthood. After World War II, a baby boom lasted from 1946 to 1964. Children born during these years flooded schools in the 1950s and 1960s. Then they moved into the labor market. Very soon, this generation will begin to reach retirement. After 1964, there was a baby bust, a sharp decline in birth rates. The average number of children per woman went down from a high of 3.8 in 1957 to the current rate of about 2.0 (Mooney, Knox, & Schacht, 2013).

The increased life expectancy, along with the baby boom followed by the baby bust, will significantly increase the median age of Americans in future years. The median age is indeed increasing dramatically. The long-term implications are that the United States will undergo a number of cultural, social, and economic changes.

The Fastest-Growing Age Group: Old-Old

As our society is having more success in treating and preventing heart disease, cancer, strokes, and other killers, more and more older people are living into their 80s and beyond. People 85 and over constitute the fastest-growing age group in the United States (Mooney et al., 2013). Older Americans are living longer, due in part to better medical care, sanitation, and nutrition. The proportion of the old-old in our society is projected to increase substantially in the next few decades as the baby boomer generation reaches age 75 and older. The number of people age 85 and older, currently 15 percent of the total older population, is the most rapidly growing segment of the U.S. population (Mooney et al., 2013).

Those who are 75 and over are creating a number of problems and difficult decisions for our society. Many of the old-old suffer from multiple chronic illnesses. Common medical problems of the old-old include arthritis, heart conditions, hypertension, osteoporosis (brittleness of the bones), Alzheimer's disease, incontinence, hearing and vision problems, and depression. The old-old with major health problems are putting strains on family resources. The old-old need more of such community help as Meals on Wheels, home health care, special busing, and homemaker services. The older an older person becomes, the higher the probability that he or she will become a resident of a nursing home. The cost to society for such care is high—more than $70,000 a year per person to provide nursing home care (Mooney et al., 2013). Despite the widespread image of families dumping aged parents into nursing homes, most frail older people still live outside institutional walls, being cared for by a spouse, child, or other relative. Some middle-aged people are now simultaneously encountering demands to put children through college and to support an aging parent in a nursing home.

"Can we afford the very old?" is a favorite conference topic for doctors, bioethicists, and other specialists. Rising health-care costs and superlongevity have ignited a controversy over whether to ration health care to the very old. For example, should people over age 75 be prohibited from receiving liver transplants or kidney dialysis? Discussion of euthanasia (the practice of killing individuals who are hopelessly sick or injured) has also been increasing. In 1984, Governor Richard Lamm of Colorado created controversy when he asserted the terminally ill have a duty to die. Dr. Eisdor Fer (quoted in Otten, 1984) stated: "The problem is age-old and across cultures. Whenever society has had marginal economic resources, the oldest went first, and the old people bought that approach. The old Eskimo wasn't put on the ice flow; he just left of his own accord and never came back" (p. 10).

•••• / Ethical Question 16.1

Do the terminally ill have a duty to end their lives as soon as they can?

EP 2.1.2

Early Retirement: The Impact of Social and Economic Forces

Maintaining a high rate of employment is a major goal in our society. One instrument used in the past to keep the workforce in line with demand was mandatory retirement at a certain age, such as 65 or 70. In 1986, Congress (recognizing that mandatory retirement was overtly discriminatory against older adults) outlawed most mandatory retirement policies. In many occupations, the supply of labor exceeds the demand. An often used remedy for the oversupply of available employees is the *encouragement* of ever earlier retirement. Even though employers can no longer force a worker to retire, many exert subtle pressures on their older employees to retire.

Many workers who retire early supplement their pension with another job, usually at a lower status. About 85 percent of Americans 65 and older are retired, even though many are intellectually and physically capable of working (Papalia & Feldman 2012). Our Social Security program supports early retirement at the age of 62. Pension plans of some companies and craft unions make it financially attractive to retire as early as 55. Perhaps the extreme case is the armed forces, which permit retirement on full benefits after 20 years of service, or as early as age 38.

Although early retirement has some advantages to society, such as reducing the labor supply and allowing younger employees to advance faster, there are also some disadvantages. For society, the total bill for retirement pensions is already huge and

still growing. For the retiree, it means facing a new life and status without much preparation or assistance. Although our society has developed education and other institutions to prepare the young for the work world, it has developed few comparable institutions to prepare older people for retirement.

In our society, we still view people's worth partly in terms of their work. People often develop their self-image in terms of their occupation. Because the later years generally provide no exciting new roles to replace the occupational roles lost on retirement, retirees cannot proudly say, "I am a ..." Instead, they must say, "I *was* a ..." The more a person's life revolves around work, the more difficult retirement is apt to be. Retirement often diminishes people's social contacts and their status and places them in a *roleless role*. People who were once valued as salespeople, teachers, accountants, barbers, or secretaries are now considered noncontributors in a roleless role on the fringe of society.

Several myths about the older worker have been widely believed by employers and the general public. Older workers are thought to be less healthy, clumsier, more prone to absenteeism, more accident-prone, more forgetful, and slower in task performance (Papalia et al., 2012). Research has shown these beliefs to be erroneous. Older workers have lower turnover rates, produce at a steadier rate, make fewer mistakes, have lower absenteeism rates, have a more positive attitude toward their work, and exceed younger employees in health and low on-the-job injury rates. However, when older workers do become ill, they usually take a somewhat longer time to recover (Papalia et al., 2012).

A key question about early retirement is the age at which people *want* to retire. Gerontologists have studied this question. Younger workers generally state they prefer to retire before age 65. Older workers indicate they desire to retire later than the conventional age of 65 (Newman & Newman, 2009). The explanation for this difference appears to be partly economic. Because Social Security benefits and pension plans are usually insufficient to provide the same standard of living as when a person was working, older people see an economic need to continue working beyond age 65. An additional explanation is sociopsychological. With retirement often being a roleless role in our society, older workers may gradually identify more and more with their work and prefer it over retirement.

Ariel Skelley/Getty Images

Retirees who have previously enjoyed social and economic success and are in good physical health are more likely to enjoy retirement.

Adjustment to retirement varies for different people. Retirees who are not worried about money and who are healthy are happier in retirement than those who miss their income and do not feel well enough to enjoy their leisure time. Many recent retirees relish the first long stretches of leisure time they have had since childhood. After a while, however, they may begin to feel restless, bored, and useless. The most satisfied retirees tend to be physically fit people who are using their skills in part-time volunteer or paid work (Papalia et al., 2012).

Workers who are pressured to retire before they want to may feel anger and resentment, and may feel out of step with younger workers. Also, workers who defer retirement as long as possible because they enjoy their work may feel that no more work is an immense loss when they are pressured to retire. On the other hand, some people's morale and life satisfaction remain stable through both working and retirement years.

Older adults who adjust best to retirement have adequate income, are healthy, are active, are better educated, have an extended social network that includes both family and friends, and usually were satisfied with their lives prior to retiring. Those having the most difficulty adjusting to retirement are those with poor health, inadequate income, and those who must adjust to other stresses (such as the death of a spouse) (Santrock, 2013b).

The two most common problems associated with retirement are adjusting to a reduced income and missing one's former job. Those who have the most difficulty in adjusting tend to be rigid or to overly identify with their work by viewing their job as their primary source of satisfaction and self-image. Those who are happiest are able to replace job prestige and financial status with values stressing self-development, personal relationships, and leisure activities.

Financial Problems of Older People

One out of 10 older people lives in poverty. A significant numbers lack adequate food, essential clothes and drugs, and perhaps a telephone in the house to make emergency calls. Only small minorities of older people have substantial savings or investments.

Poverty among older people varies dramatically by race, sex, marital status, ethnicity, and age. Women, the old-old, people of color, and those who are widowed or single are most likely to be poor (Mooney et al., 2013).

Older women are more likely to be poor than older men. Nearly half of older Hispanic women, and four out of 10 older African American women, are living in poverty (Mooney et al., 2013). Women of color were more likely to have been working in low-paying jobs with no retirement plan.

The financial problems of older people are compounded by other factors. One is the high cost of health care, as previously discussed. A second factor is inflation. Inflation is especially devastating to those on fixed incomes. Most private pension benefits do not increase after a worker retires. For example, if living costs rise annually at 3.5 percent, after 20 years, a person on a fixed pension would be able to buy only half as many goods and services as he or she could at retirement ("Will Inflation Tarnish Your Golden Years?" 1979). Fortunately, in 1974, Congress enacted an automatic escalator clause in Social Security benefits, providing a 3 percent increase in payments when the consumer price index increases a like amount. However, Social Security benefits were never intended to make a person financially independent, and it is nearly impossible to live comfortably on monthly Social Security checks.

The most important source of income for the vast majority of older people is Social Security benefits, primarily the Old Age, Survivors, Disability, and Health Insurance (OASDHI) program. This program is described later in this chapter. About 95 percent of older adults receive Social Security; for 18 percent of them, Social Security is their only income (Mooney et al., 2013). About 14 percent of Americans age 65 and older are in the paid labor force. This figure is substantially lower than in 1950, but represents an increase since 1993 (Mooney et al., 2013).

Sullivan and his associates (Sullivan, Thompson, Wright, Gross, & Spady, 1980) emphasize the importance of financial security for older persons.

Financial security affects one's entire life-style. It determines one's diet, ability to seek good health care, to visit relatives and friends, to maintain a suitable wardrobe, and to find or maintain adequate housing. One's financial resources, or lack of them, play a great part in finding recreation (going to movies, plays, playing bridge or bingo, etc.) and maintaining morale, feelings of independence, and a sense of self-esteem. In other words, if an older person has the financial resources to remain socially independent (having her own household and access to transportation and medical services), to continue contact with friends and relatives, and to maintain her preferred forms of recreation, she is going to feel a great deal better about herself and others than if she is deprived of her former style of life. (pp. 357–358)

The Social Security System

The Social Security system was not designed to be the main source of income for older people. It was originally intended as a form of insurance that would *supplement* other assets when the retirement, disability, or death of a wage-earning spouse occurred. Yet many older people do not have investments, pensions, or savings to support them in retirement, and therefore Social Security has become their major source of income.

The Social Security system was instituted in the United States in 1935. Money is paid into the system from Social Security taxes on employers and employees. In 1935, life expectancy was only somewhat over 60 years. Life expectancy, however, has increased to 78 in 2010. Social Security taxes have sharply increased in recent years, but the proportion of older people is increasing even faster. Some projections have the Social Security fund being depleted around 2020 (Santrock, 2013b).

The *dependency ratio* is the number of societal members who are under 18 or are 65 and over compared with the number of people who are between 18 and 64. With the older adults proportion of the population increasing, nonworkers will represent a ballooning burden on workers. Authorities predict that by the year 2020 the dependency ratio will decline from the current level of about three workers for every nonworking person to a ratio of about 2 to 1 (Mooney et al., 2013). This dramatic increase may lead to foundering pension plans and increased taxes as governments struggle to finance elder care programs.

Some problems now exist with the system. First, as mentioned, the benefits are too small to provide the major source of income for older people. Even with payments from Social Security included, an estimated 80 percent of retirees are now living on less than half of their preretirement income. And the monthly payments from Social Security are generally below the poverty line (Kornblum & Julian, 2012). Second, it is unlikely that the monthly benefits will be raised much. Our society faces some hard choices about keeping the Social Security system solvent in future years. Benefits might be lowered, but this would further impoverish the recipients. Social Security taxes might be raised, but there is little public support for this. The amount of salary that is subject to Social Security taxes has been rising significantly each year since 1970.

The future of the Social Security system is unclear. It is likely to continue to exist, but reduced benefits are possible. Young people are well advised to plan for retirement through savings and investments that will supplement Social Security payments.

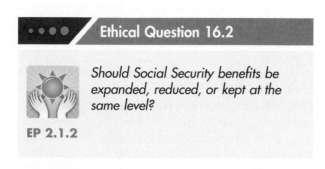

Ethical Question 16.2

Should Social Security benefits be expanded, reduced, or kept at the same level?

EP 2.1.2

Death

Preoccupation with dying, particularly with the circumstances surrounding it, is an ongoing concern of older people. For one reason, they see their friends and relatives dying. For another, they realize they've lived more years than they have left.

The older person's concern about dying is most often focused on the disability, the pain, or the long period of suffering that may precede death. People generally would like a death with dignity. They would prefer to die in their own homes, with little suffering, with mental faculties intact, and with family and friends nearby. Older people are also concerned about the cost of their final illness, the difficulties they may cause others by the manner of their death, and whether their resources will permit a dignified funeral.

In modern America, many people die in nursing homes or hospitals surrounded by medical staff (Papalia et al., 2012). Such deaths often occur without dignity. Fortunately, the hospice movement has been developing in recent years in an attempt to foster death with dignity. A hospice is a program that is designed to allow the terminally ill to die with dignity—to live their final weeks in a way they want. Hospices originated in the Middle Ages among European religious groups that welcomed travelers who were sick, tired, or hungry (Sullivan et al., 1980).

Hospices serve patients in a variety of settings—in hospitals, in nursing homes, in assisted-living facilities, and in the dying person's home. Hospices provide both medical and social services, and make extensive efforts to allow the terminally ill to spend their remaining days as they choose. Hospices sometimes have educational and entertainment programs, and visitors are welcome. Pain relievers are extensively used, so that the patient is able to live out his or her final days in relative comfort.

Hospices view the *disease*, not the patient, as terminal. Their emphasis is on helping people use the time that is left, rather than on trying to keep people alive as long as possible. Many hospice programs are set up to assist people in living their remaining days at home. In addition to medical and visiting nurse services, hospices have volunteers to help the patient and family members with such services as counseling, transportation, filling out insurance forms and other paperwork, and respite care (that is, staying with the patient to provide temporary relief for family members).

The Ethical Dilemma box raises a number of issues, including refusal of treatment, termination of treatment, and physician-assisted suicide.

Elder Abuse

A shocking way for older people to spend their final years is as victims of *elder abuse*—neglect, physical abuse, or psychological abuse of dependent older persons. The perpetrator may be the son or daughter of the older victim, a spouse, a caregiver, or some other person. Although elder abuse can occur in nursing homes and in other institutions, it is most often suffered by frail older people living with their spouses or their children. Because of problems in defining elder abuse, as well as the fact that the abuse is grossly underreported, the number abused may involve as many as 6 percent of the older population (Santrock, 2013b).

Adult children may abuse their parents for a variety of reasons. They may be responding to the stress of their own personal problems or to the stress of the time, energy, and finances needed to care for another person. They may be paying back their parent for having been abusive to them when they were younger. They may be upset with their older parent's emotional reactions, physical impairments, lifestyle, or personal habits. They may be intentionally abusing the parent to force him or her to move out of

ETHICAL DILEMMA

A Right to Die?

EP 2.1.2

The technology of life-support equipment can keep people alive almost indefinitely. Respirators, artificial nutrition, intravenous hydration, and so-called miracle drugs not only sustain life but also trap many of the terminally ill in a degrading mental and physical condition. Such technology has raised a variety of ethical questions. Do people who are terminally ill and in severe pain have a right to die by refusing treatment? Increasingly, through "living wills," patients are able to express their wishes and refuse treatment. However, does someone in a long-term coma who has not signed a living will have a right to die? How should our society decide when to continue and when to stop life-support efforts? Courts and state legislatures are presently working through the legal complexities governing death and euthanasia.

There is considerable controversy about assisted suicide in the United States. Hemlock Society founder Derek Humphry has written a do-it-yourself suicide manual. (The Hemlock Society promotes active voluntary euthanasia.) Michigan doctor Jack Kevorkian made national news by building a machine to help terminally ill people end their lives and by assisting a number of them to do so.

In the Netherlands, an informal, *de facto* arrangement made with prosecutors more than 25 years ago allows physicians there to help patients die, as long as certain safeguards are followed. The patient, for example, has to be terminally ill, in considerable pain, and mentally competent, and must repeatedly express a wish to die.

Oregon voters passed that state's Death with Dignity Act in 1994. It allows doctors to prescribe lethal drugs at the request of terminally ill patients who have less than six months to live. Doctors may only prescribe a lethal dose, not administer it.

People in favor of assisted suicide argue that unnecessary long-term suffering is without merit and should not have to be endured. They argue that people have a right to a death with dignity, which means a death without excessive emotional and physical pain and without excessive mental, physical, and spiritual degradation. They see assisted suicide as affirming the principle of autonomy—upholding the individual's right to make decisions about his or her dying process. Allowing the option of suicide for the terminally ill is perceived as the ultimate right of self-determination.

Opponents assert that suicide is, at best, unethical and, at worst, a mortal sin for which the deceased cannot receive forgiveness. They view assisted suicide as assisted murder. They assert that modern health care can provide almost everyone a peaceful, pain-free, comfortable, and dignified end to life.

Opponents believe that most terminally ill persons consider suicide not because they fear death but because they fear dying—pain, abandonment, and loss of control (all of which a hospice is designed to alleviate). Moreover, assisted-suicide legislation could easily result in a number of unintended consequences. The terminally ill might believe they have a *duty* to die in order to avoid being a financial and emotional burden to their families and to society. A health-care system intent upon cutting costs could give subtle, even unintended, encouragement to a patient to die. Relatives of a terminally ill person receiving expensive medical care may put pressure on the person to choose physician-assisted suicide to avoid eroding the family's finances. There is concern that if competent people are allowed to seek death, then pressure will grow to use the treatment-by-death option with adults in comas or with others who are mentally incompetent (such as the mentally ill and those who have a severe cognitive disability). Finally, many people worry that if the "right to die" becomes recognized as a basic right in our society, then it can easily become a "duty to die" for older people, the sick, the poor, and others devalued by society.

Some authorities have sought to make a distinction between *active* euthanasia (assisting in suicide) and *passive* euthanasia (withholding or withdrawing treatment). In many states, it is legal for physicians and courts to honor a patient's wishes to not receive life-sustaining treatment.

A case of passive euthanasia involved a Missouri woman, Nancy Cruzan. On January 11, 1983, when she was 25, her car overturned. Her brain lost oxygen for 14 minutes following the accident, and for the next several years she was in a "persistent vegetative state," with no hope of recovery. A month after the accident, her parents, Joyce and Joe Cruzan, gave permission for a feeding tube to be inserted. In the months that followed, however, the parents gradually became convinced there was no point in keeping Nancy alive indefinitely in such a hopeless condition.

In 1986, they were shocked when a Missouri state judge informed them that they could be charged with murder for removing the feeding tube. The Cruzans appealed the decision all the way to the U.S. Supreme Court, requesting the Court to overturn a Missouri law that specifically prohibits withdrawal of food and water from hopelessly ill patients. In July 1990, the Supreme Court refused the Cruzans' request that their daughter's tube be removed but ruled that states could sanction the removal if there is "clear and convincing evidence" that the patient would have wished it. Cruzan's family subsequently found other witnesses to testify that Nancy would not have wanted to be kept alive in such a condition. A Missouri judge decided that the testimony met the Supreme Court's test. The tube was disconnected in December 1990, and Nancy Cruzan died several days later.

At the present time, 10,000 Americans are in similar vegetative conditions, unable to communicate. Many of these individuals have virtually no chance to recover. Right-to-die questions will undoubtedly continue to be raised in many of these cases.

(continued)

ETHICAL DILEMMA (continued)

In June 1997, the U.S. Supreme Court ruled that terminally ill people do not have a constitutional right to doctor-assisted suicide.

In January 2006, the U.S. Supreme Court ruled that the Bush administration's attempts to stop Oregon doctors from prescribing lethal doses were improper. The immediate legal impact of the Court's ruling is clear. Oregon doctors may continue to prescribe lethal doses without fear of federal penalty.

At the time of this writing, physician-assisted suicide was legal in four states in the United States: Oregon, Washington, Vermont, and Montana. It is also legal in some other countries, including Belgium, Luxembourg, the Netherlands, and Switzerland. In the three states in the United States, there are barriers to the use of this type of suicide. For example, Pamela J. Miller (2000, p. 264) describes the processes in the state of Oregon:

To qualify to receive a prescription for medication to end life, the person must be terminally ill with six

months or less to live, and a second physician's opinion on diagnosis and prognosis is required. After the first oral request to start the process, a 15-day waiting period begins. A mental health consultation is not required, although either physician can request an evaluation by a psychiatrist or psychologist, and notification of family or friends is not required. A written request combined with another oral request is obtained, and a 48-hour waiting period begins. The prescription, generally barbiturates and antinausea medication, is then given to the terminally ill person and taken by mouth.

Do you believe that the terminally ill have a right to die by refusing treatment? Do you believe that assisted suicide should be legalized? If you had a terminally ill close relative who was in intense pain and asked you to assist her or him in acquiring a lethal dose of drugs, how would you respond? Would you be willing to help? Or would you refuse?

their home. When the older person is living with the abuser, finding alternative living arrangements is often necessary.

The typical victim is an older person in poor health who lives with someone. Papalia and her associates (2012) note that the abuser is more likely to be a spouse than a child, partly because substantially more older people live with spouses than with their children. The risk of elder abuse is substantially increased when the caregiver is depressed (Papalia, et al., 2012).

The varied forms of mistreatment of older people are typically grouped into the following seven categories:

- *Physical abuse*: the infliction of physical pain or injury, including bruising, punching, or restraining
- *Psychological abuse*: the infliction of mental anguish, such as intimidating, humiliating, and threatening harm
- *Financial abuse*: the illegal or improper exploitation of the victim's assets or property
- *Neglect*: the deliberate failure or refusal to fulfill a caretaking obligation, such as denial of food or health care, or abandoning the victim
- *Sexual abuse*: nonconsensual sexual contact with an older person
- *Self-neglect*: behaviors of a frail, depressed, or mentally incompetent older person that threaten her or his own safety or health, such as failure to eat or drink adequately or to take prescribed medications

- *Abandonment*: desertion of vulnerable elder by anyone who has assumed the responsibility for care or custody of that person.
- *Violating personal rights*: violation of an older person's rights, including the right to privacy and to make her or his personal and health decisions (Papalia et al., 2012).

One of the more notable victims of elder abuse was Mickey Rooney. He began as a child movie star and acted in more than 200 movies. In March 2011, he gave an emotional testimony on elder abuse before a U.S. senate panel. Rooney said he had been victimized for years by two of his stepchildren. He stated they bullied and threatened him, making him "effectively a prisoner in his home." He added they took his money, denied him his medication, and withheld food from him. Rooney told the senators if it can happen to him, it can happen to anyone.

Every state is mandated by the federal government to provide adult protective services similar to those provided for children. An Adult Protective Services program serves adults—primarily older people and adults with physical or mental disabilities—who are being neglected or abused. (This program is described in more detail later in this chapter.)

Housing

More than 95 percent of older people do not live in nursing homes or any other kind of institution. More than 70 percent of older men are married and live with their wives. Because women tend to outlive their spouses, more than 40 percent of women over age 65 live alone. Nearly 80 percent of older married couples maintain their own households—in apartments, mobile homes, condominiums, or their own houses. In addition, nearly half of single older people (widows, widowers, divorced, never married) live in their own homes (Papalia et al., 2012). When older people do not maintain their own households, they most often live in the homes of relatives, primarily children.

Older people who live in rural areas generally have a higher status than those living in urban areas. People living on farms can retire gradually. People whose income is in land, rather than a job, can retain importance and esteem to an advanced age.

However, almost three-fourths of Americans live in urban areas, and older people often live in poor-quality housing. At least 30 percent of older people live in substandard, deteriorating, or dilapidated housing (Mooney et al., 2013). Many older people in urban areas are trapped in decaying, low-value houses needing considerable maintenance and often surrounded by racial and ethnic groups different from their own. Many urban older people live in the urban inner cities in hotels or apartments with inadequate living conditions. Their neighborhoods may be decaying and crime-ridden, where they are easy prey for thieves and muggers.

Fortunately, many mobile home parks, retirement villages, and apartment complexes geared to the needs of older people have been built throughout the country. Many such communities for older people provide a social center, security protection, sometimes a daily hot meal, and perhaps help with maintenance. The fastest-growing housing option for older people is assisted-living facilities. Such facilities offer private living units, with the safety of around-the-clock staff.

Transportation

Many older people do not drive. Some cannot afford the cost of a car, whereas others have physical limitations that prevent them from driving and maintaining a car. The lack of convenient, inexpensive transportation is a problem faced by most older people.

Crime Victimization

Having reduced energy, strength, and agility, older people are vulnerable to being victimized by crime,

particularly robbery, aggravated assault, burglary, larceny, vandalism, and fraud. Many older people live in constant fear of being victimized, although reported victimization rates for older people are lower than rates for younger people. The actual victimization rates for older people may be considerably higher than official crime statistics indicate, because many older people feel uneasy about becoming involved with the legal and criminal justice systems. Therefore, they may not report some of the crimes they are victims of. Some are afraid of retaliation from the offenders if they report the crimes, and others dislike the legal processes they have to go through if they press charges. Some older people are hesitant to leave their homes for fear they will be mugged or for fear their homes will be burglarized while they are away.

Malnutrition

Older people are the most uniformly undernourished segment of our population (Papalia et al., 2012). Chronic malnutrition of older people exists because of transportation difficulties in getting to grocery stores; lack of knowledge about proper nutrition; lack of money to purchase a well-balanced diet; poor teeth and lack of good dentures, which greatly limit the diet; lack of incentives to prepare an appetizing meal when one is living alone; and inadequate cooking and storage facilities.

Health Problems and Cost of Care

As noted earlier, the proportion of older people in our society is increasing dramatically, and the old-old (age 85 and over) is the most rapidly growing age group. Today, there is a crisis in health care for older people. There are a variety of reasons for this.

As described in Chapter 14, older people are much more apt to have long-term illnesses. In the 1960s, the Medicare and Medicaid programs were created to pay for much of their medical costs. Due to the high costs of these programs, the Reagan-Bush administrations in the 1980s said the government could no longer pay the full costs of that care, and as a result, there were cuts in eligibility for payment and limits set for what the government will pay for a variety of medical procedures.

A national debate is raging over how to reduce the funds the federal government spends on Medicare and Medicaid, including after the passage of President

Obama's health-care plan in 2010. (Medicare and Medicaid are described later in this chapter.) One faction asserts that limits have to be set on the annual amount spent on these programs in order to keep the programs solvent. (See Highlight 16.1: The Tea Party—which wants drastic cuts in federal funding for Social Security, Medicare, and Medicaid.) Another faction claims that these programs are providing essential medical care to older people and to the poor, and that setting additional limits on funds will result in more serious untreated illnesses and a higher risk of death for these two at-risk populations.

Physicians are primarily trained in treating the young, and generally they are less interested in serving older people. As a result, when older people become ill, they often do not receive quality medical care.

Medical conditions of older people are often misdiagnosed, as physicians receive little specialized training in the unique medical conditions of older people. Many of those who are seriously ill do not get medical attention. One of the reasons physicians are not interested in treating older people is the problem of reimbursement. The Medicare program sets reimbursement limits on a variety of procedures; as a result, most physicians prefer to work with younger patients, where the fee-for-service system is much more profitable.

In addition, older people who live in the community often have transportation difficulties in getting medical care. Those living in nursing homes sometimes receive inadequate care, because some health professionals assume that such patients haven't much time to live and, as a result, providers may be less interested in providing high-quality medical care. Medical care for older people is becoming a national embarrassment because of the low quality of care that is often provided.

 HIGHLIGHT 16.1

The Tea Party Movement and Federal Funding of Social Programs

The Tea Party movement is a political movement that is generally recognized as conservative and libertarian. (The Libertarian Party is the third largest political party in the United States; it favors minimally regulated, laissez-faire markets; strong civil liberties; reduced government spending; minimally regulated migration across borders; the avoidance of foreign military or economic entanglements with other nations; and respect for freedom of travel to all foreign countries.)

The Tea Party movement endorses reduced government spending, opposition to many current taxation policies, and reduction of the federal budget deficit and the national debt. The name "Tea Party" is a reference to the Boston Tea Party, a protest by colonists who objected to a British tax on tea in 1773 and demonstrated by dumping British tea taken from docked ships into the harbor. Tea Party advocates want to sharply reduce spending on social welfare programs—including Social Security benefits, Medicare, Medicaid, unemployment insurance, and Obama care.

They also want to curtail the power of trade unions, and are against raising tax rates for millionaires.

Robert Reich asserts that the Tea Party is the rebirth of Social Darwinism.[a] Social Darwinism was based on Charles Darwin's theory of evolution. Darwin theorized that higher forms of life evolved from lower forms by the process of survival of the fittest; he had seen in the animal world a fierce struggle for survival that destroyed the weak, rewarded the strong, and produced evolutionary change. Herbert Spencer extended this theory to humanity: Struggle, destruction, and survival of the fit were thought to be essential to progress in human society as well.[b] The theory stated in its most inhumane form that the strong (the wealthy) survived because they were superior, whereas the weak (the needy) deserved to perish; it would be a mistake to help the weak survive.

Social Darwinism was used by the wealthy and powerful to argue that the government should not spend money on social programs to help the lower- and middle-income classes. The federal government rejected social Darwinism around the early 1900s. A large variety of social and educational programs (such as the 1935 Social Security Act) were created to assist all Americans. Higher-income people were taxed (along with lower income people) to invest in social programs, public schools, public transportation, public universities, and public health—programs that made us all better-off. Social Darwinism was rejected.

However, is the Tea Party movement designed to resurrect Social Darwinism?

SOURCES: (a) Robert Reich, http://www.readersupportednews.org/opinion2/277-75/7423-focus-the-rebirth-of-social. (b) Herbert Spencer (1873). *The Study of Sociology,* Ann Arbor: University of Michigan Press.

LO 16-2 Describe the Current Services to Meet These Problems and Identify Gaps in These Services

Current Services: Macro-System Responses

Present services and programs for older people are primarily maintenance in nature, as they are mainly designed to meet basic physical needs. Nonetheless, there are a number of programs, often federally funded, that provide services needed by older people. Before we briefly review many of these programs, we will look at the Older Americans Act of 1965, which set forth objectives for such programs.

Older Americans Act of 1965

The Older Americans Act of 1965 created an operating agency (Administration on Aging) within the Department of Health, Education, and Welfare (now the Department of Health and Human Services). This law and its amendments are the basis for federal aid to states and local communities to meet the needs of older people. The objectives of the act are to secure for older people:

- An adequate income
- Best possible physical and mental health
- Suitable housing
- Restorative services for those who require institutionalized care
- Opportunity for employment
- Retirement in health, honor, and dignity
- Pursuit of meaningful activity
- Efficient community services
- Immediate benefit from research knowledge to sustain and improve health and happiness
- Freedom, independence, and the free exercise of individual initiative in planning and managing their own lives (U.S. Department of Health, Education, and Welfare, 1970)

Although these objectives are commendable, they have not been realized for many older people. However, some progress has been made. Many states have offices on aging, and some municipalities and counties have established community councils on aging. Numerous universities have established centers for gerontology, which focus on research on older people

and training of students for working with older people in such disciplines as nursing, psychology, medicine, sociology, social work, and architecture. (*Gerontology* is the scientific study of the aging process from physiological, pathological, psychological, sociological, and economic points of view.) Government research grants are being given to encourage the study of older people and their problems. Publishers are now producing books and pamphlets to inform the public about older people, and a few high schools are beginning to offer courses to help teenagers understand older people and their circumstances.

Numerous programs, often federally funded and administered at state or local levels, provide funds and services needed by older people. Some of these programs are briefly described in the following sections.

Old Age, Survivors, Disability, and Health Insurance (OASDHI)

The OASDHI social insurance program[1] was created by the 1935 Social Security Act. OASDHI is usually referred to as Social Security by the general public. It is an income insurance program designed to partially replace income lost when a worker retires or becomes disabled. Cash benefits are also paid to survivors of insured workers.

Payments to beneficiaries are based on previous earnings. Rich as well as poor are eligible if insured. Benefits can be provided to fully insured workers as early as age 62—although those who seek benefits before the full retirement age receive smaller benefits. The full retirement age is gradually increasing for those who are born after 1937, as shown on the following chart:

Year of Birth	Full Retirement Age
1937 (or earlier)	65
1938	65 and 2 months
1939	65 and 4 months
1940	65 and 6 months
1941	65 and 8 months
1942	65 and 10 months
1943–1954	66

(continued)

[1]Social insurance programs are financed by a tax on employees, employers, or both. In contrast, public assistance benefits are paid from general government revenues (such as those raised by income taxes). In our society, receiving social insurance benefits is generally considered a right, whereas receiving public assistance is often stigmatized as charity.

(continued)

Year of Birth	Full Retirement Age
1955	66 and 2 months
1956	66 and 4 months
1957	66 and 6 months
1958	66 and 8 months
1959	66 and 10 months
1960 (or later)	67

Dependent husbands and wives over 62 and dependent children under 18 are also eligible for benefits. (There is no age limit on disabled children who become disabled before 18.)

Participation in this insurance program is compulsory for most employees, including the self-employed. The program is generally financed by a payroll tax (FICA, Federal Insurance Contributions Act) assessed equally to employer and employee; the self-employed are required to pay both parts. The rate has gone up gradually. Eligibility for benefits is based on the number of years in which Social Security taxes have been paid and the amount earned while working.

Supplemental Security Income (SSI)

Under the SSI program, the federal government makes monthly payments to people in financial need who are 65 years of age or older or to persons of any age who are legally blind or disabled. In order to qualify for payments, applicants must have no (or very little) regular cash income, own little property, and have little cash or few assets (such as jewelry, stocks, bonds, or other valuables) that could be turned into cash.

The SSI program became effective on January 1, 1974. The word *supplemental* in the program's name is used because, in most cases, payments supplement whatever other income may be available to the claimant. Because OASDHI monthly payments are often low, SSI sometimes supplements even that income source.

SSI provides a guaranteed minimum income (an income floor) for older people, the legally blind, and the disabled. Administration of SSI has been assigned to the Social Security Administration. Financing of the program is through federal tax dollars, primarily from income taxes.

Medicare

In 1965, Congress enacted the Medicare program (Title XVIII of the Social Security Act). Medicare helps older people pay the high cost of health care.

It has two parts: hospital insurance (Part A) and supplementary medical insurance (Part B). Everyone 65 or older who is entitled to monthly benefits under the OASDHI program gets Part A automatically, without paying a monthly premium. Nearly everyone in the United States 65 or older is eligible for Part B; Part B is voluntary, and beneficiaries are charged a monthly premium. Disabled people under age 65 who have been getting Social Security benefits for 24 consecutive months are also eligible for both Part A and Part B, effective in the 25th month of disability.

Part A helps pay for time-limited care in a hospital, in a skilled nursing facility, and for home health visits (such as visiting nurses). Coverage is limited to 150 days in a hospital and to 100 days in a skilled nursing facility. If patients are able to be out of a hospital or nursing facility for 60 consecutive days following confinement, they are again eligible for coverage. Covered services in a hospital or skilled nursing facility include the cost of meals and a semi-private room, regular nursing services, drugs, supplies, and appliances. Part A also covers home health care on a part-time or intermittent basis if beneficiaries meet the following conditions: They are homebound, in need of skilled nursing care or physical or speech therapy, and services are ordered and regularly reviewed by a physician. Finally, Part A covers up to 210 days of hospice care for a terminally ill Medicare beneficiary.

Part B helps pay for physicians' services, outpatient hospital services in an emergency room, outpatient physical and speech therapy, and a number of other medical and health services prescribed by a doctor, such as diagnostic services, X-ray or other radiation treatments, and some ambulance services.

Each Medicare beneficiary has the choice of selecting, from an alphabet soup of health plans, which plan he or she will be in. The variety of plans includes preferred provider organizations, provider service organizations, point-of-service plans, private fee-for-service plans, and medical savings accounts. (Details can be obtained from your local Social Security Administration office.)

Prescription Drug Assistance for Seniors

The cost of prescription drugs is a major concern for older people who live on fixed incomes. Individuals without a health insurance plan that covers prescription drugs and individuals with incomes just high enough to put them over the threshold for Medicaid eligibility must often pay high costs for medications out of their own pocket. Some older people make hard choices between paying for medications and essentials such as food or fuel.

In December 2003, President George W. Bush signed into law the Medicare Prescription Drug Improvement and Modernization Act of 2003. The program is designed to assist older people, especially low-income older people, to purchase prescription drugs at lower costs. (Details of the plan are complex; information can be obtained from your local Social Security Administration office.)

Medicaid

Medicaid was established in 1965 by Title XIX of the Social Security Act. Medicaid primarily provides medical care for recipients of public assistance. It enables states to pay hospitals, nursing homes, medical societies, and insurance agencies for services provided to recipients of public assistance. Many of these recipients are indigent elderly, some of whom are in nursing homes. The federal government shares the expenses with the states on a 55–45 basis for recipients of public assistance. Medical expenses covered under Medicaid include diagnosis and therapy performed by surgeons, physicians, and dentists; nursing services in the home or elsewhere; and medical supplies, drugs, and laboratory fees.

Medicaid benefits vary from state to state. The original legislation encouraged states to include coverage of all self-supporting persons whose marginal income made them unable to pay for medical care. However, this inclusion is not mandatory, and most states provide insurance coverage primarily to recipients of public assistance.

Obama's Health-Care Reform

For many years the United States, unlike most other developed countries, did not have a universal health-care system. In 2009, President Obama proposed, and Congress passed in 2010, the Health Care Reform bill. This program is also called Obamacare. Health Care Reform has numerous provisions. The provisions that most impact older persons will briefly be summarized (Barry, 2010):

● Once reform is fully implemented, **over 95 percent of Americans will have health insurance coverage**,

including 32 million who were currently uninsured in 2010.
● Health insurance companies will **no longer be allowed to deny people coverage** because of preexisting conditions—or to drop coverage when people become sick.
● Individuals and small businesses who can't afford to purchase insurance on their own will be able to pool together and **choose from a variety of competing plans with lower premiums**.
● Health care will be **more affordable for families and small businesses thanks to new tax credits**, subsidies, and other assistance—paid for largely by taxing insurance companies, drug companies, and the very wealthiest Americans.
● **Seniors on Medicare will pay less for their prescription drugs** because the legislation closes the "donut hole" gap in existing coverage. (There was a gap, prior to Health Care Reform, in the Prescription Drug Assistance for Seniors. This gap, called the donut hole, is the difference of the initial coverage limit and the catastrophic coverage threshold.)
● **Medicaid will be expanded** to offer health insurance coverage to an additional 16 million low-income people.

Food Stamps

The Food Stamp Program is designed to combat hunger. Food stamps are available to public assistance recipients and to other low-income families, including older people, who qualify. These stamps are then used to purchase groceries. The program is also called Supplemental Nutritional Assistance Program (SNAP).

Adult Protective Services

Adult protective services are offered in practically all communities, usually by human services departments. Although these services are offered widely, the public is largely unaware of them. About one in every 20 older people probably needs some form of protective services, and this proportion is expected to increase as the proportion of people over age 75 increases (Papalia et al., 2012). Protective services are for adults who are being neglected or abused or for adults whose physical or mental capacities have substantially deteriorated. The aim of adult protective services is to help older people, and adults with disabilities, meet their needs in their own home if possible. Alternative placements include foster care, group home care, and special housing units (such as apartments for older people). Services provided include homemaker services, counseling, rehabilitation, medical services, visiting nursing services, Meals on Wheels, and transportation. Highlight 16.2 illustrates some of the help that an Adult Protective Services agency might offer.

 HIGHLIGHT 16.2

Adult Protective Services

The Dodge City Human Services Department received a complaint from a neighbor of Jack and Rosella McArron that the McArrons were living in health-threatening conditions and that Mr. McArron was frequently abusing his wife.

Vincent Rudd, an Adult Protective Services worker, investigated the complaint. When he arrived at the door, Jack McArron appeared in shabby, dirty clothes with a can of beer in his hand and refused entry to Mr. Rudd. Mr. Rudd heard someone moaning in the background, so he went to the nearest service station and called the police department. Together, Mr. Rudd and a police officer returned to the McArrons. The officer informed Mr. McArron that a protective services complaint had been made and that an investigation must be made. Mr. McArron grudgingly let the officer and Mr. Rudd in.

The inside of the house appeared not to have been cleaned for years. Newspapers and dirty clothes were heaped together in piles on the floor. The dining room table was covered with dust, cigarette butts, beer cans, whiskey bottles, and dirty dishes. The plumbing was not working. Cockroaches were seen. The house had a wood-burning stove that was covered with dirt and a burned crust. At the very least, the place appeared to be a firetrap. There was a stench that was largely due to urine.

Mr. McArron appeared to be intoxicated. Mrs. McArron was found moaning in the bedroom. Mr. McArron stated that she had arthritis and had slipped on the stairs. He further stated that her demands and her behavior were driving him to drink. Her hair was greasy and appeared not to have been washed for months. She was wearing a torn nightgown that smelled of urine. She was very thin, wrinkled, and had a variety of cuts and bruises. Her mutterings were difficult to understand, but she seemed to be saying that her husband had been battering her for months.

Rosella McArron was taken to a hospital, where she spent two and a half weeks. (She was found to be 66 years old, and her husband, 69.) At first she wouldn't eat, so she was fed intravenously. After several days, she became more alert. Daily baths improved her appearance. It became clear that she had been frequently abused by her husband for more than a decade. She was also found to have severe arthritis and diabetes. In the hospital, she stated that she did not want to return to live with her husband because of the beatings. She was placed in a foster home.

The McArrons' neighbors were interviewed. They reported that Jack McArron had had a drinking problem for years and that the neighbors seldom saw him sober. The neighbors were afraid of what he might do when intoxicated. He frequently beat his wife and was loud and obnoxious, and the neighbors were fearful he might kill someone while driving under the influence. Mr. McArron was taken to a 30-day drug treatment center. Records showed he had been admitted to this center on seven previous occasions. This time, a physician found evidence that Mr. McArron was suffering from brain deterioration due to chronic alcoholism. He seemed to be paranoid as he talked about his neighbors being gangsters. He stated that they were stealing his possessions. As the days went by, he started blaming the police and protective services for kidnapping his wife and talked about getting her back. He stated, "I'm goin' lookin' for her with my shotgun, and I'll blast anyone who gets in my way." With his increasingly paranoid statements, the staff was reluctant to let Mr. McArron return to his home, as it was felt that if he became intoxicated he could be dangerous. His mental capacities were deteriorating, and he was found to have a severe case of cirrhosis of the liver. As a result, procedures were followed to have a court declare him incompetent, to appoint a younger cousin as guardian, and to place Mr. McArron in a nursing home.

After Mrs. McArron had been in the foster home for several weeks, she said that she wanted to return to live with her husband. She was informed that her husband was in a nursing home. She visited him on several occasions and became increasingly depressed about his deteriorating condition. She began talking about wanting to die. About a year and a half later, she did die—of a massive heart attack. Her husband's condition in the nursing home continued to deteriorate.

Vincent Rudd often thought about this case. It seemed that the intervention that resulted in Jack and Rosella's being separated from each other was in some way a factor in facilitating both their mental and emotional deterioration. Breaking a husband–wife bond had unexpected adverse consequences. But what were the alternatives? They seemed to be killing each other by living together. Mr. Rudd realized that intervention in social work is a matter of judgment; all anyone can do is give it his or her best shot.

Additional Programs

Additional programs for older people include the following:

- *Meals on Wheels* provides hot and cold meals to housebound recipients who are incapable of obtaining or preparing their own meals, but who can feed themselves.
- *Senior-citizen centers*, golden-age clubs, and similar groups provide leisure time and recreational activities for older people.
- *Special bus rates* reduce bus transportation costs for older people.
- *Property tax relief* is available to older people in many states.
- *Housing projects* for older people are built by local sponsors with financing assistance from the Department of Housing and Urban Development.
- *Reduced rates* at movie theaters and other places of entertainment are often offered voluntarily by individual owners.
- *Home health services* provide visiting nurse services, physical therapy, drugs, laboratory services, and sickroom equipment.
- *Nutrition programs* provide meals for older people at group eating sites. (These meals, generally provided four or five times a week, are usually luncheon meals.)
- *Homemaker services* perform household tasks that older people are no longer able to do for themselves.
- *Day-care centers* for older people provide activities that are determined by the needs of the group.
- *Telephone reassurance* is provided by volunteers, often older persons, who telephone older people who live alone. (Such calls are a meaningful form of social contact for both parties, and they also ascertain whether any serious problems have arisen that require emergency attention.)
- *Lifeline assistance* is available for people who are prone to fall and have difficulty getting back on their feet. The lifeline is a device that is worn around the neck or wrist. The fallen person presses a button, which alerts the Lifeline Response Center. The Response Center then sends help, which may be a neighbor, family member, or an ambulance.
- *Nursing homes* provide residential care and skilled nursing care when independence is no longer practical for older people who cannot take care of themselves or whose families can no longer take care of them.

- *Congregate housing facilities* are private or government-subsidized apartment complexes, hotels remodeled to meet the needs of independent older adults, or mobile home parks designed for older adults. They provide meals, housekeeping, transportation, social and recreational activities, and sometimes health care.
- *Group homes* provide housing for some older residents. A group home is usually a house owned or rented by a social agency. Employees are hired to shop, cook, do heavy cleaning, drive, and give counseling. Residents take care of many of their own personal needs and take some responsibility for day-to-day tasks.
- *Assisted-living facilities* allow older people to live semi-independently. People living in such a facility have their own rooms or apartments. Residents receive personal care (bathing, dressing, and grooming), meals, housekeeping, transportation, and social and recreational activities.
- *Foster-care homes* are usually single-family residences whose owners take in an unrelated older adult and are reimbursed for providing housing, meals, housekeeping, and personal care.
- *Continued-care retirement communities* are long-term housing facilities designed to provide a full range of accommodations and services for affluent older people as their needs change. A resident may start out living in an independent apartment; then move into a congregate housing unit with such services as cleaning, laundry, and meals; then move to an assisted-living facility; and finally move into an adjoining nursing home.
- *Nursing home ombudsman programs* investigate and act on concerns expressed by residents in nursing homes.

Nursing Homes

Nursing homes were created as an alternative to expensive hospital care and are substantially supported by the federal government through Medicaid and Medicare. About 1.8 million older people now live in extended-care facilities, making nursing homes a billion-dollar industry. There are more patient beds in nursing homes than in hospitals (Mooney et al., 2013).

Nursing homes are classified according to the kind of care they provide. At one end of the scale, there are residential homes that provide primarily room and board, with some nonmedical care (such as help in dressing). At the other end of the scale are nursing-care centers that provide skilled nursing and medical attention 24 hours a day. The more skilled and extensive the medical care given, the more expensive the home. The costs per resident average about $6,000 a month (Papalia et al., 2012) (U.S. Census Bureau, 2010). About 4.5 percent of adults 65 years of age and older reside in a nursing home at any point in time (Papalia et al., 2012).

There have been many media reports of the atrocious care that some nursing homes have provided to their residents. Patients have been found lying in their own feces or urine. Food may be so unappetizing that some residents refuse to eat it. Some homes have serious safety hazards. Boredom and apathy are common among staff as well as residents. A study in 2001 found that a third of the nursing homes in the United States had been cited by state inspectors as being abusive to residents in 1999 and 2000 ("Some Golden Years," 2001).

Numerous nursing homes fail to meet food sanitation standards and have problems administering drugs and providing personal hygiene for residents (Kornblum & Julian, 2012).

There is evidence of patients being abused in nursing homes (Kornblum & Julian, 2012). Signs of nursing home abuse include:

- Physical injuries, including broken bones, internal bleeding, bedsores, medication overdose, head injury, malnutrition, bruises, and joint dislocation
- Signs of neglect, including malnourishment, poor hygiene, soiled bedding, dehydration, and hazardous or unsanitary living conditions
- Emotional or behavioral changes, such as withdrawal, agitation, anxiety or fear, frequent crying, and strained relationships with nursing staff

At present, people of all ages tend to be prejudiced against nursing homes, even those that are well run. The average senior citizen looks at a nursing home as a human junkyard. And there is some truth to the notion that most nursing homes are places where older people wait to die.

Ethical Question 16.3

EP 2.1.2

If you were mentally competent but physically incapacitated, would you agree to being placed in a nursing home?

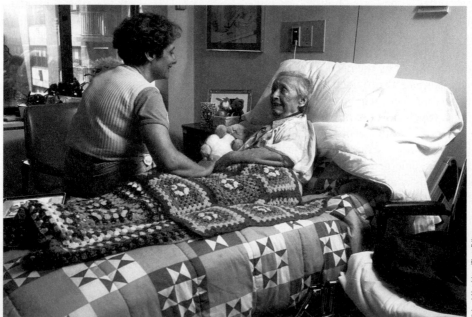

Support from family and friends is important to people living in nursing homes. Here a daughter tucks her mother's favorite afghan around her.

Richard Hutchings/PhotoEdit

The cost of care for impoverished nursing home residents is largely paid by the Medicaid program. Because the federal government has set limits on what will be reimbursed under Medicaid, certain problems may arise. There may be an effort to keep salary and wage levels as low as possible and the number of staff to a minimum. A nursing home may postpone repairs and improvements. Food is apt to be inexpensive, such as macaroni and cheese, which his high in fat and carbohydrates. Congress has mandated that every nursing home patient on Medicaid is entitled to a monthly spending allowance. However, the homes have control over these funds, and some homes keep the money.

Complaints about the physical facilities of nursing homes include not enough floor space or too many people in a room. The call light by the bed may be difficult to reach, or the toilets and showers may not be conveniently located. And the building may be in a state of decay.

Although the quality of nursing home care ranges from excellent to awful, nursing homes are needed, particularly for those requiring round-the-clock health care for an extended time. If nursing homes were abolished, other institutions such as hospitals would have to serve this need. Life in nursing homes need not be bad. When homes are properly administered, residents can expand their life experiences.

The ideal nursing home should be lively (with recreational, social, and educational programming), safe, hygienic, and attractive. It should offer stimulating activities and opportunities to socialize with people of both sexes and all ages. It should offer privacy so that (among other reasons) residents can be sexually active. It should offer a wide range of therapeutic, social, recreational, and rehabilitative services. The best care tends to be provided by larger nonprofit facilities that have a high ratio of nurses to nurse's aides (Papalia et al., 2012).

Social Work with Older People

Social work education is taking a leading role in identifying the problems of older people and is developing gerontological specializations within the curricula. Social workers are a significant part of the staff of most agencies serving older people. Some states, for example, are now requiring that each nursing home employ a social worker. Following are some of the services needed by older adults in which social workers have expertise:

- *Brokering services.* Most communities have a wide range of services available, but few people are knowledgeable about the array of services or the eligibility requirements. Older people are in special need of this brokering service, because some have difficulty with transportation and communication and others may be reluctant to ask for the assistance to which they are entitled.
- *Case management or care management services.* Social workers are trained to assess the social service needs of a client and the client's family. When appropriate, the social worker case-manages by arranging, coordinating, monitoring, evaluating, and advocating for a package of multiple services to meet the often complex needs of an older client. Common functions of most case management programs for older people include case finding, pre-screening, intake, assessment, goal setting, care planning, capacity building, care plan implementation, reassessment, and termination.
- *Advocacy.* Because of shortcomings in services for older adults in our society, social workers at times need to advocate for needed services.
- *Individual and family counseling.* Counseling interventions focus on examination of the older client's needs and strengths, the family's needs and strengths, and the resources available to meet the identified needs.
- *Grief counseling.* Older people are apt to need counseling for role loss (such as retirement or loss of self-sufficiency), loss of a significant other (such as a spouse, a child, or an adult sibling), and loss due to chronic health or mental health conditions.
- *Adult day-care services.* Social workers provide individual and family counseling, outreach and broker services, supportive services, group work services, and care-planning services for older people being served by adult day-care services.
- *Crisis intervention services.* Social workers providing crisis intervention seek to stabilize the crisis situation and connect the older person and the family to needed supportive services.
- *Adult foster-care services.* Foster care and group homes are designed to help the older person remain in the community. Social workers

providing foster care match foster families with older people and monitor the quality of life for those living in foster-care settings.

- *Adult protective services.* Social workers in adult protective services assess whether older adults are at risk for personal harm or injury owing to the actions (or inactions) of others. At-risk circumstances include physical abuse, material (financial) abuse, psychological abuse, and neglect (in which caregivers withhold medications or nourishment, or fail to provide basic care). If abuse or neglect is determined, then Adult Protective Service workers develop, implement, and monitor a plan to stop the maltreatment.
- *Self-help and therapeutic groups.* In some settings, social workers facilitate the formation of self-help groups and therapeutic groups for older people or for family members (some of whom may be caregivers). Self-help and therapeutic groups are useful for such issues as adjusting to retirement, coping with illnesses such as Alzheimer's disease, dealing with alcohol or other drug abuse, coping with a terminal illness, and coping with depression and other emotional difficulties.
- *Respite care.* Social workers are involved with the recruitment and training of respite-care workers, as well as in identifying families in need of these services. When an older person requires 24-hour at-home care, respite services allow caregivers (such as the spouse or other family members) time away from caregiving responsibilities, which alleviates some of the stress involved in providing 24-hour-a-day care.
- *Transportation and housing assistance.* Social workers operate as brokers for finding appropriate housing in the community and for arranging safe transportation services.
- *Social services in hospitals and nursing homes.* Social workers in these settings provide assessment of social needs; health education for the older person and the family; direct services (such as counseling) to the older person, the family, and significant others; advocacy; discharge planning; community liaison; participation in program planning; consultation on developing a therapeutic environment in the facility; and participation in developing care plans that maximize the older person's potential for independence.

Because the older population is the most rapidly growing age group in our society, it is anticipated that services for older people will significantly expand in the next few decades. This expansion will generate a number of new employment opportunities for social workers.

LO 16-3 Understand the Emergence of Older People as a Significant Political Force in Our Society

Older People: A Powerful Political Force

Most programs for older people are designed to maintain them at their current level of functioning rather than to enhance their social, physical, and psychological well-being. Despite all the maintenance programs available for older people, key problems remain to be solved. A high propor-

EP 2.1.8a

tion of older people do not have meaningful lives, respected status, or adequate income, transportation, living arrangements, diet, or health care. How can we defend urging people to retire when they are still productive? How can we defend the living conditions within some of our nursing homes? How can we defend our restrictive attitudes toward sexuality among older people? How can we defend providing services to older people that are limited to maintenance and subsistence? Moss and Moss (1975) comment, "Just as we are learning that black can be beautiful, so we must learn that gray can be beautiful too. In so learning, we may brighten the prospects of our old age" (p. 79).

Older people are victims of ageism. In the past, prejudice has been most effectively combated when those being discriminated against joined together for political action. It seems apparent that if major changes in the role of older people in society are to take place, they will have to be made through political action.

Older people are, in fact, increasingly involved in political activism and, in some cases, even radical militancy. A prominent organization is the AARP (formerly the American Association of Retired Persons). This group lobbies for the interests of old people at local, state, and federal levels of government.

An action-oriented group that has caught the public's attention is the Gray Panthers. This organization argues that a fundamental flaw in our society is the emphasis on materialism and on the consumption of goods and services, rather than on improving the quality of life for all citizens (including older adults). The Gray Panthers seek to end ageism and to advance the goals of human freedom, human dignity, and self-development. This organization uses social action techniques, including getting older people to vote as a bloc for their concerns. Founder Maggie Kuhn (quoted in Butler, 1975) stated, "We are not mellow, sweet old people. We have got to effect change, and we have nothing to lose" (p. 341).

Another reason older people are a powerful political group is that they are more likely to vote than the young (Kornblum & Julian, 2012). And older people will be more politically active in the future because the composition of the older population is changing. The average educational level of this population has been steadily increasing (Mooney et al., 2013). The coming generation of older people will be better educated, better informed, and more politically conscious.

Significant steps toward securing a better life for older adults have been made in the last 50 years: increased Social Security payments, enactment of the Medicare and Medicaid programs, the emergence of hospices, and the expansion of a variety of other programs. With older people becoming a powerful political bloc, we are apt to see a number of changes in future years to improve the status of older people in our society.

LO 16-4 Describe a Proposal to Provide Older People with a Meaningful, Productive Social Role in Our Society

Changing a Macro System: Finding a Social Role for Older People

As we have discussed, older adults face a variety of problems. They have a roleless role in our society and are the victims of ageism. How can these problems be combated?

In a nutshell, it would seem essential to find a meaningful, productive role for older people. At present, early retirement programs and stereotypic expectations

of older adults often result in their being unproductive, inactive, dependent, and unfulfilled. To develop a meaningful role for older people in our society, productive older adults should be encouraged to continue to work, and the expectations of older people should be changed.

Older adults who want to work and are still performing well should be encouraged to continue working past age 65 or 70. Also, older people who want to work half-time or part-time should be encouraged to do so. For example, two older persons working half-time could fill a full-time position. New roles might also be created for retired older people to be consultants in the areas where they possess special knowledge and expertise. For those who do retire, there should be educational and training programs to help them develop their interests and hobbies into new sources of income.

Working longer would have a number of payoffs for older people and for society. Older people would continue to be productive, contributing citizens. They would have meaningful roles. They would continue to be physically and mentally active. They would have higher self-esteem. They would begin to break down the stereotypes of older people being unproductive and a financial burden on society. They would be paying into the Social Security system rather than drawing from it.

In our materialistic society, perhaps the only way for older people to have meaningful roles is to be productive, either as paid workers or as volunteers. Older people face the choice (as do younger people) between having adequate financial resources through productive work or inadequate financial resources as a result of not working.

Objections to such a system may be raised by those who maintain that some older people are no longer productive. This may be true, but some younger people are also unproductive. What is needed to make the proposed system work is jobs with realistic, objective, and behaviorally measurable levels of performance. Those at any age who do not meet the performance levels should be informed about their deficiencies and be given training to meet the deficiencies. If the performance levels still are not met, discharge should be used as a last resort. For example, if a tenured faculty member is deficient in levels of performance—as measured by student course evaluations, peer faculty evaluations of teaching, record of public service, record of service to the department and to the campus, and record of publications—he or she should be informed of the deficiencies. Training and other resources to meet the deficiencies should be offered. If the performance levels do not improve to acceptable standards, dismissal proceedings would be initiated. Some colleges and universities are now moving in this direction.

In the productivity system being suggested, older people would have an important part to play. They would be expected to continue to be productive within their capacities. By being productive, they would serve as examples to counter negative stereotypes of older people.

Another objection we have heard to this new system is that older adults have worked most of their lives and deserve to retire and live in leisure with a comfortable standard of living. It would be nice if older people really had this option. However, that is not realistic. Most older people do not have the financial resources after retiring to maintain a high standard of living. Most older retirees experience sharply reduced incomes and standards of living. The choice in our society is really between working and thereby maintaining a comfortable standard of living, or retiring and having a lower standard of living.

We are already seeing older adults heading in a more productive direction. Numerous organizations have been formed to promote the productivity of older people. Three examples are the Retired Senior Volunteer Program, the Service Corps of Retired Executives, and the Foster Grandparent Program.

The *Retired Senior Volunteer Program (RSVP)* offers people over age 60 the opportunity of doing volunteer service to meet community needs. RSVP agencies place volunteers in hospitals, schools, libraries, day-care centers, courts, nursing homes, and a variety of other places.

The *Service Corps of Retired Executives (SCORE)* offers retired businesspeople an opportunity to help owners of small businesses and managers of community organizations who are having management problems. Volunteers receive no pay but are reimbursed for out-of-pocket expenses.

The *Foster Grandparent Program* employs low-income older people to provide personal care to children who live in institutions. Such children include those with developmental disabilities and those who have emotional or behavioral difficulties. Foster grandparents are given special assignments in child care, speech therapy, physical therapy, or as teachers' aides. This program has been shown to be of

considerable benefit to both the children and the foster grandparents (Atchley, 1988). The children served become more outgoing and have improved relationships with peers and staff. They have increased self-confidence, improved language skills, and decreased fear and insecurity. The foster grandparents have an additional (small) source of income, increased feelings of vigor and youthfulness, an increased sense of personal worth, a feeling of being productive, and a renewed sense of personal growth and development. For society, foster grandparents provide a vast pool of relatively inexpensive labor that can be used to do needed work in the community.

The success of these programs illustrates that older people can be productive in both paid and volunteer positions. Atchley (1988) makes the following recommendations for using older volunteers:

First, agencies must be flexible in matching the volunteer's background to assigned tasks. If the agency takes a broad perspective, useful work can be found for almost anyone. Second, volunteers must be trained. All too often agency personnel place unprepared volunteers in an unfamiliar setting. Then the volunteer's difficulty confirms the myth that you cannot expect good work from volunteers. Third, a variety of placement options should be offered to the volunteer. Some volunteers prefer to do familiar things; others want to do anything but familiar things. Fourth, training of volunteers should not make them feel that they are being tested. This point is particularly sensitive among working-class volunteers. Fifth, volunteers should get personal attention from the placement agency. There should be people (perhaps volunteers) who follow up on absences and who are willing to listen to the compliments, complaints, or experiences of the volunteers. Public recognition from the community is an important reward for voluntary service. Finally, transportation to and from the placement should be provided. (p. 216)

Ethical Question 16.4

If you were physically and mentally healthy and in your 70s, would you continue to be employed?

EP 2.1.2

HIGHLIGHT 16.3

John Glenn, One of the Many Productive Older People

John Glenn was born July 18, 1921, in Cambridge, Ohio. He entered the Naval Aviation Cadet program in March 1942 and later graduated from this program. He was commissioned in the Marine Corps in 1943. During World War II, he flew 59 combat missions; during the Korean War, he flew 63 missions. In the last nine days of fighting in Korea, Glenn downed three MIGs. He was awarded the Distinguished Flying Cross six times.

In 1959, Glenn was selected as a Project Mercury astronaut. A few years later, he became the first American to orbit the earth, and as a result, he became a national hero. He retired from the Marine Corps in 1965 and became a business executive. In November 1974, he was elected to the U.S. Senate, where he served with distinction until he retired in 1999.

John Glenn was not yet done. He offered himself as a human guinea pig by volunteering to go on a nine-day space

shuttle mission so that scientists could study the effects of space travel on an older person. Candidates for space travel of any age have to pass stringent physical and mental tests. Glenn was in such superb physical condition that he passed the examinations with flying colors. He then spent nearly 500 hours in training.

Discovery blasted off from the Kennedy Space Center at Cape Canaveral on October 29, 1998, with John Glenn on board. At age 77, he became a space pioneer—and national hero—for the second time. When *Discovery* returned to earth nine days later, Glenn, though weak and wobbly, walked out of the shuttle on his own two feet. Within four days, he had fully recovered his balance and was completely back to normal. Among other accomplishments, this flight challenged common negative stereotypes about aging.

Is there any evidence to support the hypothesis that productive activity, either paid or unpaid, is a key to aging well? Glass, Seeman, Herzog, Kahn, and Berkman (1995) compared nearly 1,200 men and women (ages 70 to 79) who showed high physical and cognitive functioning ("successful agers") with 162 medium- and low-functioning adults in the same age group ("usual agers"). Nearly all successful agers and more than nine out of 10 usual agers engaged in some form of productive activity. A key finding was that successful agers were far more productive than the usual agers. On average, the successful agers were more than three times as likely to engage in paid work, did almost four times as much volunteer work, did one-third more housework, and did twice as much yard work as the usual agers. The research supports the idea that engaging in productive activity is correlated with successful aging.

Many role models of productive older people are now emerging. These role models are challenging the formerly pervasive picture of old age as a time of inevitable physical and mental decline. Many 70-year-olds are now acting, thinking, and feeling like 50-year-olds did a decade or two ago. One of these older role models is John Glenn (see Highlight 16.3).

Chapter Summary

The following summarizes this chapter's content as it relates to the learning objectives presented at the beginning of the chapter. Chapter content will help prepare students to:

LO 16-1 Summarize the specific problems faced by older people and the causes of these problems.

People 65 and older now make up more than one-tenth of the U.S. population and are the fastest-growing age group in our society. Older people tend to encounter a number of problems in our society: low status, lack of a meaningful role, an emphasis on youth, health problems, inadequate income, inadequate housing, transportation problems, elder abuse, malnutrition, crime victimization, emotional problems (particularly depression), and concern with circumstances surrounding dying. Most older people depend on the Social Security system as their major source of income, but monthly payments are inadequate.

LO 16-2 Describe the current services to meet these problems and identify gaps in these services.

Programs for older adults include Old Age, Survivors, Disability, and Health Insurance; Supplemental Security Income; Medicare; Prescription Drug

Assistance for Seniors; Medicaid; food stamps; Adult Protective Services; Meals on Wheels; senior citizen centers; day-care centers; nursing homes; assisted-living facilities; group homes; and many additional programs.

There are a number of gaps in services. Some older persons reside in substandard nursing homes, some have serious unmet health needs, and some are living in poverty.

LO 16-3 Understand the emergence of older people as a significant political force in our society.

Older people are often politically active, and many have organized to work toward improving their status. As a result, many new programs have been created in recent years, and the rate of poverty among this age group has been decreasing in recent decades.

LO 16-4 Describe a proposal to provide older people with a meaningful, productive social role in our society.

In order to provide older people with a productive, meaningful role in our society, they should be encouraged to work (either in paid work or as volunteers) as long as they are productive and have an interest in working to maintain their standard of living. Older people benefit substantially from continuing to be productive, and society benefits also from their productivity.

COMPETENCY NOTES

The following identifies where Educational Policy (EP) competencies and practice behaviors are discussed in the chapter.

EP 2.1.7a Utilize conceptual frameworks to guide the process of assessment, intervention, and evaluation.

EP 2.1.7b Critique and apply knowledge to understand person and environment.
(All of this chapter): The content of this chapter is focused on acquiring both of these practice behaviors in working with older persons.

EP 2.1.8a Analyze, formulate, and advocate for policies that advance social well-being.
(p. 736): Material is presented on analyzing, formulating, and advocating for policies that advance social well-being for older persons.

EP 2.1.2 Apply social work ethical principles to guide professional practice.
(pp. 721, 724, 725, 734, 738): Ethical questions are posed.

WEB RESOURCES

See this text's companion website at *www.cengage brain.com* for learning tools such as chapter quizzing, videos, and more.

Bibliography

Abadinsky, H. (2011). *Drug use and abuse: A comprehensive introduction*. Belmont, CA: Wadsworth.

ABC News. (2007, April 17). *Shooter, cho, "was a loner," official says*. Retrieved from http://abcnews.go.com/US/story?id=3048534

Abels, S. L. (2001). *Ethics in social work practice: Narratives for professional helping*. Denver, CO: Love.

About.com. (2014). *Gay population statistics: How many gay people are there?*. Retrieved from http://gaylife.about.com/od/comingout/a/population.htm

Adler, J. (2006, March 27). Freud in our midst. *Newsweek*, 43–47.

Adler, N. E., David, H. P., Major, B. M., Roth, S. H., Russo, N. F., & Wyatt, G. E. (1990). Psychological factors in abortion. *American Psychologist*, 47, 41–44.

Adler, R. B., & Towne, N. (1981). *Looking out/looking in* (3rd ed.). New York: Holt, Rinehart and Winston.

Ahmad, S. (1998, March 2). Get your sex insurance now: Companies are making to buy policies to protect themselves from sex harassment suits. *U.S. News & World Report*, 61.

Akers, A. Y., Holland, C. L., & Bost, J. (2011). Inteventions to improve parental communication about sex: A systematic review. *Pediatrics*, 127, 494–510.

Alberti, R. E., & Emmons, M. L. (1976a). *Assert yourself—it's your perfect right: A guide to assertive behavior*. San Luis Obispo, CA: Impact.

Alberti, R. E., & Emmons, M. L. (1976b). *Stand up, speak out, talk back!*. New York: Pocket Books.

Alberti, R. E., & Emmons, M. L. (2001). *Your perfect right* (8th ed.). Atascadero, CA: Impact.

Alberti, R., & Emmons, M. (2008). *Your perfect right* (9th ed.). Atascadero, CA: Impact.

Albin, R. S. (1977). Psychological studies of rape. *Signs*, 3, 423–435.

Albrecht, G. (1992). *The disability business: Rehabilitation in America*. Newbury Park, CA: Sage.

Alderson, K. (2013). *Counseling LGBTI clients*. Thousand Oaks, CA: Sage.

Alinsky, S. (1969). *Reveille for radicals*. New York: Basic Books.

Alinsky, S. (1972). *Rules for radicals*. New York: Random House.

Allen, J. P. (2008). The attachment system in adolescence. In J. Cassidy & P. R. Shaver (Eds.), *Handbook of attachment: Theory, research, & clinical applications* (2nd ed., pp. 419–435). New York: Guilford.

Almeida, R. (1996). Hindu, Christian, and Muslim families. In M. McGoldrick, J. Giordano, & J. K. Pearce (Eds.), *Ethnicity and family therapy* (2nd ed., pp. 395–423). New York: Guilford Press.

Almeling, R., & Tews, L. (1999). *Post-abortion issues*. Retrieved from http://womensissues.About.com

Almquist, E. M. (1995). The experiences of minority women in the United States: Intersections of race, gender, and class. In J. Freeman (Ed.), *Women: A feminist perspective* (5th ed., pp. 573–606). Mountain View, CA: Mayfield.

Altshuler, S. J. (2007). Everything you never wanted to know about special education ... and were afraid to ask (I.D.E.A.). *Journal of Social Work in Disability and Rehabilitation*, 6(1/2), 23–34.

Al-Yagon, M. (2007). Socioemotional and behavioral adjustment among school-age children with learning disabilities: The moderating role of maternal personal resources. *The Journal of Special Education*, 40, 205–217.

Amato, P. R., Booth, A., Johnson, D. R., & Rogers, S. J. (2007). *Together: How marriage in American is changing*. Cambridge, MA: Harvard University Press.

American Academy of Family Physicians (AAFP). FamilyDoctor.org. (2010, August). *Prenatal diagnosis: Amniocentesis or CVS*. Retrieved from http://familydoctor.org/online/famdocen/home/women/pregnancy/fetal/144.html

American Academy of Pediatrics (AAP). (2007, April). *TV and your family*. Retrieved from http://www.aap.org/publiced/BR_TV.htm

American Association of Intellectual and Developmental Disabilities (AAIDD). (2013). *Definition of intellectual disability*.

Retrieved from http://aaidd.org/intellectual-disability/definition#.Uqd-E5WA1bU

American Association of Sex Educators, Counselors, and Therapists (AASECT). (1995, August). International update. *Contemporary Sexuality, 29*(8), 8–9.

American Association of Sexuality Educators, Counselors and Therapists (AASECT). (1998, November). Homophobia: Six perspectives. *Contemporary Sexuality, 52*(11), 1–9.

American Association of Sexuality Educators, Counselors and Therapists (AASECT). (2000, April). Vermont house passes "civil union" measure for same-sex couples. *Contemporary Sexuality, 34*(A), 6.

American Association of Sexuality Educators, Counselors and Therapists (AASECT). (2000, May). Big strides in gay civil unions, parental rights. *Contemporary Sexuality, 34*(5), 9.

American Association of Sexuality Educators, Counselors and Therapists (AASECT). (2001, November). Gay partners get relief after Sept. 11 terrorist attack. *Contemporary Sexuality, 35*(11), 7.

American Association of Sexuality Educators, Counselors and Therapists (AASECT). (2002, March). Pediatricians group backs gay parents. *Contemporary Sexuality, 36*(3), 10.

American Association of Sexuality Educators, Counselors and Therapists (AASECT). (2006, January). HRC: Corporate America more gay friendly. *Contemporary Sexuality, 59*(8), 9.

American Association of University Professors (AAUP). (2013). *Here's the news: The annual report on the economic status of the profession, 2012–2013*. Retrieved from http://www.aaup.org/report/heres-news-annual-report-economic-status-profession-2012-13

American Association of University Women (AAUW). (2013, Fall). *The simple truth about the gender pay gap*. Retrieved from http://www.aauw.org/research/the-simple-truth-about-the-gender-pay-gap/

American Association on Intellectual and Developmental Disabilities (AAIDD). (2011a). *Definition of intellectual disability*. Retrieved from http://www.aamr.org/content_100.cfm? navID=21

American Association on Intellectual and Developmental Disabilities (AAIDD). (2011b). *FAQ on intellectual disability*. Retrieved from http://www.Aamr.org/content_104.cfm?avID=22

American Cancer Society. (2010a). *Breast cancer*. Retrieved from http://www.cancer.org/Cancer/BreastCancer/DetailedGuide/index

American Cancer Society. (2010b). *Breast cancer in men*. Retrieved from http://www.cancer.org/Cancer/ BreastCancerinMen/DetailedGuide/breast-cancer-in-men-key-statistics

American Cancer Society. (2010c). *Estimated new cancer cases and deaths from all sites, U.S., 2010*. Retrieved from http://www.cancer.org/acs/groups/content/ @epidemiology surveilance/documents/document/ acspc-026210.pdf

American Cancer Society (ACS). (2012). *Benign breast conditions: Not all lumps are cancer*. Retrieved September 11, 2013, from http://www.cancer.org/treatment/understandingyour diagnosis/examsandtestdescriptions/forwomenfaingabreast biopsy/breast-biopsy-benign-breast-conditions

American Cancer Society (ACS). (2013a). *Chemotherapy for breast cancer*. Retrieved September 13, 2013, from http://www.cancer.org/cancer/breastcancer/detailedguide/breast-cancer-treating-chemotherapy

American Cancer Society (ACS). (2013b). *Hormone therapy for breast cancer*. Retrieved September 13, 2013, from http://www.cancer.org/cancer/breastcancer/detailedguide/breast-cancer-treating-hormone-therapy

American Cancer Society (ACS). (2013c). *How is breast cancer diagnosed?* Retrieved September 11, 2013, from http://www.cancer.org/cancer/breastcancer/detailedguide/breast-cancer-diagnosis

American Cancer Society (ACS). (2013d). *What are the key statistics about breast cancer?* Retrieved September 11, 2013, from http://www.cancer.org/cancer/breastcancer/detailed guide/breast-cancer-key-statistics

American Cancer Society (ACS). (2013e). *What are the risk factors for breast cancer?* Retrieved September 11, 2013, from http://www.cancer.org/cancer/breastcancer/detailedguide/breast-cancer-risk-factors

American Civil Liberties Union (ACLU). (2014a). *LGBT basic rights and liberties*. Retrieved from https://www.aclu.org/lgbt-rights/lgbt-basic-rights-and-liberties

American Civil Liberties Union (ACLU). (2014b). *LGBT parenting*. Retrieved from https://www.aclu.org/lgbt-rights/lgbt-parenting

American College of Nurse-Midwives. (2012). *Proportion of midwife-attended births reaches all-time high in United States*. Retrieved October 21, 2013, from http://www.midwife.org/JMWH-Midwife-Attended-Births

American Heart Association (AHA). (1984). *Cholesterol and your heart*. Dallas, TX: Author.

American Psychiatric Association (APA). (2000). *Diagnostic and statistical manual of mental disorders, text revision (DSM-IV-TR)* (4th ed.). Washington, DC: Author.

American Psychiatric Association (APA). (2013a). *Diagnostic and statistical manual of mental disorders (DSM-5)* (5th ed.). Washington, DC: Author.

American Psychiatric Association (APA). (2013b). *Intellectual disability*. Retrieved from http://www.dsm5.org/Documents/Intellectual%20Disability%20Fact%20Sheet.pdf

American Psychological Association (APA). (2001). *Publication manual for the American psychological association* (5th ed.). Washington, DC: Author.

American Psychological Association (APA). (2008). *Education, health and religious organizations unite to keep students safe*. Retrieved from http://www.apa.org/news/press/releases/2008/02/students-safe.aspx

American Psychological Association (APA). (2010). *Publication manual of the American psychological association* (6th ed.). Washington, DC: Author.

American Psychological Association (APA). (2014). *Marriage and divorce*. Retrieved from http://www.apa.org/topics/divorce/

American Society for Reproductive Medicine (ASRM). (2010). *Tests during pregnancy*. Retrieved from http://www.asrm.org/awards/index .aspx?d=3012

American Society for Reproductive Medicine. (2012a). *Age and fertility*. Retrieved from http://www.asrm.org/uploadedFiles/ASRM_Content/Resources/Patient_Resources/Fact_Sheets _and_Info_Booklets/agefertility.pdf

American Society for Reproductive Medicine. (2012b). *Fertility drugs and the risk of multiple births*. Retrieved from http://www.asrm.org/Fertility_drugs_and_the_risk_of_multiple_births/

American Society of Plastic Surgeons. (2013). *2012 Plastic surgery procedural statistics*. Retrieved September 13, 2013, from http://www.plasticsurgery.org/Documents/news-resources/statistics/2012-Plastic-Surgery-Statistics/Reconstructive-Surgery-Procedure-Trends-2012.pdf

Amini, H., Wikstrom, J., Ahlstrom, H., & Axelsson, O. (2011). Second trimester fetal magnetic resonance imaging improves diagnosis of non-Central nervous system anomalies. *Acta Obstetricia Et Gynecologica Scandinavica, 90*(4), 380–390.

Ancoli-Israel, S., & Alessi, C. (2005). Sleep and aging. *American Journal of Geriatric Psychiatry, 13*, 341–343.

Anderson, C. A., Berkowitz, L., Donnerstein, E., Huessman, R., Johnson, J. D., Linz, D., et al. (2003). The influence of media violence on youth. *Psychological Science in the Public Interest, 4*(3), 81–106.

Anderson, C. A., & Bushman, B. J. (2001). Effects of violent video games on aggressive behavior, aggressive cognition, aggressive affect, physiological arousal, and prosocial behavior: A meta-analytic review of the scientific literature. *Psychological Science, 12*, 353–359.

Anderson, J. L., Waller, D. K., Canfield, M. A., Shaw, G. M., Watkins, M. L., & Werler, M. M. (2005). Maternal obesity, gestational diabetes, and central nervous system birth defects. *Epidemiology, 16*(1), 87–92.

Anderson, P. J., De Luca, C. R., Hutchinson, E., Spencer-Smith, M. M., Roberts, G., & Doyle, L. W. (2011). Attention problems in a representative sample of extremely preterm/extremely low birth weight children. *Developmental Neuropsychology, 36*(1), 57–73.

Anderson, R. M., & Smith, B. L. (2005). Deaths: Leading causes for 2002. In Centers for Disease Control and Prevention (CDC), *National vital statistics reports* (Vol. 53, no. 17, pp. 1–92). Hyattsville, MD: National Center for Health Statistics.

Angell, B. (2008). Behavioral theory. In T. Mizrahi & L. E. Davis (Eds.), *Encyclopedia of social work* (Vol. 1, pp. 188–192). Washington, DC: NASW Press.

Apgar, V. (1958). The apgar scoring chart. *Journal of the American Medical Association, 32*, 168.

Arden, R., & Plomin, R. (2006). Sex differences in variance of intelligence across childhood. *Personality and Individual Differences, 41*, 39–48.

Arlow, J. A. (1995). Psychoanalysis. In R. J. Corsini & D. Wedding (Eds.), *Current psychotherapies* (5th ed.). Itasca, IL: Peacock.

Arnett, J. J. (2007). The long and leisurely route: Coming of age in Europe today. *A Journal of Contemporary World Affairs, 106*, 130–136.

Arnold, L. E., Chuang, S., Davies, M., Abikoff, H. B., Conners, C. K., Elliott, G. R., et al. (2004). Nine months of multicomponent behavioral treatment for ADHD and effectiveness of MTA fading procedures. *Journal of Abnormal Child Psychology, 32*(1), 39–51.

Associated Press. (2009, August 5). *Psychologists reject gay "therapy."* Retrieved from http://www.nytimes.com/2009/08/06/health/06gay.html

Association for the Prevention of Family Violence (APFV). (2010). *Association for the Prevention of Family Violence (APFV)*. Retrieved from http://www.co.walworth.wi.us/Health%20and%20Human%20Services/Intervention/apfv.aspx

Association for the Prevention of Family Violence (APFV). (2014). *About APFV*. Retrieved from http://www.apfvwalworth.com/

Atchley, R. C. (1983). *Aging: Continuity and change*. Belmont, CA: Wadsworth.

Atchley, R. C. (1988). *Social forces and aging* (5th ed.). Belmont, CA: Wadsworth.

Atkins-Burnett, S. (2010). Children with disabilities. In P. Allen-Meares (Ed.), *Social work services in schools* (6th ed., pp. 157–190). Boston: Allyn & Bacon.

Avery, A., Chase, J., Johansson, L., Litvak, S., Montero, D., & Wydra, M. (2007). America's changing attitudes toward homosexuality, civil unions, and same-gender marriage: 1977–2004. *Social Work, 52*(1), 71–79.

BabyCenter. (2005). *The Apgar score*. Retrieved from http://www.baby center.com/refcap/3 074.html

Badgly, A. M., Musselman, C., Casale, T., & Badgly-Raymond, S. (n.d.). *Heritage keepers abstinence education*. Retrieved from http://www.hhs.gov/ash/oah/oah-initiatives/teen_ pregnancy/db/programs/heritage-keepers-v2.pdf

Baer, B. L., & Federico, R. C. (1978). *Educating the baccalaureate social worker*. Cambridge, MA: Ballinger.

Bailey, J. M., Dunne, M. P., & Martin, N. G. (2000, March). Genetic and environmental influences on sexual orientation and its correlates in an Australian twin sample. *Journal of Personality and Social Psychology, 78*(3), 524–536.

Bailey, J. M., & Pillard, R. (1991). A genetic study of male sexual orientation. *Archives of General Psychiatry, 48*, 1089–1096.

Bailey, J. M., Pillard, R. C., Neale, M. C., & Agyei, Y. (1993). Heritable factors influence sexual orientation in women. *Archives of General Psychiatry, 50*(3), 217–223.

Bailey, J. M., & Zucker, K. J. (1995). Childhood sex-types behavior and sexual orientation: A conceptual analysis and quantitative review. *Developmental Psychology, 31*, 43–55.

Baillargeon, R. (1987). Object permanence in 3 V2-A'/2-month old infants. *Developmental Psychology, 23*(5), 655–664.

Bakalar, R. (2008, February 19). 5 Behaviors for longevity identified. *Wisconsin State Journal*, Al, A8.

Bales, R. F. (1965). The equilibrium problem in small groups. In A. Hare, E. Borgatta, & R. Bales (Eds.), *Small groups: Studies in social interaction* (pp. 444–476). New York: Knopf.

Balgopal, P. R. (2000). *Social work practice with immigrants and refugees*. New York: Columbia University Press.

Balgopal, P. R. (2008). Asian Americans: Overview. In T. Mizrahi & L. E. Davis (Eds.), *Encyclopedia of social work* (Vol. 1, pp. 153–160). Washington, DC: NASW Press.

Ballman, P. K. (2004, July 18). Civil unions might solve gay marriage debate. *Milwaukee Journal Sentinel*, Jl–2.

Balsam, K., Beauchaine, T., Rothblum, E., & Solomon, S. (2008). Three-year follow-up of same-sex couples who had civil unions in Vermont, same-sex couples not in civil unions, and heterosexual married couples. *Developmental Psychology, 44*, 102–116.

Bancroft, J., Herbenick, D., & Reynolds, M. (2003). Masturbation as a marker of sexual development. In J. Bancroft (Ed.),

Sexual development in childhood (pp. 156–185). Bloomington: Indiana University Press.

Bandura, A. (1965). Influence of models' reinforcement contingencies in the acquisition of imitative responses. *Journal of Personality and Social Psychology*, *1*, 589–595.

Bandura, A. (1991). Social cognitive theory of moral thought and action. In W. M. Kurtines & J. L. Gewirtz (Eds.), *Handbook of moral behavior and development: Vol. 1. Theory* (pp. 45–104). Hillsdale, NJ: Erlbaum.

Bandura, A. (2002). Selective moral disengagement in the exercise of moral agency. *Journal of Moral Education*, *31*, 101–119.

Bandura, A., Caprara, G. V., Barbaranelli, C., Pastorelli, C., & Regalia, C. (2001). Sociocognitive self-regulatory mechanisms governing transgressive behavior. *Journal of Personality and Social Psychology*, *80*, 125–135.

Banks, E. (1989). Temperament and individuality: A study of Malay children. *American Journal of Orthopsychiatry*, *59*, 390–397.

Bargad, A., & Hyde, J. S. (1991). Women's studies: A study of feminist identity development in women. *Psychology of Women Quarterly*, *15*, 181–201.

Barker, R. L. (2003). *The social work dictionary* (5th ed.). Washington, DC: NASW Press.

Barker, R. L. (2014). *The social work dictionary* (6th ed.). Washington, DC: NASW Press.

Barkley, R. A. (2006). Primary symptoms, diagnostic criteria, prevalence, and gender differences. In R. A. Barkley (Ed.), *Attention-deficit hyperactivity disorder: A handbook for diagnosis and treatment* (3rd ed., pp. 76–121). New York: Guilford.

Barnett, O., Lee, C. Y., & Thelan, R. (1997). Gender differences in attributions of self-defense and control in interpartner aggression. *Violence against Women*, *3*, 462–481.

Barnett, O., Miller-Perrin, C. L., & Perrin, R. C. (2005). *Family violence across the lifespan: An introduction* (2nd ed.). Thousand Oaks, CA: Sage.

Barnett, O. W., Miller-Perrin, C. L., & Perrin, R. D. (2011). *Family violence across the lifespan: An introduction* (3rd ed.). Thousand Oaks, CA: Sage.

Baron, A., & Cramer, D. W. (2000). Potential counseling concerns of aging lesbian, gay, and bisexual clients. In R. M. Perez, K. A. DeBord & K. J. Bieschke (Eds.), *Handbook of counseling and psychotherapy with lesbian, gay, and bisexual clients* (pp. 207–223). Washington, DC: American Psychological Association.

Baron, L., & Straus, M. A. (1989). *Four theories of rape in American society*. New Haven, CT: Yale University Press.

Barr, R. G. (2001). "Colic" is something infants do, rather than a condition they "have": A developmental approach to crying phenomena patterns, pacification and (path)genesis. In R. G. Barr, I. St James-Roberts, & M. R. Keefe (Eds.), *New evidence on unexplained infant crying* (pp. 87–104). St. Louis, MO: Johnson & Johnson Pediatric Institute.

Barret, B., & Logan, C. (2002). *Counseling gay men and lesbians: A practice primer*. Pacific Grove, CA: Brooks/Cole.

Barry, P. (2010, May). A user's guide to health care reform. *AARP Bulletin*.

Bar-Tal, D., & Saxe, L. (1976). Perceptions of similarity and dissimilarity of physically attractive couples and individuals. *Journal of Personality and Social Psychology*, *33*, 772–781.

Barth, R. P. (2008). Adoption. In T. Mizrahi & L. E. Davis (Eds.), *Encyclopedia of social work* (Vol. 1, pp. 32–44). Washington, DC: NASW Press.

Bartky, S. L. (2007). On psychological oppression. In A. Bailey & C. Cuomo (Eds.), *The feminist philosophy reader* (pp. 51–61). Boston: McGraw-Hill.

Barusch, A. S. (2012). *Foundations of social policy: Social justice in human perspective* (4th ed.). Belmont, CA: Brooks/Cole.

Basile, K. C., & Black, M. C. (2011). Intimate partner violence against women. In C. M. Renzetti, J. L. Edleson, & R. K. Bergen (Eds.), *Sourcebook on violence against women* (2nd ed., pp. 111–131). Thousand Oaks, CA: Sage.

Baumrind, D. (1971). Current patterns of parental authority. *Developmental Psychology Monographs*, *4*(1), 2.

Baumrind, D. (1978). Parental disciplinary patterns and social competence in children. *Youth and Society*, *9*, 239–276.

Baumrind, D. (1991a). Effective parenting during the early adolescent transition. In P. A. Cowan & E. M. Hetherington (Eds.), *Advances in family research* (Vol. 2, pp. 111–163). Hillsdale, NJ: Erlbaum.

Baumrind, D. (1991b). The influence of parenting style on adolescent competence and substance use. *Journal of Early Adolescence*, *11*(1), 56–95.

Baumrind, D. (1993). The average expectable environment is not good enough: A response to scarr. *Child Development*, *38*, 291–327.

Baumrind, D. (1996). The discipline controversy revisited. *Family Relations*, *45*, 405–414.

Bay-Cheng, L. Y. (2008). Human sexuality. In T. Mizrahi & L. E. Davis (Eds.), *Encyclopedia of social work* (Vol. 2, pp. 429–433). New York: Oxford University Press.

Bearman, P., & Bruckner, H. (2005). After the promise: The STD consequences of adolescent virginity pledges. *Journal of Adolescent Health*, *36*(4), 271–278.

Bearman, S. K., Presnall, K., Martinez, E., & Vaughn, N. G. (2006). The skinny on body dissatisfaction: A longitudinal study of adolescent girls and boys. *Journal of Youth and Adolescence*, *35*, 217–229.

Bearse, M. L. (2008). Native Americans: Practice interventions. In T. Mizrahi & L. E. Davis (Eds.), *Encyclopedia of social work* (Vol. 3, pp. 229–308). Washington, DC: NASW Press.

Beck, E., Burnet, K. L., & Vosper, J. (2006). Birth-order effects on facets of extraversion. *Personality and Individual Differences*, *40*(5), 953–959.

Becker, J. V., & Kaplan, M. S. (1991). Rape victims: Issues, theories, and treatment. *Annual Review of Sex Research*, *2*, 267–292.

Beckett, J. O., & Johnson, H. C. (1995). Human development. In R. L. Edwards (Ed.), *Encyclopedia of social work* (19th ed., Vol. 2, pp. 1385–1405). Washington, DC: NASW Press.

Beitchman, J. H., Zucker, K. J., Hood, J. E., DaCosta, G. A., Akman, D., & Cassavia, E. (1992). A review of the long-term effects of child sexual abuse. *Child Abuse and Neglect*, *16*(1), 101–118.

Bell, A. P., Weinberg, M. S., Martin, S., & Hammersmith, S. K. (1981). *Sexual preference*. Bloomington: Indiana University Press.

Belsky, J., & Rovine, M. J. (1988). Nonmaternal care in the first year of life and the security of infant-parent attachment. *Child Development, 59*, 157–167.

Ben-David, S., & Schneider, O. (2005). Rape perceptions, gender role attitudes, and victim-perpetrator acquaintance. *Sex Roles: A Journal of Research, 53*, 385–399.

Benjamin, A. E., Matthias, R. E., & Franke, T. M. (2000). Comparing consumer-directed and agency models for providing supportive services at home. *Health Services Research, 35*(1), 351–366.

Benjamin, L. (1991). *The black elite: Facing the color line in the twilight of the twentieth century*. Chicago: Nelson-Hall.

Bennett, L. W. (1995). Substance abuse and the domestic assault of women. *Social Work, 40*(6), 760–771.

Benson, H. (1975). *The relaxation response*. New York: Avon.

Berger, R. M. (1985). Rewriting a bad script: Older lesbians and gays. In H. Hidalgo et al. (Eds.), *Lesbian and gay issues: A resource manual for social workers* (pp. 53–58). Silver Spring, MD: NASW.

Berger, R. M., & Kelly, J. J. (1995). Gay men overview. In R. L. Edwards (Ed.), *Encyclopedia of social work* (19th ed., Vol. 2, pp. 1064–1075). Washington, DC: NASW Press.

Berk, L. E. (2006). *Child development* (7th ed.). Boston: Allyn & Bacon.

Berk, L. E. (2008a). *Infants and children* (6th ed.). Boston: Allyn & Bacon.

Berk, L. E. (2008b). *Infants, children, and adolescents* (6th ed.). Boston: Allyn & Bacon.

Berk, L. E. (2012a). *Infants and children: Prenatal through middle childhood* (7th ed.). Boston: Allyn & Bacon.

Berk, L. E. (2012b). *Infants, children, and adolescents* (7th ed.). Boston: Allyn & Bacon.

Berk, L. E. (2013). *Child development* (9th ed.). Boston: Allyn & Bacon.

Berk, L. E., & Winsler, A. (1995). *Scaffolding children's learning: Vygotsky and early childhood education. NAEYC research into practice series* (Vol. 7). Washington, DC: National Book Association for Young Children.

Berk, R. A., Fenstermaker, S., & Newton, P. J. (1988). An empirical analysis of police responses to incidents of wife battery. In G. T. Hotaling, D. Finkelhor, J. T. Kirkpatrick, & M. A. Straus (Eds.), *Coping with family violence* (pp. 158–168). Newbury Park, CA: Sage.

Berliner, K., Jacob, D., & Schwartzberg, N. (2011). Single adults and the life cycle. In M. McGoldrick, B. Carter, & N. G. Garcia-Preto (Eds.), *The expanded family life cycle: Individual, family, and social perspectives* (4th ed., pp. 163–175). Boston: Allyn & Bacon.

Berliner, L. (2011). Child sexual abuse: Definitions, prevalence, and consequences. In J. E. B. Myers (Ed.), *The APSAC handbook on child maltreatment* (3rd ed., pp. 215–232). Thousand Oaks, CA: Sage.

Berliner, L., & Elliott, D. M. (2002). Sexual abuse of children. In J. E. B. Myers, L. Berliner, J. Briere, C. T. Hendrix, C. Jenny, & T. A. Reid (Eds.), *The APSAC handbook on child maltreatment* (2nd ed., pp. 55–78). Thousand Oaks, CA: Sage.

Bernstein, D. A. (2011). *Essentials of psychology* (5th ed.). Belmont, CA: Wadsworth.

Bernstein, D. A. (2014). *Essentials of psychology* (6th ed.). Belmont, CA: Wadsworth.

Bernstein, D. A., Penner, L. A., Clarke-Stewart, A., & Roy, E. J. (2003). *Psychology* (6th ed.). Boston: Houghton Mifflin.

Bernstein, D. A., Penner, L. A., Clarke-Stewart, A., & Roy, E. J. (2008). *Psychology* (8th ed.). Boston: Houghton Mifflin.

Berube, M. S. (2002). *The American heritage college dictionary* (4th ed.). Boston: Houghton Mifflin.

Bieschke, K. J., McClanahan, M., Tozer, E., Grzegorek, J. L., & Park, J. (2000). Programmatic research on the treatment of lesbian, gay, and bisexual clients: The past, the present and the course for the future. In R. M. Perez, K. A. DeBord, & K. J. Bieschke (Eds.), *Handbook of counseling and therapy with lesbian, gay, and bisexual clients* (pp. 309–335). Washington, DC: American Psychological Association.

Bijvank, M. N., Konijn, E. A., Bushman, B. J., & Roelofsma, P. H. M. P. (2009). Age and violent-content labels make video games forbidden fruits for youth. *Pediatrics, 123*(3), 870–876. Retrieved from http://pediatrics.aappublications .org/cgi/content/abstract/123/3/870

Billingsley, A. (1993). *Climbing Jacob's ladder: The enduring legacy of African-American families*. New York: Simon and Schuster.

Bishaw, A. (2012). *Poverty: 2010 and 2011*. Retrieved September 17, 2013, from http://www.census.gov/prod/2012pubs/ acsbr11-01.pdf

Bjorklund, D. F., & Blasi, C. H. (2012). *Child & adolescent development: An integrated approach*. Belmont, CA: Wadsworth.

Blackwood, E. (1994). Sexuality and gender in native American tribes: The case of crossgender females. In A. C. Herrmann & A. M. Stewart (Eds.), *Theorizing feminism: Parallel trends in the humanities and social sciences* (pp. 301–315). Boulder, CO: Westview Press.

Blair, S. L., & Qian, Z. (1998). Family and Asian students' educational performance. *Journal of Family Issues, 19*, 355–374.

Blakemore, J. E. O., Berenbaum, S. A., & Liben, I. S. (2009). *Gender development*. New York: Psychology Press.

Blakemore, S. J., & Choudhury, S. (2006). Commentaries: Brain development during puberty: State of the science. *Developmental Science, 9*, 11–14.

Blasdell, J., & Goss, K. (2004). *Freedom of access to clinic entrances (FACE) act*. Retrieved from http://womensissues .about.com

Blaze-Gosden, T. (1987). *Drug abuse*. Birmingham, UK: David and Charles.

Blumenfeld, W. J. (Eds.). (1992). *Homophobia: How we all pay the price*. Boston: Beacon Press.

Blundo, R. (2008). Men: Practice interventions. In T. Mizrahi & L. E. Davis (Eds.), *Encyclopedia of social work* (Vol. 3, pp. 217–221). Washington, DC: NASW Press.

Boes, M., & van Wormer, K. (2002). Social work with lesbian, gay, bisexual, and transgendered clients. In A. R. Roberts & G. J. Greene (Eds.), *Social work desk reference* (pp. 619–623). New York: Oxford University Press.

Boes, M., & van Wormer, K. (2009). Social work with lesbian, gay, bisexual, and transgendered clients. In A. R. Roberts (Ed.), *Social workers' desk reference* (2nd ed., pp. 934–938). New York: Oxford.

Bogaert, A. F. (2005). Gender role/identity and sibling sex ratio in homosexual men. *Journal of Sex and Marital Therapy, 31*, 217–227.

Bohm, A. (2010). *Time to get rid of the abstinence-only zombie.* Retrieved from http://www.aclu.org/blog/reproductive-freedom/time-get-rid-abstinence-only-zombie

Boston Women's Health Book Collective. (1984). *The new our bodies, ourselves.* New York: Simon and Schuster.

Bowlby, J. (1969). *Attachment and loss* (Vol. 1). New York: Basic Books.

Boyle, S. W., Hull, G. H., Jr., Mather, J. H., Smith, L. L., & Farley, O. W. (2009). *Direct practice in social work* (2nd ed.). Boston: Allyn & Bacon.

Boyte, H. C. (1989). *People power transforms a St. Louis housing project. Occasional papers.* Chicago: Community Renewable Society.

Bradley, J. (2009). *The imperial cruise: A secret history of empire and war.* Boston: Little, Brown & Company.

Brammer, R. (2012). *Diversity in counseling* (2nd ed.). Belmont, CA: Brooks/Cole.

Brandwein, R. A. (2008). Women: Overview. In T. Mizrahi & L. E. Davis (Eds.), *Encyclopedia of social work* (Vol. 4, pp. 281–290). Washington, DC: NASW Press.

Brassard, M., Germain, R., & Hart, S. (1987). *Psychological maltreatment of children and youth.* Elmsford, NY: Pergamon.

Brazelton, H. M. (1973). Neonatal behavioral assessment scale. In *Clinics in developmental medicine* (No. 50). Philadelphia: Lippincott.

Brazelton Institute. (2005). *Understanding the baby's language.* Retrieved from http://www.brazelton-institute.com/intro.html

Brener, N. D., McMahon, P. M., Warren, C. W., & Doublas, K. A. (1999). Forced sexual intercourse and associated health-risk behaviors among female college students in the United States. *Journal of Consulting and Clinical Psychology, 67*(2), 252–259.

Breuer, J., & Freud, S. (1895). *Studies in hysteria.* London: Hogarth Press.

Bricker-Jenkins, M., & Hooyman, N. (Eds.). (1986). *Not for women only: Social work practice for a feminist future.* Silver Spring, MD: NASW Press.

Bricker-Jenkins, M., & Lockett, P. W. (1995). Women: Direct practice. In R. L. Edwards (Ed.), *Encyclopedia of social work* (19th ed., Vol. 3, pp. 2529–2539). Washington, DC: NASW Press.

Bridges, K. M. B. (1932). *Emotional development in early infancy.* Child Development, *3*, 324–341.

Bridge, J. A., Goldstein, T. R., & Brent, D. A. (2006). Adolescent suicide and suicidal behavior. *Journal of Child Psychology and Psychiatry, 47*, 372–394.

Brody, G. H., & Flor, D. O. (1998). Maternal resources, parenting practices, and child competence in rural, single-parent African American families. *Child Development, 69*, 803–816.

Brownell, P., & Fenley, R. C. (2009). Older adult immigrants in the United States: Issues and services. In F. Chang-Muy & E. P. Congress (Eds.), *Social work with immigrants and refugees: Legal issues, clinical skills, and advocacy* (pp. 277–307). New York: Springer.

Brownlee, S. (1991, August 12). Alzheimer's: Is there hope? *U.S. News & World Report*, 40–49.

Brunstein Klomek, A., Marrocco, F., Kleinman, M., Schofeld, I. S., & Gould, M. S. (2007). Bullying, depression, and suicidality in adolescents. *Journal of the American Academy of Child and Adolescent Psychiatry, 46*, 40–49.

Brush, L. D. (2000). Battering, traumatic stress, and welfare-to-work transition. *Violence against Women, 6*, 1039–1065.

Bryan, T., Burstein, K., & Ergul, C. (2004). The social-emotional side of learning disabilities: A science-based presentation of the state of the art. *Learning Disability Quarterly, 27*, 45–51.

Buhler, C. (1933). *Der menschliche, lebenslauf alpsychologishes problem.* Leipzig: Verlag von S. Herzel.

Bumiller, E. (2011, July 22). Obama ends "don't ask, don't tell policy."*The New York Times.* Retrieved from http://www.nytimes.com/2011/07/23/us/23military.html

Bumiller, E. (2012, September 19). One year later, military says gay policy is working. *The New York Times.* Retrieved from http://www.nytimes.com/2012/09/20/us/dont-ask-dont-tell-anniversary-passes-with-little-note.html?agewanted=all

Burchinal, M. R., Roberts, J. E., Riggins, R., Zeisel, S. A., Neebe, E., & Bryant, D. (2000). Relating quality of center-based child care to early cognitive and language development longitudinally. *Child Development, 71*(20), 339–357.

Burden, R. (2008). Is dyslexia associated with negative feelings of self-worth? A review and implications for future research. *Dyslexia, 14*, 188–196.

Bureau of Justice Statistics. (2010). *Criminal victimization 2009.* Retrieved from http://bjs.ojp.usdoj.gov/content/pub/pdf/cv09.pdf

Bureau of Justice Statistics (BJS). (2013). *Rape and sexual assault.* Retrieved from http://www.bjs.gov/index.cfm?y=tp&tid=317

Burgess, A. W., & Holmstrom, L. L. (1974a). Rape trauma syndrome. *American Journal of Psychiatry, 131*, 981–986.

Burgess, A. W., & Holmstrom, L. L. (1974b). *Rape: Victims of crisis.* Bowie, MD: Robert J. Brady.

Burgess, A. W., & Holmstrom, L. L. (1988, January). Treating the adult rape victim. *Medical Aspects of Human Sexuality*, 36–43.

Burke, K., & Lemire, J. (2005, February 19). *Daily news.* Retrieved from http://www.nydailynews.com/archives/news/2005/02/19/2005-02-19_cut-up_man_was_on_way_to_see.html

Burstow, B. (1992). *Radical feminist therapy: Working in the context of violence.* Newbury Park, CA: Sage.

Buss, K. A., & Goldsmith, H. H. (2007). Biobehavioral approaches to early socioemotional development. In C. A. Brownell & C. B. Kopp (Eds.), *Socioemotional development in the toddler years: Transitions and transformations* (pp. 370–395). New York: Guilford.

Butler, R. N. (1975). *Why survive? Being old in America.* New York: Harper & Row.

Byer, C. O., & Shainberg, L. W. (1994). *Dimensions of human sexuality* (4th ed.). Madison, WI: Brown and Benchmark.

Byer, C. O., Shainberg, L. W., & Galliano, G. (2002). *Dimensions of human sexuality* (6th ed.). Boston: McGraw-Hill.

California court rules gay marriage is a right. (2008, May 16). *Milwaukee Journal Sentinel*, 1A, 8A.

Cameron-Bandler, L. (1985). *Solutions.* San Rafael, CA: Future Pace.

Canadian Mental Health Association. (2013). *Youth and suicide.* Retrieved from http://www.cmha.ca/mental_health/youth-and-suicide/

Canda, E. R. (1989). Religious content in social work education: A comparative approach. *Journal of Social Work Education, 25*(1), 36–45.

Canda, E. R. (2008). Human needs: Religion and spirituality. In T. Mizrahi & L. E. Davis (Eds.), *Encyclopedia of social work* (Vol. 2, pp. 413–418). Washington, DC: NASW Press.

Canda, E. R., & Furman, L. D. (2010). *Spiritual diversity in social work practice: The heart of helping* (2nd ed.). New York: Oxford.

Caplan, P. J. (1995). *They say you're crazy.* Reading, MA: Addison-Wesley.

Carey, R. G., & Bucher, B. B. (1986). Positive practice overcorrection: Effects of reinforcing correct performance. *Behavior Modification, 10,* 73–92.

Carlson, B. E. (2008). Intimate partner violence. In T. Mizrahi & L. E. Davis (Eds.), *Encyclopedia of social work* (Vol. 2, pp. 542–546). Washington, DC: NASW Press.

Carmichael, S., & Hamilton, C. V. (1967). *Black power: The politics of liberation in America.* New York: Vintage Books.

Carrell, D. T., Wilcox, A. L., Lowry, L., Peterson, C. M., Jones, K. P., Erickson, L., et al. (2003). Elevated sperm chromosome aneuploidy and apoptosis in patients with unexplained recurrent pregnancy loss. *Obstetrics and Gynecology, 101*(6), 1229–1235.

Carroll, J. L. (2007). *Sexuality now: Embracing diversity* (2nd ed.). Belmont, CA: Wadsworth.

Carroll, J. L. (2010). *Sexuality now: Embracing diversity* (3rd ed.). Belmont, CA: Wadsworth.

Carroll, J. L. (2013a). *Discovery series: Introduction to human sexuality.* Belmont, CA: Cengage.

Carroll, J. L. (2013b). *Sexuality now: Embracing diversity* (4th ed.). Belmont, CA: Wadsworth.

Carroll, J. L. (2014). *Discovery series: Introduction to human sexuality.* Belmont, CA: CENGAGE Learning.

Carter, E. A., & McGoldrick, M. (1980). *The family life cycle: A framework for family therapy.* New York: Gardner Press.

Carter, E. A., & McGoldrick, M. (1989). Overview: The changing family life cycle—a framework for family therapy. In B. Carter & M. McGoldrick (Eds.), *The changing family life cycle: A framework for family therapy* (2nd ed., pp. 3–28). Boston: Allyn & Bacon.

Cartwright, D. (1951). Achieving change in people: Some applications of group "dynamics theory." *Human Relations, 4,* 381–392.

Casey, P. H. (2008). Growth of low birth weight preterm children. *Seminars in Perinatology, 32,* 20–27.

Cassidy, J. (1999). The nature of the child's ties. In J. Cassidy & P. R. Shaver (Eds.), *Handbook of attachment: Theory, research, and clinical applications* (pp. 3–20). New York: Guilford Press.

Catalano, S., Smith, E., Snyder, H., & Rand, M. (2009). *Female victims of violence.* Retrieved from http://bjs.ojp.usdoj.gov/content/pub/pdf/fvv.pdf

Cates, W., Jr., & Raymond, E. G. (2004). Vaginal spermicides. In R. A. Hatcher, J. Trussell, F. Stewart, A. L. Nelson, W. Cates, Jr., F. Guest, & D. Kowal (Eds.), *Contraceptive technology* (18th ed., pp. 355–363). New York: Ardent Media.

Cates, W., Jr., & Stewart, F. (2004). Vaginal barriers. In R. A. Hatcher, J. Trussell, F. Stewart, A. L. Nelson, W. Cates, Jr., F. Guest, & D. Kowal (Eds.), *Contraceptive technology* (18th ed., pp. 365–389). New York: Ardent Media.

Cattell, R. B. (1971). *Abilities: Their structure, growth, and action.* Boston: Houghton Mifflin.

Ceci, S. J. (1991). How much does schooling influence general intelligence and its cognitive components? A reassessment of the evidence. *Developmental Psychology, 27*(5), 703–722.

Ceci, S. J., Rosenblum, T., de Bruyn, E., & Lee, D. Y. (1997). A bio-ecological model of intellectual development: Moving beyond h2. In R. J. Sternberg & E. Grigorenko (Eds.), *Intelligence, heredity, and environment* (pp. 303–322). New York: Cambridge University Press.

Center for American Women and Politics. (2010). *Facts on women office holders, candidates, and voters.* Retrieved from http://www.cawp.rutgers.edu/fast_facts/index.php

Center for American Women and Politics. (2014). *Fact sheet: Women in elected office, 2014.* Retrieved from http://www.cawp.rutgers.edu/fast_facts/levels_of_office/documents/elective.pdf

Center for Reproductive Rights. (2003, July 8). *Medicaid funding for medically necessary abortions.* Retrieved from http://www.crlp.org

Center for Reproductive Rights (CRR). (2009). *Abortion.* Retrieved from http://reproductiverights.org/en/our-issues/abortion

Center for Workforce Studies. (2006). *Licensed social workers in the United States, 2004.* Washington, DC: National Association of Social Workers.

Centers for Disease Control (CDC). (2011). *Spina bifida: Data and statistics.* Retrieved from http://www.cdc.gov/ncbddd/spinabifida/data.html

Centers for Disease Control (CDC). (2012). *Suicide: Facts at a glance.* Retrieved from http://www.cdc.gov/violenceprevention/pdf/suicide-datasheet-a.pdf

Centers for Disease Control (CDC). (2013a). *2011 Assisted reproductive technology: Fertility clinic success rates report.* Retrieved from http://www.cdc.gov/art/ART2011/PDFs/ART_2011_Clinic_Report-Full.pdf

Centers for Disease Control (CDC). (2013b). *Infertility.* Retrieved from http://www.cdc.gov/nchs/fastats/fertile.htm

Centers for Disease Control (CDC). (2013c). *Infertility FAQs.* Retrieved from http://www.cdc.gov/Reproductivehealth/Infertility/#a

Centers for Disease Control (CDC). (2013d). *National prematurity awareness month.* Retrieved November 24, 2013, from http://www.cdc.gov/Features/PrematureBirth/

Centers for Disease Control (CDC). (2013e). *Preterm birth.* Retrieved from http://www.cdc.gov/Features/PrematureBirth/

Centers for Disease Control (CDC). (2013f). *Sexually transmitted diseases (STDs).* Retrieved from http://www.cdc.gov/std/default.htm

Centers for Disease Control (CDC). (2013g). *What is assisted reproduction technology.* Retrieved from http://www.cdc.gov/art/

Centers for disease Control (CDC). (2014). *Suicide prevention.* Retrieved from http://www.cdc.gov/violenceprevention/pub/youth_suicide.html

Centers for Disease Control and Prevention. (2004). *Cerebral palsy*. Retrieved from http://www.cdc.gov/ncbddd/dd/cp2.htm

Centers for Disease Control and Prevention. (2005, April 5). *2002 Assisted reproductive technology (ART) report: Section 5—ART trends, 1996–2002*. Retrieved from http://www.cdc.gov/reproductivehealth/ART02/section5.htm

Centers for Disease Control and Prevention. (2006). Youth risk behavior surveillance: United States, 2005. *Morbidity and Mortality Weekly Report, 55*, 1–108.

Centers for Disease Control and Prevention. (2008a). *Sexually transmitted diseases*. Retrieved from http://www.cdc.gov/std

Centers for Disease Control and Prevention. (2008b). *STDs today*. Retrieved from http://www.cdcnpin.org/scripts/std/std.asp

Centers for Disease Control and Prevention. (2008c). *Youth suicide*. Retrieved from http://www.cdc.gov/print.do?rl=http%3A//www.cdc.gov/ncipc/dvp/suicide/youthsuicide.htm

Centers for Disease Control and Prevention. (2009). *Infertility*. Retrieved from http://www.cdc.gov/nchs/fastats/fertile.htm

Centers for Disease Control and Prevention. (2010a). *Assisted reproductive technology*. Retrieved from http://www.cdc.gov/art/ART2007/sectionl.htm

Centers for Disease Control and Prevention. (2010b). *Autistic spectrum disorders (ASDs)*. Retrieved from http://www.cdc.gov/ncbddd/autism/facts.html and http://www.cdc.gov/ncbddd/autism/facts.html

Centers for Disease Control and Prevention. (2010c). *Birth weight and gestation*. Retrieved from http://www.cdc.gov/nchs/fastats/birthwt.htm

Centers for Disease Control and Prevention. (2010d). *Hearing loss in children*. Retrieved from http://www.cdc.gov/ncbddd/hearingloss/facts.html

Centers for Disease Control and Prevention. (2010e). *Vision impairment*. Retrieved from http://www.cdc.gov/ncbddd/dd/vision2.htm

Centers for Disease Control and Prevention. (2011). *Sexually transmitted diseases (STDs)*. Retrieved from http://www.cdc.gov/STD/

Center for Reproductive Rights (CRR). (2003, July 8). *Medicaid funding for medically necessary abortions*. Retrieved from http://www.crlp.org

CenterWatch. (2013). *Ella (ulipristal acetate)*. Retrieved from http://www.centerwatch.com/drug-information/fda-approved-drugs/drug/1112/

Chapman, G. (1992). *The five love languages: How to express heartfelt commitment to your mate*. Chicago: Northfield Publishing.

Charlesworth, R. (2014). *Understanding child development* (9th ed.). Belmont, CA: Wadsworth.

Chen, X., Hastings, P. D., Rubin, K. H., Chen, H., Cen, G., & Stewart, S. L. (1998). Child-rearing attitudes and behavioral inhibition in Chinese and Canadian toddlers: A cross-cultural study. *Developmental Psychology, 34*, 677–686.

Chen, X. K., Wen, S. W., Fleming, N., Demissie, K., Rhoads, G. G., & Walker, M. C. (2007). Teenage pregnancy and adverse birth outcomes: A large population based retrospective cohort study. *International Journal of Epidemiology, 36*, 368–373.

Chen, X. K., Wen, S. W., Yang, Q., & Walker, M. C. (2007). Adequacy of prenatal care and neonatal mortality in infants born to mothers with and without antenatal high-risk conditions. *Australian and New Zealand Journal of Obstetrics and Gynecology, 47*, 122–127.

Cherlin, A., & Furstenberg, F. F. (1986). Grandparents and family crisis. *Generations, 10*(4), 26–28.

Cherlin, A. J. (2010). Demographics trend in the United States: A review of research in the 2000s. *Journal of Marriage and Family, 72*, 403–419.

Chernin, J. M., & Johnson, M. R. (2003). *Affirmative psychotherapy and counseling for lesbians and gay men*. Thousand Oaks, CA: Sage.

Chicago Tribune. (1998, January 3). Model minority doesn't tell? 18.

ChildStats.gov. (2013). *Births to unmarried women*. Retrieved from http://www.childstats.gov/americaschildren/famsoc2.asp

Chilman, C. S. (1987). Abortion. In A. Minahan (Editor-in-Chief), *Encyclopedia of social work* (Vol. 1, pp. 1–7). Silver Spring, MD: NASW.

Chilman, C. S. (1993). Hispanic families in the United States: Research perspectives. In H. P. McAdoo (Ed.), *Family ethnicity: Strength in diversity* (pp. 141–163). Newbury Park, CA: Sage.

Chornesky, A. (1998, Spring). Multicultural perspectives on menopause and the climacteric. *Affilia*, 31–47.

Chornesky, A. (2000). The dynamics of battering revisited. *Affilia, 15*(4), 480–501.

Choudhuri, D. D., Santiago-Rivera, A. L., & Garrett, M. T. (2012). *Counseling & diversity*. Upper Saddle River, NJ: Pearson.

Christian, P. (2009). Prenatal origins of under-nutrition. *Nestle Nutrition Workshop Series: Pediatric Program, 63*, 59–73.

Christie, R., & Geis, F. (1970). *Studies in Machiavellianism*. New York: Academic Press.

Chu, S. Y., Bachman, D. J., Callaghan, W. M., Whitlock, E. P., Dietz, P. M., Berg, C. J., et al. (2008). Association between obesity during pregnancy and increased us of health care. *New England Journal of Medicine, 358*, 1444–1453.

Chumlea, W., Schubert, M., Roche, A., Kulin, H., Lee, P., Himes, J., et al. (2003). Age at menarche and racial comparisons in U.S. Girls. *Pediatrics, 111*, 110–113.

Clayton, R. R. (1975). *The family, marriage and social change*. Lexington, MA: D. C. Heath.

Clements, M. (1994, August 7). Sex in America today. *Parade Magazine*, 4–6.

Cleveland, H., & Wiebe, R. (2003, January–February). The moderation of adolescent-to-peer similarity in tobacco and alcohol use by school levels of substance use. *Child Development, 74*(1), 279–291.

Cloud, J. (1998, March 16). Harassed or hazed: Why the Supreme Court ruled that men can sue men for sex harassment. *Time*, 55.

Cloud, J. (2005, October 10). The battle over gay teens. *Time*, 43–51.

CNN. (1996). *Lesbian mom appeals decision granting child custody to convicted killer dad*. Retrieved from http://www.lectlaw.com/files/cur61.htm

CNN Money. (2013). *Average cost to raise a child*. Retrieved from money.cnn.com/2013/08/14/pf/cost-children/index.html

CNN.com. (2013). *Sandy hook shooting: What happened?* Retrieved from http://www.cnn.com/interactive/2012/12/us/sandy-hook-timeline/

Cohen, A. (1955). *Delinquent boys: The culture of the gang*. New York: Free Press.

Cohen, H. L., Padilla, Y. C., & Aravena, V. C. (2006). Psychosocial support for families of gay, lesbian, bisexual, and transgender people. In D. F. Morrow & L. Messinger (Eds.), *Sexual orientation and gender expression in social work practice: Working with gay, lesbian, bisexual, and transgender people* (pp. 153–176). New York: Columbia University Press.

Cohen, N. A. (1992). The continuum of child welfare services. In N. A. Cohen (Ed.), *Child welfare: A multicultural approach* (pp. 39–83). Needham Heights, MA: Allyn & Bacon.

Cohen, S. A. (2009). Facts and consequences: Legality, incidence and safety of abortion worldwide. *Guttmacher Policy Review, 12*(4), Retrieved from http://www.guttmacher.org/pubs/gpr/12/4/gpr120402.html

Colapinto, J. (2007). *The true story of John/Joan*. Retrieved from http://www.healthyplace.com/gender/inside-intersexuality/the-true-story-of-john-joan/menu-id-1427/

Cole, G. F., Smith, C. E., & De Jong, C. (2013). *The American system of criminal justice* (13th ed.). Belmont, CA: Brooks/Cole.

Cole, P. M., Bruschi, C. J., & Tamang, B. L. (2002). Cultural differences in children's emotional reactions to difficult situations. *Child Development, 73*, 983–996.

Cole, P. M., & Tamang, B. L. (1998). Nepal children's ideas about emotional displays in hypothetical challenges. *Developmental Psychology, 34*, 640–648.

Cole, P. M., Tamang, B. L., & Shrestha, S. (2006). Cultural variations in the socialization of young children's anger and shame. *Child Development, 77*, 1237–1251.

Coleman, J. W., & Cressey, D. R. (1984). *Social problems* (2nd ed.). New York: Harper & Row.

Coleman, J. W., & Kerbo, H. R. (2002). *Social problems* (8th ed.). Upper Saddle River, NJ: Prentice-Hall.

Colin, V. (1996). *Human attachment*. New York: McGraw-Hill.

Collier, H. V. (1982). *Counseling women*. New York: Free Press.

Comer, R. J. (2010). *Fundamentals of abnormal psychology* (6th ed.). New York: Worth.

Commission of the Council on Social Work Education (CSWE). (2002). *Glossary to educational policy and accreditation standards*. Alexandria, VA: Author.

Cook, C. A. L., Selig, K. L., Wedge, B. J., & Gohn-Baube, E. A. (1999, March). Access barriers and the use of prenatal care by low-income, inner-city women. *Social Work, 44*(2), 129–139.

Cooley, C. H. (1902). *Human nature and the social order*. New York: Scribner's.

Coon, D. (2002). *Psychology: A journey*. Belmont, CA: Wadsworth.

Coon, D. (2006). *Psychology: A modular approach to mind and behavior* (10th ed.). Belmont, CA: Wadsworth.

Coon, D., & Mitterer, J. O. (2009). *Psychology: Modules for active learning* (11th ed.). Belmont, CA: Wadsworth.

Coon, D., & Mitterer, J. O. (2011). *Psychology: A journey* (4th ed.). Belmont, CA: Wadsworth.

Coon, D., & Mitterer, J. O. (2014). *Psychology: A journey* (5th ed.). Belmont, CA: Wadsworth.

Copen, C. E., Daniels, K., & Mosher, W. D. (2013, April 4). First premarital cohabitation in the United States: 2006–2010 National survey of family growth. *National Health Statistics Reports, 64*. Retrieved from http://www.cdc.gov/nchs/data/nhsr/nhsr064.pdf

Corey, G. (2009). *Theory and practice of counseling and psychotherapy* (8th ed.). Belmont, CA: Brooks/Cole.

Corey, G. (2013). *Theory and practice of counseling and psychotherapy* (9th ed.). Belmont, CA: Wadsworth.

Costello, E. J., Sung, M., Worthman, C., & Angold, A. (2007). Pubertal maturation and the development of alcohol use and abuse. *Drug and Alcohol Dependence, 88*, S50–S59.

Council on Social Work Education. (2008). *Educational policy and accreditation standards*. Alexandria, VA: Author.

Courtenay, W. H. (2003). Key determinants of the health and well-being of men and boys. *International Journal of Men's Health, 2*(1), 1–30.

Cowger, C. D., & Snively, C. A. (2002). Assessing client strengths: Individual, family, and community empowerment. In D. Saleebey (Ed.), *The strengths perspective in social work practice* (3rd ed., pp. 106–123). Boston: Allyn & Bacon.

Cowley, A. S., & Derezotes, D. (1994, Winter). Transpersonal psychology and social work education. *Journal of Social Work Education, 30*(1), 32–41.

Cox, C. B. (2002, January). Empowering African-American custodial grandparents. *Social Work, 47*(1), 45–54.

Cox, C. B. (2005). Grandparents raising grandchildren from a multicultural perspective. In E. P. Congress & M. J. Gonzalez (Eds.), *Multicultural perspectives in working with families* (2nd ed., pp. 128–141). New York: Springer.

Crooks, R., & Baur, K. (2002). *Our sexuality* (8th ed.). Belmont, CA: Wadsworth.

Crooks, R., & Baur, K. (2011). *Our sexuality* (11th ed.). Belmont, CA: Wadsworth.

Crooks, R., & Baur, K. (2014). *Our sexuality* (12th ed.). Belmont, CA: Wadsworth.

Cross, W. E., Jr., & Fhagen-Smith, P. (1996). Nigrescence and ego identity development: Accounting for differential black identity patterns. In P. B. Pedersen, J. G. Draguns, W. J. Lonner, & J. E. Trimble (Eds.), *Counseling across cultures* (4th ed., pp. 108–123). Thousand Oaks, CA: Sage.

Crosson-Tower, C. (2008). *Understanding child abuse and neglect* (7th ed.). Boston: Allyn & Bacon.

Crosson-Tower, C. (2009). *Exploring child welfare: A practice perspective* (5th ed.). Boston: Allyn & Bacon.

Crosson-Tower, C. (2010). *Understanding child abuse and neglect* (8th ed.). Boston: Allyn & Bacon.

Crosson-Tower, C. (2013). *Exploring child welfare: A practice perspective* (6th ed.). Upper Saddle River, NJ: Pearson.

Crosson-Tower, C. (2014). *Understanding child abuse and neglect* (9th ed.). Upper Saddle River, NJ: Pearson.

Cuber, J. F., & Harroff, P. B. (1971). Five types of marriage. In A. S. Skolnick & J. H. Skolnick (Eds.), *Family in transition* (pp. 287–299). Boston: Little, Brown.

Cumming, E., & Henry, W. E. (1961). *Growing old: The process of disengagement.* New York: Basic Books.

Cummings, M. (1977). How to handle incidents of racial discrimination. In C. Zastrow & D. H. Chang (Eds.), *The personal problem solver* (pp. 200–201). Englewood Cliffs, NJ: Prentice-Hall.

Cunningham, M. (2012). *Integrating spirituality in clinical social work practice: Walking the labyrinth.* Upper Saddle River, NJ: Pearson.

Dacey, J. S., & Travers, J. F. (2006). *Human development across the lifespan* (6th ed.). Boston: McGraw-Hill.

Dacey, J. S., Travers, J. F., & Fiore, L. B. (2009). *Human development across the lifespan* (7th ed.). Boston: McGraw-Hill.

Daft, R. L. (2007). *Organization theory and design* (9th ed.). Mason, OH: South-Western.

Daft, R. L. (2010). *Organization theory and design* (10th ed.). Mason, OH: South-Western.

Daft, R. L. (2013). *Organization theory & design* (11th ed.). Mason, OH: South-Western.

Dale, C. V. (1993, March 29). *Statement to senate armed services committee.* Washington, DC: Library of Congress, Congressional Research Service.

Daniel, S. S., Walsh, A. K., Goldston, D. B., Arnold, E. M., Reboussin, B. A., & Wood, F. B. (2006). Suicidality, school dropout, and reading problems among adolescents. *Journal of Learning Disabilities, 39,* 507–514.

Daniels, H. (2005). Vygotsky and educational psychology: Some preliminary remarks. *Educational and Child Psychology, 22*(1), 6–17.

Darroch, J., Singh, S., Frost, J. J., & Study Team. (2001). Differences in teenage pregnancy rates among five developed countries: The role of sexual activity and contraceptive use. *Family Planning Perspectives, 33,* 244–250, 281.

Davis, K., & Newstrom, W. (1989). *Human behavior at work* (8th ed.). New York: McGraw-Hill.

Davis, L. V. (1995). Domestic violence. In R. L. Edwards (Ed.), *Encyclopedia of social work* (19th ed., Vol. 1, pp. 780–789). Washington, DC: NASW Press.

Dawood, K., Pillard, R. C., Horvath, C., Revelle, W., & Bailey, J. M. (2000). Familial aspects of male homosexuality. *Archives of Sexual Behavior, 29*(2), 96–97.

Deci, E. L., & Ryan, R. M. (2000). The "what" and "why" of goal pursuits: Human needs and the self-determination of behavior. *Psychological Inquiry, 11,* 227–268.

Defense of Marriage Act (DOM A) of 1996. Pub. L. 104-199, sec 1, 100 Stat. 2419 (Sep. 21, 1996), codified at 1 U.S.C. § 7 (1997).

Degangi, G. A., & Kendall, A. (2008). *Effective parenting for the hard-to-manage child: A skills-based book.* New York: Routledge.

Delgado, M. (1998a). Community asset assessments by Latino youths. In P. O. Ewalt, E. M. Freeman, & D. L. Poole (Eds.), *Community building: Renewal, well-being, and shared responsibility* (pp. 202–212). Washington, DC: NASW Press.

Delgado, M. (1998b). Strengths-based practice with Puerto Rican adolescents: Lessons from a substance abuse prevention project. In P. O. Ewalt, E. M. Freeman, & D. L. Poole (Eds.), *Community building: Renewal, well-being, and shared responsibility* (pp. 213–224). Washington, DC: NASW Press.

Delgado, M. (2000a). *Community social work practice in an urban context.* New York: Oxford University Press.

Delgado, M. (2000b). *New arenas for community social work practice with urban youth: Use of the arts, humanities, and sports.* New York: Oxford University Press.

Delgado, M. (2007). *Social work with Latinos: A cultural assets paradigm.* New York: Oxford.

Delgado, M., Jones, K., & Rohani, M. (2005). *Social work practice with refugee and immigrant youth in the United States.* Boston: Allyn & Bacon.

Delgado-Romero, E. A., Nevels, B. J., & Capielo, C. (2013). Culturally alert counseling with Latino/Latina Americans. In G. McAuliffe, Associates (Eds.), *Culturally alert counseling: A comprehensive introduction* (2nd ed., pp. 293–314). Thousand Oaks, CA: Sage.

Deming, W. E. (1986). *Out of the crisis.* Cambridge, MA: Massachusetts Institute of Technology, Center for Advanced Engineering Study.

Deparle, J. (2007, September 30). Cultivating their own gardens. *New York Times,* p. 21.

DePorto, D. (2003). Battered women and separation abuse: A treatment approach based on "knowing." In M. Kopala & M. A. Keitel (Eds.), *Handbook of counseling women* (pp. 279–306). Thousand Oaks, CA: Sage.

DePoy, E., & Gilson, S. F. (2004). *Rethinking disability: Principles for professional and social change.* Belmont, CA: Brooks/Cole.

Devore, W., & Schlesinger, E. G. (1996). *Ethnic-sensitive social work practice* (4th ed.). Needham Heights, MA: Allyn & Bacon.

Devore, W., & Schlesinger, E. G. (1999). *Ethnic-sensitive social work practice* (5th ed.). Needham Heights, MA: Allyn & Bacon.

DeWeaver, K. L. (1995). Developmental disabilities: Definitions and policies. In R. L. Edwards (Ed.), *Encyclopedia of social work* (19th ed., Vol. 1, pp. 712–720). Washington, DC: NASW Press.

Dey, J. G., & Hill, C. (2007). *Behind the pay gap.* Washington, DC: American Association of University Women.

Dhooper, S. S., & Moore, S. E. (2001). *Social work practice with culturally diverse people.* Thousand Oaks, CA: Sage.

Dickson, D. T. (1998). *Confidentiality and privacy in social work.* New York: Free Press.

Dietrich, R. S., & Cohen, I. (2006). Fetal MR imaging. *Magnetic Resonance Imagining Clinics of North America, 14,* 503–522.

Diller, J. V. (2011). *Cultural diversity: A primer for the human services* (4th ed.). Belmont, CA: Brooks/Cole.

Diller, J. V. (2015). *Cultural diversity: A primer for the human services* (5th ed.). Belmont, CA: CENGAGE Learning.

DiNitto, D. M. (2005). *Social welfare: Politics and public policy* (6th ed.). Boston: Allyn & Bacon.

DiNitto, D. M. (2007). *Social welfare: Politics and public policy* (6th ed.). Boston: Allyn & Bacon.

Dishion, T. J., Kavanagh, K., Schneiger, A., Nelson, S., & Kaufman, N. (2002). Preventing early adolescent substance use: A family-centered strategy for public middle school. In R. L. Spoth, K. Kavanagh, & T. J. Dishion (Eds.), Universal family-centered prevention strategies: Current findings and critical issues for public health impact [Special issue]. *Prevention science, 3*, 191–201.

Dobash, R. P., Dobash, R. E., Cavanagh, K., & Lewis, R. (1998). Separate and intersecting realities: A comparison of men's and women's accounts of violence against women. *Violence against Women, 4*, 382–414.

Doege, D. (2002, January 13). Surviving justice. *Milwaukee Journal Sentinel*, 1L, 3L.

Doig, W. (2008, February 26). Homophobosphere. *Advocate*, (1002), 28–31.

Doka, K. J., & Mertz, M. E. (1988). The meaning and significance of great-grandparenthood. *Gerontologist, 28*(2), 192–197.

Dolgoff, R., Harrington, D., & Loewenberg, F. M. (2012). *Ethical decisions for social work practice* (9th ed.). Belmont, CA: Brooks/Cole.

Dolgoff, R., Loewenberg, F. M., & Harrington, D. (2009). *Ethical decisions for social work practice* (8th ed.). Belmont, CA: Brooks/Cole.

Domesticviolence.org. (2007). *Cycle of violence*. Retrieved from http://www.Domesticviolence.Org/cycle-of-violence

Dotinga, R. (2013, May 16). Anti-gay bullying tied to teen depression, suicide. *U.S. News and World Report*. Retrieved from http://health.usnews.com/health-news/news/articles/2013/05/16/anti-gay-bullying-tied-to-teen-depression-suicide

Dotinga, R., & Mundell, E. M. (2010, October 8). *For many gay youth, bullying exacts a deadly toll*. Retrieved from http://www.businessweek.com/lifestyle/content/healthday/644051.html

Downs, S. W., Moore, E., & McFadden, E. J. (2009). *Child welfare and family services: Policies and practice* (8th ed.). Boston: Allyn & Bacon.

Doyle, R. (1996). *The woman who walked into doors*. New York: Vilking.

Drucker, P. F. (1954). *The practice of management*. New York: Harper.

Dubas, J. S., Graber, J. A., & Petersen, A. C. (1991). The effects of pubertal development on achievement during adolescence. *American Journal of Education, 99*, 444–460.

Duffey, T. (2005). The relational impact of addiction across the life span. In D. Comstock (Ed.), *Diversity and development: Critical contexts that shape our lives and relationships* (pp. 299–335). Belmont, CA: Brooks/Cole.

Duncan, G., & Brooks-Gunn, J. (2000). Family poverty, welfare reform, and child development. *Child Development, 71*(1), 188–196.

Dupper, D. R. (2013). *School bullying: New perspectives on a growing problem*. New York: Oxford University Press.

Duren, R. (1985, October 18). Presentation on drug abuse at University of Wisconsin –Whitewater.

Dziech, B. W., & Hawkins, M. W. (1998). *Sexual harassment in higher education: Reflections and new perspectives*. New York: Garland.

Dziegielewski, S. F., Resnick, C., & Krause, N. B. (1996). Shelter-based crisis intervention with battered women. In A. R. Roberts (Ed.), *Helping battered women: New perspectives and remedies* (pp. 159–171). New York: Oxford University Press.

Eccles, J. S., & Roeser, R. W. (2005). School and community influences on human development. In M. H. Bornstein & M. E. Lamb (Eds.), *Development science: An advanced textbook* (5th ed., pp. 513–555). Mahwah, NJ: Erlbaum.

Eckholm, R. (2014, March 22). Michigan gay marriage ban falls. *Milwaukee Journal Sentinal*, 6A.

Eisenberg, N., & Morris, A. (2004). Moral cognitions and pro-social responding in adolescence. In R. Lerner & L. Steinberg (Eds.), *Handbook of adolescent psychology* (2nd ed., pp. 155–188). New York: Wiley.

Eitzen, D. S., Zinn, M. B., & Smith, K. E. (2009). *Social problems* (11th ed.). Boston: Allyn & Bacon.

Eitzen, D. S., Zinn, M. B., & Smith, K. E. (2014). *Social problems* (13th ed.). Upper Saddle River, NJ: Pearson.

Elliot, A. J., & Thrash, R. M. (2010). Approach and avoidance temperament as basic dimensions of personality. *Journal of Personality, 78*(3), 865–906.

Ellis, A. (1957). Outcome of employing three techniques of psychotherapy. *Journal of Clinical Psychology, 13*(4), 344–350.

Ellis, A. (1962). *Reason and emotion in psychotherapy*. New York: Lyle Stuart.

Ellis, A. (1979). Rational-emotive therapy. In R. Corsini (Ed.), *Current psychotherapies* (2nd ed., pp. 185–229). Itasca, IL: Peacock.

Ekman, P., & Friesen, W. V. (1975). Unmaking the face. Englewood Cliffs, NJ: Prentice-Hall.

Emert, P. B. (2007). *Discrimination against Arab-Americans: Learning from the past*. Retrieved from www.njsbf.org/njsbf/student/respect/winter02-l.cfm

Engels, R. (2009). Early pubertal maturation and drug use: Underlying mechanisms. *Addiction, 104*(1), 67–68.

Epstein, D. (1999). In search of effective intervention in domestic violence cases: Rethinking the roles of prosecutors, judges, and the court system. *Yale Journal of Law and Feminism, 11*, 3–50.

Equal Employment Opportunity Commission (EEOC). (2008a). *Sexual harassment*. Retrieved from http://eeoc.gov/types/sexual_harassment.html

Equal Employment Opportunity Commission (EEOC). (2008b). *Sexual harassment charges*. Retrieved from http://eeoc.gov/stats/harass.html

Equal Employment Opportunity Commission (EEOC). (2010a). *Facts about sexual harassment*. Retrieved from http://www.eeoc.gov/eeoc/publications/fs-sex.cfm

Equal Employment Opportunity Commission (EEOC). (2010b). *Sexual harassment charges EEOC & FEPAs combined: FY 1997–2010*. Retrieved from http://www.eeoc.gov/eeoc/statistics/enforcement/sexual_harassment.cfm

Erez, E., & Belknap, J. (1998). In their own words: Battered women's assessment of the criminal processing system's response. *Violence and Victims, 13*, 251–268.

Erickson, M. F., & Egeland, B. (2002). Child neglect. In J. E. B. Myers, L. Berliner, J. Briere, C. T. Hendrix, C. Jenny, & T. A. Reid (Eds.), *The APSAC handbook on child maltreatment* (2nd ed., pp. 3–20). Thousand Oaks, CA: Sage.

Erickson, M. F., & Egeland, B. (2011). Child neglect. In J. E. B. Myers (Ed.), *The APSAC handbook on child maltreatment* (3rd ed., pp. 103–124). Thousand Oaks, CA: Sage.

Erikson, E. H. (1950). *Childhood and society*. New York: Norton.

Erikson, E. H. (1959). The problem of ego identity. *Psychological Issues, 1*, 101–164.

Erikson, E. H. (1963). *Childhood and society* (2nd ed.). New York: Norton.

Erikson, E. H. (1968). *Identity: Youth and crisis.* New York: Norton.

Etzioni, A. (1964). *Modern organizations.* Englewood Cliffs, NJ: Prentice-Hall.

Evans, K. M. (2013). Culturally alert counseling with African Americans. In G. McCauliffe, Associates (Eds.), *Culturally alert counseling: A comprehensive introduction* (2nd ed., pp. 125–155). Thousand Oaks, CA: Sage.

Falicov, C. J. (2011). Migration and the life cycle. In M. McGoldrick, B. Carter, & N. G. Garcia-Preto (Eds.), *The expanded family life cycle: Individual, family, and social perspectives* (4th ed., pp. 336–347). Boston: Allyn & Bacon.

Faller, K. C. (2003). *Understanding and assessing child sexual maltreatment* (2nd ed.). Thousand Oaks, CA: Sage.

Farley, J. E. (1992). *American social problems* (2nd ed.). Englewood Cliffs, NJ: Prentice-Hall.

Federal Bureau of Investigation (FBI). (2014). *Crime in the United States 2011: Forcible rape.* Retrieved from http://www.fbi.gov/about-us/cjis/ucr/crime-in-the-u.s/2011/crime-in-the-U.S.-2011/violent-crime/forcible-rape

Fellin, P. (1995). *The community and the social worker* (2nd ed.). Itasca, IL: Peacock.

Fellin, P. (2001a). *The community and the social worker* (3rd ed.). Itasca, IL: Peacock.

Fellin, P. (2001b). Understanding American communities. In J. Rothman, J. L. Erlich, & J. E. Tropman (Eds.), *Strategies of community intervention* (6th ed., pp. 118–132). Itasca, IL: Peacock.

FeralChildren.com. (2005, April 2). *Isolated, confined, wolf and wild children.* Retrieved from http://www.feralchildren.com/en/showchild.php?h=victor

Fernyhough, C. (2010). Inner speech. In H. Pashler (Ed.), *Encyclopedia of the mind.* Thousand Oaks, CA: Sage.

Fertig, A. R. (2009). Selection and the effect of prenatal smoking. *Health Economics, 19*(2), 209–226.

Fertig, A. R. (2010). Selection and the effect of prenatal smoking. *Health Economics, 19*, 209–226.

Fertilityplus. (2010). *Charting your basal body temperature information and FAQ.* Retrieved from http://www.fertilityplus.org/faq/bbt/bbtfaq.html

Field, D., Minkler, M., Falk, R. F., & Leino, E. V. (1993). The influence of health on family contacts and family functioning in advanced old age: A longitudinal study. *Journal of Gerontology, 48*, 18–28.

Finkelhor, D. (1990). Early and long-term effects of child sexual abuse: An update. *Professional Psychology: Research and Practice, 21*, 325–330.

First Star, Inc. (2013). *Child abuse and neglect stats.* Retrieved from http://www.firststar.org/library/national-statistics.aspx

Fischer, D. H. (1977, May 10). Putting our heads to the "problem" of old age. *New York Times*, 33.

Fischer, J., & Gochros, H. L. (1975). *Planned behavior change: Behavior modification in social work.* New York: Free Press.

Fiske, H. (2002, May 13). When a client commits suicide: How can you cope?. *Social Work Today, 2*(10), 9–11.

Forte, J. A., Franks, D. D., Forte, J. A., & Rigsby, D. (1996). Asymmetrical role-taking: Comparing battered and nonbattered women. *Social Work, 41*(1), 59–73.

Fouts, B., & Knapp, J. (2001). A sexual assault education and risk reduction workshop for college freshmen. In A. J. Ottens & K. Hotelling (Eds.), *Sexual violence on campus* (pp. 98–119). New York: Springer.

Fowler, J. (1981). *Stages of faith: The psychology of human development and the quest for meaning.* San Francisco: Harper & Row.

Fowler, J. (1996). *Faithful change: The personal and public challenges of postmodern life.* Nashville: Abingdon Press.

Frame, M. W. (2003). *Integrating religion and spirituality into counseling: A comprehensive approach.* Belmont, CA: Brooks/Cole.

Franzoi, S. L. (2008). *Essentials of psychology* (3rd ed.). Mason, OH: Thomson.

Fratelli, N., Papageorghiou, A. T., Prefumo, F., Bakalis, S., Homfray, T., & Thilaganathan, B. (2007). Outcome of prenatally diagnosed agenesis of the corpus callosum. *Prenatal Diagnosis, 27*, 512–517.

French, S. E., Seidman, E., Allen, L., & Aber, J. (2006). The development of ethnic identity during adolescence. *Developmental Psychology, 42*, 1–10.

Frenkel-Brunswick, E. (1970). Adjustments and reorientation in the course of the life-span. In R. G. Kuhlen & G. G. Thomson (Eds.), *Psychological studies of human development* (3rd ed., p. 47). New York: Appleton-Century-Crofts.

Freyhan, F. A. (1955). *Psychopathic personalities. Oxford loose leaf medicine.* New York: Oxford University Press.

Friebe, A., & Arck, P. (2008). Causes for spontaneous abortions: What the bugs "gut" to do with it?. *International Journal of Biochemistry and Cell Biology, 40*(11), 2348–2352.

Friedrich, W. N., Fisher, J. L., Dittner, C. A., Acton, R., Berliner, L., Butler, J., et al. (2001). Child sexual behavior inventory: Normative, psychiatric and sexual abuse comparisons. *Child Maltreatment, 6*, 37–49.

Friend, M. (2008). *Special education: Contemporary perspectives for school professionals* (2nd ed.). Boston: Allyn & Bacon.

Friend, M. (2011). *Special education: Contemporary perspectives for school professionals* (3rd ed.). Upper Saddle River, NJ: Pearson.

Fuligni, A. J., Burton, L., Marshall, S., Perez-Febles, A., Yarrington, J., Kirsch, L. B., et al. (1999). Attitudes toward family obligations among American adolescents with Asian, Latin American, and European backgrounds. *Child Development, 70*, 1030–1044.

Fullmer, E. M. (2006). Lesbian, gay, bisexual, and transgender aging. In D. F. Morrow & L. Messinger (Eds.), *Sexual orientation and gender expression in social work practice: Working with gay, lesbian, bisexual, and transgender people* (pp. 284–303). New York: Columbia University Press.

Fulmer, R. H. (2011). Becoming an adult: Finding ways to love and work. In M. McGoldrick, B. Carter, & N. G. Garcia-Preto (Eds.), *The expanded family life cycle: Individual, family, and social perspectives* (4th ed., pp. 176–192). Boston: Allyn & Bacon.

Furman, L. E. (1994, April). *Religion and spirituality in social work education.* Paper presented at the Midwest Biennial Conference on Social Work Education, St. Paul, MN.

Furman, R., Negi, N. J., & Loya, M. (2010). Introduction. In R. Furman & N. Negi (Eds.), *Social work practice with Latinos: Key issues and emerging themes* (pp. 1–14). Chicago: Lyceum.

Gacik, C. (2014). *Basic facts about the defense of marriage act.* Retrieved from http://www.frc.org/onepagers/basic-facts-about-the-defense-of-marriage-act

Gallup. (2010, May 24). *Americans' opposition to gay marriage eases slightly.* Retrieved from http://www.gallup.com/poll/128291/americans-opposition-gay-marriage-eases-slightly.aspx

Galsworthy, M. J., Dionne, G., Dale, P. S., & Plomin, R. (2000). Sex differences in early verbal and non-verbal cognitive development. *Developmental Science, 3*, 206–215.

Gambrill, E., & Gibbs, L. (2009). *Critical thinking for helping professionals* (3rd ed.). New York: Oxford.

Garbarino, J., Guttmann, E., & Seeley, J. W. (1986). *The psychologically battered child.* San Francisco: Jossey-Bass.

Garcia, B. (2009). Theory and social work practice with immigrant populations. In F. Chang-Muy & E. P. Congress (Eds.), *Social work with immigrants and refugees: Legal issues, clinical skills, and advocacy* (pp. 79–101). New York: Springer.

Garcia, B. (2011). Cultural competence with Latino Americans. In D. Lum (Ed.), *Culturally competent practice: A framework for understanding diverse groups and justice issues* (4th ed., pp. 302–357). Belmont, CA: Brooks/Cole.

Garcia Coll, C., & Pachter, L. M. (2002). Ethnic and minority parenting. In M. H. Bornstein (Ed.), *Handbook of parenting: Vol. 4. Social conditions and applied parenting* (2nd ed., pp. 1–20). Mahwah, NJ: Erlbaum.

Gardiner, H. W., Mutter, J. D., & Kosmitzki, C. (1998). *Lives across cultures: Cross-cultural human development.* Boston: Allyn & Bacon.

Garel, C. (2008). Fetal MRI: What is the future? *Ultrasound in Obstetrics and Gynecology, 31*, 123–128.

Garland, J. A., & Frey, L. A. (1973). Application of stages of group development to groups in psychiatric settings. In S. Bernstein (Ed.), *Further explorations in group work* (pp. 1–33). Boston: Milford House.

Garland, J. A., Jones, H., & Kolodny, R. (1965). A model for stages of development in social work groups. In S. Bernstein (Ed.), *Explorations in group work* (pp. 17–71). Boston: Milford House.

Garrett, M. T. (1999). Understanding the "medicine" of Native American traditional values: An integrative review. *Counseling and Values, 43*(2), 84–99.

Garvey, C. (1977). *Play.* Cambridge, MA: Harvard University Press.

Gawain, S. (1986). *Living in the light.* San Rafael, CA: Whatever Publications.

What does gay/lesbian pride mean to you? (1985, June 27). *Gay-Life,* 2.

Ge, X., Conger, R. D., & Elder, G. H., Jr. (2001). The relations between puberty and psychological distress in adolescent boys. *Journal of Research on Adolescence, 11*, 49–70.

Geller, J. (2004). The marriage mystique. In G. Kirk & M. Okazawa-Rey (Eds.), *Women's lives: Multicultural perspectives* (3rd ed., pp. 286–294). Boston: McGraw-Hill.

Gelman, D. (1988, March 7). Black and white in America. *Newsweek,* 19–21.

Gelman, D. (1993, July 26). Homoeroticism in the ranks. *Newsweek,* 28–29.

Gelman, D., Foote, D., Barrett, T., & Talbot, M. (1992, February 24). Born or bred? *Newsweek,* 46–53.

Georgiades, I., & Grieger, I. (2003). Counseling women for grief and loss: Theoretical and clinical considerations. In M. Kopala & M. A. Keitel (Eds.), *Handbook of counseling women* (pp. 220–240). Thousand Oaks, CA: Sage.

Gerhard, G. S., & Cristofalo, V. J. (1992). The limits of biogerontology. *Generations, 16*(4), 55–59.

Gibbs, L., & Gambrill, E. (1999). *Critical thinking for social workers: Exercises for the helping profession.* Thousand Oaks, CA: Pine Forge Press.

Gibbs, N. (1998). Til death do us part. In S. Ruth (Ed.), *Issues in feminism: An introduction to women's studies* (4th ed., pp. 326–333). Mountain View, CA: Mayfield.

Gilbert, M. J. (2008). Transgender people. In T. Mizrahi & L. E. Davis (Eds.), *Encyclopedia of social work* (4 ed., pp. 238–241). Washington, DC: NASW Press.

Gilford, R. (1986). Marriages in later life. *Generations, 10*(4), 16–20.

Gilligan, C. (1982). *In a different voice: Psychological theory and women's development.* Cambridge, MA: Harvard University Press.

Gilligan, C. (1996). The centrality of relationships in psychological development: A puzzle, some evidence, and a theory. In G. G. Noam & K. W. Fischer (Eds.), *Development and vulnerability in close relationships* (pp. 237–259). Hillside, NJ: Erlbaum.

Gilligan, C., & Attanucci, J. (1988). Two moral orientations. In C. Gilligan, J. V. Ward, J. M. Taylor, & B. Bardige (Eds.), *Mapping the moral domain* (pp. 73–86). Cambridge, MA: Harvard University Press.

Gilligan, C., Brown, L. M., & Rogers, A. G. (1990). Psyche embedded: A place for body, relationships, and culture in personality theory. In A. I. Rabin, R. A. Zucker, R. A. Emmons, & S. Frank (Eds.), *Studying persons and lives* (pp. 86–147). New York: Springer.

Glass, T. A., Seeman, T. E., Herzog, A. R., Kahn, R., & Berkman, L. F. (1995). Change in productive activity in late adulthood. Macarthur studies of successful aging. *Journal of Gerontology: Social Sciences, 50B,* S65–S66.

Glasser, W. (1984). *Control theory.* New York: Harper & Row.

Glasser, W. (1998). *Choice theory: A new psychology of personal freedom.* New York: Harper Perennial.

Glasser, W. (2003). *Warning: Psychiatry can be hazardous to your health.* New York: HarperCollins.

Gleitman, H. (1986). *Psychology* (2nd ed.). New York: Norton.

GlenMaye, L. (1998). Empowerment of women. In L. M. Gutierrez, R. J. Parsons, & E. O. Cox (Eds.), *Empowerment in social work practice: A sourcebook* (pp. 2–51). Belmont, CA: Brooks/Cole.

Glover, R. J. (2001). Discriminators of moral orientation: Gender role or personality?. *Journal of Adult Development, 8*(1), 1–7.

Goldenberg, H., & Goldenberg, I. (1998). *Counseling today's families* (3rd ed.). Pacific Grove, CA: Brooks/Cole.

Goldsmith, H. H., Buss, K. A., & Lemery, K. S. (1997). Toddler and childhood temperament: Expanded content, stronger genetic evidence, new evidence for the importance of environment. *Development Psychology, 33*, 891–905.

Goldstein, A. P. (1991). *Delinquent gangs: A psychological perspective.* Champaign, IL: Research Press.

Goldstein, A. P., & Huff, C. R. (Eds.). (1993). *The gang intervention handbook*. Champaign, IL: Research Press.

Goldstein, E. G. (2008). Psychosocial framework. In T. Mizrahi & L. E. Davis (Eds.), *Encyclopedia of social work* (Vol. 3, pp. 462–467). Washington, DC: NASW Press.

Goldstein, J. M., Seidman, L. J., Horton, N. J., Makris, N., Kennedy, D. N., Caviness, V. S., Jr., et al. (2001). Normal sexual dimorphism of the adult human brain assessed by in vivo magnetic resonance imaging. *Cerebral Cortex, 11*(6), 490–497.

Goleman, D. (1995). *Emotional intelligence: Why it can matter more than IQ*. New York: Bantam.

Goleman, D. (1998). *Working with emotional intelligence*. New York: Bantam.

Goleman, D. (2001). An el-based theory of performance. In C. Cherniss & D. Goleman (Eds.), *The emotionally intelligent workplace: How to select for, measure, and improve emotional intelligence in individuals, groups, and organizations* (pp. 27–44). San Francisco: Jossey-Bass.

Goleman, D. (2006). *Social intelligence: The new science of human relationships*. New York: Bantam Books.

Goleman, D. (2013). *Focus: The hidden driver of excellence*. New York: Harper Collins.

Good, G. E., & Beitman, B. D. (2006). *Counseling and psychotherapy essentials: Integrating theories, skills, and practices*. New York: Norton.

Goodman, D. D. (1998). Using the empowerment model to develop sex education for Native Americans. *Journal of Sex Education and Therapy, 23*(2), 135–144.

Gooren, L. (2006). The biology of human psychosexual differentiation. *Hormones and Behavior, 50*, 589–601.

Gordon, M. (1961, Spring). Assimilation in America: Theory and reality. *Daedalus, 90*, 363–365.

Gordon, T. (1970). *Parent effectiveness training*. New York: Wyden.

Gordon, W. (1962). A critique of the working definition. *Social Work, 7*(4), 3–13.

Graber, J. A. (2008). Pubertal and neuroendocrine development and risk for depressive disorders. In N. B. Allen & L. Sheeber (Eds.), *Adolescent emotional development and the emergence of depressive disorders* (pp. 74–91). New York: Cambridge University Press.

Graber, J. A., Seeley, J. R., Brooks-Gunn, J., & Lewinsohn, P. M. (2004). Is pubertal timing associated with psychopathology in young adulthood?. *Journal of the American Academy of Child and Adolescent Psychiatry, 43*(6), 718–126.

Greder, K. A., & Allen, W. D. (2007). Parenting in color: Culturally diverse perspectives on parenting. In B. S. Trask & R. R. Hamon (Eds.), *Cultural diversity and families: Expanding perspectives* (pp. 118–135). Thousand Oaks, CA: Sage.

Green, J. W. (1999). *Cultural awareness in the human services: A multi-ethnic approach* (3rd ed.). Boston: Allyn & Bacon.

Greenberg, J., & Becker, M. (1988). Aging parents as family resources. *Gerontologist, 28*, 786–790.

Greenberg, J. S., Bruess, C. E., & Conklin, S. C. (2007). *Exploring the dimensions of human sexuality* (3rd ed.). Sudbury, MA: Jones and Bartlett.

Greenberg, J. S., Bruess, C. E., & Conklin, S. C. (2011). *Exploring the dimensions of human sexuality* (4th ed.). Sudbury, MA: Jones and Bartlett.

Greenberg, J. S., Bruess, C. E., & Oswalt, S. B. (2014). *Exploring the dimensions of human sexuality* (5th ed.). Burlington, MA: Jones & Bartlett.

Greene, B. L. (1994). Lesbian women of color: Triple jeopardy. In L. Comas-Diaz & B. Greene (Eds.), *Women of color and mental health* (pp. 109–174). New York: Guilford.

Greene, R. R. (1999). Human behavior theory, person-in-environment, and social work method. In R. R. Greene (Ed.), *Human behavior theory and social work practice* (2nd ed., pp. 1–30). Hawthorne, NY: Aldine de Gruyter.

Greene, R. R., & Conrad, A. P. (2012). Resilience: Basic assumptions and terms. In R. R. Green (Ed.), *Resiliency: An integrated approach to practice, policy, and research* (2nd ed., pp. 29–62). Washington, DC: NASW Press.

Greene, R. R., & Livingston, N. C. (2002). A social construct. In R. R. Green (Ed.), *Resiliency: An integrated approach to practice, policy, and research* (pp. 63–93). Washington, DC: NASW Press.

Greene, R. R., & Watkins, M. (Eds.). (1998). *Serving diverse constituencies, applying the ecological perspective*. Hawthorne, NY: Aldine de Gruyter.

Greenfield, P. M., & Childs, C. P. (1991). Developmental continuity in bio-cultural context. In R. Cohen & A. W. Siegel (Eds.), *Context and development* (pp. 135–139). Hillsdale, NJ: Erlbaum.

Greenleaf, R. K. (1982). *The servant as leader*. Mahwah, NJ: Paulist Press.

Greenough, A. (2007). Late respiratory outcomes after preterm birth. *Early Human Development, 83*, 785–788.

Grolnick, W. S., Gurland, S. T., Jacob, K. F., & Decourcey, W. (2002). The development of self-determination in middle childhood and adolescence. In A. Wigfield & J. S. Eccles (Eds.), *Development of achievement motivation* (pp. 147–171). San Diego: Academic Press.

Grossmann, K., Grossmann, K. E., Spangler, G., Suess, G., & Unzner, L. (1985). Maternal sensitivity and newborns' orientation responses as related to quality of attachment in Northern Germany. In I. Bretherton & E. Waters (Eds.), *Growing points of attachment theory and research. Monographs of the society for research in child development* (Vol. 50), 1–2, Serial No. 209.

Group for the Advancement of Psychiatry. (1973). *The joys and sorrows of parenthood*. New York: Scribner's.

Grush, J. E., & Yehl, J. G. (1979). Marital roles, sex differences and interpersonal attraction. *Journal of Personality and Social Psychology, 37*, 116–123.

Guerin, E. W., Gottfried, A. W., & Thomas, C. W. (1997). Difficult temperament and behavior problems: A longitudinal study from 1.5 to 12 years. *International Journal of Behavioral Development, 21*(1), 71–90.

Guha, S. (2007). Biophysical mechanism-mediated time-dependent effect on sperm of human and monkey vas implanted polyelectrolyte contraceptive. *Asian Journal of Andrology, 9*, 221–227.

Gumpel, T. P. (2007). Are social competence difficulties by performance or acquisition deficits? The importance of self-regulatory mechanisms. *Psychology in the Schools, 44*, 351–372.

Gutheil, I. A., & Congress, E. (2000). Resiliency in older people: A paradigm for practice. In R. R. Green (Ed.), *Resiliency:*

An integrated approach to practice, policy, and research (pp. 40–52). Washington, DC: NASW Press.

Gutierrez, L. M. (1990). Working with women of color: An empowerment perspective. *Social Work, 35*(2), 149–153.

Gutierrez, L. M. (2001). Working with women of color: An empowerment perspective. In J. Rothman, J. L. Erlich, & J. E. Tropman (Eds.), *Strategies of community intervention* (6th ed., pp. 209–217). Itasca, IL: Peacock.

Gutierrez, L., GlenMaye, L., & DeLois, K. (1995). The organizational context of empowerment practice: Implications for social work administration. *Social Work, 40*, 249–257.

Guttmacher Institute. (2010a). *Abortion.* Retrieved from http://www.guttmacher.org/sections/abortion.php

Guttmacher Institute. (2010b). *U.S. Teenage pregnancies, births, and abortions: National and state trends and trends by race and ethnicity.* Retrieved from http://www.guttmacher.org/pubs/USTPtrends.pdf

Guttmacher Institute. (2011a). *Facts on American teens sexual and reproductive health.* Retrieved from http://www.guttmacher.org/pubs/FB-ATSRH.html

Guttmacher Institute. (2011b). *Sex and HIV education.* Retrieved from http://www.guttmacher.org/statecenter/spibs/spib_SE.pdf

Guttmacher Institute. (2012a, February). *Facts on American teens' sources of information about sex.* Retrieved from http://www.guttmacher.org/pubs/FB-Teen-Sex-Ed.html

Guttmacher Institute. (2012b, January). *Facts on induced abortion worldwide.* Retrieved from https://www.guttmacher.org/pubs/fb_IAW.html

Guttmacher Institute. (2013a, November 1). *Bans on "partial-birth" abortion.* Retrieved from http://www.guttmacher.org/statecenter/spibs/spib_BPBA.pdf

Guttmacher Institute. (2013b, August). *Contraceptive use in the United States.* Retrieved from http://www.guttmacher.org/pubs/fb_contr_use.html

Guttmacher Institute. (2013c, November 1). *Counseling and waiting periods for abortion.* Retrieved from http://www.guttmacher.org/statecenter/spibs/spib_MWPA.pdf

Guttmacher Institute. (2013d, June). *Facts on American teens' sexual and reproductive health.* Retrieved from http://www.guttmacher.org/pubs/FB-ATSRH.html

Guttmacher Institute. (2013e, October). *Facts on induced abortion in the United States.* Retrieved from http://www.guttmacher.org/pubs/fb_induced_abortion.html

Guttmacher Institute. (2013f, November 1). *Parental involvement in minors' abortions.* Retrieved from http://www.guttmacher.org/statecenter/spibs/spib_PIMA.pdf

Guttmacher Institute. (2013g, November 1). *Restricting state insurance coverage of abortion.* Retrieved from http://www.guttmacher.org/statecenter/spibs/spib_RICA.pdf

Guttmacher Institute. (2013h, November 1). *Sex and HIV education.* Retrieved from http://www.guttmacher.org/statecenter/spibs/spib_SE.pdf

Guttmacher Institute. (2013i, November 1). *State funding of abortion under medicaid.* Retrieved from http://www.guttmacher.org/statecenter/spibs/spib_SFAM.pdf

Haight, B. K. (1991). Reminiscing: The state of the art as a basis for practice. *Interpersonal Journal of Aging and Human Development, 33*, 1–32.

Hakim-Larson, J., Nassar-McMillan, S., & Paterson, A. D. (2013). Culturally alert counseling with middle Eastern Americans. In G. McCauliffe, Associates (Eds.), *Culturally alert counseling: A comprehensive introduction* (2nd ed., pp. 263–292). Thousand Oaks, CA: Sage.

Hall, E. T. (1969). *The hidden dimension.* Garden City, NY: Doubleday.

Hall, G., & Barongan, C. (1997). Prevention of sexual aggression: Sociocultural risk and protective factors. *American Psychologist, 52*, 5–14.

Hall, G., Nagayama, C., DeGarmo, D. S., Eap, S., Teten, A. L., & Sue, S. (2006). Initiation, desistance, and persistence of men's sexual coercion. *Journal of Consulting and Clinical Psychology, 74*, 732–742.

Hall, G., Nagayama, C., Teten, A. L., DeGarmo, D. S., Sue, S., & Stephens, K. (2005). Ethnicity, culture, and sexual aggression: Risk and protective factors. *Journal of Consulting and Clinical Psychology, 73*, 830–840.

Hall, J. (1998). How big are nonverbal sex differences? The case of smiling and sensitivity to nonverbal cues. In D. Canary & K. Dindia (Eds.), *Sex differences and similarities in communication* (pp. 155–178). Mahwah, NJ: Erlbaum.

Hall, L. (1997). Iroquois confederacy. In R. J. Vecoli (Ed.), *Gale encyclopedia of multicultural America* (Vol. 2, pp. 750–763). Boston: Thomson.

Hallahan, D. P., Kauffman, J. M., & Pullen, P. C. (2009). *Exceptional learners: An introduction to special education* (11th ed.). Boston: Allyn & Bacon.

Hallahan, D. P., Kauffman, J. M., & Pullen, P. C. (2012). *Exceptional learners: An introduction to special education* (12th ed.). Upper Saddle River, NJ: Pearson.

Hamilton, B. E., Martin, J. A., & Ventura, S. J. (2009, March 18). Births: Preliminary data for 2007. *National Vital Statistics Reports, 57*(12), 1–23.

Hancock, C. (1963). *Children and neglect—hazardous home conditions.* Washington, DC: U.S. Government Printing Office.

Hardman, M. L., Drew, C. J., & Egan, M. W. (2014). *Human exceptionality: School, community, family* (11th ed.). Belmont, CA: Wadsworth.

Hare, A. (1962). *Handbook of small group research.* New York: Free Press.

Harper-Dorton, K., & Lantz, J. (2007). *Cross-cultural practice: Social work with diverse populations.* Chicago: Lyceum.

Harris, J. F. (1999, May 15). Clinton takes Hollywood to task over kids, violence. *Milwaukee Journal Sentinel*, A3.

Harrison, A. O., Wilson, M. N., Pine, C. J., Chan, S. Q., & Buriel, R. (1994). Family ecologies of ethnic minority children. In G. Handel & G. G. Whitchurch (Eds.), *The psychosocial interior of the family* (pp. 187–210). New York: Aldine De Gruyter.

Hart, S. N., Brassard, M. R., Binggeli, N. J., & Davidson, H. A. (2002). Psychological maltreatment. In J. E. B. Myers, L. Berliner, J. Briere, C. T. Hendrix, C. Jenny, & T. A. Reid (Eds.), *The APSAC handbook on child maltreatment* (2nd ed., pp. 79–103). Thousand Oaks, CA: Sage.

Hart, S. N., Brassard, M. R., Davidson, H. A., Rivelis, E., Diaz, V., & Binggeli, N. J. (2011). Psychological maltreatment. In J. E. B. Myers (Ed.), *The APSAC handbook on child maltreatment* (3rd ed., pp. 125–144). Thousand Oaks, CA: Sage.

Harter, S. (1987). The determinants and mediational role of global self-worth in children. In N. Eisenberg (Ed.), *Contemporary topics in developmental psychology* (pp. 219–242). New York: Wiley.

Harter, S. (1988). Developmental processes in the construction of self. In T. D. Yawkey & J. E. Johnson (Eds.), *Integrative processes and socialization: Early to middle childhood* (pp. 45–78). Hillsdale, NJ: Erlbaum.

Harter, S. (1990). Processes underlying adolescent self-concept formation. In R. MonteMayor, G. R. Adams, & T. P. Gullotta (Eds.), *From childhood to adolescence: A transitional period? Advances in adolescent development* (Vol. 2, pp. 205–239). Newbury Park, CA: Sage.

Harter, S. (1993). Developmental changes in self-understanding across the 5 to 7 shift. In A. Sameroff & M. Haith (Eds.), *Reason and responsibility: The passage through childhood.* Chicago: University of Chicago Press.

Harter, S. (1998). The development of self-representations. In W. Damon & N. Eisenberg (Eds.), *Handbook of child psychology: Vol. 3. Social, emotional, and personality development* (5th ed., pp. 553–617). New York: Wiley.

Harter, S. (1999). *The construction of self: A developmental perspective.* New York: Guilford Press.

Harter, S. (2006). The development of self-representation in childhood and adolescence. In W. Damon & R. Lerner (Eds.), *Handbook of child psychology* (6th ed.). New York: Wiley.

Hartley, E. (1946). *Problems in prejudice.* New York: King's Crown Press.

Hartman, A. (1978, October). Diagrammatic assessment of family relationships. *Social Casework, 59,* 465–176.

Hartman, A. (1991). Toward redefinition and contextualization of the abortion issue. *Social Work, 36*(6), 466–167.

Harway, M. (1993). Battered women: Characteristics and causes. In M. Hansen & M. Harway (Eds.), *Battering and family therapy: A feminist perspective* (pp. 29–41). Newbury Park, CA: Sage.

Hatcher, R. A., & Nelson, A. (2004). Combined hormonal contraceptive methods. In R. A. Hatcher, J. Trussell, F. Stewart, A. L. Nelson, W. Cates, Jr., F. Guest, & D. Kowal (Eds.), *Contraceptive technology* (18th ed., pp. 391–160). New York: Ardent Media.

Hatcher, R. A., Trussell, J., Nelson, A. L., Cates, W., Stewart F. H., & Kowal, D. (1994). *Contraceptive technology* (16th rev. ed.). New York: Irvington Publishers.

Haulotte, S. M., & Kretzschmar, J. A. (2001). *Case scenarios for teaching and learning social work practice.* Alexandria, VA: Council on Social Work Education.

Healey, K. M., Smith, C., & O'Sullivan, C. (1998, February). *Batterer intervention: Program approaches and criminal justice strategies.* Washington, DC: U.S. Department of Justice.

Health Canada, Health Programs and Services Branch. (1994). *Suicide in Canada: Update of the report of the task force on suicide in Canada.* Retrieved October 18, 2011, from http://www.phacaspc.gc.ca/mh-sm/pdf/suicid_e.pdf

Healy, M. D., & Ellis, B. J. (2007). Birth order, conscientiousness, and openness to experience tests of the family-niche model of personality using a within-family methodology. *Evolution and Human Behavior, 28*(1), 55–59.

Helpguide.org. (2011). *Suicide prevention.* Retrieved from http://helpguide.org/mental/suicide_prevention.htm

Helwig, C. C., & Turiel, E. (2011). Children's social and moral reasoning. In P. K Smith & C. H. Hart (Eds.), *Wiley-Blackwell handbook of childhood social development* (2nd ed., pp. 567–583). New York: Wiley.

Henderson, A. W., Lehavot, K., & Simoni, J. M. (2009). Ecological models of sexual satisfaction among lesbian/bisexual and heterosexual women. *Archives of Sexual Behavior, 38*(1), 50–65.

Henderson, C. H., & Kim, B. (1980). Racism. In D. Brieland, L. Costin, & C. Atherton (Eds.), *Contemporary social work* (2nd ed., p. 180). New York: McGraw-Hill.

Hendricks, C. O. (2005). The multicultural triangle of the child, the family, and the school: Culturally competent approaches. In E. P. Congress & M. J. Gonzalez (Eds.), *Multicultural perspectives in working with families* (2nd ed., pp. 4–92). New York: Springer.

Henry, J. (1967, December). *Indian Historian* (Vol. 2).

Henry, W. A., III. (1993, September 10). Gay parents: Under fire and on the rise. *Time,* 66–69.

Herman, D. (1984). The rape culture. In J. Freeman (Ed.), *Women: A feminist perspective.* Palo Alto, CA: Mayfield.

Herrnstein, R. J., & Murray, C. (1994). *The bell curve: The reshaping of American life by differences in intelligence.* New York: Free Press.

Hersey, P., & Blanchard, K. (1977). *Management of organizational behavior: Utilizing human resources* (3rd ed.). Englewood Cliffs, NJ: Prentice-Hall.

Hildyard, K. L., & Wolfe, D. A. (2002). Child neglect: Developmental issues and outcomes. *Child Abuse and Neglect, 2*(3/4), 679–695.

Hill, C., Corbett, C., & St. Rose, A. (2010). *Why so few? Women in science, technology, engineering, and mathematics.* Washington, DC: American Association of University Women (AAUW). Retrieved from http://www.aauw.org/learn/research/upload/whysofew.pdf

Hill, C., & Kearl, H. (2011). *Crossing the line: Sexual harassment at school.* Retrieved from http://www.aauw.org/files/2013/02/Crossing-the-Line-Sexual-Harassment-at-School.pdf

Hill, C., & Silva, E. (2005). *Drawing the line: Sexual harassment on campus.* Retrieved from http://www.aauw.org/files/2013/02/drawing-the-line-sexual-harassment-on-campus.pdf

Hill, N. E., Bush, K. R., & Roosa, M. W. (2003). Parenting and family socialization strategies and children's mental health: Low-income Mexican-American and Euro-American mothers and children. *Child Development, 74,* 189–204.

Hill, S. A. (1999). *African American children: Socialization and development in families.* Thousand Oaks, CA: Sage.

Hines, P. M., & Boyd-Franklin, N. (1996). African American families. In M. McGoldrick, J. Giordano, & J. K. Pearce (Eds.), *Ethnicity and family therapy* (2nd ed., pp. 66–84). New York: Guilford Press.

Hirschfelder, A., & Kreipe de Montano, M. (1993). *The Native American almanac: A portrait of native America today.* New York: Prentice-Hall.

Hirschi, T. (1969). *Causes of delinquency.* Berkeley: University of California Press.

Ho, M. K. (1987). *Family therapy with ethnic minorities.* Newbury Park, CA: Sage.

Hokenstad, M. C., & Midgley, J. (1997). Realities of global interdependence: Challenges for social work in a new century. In M. C. Hokenstad & J. Midgley (Eds.), *Issues in international social work: Global challenges for a new century* (pp. 1–10). Washington, DC: NASW Press.

Holmberg, D., & Blair, K. L. (2009). Sexual desire, communication, satisfaction, and preferences of men and women in same-sex versus mixed-sex relationships. *Journal of Sex Research, 46*, 57–66.

Homan, M. S. (2011). *Promoting community change: Making it happen in the real world* (5th ed.). Belmont, CA: Brooks/Cole.

Hooyman, N. (2007). *Selected facts on aging.* Washington, DC: Gero-Ed Center, National Center for Gerontological Social Work Education.

Howard-Hamilton, M. F., & Frazier, K. (2005). Identity development and the convergence of race, ethnicity, and gender. In D. Comstock (Ed.), *Diversity and development: Critical contexts that shape our lives and relationships* (pp. 67–90). Belmont, CA: Brooks/Cole.

Hower, D. (1994, August 22). David hower's definition of total quality. *Reporter* (University of Wisconsin-Whitewater), 10.

Howes, C. (1997). Children's experiences in center-based child care as a function of teacher background and adult: Child ratio. *Merrill-Palmer Quarterly, 43*(3), 404–125.

Hoyert, D. L., Matthews, T. J., Menacker, F., Strobino, D. M., & Guyer, B. (2006). Annual summary of vital statistics: 2004. *Pediatrics, 117*, 175–180.

Huang, L. N., & Ying, Y. (1998). Chinese American children and adolescents. In J. T. Gibbs & L. N. Huang (Eds.), *Children of color: Psychological interventions with culturally diverse youth* (pp. 33–67). San Francisco: Jossey-Bass.

Huesmann, L. R., & Miller, L. S. (1994). Long-term effects of repeated exposure to media violence in childhood. In L. R. Huesmann (Ed.), *Aggressive behavior: Current perspectives* (pp. 153–186). New York: Plenum Press.

Hughes, M. (1975). *Egocentrism in preschool children.* Unpublished doctoral dissertation, Edinburgh University, Edinburgh.

Hull, G. H., Jr. (2007). Social work practice with diverse groups. In C. Zastrow (Ed.), *The practice of social work* (8th ed., pp. 324–364). Belmont, CA: Brooks/Cole.

Hull, G. H., Jr. (2010). Social work practice with diverse groups. In C. Zastrow (Ed.), *The practice of social work* (9th ed., pp. 343–390). Belmont, CA: Brooks/Cole.

Human Intelligence. (2004, July 14). *Human intelligence: Jean-marc gaspard itard.* Retrieved from http://www.indiana.edu/~intell/itard.shtml

Human Rights Campaign. (2011). *Domestic partner benefits.* Retrieved from http://www.hrc.org/issues/domestic_partner_benefits.htm

Human Rights Campaign. (2014). *Employment non-discrimination act.* Retrieved from http://www.hrc.org/laws-and-legislation/federal-legislation/employment-non-discrimination-act

Hunter College Women's Studies Collective. (1995). *Women's realities, women's choices: An introduction to women's studies* (2nd ed.). New York: Oxford University Press.

Hunter, S., & Hickerson, J. C. (2003). *Affirmative practice: Understanding and working with lesbian, gay, bisexual, and transgender persons.* Washington, DC: NASW Press.

Hutchins, T., & Baxter, V. (1980). Battered women. In N. Gottlieb (Ed.), *Alternative social services for women.* New York: Columbia University Press.

Hyde, C. A. (2008). Feminist social work practice. In T. Mizrahi & L. E. Davis (Eds.), *Encyclopedia of social work* (Vol. 2, pp. 216–221). Washington, DC: NASW Press.

Hyde, J. S. (1982). *Understanding human sexuality* (2nd ed.). New York: McGraw-Hill.

Hyde, J. S. (2002). Feminist identity development: The current state of theory, research, and practice. *Counseling Psychologist, 30*, 105–110.

Hyde, J. S. (2007). *Half the human experience* (7th ed.). Boston: Houghton Mifflin.

Hyde, J. S., & Delamater, J. D. (2008). *Understanding human sexuality* (10th ed.). Boston: McGraw-Hill.

Hyde, J. S., & DeLamater, J. D. (2011). *Understanding human sexuality* (11th ed.). New York: McGraw-Hill.

Hyde, J. S., & DeLamater, J. D. (2014). *Understanding human sexuality* (12th ed.). New York: McGraw-Hill.

Hyde, J. S., & Else-Quest, N.M. (2013). *Half the human experience: The psychology of women* (8th ed.). Belmont, CA: Wadsworth.

Infusino, P., Mercurio, M., Galasso, M. A., Gareri, P., Filardi, A., Lacava, R., et al. (1996). Multidimensional evaluation in a group of centenarians. *Archives of Gerontology and Geriatrics, 22*(Suppl. 1), 377–380.

International Association of Schools of Social Work (IASSW). (2004). *Ethics in social work, statement of principles.* Retrieved September 15, 2013, from http://www.iassw-aiets.org/uploads/file/20130506_Ethics%20in%20Social%20Work,%20Statement,%20IFSW,%20IASSW,%202004.pdf

International Association of Schools of Social Work (IASSW). (2009a). *Ethics in social work, statement of principles.* Retrieved from http://www.ifsw.org/f38000032.html

International Association of Schools of Social Work (IASSW). (2009b). *Welcome to IASSW.* Retrieved from http://www.iassw-aiets.org/

International Association of Schools of Social Work (IASSW). (2013). *About IASSW.* Retrieved September 15, 2013, from http://www.iassw-aiets.org/about-iassw

International Federation of Social Workers (IFSW). (2010). *Welcome to IFSW.* Retrieved from http://www.ifsw.org/f38000041.html

International Federation of Social Workers (IFSW). (2013a). *Statement of ethical principles.* Retrieved September 15, 2013, from http://ifsw.org/policies/statement-of-ethical-principles/

International Federation of Social Workers (IFSW). (2013b). *What we do.* Retrieved September 15, 2013, from http://ifsw.org/what-we-do/

Intersex Society of North America (ISNA). (2008a). *How common is intersex?.* Retrieved from http://www.isna.org/faq/frequency

Intersex Society of North America (ISNA). (2008b). *What do doctors do now when they encounter a patient with intersex?.* Retrieved from http://www.isna.org/faq/standard_of_care

Intersex Society of North America (ISNA). (2008c). *What does ISNA recommend for children with intersex?.* Retrieved from http://www.isna.org/faq/patient-centered

Ivey, A. E., D'Andrea, M., Ivey, M. B., & Simek-Morgan, L. (2002). *Theories of counseling and psychotherapy: A multicultural perspective* (5th ed.). Boston: Allyn & Bacon.

Ivey, A. E., & Ivey, M. B. (2008). *Essentials of intentional interviewing: Counseling in a multicultural world.* Belmont, CA: Brooks/Cole.

Ivey, A. E., Ivey, M. B., & Zalaquett, C. P. (2010). *Intentional interviewing & counseling: Facilitating client development in a multicultural society* (7th ed.). Belmont, CA: Brooks/Cole.

Ivey, A. E., Ivey, M. B., & Zalaquett, C. P. (2014). *Essentials of intentional interviewing and counseling: Facilitating client development in a multicultural society* (8th ed.). Belmont, CA: Wadsworth.

Ivey, A. E., Ivey, M. B., & Zalaquett, C. P. (2014). *Intentional interviewing: Counseling in a multicultural world* (2nd ed.). Belmont, CA: Wadsworth.

Jackson, A. W., & Davis, G. A. (2000). *Turning points 2000: Educating adolescents in the 21st century.* New York: Teachers College Press.

Jacobs, S. E., Thomas, W., & Lang, S. (1997). *Two-spirit people: Native American gender identity, sexuality, and spirituality.* Chicago: University of Illinois Press.

Jacobson, E. (1938). *Progressive relaxation* (2nd ed.). Chicago: University of Chicago Press.

Jaffee, S., & Hyde, J. S. (2000). Gender differences in moral orientation: A meta-analysis. *Psychological Bulletin, 126*, 703–726.

Jambunathan, S., Burts, D. C., & Pierce, S. (2000). Comparisons of parenting attitudes among five ethnic groups in the United States. *Journal of Comparative Family Studies, 31*, 395–406.

James, R. K., & Gilliland, B. E. (2005). *Crisis intervention strategies* (5th ed.). Belmont, CA: Brooks/Cole.

James, R. K., & Gilliland, B. E. (2013). *Crisis intervention strategies* (7th ed.). Belmont, CA: Brooks/Cole.

Jansson, B. S. (2009). *The reluctant welfare state: American social welfare policies: Past, present, and future* (6th ed.). Belmont, CA: Brooks/Cole.

Jansson, B. S. (2011). *Becoming an effective policy advocate: From policy practice to social justice* (6th ed.). Belmont, CA: Brooks/Cole.

Jansson, B. S. (2012). *The reluctant welfare state: Engaging history to advance social work practice in contemporary society* (7th ed.). Belmont, CA: Brooks/Cole.

Janus, S. S., & Janus, C. L. (1993). *The Janus report on sexual behavior.* New York: Wiley.

Jaslow, R. (2013, May 2). Suicide rates increase dramatically among middle-aged Americans. *CBS News.* Retrieved from http://www.cbsnews.com/news/suicide-rates-increase-dramatically-among-middle-aged-Americans/

Jaszyna-Gasior, M., Schoeder, J. R., Thorner, E. D., Heishman, S. J., Collins, C., Lo, S., et al. (2009). Age at menarche and weight concerns in relation to smoking trajectory and dependence among adolescent girls enrolled in a smoking cessation trial. *Addictive Behaviors, 34*, 92–95.

Jennings, V. H., Arevalo, M., & Kowal, D. (2004). Fertility awareness-based methods. In R. A. Hatcher, J. Trussell, F. Stewart, A. L. Nelson, W. Cates, Jr., F. Guest, & D. Kowal (Eds.), *Contraceptive technology* (18th ed., pp. 317–329). New York: Ardent Media.

Jensen, P. S., Arnold, L. E., Swanson, J. M., Vitiello, B., Abikoff, H. B., Greenhill, L. L., et al. (2007). 3-Year follow-up of the NIMH MTA study. *Journal of the American Academy of Child & Adolescent Psychiatry, 46*, 989–1002.

Jiao, S., Ji, G., & Jing, Q. (1996). Cognitive development of Chinese urban only children and children with siblings. *Child Development, 67*, 387–395.

Jimenez, J. (2010). *Social policy and social change: Toward the creation of social and economic justice.* Thousand Oaks, CA: Sage.

Jobes, D. A., Berman, A. L., & Martin, C. E. (1999). Adolescent suicidality and crisis intervention. In A. R. Roberts (Ed.), *Crisis intervention handbook: Assessment, treatment, and research* (pp. 131–151). New York: Oxford University Press.

Jobes, D. A., Berman, A. L., & Martin, C. E. (2005). Adolescent suicidality and crisis intervention. In A. R. Roberts (Ed.), *Crisis intervention handbook: Assessment, treatment, and research* (3rd ed., pp. 395–415). New York: Oxford.

Johnson, A. K. (1995). Homelessness. In R. L. Edwards (Ed.), *Encyclopedia of social work* (19th ed., pp. 1338–1346). Washington, DC: NASW Press.

Johnson, D. W., & Johnson, F. P. (1975). *Joining together.* Englewood Cliffs, NJ: Prentice Hall.

Johnson, D. W., & Johnson, F. P. (1987). *Joining together* (3rd ed.). Englewood Cliffs, NJ: Prentice-Hall.

Johnson, D. W., & Johnson, F. P. (1997). *Joining together* (6th ed.). Englewood Cliffs, NJ: Prentice-Hall.

Johnson, E. H. (1973). *Social problems of urban man.* Homewood, IL: Dorsey.

Johnson, J. G., Cohen, P., Smailes, E. M., Kasen, S., & Brook, J. S. (2002). Television viewing and aggressive behavior during adolescence and adulthood. *Science, 295*, 283–294.

Johnson, R. (2011a). *Gay, lesbian, bisexual, transgender and questioning youth suicide statistics.* Retrieved from http://gaylife.about.com/od/gayteens/a/gaysuicide.htm

Johnson, R. (2011b). *Inside ex-gay reparative surgery.* Retrieved from http://gaylife.about.com/od/religion/i/ex_gay_2.htm

Johnson, R. (2011c). *Why the total number of gay people in the world can't be counted.* Retrieved from http://gaylife.about.com/od/comingout/a/howmany gays.htm

Johnson, R. (2014). *Top gay stereotypes: Myths about gay men.* Retrieved from http://gaylife.about.com/od/amiga1/a/gay myths.htm

Johnson, W., & Bouchard, T. J. (2007). Sex differences in mental abilities. *Intelligence, 35*, 23–39.

Johnston, L. D., O'Malley, P. M., Bachman, J. G., & Schulenberg, J. E. (2009). *Monitoring the future national results on adolescent drug use: Overview of key findings, 2008.* Bethesda, MD: National Institute on Drug Abuse.

Johnston, L. D., O'Malley, P. M., Bachman, J. G., & Schulenberg, J. E. (2010). *Monitoring the future: National results on adolescent drug use: Overview of key findings, 2009.* Bethesda, MD: National Institute on Drug Use.

Johnston, L. D., O'Malley, P. M., Bachman, J. G., & Schulenberg, J. E. (2012). *Monitoring the future: National results on adolescent drug use: Overview of key findings, 2011.* Bethesda, MD: National Institute on Drug Use. Retrieved from http://www.monitoringthefuture.org/pubs/monographs/mtf-overview2011.pdf

Jones, A. (2008). Battering: Who's going to stop it? In A. Kesselman, L. D. McNair, & N. Schniedewind (Eds.), *Women: Images and realities* (4th ed., pp. 482–188). Boston: McGraw-Hill.

Jones, M., & Biesecker, J. (1980). *Goal planning in children and youth services.* Millersville, PA: Training Resources in Permanent Planning Projects.

Jones, R. K., Darroch, J. E., & Henshaw, S. K. (2002). Contraceptive use among U.S. Women having abortions in 2000–2001. *Perspectives on Sexual and Reproductive Health, 34*(6), 294–303.

Juran, J. M. (1989). *Juran on leadership for quality: An executive handbook.* New York: Free Press.

Just the Facts Coalition. (2008). *Just the facts about sexual orientation and youth: A primer for principals, educators, and school personnel.* Washington, DC: American Psychological Association. Retrieved from www.apa.org/pi/lgbc/publications/justthefacts.html

Kadushin, A., & Martin, J. A. (1988). *Child welfare services* (4th ed.). New York: Macmillan.

Kahn, S. (1995). Community organization. In R. L. Edwards (Ed.), *Encyclopedia of social work* (19th ed., Vol. 1, pp. 569–576). Washington, DC: NASW Press.

Kail, R. V., & Cavanaugh, J. C. (2007). *Human development: A life-span view* (4th ed.). Belmont, CA: Wadsworth.

Kail, R. V., & Cavanaugh, J. C. (2010). *Human development: A life-span view* (5th ed.). Belmont, CA: Brooks/Cole.

Kail, R. V., & Cavanaugh, J. C. (2013). *Human development: A life-span view* (6th ed.). Belmont, CA: Wadsworth.

Kail, R. V., & Cavanaugh, J. C. (2014). *Essentials of human development: A life-span view.* Belmont, CA: Wadsworth.

Kaiser Family Foundation. (2004). *Sex education in America: General public/parents survey.* Menlo Park, CA: Author.

Kalat, J. W. (2011). *Introduction to psychology* (9th ed.). Belmont, CA: Wadsworth.

Kalb, C., & Rosenberg, D. (2004, October 25). Stem cell division. *Newsweek,* 43–49.

Kalof, L., Eby, K. K., Matheson, J. L., & Kroska, R. J. (2001). The influence of race and gender on student self-reports of sexual harassment by college professors. *Gender and Society, 15,* 282–302.

Kaluger, G., & Kaluger, M. F. (1984). *Human development: The span of life* (3rd ed.). St. Louis, MO: Times Mirror/Mosby.

Kamehameha Early Education Program (KEEP). (n.d.). *Kamehameha early education program (KEEP).* Honolulu, Hawaii. Retrieved from http://www.ncrel.org/sdrs/areas/issues/educatrs/presrvce/pe#lk43.htm

Kane, T. A., Staiger, P. K., & Ricciardelli, L. A. (2000). Male domestic violence: Attitudes, aggression, and interpersonal dependency. *Journal of Interpersonal Violence, 15*(1), 16–29.

Kaplan, D. A. (1993, November 22). Take down the girlie calendars. *Newsweek,* 34.

Karger, H. J., & Stoesz, D. (2010). *American social welfare policy: A pluralist approach* (6th ed.). Boston: Allyn & Bacon.

Karger, H. J., & Stoesz, D. (2013). *American social welfare policy: A pluralist approach.* Brief edition. Upper Saddle River, NJ: Pearson.

Karlen, A. (1971). *Sexuality and homosexuality: A new view.* New York: Norton.

Katz, A. H., & Bender, E. I. (1976). *The strengths in us: Self-help groups in the modern world.* New York: Franklin-Watts.

Kaufman, S. B. (2007). Sex differences in mental rotation and spatial visualization ability: Can they be accounted for by differences in working memory capacity? *Intelligence, 35,* 211–223.

Kazdin, A. E. (2001). *Behavior modification in applied settings* (6th ed.). Belmont, CA: Wadsworth.

Kazdin, A. E. (2008a). *Behavior modification in applied settings* (6th ed., reprinted). Long Grove, IL: Waveland Press.

Kazdin, A. E. (2008b). *The kazdin method for parenting the defiant child.* New York: Mariner.

Kazdin, A. E. (2013). *Behavior modification in applied settings* (7th ed.). Long Grove, IL: Waveland.

Kelley, M. A. (2007). Building "Comunidad de Bienestar" in Puerto Rican Chicago: Community culture, development and health. *ACOSA Update, 21*(112), 3, 14.

Kelly, G. F. (2008). *Sexuality today* (9th ed.). Boston: McGraw-Hill.

Kemp, A. (1998). *Abuse in the family: An introduction.* Pacific Grove, CA: Brooks/Cole.

Kendall, D. (2007). *Social problems in a diverse society* (4th ed.). Boston: Allyn & Bacon.

Kendall, D. (2013). *Social problems in a diverse society* (6th ed.). Boston: Pearson.

Kendall-Tackett, K. A., Williams, L., & Finkelhor, D. (1993). Impact of sexual abuse on children: A review and synthesis of recent empirical studies. *Psychological Bulletin, 113,* 164–180.

Kendell, K. (2003). *Lesbian and gay parents in child custody and visitation disputes.* Retrieved March 23, 2014, from http://www.americanbar.org/publications/human_rights_magazine_home/human_rights_vol30_2003/summer2003/hr_summer03_custody.html

Kendell, K. (2003). *Lesbian and gay parents in child custody and visitation disputes.* Retrieved from http://www.abanet.org/irr/hr/summer03/custody.html

Kendler, K. S., Thornton, L. M., Gilman, S. E., & Kessler, R. C. (2000). Sexual orientation in a U.S. National sample of twin and nontwin sibling pairs. *American Journal of Psychiatry, 157,* 1843–1846.

Keniston, K. (1965). *The uncommitted.* New York: Harcourt, Brace and World.

Kenny-Benson, G. A., Pomerantz, E. M., Ryan, A. M., & Patrick, H. (2006). Sex differences in math performance: The role of children's approach to schoolwork. *Developmental Psychology, 42,* 11–26.

Kerr, M. E., & Bowen, M. (1988). *Family evaluation: An approach based on Bowen theory.* New York: Norton.

Kesler, J. T. (2000). The healthy community movement: Seven counterintuitive steps. *National Civic Review, 89*(3), 271–282.

Kesselman, A., McNair, L. D., & Schniedewind, N. (2008). *Women: Images and realities* (4th ed.). Boston: McGraw-Hill.

Kiff, S. (2012). *Under Obama administration, abstinence-only finds surprising new foothold.* Retrieved from http://www.washingtonpost.com/blogs/wonkblog/post/under-obama-administration-abstinence-only-education-finds-surprising-new-foothold/2012/05/08/gIQA8fcwAU_blog.html

Killin, M., & Smetana, J. (2008). Moral judgment and moral neuroscience: Intersections, definitions, and issues. *Child Development Perspectives, 1,* 1–6.

Kim, K. S. (2008). Strengths perspective. In T. Mizrahi & L. E. Davis (Eds.), *Encyclopedia of social work* (Vol. 4, pp. 177–181). Washington, DC: NASW Press.

Kim, K.-J., McHale, S. M., Osgood, D. W., & Crouter, A. C. (2006). Longitudinal course and family correlates of sibling relationships from childhood through adolescence. *Child Development, 77*(6), 1746–1761.

Kimmel, M. S. (2007). *The gendered society* (3rd ed.). New York: Oxford University Press.

King, J. (2013, June 4). *Hate violence against LGBT community is on dangerous rise.* Retrieved from http://colorlines.com/archives/2013/06/hate_violence_against_lgbt_is_one_a_dangerous_rise.html

Kinsey, A. C., Pomeroy, W. B., & Martin, C. E. (1948). *Sexual behavior in the human male.* Philadelphia: Saunders.

Kinsey, A. C., Pomeroy, W. B., Martin, C. E., & Gebhard, P. H. (1953). *Sexual behavior in the human female.* Philadelphia: Saunders.

Kinsey Institute. (2010). *Frequently asked sexuality questions to the kinsey institute.* Retrieved from http://www.kinseyinstitute.org/resources/FAQ.html

Kirby, D. (2001). *Emerging answers: Research findings on programs to reduce sexual risk-taking and teen pregnancy.* Washington, DC: National Campaign to Prevent Teen Pregnancy.

Kirby, D. (2007). *Emerging answers 2007: Research findings on programs to reduce teen pregnancy and sexually transmitted diseases.* Washington, DC: National Campaign to Prevent Teen and Unplanned Pregnancy. Retrieved from http://www.thenationalcampaign.org/EA2007/EA2007_sum.pdf

Kirby, D. (2007). *Emerging answers 2007: Research findings on programs to reduce teen pregnancy and sexually transmitted diseases.* Washington, DC: National Campaign to Prevent Teen and Unplanned Pregnancy. Retrieved from http://www.thenationalcampaign.org/EA2007/EA2007_full.pdf

Kirby, D., Short, L., Collins, J., Rugg, D., Kolbe, L., Howard, M., et al. (1994). School-based programs to reduce sexual risk behaviors: A review of effectiveness. *Public Health Reports, 109*(3), 339–360.

Kirk, G., & Okazawa-Rey, M. (2010). *Women's lives: Multicultural perspectives* (5th ed.). Boston: McGraw-Hill.

Kirk, G., & Okazawa-Rey, M. (2013). *Women's lives: Multicultural perspectives* (6th ed.). New York: McGraw-Hill.

Kirk, K. M., Bailey, J. M., Dunne, M. P., & Martin, N. G. (2000). Measurement models for sexual orientation in a community twin sample. *Behavior Genetics, 30*(4), 345–356.

Kirk, S., Gallagher, J., Coleman, M. R., & Anastasiow, N. (2012). *Educating exceptional children* (13th ed.). Belmont, CA: Wadsworth.

Kirk, W. G. (1993). *Adolescent suicide: A school-based approach to assessment and intervention.* Champaign, IL: Research Press.

Kirst-Ashman, K. K. (2007). *Introduction to social work and social welfare: Critical thinking perspectives* (2nd ed.). Belmont, CA: Brooks/Cole.

Kirst-Ashman, K. K. (2008). *Human behavior, communities, organizations, and groups in the macro social environment: An empowerment approach* (2nd ed.). Belmont, CA: Brooks/Cole.

Kirst-Ashman, K. K. (2010). *Social work and social welfare: Critical thinking perspectives* (3rd ed.). Belmont, CA: Brooks/Cole.

Kirst-Ashman, K. K. (2011). *Human behavior in the macro social environment: An empowerment approach to understanding communities, organizations, and groups* (3rd ed.). Belmont, CA: Brooks/Cole.

Kirst-Ashman, K. K. (2013). *Introduction to social work and social welfare: Critical thinking perspectives* (4th ed.). Belmont, CA: Brooks/Cole.

Kirst-Ashman, K. K. (2014). *Human behavior in the macro social environment: An empowerment approach to understanding communities, organizations, and groups* (4th ed.). Belmont, CA: Brooks-Cole.

Kirst-Ashman, K. K., & Hull, G. H., Jr. (2009). *Understanding generalist practice* (5th ed.). Belmont, CA: Brooks/Cole.

Kirst-Ashman, K. K., & Hull, G. H., Jr. (2012a). *Generalist practice with organizations and communities* (5th ed.). Belmont, CA: Brooks/Cole.

Kirst-Ashman, K. K., & Hull, G. H., Jr. (2012b). *Understanding generalist practice* (6th ed.). Belmont, CA: Brooks/Cole.

Kissinger, P., Trim, S., Williams, E., Mielke, E., Koporc, K., & Brosn, R. (1997). An evaluation of initiatives to improve family planning use by African-American adolescents. *Journal of the National Medical Association, 89,* 110–114.

Klein, J. D., & the Committee on Adolescence. (2005). Adolescent pregnancy: Current trends and issues. *Pediatrics, 116*(1), 281–286. Retrieved from http://pediatrics.aappublications.org/cgi/reprint/116/l/281?axtoshow=&HITS=10&hits=10&RESULTFORMAT=&fulltext=adolescent+pregnancy&andorexactfulltext=and&searchid=l&FIRSTINDEX=0&sortspec=relevance&resourcetype=HWCIT

Kliman, J. (2011). Social class and the life cycle. In M. McGoldrick, B. Carter, & N. G. Garcia-Preto (Eds.), *The expanded family life cycle: Individual, family, and social perspectives* (4th ed., pp. 75–88). Boston: Allyn & Bacon.

Knapp, M. L., & Hall, J. A. (1992). *Nonverbal communication in human interaction* (3rd ed.). Fort Worth, TX: Harcourt Brace.

Knapp, M. L., & Hall, J. A. (2010). *Nonverbal communication in human interaction* (7th ed.). Belmont, CA: Wadsworth.

Knopf, R. (1979). *Surviving the BS (bureaucratic system).* Wilmington, NC: Mandala Press.

Koch, M. O., Dotson, V., Troast, T. P., & Curtis, L. A. (2006). In C. Zastrow (Ed.), *Strategies for working with specific social work groups* (pp. 26–42). Belmont, CA: Brooks/Cole.

Koenig, H. G., George, L. K., & Siegler, I. C. (1988). The use of religion and other emotion-regulating coping strategies among older adults. *Gerontologist, 28,* 303–310.

Koenig, H. G., Kvale, J. N., & Ferrel, C. (1988). Religion and well-being in later life. *Gerontologist, 28,* 18–28.

Kohlberg, L. (1963). The development of children's orientations toward a moral order. Part 1: Sequence in the development of moral thought. *Vita Humana, 6,* 11–35.

Kohlberg, L. (1968, April). The child as a moral philosopher. *Psychology Today,* 25–30.

Kohlberg, L. (1969). *Stages in the development of moral thought and action.* New York: Holt, Rinehart and Winston.

Kohlberg, L. (1978). Revisions in the theory and practice of moral development. In W. Damon (Ed.), *New directions for child development: Moral development* (pp. 83–87). New York: Wiley.

Kohlberg, L. (1981a). *The philosophy of moral development*. New York: Harper & Row.

Kohlberg, L. (1981b). *Essays on moral development*. San Francisco: Harper & Row.

Kolko, D. J. (2002). Child physical abuse. In J. E. B. Myers, L. Berliner, J. Briere, C. T. Hendrix, C. Jenny, & T. A. Reid (Eds.), *The APSAC handbook on children maltreatment* (2nd ed., pp. 21–54). Thousand Oaks, CA: Sage.

Kondrat, M. E. (2008). Person-in-environment. In T. Mizrahi & L. E. Davis (Eds.), *Encyclopedia of social work* (Vol. 3, pp. 348–354). Washington, DC: NASW Press.

Konijn, E. A., Bijvank, M. N., & Bushman, B. J. (2007). I wish I were a warrior: The role of wishful identification in effects of violent video games on aggression in adolescent boys. *Developmental Psychology, 43*, 1038–1044.

Kopels, S. (1995, Fall). The Americans with disabilities act: A tool to combat poverty. *Journal of Social Work Education, 31*(3), 337–346.

Kornblum, W., & Julian, J. (2001). *Social problems* (10th ed.). Upper Saddle River, NJ: Prentice-Hall.

Kornblum, W., & Julian, J. (2012). *Social problems* (14th ed.). Upper Saddle River, NJ: Pearson.

Kosberg, J. I., & Adams, J. I. (2008). Men: Overview. In T. Mizrahi & L. E. Davis (Eds.), *Encyclopedia of social work* (Vol. 3, pp. 205–214). Washington, DC: NASW Press.

Koss, M. P. (1992). The underdetection of rape: Methodological choices influence incidence estimates. *Journal of Social Issues, 48*(1), 61–75.

Koss, M. P. (1993). Rape: Scope, impact, interventions, and public policy responses. *American Psychologist, 48*, 1062–1069.

Koss, M. P., Goodman, L. A., Browne, A., Fitzgerald, L. G., Keita, G. P., & Russo, N. F. (1994). *No safe haven: Male violence against women at home, at work, and in the community*. Washington, DC: American Psychological Association.

Kotz, D. (2000, September, 15). Sex, health & happiness. *U.S. News & World Report*, pp. 50–52.

Kramer, L. (2005). *The sociology of gender: A brief introduction* (2nd ed.). Los Angeles: Roxbury.

Kraus, M. W., & Keltner, D. (2009). *Rich man, poor man: Study shows body language can indicate socioeconomic status*. Retrieved from http://www.psychologicalscience.org/media/2009/ kraus.cfn

Kretzmann, J. P., & McKnight, J. L. (1993). *Building communities from the inside out*. Chicago: ACTA Publications.

Kristensen, J., Vestergaard, M., Wisborg, I. K., Kesmodel, U., & Secher, N. J. (2005). Pre-pregnancy weight and the risk of stillbirth and neonatal death. *British Journal of Obstetrics and Gynecology, 112*, 403–408.

Kübler-Ross, E. (1969). *On death and dying*. New York: Macmillan.

Kurdek, L. A. (2005). What do we know about gay and lesbian couples?. *Current Directions in Psychological Science, 14*(5), 251–254.

Kurpius, S. E., Kerr, B., & Harkins, A. (2005). *Handbook for counseling girls and women: Vol. 1. Talent, risk, and resiliency*. Mesa, AZ: Nueva Science Press.

Kuypers, J., & Benston, V. (1973). Competence and social breakdown: A social-psychological view of aging. *Human Development, 16*(2), 37–49.

Lacayo, R. (2001, August 20). How bush got there. *Time*, 17–23.

Lachance, J., & Mazzocco, M. M. M. (2006). A longitudinal analysis of sex differences in math and spatial skills in primary school age children. *Learning and Individual Differences, 16*, 195–216.

Ladd, G. W., Buhs, E., & Troop, W. (2002). School adjustment and social skills training. In P. K. Smith & C. H. Hart (Eds.), *Blackwell handbook of childhood social development* (pp. 394–415). Malden, MA: Blackwell.

Laifer-Narin, S., Budorick, N. E., Simpson, L. L., & Platt, L. D. (2007). Fetal magnetic resonance imaging: A review. *Current Opinion in Obstetrics and Gynecology, 19*, 151–156.

Laird, J. (1995). Lesbians: Parenting. In R. L. Edwards (Ed.), *Encyclopedia of social work* (19th ed., Vol. 2, pp. 1604–1616). Washington, DC: NASW Press.

Land, H. (1995). Feminist clinical social work in the 21st century. In N. Van Den Bergh (Ed.), *Feminist practice in the 21st century* (pp. 3–19). Washington, DC: NASW Press.

Lane, H. (1976). *The wild boy of Aveyron*. Cambridge, MA: Harvard University Press.

Lankton, S. (1980). *Practical magic*. Cupertino, CA: Meta Publications.

Lapsey, D. K. (2005). Stage theories generated by Kohlberg. In M. Killen & J. Smetana (Eds.), *Handbook of moral development*. Mahwah, NJ: Erlbaum.

LaSala, M. C. (2004). Monogamy of the heart: Extradyadic sex and gay male couples. *Journal of Gay & Lesbian Social Services: Issues in Practice, Policy & Research, 17*(3), 1–24.

Lamanna, M. A., & Reidmann, A. (2009). *Marriages, families, & relationships: Making choices in a diverse society* (10th ed.). Belmont, CA: Cengage.

Latham, G. P., & Budworth, M. H. (2007). The study of work motivation in the 20th century. In L. L. Koppes (Ed.), *Historical perspectives in industrial and organizational psychology* (pp. 353–381). Mahwah, NJ: Erlbaum.

Laufersweiler-Dwyer, D. L., & Dwyer, G. (2005). Rapists. In F. P. Reddington & B. W. Kreisel (Eds.), *Sexual assault: The victims, the perpetrators, and the criminal justice system* (pp. 205–231). Durham, NC: Carolina Academic Press.

Laumann, E., Gagnon, J., Michael, R., & Michaels, S. (1994). *The social organization of sexuality*. Chicago: University of Chicago Press.

Lavelle, M. (1998, July 6). The new rules of sexual harassment: The Supreme Court defines what harassment is and who can be held responsible. *U. S. News & World Report*, 31.

Leacock, E. (1971). *The culture of poverty: A critique*. New York: Simon and Schuster.

Leadbeater, B. J., Kupperminc, G. P., Blatt, S. J., & Hertzog, C. (1999). A multivariate model of gender differences in adolescents' internalizing and externalizing problem. *Developmental Psychology, 35*, 1268–1282.

LeClaire, J. (2013, April 12). *Attacking abortion clinics is not the pro-life answer*. Retrieved November 26, 2013, from http://

www.charismanews.com/opinion/39069-attacking-abortion-clinics-is-not-the-pro-life-answer

Lee, J. A. (Ed.). (1991). *Gay midlife and maturity*. New York: Harrington Park Press.

Lee, J. A. B. (2001). *The empowerment approach to social work practice: Building the beloved community*. New York: Columbia University Press.

Lee, V. E., & Smith, J. (2001). *Restructuring high school for equity and excellence: What works*. New York: Teachers College Press.

Lee, Y. S., Cheng, A. W., Ahmed, S. F., Shaw, N. J., & Hughes, I. A. (2007). Genital anomalies in Klinefelter's syndrome. *Hormonal Research, 68*, 150–153.

Lefrancois, G. R. (1999). *The lifespan* (6th ed.). Belmont, CA: Wadsworth.

Lein, L. (2008). Child care services. In T. Mizrahi & L. E. Davis (Eds.), *Encyclopedia of social work* (Vol. 1, pp. 240–243). Washington, DC: NASW Press.

Leland, J. (2000, March 20). Shades of gay. *Newsweek*, 46–49.

Lemish, D. (2007). *Children and television: A global perspective*. New York: Blackwell.

Lemon, N. K. D. (2002, October/November). Sonoma county, California, sheriffs department settles domestic violence murder case for $1 million. *Domestic Violence Report, 8*(1), 11–12, 14–16.

Leong, F. T. L., Lee, S., & Chang, D. (2008). Counseling Asian Americans: Client and therapist variables. In P. B. Pedersen, J. G. Draguns, W. J. Lonner, & J. E. Trimble (Eds.), *Counseling across cultures* (6th ed., pp. 113–128). Thousand Oaks, CA: Sage.

Leon-Guerrero, A. (2009). *Social problems: Community, policy, and social action* (2nd ed.). Thousand Oaks, CA: Pine Forge.

Leon-Guerrero, A. (2011). *Social problems: Community, policy, and social action* (3rd ed.). Thousand Oaks, CA: Pine Forge.

LeVay, S. (1991). A difference in hypothalamic structure between heterosexual and homosexual men. *Science, 253*, 1034–1037.

LeVay, S. (1996). *Queer science: The use and abuse of research into homosexuality*. Cambridge, MA: MIT Press.

LeVay, S., & Valente, S. M. (2006). *Human sexuality* (2nd ed.). Sunderland, MA: Sinauer.

LeVine, E. S., & Sallee, A. L. (1999). *Child welfare: Clinical theory and practice*. Dubuque, IA: Eddie Bowers.

Levin, I. (2004). Living apart together: A new family form. *Current Sociology, 52*(2), 223–240.

Levinson, D. (1986). A conception of adult development. *American Psychologist, 41*(1), 3–13.

Levinson, D. J., Darrow, C. N., Klein, E. B., Levinson, M. H., & McKee, B. (1974). The psychosocial development of men in early adulthood and the mid-life transition. In D. F. Ricks, A. Thomas, & M. Roff (Eds.), *Life history research in psychopathology*. Minneapolis: University of Minnesota Press.

Levinson, D. J., & Levinson, J. D. (1978). *The seasons of a man's life*. New York: Knopf.

Levinson, D. J., & Levinson, J. D. (1996). *The seasons of a woman's life*. New York: Knopf.

Lewis, J. S., & Harrell, E. B. (2012). Resilience and the older adult. In R. R. Green (Ed.), *Resiliency: An integrated approach to practice, policy, and research* (2nd ed., pp. 335–351). Washington, DC: NASW Press.

Lewis, L. A. (1984). The coming-out process for lesbians: Integrating a stable identity. *Social Work, 29*(5), 464–468.

Lewis, M. A., Neighbors, C., Lindgren, K. P., Buckingham, K. G., & Hoang, M. (2010). *Social influences on adolescent and young adult alcohol use*. Hauppauge, NY: Nova Science Publishers.

Lewis, O. (1966). The culture of poverty. *Scientific American, 215*(10), 19–25.

LGBT Hate Crimes Project. (2010). *Sakia gunn*. Retrieved from http://www.lgbthatecrimes.org/doku.php/sakia_gunn

Liederman, D. S. (1995). Child welfare overview. In R. L. Edwards (Ed.), *Encyclopedia of social work* (19th ed., Vol. 1, pp. 424–433). Washington, DC: NASW Press.

Lightfoot, E. (2009a). Case management policies and programs with the developmentally disabled. In A. R. Roberts (Ed.), *Social workers' desk reference* (2nd ed., pp. 759–764). W York: Oxford.

Lightfoot, E. (2009b). Social policies for people with disabilities. In J. Midgley & M. Livermore (Eds.), *The handbook of social policy* (2nd ed., pp. 445–162). Thousand Oaks, CA: Sage.

Lin, C., & Liu, W. T. (1999). Intergenerational relationships among Chinese immigrant families from Taiwan. In H. P. McAdoo (Ed.), *Family ethnicity* (2nd ed., pp. 235–251). Thousand Oaks, CA: Sage.

Lindberg, C. A. (2007). *The Oxford college dictionary*. New York: Oxford.

Lippa, R. (2008). The relationship between childhood gender nonconformity and adult masculinity-femininity and anxiety in heterosexual and homosexual men and women. *Sex Roles, 59*, 684–693.

Liptak, A. (2013, November 19). *Justices reject bid to block Texas law on abortions*. Retrieved November 25, 2013, from http://www.nytimes.com/2013/11/20/us/supreme-court-rejects-bid-to-block-texas-abortion-law.html?r=0

Lloyd, G. A. (1995). HIV/AIDS overview. In R. L. Edwards & J. G. Hobbs (Editors), *Encyclopedia of social work* (19th ed., pp. 1257–1290). Washington, DC: NASW Press.

London, S. (2004). Risk of pregnancy-related death is sharply elevated for women 35 and older. *Perspectives on Sexual and Reproductive Health, 36*, 87–88.

Longres, J. F. (2008). Diversity in community life. In J. Rothman, J. L. Erlich, & J. E. Tropman (Eds.), *Strategies of community intervention* (7th ed., pp. 77–106). Peosta, LA: Eddie Bowers.

Longres, J. F., & Aisenberg, E. (2008). Latinos and Latinas: Overview. In T. Mizrahi & L. E. Davis (Eds.), *Encyclopedia of social work* (Vol. 3, pp. 31–41). Washington, DC: NASW Press.

Longres, J. F., & Fredriksen, K. I. (2000). Social work practice with lesbians and gay men. In P. Allen-Meares & C. Garvin (Eds.), *The handbook of social work practice* (pp. 477–198). Thousand Oaks, CA: Sage.

Lorber, J. (2005). *Gender inequality: Feminist theories and politics* (3rd ed.). Los Angeles: Roxbury.

Lorber, J. (2010). *Gender inequality: Feminist theories and politics* (4th ed.). New York: Oxford.

Lorber, J., & Moore, L. J. (2011). *Gendered bodies: Feminist perspectives* (2nd ed.). New York: Oxford.

Lorenz, F. O., Wickrama, K. A., Conger, R. D., & Elder, G. H. (2006). The short-term and decade-long effects of divorce on women's midlife health. *Journal of Health and Social Behavior*, *47*, 117–125.

Lott, B. (1987). *Women's lives: Themes and variations in gender learning.* Belmont, CA: Brooks/Cole.

Lott, B. (1994). *Women's lives: Themes and variations in gender learning* (2nd ed.). Pacific Grove, CA: Brooks/Cole.

Loukas, A., & Robinson, S. (2004). Examining the moderating role of perceived school climate in early adolescent adjustment. *Journal of Research on Adolescence*, *14*, 209–233.

Lu, Y. E. (2008). Asian Americans: Chinese. In T. Mizrahi & L. E. Davis (Eds.), *Encyclopedia of social work* (Vol. 1, pp. 164–166). Washington, DC: NASW Press.

Luckasson, R., Borthwick-Duffy, S., Buntinx, W. H. E., Coulter, D. L., Craig, E. M., Reeve, A., et al. (2002). *Mental retardation: Definition, classification, and systems of supports.* Washington, DC: American Association on Mental Retardation.

Lum, D. (2000). *Social work practice and people of color: A process-stage approach* (4th ed.). Pacific Grove, CA: Brooks/Cole.

Lum, D. (2003). *Culturally competent practice: A framework for understanding diverse groups and justice issues* (2nd ed.). Belmont, CA: Brooks/Cole.

Lum, D. (Ed.). (2005). *Cultural competence, practice stages, and client systems: A case study approach.* Belmont, CA: Brooks/Cole.

Lum, D. (2007). *Culturally competent practice: A framework for understanding diverse groups and justice issues* (3rd ed.). Belmont, CA: Brooks/Cole.

Lum, D. (2011). A framework for cultural competence. In D. Lum (Ed.), *Culturally competent practice: A framework for understanding diverse groups and justice issues* (4th ed., pp. 123–135). Belmont, CA: Brooks/Cole.

Lynne, S. D., Graber, J. A., Nichold, T. R., Brooks-Gunn, J., & Botvin, G. J. (2007). Links between pubertal timing, peer influences, and externalizing behaviors among urban students followed through middle school. *Journal of Adolescent Health*, *40*(2), 181.e7–181.e13.

Maag, J. W., & Reid, R. (2006). Depression among students with learning disabilities: Assessing the risk. *Journal of Learning Disabilities*, *39*, 3–10.

MacKay, A. P., Berg, C. J., & Atrash, H. K. (2001). Pregnancy-related mortality from preeclampsia and eclampsia. *Obstetrics and Gynecology*, *97*(4), 533–538.

Mackelprang, R. M. (2008). Disability: Overview. In T. Mizrahi & L. E. Davis (Eds.), *Encyclopedia of social work* (Vol. 2, pp. 36–43). Washington, DC: NASW Press.

Mackelprang, R. W., & Salsgiver, R. O. (2009). *Disability: A diversity model approach in human service practice* (2nd ed.). Chicago: Lyceum.

Macklem, G. O. (2003). *Bullying and teasing: Social power in children's groups.* New York: Kluwer Academic/Plenum.

Madsen V. Women's Health Center. (93-880), 512 U.S. 753 (1994).

Madom, S., Jussim, L., & Eccles, J. (1997). In search of the powerful self-fulfilling prophecy. *Journal of Personality and Social Psychology*, *72*, 791–809.

Magana, S., & Ybarra, M. (2010). Family and community as strengths in the Latino community. In R. Furman & N. Negi (Eds.), *Social work practice with Latinos: Key issues and emerging themes* (pp. 69–84). Chicago: Lyceum.

Magness, P. W., & Page, S. P. (2011). *Colonization after emancipation.* Columbia: University of Missouri Press.

Mahoney, M., Simone, K., & Simon-Rusinowitz, L. (2000). Early lessons from the case and counseling demonstration and evaluation. *Demonstration and Evaluation*, *25*(3), 41–46.

Maier, R. A. (1984). *Human sexuality in perspective.* Chicago: Nelson-Hall.

Malamitsi Puchner, A., & Boutsikou, T. (2006). Adolescent pregnancy and perinatal outcome. *Pediatric Endocrinology Reviews*, *5*(1), 170–171.

Malamuth, N. M. (1998). The confluence model as an organizing framework for research on sexually aggressive men: Risk moderators, imagined aggression and pornography consumption. In R. Green & E. Donnserstein (Eds.), *Aggression: Theoretical and empirical reviews* (pp. 229–245). New York: Academic Press.

Malamuth, N. M., Sockloskie, R. J., Koss, M. P., & Tanaka, J. S. (1991). Characteristics of aggressors against women: Testing a model using a national sample of college students. *Journal of Consulting and Clinical Psychology*, *59*, 670–781.

Mallon, G. P. (2008). Gay families and parenting. In T. Mizrahi & L. E. Davis (Eds.), *Encyclopedia of social work* (Vol. 2, pp. 241–247). Washington, DC: NASW Press.

Mamie, A., & Cuimingliam, G. (2008). *From clients to citizens.* Warwickshire, UK: Practical Action Publishing.

Mangione, R., Fries, N., Godard, P., Capron, C., Mirlesse, V., Lacombe, D., et al. (2011). Neurodevelopmental outcome following prenatal diagnosis of an isolated anomaly of the corpus callosum. *Ultrasound in Obstetrics & Gynecology*, *37*(3), 290–295.

Manlove, J., & Terry-Humen, E. (2007). Contraceptive use patterns within females' first sexual relationships: The role of relationships, partners, and methods. *Journal of Sex Research*, *44*, 3–16.

March of Dimes Foundation. (2009). *Teenage pregnancy.* Retrieved from http://www.marchofdimes.com/medicalresources_teenpregnancy.html

March of Dimes Foundation. (2010a). *Low birth weight.* Retrieved from http://www.marchofdimes.com/baby/medical resources_lowbirthweight.html

March of Dimes Foundation. (2010b). *Your premature baby.* Retrieved from http://www.marchofdimes.com/baby/premature_indepth.html

March of Dimes. (2012). *Low birthweight.* Retrieved from http://www.marchofdimes.com/baby/low-birthweight.aspx

Marcia, J. E. (1980). Identity in adolescence. In J. Adelson (Ed.), *Handbook of adolescent psychology* (pp. 159–187). New York: Wiley.

Marcia, J. E. (1991). Identity and self-development. In R. M. Lerner, A. C. Petersen, & J. Brooks-Gunn (Eds.), *Encyclopedia of adolescence* (Vol. 1, pp. 529–534). New York: Garland Publishing.

Marcia, J. E. (2002). Identity and psychosocial development in adulthood. *Identity*, *2*(1), 7–28.

Marcia, J. E., & Carpendale, J. (2004). Identity: Does thinking make it so? In C. Lightfoot, C. Lalonde, & M. Chancler (Eds.), *Changing conceptions of psychological life* (pp. 113–126). Mahwah, NJ: Erlbaum.

Margalit, M. (2006). Loneliness, the salutogenic paradigm and learning disabilities: Current research, future directions, and interventional implications. *Thalamus*, *24*, 38–48.

Markus, H., & Nurius, P. S. (1984). Self-understanding and self-regulation in middle childhood. In W. A. Collins (Ed.), *Development during middle childhood: The years from six to twelve* (pp. 147–183). Washington, DC: National Academy Press.

Marshall, D. S. (1980). Too much in mangaia. In C. Gordon & G. Johnson (Eds.), *Readings in human sexuality: Contemporary perspectives* (2nd ed.). New York: Harper & Row.

Martin, C. L., & Fabes, R. (2009). *Discovering child development* (2nd ed.). Boston: Houghton Mifflin.

Martin, J. A., Hamilton, B. E., Sutton, P. D., Ventura, S. J., Menacker, F., Kirmeyer, S., et al. (2009, January 7). Births: Final data for 2006. *National Vital Statistics Reports, 57*(7), 1–104. Retrieved from http://www.cdc.gov/nchs/data/nvsr/nvsr57/nvsr57_07.pdf

Martin, J. A., Hamilton, B. E., Sutton, P. D., Ventura, S. J., Menacker, F., & Munson, M. L. (2005, September). Births: Final data for 2003. *National Vital Statistics Reports, 54*(2), 1–116.

Martin, J. A., Hamilton, B. E., Ventura, S. J., Osterman, M. H. S., Wilson, E. C., & Matthews, T. J. (2012). *National Vital Statistics Reports, 61*(1). Retrieved October 21, 2013, from http://www.cdc.gov/nchs/data/nvsr/nvsr61/nvsr61_01.pdf

Martin, J. I. (2008). Gay men: Overview. In T. Mizrahi & L. E. Davis (Eds.), *Encyclopedia of social work* (Vol. 2, pp. 247–256). Washington, DC: NASW Press.

Martin, S. E. (1995). Sexual harassment: The link joining gender stratification, sexuality, and women's economic status. In J. Freeman (Ed.), *Women: A feminist perspective* (5th ed., pp. 22–46). Mountain View, CA: Mayfield.

Martinez-Brawley, E. M. (1995). Community. In R. L. Edwards (Ed.), *Encyclopedia of social work* (19th ed., Vol. 1, pp. 539–548). Washington, DC: NASW Press.

Maslova, E., Bhattacharya, S., Lin, S. W., & Michels, K. B. (2010). Caffeine consumption during pregnancy and risk of preterm birth: A meta-analysis. *American Journal of Clinical Nutrition, 92*, 1120–1132.

Maslow, A. H. (1954). *Motivation and personality*. New York: Harper & Row.

Maslow, A. H. (1968). *Toward a psychology of being* (2nd ed.). Princeton, NJ: Van Nostrand.

Maslow, A. H. (1971). *The farther reaches of human nature*. New York: Viking.

Mason, G. (2002). *The spectacle of violence: Homophobia, gender, and knowledge*. London: Routledge.

Masters, W. H., & Johnson, V. E. (1966). *Human sexual response*. Boston: Little, Brown.

Masters, W. H., Johnson, V. E., & Kolodny, R. C. (1995). *Human sexuality* (5th ed.). New York: HarperCollins.

Maultsby, M. C., Jr. (1975). *Help yourself to happiness*. Boston: Herman.

Mayer, A. (1983). *Incest: A treatment manual for therapy with victims, spouses and offenders*. Holmes Beach, FL: Learning Publications.

Mayo Clinic. (2013a). *Breast cancer: Treatment and drugs*. Retrieved September 11, 2013, from http://www.mayoclinic.com/health/breast-cancer/DS00328/DSECTION=treatments-and-drugs

Mayo Clinic. (2013b). *Female infertility*. Retrieved from http://www.mayoclinic.com/health/female-infertility/DS01053

Mayo Clinic. (2013c). *Pregnancy tests*. Retrieved from http://www.mayoclinic.com/health/home-pregnancy-tests/PR00100

Mayo Foundation for Medical Education and Research (MFMER). (2009). *Stages of labor: Baby, it's time!*. Retrieved from http://www.mayoclinic.com/health/stages-of-labor/PR00106/METHOD=print

Mayo Foundation for Medical Education and Research. (2010a). *Female infertility*. Retrieved from http://www.mayoclinic.com/health/female-infertility/DS01053/DSECTION=risk-factors

Mayo Foundation for Medical Education and Research. (2010b). *Home pregnancy tests: Can you trust the results?*. Retrieved from http://www.mayoclinic.com/health/home-pregnancy-tests/PR00100

McAdoo, H. P. (2007). *Black families* (4th ed.). Thousand Oaks, CA: Sage.

McAnulty, R. D., & Burnette, M. M. (2003). *Fundamentals of human sexuality: Making healthy decisions*. Boston: Allyn & Bacon.

McCabe, M. P., & Wauchope, M. (2005). Behavioral characteristics of men accused of rape: Evidence for different types of rapists. *Archives of Sexual Behavior, 34*(2), 241–253.

McCammon, S., & Knox, D. (2007). *Choices in sexuality* (3rd ed.). Mason, OH: Thomson.

McCammon, S., Knox, D., & Schacht, C. (1993). *Choices in sexuality*. Minneapolis: West.

McCoy, D. (2006). *Gay adoption next big hurdle says media analysts*. Retrieved from http://www.proudparenting.com/page.cfm?ectionis=75&typeofsite=storydetail&ID=805

McCrary, J., & Gutierrez, L. (1979/80). The homosexual person in the military and in national security employment. *Journal of Homosexuality, 51*(1, 2), 115–146.

McFadden, R. D. (2008, December 9). Attack on Ecuadorean brothers investigated as hate crime. *The New York Times*. Retrieved from http://www.nytimes.com/2008/12/09/nyregion/09assault.html

McGoldrick, M. (2011). Becoming a couple. In M. McGoldrick, B. Carter, & N. G. Garcia-Preto (Eds.), *The expanded family life cycle: Individual, family, and social perspectives* (4th ed., pp. 193–210). Boston: Allyn & Bacon.

McGregor, D. (1960). *The human side of enterprise*. New York: McGraw-Hill.

McHugh, M. C. (1993). Studying battered women and batterers: Feminist perspectives on methodology. In M. Hansen & M. Harway (Eds.), *Battering and family therapy: A feminist perspective* (pp. 54–68). Newbury Park, CA: Sage.

McInnis-Dittrich, K. (2009). *Social work with older adults* (3rd ed.). Boston: Allyn & Bacon.

McInnis-Dittrich, K. (2014). *Social work with older adults* (4th ed.). Upper Saddle River, NJ: Pearson.

McIntosh, P. (1988). *White privilege: Unpacking the invisible knapsack*. Wellesley College, MA: Wellesley College Center for Research on Women.

McKnight, J., & Block, P. (2010). *The abundant community: Awakening the power of families and neighborhoods*. San Francisco: Berrett-Koehler.

McLaughlin, E. (2006). *Artificial insemination*. Retrieved from http://uimc.discovery hospital.com/main.php?d=3127

McWhirter, J. J., McWhirter, B. T., McWhirter, E. H., & McWhirter, R. J. (2007). *At risk youth* (4th ed.). Belmont, CA: Brooks/Cole.

McWhirter, J. J., McWhirter, B. T., McWhirter, E. H., & McWhirter, R. J. (2013). *At risk youth: A comprehensive response for counselors, teachers, psychologists, and human service professionals* (5th ed.). Belmont, CA: Brooks/Cole.

Mead, M. (1935). *Sex and temperament in three primitive societies.* New York: Morrow.

Meadan, H., & Halle, J. W. (2004). Social perceptions of students with learning disabilities who differ in social status. *Learning Disabilities Research and Practice, 19*, 71–82.

Meadows, M. (2004, November/December). Facing infertility. *FDA Consumer magazine.* Retrieved from http://www.fda.gov/dfac/features/2004/604_baby.html

Melby, T. (2008, May). Should rapists ever be free?. *Contemporary Sexuality, 5*(6), 1, 4–6.

Menec, V. H. (2003). The relation between everyday activities and successful aging: A 6-year longitudinal study. *Journal of Gerontology: Social Sciences, 58B*, 74–82.

Menna, A. (2011). *Rape trauma syndrome: The journey to healing belongs to everyone.* Retrieved from http://www.giftfromwithin.org/html/journey.html

Merton, R. K. (1949). Discrimination and the American creed. In R. M. MacIver (Ed.), *Discrimination and national welfare* (pp. 99–126). New York: Harper.

Merton, R. K. (1968). *Social theory and social structure.* New York: Free Press.

Messinger, L. (2006). Social welfare policy and advocacy. In D. F. Morrow & L. Messinger (Eds.), *Sexual orientation and gender expression in social work practice: Working with gay, lesbian, bisexual, and transgender people* (pp. 427–459). New York: Columbia University Press.

Messinger, L., & Brooks, J. W. (2008). Lesbians: Overview. In T. Mizrahi & L. E. Davis (Eds.), *Encyclopedia of social work* (Vol. 3, pp. 71–79). Washington, DC: NASW Press.

Meyer, C. (1987). Direct practice in social work: Overview. In A. Minahan (Ed.), *Encyclopedia of social work* (Vol. 1, pp. 409–122). Silver Spring, MD: NASW.

Michael, R. T., Gagnon, J. H., Laumann, E. O., & Kolata, G. (1994). *Sex in America: A definitive survey.* Boston: Little, Brown.

Midgley, J. (1995). *Social development: The developmental perspective in social welfare.* Thousand Oaks, CA: Sage.

Midgley, J., & Livermore, M. (1997, Fall). The developmental perspective in social work: Educational implications for a new century. *Journal of Social Work Education, 33*(3), 573–585.

Miley, K. (1992, April). *Religion and spirituality as Central social work concerns.* Paper presented at the Midwest Biennial Conference on Social Work Education, LaCrosse, WI.

Miller, P. J. (2000, May). Life after death with dignity: The Oregon experience. *Social Work, 45*(3), 263–271.

Miller, R. L., Jr. (2008). Gay men: Practice interventions. In T. Mizrahi & L. E. Davis (Eds.), *Encyclopedia of social work* (Vol. 2, pp. 256–260). Washington, DC: NASW Press.

Miller, S. L., Iovanni, L., & Kelley, K. G. (2011). Violence against women and the criminal justice response. In C. M. Renzetti, J. L. Edleson & R. K. Bergen (Eds.), *Sourcebook on violence against women* (2nd ed., pp. 267–287). Thousand Oaks, CA: Sage.

Miller, W. B. (1958). Lower class culture as a generating milieu of gang delinquency. *Journal of Social Issues, 14*(3), 5–19.

Miller, W. R., & Rollnick, S. (1981). *Motivational interviewing: Preparing people to change addictive behavior.* New York: Guilford Press.

Miller-Perrin, C. L., & Perrin, R. D. (1999). *Child maltreatment: An introduction.* Thousand Oaks, CA: Sage.

Miller-Perrin, C. L., & Perrin, R. D. (2007). *Child maltreatment: An introduction* (2nd ed.). Thousand Oaks, CA: Sage.

Miller-Perrin, C. L., & Perrin, R. D. (2013). *Child maltreatment: An introduction* (3rd ed.). Thousand Oaks, CA: Sage.

Miltenberger, R. G. (2008). *Behavior modification: Principles and procedures* (4th ed.). Belmont, CA: Wadsworth.

Miltenberger, R. G. (2012). *Behavior modification: Principles & procedures* (5th ed.). Belmont, CA: Wadsworth.

Mindell, C. L. (2007). Religious bigotry and religious minorities. In G. A. Appleby, E. Colon, & J. Hamilton (Eds.), *Diversity, oppression, and social functioning: Person-in-environment assessment and intervention* (2nd ed., pp. 227–246). Boston: Allyn & Bacon.

Minnes, S., Lang, A., & Singer, L. (2011). Prenatal tobacco, marijuana, stimulant, and opiate exposure: Outcomes and practice implications. *Addiction Science & Clinical Practice, 6*(1), 57–70.

Mish, F. C. (Ed.). (1995). *Merriam- Webster's collegiate dictionary* (10th ed.). Springfield, MA: Merriam-Webster.

Mish, F. E. (2008). *Merriam-webster's collegiate dictionary* (11th ed.). Springfield, MA: Merriam-Webster, Inc.

Misiewicz, G. L. (2012). *African American grandparents raising grandchildren.* Retrieved from http://sophia.stkate.edu/cgi/viewcontent.cgi?rticle=1060&context=msw_papers

Mitchell, K. J., Wolak, J., & Finkelhor, D. (2007). Trends in youth reports of sexual solicitations, harassment and unwanted exposure to pornography on the internet. *Journal of Adolescent Health, 40*, 116–126.

Mondics, C. (2003, April 21). Advocacy groups seek santorum's ouster for remarks on gay sex. *Knight Ridder Newspapers*, K4893.

Money, J. (1987). Sin, sickness, or status: Homosexual gender identity and psychoneuroendocrinology. *American Psychologist, 42*, 384–399.

Montague, A. (1964). *Mans most dangerous myth: The fallacy of race* (4th ed.). Cleveland, OH: World.

Montgomery, N. (2013, February 24). *Will abortion law change help female troops?.* Retrieved November 25, 2013, from http://www.stripes.com/news/will-abortion-law-change-help-female-troops-1.209513

Mooney, L. A., Knox, D., & Schacht, C. (2007). *Understanding social problems* (5th ed.). Belmont, CA: Wadsworth.

Mooney, L. A., Knox, D., & Schacht, C. (2009). *Understanding social problems* (6th ed.). Belmont, CA: Wadsworth.

Mooney, L. A., Knox, D., & Schacht, C. (2013). *Understanding social problems* (8th ed.). Belmont, CA: Wadsworth.

Moore, S. E. (2008). African Americans: Practice interventions. In T. Mizrahi & L. E. Davis (Eds.), *Encyclopedia of social work* (Vol. 1, pp. 81–85). Washington, DC: NASW Press.

Moore, S., & Rosenthal, D. (2006). *Sexuality in adolescence: Current trends.* London: Routledge.

Mor Barak, M. (2005). *Managing diversity: Toward a globally inclusive workplace.* Thousand Oaks, CA: Sage.

Morales, A. T., Sheafor, B. W., & Scott, M. E. (2010). *Social work: A profession of many faces.* Boston: Pearson.

Morales, J. (1995). Gay men: Parenting. In R. L. Edwards (Ed.), *Encyclopedia of social work* (19th ed., Vol. 2, pp. 1085–1095). Washington, DC: NASW Press.

Morrow, D. F. (2006a). Coming out as gay, lesbian, bisexual, and transgender. In D. F. Morrow & L. Messinger (Eds.), *Sexual orientation and gender expression in social work practice: Working with gay, lesbian, bisexual, and transgender people* (pp. 129–149). New York: Columbia University Press.

Morrow, D. F. (2006b). Gay, lesbian, bisexual, and transgender adolescents. In D. F. Morrow & L. Messinger (Eds.), *Sexual orientation and gender expression in social work practice: Working with gay, lesbian, bisexual, and transgender people* (pp. 177–195). New York: Columbia University Press.

Morrow, D. F. (2006c). Sexual orientation and gender identity expression. In D. F. Morrow & L. Messinger (Eds.), *Sexual orientation and gender expression in social work practice: Working with gay, lesbian, bisexual, and transgender people* (pp. 3–17). New York: Columbia University Press.

Morrow, D. F. (2008). Lesbians: Practice interventions. In T. Mizrahi & L. E. Davis (Eds.), *Encyclopedia of social work* (Vol. 3, pp. 79–87). Washington, DC: NASW Press.

Morrow, D. F., & Tyson, B. (2006). Religion and spirituality. In D. F. Morrow & L. Messinger (Eds.), *Sexual orientation and gender expression in social work practice: Working with gay, lesbian, bisexual, and transgender people* (pp. 384–104). New York: Columbia University Press.

Morse, S. B., Zheng, H., Tang, Y., & Roth, J. (2009). Early school-age outcomes of late preterm infants. *Pediatrics, 123*, e622–e629.

Mortensen, L. H., Diderichsen, F., Davey Smith, G., & Nybo Andersen, A. M. (2009). Time is on whose side? Time trends in the association between maternal social disadvantage and offspring fetal growth. A study of 1,409,339 births in Denmark, 1981–2004. *Journal of Epidemiology and Community Health, 63*(4), 267–268.

Mosak, H. H. (1995). Adlerian psychotherapy. In R. J. Corsini & D. Wedding (Eds.), *Current psychotherapies* (5th ed., pp. 51–94). Itasca, IL: Peacock.

Mosak, H. H., & Maniacci, M. (2011). Adlerian psychotherapy. In R. S. Corsini & D. Wedding (Eds.), *Current psychotherapies* (9th ed., pp. 67–112). Belmont, CA: Brooks/Cole.

Moser, C. (1992). Lust, lack of desire, and paraphilias: Some thoughts and possible connections. *Journal of Sex and Marital Therapy, 18*, 65–69.

Moses, A. E., & Hawkins, R. O. (1982). *Counseling lesbian women and gay men: A life-issues approach.* St. Louis: Mosby.

Moss, G., & Moss, W. (1975). *Growing old.* New York: Pocket Books.

Moster, D., Lie, T. L., & Markestad, T. (2008). Long-term medical and social consequences of preterm birth. *New England Journal of Medicine, 359*, 262–273.

MSN Money. (2010). *The cost of raising children.* Retrieved from http://moneycentral .msn.com/articles/family/kids/tlkidscost.asp

Mulder, E. J., Robles de Medina, P. G., Huizink, A. C., van den Bergh, B. R., Buitelaar, J. K., & Visser, G. H. (2002). Prenatal maternal stress: Effects on pregnancy and the (unborn) child. *Early Human Development, 73*, 1–14.

Mulrine, A. (2004, September 24). Making babies. *U.S. News & World Report*, 61–67.

Munk-Olsen, T., Laursen, T. M., Pedersen, C. B., Lidegaard, Ø., & Mortensen, P. B. (2011). Induced first-trimester abortion and risk of mental disorder. *New England Journal of Medicine, 364*, 332–339.

Murphy, Y., Hunt, V., Zajicek, A. M., Norris, A. N., & Hamilton, L. (2009). *Incorporating intersectionality in social work practice, research, policy, and education.* Washington, DC: NASW Press.

Murry, V. (1996). An ecological analysis of coital timing among middle-class African American adolescent females. *Journal of Adolescent Research, 11*, 261–279.

Mwalimu, I. (1975). Dying as the last stage of growth. In E. Kübler-Ross (Ed.), *Death: The final stage of growth* (pp. 147–163). Englewood Cliffs, NJ: Prentice-Hall.

Myrdal, G. (1944). *An American dilemma.* New York: Harper & Row.

Nabet, C., Lelong, N., Ancel, P. Y., Saurel-Cubizolles, M. J., & Kaminski, M. (2007). Smoking during pregnancy according to obstetric complications and parity: Results of the EURO-POP study. *European Journal of Epidemiology, 22*, 715–721.

Nabha, A., & Blasdell, J. (2002). *Public funding for abortion: Medicaid and the Hyde Amendment. National Abortion Federation.* Retrieved from http://womensissues.about.com

Nairne, J. S. (2011). *Psychology* (5th ed.). Belmont, CA: Wadsworth.

Nairne, J. S. (2014). *Psychology* (6th ed.). Belmont, CA: Wadsworth.

Nanda, S. (2001). *Gender diversity: Crosscultural variations.* Prospect Heights, IL: Waveland Press.

Nansel, T. R., Overpeck, M., Pilla, R., Ruan, W., Simons-Morton, B., & Scheidt, P. (2001). Bullying behaviors among U.S. Youth. *Journal of the American Medical Association, 285*, 2094–2100.

National Abortion Federation (NAF). (2004). *Parental involvement.* Retrieved from http://www.prochoice.org/about_abortion/violence/2003.html

National Abortion Federation (NAF). (2010). *Clinic violence.* Retrieved from http://www.prochoice.org/about_abortion/violence/violence_statistics.html

National Association of Social Workers (NASW). (1982). *Standards for the classification of social work practice.* Washington, DC: Author.

National Association of Social Workers (NASW). (1984). *Practice digest.* New York: NASW.

National Association of Social Workers (NASW). (1999). *The National Association of Social Workers code of ethics.* Washington, DC: Author.

National Association of Social Workers (NASW). (2001). *NASW standards for cultural competence in social work practice.* Washington, DC: Author.

National Association of Social Workers. (2008a). *Code of ethics.* Washington, DC: Author.

National Association of Social Workers. (2008b). *Code of ethics for social workers.* Washington, DC: Author.

National Association of Social Workers. (2009). *Social work speaks: National association of social workers policy statements 2009–2012* (8th ed.). Washington, DC: Author.

National Association of Social Workers (NASW). (2012). *Social work speaks: National Association of Social Workers policy statements 2012–2014* (9th ed.). Washington, DC: NASW Press.

National Cancer Institute (NCI). (2013a). *Breast cancer treatment*. Retrieved from http://www.cancer.gov/cancertopics/ pdq/treatment/breast/Patient/page5

National Cancer Institute (NCI). (2013b). *Radiation therapy for cancer*. Retrieved from http://www.cancer.gov/cancertopics/ factsheet/Therapy/radiation

National Center for Education Statistics. (2009). *Digest of education statistics: 2009 tables and figures*. Retrieved from http://nces.ed.gov/programs/digest/d09/tables/ dt09_054.asp

National Center for Health Statistics. (2002). *Health United States, 2002*. Hyattsville, MD: U.S. Department of Health and Human Services.

National Center for Health Statistics. (2007). *Health, United States, 2007 with chartbook on trends in the health of Americans*. Hyattsville, MD: Author.

National Coalition of Anti-Violence Programs (NCAVP). (2013). *Lesbian, gay, bisexual, transgender, queer, and HIV-affected hate violence in 2012*. Retrieved from http://www.avp.org/ storage/documents/ncavp_2012_hvreport_final.pdf

National Committee on Pay Equity. (2007). Questions and answers on pay equity. In A. Kesselman, L. D. McNair, & N. Schniedewind (Eds.), *Women: Images and realities* (4th ed., pp. 185–187). Boston: McGraw-Hill.

National Committee on Pay Equity. (2014). *National committee on pay equity*. Retrieved from http://www.pay-equity.org/

National Conference of State Legislators (NCSL). (2014). *Defining marriage: State defense of marriage laws and same sex marriage*. Retrieved from http://www.ncsl.org/research/ human-services/same-sex-marriage-overview.aspx

National Conference of State Legislatures (NCSL). (2011). *Same-sex marriage, civil unions and domestic partnerships*. Retrieved from http://www.ncsl.org/default.aspx? tabid=16430

National Gay and Lesbian Task Force. (2005). *Why civil unions are not enough*. Retrieved from http://www.thetaskforce.org/ node/945/print

National Gay and Lesbian Task Force. (2007a). *Adoption laws in the U.S.* Retrieved from http://www.thetaskforce.org/reports _and_research/issue_maps

National Gay and Lesbian Task Force. (2007b). *Anti-gay marriage measures in the U.S.* Retrieved from http://www.the taskforce.org/reports_and_research/issue_maps

National Gay and Lesbian Task Force. (2008a). *Discrimination in the military*. Retrieved from http://www.thetaskforce.org/ node/1951/print

National Gay and Lesbian Task Force. (2008b). *Hate crime laws in the U.S.* Retrieved from http://www.thetaskforce.org/ reports_and_research/issue_maps

National Gay and Lesbian Task Force. (2008c). *Marriage/partner recognition*. Retrieved from http://www.thetaskforce.org/ node/601/print

National Gay and Lesbian Task Force. (2008d). *Nondiscrimination*. Retrieved from http://www.thetaskforce.org/node/602/ print

National Gay and Lesbian Task Force. (2008e). *Relationship recognition for same-sex couples in the U.S.* Retrieved from http://www.thetaskforce.org/reports_and_research/issue_maps

National Gay and Lesbian Task Force. (2008f). *State nondiscrimination laws in the U.S.* Retrieved from http://www.the taskforce.org/reports_and_research/issue_maps

National Gay and Lesbian Task Force. (2011). *Challenges facing LGBT elders*. Retrieved from http://www.thetaskforce.org/ issues/aging/challenges

National Institute of Mental Health (NIMH). (2010). *Suicide in the U. S.: Statistics and prevention*. Retrieved from http:// www.mentalhealth.gov/health/publications/suicide-in-the-us-statistics-and-prevention/index.shtml

National Institutes of Health (NIH). (2010). *Stem cell information*. Retrieved from http://stemcells.nih.gov/

National Institutes of Health (NIH). (2011). *Birth control*. Retrieved from http://www.nlm.nih.gov/medlineplus/ birthcontrol.html

National Institutes of Health (NIH). (2012). *Chorionic villus sampling*. Retrieved October 20, 2013, from http://www.nlm .nih.gov/medlineplus/ency/article/003406.htm

National Institutes of Health (NIH). (2013a). *Intersex*. Retrieved from http://www.nlm.nih.gov/medlineplus/ency/article/ 001669.htm

National Institutes of Health (NIH). (2013b). *Stem cell information*. Retrieved from http://stemcells.nih.gov/Pages/Default .aspx

National Joint Committee on Learning Disabilities. (2010). *National Joint Committee on Learning Disabilities*. Retrieved from http://www.ldonline.org/pdfs/njcld/NJCLDDefinition of LD.pdf

National Organization on Disability. (2004). *Harris survey of Americans with disabilities: 2004*. Washington, DC: Author

National Organization on Disability. (2011). *NOD/Harris surveys*. Retrieved from http://www.nod.org/research_ publications/nod_harris_survey/

National Women's Health Information Center (NWHIC). (2009). *Infertility*. Retrieved from http://www.womenshealth .gov/faq/infertility.cfm#a

National Women's Health Information Center (NWHIC). (2010a). *Labor and birth*. Retrieved from http://www. womenshealth.gov/pregnancy/childbirth-beyond/labor-birth .cfm

National Women's Health Information Center (NWHIC). (2010b). *Pregnancy tests*. Retrieved from http://www .womens health.gov/faq/pregnancy-tests.cfm

Nelson, C. A., Thomas, K., & deHaan, M. (2006). Neural bases of cognitive development. In W. Damon, R. Lerner, D. Kuhn, & R. S. Siegler (Eds.), *Handbook of child psychology: Vol. 2. Cognition, perception, and language* (6th ed., pp. 3–57). Hoboken, NJ: Wiley.

Nelson, K. (2007). *Young minds in social worlds: Experience, meaning, and memory*. Cambridge, MA: Harvard University Press.

Nelson, K., Mattingly, M., & Schmitt, F. A. (2007). Out-of-body experience and arousal. *Neurology, 68*, 94–95.

Nemec, S. F., Nemec, U., Weber, M., Kasprina, G., Brugger, P. C., Krestan, C. R., et al. (2011). Male sexual development in utero: Testicular descent on prenatal magnetic resonance imaging. *Ultrasound in Obstetrics and Gynecology, 38*(6), 688–694.

Netting, F. E., & O'Connor, M. K. (2003). *Organization practice: A social worker's guide to understanding human services.* Boston: Allyn & Bacon.

Netting, F. E., Ketner, P. M., & McMurtry, S. L. (1993). *Social work macro practice.* New York: Longman.

Neugarten, B., & Weinstein, K. (1964). The changing American grandparent. *Journal of Marriage and the Family, 26,* 199–205.

Nevid, J. S. (2009). *Essentials of psychology* (2nd ed.). Boston: Houghton Mifflin.

Nevid, J. S. (2013). *Psychology: Concepts and applications* (4th ed.). Belmont, CA: Wadsworth.

Newcomb, A. F., Bukowskik, W. M., & Pattee, L. (1993). Children's peer relations: A meta-analytic review of popular, rejected, neglected, controversial, and average sociometric status. *Psychological Bulletin, 113*(1), 99–128.

Newman, B. M., & Newman, P. R. (2009). *Development through life: A psychosocial approach* (10th ed.). Belmont, CA: Wadsworth.

Newman, B. M., & Newman, P. R. (2012). *Development through life: A psychosocial approach* (11th ed.). Belmont, CA: Wadsworth.

New Media Learning. (2007). *Preventing sexual harassment.* Retrieved from http://training.newmedialearning.com/psh/aurora/index.htm

Nichols, W. R. (1999). *Random house Webster's college dictionary.* New York: Random House.

Nohr, E. A., Bech, B. H., Davies, M. J., Fryenberg, M., Henriksen, T. B., & Olsen, J. (2005). Prepregnancy obesity and fetal death: A study with the Danish national birth cohort. *Obstetrics and Gynecology, 106,* 250–259.

NOLO Law for All. (2014a). *Issues affecting same-sex couples FAQ.* Retrieved from http://www.nolo.com/legal-encyclopedia/issues-affecting-same-sex-couples-faq-32292-4.html

NOLO Law for All. (2014b). *Sexual orientation discrimination: Your rights.* Retrieved from http://www.nolo.com/legal-encyclopedia/sexual-orientation-discrimination-rights-29541.html

Norman, E. (2000). Introduction: The strengths perspective and resiliency enhancement—a natural partnership. In E. Norman (Ed.), *Resiliency enhancement: Putting the strengths perspective into social work practice* (pp. 1–16). New York: Columbia University Press.

Norman, N. D. (2005). Generalist practice with people of color. In J. Poulin (Ed.), *Strengths-based generalist practice: A collaborative approach* (pp. 398–130). Belmont, CA: Brooks/Cole.

Northouse, P. G. (2010). *Leadership: Theory and practice* (5th ed.). Thousand Oaks, CA: Sage.

Norton, D. G. (1978). Incorporating content on minority groups into social work practice courses. In *The dual perspective.* New York: Council on Social Work Education.

NPR. (2008a, April 20). *NIU gunman had "stopped taking medication."* Retrieved from http://www.npr.org/templates/story/story.php?toryID=19096619

NPR. (2008b, April 20). *NIU gunman had "stopped taking medication."* Retrieved from http://www.npr.org/templates/story/story.php?toryID=19073303

Nugent, A. (2014). *Top 10 gay stereotypes that just need to stop.* Retrieved from http://www.sundance.tv/top-ten/top-ten-gay-stereotypes-that-should-stop#/8

O'Brien, F., Azrin, N. H., & Bugle, C. (1974). Training profoundly retarded children to stop crawling. *Journal of Applied Behavior Analysis, 5,* 131–137.

O'Donnell, L., Myint-U, A., O'Donnell, & C. R., Stueve, A. (2003). Long-term influence of sexual norms and attitudes on timing of sexual initiation among urban minority youth. *Journal of School Health, 23*(2), 68–75.

O'Keefe, E. (2011). *Fight for gays in the military isn't ending any time soon.* Retrieved from http://voices.washingtonpost.com/federal-eye/2011/02/fight_for_gays_in_the_military.html

O'Sullivan, L. (2005). Sexual coercion in dating relationships: Conceptual and methodological issues. *Sexual and Relationship Therapy, 20,* 3–11.

Obenauer, S., & Maestre, L. A. (2008). Fetal Mr. Of lung hypoplasia: Imaging findings. *Clinical Imaging, 32,* 48–50.

Office of Adolescent Health, U.S. Department of Health and Human Services. (2013). *Trends in teen pregnancy and childbearing.* Retrieved from http://www.hhs.gov/ash/oah/adolescent-health-topics/reproductive-health/teen-pregnancy/trends.html

Okun, B. F., & Rappaport, L. J. (1980). *Working with families: An introduction to family therapy.* North Scituate, MA: Duxbury.

Older Americans Act of 1965, as amended, text and history. (1970, November). Washington, DC: U.S. Department of Health, Education, and Welfare.

Omachonu, V. K., & Ross, J. E. (1994). *Principles of total quality.* Delray Beach, FL: St. Lucie Press.

Ossana, S. M. (2000). Relationship and couples counseling. In R. M. Perez, K. A. DeBord, & K. J. Bieschke (Eds.), *Handbook of counseling and psychotherapy with lesbian, gay, and bisexual clients* (pp. 275–302). Washington, DC: American Psychological Association.

Otten, A. S. (1984, July 30). Ever more Americans live into 80s and 90s, causing big problems. *Wall Street Journal, 1,* 10.

Ou, Y., & McAdoo, H. P. (1999). The ethnic socialization of Chinese American children. In H. P. McAdoo (Ed.), *Family ethnicity* (2nd ed., pp. 252–276). Thousand Oaks, CA: Sage.

Ouchi, W. (1981). *Theory Z: How American business can meet the Japanese challenge.* Reading, MA: Addison-Wesley.

Kinnunen, L. H., Moltz, H., Metz, J., & Cooper, M. (2004). Differential brain activation in exclusively homosexual and heterosexual men produced by the selective serotonin reuptake inhibitor, fluoxetine. *Brain Research, 1024*(1–2), 251–254.

Pace, P. R. (2010, June). Salary survey released. *NASW News, 55*(6), 8.

Paniagua, F. A. (2005). *Assessing and treating culturally diverse clients* (3rd ed.). Thousand Oaks, CA: Sage.

Papalia, D. E., & Feldman, R. D. (2012). *Experience human development* (12th ed.). New York: McGraw-Hill.

Papalia, D. E., Feldman, R. D., & Martorell, G. (2012). *Experience human development* (12th ed.). New York: McGraw-Hill.

Papalia, D. E., & Olds, S. W. (1981). *Human development* (2nd ed.). New York: McGraw-Hill.

Papalia, D. E., & Olds, S. W. (1992). *Human development* (5th ed.). New York: McGraw-Hill.

Papalia, D. E., Olds, S. W., & Feldman, R. D. (1998). *Human development* (7th ed.). New York: McGraw-Hill.

Papalia, D. E., Olds, S. W., & Feldman, R. D. (2004). *Human development* (9th ed.). Boston: McGraw-Hill.

Papalia, D. E., Olds, S. W., & Feldman, R. D. (2007). *Human development* (10th ed.). Boston: McGraw-Hill.

Papalia, D. E., Olds, S. W., & Feldman, R. D. (2009). *Human development* (11th ed.). New York: McGraw-Hill.

Parke, R. D., & Buriel, R. (2006). Socialization in the family: Ethnic and ecological perspectives. In N. Eisenberg, W. Damon, & R. M. Lerner (Eds.), *Handbook of child psychology: Vol. 3. Social, emotional, and personality development* (6th ed., pp. 429–504). Hoboken, NJ: Wiley.

Parker, K. (2011). *A portrait of stepfamilies.* Retrieved from http://pewsocialtrends.org

Parks, C. A., & Humphreys, N. A. (2006). Lesbian relationships and families. In D. F. Morrow & L. Messinger (Eds.), *Sexual orientation and gender expression in social work practice: Working with gay, lesbian, bisexual, and transgender people* (pp. 216–242). New York: Columbia University Press.

Parrott, D., & Peterson, J. (2008). What motivates hate crimes based on sexual orientation? Mediating effects of anger on antigay aggression. *Aggressive Behavior, 34,* 306–318.

Parten, M. (1932). Social participation among preschool children. *Journal of Abnormal and Social Psychology, 27,* 243–269.

Pasupathi, M., & Staudinger, U. M. (2001). Do advanced moral reasoners also show wisdom?. *International Journal of Behavioral Development, 25*(5), 401–115.

Patchner, L. S., & DeWeaver, K. L. (2008). Disability: Neurocognitive disabilities. In T. Mizrahi & L. E. Davis (Eds.), *Encyclopedia of social work* (Vol. 2, pp. 43–49). Washington, DC: NASW Press.

Patterson, G. R. (1975). *Families: Applications of social learning to family life.* Champaign, IL: Research Press.

Patterson, G. R., DeBaryshe, B. D., & Ramsey, E. (1989). A developmental perspective on antisocial behavior. *American Psychologist, 44,* 329–335.

Patterson, W. M., Dohn, H. H., Bird, J., & Patterson, G. A. (1983). Evaluation of suicidal patients: The SAD PERSONS scale. *Psychosomatics, 24*(4), 343–349.

Pauli-Pott, U., Mertesacker, B., & Beckmann, D. (2003). Ein fragebogen zur erfassung des fruhkindlichen temperaments im elternurteil. *Zeitschrift Fur Kinder- Und Jugendpsychiatrie Und Psychotherapie, 31*(2), 99–110.

Paus, T. (2003). Mapping brain maturation and cognitive development during adolescence. *Trends in Cognitive Sciences, 9,* 60–68.

Peck, R. C. (1968). Psychological development in the second half of life. In B. L. Neugarten (Ed.), *Middle age and aging* (pp. 78–103). Chicago: University of Chicago Press.

Pecora, N., Murray, J. P., & Wartella, E. A. (2007). *Children and television: Fifty years of research.* Mahwah, NJ: Erlbaum.

Pecora, P. J., Whittaker, J. K., Maluccio, A. N., Barth, R. P., DePanfilis, D., & Plotnick, R. D. (2010). *The child welfare challenge: Policy, practice, and research* (3rd ed.). New Brunswick, NJ: Transaction Publishers.

Peplau, L. A. (2003). Human sexuality: How do men and women differ?. *Current Directions in Psychological Science, 12*(2), 37–40.

Perloff, J. D., & Jaffee, K. D. (1999, March). Late entry into prenatal care: The neighborhood context. *Social Work, 44*(2), 116–128.

Perls, T. T., Hutter-Silver, M., & Lauerman, J. F. (1999). *Living to 100: Lessons in living to your maximum potential at any age.* New York: Basic Books.

Perren, S., & Alsaker, F. D. (2006). Social behavior and peer relationships of victims, bully victims, and bullies in kindergarten. *Journal of Child Psychology and Psychiatry, 47*(1), 45–57.

Peskin, H. (1967). Pubertal onset and ego functioning. *Journal of Abnormal Psychology, 72,* 1–15.

Peters, H. (1982). The legal rights of gays. In A. E. Moses & R. O. Hawkins (Eds.), *Counseling lesbian women and gay men: A life issues approach* (pp. 21–24). St. Louis: Mosby.

Petretic-Jackson, P. A., & Jackson, T. (1996). Mental health interventions with battered women. In A. R. Roberts (Ed.), *Helping battered women: New perspectives and remedies* (pp. 188–121). New York: Oxford University Press.

Petrini, J. R., Dias, T., McCormick, M. C., Massolo, M. L., Green, N. S., & Escobar, G. J. (2009). Increased risk of adverse neurological development for later preterm infants. *Journal of Pediatrics, 154,* 169–176.

Pew Forum on Religion and Public Life. (2010). *Most continue to favor gays serving openly in military.* Retrieved from http://pewforum.org/Gay-Marriage-and-Homosexuality/Most-Continue-to-Favor-Gays-Serving-Openly-in-Military.aspx

Pew Research Center (2007, March 22). *Trends in political values and core attitudes: 1987–2007.* Washington, DC: Pew Research Center for People and the Press. Retrieved from www.people-press.org/files/legacy-pdf/312pdf.

Pew Research Center. (2013). *10 Findings about women in the workplace.* Retrieved from http://www.pewsocialtrends.org/2013/12/11/10-findings-about-women-in-the-workplace/

Pew Research Center. (2014). *Gay marriage around the world.* Retrieved from http://www.pewforum.org/2013/12/19/gay-marriage-around-the-world-2013/

Pfeiffer, K. (2009). *Teen moms aren't likely to get married.* Retrieved from http://www.suite101.com/content/teen-parents-arent-likely-to-get-married-a106497

Phenice, L. A. (1999). Native Hawaiian families. In H. P. McAdoo (Ed.), *Family ethnicity* (2nd ed., pp. 107–118). Thousand Oaks, CA. Sage.

Phillips, W. (1996). Culturally competent practice understanding Asian family values. *The Roundtable: Journal of the National Resource Center for Special Needs Adoption, 10*(1), 1–3.

Phinney, J. (1989). Stages of ethnic identity development in minority group adolescents. *Journal of Early Adolescence, 9,* 34–49.

Phinney, J. S. (2005). Ethnic identity development in minority adolescents. In C. B. Fisher & R. M. Lerner (Eds.), *Encyclopedia of applied developmental science* (Vol. 1, pp. 420–123). Thousand Oaks, CA: Sage.

Piaget, J. (1952). *The origins of intelligence in children.* New York: International Universities Press.

Piaget, J. (1972). Intellectual development from adolescence to adulthood. *Human Development, 15,* 1–12.

Pianta, R. C. (2006). Classroom management and relationships between children and teachers: Implications for research and practice. In C. M. Evertson & C. S. Weinstein (Eds.), *Handbook of classroom management: Research, practice, and contemporary issues* (pp. 685–709). Mahwah, NJ: Erlbaum.

Pianta, R. C., & Stuhlman, M. W. (2004). Teacher-child relationships and children's success in the first years of school. *School Psychology Review, 33,* 444–458.

Pierrehumbert, B., Ramstein, T., Karmaniola, A., Miljkovitch, R., & Halfon, O. (2002). Quality of child care in the preschool years. *International Journal of Behavioral Development, 26*(5), 385–396.

Pillemer, K., & Moore, D. W. (1989). Abuse of patients in nursing homes: Findings from a survey of staff. *Gerontologist, 29,* 314–320.

Pinderhughes, E. (1982). Afro-American families and the victim system. In M. McGoldrick, J. K. Pearce, & J. Giordana (Eds.), *Ethnicity and family therapy* (p. 108–122). New York: Guilford Press.

Pinkney, A. (1972). *The American way of violence.* New York: Random House.

Planned Parenthood. (2006). *Global illegal abortion: Where there is no "Roe": An examination of the impact of illegal abortion around the world issue brief.* Retrieved from http://www.plannedparenthood.org/issues-action/global-inequality/global-abortion-6480.htm

Planned Parenthood. (2007). *There's no place like home … for sex education.* Retrieved from http://www.noplacelikehome.org/nativeamerican.php

Planned Parenthood. (2008a). *The abortion pill.* Retrieved from http://www.plannedparenthood.org/health-topics/abortion/abortion-pill-medication-abortion-4354.htm

Planned Parenthood. (2008b). *Abortion procedures.* Retrieved from http://www.plannedparenthood.org/health-topics/abortion/abortion-procedures-4359.htm

Planned Parenthood. (2008c). *Birth control.* Retrieved from http://www.plannedparenthood.org/health-topics/birth-control-4211.htm

Planned Parenthood. (2010). *Abortion.* Retrieved from http://www.plannedparenthood.org/health-topics/abortion-4260.asp

Planned Parenthood. (2011). *Birth control.* Retrieved from http://www.plannedparenthood.org/health-topics/birth-control-4211.htm

Planned Parenthood. (2013). *Abortion.* Retrieved December 2, 2013, from http://www.plannedparenthood.org/health-topics/abortion-4260.asp

Planned Parenthood. (2014). *Birth control.* Retrieved from http://www.plannedparenthood.org/health-topics/birth-control-4211.htm

Plotnik, R., & Kouyoumdjian, M. (2011). *Introduction to psychology* (9th ed.). Belmont, CA: Cengage.

Polansky, N. F., Chalmers, M. A., Buttenwieser, E., & Williams, D. P. (1991). *Damaged parents: An anatomy of child neglect.* Chicago: University of Chicago Press.

Polansky, N. F., Holly, C., & Polansky, N. A. (1975). *Profile of neglect: A survey of the state of knowledge of child neglect.* Washington, DC: Department of Health, Education, and Welfare.

Pollack, A. E., Carignan, C. S., & Jacobstein, R. (2004). Female and male sterilization. In R. A. Hatcher, J. Trussell, F. Stewart, A. L. Nelson, W. Cates, Jr., F. Guest, & D. Kowal (Eds.), *Contraceptive technology* (18th ed., pp. 531–573). New York: Ardent Media.

PollingReport.com. (2010). *Same sex marriage, gay rights.* Retrieved from http://www.pollingreport.com/civil.htm

PollingReport.com. (2014). *Same-sex marriage, gay rights.* Retrieved from http://www.pollingreport.com/civil.htm

Pollio, E., Deblinger, E., & Runyon, M. K. (2011). Mental health treatment for the effects of child sexual abuse. In J. E. B. Myers (Ed.), *The APSAC handbook on child maltreatment* (3rd ed., pp. 267–288). Thousand Oaks, CA: Sage.

Poniewozik, J. (2005, March 25). The decency police. *Time,* 24–31.

Porath, A. J., & Fried, P. A. (2005). Effects of prenatal cigarette and marijuana exposure on drug use among offspring. *Neurotoxicology and Teratology, 27,* 267–277.

Potocky, M. (2008). Immigrants and refugees. In T. Mizrahi & L. E. Davis (Eds.), *Encyclopedia of social work* (Vol. 3, pp. 441–445). Washington, DC: NASW Press.

Powell, G. J. (Ed.). (1983). *The psychosocial development of minority group children.* New York: Brunner/Mazel.

Powell, T. J. (1987). *Self-help organizations and professional practice.* Silver Spring, MD: NASW.

Premack, D. (1965). Reinforcement theory. In D. Levine (Ed.), *Nebraska symposium on motivation* (Vol 13, pp. 123–180). Lincoln: University of Nebraska Press.

Preto, N. G. (2011). Transformation of the family system during adolescence. In M. McGoldrick, B. Carter, & N. G. Garcia-Preto (Eds.), *The expanded family life cycle: Individual, family, and social perspectives* (4th ed., pp. 232–246). Boston: Allyn & Bacon.

Preto, N. G., & Blacker, L. (2011). Families at midlife: Launching children and moving on. In M. McGoldrick, B. Carter, & N. G. Garcia-Preto (Eds.), *The expanded family life cycle: Individual, family, and social perspectives* (4th ed., pp. 247–260). Boston: Allyn & Bacon.

Priess, H., Lindberg, S., & Hyde, J. S. (2009). Adolescent gender-role identity and mental health: Gender intensification revisited. *Child Development, 80,* 1531–1544.

Prochaska, J. O., DiClemente, C. C. (1982). Trans-theoretical therapy—toward a more integrative model of change. *Psychotherapy: Theory, Research and Practice, 19*(3), 276–288.

ProCon.org. (2014). *Gay marriage.* Retrieved from http://gaymarriage.procon.org/view.resource.php?esourceID=004857

Putnam, S. P., Gartstein, M. A., & Rothbart, M. K. (2006). Measurement of fine-grained aspects of toddler temperament: The early childhood behavior questionnaire. *Infant Behavior & Development, 29,* 386–401.

Raines, J. C. (2006). Improving educational and behavioral performance of students with learning disabilities. In C. Franklin, M. B. Harris, & P. Allen-Meares (Eds.), *The school services sourcebook: A guide for school-based professionals* (pp. 178–195). New York: Oxford.

Ramirez, O. (1998). Mexican American children and adolescents. In J. T. Gibbs & L. N. Huang (Eds.), *Children of color: Psychological interventions with culturally diverse youth* (pp. 215–239). San Francisco: Jossey-Bass.

Raneri, L., & Wiemann, C. (2007). Social ecological predictors of repeat adolescent pregnancy. *Perspectives on Sexual and Reproductive Health, 39,* 1036–1042.

Raskin, N. J., & Rogers, C. R. (1995). Person-centered therapy. In R. J. Corsini & D. Wedding (Eds.), *Current psychotherapies* (5th ed., pp. 128–161). Itasca, IL: Peacock.

Raskin, N. J., Rogers, C. R., & Witty, M. C. (2011). Client-centered therapy. In R. S. Corsini & D. Wedding (Eds.), *Current psychotherapies* (9th ed., pp. 148–195). Belmont, CA: Brooks/Cole.

Rathus, S. A. (2010). *HDEV*. Belmont, CA: Wadsworth.

Rathus, S. A. (2011a). *CDEV*. Belmont, CA: Wadsworth.

Rathus, S. A. (2011b). *Childhood & adolescence: Voyages in development* (4th ed.). Belmont, CA: Wadsworth.

Rathus, S. A. (2013). *Discovery series introduction to life span.* Belmont, CA: Wadsworth.

Rathus, S. A. (2014a). *Childhood: Voyages in development.* Belmont, CA: Wadsworth.

Rathus, S. A. (2014b). *Childhood & adolescence: Voyages in development* (5th ed.). Belmont, CA: Wadsworth.

Rathus, S. A. (2014c). *HDEV* (3rd ed.). Belmont, CA: Wadsworth.

Rathus, S. A. (2014d). *PSYCH* (3rd ed.). Belmont, CA: Wadsworth.

Rathus, S. A., Nevid, J. S., & Fichner-Rathus, L. (2011). *Human sexuality in a world of diversity* (8th ed.). Boston: Allyn & Bacon.

Rathus, S. A., Nevid, J. S., & Fichner-Rathus, L. (2014). *Human sexuality in a world of diversity* (9th ed.). Upper Saddle River, NJ: Pearson.

Reamer, F. G. (1995). Ethics and values. In R. L. Edwards (Ed.), *Encyclopedia of social work* (19th ed., Vol. 1, pp. 893–902). Washington, DC: NASW Press.

Reamer, F. G. (2013). *Social work values and ethics* (4th ed.). New York: Columbia University Press.

Rees, S. (1998). Empowerment of youth. In L. M. Gutierrez, R. J. Parsons, & E. O. Cox (Eds.), *Empowerment in social work practice: A sourcebook* (pp. 130–145). Pacific Grove, CA: Brooks/Cole.

Register, E. (1993). Feminism and recovering from battering: Working with the individual woman. In M. Hansen & M. Harway (Eds.), *Battering and family therapy: A feminist perspective* (pp. 93–104). Newbury Park, CA: Sage.

Regulus, T. A. (1995). Gang violence. In R. L. Edwards & J. G. Hopps (Eds.), *Encyclopedia of social work* (19th ed., Vol 2, pp. 1045–1054). Washington, DC: NASW Press.

Reichert, E. (2007). *Challenges in human rights: A social work perspective.* New York: Columbia University Press.

Reicherzer, S. (2005). Coming out and living across the life span. In D. Comstock (Ed.), *Diversity and development* (pp. 161–183). Belmont, CA: Brooks/Cole.

Reis, S., & Housand, A. M. (2008). Characteristics of gifted and talented learners: Similarities and differences across domains. In F. A. Karnes & K. R. Stephens (Eds.), *Achieving excellence: Educating the gifted and talented* (pp. 62–81). Upper Saddle River, NJ: Merrill.

Renninger, L., Wade, J., & Grammer, K. (2004). Getting that female glance: Patterns and consequences of male nonverbal behavior in courtship contexts. *Evolution and Human Behavior, 25*, 416–431.

Renzetti, C. M., & Curran, D. J. (2003). *Women, men, and society* (7th ed.). Boston: Allyn & Bacon.

Renzetti, C. M., Curran, D. J., & Maier, S. L. (2012). *Women, men, and society* (6th ed.). Boston: Pearson.

Research America. (2013). *Voters favor expanding funding for stem cell research.* Retrieved November 26, 2013, from http://www.researchamerica.org/stemcell_issue?clid=CIj-4OeKg7sCFWTxOgodvkMAKA

Rhodes, M. L. (1985). Gilligan's theory of moral development as applied to social work practice. *Social Work, 30*, 101–105.

Richardson, L. (2007). Gender stereotyping in the English language. In V. Taylor, N. Whitter, & L. J. Rupp (Eds.), *Feminist frontiers* (7th ed., pp. 99–103). Boston: McGraw-Hill.

Richters, J. E., Arnold, L. E., Jensen, P. S., Abikoff, H., Conners, C. K., Greenhill, L. L., et al. (1995). NIMH collaborative multisite multimodal treatment study of children with ADHD: I. Background and rationale. *Journal of the American Academy of Child and Adolescent Psychiatry, 34*(8), 987–1000.

Riessman, F. (1965). The "helper therapy" principle. *Journal of Social Work, 10*(2), 27–34.

Rind, B., Tromovitch, P., & Bauserman, R. (1998). A meta-analytic examination of assumed properties of child sexual abuse using college samples. *Psychological Bulletin, 124*, 22–53.

Robbins, S. P., Chatterjee, P., & Canda, E. R. (2006). *Contemporary human behavior theory: A critical perspective for social work* (2nd ed.). Boston: Allyn & Bacon.

Robbins, S. P., Chatterjee, P., & Canda, E. R. (2012). *Contemporary human behavior theory: A critical perspective for social work.* Boston: Allyn & Bacon.

Roberts, A. R. (1996a). Introduction: Myths and realities regarding battered women. In A. R. Roberts (Ed.), *Helping battered women: New perspectives and remedies* (pp. 3–12). New York: Oxford University Press.

Roberts, A. R. (1996b). Police responses to battered women: Past, present, and future. In A. R. Roberts (Ed.), *Helping battered women: New perspectives and remedies* (pp. 85–95). New York: Oxford University Press.

Roberts, A. R. (1999). An overview of crisis theory and crisis intervention. In A. R. Roberts (Ed.), *Crisis intervention handbook: Assessment, treatment, and research* (pp. 3–30). New York: Oxford University Press.

Roberts, A. R. (2005). Briding the past and present to the future of crisis intervention and crisis management. In A. W. Roberts (Ed.), *Crisis intervention handbook: Assessment, treatment, and research* (3rd ed., pp. 3–34). New York: Oxford University Press.

Robertson, I. (1980). *Social problems* (2nd ed.). New York: Random House.

Robinson, B. A. (2003, January 17). *Decriminalizing same-sex behavior.* Retrieved from http://www.religioustolerance.org/hom_laws2.htm

Robinson, B. A. (2005, December 11). *Criminalizing same-sex behavior.* Retrieved from http://www.religioustolerance.org/hom_lawsl.htm

Roeder, K. (2002, Fall). Ethics: Practicing with honorable spirit: The use and non-use of spirituality in social work practice. *The New Social Worker, 9*, 10–12.

Roethlisberger, F. J., & Dickson, W. J. (1939). *Management and the worker.* Cambridge, MA: Harvard University Press.

Rogers, C. R. (1959). A theory of therapy, personality and interpersonal relationships, as developed in the client-centered framework. In S. Koch (Ed.), *Psychology: A study of a science* (Vol. 3). New York: McGraw-Hill.

Rogers, J. K., & Henson, K. D. (2007). Hey, why don't you wear a shorter skirt? In S. M. Shaw & J. Lee (Eds.), *Women's voices: Feminist visions* (3rd ed., pp. 486–497). Boston: McGraw-Hill.

Rogers, P. (1993, February 15). How many gays are there? *Newsweek*, 46.

Roid, G. H. (2003). *Stanford-Binet intelligence scales, fifth edition, examiner's manual.* Itasca, IL: Riverside.

Roisman, G., Clausell, E., Holland, A., Fortuna, K., & Elieff, C. (2008). Adult romantic relationships as contexts of human development: A multimethod comparison of same-sex couples with opposite-sex dating, engaged, and married dyads. *Developmental Psychology, 44,* 91–101.

Rolland, J. S. (2011). Chronic illness and the life cycle. In M. McGoldrick, B. Carter, & N. G. Garcia-Preto (Eds.), *The expanded family life cycle: Individual, family, and social perspectives* (4th ed., pp. 348–367). Boston: Allyn & Bacon.

Romano, A. (2007, April 30). Making of a massacre. *Newsweek,* 22–35.

Roopnarine, J. L., & Evans, M. E. (2007). Family structural organization, mother-child and father-child relationship and psychological outcomes in English-speaking African Caribbean and Indo Caribbean families. In M. Sutherland (Ed.), *Psychological development in the caribbean.* Kingston, Jamaica: Ian Randle.

Roopnarine, J. L., Krishnakumar, A., Metindogan, A., & Evans, M. (2006). Links between parenting styles, parent-child academic interaction, parent-school interaction, and early academic skills and social behaviors in young children of English-speaking Caribbean immigrants. *Early Childhood Research Quarterly, 21,* 238–252.

Roosevelt, F. D. (1937, January 20). *Second inaugural address.*

Rosenbaum, J. E. (2009). Patient teenagers? A comparison of the sexual behavior of virginity pledgers and matched nonpledgers. *Pediatrics, 123*(1), 110–120. Retrieved from http://pediatrics.aappublications.org/content/123/1/e110. full

Rosenhan, D. (1973). On being sane in insane places. *Science, 179,* 250–257.

Rosenthal, M. S. (2013). *Human sexuality: From cells to society.* Belmont, CA: CENGAGE Learning.

Rothbart, M. K., Ellis, L. K., & Posner, M. I. (2004). Temperament and self-regulation. In R. F. Baumeister & K. D. Vohs (Eds.), *Handbood of self-regulation: Research, theory, and applications* (pp. 357–370). New York: Guilford.

Rothbart, M. K., & Mauro, J. A. (1990). Questionnaire approaches to the study of infant temperament. In J. W. Fagen & J. Colombo (Eds.), *Individual differences in infancy: Reliability, stability, and prediction* (pp. 411–129). New York: Guilford.

Rothbaum, F., Morelli, G., Pott, M., & Liu-Constant, Y. (2000). Immigrant-Chinese and euro-American parents' physical closeness with young children: Themes of family relatedness. *Journal of Family Psychology, 14,* 334–348.

Rothbaum, F., Weisz, J., Pott, M., Miyake, K., & Morelli, G. (2000). Attachment and culture: Security in the United States and Japan. *American Psychologist, 55,* 1093–1104.

Rothman, J. (1987). Community theory and research. In *Encyclopedia of social work* (Vol. 1, pp. 308–316). Silver Spring, MD: NASW.

Rothman, J. (2001). Approaches to community intervention. In J. Rothman, J. L. Erlich, & J. E. Tropman (Eds.), *Strategies of community intervention* (6th ed., pp. 27–64). Itasca, IL: Peacock.

Rothman, J. (2007). Multi modes of intervention at the macro level. *Journal of Community Practice, 15*(4), 11–40.

Rothman, S. M. (1978). *Woman's proper place.* New York: Basic Books.

Rozee, P. D., & Koss, M. P. (2000). Rape: A century of resistance. *Psychology of Women Quarterly, 25,* 295–311.

Rubin, A., & Babbie, E. (2011). *Research methods for social work* (7th ed.). Belmont, CA: Brooks/Cole.

Rubin, A., & Babbie, E. R. (2014). *Research methods for social work* (8th ed.). Belmont, CA: Brooks/Cole.

Rubin, K. H., Bukowski, W., & Parker, J. G. (1998). Peer interactions, relationships, and groups. In W. Damon & N. Eisenberg (Eds.), *Handbook of child psychology: Vol. 3. Social, emotional, and personality development* (5th ed., pp. 619–700). New York: Wiley.

Rubin, K. H., Bukowski, W., & Parker, J. G. (2006). Peer interactions, relationships, and groups. In W. Damon, R. M. Lerner, & N. Eisenberg (Eds.), *Handbook of child psychology: Vol. 3. Social, emotional, and personality development* (6th ed., pp. 571–645). New York: Wiley.

Rubin, Z. (1973). *Liking and loving.* New York: Holt, Rinehart and Winston.

Runyon, M. D., & Urquiza, A. J. (2011). Child physical abuse. In J. E. B. Myers (Ed.), *The APSAC handbook on child maltreatment* (3rd ed., pp. 195–212). Thousand Oaks, CA: Sage.

Russell, S. T., & Joyner, K. (2001). Adolescent sexual orientation and suicide risk: Evidence from a national study. *American Journal of Public Health, 91,* 1276–1281.

Ruth, S. (1998). *Issues in feminism* (4th ed.). Mountain View, CA: Mayfield.

Rutter, M. (1983). Stress, coping, and development: Some issues and some questions. In N. Garmezy & M. Rutter (Eds.), *Stress, coping, and development in children* (pp. 1–42). New York: McGraw-Hill.

Ryan, R. M., & Deci, E. L. (2000a). Self-determination theory and the facilitation of intrinsic motivation, social development, and well-being. *American Psychologist, 55,* 68–78.

Ryan, R. M., & Deci, E. L. (2000b). When rewards compete with nature: The undermining of intrinsic motivation and self-regulation. In C. Sansone & J. M. Harackiewicz (Eds.), *Intrinsic and extrinsic motivation: The search for optimal motivation and performance* (pp. 13–54). San Diego: Academic Press.

Ryan, W. (1976). *Blaming the victim.* New York: Vintage.

Sable, M. R., & Kelly, P. J. (2008). Reproductive health. In T. Mizrahi & L. E. Davis (Eds.), *Encyclopedia of social work* (Vol. 3, pp. 506–512). Washington, DC: NASW Press.

Sachs, A. (1993, November 22). 9-Zip! i love it!. *Time,* 44–45.

Saleebey, D. (2009). *The strengths perspective in social work practice* (5th ed.). Boston: Allyn & Bacon.

Saleebey, D. (2013). *The strengths perspective in social work practice* (6th ed.). Upper Saddle River, NJ: Pearson.

Salmivalli, C., & Peets, K. (2009). Bullies, victims, and bully-victim relationships in middle childhood and adolescence. In K. H. Rubin, W. M. Bukowski, & B. Laursen (Eds.), *Handbook of peer interactions, relationships, and groups* (pp. 322–340). New York: Guilford.

Salmivalli, C., Peets, K., & Hodges, E. V. E. (2011). Bullying. In P. K. Smith & C. H. Hart (Eds.), *Wiley-Blackwell handbook of childhood social development* (2nd ed, pp. 510–528.). New York: Wiley.

Samuelson, P. (1980). Quoted in P. Blumberg, *Inequality in an age of decline*. New York: Oxford University Press.

Sanchez, T. W., & Jones, S. (2010). The diversity and commonalities of Latinos in the United States. In R. Furman & N. Negi (Eds.), *Social work practice with Latinos: Key issues and emerging themes* (pp. 31–44). Chicago: Lyceum.

Sandhu, D. S., & Madathil, J. (2013). Culturally alert counseling with South Asian Americans. In G. McAuliffe, Associates (Eds.), *Culturally alert counseling: A comprehensive introduction* (2nd ed., pp. 315–344). Thousand Oaks, CA: Sage.

Sandler, B. (2008). In case of sexual harassment: A guide for women students. In A. Kesselman, L. D. McNair, & N. Schniedewing (Eds.), *Women: Images and realities* (4th ed., pp. 206–208). Boston: McGraw-Hill.

Santiago-Rivera, A. L., Arredondo, P., & Gallardo-Cooper, M. (2002). *Counseling Latinos and la familia: A practical guide.* Thousand Oaks, CA: Sage.

Santo, J. L., Portuguez, M. W., & Nunes, M. L. (2009). Cognitive and behavioral status of low birth weight preterm children raised in a developing country at preschool age. *Journal of Pediatrics, 85*, 35–41.

Santrock, J. W. (2008). *Life-span development* (11th ed.). Boston: McGraw-Hill.

Santrock, J. W. (2010a). *Adolescence* (13th ed.). New York: McGraw-Hill.

Santrock, J. W. (2010b). *Children* (11th ed.). New York: McGraw-Hill.

Santrock, J. W. (2010c). *A topical approach to life-span development* (5th ed.). New York: McGraw-Hill.

Santrock, J. W. (2012a). *Adolescence* (14th ed.). New York: McGraw-Hill.

Santrock, J. W. (2012b). *A topical approach to life-span development* (6th ed.). New York: McGraw-Hill.

Santrock, J. W. (2013a). *Children* (12th ed.). New York: McGraw-Hill.

Santrock, J. W. (2013b). *Life-span development* (12th ed.). New York: McGraw-Hill.

Sapiro, V. (1999). *Women in American society* (4th ed.). Mountain View, CA: Mayfield.

Sapiro, V. (2003). *Women in American society: An introduction to women's studies* (3rd ed.). Boston: McGraw-Hill.

Sardar, Z. (2000, July 30). More hackneyed than Bollywood. *New Statesman, 14*, 14–16.

Saskatchewan Psychology Portal. (n.d.). *Psychology 30: Human development: The wild boy of aveyron.* Retrieved from http://sesd.sk.ca/psychology/psych30/wild_boy_P30.htm

Saunders, D. G. (1995). Domestic violence: Legal issues. In R. L. Edwards (Ed.), *Encyclopedia of social work* (19th ed., Vol. 1, pp. 789–795). Washington, DC: NASW Press.

Savic, I., & Lindstrom, P. (2008, June 16). PET and MRI Show differences in cerebral asymmetry and functional connectivity between homo- and heterosexual subjects. *Proceedings of the National Academy of Sciences.* Retrieved from http://www.pnas.org/content/105/27/9403.full?id=d391ac55-88e7-43d2-8425-c90e3af9019e

Savin-Williams, R. C. (2001). Suicide attempts among sexual-minority youths: Population and measurement issues. *Journal of Consulting and Clinical Psychology, 69*, 983–991.

Schaefer, R. T. (2008). *Racial and ethnic groups* (11th ed.). Upper Saddle River, NJ: Prentice Hall.

Schaefer, R. T. (2012). *Racial and ethnic groups* (13th ed.). Boston: Pearson.

Schaffer, H. R. (1996). *Social development.* Cambridge, MA: Blackwell.

Scharf, M., Shulman, K. S., & Avigad-Spitz, L. (2005). Sibling relationships in emerging adulthood and in adolescence. *Journal of Adolescent Research, 20*(1), 64–90.

Scheflen, A. (1974). *How behavior means.* Garden City, NY: Anchor.

Scheff, T. (1966). *Being mentally ill.* Chicago: Aldine

Schick, F. L. (Ed.). (1986). *Statistical handbook on aging Americans.* Phoenix: Oryx.

Schiele, J. H. (1996, May). Afrocentricity: An emerging paradigm in social work practice. *Social Work, 41*, 284–294.

Schiller, L. Y. (1995). Stages of development in women's groups: A relational model. In R. Kurland & R. Salmon (Eds.), *Group work practice in a troubled society: Problems and opportunities* (pp. 117–138). Binghamton, NY: Haworth.

Schmid, M., Kasprian, G., Marschaleck, J., Posch, A., Balassy, C., & Prayer, D. (2011). Maternal smoking and fetal lung volume—an in utero MRI Investigation. *Prenatal Diagnosis, 31*(5), 491–495.

Schmidt, L. A., Miskovic, V., Boyle, M. H., & Saigal, S. (2008). Shyness and timidity in young adults who were born at extremely low birth weight. *Pediatrics, 122*, e181–e187.

Schneider, B. H., Atkinson, L., & Tardif, C. (2001). Child-parent attachment and children's peer relationships: A quantitative review. *Developmental Psychology, 37*, 86–100.

Schwaber, F. H. (1985). Some legal issues related to outside institutions. In H. Hidalgo, T. Peterson, & N. J. Woodman (Eds.), *Lesbian and gay issues: A resource manual for social workers* (pp. 92–99). Silver Spring, MD: NASW.

Schwartz, D., Kelly, B. M., Duong, M., & Badaly, D. (2010). Contextual perspective on intervention and prevention efforts for bully/victims problems. In E. M. Vernberg & B. K. Biggs (Eds.), *Preventing and treating bullying and victimization* (pp. 17–44). New York: Oxford University Press.

Seaward, B. L. (2009). *Managing stress* (6th ed.). Sudbury, MA: Jones & Bartlett.

Seaward, B. L. (2012). *Managing stress* (7th ed.). Sudbury, MA: Jones & Bartlett.

Segal, E. A. (2010). *Social welfare policy and social programs: A values perspective* (2nd ed.). Belmont, CA: Brooks/Cole.

Segal, S. P. (2008). Deinstitutionalization. In T. Mizrahi & L. E. Davis (Eds.), *Encyclopedia of social work* (Vol. 2, pp. 10–20). Washington, DC: NASW Press.

Segovia, A., Garcia-Falgueras, A., Carrillo, B., Collado, P., Pinos, H., Perez-Laso, C., et al. (2006). Sexual dimorphism in the vomeronasal system of the rabbit, *Brain Research, 1102*(1), 52–62.

Selye, H. (1956). *The stress of life.* New York: McGraw-Hill.

Selye, H. (1974). *Stress without distress.* New York: Signet.

Seroczynski, A. D., Jacquez, F. M., & Cole, D. (2003). Depression and suicide during adolescence. In G. Adams & M. Berzonsky (Eds.), *Blackwell handbook of adolescence.* Malden, MA: Blackwell.

Serpell, R. (2003, February). Cited in E. Benson, intelligence across cultures. *Monitor on Psychology,* 56–58.

Servicemembers Legal Defense Network (SLDN). (2005a, June 13). *New data reveals military losing mission critical specialists under "don't ask, don't tell."* Retrieved from http://www.sldn.org/templates/press/record.html?ecord+2204

Servicemembers Legal Defense Network (SLDN). (2005b, July 25). *As army misses annual recruiting goal, new data shows military could attract as many as 41,000 gay recruits by lifting ban.* Retrieved from http://www.sldn.org/templates/press/record.html?ecord+2299

Servicemembers' Legal Defense Network (SLDN). (2011). *Next steps for "don't ask, don't tell" repeal.* Retrieved from http:// www.sldn.org/pages/next-steps-for-dont-ask-dont-tell-repeal

Sex education in America: General public/parents survey. (2004). Washington, DC: National Public Radio, Kaiser Family Foundation, Kennedy School of Government.

Shaffer, D. R., & Kipp, K. (2010). *Developmental psychology: Childhood & adolescence* (8th ed.). Belmont, CA: Wadsworth.

Shattuck, R. (1980). *The forbidden experiment: The story of the wild body of aveyron.* New York: Quartet Books.

Shaw, S. M., & Lee, J. (2001). *Women's voices, feminist visions: Classic and contemporary readings.* Mountain View, CA: Mayfield.

Shaw, S. M, & Lee, J. (2009). *Women's voices: Feminist visions: Classic and contemporary readings* (4th ed.). Boston: McGraw-Hill.

Shaw, S. M., & Lee, J. (2012). *Women's voices/Feminist visions: Classic and contemporary readings* (5th ed.). New York: McGraw-Hill.

Sheafor, B. W., & Horejsi, C. R. (2006). *Techniques and guidelines for social work practice* (7th ed.). Boston: Allyn & Bacon.

Sheafor, B. W., & Horejsi, C. R. (2009). *Techniques and guidelines for social work practice* (8th ed.). Boston: Allyn & Bacon.

Sheafor, B. W., & Horejsi, C. R. (2012). *Techniques and guidelines for social work practice* (9th ed.). Boston: Allyn & Bacon.

Shearer, B., Mulvihill, B., Klerman, L., Wallander, J., Hovinga, M., & Redden, D. (2002). Association of early childbearing and low cognitive ability. *Perspectives on Sexual and Reproductive Health, 34,* 236–243.

Sheehan, G. (2008). Building the Mercado Central: Asset Based Community Development and community entrepreneurship in the USA. In A. Mathie & G. Cunningham (Eds.), *From clients to citizens* (pp. 78–93). Warwickshire, UK: Practical Action Publishing.

Shernoff, M. (1995). Gay men: Direct practice. In R. L. Edwards (Ed.), *Encyclopedia of social work* (19th ed., Vol. 2, pp. 1075–1085). Washington, DC: NASW Press.

Shireman, J. (2003). *Critical issues in child welfare.* New York: Columbia University Press.

Shulman, L. S. (2005, Summer). Signature pedagogies in the professions. *Daedelus,* 52–159.

SIECUS (Sexuality Information and Education Council of the United States). (2004). *Guidelines for comprehensive sexuality education* (3rd ed.). New York: Author.

SIECUS. (2005a). *Comprehensive sexuality education and emergency contraception: Working together to prevent unintended pregnancy.* Retrieved from http://www.siecus.com

SIECUS. (2005b). *The five most egregious uses of welfare's Title V abstinence-only-until-marriage funds.* Retrieved from www.siecus.com

SIECUS. (2005c). *Frequently asked questions.* Retrieved from http://www.siecus.com

SIECUS. (2005d). *"I swear I won't!" a brief explanation of virginity pledges.* Retrieved from http://www.siecus.com

SIECUS. (2005e). *In good company: Who supports comprehensive sexuality education?.* Retrieved from http://www.siecus.com

SIECUS. (2005f). *In their own words: What abstinence-only-until-marriage programs say.* Retrieved from http://www.siecus.com

SIECUS. (2005g). *Information updates: Availability of EC without a prescription does not increase unsafe sexual practices.* Retrieved from http://www.siecus.com

SIECUS. (2005h). *Information updates: Consumer reports shows condoms to be reliable.* Retrieved from http://www.siecus.com

SIECUS. (2005i). *Information updates: Survey provides additional insight about teen sexual health, behaviors, and attitudes.* Retrieved from http://www.siecus.com

SIECUS. (2005j). *Lesbian, gay, bisexual, transgender, and questioning (LGBTQ) youth.* Retrieved from http://www.siecus.com

SIECUS. (2005k). *On our side: Public support for comprehensive sexuality education.* Retrieved July 22, 2005, from http://www.siecus.com

SIECUS. (2005l). *Policy update—June 2005.* Retrieved from http://www.siecus.com

SIECUS. (2005m). *What the research says.* Retrieved from http://www.siecus.com

SIECUS. (2007a). *On our side: Public support for comprehensive sexuality education.* Retrieved from http://www.siecus.org/policy/public_support.pdf

SIECUS. (2007b). *What the research says.* Retrieved from http://www.siecus.org/policy/research_say s.pdf

SIECUS. (2008, April 23). *Statement of sexuality information and education council of the United States (SIECUS) on the public health and ethical concerns regarding abstinence-only-until-marriage programs and the need for comprehensive sexuality education.* Retrieved from http://siecus.org/media/press/press0170.html

SIECUS. (2010). *SIECUS fact sheets: Who supports comprehensive sexuality education?.* Retrieved from http://www.siecus.org/index.cfm?useaction=Page.ViewPage&PageID=1198

SIECUS. (2011). *Sexuality education Q & A.* Retrieved from http://www.siecus.org/index.cfm?useaction=page.viewpage&pageid=521&grandparentID=477&parentID=514

Siegel, R. K. (1981, January). Accounting for "afterlife" experiences. *Psychology Today,* 66–69.

Sigelman, C. K., & Rider, E. A. (2006). *Life-span human development* (5th ed.). Belmont, CA: Wadsworth.

Sigelman, C. K., & Rider, E. A. (2009). *Life-span development* (6th ed.). Belmont, CA: Wadsworth.

Sigelman, C. K., & Rider, E. A. (2012). *Life-span human development* (7th ed.). Belmont, CA: Wadsworth.

Signore, R. J. (2004). Bradley method offers option for natural childbirth. *American Family Physician, 70*, 650.

Simon, J. P. (1996). Lebanese families. In M. McGoldrick, J. Giordano, & J. K. Pearce (Eds.), *Ethnicity and family therapy* (2nd ed., pp. 364–375). New York: Guilford Press.

Sindler, A. P. (1978). *Bakke, Defunis, and minority admissions: The quest for equal opportunity*. New York: Longmans, Green.

Singh, D., Vidaurri, M., Zambarano, R. J., & Dabbs, J. M., Jr. (1999). Lesbian erotic role identification: Behavioral, morphological, and hormonal correlates. *Journal of Personality and Social Psychology, 76*, 1035–1049.

Singh, S., & Darroch, J. (2000). Adolescent pregnancy and childbearing levels and trends in developed countries. *Family Planning Perspectives, 32*, 14–23.

Sinnott, J. (1996). The developmental approach: Postformal thought as adaptive intelligence. In F. Blanchard-Fields & T. M. Hess (Eds.), *Perspectives on cognitive change in adulthood and aging* (pp. 358–383). New York: McGraw-Hill.

Slattery, D., Badia, E., & Kemp, J. (2013, May 18). *Gunman shoots 32-year-old Mark Carson dead in bias attack*. Retrieved from http://www.nydailynews.com/new-york/gunman-shoots-32-year-old-man-dead-greenwich-village-bias-attack-officials-article-1.1347776

Smetana, J. (2005). Social domain theory. In M. Killen & J. Smetana (Eds.), *Handbook of moral development* (pp. 119–154). Mahwah, NJ: Erlbaum.

Smith, A. (2005). Beyond pro-choice versus pro-life: Women of color and reproductive justice. *NWSW Journal, 17*(1), 119–140.

Smith, A. E., Jussim, L., & Eccles, J. S. (1999). Do self-fulfilling prophecies accumulate, dissipate, or remain stable over time? *Journal of Personality and Social Psychology, 77*, 548–565.

Smith, B. (1995). Myths to divert black women from freedom. In S. Ruth (Ed.), *Issues in feminism* (3rd ed.). Mountain View, CA: Mayfield.

Smith, D. S., & Tyler, N. C. (2010). *Introduction to special education: Making a difference* (7th ed.). Upper Saddle River, NJ: Merrill.

Smith, M., Segal, J., & Robinson, L. (2013). *Suicide prevention: How to help someone who is suicidal*. Retrieved from http://helpguide.org/mental/suicide_prevention.htm

Smithbattle, L. (2007). Legacies of advantage and disadvantage: The case of teen mothers. *Public Health Nursing, 24*, 238–252.

Smolowe, J. (1995a, July 31). Noble aims, mixed results. *Time*, 54–55.

Snarey, J. (1987, June). A question of morality. *Psychology Today*, 6–8.

Sohn, Y.-S., Kim, M.-J., Kwon, J.-K., Kim, Y.-H., & Park, Y.-W. (2007, August 31). The usefulness of fetal MRI for prenatal diagnosis. *Yonsei Medical Journal, 48*(4), 671–677. Retrieved from http://www.ncbi.nlm.nih.gov/pmc/articles/PMC2628062/

Solomon, A. (1988). Integrating infertility crisis counseling into feminist practice. *Reproductive and Genetic Engineering, 1*, 41–19.

Solomon, B. B. (1983). Social work with Afro-Americans. In A. Morales & B. W. Sheafor (Eds.), *Social work: A profession of many faces* (3rd ed.). Boston: Allyn & Bacon.

Some golden years. (2001, August 13). *U.S. News & World Report*, 8.

Spake, A. (2002, July 22). The hormone conundrum. *U.S. News & World Report*, 36–37.

Spakes, P. (1992). National family policy: Sweden versus the United States. *Affilia: Journal of Women and Social Work, 7*(2), 44–60.

Sparks, A., & Syrop, C. H. (2005). *Intracytoplasmic sperm injection (ICSI)*. Retrieved from http://www.vh.org/adult/patient/obgyn/assistedreproductivetechnology/icsi.html

Spear, L. P. (2000). The adolescent brain and age-related behavioral manifestations. *Neuroscience and Biobehavioral Reviews, 24*, 417–163.

Spear, L. P. (2003a). *Alcohol's effects on adolescents*. Retrieved from http://pubs.niaaa.nih.gov/publications/arh26-4/287-291.htm

Spear, L. P. (2003b). Neurodevelopment during adolescence. In D. Cicchetti & E. Walker (Eds.), *Neurodevelopmental mechanisms in psychopathology* (pp. 62–83). New York: Cambridge University Press.

Spears, L. C., & Lawrence, M. (2004). *Practicing servant-leadership: Succeeding through trust, bravery, and forgiveness*. Westfield, IN: Robert K. Greenleaf Center for Servant Leadership.

Spencer, H. (1873). The study of sociology. Ann Arbor, MI: University of Michigan Press.

Spergel, I. A. (1995). *The youth gang problem: A community approach*. New York: Oxford University Press.

Spiegler, M. D., & Guevremont, D. C. (2010). *Contemporary behavior therapy* (5th ed.). Belmont CA: Wadsworth.

Spitz, R. (1945). Hospitalization: Genesis of psychiatric conditions in early childhood. *Psychoanalytic Study of the Child, 1*, 53.

Spock, B. (1976). *Baby and child care*. New York: Pocket Books.

Spock, B., & Rothenberg, M. B. (1985). *Baby and child care*. New York: Pocket Books.

Spranger, E. (1928). *Types of men*. New York: Hafner.

Srabstein, J. C., McCarter, R. J., Shao, C., & Huang, Z. J. (2006). Morbidities associated with bullying behaviors in adolescents: School based study of American adolescents. *International Journal of Adolescent Medicine and Health, 18*, 587–596.

Starkman, N., & Rajani, N. (2002). The case for comprehensive sex education. *AIDS Patient Care and STDs, 16*(1), 313–318.

Stattin, H., & Magnusson, D. (1990). *Pubertal maturation in female development: Paths through life* (Vol. 2). Hillsdale, NJ: Erlbaum.

Stein, R. (2010). *Health bill restores $250 million in abstinence-education funds*. Retrieved from http://www.washingtonpost.com/wp-dyn/content/article/2010/03/26/AR2010032602457.html

Steinberg, L. (2004). *The 10 basic principles of good parenting*. New York: Simon and Schuster.

Steinberg, L. (2006, February). Cognitive and affective development in adolescence. *Trends in Cognitive Sciences, 9*(2), 69–74.

Steinberg, L., Bornstein, M. H., Vandell, D. L., & Rook, K. S. (2011a). *Lifespan development: Infancy through adulthood*. Belmont, CA: Wadsworth.

Steinberg, L., Vandell, D. L., & Bornstein, M. H. (2011b). *Development: Infancy through adolescence*. Belmont, CA: Wadsworth.

Sternberg, R. J. (1984). A contextualist view of the nature of intelligence. *International Journal of Psychology*, *19*, 307–334.

Sternberg, R. J. (1985). *Beyond IQ: A triarchic theory of human intelligence*. New York: Cambridge University Press.

Sternberg, R. J. (1986). *Intelligence applied: Understanding and increasing your intellectual skills*. New York: Harcourt Brace Jovanovich.

Sternberg, R. J. (1987, September 23). The uses and misuses of intelligence testing: Misunderstanding meaning, users over-rely on scores. *Educational Week*, 28.

Sternberg, R. J. (1990). *Metaphors of mind: Conceptions of the nature of intelligence*. New York: Cambridge University Press.

Sternberg, R. J. (1996). *Successful intelligence*. New York: Simon and Schuster.

Sternberg, R. J. (1997). A triarchic view of giftedness: Theory and practice. In N. Colangelo & G. A. Davis (Eds.), *Handbook of gifted education* (2nd ed., pp. 43–53). Boston: Allyn & Bacon.

Sternberg, R. J. (2000a). Cross-disciplinary verification of theories: The case of the triarchic theory. History of Psychology, *5*(2), 177–179.

Sternberg, R. J. (2000b). *Handbook of intelligence*. New York: Cambridge University Press.

Sternberg, R. J. (2004). Culture and intelligence. *American Psychologist*, *59*, 325–338.

Sternberg, R. J. (2008). The triarchic theory of successful intelligence. In N. Salkind (Ed.), *Encyclopedia of educational psychology*. Thousand Oaks, CA: Sage.

Sternberg, R. J. (2009). *Cognitive psychology* (5th ed.). Belmont, CA: Wadsworth.

Sternberg, R. J., & Yang, S. (2003, February). Cited in E. Benson, intelligence across cultures. *Monitor on Psychology*, 56–58.

Stipek, D. J. (1997). Success in school—for a head start in life. In J. Burack & S. S. Luthar (Eds.), *Developmental psychopathology: Perspectives on adjustment, risk, and disorder* (pp. 75–92). New York: Cambridge University Press.

Stone, A. (2006, February 20). *Drives to ban gay adoption heat up in 16 states*. Retrieved from http://www.usatoday.com/news/nation/2006-02-20-gay-adoption_x.htm

Storms, M. C. (1980). Theories of sexual orientation. *Journal of Personality and Social Psychology*, *38*, 783–792.

Storms, M. D. (1981). A theory of erotic orientation development. *Psychological Review*, *88*, 340–353.

Stothard, K. J., Tennant, P. W. G., Bell, R., & Rankin, J. (2009). Maternal overweight and obesity and the risk of congenital anomalies: A systematic review and meta-analysis. *Journal of the American Medical Association*, *301*, 636–650.

Stout, H. R. (1885). *Our family physician*. Peoria, IL: Henderson & Smith.

Stout, K. D., & McPhail, B. (1998). *Confronting sexism and violence against women: A challenge for social work*. New York: Longman.

Streeter, C. L. (2008). Community: Overview. In T. Mizrahi & L. E. Davis (Eds.), *Encyclopedia of social work* (Vol. 1, pp. 347–355). Washington, DC: NASW Press.

Stuart, R. B. (1970). *Trick or treatment*. Champaign, IL: Research Press.

Stuart, R. B. (1983). *Couple's pre-counseling inventory*. Champaign, IL: Research Press.

Sue, D., Sue, D. W., Sue, D., & Sue, S. (2013). *Understanding abnormal behavior* (3rd ed.). Belmont, CA: Wadsworth.

Sue, D. W. (2006). *Multicultural social work practice*. Hoboken, NJ: Wiley.

Sue, D. W., & Sue, D. (1990). *Counseling the culturally different: Theory and practice*. New York: Wiley.

Sue, D. W., & Sue, D. (2008). *Counseling the culturally diverse: Theory and practice* (5th ed.). Hoboken, NJ: Wiley.

Suitor, J. J., & Pillemer, K. (1988). Explaining intergenerational conflict when adult children and elderly parents live together. *Journal of Marriage and the Family*, *50*, 1037–1047.

Sullivan, C. M., & Gillum, T. (2001). Shelters and other community-based services for battered women and their children. In C. M. Renzetti, J. O. Edleson, & R. K. Bergen (Eds.), *Sourcebook on violence against women* (pp. 247–260). Thousand Oaks, CA: Sage.

Sullivan, T. J., Thompson, K., Wright, R., Gross, G., & Spady, D. (1980). *Social problems*. New York: Wiley.

Sundel, M., & Sundel, S. S. (2005). *Behavior change in the human services* (5th ed.). Thousand Oaks, CA: Sage.

Sutherland, E. H., & Cressey, D. R. (1970). *Criminology* (8th ed.). Philadelphia: Lippincott.

Swaab, D. F. (2004). Sexual differentiation of the human brain: Relevance for gender identity, transsexualism and sexual orientation. *Gynecological Endocrinology*, *19*(6), 301–312.

Swearer, S. M., Espelage, D. L., & Napolitano, S. A. (2009). *Bullying prevention and intervention*. New York: Guilford.

Swigonski, M. E. (1995, Winter). Claiming a lesbian identity as an act of empowerment. *Affilia*, *10*(4), 413–425.

Swigonski, M. E. (2006). Violence, hate crimes, and hate language. In D. F. Morrow & L. Messinger (Eds.), *Sexual orientation and gender expression in social work practice: Working with gay, lesbian, bisexual, and transgender people* (pp. 364–383). New York: Columbia University Press.

Symanski, D. (2009). Examining potential moderators of the link between heterosexist events and gay and bisexual men's psychological distress. *Journal of Counseling Psychology*, *56*, 142–151.

Szasz, T. S. (1961a). *The myth of mental illness*. New York: Hoeber-Harper.

Szasz, T. S. (1961b). The myth of mental illness. In J. R. Braun (Ed.), *Clinical psychology in transition* (pp. 15–32). Cleveland, OH: Howard Allen.

Tafoya, R., & Rowell, R. (1988). Counseling gay and lesbian Native Americans. In M. Shernoff & W. Scott (Eds.), *The sourcebook on lesbian/gay health care* (2nd ed., pp. 63–67). Washington, DC: National Lesbian/Gay Health Foundation.

Tarasoff v. Regents of University of California, 1975

Tarasoff v. Regents of University of California. (1975). *University of Pittsburgh Law Review*, *37*, 159–164.

Task Force for Child Survival and Development. (2004a). *About us*. Retrieved from http://www.taskforce.org/aboutus.asp

Task Force for Child Survival and Development. (2004b). *Suicide prevention*. Retrieved from http://www.taskforce.org

Task Force for Child Survival and Development (TFCSD). (2011). *Task force for child survival and development*. Retrieved October 18, 2011, from http://www.sph.emory.edu/cms/departments_centers/centers/tfcsd.html

Task Force for Child Survival and Development (TFCSD). (2014). *Emory Robbins School of Public Health*. Retrieved from http://www.sph.emory.edu/departments_centers/centers/tfcsd.html

Taylor, F. W. (1947). *Scientific management*. New York: Harper & Row.

Taylor, R. D., & Lopez, E. I. (2005a). Family management practice, school achievement, and problem behavior in African American adolescents: Mediating processes. *Journal of Applied Developmental Psychology*, *26*, 39–49.

Taylor, R. D., & Lopez, E. I. (2005b). *Perceived school experiences, school engagement and achievement among African-American adolescents*. Atlanta, GA: Society for Research in Child Development.

Teen Lifeline. (2005). *Welcome to teen lifeline*. Retrieved from http://www.teenlifeline.org

Teen Lifeline. (2013). *Teen lifeline*. Retrieved from http://www.teenlifeline.org/index.htm

Teunissen, H. A., Adelman, C. B., Prinstein, M. J., Spijkerman, R., Polen, E. A. P., Engels, R. C. M. E., et al. (2011). The interaction between pubertal timing and peer popularity for boys and girls. *Journal of Abnormal Child Psychology*, *39*(3), 413–423.

Tharp, R. G., Jordan, C., Speidel, G. E., Hu-Pei Au, K., Klein, T. W., Calkins, R. P., et al. (2007). Education and Native Hawaiian children: Revisiting KEEP. *Hulili*, *4*(1), 269–317. Retrieved from http://www.ksbe.edu/spi/Hulili/vol_4/education_and_native_hawaiian_children.pdf

Thomas, A., & Chess, S. (1977). *Temperament and development*. New York: Brunner/Mazel.

Thomas, A., & Chess, S. (1989). Temperament and personality. In G. A. Kohnstamm, J. E. Bates, & M. K. Rothbart (Eds.), *Temperament in childhood* (pp. 187–247). Chichester, England: Wiley.

Thomas, A., & Chess, S. (1991). Temperament in adolescence and its functional significance. In R. M. Learner, A. C. Petersen, & J. Brooks-Gunn (Eds.), *Encyclopedia of adolescence* (Vol. 2). New York: Garland.

Thomas, J. L. (1986). Gender differences in satisfaction with grandparenting. *Psychology and Aging*, *1*(3), 215–219.

Thompson, L., & Walker, A. J. (1989). Women and men in marriage, work, and parenthood. *Journal of Marriage and the Family*, *51*, 845–872.

Thompson, R. A. (1998). Early sociopersonality development. In W. Damon & N. Eisenberg (Eds.), *Handbook of child psychology: Vol. 3. Social, emotional, and personality development* (5th ed., pp. 25–104). New York: Wiley.

Thorman, G. (1982). *Helping troubled families: A social work perspective*. New York: Aldine.

Thorndike, E. L. (1920). Intelligence and its uses. *Harper Magazine*, *140*, 227–235.

Thurstone, L. L. (1938). Primary mental abilities. *Psychometric Monographs*, 11.

Tinzmann, M. B., Jones, B. F., Fennimore, T. F., Bakker, J., Fine, C., & Pierce, J. (1990). *What is the collaborative classroom?*. Oak Brook: North Central Regional Education Laboratory. Retrieved from http://www.ncrel.org/sdrs/areas/rpLesy s/collab.htm

Toseland, R. W., & Rivas, R. F. (2005). *An introduction to group work practice* (5th ed.). Boston: Allyn & Bacon.

Toseland, R. W., & Rivas, R. F. (2009). *An introduction to group work practice* (6th ed.). Boston: Allyn & Bacon.

Toseland, R. W., & Rivas, R. F. (2012). *An introduction to group work practice* (7th ed.). Boston: Allyn & Bacon.

Toufexis, A. (1989, January 30). Shortcut to the Rambo look. *Time*, 78.

Tozer, E. E., & McClanahan, M. K. (1999). Treating the purple menace: Ethical considerations of conversion therapy and affirmative alternatives. *Counseling Psychologist*, *27*(5), 722–743.

Treguer, A. (1992). The Chicanos—muralist with a message. *UNESCO Courier*, *45*, 22–24.

Trenholm, C., Devaney, B., Fortson, K., Quay, L., Wheeler, J., & Clark, C. (2007). *Impacts of four Title V, Section 510 abstinence education programs, final report*. Princeton, NJ: Mathematica Policy Research. Retrieved from http://aspe.hhs.gov/hsp/abstinence07/

Trepka, M. J., Kim, S., Pekovic, V., Zamor, P., Velez, E., & Gabaroni, M. V. (2008). High-risk sexual behavior among students of a minority-serving university in a community with a high HIV/AIDS prevalence. *Journal of American College Health*, *57*(1), 77–84.

Triulzi, F., Manganaro, L., & Volpe, P. (2011). Fetal magnetic resonance imaging: Indications, study protocols and safety. *La Radiologiz Medica*, *116*(3), 337–350.

True, M. M., Pisani, L., & Oumar, F. (2001). Infant-mother attachment among the Dogon of Mali. *Child Development*, *72*, 1451–1466.

Trussell, J. (2004). The essentials of contraception: Efficacy, safety, and personal considerations. In R. A. Hatcher, J. Trussell, F. Stewart, A. L. Nelson, W. Cates, Jr., F. Guest, & D. Kowal (Eds.), *Contraceptive technology* (18th ed., pp. 221–252). New York: Ardent Media.

Tucker, J. S., Ellickson, P. L., & Klein, M. S. (2003). Predictors of the transition to regular smoking during adolescence and young adulthood. *Journal of Adolescent Health*, *32*(4), 314–324.

Tuckman, B. (1965). Developmental sequence in small groups. *Psychological Bulletin*, *63*, 384–399.

Tully, C., & Nibao, J. (1979). Homosexuality: A social worker's imbroglio. *Journal of Sociology and Social Welfare*, *7*(3), 154–168.

Tully, C. T. (1992). Research on older lesbian women: What is known, what is not known, and how to learn more. In N. J. Woodman (Ed.), *Lesbian and gay lifestyles: A guide for counseling and education* (pp. 235–264). New York: Irvington Press.

Tully, C. T. (1995). Lesbians overview. In R. L. Edwards (Ed.), *Encyclopedia of social work* (19th ed., Vol. 2, pp. 1591–1596). Washington, DC: NASW Press.

Tully, C. T. (2000). *Lesbians, gays, and the empowerment perspective*. New York: Columbia University Press.

Tully, C. T. (2001). Gay and lesbian persons. In A. Gitterman (Ed.), *Handbook of social work practice with vulnerable and resilient populations* (2nd ed., pp. 582–627). New York: Columbia University Press.

Turner, J. S., & Rubinson, L. (1993). *Contemporary human sexuality*. Englewood Cliffs, NJ: Prentice-Hall.

U.S. Census Bureau. (1982, July). Money income and poverty status of families and persons in the United States: 1981.

Current population reports (Series P-60, No. 134). Washington, DC: Government Printing Office.

U.S. Census Bureau. (2009). *Statistical abstract of the United States: 2010* (129th ed.). Washington, DC: U.S. Government Printing Office.

U.S. Census Bureau. (2011). *Statistical abstract of te United States: 2012*. Washington, DC: U.S. Government Printing Office.

U.S. Census Bureau. (2012). *Statistical abstract of the United States: 2013* (132nd ed.). Washington, DC: US Government Printing Office.

U.S. Census Bureau. (2013). *Profile American facts for features: Anniversary of Americans with disabilities act: July 26*. Retrieved from http://www.census.gov/newsroom/releases/archives/facts_for_features_special_editions/cb13-ff15.html

U.S. Department of Education. (2005). National assessment of education progress (NAEP). *The nation's report card, mathematics 2005*. Washington, DC: Office of Educational Research and Improvement, National Center for Education Statistics.

U.S. Department of Education. (n.d.). *Building the legacy: IDEA 2004*. Retrieved from http://idea.ed.gov/explore/view/p/%2Croot%2Cregs%2C300%2CA%2C300%252E8%2C

U.S. Department of Health, Education, and Welfare. (1970). *Older Americans Act of 1965, as amended, text and history*. Washington, DC: U.S. Government Printing Office.

U.S. Department of Health and Human Services. (2004). *National survey results on drug use from the monitoring the future study 2003: Vol. 1. Secondary school students*. Washington, DC: Government Printing Office.

U.S. Department of Justice. (2005). *A guide to disability rights laws*. Retrieved from http://www.ada.gOv/cguide.htm#anchor62335

U.S. Equal Opportunity Commission (EEOC). (2014). *Facts about sexual harassment*. Retrieved from http://www.eeoc.gov/eeoc/publications/fs-sex.cfm

U.S. Equal Opportunity Commission (EEOC). (2014). *Sexual harassment charges EEOC & FEPAs combined: FY 1997-FY 2011*. Retrieved from http://www.eeoc.gov/eeoc/statistics/enforcement/sexual_harassment.cfm

U.S. Merit Systems Protection Board (MSPB). (1981). *Sexual harassment in the federal workplace: Is it a problem?* Washington, DC: Government Printing Office.

U.S. National Library of Medicine. (2010). *Chorionic villus sampling*. Retrieved from http://www.nlm.nih.gov/medlineplus/ency/article/003406.htm

U.S. News & World Report. (1979, February 26). Will inflation tarnish your golden years? 57.

United Nations. (1948). *Universal declaration of human rights*. GA Res. 2200 AXXI, adopted December 10, 1948. New York: Author.

United Nations Program on HIV/AIDS. (1997). *Impact of HIV and sexual health education on the sexual behavior of young people*. Geneva: Author.

University of Kentucky Center for Research on Violence Against Women. (2011). *Top ten series: Top ten things advocates need to know*. Retrieved from http://www.uky.edu/CRVAW/files/TopTen/07_Rape_Prosecution.pdf

Valencia, M. J. (2014, January 20). *Gay married man says catholic school rescinded job offer*. Retrieved from http://www.bostonglobe.com/metro/2014/01/29/dorchester-man-files-discrimination-against-catholic-school-says-lost-job-because-was-gay-married/0KswVITMsOrruEbhsOsOeN/story.html

van Den Akker, O. B. A. (2001). Adoption in the age of reproductive technology. *Journal of Reproductive & Infant Psychology, 19*, 147–159.

van Den Bergh, N., & Cooper, L. B. (Eds.). (1986). *Feminist visions for social work*. Silver Spring, MD: NASW.

van Hook, M., Hugen, B., & Aguilar, M. (2001). *Spirituality within religious traditions in social work practice*. Belmont, CA: Brooks/Cole.

van IJzendoorn, M. H., & Sagi, A. (1999). Cross-cultural patterns of attachment. In J. Cassidy & P. R. Shaver (Eds.), *Handbook of attachment: Theory research and clinical applications* (pp. 713–734). New York: Guilford Press.

van Wormer, K., Wells, J., & Boes, M. (2000). *Social work with lesbians, gays, and bisexuals: A strengths perspective*. Boston: Allyn & Bacon.

Vandell, D. L. (2004). Early child care: The known and the unknown. *Merrill-Palmer Quarterly, 50*(3), 387–414.

Vander Zanden, J. W., Crandell, T. L., & Crandell, C. H. (2007). *Human development* (8th ed.). New York: McGraw-Hill.

Villani, S. (2001). Impact of media on children and adolescents: A 10-year review of the research. *Journal of the American Academy of Child and Adolescent Psychiatry, 40*(4), 392–401.

Violence Against Women Act (VAWA) of 1994. Title IV, §§ 40001-40703 of the Violent Crime Control and Law Enforcement Act, Pub. L. 103-322, Sept. 13, 1994, 108 Stat. 1796.

Voyer, D., Postma, A., Brake, B., & Imperato-McGinley, J. (2007). Gender differences in object location memory: A meta-analysis. *Psychonomic Bulletin and Review, 14*, 23–38.

Vygotsky, L. S. (1934/1986). *Thought and language* (A. Kozulin, Trans.). Cambridge, MA: MIT Press.

Vygotsky, L. S. (1978). *Mind in society*. Cambridge, MA: Harvard University Press.

Wachs, T. D. (2006). The nature, etiology, and consequences of individual differences in temperament. In L. Baiter & C. S. Tamis-LeMonda (Eds.), *Child psychology: A handbook of contemporary issues* (2nd ed., pp. 27–52). New York: Psychology Press.

Waddy, S. (2013). *Moving the ball forward on comprehensive sex education*. Retrieved from https://www.aclu.org/blog/reproductive-freedom/moving-ball-forward-comprehensive-sex-education

Walker, L. (1995). Sexism in Kohlberg's moral psychology? In W. M. Kurtines & J. L. Gewirtz (Eds.), *Moral development: An introduction*. Boston: Allyn & Bacon.

Walker, L. (2005). Gender and morality. In M. Killen, & J. Smetana (Eds.), *Handbook of moral development* (pp. 93–115). Mahwah, NJ: Erlbaum.

Walker, L. E. (1979). *The battered woman*. New York: Harper & Row.

Walker, L. J., & Frimer, J. A. (2011). The science of moral development. In M. K. Underwood & L. Rosen (Eds.), *Social development* (pp. 235–262). New York: Guilford.

Walker, L. S. (2009). *The battered woman syndrome*. New York: Springer.

Walsh, F. (2011). Families in later life: Challenges, opportunities, and resilience. In M. McGoldrick, B. Carter, & N. G. Garcia-Preto (Eds.), *The expanded family life cycle: Individual, family, and social perspectives* (4th ed., pp. 261–277). Boston: Allyn & Bacon.

Walther, C. S., & Poston, D. L., Jr. (2004). Patterns of gay and lesbian partnering in the larger metropolitan areas of the United States. *Journal of Sex Research, 41*(2), 201–214.

Ward, C. A. (1995). *Attitudes toward rape: Feminist and social psychological perspectives*. Thousand Oaks, CA: Sage.

Wark, G. R., & Krebs, D. L. (1996). Gender and dilemma differences in real-life moral judgment. *Developmental Psychology, 32*(2), 220–230.

Wark, G. R., & Krebs, D. L. (2000). The construction of moral dilemmas in everyday life. *Journal of Moral Education, 29*, 5–21.

Waskow, A. I. (1967). *From race riot to sit-in*. Garden City, NY: Doubleday.

Watson, J. B. (1919). Psychology from the standpoint of a behaviorist. Philadelphia: Lippincott.

Watson, D. L., & Tharp, R. G. (1973). *Self-directed behavior*. Monterey, CA: Brooks/Cole.

Watson, J. (2011, August 13). *Don't ask, don't tell repeal: Gay military personnel have tough time returning to service. Huff Post Politics*. Retrieved from http://www.huffingtonpost.com/2011/08/13/dont-ask-dont-tell-repeal_n_926305.html

Watson, J. C., Goldman, R. N., & Greenberg, L. S. (2011). Humanistic and experiential theories in psychotherapy. In J. C. Norcross, G. R. Vandenbos, & D. K. Freedheim (Eds.), *History of psychotherapy* (2nd ed., pp. 141–172). Washington, DC: American Psychological Association.

Waxman, H. A. (2004, December). *The content of federally funded abstinence-only education programs*. Washington, DC: U.S. House of Representatives.

Weaver, A., Byers, E. S., Sears, H., Cohen, J., & Randall, H. (2002). Sexual health education at school and at home: Attitudes and experiences of New Brunswick parents. *Canadian Journal of Human Sexuality, 11*, 19–32.

Weaver, H. N. (2005). *Explorations in cultural competence: Journeys to the four directions*. Belmont, CA: Brooks/Cole.

Weaver, H. N. (2008). Native Americans: Overview. In T. Mizrahi & L. E. Davis (Eds.), *Encyclopedia of social work* (Vol. 3, pp. 295–299). Washington, DC: NASW Press.

WebbMD. (2013). *Benign breast lumps*. Retrieved September 13, 2013, from http://www.webmd.com/breast-cancer/benign-breast-lumps

Webster's collegiate dictionary (10th ed.). (1995). Springfield, MA: Merriam-Webster.

Weed, S. E., Birch, P. J., Ericksen, I. H., & Olsen, J. A. (2011). *Testing a predictive model of youth sexual intercourse initiation*. Unpublished manuscript.

Week, S. E. (2008). Marginally successful results of abstinence-only program erased by dangerous errors in curriculum. *American Journal of Health Behavior, 32*, 60–73.

Wedding, D., & Corsini, R. J. (2014). Current psychotherapies (10th ed.). Belmont, CA: Brooks/Cole.

Wegscheider, S. (1981). Another chance: Hope and health for the alcoholic family. Palo Alto, CA: Science and Behavior Books.

Weichold, K., Silbereisen, R. K., & Schmitt-Rodermund, E. (2003). Short-term and long-term consequences of yearly versus late physical maturation in adolescents. In D. Hayward (Ed.), *Gender differences at puberty* (pp. 241–276). New York: Cambridge University Press.

Weil, M. O., & Gamble, D. N. (1995). Community practice models. In R. L. Edwards (Ed.), *Encyclopedia of social work* (19th ed., Vol. 1, pp. 577–594). Washington, DC: NASW Press.

Weisz, A. N., & Black, B. M. (2002). Gender and moral reasoning: African American youth respond to dating dilemmas. *Journal of Human Behavior in the Social Environment, 5*, 35–52.

Welch, K. (2011). *THINK: 2011 human sexuality*. Boston: Allyn & Bacon.

Weng, S., Odouli, R., & Li, D. K. (2008). Maternal caffeine consumption during pregnancy and the risk of miscarriage: A prospective cohort study. *American Journal of Obstetrics and Gynecology, 198*, e1–e8.

Wertheimer, D. M. (1988, January). Victims of violence: A rising tide of anti-gay sentiment. USA Today Magazine, 52–54.

Wermiel, S., & McQueen, M. (1989, July 5). Turning point? *Historic court ruling will widen disparity in access to abortion.* Wall Street Journal, 1.

West, M. S., & Curtis, J. W. (2006). *AAUP faculty gender equity indicators 2006*. Washington, DC: American Association of University Professors (AAUP).

Westberg, G. (1962). *Good grief*. Philadelphia: Fortress.

Westhoff, C., Picardo, L., & Morrow, E. (2003). Quality of life following early medical or surgical abortion. *Contraception, 67*(1), 41–17.

Westling, E., Andrews, J. A., Hampson, S. E., & Peterson, M. (2008). Pubertal timing and substance use: The effects of gender, parental monitoring, and deviant peers. *Journal of Adolescent Health, 42*, 555–563.

Wheeler, J., Newring, K., & Draper, C. (2008). Transvestic fetishism: Psychopathology and theory. In D. Laws & W. O'Donohue (Eds.), *Sexual deviance: Theory, assessment and treatment* (2nd ed., pp. 272–285). New York: Guilford Press.

White, J. W., Donat, P. L. N., & Bondurant, B. (2009). A developmental examination of violence against girls and women. In J. W. White (Ed.), *Taking sides: Clashing views in gender* (4th ed., pp. 120–130). Boston: McGraw-Hill.

White, M. (1995). *Stranger at the gate: To be gay and Christian in America*. New York: Simon and Schuster.

Whiting, B. B., & Edwards, C. P. (1988). *Children of different worlds*. Cambridge, MA: Harvard University Press.

Wikan, U. (1977). Man becomes woman: Transsexualism in Oman as a key to gender roles. *Man, 12*, 304–391.

Wilber, K. (2006). *Integral spirituality*. Boston: Integral Books.

Wilensky, H., & Lebeaux, C. (1965). *Industrial society and social welfare*. New York: Free Press.

Williams, M. B. (2013, January 30). Another bullied gay teen commits suicide. *Salon*. Retrieved from http://www.salon.com/2013/01/30/another_bullied_gay_teen_commits_suicide/

Williams, P., & McClam, E. (2013, June 26). *Supreme Court strikes down Defense of Marriage Act, paves way for gay marriage to resume in California.* Retrieved from http://nbcpolitics.nbcnews.com/_news/2013/06/26/19151971-supreme-court-strikes-down-defense-of-marriage-act-paves-way-for-gay-marriage-to-resume-in-california?ite=

Williams, W. L. (1986). *The spirit and the flesh: Sexual diversity in American Indian culture*. Boston: Beacon Press.

Wilson, B. J. (2008). Media and children's aggression, fear, and altruism. *The Future of Children, 18*, 87–118.

Wilson, F. L. (1995). The effects of age, gender, and ethnic/cultural background on moral reasoning. *Journal of Social Behavior and Personality, 10*(1), 67–78.

Wilson, G. T. (2011). Behavior therapy. In R. S. Corsini & D. Wedding (Eds.), *Current psychotherapies* (9th ed., pp. 235–275). Belmont, CA: Brooks/Cole.

Wilson-Costello, D., Friedman, H., Minich, N., Siner, B., Taylor, G., Schulchter, M., et al. (2007). Improved neurodevelopmental outcomes for extremely low birth weight infants in 2000–2002. *Pediatrics, 119,* 37–45.

Wind, R. (2012). *Sex education linked to delay in first sex.* Retrieved from http://www.guttmacher.org/media/nr/2012/03/08/

Windle, M., Spear, L. P., Fuligni, A. J., Angold, A., Brown, J. D., Pine, D., et al. (2008). Transitions into underage and problem drinking: Developmental processes and mechanisms between 10 and 15 years of age. *Pediatrics, 121*(Suppl. 4), S273–S289.

Winkelman, M. (2005). *Cultural awareness, sensitivity and competence.* Peosta, IA: Eddie Bowers.

Winton, M. A., & Mara, B. A. (2001). *Child abuse and neglect: Multidisciplinary approaches.* Boston: Allyn & Bacon.

Wolf, D. (1979). *The lesbian community.* Berkeley: University of California Press.

Women Organized Against Rape (WOAR). (2011). *How to reduce risk.* Retrieved from http://www.woar.org/resources/sexual-assault-prevention.html

Women Organized Against Rape (WOAR). (2014). *How to reduce risk.* Retrieved from http://www.woar.org/resources/sexual-assault-prevention.php

Women's Resource Center of the New River Valley. (2013). *The three-phase cycle of domestic violence.* Retrieved from http://www.wrcnrv.org/helpingYou/dv_3phaseCycle.shtml

Wong, I. (2008). Homelessness. In T. Mizrahi & L. E. Davis (Eds.), *Encyclopedia of social work* (Vol. 2, pp. 377–383). Washington, DC: NASW Press.

Woodman, N. J. (1995). Lesbians: Direct practice. In R. L. Edwards (Ed.), *Encyclopedia of social work* (19th ed., Vol. 2, pp. 1597–1604). Washington, DC: NASW Press.

Woodward, K. L. (1995, April 10). Life, death and the pope. *Newsweek,* 56–66.

Woodward, E. H., & Gridina, N. (2001). *Media in the home.* Philadelphia: Annenberg Public Policy Center.

World-Herald News Service. (2011, January 6). Omaha high-school student kills administrator, wounds another before killing self. *The Tribune.* Retrieved from http://www.amestrib.com/articles/2011/01/06/ames_tribune/news/doc4d24f60ceaab5438288380.txt

Xiong, X., Wightkin, J., Magnus, J. H., Pridjian, G., Acuna, J. M., & Buekens, P. (2007). Birth weight and infant growth: Optimal infant weight gain versus optimal infant weight. *Maternal and Child Health, 11,* 57–62.

Yarber, W. L., & Sayad, B. W. (2013). *Human sexuality: Diversity in contemporary America* (8th ed.). New York: McGraw-Hill.

Yessian, M. R., & Broskowski, A. (1983). Generalists in human-service systems: Their problems and prospects. In R. M. Kramer & H. Specht (Eds.), *Readings in community organization practice* (3rd ed., pp. 180–193). Englewood Cliffs, NJ: Prentice-Hall.

Yochelson, S., & Samenow, S. E. (1976). *The criminal personality: Vol. 1. A profile for change.* New York: Aronson.

Yousef, N. (2001). Savage or solitary? The wild child and Rousseau's man of nature. *Journal of the History of Ideas, 62*(2), 245–263. Retrieved from http://www.feralchildren.com/en/pager.php?f=yousef 2001

Zastrow, C. (1999). *The practice of social work* (6th ed.). Belmont, CA: Brooks/Cole.

Zastrow, C., & Navarre, R. (1979, Fall). Self-talk: A new criminological theory. *International Journal of Comparative and Applied Criminal Justice,* 167–176.

Zayas, L. H. (2011). *Latinas attempting suicide: When cultures, families, and daughters collide.* New York: Oxford.

Zayas, L. H., Kaplan, C., Turner, S., Romano, K., & Gonzalez-Ramos, G. (2000). Understanding suicide attempts by adolescent Hispanic females. *Social Work, 45*(1), 53–63.

Zea, M. C., Reisen, C. A., & Diaz, R. M. (2003). Methodological issues in research on sexual behavior with Latino gay and bisexual men. *American Journal of Community Psychology, 31,* 281–291.

Zuckerman, M. (2011). Personality science: Three approaches and their applications to the causes and treatment of depression. In M. Zuckerman (Ed.), *Three approaches and their applications to the causes and treatment of depression* (pp. 47–77). Washington, DC: American Psychological Association.

Zuravin, S. J., & Taylor, R. (1987). *Family planning behaviors and child care adequacy.* Final report submitted to the U.S. Department of Health and Human Services, Office of Population Affairs (Grant FPR 000028001-1).

Zurbriggen, E. L. (2010). Rape, war, and the socialization of masculinity: Why our refusal to give up war ensures that rape cannot be eradicated. *Psychology of Women Quarterly, 34,* 538–549.

Zusman, J. (1966). Some explanations of the changing appearance of psychotic patients: Antecedents of the social breakdown syndrome concept. *Millbank Memorial Fund Quarterly, 64*(1), 20.

Zweigenhaft, R. L., & Von Ammon, J. (2000). Birth order and civil disobedience: A test of sulloway's "born to rebel" hypothesis. *Journal of Social Psychology, 140*(5), 624–627.

Name Index

A

AARP, 613, 736
AASECT, (American Association of Sex Educators, Counselors and Therapists), 105, 622, 637, 639, 640
Abadinsky, H., 533, 535, 537, 547
ABC News, 229
Abels, S. L., 342
Aber, J., 342
Abikoff, H., 173
About.com, 626
Abramovitz, M., 586
Abundant Community, 16–17
Action, R., 246
Acuna, J. M., 76
Adams, J. I., 435
Adelman, C. B., 301
Adenauer, Konrad, 657
Adler, Alfred, 118, 119, 173
Adler, J., 114
Adler, R. B., 509
Administration of Aging, 729
Adorno, T. W., 265
Adult Children of Alcoholics, 546
AFDC (Aid to Families with Dependent Children), 585
Affordable Care Act, 313
Aguilar, M., 354
Ahlstrom, H., 69
Ahmad, S., 441
Ahmed, S. F., 428
Aid to Families with Dependent Children (AFDC), 585
Aisenberg, E., 219, 433
Akers, A. Y., 307
Akman, D., 246
Al-Anon, 315, 546

Alateen, 315, 541
Alberti, R. E., 358
Albin, R. S., 447
Albrecht, G., 171
Alcoholics Anonymous (AA), 541, 542–543, 596
Alderson, K., 362, 626, 631, 644, 646, 648
Alessi, C., 11
Alinsky, Saul, 47
All Handicapped Children Act (PL. 94–142) (1975), 171. See Individuals with Disabilities Education Act
Allen, L., 342
Allen, W. D., 190
Almeida, R., 192
Almquist, E. M., 644
Alsaker, F. D., 227
Altshuler, S. J., 171
Al-Yagon, M., 169
Alzherimer, Dr. Alois,
American Academy/Association of Pediatrics (AAP), 229, 315, 623
American Association on Intellectual Developmental Disabilities (AAIDD), 160
American Association of Sex Educators, Counselors, and Therapists (AASECT), 105, 622, 637, 639, 640
American Association of University Professors, 440
American Association of University Women (AAUW), 437, 438, 443
American Cancer Society (ACS), 412, 472, 473, 474, 475, 476
American Civil Liberties Union (ACLU), 633, 639
American College of Nurse-Midwives, 73

American Counseling Association, 623
American Foundation for AIDS Research, 315
American Heart Association (AHA), 477
American Medical Association, 315
American Psychiatric Association (APA), 158, 159, 160, 172, 391, 392, 393, 520, 522, 623, 630, 641, 678
American Psychological Association (APA), 192, 315, 432, 623
American Public Health Association, 315
American Self-Help Group Clearinghouse, 409
American School Counselor Association, 623
American Society of Plastic Surgeons, 475
American Society for Reproductive Medicine (ASRM), 102, 103, 104
Americans with Disabilities Act (ADA), 163, 496
Amini, H., 69
Anastasiow, N., 161
Ancoli-Israel, S., 11
Anderson, C. A., 229
Anderson, Dame Judith, 657
Anderson, P. J., 76
Anderson, R. M., 360
Angold, A., 301
Apgar, K., 356
Apgar, V., 75
Aravena, V. C., 647
ARC of the U.S., 409
Arck, P., 72
Arden, R., 436
Arevalo, M., 328
Aristotle, 416
Arlow, J. A., 114

Arnett, J. J., 190
Arnold, E. M., 169
Arnold, L. E., 173
Arredondo, P., 219
Associated Press, 623
Association of Black Social Workers, 291
Association for the Prevention of Family
    Violence (APFV), 462
Atchley, R. C., 697, 738
ATEC (Automated Tissue Excision and
    Collection), 474
Atkins-Burnett, S., 173
Atkinson, L., 150
Attanucci, J., 347
Automated Tissue Excision and
    Collection (ATEC), 474
Aveyron, wild boy of, 1
Avigad-Spritz, L., 221
Axelsson, O., 69
Azrin, N. H., 209

B

Babbie, E., 354
Bachman, D. J., 67
Bachman, J. G., 303, 305
Badaly, D., 227
Badia, E., 640
Baer, B. L., 5
Bailey, J. M., 627, 629
Baillargeon, R., 138
Bakalar, R., 673
Bakke, Alan, 279
Balassy, C., 69
Bales, R. F., 415, 421
Balgopal, P. R., 220, 221, 433
Ballman, P. K., 637
Bancroft, J., 306
Bandura, A., 197, 349, 350
Banks, E., 148
Barbaranelli, C., 349
Bargad, A., 126
Barker, R. L., 20, 25, 34, 45, 46, 49, 50,
    53, 181, 263, 630
Barkley, R. A., 172
Barnett, O. W., 32, 237, 238, 239, 240,
    241, 455, 456, 457, 458, 459, 460,
    461
Baron, A., 648
Baron, L., 447
Barret, B., 341
Barrett, T., 629
Barry, P., 731
Bar-Tal, D., 517
Barth, R. P., 104, 241, 242
Bartky, S. L., 434
Barusch, A. S., 639
Basile, K. C., 457, 458, 459
Baumrind, D., 215, 217
Baur, K., 94, 224, 244, 245, 305, 306, 307,
    308, 310, 316, 319, 320, 321, 322,

326, 327, 328, 329, 330, 428, 430,
    431, 433, 434, 447, 448, 449, 450,
    451, 464, 472, 488, 621, 627, 629,
    631, 632, 633, 639, 642, 643
Baxter, V., 461
Bay-Cheng, L. Y., 425
Bays, L., 268
Bearman, P., 312
Bearman, S. K., 300
Bearse, M. L., 220
Beck, E., 222
Becker, M., 702
Beckett, J. O., 23, 58, 285, 286
Beckmann, D., 146
Beitchman, J. H., 246
Beitman, B. D., 120
Belknap, J., 459
Bell, A.P., 629
Bell, Jadin, 362
Bell, R., 67
Belsky, J., 557
Ben-David, S., 451
Bender, E. I., 408
Benjamin, A. E., 165
Benjamin, L., 268
Bennett, L. W., 457
Benson, H., 681
Benston, V., 698
Berenbaum, S. A., 348
Berg, C. J., 67
Berger, R. M., 626, 628, 635, 639, 648
Berk, L. E., 10, 66, 67, 75, 76, 130, 141,
    142, 145, 146, 147, 150, 151, 217,
    228, 303, 304, 360, 362
Berk, R. A., 459
Berkman, L. F., 739
Berkowitz, L., 229
Berliner, L., 193, 243, 244, 245, 246
Berman, A. L., 367, 368, 369
Berman, C., 588
Bernstein, D. A., 148, 155, 431
Berube, M. S., 92n8, 94
Bhattacharya, S., 67
Bieschke, K. J., 622, 623
Biesecker, J., 16
Bijvank, M. N., 229
Billingsley, A., 286
Binggeli, N. J., 241
bin Laden, Asama, 261
Bird, J., 362, 365, 366
Bishaw, A., 25
Bjorklund, D. F., 68, 303
Black, B. M., 348
Black, M. C., 457, 458, 459
Blacker, L., 191
Blackwood, E., 430
Blair, K. L., 632
Blair, S. L., 221
Blakemore, J. E. O., 348
Blakemore, S. J., 302

Blanchard, K., 416
Blasdell, J., 92
Blasi, C. H., 68, 303
Blatt, S. J., 301
Blaze-Gosden, T., 533
Block, P., 16
Bloom, L. Z., 356
Blundo, R., 435
Boes, M., 341, 634, 644, 645, 647, 648
Bogaert, A. F., 627
Bonds, Barry, 538
Bondurant, B., 456, 459
Bornstein, M. H., 65, 67, 68, 75, 137, 139,
    140, 146, 148, 226, 227, 232, 251,
    360, 364
Boston Women's Health Book Collective,
    642, 643
Botvin, G. J., 301
Bouchard, T. J., 436
Boutsikou, T., 76
Bowen, M., 595
Bowlby, J., 147
Boyle, S. W., 353, 623
Bradley, J., 266
Brake, B., 436
Brammer, R., 433
Brandwein, R. A., 440
Brassard, M. R., 240, 241
Braun, Ryan, 538
Brazell, RaShawn, 640
Brazelton, H. M., 75
Brazelton, Institute, 75
Brener, N. D., 447
Brent, D. A., 360
Breuer, J., 117
Bricker-Jenkins, M., 123, 124
Bridge, J. A., 360
Bridges, K. M. B., 144
Broderick, A. M., 409
Brody, G. H., 217
Brook, J. S., 229
Brooks, J. W., 621, 630, 632, 646
Brooks-Gunn, J., 232, 301
Broskowski, A., 53
Brosn, R., 307
Brown, J. D., 301
Brown, L. M., 347
Brown v. Board of Education, 272, 292
Brownell, P., 191
Brownlee, S., 670
Bruckner, H., 312
Bruess, C. E., 64, 65, 94, 102, 103, 104,
    299, 306, 311, 312, 313, 315, 317,
    321, 329, 330, 430, 446, 449, 452,
    453, 455, 619, 620, 622, 627, 634,
    638, 650
Brugger, P. C., 69
Brunstein Klomek, A., 227
Bruschi, C. J., 130
Brush, L. D., 456

Bryan, T., 169
Bucher, B. B., 210
Buckingham, K. G., 304
Budworth, M. H., 221
Buekens, P., 76
Bugle, C., 209
Buhler, C., 471
Buhs, E., 226
Bukowski, W., 224, 227
Bukowskik, W. M., 225
Bumiller, E., 636
Burchinal, M. R., 150
Burden, R., 169
Bureau of Indian Affairs (BIA), 192
Bureau of Justice Statistics, 446, 449
Burgess, A. W., 453
Buriel, R., 217, 221
Burke, K., 640
Burnet, K. L., 222
Burnette, M. M., 243, 620
Burns, George, 657
Burstein, K., 169
Burstow, B., 458, 462
Burton, L., 221
Burts, D. C., 217
Bush, President George H. W., 291, 358, 727
Bush, President George W., 93, 94, 292, 312, 313, 726, 731
Bush, K. R., 217
Bushman, B. J., 229
Buss, K. A., 146
Butcher, Susan, 502
Butler, J., 246
Butler, R. N., 737
Butler, Robert, Jr., 229
Buttenwieser, E., 240
Byers, E. S., 311

C
Caesar, Julius, 416
Calkins, R. P., 232
Callaghan, W. M., 67
Cameron-Bandler, L., 577
Canadian Association of Social Workers (CASW), 19
Canadian Mental Health Association, 360
Canda, E. R., 131, 351, 353, 354
Capielo, C., 219
Caplan, P. J., 393
Caprara, G. V., 349
Capron, C., 69
Carey, R. G., 210
Carlson, B. E., 456, 457, 459
Carmichael, S., 263
Carpendale, J., 339
Carrell, D. T., 72
Carrillo, B., 303
Carroll, J. L., 70, 72, 88, 104, 106, 109, 307, 312, 313, 317, 319, 320, 321,

322, 329, 330, 428, 430, 431, 432, 453, 626, 627, 628, 630, 639, 641, 646, 648
Carson, Mark, 640
Carter, B., 189, 190, 191, 215
Carter, E. A., 189
Carter, President Jimmy, 703, 704
Cartwright, D., 561
Cassavia, E., 246
Cassidy, J., 149
Catalano, S., 449
Cates, W., Jr., 326
Catholic Campaign for Human Development, 284
Cattell, R. B., 153, 175
Cavanagh, K., 456
Cavanaugh, J. C., 11, 66, 67, 68, 92, 139, 140, 141, 143, 145, 147, 148, 149, 157, 172, 173, 221, 222, 228, 302, 342, 347, 360, 365, 367, 552, 558, 588, 700
Caviness, V. S., Jr., 303
Ceci, S. J., 157
Cen, G., 148
Center for American Women in Politics (CAWP), 440
Center for Disease Control (CDC), 75, 76, 101, 102, 104, 105, 106, 167, 316, 317, 318, 319, 360, 363, 364, 365, 366
Center of Reproductive Rights (CRR), 89
CenterWatch, 324
Chalmers, M. A., 240
Chan, S. Q., 217
Chang, D., 220, 221
Chanel, Coco, 657
Chapman, G., 489
Charlesworth, R., 70
Chatterjee, P., 351
Chen, H., 148
Chen, X., 148
Chen, X. K., 76
Cheng, A. W., 428
Cherlin, A. J., 182, 702
Chernin, J. M., 642
Chess, S., 146
Childs, C. P., 148
Childstats.gov, 182
Chilman, C. S., 98, 219
Chornesky, A., 458, 459, 483
Choudhuri, D. D., 131
Choudhury, S., 302
Christian, P., 76
Christie, R., 417
Chu, S. Y., 67
Churchill, Winston, 417
CIA, 635
Clark, C., 312
Clarke-Stewart, A., 148, 431
Clayton, R. R., 551

Clemens, Roger, 538
Clinton, President Bill, 229, 291, 292, 585, 635
Cloud, J., 441
CNN.com, 229, 639
CNN Money, 558
Coburn, K., 356
Cohen, A., 405
Cohen, H. L., 647
Cohen, J., 311
Cohen, N. A., 240
Cohen, P., 229
Cohen, S. A., 90, 97
Cohen, Wilbur, 49
Colapinto, J., 426
Cole, G. F., 401
Cole, P. M., 130
Coleman, J. W., 256, 547, 561, 563, 564
Coleman, M. R., 161
Colin, V., 149
Collado, P., 303
Collier, H. V., 453, 464
Collins, J., 314
Columbine High School, 229, 402
Columbus, 264
Comer, R. J., 391, 393
Commission of the Council on Social Work Education, 181
Confucius, 217, 416
Conger, R. D., 301, 487
Congress, E., 18
Conklin, S. C., 64, 65, 94
Conners, C. K., 173
Conrad, A. P., 18
Cook, C. A. L., 71
Cooley, C. H., 267, 338, 393, 562, 690
Coon, D., 116, 118, 143, 150, 155, 349, 361, 362, 363, 364, 365
Cooper, M., 627
Cooper, L. B., 122, 123
Copen, C. E., 182
Corbett, C., 438
Corey, G., 121, 248
Coronado, 264
Corsini, R. J., 248
Costello, E. J., 301
Council on Social Work Education (CSWE), 5, 7, 11, 12, 13, 19, 20, 24, 25, 55, 58, 59, 130, 284, 290, 566, 694
Courtenay, W. H., 435
Cowger, C. D., 14
Cowley, A. S., 353
Cox, C. B., 191
Cramer, D. W., 648
Crandell, C. H., 141, 142
Crandell, T. L., 141, 142
Cressey, D. R., 256, 404, 561, 563, 564
Cristofalo, V. J., 666
Crooks, Hulda, 657

Crooks, R., 94, 224, 244, 245, 305, 306, 307, 308, 310, 316, 319, 320, 321, 322, 326, 327, 328, 329, 330, 428, 430, 431, 433, 434, 447, 448, 449, 450, 451, 464, 472, 488, 621, 627, 629, 631, 632, 633, 639, 642, 643
Cross, W. E. Jr., 342
Crosson-Tower, C., 31, 32, 104, 234, 235, 236, 239, 240, 241, 242, 243, 244, 245, 246, 247, 248, 307
Crouter, A. C., 221
Cruzan, Joe/Joyce, 725
Cruzan, Nancy, 725
Cuber, J. F., 572
Cullen, D., 402
Cumming, E., 697
Cummings, M., 259, 281
Cunningham, G., 283
Curran, D. J., 431, 442, 444, 456, 457, 458, 459, 460
Curtis, L. A., 384, 385, 386, 387, 388, 389

D

D'Andrea, M., 120
Dabbs, J. M., Jr., 629
Dacey, J., 73, 138, 143, 348
Dacey, J. S., 216
DaCosta, G. A., 246
Daft, R. L., 50, 600
Dale, C. V., 633, 635
Dale, P. S., 436
Daniel, S. S., 169
Daniels, H., 143
Daniels, K., 182
Danielson, P., 269
Darrow, C. N., 471, 503
Darwin, Charles, 719, 728
Davey Smith, G., 76
Davidson, H. A., 241
Davis, G. A., 231
Davis, K., 601, 604
Davis, L., 410
Davis, L. V., 456, 457
Davis, M., 501, 680
Dawood, K., 627
Death with Dignity Act, 725
DeBaryshe, B. D., 382
Deblinger, E., 246, 248
de Bruyn, E., 157
Deci, E. L., 231
Decourcey, W., 231
Deep Water Horizon, 502
Defense of Marriage Act (DOMA), 636
Degangi, G. A., 195, 202
DeGarmo, D.S., 451
deHaan, M., 139, 140
DeJong, C., 401
DeLamater, J. D., 64, 65, 67, 70, 97, 102, 104, 105, 122, 123, 222, 224, 297,

299, 300, 306, 308, 310, 311, 317, 318, 320, 321, 329, 330, 436, 447, 449, 451, 453, 482, 483, 485, 486, 487, 488, 489, 490, 491, 495, 527, 624, 626, 628, 639, 664, 665
Delgado, M., 45, 193, 219, 344, 345
Delgado-Romero, E. A., 219
DeLois, K., 191
De Luca, C. R., 76
Deming, W. E., 605
Demissie, K., 76
DePanfilis, D., 241, 242
DePorto, D., 462
DePoy, E., 163
Derezotes, D., 353
De Valera, Eamon, 657
Devaney, B., 312
Devore, W., 130, 131, 274, 285, 286
DeWeaver, K. L., 161, 163
Dhooper, S. S., 192, 219, 286
Diagnostic and Statistical Manual-IV (DSM), 158, 159, 160, 391, 393, 520, 522
mental disorders, 392–393
Diaz, R. M., 621
Diaz, V., 241
Dickson, D. T., 496
Dickson, W. J., 602
DiClemente, C. C., 544
Diderichsen, F., 76
Dietz, P. M., 67
Diller, J. V., 131, 191, 219, 221, 433
DiNitto, D. M., 94
Dionne, G., 436
Dishion, T. J., 304
Dittner, C. A., 246
Dively, M. et al., 623
Dobash, R. E., 456
Dobash, R. P., 456
Doege, D., 454, 458
Dohn, H. H., 362, 365, 366
Doig, W., 631
Dolgoff, R., 19, 99–100
Donat, P. L. N., 456, 459
Donnerstein, E., 229
Dotinga, R., 362
Dotson, V., 384, 385, 386, 387, 388, 389
Douglas, K. A., 447
Douglass, Frederick, 281
Downs, S. W., 31, 238, 239, 240, 307, 308
Doyle, L. W., 76
Doyle, R., 458
Draper, C., 430
Drechsler, 546
Drew, C. J., 156, 172
Drucker, P. F., 605
Dubas, J. S., 302
Duffey, T., 352
Duncan, G., 232

Dunne, M. P., 627
Duong, M., 227
Dupper, D. R., 227
Duren, Ryne, 539
Durkheim, Emile, 559
Dwyer, G., 451
Dykstra, Lenny, 538

E

Eccles, J. S., 230, 231
Eckholm, R., 637
Eddy, Mary Baker, 657
Educational Policy and Accreditation Standards (EPAS), 5, 7, 55, 58, 271, 284, 290, 694
Edwards, C. P., 218
Egan, M. W., 156, 172
Egeland, B., 237, 238, 239
Eisenberg, N., 348
Eitzen, D. S., 12
Ekman, P., 515
Elder, G. H., 487
Elder, G. H., Jr., 301
Ellickson, P. L., 305
Elliot, A. J., 146
Elliott, D. M., 243, 244, 246
Ellis, A., 268, 394
Ellis, B. J., 221
Ellis, L. K., 146
Else-Quest, N. M., 123, 124, 125, 126, 347, 349, 431, 432, 436, 456, 457, 458, 459, 465
Emert, P. B., 261
Emmons, M. L., 358
Employment Non-Discrimination Act (ENDA), 635
Enchiridion, 394
Engels, R., 301
Epictetus, 394
Epstein, D., 461
Equal Employment Opportunity Commission (EEOC), 291, 440, 441, 444, 445, 466
Erez, E., 459
Ergul, C., 169
Erickson, L., 72
Erickson, M. F., 237, 238, 239
Erikson, E. H., 114, 334, 335, 338, 340, 341, 371, 499, 500, 501, 547, 559, 689
Eshelmen, E. R., 501, 680
Etzioni, A., 603
Evans, K. M., 433
Evans, M. E., 217

F

Fabes, R., 145, 146, 228, 230, 303
Falicov, C. J., 193
Falk, R. F., 701
Faller, K. C., 246

Family and Medical Leave Act, 590
Farley, J. E., 569
Farley, O. W., 353, 623
Federal Bureau of Investigation (FBI), 447, 635
Federal Insurance Contributions Act (FICA), 730
Federico, R. C., 5
Feldman, R. D., 1, 66, 68, 136, 138, 145, 146, 148, 150, 152, 217, 224, 225, 232, 341, 379, 431, 456, 457, 458, 471, 472, 479, 481, 484, 507, 551, 552, 553, 556, 576, 580, 581, 583, 584, 588, 589, 658, 659, 660, 661, 662, 665, 666, 667, 671, 674, 689, 691, 697, 699, 700, 701, 713, 721, 722, 724, 726, 727, 731, 734, 735
Fellin, P., 38, 41, 42
Fenley, R. C., 191
Fenstermaker, S., 459
Fer, Dr. Eisdor, 720
FeralChildren.com, 2
Fernyhough, C., 143
Ferrel, C., 693
Fertig, A. R., 76
Fertility Clinic Success Rate and Certification Act, 106
Fertilityplus, 102
Fhagen-Smith, P., 342
FICA (Federal Insurance Contributions Act), 730
Fichner-Rathus, L., 64, 65, 67, 68, 106, 107, 244, 246, 299, 306, 307, 308, 310, 317, 319, 442, 445, 451, 453, 620, 621, 629, 631, 632
Field, D., 701
Filardi, A., 673
Finkelhor, D., 245
Fiore, L., 73, 138, 143, 348
First Star, Inc., 234
Fischer, D. H., 698
Fischer, J., 203
Fisher, J. L., 246
Fleming, N., 76
Flor, D. O., 217
Foote, D., 629
Ford Motor Co., 606
Fortson, K., 312
Fouts, B., 451
Fowler, J., 132, 350, 351, 352, 353, 371
Frame, M. W., 132, 350, 351, 352, 353
Franke, T. M., 165
Franklin, Benjamin, 657
Franzoi, S. L., 303
Frazier, K., 343
Fredriksen, K. I., 631, 648
Freeman-Longo, R., 268
Freire, P., 315
French, S. E., 342
Frenkel-Brunswick, E., 265, 690

Freud, S., 114, 115, 117, 118, 119, 120, 127, 147, 173, 334, 509
Frey, L. A., 413, 414
Freyhan, F. A., 268
Friebe, A., 72
Friedman, H., 76
Friedrich, W. N., 246
Friend, M., 68n1, 156, 158, 164, 165, 166, 167, 168, 169, 170, 172, 173
Fries, N., 69
Friesen, W. V., 515
Fromm, Erich, 118, 173
Fuligni, A. J., 221, 301
Fullmer, E. M., 648
Fulmer, R. H., 190
Furman, L. E., 694
Furman, L. D., 131, 351, 354
Furman, R., 219
Furstenberg, F. F., 702

G

Gaciki, C., 636
Gagnon, J., 306
Galasso, M. A., 673
Galinsky, M., 410
Gallagher, J., 161
Gallardo-Cooper, M., 219
Galsworthy, M. J., 436
Gamble, D. N., 45
Gambrill, E., 19, 25, 58, 118
Gandhi, 346, 417, 501
Garbarino, J., 240
Garcia, B., 45, 46, 193
Garcia Coll, C., 217
Garcia-Falgueras, A., 303
Garcia-Preto, N. G., 189, 190, 191, 215
Gardiner, H. W., 190
Gareri, P., 673
Garland, J. A., 412, 413, 414
Garrett, M. T., 131, 192
Garstein, M. A., 146
Garvey, C., 223
Gates, Bill, 563
Gawain, S., 499, 522, 523, 548
Ge, X., 301
Gebhard, P. H., 624
Geis, F., 417
Geller, J., 432
Gelman, D., 273, 629, 635
George, L. K., 693
Georgiades, I., 109
Gerhard, G. S., 666
Germain, R., 240
Giambi, Jason, 538
Gibbs, L., 19, 25, 58, 118
Gibbs, N., 456
Gibelman, M., 439
Gilbert, M. J., 425
Gilford, R., 699
Gilligan, C., 123, 345, 347, 348, 349, 371

Gilliland, B. E., 365, 368
Gillum, T., 461, 462
Gilman, S. E., 627
Gilson, S. F., 163
Glass, T. A., 739
Glasser, W., 499, 518, 519, 520, 522, 548
Gleitman, H., 522
Glenmaye, L., 123, 191
Glenn, John, 739
Glover, R. J., 348
Gochros, H. L., 203
Godard, P., 69
Gohn-Baube, E. A., 71
Goldenberg, H., 218
Goldenberg, I., 218
Goldman, R. N., 121
Goldsmith, H. H., 146
Goldstein, A. P., 402, 404, 405
Goldstein, E. G., 130
Goldstein, J. M., 303
Goldstein, T. R., 360
Goldston, D. B., 169
Goleman, D., 502, 507, 508, 548
Gonal, F., 104
Gonzalez-Ramos, G., 366
Good, G. E., 120
Goodman, D. D., 315
Gooren, L., 627
Gordon, M., 292
Gordon, T., 380, 381, 599
Gordon, W., 23
Goss, K., 92
Gottfried, A. W., 146
Gould, M. S., 227
Graber, J. A., 301, 302
Grammar, K., 512
Grandma Moses, 657
Gray Panthers, 737
Greder, K. A., 190
Green, J. W., 45
Greenberg, J., 702
Greenberg, J. S., 64, 65, 94, 102, 103, 104, 299, 306, 311, 312, 313, 315, 317, 321, 329, 330, 430, 446, 449, 452, 453, 455, 619, 620, 622, 627, 634, 638, 650
Greenberg, L. S., 121
Greene, B. L., 644
Greene, R. R., 18, 23
Greenfield, P. M., 148
Greenhill, L. L., 173
Greenleaf, R. K., 419
Gridina, N., 228
Grieger, I., 109
Grolnick, W. S., 231
Gross, G., 277, 562, 657, 723, 724
Grossmann, K., 151
Grossmann, K. E., 151
Group for the Advancement of Psychiatry, 557

Grush, J. E., 551
Grzegorek, J. L., 622, 623
Guerin, D. W., 146
Guerin, Madame, 2
Guevremont, D. C., 195, 203, 206, 209
Guha, S., 330
Gumpel, T. P., 169
Gunn, Sakia, 640
Gurland, S. T., 231
Gutheil, I. A., 18
Gutierrez, L., 191, 635
Gutierrez, L. M., 14, 25, 58, 123, 406
Guttmacher Institute, 89, 90, 91, 94, 95, 96,
  97, 307, 310, 311, 312, 313, 315, 320
Guttmann, E., 240

H

Habitat for Humanity, 704
Haight, B. K., 690
Hakim-Larson, J., 433
Halfon, O., 150
Hall, E. T., 513
Hall, G., 451
Hall, J., 436
Hall, J. A., 479, 509, 510, 512, 515, 516,
  517
Hall, L., 192
Hallahan, D. P., 71, 156, 159, 161,
  163, 164, 165, 166, 168, 169, 170, 172
Halle, J. W., 170
Hamilton, B. E., 73, 76
Hamilton, C. V., 263
Hamilton, L., 126
Hammersmith, S. K., 629
Hancock, C., 238
Hardman, M. L., 156, 172
Hardy, Charles, 442
Hare, A., 418
Harkins, A., 361
Harper-Dorton, K., 633
Harrell, E. B., 18
Harrington, D., 19, 99–100
Harris, Eric, 402
Harris, J. F., 229
Harris, O., 588
Harris, Teresa, 442
Harris v. McRae, 88
Harrison, A. O., 217
Harroff, P. B., 572
Hart, S. N., 240, 241
Harter, S., 152
Hartley, E., 267
Hartman, A., 88, 592
Harvard University, 280
Harway, M., 456
Hastings, P. D., 148
Hatcher, R. A., 322
Haulotte, S. M., 15
Hawkins, R. O., 639, 642, 643, 646, 647,
  648

Hawthorne Works, 602
Head Start, 129n2
Healey, K. M., 460
Health Canada, 369, 370
Healy, M. D., 221
Helwig, C. C., 346
Hemlock Society, 725
Henderson, A. W., 632
Henderson, Russell, 640
Henderson, C. H., 272
Hendricks, C. O., 342
Henry, J., 264
Henry, W. E., 697
Henson, K. D., 445
Herbenick, D., 306
Herman, D., 448
Herrnstein, R. J., 262
Hersey, P., 416
Hertzog, C., 301
Herzog, A. R., 739
Hickerson, J. C., 362, 639, 647
Higher Educational Amendments, 441
Hildyard, K. L., 239
Hill, C., 438, 443, 444
Hill, N. E., 217
Hill, S. A., 433
Hirschfelder, A., 192
Hirschi, T., 405
Hitler, Adolf, 256, 402, 417
Ho, M. K., 220
Hoang, M., 304
Hodges, E. V. E., 227
Hoffman-LaRoche, 529
Holland, C. L., 307
Holly, C., 240
Holmberg, D., 632
Holmstrom, L. L., 453
Homan, M. S., 18, 36, 38, 39, 42, 43, 58
Hood, J. E., 246
Hooyman, N., 124, 719
Horejsi, C. R., 23, 212, 364, 368
Horton, N. J., 303
Horvath, C., 627
Housand, A. M., 156
Howard, M., 314
Howard, Tony, 502
Howard-Hamilton, M. F., 343
Hower, D., 606
Howes, C., 150
Huang, L. N., 433
Huang, Z. J., 227
Huesmann, L. R., 229
Huessman, R., 229
Huff, C. R., 405
Hugen, B., 354
Hughes, I. A., 428
Hughes, M., 138
Hull, G. H., Jr., 16, 23, 193, 288, 289, 290,
  353, 369, 424, 623
Human Genome Project, 667

Human Intelligence, 2
Human Rights Campaign, 635
Humphreys, N. A., 639
Humphry, Derek, 725
Hunt, V., 126
Hunter College Women's Studies
  Collective, 122, 123, 644
Hunter, S., 362, 639, 647
Hu-Pei Au, K., 232
Hutchins, T., 461
Hutchinson, E., 76
Hutter-Silver, M., 673
Hyde Amendment, 91
Hyde, C. A., 109, 123, 124
Hyde, J. S., 64, 65, 67, 70, 97, 102, 104,
  105, 122, 123, 124, 125, 126, 222,
  224, 297, 299, 300, 306, 308, 310,
  311, 317, 318, 320, 321, 329, 330,
  347, 349, 431, 432, 436, 447, 449,
  451, 453, 456, 457, 458, 459, 465,
  482, 483, 485, 486, 487, 488, 489,
  490, 491, 495, 527, 624, 626, 628,
  639, 664, 665

I

Iditarod Trail Dog Race, 502
Immigration and Naturalization Service
  (INS), 15, 283
Imperato-McGinley, J., 436
Indian Gaming Regulatory Act, 282
Individuals with Disabilities Act, 171
Individuals with Disabilities Education
  Improvement Act (IDEA), 171
Infusino, P., 673
Institute of Medicine, 315
International Association of Schools of
  Social Work (IASSW), 20, 55, 59, 60
International Federation of Social Work-
  ers (IFSW), 20, 55, 59, 60
Intersex Society of North America
  (ISNA), 428, 429
Iovanni, L., 460
Itard, Jean-Marc Gaspard, 2
Ivey, A. E., 120, 212
Ivey, M. B., 120, 212

J

Jackson, A. W., 231
Jackson, Jesse, 288
Jackson, T., 462
Jacob, D., 193
Jacob, K. F., 231
Jacobs, S.E., 430
Jacobson, E., 681
Jaffee, K. D., 71
Jaffee, S., 349
Jambunathan, S., 217
James, R. K., 365, 368
Jansson, B. S., 49, 129
Janzen, C., 588

Jennings, V. H., 328
Jensen, P. S., 173
Ji, G., 222
Jiao, S., 222
Jim Crow laws, 259, 272
Jimenez, J., 162, 163
Jing, Q., 222
Joan of Arc, 352
Job Corps, 129n3
Jobes, D. A., 367, 368, 369
Johnson, A. K., 51
Johnson, D. W., 406, 411, 415, 416, 418
Johnson, E. H., 260, 262
Johnson, F. P., 406, 411, 415, 416, 418
Johnson, H. C., 23, 58, 285
Johnson, J. D., 229
Johnson, J. G., 229
Johnson, President Lyndon B., 49
Johnson, M. R., 642
Johnson, R., 620, 623, 626, 645
Johnson, V. E., 299, 453, 454, 626, 663
Johnson, W., 436
Johnston, L. D., 303, 305
Jones, A., 456, 460
Jones, H., 412
Jones, K., 45, 193
Jones, K. P., 72
Jones, M., 16
Jones, S., 219
Jones, Reverend Terry, 261
Jordan, C., 232
Julian, J., 25, 265, 279, 280, 524, 526, 527, 529, 534, 535, 536, 552, 564, 565, 566, 576, 579, 586, 717, 723, 734, 737
Jung, Carl, 118, 173
Juran, J. M., 605
Jussim, L., 230
Just the Facts Coalition, 623
Justice, David, 538

K

Kadushin, A., 233
Kahn, R., 739
Kahn, S., 53
Kail, R. V., 11, 66, 67, 68, 92, 139, 140, 141, 143, 145, 147, 148, 149, 157, 172, 173, 221, 222, 228, 302, 342, 347, 360, 365, 367, 552, 558, 588, 700
Kaiser Family Foundation, 311
Kalat, J. W., 155
Kalb, C., 93
Kaluger, G., 487, 580
Kaluger, M. F., 487, 580
Kamehameha Early Education Program (KEEP), 232
Kanie, Gin, 657
Kaplan, C., 366
Kaplan, D. A., 442

Karenga, M. R., 275
Karger, H. J., 162
Karlen, A., 622
Karmaniola, A., 150
Kasen, S., 229
Kasprian, G., 69
Kasprina, G., 69
Katz, A. H., 408
Kauffman, J. M., 71, 156, 159, 161, 163, 164, 165, 166, 168, 169, 170, 172
Kaufman, N., 304
Kaufman, S. B., 436
Kavanagh, K., 304
Kazdin, A. E., 119, 195, 196, 197, 200, 202, 203, 207, 208, 209, 213, 214
Kazmierczak, Stephen, 229
Kearl, H., 443
KEEP (Kamehameha Early Education Program), 232
Kelley, G., 460
Kelley, M. A., 45
Kelly, B. M., 227
Kelly, G. F., 70, 97, 130, 306, 329, 447, 621, 626, 630, 635, 639
Kelly, J. J., 626, 628
Kelly, P. J., 70
Keltner, D., 512
Kemp, J., 640
Kendall, A., 195, 202
Kendall, D., 425, 432
Kendell, K., 639
Kendler, K. S., 627
Keniston. K., 268
Kennedy, D. N., 303
Kennedy, President John F., 416, 705
Kenny-Benson, G. A., 436
Kerbo, H. R., 547
Kerr, B., 361
Kerr, M. E., 595
Kesler, J. T., 43
Kesselman, A., 184
Kessler, R. C., 627
Ketner, P. M., 603
Kevorkian, Dr. Jack, 725
Kiff, S., 312
Killin, M., 346
Kim, B., 272
Kim, K-J., 221
Kim, K. S., 131
King, J., 641
King, Martin Luther, Jr., 272, 277, 278, 288, 346, 352, 416, 501
King, Rodney, 257–258, 277
Kinnunen, L. H., 627
Kinsey, A. C., 488, 622, 624, 625, 626
Kinsey Institute for Sex Research, 305, 306, 307, 629
Kipp, K., 68, 142, 144, 230, 231
Kirby, D., 312, 314

Kirk, G., 89, 125, 184, 432, 437, 439, 444, 449, 456, 458, 459, 460
Kirk, K. M., 627
Kirk, S., 161
Kirsch, L. B., 221
Kirst-Ashman, K. K., 11, 16, 23, 39, 50n3, 53, 126, 369, 424
Kissinger, P., 307
Klebold, Dylan, 402
Klein, E. B., 471, 503
Klein, J. D. and the Committee on Adolescence, 308
Klein, M. S., 305
Klein, T. W., 232
Kleinman, M., 227
Kliman, J., 191
Knapp, J., 451
Knapp, M. L., 479, 509, 510, 512, 515, 516, 517
Knoblauch, Chuck, 538
Knopf, R., 607, 608
Knox, D., 182, 382, 383, 387, 388, 400, 401, 403, 424, 429, 447, 451, 452, 464, 478, 495, 563, 564, 579, 580, 581, 584, 589, 620, 671, 692, 717, 720, 722, 723, 727, 733, 734
Koch, M. O., 384, 385, 386, 387, 388, 389
Koenig, H. G., 693
Kohlberg, L., 114, 123, 345, 346, 347, 348, 349, 371
Kolbe, L., 314
Kolko, D. J., 32, 236
Kolodny, R., 412
Kolodny, R. C., 299, 453, 454, 626
Kondrat, M. E., 425
Konijn, E. A., 229
Koop, C. E., 535
Kopels, S., 163
Koporc, K., 307
Kornblum, W., 25, 265, 279, 280, 524, 526, 527, 529, 534, 535, 536, 552, 564, 565, 566, 576, 579, 586, 717, 723, 734, 737
Kosberg, J. I., 435
Kosmitzki, C., 190
Koss, M. P., 447, 451
Kotz, D., 664
Kouyoumdjian, M., 157
Kowal, D., 328
Kramer, L., 426
Kraus, M. W., 512
Krauthammer, Charles, 532
Krebs, D. L., 348, 349
Kreipe de Montano, M., 192
Krestan, C. R., 69
Kretzmann, J. P., 16, 17, 282
Kretzschmar, J. A., 15
Krishnakumar, A., 217
Kübler-Ross, E., 102, 706, 707
Kuhn, Maggie, 737

Ku Klux Klan, 257, 267, 291, 403
Kupperminc, G. P., 301
Kurdek, L. A., 632
Kurpius, S. E., 361
Kuypers, J., 698
Kvale, J. N., 693

L
Lacava, R., 673
Lacayo, R., 93
Lachance, J., 436
Lacombe, D., 69
Ladd, G. W., 226
Laird, J., 646, 647
Lamanna, M. A., 215, 216
Lamm, Gov. Richard, 720
Land, H., 123
Lane, H., 2
Lang, A., 67
Lang, S., 430
Lankton, S., 511
Lantz, J., 633
Lanza, Adam, 229
La Raza Unida, 45
Latham, G. P., 221
Lauerman, J. F., 673
Laufersweiler-Dwyer, D. L., 451
Laumann, E., 306
Laursen, T. M., 97
Lavell, M., 442
Lawrence, M., 419
Lawrence et al., v. Texas, 633
Leacock, E., 569
Leadbeater, B. J., 301
Lebeaux, C., 611, 613
LeClaire, J., 92
Lee, D. Y., 157
Lee, J., 92, 184, 432, 434, 436, 437, 439,
    442, 456, 457, 458
Lee, J. A., 648
Lee, J. A. B., 14
Lee, S., 220, 221
Lee, V. E., 231
Lee, Y. S., 428
Lefrancois, G. R., 262, 472, 482, 582, 583,
    584, 587, 673
Lehavot, K., 632
Lein, L., 184
Leino, E. V., 701
Lemire, J., 640
Lemish, D., 228
Lemon, N. K. D., 460
Leong, F. T. L., 220, 221
Leon-Guerrero, A., 12, 425
LeVay, S., 627, 630, 634
Levin, I., 182
LeVine, E. S., 32, 248
Levinson, D., 265, 499, 503, 504, 505, 506
Levinson, D. J., 471, 487, 503, 506, 547,
    556

Levinson, J. D., 503, 506, 556
Levinson, M. H., 471, 503
Lewin, K., 418
Lewinsohn, P. M., 301
Lewis, J. S., 18
Lewis, M. A., 304
Lewis, O., 568
LGBT Hate Crimes Project, 640
Liben, I. S., 348
Lidegaard, O., 97
Lie, T. L., 76
Lightfoot, E., 161, 162, 165, 171
Lin, C., 217
Lin, S. W., 67
Linares, Juan, 283
Lincoln, President Abraham, 254, 266,
    272
Lindberg, C. A., 3
Lindberg, S., 431
Lindgren, K. P., 304
Linz, D., 229
Lippa, R., 629
Lippitt, R., 418
Liptak, A., 89, 90
Liu, W. T., 217
Liu-Constant, Y., 221
Livermore, M., 614
Livingston, N. C., 18
Lloyd, G. A., 492
Lock, M., 483
Lockett, P. W., 123, 124
Loewenberg, F. M., 19, 99–100
Logan, C., 341
London, S., 68
Longres, J. F., 40, 219, 433, 631, 648
Lopez, E. I., 230
Lorber, J., 124, 125, 126, 184, 425, 426,
    464
Lorenz, F. O., 487
Lott, B., 224, 453, 464
Loukas, A., 230
Lowry, L., 72
Loya, M., 219
Lu, Y. E., 433
Lum, D., 11, 12, 25, 46, 57, 131, 192, 434
Lynne, S. D., 301

M
Maag, J. W., 169
Machiavelli, Niccolò, 417
Mackelprang, R. W., 163, 165, 171
Madara, E. J., 409
Madathil, J., 221
Madom, S., 230
*Madsen et al. v. Women's Health Center,
    Inc.*, 92
Magana, S., 219
Magness, P. W., 266
Magnus, J. H., 76
Mahoney, M., 165

Maier, R. A., 490, 630
Maier, S. L., 431, 442, 444, 456, 457, 458,
    459, 460
Major League Baseball of Biogenesis of
    America, 538
Makris, N., 303
Malamitsi Puchner, A., 76
Malamuth, N. M., 451
Mallon, G. P., 626, 631, 632, 646
Maluccio, A. N., 241, 242
Mammotome, 474
Manganaro, L., 69
Mangione, R., 69
Maniacci, M., 119
Mara, B. A., 241
March of Dimes,75, 76, 308
Marcia, J. E., 334, 339, 340, 341, 343, 371
Margalit, M., 169
Markestad, T., 76
Markus, H., 151
Marrocco, F., 227
Marschaleck, J., 69
Marshall, S., 221
Martin, C. E., 367, 368, 369, 622, 624,
    625, 626
Martin, C. L., 145, 146, 228, 230, 303
Martin, J. A., 73, 76, 233
Martin, J. I., 621, 642
Martin, N. G., 627
Martin, S., 629
Martin, S. E., 445
Martinez-Brawley, E. M., 39, 40
Martinez, E., 300
Martorell, G., 379, 507, 551, 552, 553,
    556, 576, 580, 581, 583, 584, 588,
    589, 659, 660, 661, 662, 665, 666,
    667, 671, 674, 689, 691, 697, 699,
    700, 701, 713, 721, 722, 724, 726,
    727, 731, 734, 735
Maslova, E., 67
Maslow, A. H., 499, 505, 507, 548
Mason, G., 641
Massachusetts Bay Pilgrims, 257
Masters, W. H., 299, 453, 454, 626, 663
Mather, J. H., 353, 623
Mathie, A., 283
Matlovich, Leonard, 635
Matthews-Simonton, S., 675
Matthews, T. J., 73
Matthias, R. E., 165
Mattingly, M., 713
Maugham, W. Somerset, 657
Maultsby, M. C., Jr., 395
Mauro, J. A., 146
Mayan society, 705
Mayer, A., 244
Mayer, J., 507
Mayo Clinic, 65, 101, 102, 104, 474, 475
Mayo Foundation for Medical Education
    and Research (MRMER), 72

Mazzocco, M. M. M., 436
McAdoo, H. P., 217, 232
McAnulty, R. D., 243, 620
McCabe, M. P., 451
McCammon, S., 424, 429, 447, 451, 452, 464, 620
McCarter, R. J., 227
McClam, E., 636
McClanahan, M., 622, 623
McClelland, 507
McCoy, D., 646
McCrary, J., 635
McFadden, E. J., 31, 238, 239, 240, 307, 308
McFadden, R. D., 641
McGoldrick, M., 189, 190, 191, 215
McGregor, D., 603
McGwire, Mark, 538
McHale, S. M., 221
McInnis-Dittrich, K., 649
McIntosh, P., 260
McKay, M., 501, 680
McKee, B., 471, 503
McKinney, Aaron, 640
McKnight, J., 16, 17, 282
McMahon, P. M., 447
McMurtry, S. L., 603
McNair, L. D., 184
McPhail, B., 444
McQueen, M., 89
McWhirter, B. T., 304, 361, 362, 364, 365, 367, 368
McWhirter, E. H., 304, 361, 362, 364, 365, 367, 368
McWhirter, J. J., 304, 361, 362, 364, 365, 367, 368
McWhirter, R. J., 304, 361, 362, 364, 365, 367, 368
Mead, George Herbert, 562
Mead, M., 379
Meadan, H., 170
Meadows, M., 103
Medicare Prescription Drug Improvement and Modernization Act, 731
Menacker, F., 73
Menec, V. H., 697
Menna, A., 453
Mercado Central, 283, 284
Mercurio, M., 673
Mertesacker, B., 146
Merton, R. K., 258, 269, 404, 559
Messinger, L., 621, 630, 632, 646
Metindogan, A., 217
Metz, J., 627
Meyer, C., 23
Michael, R., 306
Michaels, S., 306
Michelangelo, 657
Michels, K. B., 67
Midgley, J., 614

Mielke, E., 307
Miley, K., 694
Miljkovitch, R., 150
Miller, L. S., 229
Miller, P. J., 726
Miller, R. L., Jr., 341, 621
Miller, S. L., 460
Miller, W. B., 404
Miller, W. R., 544
Miller-Perrin, C. L., 32, 236, 237, 238, 245, 246, 248, 455, 456, 457, 458, 459, 460, 461
Miltenberger, R. G., 195, 196, 197, 202, 204, 206, 207, 208, 209, 214
Mindell, C. L., 192
Minich, N., 76
Minkler, M., 701
Minnes, S., 67
Miranda, Salvador, 283
Mirlesse, V., 69
Mish, F. C., 123, 424, 441n1, 453
Mish, F. E., 68
Misiewicz, G. L., 191
Mitchell, Sen. George, 538
Mitchell, K. J., 245
Mitterer, J. O., 143, 150, 155, 349, 361, 362, 363, 364, 365
Miyake, K., 151
Moltz, H., 627
Money, J., 428
Monroe, Marilyn, 389
Montague, A., 260, 262
Mooney, L. A., 182, 382, 383, 387, 388, 400, 401, 403, 457, 478, 495, 563, 564, 579, 580, 581
Moore, E., 31, 238, 239, 240, 307, 308
Moore, L. J., 425
Moore, S., 300
Moore, S. E., 192, 219, 286, 433
Mor Barak, M., 270
Morales, A. T., 102, 103
Morales, J., 631, 639, 644, 647
Morelli, G., 151, 221
Morris, A., 348
Morrow, D. F., 341, 620, 623, 631, 642, 643
Mortensen, L. H., 76
Mortensen, P. B., 97
Mosak, H. H., 119
Moser, C., 620
Moses, A. E., 639, 642, 643, 646, 647, 648
Mosher, W. D., 182
Moss, G., 717, 736
Moss, W., 717, 736
Moster, D., 76
Mother Teresa, 352
Mothers Against Drunk Driving, 526
Mulrine, A., 105
Mulder, 68
Mundell, E. M., 362

Munk-Olsen, T., 97
Munson, M. L., 73
Murphy, Y., 126
Murray, C., 262
Murray, J. P., 228
Murry, V., 307
Mutter, J. D., 190
Mwalimu, I., 712
Myrdal, G., 259

N

Nagayama, C., 451
Nairne, J. S., 297, 360, 363, 364
Nanda, S., 430
Nansel, T. R., 227
Narcotics Anonymous, 541
Narita, Kin, 657
Nassar-McMillan, S., 433
NASW National Committee on Lesbian and Gay Issues, 650
National Abortion Federation (NAF), 90, 92
National Advisory Commission on Civil Disorders, 273
National Association of School Psychologists, 623
National Association of Social Workers (NASW), 6, 19, 20, 21, 24, 55, 59, 88, 128, 270, 287, 290, 440, 618, 623, 624, 650
National Cancer Institute (NCI), 474, 475
National Center for Education Statistics, 156
National Coalition of Anti-Violence Programs (NCAVP), 641
National Commission on Causes and Prevention of Violence, 277
National Committee on Lesbian and Gay Issues, 650
National Committee on Pay Equity (NCPE), 437, 438
National Conference of State Legislatures (NCSL), 636, 637
National Gay and Lesbian Task Force, 409, 633, 637, 648
National Institute of Child Health and Welfare Development, 150
National Institute of Mental Health (NIMH), 173, 361, 363, 364, 365
National Institutes of Health (NIH), 70, 93, 321, 323, 324, 325, 428
National Joint Committee on Learning Disabilities (NJCLD), 164, 165, 166
National Organization on Disability, 163
National Organization for Women (NOW), 124
National Urban League, 273
National Women's Health Information Center (NWHIC), 72, 73, 102, 103
Native American Church, 534

Navarre, R., 401
Negi, N. J., 219
Neighbors, C., 304
Neighborhood Development Center, 283
Nelson, A., 322
Nelson, C. A., 139, 140
Nelson, K., 144, 713
Nelson, S., 304
Nemec, S. F., 69
Nemec, U., 69
Netting, F. E., 123, 603
Neugarten, B., 702
Nevels, B. J., 219
Nevid, J. S., 64, 65, 67, 68, 106, 107, 244,
    246, 299, 306, 307, 308, 310, 317,
    319, 364, 442, 445, 451, 453, 620,
    621, 629, 631, 632
Newcomb, A. F., 225
Newman, B. M., 67, 68, 143, 149, 150,
    228, 229, 300, 301, 304, 347, 674,
    721
Newman, P. R., 67, 68, 143, 149, 150,
    228, 229, 300, 301, 304, 347, 674,
    721
New Media Learning, 445
Newring, K., 430
Newstrom, W., 601, 604
Newton, P. J., 459
Nibao, J., 633
Nichold, T. R., 301
Nichols, W. R., 12, 122
Nicholson Callahan, B., 356
Nixon, President Richard, 346
Nobel Peace Prize, 704
No-Doz, 529
NOLO, 635, 636, 637
Norman, E., 18
Norman, N. D., 132
Norris, A. N., 126
Northern Illinois University, 229
Norton, D. G., 285
Northouse, P. G., 156
NPR, 229
Nugent, A., 620
Nunes, M. L., 76
Nurius, P. S., 151
Nursing Home Ombudsman Program,
    733
Nybo Andersen, A. M., 76

O

O'Brien, F., 209
O'Connor, M. K., 123
O'Connor, Justice Sandra Day, 442
O'Keefe, E., 635
O'Malley, P. M., 303, 305
O'Sullivan, C., 460
O'Sullivan, L., 447
Obama, President Barack, 93, 191, 273,
    292, 312, 313, 586, 636, 727–728, 731

Office of Adolescent Health, 307
Okazawa-Rey, M., 89, 125, 184, 432, 437,
    439, 444, 449, 456, 458, 459, 460
Okun, B. F., 598
Old Age, Survivors, Disability, and
    Health Insurance (OASDHI), 723,
    729–730
Older Americans Act, 729
Olds, S. W., 1, 136, 378, 506, 659, 700
Omachonu, V. K., 605
Oncale, Joseph, 441
Osgood, D. W., 221
Ossana, S. M., 632
Osterman, M. H. S., 73
Oswalt, S. B., 102, 103, 104, 299, 306, 311,
    312, 313, 315, 317, 321, 329, 330,
    430, 46, 449, 452, 455, 619, 620, 622,
    627, 634, 638, 650
Otten, A. S., 720
Ou, Y., 217
Ouchi, W., 604
Oumar, F., 151
Overpeck, M., 227

P

Pace, P. R., 440
Pachter, L. M., 217
Padilla, Y. C., 647
Page, S. P., 266
Palmeiro, Rafael, 538
Paniagua, F. A., 219, 220
Papalia, D. E., 1, 66, 68, 136, 138, 145,
    146, 148, 150, 152, 217, 224, 225,
    232, 341, 378, 379, 431, 456, 457,
    458, 471, 472, 479, 481, 484, 506,
    507, 551, 552, 553, 556, 576, 580,
    581, 583, 584, 588, 589, 658, 659,
    660, 661, 662, 665, 666, 671, 674,
    689, 691, 697, 699, 700, 701, 713,
    721, 722, 724, 726, 727, 731, 734,
    735
Parents Anonymous, 32
Parents Without Partners, 583
Park, J., 622, 623
Parke, R. D., 221
Parker, J. G., 224, 227
Parker, K., 182
Parks, C. A., 639
Parks, Rosa, 277, 278
Parrott, D., 641
Parsons, Talcott, 559
Parten, M., 223, 224
Pastorelli, C., 349
Pasupathi, M., 349
Patchner, L. S., 163
Paterson, A. D., 433
Patrick, H., 436
Pattee, L., 225
Patterson, G. A., 362, 365, 366
Patterson, G. R., 210, 382

Patterson, W. M., 362, 365, 366
Patton, General George, 416–417
Pauli-Pott, U., 146
Paus, T., 302
Pearlman, J., 356
Peck, R. C., 499, 501, 547, 689, 690
Pecora, P. J., 228, 241, 242
Pedersen, C. B., 97
Peets, K., 227
Pelosi, Congresswoman Nancy, 440
Penner, L. A., 148, 431
Perez-Febles, A., 221
Perez-Laso, C., 303
Perloff, J. D., 70
Perls, T. T., 673
Perrin, R. C., 237, 238, 239, 240, 241, 455,
    456, 457, 458, 459, 460, 461
Perrin, R. D., 32, 236, 237, 238, 245, 246,
    248
Perrin, S., 227
Personal Responsibility Education Pro-
    gram (PREP), 313
Personal Responsibility and Work
    Opportunity Reconciliation Act, 585
Perterson, C. M., 72
Peskin, H., 301
Peters, H., 638
Petersen, A. C., 302
Peterson, J., 641
Petretic-Jackson, P. A., 462
Pettitte, Andy, 538
Pfeiffer, K., 307
Phenice, L. A., 232
Phillips, W., 220
Phinney, J., 342, 343
Piaget, J., 113, 129, 132, 133, 134, 135,
    136, 137, 138, 141, 143, 144, 174,
    352, 371
Pianta, R. C., 230
Picasso, Pablo, 657
Pierce, S., 217
Pierrehumbert, B., 150
Pilgrims, 523
Pilla, R., 227
Pillard, R. C., 627
Pillemer, K., 702
Pinderhughes, E., 267
Pine, C. J., 217
Pine, D., 301
Pinel, Philippe, 2
Pinkney, A., 257
Pinos, H., 303
Pisani, L., 151
Planned Parenthood, 65, 91, 96, 97, 315,
    320n1, 321, 322, 323, 324, 325, 326,
    327, 328, 329
Planned Parenthood v. Casey, 88
Plomin, R., 436
Plotnick, R. D., 241, 242
Plotnik, R., 157

Polansky, N. A., 240
Polansky, N. F., 240
Polen, E. A. P., 301
PollingReport.com, 637
Pollio, E., 246, 248
Pomerantz, E. M., 436
Pomeroy, W. B., 622, 624, 625, 626
Poniewozik, J., 229
Portuguez, M. W., 76
Posch, A., 69
Posner, M. I., 146
Postma, A., 436
Potocky, M., 193
Pott, M., 151, 221
Powell, G. J., 274
Powell, T. J., 408
Prayer, D., 69
Premack, D., 204
Presnall, K., 300
Preto, N. G., 191
Pridjian, G., 76
Priess, H., 431
Prinstein, M. J., 301
Prochaska, J. O., 544
ProCon.org, 632
Proposition 209, 280
Pullen, P. C., 71, 156, 159, 161, 163, 164,
    165, 166, 168, 169, 170, 172
Putnam, S. P., 146

Q
Quay, L., 312
Qian, Z., 221

R
Rainbow Retreat, 461
Raines, J. C., 171
Ramirez, O., 433
Ramsey, E., 382
Ramstein, T., 150
Rand, M., 449
Randall, H., 311
Rankin, J., 67
Rappaport, L. J., 598
Raskin, N. J., 120
Rathus, S. A. 64, 65, 67, 68, 70, 106, 107,
    139, 140, 141, 146, 215, 216, 221,
    224, 226, 228, 230, 231, 244, 246,
    299, 301, 306, 307, 308, 310, 317,
    364, 365, 442, 445, 451, 453, 620,
    621, 629, 631, 632, 642
Reagan, President Ronald, 79, 291, 657,
    727
Reamer, F. G., 13
Reboussin, B. A., 169
Rees, S., 383
Regalia, C., 349
Register, E., 462
Regulus, T. A., 401, 403, 404, 406
Reich, Robert, 728

Reichert, E., 284, 285
Reicherzer, S., 633
Reid, R., 169
Reis, S., 156
Reisen, C. A., 621
Renninger, L., 512
Renzetti, C. M., 431, 442, 444, 456, 457,
    458, 459, 460
Research America, 93
Retired Senior Volunteer Program
    (RSVP), 738
Revelle, W., 627
Reynolds, M., 306
Rhoads, G. G., 76
Rhodes, M. L., 349
Richardson, L., 429
Richters, J. E., 173
Riddleberger, P., 409
Rider, E. A., 66, 146, 147, 148, 150, 297,
    301, 302, 349, 350, 360, 361, 436
Riedmann, A., 215, 216
Riessman, F., 409
Rivas, R. F., 16
Rivelis, E., 241
Road Scholar, 673
Robbins, S. P., 351
Roberts, A. R., 367
Roberts, G., 76
Robinson, B. A., 633
Robinson, L., 367
Robinson, S., 230
Rock County Coroner's Office, 363
Rodriguez, Alex, 538, 563
Roe v. Wade, 88
Roeder, K., 354
Roelofsma, P. H. M. P., 229
Roeser, R. W., 230, 231
Roethlisberger, F. J., 602
Rogers, A. G., 347
Rogers, C. R., 119, 120, 150, 173
Rogers, J. K., 445
Rogers, P., 626
Rogoff, B., 144
Rohani, M., 45, 193
Roid, G., 155
Rolland, J. S., 190
Rollnick, S., 544
Romano, A., 229
Romano, K., 366
Rook, K. S., 65, 67, 68, 75, 137, 139, 140,
    146, 148
Rooney, Mickey, 726
Roopnarine, J. L., 217
Roosa, M. W., 217
Roosevelt, President Franklin D., 49, 565
Rosellini, L., 535
Robenbaum, J. E., 312
Rosenberg, D., 93
Rosenblum, T., 157
Rosenhan, D., 393

Rosenthal, D., 300
Rosenthal, M. S., 430, 448, 449, 452, 454,
    455, 626, 646, 648
Ross, J. E., 605
Rothbart, M. K., 146
Rothbaum, F., 151, 221
Rothenberg, M. B., 216
Rothman, J., 39, 43, 49, 58, 431
Rovine, M. J., 557
Rowell, 644
Roy, E. J., 148, 431
Rozee, P. D., 451
Ruan, W., 227
Rubin, A., 354
Rubin, K. H., 148, 224, 227
Rubin, Z., 551
Rubinstein, Arthur, 657
Rugg, D., 314
Runyon, M. D., 236
Runyon, M. K., 246, 248
Russell, Bertrand, 657
Ruth, S., 429
Ryan, A. M., 36
Ryan, W., 569

S
Sable, M. R., 71
Sachs, A., 442
Sagi, A., 151
Sagrado Corazon, 283
Saleebey, D., 14, 15, 131
Sallee, A. L., 32, 248
Salmivalli, C., 227
Salovey, P., 507
Salsgiver, R. O., 163, 165, 171
Samenow, S. E., 268, 269
Samuelson, P., 564
Sanchez, T. W., 219
Sandhu, D. S., 221
Sandler, B., 445
Sandy Hook Elementary School, 229
Sanford, N., 265
Santiago-Rivera, A. L., 131, 219
Santo, J. L., 76
Santrock, J. W., 10, 67, 68, 69, 70, 71, 73,
    74, 75, 76, 143, 145, 146, 166, 217,
    218, 221, 222, 227, 229, 274, 301,
    302, 305, 341, 346, 347, 348, 368,
    487, 552, 553, 556, 657, 659, 660,
    661, 662, 666, 667, 668, 671, 672,
    673, 674, 690, 693, 701, 702, 718,
    719, 722, 723, 724
Sapiro, V., 436, 456, 457
Sappho, 622
Sardar, Z., 270
Saskatchewan Psychology Portal, 2
Saxe, L., 517
Sayad, B. W., 64, 67, 68, 69, 97, 104, 107,
    109, 222, 300, 306, 308, 425, 429,
    431, 434, 449, 451, 452, 453

Schacht, C., 182, 352, 383, 387, 388, 400, 401, 403, 434, 457, 478, 495, 563, 564, 579, 580, 581, 584, 589, 671, 692, 717, 720, 722, 723, 727, 733, 734
Schaefer, R. T., 261, 262, 264, 267, 270, 271, 273, 274, 277, 278, 281, 282, 288, 692, 693
Scharf, M., 221
Scheff, T., 563
Scheflen, A., 511, 512
Scheidt, P., 227
Schiele, J. H., 276
Schiller, L. Y., 414, 421
Schlesinger, E. G., 130, 131, 274, 285, 286
Schmid, M., 69
Schmitt, F. A., 713
Schneider, B. H., 150
Schneider, O., 451
Schneiger, A., 304
Schniedewind, N., 184
Schofeld, I. S., 227
Schopler, J., 410
Schorr, A. L., 586
Schulchter, M., 76
Schulenberg, J. E., 303, 305
Schwaber, F. H., 639
Schwartz, D., 227
Schwartzberg, N., 193
Schweitzer, Albert, 657
Scott, M. E., 402, 403
Sears, H., 311
Seaward, B. L., 477, 675, 676, 682, 683
Seeley, J. W., 240
Seeman, T. E., 739
Segal, E. A., 162
Segal, J., 367
Segal, S. P., 163
Segovia, A., 303
Seidman, E., 342
Seidman, L. J., 303
Selig, Bud, 538
Selig, K. L., 71
Selye, H., 675, 677
Serpell, R., 157
Service Corps of Retired Executives (SCORE), 738
Servicemen Legal Defense Network (SLDN), 636
Sesame Street, 229
Seung-Hui, Cho, 229
Sex Education in America, 311
Sex, Respect, Parent Guide, 312
Sexuality Information and Education Council of the United States (SIE-CUS), 311, 312, 313, 314, 315
Shaffer, D. R., 68, 142, 144, 230, 231
Shao, C., 227
Shattuck, 2
Shaw, George Benard, 657
Shaw, N. J., 428

Shaw, S., 92, 184, 432, 434, 436, 437, 439, 442, 456, 457, 458
Sheafor, B. W., 23, 212, 364, 368, 402, 403
Sheehan, G., 283
Sheffield, Gary, 538
Shepard, Matthew, 640
Sher Institutes for Reproductive Medicine, 105
Shernoff, M., 621, 644
Shireman, J., 237, 241
Short, L., 314
Shrestha, S., 130
Shulman, K. S., 221
SIECUS (Sexuality Information and Education Council of the United States), 311, 312, 313, 314, 315
Siegel, R. K., 713
Siegler, I. C., 693
Sigelman, C. K., 66, 146, 147, 148, 150, 297, 301, 302, 349, 350, 360, 361, 436
Silva, E., 443, 444
Simek-Morgan, L., 120
Siminton, O. C., 675
Simon, J. P., 192
Simon-Rusinowitz, L., 165
Simone, K., 165
Simoni, J. M., 632
Simons-Morton, B., 227
Sindler, A. P., 279
Siner, B., 76
Singer, L., 67
Singh, D., 629
Skinheads, 257, 403
Skinner, Tom, 363
Slattery, D., 640
Smailes, E. M., 229
Smetana, J., 346
Smith, A. E., 230
Smith, B., 644
Smith, B. L., 360
Smith, C., 460
Smith, C. E., 401
Smith, D. S., 156, 167, 168, 169, 172
Smith, E., 449
Smith, J., 231
Smith, K. E., 12
Smith, L. L., 353, 623
Smith, M., 367
Smithbattle, L., 68
Smolowe, J., 162
Snarey, J., 347
Snively, C. A., 14
Snyder, H., 449
Social Security Act (1935), 49, 657, 723, 728, 729
Social Security Administration, 730
Sockloskie, R. J., 451
Solomon, A., 109
Solomon, B. B., 274

Some Golden Years, 734
Spady, D., 277, 562, 657, 723, 724
Spake, A., 484, 485
Spakes, P., 184
Spangler, G., 151
Sparks, A., 106
Spear, L. P., 301, 302
Spears, L. C., 419
Speidel, G. E., 232
Spencer, Herbert, 728
Spencer-Smith, M. M., 76
Spergel, I. A., 405, 406
Spiegler, M. D., 195, 203, 206, 209
Spijkerman, R., 301
Spitz, R., 489, 512
Spock, Dr. Benjamin, 216, 217
Spranger, E., 610
Srabstein, J. C., 227
Statistical Abstract of the U.S.: 2012, 95, 437, 439
Statistics Canada, 456
Students Against Drunk Driving, 526
Staudinger, U. M., 349
Stein, R., 312
Steinberg, L., 65, 67, 68, 75, 137, 139, 140, 146, 148, 226, 227, 232, 251, 302, 360, 364
Stephens, K., 451
Sternberg, R. J., 153, 154, 157
Stewart, F., 326
Stewart, Josephine, 650
Stewart, S. L., 148
Stipek, D. J., 230
Stoesz, D., 162
Stone, A., 646
Stonewall, 640
Storms, M. C., 625
Storms, M. D., 625, 628
Stothard, K. J., 67
Stout, H. R., 306
Stout, K. D., 444
Straus, M. A., 447
Streeter, C. L., 39, 41
St. Rose, A., 438
Strong, B., 464
Stuart, R. B., 129, 598
Stuhlman, M. W., 230
Sucuzhanay, Jose, 640
Sue, D., 131, 191, 219, 220, 221, 343, 362, 364, 365, 367
Sue, D. W., 131, 191, 219, 220, 221, 343, 362, 364, 365, 367
Sue, S., 362, 364, 365, 367, 451
Suess, G., 151
Suitor, J. J., 702
Sullivan, C. M., 461, 462
Sullivan, Harry Stack, 118, 119, 173
Sullivan, T. J., 277, 562, 570, 657, 723, 724
Sundel, M., 195, 196, 197, 207, 208, 209, 214

Sundel, S. S., 195, 196, 197, 207, 208, 209, 214
Sundowner Offshore Services, 441
Sung, M., 301
Supplemental Nutrition Assistance Program (SNAP), 731
Supplemental Security Income (SSI), 730
Sutherland, E. H., 404
Sutton, P. D., 73
Swaab, D. F., 627
Swigonski, M. E., 641, 642
Symanski, D., 631
Syrop, C. H., 106
Szasz, T. S., 391

T

Tafoya, R., 644
Talbot, M., 629
Tamang, B. L., 130
Tamoxifen, 475
Tanaka, J. S., 451
Tarasoff v. Regents of the University of California, 496
Tardif, C., 150
Task Force for Child Survival and Development (TFCSD), 370
Task Force on Suicide in Canada, 369
Taylor, F. W., 602
Taylor, G., 76
Taylor, R., 238
Taylor, R. D., 230
Teen Lifeline, 370
Tejada, Miguel, 538
Temporary Assistance to Needy Families (TANF), 585–586
Ten Percent Society, 626
Tennant, P. W. G., 67
Teten, A. L., 451
Teunissen, H. A., 301
Tharp, R. G., 232, 681
Thelan, R., 456
Thomas, A., 146
Thomas, C. W., 146
Thomas, J. L., 702
Thomas, K., 139, 140
Thomas, W., 430
Thompson, K., 277, 562, 657, 723, 724
Thompson, L., 556
Thompson, R. A., 149
Thorman, G., 597
Thorndike, E. L., 508
Thornton, L. M., 627
Thrash, R. M., 146
Thurstone, L. L., 152
Tinzmann, M. B., 232
Title IX-Higher Education Amendment, 441
Title IXa, 156
Title XVIII of the Social Security Act, 730
Title XIX of the Social Security Act, 731
Tolman, R. M., 456

Tolstoy, Leo, 657
Toseland, R. W., 16
Toufexis, A., 537
Tower, 32
Towne, N., 509
Tozer, E., 622, 623
Travers, J., 73, 138, 143, 216, 348
Treguer, A., 345
Trenholm, C., 312
Trim, S., 307
Triulzi, F., 69
Troast, T. P., 384, 385, 386, 387, 388, 389
Troop, W., 226
True, M. M., 151
Tucker, J. S., 305
Tuckman, B., 414
Tully, C., 633
Tully, C. T., 620, 626, 631, 635, 644, 648
Turiel, E., 346
Turner, S., 366
Twain, Mark, 378
Tyler, N. C., 156, 167, 168, 169, 172
Tyson, B., 623

U

United Nations, 284, 285, 614
United Nations Program on HIV/AIDS, 314
Universal Declaration of Human Rights, 284
University of California at Davis, 279
University of Kentucky Center for Research on Violence Against Women, 454
University of Wisconsin Board of Regents, 441n3
Unzner, L., 151
Urquiza, A. J., 236
U. S. Census Bureau, 45, 68, 73, 92, 94, 95, 163, 181, 182, 184, 218, 232, 360, 432, 434, 437, 438, 439, 440, 478, 486, 565, 668, 719, 720, 734
U. S. Department of Agriculture, 536
U. S. Department of Education, 161, 165, 436, 440
U. S. Department of Health, Education and Welfare, 729
U. S. Department of Health and Human Services, 161, 729
U. S. Department of Justice, 162
U. S. Food and Drug Administration (FDA), 96
U. S. State Department, 507
U. S. Supreme Court, 442

V

Valdez, Carl, 283
Valencia, M. J., 635
Valente, S. M., 630, 634
Van Den Akker, O. B. A., 103

Van Den Bergh, N., 122, 123
Van Hook, M., 354
Van Ijzendoorn, M. H., 151
van Wormer, K., 341, 634, 644, 645, 647, 648
Vandell, D. L., 65, 67, 68, 75, 137, 139, 140, 146, 148, 150, 226, 227, 232, 251, 360, 364
Vander Zanden, J. W., 141, 142
Vaughan, Clark, 543
Vaughn, N. G., 300
Ventura, S. J., 73, 76
Vgotsky, L. S., 113, 141, 142, 143, 144, 174
Vidaurri, M., 629
Villani, S., 228
Violence against Women Act (VAWA), 460
Virginia Tech, 229
Visher, E. B., 588
Visher, J., 588
Volpe, P., 69
Von Ammon, J., 222
von Goethe, Johann Wolfgang, 657
Vosper, J., 222
Voyer, D., 436

W

Wade, J., 512
Walker, A. J., 556
Walker, L., 349
Walker, L. E., 457, 459
Walker, L. J., 346
Walker, L. S., 457, 458, 462
Walker, M. C., 76
Walsh, A. K., 169
Walsh, F., 191
Ward, C. A., 447
Wark, G. R., 348, 349
Warren, C. W., 447
Wartella, E. A., 228
Waskow, A. I., 257
Watergate, 346
Watkins, M. L., 23
Watson, D. L., 681
Watson, J. B., 144
Watson, J. C., 121
Wauchope, M., 451
Waxman, H. A., 312
Weaver, A., 311
Weaver, H. N., 45, 46, 218, 219, 220
WebbMD, 472
Weber, M., 69
Webster v. Reproductive Health Services, 88
Wedding, D., 248
Wedge, B. J., 71
Week, S. E., 312
Wegscheider, S., 539, 540
Weil, M. O., 45

Weinberg, M. S., 629
Weinstein, K., 702
Weisz, A. N., 348
Weisz, J., 151
Welch, K., 307
Welfare Reform Act, 585
Wells, J., 341, 634, 644, 647, 648
Wen, S. W., 76
Wermiel, S., 89
Wertheimer, D. M., 641
Westberg, G., 706, 707
Western Electric Company, 602
Wheeler, J., 312, 430
White, B. J., 409
White, J. W., 456, 459
White, M., 623
White, R. K., 418
Whiting, B. B., 218
Whitlock, E. P., 67
Whittaker, J. K., 241, 242
Wickrama, K. A., 487
Wightkin, J., 76
Wikan, U., 430
Wikstrom, J., 69
Wilber, K., 354
Wilcox, A. L., 72
Wilensky, H., 611, 613
Williams, D. P., 240
Williams, E., 307
Williams, M. B., 362
Williams, P., 636

Williams, W. L., 430
Wilson, B. J., 228, 229
Wilson, M. N., 217
Wilson, F. L., 349
Wilson, G. T., 119, 195
Wilson-Costello, D., 76
Wind, R., 313
Windle, M., 301
Winkelman, M., 12
Winsler, A., 141
Winton, M. A., 241
Wisconsin Fair Employment Act, 441n2
Witty, M. C., 120
Wolak, J., 245
Wolf, D., 647
Wolfe, D. A., 239
Women Organized Against Rape
    (WOAR), 450
Women's Resource Center, 457
Wong, I., 51
Wood, F. B., 169
Woodman, N. J., 646
Woods, Tiger, 263
Woodward, E. H., 228
Woodward, K. L., 98
World Trade Center, 261
Worthman, C., 301
Wright, R., 277, 562, 657, 723, 724

X

Xiong, X., 76

Y

Yang, S., 157
Yarber, W. L., 64, 67, 68, 69, 97, 104, 107,
    109, 222, 300, 306, 308, 425, 429,
    431, 434, 449, 451, 452, 453, 464
Yarrington, J., 221
Yates, Dr. Laurel, 673
Ybarra, M., 219
Yehl, J. G., 551
Yessian, M. R., 53
Ying, Y., 433
Yochelson, S., 268, 269
Yousef, N., 2

Z

Zajicek, A. M., 126
Zalaquett, C. P., 212
Zambarano, R. J., 629
Zastrow, C., 119n1, 382, 394, 401, 546,
    554
Zayas, L. H., 366
Zea, M. C., 621
Zinn, M. B., 12
Zucker, K. J., 246, 629
Zuckerman, M., 146
Zukor, Adolph, 657
Zuravin, S. J., 238
Zurbriggen, E. L., 447
Zusman, J., 698
Zweigenhaft, R. L., 222

Subject Index

A

ABC approach/AIDS, 494
ABCs of behavior, 197–198
abandonment, 239
Ability levels of men and women, 435–436
abortion, 85
    anti-, 88
    arguments for and against, 97–98
    condition of fetus, 91–92
    condition of mother, 91
    court decisions/government
        restrictions regarding, 86, 88
    dilation and evacuation, 96
    effects on women and men, 97
    empowerment and, 98–99
    ethical dilemmas related to, 99–101
    facts about, 95
    Hyde amendment, 91
    illegal, 96–97
    impacts of macro policies on, 88–94
    impacts of social and economic forces,
        85–101
    importance of context and timing of,
        97
    incidence of, 95
    intact dilation and extraction, 94
    international perspectives on, 90
    late-term, 94
    limiting financial support for, 91
    mandatory counseling for, 89
    medication, 96
    methods of, 96
    NASW policy on, 87
    reasons for, 95
    restricting access to, 89–91
    social work roles and, 98–99
    spontaneous, 72, 484

stem cell research, 92–94
teen, 89, 307
U.S. military and, 91
vacuum aspiration, 96
and viability, 66
violence against clinics, 92
abstinence-only programs, 312–313
abuse. *See* child abuse; elder abuse
academic difficulties, 168
accidental training, 210, 211
acclaim, 12
accommodation, 133
accountability, 52
acculturation, 366, 434
accumulation theory, 666
Accutane, 67
acquaintance rape. *See* date rape
acquired immunodeficiency syndrome.
        See AIDS/HIV
action stage of change, 544
active commitment, 126–127
active euthanasia, 725
active listening, 212–213, 380
activism, 277–278
activist role, 47, 48
activities, 204
activity theory, 696–697
acute stress disorder, 678
adaptation, 34, 35, 133
adaptive assessment
    at age 4 months, 79
    at age 8 months, 80
    at age 1 year, 80
    at age 18 months, 81
    at age 2 years, 81–82
    at age 3 years, 82
    at age 4 years, 83

at age 5 years, 83
at ages 6 to 8 years, 84
at ages 9 to 11 years, 85
adaptive functioning, 158
addictive disorders, 392
addiction, 538
adjourning stage, 414
adjudication, 243
ad hoc committee, 407
Adlerian analysis, 114
adolescence
    abstinence-only sex education
        programs, 312–313
    and assertiveness, 355–359
    body image and self-concept, 300–301
    brain development, 302–303
    contraception, 310
    crime and delinquency, 400–401
    definition of, 297
    and depression, 301
    diversity, 130, 191, 299, 307
    gender intensification/stereotypes, 431
    growth spurt, 298
    health and substance use/abuse,
        303–305
    herd drive, 379
    Hispanic females and suicide, 366
    gangs,, 401–404
    gender intensification, 431
    gender-role stereotyping in, 431–432
    homeless, 382–383
    identity formation, 334–345
    lesbian and gay, 341, 645–646
    life events, 305
    masturbation, 306
    maturation, 301–302
    menarche, diversity and, 299

moral development, 123, 345–350
peer group systems, 379, 382
psychological reactions to physical changes, 300–305
proof of puberty, 298–300
puberty, 297
racial and cultural identity development model, 343
reasons teens get pregnant, 310
rebellion in, 379
secular trend, 298
sex characteristics, 298
sex education and empowerment, 310–315
sex education and Native Americans, 315
sex education and parents, 311–312
sexual activity, 305–315
sexually transmitted infections (STIs), 316–320
social development changes in, 378–383
social problems, 383–388
social work with groups, 406–411
substance use and abuse, 303–305
suicide, 360–370, 645
teenage fathers, 308–310
teenage mothers, 68
unplanned pregnancy in, 307–308
adoption, 104, 307
adrenal glands, 302
adrenalin, 530
adult children, parenting of, 701–702
adult day care, 735
adult foster care, 735
adulthood
gender-role socialization, 432, 434–435
adult protective services, 726, 731–732, 736
adults, single, 193
advocacy
legal, 462
policy, 49
self, 165
social, 49
advocate role, 54
and abortion, 98–99
with battered women, 462, 463
against discrimination, 291
and family problems, 600
in feminist theories, 124
with gangs, 406
and infertility, 108
for LGBT clients, 649
with older people, 735
and people with ADHD and learning disabilities, 173
and people with developmental disabilities, 164
person-in-environment focus, 24
prenatal care, 71
in social action model, 47, 48
aesthetic value orientation, 610

affirmative action, 278–280
afterbirth, 73
afterlife, 713
Africa
and AIDS, 495
infants in, 151
parents in East, 148
African Americans
adolescence, 191, 301, 307
and adolescent sexual activity, 307
Afrocentric perspective, 274, 276
and breast cancer, 473
and death, 478
economic inequality for, 437
ethnic identity, 342
gender-role socialization and, 429, 433
grandparents, 191
history and culture of, 272–273
and hypertension, 472
identity development, 191
infant mortality rate, 285
institutional racism, 264
and Kwanzaa, 274, 275
menarche, 299
one-parent families, 583
parenting, 217
poverty and female, old, 692, 722
and religion/spirituality, 273, 288–289, 693
Rosa Parks & civil rights movement for, 277–278
and schools, 232–233, 272
and self-concept, 274
sexual activity, 307
and sexual orientation, 644
sickle-cell anemia, 667
single-parenting, 273
slavery, 254, 257, 272
stereotyping, 271
strengths of, 273, 286
and suicide, 360
surrogate parenting, 191
victim system, 267
violence against, 257
worldview, 131, 274, 276
Afrocentric perspective, 274, 276
age
characteristics of different levels of, 78
and pregnancy, 68
and productivity, 657
ageism
definition of, 691
and low status, 691
agency services for LGBT clients, 650
aging. See also later adulthood; older adults
adjusting to, 191–192
and diversity, 192
double standard of, 479
factors that influence, 666–670
fear of, 485

genetic theories on, 666
health practices and longevity, 668
lesbian and gay men, 648–649
new view on, 658
nongenetic cellular theories on, 666
physiological theories on, 666
the process of, 658–665
senility, 661
and sexual response, 664
theories for successful, 696–698
values and, 661
what causes, 665–666
and woman's fertility, 102
agitator role, 47, 48
aggressive communication, 356–358
AI (artificial insemination), 104–105, 107
AIDS/HIV, 319
and Americans with Disabilities Act, 496
causes, 492
diagnosis, 493
discrimination and oppression, 494–495
and drug abuse, 532, 534
duty to inform, 496
effects of, 493
gay and lesbian people and, 649–650
a global epidemic, 495
HAART, 494
how is it contracted, 492–493
impact on family life cycle, 190
people living with, 491–496
and pregnancy, 69
professional values and, 495–496
social and economic forces and, 494–495
treatment and prevention of, 494
Vida Sida, 45
AIDS-dementia complex, 493
alarm phase, 675, 676
Alaskan Natives and suicide, 360
alcohol/alcoholism, 524, 667
an AA meeting, 541
and adolescents, 303–305
codependency, 546
denial, 539, 540, 544–546
dependence on, 477, 538–539
drinking age, 526
effects of, 525, 526–527
facts and effects, 525
interactions in families, 539–540
motivational interviewing, 544–546
and pregnancy, 67–68
reasons people use and abuse, 538–539
risk factors, 304
self-help groups, 541, 546
social work roles, 405, 544, 546
treatment, 540–546
who drinks, 524, 526
in young adulthood, 476–477
Alianza Escolar program, 45
alpha-fetoprotein (AFP), 70

alternatives, identifying and evaluating, 7
Alzheimer's disease, 93n9, 667, 669–670
American Indian. *See* Native Americans
American Muslims, 261–262
amniocentesis, 69
amphetamines, 525, 529–530
amyl nitrate, 525, 532
amyloid, 670
amyloid precursor protein (APP), 670
anabolic steroids, 525, 537–538
analgesics, 533
anal stage, 116
analyst/evaluator role. *See also* evaluator
   role
   and discrimination, 291
   with gangs, 406
   in infertility counseling, 108
   in social planning model, 44
analytic psychology, 118
androgens, 428, 485
androgeny, 465
anemia, 67, 104
anger rapist, 451
Anglo-conformity, 292
angry cry, 145
anomie, 404
anomie theory, 404
anorexia nervosa, 383–385, 392
Antabuse, 543
antagonistic response, 527
antecedents, 197
antianxiety drugs, 678
anticipate, RAP framework, 410
anticipation stage, 557
antidepressant medications, 67
antihomosexual/antigay, 630
antiretroviral drugs, 494
antisocial acts, 391
anxiety disorders, 392
anxiety reduction, 248
anxious-avoidant attachment, 149, 151
anxious-resistant attachment, 149, 151
apartheid, 267
Apgar scale, 75
appreciation stage, 577
Arabs/Arab Americans, 256
   discrimination against, 261–262
   gender-role development, 433
arbitrator and mediator role, 419
Aricept, 670
aromatese inhibitors, 475
artificial insemination (AI), 104–105, 107
Asia and AIDS, 495
Asian Americans, 220–221
   and adolescent sexual activity, 307
   and breast cancer, 473
   ethnic identity, 342
   families, 220–221
   and gender-role development, 433
   hierarchical relationships, 221
   identity development, 191, 340, 343

and interdependence, 221, 340
   patriarchal hierarchy in, 221, 433
   and sexual orientation, 644
   stereotyping, 270
Asian Indians, 220
Asian Pacific Island families, 217, 220
Asperger syndrome, 167
assertive communication, 356–358
assertiveness, 574
   advantages of, 358
   definition of, 355
   empowerment through, 355–359
   relevance of, 355–356
   rights, 356
   in social work practice, 359
   and suicide, 355
assertiveness training, 358–359
   definition of, 355
   empowerment through, 355–359, 464
assessment
   bio-psycho-social, 21–22
   of child abuse, 31–32, 242
   definition of, 3, 4
   of developmental milestones, 79–85
   of deviant behavior, 398–399
   of family systems, 590–600
   of human behavior, 31
   importance of, 6
   of infertility, 103
   instruments, 592–597
   newborn, 74–75
   prenatal, 69–70
   relationship between knowledge and,
      546–547
   of strengths, 17
   of unwanted emotions, 394
asset-based community development,
   281–284
assimilation, 133, 218, 257, 292
assisted-living facilities, 733
Assisted Reproductive Technology
   (ART), 105–106, 107
assisted suicide/death, 725–726
associative play, 223
attachment, 147
   cross-cultural differences in, 151
   and day care, 150
   long-term effects of, 150
   patterns of, 149–150
   qualities of, 149
   stages of, 147
attention
   negative, 139, 210
   parental, 212–213
   selective, 139
attention-deficit hyperactivity disorder
   (ADHD), 76n5, 172–173, 667
   social work roles with, 173
   treatment for, 172–173
attraction/infatuation stage, 577
auditory processing difficulties, 168

auditory systems, 511
Australia,
   and low birth weight, 76
   and suicide rate, 360
authoritarianism, 265
authoritarian leaders, 418
authoritarian parenting, 215
authoritarian personality, 265
authoritative parenting, 216
autism, 2, 167
autistic spectrum disorders (ASD), 167
autocratic model, 600
autonomy, 183
autonomy versus shame and doubt stage,
   335
AZT (azidothymidine), 69
azithromycin, 316
Aztecs, 345

B

Babinski reflex, 77
baby, coming of a new, 216–217
baby boomers, 720
Bales model, 415
Bali, 705
barbiturates, 525, 527
barrio, code of the, 403
basal body temperature method, 102, 328
baseball, drug use in, 538
baseline, 212
basic cry, 145
basic trust versus basic mistrust stage, 335
battered woman syndrome, 455
battered women, 455–463
   abusive perpetrator, 456–457
   battering cycle, 457
   community responses to empower,
      459–463
   counseling strategies to empower,
      462–463
   in gay and lesbian relationships, 459
   incidence of, 456
   myths about, 455
   reasons for staying, 457–459
   shelters, 461–462
   strategies for empowerment and
      sexual equality, 465
batterer's intervention programs, 462
battering
   cycle, 457
   definition of, 455
   in gay and lesbian relationships, 459
Baumrind system, 217
behavior, 197
   ABCs of, 197–198
   changing deviant, 398–399
   consequences of recurring, 198
   goal-directed, 134
   indicators of abuse, 236
   measuring improvement of, 211–212
   our thinking determines our, 400

play, 223
preening, 512
shaping, 207
specific terminology, 210
total, 519
behavior checklist/chart, 212
behavior modification, 172–173, 195,
208–209, 599
behavioral and emotional problems,
390–394
behavioral theories, 119
with Alzheimer's clients, 670
on drug use, 539
See also learning theories
Belgium, 726
belongingness and love need, 505
benign lumps, 473
berdache, 430
bereavement, cultural-historical context
of death and, 705
binge-eating disorder, 392
biofeedback, 681–682
biological development, 8
biological insults, 667
biological theories
on drug use, 539
on homosexuality, 627–628
biopsy, 474
bio-psycho-social assessments, values and
ethics applied to, 21–22
bio-psycho-social development, 9–10
bipolar disorder, 91, 392
birth control patch, 322–323
birth control pill, 66, 320–322
and breast cancer, 473
birth control sponge, 327
birth defects, 75
birth order, 221–222
birth process, 72–77
natural, 73–74
premature, 75–77
positions, 73, 74
stages of labor, 72–73
birth weight, 75–77
international perspective, 76
low, 75–77, 308
bisexuality. *See also* gay men; lesbian
Code of Ethics (NASW), 618
definition of, 622–626
and homosexuality, 619–626
Blackfoot children, 342
blaming the victim in poverty, 566, 569,
612
blastocyst, 65
blended families, 182, 584, 586–589
blindness, 167
blood poisoning, 70
board of directors, 50n3, 407
bodegas, 219
body beautiful cult, 479

body image and self-concept, 300–301
body orientation, 510
body posture, 358
body transcendence, 689–690
Bolivian forest, 717
BOOM (becoming one's own man) phase,
504
Boston Tea Party, 728
botanicas, 219
Botswana, 145
boundaries, 27, 35, 183, 186, 189
boycotts, 47
brain, hemispheres, 522
brain development and adolescence,
302–303
brain (anatomical) factors, 627
Braxton-Hicks contractions, 72
Brazelton Neonatal Behavioral
Assessment Scale, 75
Brazil, 283
BRCA1 and 2 genes, 472
breast cancer, 472–476, 667
benign lumps, 472
early detection of, 476
incidence of, 472
risk factors, 472–473
suspicion of, 473
symptoms, 472
treatment of, 474–475
breast reconstruction, 475
breast self-examination (BSE), 476
breasts, development of, 299–300
breech presentation, 73, 74
broker role, 53–54
and abortion, 98
and addiction, 544
and codependency, 546
and discrimination, 291
with family problems, 599
and gangs, 405
and grief management, 709
and infertility, 108
with older people, 735
and people with ADHD and learning
disabilities, 173
and people with developmental
disabilities, 164
in person-in-environment focus, 24
with pregnant women, 76
in social action model, 47, 48
and stress management, 683
Buddhism, 130, 696
bulimia nervosa, 385–387, 392
bullying, 226–228, 362
bureaucracy, 606–609
behavior patterns in a, 608
how to survive, 608–609
value conflicts, 607
burnout, 501
bus rate reductions, 733

business, minority-owned, 281
butyl nitrate, 525, 532

C
caffeine, 525, 529
calendar method, 328
Cambodians, 220
and abortion, 90
Canada
asset-based community development,
283
battering and sexual assault in, 456
Canadian Association of Social
Workers' Code of Ethics, 19
death rate in, 478
infants/mothers in, 148
sex education, 311
suicide, 360, 369–370
teen pregnancy, 307
women and menopause in, 483
cancer, therapy group for spouses of
adults with, 412
cannabis, 525, 536
care perspective, 347
career-long learning, 302
Caribbean families, 217
cartoons and violence, 228
case/care manager, 173, 405, 735. *See also*
manger role
case worker, 7
casinos, Native American, 282
caste system, 272
castration anxiety, 117
catalyst role, 43
cataracts, 658–659
Cattell's fluid and crystallized intelligence,
153
caucus, 575
celibacy, 491
centenarians, 673
centration, 135
cephalocaudal development, 78
cephalopelvic disproportion, 153
cerebral palsy, 167
cerebrum, 522
cervical cancer, 319
cervical cap, 326–327
cervical mucus (ovulation) method,
328
cervix, 317
cesarean (C) section, 73
challenge and change stage, 414
chancre, 317
change-of-life babies, 484
charisma, 416
charismatic leader, 416
chemical substance. *See* substance use and
abuse
chemotherapy, 475
Cherokee nation, 257, 315

Chicano/Chicana, 45–46, 288, 345
Chicano Initiative (CI), 46
chief enabler, 540
child abuse. *See also* child maltreatment;
  child neglect
    behavioral indicators of, 31–32, 236
    case example of, 29–33
    characteristics of abusers, 236–237
    characteristics of physical, 234–236
    diverse cultural contexts, 235
    environmental factors, 32
    and family social functioning, 32
    physical indicators of physical, 31
    resources for, 32
childbirth. *See* birth process
    natural, 73–74
child care, 590
child custody. *See* custody
childless couples, 107, 557–558
child maltreatment, 233–249
    characteristics of abusers, 236–237
    characteristics of neglect, 238–240
    characteristics of neglectful parents,
      240
    characteristics of perpetrators of psy-
      chological maltreatment, 241
    characteristics of physically abused
      victims, 234–236
    characteristics of psychologically
      maltreated, 241
    child protective services (CPS), 241–242
    cultural context: discipline or abuse,
      235
    definition of, 233
    ethical questions, 33
    incidence of, 234
    involvement of courts, 243
    macro system response, 241–242, 243,
      249
    neglect, 237–238
    physical child abuse, 31, 234–237
    psychological maltreatment, 240–241
    sexual abuse, 243–249. (*See also* sex-
      ual abuse)
    social work role, 242–243, 247–249
    treatment of, 242–243, 247–249
child neglect, 237–240
    characteristics of, 238–240
    characteristics of parents, 240
child protective services (CPS), 234, 241
children
    attachment, 147, 149–150, 151
    and attention deficit hyperactivity
      disorder, 76n5, 172–173
    birth order, 221–222
    bullying, 226–228
    categories of temperament, 146–147
    communication between parents and,
      380–382
    cultural values and, 190, 217–221, 232
    day care, 184

development from 4 months to 11
    years, 79–85
  disabilities that affect, 167
  of divorce, 580–583
  domestic violence services, 462
  educating about sexual abuse, 247, 249
  family life cycle, 190
  first-born, 221
  gender-role socialization, 222
  gender-role stereotyping in, 431
  influence of television/media on, 228–230
  later-born, 221–222
  launching, 191
  and learning disabilities, 164–172
  life events that affect, 215–222
  only, 222
  parenting styles for, 215–216
  play, 222–226
  peer group and popularity, 224–226
  school environment and, 230–233
  sibling subsystems, 216–217, 221
  social environment, 230–233
  socialization of, 180
  teacher's impact, 230
China
  and abortion, 90
  and AIDS, 495
  and dealing with death, 705
  high status for older people in, 719
  one-child policy, 433
Chinese/Chinese Americans, 220, 221, 271
  approach to medicine, 672
  gender-role socialization, 433
  infants/mothers, 148
  parenting, 217, 299
  violence against, 257
chlamydia, 102, 316
choice theory, 518–522
cholesterol, 477
cholinesterase inhibitors, 670
chorionic villi, 70
chorionic villi sampling (CVS), 69, 70
Christianity, 261, 695
chromosome, 64
church, 693. *See* religion; spirituality
cilia, 64
cinco de Mayo, 219
cirrhosis, 477, 526
civil rights, 20
civil rights movement/laws, 47, 277
  Rosa Parks and, 277, 278
  and sexual harassment, 440
civil union, 637
Civil War, 257, 266, 272
classic autism, 167
classical conditioning. *See* respondent
  conditioning
classification, 135
classroom environment, 230–233
client-centered therapy. *See* person-
  centered therapy

climacteric. *See* menopause; male
  climacteric
clinical breast exam (CBE), 476
clitoris, 299, 663
Clomid, 104
clothing, 513
closed-channel thinking, 268, 269
club sociales, 219
cocaine, 525, 530–531
code of the barrio, 403
Code of Ethics, 19
  and abortion, 99
  on discrimination, 270, 290
  ethical principles, 19
  ethical responsibilities, 21
  evaluation of theory, 128
  and Gilligan's theory, 349
  self-determination, 618
  sexual orientation, 618
codependency, 546
cognition, 129, 144, 197, 398–399
cognitive ability, developing, 135–136
cognitive-behavioral therapy, 248, 623,
  678
cognitive characteristics, 167–168
cognitive development, 129, 132–144
  critical thinking about, 137–138,
    143–144
  Piaget's theory, 129, 132–138
  Piaget's four stages of, 133–137
  information-processing, conception
    of, 138–141
  Vygotsky's theory of sociocultural,
    141–144
cognitive functioning and middle adulthood, 482
cognitive training, 170
cohabitation, 182, 553, 555
collective unconscious, 118
collectivism, 142
collegial model, 604
collisions of values, 381–382
Colombia
  and abortion, 90
  and drugs, 529, 533
color, people of, 11
comadrazgo, 288
Comanche, 192
combined hormone therapy, 473
combined pill, 320–321
coming out, 341, 642–645, 647
committee, 407
common-law marriage, 555
communication
  in families, 183
  male/female differences in, 436
  nonassertive, assertive, and aggressive,
    356–358
  between parents and children, 380–382
  verbal and nonverbal, 509–518,
    590–591

communities
 and racial and cultural identity
  development, 344–345
 resiliency in, 18
community
 abundant, 16–17
 definition of, 36, 38
 empowerment, 16, 369–370
 gay and lesbian, 634
 strengths of, 16, 17
community-based services, 164
community capacity development, 49
community change models, 43–49
 characteristics of, 48
 contemporary conceptual frameworks, 49
 locality development model, 43–44, 48
 social action model, 47–48
 social planning model, 44, 46–47, 48
community conceptual frameworks,
  38–43
 human ecology perspective, 41–42
 sociopsychological perspective, 40
 social systems perspective, 42–43
 structural perspective, 39–40
community development
 asset-based, 281–284
 deficiency model, 281–282
 Latino and Hispanic, 45–46
 social work roles and, 43
 See also locality development
community disengagement theory, 697
community disorganization and gangs,
  406
community macro systems
 discrimination and oppression in, 264
 human behavior and, 38–49
 responses to empower battered
  women, 459–463
 strategies to promote social and
  economic justice, 276–281
community mobilization, 406
community organizer, 7
community residential facilities (CRFs),
  164
community system, 30, 32, 52
community theory, 37–38
community of wellness, 45
como familial, 219
compadrazo, 219, 288
compatibility theory, 551
compensation, 116
competencies, 5, 55–57
competition, 41
 and exploitation, 265–266
complementary needs theory, 551
componential element, 153
compulsions, 118
compulsive overeating, 387–388, 392
Comunidad de Bienestar, 45
conception, 64–65

conceptus, 65
concordance rate, 391, 627
concrete operations period, 136
concurrent disabilities, 167
conditioned stimulus, 195, 202
conditions of worth, 120
condom, 325
 female, 325–326
confidentiality, 19
conflict, 381, 573
conflict gangs, 402–403
conflict-habituated relationship, 572
conflict perspective/theory, 560–561
 on poverty, 571
conflict resolution strategies, 410, 573–576
conformity stage, 343
confrontation, 47
congregate housing facilities, 733
congruence in values theory, 551
congruent, 121
congruent communication, 591
conjunctive faith, 352
conscience, 115
conscious, 114
consequence
 of punishment, 207–208
 and recurring behavior, 198
conservation, 132, 133, 136
conservative perspective, 611–612
consultant role, 24, 173, 382, 683
consumables, nonfood, 203–204
consumer-directed approach, 165
contemplation stage of change, 544
contemporary life events approach, 487
contextual element, 153
continued-care retirement communities,
  733
continuous reinforcement, 206
contraception, 320–330
 birth control patch, 322–323
 birth control pills, 320–322, 473
 birth control sponge, 327
 cervical cap, 326–327
 contraceptive sponge, 327
 depo-provera injections, 323
 diaphragm, 326–327
 emergency contraception (EC), 323–324
 female condom, 325–326
 fertility awareness methods, 328–329
 hormonal implants, 323
 intrauterine device (IUD), 327–328
 male condom, 325
 methods of the future, 329–330
 spray-on, 330
 sterilization, 329
 vaginal ring, 322–323
 vaginal spermicides, 324–325
 withdrawal, 328
contraceptive sponge, 327
contraceptive vaccines, 329
contracts, 29

controller of internal relations role, 419
control theories, 405
conventional level, 345–346
conversion therapy, 623
cooperation, social, 220
cooperative play, 223
Copper T, 327
coordinator role, 173
 in communities and organizations, 53
 with people with developmental disabilities, 164
 against discrimination, 291
 in locality development, 43, 48
 in person-in-environment focus, 24
coping, 34–35, 128, 340
 with grief, 708
 in later adulthood, 704
 poor skills for, 237
coping strategies, 546
core needle biopsy, 474
corrupting behavior, 241
Council on Social Work Education. *See*
  competencies; Educational Policy
  and Accreditation Standards (EPAS)
  goals/purpose of social work, 24–25
counselor role, 405
 and addiction, 544
 and codependency, 546
 and discrimination, 291
 for empowering battered women,
  462–463
 and grief management, 708
 with LGBT people, 650
 with older people, 735
 and stress management, 683
Couple's Pre-Counseling Inventory, 598
courts and child maltreatment, 243
Cowper's glands, 328, 663
crack, 525, 531–532
 babies, 532
creative disorder, politics of, 277
Creek tribe and older adults, 717
crime
 causes and treatment, 401
 and delinquency, 400–401
 hate/message, 641
 older victims, 727
criminal justice and racism, 264
criminal gangs, 402
criminal thinking, is racial discrimination
  based on, 268–269
 overview of, 268
 thinking errors, 269
crisis intervention, 369–370, 735
crisis telephone lines, 370, 462
critical thinking
 definition of, 19, 25, 118
 ethical issues, 18, 21–22
 evaluation of Fowler's theory, 352–353
 evaluation of Gilligan's theory,
  348–349

evaluation of identity formation theories, 340
evaluation of Kohlberg's theory, 346–347
evaluation of learning theory, 195
evaluation of Piaget's theory, 137–138
evaluation of psychodynamic theory, 118
evaluation of theory, 127–128
evaluation of Vygotsky's theory, 143–144
relevance of theory to social work, 127–129
cross-cultural, 12
    attachment differences, 151
    context of death and bereavement, 705
    gender-role development, 433–434
    infants' expectations and temperament, 148
    longevity differences, 673
    nonverbal communication, 510
    orientation, 12
    social work, 287
    women's experience with menopause, 483
Crow tribe and older members, 717
crying, types of, 144–145
crystallized intelligence, 153
C-section. See cesarean section
Cuba/Cuban Americans, 218
    and abortion, 90
    families, 218
cult/occult gang, 403
cultural biases and IQ tests, 157
cultural competency, 11–13, 25
    definition of, 12
cultural context and parenting style, 217
cultural differences
    bereavement and death, historical context, 705
    in families, 218–221
    in menopause, 483
    in nonverbal communication, 510
cultural feminism, 124
cultural identity, 342
cultural lag, 560
cultural pluralism, 218, 292
cultural values, 218
    and children, 190
    and educational programming, 232
culturally competent practice, 286–290
culture, 130
    African American history and, 272–273
    definition of, 12
    and interdependence/independence, 142
    learning group, 288–289
    race, ethnicity, and identity development, 340–345
culture of poverty theory, 568–569
curandera, 16
curettage, 96

custodial model, 600–602
custody, 576, 580
    joint, 576, 580
    legal, 580
    lesbian and gay parents and child, 639–640
cycle of poverty, 567, 568
cystic fibrosis, 667
cysts, 472

D
date rape, 452
    drugs, 449, 529
day care
    aspects of good, 150
    and attachment, 150
    and families, 184
    for older people, 733, 735
death, 724
    accepting the prospect of, 688
    assisted suicide/death, 725–726
    and bereavement, cultural-historical context of, 705
    celebration of life funerals, 709
    dealing with, 192–193
    differential incidence of, 478
    with dignity, 192–193
    diseases and causes of, 666–670
    and diversity, 725
    drug-related, 528
    feeding tube questions and, 712
    funerals, 705, 709
    grief management and, 704–713
    grieving process, 706–707
    hospice, 724
    how to become comfortable with your own eventual, 710, 712–713
    how to relate to a person facing, 709–710
    how to relate to survivors, 710
    impacts of social forces, 705–706
    Kübler-Ross model, 706, 707
    leading causes of, 668
    life after life, 713
    poverty and, 478
    questions about, grief, dying, and, 711
    right to, 725–726
    social work and, 708–710
    of a spouse, 687, 699
    Westberg model, 706–707
    of young adults, 478
decision-making groups, 407–408
deconstruction, 125
deep-breathing relaxation, 680
de facto discrimination, 259
defense mechanisms, 115–116, 121, 265, 539
deferred gratification, 569
deinstitutionalization, 163–164
de jure discrimination, 259
delegating behavior, 416

delinquency, crime and, 400–401
delinquent gangs, 401–404
delirium tremens (DTs), 527
democratic leadership, 418
democratic party, 611
denial, 116, 539, 540, 544
dental dam, 319
dependence
    drug, 538–539
    movement to independence, 378–379
dependency ratio, 723
depo-provera injections, 323
depressant drugs, 524–529
depression
    in adolescence, 301
    and eating disorders, 388
    and estrogen cycle, 301
    in later adulthood, 691–693
    and male climacteric, 486
depressive disorder, 364, 392
designated leader, 419
Desoxyn, 530
despair, 336, 689
detached worker, 405
deterioration of brain, personality changes, 391
development
    bio-psycho-social, 9
    cephalocaudal/proximodistal, 78
    emotional, 144–150
    theories of psychological, 114–127
developmental lags, 32, 236
developmental milestones, 10–11, 77–79
    growth as a continuous orderly process, 78
    nature-nurture controversy, 78–79
    profiles of normal, 79–85
    relevance to social work, 79
developmental perspective, 613
developmental tasks of later adulthood, 687–689
    theoretical concepts about, 689–696
deviant behavior, 398–399
deviant subcultures theory, 404
devitalized relationship, 572
diaphragm, 326–327
die, right to, 725–726
diet, 674. See also nutrition
differential association theory, 404
differentiation, 29, 32, 35, 188–189
differentiation stage, 413–414
difficult children, 146
diffused identity, 342
dilation, 72
dilation and evacuation (D & E), 96
direct instruction, 170
direct sperm injection, 106, 107. See intracytoplasmic sperm injection
disappointment/disillusionment stage, 577
disarming, 574
discipline or abuse, 235

discrepancy, develop, 545
discrimination
    affirmative action programs, 278–280
    AIDS, 494–495
    against Arab Americans and
        American Muslims, 261–262
    aspects/impacts of social and
        economic forces, 258–259
    is it based on criminal thinking, 268–269
    defacto/dejure, 259
    definition of, 11, 258, 424
    effects and costs of, 267, 270
    effects on development of self-concept,
        274
    effects on human growth and
        development, 267, 270
    and employment of GLBT people,
        633, 635
    and employment of older people, 718
    evaluation of theories, 267
    homophobia, 630
    institutional, 263–264
    in macro systems, 263–264
    NASW policy on oppression and, 290
    prejudiced/nonprejudiced, 258, 269
    is the problem of whites, 259–260
    racial and ethnic, 259–260
    reverse, 279
    social work roles for countering,
        290–291
    sources of prejudice and, 264–267
    types of, 258
diseases and causes of death, 666–670
disengagement stage, 557
disengagement theory, 10, 697
disorder, politics of, 277
disorganized attachment, 149–150
disposition, 243
disruptive, impulse-control and conduct
    disorders, 392
dissociative disorders, 392
dissonance stage, 343
distant figure grandparents, 702
distress, 677
distributed-functions approach, 418–419
diversity, 10, 11–13, 25
    effects of abortion on women and
        men, 97
    in adolescent sexual activity, 307
    AIDS, a global epidemic, 495
    Americans with Disabilities Act,
        162–163
    Arab Americans and American
        Muslims, discrimination against,
        261–262
    aspects of, 10
    attachment differences, 151
    battering in gay and lesbian
        relationships, 459
    cross-cultural differences in
        attachment, 151

cross-cultural diversity in expectations
    and temperament, 148
cross-cultural perspective on gender-
    role development, 433–434
cross-cultural research on centenar-
    ians, 673
cultural biases and IQ tests, 157
cultural context and parenting style, 217
death and bereavement, cultural-
    historical context of, 705
death, differential incidence of, 478
disabilities that can affect children, 167
discipline or abuse and diverse cultural
    contexts, 235
educational programming and cultural
    values, 232
empowerment through appreciation of
    strengths, 218–221
empowerment and a consumer-
    directed approach, 165
empowerment through sex education
    for Native Americans, 315
ethnic and cultural differences in
    families, 218–221
ethnicity and sexual orientation, 644
evidence-based practice, spirituality
    and, 354
family life cycle, 190–194
in feminism, 124–126
feminist perspective on infertility
    counseling and empowerment, 109
gay and lesbian pride, 634
gender expression, 430
gender/racial comparison of median
    weekly earnings, 437
high status of older people in other
    countries, 719
homophobia, 630–631
intellectual disabilities, 159–160
international perspectives on abortion
    policy, 90
intersectionality and, 125–126
Kwanzaa, 275
Latino and Hispanic communities,
    45–46
lesbian and gay adolescents and
    empowerment, 341
lesbian and gay people, social work
    with, 650
Levinson's theories applied to women,
    506
and menarche, 299
menopause, cultural differences in
    women's experience of, 483
multicultural, 271
personal income disparities, 563
poverty perpetuates poverty, 567
productivity of noted older people, 657
and psychological theories, 130–132
race, culture, ethnicity, and identity
    development, 340, 342–345

racial discrimination based on crimi-
    nal thinking, 268–269
RAP framework for leading
    multiracial groups, 410
Rosa Parks and Civil Rights
    Movement, 278
and schools, 232
social work with LGBT people—
    optimal well-being, 650
sociocultural learning, 142
spirituality, 132, 350–351
spirituality and religion, 694–696
strengths perspective, 132
and suicide, 360, 366
suicide and adolescent Hispanic
    females, 366
transsexual and transgender people,
    624
triple jeopardy: being female, African
    American, and old, 692
violence against minorities in the U.S.,
    257–258
Vygotsky's theory, 142
women and sexual equality, strategies
    for empowering, 465
worldview, 131–132
divorce, 576–583
    children of, 580–583
    consequences of, 579–580
    facts about, 184, 579
    marriage counseling, 583
    mediation, 583
    reasons for, 576, 578–579
    sex following, 490–491
    social work roles, 583
Dogan mothers, 151
domestic partnership, 637
domestic violence, 455–463. *See also* bat-
    tered women
dominant/sustaining system, 285–286
Dominican, 46, 218
Don't ask, don't tell, don't pursue repeal,
    635–636
dopamine, 302
Down syndrome, 68n1, 70, 75, 484, 670
doxycycline, 316
drag kings, 430
drag queens, 430
dream, 503, 506
drug abuse, 525. *See also* substance abuse
    definition of, 524
drug addiction, definition of, 538
drug tourism, 547
drugs
    date rape, 449, 529
    definitions of, 524
    medication, and pregnancy, 67
DTs (delirium tremens), 527
dual perspective, 285–286
ductogram, 474
Dutch drug policy, 547

E

early adulthood era/transition, 503
early retirement, 721–722
East Africa, 148
easy children, 146
eating disorders, 383–388, 392
    causes of, 388–389
    impacts of social forces, 389
    interrelationships among, 388
    set point theory, 389
    treatment of, 389–390
eclampsia, 71
ecological perspective, concepts of, 33–35, 128
ecomap, 592–595
economic forces
    abortion, 85–101
    and AIDS discrimination and oppression, 494–495
    early retirement, 721–722
    legal empowerment and social justice—lesbian and gay people, 633–650
    lesbian and gay people, 633–650
    and older adults, 719
    prejudice, discrimination and oppression, 258–259, 267, 270
    and poverty, 563–572
economic independence, 379
economic inequality, 563
    between men and women, 437–440
economic justice
    Americans with Disabilities Act, 162–163
    community strategies to promote, 276–281
    definition of, 25
    macro systems, families, social and, 183–184
economic value orientation, 610
ecosystems theory, 23–35
    concept summary, 35
    definition, 23
ecstasy, 525, 535
ectopic pregnancy, 70, 72, 101, 322
Ecuador, 46
    asset-based community development, 283
educational groups, 407
educational neglect, 238–239
Educational Policy and Accreditation Standards. See EPAS
educational programming, 232
educator/teacher role, 53
    and abortion, 98
    and addiction, 544
    and codependency, 546
    and discrimination, 291
    with gangs, 405, 406
    and infertility, 108
    with people with developmental disabilities, 164

and stress management, 683
egalitarianism, 123
ego, 114, 115, 117
ego psychologists, 118
egocentrism, 134–135, 138
ego integrity versus despair stage, 336
Egypt
    asset mobilization, 283
    death in, 705
EI test, 507
eighteen-month olds, 81
eight-month olds, 79–80
eight-year olds, 84–85
85/15 rule, 606
ejaculation, 64
elaboration, 141
elder abuse, 724, 726
elderly. See aging; later adulthood; older adults
electra complex, 117, 118
eleven-year olds, 85
elimination disorders, 392
Ella, 324
El Salvador and abortion, 90
embeddedness, 126
embryo, 65
embryo and transplants, 106, 107
embryonic stem cells, 93
embryonic stem cell lines, 93
emergency contraception (EC), 323–324
emotion, 144–145
emotional and behavioral problems, 390–394
    assessing and treating, 394–400
    changing unwanted, 395–399
    destructive ways to change, 398
    major mental disorders, 392–393
    rational self-analysis, 394–398
emotional development, 144–150
emotional flexibility versus emotional impoverishment, 501
emotional independence, 379
emotional intelligence (EI), 507–508
emotional love languages, 489
emotions, 144
    infants', 144–145
    thinking determines, 400
empathy, 544, 573–574
    lack of, 268, 269
    of servant leader, 419
empirical research and spirituality, 354
employee assistance programs, 526
employment
    LGBT, 633, 635
    held by women, 439
empowerment, 13–16
    and abortion, 98–99
    and alcoholic client, 546
    and assertiveness and assertiveness training, 355–359
    for battered women, 459–463

community, 16
community suicide prevention and crisis intervention, 369–370
and consumer-directed approach, 165
counseling rape survivors, 453–455
definition of, 14, 25, 123, 406
ethnic and cultural differences in families and, 218–221
ethnic and racial groups and, 286
feminist perspective, 109, 123
gay and lesbian pride and community, 634
through groups, 16, 406–419
of homeless youth, 382–383
individual, 16
and infertility, 107–108
Latino and Hispanic communities promote, 45–46
lesbian and gay adolescents, 341
lesbian and gay legal, 633–650
lesbian and gay parents, 646–648
organizational, 16
for people with intellectual disabilities, 158–164, 165
practice, 191
for rape survivors, 453–455
self-concept, self-esteem, and, 150–152
and sex education, 310–315
through sex education for Native Americans, 315
through social work with groups, 406–419
through spiritual development, 353–354
stress management, 677–683
suicide prevention, 369–370
types of, 16
for women, 463–464, 465
empty-nest syndrome, 191, 486
empty-shell marriages, 100, 372–376, 583
enabler role
    and abortion, 98
    and gangs, 406
    and infertility, 107–108
    in locality development, 43, 48
    in organizations and communities, 53
    with people with developmental disabilities, 164
    and person-in-environment focus, 24
    analytic psychology, 118
encounter groups, 411
endometrial cancer, 322
endometriosis, 102
endometrium, 322
energy, definition of, 33–34, 35
entropy, 29, 31, 35, 188, 189
    negative, 29, 33, 35, 188, 189
environment
    definition of, 3
    nonverbal communication, 517–518
    shifting, 51–52
environmental factors

and aging, 667
and child abuse, 32
and substance abuse, 304
EPAS (Educational Policy and Accreditation Standards)
competencies, 5, 55–57
on diversity, 271, 290–291
generalist social work definition, 7
on human rights, 284
on marginalization, 566
on racism, 290–291
on social and economic justice, 290–291
on spirituality, 694
epididymis/epididymitis, 316
epilepsy/seizure disorder, 167
episiotomy, 72
epistemology, 125
equifinality, 29, 32, 35, 188, 189
equilibrium, 559
eras and transitional periods, 503–505
erectile dysfunction, 665
Erikson's psychosocial theory, 334–339, 559
concept summary, 336
critical thinking about, 340
evaluation of, 340
during young and middle adulthood, 500–501
escape, politics of, 277
Eskimos, 717, 721
espiritismo, 644
estrogen, 298
cycle and depression, 301
synthetic, 320
ether, 526
ethical dilemmas, 19, 25
and morality, 350
related to abortion, 99–101
blaming the poor, 612
duty to inform about HIV, 496
feeding tube, whether to insert, 712
genetic testing, 667
to marry if not in love, 551
Native American casinos, 282
punishing or treating drug users, 547
a right to die, 725–726
ethical issues, 18–22
disengagement theory, 697
about homosexuality theories, 629
ethical principles, 19
screen, 99–101
ethical questions
abortion, 92
affirmative action, 280
age of first sexual intercourse, 307
ageism, 479
artificial insemination, 105
availability of contraception, 329
child maltreatment, 33
child neglect, 240
classroom environment, 231

comfortable with your own death, 712
controlling people, 520
conversion therapy, 623
crime, 400
cultural competence, 286
custody of children, 580
day care, 184
discipline/abuse by parents, 236
disengagement, 697
divorce or empty-shell marriage, 572
domestic violence, 461
dream of the future, 504
drug/alcohol abuse, 530
eating disorders, 389
economic inequality, 42
embryonic stem cell research, 94
emphasis on physical appearance, 301
employment for people 50 or older, 479
employment in your 70's, 738
ethnic groups and intelligence, 262
extramarital affairs, 490
Fabian and sociopsychological perspective, 40
feminism, 126
gender assignment, 429
gender-related behavior, 436
grounding in child management, 215
helping people who abuse drugs, 537
HIV, a global perspective, 496
HIV/AIDS, 494
how long do you want to live, 671
how many children do you want, 558
identity formation, 339
intact dilation and extraction, 94
intellectual disabilities, 161
IQ tests, 156
Joe, adolescent alcohol and other substance abuse, 305
knowing when you will die, 671
labeling, 393
lesbian and gay marriage, 639
lesbian, gay, bisexual, and transgender discrimination in employment, 635
lesbian, gay, bisexual, and transgender, violence against, 642
life review, 690
love relationships, 555
mainstreaming people with intellectual disabilities, 164
mate swapping, 490
morality, 345
morality and Waldo, 350
negative attitudes toward being old, 691
nursing homes, 734
one true religion, 266
parenting style, 216
physical attraction, 516
physical care, 471
poverty, functional for society, 570
pregnant women and illegal drug use, 67

punishment as behavior modification, 210
racist jokes, 281
rape—consequences, 455
rape, why men do it, 452
religious beliefs, 266, 693
revolt against/work within power structures, 561
self-fulfilling prophecy, 504
self-talk, 399
senility and older people, 661
sex education, 315
sexual harassment, 444
sexuality and older people, 663
Social Security benefits, 724
spanking for discipline, 236
spirituality and religion, 353
stem cell research, 92–94
stereotypes about lesbian or gay people, 621
substance abuse, 537
suicide, 366
surrogate motherhood, 107
terminal illness—duty to die, 721
terminal illness—right to die, 370
time outs in child management, 215
transgender surgery, 624
value orientations, 610
Victor, the French child from the wild, 3
violence on television, 230
why are people lesbian, gay, or bisexual, 630
why are people poor, 568
withdrawal in later adulthood, 697
ethics. *See also* Code of Ethics
of caring, 348
definition of, 3n1, 19
situational, 647
and values in bio-psycho-social assessment, 21–22
and values for cultural competence, 287
Ethics in Social Work, Statement of Principles, 20
Ethiopia and abortion, 90
ethnic and cultural differences in families, 218–221
ethnic discrimination, 259–260
ethnic groups, 255
social work with, 285–291
ethnic identity, 342
ethnic and race relations, future of U.S., 291–292
ethnic and racial discrimination, 258
ethnic-sensitive practice, 285–286
ethnic stereotypes, 259
ethnicity
race, culture, and identity development, 340–345
race, and schools, 232–233
and sexual orientation, 644
ethnocentric ideologies, 256

ethnocentrism, 255–256
Eurocentric theories, 274–275
European cultures and nonverbal
    communication, 510
euthanasia, 720, 725
evaluation, 7
    of culture of poverty theory, 568–569
    of discrimination theories, 267
    of disengagement theory, 697
    of Fowler's theory, 352–353
    of Gilligan's theory, 348–349
    of identity formation theories, 340
    of Kohlberg's theory, 346–347
    of learning theory, 195
    of Levinson's theories to women, 506
    of models of the grieving process, 707
    of outcomes, 52
    of Piaget's theory, 137–138
    of psychodynamic theory, 118
    of theories about homosexuality, 628
    of theories of aging, 666
    of theory, 127–128
    of Vygotsky's theory, 143–144
evaluator role, 53, 108, 164, 406
evidence-based practice, 290
    and spirituality, 354
excitement, 144, 663
executive role, 419
exemplar role, 419
exercise, 673, 682
exhaustion phase, 676
expectation stage, 577
expectations and temperament, 148
experiential element, 153
expert role, 44, 48, 419
exploitation and competition, 265–266
exposure therapy, 248
expulsion, 72
extended family, 219, 288
external control psychology, 521
extensive support, 161
external group representative, 419
extinction, 200–201, 202, 213
extinction burst, 201
extragenital physical responses, 664
extramarital sexual relationships, 488–490
eye-accessing eyes, 511
eye contact, 288, 358, 510
eye expressions, 515
eye movement desensitization and repro-
    cessing (EMDR), 678
eyesight, 471

F

facial expressions, 358–359, 515–516
facilitator/group facilitator role, 54
    and addiction, 544
    and codependency, 546
    with gangs, 406
    and grief management, 709
    with learning disabilities, 173

in locality development, 44, 48
in social planning model, 44
and stress management, 683
fact gatherer, 44
faith, monotheistic, 261
faith-based organizations, 354
faith development, Fowler's theory of,
    350–353
faith healers, 219
fallopian tube, 64, 70
false labor, 72
families, 181
    assessment, 590–600
    autonomy, 183
    blended, 182, 584, 586–589
    birth order, family size, and spacing,
        221–222
    child abuse in, 29–33
    communication in, 183
    cultural context and parenting style,
        217
    and day care, 184
    drug abuse, 539–540
    effective communication in, 380–382
    and end of life, 191–192
    ethnic and cultural differences in, 218–221
    gender role socialization, 222
    interaction in, 380–382
    issues and adolescent suicide, 361
    macro systems and, 183–184
    mezzo system problems, 572–590
    mothers working outside the home,
        589–590
    new baby, 216–217
    norms in, 591–592
    nuclear, 181
    one-parent, 583–584
    roles in chemically dependent, 540
    sandwich generation, 590
    school environment, 200–233
    sibling subsystems/interactions, 187,
        216–217, 221
    single-parent, 181, 182, 273
    social and economic justice, 183–184
    social environment, 222–233
    step-, 181–182
    strengths of, 15, 17
    systems theory application, 184–189
    types of, 181–182
    unmarried cohabitation, 182
familism, 288
family counseling, 735
family domain, 366
family environment, 180–185
family functioning, positive, 182–183
family groups, membership in, 181–182
family hero, 540
family life cycle, 189, 194
    diverse perspectives on, 190–194
family norms, 591–592
family size, 221

family social functioning, 32
family spacing, 221
family structure, variations in, 181–182
family systems, 30
    assessing and intervening in, 590–600
    assessment instruments, 592–597
    dynamics of, 184–185
    membership in, 215–216
    mezzo problems, 572–590
    personal lifestyles, 550–558
    relationships in later adulthood,
        700–702
    social work roles, 597–600
    theoretical approach to drug abuse,
        539–540
    verbal and nonverbal communication
        in, 590–591
family therapy, 185, 598
family violence. *See* battered women
fantasy play, 223
fascism, 265
fear, 144
fear of fear, 268, 269
feedback, 28, 33, 35, 187, 189
    negative, 28, 187–188
    positive, 28, 187
feeding and eating disorders, 392
feeding tube, whether to insert a, 712
female condom, 325–326
female-dominated professions, 439
female impersonators, 430
female infertility, 102
female/male differences, 435–437
female menopause. *See* menopause
female-to-male surgery, 624
FemCap, 326
feminine speech, 436
femininity, 432
feminism
    categories of, 124–125
    definition of, 122
    diversity in, 124–126
    ethical questions, 126
    future, 126
feminist identity development, 126
feminist perspective
    on infertility counseling, 109
    on rape, 448
feminist theories, 122–127
    principles of, 122–124
fencer pose, 77
fertility and aging, 102
fertility awareness methods (rhythm
    method), 328–329
fertility computers, 330
fertility drugs, 104
fertilization, 64
fetal alcohol effects (FAE), 68
fetal alcohol syndrome (FAS), 67–68, 527
fetal development, 65–66
fetal MRI, 69

fetal tissue, 92
fetus, 65
fibroadenoma, 472
fibromyalgia, 91
field education, 57
fight or flight reaction, 675–676, 677
Filipinos, 220, 221, 271, 343, 430
fimbriae, 64
fine needle aspiration biopsy (FNAB), 474
Finland, 76, 360
First Nations people. *See* Native
    Americans
first trimester, 65–66
five-year olds, 83–84
fixated development, 115, 117
flashbacks, 534
fluid intelligence, 153
focus group, 46, 344, 408
folic acid, 67
folk healing, 288
food stamps, 731
foreclosure, 339, 342
foreclosed identity, 342
forgiving strategy, 574–575
formal figure grandparents, 702
formal operations period, 136–137
formication, 531
forming stage, 414
foster-care homes, 733, 735
Foster Grandparent Program, 738
foundation knowledge, 5–8
four-month olds, 79
four-year olds, 82–83
Fowler's faith development theory,
    350–352
    critical thinking/evaluation of, 352–353
France
    and low birth weight, 76
freedom need, 519
Freedom of Access to Clinic Entrances
    (FACE) Act, 92
frustration-aggression, 265
full-term pregnancy, 76
fun need, 519
fun-seeker grandparenting, 702
functional leadership approach, 419
functionalist perspective, 559–560
    on poverty, 569–571
funerals, 705
    celebration of life, 709

G

gag rule and abortion, 91
galactogram, 474
Gamete Intrafallopian Transfer (GIFT),
    106, 107
gamma hydroxyl butyrate (GHB), 449, 529
gang group worker, 405
gangs, 401–406
    contradictions in conceptualizing,
        403–404

Morales's classification, 402–403
    social work roles and intervention,
        405–406
    sociological theories, 404–405
    street/detached worker, 405–406
    types of, 402–403
Garland, Jones, and Kolodny model,
    412–414
gay gene, 627
gays and lesbians
    adolescents, 341, 645–646
    adolescents and suicide, 362
    AIDS and, 492, 493, 649–650
    battering in relationships of, 459
    child custody and visitation rights,
        639–640
    coming out, 341, 642–645, 647
    conceptual frameworks, 626–631
    definition of, 622
    employment, 633, 635
    empowerment of adolescents, 341
    ethnicity and, 644
    finances, 636–639
    future of rights for, 640
    global same-sex marriage, 638
    homophobia, 341
    joining of families, 190
    in later adulthood, 648–649, 700
    legal empowerment and social justice,
        633–640
    lifestyles, 631–633
    and the military, 635–636
    NASW policy, 618
    numbers of, 626
    parents, empowering, 646–648
    pride, 634
    relationships, 631–632, 636–639
    same-sex marriage, 636–639
    self-identity exploration, 645
    sexual harassment, 441
    sexual interaction, 633
    significant issues and life events for,
        633–650
    social work and, 650
    stereotypes about, 620
    ten percent society, 626
    violence against, 640–642
gender, 425–429
    complexity of, 426–429
    definition of, 425
    differences in play, 224
    economic inequality, 437–440
    parental preferences of, 556
    social construction of, 425–426
gender dysphoria, 392
gender expression
    complexity of, 426–429
    definition of, 425
gender identity
    complexity of, 426–429
    definition of, 425, 620, 622

gender intensification, 431
gender nonconformity, 629
gender/racial comparison of earnings, 437
gender-role development, cross-cultural
    perspectives on, 433–434
gender-role socialization, 123, 222, 425, 433
gender-role stereotypes, 465
    adolescence, 431–432
    adulthood, 432, 434–435
    batterers, 456
    childhood, 431
    and intimacy, 500
    of men, 435
    modern, 596
    traditional, 429–435, 596
gender roles, 123
    definition of, 123, 425
    in Hispanic families, 219
    Mexican American women, 286
    Puerto Rican, 286
gender segregation, 124
gender spectrum, 430
gender splitting, 506
gender status, 425
general adaptation syndrome (GAS),
    675–676
general manager role. *See* manager role
general-purpose organizations, 408
generalist practice. *See* social work
generalization, 168
generativity, 336, 501
generativity versus stagnation stage, 336,
    501
genetic determinism, 667
genetic factors
    on homosexuality, 627
    a learning disabilities, 169
genetic mutations, 472
genetic testing, 667
genetic theories, 666
genital herpes, 318–319
genital stage, 117
genital warts. *See* human papilloma virus
genogram, 595–597
German measles and pregnancy, 68
Germany
    infants in, 151
    teenage pregnancy in, 307
gerontologists, 657
gerontology, 729
gestation, 65
gestures, 358, 510–512
GHB (gamma hydroxybutyrate), 449, 529
giftedness, 156
Gilligan's moral development model, 347–349
    concept summary, 349
    critical thinking/evaluation of, 348–349
    ethical application to client situations,
        349
glass ceiling, 124, 281, 439
glaucoma, 659, 667

global issues, 20
global epidemic-AIDS, 495
global recession, 567
global same-sex marriage, 638
global self-worth, 152
goal-directed behavior, 134
goals
    of social work, 24–25
    vagueness of, 52
gonorrhea, 316–317
good-person self-image, 268, 269
goodness as self-sacrifice level, 348
grandparenthood, 702
grasping reflex, 77
great-grandparenthood, 702
great person theory. See trait approach
Great Society, 49
Greece, 360, 705
grief management
    celebration of life funerals, 709
    counseling, 708–709
    cultural-historical context of, 705
    and death education, 704–713
    feeding tube, whether to insert a, 712
    grieving process, 706–707
    how to cope with, 708
    how to relate to a dying person,
        709–710
    how to relate to survivors, 710
    impact of social forces, 705–706
    Kübler-Ross model, 706, 707
    life after life, 713
    questions about death, dying, and, 711
    social work and, 708–709, 735
    Westberg model, 706–707
    And your own death, 710, 712–713
    See also death
grounding, 215
group development models, 411–415
group facilitator. See facilitator role
group homes
    for older people, 733
    for people with intellectual disabilities,
        164
group worker, 7
groups
    culture of, 288–289
    definition of, 406
    differences, 13
    empowerment through, 16, 406–419
    membership and values, 13
    multiracial, 410
    strengths of, 15–16, 17
    support, 16
    task and maintenance roles in, 415–416
    types of, 407–411
growth process, 78
growth spurt, 298
Guamanians, 220
gut feelings, 523
gypsies, 256

H
HAART (highly active antiretroviral
    therapy), 494
habit disturbance organizations, 408
habituation stage, 577
hair growth, 299
hallucinogens, 525, 534
hangover, 526
harmony with nature concept, 220, 232
hashish, 525, 536
hate/message crimes, 260, 640–642
Hawaiians, 220, 232
Hawthorne effect, 603
HCG. See Human chorionic gonatropin
health/health care
    adolescent, substance abuse and, 303–305
    lifestyle, 476–477
    and marriage, 553
    middle adulthood, 479
    practices and longevity, 668
    problems for older adults, 727–728
    young adulthood, 471–472
health-care reform, 586, 731
hearing problems, 167
helper therapy principle, 409, 411
helping network, 16
hemophilia, 104n11
hemp plant, 536
herd drive, 379
hermaphrodite, 428
heroin, 525, 533–534
herpes simplex virus, 318
herpes zoster, 493
heteroeroticism, 625
heterosexism, 625
HGH (human growth hormone), 538
hierarchical relationship, 221
hierarchy of needs, 505, 507
hierarchy of principles, 99
highly active antiretroviral therapy
    (HAART), 494
hijab, 261
Hindu
    children, 130
    death and bereavement, 705
    perception and treatment of death, 192
hijra, 430
Hispanics
    adolescence, 301
    adolescent sexual activity, 307
    breast cancer, 473
    cultural themes, 219
    definition of term, 45–46
    discipline of children, 235
    economic inequality, 437
    ethnic identity, 342
    families, 217, 218–219
    gangs, 403
    gender roles of, 219
    and Latino communities' strengths
        and empowerment, 45–46

menarche, 299
poverty and older women, 722
schools, 232–233
and sexual orientation, 644
suicide and adolescent females, 360, 366
history
    culture of African Americans,
        272–273
    and death and bereavement, 705
    and prejudice/discrimination, 265
HIV (human immunodeficiency virus),
    319, 491–496
    and pregnancy, 69
    effects of, 493
    See also AIDS/HIV
holistic concept, 672
Holland, death rates in, 478
home health services, 733
homeless, empowerment of youth, 382–383
homemaker services, 733
homeostasis, 27, 35, 189
    in families, 185–186, 188
    in later adulthood, 661–662, 675
home pregnancy tests (HPTs), 65
homoeroticism, 625
homogamy theory, 551
homophobia, 341, 622, 630
    discrimination and impacts of, 630
homosexuality, 341, 391
    biological theories on, 627–628
    and bisexuality, 619–626
    brain (anatomical) factors, 627
    concept of, 621–622, 625
    continuum, 624–625
    definition of, 618, 621, 622
    ethical issues related to theories, 629
    evaluation of theory, 628
    genetic factors, 627
    hormonal factors, 627–628
    interactionist theory, 628
    Kinsey's research on, 624, 625, 626, 629
    Lawrence et al. v. Texas, 633
    personality pie, 621
    psychosocial theories, 628
    research on origin, 629
    Storms's conceptualization, 625
    See also gays/lesbians; sexual
        orientation
honeymoon stage, 557
hope, conveying, 545
Hopi, 219, 705, 717
hormonal factors on homosexuality,
    627–628
hormonal implants, 323, 329, 627–628
hormonal injection, 323
hormonal IUDs, 327–328
hormone replacement therapy (HRT),
    484–485
hormones, 297–298, 329
hormone therapy, 475
hospice, 724

hospital social services, 736
hot flash, 482–483
household, 181
housing
    assistance/projects, 733, 736
    for older people, 726–727
human behavior
    assessment of, 31–32
    choice theory of, 518–522
    community macro systems, 38–49
    definition of, 3
    ecosystems theory, 23, 27–35
    important concepts, 11–22
    and intuition, 522–523
    multiple systems, 35–38
    in organizational macro systems, 49–52
    person-in-environment perspective, 22–23
    sociological theories, 558–563
human chorionic gonadotropin (HCG), 65
human development and growth, 77–79, 141
    effects of discrimination on, 270
    See also developmental milestones
human ecology perspective, 41–42
human growth and development, effects
    of discrimination, 267, 270
human growth hormone (HGH), 538
human immunodeficiency virus. *See* HIV
    (human immunodeficiency virus)
human papillomavirus (HPV), 319
human relations model, 602–603
human reproduction, 63–77
human rights, 20–21
    definition, 20, 25, 284–285
    and EPAS, 284
    list of basic, 284–285
    and sexual harassment, 441
    and social justice, 284–285
human services, 50
    organizations, 601. (*See also*
        organizations)
humanistic therapists, 121
hungry cry, 145
Huntington's disease, 667
hydrocephalus, 75
hyperactivity, 172, 530
hyperkinesis, 530
hypertension, 479
hypervigilance, 236
hypothalamus, 483, 627
hypothetical-deductive reasoning, 137
hysterosalpinography, 103

I

ice. *See* methamphetamine hydrochloride
id, 114, 115
ideal mate theory, 551
ideal self, 120, 122
identification, 116, 117
identity achievement, 267, 339
identity confusion, 338
identity crisis, 480

identity diffusion, 339
identity formation, 191, 334–340
    critical thinking/evaluation of theory,
        340
    Erikson's psychosocial theory, 334–339
    how to determine who you are, 337
    implications in adolescence, 337
    lesbians and gay adolescents, 341
    Marcia's categories of, 339
    race, culture, ethnicity, and, 340–345
    racial and cultural model, 343–344
identity versus role confusion stage, 336
ideologist role, 419
ideology, 266
ignoring behavior, 241
Ik of Uganda, 717
illegal abortions, 96–97
illegal aliens, 193
imagery relaxation, 680
I-messages, 380–381, 574
immigrants, 193
immigration status, 193–194
immunocontraceptives, 329
Implanon, 323
implementation, 7
implementer role, 44
impulsivity, 172, 362
inattention, 172
incest, 243–244
income
    definition of, 563
    disparities, 563
    gender/racial comparison, 437
    and pregnancy, 68
    retirement and lower, 687
incongruence, 120–121, 122
incongruent communication, 591
incontinence, 662
independence
    movement from dependence to, 378–379
    types of, 379
    versus interdependence, 142
India
    abortion in, 90
    and AIDS, 495
    asset-based community development,
        283
    birth weight, 76
    hjira, 430
    and public cremation, 705
    two-spirits/berdache, 430
individual education program (IEP), 171,
    173
individual empowerment/strengths,
    15–16, 17
individual psychology, 118
individual racism, 263
individualism, 142, 579
    ideology of, 566
individualized family service plan (IFSP),
    173

individuative-reflective faith, 352
Indonesians, 271
industry versus role confusion stage, 336
inequality gap, 12
infancy and childhood, 8
infant mortality rate, 264, 285, 565, 719
infants
    attachment, 147–150
    exposed to crack, 532
    emotions, 144–145
    preterm, 75–77
    teenage pregnancy and low birth-
        weight, 76
    and temperament, 145–147
    See also children
inferiority, countering, 265
infertility, 101–109
    aging and, 102
    alternatives for, 104–107
    assessment of, 103
    causes of, 102
    concept summary, 107
    definition of, 101
    effects of macro systems on, 108
    empowerment and, 107–109
    feminist perspective, 109
    psychological reactions to, 102–103
    social work roles, 107–108
    treatment of, 103
information organization, 168
information-processing concept, 138–141
    strategies for, 140–141
initiator/program initiator role, 54
    and addiction, 544
    and codependency, 546
    and discrimination, 291
    and gangs, 406
    and grief management, 708
    with people with developmental dis-
        abilities, 164
    and stress management, 683
initiative versus guilt stage, 335–336
injury to others, failure to consider, 268,
    269
inner focus, 502
inner speech, 143
input, 28, 30, 31, 32, 33, 35
    in families, 186, 189
inquiry, 574
insecurity/inferiority, countering, 265
instant gratification, 268
institution, 12n2
institutional discrimination, 263–264
    mass media appeals to change, 276–277
institutional racism, 263, 264
institutional view, 612–613
intact dilation and extraction (D & X), 94
integration, ecological concept of
    human ecology perspective, 41
integrative awareness stage, 343
integrative thinking, 481

integrator/coordinator role, 291
integrity, 689
integrity versus despair, 689
intellectual disability, 71n4
    Americans with Disabilities Act,
        162–163
    categories of, 158–160
    definition of, 158–160
    empowerment and, 158–164
    macro system responses, 161–164
    people with, 159–160
    social work roles, 164
    support systems for, 161
intellectual functioning
    in later adulthood, 660–661
    in middle adulthood, 481–482
intelligence/intelligence testing, 152–157
    Cattell's fluid and crystallized, 153
    cultural biases and, 157
    definition of, 152
    emotional, 507–508
    IQ, 154–155
    problems with, 157
    special needs, 156–157
    Stanford-Binet, 155
    Steinberg's triarchic theory of, 153–154
    terminal drop in, 661
    Wechsler, 155–156
interaction, play and, 223
interactional model, 391, 393–394
interactionist perspective/theories, 561–563
    about drug use, 539
    about homosexuality, 628
    on poverty, 571–572
interconnections, 42
intercultural relations, 12
interdependence, 35
    and Asian Americans, 221, 340
    and Native Americans, 340
    versus independence, 142
interface, 28–29, 30, 31, 33
intermittent reinforcement, 206–207
intermittent support, 161
internal control psychology, 519
international perspectives
    on abortion policy, 90
    on drugs, 547
    on human rights and social justice,
        20–21, 284–285
    on low birth-weight infants, 76
    same-sex marriage, 638
    on suicide, 360
Internet and sexual predators, 245
interpersonal intelligence, 509
intersectionality, 125–126, 271
intersex, 428
intervention, 7
    with delinquent gangs, 405–406
    in family systems, 185, 590–600
    with suicidal people, 369–370
    techniques of, 289–290

intimacy, 336, 500
intimacy stage, 413
intimacy versus isolation stage, 336, 500
intimate zone, 513–514
intracytoplasmic sperm injection (ICSD),
    106, 107
intrauterine device (IUD), 324, 327–328,
    330
intrauterine insemination (IUI), 104–105,
    107
introjection, 120
introspection stage, 343
intuition, 522–523
intuitive-projective faith, 351
in vitro fertilization (IVF), 93n10, 105, 107
IQ. *See* Intelligence/testing
Iranians, 271
    and abortion, 90
Iraq, 256
Ireland and abortion, 90
irreversibility, 135
Islam, 261–262, 695–696
    and death and bereavement, 705
Israel, 256, 347
isolation, 241, 336, 341, 500
Italy, 307, 360, 673
IUD (intrauterine device), 324, 327–328, 330

J
Japan
    and adolescent sexuality, 130
    death in, 705
    high status for older people in, 658, 719
    and suicide, 360
    theory Z, 604
    women and menopause in, 483
Japanese/Japanese Americans, 256
    families, 220, 221
    infants, 151
    relocation camps, 201
jaundice, 322
joint custody, 576, 580
Judaism/Jews, 694–695
    and death, 192
    mass execution, 256
    and women, 131
Jungian analysis, 114
juvenile courts, 400–401
justice perspective, 347
juvenile diabetes, 92n8
juvenile gangs, 401–406
juvenile probation, 405

K
Kaposi's sarcoma, 493
karma, 192
Kenya, 283
ketamine hydrochloride (Special K), 449
kinesthetic system, 511
Kinsey's sexual behavior scale, 624–625
kinship, 273

Kiribati, 142
Klinefelter's syndrome, 428
knowledge
    foundation, 5–8
    relationship with assessment, 546–547
Kohlberg's theory of moral development,
    345–347
    concept summary, 346
    critical thinking/evaluation of, 346–347
Koreans, 76, 220, 221, 271
Kübler-Ross model, 706, 707
!Kung people, 145
Kurds, 256
Kwanzaa, 274, 275
Kwell, 318

L
labeling, 338–339, 393, 560, 562
    in juvenile courts, 401
    of older people, 698
labia, 428, 663
labor
    false, 72
    stages of, 72–73
laissez-faire leadership, 418
Lakota Sioux, 483
Lamaze method, 74
language
    common, 219
    difficulties, 168
    of love, 489
    paralanguage, 516
    sexist/nonsexist, 444, 446
language assessment
    at age 4 months, 79
    at 8 months, 79–80
    at 1 year, 81
    at 18 months, 81
    at 2 years, 82
    at 3 years, 82
    at 4 years, 83
    at 5 years, 83
    at 6 to 8 years, 84–85
    at 9 to 11 years, 85
Laotians, 220
laparoscopy, 103
late adulthood era, 503
late-term abortion. *See* intact dilation and
    extraction
latency stage, 117
latent functions/dysfunctions, 560
later adulthood. *See also* older adults
    Alzheimer's disease, 669–670
    causes of aging, 665–666
    causes of death, 668
    cross-cultural research on centenar-
        ians, 673
    definition of, 657
    developmental tasks of, 687–689
    developmental tasks of, theoretical
        concepts about, 689–693

diseases and causes of death in, 666–670
and diversity, 192–193
empowerment approaches to stress management in, 677–683
factors that influence aging process, 666–669
genetic testing, 667
grief management and death education, 704–713
guidelines for positive psychological preparation for, 703–704
health practices and longevity, 668
homeostasis in, 661–662
impacts of life events in, 699–702
intellectual functioning in, 660–661
law of attraction, 680
lesbians and gay men in, 648–649
life expectancy in, 666, 671–672
muscular structure changes in, 662
myth of senility, 661
nervous system changes in, 662
new way of viewing, 658
old-old, 657
physiological and mental changes in, 658–665
productivity, 657
psychomotor skills in, 659–660
reserve capacity in, 663
self-concept, 682
senescence, 658
sense changes in, 658–659
sexuality and sexual response in, 663–664
social work and, 683
strengths perspective for successful, 696–698
strengths perspective, wellness and, 672–683
stress and stress management in, 675–683
theories of successful, 696
traumas and stress disorders, 678
values and sexuality in, 664–665
wellness: the strengths perspective, 672–683
what is, 657–658
young-old, 657
Latino/Latinas. *See also* Chicano/ Chicana; Hispanics; Mexican Americans
adolescents, 191
and death, 478
and Hispanic communities, 45–46
identity development, 191
Mercado Central, 283–284
Murals, 345
laughing phase, 145
law of attraction, 680
law of requisite variety, 575
leadership, 419

leadership roles, 419
leadership style approach, 418
leadership theories, 416–419
distributed-functions approach, 418–419
Machiavellianism, 417
position approach, 417–418
servant, 419–420
situational, 416
style approach, 418
trait approach, 416–417
learned helplessness reaction, 169
learning disabilities, 164–172
academic characteristics, 168–169
causes of, 169
cognitive characteristics, 167–168
definition of, 164–165, 166
effects on children, 169–170
and low birth weight, 75–77
policies for social justice, 171–172
problems involved, 166–167
treatment for, 170–171
learning objectives
chapter 1, 4–5, 57–58
chapter 2, 63, 108–110
chapter 3, 113, 173–175
chapter 4, 179–180, 249–251
chapter 5, 255, 292–293
chapter 6, 296, 330–331
chapter 7, 334, 371
chapter 8, 378, 420–421
chapter 9, 424, 464–467
chapter 10, 470, 496–497
chapter 11, 499, 547–548
chapter 12, 550, 615–616
chapter 13, 619, 650–651
chapter 14, 656, 683–684
chapter 15, 686, 713–714
chapter 16, 717, 739–740
learning theory, 119, 194–215, 559
ABCs of behavior, 197–198
application to practice, 201–210
behavior modification, 195
consequences and recurring behavior, 198
critical thinking/evaluation of, 195
definition of, 195, 202
extinction, 200–201, 202
and family problems, 599
modeling, 196, 202
and moral development, 349–350
operant conditioning, 197, 202
importance of parental attention, 212–213
punishment, 199–200, 201, 202
reinforcement, 198–199, 201, 202
respondent conditioning, 195–196, 202
Lebanese families and death, 192
left brain, 522
legal advocacy, 462
legal custody, 580
legal empowerment, 633–650

lesbians and gays
adolescents, 341, 645–646
adolescents and suicide, 362
AIDS and, 492, 493, 649–650
battering in relationships of, 459
child custody and visitation rights, 639–640
coming out, 341, 642–645, 647
conceptual frameworks, 626–631
definition of, 622
employment, 633, 635
empowerment of adolescents, 341
ethnicity and, 644
finances, 636–639
future of rights for, 640
global same-sex marriage, 638
homophobia, 341
joining of families, 190
in later adulthood, 648–649, 700
legal empowerment and social justice, 633–640
lifestyles, 631–633
and the military, 635–636
NASW policy, 618
numbers of, 626
parents, empowering, 646–648
pride, 634
relationships, 631–632, 636–639
same-sex marriage, 636–639
self-identity exploration, 645
sexual harassment, 441
sexual interaction, 633
significant issues and life events for, 633–650
social work and, 650
stereotypes about, 620
ten percent society, 626
violence against, 640–642
Lesbos, 622
letting go strategy, 574
Levinson's theories for men, 503–505
applied to women, 506
levonorgestrel, 324
LGBTQ/LGBTI, 626
liberal feminism, 124
liberal perspective, 612–613
libertarian party, 728
libido, 115
Librium, 528
lice, pubic, 318
life
key to success in, 502
meaning of, 546
nearing end of, 191–193
transitional points of, 130
life after life, 713
life cycle, family, 189–194
diverse perspectives on, 190–194
life eras, 503
life events, 9–10, 85
assertiveness and suicide, 355

on children, 215–222
 for lesbian and gay people, 633–650
 impact on older people, 699–702
 of women, 437
life expectancy, 264, 270, 666, 671–672
 for married/unmarried people, 553
 and poverty, 565
 and social security, 723
 and stress management, 675
lifeline assistance, 733
life review, 690
life satisfaction, 690
life-span
 development, 8–11
 extending the, 666
life structure concept, 503
lifestyle
 and good health, 476–477
 lesbian and gay, 631–633
 organizations, 408
 personal, 550–558
life-support equipment, 725
limited support, 161
listening, active, 212–213, 380
living wills, 725
locality development model, 43–44
Locker Room, 532
logical thinking, barriers to, 134–135
long-term memory, 140
longevity
 cross-cultural research on, 673
 and health practices, 668
looking-glass self, 267, 338, 393, 562, 690
lost child, 540
love
 analyzing relationships, 577–578
 five languages of, 489
 and marriage, 551
 relationship stage, 506
 romantic versus rational, 554, 576
love and belonging need, 505, 519
LSD (lysergic acid diethylamide), 525,
 534–535
lumpectomy, 474
lumps, benign, 472
lung cancer, 305
Luxembourg, 726
lynch mobs, 257

M

Machiavellianism, 417
Machiavellian leaders, 417
machismo, 288
macro system problems
 crime and delinquency, 400–401
 cycle of poverty, 567, 568
 delinquent gangs, 401–404
macro systems
 abortion policies, 86, 88–94
 affirmative action programs, 278–280
 child protective services (CPS), 241–242

civil rights laws, 277
court involvement and maltreatment,
 243
definition of, 36, 558
discrimination and oppression in,
 263–264
effects on infertility, 108
families, 183–184
human behavior and community, 36,
 38–49
human behavior and organizational,
 36, 49–52
interactions between micro and, 36–38
and prenatal care, 70
responses to child maltreatment, 241–243
response to empower battered women,
 459–463
responses to intellectual disabilities,
 161–164
response to older people, 718–719,
 729–735, 737–739
response to sexual abuse, 249
response to sexual harassment, 442
social system theories in, 558–563
social work with gangs, 406
social work roles in, 52–54, 242–243
macular degeneration, 659
magic mushrooms, 534
magnetic resonance imaging (MRI), 69, 473
mainlining, 533
mainstreaming, 164
maintenance roles, 415–416
maintenance stage of change, 544
Malaysian infants, 148
male climacteric, 485–486
male condom, 325
male-dominated professions, 439
male/female differences, 435–437
male infertility, 102
male-to-female surgery, 624
Mali, 151
malnutrition, 66, 727
mammogram, 473, 476
management by objectives (MBO), 605
manager role, 53, 164
mandatory retirement, 721
Mangaia, 297
manic-depressive psychosis. *See* bipolar
 disorder
manifest functions/dysfunctions, 559
Marcia's categories of identity, 339,
 342–343
 critical thinking/evaluation of theory,
 340
marginalization, 131, 566
marijuana (cannabis sativa), 525, 536–537
 medical, 537
marital property, 555
marriage, 182, 551–553, 555
 benefits of, 552–553
 common-law, 555

empty-shell, 500, 572–576, 583
extramarital sexual relationships, 488–490
family life cycle stage, 190
guidelines for a happy, 555
later or not at all, 182
and older people, 699
predictors of successful, 552
same-sex, 636–639
sex in, 487–488
when not in love, 551
why people choose each other in, 551
marriage counseling, 583
Marxist/socialist feminism, 124
Masai parents, 148
mascot, 540
masculine speech, 436
masculinity, 432, 435, 436
Maslow's hierarchy of needs, 505, 507
mass media, 276–277
mastectomy, 474–475
masturbation, 306, 488
material reinforcers, 203–204
maternal blood tests, 69, 70
maternal deprivation, 589, 590
maternal stress, 68
mate swapping, 490
matrilineal descent, 131, 219
maturation
 early and late in boys, 301–302
 early and late in girls, 302
Mayans, 148
 and death, 705
 women and menopause, 483
MDMA (ecstasy), 525, 535
Meals on Wheels, 675, 733
meaning of life, 546
measurement of improvement, 211–212
media, influence of TV and other,
 228, 230
mediation, 575, 583
mediator role, 53, 108, 173, 406
Medicaid, 88n6, 731
 and abortion, 91
Medicare, 49, 728, 730
medical marijuana, 537
medical model, 127–129, 391–394
medication abortion, 96
medication and drugs during pregnancy, 67
medication-induced movement disorders,
 393
melting pot, 218, 292
memory
 long-term, 140
 and recall, 139–140, 168
 sensory, 139–140
 short-term, 139–140
 working, 139
men
 differences between women and, 435–437
 economics inequality between women
 and, 437–440

effects of abortion on women and, 97
gender-role stereotyping, 434–435
Levinson's theories, 503–505
special issues and needs of, 435
menarche, 298, 299
menopause, 473, 482–485
cultural differences in women's
experience of, 483
male climacteric, 485–486
menstruation, 298–299
mental activity, 673
mental disorders, 392–393
mental flexibility versus mental rigidity, 502
mental hardware/software, 139
mental illness, 128, 391
myth, 391, 393–394
mental retardation. *See* intellectual disability
mentor, 504, 506
Mercado Central, 283–284
merchant clubs, 288
mescaline, 525, 534, 535
message/hate crimes, 641
messages
double, 591
I/you, 380–381, 574
nonverbal, 509
methamphetamine hydrochloride (meth),
530
methaqualone (Quaalude), 528
Mexican Americans, 45, 217, 218
gender-role socialization, 286, 433
and moratorium, 342–343
Mexico, 148
and drugs, 529
historical context of death, 705
Mayan women and menopause, 483
Mexico city, 90
mezzo systems
abortion and, 86
definition of, 36
empowerment through social work,
406–419
family problems, 572–590
and gang intervention, 405–406
nonverbal communication, 509–518
microbicides, 329–330
Micronesia, 157
micro systems, 559
definition of, 36
and gang intervention, 405–406
interactions with macro systems,
36–38
middle adulthood, 477, 479–491
age span of, 477
AIDS and, 491–496
assessing and intervening in family
systems in, 590–600
and diversity, 191
double standard of aging in, 479
era, 503
extramarital relationships, 488–490

families in late, 191–192
family mezzo system problems in,
572–590
female menopause, 482–484
gender-role stereotypes, 432, 434–435
generativity versus stagnation, 501
health changes in, 479
identity crisis in, 480
intellectual functioning in, 481–482
macro social system theories on, 558–563
male climacteric, 485–487
management by objectives, 605
midlife crisis, 191, 485–487
Peck's theory of psychological development, 501–503
personal lifestyles, 550–558
physical changes in, 477, 479–482
physical strength and reaction time
changes, 480–481
poverty in, 563–572
psychological development, 500–505
sense organ changes in, 480
sexual functioning in, 487–491
social work with organizations, 600–609
value orientations in organizational
decision making, 609–610
middle childhood, 151
Middle East, 256
midlife crises, 191, 465, 486–487, 505
midwifery, 73
mifepristone, 96
migration, 193
military and gay and lesbian people, 635
Miltown, 528
mind, conception of, 114–115
mind-altering substance, 303
minimization, 539
minipill, 321
minorities
greater interaction between majority
groups and, 277
violence against, 257–258
minority-owned businesses, 281
Mirena, 327
miscarriage, 72, 75. *See also* spontaneous
abortion
misoprostol, 96
modeling, 196–197, 202
modified radical mastectomy, 474
Mohegan tribe, 257
Mongolia, 90
monotheistic faith, 261
moral code, 337
moral development, 123, 345–350
Gilligan's approach to, 123, 347–349
Kohlberg's theory of, 345–347
social learning theory perspective on,
349–350
and women, 123, 347–349
morality, 345
of justice, 348

of nonviolent responsibility level,
348
moratorium, 339, 342–343
morning sickness, 66
Moro reflex, 77
Morocco, 283
morphine, 525, 533
mosques, 261
mothers
increased employment of, 182
working outside the home, 589–590
motility, 102
motivational interviewing, 544–546
motor assessment
at age 4 months, 79
at age 8 months, 79–80
at age 1 year, 80
at age 18 months, 81
at age 2 years, 81
at age 3 years, 81
at age 4 years, 81–82
at age 5 years, 83
at age 6 to 8 years, 84
at age 9 to 11 years, 85
mourning and diversity, 192
MRI. *See* magnetic resonance imaging
multicultural diversity, 271
multiculturalism, stereotyping and,
270–271
multiple personality disorder. *See*
dissociative identity disorder
multiracial groups, RAP framework for,
410
mummification, 705
murals, 344–345
muscular dystrophy, 70n2
mushrooms, magic, 534
Muslims/American Muslims, 262.
See also Islam
gender-role development, 433
mutual respect, 220
mutuality and interpersonal empathy
stage, 414
myotonia, 663
mythic-literal faith, 351

N

narcissistic rapist, 451
narcotics, 525, 533–534
National Association of Social Workers
(NASW)
and cultural competence, 287
Code of Ethics (*See* Code of Ethics)
conversion therapy, 623
on cultural competence, 287
goals of social work, 24–25
human rights, 20
income inequality, 440
policy on abortion, 87
self-determination, 618, 650
sexual orientation, 618

on transgender and gender identity issues, 624
Native Americans. *See also* specific tribes
and aging, 192
attempts to exterminate, 256, 257
berdache/two-spirits, 430
breast cancer among, 473
casinos-a benefit or a detriment, 282
cooperation, 220
and death, 478, 705
empowerment through sex education for, 315
ethnic identity, 342
importance of extended families, 219
and eye contact, 288, 510
families, 219–220
500 specific groups, 218, 271
forced assimilation, 257
harmony with nature, 220
interdependence, 340
institutional racism, 264
mutual respect, 220
noninterference, 220
peyote, psilocybin and, 534
and poverty, 566
and self-determination, 290
and sexual orientation, 644
spirituality, 220
and suicide, 360
time concept, 220
tribes, 218, 271
violence against, 257
women and menopause, 483
natural childbirth, 73–74
natural support network, 16, 288
nature, harmony with, 220, 232
nature-nurture controversy, 2, 78–79, 222, 436
Navajo, 131, 220, 232
nazism, 402
near-death experiences, 713
needs
Glasser's innate, 519
Maslow's hierarchy of, 505, 507
survey, 281
negative attention, 210
negative entropy, 29, 31, 33, 35, 188, 189
negative feedback, 28, 187–188
negative reinforcement, 199, 202
negative self-concept, 151
negotiation, in families, 183
negotiator role, 54, 164, 406
in social action model, 47, 48
neighborhood watch programs, 18
neo-Freudian psychoanalytic developments, 118–119
neonates, early functioning of, 77
neo-nazi groups, 403
Nepal, 130
and abortion,
and public cremation, 705

Nesterone, 330
Netherlands, 360, 547, 725, 726
networks, support/helping, 16
net worth, 564
neurocognitive disorders, 392
neurodevelopmental disorders, 392
neuro-linguistic programming (NLP), 511
never married, people who have, 700
and sex, 491
newborn
assessment, 74–75
reflexes, 77
New Bridges program, 344
New Deal program, 49
New Guinea, 347
New Zealand, 76, 360
nexplanon, 323
Next Choice, 324
Nicaragua, 90
nicotine. *See* tobacco
9/11, discrimination after, 261–262
nine- to 11-year olds, 85
nocturnal emissions, 300
no-lose problem solving, 381
nonassertive communication, 356–358
non-blaming messages, 380, 574
nondiscriminators, prejudiced/nonprejudiced, 258, 269
nonfood consumables, 203–204
nongenetic cellular theories, 666
nongonococcal urethritis (NGU), 316
noninterference, 220
nonorganic failure-to-thrive syndrome (NFTT), 239
nonsexist language, 446
nonspecific urethritis (NSU), 316
nonverbal communication, 509–518
body orientation, 510
clothing, 513
cultural awareness, 510
and the environment, 517–518
eye-accessing eyes, 511
facial expressions, 515
in family systems, 590–591
functions of, 509
gestures, 510–512
personal space, 513–514
physical appearance, 516–517
posture, 510
preening behavior, 512
territoriality, 515
touching, 512
voice, 515–516
normalization, 164
norming stage, 414
non-blaming messages
norm of noninterference, 702
norms, 591–592
North American babies, 145
Norway, 76
nuclear family, 181
Nuevo Puente, 344

nursing homes, 665, 720, 733–735, 736
nurturing, 512
nurturing system, 286
nutrition, 66, 674–675, 733
NuvaRing, 322

O
Obama's health-care reform, 727–728, 731
obesity, 387–388
object permanence, 134, 137
observational learning, 196
obsessions, 118
obsessive-compulsive disorder, 91, 392
occult gangs, 403
oedipus complex, 117, 118
oil rig explosion, 502
old-old group, 657, 720–721
older people. *See also* aging; later adulthood
adult protective services, 731–732
African American females, 692
ageism and low status, 691
Chicano, 288
coping with illness, 687
crime victimization of, 727
current services, 729–735
and death, 704–713, 724
death of a spouse, 699
depression, 691–693
developmental milestones, 10–11
developmental tasks, 687–689
diseases and causes of death among, 666–670
disengagement theory, 697
early retirement, 721–722
elder abuse, 724, 726
emphasis on youth, 719
family system relationships and, 700–702
fastest growing—old-old, 720–721
financial problems of, 722–723
finding a social role for, 737–739
gay and lesbian, 648–649, 700
grandparenthood, 702
great-grandparenthood, 702
grief management, 704
health-care reform, 731
health problems and cost of care for, 727–728
high status in other countries, 719
housing for, 726–727
impacts of life events on, 699–702
increasing numbers of, 719–720
life review/satisfaction, 690
macro system responses to, 729–735, 737–739
malnutrition, 727
marriage for, 699
Native American, 192, 717
never married, 700

nursing homes, 733–735
parenting adult children, 701–702
a population-at-risk, 717–718
a powerful political force, 736–737
prescription drug assistance, 730–731
problems faced by, 718–728
remarriage for, 700
right to die, 725–726
retirement, 687
social breakdown, 698
social security system and, 723–724
social work with, 735–736
spirituality/religion and, 693–696
strengths perspective, 703–704
successful aging for, 696–698
theoretical concepts about
developmental tasks for, 689–696
transportation, 727
in U.S. population, 719–720
widowhood, 700
Oman, 430
Oneida, 192
one-parent families, 583–584, 589
one true religion belief, 206, 266
one-year olds, 80–81
onlooker play, 223
operant conditioning, 197–198, 202
opiates, 533
opium, 525, 533
oppression, 11–13
AIDS, 494–495
aspects of social and economic forces,
259
definition of, 11, 25, 259
and discrimination, 258–259
effects and costs of, 267, 270
in organizational/community macro
systems, 263–264
oral contraception. *See* birth control pills
oral language difficulties, 168
oral stage, 116
organization of book, 8–11
organization strategy, 140
organizational empowerment, 16–17
organizational macro systems
discrimination and oppression in,
263–264
human behavior in, 49–52
organizational theory, 37
organizations, 49
analyzing, 601
definition of, 36–37, 50–51, 600
discrimination and oppression in,
263–264
faith-based, 354
liberal, conservative, and developmental perspectives on, 611–614
management styles in, 600–606
models and theories of, 600–609
problems in social service, 51–52
resiliency in, 18

social work with, 52–54, 600–609
strengths in, 16, 17
surviving and thriving in, 606–609
value orientations and decision making in, 609–610
orgasm stage, 663
orientation to personal survival level, 348
Ortho Evra, 322
osteoporosis, 484
other focus, 502
other-/self-directed adolescents, 379
outcome versus output, 28
outer focus, 502
output, 28, 34, 35, 187, 189
versus outcome, 28
outsourcing, 563
ovarian cancer/cysts, 322
ovaries, 298
ovulation, 64
ovulation method, 328
ownership, 268, 269

P

pain cry, 145
ParaGard intrauterine device, 324, 327–328
paralanguage, 516
parallel play, 223
paraphilic disorders, 393
parental attention, importance of,
212–213
parental factors and substance abuse, 304
parental subsystem, 30
Parent Effectiveness Training, 32,
380–382, 599
parenting, 556–557
adult children, 701–702
cultural context, 190, 217, 235
as developmental process, 557
effective communication with
children, 380–382
economic hardship, 190
gender preferences, 556
lesbian and gay, 639–640, 646–648
poor skills, 248
and sex education, 311–312
styles of, 215–216
teenage fathers, 308–310
and temperament, 146–147
Parkinson's disease, 92n7
partial-birth abortion. *See* intact dilation
and extraction
partial mastectomy, 474
participating behavior, 416
partisan role, 47, 48
passive acceptance, 126
passive euthanasia, 725
passive-congenial relationship, 572
passive smoking, 535
paternal deprivation, 590
path analysis, 629
patriarchal hierarchy, 221, 433

patriarchy, end of, 123
Pavlovian conditioning. *See* respondent
conditioning
PCP (phencyclidine), 525, 534
Peck's psychological development theories, 501–503
pedophile, 244
Peer Counseling Hotline, 370
peer-helping program, 370
peers
adolescent suicide and pressure from, 360
group and popularity of, 224–226
interaction in group systems with, 379,
382
pressure of, 304, 305
social aspects of play with, 222–226
pelvic inflammatory disease (PID), 102,
316, 317
penis envy, 117
Pentagon, 261
people as individuals, 437
people of color, 11
Pequot tribe, 257
perceptions, 122, 168, 518
perceptual difficulties, 168
performing stage, 414
permissive parenting, 215
person-centered therapy, 119–122
personal characteristics and substance
abuse, 304
person-in-environment, 22–23, 24, 144
person is political, 123
personal disabilities, 391
personal income disparities, 563
personality, 114, 145
personality development, 114–127
personality disorders, 392
personality pie, 621
personality theory, 114
personal space, 513–514
personal zone, 514
Peruvian mothers, 145, 299
pervasive support, 161
petition, 243
peyote, 525, 534
phallic stage, 116–117
phencyclidine (PCP), 535
phenomenological/self theories, 119–122
concept summary, 122
Philippines, 283
phimosis, 426
phobias, 195–196
phrenology, 152
physical appearance, 479, 516–517
psychological reactions to changes in,
300–305
physical child abuse. *See* child abuse
physical dependence, 538
physical exercise, 673, 682
physical development/functioning, 471,
477–481

changes during adolescence, 297–300
changes during later adulthood, 658–659
changes during middle adulthood, 477
physical-handicap organizations, 408–409
physical neglect, 237
physical strength, 480–481
physician-assisted suicide, 725–726
physiological functioning/needs, 505
impact of thoughts on, 521
physiological theories on aging, 666
Piaget's theory. See cognitive
development
pictures/perceptions, 518
Pilgrims, 257
pill, the, 66, 320–323
and breast cancer, 473
placenta, 65, 73
Plan B One-Step, 324
planner role, 24, 419
in social planning model, 44, 48
planning, 7
planning and policy practice, 49
plateau stage, 557, 663
play
gender differences in, 224, 431
and interaction, 223
levels of social, 223
social aspects of, 222–226
play assessment
at age 8 months, 80
at age 1 year, 80
at age 18 months, 81
at age 2 years, 81
at age 3 years, 82
at age 4 years, 83
at age 5 years, 83
at age 6 to 8 years, 84
at age 9 to 11 years, 85
pleasurable goodies, 683
pneumocystic carinii pneumonia, 493
Poland and abortion, 90
policy, 87
policy advocacy, 49
policy developer role, 24
policy practice, 49
policymaker role, 419
political identity, 383
political value orientation, 610
politics of creative disorder, 277
politics of disorder, 277
politics of escape, 277
Polynesians, 705
poor. See poverty
poppers, 532
popularity and peer group, 224–226
populations-at-risk, 11–13
definition of, 11, 25
older people, 717–718
people living with AIDS, 491–496
Portugal and abortion, 90
position approach, 417

positive family functioning, 182–183
positive feedback, 28, 187
positive regard, need for, 120, 122
positive reinforcement, 119, 198–199,
202–203
using, 206
positive self-concept, 151
positive thinking, 667, 679
postabortion syndrome, 97
postconventional level, 346
postmodern feminism, 125
posttraumatic stress disorder, 97, 453, 678
rape trauma syndrome, 453
and sexual abuse, 246
posture, 510
postvention/prevention of suicide, 369–370
poverty, 563–572
adolescent sexual activity and, 307
blaming the victim in, 566, 569, 612
causes of, 566–567
and child neglect, 238
conflict theory applied to, 571
culture of, 568–569
cycle of, 567, 568
and death rate, 478
definition of, 25
is functional, 569–571
impacts of social and economic forces,
563–572
infant mortality, 565
ideology of individualism, 566
interactionist theory applied to, 571–572
and life expectancy, 565
and low birth-weight infants, 76
older adults, 717
older African American women and, 692
one-parent families and, 584
perpetuates poverty, 567
personal income disparities, 563
the problem of, 564–565
and the rich and the poor, 563–564
who lives in, 565–566
poverty line, 564, 723
power, 12–13
power elite, 13
power need, 519
power thrust, 268
powerlessness, 383
power and control stage, 413
power rapist, 451
preadulthood era, 503
preaffiliation stage, 413, 414
preattachment, 148
preconscious, 114
precontemplation stage of change, 544
preconventional level, 345, 346
preeclampsia, 70
preening behavior, 512
prefrontal cortex, 302–303
pregnancy
the birth process, 72–77

diagnosis of, 65
ectopic, 70, 72, 101, 322
fetal alcohol effects (FAE), 68
fetal alcohol syndrome (FAS), 67–68
fetal development during, 65–66
full-term, 76
prenatal assessment, 69–70
prenatal influences, 66–69
problem, 70
single women and, 87
smoking during, 535
social work roles with women during, 71
unplanned, 8, 85, 307–310
teenage, 69, 307–310
trimesters during, 65–66
prejudgments, 13
prejudice, 258, 414
aspects of social and economic forces,
258
self-awareness of, 289
sources of discrimination and, 264–267
types of, 258
prejudiced discriminator, 258, 269
prejudiced nondiscriminator, 258, 269
Premack Principle, 204
prematurity, 75–76
premoral level, 345, 346
prenatal care
assessment, 69–70
influences, 66–69
macro environment obstacles to, 70
preoperational thought period, 134–136
preparation stage of change, 544
presbycusis, 471, 480
presbyopia, 471, 480
prescription drug assistance for seniors,
730–731
prestige, 12
preterm babies, 75–76
primal or undifferentiated faith, 351
primary group, 181
primary reinforcers, 203
primary sex characteristics, 298
private speech, 143
privilege, 12
problem-solve, RAP framework, 410
problem solving
capacities, 481
groups, 407–408
marriage counseling, 583
no-lose, 381
teacher of, 43, 48
problem-solving approach, 573
process
equal to product, 123
vagueness of, 52
pro-choice, 88
productivity and age, 657
progesterone, 298, 320
progestin, 320
program developer, 24, 44, 48

progressive muscle relaxation, 681
projection, 116, 265, 539
property tax relief, 733
prophylactic. *See* condom
propinquity theory, 551
prostaglandins, 96
prostate gland, 298
protection dimension, 18
protests, 47
proximal development zone, 142
proximodistal development, 78
pseudohermaphrodite, 428
psilocin, 525, 534
psilocybin, 525, 534
psychoanalysis, 114
   defense mechanisms in, 116
psychodynamic theory, 114–118
   critical thinking about, 118
psychoeducation, 248
psychological abuse, 240
psychological adjustments, 689–690
psychological dependence, 538
psychological development, 8–9, 113
   behavioral theories, 119
   critical thinking about relevance to
      social work, 127–129
   Erikson's eight stages of, 334–339
   feminist theories, 122–127
   neo-Freudian psychodynamic, 118–119
   Peck's advances, 501–503
   phenomenological theories, 119–122
   psychodynamic theory, 114–118, 119
   sensitivity to diversity, 130–131
   theories about personality, 114–127
psychological domain, 366
psychological maladjustment, 121, 122
psychological maltreatment, 240–241
psychological neglect, 240
psychological variables and adolescent
   suicide, 361–362
psychology
   analytic/individual, 118
   collective/individual, 118
   definition of, 113
psychomotor skills, 659–660
psychopathological development, 117–118
psychosexual development, 115–117
psychosocial dwarfism (PSD), 240
psychosocial moratorium, 338
psychosocial theories, 334–336, 628
psychotic disorders, 392
psychotropic drugs, 91
puberty, 297
   proof of, 298–300
pubic lice, 318
public day care, 184
public zone, 513
Puerto Rican cultures, 130, 218
   Comunidad de Bienestar, 45
   and gender roles, 286
   and Nuevo Puente program, 344

parenting, 235
   youth, 344
punishment, 199–200, 202
   effectiveness of, 208
   nature of, 208
   potential negative consequences of, 207
   suggestions for using, 209
   use of, 207–210
purveyor of rewards and punishment, 419
put-down messages, 380, 574

O

quaalude, 525, 528–529
quality circle, 604
Quran, 261

R

race, 256
   and adolescent sexual activity, 307
   culture, ethnicity, and identity devel-
      opment, 340–345
   differences in definition, 262
   ethnicity, and schools, 232–233
   and racism, 256
   is a social concept, 260, 262–263
race-blind policies, 280
race and ethnic relations, future of U.S.,
   291–292
race riots, 257, 277
racial and cultural identity development
   model, 343–345
racial and ethnic discrimination, 259–260
racial and ethnic stereotypes, 259
racial and ethnic groups, social work
   practice with, 285–291
racial discrimination
   based on criminal thinking, 268–269
racial/gender comparison of earnings, 437
racial stereotypes, 259
racism, 256, 268
   individual, 263
   institutional, 263–264
   institutional values and, 263–264
racist beliefs, errors in, 268–269
racist jokes/remarks, 281, 289
radiation therapy, 475
radical feminism, 125
radical mastectomy, 475
RAP framework, 409, 410
rape, 446–455
   attempted, 446
   common myths about, 448–449
   counseling survivors of, 453–455
   date, 449, 452, 529
   definition of, 446
   emotional issues, 453–454
   empowerment for survivors of, 453–455
   incidence of, 447
   medical status after a, 455
   prevention, 450
   reporting to police about, 454–455

   survivors' reactions to, 452–453
   theoretical views of, 447–448
rape trauma syndrome, 453
rapist, profile of a, 449, 451
rapist psychopathology perspective, 448
rationalization, 116, 539
rational self-analysis (RSA), 394–399, 412
rational therapy, 268, 394–400, 521, 678
rational versus romantic love, 554
reaction formation, 117
reaction time, 480–481
readiness to change ruler, 545
real self, 120, 122
rebellion, adolescent, 379
recession, global, 567
recidivism rate, 401
reciprocal relationships, 148
recognize, RAP framework,
reconstruction period, 257, 266
recreation groups, 407
recreation-skill groups, 407
recurring behavior, consequences of, 198
recurring-phase model, 415
reflex smiling, 145
reflexes, newborn, 77
reform approach, 129
refugees, 193
regression, 116
reinforcement, 198–199, 202
   schedules of, 207
   time-out from, 213–215
reinforcers
   types of, 203–205
   versus rewards, 205–206
rejection, 240
relational base, establishing, 414
relational problems, 393
relationship, in systems theories, 28, 32, 35
relationship management, 508
relationships
   analyzing love, 577–578
   close personal, 703–704
   in empty-shell marriage, 572–576
   family system, 219, 700–702
   lesbian and gay, 631–632, 636–639, 700
   problems in, 519
   theories about why people choose, 551
relaxation techniques, 680–682
religion
   African Americans and, 273, 288–289
   belief in one true, 266, 694
   definition of, 350, 694
   in later adulthood, 693
   and sexual orientation, 644
   and spirituality, 693–696
religious value orientation, 610
remarriage, 700
reorientation therapy, 623
reparative therapy, 623
repetition, 140
representation, 134

representative group, 408
reproduction, 63–77
repression/repressed barrier, 114–115, 116, 117
Repronex, 104
republican party, 611
research, 127–128
reserve capacity, 477, 663
reservoir of family wisdom grandparents, 702
residual view, 611, 612
resiliency, 13, 17–18
    definition of, 18, 25
    dimensions of, 18
    using strengths, 17–18
resistance, roll with, 545
resistance phase, 676
resistance and immersion stage, 343
resolution stage, 663
respect, mutual, 220
respite care, 736
respondent conditioning, 195–196, 202
responsible performance, disregard for, 268
retirement, 687
    early, 721
    living with spouse in, 687
    and lower income, 687
retreatist gangs, 403
retrovirus, 492
revelation, 126
reverse discrimination, 279, 280
rewards versus reinforcers, 205–206
Rh factor incompatibility, 71, 72
RhoGAM, 71
rhythm method. *See* fertility awareness methods
rich and poor, 563–564
right brain, 522
rights, assertive, 356
risk dimension, 18
Ritalin, 172, 530
rock, 531
Rogerian counseling, 120
rohypnol, 449, 529
roleless role, 484, 721
role confusion, 336
role-playing, 196
role reversal, 573
roles
    definition of, 52
    in families with chemical dependency, 540
    maintenance, 415–416
    in systems theories, 28, 35
    task, 415
    See also social work, roles of; social worker roles
Romania, 705
romantic versus rational love, 554, 576
roofie, 449
rooting reflex, 77

RU-486, 96. *See also* mifepristone
Rubella and pregnancy, 68
running-out-of-program theory, 666
Rush, 532
Russians and abortion, 90

S
sadistic rapist, 451
SAD PERSONS scale, 363–366
    how to use, 365–366
safety needs, 505
safety plan, 463
same-gender harassment, 441
same-sex marriage, 636–639
Samoans, 220, 379
sandwich generation, 590
scabies, 318
scaffolding, 142, 143
scapegoat, 265, 540
    leader role, 419
schema, 132–133
Schiller model, 414–415
scientific management model, 602
schizoaffective disorder, 392
schizophrenia, 391, 392
schizotypal disorder, 392
school environment, 230–233
    Brown v. Board of Education, 272, 292
    educational programming and cultural values, 232
    effective, 230–231
    race and cultural identity development and, 344–345
    race, ethnicity, and, 232–233
    sexual harassment, 443
    teacher's impact, 230
school social worker, 405
Scotland, 510
scrotum, 428, 663
Seasonale, 321
second prohibition, 536
second trimester, 66
secondary reinforcers, 203–206
secondary sex characteristics, 297, 298
secular trend, 298
secure attachment, 149, 151
segregation, human ecology perspective, 41
seizure disorders. *See* epilepsy
selective attention, 139
self, real/ideal, 120, 122
self-actualization, 120, 122, 505, 507
self-advocacy, 165
self-awareness, 144, 287, 289, 507
self-concept, 120, 122, 274
    body image and, 300–301
    effects of discrimination on development of, 274
    effects of positive and negative, 151
    in older people, 688
    self-esteem, and empowerment, 150–152

strategy to improve, 682
self-determination
    and abortion, 87, 97
    and death, 725–726
    and gangs, 406
    NASW policy on gay and lesbian clients and, 618, 650
    and Native Americans, 290
    and people with intellectual disabilities, 164
    and people with learning disabilities, 165
self-differentiation, 689
self-/other-directed adolescents, 379
self-efficacy, 545
self-esteem, 150, 464, 507
    in later adulthood, 690
    low, 169, 236, 267, 301, 361, 565
    self-concept, empowerment and, 150–152
self-fulfilling prophecy, 154, 157, 230, 562
self-help groups, 401, 408–409, 583, 736
self-identity
    in later adulthood, 704
    and sexual orientation, 645
self-image, 268, 269, 513
self-instruction, 170
self management, 507
self-regard, sense of, 120, 122
self-talk, 268, 394–399, 523
    explanation for Columbine massacre, 402
    and criminal activity, 401
    romantic love versus rational love, 554
self theories. *See* phenomenological theories
self-transcendence, 690
self-worth, 120, 152
selling behavior, 416
senescence, 658
senility, myth of, 661
senior-citizen centers, 733
sense organs
    changes in later adulthood, 658–659
    changes in middle adulthood, 480
sensitivity groups, 411
sensorimotor period, 134
sensory memory, 139–140
sensory systems, 511
sentinel lymph node, 474
separation stage, 414, 415
September 11th terrorist attacks, 261–262
sequential-stage perspective, 415
seraphine, 104
serax, 528
seriation, 135
serotonin, 302
servant leadership approach, 419–420
set point theory, 389
sex, 425
    extramarital, 488–490
    following divorce, 490–491

in marriage, 487–488
and the never married, 491
in widowhood, 491
sex characteristics, 297, 298, 426
sex chromosomes, 428
sex discrimination, 440
sex education
abstinence-only, 312–313
comprehensive, 313–315
current policy and, 312
and empowerment, 310–311
empowerment for Native Americans, 315
by parents, 311–312
sexism, 123, 424, 465
sexist language, 444, 446
sexual abuse, 243–249
characteristics of victims, 245–246
definition of, 243
dynamics of child, 244–245
educating children about, 249
incest, 243
Internet and predators, 245
long-term effects of, 246–247
macro system response, 249
pedophile, 244
phases of, 244
prevention of, 249
risk factors, 244–245
social work role, 247–249
talking to child victims of, 247
treatment of, 247–249
sexual activity
in adolescence, 305–310
in later adulthood, 663–665
racial and other differences in adolescent, 307
unplanned pregnancy, 307–310
sexual assault
definition of, 446
rape and, 446–455
suggestions for talking to child victims, 247
See also rape
sexual dysfunctions, 392
sexual equality, 465
sexual functioning in middle age, 487–491
celibacy, 491
following divorce, 490–491
extramarital relationships, 488–490
in marriage, 487–488
among never-married, 491
in widowhood, 491
sexual harassment, 440–444, 445
confronting, 445
definition of, 441
in educational settings, 443
effects of, 443–444
extent of, 442
macro system response to, 442
same-gender, 441

in the workplace, 442
sexual interaction, gay/lesbian, 633
sexual intercourse, percent by age group engaging in, 488
sexuality
and diversity, 130
sexual response and later adulthood, 663–665
values and, 664–665
sexually transmitted diseases (STDs). See sexually transmitted infections
sexually transmitted infections (STIs), 316–320, 472
and infertility, 101
and pregnancy, 68–69
preventing, 319–320
sexual orientation, 619–626
and adolescence, 341
conceptual frameworks concerning, 626–631
definition of, 619, 620, 622
ethnicity and, 644
personality pie, 621
self-identity and, 645
shaping behavior, 207
shelters for battered women, 461–462
Shiites, 256
shingles, 493
Shiva, 192
short-term/working memory, 139–140
sibling interaction, 217, 221
sibling subsystem, 30, 216–217, 221–222
sickle-cell anemia, 667
signature pedagogy, 57
significant-other organization, 409
signification process, 642
simple mastectomy, 474
Singapore, 90, 360
single adults, 193
single fathers, 308
single-parent family, 181, 182, 583–584, 589
single women and pregnancy, 87
single life, 555
Sioux, 220
Siriono people, 717
situational ethics, 647
situational theory, 416
six- to 8-year olds, 84 85
skin changes, 300
skinheads, 257
skin-sparing mastectomy, 474
Skyla, 327
slavery, 254
sleep/wake disorders, 392
sleep patterns, 674
slow-to-warm-up children, 146
smiling, types of, 145
smoking
passive, 535
and pregnancy, 68, 101, 535
snorting, 531

social action model, 47–48
social activist, 47
social advocacy, 49
social agency, 50
social assessment
at age 4 months, 79
at age 8 months, 80
at age 1 year, 80–81
at age 18 months, 81
at age 2 years, 82
at age 3 years, 82
at age 4 years, 83
at age 5 years, 83
at age 6 to 8 years, 84
at age 9 to 11 years, 85
social awareness, 507
social behavioral theory, 119
social bonding, 405
social breakdown syndrome, 698
social change, 560
social class, 41, 191
social clubs, 288
social competence, 152, 169
social concept, race as a, 260, 262–263
social construction of gender, 425–426, 435
social cooperation, 220
social Darwinism, 268, 728
social development, 9, 10
changes in adolescence, 378–383
social disorganization, 560
social/emotional characteristics, 168–169
social environment, 128, 129
definition of, 3, 33, 35
and families, 222–233
multiple systems in, 35–38
social forces, 51–52
and abortion, 85–101
and AIDS discrimination and oppression, 494–495
prejudice, discrimination and oppression, 258–259
death, impact of, 705–706
and early retirement, 721–722
impact on eating disorders, 389
legal empowerment and social justice—homosexuality, 633–640
and older people, 719
on poverty, 563–572
and prejudice, discrimination and oppression, 267, 270
social independence, 379
social insurance, 729n1
social intelligence, 508–509
social isolation, 236
social justice
community strategies to promote, 276–281
definition of, 20, 25, 284
and human rights, 20, 284–285
macro systems, families, economic and, 183–184

and people with intellectual disabilities, 162–163
and people with learning disabilities,
171–172
social learning, 119
social learning theory/moral development,
349–350
social value orientation, 118, 610
social planning model, 44, 46–47, 48
social play, 222–226
social policy, 406
police and battered women, 459
race-blind, 280
social problems, 383–388
social reconstruction syndrome theory, 698
social reinforcers, 204–205
social security system, 723–724
Old Age, Survivors, Disability, and
Health Insurance (OASDHI), 723,
729–730
social service organizations, 51–52
social services, 49
social smiling, 145
social solidarity, 49
social stratification, 563
social systems perspective, 42
social systems theories, 558–563
social welfare, 50
social work
advanced, 57
and AIDS, 495–496
application of learning theory to, 201
application of theory to, 289–290
assertiveness approaches to, 359
assessment, 5–8, 546–547
culturally competent, 286–290
definition of, 6
and empowerment through spiritual
development, 353–354
and empowerment through groups,
406–419
ethics, international, 20
ethnic-sensitive, 285–286
evidence-based, 290
and spiritual, 354
and faith-based organizations, 354
field education, 57
foundation knowledge of, 5–8, 546–547
gender wage gap in, 439–440
generalist, 7, 57
goals of, 24–25
with groups, 406–420
hospital, 736
and human development, 79
human rights issues, 20, 284
international, 20
knowledge, 5–8
LGBT people, 650
major thrusts of, 6
and medical model, 127–129
with men, 435

and motivational interviewing, 544–546
with older people, 735–736
with organizations, 600–609
process of, 6
professional values and AIDS, 495–496
with racial and ethnic groups, 285–291
with rape survivors, 453–455
relevance of theory to, 127–129
roles. (*See* social work roles)
social justice issues, 20
and spirituality/religion, 694
strengths-based, 132
with suicidal people, 368
theory and values, 127
values, 13, 289
wage inequality, 439–440
with women, 463–464, 465
social work roles
and abortion, 86, 98–99
and addiction, 544
and ADHD, 173
and child maltreatment, 242, 247–249
and codependency, 546
and community change, 43, 44, 47, 48
for countering discrimination, 290–291
and intellectual/developmental disabilities, 164
and family problems, 597–600
and gangs, 405–406
and grief management, 708–709
and infertility, 107–108
and lesbian and gay parents, 646–648
and lesbian and gay people, 642–650
and marriage counseling, 583
with older people, 735–736
in organizational and community
systems, 52–54
in person-in-environment focus, 24
and pregnant women, 71, 76
and sexual abuse, 247–249
and stress management, 683
social zone, 514
socialist feminism, 124–125
socialization, 123
definition of, 180
family, 183
gender-role, 123, 222, 433
intimacy, 500
socialization groups, 409
socialization patterns, 266
socializing versus sexualizing, 501
sociocultural cognitive development, 141–142
socioeconomic class
and gestures, 512
and pregnancy, 68
and schools, 232
sociogram, 225–226
sociological theories
application to gangs, 404–406
about human behavior, 558–563
sociometry, 225

sociopsychological perspective, 40
sodomy laws, 633
solitary play, 223
solution message, 380, 574
solving circle, 520
somatic symptoms, 392
South Africa
and abortion, 90
apartheid, 267
asset-based community development,
283
Southeast Asia, 144, 221, 533
South Pacific, 297, 379
Soviet Union and abortion, 90
space, personal, 513–514
Spain, 360
special K (ketamine hydrochloride), 449
special needs and IQ tests, 156–157
specificity, 210
speech
feminine/masculine, 436
inner/private, 143
speed. *See* methamphetamine
hydrochloride
speeding. *See* amphetamines
sperm, 64
bank, 104, 105
motility, 102
spermicide, 324–325
spina bifida, 70n2, 75
spirituality
definition of, 350, 694
and diversity, 132
evidence-based practice and, 354
Fowler's faith development theory,
350–353
importance to Native Americans, 220
and later adulthood, 693
religion and, 693, 696
and sexual orientation, 644
social work and empowerment
through, 353–354
spontaneous abortion, 72, 484
spouse abuse. *See* battered women
spray-on contraception, 330
stage theorists, 487
stages of change model, 544–546
stagnation, 336, 501
Stanford-Binet IQ test, 155
startle response. *See* Moro reflex
status, 12–13
ageism and low, 691
detecting differences in, 510
status offenses, 400
stem cell research, 92–94
stepfamilies, 181–182, 500, 586–589
stepping reflex, 77
stereotypes, 13, 423
gender-role, 429–435, 465, 500, 596
about later adulthood, 658, 691
about lesbian and gay people, 620

about physical appearance, 517
racial and ethnic, 259
self-awareness of, 289
stereotyping and multiculturalism, 270–271
sterilization/sterility, 317, 329, 330
Sternberg's triarchic theory of intelligence, 153–154
steroid use, 525, 537–538
stigma, mastery of, 648–649
stimulants, 525, 529–533
and ADHD, 172
stimulus, 195, 202
Stonewall, remember, 640
storming stage, 414
Storms's sexual orientation conceptualization, 625
strategic planning and budgeting (SPB), 605
street worker, 405
strengths, 15–16
assessing your, 17
community, 16
ethnic and cultural differences in families, 218–221
Latino and Hispanic communities promote, 45–46
multiple sources of, 15–16
spirituality, 350–351
strengths perspective, 13–16, 286
and African Americans, 286
becoming comfortable with own death, 710, 712–713
and diversity, 132
in later adulthood, 703–704
principles of, 14
successful aging theories and, 696–698
and wellness, 672–683
streptomycin, 67
stress, 675
application of theory, 677, 683
conceptualizing, 675–677
disorders and traumas, 678
empowerment approaches to managing, 677–683
general adaptation syndrome (GAS), 675
signals, 679
social work and managing, 683
and stress management, 675–683
and stress-related illnesses, 676
and suicide, 360–361
and young adults, 477
stressor, 675, 676
stress theory, 666
stroking, 574
structural perspective, 39–40
structure, 39
style approach, 418
subculture theory, 404–405
sublimation, 116
subprime mortgage loans, 567

sub-Saharan Africa & AIDS, 495
substance-related disorders, 392
substance use and abuse, 523–547.
See also drugs
an AA meeting, 542–543
and adolescent health, 303–305
and AIDS, 534
alcohol, 303–305, 524–527
anabolic steroids, 525, 537–538
babies addicted to crack, 532
cannabis, 525
codependency, 546
date rape, 529
deaths of famous people related to, 528
dependence, 538–539
depressant drugs, 524–529
drugs of abuse, facts and effects, 525
Dutch policy, 547
hallucinogens, 525, 534–535
interaction in family systems, 539–540
marijuana, 525, 536–537
mind-altering, 303
motivational interviewing and denial, 544–546
narcotics, 525, 533–534
performance-enhancing drugs in baseball, 538
reasons for, 538
relationship between knowledge and assessment, 546–547
specific drugs, 524–538
stimulants, 525, 529–534
theories about, 539–540
tobacco, 305, 525, 535–536
treatment, 540–544
substitute child care, 239
subsystems, 30
definition of, 27, 35, 186, 189
sibling, 30, 216–217, 221–222
subtext, 125
sucking reflex, 77
suction curettage, 96
Sudan, 76
suicide, 360–370, 398
and adolescent Hispanic females, 366
assisted, 725–726
barbiturates, 528
Canadian task force on, 369–370
causes of adolescent, 360–362
community empowerment, 369–370
crisis intervention, 369–370
guidelines for helping, 367–369
incidence of, 360
integrative model, 366
international perspectives, 360
lesbian and gay adolescents and, 362, 645
notes, 363
among older men, 689
prevention and crisis intervention, 369–370

professional counseling of, 368–369
reactions to threat, 367–368
SAD PERSONS scale, 363–366
symptoms, 362–365
a victim of, 361
superego, 114, 115, 118
supervision of children and neglect, 237–238, 239
supervisor role, 24
suicide prevention task force, 369
Sunnis, 256
support networks, natural/helping, 16, 288, 462
supported living, 164
supportive relationships, 545
support systems and intellectual disabilities, 161
surgery for infertility, 104
surgical biopsy, 474
surrogate motherhood, 106–107
surrogate parent grandparents, 191, 702
survival need, 519
sustaining/dominant systems, 285–286
Sweden, 76
swimming reflex, 77
Switzerland, 726
symbolic representation, 134
symbols, 562
symptothermal method, 329
synergistic interaction, 527
synthesis, 126
synthetic-conventional faith, 351–352
synthetic drugs, 530
synthetic estrogen, 320
syphilis, 317–318
systematic desensitization, 195, 202
system, definition of, 23, 32, 185, 189
systems, 129
community, 30
definition of, 35, 185, 189
discrimination in, 263–264
dominant/sustaining, 285–286
family, 30, 184–185
micro, mezzo, macro, 36–38
multiple, 35–38
nurturing, 286
peer group, 379, 382
systems theories, 129
application to child abuse case, 29–33
application to families, 184–189
key concepts in, 23, 27–33, 35

T

Tahitian Islands, 705
Taiwan, 90, 157
talk story, 232
task force, 369, 407
task groups, 407
task roles, 415
tea party movement, 728
teacher/educator role, 43, 48

teachers, impact of, 230
technological advances, 560
teenage. *See* adolescence
teenage fathers, 308–310
teenage pregnancy, 68, 307–310
    and low birth-weight infants, 68
telephone reassurance, 733
television/media, influence of, 228–230
telling behavior, 416
temperament, 145
    cross-cultural diversity and, 148
    infants and, 145–147
    and parenting, 147
teratogens, 67, 169
terminal drop, 661
termination, 7
termination stage, 578
terminology, behaviorally specific,
    210–211
territoriality, 515
terrorists, 263
terrorizing behavior, 241
testes, 298, 485
testosterone, 298, 485
test-tube babies, 105
tetracycline, 67
text, 125
Thailand and abortion, 90
thalidomide babies, 67
theoretical value orientation, 610
theoretical perspectives
    by chapter, 26
theory
    application to gangs, 404–406
    application to practice, 289–290
    critical thinking about social work
        and, 127–129
    definition of, 22
    ethical issues related to, 629
    evaluation of, 127–128, 666
    relevance to social work, 127–129
theory of differential association, 404
theory X, 603–604
theory Y, 603–604
theory Z, 604–605
therapy groups, 409, 411, 736
    for spouses of adults with cancer, 412
thinking
    determines our behavior/emotions, 400
    errors, 268–269
third trimester, 66
three-year olds, 82
threshold/perceptual reorientation stage,
    577
time, concept of, 220
time-out from reinforcement, 213–215
time perspective, lack of, 268
tobacco, 525, 535
    adolescent use, 305
    civil settlement, 536
    passive smoking, 535

risk factors, 305, 535
Today Sponge, 327
token reinforcers, 205
tokens, 205
tolerance, 538
tonic neck reflex, 77
total mastectomy, 474
total quality management (TQM),
    605–606
touching, 512
toxemia, 70–71, 72
toxic shock syndrome (TSS), 326
trait approach, 416–417
tranquilizers, 525, 528
transactions, definition of, 33, 35
transgenderism, 430
transgender people, 430, 624
transitional housing programs, 462
transitional points of life, 130, 503–505
transman, 430
transportation and older adults, 727, 736
transsexual people, 430, 624
transtheoretical model of change, 544
transverse presentation, 73, 74
transvestites, 430
transwoman, 430
transyouth, 430
tranxene, 528
traumas, 678
triarchic theory of intelligence, 153–154
trichomoniasis, 318
trimesters of pregnancy, 65–66
triphasic pill, 321
triple jeopardy, 644, 692
trust
    lack of, 268
    stage, 335
    walk, 411
tubal ligation, 329
tubal pregnancy. *See* ectopic pregnancy
Tuckman model, 414
tumors, 472
Tunisia and abortion, 90
Turkey
    and abortion,
    and drugs,
Turks, 271
Two-spirits, 430
two-year olds, 81–82

U
Uganda, 717
ulipristal acetate, 324
ultrasound/sonography, 69, 473–474
ultimacy, 351
unconditioned reinforcers, 203
unconditioned stimulus, 195, 202
unconscious, 114, 118
undocumented immigrants, 193
unity and diversity, 124
universalizing faith, 352

unoccupied behavior, 223
unplanned pregnancy, 8, 86, 307–310
unprejudiced discriminator, 258, 269
unprejudiced nondiscriminator, 258

V
vacuum aspiration, 96
vacuum-assisted biopsies, 474
vacuum curettage, 96
vaginal ring, 322–323, 330
vaginal spermicides, 324–325
vagueness of goals/process, 52
valium, 528
values
    and abortions, 86–87
    and aging, 661
    AIDS and professional, 495–496
    collisions of, 381–382
    conflicts between helping professionals
        and bureaucracies, 607
    cultural, 218, 232
    definition of, 18–19
    ethics in bio-psycho-social assess-
        ments, 21–22
    institutional, 263–264
    group, 13
    orientations in organizations, 609–610
    racism and institutional, 263–264
    self-awareness of, 289
    and sexuality, 664–665
    social work, 13
valuing process equally with product, 123
valuing wisdom versus valuing physical
    power, 501
varicocele, 102
vas deferens, 329, 330
vasectomy, 329
vasocongestion, 663
venereal diseases (VD). *See* sexually
    transmitted infections
verbal communication, 590–591
verification stage, 577–578
vertex presentation, 73, 74
vestibular senses, 659
viability, 66
Viagra, 664, 665
victim-precipitated rape, 447–448
victim stance, 268, 269
victim system, 267
video games, violence of, 228–230
Vietnamese, 220, 235
    and abortion, 90
    and discipline, 235
victim, blaming the, 566, 569
victim-precipitated rape, 447–448
victim system, 267
violence
    against abortion clinics, 92
    bullying, 226–228
    against lesbian and gay people,
        640–642

against minorities in the U.S., 257–258
against women, 456
hate crimes, 260
on television/media, 228–230
virginity pledge, 312
virus, 492
vision impairment, 167, 658
visual acuity, 471
visual system, 511
voice tone, 300, 359, 515–516
volunteerism, 738
vulnerability, 18
vulva, 306
Vygotsky's theory, 141–144

W

wage inequality, 437–440
Wappinger tribe, 257
war on poverty, 49
Watergate break-in, 346
wealth, 12–13, 563
Wechsler, tests, 155–156
well-being, promoting optimal, 650
wellness, strengths perspective, 672–683
Westberg model, 706–707
wet dream. See nocturnal emissions
white privilege, 260
white supremacy, 260
widowhood, 491, 700
wild boy of Aveyron, 1
win-lose approach, 381
win-lose conflict, 573
withdrawal, 527
    method of contraception, 328
    women
    abortion, 97, 98
    achieving sexual equality, 465
    African American older, 692
    battered, 455–463
    differences between men and, 435–437

economic inequality, 437–440
employment positions held by, 439
empowering, 459–464
and fertility/infertility, 102
gender-role stereotypes in, 432, 434
Gilligan's approach to moral
    development, 123, 347–349
income comparisons, 437
Levinson's theories applied to, 506
menopause, 482–485
moral development of, 123
mothers working outside the home,
    589–590
rape and sexual assault, 446–455
sexual harassment, 440–444, 445
significant issues and events, 437
as single parents, 182
suicide and Hispanic, 366
women's liberation, 125
women's movement, 426
work
    key to success at, 502
    myths about older people and, 721
work ethic, 117
working memory, 139, 140
working mothers, 182, 589–590
World War II, 265, 272, 614
worldview, 121, 131–132, 274, 276
worth, conditions of, 120
written language difficulties, 168
xani-th, 430
X chromosome, 64, 428, 556
XX chromosome, 428

Y

Y chromosome, 64, 428, 556
you-messages, 380, 574
young adulthood, 471–477
    age span, 471
    AIDS/HIV and, 191–450

assessing and intervening in family
    systems in, 590–600
breast cancer, 472–476
differential incidence of death in, 478
family mezzo system problems in,
    572–590
gender-role stereotypes, 432, 434–435,
    465
health status during, 471–472
intimacy versus isolation, 500
leaving home, 190
liberal, conservative, and develop-
    mental perspectives on, 611–614
lifestyle and good health in, 476–477
macro social system theories on,
    558–563
management by objectives, 605
personal lifestyles, 550–558
physical development during, 471
poverty in, 563–572
social work with organizations, 600–609
value orientations in organizational
    decision making, 609–610
young-old, 657
youth
    emphasis on, 719
    empowerment of homeless, 382–383
    Puerto Rican program, 344
youth gangs, 401–404

Z

Zambia
    abortions, 90
    IQ tests, 157
Zinacantecos, 148
zone of proximal development, 142
zones of space, 513–514
zygote, 64
Zygote Intrafallopian Transfer (ZIFT),
    106, 107

Human Diversity Content

Appreciation of diversity is a major theme in social work education. This text infuses diversity in every chapter. The following material summarizes the diversity content that is covered. Because this book assumes a chronological approach to the life span, it is assumed that some dimensions of diversity are intrinsically covered, including those related to clients' age, gender, and family structure (see "Mezzo Systems" for content on families). Many of the content areas cited below are included as "Spotlights on Diversity."

Chapter 1
Introduction to Human Behavior and the Social Environment
- Diversity, oppression, and populations-at-risk
- Culture and the importance of cultural competency
- Empowerment, the strengths perspective, and resiliency
- Latino and Hispanic communities' promotion of strengths and empowerment

Chapter 2
Biological Development in Infancy and Childhood
- International perspectives on abortion policy
- Psychological effects of abortion on women and men
- Social work roles and empowering women
- A feminist perspective on infertility counseling and empowerment

Chapter 3
Psychological Development in Infancy and Childhood
- Sensitivity to diversity when examining psychological theories
- Diversity in feminist conceptual frameworks
- Intersectionality and gender
- Feminist identity development
- Cross-cultural diversity in expectations and temperament
- Cross-cultural differences in attachment
- Sociocultural cognitive development
- Sociocultural learning of interdependence versus independence
- Cultural biases and IQ tests
- People who have intellectual disabilities: A population-at-risk
- The Americans With Disabilities Act: The pursuit of social and economic justice
- People with learning disabilities: A dimension of diversity
- Other disabilities that can affect children
- Empowerment and a consumer-directed approach for people with disabilities

Chapter 4
Social Development in Infancy and Childhood
- Membership in family groups: Variations in family structure
- Diverse perspectives on the family life cycle
- The effects of immigration status on families
- Cultural context and parenting style
- Ethnic and cultural differences in families
- Concepts important in Native American families
- Gender-role socialization
- Gender differences in play
- Race, ethnicity, and schools
- Educational programming that responds to cultural values
- Diverse cultural contexts for discipline and abuse of children

Chapter 5
Ethnocentrism and Racism

Although the entire chapter addresses diversity in terms of class, color, culture, ethnicity, national origins, and populations-at-risk, the following content is of special significance.

- Ethnic groups and ethnocentrism
- Race and racism
- Violence against minorities in the United States
- Aspects of social and economic forces: prejudice, discrimination, and oppression
- Racial and ethnic stereotypes
- Racial and ethnic discrimination is the problem of whites
- White privilege
- Hate crimes
- Race is a social concept
- Institutional values and racism: Discrimination in systems
- Discrimination and oppression in organizational macro systems
- Discrimination and oppression in community macro systems
- Sources of prejudice and discrimination
- Is racial discrimination based on criminal thinking?
- Impacts of social and economic forces: The effects and costs of discrimination and oppression
- The effects of discrimination on human growth and development
- History and culture of African Americans
- Effects of discrimination on development of self-concept
- The Africentric perspective and world-view
- Kwanzaa
- Discrimination against Arab Americans and American Muslims
- Stereotyping and multiculturalism
- Intersectionality of multiple factors
- Human rights and social justice
- Community strategies to promote social and economic justice
- Civil rights laws: Changing the legal macro system
- Rosa Parks's act of courage sparked the civil rights movement
- Affirmative action: A macro system response
- Confronting racist remarks and actions
- Minority-owned businesses
- Asset-based community development
- Social work practice with racial and ethnic groups
- Ethnic-sensitive practice
- Empowerment
- Strengths perspective
- Culturally competent practice
- The future of American race and ethnic relations
- A dream of the end of racism

Chapter 6
Biological Development in Adolescence
- Diversity and menarche
- Gender differences in maturation
- Racial and other differences in adolescent sexual activity
- Empowerment through sex education for Native Americans

Chapter 7
Psychological Development in Adolescence
- Race, culture, ethnicity, and identity development
- Communities and schools can strengthen racial and cultural identity development for adolescents
- Empowering lesbian and gay adolescents
- Moral development and women: Gilligan's approach